D1378269

Handbook of Contemporary Developments in World Ecology

Handbook of Contemporary Developments in World Ecology

Edited by Edward J. Kormondy and J. Frank McCormick

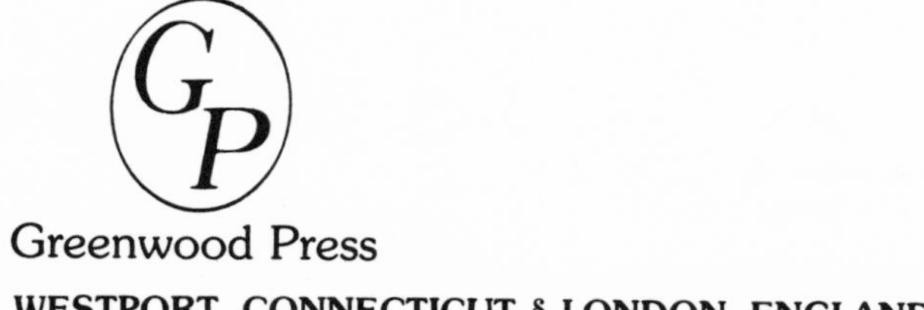
Greenwood Press
WESTPORT, CONNECTICUT § LONDON, ENGLAND

Library of Congress Cataloging in Publication Data
Main entry under title:

Handbook of contemporary developments in world ecology.

Bibliography: p.
Includes index.
1. Ecology. I. Kormondy, Edward John, 1926–
2. McCormick, J. Frank, 1935–
QH541.H243 574.5 80-1797
ISBN 0-313-21381-X (lib. bdg.)

Library of Congress Catalog Card Number: 80-1797
ISBN: 0-313-21381-X

First published in 1981

Greenwood Press
A division of Congressional Information Service, Inc.
88 Post Road West, Westport, Connecticut 06881

Distributed in the United Kingdom and Europe by
Aldwych Press, Ltd., London

Printed in the United States of America

10 9 8 7 6 5 4 3 2 1

Contents

ASIA

Figures

Tables

Preface

In undertaking this project, we were persuaded of the need for an international and globally regional perspective on developments of concepts and methodology in contemporary ecology. We were interested in tracing the emergence of ecology as a distinct science, a phenomenon that in large measure, in our view, has occurred since World War II. Although there have been a substantial number of surveys of particular aspects of ecological theory or methodologies and of generalizations based on worldwide data, there have been virtually no nationally based historical reviews of the science as a whole. Approximately once each decade, ecologists and ecological societies seriously question where the science is going in terms of philosophy, concepts, methodologies, and applications. In preparation for this recurrent exercise, we offer this analysis of where we are and how we got here.

Invitations to participate in this project were extended to ecologists throughout the world. Some were known to one or the other of us or had been brought to our attention. In other cases, we sent a letter to persons involved in international projects or to senior government or academy of science representatives, asking them to identify persons for us to contact. In a number of cases, individuals who themselves were unable to participate facilitated our effort by recruiting authors for us. In addition to the national perspective essays, we sought some essays dealing integratively with international and applied dimensions of the field.

As a result of our efforts, thirty-four countries are represented in this volume. Some of the individuals we contacted did not respond to our letters, and two advised they did not feel enough had transpired to warrant an essay. Eight additional authors agreed to prepare essays but did not do so. Of this latter group, three advised us very late that they would not be able to fulfill their commitment, and one of these tried, in vain, to recruit someone. This group of eight accounts for the recognizable absence of contributions from such countries as Canada, Finland, France, India, Ireland, and Spain. While recognizing that this task is essentially "voluntary" work, we admit to some disappointment concerning those who failed to respond.

Each author was asked to address the following points insofar as they pertained or seemed appropriate to an essay of some five thousand words: historical antecedents and intellectual traditions; significant advances in theory and methodology; major trends in theoretical and applied research; interactions with other disciplines; sources and levels of government and private support; teaching and training at undergraduate and graduate levels; major native language journals and societies, and foreign language journals routinely consulted; major research papers, briefly annotated. Different emphases and/or omissions by the authors reflect their particular bias and experience; the result is that each essay is unique rather than stereotyped. Several essays considerably exceeded the suggested length and in only a few cases were these shortened, the authors being dutifully notified. All the essays were edited to provide some degree of consistency in styling and to improve language use.

The essays have been arranged according to major world regions and are in alphabetical order within a region. The topical or thematic essays are also arranged in alphabetical order.

This volume would not exist, of course, were it not for the willingness of these authors to prepare their respective essays. We are grateful to them and appreciate the timeliness with which most completed their task. We also acknowledge the assistance of the many persons in various countries who assisted in identifying potential authors. In this regard, we particularly acknowledge the assistance of Vernon C. Gilbert, International Science and Technology Institute, not only for identifying contacts in a number of countries, but also for being willing, very late in the project, to prepare the essay on international programs. Ariel Lugo made helpful suggestions on several aspects of the project. George Bowen and Tricia Gregory compiled the information that appears in the appendices. To all these persons we express our appreciation. We believe they have provided a most worthwhile contribution to understanding the state of contemporary ecology.

EDWARD J. KORMONDY
J. FRANK MCCORMICK

Introduction

Edward J. Kormondy and J. Frank McCormick

The period since the end of World War II has been one of most rapid advancement in science (and in culture in general); advancement has been particularly accelerated in the life sciences. While developments in molecular and cellular biology headlined the first two intervening decades, ecosystem ecology and, more recently, sociobiology were emerging at the population level of life's organizational hierarchy. These new disciplines emerged not primarily from within biology sensu stricto but from interdigitations of the physical and chemical sciences and mathematics; in the instances of ecology and sociobiology, there were interactions with the social sciences as well. Truly interdisciplinary, these emerging new arenas of intellectual activity have forced the development of new constructs and methodologies, new applications, and training and educational programs. They have also presented new challenges in communicating the impact of their sometimes esoteric findings to the public at large and especially to funding and regulatory agencies.

Ecology has been in the midst of this change, moving from a largely organism-centered and qualitatively descriptive discourse to that of a system of dynamically interacting and interrelated parts capable of being quantitatively analyzed and modelled. From its origins in the natural history observations recorded in the early literature of Greece and Rome in the West and of Confucius and Tao in the East, one can trace the evolution of ecology through the works of early biogeographers like von Humboldt, Wallace, and Darwin, and later Schimper and Warming. Floristic and faunistic cataloging became increasingly correlated with geography, climate, and soil. Although emphasizing the post-World War II period, most of the contributors to this volume have characterized the beginnings of ecology in their respective countries as having had these kinds of roots. Subsequently, there tends to be two major tacks, that of phytosociology being predominant, and of plant physiology with an ecological bias. Much later came considerations of the structure and dynamics of the total community of organisms, plants, animals, and microbes.

RISE OF MODERN ECOLOGY

Most historians of science mark the rise of modern ecology with the introduction and elaboration of the ecosystem concept attributed to Anglo-American sources: the bioeconomic food chain/pyramid concepts of Elton; the ecosystem model of Tansley; and the energetic trophic dynamics of Transeau/Juday/Lindeman. While this is not the forum in which to articulate the particular paradigms of ecosystem ecology, the authors of these essays either imply or assume contemporary ecology to be a discrete science of the ecosystem. We concur that there is a more or less circumscribed body of knowledge that can be isolated as being ecological and concerned with the flow of energy and nutrients, the interactions of populations in that flow, and the interactions of mathematically describable attributes, even if not well understood, such as diversity, stability, and evolution. This new ecology, while having its roots in the tangible plants, animals, and microbes that constitute the biotic components of an ecosystem, has reached highly sophisticated levels of abstraction that would surely be baffling, if not overwhelming, to modern ecology's early and mid-twentieth-century forebears.

There is another approach to assessing the emergent/emerging status of ecology as a science: the ubiquity of its particular theoretical constructs and methodologies. This is well reflected in these essays, conveying the adage that science knows no national boundaries. In the instance of contemporary ecology, as with perhaps all science, much of this is owing to the speed of twentieth-century communication through such vehicles as nearly instantaneous access to current literature, numerous international conferences and symposia, and international research projects. Virtually all ecology any place in the world can be or is au courant.

Further contributing to the omnipresence of ecosystem ecology is the source of educational preparation and advanced training of ecologists. Until quite recently, as many of these essays indicate, there were no advanced study opportunities available in ecology in a number of countries, with the consequence that students were sent abroad, primarily to English and American universities where ecosystem ecology played an ever-increasing role in the science. In some instances, authors attribute the emphasis on ecosystem ecology to the importation of persons trained in that approach, people who came both to teach and conduct research. Yet a further contribution has been the influence of Anglo-American textbooks, now increasingly being replaced by native-developed ones.

It is gratifying to note the availability today of courses in ecology in most countries and the opportunities for advanced major study in some. However, several authors note the absence of contributions to ecological theory and methods, attributing this both to the paucity of trained ecologists and particularly to the absence of specialists in adjunctive and cognate disciplines, such as statistics, computer science, pedology, and climatology.

At the outset of this project, we anticipated the survey would show that contemporary ecology on a worldwide basis would be found to be pluralistic. A critical reading of these essays indicates that multiple focuses are not characteristic of the world scene. Instead, there is a spectrum of activity in most countries, which includes vegetation analysis, ecophysiology, and ecosystem analysis, with varying degrees of emphasis on these areas. Largely because of cooperation in international programs like the International Biological Program (IBP), virtually all countries have been involved in productivity studies, fewer in studies on decomposition and mineral cycling, and many fewer on ecosystem modelling. Although a number of countries with younger traditions in science and ecology report considerable current emphasis on vegetation analysis and mapping, such studies are typically concurrent with ones on productivity and decomposition, or both.

Factors in the Rise of Modern Ecology

Applications. Applied ecology has not played a uniformly influential role in the development of ecology around the world. In those countries in which there has been a long-established tradition in life science, within which ecology developed as a subset and from which it has emerged, there was relatively little impact from practical applications in forestry, agriculture, and fisheries; in fact, in most instances they moved in parallel with little or no intellectual or methodological interchange. In most of these same countries, there was insignificant impact to the science from environmental degradation and pollution. By contrast, in a number of countries, including those with and without strong intellectual traditions in science, the development of ecology results directly from the need for knowledge to effectively manage limited natural resources, such as forests, water, soil, fish, and food crops. In yet other instances, the primary impetus has come from the need to stay and correct environmental pollution and degrading land use. Particularly in insular and peninsular countries such as Iceland, Korea, and Taiwan are these applied impacts on ecology emphasized, as is the indistinguishable line between basic and applied research. Where survival and livelihood are at stake, there is crucial importance to understanding the dynamics of the system that provides such support.

In their article on Israel, Slobodkin and Loya describe the "curious relation between ecological, political, and philosophical thought" in the development of ecology, suggesting that such relations exist in all countries but are usually not so clearly seen for various reasons of complexity. That there is an interaction of a particular people and their particular landscape and their particular literature is well described by Slobodkin and Loya, and if one teases most of the other essays, similar conclusions result.

Political Influences. Not the least of political influences in the development of ecology has been that of changing national boundaries and dominations. Austria was once considerably involved in plankton research when the boundaries of the Austro-Hungarian Empire extended to the sea. The Congo was studied intensively by Belgians and Indonesia by the Dutch when these areas were parts of their respective colonial domains. Taiwan experienced a serious vacuum in science (and other areas) when the Japanese vacated the island in 1945 after fifty years of domination. Other instances are described or hinted at by other authors.

No less significant was the negative impact of World War II. It not only brought a halt to virtually all ecological and other scientific work, but also resulted in the loss of trained professionals, laboratories, and equipment. In the immediate postwar recovery period, the resurgence of science in general and of ecology in particular in many countries took second seat to other more pressing societal needs, typically compounded by shaky economies. Almost all of the writers from countries most directly affected by World War II speak of the devastating impact of that war on advancements in the field.

An additional political influence derives from the source of research funding. In all instances, this support is largely, sometimes exclusively, governmental with smaller amounts from international organizations, such as UNESCO, FAO, and WHO, and from private philanthropies, such as the Ford Foundation, Rockefeller Foundation, and World Wildlife Fund. In the case of governmentally derived funding, the allocation is often directed to meet national needs as determined by the central government through its ministries, cabinets, and legislatures, or through powerful academies of science. Directly, as well as indirectly, such control of research and training funding cannot be dismissed as not having powerful impact on the development of the discipline.

Intellectual Influences. We have already pointed out that, in those countries in which there was a strong intellectual tradition in science, applied concerns generally did not have much of a stimulating influence in ecology. But, as several authors note, these intellectual traditions have also had their detrimental effects in preventing the introduction and advancement of new ideas. The role of the "chair" in Western universities and in those whose organizational pattern derives therefrom is implicitly or explicitly recognized as being of singular importance in the development of ecology, sometimes advancing it, but most often restraining it.

The influences of schools of thought, designated as Uppsala, Zurich-Montpellier, individualistic, and continuum, while not necessarily ascribed to "chairs," are exemplary of strongly held and practiced intellectual ecological traditions that have had pervasive influence and strong impact on the training of future ecologists and the direction of research.

The role of professional societies and of native language journals specifically devoted to ecology as factors in the development of ecology is ambiguous. Only one or two authors lament the lack of native language journals in ecology, and most authors see the availability of outlets in other types of native language journals as amply fulfilling the needs for professional communication. Similarly, in a number of countries, ecology groups are subsections of the established societies and academies, yet they satisfactorily meet the needs for professional association. A review of significant publications in each essay gives credence to the point that regardless of available native outlets for publication, scientists in virtually all countries seek to publish in journals with international circulation. At least one author has acknowledged the importance of such publication in personal professional advancement.

Ecological Influences. As will be abundantly clear from these essays, the particular environments of the respective countries have had a remarkable focusing effect and, in some cases, a strong impact on the development of theory and method. One reads of the sharply bounded ecosystems of Switzerland having had considerable influence on Braun-Blanquet whose system, as authors of several tropical countries note, is very difficult to apply where vegetation boundaries are indistinct. Similarly described is the strong influence of climate and the importance of insect pests in Australia on the population theories developed by Andrewartha and Birch. By the same token, advances in knowledge of particular ecosystems has come from ecologists who have taken advantage of sometimes unique environments in their own backyard—the Nile in Sudan, the sand dunes on the northwest coast of the Netherlands, the deserts of Egypt, and the tundra in many northern countries. Similarly, the economic importance of ecologically dominant components, such as fish, forests, and crops, as well as their pests and parasites, has had singular influence in many countries on the direction and intensity of ecological work.

CONCLUSION

As will be evident to the reader, the authors have taken quite understandably parochial views of ecological development in their respective countries. Although virtually all authors have cast their particular review in a larger context, the focus is decidedly internal, historical, and nationalistic in giving primary recognition to the work of native scientists. Several authors are remarkably candid about shortcomings in the exercise of ecology itself, as well as with regard to external support and acceptance.

The unique quality of these essays, even though they have, for the most part, addressed the same set of issues, does not permit more than the broad perspectives offered in the foregoing paragraphs. No summary or set of conclusions is warranted or justified at this stage of the emergence of ecology on a global or regional scale. Our intent has been to identify distinct characteristics by nation and geographic region, rather than assimilate a global status of the science. Perhaps this review, along with other studies synthesizing particular research areas, will form part of a developing literature on the recent emergence of ecology upon which a truly critical assessment of its distinctness as a science can be made.

The Americas

1

BRAZIL

José G. Tundisi

HISTORICAL BACKGROUND

Ecological studies in Brazil developed as a diversification of botany and zoology mainly after 1945. Prior to that time, ecology was primarily associated with practical problems in agriculture and medicine; its roots then are in an applied approach. Since 1943, the Department of Botany at São Paulo University has emphasized autecological research related to physiologic problems of the "cerrado" trees. In the Departments of Botany and Zoology of the Biosciences Institutes at São Paulo University, many courses in ecology were given for the bachelor's degree and as a postgraduate option.

At the same time, other institutions in São Paulo State and several regions of Brazil developed some connection with ecological studies. This was the case for many Faculties of Agronomy, which needed environmental data for their courses and research. Also, baccalaureate courses in sanitary engineering and research in public health extensively used ecological information. A baccalaureate course in ecology, as well as a postgraduate program, was established in 1969 at the University of Rio de Janeiro, but this was discontinued around 1972.

From 1970 onward, the new research groups interested in developing a broad ecological approach produced an increase in scientific activity in this field. This also accelerated the development of qualified personnel in ecology.

THE GROWTH AND DISTRIBUTION OF POPULATION IN BRAZIL

So that Brazil's needs in ecology may be understood and a background provided for further analysis of this problem, it is worth showing the main trends in the growth of population in Brazil. During the period from 1870 to 1970, Brazil's population increased tenfold, from 10 to 100 million; it is projected to reach some 230 million by the year 2000. The growth of urban population between 1940 and 1970 has been fivefold, from about 12 to 55 million, whereas the rural population increased only 60 percent, or from 25 to 40 million. Thus, more than 50 percent of the total population in Brazil is now concentrated in urban centers.

The population is distributed so that there are vast areas, notably in the northwest, with less than 1 inhabitant/km^2 and the large central area with less than 10 individuals/km^2. The eastern portion has densities largely of 20–100/km^2 with localized centers where the density exceeds 200/km^2.

This pattern of population growth and distribution is the cause of several problems with many ecological consequences. For example, the agglomeration of population in urban centers has considerably increased atmosphere and water pollution in the south and southeast, where the demand for energy for industrial purposes has also increased. This, in turn, produced several problems related to the building of reservoir systems, with consequences for both basic and applied ecology. The buildup of a large network of roads to improve communication and transportation among these centers was the other major cause of ecological change. Other consequences of industrial and agricultural developments and the concentration of people in urban centers are erosion of agricultural lands, propagation of endemic diseases, and large modifications of forest systems.

THE NATURAL REGIONS OF BRAZIL

Four large-scale vegetation types are recognized in Brazil: the Amazon tropical rain forest in northern Brazil; the "cerrado" mainly in central Brazil; the "caatinga" or semiarid vegetation of the northeast; and the Atlantic forest along the coast and the Araucaria forest in some areas in the south (Hueck 1966).

Two major hydrographic basins occur in Brazil: the Rio de La Plata basin, extending from true desert to the most populated areas in southern Brazil and northern Argentina (Bonetto 1975); and the Amazon basin, mostly covered by tropical rain forest. Sparse human populations and areas still relatively undisturbed by human influences or industrial activities are characteristic of the Amazon basin region (Sioli 1975).

PRESENT SITUATION OF ECOLOGICAL RESEARCH

Major Research Groups and Recent Research Developments

Since about 1970, four major groups have started programs of ecological research in Brazil. These are the following:

University of Campinas: In São Paulo State. Main research lines: theoretical ecology; biology of populations; plant ecophysiology; biological control of pests; chemical ecology; climatology; human ecology; ethology; and genetics and evolution of birds, insects, plants, and microorganisms.

Federal University of São Carlos: In São Paulo State. Main research lines: typology of lakes and reservoirs; basic and applied limnology; aquaculture; ecology of populations of insects and fishes; population dynamics; integrated control of pests; ecological genetics; and conservation of natural resources.

University of Brasilia: In the Federal District at Brasilia. Main research lines: plant and animal ecology; microclimatology; population ecology; and limnology.

Instituto Nacional de Pesquisas da Amazonia (INPA): At Manaus, Amazon State. Main research lines: nutrient cycles in forests; human ecology; control and water balance of small watershed; aquatic microbiology; and limnology.

Two other groups emerged in 1976–1977, the Federal University of Minas Gerais in Minas Gerais State and the Federal University of Rio Grande do Sul in Rio Grande do Sul State. Furthermore, many other research groups, interested primarily in zoological, botanical, and agricultural research, have developed an interest in ecological problems. These groups are at University of São Paulo and other institutions in Brazil (see List of University Departments below).

The main groups developing ecological research have, at present, relatively good scientific communication. Travel grants and opportunity for joint work with specific programs at each region have been increased recently as well.

"Cerrado" Ecology

Studies on "cerrado" ecology have been developed mainly at the University of São Paulo. The cerrado occupies more than 1.5 million km^2 extending from the southern tropics nearly to the equator. Several studies have been carried out since 1943. Ravitscher et al. (1943) provided background information on soil composition and vegetation; Ferri (1971) produced basic research on water economy and made a comparison with "caatinga" vegetation. Goodland (1971) analyzed oligotrophy and the role of aluminum in the cerrado, showing that aluminum in the cerrado soil may decrease the availability of phosphate, calcium, magnesium, nitrogen, potassium, and possibly other nutrients; he concluded that one of the principal effects of aluminum is mineral deficiency. Goodland and Pollard (1973) studied fertility gradients. Ferri (1977) summarized the existing information on the cerrado, indicating that most of the knowledge on this vegetation will be based on understanding water balance problems. Several contributions on soils (Alvim and Araujo 1952) developed as a result of ecophysiologic studies, and botanical, phytogeographic, and geographic information was reviewed by Rizzini (1976).

At the Second Symposium on the Cerrado, Laboriau (1966) summarized the state of knowledge from the research carried out to that date. It was concluded that a synecological approach was needed and that emphasis should be on phytosociological studies.

Recent studies by Coutinho (1976) have demonstrated the role of fire in the flowering of cerrado species. One of the main conclusions of this work is that fire or drought acts as a "synchronizing factor for flowering within the population, performing an important genetic evolutionary role for these species."

Recent studies along this line deal with atmospheric precipitation of certain mineral nutrients in an area of cerrado at São Paulo State, and the possible influence of fires on it. The input of nutrients by atmospheric precipitation seems to be highly significant for the mineral nutrition of the vegetation layer (Coutinho in press).

At present, renewed interest in cerrado ecology arises from the possibilities of exploitation of its considerable potential for agricultural use because of its location and topography. The Fourth Symposium on the Cerrado summarized the applied work in progress, as well as providing a background for use of the fundamental research.

TRAINING OF QUALIFIED PERSONNEL

The urgent need for the creation of programs for training qualified personnel in ecology at a postgraduate level has been recognized by many federal and state agencies that supply funds for research and grants for students at MsC. and Ph.D. levels. Thus, the Conselho Nacional de Desenvolvimento Científico e Technológico (CNPq-National Research Council) has begun to support postgraduate courses in ecology through grants for research and for postgraduate students. Also in São Paulo State, the FAPESP (Fundação de Amparo à Pesquisa do Estado de São Paulo-State Foundation) has provided financial support on the same basis. For applied work in ecology, the federal agency FINEP (Financiadora de Projetos) has been actively supportive since 1972.

An analysis of the four programs active since 1976 shows that the basic curriculum for training in ecology has developed mainly as a diversification of the research interests of the existing groups and the available professionals in the field. In general, the courses provide students with fundamental ecological theory, and a background in zoology, botany, and genetics; subjects to be incorporated include statistics, systems analysis, climatology, and biogeography. It is of significance that most of the present curricula have emphasized the importance of an ecosystem approach and have introduced methods of studying the functioning of tropical ecosystems. Also, the time dedicated to field and practical work shows that the present training in ecology is taking into account the need to produce scientists familiar with field problems in various regions of the country.

The present number of MsC. and Ph.D. students enrolled is approximately 150. This is insufficient for the needs of Brazil in ecology, but this number represents the first generation of ecologists trained in Brazil, with programs developed in Brazilian universities.

The prospects for employment of these ecologists include: (1) as research scientists in the universities and in new groups of ecology in areas of scientific and educational interests; (2) as advisors for industry and government agencies, contributing to the planning of environmental protection and the control of pollution and environmental stresses; and (3) as research workers in government institutes or private industries providing data in basic and applied ecology.

The development of undergraduate curricula in ecology began in 1969–1970. These courses were mainly options of the biological sciences or natural sciences degree. As a result, a considerable number of courses in taxonomy, zoology, and botany was included. At present, there are five BsC. courses in biology that have options in ecology. A curriculum for a BsC. program in ecology was studied at the Ministry of Education, but has not been put into operation yet. A BsC. degree on nature conservancy started in 1976 at UNESP (Rio Claro Faculty, São Paulo State).

An analysis of the existing research and the activities in the training centers shows that there are several lines of investigation in ecology with a reasonable degree of diversification. In many regions of Brazil, research problems are being tackled that have high scientific relevancy and that can have considerable impact on the existing knowledge of tropical ecosystems. However, certain basic connections are lacking. Ecology, as noted earlier, has been mainly derived from the natural sciences, agriculture, and medical groups in Brazil. Relationships with physics, chemistry, and biochemistry are poor. With the background given by the study of genetics, many relationships between genetics and ecology were developed. At present, there are several groups starting on projects in ecological genetics and related subjects, giving new dimensions to pure and applied work. Sanitary engineering and tropical medicine have relatively good connections with ecology, chiefly from earlier work on applied problems (Andrade and Freitas 1971). Studies on fish population dynamics (Santos 1968) provided many important relationships with ecological work in limnology and marine ecology.

At the University of São Paulo, the Institute of Geography is developing extensive research on climatology and general geographic aspects related to landscape modification and urban planning. A good deal of information also exists on the natural organization of landscape and on paleogeography. The use of computer sciences in connection with ecological problems is still embryonic. This means that a more dynamic approach is needed, in particular, the introduction of synecological studies that could provide more interfaces and help considerably in the development of ecological problems.

Historically, ecology in Brazil used existing botanical and zoological information to a considerable extent. As a consequence, the traditional division between plant and animal ecology still persists with very little exchange between the two approaches. This has resulted in the development of two main intellectual directions in ecological work. The need for an integrated effort, mainly in terrestrial ecology, has been emphasized in recent suggestions for improvement of the field. Possibly, the postgraduate courses now in progress will be a useful tool in concentrating efforts to introduce a synecologic approach and to produce further scientific advances.

MAJOR THRUSTS IN THE FIELD

When the development of ecology in Brazil is considered, it must be stressed that few conceptual advances have been made. Ecological research is still, in many cases, in a descriptive state. This is a result of the lack of knowledge in the basic botany, zoology, and biology of the diverse and complex communities that occur in the Neotropical region. However, some major advances were made in certain problems, and these are worth stressing, namely, development of the refugia theory; studies on primary production of phytoplankton of aquatic communities; introduction of synecologic approach in limnology; and synthesis on the phytogeographic and climatic regions of Brazil.

Development of the Refugia Theory

Vanzolini (1970) and Vanzolini and Williams (1970), in studying the geographic distribution of species of lizards and correlating this information with paleogeographic and paleoclimatologic data, determined regions of refugia of fauna. Haffer (1969), working with Amazonian birds, came to similar conclusions. Studying the geographic patterns of evolution and differentiation of species of Neotropical Lepidoptera (Nymphalidae) and using climatological, palynologic, and botanical information, Brown (1977) proposed thirty-eight forest refuges and fifty principal forest centers of evolution.

The development of the refugia theory produced many areas of interface with paleoclimatology, botany, zoogeography, and theoretical ecology; its development can be considered a major achievement in terrestrial ecology in Brazil. There are still many problems to be solved, but the scientific information resulting from this work gave a strong basis for further studies with an interdisciplinary effort.

The location of these refuges based on extensive examination of zoological data and ecological information also gave an important background for theories in conservation ecology, indicating the need for preservation of the primary habitats constituting biotic and ecological reserves. Recent work in the Amazon region proposes the establishment of ecological reserves corresponding broadly to areas of forest refuges.

During 1978–1980, there were intensive efforts along this line that resulted in the consolidation of the refugia theory. Interdisciplinary work with ecologists and geographers produced considerable information on the geographic definition of regions in the Neotropical forest, which has retained a relative ecological stability and continuity during the climatic fluctuations of the past 20,000 years.

Relationships among climate, topography, soils, vegetation, and processes of regional biotic evolution were used to develop two separate approaches, one genetic and the other paleo-ecological (Brown 1979; Brown and Ab'Saber 1979).

Studies on Primary Production of Phytoplankton of Aquatic Ecosystems

The studies in this field started with work by Teixeira (1963) and by Teixeira and Tundisi (1967). Until 1960, no effort was made to study the primary production of marine or lacustrine ecosystems. The research carried out at the Lagunar region of Cananeia (25° south latitude), an estuarine environment amid extensive mangrove vegetation, produced a major advance in the understanding of primary production of phytoplankton and the limiting and controlling factors. Particular attention was given to the basic aspects of nutrient limitation and recycling, light/photosynthesis responses of the phytoplankton community (Teixeira 1969), and comparative problems in estuarine, coastal, and oceanic waters (Tundisi et al. 1978). This research provided the opportunity to develop many connections in, for example, culture work in phytoplankton, nutritional studies of certain species in pure culture, enrichment experiments, and biossay techniques (Teixeira and Vieira

1976). Investigations on the structure of aquatic ecosystems, seasonal cycle, and succession of aquatic communities also resulted from this work. Subsequently, Tundisi (In press *a*) made revisions on several ecological aspects of the Langunar region of Cananeia, the nutrient cycle, and the seasonal cycle of events in terms of coupling climatological/hydrological and biological factors.

Synecologic Approach in Limnology

Limnological work on the Amazon river and lakes has been carried out extensively by the Max Planck Institute in collaboration with INPA (Junk 1970; Schmidt 1973). Other limnological contributions were made mainly by the Department of Zoology, Biosciences Institute, University of São Paulo (Zago 1976). Integrated limnological work, started in 1971 in southern Brazil, is another important development in ecology. A program of research in the shallow turbulent Broa Reservoir in São Paulo State was set up to produce a complete descriptive and dynamic study of this ecosystem and to provide a scientific basis for the training of personnel in ecology (Tundisi 1977; Tundisi et al. 1977). This research, now in its seventh year, has had several results related to the typology of lakes and reservoirs in Brazil, and how limiting factors function in lakes and reservoirs and the effects of these factors on the communities. Figure 1.1 shows the Broa ecosystem model as it is in the present state of knowledge. This model also gave background data for the introduction of systems analysis into Brazilian ecology.

This synecologic approach in limnology reached maximum development during 1979, when a project on the typology of reservoirs was developed (Tundisi In press *b*). Fifty-two reservoirs in São Paulo State (southern Brazil) were investigated by means of the same methodology and with simultaneous collection of material. The typology of reservoirs introduced a new approach to limnology and ecology in Brazil, mainly through the large-scale comparison of ecosystems and multivariate analysis. Also, some specific problems in terms of the evolution of reservoirs (Matsumura-Tundisi et al. In press), and circulation problems and their biological effects (Arcifa and Froelich. In press), were studied. Development of limnological research in several lake systems in Brazil progressed relatively well in 1978–1979 (Tundisi et al. In press).

Synthesis of the Phytogeographic and Climatic Regions of Brazil

Ab'Saber (1971), after several years of field observations and work on geomorphology and the natural organization of landscape, gave an extensive review on this subject. In connection with a series of paleogeographic and geomorphologic studies, he reconstituted the earlier climatic and vegetation types from 13,000 to 18,000 years ago (Ab'Saber 1977). A synthesis on present natural regions and their reconstitution opens a series of interfaces in

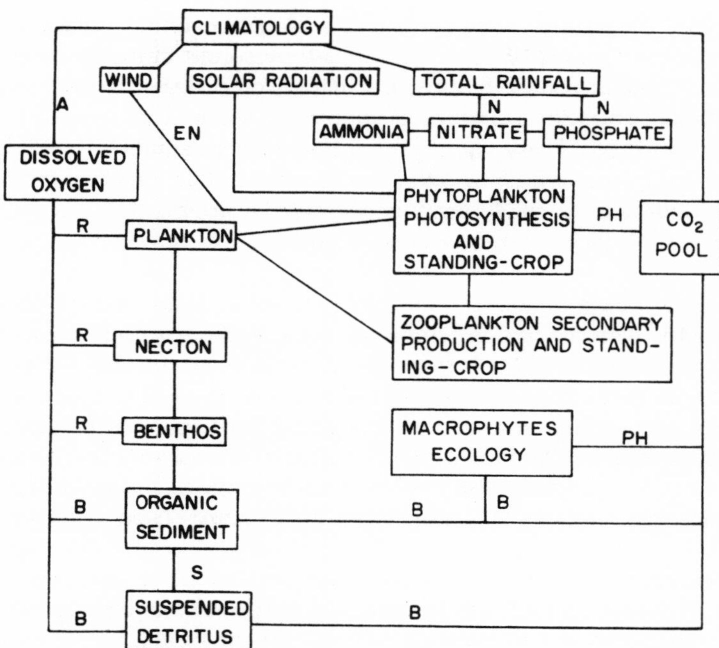

Figure 1.1 The Broa Ecosystem Model (from Tundisi, 1977)

A = AERATION
R = RESPIRATION
S = SEDIMENTATION
PH = PHOTOSYNTHESIS
EN = WIND EFFECT ON NUTRIENT INPUT
N = NUTRIENT INPUT THROUGH RAINFALL
B = BACTERIAL DECOMPOSITION

many directions, producing a considerable advance in understanding terrestrial ecological problems. Also, this synthesis gave the basis for creating the national park and reserve system and produced a scientific background for establishing conservation units in Brazil.

Recently, the special secretary for environment (SEMA) has launched a program of twenty-one ecological stations in Brazil, taking into account representative ecosystems. A research program was also established to provide a framework of comparative ecological studies in these stations (Tundisi 1979).

PERSPECTIVES FOR FUTURE DEVELOPMENTS

Problems to Be Solved

Even when considering the recent research achievements and the formal training of qualified scientists, some fundamental problems still remain to be solved.

Qualified Personnel: The number of ecologists needed in Brazil is considerably greater than the number of qualified personnel currently operating in this field. There are only a few interdisciplinary groups of ecologists and other scientists working with a synecologic approach within a framework of broad ecological research. Presently, not more than thirty scientists at the Ph.D. level are working in ecology. Even with the efforts toward the qualification of more professionals, the scientific production and development of programs will suffer from this lack for some time to come.

Methods: By tradition, probably because most of the present generation of ecologists were trained in temperate regions, the methods used are very much those developed for research in those regions. There have been few advances in techniques in ecology specifically in Brazil. Because the subject has been approached from various disciplines, such as medicine, agriculture, sanitary engineering, and the natural sciences, there is a variety of techniques, which were not properly discussed and interchanged. This diversification of methodology imposes some restrictions on the comparison of results.

Publications: There are no specialized publications in ecology in Brazil that could serve as a synthesis of work in progress. All the papers published in ecology are scattered in international journals or local journals of general scientific interest.

International Cooperation: There are few programs involving international cooperation in progress. Major cooperation is among scientists within their individual plans, but there is little cooperation at an institutional level. Only at certain universities and institutes, such as INPA and Max Planck Institute, does this occur, but such cooperation is insufficient to provide good scientific contact with the international community working in ecology.

Scientific Meetings: Few scientific meetings on ecology have been held. The introduction of a section in ecology at the yearly meetings of the Sociedade Brasileira para o Progresso da Ciência (SBPC) was an important achievement. Clearly, there is a need for more exchange of information among the groups working in Brazil. The recent creation of a Brazilian Society of Ecology may help to develop the needed communication among the ecologists in Brazil.

Financial Support: Support to the existing programs is relatively good. Federal and state agencies, as well as private industries, are giving financial help to pure scientific research and applied problems in ecology. The continuation of this support in the future is basic to the development of the field.

Regions to Be Studied

A number of important systems in Brazil need to be studied through an integrated, synecologic approach.

Aquatic Ecology: natural lakes of the Amazon River; River Doce Valley lakes; natural lakes and terrestrial interactions at the Pantanal (Mato Grosso State); reservoirs in the south and the northeast; estuaries and coastal waters.

Terrestrial Ecology: ecology of rain forest in the Amazon; ecology of semiarid vegetation; ecology of cerrado; ecology of "Floresta Atlantica"; ecology of Araucaria forest in southern Brazil.

Basic Research

Numerous perspectives for future research in tropical ecosystems were given by Farnworth and Golley (1974). Many of the research lines proposed by these authors could be developed in Brazil by taking into account the problems considered, as well as the existing background information.

Intensification of Synecologic Studies: Topics for study should include comparative aspects of energy flux and maximum rates of production in terrestrial and aquatic ecosystems; recycling of nutrients, and species succession in communities; interactions of climatological and ecological studies, such as cycles of organic production, biomass, and climatological trends. In parallel with this synecological approach, autecological studies should be expanded, mainly regarding mechanisms of operation at the interspecific and intraspecific level. Competition, predator-prey relationships, and biological cycles of the more representative species of the community are basic, important problems to be tackled.

Stability and Diversity: There are few investigations on the problem of stability and diversity of ecosystems in Brazil. This line of research should develop bearing in mind the possible effects of pollution and environmental stresses on organisms and communities.

Taxonomy: Many surveys of the flora and fauna in Brazil have been carried out. Taxonomic studies should progress in integration with geographic distribution and evolutionary problems.

Theoretical Ecology: Concentration on theoretical ecology including the further analysis of experimental findings and fieldwork would be of considerable interest. This could improve the state of knowledge of structure and function of tropical ecosystems, as well as producing original contributions on systems analysis of these ecosystems based on experimental data.

Applied Ecology

Preservation and conservation of natural resources are important subjects in the present development of Brazil. Pollution problems in the major cities are aggravating, even when measures are reinforced by law. Research in applied ecology could consider emphasizing the following problems:

Pollution: Important areas for study include air, water, and soil pollution; pollution problems coupled with utilization of water for irrigation; effects of pollutants on species and communities of aquatic and terrestrial ecosystems; and effects of thermal pollution on aquatic organisms. (Developments in 1979 in the study of air pollution include the start of research in suspended particles and chemical analysis of air pollutants by a research group at São Paulo University.)

Eutrophication: Effects of eutrophication on aquatic (freshwater and marine) ecosystems and typology of lakes and reservoirs in relation to eutrophication stages are two areas in which research would be valuable.

Water Resources: Topics of interest include the preservation and multiple use of reservoirs and water resources; quantitative aquaculture; and research on agro-ecosystems.

Studies in Human Ecology: The concentration of more than 50 percent of the population of Brazil in urban centers, mainly in the south, has produced many problems concerned with the quality of life in these centers. The development of this line of research could help in the planning of these major cities, as well as giving useful information on the basic sanitary and health conditions of the population. These studies also could provide the background for predicting the results of human activity in tropical ecosystems.

Conservation Ecology

The effects of rapid economic growth in some areas of Brazil have produced, as mentioned, extensive ecological alterations. For example, the rate of deforestation in Brazil has been accelerated in the last few years (Ferri 1974). Several measures have been taken to protect areas from damage and to introduce ecological planning in the process of development. These were: the creation of Secretaria do Meio Ambiente (SEMA) (Special Agency for the Environment); an increase of controls on industries that severely polluted air, water, and soil; an increase in the number of national parks and national protected areas; and the stimulation of ecological education at the primary and high school levels, as well as the support of ecology programs at the BsC. level.

These efforts need expansion and have to be continued by trained ecologists. To improve programs of environmental conservation, there needs to be protection of endangered species; research programs to evaluate effects of internal migrations and tourism on environmental degradation; and zonation of the country into areas suitable for production of energy, those subjected to heavy pollution, and others to be preserved. Continuous monitoring of polluted areas and basic research on pollution effects are important measures that should be taken as part of a broad general plan of conservation ecology for Brazil.

As in many other countries, an "environmental movement" is now in progress in Brazil. Societies of ecology and the Nature Conservancy are being created in several states and cities and are actively engaged in popular programs of environmental protection of regional or local ecosystems. The increasing social importance of this movement, at least in the more developed areas of the country, could be a tool to produce conservation programs on a scientific basis.

Recent Developments in Conservation Ecology in Brazil (1978–1980)

During 1978–1980, two major problems were the object of intensive discussion at universities in Brazil and in conservation societies as well, the energy problem and the development of the Amazon basin.

There is at present an intensive program to develop the production of alcohol as a substitute for gasoline, and the number of new plants to process sugar cane has increased considerably. Because of this, pollution problems resulting from discharges into the soil, rivers, and reservoirs will also increase. The introduction of two nuclear energy plants on the coast has been the object of many discussions, with local and national conservation societies taking a firm stand against the plants.

The Amazon basin is, at present, the largest undisturbed forest ecosystem in the world. Its area of approximately 7×10^6 km^2 occupies more than 35 percent of South America. The basic problem in the development of the basin is the lack of information about its natural resources and the interaction of terrestrial and aquatic ecosystems. A series of papers published in *Interciencia* (1978) deals with several problems in the Amazon basin.

One of the main points in this discussion is the model of development. As opposed to large development plans, there are propositions of small-scale, self-sustaining communities that take into account local knowledge and produce less harm to the environment. The Brazilian Society for Progress in

Science has recently produced a document representing the position of its 16,000 members on the Amazon basin problem (Comissão de Estudos de Problemas Ambietais 1980).

In recent years, the whole discussion in Brazil, in terms of conservation, has been centered around the dilemma between conservation and development and the strategies to deal with each.

INSTITUTIONS AND UNIVERSITY DEPARTMENTS

Institutions

Research institutes, museums, and government agencies with publications on ecological problems and with research interests in ecology are the following: Museu Nacional, Rio de Janeiro; Museu de Zoologia da Universidade de São Paulo; Museu Goeldi, Belém; Fundação Zoobotânica, Rio Grande do Sul; Museu de Biologia Prof. Mello-Leitão, Santa Teresa, ES.; Departamento de Zoologia, Universidade Federal do Paraná; Departamento de Botânica, Universidade de São Paulo, Instituto de Biociências; Departamento de Zoologia, Universidade de São Paulo, Instituto de Biociências; Departamento de Hidráulica e Saneamento, Universidade de São Paulo, EESC; Secretaria Especial do Meio Ambiente, Ministério de Interior; Instituto Agronômico de Campinas; Instituto Biológico, São Paulo; Instituto Botânico, São Paulo; Instituto Florestal, São Paulo; Instituto Oswaldo Cruz, Rio de Janeiro; Instituto Brasileiro de Desenvolvimento Florestal; Fundação Brasileira para a Conservação da Natureza; Associação Brasileira para a Prevenção da Poluição do Ar.; Associação Gaúcha para a Proteção dos Ambientes Naturais; Sociedade Ornitológica Mineira; Instituto Butantan, São Paulo; Centro de Pesquisas "René Rachou," Belo Horizonte; Instituto Evandro Chagas, Belém; Instituto Oceanográfico, Departamento de Oceanografia Biológica, Universidade de São Paulo; Instituto de Geografia, Universidade de São Paulo; Projecto RADAMBRASIL, Belém; Projecto Cabo Frio; CEPEC/CEPLAC, Itabuna, Bahia; Secretaria de Ciência e Technologia do Estado de Minas Gerais, CETEC; CETESB, São Paulo; and Fundação Estadual de Engenharia do Meio Ambiente, Rio de Janeiro.

Universities

University departments and institutes with integrated programs and postgraduate courses in ecology are: University of Campinas (UNICAMP)—Departments of Zoology, Biology, and Botany; Federal University at São Carlos—Department of Biological Sciences; University of Brasilia—Department of Biology; Federal University Rio Grande do Sul—Department of Zoology; and Instituto Nacional de Pesquisa da Amazonia (INPA) of the

University of Amazonas. A Department of Ecology was recently created at the Biosciences Institute, University of São Paulo.

JOURNALS

International

International journals currently used in Brazil as support for research in ecology and related subjects include: *Ecology, Ecological Monographs, Oecologie, Limnology and Oceanography, Freshwater Biology, Bulletin of Marine Science, Journal of Ecology, Journal of Animal Ecology, Botanical Reviews, Biological Reviews, Physiologia Plantarum, Amazoniana, Journal of Entomology, Journal of Experimental Zoology, Journal of Applied Ecology, Archiv für Hydrobiologie, Australian Journal of Ecology, Canadian Journal of Zoology, Oecologia Aquática, Hydrobiologia, Oikos, Aquatic Sciences and Fisheries Abstracts, Archives of Microbiology, Bulletin of the Fisheries Research Board of Canada, Canadian Journal of Botany, Cahiers Orstom: Serie Hydrobiologique, Ekologia Polska, Hydrobiologica Journal, International Revue Der Gesanten Hydrobiol, Japanese Journal of Limnology, Journal of Experimental Botany, Journal of Phycology, Marine Biology, New Phytologist, Hydrobiologia,* and *Entomological Review.*

National

Scientific publications with data on the ecology of Brazil are: *Amazoniana, Acta Amazonica, Biotropica, Tropical Ecology, Revista de Biologia Tropical,* and *Boletim do Instituto Oceanográfico, Universidade de São Paulo, Série Oceanografia Biológica.*

ACKNOWLEDGMENTS

Most of this review is based on a document prepared for the National Research Council of Brazil (CNPq) that contains an analysis of the situation of ecology in Brazil up to December 1977. To this document, the members of the Advisory Committee contributed suggestions, criticism, and discussion. These members were J. C. Mello Carvalho, Dalcy O. Albuquerque, Dardano A. Lima, and Moacyr Maestri.

Dr. K. S. Brown discussed many central ideas with me on several occasions and provided information and constructive criticism on the present situation of ecology in Brazil.

My own papers cited in the text were the result of research supported by the Conselho Nacional de Desenvolvimento Científico e Technológico (CNPq), FAPESP, Organization of American States, CETEC, CAPES,

Japan Society for the Promotion of Science, and the Brazilian Academy of Sciences.

REFERENCES CITED

Ab'Saber, A. 1971. A organização das apisagens inter e subtropicais brasileiras. In *III Simpósio sobre o Cerrado,* ed. M. Ferri. Edgard Blücher and Editora Universidade de São Paulo. (Describes and discusses the natural regions of Brazil on the basis on field observations, paleogeographic, and paleobotanical information.)

______. 1977. Espaços ocupados pela expansão dos climas secos na América do Sul, por ocasião dos períodos glaciais Quaternários. *Inst. Geogr. USP. Paleoclimas,* vol. 3. (Discusses the paleogeographic and paleoecological landscapes of South America in the Quaternary.)

Andrade, M. R. and J. R. Freitas. 1971. Observações ecológicas sobre o *Australorbis glabratus* em Belo Horizonte, Minas Gerais. I. Densidade e vitalidade dos caramujos (Pulmonata, Planorbidae). *Rev. Bras. Biol.* 21:419–433. (Ecological observations on *Australorbis glabratus* with remarks on life cycle, distribution, and concentration of individuals in selected environments.)

Alvim, P. T. and W. A. Araujo. 1952. El suelo como fator ecológico en el desarollo de la vegetacion en el centro-oeste del Brasil. *Turrialba* 2:153–160. (Discusses the importance of soil types as substrata in the "cerrado" of Central Brazil.)

Arcifa, M. A. and Froelich. In press. Circulation patterns and their influence on physical, chemical and biological conditions in nine reservoirs in Southern Brazil. *Verh. Verein Int. Lim.* (This paper analyzes the influence of thermal stratification and destratification on the vertical distribution of chemical factors, such as dissolved ions, inorganic nutrients, and dissolved oxygen, and the communities. It relates circulation patterns with nutrient cycling and primary production levels.)

Bonetto, A. 1975. Hydrologic regime of the Paraná river and its influence on ecosystems. In *Coupling of land and water systems,* ed. A. D. Hasler, pp. 175–197. (A description of the hydrobiological and ecological conditions of the Paraná system with data on water chemistry, communities, and general ecological relationships.)

Brown, K. S. Jr. 1977. Centros de evolução, refúgios quaternários e conservação de patrimônios genéticos na região neotropical: padrões de diferenciação em Ithomiinae (Lepidoptera: Nymphalidae). *Acta Amazônica* 7:75–138. [This paper analyzes the geographic patterns of evolution and differentiation, under selective pressure of Mullerian mimicry, of species of Neotropical Helicomiini and Ithomiinae (Lepidoptera: Nymphalidae). It indicates 50 principal forest centers of evolution and endemism and 38 refuge areas. Suggestions for maintenance of biological reserves based on these refuges are given.]

______. 1979. Ecologia geografica e evolução nas florestas neotropicais. D.Sc. thesis, Unicamp. (This thesis deals with geographic ecology and evolution in the Neotropical forests. It is a synthesis of the genetic and paleoecological approaches to the problem of definition of regions in the Neotropical forests that retained a relative ecological stability and continuity during climatic fluctuations of the past 20,000 years. The genetic analysis was based on regional patterns of differentiation of the wing color patterns in two groups of aposematic Neotropical forest butterflies, Heliconiini and Ithimiinae (Nymphalidae). Information about local populations and ecological conditions was obtained during 14 years of fieldwork.)

——— and A. Ab'Saber. 1979. Ice-age forest refuges and evolution in the Neotropics: correlation of paleoclimatological, geomorphological and pedological data with modern biological endemism. *Inst. Geogr. USP, Paleoclimas* 5:1–30. (This paper is a synthesis correlating paleoclimatological, geomorphological, and pedological data with biological data, showing that the centers of biotic endemism evolved in harmony with local conditions during periods of dry climates in the recent past.)

Comissão de Estudos de Problemas Ambientais. Sociedade Brasileira para o Progresso da Ciência (SBPC) 1980. A SBPC e a Amazonia. *Cienc. Cult.* (São Paulo) 32:246–251. (This document was prepared by a group of ecologists with an analysis of the conservation problems in the Amazon basin and giving perspectives for future developments. It gives a critical analysis of the large-scale projects and presents several propositions for conservation, rational exploitation in agroecosystems and fisheries, and maintenance of national parks and reserves.)

Coutinho, L. M. 1976. Contribuição ao conhecimento do papel ecológico das queimadas na floração de espécies do cerrado. D.Sc. thesis, Dep. Botânica, Universidade de São Paulo. (This paper contributes toward clarifying the ecological role played by fires in the flowering of cerrado species. The main factors studied were air temperature, recycling of nutrients, primary production, and succession stages. A discussion on the present concepts of "cerrado" is included.)

———. In press. Ecological aspects of fire in the cerrado. III. The atmospheric precipitation of mineral nutrients. *Rev. Bras. Bot.* (The paper deals with atmospheric precipitation of nutrients in the "cerrado" vegetation and its importance on nutrient cycling. Input of nutrients by atmospheric precipitation is highly significant for the mineral nutrition of vegetation.)

Farnworth, E. G. and F. B. Golley. 1974. *Fragile ecosystems. Evaluation of research and applications in the neotropics.* Berlin-Heidelberg-New York; Springer-Verlag. (The authors present an extensive analysis of the research problems and future perspectives for tropical regions.)

Ferri, M. 1971. *III Simpósio sobre o cerrado.* São Paulo: Edgard Blücher and Ed. Universidade de São Paulo. (This symposium deals with several aspects of botanical, autecological, and physiologic work carried out in the cerrado mainly from 1966 to 1971.)

———. 1974. Information about the consequences of accelerated deforestation in Brazil. Proceedings of the First International Congress of Ecology, pp. 355–360. Wageningen, Netherlands: Centre for Agricultural Publishing and Documentation. (This work describes the ecological effects of deforestation in Brazil.)

———. 1977. Ecologia dos cerrados. In *IV Simpósio sobre o cerrado: bases para a utilização agropecúaria,* ed. M. G. Ferri, pp. 15–33. São Paulo: Editora Universidade de São Paulo/Itatiaia. (This is an extensive review of the ecological problems of the cerrado studied up to 1977.)

Goodland, R. J. A. 1971. Oligotrofismo e alumínio no cerrado. In *III Simpósio sobre o cerrado,* ed. M. G. Ferri, pp. 44–60. São Paulo: Edgard Blücher and Editora Universidade de São Paulo. (An analysis of the role of aluminum and oligotrophy in the "cerrado" is presented.)

______ and R. Pollard. 1973. The Brazilian cerrado vegetation: a fertility gradient. *J. Ecol.* 61:219–224. (The physiognomic gradient of cerrado vegetation from stands of small, widely scattered trees through "orchard" to well-developed woodland in central Brazil was found to parallel a soil fertility gradient.)

Haffer, J. 1969. Speciation in Amazonian forest birds. *Science* 165:131–137. (The author discusses the differentiation of Amazonian birds from the refuges and determined areas of refuges based on climatological and topographical data.)

Hueck, K. 1966. *Die wälder Sudamerikas. Zusanmentzung und Wirtschaftliche Bedentung.* Stuttgart. (A descriptive account and ecological observations on the main vegetation types of South America is presented.)

Interciencia. 1978. Amazon basin ecosystems. 3(4):193–263. (In this issue, eight articles on natural science aspects of the Amazon basin were published. The articles discuss the problems of origin and distribution of rains, origin and evolution of the Amazon flora, nutrient cycling, soils, agroecosystems, and phytochemistry. A review article on the future of the Amazon basin is also included.)

Junk, W. J. 1970. Investigations on the ecology and production biology of the "floating meadows" (Paspalo-Echinochlaetun) on the middle Amazon. I. The floating vegetation and its ecology. *Amazoniana* 2:449–495. (The author describes the ecological interactions and mechanisms of production in the "floating meadows" of the Amazon River.)

Laboriau, L. G. 1966. Revisão da situação da ecologia vegetal nos cerrados. *An. Acad. Bras. Ciênc.* 38, Suppl.:5–38. (This supplement presents an extensive analysis of the status of the ecology of the cerrado up to 1966, with considerations on autecologic and synecologic studies, and future perspectives for research.

Matsumura-Tundisi, T., K. Hino, and S. M. Claro. In press. Limnological studies in 23 reservoirs in southern Brazil. *Verh. Verein. Int. Lim.* (This paper discusses comparative limnological research carried out during 1979 in 23 reservoirs in São Paulo State. It deals with problems of stratification and destratification processes, vertical distribution of nutrients, chlorophyll *a,* and the distribution of different groups of zooplankton in connection with chemical and biological characteristics of the reservoirs. Primary production processes and recycling of nutrients are also discussed.)

Ravitscher, F. K., M. G. Ferri, and M. Rachid. 1943. Profundidade dos solos e vegetação em campos cerrados do Brasil meridional. *An. Acad. Bras. Ciênc.* 15:267–294. (A description is given of the soil depth, root systems of the cerrado plants, and list of species representative of the cerrado of southern Brazil.)

Rizzini, C. T. 1976. *Tratado de fitogeografia do Brasil: aspectos ecológicos.* São Paulo: Editora da Universidade de São Paulo. (The author discusses the ecological problems in the study of distribution and characteristics of vegetation in Brazil. He describes phytosociological and floristic problems associated with distribution, giving the main floristic systems of Brazil.)

Santos, E. P. 1968. Estudo populacional do goete (*Cynoscion petranus* Ribeiro, 1915). *Bol. Inst. Ocean. Univ. São Paulo* 17:17–31. (These studies on population dynamics and population distribution of a species of coastal marine fish develop certain relationships with ecological information.)

Schmidt, G. W. 1973. Primary production of phytoplankton in three types of Amazonian waters. III. Primary productivity of phytoplankton in a tropical food plain lake of central Amazonian, Lago do Castanho, Brazil. *Amazoniana* 4:379–404. (This presents studies on the seasonal cycle of primary production of phytoplankton in a clear-water lake in the Amazon region, with an account of the ecological conditions, limiting, and controlling factors.)

Sioli, H. 1975. Amazon tributaries and drainage basins. In *Coupling of land and water systems,* ed. A. D. Hasler, pp. 199–213. Ecological Studies Vol. 10. Berlin-Heidelberg-New York: Springer-Verlag. (This review on the river ecology in the Amazon region includes remarks on the interactions between terrestrial/aquatic ecosystems and drainage basins.)

Teixeira, C. 1963. Relative rates of photosynthesis and standing-stock of the netplankton and nannoplankton. *Bol. Inst. Ocean. Univ. São Paulo* 13:53–60. (This study compares the contribution of each fraction of phytoplankton to the total standing-stock and primary production.)

———. 1969. Estudos sobre algunas características do fitoplancton da região Lagunar de Cananéia e seu potencial fotossintético. Ph.D. thesis, Universidade São Paulo. (The thesis offers findings on the light/photosynthesis response of the phytoplankton community, primary production, and ecological conditions in a mangrove swamp of the estuarine type.)

——— and J. Tundisi. 1967. Primary production of phytoplankton in equatorial waters. *Bull. Mar. Sci.* 17:884–891. (The authors make a comparison of the rates of primary production and qualitative and quantitative composition of the phytoplankton at a series of stations from the Amazon area to 10° north latitude. They remark on ecological conditions and selective effects on the phytoplankton composition.)

——— and A. A. H. Vieira. 1976. Nutrient experiment using *Phaeodactylum tricornutum* as an assay organism. *Bol. Inst. Ocean. Univ. São Paulo* 25:29–42. (Experimental research was carried out in tropical oligotrophic waters using a strain from coastal waters of Brazil *Phaeodactylum tricornutum* cultivated in pure culture.)

Tundisi, J. 1977. Produção primária, "standing-stock," fracionamento do fitoplancton e fatores ecológicos em ecossistema lacustre artificial (Represa do Broa). D.Sc. thesis, Universidade de São Carlos. (The ecological factors, the seasonal cycle of primary production and standing-stock of phytoplankton, and zooplankton seasonal succession were studied in a shallow turbulent reservoir, Broa Reservoir.)

———. 1979. Programa Integrado de Pesquisas nas Estações ecológicas para o Brasil. *Interfacies: Escritos e Documentos.* No. 2:1–17. (This paper proposes a program of research for the ecological stations of SEMA in Brazil.)

———. In press *a.* Ecological studies at the lagunar region of Cananeia: a review. *Bol. Inst. Ocean. Univ. São Paulo.* (The author describes and discusses scientific

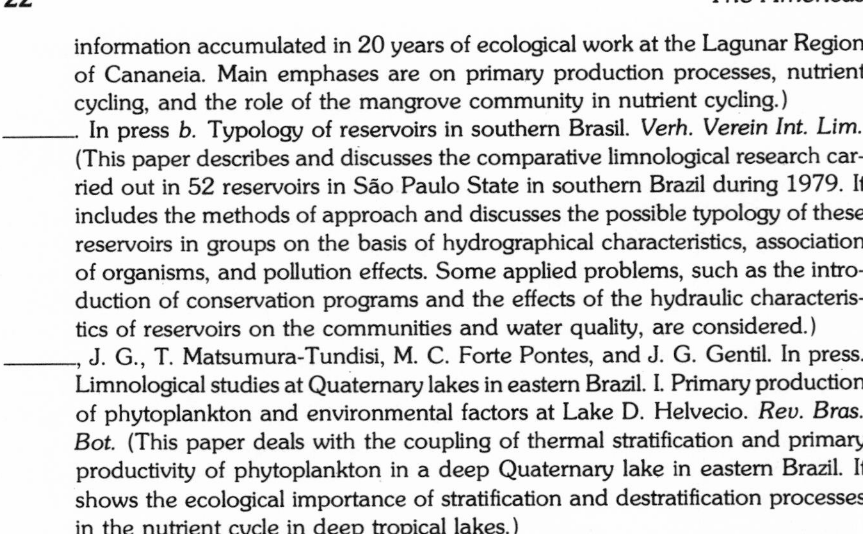

information accumulated in 20 years of ecological work at the Lagunar Region of Cananeia. Main emphases are on primary production processes, nutrient cycling, and the role of the mangrove community in nutrient cycling.)

———. In press *b*. Typology of reservoirs in southern Brasil. *Verh. Verein Int. Lim.* (This paper describes and discusses the comparative limnological research carried out in 52 reservoirs in São Paulo State in southern Brazil during 1979. It includes the methods of approach and discusses the possible typology of these reservoirs in groups on the basis of hydrographical characteristics, association of organisms, and pollution effects. Some applied problems, such as the introduction of conservation programs and the effects of the hydraulic characteristics of reservoirs on the communities and water quality, are considered.)

———, J. G., T. Matsumura-Tundisi, M. C. Forte Pontes, and J. G. Gentil. In press. Limnological studies at Quaternary lakes in eastern Brazil. I. Primary production of phytoplankton and environmental factors at Lake D. Helvecio. *Rev. Bras. Bot.* (This paper deals with the coupling of thermal stratification and primary productivity of phytoplankton in a deep Quaternary lake in eastern Brazil. It shows the ecological importance of stratification and destratification processes in the nutrient cycle in deep tropical lakes.)

———, M. T. Tundisi, O. Rocha, J. G. Gentil, and N. Nakamoto. 1977. Primary production, standing-stock of phytoplankton and ecological factors in a shallow tropical reservoir. (Represa do Broa, São Carlos, Brasil). *Sem. Medio Ambiente y Represas* 1:138–172. (This offers a summary of the seasonal cycle of primary production, climatological and hydrological factors, and the limiting factors in primary production in a shallow reservoir.)

———, C. Teixeira, T. Matsumura-Tundisi, M. B. Kutner, and L. Kinoshita. 1978. Plankton studies in a mangrove environment. IX. Comparative studies with oligotrophic coastal waters. *Rev. Bras. Biol.* 38:301–320. (This is a comparative ecological study of the primary production rates, assimilation rates, nutrient cycling, and environmental factors in an estuarine region of the mangrove type and a coastal region.)

Vanzolini, P. E. 1970. Zoologia sistemática, geografia e a origem das espécies. *Inst. Geogr. Univ. São Paulo, Série Teses e Monografias* 3:1–56. (The author discusses the relationships between zoological and geographic work, gives examples of geographic distribution of terrestrial vertebrates, and emphasizes the importance of zoogeographic studies for the development of theories of evolution of the tropical fauna. He gives an indication of refuge areas mainly in the Amazon region, based on zoological data.)

——— and E. E. Williams. 1970. South American anoles: the geographic differentiation and evolution of the *Anolys chrysolepis* species group (Fauria, Iguanidae). *Arg. Zool. São Paulo* 19:1–298. (These authors discuss ecological data on the geographic distribution of the *Anolys chrysolepis* groups and propose refuge areas.)

Zago, M. S. A. 1976. The planktonic cladocera (Crustacea) and aspects of the eutrophication of Americana reservoir, Brazil. *Bol. Zool. São Paulo* 1:105–145. (This is an account of the seasonal distribution of cladocera and the ecological conditions related to eutrophication in a reservoir in São Paulo State.)

2

COSTA RICA

Luis A. Fournier-Origgi

INTRODUCTION

Ecology as a science is of recent origin, but the history of scientific thought demonstrates that long ago many philosophers and scientists became aware of the importance of environmental knowledge and that judicious management of natural resources advanced the welfare of mankind.

In Costa Rica, the situation is quite similar to that of other regions. By the time of discovery by Columbus in 1502, there were approximately 27,000 inhabitants living in dynamic balance with the natural environment. They practiced a shifting cultivation of a few crops, such as beans, casava, corn, cotton, and some fruits; their diet was supplemented with proteins from fish and game. With the arrival of the Spanish Conquistadores, the environment began to change. Everything they saw, especially the luxuriant tropical forests, presented new and threatening challenges, something to be conquered and annihilated. The majority of the Conquistadores came from the arid regions of the Castillian plateau and from Extremadura where trees and forests were rare sights; for those from other parts of Spain, forests had long ago given way to orderly rows of cultivated fields and orchards. Not surprisingly, the famous Spanish naturalist Gonzalo Fernández de Oviedo referred to the rain forests of America as "El mare magno e oculto," the great and dark sea. He was overwhelmed by the immensity of the individual trees and the seemingly endless forests.

For many years, the Spanish concept of treatment of tropical forests as something to be cleared away had little effect in Costa Rica because the population increase was slow and there was always available land for agriculture. This idyllic balance between man and his environment was soon to change. At the beginning of this century, the population of Costa Rica was less than three hundred thousand; it jumped to nearly two million in less than eighty years and is predicted to double again within the next twenty-five years. In 1900, 90 percent of the country was covered by forests; today, that area has been reduced to 35 percent. Therefore, it is really in the last decade that we have started to focus attention on the environment and finally realized that something must be done in order to avert an irreversible disaster. On the other hand, even during colonial times and the beginning of the republic, a few visionaries were advocating rational use of the environment. In 1775, the Spanish governor of the province of Costa Rica, don Juan Fernández de Bobadilla, issued the following proclamation: "Whereas it has been observed that every summer some people, fully aware of their disorderly behavior, and with impunity, set fire to the fields of this province, causing serious damage to farmers, since this practice is followed by sterility of the fields . . . I therefore order and command that no person shall set fire to fields and forests."

During the nineteenth century, there was much legislative action directed toward the protection of large patches of natural forests in the neighborhood of several towns of the central valley. And, in 1906, the Costa Rican Congress suggested that the executive branch enact forestry legislation (Retana 1976).

In 1939, the botanist José María Orozco wrote in his annual report to the director of the School of Agriculture the following (Orozco 1940): "From now on, we should direct our efforts toward the improvement and conservation of our forests, paying special attention to the following points: (1) study and classification of the different forest types; (2) protection of forests; (3) study of the impact of man on forests (highways, logging, fires, agriculture, and grazing); (4) study of the relationship between water and vegetation; and (5) erosion."

These few examples taken from the history of the development of science in this country (Saénz, 1970) give evidence that at least some Costa Ricans were interested in ecological problems and the rational use of nature long before 1940. This way of thinking is now permeating into the different strata of our society; our people are becoming aware that the future of the country will depend on the rational use of the environment.

DEVELOPMENT OF ECOLOGICAL IDEAS AND TRENDS

As mentioned above, the application of ecology to conservation has been a major concern in this country; fortunately, during the last two decades, ecological research has been enriched by the efforts of local and foreign scientists. Among the different trends recently developed in the country, the following seem to be the best oriented: classification of natural environments and land-use planning; study of forest phenology; study of forest succession; and ecology of reproductive biology.

Classification of Natural Environments and Land-Use Planning

Dr. Leslie R. Holdridge and his co-workers developed a life zones or plant formations classification system based mainly on climatic parameters (Holdridge 1965, 1967; Holdridge et al. 1971). The parameters used for classification of the life zones are biotemperature, precipitation, and potential evapotranspiration; soil characteristics, atmospheric humidity, and water level are considered for the separation of associations. Recent additions to this system are the complexity index and the idealized profile of vegetation (Holdridge et al. 1971). The formula for the complexity index is as follows:

$$\text{C.I.} = 10^{-3}\, hbds$$

where, in natural mature forest associations: h = height of stand in meters; b = basal area in square meters per 0.1 hectare; d = number of trees per 0.1 hectare; s = number of tree species per 0.1 hectare. In all cases, only trees 10 cm or larger (dbh) are considered. This system has been used in Costa Rica and other countries of Latin America for land-use planning and forest management.

The interest in nature conservation has promoted the establishment and development of national parks and forest reserves as well as the preservation of many small patches of natural forest under private control in different life zones of the country (Chaverri 1979; Fournier and Herrera de Fournier 1979). Boza (1978) has published a comprehensive summary of the salient features of the Costa Rican National Park System, which covers 2.5 percent of the country. And recently, Gonzalez (1979) gave an account of the system of forest reserves, twenty of which, covering over 20 percent of our territory, have been established by the Forest Service.

Study of Forest Phenology

The first phenological work published in Costa Rica was that of Fournier and Salas (1966), a study of the variation on tree flowering in a forest community in the Pacific middle lands demonstrating that in this area most trees bloom during the dry season. Many other phenological studies followed, covering different types of forests (Daubenmire 1972; Fournier 1976*a;* Frankie et al. 1974), and the behavior of individual tree species (Fournier 1967). These studies included the variation not only of flowering but also of other phenological characteristics, such as fruiting, leaf flushing, and leaf fall. For the quantitative evaluation of these characteristics, Fournier and his co-workers developed simple methods, based on the size of the sample and frequency of observation (Fournier and Charpantier 1975) and on a field scale for the determination of the phenological stage of the community, the species, or the individual tree (Fournier 1974). Another contribution to methodology is the dendrophenograph, a graphic representation of tree phenology that includes a horizontal scale for time and four vertical scales representing the percentage of leaf flushing, leaf fall, flowering, and fruiting (Fournier 1976*b*).

Recently, Fournier (1980) presented a report on flowering phenology of coffee trees, resulting from ten years of observations in Ciudad Colón, Costa Rica. This paper notes the importance of phenological knowledge for a better understanding of morphological and physiologic data on the origin and development of flower buds in this important tropical crop. The methods proposed by Fournier (1974, 1976*b*) have also been used in Brasil by Piccolo and Gregolim (1980) to prepare a phenological study of *Melia azedarach.*

Study of Forest Succession

The study of forest succession has attracted the attention of Costa Rican ecologists for more than twenty years. One of the first workers in this field was Dr. Gerardo Budowski, chairman of the Department of Forestry of the Tropical Agronomic Center for Research and Teaching (CATIE). This researcher, in his studies in the Atlantic lowlands of Costa Rica and Panama (Budowski 1963, 1965), recognized four principal stages in the course of forest succession based on more than twenty physiognomic, floristic, ecological, dendrologic, and physiologic characteristics: pioneer, early secondary, late secondary, and climax. He also found that the successional position of a given species varies according to climatic conditions at the site. Some late secondary species of wet areas are thus climax species in drier places.

Recently, Herrera de Fournier (1977) studied litter production and decomposition, fauna, soil respiration, and soil biota in three successional forests and a pasture in the Pacific middle lands. Fournier and Herrera de Fournier (1977), in a report of twenty-one years of forest regeneration by succession, suggested that this is an adequate approach for reforestation in devastated areas, especially those set apart as protected forests.

Ecology of Reproductive Biology

Phenological works carried out in Costa Rica have promoted the development of other ecological trends, e.g., the study of reproductive biology, among which the work of Stiles (1975) on flowering phenology and hummingbird pollination of some Costa Rican *Heliconia* species, and the study of fig wasp mechanisms of pollen transfer (Ramírez 1969) are worth mentioning. The studies of Salas (1973) on bat pollination of bromeliads and the pollination system of *Ingà vera spuria* (Salas 1974) are also examples of the type of work that is being developed by this group.

Recently, Stiles (1979) published a study of a community of twenty-two species of hummingbirds and over forty-five species of ornithophilous plants carried out over a seven-year period in the humid Caribbean lowlands of Costa Rica. This work shows that there are two approximately equal blooming peaks of hummingbird flowers per year, during the dry season (March) and early in the rainy season (July–August), with a severe scarcity of flowers during the period between November and January at the end of the rainy season. Habitat shifts of hummingbirds are closely associated with flowering of preferred food plants as is the differential habitat use by the sexes of some species. Migration of some species into and out of the area of study reflects the cycle of flower abundance. In general, the breeding season of the hummingbirds coincides with the first peak and molting season with the second peak of flowering.

Other Developing Trends in Ecology

Besides the four well-established ecological trends discussed above, there are several others that are now in an active developmental stage. The most outstanding among these are: ecology of stingless bees (Dr. Alvaro Wille); ecology of spiders (Dr. Carlos Valerio); ecology of birds (Dr. Gary Stiles); ecology of fishes (Mr. and Mrs. William Bussing); ecology of snakes, lizards, and amphibians (Dr. Douglas Robinson); marine ecology (Dr. Manuel M. Murillo and Mr. Carlos Villalobos); and pollution ecology (Dr. Alfonso Mata and his co-workers).

RELATIONS AND INTERACTIONS WITH OTHER DISCIPLINES

The founding of the University of Costa Rica initiated a process of integration and interaction of the different teaching and research units of natural and agricultural sciences. Today, these ecological research programs are channelled through the School of Biology of the College of Science with the support of other academic units. A relatively rich herbarium and a good museum of zoology exist at the School of Biology, and there is an entomological museum at the College of Agronomy; both act as supporting units for ecological research. An older and larger herbarium at the National Museum houses valuable collections, some dating from the last century. The National Museum also possesses a small but valuable collection of botanical and zoological publications. Other academic units of the University of Costa Rica, available for ecological research, are: Laboratory of Plant Physiology and Soil Chemistry (College of Agronomy); Laboratory of Soil Physics and Soil Survey (College of Agronomy); Laboratory of Statistics and Experimental Design (College of Agronomy); Computer Center (College of Engineering); Laboratory of Cell Physiology and Virology (vice-president of research); Laboratory of

Electronic Microscopy (vice-president of research); and Library (vice-president of research).

Besides the library facilities of the University of Costa Rica, scholars make use of the collections of the Orthon Memorial Library at the Interamerican Institute of Agricultural Sciences at Turrialba and the library of the National University at Heredia.

The Organization for Tropical Studies (OTS), an international group of twenty-eight North American and Latin American universities interested in teaching and research in tropical ecology, deserves special mention. This organization, with its various field stations open to local and foreign scientists, has always taken an active part in ecological programs.

The facilities of the National Parks Service of the Ministry of Agriculture, strategically located in different life zones of the country, have also been extensively used as field stations.

SOURCES AND LEVELS OF GOVERNMENTAL AND PRIVATE SUPPORT

The three national institutions of higher learning, the University of Costa Rica, the National University, and the Costa Rican Institute of Technology, obtain their financial support from the central government. These institutions devote a certain amount of their funds to research programs, but they also obtain economic support from the National Council of Research in Science and Technology (CONICIT), a specialized government agency. Although no information is currently available as to the funds allocated to the different fields of research, these data are being compiled and will soon be made public. However, a preliminary estimate by the author indicates that in 1980, Costa Rica will be spending $20 million on research, and 20 percent of this figure will be devoted to ecology and related fields.

Two other institutions with research programs in ecology are the Tropical Agronomic Center for Teaching and Research (CATIE) and the Tropical Science Center (TSC). CATIE is sponsored by the Interamerican Institute of Agricultural Science (an agency of the Organization of American States), the government of Costa Rica, and other Latin American governments. The Tropical Science Center, a nonprofit organization devoted mainly to research in applied ecology, is funded by contracts with the governments of Costa Rica and other Latin American countries. Both institutions have cooperative research programs with such groups as the Agency for International Development and the Food and Agriculture Organization of the United Nations.

TEACHING OF ECOLOGY

Although Costa Rica was known in colonial times as the "most miserable of Spain's Colonies in the New World," great advances have been made since then in education and economic development. Prior to the 1840s, the youth of Costa Rica were forced to attend the universities of Nicaragua and Guatemala for advanced studies. In 1844, President José María Castro Madriz founded the University of Santo Tomás, which began the teaching of theology, law, and medicine; later, in 1881, civil engineering was included in the curriculum. However, the existence of this university was ephemeral since it was closed down in 1888 by President Bernardo Soto, under the pressure of his Minister of Education, Mauro Fernández, who argued that instead of a university the country needed a good system of high schools (Monge 1975).

The arrival, during these years, of many European and North American scientists had a positive effect in the development of the sciences. Also, the country was experiencing rapid economic development due to increasing coffee trade with Europe, with the consequent increase in cultural interchange. Coffee planters now had the option of sending their sons to the best European universities.

At the end of last century, Dr. Henri Pittier, a Swiss scientist, came to Costa Rica and remained for several years. He founded the National Meteorological Observatory and initiated a series of studies on climatology, botany, zoology, ethnology, and anthropology, the foundations of modern Costa Rican science.

In 1927, after many failures, the government established a School of Agriculture, under the direction of a Costa Rican graduated from an American university. At that time, there was no university in Costa Rica, but there were two other schools of higher learning, the School of Law and the School of Pharmacy, both under the administration of their respective professional associations. The new School of Agriculture joined efforts with the School of Pharmacy in the advancement of the biological and physical sciences. Finally, in 1940, President Rafael Angel Calderón Guardia, strongly influenced by his Minister of Education, Luis Demetrio Tinoco, founded the University of Costa Rica.

Three years after the establishment of the University of Costa Rica, the Organization of American States founded the Interamerican Institute of Agricultural Sciences in Turrialba, for research and education in tropical agriculture and forestry. With this idea in mind, the center opened a graduate program leading to a master's degree. Since its very beginning, there has been great emphasis on ecology per se as a means of solving many agricultural problems.

In 1956, the University of Costa Rica opened the College of Arts and Sciences, divided into departments including a Department of Biology, the precursor of the present School of Biology. Before this, teaching and research in biology were done independently at different schools and departments of the university. During the first fifteen years, research work was limited, and, therefore, one of the objectives of the new Department of Biology was promotion of research. One of the department's first chairmen, Dr. Rafael L.

Rodríguez, a graduate of the University of California at Berkeley, devoted his best efforts to the department, fighting for funds, physical facilities, and scholarships for the academic training of the staff. In 1961, general ecology was taught for the first time; in 1965, the department offered plant ecology, and since then, many other ecology courses have been incorporated into the curriculum. The present School of Biology of the College of Sciences offers three degrees in the area of ecology: Bachiller en Ordenamiento de Vida Silvestre (Bachelor in Wildlife Management), Licenciado en Ecología, and Magister Scientia in Ecology.

The National University, founded in 1973, has a School of Environmental Sciences that offers a Bachelor's degree in forestry with strong emphasis in ecology.

JOURNALS

Major Native Language Journals

There are four major local journals used by Costa Rican ecologists to communicate the results of their research (Table 2.1); however, some scientists also publish in and make use of foreign journals.

Major Foreign Publications Consulted

The following list includes the publications most frequently consulted by Costa Rican ecologists: *Acta Científica Venezolana, Acta Amazonica, Adan-*

Table 2.1. Major Native-language Science Journals Publishing Work by Costa Rican Ecologists

Name of the Publication	Year of Establishment	Publisher
Agronomía costarricense	1977	Universidad de Costa Rica, Ministerio de Agricultura y Ganadería, Colegio de Ingenieros Agrónomos
Brenesia	1973	Costa Rican National Museum
Revista de Biologia Tropical	1953	Universidad de Costa Rica
Revista Turrialba	1950	Interamerican Institute of Agricultural Sciences

sonia, Advances in Ecological Research, Advances in Marine Biology, American Midland Naturalist, American Naturalist, American Journal of Botany, American Scientist, Annual Review of Ecology and Systematics, Botanical Gazette, Caribbean Forester, Canadian Journal of Botany, Ceiba, Condor, Copeia, Ecological Monographs, Ecology, Evolution, Fieldiana Botany, Fieldiana Zoology, Forest Science, Annual Review of Entomology, Annual Review of Plant Pathology, Annual Review of Plant Physiology, Annals of the Missouri Botanical Garden, Arquivos do Instituto Biológico, Australian Journal of Botany, Biotropica, Bois et Forests des Tropiques, Boletín—Latín American Forest Institute, Boletín—Brasilian Forest Service, Bulletin of Marine Sciences, Hilgardia, Ibis, Interciencia, Indian Forester, Journal of Ecology, Journal of the Linnaean Society, Journal of Experimental Biology, Journal of Economic Entomology, Journal of Herpetology, Journal of Animal Ecology, Journal of Mammology, Journal of Ornithology, Journal of Tropical Ecology, Journal of Zoology, Malayan Forester, Montes, Nature, Oikos, Planta, Proceedings United States National Museum, Quarterly Review of Biology, Revista Ceres, Revista de Facultad de Agronomía de Colombia, Revista Forestal Venezolana, Science, Scientific American, Taxon, Torreya, Tropical Woods, and *Unasylva.*

SOCIETIES

Costa Rican ecologists are associated with the Colegio de Biólogos de Costa Rica (Costa Rican Society of Biologists), an organization devoted to the advancement of biological sciences. Besides this professional organization, there is another group of Costa Ricans interested in conservation, Asociación Costarricense para la Conservación de la Naturaleza (ASCONA). This association includes not only biologists, but also persons in other technical and scientific disciplines, as well as farmers and businessmen.

SUMMARY AND OUTLOOK

Ecology had a dynamic development in Costa Rica during the period from 1945 to 1975, largely due to the establishment of the Department of Biology of the University of Costa Rica, which created a critical mass of human and physical facilities devoted to education and research in biology. The advance of ecology was also favored by the following events that took place during this period: (1) realization by national and foreign scientists of the existence of a tremendous diversity of natural environments within reduced geographic boundaries; (2) improvement of the system of higher learning; (3) availability of more funds for research and teaching; and (4) a better understanding by the general population of the basic and practical importance of ecology.

Today, besides the interest in conservation of natural resources that some Costa Ricans have shown throughout our history, it is possible to identify the following trends of ecological research: classification of natural environments and land-use planning; study of forest phenology; study of forest succession; and ecology of reproductive biology. Moreover, other ecological aspects are now in an active developmental stage, such as the ecology of spiders, fish, amphibians, reptiles, birds, and stingless bees; marine ecology; and pollution control.

As previously mentioned, there is no doubt that Costa Ricans are now more aware that research in ecology would be valuable for future development of the country. Pollution is becoming a problem in our marine and continental waters, as well as in cities and on agricultural lands. Problems of air and water pollution have been detected already (Cordero et al. 1979; Méndez and Fournier 1980). On the other hand, the Ministry of Public Health is developing several air pollution control stations in the metropolitan area of the city of San José, and the ministry is also strengthening pollution control regulations. In addition, the Ministry of Agriculture is limiting the use of agricultural chemicals.

Last year, the government issued a decree reducing the income tax of those persons and companies that made investments in reforestation. This law has promoted the establishment of many companies that are making important investments in forest plantations in different parts of the country. Formerly, most timber came from natural forests, but as those are becoming depleted, future supplies of forest products will depend mainly on plantations. This increase in forest plantations will demand more research in forest ecology and, therefore, it seems likely that this field will need attention in the near future.

Agroforestry, an ecological form of land use, is becoming popular in Costa Rica. For example, some important timber trees are being planted with coffee trees or on pasture land, *Cordia alliodora* on the Atlantic side of the country and *Alnus acuminata* in the highlands. Recently a workshop in agroforestry was sponsored by the Tropical Agricultural Center for Research and Teaching and the United Nations University (Salas de las 1979).

The current Costa Rican government is deeply interested in a rational use of marine resources, and this official position has encouraged research in marine ecology and related fields.

It is rewarding to observe that even politicians are now taking advantage of ecological issues for their activities, something unknown five years ago. I think that the next decade will be of great importance in Costa Rica for both basic and applied ecology.

ACKNOWLEDGMENT

I want to express my sincere thanks to Mr. Manuel Chavarría, editor of *Revista de Biología Tropical,* for his critical review of the manuscript and valuable suggestions.

REFERENCES CITED

Boza, M. 1978. *Los parques nacionales de Costa Rica.* Madrid: Omnia. Industrias Gráficas.

Budowski, G. 1963. Forest succession in tropical lowlands. *Turrialba* 13:42–44.

———. 1965. Distribution of tropical American rain forest species in the light of successional process. *Turrialba* 15:40–42.

Chaverri, A. 1979. Análisis de un sistema de reservas biológicas privadas en Costa Rica. M.S. thesis, Turrialba, Universidad de Costa Rica and Centro Agronómico Tropical de Investigación y Enseñanza.

Cordero, A., B. Chacón, and A. Rodríguez. 1979. Contaminación del río Bermúdez, Alajuela. *Agron. Costarric.* 3:100–113.

Daubenmire, R. 1972. Phenology and other characteristics of tropical semideciduous forests in North-Western Costa Rica. *J. Ecol.* 60:147–170.

Fournier, L. A. 1967. Estudio preliminar sobre la floración en el roble de sabana *Tabebuia pentaphylla. Rev. Biol. Trop.* 15:259–267.

———. 1974. Un método cuantitativo para la medición de características fenológicas en árboles. *Turrialba* 24:422–423.

———. 1976*a*. Observaciones fenológicas en el bosque húmedo de premontano de San Pedro de Montes de Oca, Costa Rica. *Turrialba* 26:54–59.

———. 1976*b*. El dendrofenograma, una representación gráfica del comportamiento fenológico de los árboles. *Turrialba* 26:96–97.

———. 1980. Determinación cuantitativa de la floración en Café, *Coffea coffea arabica* L. *Turrialba*.

——— and C. Charpantier. 1975. El tamaño de la muestra y la frecuencia de las observaciones en el estudio de las características fenológicas de los árboles tropicales. *Turrialba* 25:45–48.

——— and M. E. Herrera de Fournier. 1977. La sucesión ecológica como un método eficaz para la recuperación del bosque en Costa Rica. *Agron. Costarric.* 1:23–29.

——— and M. E. Herrera de Fournier. 1979. Importancia científica, económica y cultural de un sistema de pequeñas reservas naturales en Costa Rica. *Agron. Costarric.* 3:53–55.

——— and S. Salas. 1966. Algunas observaciones sobre la dinámica de la floración en el bosque tropical húmedo de Villa Colón. *Rev. Biol. Trop.* 14:75–85.

Frankie, G. W., H. G. Baker, and P. A. Opler. 1974. Comparative phenological studies of trees in tropical wet and dry forests in the lowlands of Costa Rica. *J. Ecol.* 62:881–919.

González, R. 1979. Establecimiento y desarrollo de reservas forestales en Costa Rica. *Agron. Costarric.* 3:161–166.

Herrera de Fournier, M. E. 1977. La producción, descomposición del mantillo y cambios en la biota del suelo en varias etapas de la sucesión en Ciudad Colón. Thesis, San Pedro de Montes de Oca, Universidad de Costa Rica.

Holdridge, L. R. 1965. The tropics, a misunderstood ecosystem. *Assoc. Trop. Biol. Bull.* No. 5:21–30.

———. 1967. *Life zone ecology,* 2d ed. San José, Costa Rica: Tropical Science Center.

——— *et al.* 1971. *Forest environments in tropical life zones; a pilot study*. Oxford: Pergamon Press.

Méndez, O. and L. A. Fournier. 1980. Los líquenes como indicadores de la contaminación atmosférica en el área metropolitana de San José, Costa Rica. *Rev. Biol. Trop.* 28:31–39.

Monge, C. 1975. *La educación superior en Costa Rica.* San José: Costa Rica Consejo Nacional de Rectores, Oficina de Planificación de la Educación Superior.

Orozco, J. M. 1940. Informe de la Sección de Botánica y Forestal. In *Informe Anual de 1939,* pp. 40–52. Costa Rica, Centro Nacional de Agricultura.

Piccolo, A. L. G. and M. I. Gregolim. 1980. Fenología de *Melia azederach* L. no sul do Brasil. *Turrialba* 30:107–109.

Ramírez, W. L. 1969. Fig wasps: mechanism of pollen transfer. *Science* 16:580–581.

Retana, G. 1976. Análisis de la Dirección General Forestal del Ministerio de Agricultura y Ganadería de Costa Rica. Thesis, San Pedro de Montes de Oca, Facultad de Agronomía, Universidad de Costa Rica.

Saénz, A. 1970. *Historía agrícola de Costa Rica.* Publicaciones de la Universidad de Costa Rica, Serie Agronomía No. 12.

Salas, S. 1974. Análisis del sistema de polinización de *Inga vera* subspecie *spuria.* Thesis, San Pedro de Montes de Oca, Escuela de Biología, Universidad de Costa Rica.

———. 1973. Una bromeliácea costarricense polinizada por murciélagos. *Brenesia* 2:5–10.

Salas de Las, G., ed. 1979. *Taller de Sistemas Agroforestales en América Latina.* Turrialba, Costa Rica: Centro Agronómico Tropical de Investigación y Enseñanza.

Stiles, G. 1975. Ecology, flowering phenology and hummingbird pollination of some Costa Rican *Heliconia* species. *Ecology* 56:285–301.

———. 1979. El ciclo anual en una comunidad coadaptada de colibries y flores en el bosque tropical muy húmedo de Costa Rica. *Rev. Biol. Trop.* 27:75–101.

3

MEXICO

José Sarukhán

This is a personal vision of the origins, development, and actual status of ecology in Mexico. In order to lessen the subjectivity inherent in a personal view, I have imposed the following limits: (a) only the most relevant biological and natural history was included as pertinent to the origin of ecology in Mexico; (b) only research that is directly ecological, that has been produced within research groups, or that has had an important influence in the further development of ecology is included; and (c) only research carried out by Mexican ecologists in Mexico has been considered, since it is more interesting to analyze the development of a corps of Mexican ecologists than to refer only to the production of ecological information about Mexico.

MARINE AND AQUATIC ECOLOGY

The area of ecology that has had the most recent development, marine and aquatic ecology, was originally the pursuit of isolated individuals. It has experienced a major stimulus in the last five to seven years from federal and international agencies interested in the exploitation of marine and freshwater resources. As a result, a number of young biologists have been attracted to the field, many of whom are still in the stages of postgraduate training or, having completed it, are just starting to develop their research. Although there is no ecological tradition in this area, it is vigorously starting to form.

Basic Research

Most of the basic research is still in a phase of description of the physical and biological components of these ecosystems. Maria Elena Caso's extensive monograph on echinoderms (Caso 1961, 1978), the works of Alvarez del Villar (1970), Berdegué (1956) and De Buen (1940) on fishes, as well as the contributions of Osorio Tafall (1943, 1944, 1946), are considered important infrastructural elements for the development of this field. Two other contributions deserve special mention: the work of Ramírez-Granados (1958), which represents the first study with an essentially ecological approach for coastal lagoons; and the influence of Enrique Rioja, both as an author (Rioja 1954) and as a research trainer in the 1940s and 1950s.

Over the last two decades, some important investigations have been carried out for estuarine ecosystems, e.g., Ayala-Castañares (1969), Villalobos et al. (1966, 1969), Villalobos (1971), Chávez (1972, 1980), H. Chávez (1963), Stuardo and Martínez (1975), Castro-Aguirre (1978), and De Lachica (1979). Important studies on coral reefs are those of Bonet (1967), Kormicker et al. (1959), Villalobos (1971), and Chávez et al. (1970). A recent group has actively started research on estuarine and coastal lagoon ecology at the Centro de Ciencias del Mar y Limnología, at the University of México, under A. Yáñez-Arancibia, dealing both with trophic and structural aspects of these systems (e.g., Yáñez-Arancibia 1976, 1978; Yáñez-Arancibia and Nugent 1976).

Joint research by workers at both the Escuela Nacional de Ciencias Biológicas (at the Polytechnic Institute) and the Centro de Ciencias del Mar y Limnología (at the University of México) has dealt with aspects of the structure and composition of littoral communities of the coast of Veracruz (e.g., Turcott; Santoyo and Signoret; Hidalgo and Chávez; Chávez and Parra-Alcocer; Chávez et al.; and Bautista-Gil and Guadarrama, all in press).

Applied Research

Most of the little research that has been carried out on marine ecology is focused directly on the solution of urgent economic problems. Thus, some important studies on fisheries are strongly oriented toward defining short-term optimal catch policies. The main antecedents of this applied focus are the works of Chapa-Saldaña (1956, 1975) on shrimps and of Ramírez-Granados (1958) on sardines. Some important studies have been produced at the Instituto Nacional de Pesca, e.g., Doi et al. (1977) on abalones. An important study on shrimp fisheries (Lluch 1976), produced at the same place, is based on more practical fishery data; however, it lacks basic, ecological information that would give better predictive powers to the proposed models. The efforts of research in this field are summarized in the proceedings of three symposia carried out in 1976 (Instituto Nacional de Pesca 1976*a, b, c*).

TERRESTRIAL ANIMAL ECOLOGY

In the development of the natural history of Mexico, botanical studies have predominated zoological studies since precolonial times. Although I would not suggest that the native populations of ancient Mexico were relatively ignorant about their surrounding fauna, it is clear through what was saved from the conquerors' destructive zeal that the Indians' knowledge of plants and of the plants' ecological implications, on which the people depended so heavily for their daily sustenance, was truly great. Testimonies of this knowledge are the numerous cultivars developed in the Mesoamerican area and the sophisticated way in which the natural resources were exploited. The predominance of plant over animal natural history continued through colonial times. Because of this emphasis and other circumstances, animal ecology has been relatively less developed than plant ecology in Mexico.

Basic Research

At the initial stages of what has become animal ecology, the work of Alfonso L. Herrera (1888, 1890) is considered an important early contribution to the understanding of several biogeographic problems. A considerable amount of basic biological literature has been produced, of which Villa's work on Mexican bats (1966), Phillips' on birds (1961), and Alvarez del Toro's on reptiles (1960) deserve special mention. More recently, the zoogeographic accounts by Gonzalo Halffter (1964, 1974, 1976), mostly in relation to the Mexican entomofauna, are basic sources of information for both taxonomists and ecologists. Barrera's initial work on the zoogeography of part of tropical Mexico (1962) is also worth mentioning.

Although much of the zoological literature, which is predominantly taxonomic, contains references to environmental parameters or, at best, general descriptions of the environments of collecting localities, very little of this can be considered as research seriously aimed at studying ecological problems. Ecological research on terrestrial animals is rather restricted to a few groups and centers of activity. Gonzalo Halffter's research group constitutes an active center of basic ecological research, particularly on insect ecology and behavior. Formerly at the Escuela Nacional de Ciencias Biológicas, Instituto Politécnico Nacional, this research group is presently at the Instituto de Ecología and Museo de Historia Natural de la Ciudad de México (Chapultepec Park). Recently, research on the population ecology of several vertebrates (white-tailed deer and desert turtle) has been started at the Instituto de Ecología.

Applied Research

A widely known monograph on dung beetles (Halffter and Matthews 1966), which has been basic for many applied ecology problems of pasture lands, and studies on the ethology of scarabids (Halffter, Halffter and López 1974) are examples of applied research being done by Halffter's group. Basic entomological studies on economic problems are also being carried out at the Rama de Entomología, Colegio de Postgraduados, Escuela Nacional de Agricultura, and at some agricultural research stations throughout the country, particularly in the northwest.

TERRESTRIAL PLANT ECOLOGY

Several floristic and phytogeographic studies serve as basic infrastructure for the development of modern-day plant ecology in Mexico, but a fair proportion of the plant ecology research that is being carried out is still in the form of synecological, descriptive surveys. One of the basic studies in this sense is Standley's *Trees and Shrubs of Mexico* (1920–1926), which is the nearest work to a still nonexistent flora of Mexico. On the phytogeographic aspects, the most relevant studies have been contributed by Sharp (1953), Miranda (1959), and particularly Rzedowski (1962, 1965, 1972*a*, *b*), constituting much of the conceptual framework for vegetation studies, although interest in this area dates back to the first three decades of this century (e.g., Ochoterena 1918).

Historical Background

Plant ecology developed primarily from the work of taxonomists or of persons who began their studies with an initial interest in taxonomy but afterwards defined their fields solely or predominantly within some aspect of ecology. This pattern does not apply, however, to the most recent generations of ecologists, who deal immediately with purely ecological problems. Although this trend has the advantage of centering young people into ecology from the beginning, it has often had the effect of making them rather hopeless at solving the most basic problems of taxonomic identification. This is mostly due to the unfortunate deterioration of taxonomy as a subject in the curriculum; this situation applies equally to botanists and zoologists.

The main body of plant ecology studies was done in the mid-1950s, mostly as an extension of phytogeographic and floristic studies, either by the phytogeographers themselves or by their first students. This initial stage of plant ecology is clearly characterized by "vegetation survey" studies. Several of these studies had a significant impact, both by influencing further research on plant ecology and by serving as a basis for a more analytical approach in ecology. Characteristically, all these studies were initially qualitative, becoming more quantitative later on. Such is the case of Faustino Miranda's work (e.g., 1948, 1952–1953, 1957, 1959) in much of the tropical area of Mexico as well as in some temperate and arid zones of the country (e.g., 1950, 1955; García, Soto, and Miranda 1960). Miranda's phytogeographic and ecological studies culminated in the first comprehensive and detailed description of the vegetation types of Mexico, based mostly on physiognomic and ecological data (Miranda and Hernández 1963). His important taxonomic work, however, never crystallized in the same manner, as a result of his untimely death in 1964. Much of the present development of plant ecology, particularly of the tropics, can be attributed to direct or indirect influence of Miranda.

Ecological studies on the arid zones of Mexico, although comparatively less advanced than those of the tropic zones, progressed considerably as a result of Jerzy Rzedowski's (1957 and 1961) detailed ecological surveys of such zones as the states of San Luis Potosí and Zacatecas; his studies are the most complete accounts yet published of the origins and relations of the Mexican flora, including detailed analyses of certain families like the Compositae (Rzedowski 1962, 1965, 1972*a, b*). His latest contribution to the study of the ecology of Mexican plants has been his book *Vegetation of Mexico,* at present the most up-to-date and authoritative work on the subject (Rzedowski 1978).

Role of CEED

Perhaps the single most important factor in the development of most of the ecologists and much of ecology in Mexico was the existence, during the late 1950s and 1960s, of the Comisión de Estudios sobre la Ecología de Dioscoreas (CEED) within the Instituto Nacional de Investigaciones Forestales (INIF), which is under the Secretaría de Agricultura y Recursos Hidráulicos. In 1959, stimulated by INIF, Faustino Miranda, Efraím Hernández X., and Arturo Gómez-Pompa (Miranda et al. 1967) conceived and created CEED, outlining its aims, methodology, and structure. Initially, the research group operated under the direction of Gómez-Pompa, who gave it a dynamic character.

Among its direct aims was the study of the natural productivity of *Dioscorea composita,* for a long time the world's most important source of natural steroids and a native component of primary and secondary vegetation of the hot, humid tropics of Mexico. Interestingly, however, it was the secondary objectives of CEED, such as the survey of vegetation of most of the tropical rain forest communities of Mexico, that really meant a major contribution to Mexican ecology through the ecological training of many students. It was in

CEED that many of the present-day, active plant ecologists were trained, either directly or indirectly, and it was by CEED that a substantial part of the ecological studies in the tropics was sponsored. Besides descriptive studies of vegetation, CEED started research studies on the dynamics of secondary vegetation, studies which, although not widely known internationally because of their place of publication, were among the most original in their field at the time and are still considered basic for this type of study in Mexico (Sarukhán 1964, 1968; Sousa Sánchez 1964).

CEED stimulated the development of several groups and ideas even after its activity decreased abruptly at the beginning of the 1970s. The results of its influence are wide-ranging, since a number of those research groups are still active or have germinated into new groups, which themselves are training young ecologists. The following are the outstanding examples of the influence of CEED:

1. The research group on "Regeneration of Tropical Rain Forests" and "Flora of Veracruz" was led by Arturo Gómez-Pompa, roughly from 1970 to 1976, and, to an extent, continued several research lines of CEED at the botany department, Institute of Biology, UNAM (Gómez-Pompa 1966). Perhaps the best-known product of this group was the summary of many ideas on the dynamics of secondary vegetation (Gómez-Pompa 1971) and of seed soil populations in a paper proposing the tropical rain forest as a non-renewable resource (Gómez-Pompa et al. 1972). Some of the young ecologists of this group have contributed to knowledge on the ecophysiology of seeds of tropical species (Vázquez-Yanes 1976*a*) and have made preliminary attempts at describing seed banks in soils of primary and secondary vegetation in the tropics (Guevara and Gómez-Pompa 1972). A recent volume summarizing much of the work of this group (Gómez-Pompa et al. 1976) covers the dynamics of secondary succession, viability and germination of seeds of tropical plants, allelopathy of species of secondary vegetation, seed dispersal by birds, growth of plants at juvenile stages, and aspects of human ecology related to the use of natural resources. Several of the members of this group have recently started their own research groups and work at different intensities depending on the nature of the institution to which they are attached.

With government support from the Consejo Nacional de Ciencia y Tecnología (CONACyT) and also from the UNAM, Gómez-Pompa founded the Instituto de Investigaciones sobre Recursos Bióticos (INIREB) in Xalapa, Veracruz in 1975. The institute devotes most of its efforts to research on practical problems of policies of land and natural resource utilization in the tropics, looking for alternative unconventional forms of land use. The creation of INIREB was envisaged also as a means of decentralizing research from Mexico City and training people from the provinces in situ.

2. A relatively new (1974) research group on plant population ecology was

led by José Sarukhán also at the botany department, Instituto de Biología, UNAM. This group originated from interest in the dynamic aspects of tropical vegetation and has a strong plant demographic influence as a result of its leader's research training (e.g., Sarukhán and Harper 1973; Sarukhán and Gadgil 1974). The group operates as a "research school" in the sense of having such elements as internal development plans, postgraduate training programs in operation, and internal research seminars. It is composed of people who range in their experience from research associates and graduate students to undergraduate part-time assistants. Three main research programs are being pursued. The first started between 1974 and 1975 on the comparative demography of trees of Mexico, including studies on the mechanisms of population regulation of selected species of single-species temperate (conifer) forests, species-rich tropical rain forests, and species-rich tropical deciduous forests. A general account of the portions on the tropics with preliminary results can be found in Sarukhán (1977, 1980). Besides detailed studies on the demography of the species involved, with the aim of modelling the systems (Franco and Sarukhán 1980), research is being carried out on energy allocation strategies in plants and the relation of those strategies to demography (Piñero 1979), productivity of the tropical deciduous forests, growth rates of arboreal species of the deciduous forests, and the reproductive potential of all arboreal species of the deciduous forests. The second research program, started in 1976, is on the adaptive strategies of the wild and cultivated populations of the *Phaseolus coccineus* complex, with emphasis on the selective forces acting on these different populations and their adaptive responses to such forces (Fernández 1979). The third project, begun in early 1977, is on the biology of weeds of the Valley of Mexico. Another group, under Rodolfo Dirso, is studying the impact of herbivores on the demography of the temperate and tropical plants in the systems described above and is making a comparative study of herbivore effects on seedling communities of tropical forests.

3. Several other lines of research have resulted from CEED, such as paleo-ecological interpretations of the actual status of tropical vegetation in Mexico (Toledo 1976) and studies on the man-resource interrelationships that have led to the recent development of a fresh and challenging branch of human ecology in the tropics (Martínez-Alfaro 1972; Caballero 1976), primarily under the direction of Victor M. Toledo at the botany department, Institute of Biology, UNAM. At the same department, studies on plant-animal interrelations, specifically with aspects of plant pollination by animals, are continuing (e.g., Sousa Sánchez 1969; Toledo 1975, 1977; Cruden and Toledo 1977). Likewise, research on the ecophysiology of seeds by Vázquez-Yanes (1976*b*, 1980) at the Departamento de Botánica, Instituto de Biología, UNAM, promises to start a whole new branch of ecology in Mexico.

Institutions concerned primarily with applied problems have also benefitted amply from the work carried out at CEED. Researchers who sought to determine the cattle-carrying capacity of grazing lands in Mexico (e.g., COTECOCA 1968) based their methodology for the tropical and subtropical areas of México on that used by CEED for its studies of vegetation. Likewise, the Dirección de Estudios del Territorio Nacional (DETENAL), a government office in charge of the natural resources inventory, land planning, and map production including topographic, edaphic, and actual land-use information, has derived great benefits from the experience obtained through some ten years in CEED. In fact, the first integrated vegetation map of Mexico (Flores Mata et al. 1971) was produced largely on field information, published and unpublished, obtained by CEED for much of the tropical and subtropical areas of Mexico.

Other Research Activity

Other research groups in plant ecology operate at different research and teaching institutions in Mexico, some on a modest scale. A great deal of the research done by these groups appears as theses (equivalent to the B.S. level) or as internal reports and has not been published in journals; often these are valuable pieces of research. The only group working on aquatic plant ecology is carrying out its research at the botany department, Institute of Biology, UNAM, under Antonio Lot-Helgueras; very little of their work has reached the printed form (Lot-Helgueras et al. 1975; Lot et al. 1979; Orozco and Lot-Helgueras 1976). At the same department, a small group, led by Francisco González-Medrano, has been working at a basic level on the ecology and floristics of several semiarid areas of Mexico, particularly the state of Tamaulipas and some areas of central Mexico (González-Medrano et al. 1976).

Another center where a certain amount of ecological study has been conducted, mostly on arid areas of the country, is the Department of Botany, Escuela Nacional de Ciencias Biológicas, Instituto Politécnico Nacional. Much of the work has been carried out as a result of government contracts and is not published. However, other important studies have been published on the vegetation and ecology of the Pacific Coast and of Mexican grasslands, as well as on the ecology of pine forests (Rzedowski and McVaugh 1966; Rzedowski 1975; Rzedowski et al. 1977).

The INIF, which started operations about 1957, has produced, besides the activities of CEED, a certain amount of ecological work intermittently, mainly dealing with aspects of forest ecology. Again, little of this work has been published. Among the most relevant studies are Vázquez-Soto's study of the tropical vegetation of the Yucatán Peninsula (1963), Madrigal's on the ecology of fir forests (1967), and Vela's on the ecology of *Pinus patula* (1976).

Applied and Other Research

Agriculturally oriented ecology as such is virtually nonexistent, although a considerable body of agricultural research with ecological implications exist, which will not be dealt with in this paper. However, it is important to mention a few ecological studies dealing with agricultural problems; these studies constitute excellent examples of a potentially rich area of research but, sadly, were not pursued further. These are the studies by Efraim Hernández X. on the distribution, ecology, productivity, and exploitation of the oil palm *Scheelea liebmanii* (1947) and his classic study of Mayan agricultural systems (1958).

At the present moment, ecological research at the Escuela Nacional de Agricultura, Colegio de Postgraduados, Chapingo, is aimed at the ecology of arid-zone grasslands in the state of San Luis Potosí.

Institutions like the Inventario Nacional Forestal (National Forest Inventory) and the Dirección de Estudios del Territorio Nacional (DETENAL) are carrying out basic natural resources inventories, using modern techniques such as satellite imagery. Such research may be considered, up to a point, as basic infrastructure for future, more detailed ecological studies.

Very few other ecological research groups are established besides those enumerated. One of these is in the Facultad de Ciencias, Universidad Nacional Autónoma de México (UNAM) with interest on seed ecophysiology, seed ecology, sand dune ecology, and human ecology, all in the tropics.

Paleo-ecology has also had a certain degree of development, particularly with the initial work of Frederico Bonet (1967) and lately of L. González-Quintero (1974).

SCIENTIFIC SOCIETIES AND PUBLICATIONS

Of the main scientific societies in Mexico, the oldest in the biological sciences is the Sociedad Mexicana de Historia Natural (SMHN), initially founded in 1868. It was restarted in 1936 by Enrique Beltrán, long-time director of the Instituto Mexicano de Recursos Naturalez Renovables (IMRNR), an institution which promoted many important initial ecological studies like those of Miranda and Hernández in plant ecology. Membership in the society numbers about 300.

The Sociedad Botánica de México (SBM), founded by Maximino Martínez, Miranda, and other botanists in 1941, has been an active association, particularly in the last fifteen to twenty years, having organized seven national and the first Latin American botanical congresses. Its membership numbers about 600.

The Sociedad Mexicana de Entomología (SME) founded in 1952, has sponsored thirteen national congresses. Its membership numbers about 250.

The major journals publishing results of ecological research are: the *Publicaciones* of the IMRNR, started in 1953; the *Boletín de la Sociedad Botánica de México* (published since 1944 by the SBM); *Folia Entomológica Mexicana* (published since 1961 by the SME); *Anales del Instituto de Biología* (*Series Botánica y Zoología,* published since 1930 by the Instituto de Biología, UNAM); *Biótica* (published since 1976 by the INIREB, Xalapa, Ver.); *Anales de la Escuela Nacional de Ciencias Biológicas* (published since 1938 by the IPN); *Revista de la Sociedad Mexicana de Historia Natural* (published since 1939 by the SMHN) and *Ciencia, México* (published since 1940).

FUTURE PERSPECTIVES OF ECOLOGY

Any projection of the future of ecology in Mexico should include two relevant aspects. The first is the growing involvement of ecologists with problems related to the growth and development of the country, which obviously impinge seriously on many ecological matters. Many active ecologists have continuously raised their voices, sometimes with laudable persistence, against developmental policies that clearly lack consideration of ecological principles and that, therefore, will be and have already been detrimental to the country and its population. In this regard, A Gómez-Pompa and G. Halffter, through their respective institutions, and Enrique Beltrán (for a long time through the IMRNR) have played an outstanding role. Responsiveness from the government has been mild at best, often apathetic. However, a few actions, like the support of ecological research through the CONACyT and other recent demonstrations of official interest regarding conservation of natural areas, may be interpreted as encouraging signs. Perhaps ecology will be able to play its potentially important role in helping to devise ecologically sound and politically acceptable propositions for development in the country through the pursuit of solid, applied ecological research. Perhaps ecology will move from its currently rhetorical role in dealing with these problems.

A second aspect is the promising structure of ecological research, particularly plant ecology, in terms of the groups that are building up and actively pursuing original, sound, and important lines of research and that are training the upcoming generations of younger ecologists, both at home and abroad. If this trend continues, many active research groups will be established that will both continue and augment the first-rate, original research lines that have already been initiated in Mexico.

ACKNOWLEDGMENTS

While the responsibility of the paper remains mine, it is a pleasure to acknowledge the help and information given by the following persons: E.

Chávez, G. Green, G. Halffter, E. Hernández X., L. A. Pérez, M. Sousa, and A. Yáñez-Arancibia.

REFERENCES CITED

Alvarez del Toro, M. 1960. *Los reptiles de Chiapas.* Chiapas: Ed. del Gobierno del Estado, Tuxtla Gutiérrez.

Alvarez del Villar, J. 1970. *Peces Mexicanos (claves).* México: Secretaría de Industria y Comercio, Instituto Nacional de Investigaciones Biológico-Pesqueras.

Ayala-Castañares, A. 1969. Datos comparativos de la geología marina de tres lagunas litorales del Golfo de México. *An. Inst. Biol. UNAM* (Serie Cienc. del Mar y Limnol.) 40:1–10.

Barrera, A. 1962. La Península de Yucatán como provincia biótica. *Rev. Soc. Mex. Hist. Nat.* 23:71–105.

Bautista-Gil, M. L., and R. Guadarrama. In press. Datos acerca de la distribución y abundancia de los foraminíferos del bentos marino cercano a Laguna Verde, Veracruz (México). *An. Inst. Biol. UNAM.*

Berdegué, J. 1956. *Peces de importancia comercial en la costa Noroccidental de México.* México: Secretaría de Marina, Dir. Gral. de Pesca e Industrias Conexas.

Bonet, F. 1967. Biogeología subsuperficial del arrecife Alacranes, Yucatán. *UNAM. Inst. de Geología. Bol.* 80:1–192.

Caballero, J. 1976. *El costo ecológico del uso de la tierra en un ejido del trópico mexicano.* Thesis, Facultad de Ciencias, UNAM.

Caso, M. E. 1961. *Estado actual de los conocimientos acerca de los Equinodermos de México.* Doctoral thesis, Fac. de Ciencias, UNAM.

———. 1978. Los equinoideos del Pacífico de México, I y II. *Centro Cienc. del Mar y Limnol. UNAM Publ. Esp.* 1:1–244.

Castro-Aguirre, J. L. 1978. *Catálogo sistemático de los peces marinos que penetran a las aguas continentales de México, con aspectos zoogeográficos y ecológicos.* Depto. de Pesca. Serie Científica No. 19.

Chapa-Saldaña, H. 1956. *La distribución geográfica de los camarones del noroeste de México y el problema de las artes fijas de pesca.* Veracruz: Sría. de Marina.

———. 1975. Breve estudio comparativo de la pesquería de camarón de alta Mar en Mazatlán (1953–1973). *Mem. Simp. Lat. Ocean. (México),* pp. 25–56.

Chávez, E. A. 1972. Acerca de la ictiofauna del estuario del Río Tuxpan y sus relaciones con la temperatura y la salinidad. In *Mem. IV Congr. Nac. Ocean. (México),* ed. Carranza, pp. 177–199.

———. 1980. Análisis de la comunidad de una laguna costera en la costa sur occidental de México. *An. Centro Cienc. del Mar y Limnol. UNAM* 6(2):19–48.

———, E. Hidalgo, and M. L. Sevilla. 1970. Datos acerca de las comunidades bentónicas del arrecife de Lobos. *Ver. Rev. Soc. Mex. Hist. Nat.* 31:211–280.

——— and M. L. Parra-Alcocer. In press. Datos acerca de la abundancia y diversidad de la bentofauna Marina de la región de Laguna Verde, Veracruz, México. *Mem. IV Congr. Nac. Ocean. (México).*

———, Z. Chávez-Alarcón, and M. J. Parra-Alcocer. In press. Contribución al conocimiento de las comunidades de la zona de mareas en la costa rocosa cercana a Laguna Verde, Veracruz (México). *Mem. IV Congr. Nac. Ocean. (México).*

Chávez, H. 1963. Contribución al conocimiento de la biología de los robalos, chucumite y constantino (*Centropomus* spp.) del Estado de Veracruz (Pisces: Centropomidae). *Ciencia* (México City) 22:141–160.

COTECOCA. 1968. *Coeficientes de agostadero de la República Mexicana. Región del Estado de Tabasco, Norte de Chiapas y Suroeste de Campeche.* México: Secretaría de Agricultura y Ganadería.

Cruden, R. W. and V. M. Toledo. 1977. Oriole pollination of *Erythrina breviflora* (Leguminosae): Evidence for a polytypic view of ornithophily. *Plant Syst. Evol.* 126:393–403.

De Buen, F. 1940. Lista de peces de agua dulce de México. En preparación de su catálogo. *Trabajos Est. Limnol. Pátzcuaro* 2:1–66.

De Lachica, F. 1979. Diversidad espacial y temporal de la bentocenosis del estuario del río Coatzacoalcos, Veracruz, México. In *Estudio Científico e Impacto Humano en el ecosistema de Manglares.* Informes de la UNESCO sobre Ciencias del Mar 9 (Resumen).

Doi, T., S. A., Guzmán del Proo, V. Marín, M. Ortíz, J. Camacho, and T. Muñoz. 1977. *Análisis de la población y diagnóstico de la pesquería de abulón amarillo* (Haliotis corrugata) *en el área de Punta Abreojos e Isla Cedros, B.C.* Depto. de Pesca, Serie Científica No. 18.

Fernández, P. 1979. *Ciclos de vida comparativos de Poblaciones de* Phaseolus coccineus *L. (Leguminosae).* Doctoral Thesis, Facultad de Ciencias, UNAM.

Flores Mata, G. et al. 1971. *Tipos de vegetación de la República Mexicana.* México: Secretaría de Recursos Hidráulicos, Dirección de Agrología. [This is the first complete vegetation map of Mexico, compiled from many sources, especially from Miranda, Rzedowski, and CEED (see text).]

Franco, M. and J. Sarukhán. 1980. *Un modelo de simulación de la productividad forestal de un bosque de pino.* México: Ed. Esp. Subsría. For. y de la Fauna.

García, E., C. Soto, and F. Miranda. 1960. *Larrea* y clima. *An. Inst. Biól. Univ. Méx.* 31:133–171.

Gómez-Pompa, A. 1966. Estudios botánicos en la región de Misantla, Veracruz. *Pub. Inst. Mex. Rec. Nat. Renov., México.*

______. 1971. Posible papel de la vegetación secundaria en la evolución de la flora tropical. *Biotropica* 3:125–135.

______, C. Vázquez-Yanes, and S. Guevara. 1972. The tropical rain forest: A nonrenewable resource. *Science* 177:762–765. (This constitutes an overview of various aspects of tropical rain forest dynamics in relation to ever growing disturbance by human activities.)

______ et al., eds. 1976. *Regeneración de Selvas.* México: CECSA.

González-Quintero, L. 1974. El pleistoceno de México. Inst. Nal. de Antropología e Historia, Depto. de Prehistoria, *Cuadernos de Trabajo* 2:1–17.

González-Medrano, F. et al. 1976. Estudios ecológicos en la zona de Las Adjuntas, porción central de Tamaulipas, México. I. La metodología del estudio de la vegetación. *Biótica* 1:71–79.

Guevara, S. and A. Gómez-Pompa. 1972. Seeds from surface soils in a tropical region of Veracruz, México. *J. Arnold Arbor. Harv. Univ.* 53:312–335. (This is one of the few first attempts at studying and analyzing tropical rain forest seed banks, with a discussion of its floristic composition.)

Halffter, G. 1964. La entomofauna Americana, ideas acerca de su origen y distribución. *Folia Entomol. Mex.* 6:1–108.

———. 1974. Elements anciens de l'entomofaune neotropicale: ses implications biogeographiques. *Quaestiones Entomol.* 10:223–262.

———. 1976. Distribución de los insectos en la zona de transición Mexicana. Relaciones con la entomofauna de Norteamérica. *Folia Entomol. Mex.* 35:1–64. (These three papers by Halffter are of basic importance for the zoogeography of Mexico.)

———, V. Halffter, and Y. López. 1974. *Phanaeus* behavior I. Food transportation and bisexual cooperation. *Environ. Entomol.* 3:341–345.

——— and E. G. Matthews. 1966. The natural history of dung beetles of the subfamily Scarabaeinae (Coleoptera: Scarabaeidae). *Folia Entomol. Mex.* 12–14: 1–312. (This monograph is a basic reference work for all studies on dung beetles and grassland ecology in many parts of the world.)

Hernández X., E. 1947. La Scheelea liebmannii, su distribución y producción. *An. Inst. Biól. Méx.* 18:43–70.

———. 1958. La agricultura. In *Los recursos naturales del Sureste y su aprovechamiento* Vol. 2, pp. 3–57. México: Ediciones del Inst. Mex. Rec. Nat. Renov. (The most important agroecological study at the general level in Mexico and basic to understanding patterns and customs of traditional agriculture in the tropics.)

Herrera, A. 1888. Apuntes de ornitología. La migración en el Valle de México. *La Naturaleza,* 2a. Ser. 1:165–169.

———. 1890. El Valle de México considerado como provincia zoológica. *La Naturaleza,* 2a. Ser. 1:343–378.

Hidalgo, E. and E. A. Chávez. In press. Estudio de la macrofauna de las playas cercanas a Laguna Verde, Veracruz, México. *Depto. de Pesca, Serie Científica* No. 18.

Instituto Nacional de Pesca. 1976*a*. *Memorias del primer Simposio Nacional de Recursos Pesqueros Masivos de México,* 2 vols.

———. 1976*b*. *Memorias del Simposio sobre Biología y Dinámica Poblacional de Camarones,* 2 vols.

———. 1976*c*. *Memorias de la Reunión sobre los Recursos de Pesca Costera de México.*

Kormicker, L. S., F. Bonet, R. Cann, and C. Hoskin. 1959. Alacran Reef, Campeche Bank, México. *Publ. Inst. Mar. Sci.* (Texas) 6:1–22.

Lluch, B. D. 1976. *Diagnóstico, modelo y régimen óptimo de la pesquería de camarón en el Noroeste de México.* Doctoral Thesis, Escuela Nacional de Ciencias Biológicas, Instituto Politécnico Nacional.

Lot-Helgueras, A., C. Vázquez-Yanes, and F. Menéndez. 1975. Physiognomic and floristic changes near the northern limit of mangroves in the Gulf Coast of

Mexico. In *Proceedings of the International Symposium on the Biological Management of Mangroves,* Vol. 1, pp. 52–61.

Lot, A., A. Novelo, and A. Quiroz. 1979. The chinampa: an agricultural system that utilizes aquatic plants. *J. Aquat. Plant Manage.* 17:74–75.

Madrigal, X. 1967. Contribución al conocimiento de la ecología de los bosques de oyamel, *Abies religiosa* (H.B.K.). Schl. et Cham., en el Valle de México. *Bol. Téc. Inst. Nac. Invest. For. Méx.* Vol. 18.

Martínez-Alfaro, M. A. 1972. Ecología humana del ejido "Benito Juárez" o Sebastopol, Tuxtepec, Oax. *Publ. Esp. Inst. Nac. Inv. For. Mex.* 1:1–156.

Miranda, F. 1948. Observaciones botánicas en la región de Tuxtepec, Oax. *An. Inst. Biol. Univ. Méx.* 19:105–136.

______. 1952–1953. *La vegetación de Chiapas.* Tuxtla Gutiérrez: Imprenta del Gobierno del Estado.

______. 1955. Formas de vida y el problema de la delimitación de las zonas áridas de México. In *Mesas redondas sobre problemas de las zonas áridas de México.* Publ. Inst. Mex. Rec. Nat. Renov., pp. 85–109.

______. 1957. Vegetación de la vertiente del Pacífico de la Sierra Madre de Chiapas (México) y sus relaciones florísticas. *Proc. 8th Pacif. Sci. Congr.* 4:438–453.

______. 1959. Estudios acerca de la vegetación. In *Los recursos naturales del sureste y su aprovechamiento.* Edic. Inst. Mex. Rec. Nat. Renov. Vol. 2, pp. 215–271.

______, A. Gómez-Pompa, and E. Hernández X. 1967. Un método para la investigación de las regiones tropicales. *An. Inst. Biol. UNAM* (Ser. Bot.) 38:101–110.

______ and E. Hernández X. 1963. Los tipos de vegetación de México y su clasificación. *Bol. Soc. Bot. Méx.* 28:29–179.

______ and A. J. Sharp. 1950. Characteristics of the vegetation in certain temperate regions of eastern Mexico. *Ecology* 31:313–333.

Ochoterena, I. 1918. Las regiones geográfico-botánicas de México. *Bol. Soc. Mex. Geogr. Estad.* 8:221–231.

Orozco, A. and A. Lot-Helgueras. 1976. La vegetación de las zonas inundables del Sureste de Veracruz. *Biótica* 1:1–44.

Osorio-Tafall, B. 1943. El Mar de Cortés y la productividad fitoplanctónica de sus aguas. *An. Esc. Nac. Cienc. Biol.* 3:73–118.

______. 1944. Biodinámica del lago de Pátzcuaro. I. Ensayo de interpretación de sus relaciones tróficas. *Rev. Soc. Mex. Hist. Nat.* 5:197–227.

______. 1946. Contribución al conocimiento del Mar de Cortés. *Bol. Soc. Mex. Geogr. Estad.* 62:89–130.

Phillips, A. R. 1961. Emigraciones y distribución de aves terrestres en México. *Rev. Soc. Mex. Hist. Nat.* 22:295–311.

Piñero, D. 1979. *El presupuesto energético y sus consecuencias demográficas en una palma tropical.* M.S. thesis, Facultad de Ciencias, UNAM, México.

Ramírez-Granados, R. 1958. Aspectos biológicos y económicos de la pesquería de sardina, *Sardinops caerulea* (Girard, 1854), en aguas mexicanas del Pacífico. Veracruz: Sría. de Marina.

Rioja, E. 1954. Contribución al estudio de las esponjas de agua dulce de México. *An. Inst. Biol. Univ. Méx.* 24:425–433.

Rzedowski, J. 1957. Vegetación de las partes áridas de los estados de San Luis Potosí y Zacatecas. *Rev. Soc. Méx. Hist. Nat.* 18:49–101.

———. 1961. *La vegetación del Estado de San Luis Potosí.* Doctoral thesis. Facultad de Ciencias, UNAM. (This study of vegetation of semi-arid lands influenced much of the research on plant ecology done for these three areas in Mexico.)

———. 1962. Contribuciones a la fitogeografía florística e histórica de México. I. Algunas consideraciones acerca del elemento endémico en la Flora Mexicana. *Bol. Soc. Bot. Méx.* 27:52–65.

———. 1965. Relaciones geográficas y posibles orígenes de la Flora de México. *Bol. Soc. Bot. Méx.* 29:121–177.

———. 1972*a*. Contribución a la fitogeografía florística e histórica de México. II. Afinidades geográficas de la flora fanerogámica de diferentes regiones de la República Mexicana. *An. Esc. Nac. Cienc. Biol. Mex.* 19:45–48.

———. 1972*b*. Contribuciones a la fitogeografía florística e histórica de México. III. Algunas tendencias en la distribución geográfica y ecológica de las Compositae mexicanas. *Ciencia* (Méx. City) 27:123–132. (This series of four papers are the basis for the understanding of origins, relations, and evolution of Mexican flora and vegetation.)

———. 1975. An ecological and phytogeographical analysis of the grasslands of Mexico. *Taxon* 24:67–80.

———. 1978. *Vegetación de México.* México: Limusa.

——— and R. McVaugh. 1966. La vegetación de la Nueva Galicia. *Contrib. Univ. Mich. Herb.* 9:1–123.

———, L. Vela G., and X. Madrigal. 1977. Algunas consideraciones acerca de la dinámica de los bosques de coníferas en México. *Ciencia For.* 2:15–35.

Santoyo, H. and M. Signoret. In press. *Ciclo estacional del fitoplancton en la región litoral adyacente a la laguna Verde.* Veracruz: Sría. de Marina.

Sarukhán, J. 1964. Estudio sucesional de una área talada en Tuxtepec, Oaxaca. *Publ. Esp. Inst. Nac. Invest. For. Méx.* 3:107–172.

———. 1968. *Análisis sinecológico de las selvas de* Terminalia amazonia *en la Planicie Costera del Golfo de México.* M.S. thesis. Colegio de Postgraduados, Escuela Nacional de Agricultura, Chapingo, México. (These and Sousa [1964] are basic for the study of secondary vegetation in the hot-humid tropics and were among the first to be carried at the world level. Sarukhán's 1968 study is an attempt at describing the general dynamics and structure of a tropical rain forest community in most of its area of distribution in Mexico.)

———. 1977. Studies on the demography of tropical trees. In *Tropical trees as living systems,* eds. P. B. Tomlinson and M. H. Zimmermann. Cambridge: Cambridge University Press.

———. 1980. Problems and perspectives of plant demography in the tropics. In *Plant population dynamics and demography,* ed. O. Solbrig, pp. 161–188. Oxford: Blackwell's Scientific Publishers.

——— and M. Gadgil. 1974. Studies on plant demography: *Ranunculus repens, R. bulbosus* and *R. acris.* III. A mathematical model incorporating multiple modes of reproduction. *J. Ecol.* 62:921–936.

——— and J. L. Harper. 1973. Studies on plant demography: *Ranunculus repens, R. bulbosus* and *R. acris.* I. Population flux and survivorship. *J. Ecol.* 61:675–716.

Sharp, A. J. 1953. Notes on the flora of Mexico: World distribution of the woody dicotyledoneous families and the origin of the modern vegetation. *J. Ecol.* 41:374–380.

Sousa Sánchez, M. 1964. Estudio de la vegetación secundaria en la región de Tuxtepec, Oaxaca. *Publ. Esp. Inst. Nac. Invest. For. Méx.* 3:91–105.

______. 1969. Influencia de las aves en la vegetación de la Laguna del Majahual en Los Tuxtlas, Veracruz. *Bol. Soc. Bot. Méx.* 30:97–112.

Standley, P. C. 1920–1926. *Trees and shrubs of Mexico.* Contr. U.S. Nat. Herb. Vol. 23, parts 1–5. Washington, D.C.

Stuardo, J. and A. Martínez. 1975. Resultados generales de una prospección de los recursos biológicos y pesqueros del sistema lagunero costero de Guerrero, México. *Acta Politéc. Mex.* 16(72):99–115.

Toledo, Víctor M. 1975. La estacionalidad de las flores utilizadas por los colibríes de una selva tropical húmeda en México. *Biotrópica* 7:63–70.

______. 1976. *Los cambios climáticos del pleistoceno y sus efectos sobre la vegetación tropical cálida y húmeda de México.* M.S. thesis, Facultad de Ciencias, UNAM.

______. 1977. Pollination of some rain forest plants by non-hovering birds in Veracruz, México. *Biotrópica* 9:262–267.

Turcott, V. In press. *Variación estacional del zooplancton en el área costera adyacente a la Laguna Verde.* Veracruz: Sría. de Marina.

Vázquez-Soto, J. 1963. Clasificación de las masas forestales de Campeche. *Bol. Tec. Inst. Nac. Inv. For. Méx.* 10.

Vázquez-Yanes, C. 1976*a*. Estudios sobre la ecofisiología de la germinación en una zona cálido-húmeda de México. In *Regeneración de selvas,* eds. A. Gomez-Pompa et al., pp. 279–387. México: CECSA.

______. 1976*b*. Seed dormancy and germination in secondary vegetation tropical plants: The role of light. *Comp. Physiol. Ecol.* 1:30–34.

______. 1980. Light quality and seed germination in *Cecropia obtusifolia* and *Piper auritum* from a tropical rain forest in Mexico. *Phyton* 38:33–35.

Vela, L. 1976. Contribución a la ecología de *Pinus patula* Schl. et Cham. Thesis, Escuela Nacional de Ciencias Biológicas, IPN.

Villa, B. 1966. *Los murciélagos de México.* México: Ed. Universidad Nacional Autónoma de México.

Villalobos, A. 1971. Estudios ecológicos en un arrecife coralino en Veracruz, México. In *Symp. Inv. Resour. Caribb. Sea and Adjacent Regions,* pp. 531–546. New York: UNESCO-FAO.

______, J. A. Suárez-Caabro, S. Gómez, G. de la Lanza, M. Aceves, F. Manrique, and J. Cabrera. 1966. Considerations on the hydrography and productivity of Alvarado lagoon, Veracruz, México. *Proceedings of the Gulf and Caribbean Fisheries Institute.* 19th Annual Ses., pp. 75–85.

______, J. Cabrera, S. Gómez, V. Arenas, and G. de la Lanza. 1969. Relación entre postlarvas planctónicas de *Penaeus* sp. y caracteres ambientales en la laguna de Alvarado, Veracruz, México. *Mem. Simp. Intern. Lagunas Costeras.* UNAM-UNESCO Nov. 28–30, 1967, México, pp. 601–620.

Yáñez-Arancibia, A. 1976. Fish culture in coastal lagoons: Perspectives in Mexico. *Progress in marine research in the Caribbean and adjacent regions.* CICAR-II Symposium, FAO-UNESCO-WMO, July 12–16, 1976.

———. 1978. Taxonomía, ecología y estructura de las comunidades de peces en lagunas costeras con bocas efímeras del Pacífico de México. *Centro Cienc. del Mar y Limnol. UNAM Publ. Esp.* 2:1–306.

——— and R. S. Nugent. 1976. Some ecological relationships of nektonic communities in nine coastal lagoons on the Pacific Coast of Mexico. Paper read at the 39th Annual Meeting American Society of Limnology and Oceanography, Savannah, Georgia.

4

PUERTO RICO

Herminio Lugo Lugo

INTRODUCTION

Puerto Rico is the smallest of the Greater Antilles, located between 17°54′ and 18°31′ north latitude and 65°15′ and 67°15′ west longitude. It was discovered in 1493 by Christopher Columbus on his second voyage to the New World. Then, tropical ecosystems, such as the mangroves, flourished in Puerto Rico along the coasts; there were dense tropical rain forests in the central mountains and on the northern plains, sand dunes along the northern beaches, "haystack" hills from Carolina to Aguadilla, xerophytic forests and scrub vegetation on the southern side, and magnificent coral reefs in the shallow waters of the coasts. Flocks of tropical birds, such as the Puerto Rican parrot [*Amazona vittata vittata* (Boddaert)], were a vital component of the tropical forests then in existence in Puerto Rico.

Five centuries later, the mangroves have been drastically reduced; the rain forests are limited to the crests of the highest mountains and the Caribbean National Forest; the sand dunes have almost disappeared; the southern part of the island has been largely denuded of xerophytic vegetation; and the Puerto Rican parrot is nearly extinct with only sixteen to twenty individuals remaining. The vegetation of the island has been dramatically changed by the introduction of exotic plant species for agricultural and ornamental purposes.

Intensive agriculture, rapid urban development, increasing industrial potential, and intense human activities have been important factors in the disappearance of natural ecosystems in Puerto Rico. The island, with its almost four million inhabitants, is considered to be the second most densely populated country in the New World. The negative impact on the environment as a result of the human population explosion has produced a tremendous stress in the natural ecosystems of the island.

The scientific studies carried out in Puerto Rico up to the early 1920s were mainly exploratory, consisting mostly of the identification of plant and animal species. The only prominent scientific treatise written during the nineteenth century was Agustin Stahl's *Flora of Puerto Rico.* His observations on our vegetation appeared in separate booklets between 1883 and 1888. In 1934, these were combined and published in three volumes. In 1899, the U.S. Fish Commission published in their bulletin a paper on their investigations of the aquatic resources and fisheries of Puerto Rico.

Other descriptive publications of the first quarter of the twentieth century were Urban's *Plant Geography of Puerto Rico* in 1911, Murphy's *Forests of Porto Rico* in 1916, Wolcott's *Entomologia Economica Puertorriqueña* in 1924, Britton and Wilson's *Descriptive Flora of Puerto Rico* in 1925, and the *Scientific Study of Porto Rico and the Virgin Islands,* a treatise in 18 volumes published from 1916 to 1943. This publication presents the findings of a group of scientists who visited Puerto Rico under the auspices of the New York Academy of Sciences and under the direction of N. L. Britton.

The first ecological study of the island carried out by Gleason and Cook is presented in Vol. VII of the *Scientific Survey of Porto Rico and the Virgin Islands.* Other important recent ecological contributions are Dansereau's *Studies of the Vegetation of Puerto Rico* in 1966; Ewel and Witmore's *Ecological Life Zones of Puerto Rico and the Virgin Islands;* the studies on forest ecology carried out by the U.S. Forest Service of the U.S. Department of Agriculture; Odum's *A Tropical Rain Forest* in 1970; the *Flora of Mona and Monito Islands* in 1977 by Woodbury et al.; *An Ecological Guide to the Littoral Fauna and Flora of Puerto Rico* by Barbara Mathews in 1967; and Almy's *Shallow-Water Stony Corals of Puerto Rico* in 1963.

In 1903, the federal government set aside the forest on the Luquillo Mountains as the Caribbean National Forest; similarly, the state government set aside, from 1918 to 1922, the forests in San Juan, Aguirre, Boquerón, Guánica, Mona, and Maricao, and from 1935 to 1943, the Carite, Toro Negro, Guilarte, Río Abajo, and Guajataca forests as state reservations. These governmental actions are important because these forests represent a network of ecosystems in fairly natural conditions.

Springing from the population explosion, the industrial developments of the last decades, and the rapid deterioration of our natural ecosystems, interest in ecology and environmental problems in Puerto Rico has increased greatly. Changes in the attitude of the people are already producing a better climate for the solution of our environmental problems.

CONTRIBUTIONS OF EDUCATIONAL INSTITUTIONS

The Universities and Colleges

As a subject at the university level, ecology was first taught in 1935 at the Polytechnic Institute of Puerto Rico (now Inter American University). The late Dr. Ismael Vélez, who taught this course with emphasis on field trips, can be considered a pioneer in the teaching of modern ecology in Puerto Rico. Since the first course at Inter American University, ecology has become a favorite course on most of the university campuses in Puerto Rico. Courses in ecology were first taught at the campuses of the University of Puerto Rico at Río Piedras and Mayaguez during the mid-1950s. At present, any student obtaining a degree in science from any public or private university in Puerto Rico has taken at least a one-semester course in ecology.

At Mayaguez, the creation of the Department of Marine Sciences with programs leading to the M.S. and Ph.D. in these fields has provided the opportunity to study the ecological problems of marine ecosystems in Puerto Rico. The establishment of an educational nuclear reactor and the organization of the zoological park of the University of Puerto Rico at Mayaguez has further enhanced interest in nature and its problems.

The biology department of the Río Piedras campus of the University of Puerto Rico offers the richest program in ecology in Puerto Rico. The general course, Environmental Biology, has grown from one section in 1955 to twenty sections today and is offered to approximately 450 students annually. Additional course titles are Plant Communities, Population Biology, Marine Ecology, Animal Behavior, and Ecology of Puerto Rico. These are offered as part of the regular curriculum for science students working toward a major in biology. Graduate students in biology working toward the M.S. degree can, if they want, do their research and thesis on ecological problems in Puerto Rico. The schools of architecture, social sciences, and law also offer courses related to human ecology and to environmental law.

Under the auspices of the National Science Foundation, a new program leading to a B.S. in environmental management was started in 1976–1977 at the University of Puerto Rico. This multidisciplinary program is open to sophomore students who devote their remaining university years to studying environmental management, air and water pollution, solid wastes disposal, economics, environmental law, geography, meteorology, geology, and energy and natural resources conservation. The new program aims at the training of leaders in the search for solutions to environmental management problems in Puerto Rico and other tropical countries. Graduates of this program are already doing fieldwork in different ecological aspects in private and public institutions of Puerto Rico.

For eight years, the medical science campus of the University of Puerto

Rico has offered a program leading to the M.S. degree in environmental health. It has also incorporated in its medical curriculum a course on man and the environment, which has to be taken by all students working toward a doctorate in medicine.

The central administration of the University of Puerto Rico is taking the necessary steps to become a leader in the search for solutions to environmental problems on the island. It sponsors seminars, open discussions, and radio and television programs to increase the public's information about the energy problems of our modern society. For several years, a committee of scientists chosen from the different campuses has been considering the energy problems that affect Puerto Rico. In cooperation with the President's office and in response to the serious worldwide energy crisis, members of the Faculty of Natural Sciences at the Río Piedras campus have undertaken research toward the development of an electric automobile.

University officials have proposed the conversion of the Humacao College into a center for the study of marine sciences, while the Cayey campus would concentrate on terrestrial ecosystems. The botanical garden of the University of Puerto Rico at Río Piedras, the zoological park at Mayaguez, and the arboretum to be developed at the Cayey campus would be centers of both educational and recreational activities for the people of Puerto Rico interested in nature.

The Administration of Junior Colleges of the University of Puerto Rico instituted in 1975 a televised course on man and his environment. The course may be taken with or without credit by university students or by citizens who are interested in environmental problems. Grades and credits are offered to all persons officially registered in the course who participate in all the academic activities involved. Professors and students from the six regional colleges of the University of Puerto Rico participate in this joint educational effort.

The Public Schools

Consciousness of the ecological problems of Puerto Rico and the modern world is developed in students of the public school system from the moment they enter the first grade until they graduate from high school. From the first grade when students start to develop concepts on how to improve the surrounding environment, the curriculum grows in complexity up to the high school level. At the junior high school level, the students consider the impact of humans on the environment and Puerto Rican ecosystems. In high school, the students receive an intensive course on both terrestrial and aquatic ecosystems and consider topics on human ecology, such as urban ecology. The biology course offered at the junior and senior high schools in Puerto Rico is the Biological Sciences Curriculum Study (BSCS) with the ecological approach. The interest in the environment is evidenced by the increase in the number of projects presented at science fairs by students from private and public high schools of Puerto Rico.

CONTRIBUTIONS OF FEDERAL AND STATE GOVERNMENT AGENCIES

State Agencies

The Experimental Station of Puerto Rico at Río Piedras is the research unit of the Mayaguez campus of the University of Puerto Rico. Since 1916, the institution has been doing active research in applied ecological aspects of agriculture. At present, there are about 160 research projects involved in advancing the cultivation of the main agricultural crops of the island. The findings of this research have been published for the last sixty years in the *Journal of Agriculture of the University of Puerto Rico* and in the *Bulletins of the Experimental Station,* of which about 250 have already been printed. The Agricultural Extension Service is the unit responsible for the dissemination of educational information to the people of Puerto Rico, using the findings of the research developed at the experimental station.

Federal Agencies

The Federal Experimental Station (now Mayaguez Institute of Tropical Agriculture) was started as an institution to do research in agricultural problems of Puerto Rico, but now specializes in international agriculture. The findings of the research carried on in tropical agriculture are used to strengthen U.S. international policies with tropical countries through advice in the scientific phase of agriculture.

The Institute of Tropical Forestry of the Forest Service, U.S. Department of Agriculture, at Río Piedras has also made sound contributions to the advancement of ecological research in Puerto Rico. The institute has studied the dwarf forests of the Luquillo Mountains and the silviculture of natural forests. Since 1957, it has continued a program to save the Puerto Rican parrot from extinction. From 1957 to 1959 and again in 1979, it made island-wide forest inventories; it made inventories of the Caribbean National Forest in 1937, 1948, and 1966; and it has kept growth records in primary and secondary forests throughout the island from 1943 to the present. Staff of the institute also produced a *Life Zone Map of Puerto Rico* and several volumes on the trees of Puerto Rico. The forest service personnel are also actively working in a program of reforestation and conservation of Puerto Rican forests and doing research on the introduction of trees from other tropical countries. Over 400 species of native and exotic trees have been tested for silvicultural promise.

One of the newly introduced species, which has been violently opposed by some environmentalists in Puerto Rico, is the honduran pine, *Pinus caribea hondurensis.* Civic organizations like the Puerto Rico Medical Association and the Evangelical Council of Puerto Rico recently held a two-day seminar to show their opposition to the introduction of this Central American species. Opposition to this species is based on possible negative ecological effects on Puerto Rican ecosystems.

The Center for Energy and Environment Research (CEER), formerly the Puerto Rico Nuclear Center of the University of Puerto Rico, is actively performing research on alternative sources of energy, including solar energy, biomass, and thermal gradients in the deep ocean waters on the south coast of Puerto Rico. The center aids in the national effort to achieve energy independence and serves as a focal point for energy and environmental research in Puerto Rico. CEER also cooperates with other countries in the tropical and subtropical zones by providing consultations and training to students and personnel from Latin America and the Caribbean. The center's major research in ecology-related fields encompasses marine and terrestrial ecology, environmental assessment, energy conservation, solar engineering, and ocean thermal energy utilization. From 1974 through 1980, CEER has published eighteen scientific papers on human ecology, forty-four on marine biology, and twenty-five on terrestrial ecology. Seventy-nine other papers were published on topics related to nuclear science and agronomy. It is anticipated that, with the new orientation, CEER will stimulate further research in environmental sciences with emphasis on energy problems.

The terrestrial ecology section of CEER has developed an intensive research program in Puerto Rico. A group of scientists from different federal and state agencies carried out one of the most complete studies in the world on a tropical rain forest. In the study at El Verde, the researchers sought to determine how a rain forest works as a system and under stress. Using modern and classical techniques, they emphasized population ecology, mineral cycling, metabolism, and other functions of the complex living structure. The disordering stress of the radiation experiment was a tool for the study of mechanisms that maintain order, mechanisms that may reach their greatest development in a tropical forest. The metabolism of a natural rain forest was measured. The ecological findings of this project were edited by H. T. Odum (1970) in a volume that includes 106 scientific papers.

Funds for the development of research on wildlife and sportfishing are provided by the U.S. Department of Interior through the Fishing and Wildlife Service. These funds have been used by the Commonwealth Department of National Resources for ecological research on estuaries, the dry forest at Guánica, the limestone hills at Río Abajo, population studies on wild animals and their effect on the vegetation at the Mona Island, the aquatic effect of sedimentation on coral reefs, as well as studies on the ecology of pigeons and other bird species in Puerto Rico. Today, the Department of Natural Resources is preparing a comprehensive review of knowledge on the natural resources of Puerto Rico. This review will take three years and will culminate in the publication of an encyclopedia of natural resources of Puerto Rico.

During the decade of the 1960s, government studies showed that about a dozen agencies of the Commonwealth of Puerto Rico, half a dozen federal agencies, and all the seventy-eight municipalities on the island were involved in the search for solutions to pollution problems. This situation led to the organization of these agencies, so that effective solutions to pollution problems could be achieved. The first official step toward this goal was taken on June 28, 1968, when a law was approved creating the Natural Resources Area as part of the Department of Public Works. However, government officials were conscious that a high-level organization was needed if Puerto Rico was going to move toward environmental protection by legal force and to provide the necessary power to develop a public environmental policy. In response to these concerns, the law on public environmental policy was approved on June 18, 1970. This law provided for the establishment of an Environment Quality Board that answered to the governor and was responsible for the establishment of the environmental policies of the island with power to impose on public agencies the responsibilities to protect the natural environments of Puerto Rico.

The powers lodged in the Environmental Quality Board by the 1970 law are similar to those exercised by the Federal Council on Environmental Quality and by the National Environmental Policy Act that was approved by the U.S. Congress in 1969. The Environmental Quality Board investigates and identifies the conditions and tendencies of the environment, evaluates government and private activities in the light of public environmental policy, and makes specific recommendations to the governor. The control functions bestowed by the law convert the board into a regulatory agency with quasi-judicial and quasi-legislative powers to act on behalf of the Puerto Rican environment. Besides these controlling functions, the Environmental Quality Board has developed an intensive educational campaign for government officials at different administrative levels, for private enterprises, and for the general public of the island.

The Environmental Quality Board produces for distribution among the people of Puerto Rico numerous scientific papers and studies on environmental problems. Among these, worth mentioning is the study published in two volumes in 1973 entitled *Mona and Monito Islands, an Assessment of Their Natural and Historical Resources.* The study, carried out by a group of scientists attached to different federal and state government institutions, includes climate, soils, geology, water resources, marine life, terrestrial vegetation, and the fauna of these islands. In December 1974, the board held a seminar workshop on environmental education at the University of Puerto Rico at Río

Piedras. The workshop's discussions and a directory listing federal, state, and civic agencies involved in the environmental problems of Puerto Rico were published by the board in 1975.

On June 20, 1972, the Department of Natural Resources was created by law to stimulate the use and conservation of the natural resources of Puerto Rico. One of the main developments of the newly organized department is the scientific research section, which obtains basic information about ecosystems that is then used to plan the development and conservation of our natural resources. The department has also created the Geological Service of Puerto Rico, which seeks a rational policy for the effective use of our nonrenewable resources in order to minimize the negative consequences that adversely affect the welfare of Puerto Ricans. The Department of Natural Resources coordinates its activities with other local and federal government agencies. In addition, the department oversees two other corporations for mining and fishing.

With a research budget exceeding $500,000 per year, the Department of Natural Resources represents the most powerful force in the island's research efforts. The department sponsors an annual symposium, now in its eighth year, the proceedings of which are published. The department has also produced comprehensive publications summarizing knowledge on beach ecosystems, coral reefs, mangroves, lakes, estuaries, caves, critical natural areas, and terrestrial ecosystems such as the Guánica subtropical forest and the Río Abajo limestone forest. Management plans for all state forests, including Mona Island and the coastal zone, have also been published. All these studies have been supported by federal funds from the Coastal Zone Management Program and from the U.S. Department of Interior. These publications are available from the Assistant Secretary of Scientific Investigations, Department of Natural Resources, P.O. Box 5887, San Juan, Puerto Rico 00906.

At present, the main projects for future use of natural resources include copper mining on the Utuado-Adjuntas area and the exploration for possible petroleum deposits on the northern coast. The probability of the development of these natural resources has stirred up public debate about environmental conservation. In Puerto Rico, the economic, social, and environmental factors are perceived differently in this debate by the leaders of the three political parties, the views of none having thus far prevailed. Detailed studies by the Department of Natural Resources on the effect on natural ecosystems and the economy of the island, and the changes that will be produced in the behavior of the people of Puerto Rico by development of the natural resources, are being carried out before actual development begins.

The Puerto Rico Water Resources Authority has also performed research on the pollution problems of the Grande de Loíza River and the possible effects of the discharges of the Barceloneta sewage treatment plant on the marine life of the region.

CONTRIBUTIONS OF CIVIC ORGANIZATIONS

Clearly, both federal and state agencies and the educational system have played an important role in ecological developments in Puerto Rico. However, the role played by the fourteen civic organizations included in the directory prepared by the Environmental Quality Board in 1975 cannot be overlooked. They have made a meritorious contribution through their educational programs toward the preservation of our natural environment. The proliferation of such organizations, as well as the fragmentary activities that each develops, make it a very difficult job to evaluate the magnitude of their contribution. The unifying factor in all of these organizations is their interest in the conservation of the natural ecosystems in Puerto Rico through an educational campaign among their members conducted through seminars, lectures, field trips, press releases, and special projects for the betterment of our land, air, and water resources.

Although none of these organizations by itself can claim a very extensive conservation program, the combined effort of all of these civic associations really represents an impressive effort to awaken the people of Puerto Rico to the problems of environmental conservation. Five of these organizations can be identified as having had significant impact.

Conservation Trust of Puerto Rico

Composed of prominent leaders, the trust is mainly concerned with acquiring natural areas of ecological importance to be preserved for future generations. The trust receives funds from industry through a fixed formula based on profits and administers these funds to buy property for nature protection. One significant purchase is the San Cristobal Canyon.

Institute of Environmental Studies of the Bar Association of Puerto Rico

This is a militant group in matters of environmental problems. Once it completes the necessary studies of an environmental situation, it issues public releases of its conclusions and, if necessary, goes to the courts to enforce environmental laws.

Misión Industrial

This organization studies the effects of pollution on humans and makes recommendations about ways to reduce pollution levels in the environment. This group took the U.S. Navy to court in the bombing of Vieques Island and the DuPont Corporation to court in pollution of the Manatí River. It is the leading watchdog group on mining and oil exploration in Puerto Rico.

Natural History Society

This is one of the oldest civic organizations dealing with conservation of natural resources and protection of natural ecosystems. On certain occasions, it has gone to the courts as a defender of the natural resources of the island. For example, it is the major defender on behalf of Mona Island, which is known for its giant iguanas and a number of other endangered species.

Servicios Legales

A quasi-civic group, this organization receives funds from the government to represent largely indigent individuals and groups against both industry and the government. It has joined forces with other groups in several significant environmental cases, including the defense of the mangroves of Vacia Talega, the largest swamps in Puerto Rico.

Another cluster of civic environmental groups includes the Improvement Fund Association, which aims to create environmental consciousness among its members through publications and field trips; League of Women Voters, which has an environmental quality committee working toward solution of environmental problems; Puerto Rico Lung Association, actively involved in air pollution problems and also in reforestation programs; and the Puerto Rico Planning Society, acting as a forum for correct use of land in the island. Groups that tend to focus on local problems include Boy Scouts of America, aiming at both pollution and protection; Condado Association, improving the aesthetics in San Juan; Cuidar, preserving the mangroves on the Piñones-Vacía Talega area in Carolina; Enceste, combining private and public interests in common environmental problems; and Lions Clubs, especially involved in disposal of solid wastes in public places.

CLOSING REMARKS

Several remarks about the present situation and future perspectives of environmental problems in Puerto Rico should be made. About 90 percent of the terrestrial ecosystems of Puerto Rico have now been modified in some degree by agricultural practices and plant importation. Forests, which formerly covered 100 percent of the island, had been reduced to 4 percent; with the recent decline of agriculture, they have returned to a coverage of about 40 percent. Virtually all the original plant species remain, showing that, in spite of ecosystem interruption, the tropical environment has provided favorable conditions for their preservation. However, there are about 400 endemic and non-endemic plant species in Puerto Rico that are endangered. About twenty-eight animal species are close to extinction, and there are forty-eight rare and endangered species at the present time.

All the rivers in Puerto Rico are polluted, at least near their outlet into the sea. However, some of them are less polluted now than when the rural population was widely dispersed on the island. Some of the estuaries are polluted, causing a deterioration of coastal coral reefs. Air pollution is evident, especially around the large metropolitan areas and industrial centers. Unfortunately, only about 4 percent of Puerto Rico is under legal protection against destruction.

Surprisingly, in spite of the budget limitations of the government agencies in Puerto Rico, developments in ecology during the last two decades have been considerable. As consciousness in the public increases, government officials respond by widening the scope of the programs dealing with environmental problems.

A bright environmental future may be a reality in Puerto Rico. Consciousness among the people about population density and the conservation of our natural resources is improving. The educational campaign of our civic organizations on environmental problems, research and leadership in the universities, greater attention to ecology in public and private school systems in the island, and the actions of federal and state government agencies have brought an awakening of the people of Puerto Rico to the seriousness of our environmental problems. It is hoped that we will continue to preserve the natural aspects of our tropical environment in spite of the pressure exerted by a rapidly growing population with ever-increasing expectations.

MAJOR SCIENTIFIC PERIODICALS IN PUERTO RICO

Bulletins. Publications of the Agricultural Experimental Station of the University of Puerto Rico.

Caribbean Forester. A publication of the U.S. Forest Service, published in San Juan, Puerto Rico from 1939 to 1963.

Caribbean Journal of Sciences. Published by the Institute of Caribbean Science, Faculty of Arts and Sciences, University of Puerto Rico at Mayaguez, since 1961.

Journal of Agriculture. Published since 1917 by the Agricultural Experimental Station of the University of Puerto Rico.

Research Papers. Published irregularly to publicize important research done in tropical forests by the U.S. Forest Service at Río Piedras, Puerto Rico.

Revista de Agricultura de Puerto Rico. An official publication of the Puerto Rico Department of Agriculture.

ACKNOWLEDGMENTS

The author expresses his gratitude to Dr. Frank Wadsworth and Mr. Roy Woodbury for their sound advice in the preparation of this paper. Acknowledgments are also given to educational and governmental institutions and private agencies, which were kind enough to provide information regarding the ecological history of Puerto Rico.

MAJOR ECOLOGICAL PUBLICATIONS OF PUERTO RICO

Almy, C. C., Jr. and C. Carrión-Torres. 1963. Shallow water and stony corals of Puerto Rico. *Caribb. J. Sci.* 3:133–162.

Biaggi, V. 1970. *Las aves de Puerto Rico.* Río Piedras, P.R.: Editorial Universitaria.

Britton, N. L., et al. 1916–1943. *Scientific survey of Porto Rico and the Virgin Islands,* 18 volumes. New York: New York Academy of Sciences.

Dansereau, P. 1966. *Studies on the vegetation of Puerto Rico.* Institute of Caribbean Sciences, Special Publication No. 1. Mayaguez: University of Puerto Rico.

Ewel, J. S. and J. L. Whitmore. 1973. *Ecological life zones of Puerto Rico and the Virgin Islands.* Río Piedras, P.R.: Forest Service, U.S. Department of Agriculture.

Holdridge, L. R. 1942. *Trees of Puerto Rico,* 2 volumes. Río Piedras, P.R.: Forest Service, U.S. Department of Agriculture.

Little, E. L. and F. H. Wadsworth. 1964. *Common trees of Puerto Rico and the Virgin Islands,* Vol. I and Little, E. L., R. O. Woodbury, and F. H. Wadsworth. 1974. *Common trees of Puerto Rico and the Virgin Islands,* Vol. II. Washington, D.C.: Forest Service, U.S. Department of Agriculture. (Two volumes on the classification, botanical description, geographical distribution and uses of our common trees.)

Martorell, L. F. 1976. *Annotated food plant catalog of the insects of Puerto Rico.* Río Piedras, P.R.: Agricultural Experimental Station, University of Puerto Rico. (Plant descriptions and the insects feeding on them. Although it is not written from the ecological point of view, it provides information on energy transfer.)

Mathews, B. M. 1967. *An ecological guide to the littoral fauna and flora of Puerto Rico.* San Juan, P.R.: Department of Education Press.

Murphy, L. S. 1916. *Forests of Puerto Rico.* Bulletin No. 354. Washington, D.C.: U.S. Department of Agriculture. (Past, present and future of the forests of Puerto Rico as well as their physical and economical environment.)

Odum, H. T. 1970. *A tropical rain forest—A study of irradiation and ecology at El Verde, Puerto Rico.* Washington, D.C.: U.S. Atomic Energy Commission. (The most extensive ecological study of a tropical rain forest prepared by a battery of ecologists, botanists, zoologists, foresters, engineers, radiation biologists, and microbiologists.)

Petrunkevitch, A. 1929. *The spiders of Porto Rico.* Connecticut Academy of Arts and Sciences. New Haven: Yale University Press. (Classification, description and geographic distribution of spiders.)

Stahl, A. 1934. *La flora de Puerto Rico.* 3 volumes. San Juan, P.R.: Imprenta Venezuela. (The most complete work on the classification of the plants of the nineteenth century.)

U.S. Fish Commission. 1899. *Investigations of the aquatic resources and fisheries of Porto Rico.* Bulletin No. 20. Washington, D.C.: Government Printing Office.

Vélez, I. and J. van Overbeek. 1950. *Plantas indeseables en los cultivos tropicales.* Río Piedras, P.R.: Editorial Universitaria. (Botanical description, the common and scientific names, geographical distribution of the common tropical weeds.)

Wolcott, G. N. 1924. *Entomología económica Puertorriqueña.* Bulletin No. 32. Río Piedras, P.R.: Agricultural Experimental Station. (Description, classification, life cycles, and geographic distribution of the insects of Puerto Rico.)

Woodbury, R. O., L. Martorell, and J. G. García. 1977. *The flora of Mona and Monito Islands.* Bulletin No. 252. Río Piedras, P.R.: Agricultural Experimental Station. (An ecological and systematic study of the vegetation of these islands.)

———. 1975. *Rare and endangered animals of Puerto Rico;* and *Rare and endangered plants of Puerto Rico.* San Juan, P.R.: Soil Conservation Service, U.S. Department of Agriculture.

———. 1974. Puerto Rico y el mar. San Juan, P.R.: University of Puerto Rico and the Economic Development Administration. (A report to the Governor of Puerto Rico on marine environments, living resources and research developed on the use of our ocean natural resources.)

5

UNITED STATES

Robert L. Burgess

INTRODUCTION

Since the close of the Second World War, the science of ecology in the United States has undergone massive development. With the return of millions of fighting men, college and university enrollments swelled, faculties grew, and curricula expanded. Of course, ecology was not the only science to benefit, but significantly, ecological courses began to be taught in numerous schools for the first time, often as necessary adjuncts to programs in forestry, wildlife, fisheries, and range management.

Ecology has also been notably affected by new federal agencies, new programs within old-line bureaucracies, a spate of environmental legislation, both state and national, in the last two decades, and a number of new institutional programs. In addition, new societies, new journals, and new social problems have all had an impact on the growth, development, and recognition of ecology and ecologists and their role in a modern, high technology, energy-intensive civilization.

This review attempts to outline and highlight a series of these developments but cannot delve too deeply into the various subdivisions of ecological science. Therefore, the ontogeny of population ecology, mathematical and theoretical ecology, evolutionary and genetic ecology is woven into the institutional rubric on which the development of ecological science in the United States has had to build, and with which the active scientists, at times, have had to contend.

This period in the development of ecology is exemplified by a rather astonishing interest in the historical roots of the science. Within the last few years, several major books and papers have appeared that reflect this phenomenon (Egerton 1976; McIntosh 1974, 1975, 1976; Burgess 1977; Egerton and McIntosh 1977; Cook 1977; Worster 1977). While earlier works were available (e.g., Gleason 1936; Allee et al. 1949; Brewer 1960; Major 1969; Darnell 1970; Sears 1956, 1969), the recent spate of activity seems to be related to three events. First of all, the bicentennial observance of the United States of America was a prime force in providing a focus for historical documentation. Science, along with most other disciplines, received its share of attention, certainly augmented by a vocal and continuing concern for the environment. The Oklahoma Press volume (Taylor and White 1976) is a good example, and Marschner's excellent map of the original vegetation of Minnesota (Marschner 1976) was a bicentennial marker for the North Central Forest Experiment Station of the U.S. Forest Service. The bicentennial also created a milieu in which both historians and ecologists could flourish, perhaps for the first time, and recently, the two groups have begun to talk to each other.

Secondly, the founders of American ecology were beginning to disappear, at a time when most of their memories and reminiscences remained unrecorded. Within the last dozen years, Victor E. Shelford, Orlando Park (Engelmann 1970), Henry J. Oosting (Billings 1970), LaMont C. Cole (Anon. 1978), William S. Cooper (Lawrence 1979), B. W. Wells (Cooper 1979), and Henry A. Gleason (Muller 1975; McIntosh 1975) have died, while many more have retired into relative obscurity. There has been a recognized need in most disciplines to tap these historical sources before it is too late, and I suspect that an undercurrent in ecology responds similarly.

Finally, the science of ecology has reached a degree of maturity (McIntosh 1976; Nelkin 1976). Ecology has become a household word, even if not totally understood or even used correctly by the masses. Courses in ecology are offered on most campuses, jobs for graduates continue to expand, there are more and more texts and reference volumes available, and perhaps most important, there is a growing body of theory on which to build. With maturity, ecology has become respectable, and while still a predominantly synthetic science drawing data from a broad array of disciplines, few would deny that ecology has taken its place in the community of sciences.

The past three decades are characterized by an increasing institutional impact, on science in general and on ecology in particular. Federal agencies, regulatory bodies, and international programs have tended to chart the course of the science. An ever-growing body of environmental legislation, at federal, state, and local levels, has created needs and directed research into new areas. All of these are important aspects of the development of ecology in postwar America.

SCHOOLS AND CURRICULA

From what has been called a "twin birth" at the universities of Chicago and Nebraska at the turn of the century, ecological training had spread to a number of other universities by the start of World War II. Animal ecology was strong at Illinois, Duke, Arizona, Cornell, and California, while Yale, Michigan, Duke, Tennessee, Minnesota, and others had developed comprehensive programs in plant ecology. Textbooks could be counted on the fingers of one hand (Egler 1951), and while research productivity was relatively large for both the numbers of people involved and the research dollars available, relatively few "ecologists" were being trained, either at graduate or undergraduate levels.

The hiatus of World War II left a significant gap in continuity, and following V-J day in August of 1945, many faculty returned to their institutions to find thousands of GIs clamoring for an education, graduate students whose development had been grossly interrupted, and curricula that were generally in shambles. As an example, John T. Curtis had left Wisconsin in 1943, from a basic position in plant physiology, to work on *Cryptostegia* production in Haiti as an alternative source of rubber. While there, his interest in vegetation was stimulated by the writings of H. A. Gleason and the interesting problems of Haitian forests, which resulted in a little read but often cited paper published in the *Caribbean Forester* (Curtis 1947). Returning to Wisconsin, he filled an ecological vacuum, and immediately attracted students returning from the war whose education had been temporarily suspended. Forest Stearns, Grant Cottam, and Max Partch exemplified this group, soon followed by Robert P. McIntosh, Richard T. Ward, and Robert T. Brown. This scenario was probably repeated in a dozen universities, as the U.S. educational community began to put the pieces back together. Within a decade, Rutgers, California, Wisconsin, Duke, Illinois, Missouri, Texas, Tennessee, Michigan, and Michigan State had all emerged as strong centers of ecological teaching and research.

The highly successful *Fundamentals of Ecology* by Eugene P. Odum (1953) gave both a boost to the teaching of ecology in colleges and universities and a foundation for the establishment of the Institute of Ecology at the University of Georgia. The text did some other things as well. It brought both animal and plant ecology into a common framework, and building on Lindemann's (1942) concepts, stressed energy flow and "functional ecology." These, in turn, fostered the "ecosystem level" research thrust that has permeated the 1960s and 1970s. Analyses of functional groups, guilds, and trophic levels, however, further sounded the knell for taxonomic erudition in ecology, a trend that has continued to the present (Wilson 1971; Isely 1972). In sum, Odum's text, now in its third edition and translated into over twenty languages, has been a huge success, and the logic, concepts, integration, and use of mathematics as a universal language have probably done more to influence ecological development in both teaching and research than any other single factor in the last thirty years.

By the late 1950s, partly in response to swelling enrollments and changing social needs, many academic institutions were initiating or consolidating major changes in emphasis and organization, often coupled with changes in nomenclature. Gone were the "normal" schools, along with most of the agricultural and mechanical (A and M) institutions. As examples, Arizona State University had completed its evolution from a Territorial Normal School, Oklahoma A&M had become Oklahoma State University, and the North Dakota Agricultural College had grown into the North Dakota State University. In some, the historic name was preserved (e.g., Texas A&M College simply became Texas A&M University). In some cases, postal name changes accompanied the reordering, as State College, Pennsylvania became University Park, and College Station became University Station, Mississippi.

These new institutions often expanded their basic biology curricula and added ecologists to their staffs, mostly still segregated into botanical and zoological departments. While it is almost impossible to obtain data from the more than 2,000 four-year colleges and universities in the United States, it is probably safe to say that by 1960, between 75 and 90 percent of these schools were offering at least one course in "ecology," and many of the universities were pushing for authorization to grant advanced degrees, in many of which ecology was an available discipline.

In the decade of the 1960s, when the postwar "baby boom" hit the colleges, growth in enrollment, broadening of curricula, and the availability of research money all contributed to expanded involvement with ecology. Many schools had numbers of ecologists, if one can judge by lists of members of the Ecological Society of America. More and more specialized courses were being offered, to the point that in some universities, twenty to thirty credit hours were available in "ecological" course work.

By 1960, the University of Saskatchewan (Canada) was offering a degree program in plant ecology, to my knowledge, the first to do so. It would be another ten years before U.S. institutions began to move away from the traditional Master of Science and Doctor of Philosophy degrees in botany and zoology. Today, a number of schools offer advanced degrees in "environmental science," many of which are strongly ecological, but most stress a multidisciplinary approach by including courses such as civil engineering, resource economics, rural and urban sociology, and public relations, in addition to the more traditional exposure to geology, soils, statistics, and basic biology.

THE GROWTH OF RESEARCH SUPPORT

Until World War I, money for research, particularly ecological research, was difficult to find. Tiny sums from federal agencies like the Departments of

Interior or Agriculture were the rule, if one was lucky enough to obtain such a grant. Elery Becker, later to edit the *Journal of Parasitology,* told of approaching the Iowa legislature in 1917 for funds to provide a research animal. Fifty dollars were eventually granted, and Dr. Becker, thinking to the future, bought what he thought was a pregnant goat. Within two months, the goat had died from a massive abdominal tumor, taking with her the entire research grant.

World War II, however, demonstrated the efficacies of large federal support for research, exemplified by, among others, the Manhattan Project, the development of the sulfanilamides and penicillin, and the engineering marvels of rocketry and the jet engine. By 1947, both the Atomic Energy Commission (AEC) and the Office of Naval Research (ONR) were sponsoring ecological research in several universities. The big impetus came, however, with the establishment of the National Science Foundation (NSF) in 1950. In the thirty years since its inception, NSF has been a major source of the research money available to the ecological sciences.

The definition of "ecological research" is, of course, subject to interpretation. The report of the ad hoc Committee on Ecological Research (CEQ-FCST 1974) lists the Department of Commerce as the leading agency supporting ecological science in fiscal year (FY) 1973, indicating an ecological research budget of $40.45 million. Much of this, however, was earmarked for the National Weather Service (meteorological and climatological research) and the National Marine Fisheries Service (NMFS) which is heavily oriented toward the management, including harvest, of marine protein from coastal and oceanic fisheries. Very little of this sum was allocated for external research, either in universities, industry, or private agencies. Similarly, the Department of Agriculture, including the Forest Service, Soil Conservation Service, and Agricultural Research Service, had a 1973 ecological research budget of $32.48 million, but again, most of this total was for in-house support of experiment stations, and the Hatch and Pittman-Robertson funds allocated to state land grant institutions. Only a small amount was available to independent investigators for basic research in ecology.

The AEC, for many years a major supporter of ecological research, had an annual budget of $10 million, a portion of which was specifically included for university support in response to unsolicited proposals. In the early 1950s, the AEC had asked a group of ecologists, including E. P. Odum and Thomas Park, to serve as advisors to its research program on the fate of radionuclides in the environment. By 1953, John Wolfe had left Ohio State for AEC headquarters, and the first AEC ecologist had been hired at Oak Ridge National Laboratory. Wolfe succeeded in implanting the need for long-range ecological research into AEC thinking (Larson 1971), and the results are clearly evident in the early papers from Brookhaven, Hanford, and Argonne, as well as Oak Ridge, National Laboratories.

The National Science Foundation gave its first grant for ecological research in 1952 to G. W. Prescott of Michigan State University—$3,900 for an "Ecological Survey of Arctic and Alpine Algae in Relation to Glaciation and the Disjunctive Distribution of Phanerogams." This was followed later in the same year by grants of $9,700 for a two-year study of "Phytogeography of the American Arctic and Subarctic" to Ernst C. Abbe of the University of Minnesota; $7,500 for three years to C. Clayton Huff, University of New Mexico, for "Effect of Elevation on Distribution of Insect and Arachnid Groups"; and $3,960 to Basile J. Luyet, St. Louis University, for "Survival of Vitrified and Dried Tissues and Organisms." The first-year total of $25,060 dropped to $7,500 for two awards in FY 1953, and rose to $43,200 for seven grants in 1954, including $2,200 for a continuation of Prescott's work on arctic and alpine algae. A large budget increase in FY 1955 is reflected in an expenditure of $212,200 for twenty-five awards in environmental biology.

The amounts (and numbers of awards) have increased through the years, along with a number of organizational changes (Fig. 5.1). Until 1969, environmental and systematic biology shared a budget that reached $10 million per year in the late 1960s (National Science Board 1971). Biological oceanography, funded for two years in the program, was transferred to the Division of Environmental Sciences when the International Biological Pro-

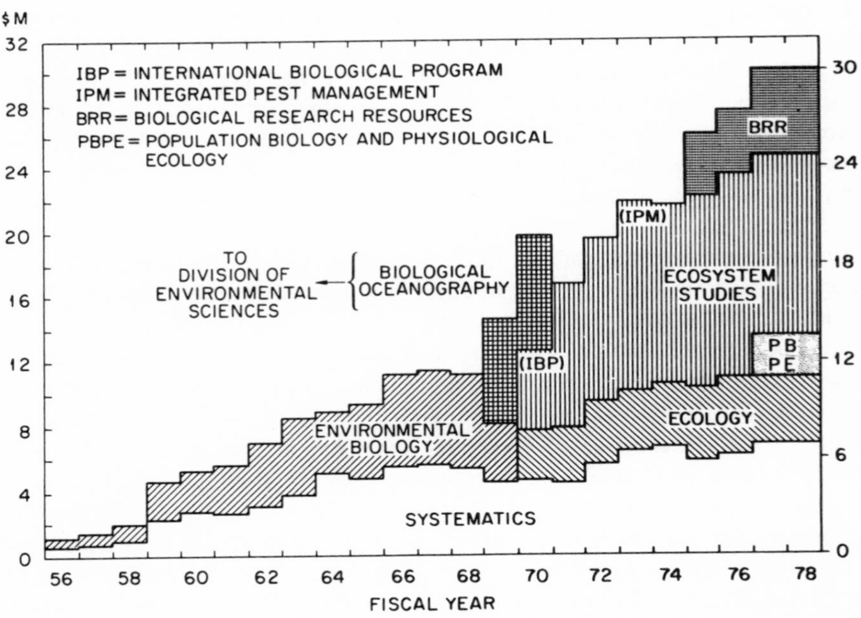

Figure 5.1 Temporal History of Both the Developmental Organization and the Fiscal Year Funding of Environmental Biology Programs in the National Science Foundation. (Courtesy of the National Science, Foundation, modified)

gram (IBP) began. The current budget of over $30 million annually has built heavily on the evolution of IBP into an Ecosystem Studies Program, the recent organization of a program in biological research resources—to cover museums, herbaria, biological stations, experimental ecological reserves, and long-term ecological measurement activities—and an incipient split off of population biology and physiologic ecology (Fig. 5.1).

THE ECOLOGICAL SOCIETY OF AMERICA

Since its founding in 1915, the Ecological Society of America (ESA) has been the principal professional focus for ecologists and ecological science in the United States. Both qualitative and quantitative changes in ESA reflect the development of ecology during the past three decades (Simkins 1971), including changes in membership, activity, and journals. *Ecology* and *Ecological Monographs* still constitute a major outlet for research papers in the field, and their content largely mirrors most developments in the discipline.

In 1942, ESA had 684 paid members, a figure that increased only to 711 by 1947. Since then, the rise in the membership curve has been steep and continuous. In 1953, the society membership passed 1,000 members, reached 2,000 in 1960, 3,000 in 1966, and doubled to 6,047 members in 1979 (Burgess 1977). Rather obviously, this increase reflects concurrent developments: the rise in university enrollments, expansion of curricula, the augmentation of graduate degree programs, the increased research support for ecology, the growing public awareness, and the passage of a great deal of environmental legislation. In short, the American population of practicing ecologists had multiplied several-fold since the end of World War II.

The society currently has three real classes of membership, Associate, Active, and Sustaining. A few Life members remain, dating to the period before such memberships were dropped. Emeritus status is available for those with thirty years of continuous membership, to whom journals are available at cost. Student memberships are available in both Active and Sustaining categories, for a maximum of three years at a reduced rate. Finally, Family memberships cover those few cases in which more than one person in a household wishes to become a member. Associate members receive only the *Bulletin of ESA,* Active members receive *Ecology* as well as the *Bulletin,* while Sustaining members also receive *Ecological Monographs.* The category of membership is thus a function of the amount of money paid to the society.

In 1972, in conjunction with incipient moves toward both a Code of Ethics and some type of professional certification, the membership was analyzed and a functional categorization was proposed. This included Professional Ecologists (those trained in and currently practicing the science as teachers, researchers, consultants, or administrators), Adjunct Professionals (those trained in other fields, e.g., hydrologists, meterologists, and soil scientists), Paraprofessionals (those, primarily students, on the way to becoming professionals), and Associates (all others). While not adopted, this breakdown offers a reasonable current interpretation of ESA's composition, with a preponderance, of course, of professional ecologists.

Six sectional affiliations are available to ESA members, based on interest and expression of a desire to be a section member. Three sections of long standing (Animal Behavior: 1,151 members in 1979, Aquatic Ecology: 1,939, and Physiological Ecology: 1,444) have been joined recently by three newer sections. The Applied Ecology Section was formalized in 1972 in response to the burgeoning of a new class of consulting ecologists, plying their trade in the public sector, as well as those working for various mission-oriented government agencies. With 2,584 nominal members, it is now the largest section of ESA. Two small sections, Paleoecology with 304 members and International Affairs with 264, were instituted in 1975 and 1978, respectively. ESA members may claim affiliation with more than one section, and many of them do. Thus, it is possible for a single individual to "belong" to all six sections. No tabulation of this overlap has been attempted. Conversely, many members claim no sectional affiliation. Both of these above facts make any addition of sectional memberships relatively meaningless.

Involvement of the Ecological Society of America in public affairs has been a continuing thrust, although one that often has generated much internal polemic discourse over virtually every issue (Hollander 1976). Since its founding in 1915, ESA was continually interested in the preservation of natural areas for scientific research and teaching purposes. A series of committees served for almost three decades to make recommendations, conduct inventories (Shelford 1926), or to contribute to policy decisions of government agencies (Burgess 1977). At the close of World War II, strong support, led by Victor E. Shelford, was marshalled for ESA to become involved in land acquisition and protection. Many midwestern and western ecologists shared these views. A powerful conservative block in the east, however, held that such activity was beyond the scope and the corporate charter of ESA, and another mechanism had to be found for preserving natural areas. The result was the formation of the Ecologists' Union (Dexter 1978) that rapidly evolved into The Nature Conservancy. This new organization, a private, nonprofit membership group, has been remarkably successful in identifying, acquiring, and managing (or arranging for management) hundreds of natural areas in almost all of the states. Originally a spin-off of the Ecological Society, The Nature Conservancy continues to be a powerful force in preserving a priceless American heritage.

Three indices of ecological growth are available from the scientific literature. Table 5.1 is a skeletal analysis of thirty-five volumes of *Ecology,* the major American journal in the field, and an official organ of the Ecological Society of America. The five volumes from 1945 through 1949 (volumes 24–29) averaged 476 pages per year, and carried fifty-eight papers, including the shorter "Notes and Comment." The increase in size of the journal has

Table 5.1. **Growth of American Ecology from 1945–1979 Exemplified by *Ecology***

Period	Av. no. of pages[1]	Av. no. of papers[2]
1945–1949	476	58
1950–1954	698	81
1955–1959	760	122
1960–1964	846	129
1965–1969	1,085	154
1970–1974	1,279	150
1975–1979	1,379	129

[1]Based on total pages, including "Reviews" and "Index."

[2]Including "Notes and Comment" (1945–1960) and "Reports" (1961–1969). This section of short papers was abandoned from 1970 (Vol. 51) until reinstituted in 1979 with Vol. 60, no. 3. "Reviews" are not included.

Note: *Ecology*, the major journal of the Ecological Society of America, was published quarterly from its inception in 1920 until 1965 (volume 46) when it became bimonthly, six issues per year. Size of the printed portion of each page was 13 × 20.5 cm until 1954 (volume 35), when size was increased to 15.5 × 22.5 cm.

been steady, with a volume averaging 1,379 pages per year over the last five years. The number of articles has dropped, however, after a peak in the decade from 1965 to 1974.

While total pages is a standard index, two other changes are worthy of note. Until 1965, *Ecology* had been published quarterly, but went to bimonthly (six issues per year) with volume 46. The change was instituted as a response to the growing number of submitted manuscripts (generated by an ever-increasing number of working ecologists), and the consequent rise in the rejection rate for *Ecology*. The sharp jump in both number of pages and number of papers between 1960–1964 and 1965–1969 is a reflection of this change (Table 5.1). The other change, more subtle but probably equally significant, occurred in 1954 (volume 35). This was a major increase in the size of the printed page, from 13 × 20.5 cm to 15.5 × 22.5 cm. The approximately 30 percent increase in the amount of printed material per page led, of course, to greater information content in each volume, irrespective of any increase in number of pages. As Table 5.1 shows, however, the measure only delayed a rather inevitable growth in pages and issues per volume.

A second indicator resides in the new scientific journals in ecology and closely related fields that have arisen since the end of World War II (Table 5.2). All of the listed journals publish in English; many are organized, edited, and printed in the United States; and most have American ecologists serving on their editorial boards. Even though the listing is not exhaustive, Table 5.2

Table 5.2. **Partial List of Ecological/Environmental Journals that Have Originated since 1945**

Title	Year of origin
Agriculture and Environment	1975
Agro-Ecosystems	1975
Arctic and Alpine Research	1969
Australian Journal of Ecology	1976
Biological Conservation	1969
Bioscience	1951
Chesapeake Science	1960
Ecological Modelling	1975
Environment International	1978
Environmental Conservation	1974
Environmental and Experimental Botany	1961
Environmental Management	1977
Environmental Science and Technology	1967
Environmental Review	1976
Forest Ecology and Management	1976
Forest Science	1955
Human Ecology	1973
International Journal of the Environment	1979
International Journal of Environmental Studies	1967
Journal of Applied Ecology	1964
Journal of Arid Environments	1978
Journal of Biogeography	1974
Journal of Environmental Management	1972
Journal of Environmental Quality	1972
Journal of Experimental Marine Biology and Ecology	1948
Journal of Range Management	1948
Journal of Soil and Water Conservation	1946
Limnology and Oceanography	1955
Microbial Ecology	1974
Oecologia	1961
Oikos	1950
Palaeogeography, Palaeoclimatology, Palaeoecology	1957
Pedobiologia	1961
Phytocoenologia	1973
Prairie Naturalist	1969
Protection Ecology	1977
Quaternary Research	1970
Science of the Total Environment	1972
Southwestern Naturalist	1956
Tropical Ecology	1960

(*continued*)

Table 5.2—Continued

Title	Year of origin
Urban Ecology	1975
Vegetatio	1948
Water, Air, and Soil Pollution	1970
Water Research	1967
Water Resources Research	1965

still portrays both the growth and the breadth of the science of ecology. Only five journals were added in the five years following the war, while twenty-two (almost half) have begun publication since 1970. In contrast to prewar ecology, relatively few of the newer journals are official publications of scientific societies. Most are commercial ventures that were initially launched in response to the burgeoning growth of the science.

The breadth is indicated by environmental focuses (*Arctic and Alpine Research, Journal of Arid Environments*), taxonomic considerations (*Human Ecology, Microbial Ecology*), regional concerns (*Chesapeake Science, Prairie Naturalist*), and many in a variety of applied areas (*Agro-Ecosystems, Environmental Conservation, Forest Ecology and Management*). This response to the recognized and widespread needs of the growing and diversified ecological community means that outlet and exposure potential has perhaps tripled in the last three and one-half decades. In turn, increased numbers of journals have created bibliographical problems, placed stress on library space and budgets, and have led, at least indirectly, to an increased number of computerized abstracting services (Blackburn 1973). *Ecological Abstracts,* published by Geo Abstracts, Ltd. in Norwich, England, annually searches about 700 journals for ecological articles. The resultant computerized files produce six issues per year (plus a comprehensive index volume) containing approximately 5,000 abstracts, all categorized according to general subject matter, keyworded, and indexed by subject and author. The same firm also publishes Geo Abstracts in seven sections, of which A (Landforms and the Quaternary), B (Climatology and Hydrology), and G (Remote Sensing, Photogrammetry, and Cartography) are of direct importance to ecologists.

More recently, the Commonwealth Agricultural Bureau in Farnham Royal, Slough, England has added *Arid Lands Abstracts* to its list of computerized abstracting and information dissemination services. With the first issue due in early 1980, this promises to be a welcome adjunct to the continuing need for literature search, collation, abstracting, and synthesis. While the above do not constitute forays in American ecology, they are indispensable to ecological research and teaching in the United States. As the body of literature has grown, it has become ever more difficult to keep abreast of the myriad developments in the science, and these abstracts, widely available to American ecology, perform a valuable service in the continued quest for ecological knowledge and understanding.

Finally, several series of books dealing with ecological science have begun publication in the last two decades (Table 5.3). The first of the hardcover series, *Advances in Ecological Research,* was a welcome addition. It carried, by invitation, major review papers and expositions of new research thrusts. During the 1960s, publication was almost annual, but more recently the sequence has lagged considerably. Part of the slack was taken up by the *Annual Review of Ecology and Systematics.* This series is truly annual, and publishes much the same kinds of material as *Advances in Ecological Research,* but interspersed, of course, with major reviews in taxonomy and systematics.

The most successful series has been Springer's *Ecological Studies,* with thirty-three volumes in ten years. It has become an elite outlet for book-length works in ecology, and many American authors openly look to Springer-Verlag as a major publisher in the field. Both international series and those of the United States are documenting the IBP (Table 5.3). Although other nations (notably the Japanese and the Soviet Union) are publishing IBP synthesis series, the Cambridge volumes plus the US/IBP series carry an obvious major contribution from American ecologists.

Dowden, Hutchinson, and Ross began to produce "Benchmark Papers" in a variety of scientific disciplines, adding ecology in 1976 with Frank Golley as series editor. These are essentially anthologies of reprinted papers with explanatory, interpretive, and editorial material added by the individual volume editors. Choices of inclusions are always subject to criticism, and many papers suffer from a degree of emasculation in the reprint process, but generally the series has been well received by the ecological community.

Elsevier's recent ambitious undertaking on Ecosystems of the World (with David W. Goodall as series editor) promises a global ecosystem library in a projected fifty volumes. Unfortunately, the publisher's reputation for high-priced books is not alleviated in this series, as the second volume (in two parts) retails at $166.00. A full set could thus cost the equivalent of a small automobile or a year's tuition at a major university.

Of the series listed in Table 5.3, only the two IBP series and *Ecosystems of the World* have finite termination plans. The others, plus perhaps more still to be instituted, will be part of American ecology for many years to come.

THE INTERNATIONAL BIOLOGICAL PROGRAM

In all probability, the single most important event for U.S. ecology in the last thirty years was the participation in the International Biological Program

Table 5.3. **Recently Established Series of Hardbound Volumes in Ecology and Related Sciences, All with Major Contributions from United States Ecologists**

Series	Publisher	Starting Date	Volumes through 1979
Advances in Ecological Research	Academic Press, New York	1962	10
Ecological Studies	Springer-Verlag, Berlin-Heidelberg-New York	1970	33
Annual Review of Ecology and Systematics	Annual Reviews, Inc., Palo Alto, CA	1970	9
Zoophysiology and Ecology	Springer-Verlag, Berlin-Heidelberg-New York	1971	12
International Biological Programme	Cambridge University Press, Cambridge and New York	1975	8
Developments in Agricultural and Managed-Forest Ecology	Elsevier Scientific Publishing Co., Amsterdam and New York	1975	7
US/IBP Synthesis Series	Dowden, Hutchinson, and Ross, Inc., Stroudsburg, PA	1976	11
Benchmark Papers in Ecology	Dowden, Hutchinson, and Ross, Inc., Stroudsburg, PA	1976	9
Ecosystems of the World	Elsevier Scientific Publishing Co., Amsterdam and New York	1977	2

(IBP). Planned and organized through a series of ICSU (International Council of Scientific Unions) and IUBS (International Union of Biological Sciences) meetings, IBP settled on a general theme of "Biological Productivity and Human Welfare" (Worthington 1975).

In the United States, an ad hoc committee for the IBP was appointed in late 1963 by Frederick Seitz, then president of the National Academy of Sciences. A series of formative meetings, both national and international, paved the way for a major breakthrough at Williamstown, Massachusetts in October 1966. Led by Frederick Smith, then of the University of Michigan, national subcommittees for terrestrial and freshwater productivity coalesced to develop an integrated research program called "Analysis of Ecosystems" (Blair 1977). Within this program, six "biome" studies were originally proposed, but only five (desert, eastern deciduous forest, western coniferous forests, grassland, and tundra) ever came to fruition, a tropical forest program failing to obtain necessary funding. In addition, subsequent strategy meetings spawned additional programs on the origin and structure of ecosystems, Eskimo populations, aerobiology, upwelling ecosystems, and adaptations of high altitude peoples. The point is that the total emphasis was heavily ecological, and consequently, the programs were staffed predominantly with ecologists.

Funded primarily through the National Science Foundation, the IBP had a line budget that reached $12 million per year, with the greatest share going into the five major biome programs (Table 5.4). Large teams of research scientists were assembled, proposals drafted, data gathered, and models developed. While the holistic view had permeated much of ecology for several decades, the biome programs focused on analysis of total systems, including abiotic parameters, trophic levels, energy flows, nutrient cycling, and biomass storage. Evaluations (Battelle Columbus Laboratories 1975; Mitchell et al. 1976) have stressed that these programs resulted in more emphasis on between-compartment exchanges of energy and materials than was normal in American ecology. Models, ranging from process to total system levels, were developed in each program. Many of these have been used in various applications to current problems, but all contributed to an increased understanding not only of the structure and function of ecosystems, but also of the idiosyncracies and pitfalls inherent in attempts to express ecosystem diversity in the rigid language of mathematics.

Irrespective of the criticisms of IBP (and there are many), the United States effort can claim at least three major contributions. First of all, well over 2,000 research papers have already been published in the open literature. In addition, a US/IBP Synthesis Series is being published by Dowden, Hutchinson, and Ross (e.g., Blair 1977), which will total approximately twenty volumes. An International Synthesis Series (e.g., Worthington 1975) (Table 5.3) is also underway at Cambridge University Press, with major contributions from U.S. ecologists in many of its volumes. Thus, the US/IBP, with all of its dollars, has already augmented our ecological knowledge to a significant degree.

Table 5.4. **Funding for Ecological Programs in the US/IBP (modified from USNC/IBP 1974)**

Program	Funding ($\$ \times 10^6$)						
	1968	1969	1970	1971	1972	1973	Total
Grasslands biome	0.424	0.451	1.80	1.80	2.05	2.00	8.525
Eastern deciduous forest biome	—	0.04	0.37	1.67	2.03	2.14	6.250
Coniferous forest biome	—	0.08	0.048	0.63	1.27	1.50	3.528
Desert biome	—	0.02	0.645	1.41	1.50	1.50	5.075
Tundra biome	—	—	0.452	1.14	1.44	1.25	4.282
Origin and structure of ecosystems	0.162	0.231	0.300	0.800	0.908	1.068	3.469
Upwelling ecosystems	—	0.094	0.268	0.348	0.315	0.838	1.881
Aerobiology	—	0.051	0.129	0.155	0.185	0.470	0.990
Conservation of ecosystems	—	—	0.004	0.053	0.055	0.080	0.192

Table 5.5. **Training Resulting from Some Ecological Programs in the US/IBP (modified from USNC/IBP 1974)**

Program	Students supported at PhD level	PhDs in systems or environmental science	PhDs from other disciplines trained at post-doctoral level	Foreign students supported	Foreign senior scientists collaborating at US / IBP sites
Grasslands biome	55	14	3	2	11
Eastern deciduous forest biome	43	43	4	4	5
Coniferous forest biome	11	5	3	3	4
Desert biome	27	3	5	6	2
Tundra biome	11	0	0	1	2
Origin and structure of ecosystems	49	29	1	21	19
Upwelling ecosystems	7	3	0	1	1
Aerobiology	4	4	2	0	0

Secondly, the US/IBP made major contributions to the training of ecological scientists (Table 5.5), at a time when an increasing environmental concern was creating a demand for ecological manpower. The nation now has a well-trained cadre of systems ecologists in academia, industry, and government that owes its existence, in part, to the impetus provided by the IBP.

Finally, perhaps the most important and long-term development attributed to the IBP was the establishment of the Ecosystem Studies Program in the National Science Foundation (Fig. 5.1). In the recent post-IBP period, many of the lessons learned during IBP have been implemented, to a point where American ecology is far stronger in its conceptual base, research strategies, data analysis, and model development as well as its funding stability, than it ever could have been without the International Biological Program.

(For further discussion of the IBP, see Chapter 37 by Gilbert and Christy in this volume.)

MATHEMATICAL ECOLOGY

Mathematical ecology really had its beginnings in the research and writings of Pierre-Francois Verhulst in the nineteenth century (Verhulst 1838; Hutchinson 1978). No major breakthrough or further building on this initial work is evident in the literature until the classical publications of Lotka and Volterra in the 1920s (Scudo and Ziegler 1978). Even then, it was to be many years before major utilization and expansion, definition, and application of the Lotka-Volterra models began to appear in ecology. Fisheries biologists and entomologists (Watt 1962) were applying the techniques to unique resource management problems, but the experimentation that has been the keystone of theoretical ecology was still lacking. In G. Evelyn Hutchinson's laboratory at Yale (Edmondson 1971), the initial work of Raymond Lindeman (Lindeman 1942; Cook 1977) began to flower with the advent of Robert MacArthur, who applied many mathematical concepts and techniques to perplexing problems inherent in the growing body of empirical data. In a short but productive career, the contributions of MacArthur range from the early "broken stick" model of niche overlap to sophisticated theories of species packing, island biogeography, and geographical ecology (MacArthur 1957, 1960, 1972; MacArthur and Levins 1964; MacArthur and Wilson 1963, 1967; Fretwell 1975).

Mathematical modelling had early precedents in demography, oceanography, and geochemistry (Hutchinson 1947, 1957), but the incipient catchphrase around 1950 could hardly portend the great wave of activity that would characterize American ecology by the 1970s. Extending analyses of income and loss rates of litter and soil nitrogen, Olson (1958) dated the classic dune successions around Lake Michigan, and his analyses challenged the old paradigm of the convergence of mesic "climax" ecosystems. By the late

1950s, the use of new computing tools, both analog and digital, was beginning to permeate several aspects of ecological and limnological research. At Oak Ridge National Laboratory, Olson (1960, 1963) was experimenting both with mathematical formulations of ecological processes and with implementation of simulations on early-generation computers (Olson 1963; Neel and Olson 1962); field experiments with radioactive tracers (Olson 1965; Weller and Olson 1967) illustrated a transition to a more complete ecosystem analysis.

Meanwhile, the Ford Foundation enabled the nearby University of Tennessee to strengthen the growing synergism with Oak Ridge National Laboratory through part-time professorial appointments of Oak Ridge staff. Extending a 1963 seminar course in systems ecology, Olson, Bernard C. Patten, and George M. Van Dyne developed a two- or three-quarter sequence in systems ecology, which continues to have wide influence through students of H. H. Shugart. During the early period, Thomas Kerlin, professor of nuclear engineering at Tennessee, provided a series of matrix analysis codes that were soon adapted to food chain dynamics and other analyses (Kaye and Ball 1969).

Stemming from discussions at the 1965 Ecological Society of America meetings at the University of Illinois, Kenneth E. F. Watt (1965) and Alice Witherow, then director of the Advanced Sciences Education Program at the National Science Foundation, encouraged pre- and postdoctoral stipend support and the teaching of systems ecology to fill a recognized national need (Patten 1966). As students and staff combined theory, data analysis, and system simulation at Davis, California; Knoxville and Oak Ridge, Tennessee; and then Athens, Georgia; Fort Collins, Colorado; and at a growing number of "systems ecology" activities, a fuller integration with basic and applied ecology was underway through the 1970s, which has yet to run its course (Van Dyne 1980).

Meanwhile, several of G. Evelyn Hutchinson's students developed traditions that carried a strong systems orientation in diverse directions (Kohn 1971; Riley 1971). For example, L. B. Slobodkin and other population ecologists used simplified laboratory microcosms to illustrate principles of broader application. H. T. Odum used early resistance analogs of energy flow (1960) as a provocative stimulus to experimentation (Odum and Pigeon 1970) and in a wide variety of field studies of technological and social importance (e.g., Odum 1971).

Frederick Smith shifted successively from theory of populations to the orchestration of an ambitious "ecosystem analysis" program by which the National Science Foundation and several other agencies supported much of the United States participation in the International Biological Program (Smith 1970). Smith then moved into a new and quite distinct professional role at the Harvard Graduate School of Design while continuing to have many half-visible roles in bridging the academic and government establishments in environmental science.

International connections in systems ecology, important throughout this period, are reflected in many of the chapters of this volume. C. F. Holling provided one of the strongest focuses of theoretical and resource-oriented systems work at the University of British Columbia and elsewhere in Canada; he continued to stimulate and participate in such work at the International Institute for Applied Systems Analysis in Vienna. K. Shinozaki and K. Hozumi of Japan visited Holling while en route from the Tenth International Botanical Congress in Seattle to participate in the Knoxville/Oak Ridge seminar course in 1969 and have influenced active systems ecology work in Japan.

Ecosystem analysis and continued planning at the Botanical Congress in Montreal (1959), at Oak Ridge/Great Smoky Mountains meetings in 1959 and 1961, and several IBP meetings in Europe (1963–1971) helped to link fieldwork on chemical cycles in ecosystems in several countries with modelling of both energy flow and nutrient cycling. David Goodall's work in Australia and Africa, as well as his role as director of the Desert Biome Program (US/IBP) while in the United States, illustrates numerous connections of statistical ecology with ecosystem modelling (Goodall 1952, 1970, 1972). Additional aspects of statistical ecology were reviewed at a meeting at Yale in 1969, also subsidized by the Ford Foundation.

Robert H. Whittaker's constructive participation in many planning developments, his early work on phosphorus tracers at the Hanford Laboratories (Whittaker 1961), and vigorous fieldwork in contrasting biogeographic regions epitomize the trend toward integrating systems analysis with the major traditions of previous plant and animal ecology. During the 1970s, the results of these early forays into a linkage between mathematics and ecology have blossomed to a point where training in advanced mathematics and computer science is part of the ecological curriculum in most American graduate universities.

Bernard C. Patten left Oak Ridge National Laboratory in 1968 to establish a major school in ecosystem modelling at the University of Georgia, while George Van Dyne was instrumental in building a natural resource application program, heavily dependent on simulation modelling, at Colorado State University. Robert V. O'Neill and H. Henry Shugart (a student of Patten's) have, with a number of other scientists, continued the strong thrust at Oak Ridge National Laboratory (Shugart 1978; Shugart and O'Neill 1979). There are many others as well (O'Neill et al. 1975).

Kenneth E. F. Watt compiled the first text on ecological modelling while at California (Watt 1966). C. S. Holling, Carl Walters, Dennis Chitty, and their colleagues have established a strong program at the University of British Columbia. Similarly, Simon A. Levin, Richard B. Root, Robert H. Whittaker, and others have developed Cornell University into a major center of mathematical modelling. Utah State, Wisconsin, Michigan State, Rensselaer Polytechnic Institute, Texas A&M, and several other institutions have contributed to the development and have made major use of simulation models both in resource management and in theoretical ecology. On the other hand, temperance in mathematical ecology has been cautioned, exemplified best perhaps by Beals (1973), and especially by Slobodkin's (1974) classic caveat, "I wish they would stop developing biological nonsense with a mathematical certainty."

Certainly, within the past decade, a major impetus was provided by the International Biological Program (IBP). In the United States, early planning centered on the development of ecosystem models that could be used to address most of the world's environmental problems. Much has been written about this unrealistic goal, some based on inadequate information (Battelle Columbus Laboratories 1975; Mitchell et al. 1976; National Academy of Sciences 1975). In reality, most of the US/IBP studies, by the time initial plans were firm, had strongly modified this "total ecosystem" view into programs much more realistic, much more attainable, and much less fraught with both conceptual and data-based pitfalls (Auerbach et al. 1977). Consequently, the programs embarked on the development of a large series of process and subsystem models, many of which were heuristic and utilitarian, and all of which were stepping-stones to the larger, more comprehensive system models that followed.

It has been argued that the expenditure of over $50 million for the US/IBP has been somewhat less than successful, but the state of the art in ecosystem modelling could only have been brought to where it is today under the aegis of a major integrated research program (Van Dyne 1980).

THE ENVIRONMENTAL REVOLUTION

One of the major forces driving ecology in recent years was the rise of the so-called environmental movement, a groundswell of awareness, concern, and action focused heavily on increases in air and water pollution, loss of open space, vanishing species, human population growth, and later, the energy crisis. To be sure, the roots were there in prewar America, in the Sierra Club, the Wilderness Society, Audubon Society, the Izaak Walton League, and several other organizations, but realization of the magnitude of the problems and massive response by the lay public were largely absent.

By the late 1960s, preoccupation with environmental problems was evident in the press, on television, on college and university campuses, and in the halls of Congress. Qualities in the early writings of Thoreau, Emerson, White, and Muir were augmented and synthesized in the deathless prose of Aldo Leopold (1948), words and thoughts that tapped and probed deep psychological feelings in the U.S. populace. While earlier warnings had been sounded (Vogt 1948; Osborn 1948; Brown 1954), a great deal of new fervor was stimulated by Rachel Carson's *Silent Spring* (1962) and Paul Ehrlich's *The Population Bomb* (1968), both of which enjoyed immense popularity and climbed to the top of "best seller" lists. Carson's prose captured the hearts and minds of her readers, succeeding where others (e.g., F. Wentworth Day's *Poison on the Land,* 1957) had failed. For the first time, scientists, sociologists, politicians, and the public began to take a hard look at the potential dangers inherent in uncontrolled use of synthetic chemicals. Ehrlich, expounding the need for "zero population growth," brought the importance of the problem to millions of Americans, not only through his small book, but also by lecture and television appearances, and a rash of multimedia expressions of interest in the rationale for and potential long-range consequences of continued growth. The turning point, when people had had enough, came in 1969, a year that included the Santa Barbara oil spill, the seizure of eleven tons of coho salmon in Wisconsin and Minnesota because of excessive DDT concentrations, application for permission to build a trans-Alaska pipeline, and the burning of the Cuyahoga River in Cleveland.

All of this activity and concern resulted in an "Earth Day," observed on hundreds of college campuses April 20, 1970. Slogans, speeches, debates, and demonstrations all served to alert local audiences to the magnitude and the gravity of the "environmental crisis." In turn, Earth Day spawned "environmental teach-ins;" workshops; much environmental education legislation in state houses, public education offices, and school boards; and a great deal of activism, ranging from anti-litter campaigns to major lawsuits. Earth Day was repeated in the spring of both 1971 and 1972 as a national event, but by 1973 had all but disappeared. Its legacy, however, lay in the tripling of membership rosters in most of the old-line organizations (such as Audubon, Sierra Club, and the National Wildlife Federation), as well as providing impetus, bodies, and dollars for new ones. These included Friends of the Earth, Environmental Action, Earth Awareness Foundation, the Northern Environmental Council, and many others.

On balance, the environmental movement has had a lasting impact on the development of ecology in the United States (Fleming 1972). It has made ecology a household word, created the pressures requisite to a host of environmental legislation, and in turn, has expanded both the need for ecologists and the role they must play in shaping the future of the nation.

MORE NATURAL AREA PROGRAMS

From an early and continuing interest in natural areas, exemplified by ESA committees established (shortly after the society was incorporated) for the preservation of plant and animal communities, American ecologists have been concerned with the need to maintain areas where "natural ecosystem" structure and function could be described, analyzed, and understood. Such areas have been viewed as "standards," "baselines," and "experimental controls" for ecological research, in addition to any recreational, educational, or aesthetic considerations.

In the 1920s, probably under some stimulus from Aldo Leopold and others, the U.S. Forest Service designated a number of "wild" and "primitive" areas, the distinction being primarily one of size. Description and inventory of many of these areas appeared in Shelford (1926), still perhaps the best single work on natural areas, although more than fifty years out of date. The establishment of The Nature Conservancy in 1950 has already been mentioned, and for three decades, this organization has built an exemplary record of land preservation. Within the last fifteen years, however, a number of other efforts have been made, instigated and manned primarily by American ecologists.

In the 1960s, largely with leadership from the U.S. Forest Service, came the establishment of the Federal Committee on Research Natural Areas. Representatives were named from the various agencies that were either landholders (e.g., Forest Service, Bureau of Land Management) or had some responsibility for natural resource management or enforcement (e.g., National Water Council, Corps of Engineers). After 1970, the Environmental Protection Agency and the Council on Environmental Quality were major additions to the group. The committee reactivated the inventory of federal areas that were designated for research purposes (Federal Committee on Research Natural Areas 1968; Federal Committee on Ecological Reserves 1977) and has since issued supplements to the inventory, as well as policy recommendations and guidelines for the federal agency family regarding natural area research programs, management, and utilization. A major landmark in this activity was the publication of an expanded inventory for Oregon and Washington (Franklin et al. 1972), which provides a model that might well be emulated for all regions of the United States.

The National Park Service of the U.S. Department of Interior began a series of "theme studies" in the early 1970s. These were planned as attempts to identify and inventory the remaining areas of America's natural heritage. Three volumes have appeared to date, two (of five scheduled) on the eastern deciduous forest (Waggoner 1975; Lindsey and Escobar 1976) and a single volume covering the inland wetlands of the United States (Goodwin and Niering 1975).

Considerable controversy still rages in the ecological community over activities of this nature, one that filters down to state and local levels, as well as flourishing on the national scene. One school of thought proposes working in silent, covert ways to identify, describe, and determine the status of natural areas in regional settings; establish priorities for acquisition; obtain options; and eventually acquire title to such lands. Problems with this approach are primarily those concerned with a lack of knowledge on the part of both individuals and organizations that are in a position to help. In contrast, a second philosophy (exemplified by the two programs discussed above) attempts to publish inventories of "potential" natural areas (i.e., those not currently preserved or protected) in order to alert ecologists, administrators, legislative bodies, state and federal agencies, and the general public to the regional importance and status of such areas. Detractors point to the possible increases in land valuation with the knowledge that somebody wants (or might want) those idle acres. Certainly, over the past ten years or so, natural increases in the value of real estate, coupled with a steep, inflationary spiral in the national economy, make it doubtful that land speculation in potential natural area tracts has become a significant problem.

In 1968, the advent of the US/IBP included a Conservation of Ecosystems (CE) program component that surveyed potential natural areas in terrestrial, freshwater, estuarine, and marine categories. While seriously underfinanced throughout its duration, the CE program surveyed, inventoried, and computerized information on 420 federal areas, 2,280 nonfederal terrestrial areas, and 453 freshwater areas, all of which met a stringent list of quality criteria for natural area designation (Darnell et al. 1974). The total activity was unique in several ways. It was the first attempt in the United States to focus on the need for estuarine and marine areas as examples of representative ecosystem types. The CE program also used questionnaires, pleas for assistance published in scientific journals (Peter 1971; Lemon 1974), and a rather large number of scientific volunteers. Consequently, information on individual states and regions was relatively well standardized prior to computerization of the inventory. Finally, by using Küchler's (1964) vegetation types as a nationwide framework, the CE program tried to assess the adequacy of its inventory. This was accomplished both by analysis of types not represented and through an estimation of the number of areas potentially missed in each region. Both the use of the Küchler classification and an assessment of adequacy have since been incorporated in other similar efforts (below).

After Earth Day 1970 and subsequent recognition of real and potential problems in population, food supply, energy, and general resource availability, many ecologists began to modify the old concept of "preserved natural areas" to one of "manipulated" or "experimental natural areas." In these locations, major experimental treatments could be imposed without risking either loss of experimental equipment and materials in essentially uncontrolled areas or a potential public backlash to apparently degrading practices on public lands, such as clearcutting of forests or disposal of municipal sewage wastes. This recognition spawned two programs, one by the Atomic Energy Commission (AEC), the other by the National Science Foundation.

In the early 1970s, the AEC began to discuss establishment of a series of National Environmental Research Parks (NERP) at several of its government-owned national laboratories. In several areas, ecological research had been supported for many years, and new problems of energy and environment gave special impetus to the deliberations. The first NERP was established in 1974 at the 122,000-hectare Savannah River Reservation in northern Georgia. Since then, additional NERPs have been officially established on AEC (later the Energy Research and Development Administration and now the Department of Energy) reservations at Hanford, Washington (the ALE-Arid Lands Ecosystems-Reserve at the Pacific Northwest Laboratory); at the Idaho National Engineering Laboratory in southeastern Idaho; and at Los Alamos Scientific Laboratory in northern New Mexico (National Environmental Research Park Symposium 1975; Kitchings and Tarr 1978). Largely because of local problems, neither the Oak Ridge Reservation* in east Tennessee nor Brookhaven National Laboratory on Long Island has been designated as a NERP, in spite of long and continuing records of strong ecological research programs and demonstrated needs for increased research of the kind that the NERPs are uniquely qualified to support.

The National Science Foundation sponsored a two-year project to survey "experimental ecological reserves" (Lauff and Reichle 1979; National Science Foundation 1977), again building on the recognized need for manipulative research in natural or seminatural ecosystems. Working from a series of applications submitted by area managers, the program recommended the establishment and funding of a series of Experimental Ecological Reserves. The initial list of seventy-one reserves (National Science Foundation 1977) includes areas from federal and stage agencies, universities, and consortia, and utilized Küchler's (1964) classification to ensure maximum distribution, both geographically and by major vegetation type. The program has been augmented by two recent NSF-supported conferences on long-term ecological measurement (Botkin 1977, 1978), and a follow-up grant to The Institute of Ecology for continued exploration of the needs, mechanisms, and integration of a national system of Experimental Ecological Reserves.

Internationally, the Man and the Biosphere (MAB) program became the logical successor to the IBP. MAB, set in the United Nations (UNESCO), is an organization of governments, rather than an organization of scientists as was the IBP. Consequently, among other differences, the National Committee for MAB resides in the U.S. Department of State, whereas the National Committee for the IBP was an arm of the National Academy of Sciences. MAB is structured around thirteen "themes," or "projects," some geographical (e.g., temperate forests), and some conceptual (e.g., Conservation of Natural Areas and of the Genetic Material They Contain—Project 8, Perception of Environmental Quality—Project 13). MAB 8 includes the so-called Biosphere

*The Oak Ridge National Environmental Research Park, comprising 5,500 hectares, was approved 5 June and dedicated 2 October 1980 by the U. S. Department of Energy.

Reserve Program, where nations designate specific areas as part of an international network and agree to preservation in perpetuity. In the U.S., twenty-eight biosphere reserves have received official designation (Franklin 1977; Risser and Cornelison 1979), ranging from Alaska to Puerto Rico and the Virgin Islands and from Hubbard Brook Experimental Forest in the northeast to several reserves in California. As the list of established reserves grows, concern for ecologically relevant research and monitoring programs is apparent. Two workshops have been held to frame a program of environmental monitoring in biosphere reserves, one that can be mounted internationally regardless of the level of sophistication of the nation or the quantity and quality of its cadre of scientists. (Also see Chapter 37 by Gilbert and Christy in this volume.)

Also, a bilateral U.S./U.S.S.R. environmental agreement covers biosphere reserves in the two countries. A major symposium was held in the Soviet Union in 1976 (Franklin and Krugman 1979), and a reciprocal symposium is scheduled in the United States in the spring of 1980.

Two other well-intentioned, though abortive, attempts at institutional ecology need to be discussed at this stage. In 1966, Senate bill S.2282 was introduced in the United States Senate, 89th Congress, to provide for a federal program within the Department of the Interior to conduct ecological research and surveys. Patterned after the U.S. Geological Survey and borrowing a legacy from the defunct U.S. Biological Survey, the bill proposed to establish a professional ecological agency to handle inventories, baseline studies, environmental monitoring, mapping, and other research in ecological themes related to the national interest. The hearings, held in April 1966, were attended by a great many prominent ecologists, all of whom offered strong arguments in favor of the proposed legislation. Although the bill failed passage and the hearings transcript is thirteen years old, the 160-page record (Committee on Interior and Insular Affairs 1966) still provides a strong rationale for a means to address the complex problems of environment, technology, and society that are even more crucial today.

In 1970, Senator Howard Baker of Tennessee and Senator Edmund Muskie of Maine introduced S.3410 in the second session of the 91st Congress. Cited as the "National Environmental Laboratory Act of 1970," the proposed legislation was "to establish a structure that will provide integrated knowledge and understanding of the ecological, social, and technological problems associated with air pollution, water pollution, solid waste disposal, general pollution, and degradation of the environment, and other related problems." The bill authorized the establishment of up to six regional environmental laboratories, the appropriation of $50 million per year for five years to be deposited in a special trust fund to ensure perpetual maintenance of long-term research, and an additional appropriation not to exceed $200 million for any single regional laboratory (Committee on Public Works 1971).

In December of 1970, Senator Bellmon submitted a similar bill, S.4599, to "establish environmental laboratories within the states, regions, and nation pursuant to policies and goals established in the National Environmental Policy Act of 1969." Then, in March 1971, Senators Baker and Muskie introduced S.1113 to the 92nd Congress, essentially identical to the bill submitted the previous year. The Baker/Muskie legislation proposed maximum use of both facilities and staff at existing national laboratories operated under the aegis of the Atomic Energy Commission. Thus, the large research and development facilities already present at Brookhaven, Argonne, Oak Ridge, Hanford, Livermore, and elsewhere would reprogram to meet the requirements and the spirit of the National Environmental Laboratory (NEL) legislation. In contrast, Bellmon's bill focused on the Environmental Protection Agency as a means to create, de novo, a series of state and regional centers to "combine or coordinate the research capability of educational institutions," in addition to its own staff administrative and research functions. As had been true for the research and surveys proposal in 1966, the mix of NEL proposals received strong support from the American ecological community. None of the bills passed in Congress, however, so the possible results of enactment are obviously open to conjecture. It would appear, though, that one or both of these major acts would have immeasurably strengthened the total ecological research apparatus in the United States.

FEDERAL ENVIRONMENTAL LEGISLATION

For at least 100 years, the Congress of the United States has enacted various kinds of "environmental" legislation, laws that either pertain to, regulate, or provide for some sort of administrative control of the nation's land, water, air, and biotic resources. Since 1950, however, a number of highly significant and far-reaching acts have been passed (Table 5.6), all of which have affected the postwar development of American ecology. Many of these laws require ecological expertise, many call for research or assessment activity, and most have contributed to the growing job market for trained ecologists. Subjectively, the most important pieces of federal legislation are the Wilderness Act, the National Environmental Policy Act (NEPA), the Endangered Species Act, and more recently, the Resource Conservation and Recovery Act (RCRA), the Toxic Substances Control Act (TOSCA), and the Surface Mining Control and Reclamation Act (Table 5.6).

NEPA far outdistances the others in its impact on the ecological community. By establishment of the Council on Environmental Quality, the act created a heretofore unrecognized need for ecological expertise in the public sector, in large measure directly responsible for scientific input into the decision-making process. Most importantly, Section 102(c) required the

Table 5.6. Major Federal Environmental Legislation Enacted since 1945 (not including amendments)

Year	General Title	Public Law
1950	Fish Restoration Act	81-681
1953	Outer Continental Shelf Lands Act	82-212
1954	Watershed and Flood Protection Act	83-544
1956	Fish and Wildlife Act	84-1024
1964	Wilderness Act	88-577
1965	Land and Water Conservation Act	88-578
1965	Fish and Wildlife Coordination Act	89-72
1965	Water Resources Planning Act	89-80
1966	National Historic Preservation Act	89-665
1968	Estuary Protection Act	90-454
1969	National Environmental Policy Act	91-190
1970	Clean Air Act	91-604
1970	Solid Waste Disposal Act	91-512
1972	Coastal Zone Management Act	92-583
1972	Environmental Pesticide Control Act	92-516
1972	Water Pollution Control Act	92-500
1972	Marine Protection, Research, and Sanctuaries Act	92-532
1972	Noise Control Act	92-574
1973	Endangered Species Act	93-205
1974	Renewable Resources Planning Act	93-378
1974	Safe Drinking Water Act	93-523
1976	Resource Conservation and Recovery Act	94-580
1976	Toxic Substances Control Act	94-469
1977	Clean Water Act	95-217
1977	Surface Mining Control and Reclamation Act	95-87

preparation of the now well known "environmental impact statement," a document analyzing and assessing the short- and long-term consequences of federal actions affecting American environments.

Early impact statements were often cumbersome, highly speculative, and rather unscientific. Until federal agencies were able to build staffs of ecologists, statements were often the work of engineers, bureaucrats, administrators, and general biologists, although some subcontracting to university-based ecologists was evident. Many agencies were treating NEPA requirements as simply more bureaucratic stipulation, but the landmark decision on Calvert Cliffs (*Maryland* v. *AEC*) had far-reaching consequences. The Maryland Supreme Court ruled that environmental impact statements had to address the spirit, as well as the letter, of the law. The AEC responded by assigning impact statement preparation work to several of its national laboratories and augmenting their staffs with qualified ecologists to do the work. Other federal agencies soon followed suit.

Led by California, a number of states soon enacted their own, state-level versions of NEPA, and consequently, not much could be done for technological "progress" without forthright consideration of the environmental consequences. All of this activity spawned, almost immediately, a new breed of ecologist, the "consultant," available for hire to utilities, petroleum corporations, construction firms, or any other elements of the private sector that was faced with NEPA requirements but lacked staff ecologists.

At least four additional developments can be traced directly to the National Environmental Policy Act of 1969. As mentioned above, the Ecological Society of America organized and authorized an Applied Ecology Section, composed predominantly of federal and state agency employees and members of environmental (or engineering) consulting firms, virtually all of which were involved in some way with NEPA. Secondly, a National Association of Environmental Professionals (NAEP) was formed in 1975. Because NAEP has a more applied and less research-oriented emphasis than ESA, membership is primarily composed of engineers, environmental chemists, and so forth, and ecologists are a minority of the current membership of approximately 500.

Both of the above movements gave rise to certain ethical concerns, and by 1972 ESA had appointed a Committee on Ethics. This group set about to draft a Code of Ethics for the society, finally adopted in 1975. While adherence to the code is strictly voluntary, it does provide a standard for individual deportment of ecologists, particularly those involved in consulting work.

Finally, a move toward a civil service rating for ecologists was consummated in 1978. Interestingly, the first issue of *Ecology,* published in January 1920, carried a note stating that ESA was working with government officials to establish ecological ratings for civil service. The movement languished for five decades, however, until resurrected at the beginning of the 1970s. In the fifty-year interim, many ecologists were classified as foresters, range managers, and wildlife biologists, simply because ecology was still unrecognized by the U.S. Civil Service Commission. Dr. Beatrice Willard led the early efforts as a member of the Council on Environmental Quality during the Nixon administration. Later, Dr. J. Frank McCormick, of the University of Tennessee, went to Washington as a senior ecologist with the Office of Biological Services, U.S. Department of the Interior. Working with several other Washington-based ecologists, McCormick was instrumental in completing the process to place ecological classifications within the federal civil service system.

Both RCRA and TOSCA have engendered a need for environmental chemists and engineers, but always with an ecological oversight. Concerned with mechanisms of transport, chronic (as well as acute) effects, testing protocols, and regulatory functions, these laws may well lead to still other kinds of "new" ecologists, biologically trained, but with an in-depth technological expertise that will permit them to function in an increasingly complex world whose problems, already great, may soon be insurmountable. It may be frightening even to think that in ecology may lie the salvation of mankind, but without continued ecosystem function, including the carbon fixation, energy flow, and nutrient cycling that are so much a touchstone of our science, there is no future.

SUMMARY

The past three decades of American ecology have witnessed a rapid expansion and an increased diversity in the institutions that relate to the science. Schools and curricula, legal and social constraints, changing technology, resource depletion, and public awareness have all played significant roles in the massive changes that ecology has experienced since World War II. In the foregoing pages, some of this institutional framework has been examined, albeit often superficially. This results, at least in part, from a strong desire to neither duplicate nor overlap too much with the excellent recent reviews of ecological development that have appeared (McIntosh 1974, 1975, 1976; Egerton and McIntosh 1977).

Spearheaded by the National Science Foundation, a large family of federal agencies now supports ecological science through a broad spectrum of programs, often narrowly defined and mission-oriented, but nevertheless important in any review of ecology. Environmental legislation, particularly the National Environmental Policy Act of 1969, has had a major impact on ecology, including new societal concerns, assessment that often follows analysis and synthesis, and a raison d'être for a large and prolific corps of private consulting ecologists.

The Ecological Society of America has enjoyed major growth, and now seeks a voice in public affairs commensurate with its size and self-image. Only time will tell if this comes to pass. Finally, new national and international programs continue to provide vehicles for ecological research and application of results.

It is hoped that this review will be but another stepping-stone in the continuing effort to adequately document the development of ecology, particularly ecology in the U.S. As ecology takes its rightful place in the community of sciences, let it not be said that, "we know not from whence we came," but that a self-conscientiousness and a commensal and catholic understanding of our history will be commonplace as the science of ecology, worldwide, moves ever closer to its own centennial.

REFERENCES CITED

Allee, W. C., A. E. Emerson, O. Park, T. Park, and K. P. Schmidt. 1949. *Principles of animal ecology*. Phila.: W. B. Saunders Co.

Anonymous. 1978. Resolution of respect—LaMont C. Cole. *Bull. Ecol. Soc. Am.* 59:171–172.

Auerbach, S. I., R. L. Burgess, and R. V. O'Neill. 1977. The biome programs: Evaluating an experiment. *Science* 195:902–904.

Battelle Columbus Laboratories. 1975. *Evaluation of three of the biome studies programs funded under the Foundation's International Biological Program (IBP).* Final report to the National Science Foundation. Columbus, Ohio: Battelle Columbus Laboratories.

Beals, E. W. 1973. Ordination: Mathematical elegance and ecological naivete. *J. Ecol.* 61:23–36.

Billings, Dwight. 1970. Resolution of respect—Henry J. Oosting, 1903–1968. *Bull. Ecol. Soc. Am.* 51:16–17.

Blackburn, T. R. 1973. Information and the ecology of scholars. *Science* 181:1141–1146.

Blair, W. Frank. 1977. *Big biology—the US/IBP.* Stroudsburg, PA.: Dowden, Hutchinson, and Ross, Inc.

Botkin, Daniel B. (chm.). 1977. *Long-term ecological measurements.* Report of a conference, Woods Hole, Massachusetts, March 16–18, 1977. Washington, D. C.: National Science Foundation.

______. 1978. *A pilot program for long-term observation and study of ecosystems in the United States.* Report of a second conference on long-term ecological measurements, Woods Hole, Massachusetts, February 6–10, 1978. Washington, D.C.: National Science Foundation.

Brewer, Richard. 1960. A brief history of ecology. Part I. Prenineteenth century to 1919. *Occasional Papers of the C. C. Adams Center for Ecological Studies* 1:1–18.

Brown, Harrison. 1954. *The challenge of man's future.* New York: Viking Press.

Burgess, R. L. 1977. The Ecological Society of America: Historical data and some preliminary analyses. In *History of American ecology,* eds. F. N. Egerton and R. P. McIntosh, pp. 1–24. New York: Arno Press.

Carson, R. 1962. *Silent spring.* Boston: Houghton Mifflin Co.

CEQ-FCST. 1974. *The role of ecology in the federal government.* Report of the committee on ecological research. Washington, D.C.: Council on Environmental Quality and Federal Council for Science and Technology.

Committee on Interior and Insular Affairs. 1966. *Ecological research and surveys.* Hearing before the Committee on Interior and Insular Affairs, United States Senate, 89th Congress, 2nd Session, on S.2282. Washington, D.C.: U.S. Government Printing Office.

Committee on Public Works. 1971. *National Environmental Laboratories. A compilation of comments and materials related to a proposed environmental laboratory.* Committee on Public Works, United States Senate. Washington, D.C.: U.S. Government Printing Office.

Cook, Robert E. 1977. Raymond Lindeman and the trophic-dynamic concept in ecology. *Science* 198:22–26.

Cooper, Arthur W. 1979. Dr. Bertram Whittier Wells (1884–1978). *Veröff. Geobot. Inst. ETH, Stift. Rübel, Zurich* 68:7–10.

Curtis, John T. 1947. The palo verde forest type near Gonivaves, Haiti, and its relation to the surrounding vegetation. *Caribb. For.* 8:1–26.

Darnell, R. M. 1970. The new ecology. *BioScience* 20:746–748.

———, Paul C. Lemon, John M. Neuhold, and G. Carleton Ray. 1974. *Natural areas and their role in land and water resource preservation.* Final report to the National Science Foundation, US/IBP Program for Conservation of Ecosystems. Washington, D.C.: American Institute of Biological Sciences.

Day, J. Wentworth. 1957. *Poison on the land.* New York: Philosophical Library, Inc.

Dexter, Ralph W. 1978. History of the Ecologists' Union—spinoff from the ESA and prototype of The Nature Conservancy. *Bull. Ecol. Soc. Am.* 59:146–147.

Edmondson, Y. H. 1971. Some components of the Hutchinson legend. *Limnol. Oceanog.* 16:157–161.

Egerton, Frank N. 1976. Ecological studies and observations before 1900. In *Issues and ideas in America,* eds. B. J. Taylor and T. J. White, pp. 311–351. Norman, OK: University of Oklahoma Press.

——— and Robert P. McIntosh, eds. 1977. *History of American ecology.* New York: Arno Press.

Egler, Frank E. 1951. A commentary on American plant ecology, based on the textbooks of 1947–1949. *Ecology* 32:673–694.

Ehrlich, P. R. 1968. *The population bomb.* New York: Ballantine Books.

Engelmann, Manfred. 1970. Resolution of respect—Orlando Park, 1901–1969. *Bull. Ecol. Soc. Am.* 51:16–19.

Federal Committee on Ecological Reserves. 1977. *A directory of research natural areas on federal lands of the United States of America.* Washington, D.C.

Federal Committee on Research Natural Areas. 1968. *A directory of research natural areas on federal lands of the United States of America.* Washington, D.C.

Fleming, D. 1972. Roots of the new conservation movement: Perspectives. *Am. Hist.* 6:7–94.

Franklin, Jerry F. 1977. *The biosphere reserve program in the United States.* Science 195:262–267.

———, F. C. Hall, C. T. Dyrness, and C. Maser. 1972. *Federal research natural areas in Oregon and Washington: A guidebook for scientists and educators.* Portland, OR.: USDA Forest Service, Pacific Northwest Forest and Range Experiment Station.

——— and Stanley L. Krugman, eds. 1979. *Selection, management and utilization of biosphere reserves.* Gen. Tech. Rept. PNW-82, Portland, OR.: USDA Forest Service, Pacific Northwest Forest and Range Experiment Station.

Fretwell, S. D. 1975. The impact of Robert MacArthur on ecology. *Annu. Rev. Ecol. Syst.* 6:1–13.

Gleason, H. A. 1936. Twenty-five years of ecology, 1910–1935. *Mem. Brooklyn Bot. Gard.* 4:41–49.

Goodall, D. W. 1952. Quantitative aspects of plant distribution. *Biol. Rev.* 27:194–245.

———. 1970. Statistical plant ecology. *Annu. Rev. Ecol. Syst.* 1:55–98.

———. 1972. Building and testing ecosystem models. In *Mathematical models in ecology,* ed. J. N. R. Jeffers, pp. 173–194. Oxford: Blackwell Scientific Publishers.

Goodwin, Richard H. and William A. Niering. 1975. *Inland wetlands of the United States, evaluated as potential registered natural landmarks.* Washington, D.C.: National Park Service.

Hollander, Rachelle. 1976. Ecologists, ethical codes, and the struggles of a new profession. *Hastings Cent. Rep.* 6:45–46.

Hutchinson, G. E. 1947. The problems of oceanic geochemistry. *Ecol. Monogr.* 17:299–307.

______. 1957. A treatise on limnology. Vol. 1. Geography, physics and chemistry. New York: John Wiley and Sons.

______. 1978. *An introduction to population ecology.* New Haven: Yale University Press.

Isley, Duane. 1972. The disappearance. *Taxon* 21:3–12.

Kaye, S. V. and S. J. Ball. 1969. Systems analysis of a coupled compartment model for radionuclide transfer in a tropical environment. In *Proceedings of the Second National Symposium on Radioecology,* eds. D. J. Nelson and F. C. Evans, pp. 731–739. Ann Arbor: U.S. Atomic Energy Commission.

Kitchings, J. T. and N. E. Tarr, eds. 1978. *National Environmental Research Park Symposium: Natural resource inventory, characterization, and analysis.* ORNL-5304, Oak Ridge, TN.: Oak Ridge National Laboratory.

Kohn, Alan J. 1971. Phylogeny and biogeography of *Hutchinsonia:* G. E. Hutchinson's influence through his doctoral students. *Limnol. Oceanogr.* 16:173–176.

Küchler, A. W. 1964. *Potential natural vegetation of the conterminous United States.* Spec. publ. 36 (map and manual). New York: American Geographical Society.

Larson, Clarence E. 1971. Not in retrospect. In *Radionuclides in ecosystems. Proceedings of the Third National Symposium on Radioecology.* CONF-710501. Oak Ridge, TN.: Oak Ridge National Laboratory.

Lauff, George H. and D. E. Reichle. 1979. Experimental ecological reserves. *Bull. Ecol. Soc. Am.* 60:4–11.

Lawrence, Donald B. 1979. William Skinner Cooper (1884–1978). *Bull. Ecol. Soc. Am.* 60:18–19.

Lemon, Paul C. 1974. AIBS Conservation of Ecosystems Program. *BioScience* 24:249–253.

Leopold, Aldo. 1948. *A Sand County almanac.* New York: Oxford University Press.

Lindsey, Alton A. and Linda K. Escobar. 1976. *Eastern deciduous forest, Volume 2. Beech-maple region.* Inventory of natural areas and sites recommended as potential natural landmarks. Washington, D.C.: National Park Service.

Lindeman, R. L. 1942. The trophic-dynamic aspect of ecology. *Ecology* 23:399–418.

MacArthur, R. H. 1957. On the relative abundance of bird species. *Proc. Nat. Acad. Sci. U.S.A.* 43:293–295.

______. 1960. On the relative abundance of species. *Am. Nat.* 94:25–36.

______. 1972. *Geographical ecology.* New York: Harper and Row.

______ and R. Levins. 1964. Competition, habitat selection, and character displacement in a patchy environment. *Proc. Natl. Acad. Sci. U.S.A.* 51:1207–1210.

______ and E. O. Wilson. 1963. An equilibrium theory of insular zoogeography. *Evolution* 17:373–387.

______ and E. O. Wilson. 1967. *The theory of island biogeography.* Princeton, N.J.: Princeton University Press.

Major, J. 1969. Historical development of the ecosystem concept. In *The ecosystem concept in natural resource management,* ed. G. M. Van Dyne, pp. 9–22. New York: Academic Press.

McIntosh, R. P. 1974. Plant ecology 1947–1972. *Ann. Mo. Bot. Gard.* 61:132–165.

______. 1975. H. A. Gleason—"individual ecologist" 1882–1975; his contributions to ecological theory. *Bull. Torrey Bot. Club* 102:22253–273.

______. 1976. Ecology since 1900. In *Issues and ideas in America,* eds. Benjamin J. Taylor and Thurman J. White, pp. 353–372. Norman, OK.: University of Oklahoma Press.

Marschner, Francis J. 1976. The original vegetation of Minnesota. USDA Forest Service, North Central Forest Experiment Station, St. Paul, Minnesota. (map, in color, at 1:500,000).

Mitchell, Rodger, Ramona A. Mayer, and Jerry Downhower. 1976. An evaluation of three biome programs. *Science* 192:859–865.

Muller, C. H. 1975. Henry Allan Gleason, 1882–1975. *Bull. Ecol. Soc. Am.* 56:25.

National Academy of Sciences. 1975. *An evaluation of the International Biological Program.* Committee to Evaluate the IBP, Assembly of Life Sciences, NAS, Washington, D.C.

National Environmental Research Park Symposium. 1975. Snake River Regional Studies Center, College of Idaho, Caldwell, ID.

National Science Board. 1971. *Environmental science. Challenge for the seventies.* National Science Foundation, Washington, D.C.

National Science Foundation. 1977. Experimental ecological reserves. A proposed national network. Washington, D.C.

Neel, R. B. and J. S. Olson. 1962. Use of analog computers for simulating the movement of isotopes in ecological systems. ORNL-3172. Oak Ridge, TN.: Oak Ridge National Laboratory.

Nelkin, Dorothy. 1976. Ecologists and the public interest. *Hastings Cent. Rep.* 6:38–44.

Odum, E. P. 1953. *Fundamentals of ecology.* Philadelphia: W. B. Saunders Co.

Odum, H. T. 1960. Ecological potential and analogue circuits for the ecosystem. *Am. Sci.* 48:1–8.

______. 1971. *Environment, power and society.* New York: John Wiley and Sons.

______ and R. F. Pigeon, eds. 1970. A tropical rain forest. A study of radiation and ecology at El Verde, Puerto Rico. Div. Techn. Inform., U.S. Atomic Energy Commission.

Olson, J. S. 1958. Rates of succession and soil changes on southern Lake Michigan sand dunes. *Bot. Gaz.* 119:125–170.

______. 1960. Forest studies. pp. 167–185. In *Health Physics Division annual progress report, 1959–1960.* ORNL-2994. Oak Ridge, TN.: Oak Ridge National Laboratory.

______. 1963. Analog computer models for movement of isotopes through ecosystems. In *Proceedings of the First National Symposium on Radioecology,* eds. V. Schultz and A. W. Klement, pp. 121–125. New York: Reinhold Publishing Co.

______. 1965. Equations for cesium transfer in a *Liriodendron* forest. *Health Phys.* 11:1385–1392.

O'Neill, R. V., N. Ferguson, and J. A. Watts. 1975. *A bibliography of mathematical modeling in ecology.* EDFB/IBP-75/5. Oak Ridge, TN.: Oak Ridge National Laboratory.

Osborn, Fairfield. 1948. *Our plundered planet.* Boston: Little, Brown and Co.

Patten, Bernard C. 1966. Systems ecology: A course sequence in mathematical ecology. *BioScience* 16:593–598.

Peter, Walter G. 1971. AIBS to document U.S. ecosystems. *BioScience* 21(3):242–243.

Riley, Gordon A. 1971. Introduction [to special issue commemorating the retirement of G. E. Hutchinson]. *Limnol. Oceanogr.* 16:177–179.

Risser, Paul G. and Kathy D. Cornelison. 1979. *Man and the biosphere.* Norman, OK.: University of Oklahoma Press.

———. 1969. Plant ecology. In *A short history of botany in the United States,* ed. Joseph Ewan, pp. 124–131. New York: Hafner Publishing Co.

Scudo, Francesco M. and James R. Ziegler, eds. 1978. *The golden age of theoretical ecology: 1923–1940.* A collection of works by V. Volterra, V. A. Kostitzain, A. J. Lotka, and A. N. Kolmogoroff. Lecture Notes in Biomathematics 22. Berlin-Heidelberg-New York: Springer-Verlag.

Sears, Paul B. 1956. Some notes on the ecology of ecologists. *Sci. Monogr.* 83:22–27.

Shelford, V. E. 1926. *Naturalists' guide to the Americas.* Baltimore: Williams and Wilkins Co.

Shugart, H. H., ed. 1978. *Time-series and ecological processes.* Philadelphia: SIAM Press, Society for Industrial and Applied Mathematics.

——— and R. V. O'Neill, eds. 1979. *Systems ecology.* Benchmark Papers in Ecology, vol. 9. Stroudsburg, PA.: Dowden, Hutchinson, and Ross, Inc.

Simkins, Tania. 1971. Association profile: The Ecological Society of America. *Assoc. Soc. Mgt.* Oct./Nov.: 27–30, 110–114.

Slobodkin, L. B. 1974. Comments from a biologist to a mathematician. In *Proceedings of the SIAM-SIMS Conference, Alta, Utah,* ed. S. A. Levin, pp. 318–329. Philadelphia: Society for Industrial and Applied Mathematics.

Smith, Frederick E. 1970. Analysis of ecosystems. In *Analysis of temperate forest ecosystems,* ed. D. E. Reichle, pp. 7–18. Berlin-Heidelberg-New York: Springer-Verlag.

Taylor, Benjamin J. and Thurman J. White, eds. 1976. *Issues and ideas in America.* Norman, OK.: University of Oklahoma Press.

Van Dyne, George M. 1980. Systems ecology: The state of the art. In *Environmental Sciences Laboratory Dedication, February 26–27, 1979.* ORNL Report. Oak Ridge, TN.: Oak Ridge National Laboratory (in press).

Verhulst, P. F. 1838. Notice sur la loi que la population suit dans son accroissement. *Corresp. Math. et Phys.* 10:113–121.

Vogt, William. 1948. *Road to survival.* New York: Wm. Sloan Associates, Inc.

Waggoner, Gary S. 1975. *Eastern deciduous forest, Volume 1. Southeastern evergreen and oak-pine region.* Inventory of natural areas and sites recommended as potential natural landmarks. Washington, D.C.: National Park Service.

Watt, K. E. F. 1962. Use of mathematics in population ecology. *Annu. Rev. Entomol.* 7:243–260.

———. 1965. An experimental graduate training program in biomathematics. *BioScience* 15:777–780.

———, ed. 1966. *Systems analysis in ecology.* New York: Academic Press.

Weller, H. D. and J. S. Olson. 1967. Prompt transfers of cesium-137 to the soils of a tagged *Liriodendron* forest. *Ecology* 48:15–25.

Whittaker, Robert H. 1961. Experiments with radiophosphorus tracer in aquarium microcosms. *Ecol. Monogr.* 31:157–188.

Wilson, E. O. 1971. Commentary—the plight of taxonomy. *Ecology* 52(5):741.

Worster, Donald. 1977. *Nature's economy. The roots of ecology.* San Francisco: Sierra Club Books.

Worthington, E. B. 1975. *The evolution of IBP.* International Biological Programme 1. Cambridge: Cambridge University Press.

Europe

6

AUSTRIA

Wilhelm Kühnelt

BACKGROUND: HISTORICAL ANTECEDENTS

Long before Ernst Haeckel coined the term *ökologie* (ecology) in 1869, Austrian scientists had published pertinent ecological data. In 1853, Ludwig K. Schmarda, the first professor of zoology at an Austrian university (Graz), published his textbook, *Die geographische Verbreitung der Tiere* (The Geographic Distribution of Animals). Several chapters of some sixty pages covered the influence on animals of such environmental factors as temperature, light, air, electricity, general climate, seasonal changes, food, seawater, fresh water, and dry land. Although some of these statements did not hold true, the whole treatise is a very comprehensive account of contemporary knowledge of these matters.

Josef R. Lorenz summarized his results obtained over many years in a book, *Physicalische Verhältnisse und Verteilung der Organismen im quarnerischen Golf* (Physical Conditions and Distribution of the Organisms within the Gulf of the Quarnero), published in 1863. At first glimpse, this report looks like a merely local paper. Closer consideration reveals many facts being reported for the first time. Besides considerable and painstaking oceanographic data, about one-half of the book was devoted to the composition of the animal communities in relation to environmental conditions (e.g., depth below sea level and kind of bottom). Modern reports on these conditions do not differ considerably from this early report. It is of special interest to note that the floating organisms (in Lorenz' term, "schwebende Tiere") were also treated at length. He did not include the plankton as we define it today, but did cover the nekton and the macroplankton (e.g., jellyfish and other pelagic animals).

Still earlier records of an ecological nature were published by botanists. For example, F. Unger described, in 1836, the different composition of alpine vegetation according to the composition of the soils (limestone or siliceous).

Another aspect of ecology was treated by Anton Kerner in his book *Pflanzenleben* (Plant Life) (1887, second edition, 1896). His main interest centered around the correlation of structure of plants and environmental conditions. In modern terms, we would call this *Lebensformen* (life forms). His very careful analyses of these features are worthwhile studying even today.

Adolf Steuer, in his *Planktonkunde* (planktology), assembled practically everything known on the subject at the time of publication in 1906. Much of the material constitutes pure ecology. Othenio Abel, a well-known paleontologist, included in his book *Paläobiologie* in 1912 many data on the ecology of vertebrates in a similar way as Kerner had treated plants.

The time from 1914 to about 1930 was not very favorable for the development of ecological science in Austria. In 1918–1919, Austria lost connection with the sea, the Zoologische Station at Triest was closed, and the German laboratory at Rovigno did not function properly under Italian rule. Ecological research was not highly regarded at our universities and led a rather latent life. An outstanding person who tried to fill this vacuum was Franz Werner. Herpetologist by training, he had an excellent knowledge of insects, especially Orthoptera, and wrote several papers of an ecologically faunistic character (e.g., his paper on the fauna of the "Kamptal" in lower Austria, 1927). Most importantly, he awakened an interest in ecology among his pupils, including this writer.

Finally, the difficulties at our scientific institutions have been overcome. In 1940, Franz Ruttner, director of the Biologische Station, Lunz am See, published an outstanding book, *Grundriss der Limnologie* (Outlines of Limnology), which appeared in a second edition in 1960. The main purpose of this book was to emphasize the role of the physical and chemical properties of fresh water for the life of aquatic plants and animals.

One decade later, Kühnelt was able to publish a comprehensive account of a newly developed branch of ecology, soil biology (1950). Not long before that, knowledge of soil organisms was limited merely to bacteria, microscopic fungi, and earthworms, the latter having been treated by Charles Darwin. From about 1930 on, an increasing number of scientists accumulated data on other important soil animals and their dependence on environmental conditions within the soil. Kühnelt's book played perhaps the same role for soil ecology as Steuer's *Planktonkunde* did for planktology. (Translations into Spanish, 1955, and English, 1961 and 1976, are available.)

A specialized field of marine research is covered in a 1966 monograph on the biology of marine caves by R. Riedl. A general textbook on ecology (*Grundriss der Ökologie*) has also been published by Kühnelt in 1965 (second edition 1970) (French edition 1969).

The plant physiologist Richard Biebl emphasized the cellular aspect of plant ecology within his unfinished report on *Protoplasmatische Ökologie* (1962), which is highly regarded at the international level. Walter Larcher, from the University of Innsbruck, is the author of a rather short but impressive book on plant ecology, *Ökologie der Pflanzen,* published in 1973. He treated the metabolic cycles of carbon, nitrogen, minerals, and water, as well as summarizing the problems of resistance toward detrimental influences.

INTELLECTUAL TRADITIONS

Marine Ecology

In the field of marine ecology and oceanography, Adolf Steuer must be named first. He became assistant at the Zoologische Station at Triest in 1900, went to Innsbruck in 1904, and accepted the post of a director of the Deutsch-Italienisches Institut für Meeresbiologie in Rovigno in 1931. His lectures and practical courses attracted many students to marine biology.

In 1948, a group of enthusiastic students started an expedition to the Tyrrhenian Sea to use the skin-diving method for research of the littoral benthos of rocky shores (Riedl 1962). From this group, Rupert Riedl and Wolfgang Wieser are still doing work in marine ecology. Riedl, who was assistant at the zoology department of the University of Vienna, later became Professor at the Department of Zoology, University of North Carolina, and returned to Vienna in 1971 as head of the department. He trained many students in marine ecology in Chapel Hill and in Vienna, and through occasional practical courses at Rovinj. Wolfgang Wieser, who is head of the Department for Zoo-physiology at the University of Innsbruck, is also still active with his students in marine littoral research, mostly limited to the uppermost part of sandy beaches.

Freshwater Ecology

In the field of freshwater ecology and limnology, the outstanding Franz Ruttner was a founder of a school in the best sense of the word. Many students who were participants of his practical courses at Lunz have been induced to do work in limnology. Together with his friend Vinzenz Brehm, Ruttner inspired a group of young students to carry out an expedition to Lake Niriz in eastern Iran (1950–1952) to investigate the limnological features of this remarkable salt lake. The participants were Jens Hemsen, Heinz Löffler, and Ferdinand Starmühlner. Löffler became an outstanding limnologist whose investigations will be treated later. The Biologische Station Lunz am See became a center of limnogical research under the influence of Ruttner, and his tradition continued with his successors Ingo Findenegg, Heinz Löffler, and Gernot Bretschk.

At Innsbruck, the limnological tradition started with Otto Steinböck, whose former pupil, R. Pechlaner, has enlarged his activities during the last decade (see also International Programs).

Terrestrial Ecology

In terrestrial ecology, the difference between botanical and zoological research is still much more marked than in oceanography and limnology. Therefore, the schools must be treated separately.

Plant Ecology

Starting about 1935 at Innsbruck, a group developed around A. Pisek and E. Cartellieri in comparative ecophysiology, while H. Gams worked on the ecology and distribution of plant communities. Later, W. Tranquillini studied the ecophysiology of trees at timberline, subsequently approaching the ecological point of view in a similar way as Lundegårdh did in 1923. Pisek's successor, Walter Larcher, is an outstanding ecologist whose main topic is how plants can live under the severe conditions of alpine climate. To assist him in these studies, he has assembled around him a group of capable scientists (see also International Programs).

The approach from pure physiology to ecology was also the same in Vienna. At the beginning of the twentieth century, Hans Molisch founded a school in plant physiology, but he was also aware of facts that must be considered to be pure ecology. His successor, Karl Höfler, although a prominent cell physiologist, went farther into ecology, and his successor, Richard Biebl, connected these two branches to his famous "protoplasmatische Ökologie" (protoplasmatic ecology). In addition, he became interested in ecological field studies, especially in the turnover of nutrients and energy (see also International Programs). His former pupil, Karl Burian, continued with these activities and was able to gather around him several capable and interested research workers.

Animal Ecology

In the zoology branch of terrestrial ecology, Heinz Janetschek, of Innsbruck, must be named. Around 1950, he started work on the colonization of soil recently made free by melting glacier ice. Later, he extended his studies to other animal communities in the high alpine region. As head of the Department of Zoology, he was able to induce students to build a working group (see also International Programs).

Since the physiologic tradition did not exist at the zoology department of the University of Vienna, the ecological line of research developed independently, aided by Professor Franz Werner as noted above. Here, Herbert Franz must be named. He studied simultaneously at the Faculty of Agriculture and at the university, and became interested in faunistic and ecological work. As head of the department at the Bundesanstalt für alpine Landwirtschaft at Admont (Styria), he has carried out important work in applied ecology, notably in soil biology, and also in faunistics and ecological zoogeography. As a lecturer and later professor at the University of Graz, he has found students interested in these fields. His appointment at the University of Agriculture at Vienna enabled him to extend his activities and to participate in well-organized research in the framework of international programs.

Wilhelm Kühnelt, who started at Vienna, went to Graz in 1950, and returned in 1953 to Vienna, also developed his interest in ecology in the zoology department of Vienna. A decade of work within the framework of the biometeorologic program at Lunz am See served as a training period. As head of the Department of Zoology of Graz and later of Vienna, he tried to induce students to join his activities. Several of them who were together with him as assistants are now heads of department of several universities (Fritz Schremmer, Heidelberg until 1976; Reinhard Schuster, Graz; and Harald Nemenz, Vienna) (see also International Programs).

SIGNIFICANT ADVANCES IN THEORY AND METHODOLOGY

In biological oceanography, the use of the skin-diving method was a real breakthrough. Hans Hass's practice in skin-diving dates to 1937, a time in which only about a dozen people around the world applied it. On the recommendation of Kühnelt, Hass used this method to gather the material for his doctoral thesis (*Zoologica* 101, 1948). Rupert Riedl, a former pupil of Hass, applied this method extensively from about 1948 on. (See Tyrrhenia expedition.) He also constructed a sledge-dredge, which can operate in depths inaccessible to skin divers, but which is limited to rather flat, muddy bottoms. Also, automatic photocameras ("Aqua-rover") have been adapted to submarine research (Riedl 1955, 1956).

In the field of limnology, there have been important new findings. O. Steinböck discovered, in 1953, a new type of high-alpine lake, the kryoeutrophic lake, which is caused by allochthonous organic substances (mostly dead plant remains) being blown into the lake by wind. Thus, a lack of oxygen develops in the deeper layers and the bottom fauna accords with these conditions (Steinböck 1953). I. Findenegg discovered, in 1933, another new type of lake, the meromictic lake, in which the usual spring and autumn water circulation only partly occurs (Findenegg 1937). For this outstanding finding, he was awarded the Einer Naumann medal; he was the seventh man on whom this honor was conferred.

H. Löffler has found an interesting change of habitat in some plankton crustaceans in connection with climate. Many small planktonic animals that live under temperate climatic conditions in small ponds or only at the edge of larger water bodies penetrate within the tropics into big lakes.

In terrestrial ecology, the term *epeirology* was introduced by Kühnelt (1960) to have a single internationally applicable word as a counterpart to oceanography and limnology. H. Gams (1931/2) proposed to characterize the water conditions of different habitats by the term *Hygrische Kontinentalität,* an index built from the height above sea level and the annual rainfall. H. Franz (1952) proposed, as a supplement to the two "ecological laws" proposed by Thienemann, a "third ecological law," which states that the number of species and the stability toward changes increase with the time the community is left undisturbed.

Kühnelt was able to detect an interesting shift of mites and collembolas in connection with climate. Many of these animals, which live under temperate climatic conditions in moss or lichen covers on tree trunks, occur under warmer climates in the uppermost layers of soil proper.

Several findings are not limited to one part of ecology but apply to the whole. For example, in 1904, Raunkiaer coined the term *Lebensform* (life form) for the different ways higher plants hibernate. Kühnelt (1940) extended this term to all characteristics of organisms that can be brought in connection with any ecological factor (e.g., anaerobic–aerobic and poikilotherm—homoiotherm). Further, and as a result of his activities within the framework of the bioclimatic program at Lunz, Kühnelt (1943) developed the concept of *bioklimatische Leitform* (bioclimatic indicator). He observed that, along a vertical transect on a mountain slope, a characteristic arrangement of animal species occurs. From among these, the least mobile species were selected and their dependence on climatic factors studied. In such a way, a system of bioclimatic indicators has been established that allows making some assertions about the conditions in places where climatological measurements have not been carried out. This does not mean that numerical data may be predicted from the faunal composition but rather that places with the same or nearly the same set of indicator species may also have very similar conditions.

MAJOR EMPHASES IN THEORETICAL AND APPLIED RESEARCH

Although not intended to serve as an ecological field station, the Zoologische Station at Triest, nevertheless, deserves mention. Originally, its purpose was to provide the zoology department of the University of Vienna with living animals from the Adriatic Sea, but during the time when Adolf Steuer was an assistant at this station, it developed into an important center of plankton research. In 1953, a research station for subalpine forest research was founded at Innsbruck, and a high-alpine research station has been established at Obergurgl. However, the most significant contributions to ecology came from the Biologische Station at Lunz.

The Biological Station at Lunz

In his introductory lecture at the University of Vienna, the famous botanist Richard Wettstein stressed that a biological field station should be erected in the Austrian Alps. Seemingly independent but perhaps in some mental connection, a rich landlord, Carl Kupelwieser, founded the Biologische Station Lunz near Lunz am See, lower Austria, in his castle Seehof in 1906. The time was not then favorable for an official foundation by the government. During the first years and until 1908, Richard Woltereck, a well-known freshwater biologist, served as the director. From 1908 until 1961, Franz Ruttner, a friend of Carl Kupelwieser, was director of the station. During this long and practically uninterrupted period, Ruttner carried out an important program in freshwater ecology. The physiographic data of the three lakes situated within the "Seetal" were carefully investigated, the geological properties of the lake basins studied, and especially the plankton identified and counted over more than twenty years (1929–1930). Together with his collaborators Vinzenz Brehm and Karl Krawany, Ruttner studied the many and different streams, brooks, and ponds, publishing a report, "Die Biozönosen der Lunzer Gewässer," in 1927 (Brehm and Ruttner 1926).

In addition to these purely limnological studies, another branch of research developed. Ruttner became aware of the fact that meteorologic influences, especially the direction and strength of wind, are responsible for seasonal changes within lakes. These influences were studied jointly with the meteorologist S. Exner. Furthermore, during the pertinent talks, Ruttner and Exner became interested in the microclimatic differences at various heights of the Seetal, where the three lakes are situated. In order to have the simplest conditions, they chose a transect from the Mittersee (800 m) to the summit of the Hetzkogel (1,581 m), along which four stations were placed for the measurement of microclimatic differences. The results were promising in such a way that an extension of the research program was planned for a number of years.

After Exner's death, Wilhelm Schmidt, head of the central meteorologic station of Austria, agreed with Ruttner on the following program: Within the mountain area of Lunz, three transects should be made, by means of a dozen small meteorologic stations containing thermographs, hygrographs, ombrometers, and thermometers (maximum-minimum) 50 cm, 30 cm, and 5 cm above ground, and 5 cm, 10 cm, and 30 cm below ground. Each transect would be studied for three years. Since both biological and meterologic research were planned, a botanist, Helmut Gams from Innsbruck, and Kühnelt as a zoologist, were chosen to carry out the necessary observations. In the beginning, a chemist, J. Müller, and a soil scientist, Karl Furlani, were named but they soon left the program. The microclimatic stations worked well even under the most difficult conditions, such as temperatures of 52°C below zero, hailstorms, and heavy snow. Thanks to Josef Aigner, who went out every week to change the recording strips, very valuable data were collected.

Botanical and zoological data were accumulated, but during the preparation of the final report, Wilhelm Schmidt died. Disagreement between his successors at the central meteorologic station prevented the evaluation and publication of the results. The biologists, now left alone, were able only to publish their own results without the necessary meteorologic and bioclimatic data. Gams published the botanical results in several small papers, and Kühnelt succeeded in writing a whole chapter within a book edited by Eduard Stepan (1948) on the Ybbs valley, to which the region of Lunz belongs. It is deplorable that this much more comprehensive and sophisticated program than that on Mount Marcy (Adams et al. 1920) could not be published in an appropriate form. Nevertheless, the impact of the program on other interested research workers was sufficient to induce further pertinent work: Franz Sauberer, a meteorologist, carried out many interesting investigations of special phenomena; Erwin Schimitschek (1969), of the Agricultural University of Vienna, together with his collaborators carried out important research in applied ecology (e.g., he investigated the microclimatic conditions under which bark beetles grow best by placing fresh logs on the ground and comparing the development of the beetles with the temperature below the bark); other investigators, like J. Dissmann, have studied tree ring growth under different microclimatic conditions.

RELATIONS AND INTERRELATIONS WITH OTHER DISCIPLINES

As in nearly every other country, the botanical and the zoological branches of ecology developed independently in Austria. Direct interrelations arose late. As an example, during the bioclimatic program of Lunz, fruitful talks and practical cooperation occurred between the botanist H. Gams and the zoologist W. Kühnelt. Around 1940, another contact was established between a former pupil of Braun-Blanquet, Erwin Aichinger, and Kühnelt to find whether the plant associations of Braun-Blanquet had a zoological counterpart. The answer is that a partial coincidence occurs, but certain animal communities seem to be independent from well-defined plant associations.

A close cooperation between plant ecology and microclimatology has been reached at the University of Innsbruck where W. Larcher works with A. Cernusca (see also International Programs). Contact of ethology and ecology occurred twice: during the marine Tyrrhenia expedition in 1948, etho-ecological relations were established between Erich Abel (ethologist) and Rupert Riedl and his collaborators (as ecologists); etho-ecological relations were carefully studied also by Otto Koenig in connection with his studies on the birds in the reed belt of Lake Neusiedlersee (1952).

A good interrelation between soil science (Walter Kubiena) and soil biology (Kühnelt) started about 1940. Several reports on this topic were published as doctoral theses at the zoology department of the University of Vienna (e.g., Schaller, Riha).

An interesting cooperation between ecology (W. Moser of Innsbruck) and the International Institute for Systems Analysis (IIASA) at Laxenburg has yielded sizable results, which appear in a paper jointly written by both parties (Modell Obergurgl).

SOURCES AND LEVELS OF GOVERNMENT AND PRIVATE SUPPORT

It is impossible to give exact support figures for the different periods treated within this paper. Fortunately, a seemingly exact report is available for 1974, comprising the different sources of support spent for "ecological" research in the widest possible sense of the word, including also applied ecology. The total amount of money (in Austrian shillings) spent for ecological research in 1974 was 94.32 million: 15.49 million was used for installations, 77.63 for current work. The sources of support were the following: 82.18 million came from government institutions of the central government, the governments of the countries (Bundesländer), and the city governments; 8.97 million came from different research councils; 4.44 million from international projects; and 18.73 million from private sources.

TEACHING AND TRAINING OF ECOLOGY AT UNDERGRADUATE AND GRADUATE LEVELS

Ecology is included in the normal curriculum of students of biology at the universities of Vienna, Innsbruck, and occasionally Graz, and now also at Salzburg. Perhaps the first lectures in ecology were given by the botanist Karl Höfler in Vienna; Kühnelt started his activities later, about 1936–1937. Practical demonstrations were carried out as well in botany and in zoology from 1940 on.

Limnological courses during the long vacation term started at Lunz under the direction of Franz Ruttner in 1912. There was a cycle of two courses, one devoted to plankton, the other to the littoral communities and running water. Today, there are many highly specialized courses given during the summer months under the direction of Heinz Löffler and his collaborators. Practical courses in terrestrial ecology have been given at the Biological Station at Lunz by Kühnelt and his staff since 1954 as well as in the Alpine Forschungsstätte Obergurgl by the biologists of the University of Innsbruck.

From 1966 on, interdisciplinary courses on ecosystem ecology have been offered by a group of scientists directed by A. Cernusca at the University of Innsbruck.

As far as postgraduate courses are concerned, international limnological courses are sponsored by UNESCO under the direction of H. Löffler.

MAJOR NATIVE LANGUAGE JOURNALS AND SOCIETIES

There is neither a society for ecology nor a journal exclusively devoted to ecology in Austria except for a small leaflet, "Berichte der Arbeitsgemeinschaft für ökologische Entomologie in Graz," edited by Johann Gepp. All other Austrian journals accept ecological papers (e.g., the *Sitzungsberichte der österreichischen Akademie der Wissenschaften*) especially in connection with international programs. Another journal in which ecological papers currently appear is *Verhandlungen der zoologisch-botanischen Gesellschaft, Wien.*

Since 1975, the Kärntner Institut für Seenforschung has published yearly reports. The Österreichisches Bundesinstitut für Gesundheitswesen und Umweltschutz has published since 1979 a *Review,* which contains articles of ecological significance. The same is true for the Institut für Umweltwissenschaften und Naturschutz, originally at the Ludwig Boltzmanngesellschaft, and since 1978, converted into an institute of the Austrian Academy of Sciences. The Bundesminsterium für Gesundheit und Umweltschutz has published since 1979 *Forschungsberichte.* Of the latter, of note is "Anthropogene beeinflussung der Vegetation in Österreich" by R. Schininger and K. Burian.

FOREIGN LITERATURE ROUTINELY CONSULTED

Since the major reference journals (e.g., *Biological Abstracts, Berichte über die wissenschaftliche Biologie*) are currently available at our university libraries and biological departments, nothing further need be said within this paragraph.

AUSTRIAN PARTICIPATION IN INTERNATIONAL PROGRAMS

At the beginning of the International Biological Program (IBP) in 1964, the Austrian national committee proposed the following projects:

Section PT (terrestrial productivity): Plant productivity studies in the high-alpine region of "Hoher Nebelkogel" at 3,184 m in northern Tirol were planned by W. Larcher and carried out by W. Moser. Plant productivity studies at the tree line of the "Patscher Kofel" near Innsbruck were carried out by W. Larcher and his staff. Primary productivity study in the reed belt of Lake Neusiedlersee was carried out by R. Biebl and his successor K. Burian, and studies on secondary productivity in the same place were carried out by W. Kühnelt and his staff.

Section PF: Productivity of a high mountain lake (Finstertalersee) in northern Tirol was studied by R. Pechlaner and his staff. Productivity of several pre-alpine lakes in Kärnten was studied by I. Findenegg and his staff. Productivity of Lake Neusiedlersee was studied by H. Löffler and his staff.

Rather isolated projects were proposed and carried out in Section PP by R. Biebl and in HA by E. Breitinger.

Two final reports were published in 1974 and 1979. The former, written in German by H. Löffler and based on many contributions from his collaborators, was entitled *Der Neusiedlersee (Naturgeschichte eines Steppensees)*. The other report, written in English, *Neusiedlersee, the Limnology of a Shallow Lake in Central Europe,* was edited by H. Löffler from many isolated contributions. Austria is also engaged in the preparation of the international synthesis volume on wetlands.

In contrast to the smooth-running IBP, the establishment and implementation of the MAB (Man and the Biosphere program) were beset with numerous difficulties. Ultimately, the government was ready to sponsor only two projects: high-alpine research under the direction of H. Franz, and eutrophication of lakes under the direction of H. Löffler. The Academy of Sciences succeeded in sponsoring a third project, on urban ecology, originally started by R. Biebl and now conducted by his successors K. Burian and W. Kühnelt. A preliminary publication of the group on high-alpine research was noteworthy because of the cooperation with computer scientists (Modell Obergurgl). An Austrian group, headed by H. Löffler, is also participating in the Organization for Economic Co-operation and Development program on eutrophication of Lake Attersee.

Bi- or trilateral cooperation exists between Austria, Italy, and Yugoslavia regarding the eutrophication of the northern part of the Adriatic Sea, in a program established by R. Riedl and his staff.

APPLIED ECOLOGY

In the field of fisheries, the outstanding work of Einsele on productivity, food, and conditions of life in salmonids of the genus *Coregonus,* which are of practical importance within Austrian lakes, must be mentioned.

In the field of forestry, the work of Helmut Friedel (1966) is noteworthy. In his paper, "Development of the alpine timberline in relation to the surrounding mountain land slope configuration," he assembled data that had been gathered during his long and intensive studies. This material serves well the understanding of the real conditions that cause the phenomenon of timberline under climatic aspects. This work has been carried out at the Forschungsstelle für subalpine Waldforschung.

Erwin Schimitschek assembled in his book, *Grundzüge der Waldhygiene* (1969), the results of research carried out together with collaborators over a decade on the susceptibility of European forest trees to diseases and parasites. He found that some of the most effective factors were planting outside the climatic range of the species, changes in the groundwater table, and human influences.

In his book, *Forstökologie* (1952), Franz Hartmann gives a comprehensive account on the different soil groups and their influence on the trees rooting within it.

In agricultural research, H. Franz (1945) made a notable finding regarding the usual way of manuring. Usually, stable manure is brought to the field, but the rich community of microorganisms and small animals cannot continue to metabolize the manure under changed climatic conditions on the field. So it is recommended that the manure be left stored to enable the organisms to finish their work and to metabolize the whole matter. It is this "compost" that should be brought out to the fields.

A major breakthrough was accomplished by Gernot Graefe in 1969 who succeeded in recovering most of the energy stored in grape mark (husks) in a rotting process. The energy can be used for heating greenhouses and inhabited buildings, as well as for heating water. Since the yearly amount of grape mark harvested in eastern Austria equals roughly 80,000 tons and one kg of dry substance can give up about 20,000 k Joule, this method of energy production cannot be neglected.

During the past years, applied ecology has become an important subject far beyond the special aspects discussed above. Awakened by the imminent danger of environmental destruction, nearly the whole population is now aware of ecological facts. Different groups, however, react differently to these facts. Politicians feel that their positions are in danger and make lavish promises in order to persuade the voters. Industrialists, who are, in many cases, responsible for the deterioration of the environment, either deny their responsibility or hire so-called experts to demonstrate that industrial pollution and landscape destruction are negligible and, in most cases, the individual citizen is responsible for the observed damages. The evidence of these experts is either sent to the authorities or freely distributed among the population in order to impress them.

Other industrialists develop an environmental technology to invent costly gadgets that may serve to diminish the damages; in every case, the gadgets are profitable for the producers. Under these circumstances, it is not surprising that individuals, groups, associations, and even political parties make applied ecology their (mostly unpaid) occupation. The literature that results cannot be treated adequately here, in spite of the fact that many of these papers are scientifically correct, often also contribute new facts, and are in general worth reading. The organs of publication run the whole gamut from pamphlets to single articles in newspapers; little leaflets printed on recycled paper (e.g., *Die Umwelt,* private publication, Vienna since 1971); little journals of small local organizations (e.g., *Öko-Linz, Zeitschrift für Ökologie, Natur- und Umweltschutz der naturkundlichen Station der Stadt Linz*); and symposium volumes (e.g., *Österreichisches Forum für Natur- und Umweltschutz, Altmünster, Oberösterreich* since 1969).

Even international symposia on these topics have been held in Austria with important contributions from Austrian scientists. These include *Mensch und Natur in der europäischen Grosstadt* Europagespräch 1970 in Wiener Schriften, Verlag für Jugend und Volk; and *Natur und Mensch im Alpenraum,* 3rd europäischer Kurs über angewandte Ökologie, Innsbruck, 1975, herausgegeben vom Institut für Umweltwissenschaften und Naturschutz.

There is an immense number of organizations that are, in some way, concerned with applied ecology in Austria. An incomplete list of them has been published by the European Information Center for Nature Conservation under the name *Directory of organizations concerned with the environment in Europe* (Strassburg 1977).

REFERENCES CITED

Adams, C. C., G. P. Burns, T. L. Hankinson, B. Moore, and N. Taylor. 1920. Plants and animals of Mount Marcy, New York. *Ecology* 1:71–94, 204–233, 274–288.

Brehm, V. and F. Ruttner. 1926. Die Biozönosen der Lunzer Gewässer. *Int. Rev. Hydrobiol.* 16:281–391.

Findenegg, I. 1937. Holomiktische und meromiktische Seen. *Rev. Hydrobiol.* 35:586–610.

Franz, H. 1945. Über die Bedeutung von Kleintieren für die Rotte von Stallmist und Kompost. *Pflanzenbau.* 20:145–70.

———. 1950. *Bodenzoologie als Grundlage der Bodenpflege.* Berlin: Akademieverlag.

———. 1952. Dauer und Wandel der Lebensgemeinschaften. *Schr. Ver. Verbr. Naturwiss. Kenntnisse.* 93:27–45.

Friedel, H. 1966. Verlauf der alpinen Waldgrenze im Rahmen anliegender Gebirgsgelände. *Mitt. Forstl. Bundes-versuchsanst. Wien* 1966:81–172.

Hartmann, F. 1952. *Forstökologie.* Vienna: Georg Fromme & Co.

Koenig, O. 1952. Ökologie und Verhalten der Vögel des Neusiedlersee-Schilfgürtels. *J. Ornithol.* 93:207–289.

Kühnelt, W. 1940. *Aufgaben und Arbeitsweise der Ökologie der Landtiere. Der Biologe.* 9:108–117. Munich-Berlin: J. Lehmann.

______. 1943. Die Leitformenmethode in der Ökologie der Landtiere. *Biologia Generalis* 17:106–146.

______. 1948. Die Landtierwelt des Lunzer Gebietes. In *Das Ybbstal,* ed. E. Stepan, Vol. 1, pp. 90–154. Vienna-Göstling: Heimatkundlicher Verlag.

______. 1950. *Bodenbiologie.* Vienna: Herold. [Spanish edition 1957. (Biologia del Suelo) Consejo superopr de investigaciones cientificas; English edition 1961, 1976. Soil Biology. London: Faber & Faber.]

______. 1960. Inhalt und Aufgaben der Festlandsökologie (Epeirologie). *Anz. Oesterr. Akad. Wiss. Math. Natwiss. Kl.* 1960:52–61.

______. 1965. *Grundriss der Ökologie.* Jena: Gustav Fischer. (2d edition 1970. Gustav Fischer, Jena and Stuttgart. French edition 1969. *Ecologie Générale.* Masson et Cie.)

Larcher, W. 1973. *Ökologie der Pflanzen.* Stuttgart: Eugen Ulmer.

Löffler, H., ed. 1974. *Der Neusiedlersee* (*Naturgeschichte eines Steppensees*). Vienna: Verlag Molden.

Löffler, H., ed. 1979. *Neusiedlersee, the limnology of a shallow lake in Central Europe.* The Hague: W. Junk.

Riedl, R. 1955. Aufsammlung tiefer Meeresböden in abgegrenzten Schichten und Flächen. *Arch. Hydrobiol.* 51:189–208.

______. 1956. Automatische Photographie von Meeresböden für Ökologisch faunistische Zwecke. *Oesterr. Zool. Z.* 6:532–541.

______. 1962. Probleme und Methoden der Erforschung des litoralen Benthos. *Verh. Dtsch. Zool. Ges.* 1962:505–567.

______. 1966. *Biologie der Meereshöhlen.* Hamburg-Berlin: Paul Parey.

Ruttner, F. 1929-1930. Das Plankton des Lunzer Untersees. *Int. Rev. Hydrobiol.* 23:1–287.

______. 1940. *Grundriss der Limnologie.* Berlin: Walter de Gruyter & Co. (2d and 3d eds., 1952, 1962).

Schmitschek, E. 1969. *Grundzüge der Waldhygiene.* Hamburg-Berlin: Paul Parey.

Steinböck, O. 1953. Ein neuer Seetyp, der kryoeutrophe See. *Mem. Ist. Ital. Idrobiol.* 7:153–163.

Werner, F. 1927. Zur kenntnis der Fauna einer xerothermischen Lokalität in Niederösterreich (unteres Kamptal). *Z. Morphol. Oekol. Tiere* 9:1–96.

7

BELGIUM

Philippe F. Bourdeau

ECOLOGICAL RESEARCH

Terrestrial Ecology

Ecological research as such started in Belgium (and what was then the Belgian Congo, now Zaire) in the late 1930s. In those days, the emphasis was on the phytosociological interpretation of terrestrial vegetation, based on the teachings of Braun-Blanquet and the Zurich-Montpellier school. After the initial work of R. Mosseray and of J. Massart, best noted for his contribution to phytogeography, J. Louis and J. Lebrun published a basic paper on the plant communities of Belgium (1942). Thereafter, they established the Center for Ecological and Phytosociological Research where many Belgian and foreign botanists were trained. After Louis's untimely death in 1947, J. Lebrun, A. Noirfalise, P. Heinemann, and C. vander Berghen co-authored a compendium on the plant associations of Belgium (1949).

In 1950, the center initiated a vegetation cartography program in parallel with a soil-mapping project undertaken by pedologists. The aim was not to map systematically the whole territory but to survey and map the most representative areas from the viewpoint of diversity of vegetation and forest cover. About twenty maps (scale 1/20,000) were eventually produced and more than seventy major papers were published by the center between 1942 and 1972.

In the Belgian Congo, Lebrun and Louis did pioneering work in the savanna and the equatorial rain forest, respectively. The classic paper by

Lebrun (1947) on the alluvial plain of the Rwindi in the Albert National Park was the first successful application of Braun-Blanquet's method to tropical vegetation. Several younger botanists followed in their footsteps in describing and mapping the major vegetation types of the Congo. Among them were R. Germain, W. Mullenders, R. Devred, A. Schmitz, J. Leonard, A. Leonard, P. Gerard, C. Evrard, and L. Liben, all working at the INEAC (Institut National pour l'Etude Agronomique de Congo Belge) or at IRSAC (Institut pour la Recherche Scientifique en Afrique Centrale), both of which promoted basic and applied research in botany and zoology in central Africa. A general ecological classification of the Congo forests was published by Lebrun and Gilbert in 1954.

At the Université Catholique de Louvain, by 1956, Lebrun and his successor, J. R. de Sloover, also developed a research program on the ecophysiology of cultivated and wild tropical species (coffee, peanut, water hyacinth) using plant growth chambers. At the same institution, P. Lebrun initiated research on the ecology of microarthropods (mainly Acarine) in soils, forests, and fresh water, publishing results of these studies in 1971.

In addition to vegetation typing and mapping, A. Noirfalise and his co-workers at the Faculté des Sciences Agronomiques in Gembloux undertook research in applied ecology (forestry and grasslands) and on the ecophysiology of evapotranspiration (Lebrun et al. 1949). Emphasis was placed on forest productivity in relation to site properties and on primary and secondary productivity in pastures as affected by floristic composition and farming practices. For the evapotranspiration studies, water transfer under unsaturated conditions is evaluated in a unique aerodynamic simulation tunnel.

P. Duvigneaud (1946), at the Université Libre de Bruxelles, proposed to replace the characteristic species for the association, alliance, and order of the Zurich-Montpellier school with groups of species characteristic of certain ecological factors, the so-called ecological groups. The plant association is then determined by the abundance-dominance of these groups. This concept, related to that of Aichinger and other central European workers, was applied successfully to various types of vegetation by Duvigneaud (1953) and later by his associate M. Tanghe.

Duvigneaud, Simone Denaeyer-de Smet, A. Galoux, and co-workers established, in 1959, the Center of General Ecology for the integrated study of productivity and biogeochemical cycles in various ecosystems. Together with colleagues from other Belgian universities and research institutes, they succeeded in making an important contribution to the International Biological Program (IBP), terrestrial productivity section. The Virelles forest, which was well instrumented and extensively studied, was selected as a pilot station for deciduous forests in the temperate zone. It provided data for the "Oak Ridge energy flux model," developed by the Oak Ridge National Laboratory Ecology Division. The Belgian IBP program included also the "Mirwart project," in which productivity and mineral cycling were studied in a series of ecosystems ranging from coniferous and beech forests to fields and pastures, all established on the same parent material. The project yielded a wealth of information, showing, for example, the similarity, in quantitative terms, of these systems with their ecological analogs elsewhere in Europe (Duvigneaud and Denaeyer-de Smet 1975; Duvigneaud and Kesternont 1977).

The Brussels group is also working on the ecology and genecology of plants growing on soils with abnormal chemistry (high copper, zinc, lead or gypsum content) and serpentine soils (Lefebvre 1976). More recently, this group initiated activities in the regional mapping of ecosystems, in the cartography of carbon cycling (as a part of the SCOPE International Carbon Center located in Hamburg, Lund, and Brussels), and in urban ecology. Duvigneaud (1980) has also published recently a basic ecology textbook in French.

Aquatic Ecology

The study of aquatic environments was stimulated in the late 1960s by concern over pollution. Under government sponsorship, in particular the Ministry for Scientific Policy Programmation, integrated programs for the study of the pollution of rivers and streams, and of the North Sea were launched aiming at the establishment of "management models" for these environments. Thus, an ambitious national project was started in 1970 to establish a mathematical model for the North Sea and Scheldt Estuary. The project was made possible through the coordination of the activities of oceanographers in several universities and research institutes. Initial results have been published in Nihoul and de Coninck (1977). The basis is a hydrodynamic model, developed by J. Nihoul at Liège University, to which chemical and biological models are connected. Plankton ecology was studied by P. Polk and co-workers at the Vrije Universiteit Brussels. They have worked out a yearly budget of the carbon cycle in the southern part of the North Sea. They found, for example, that grazing of phytoplankton by zooplankton is much less intensive than generally assumed and that there is a heavy mortality of phytoplankton during the night, hence the increased importance of bacteria in this ecosystem. L. de Coninck and associates of the Rijksuniversiteit Gent, working on the North Sea benthos and microfauna, found that the latter was considerably more important in terms of secondary productivity.

A simplified marine ecosystem, the Ostend sluice-dock, is being studied intensively by Polk, Persoone and others cooperating in the Instituut voor Zeewetenschappelijk Onderzoek (Institute for Marine Scientific Research), an inter-university establishment in Bredene. Investigations on the plankton, benthos, microbes, zooplankton, and sediments of the sluice-dock have yielded results helpful in understanding the North Sea system (Podamo 1976).

With regard to freshwater environments an integrated effort was mounted to investigate a heavily polluted stream, the Sambre, as well as the Meuse river (Anon. 1975). In this framework, L. de Coninck (Ghent) studied the benthos and zooplankton, while J. Lambinon, J. P. Descy and A. Empain, all at the University of Liège, designed a system of pollution assessment based on populations of benthos algae (diatoms) and bryophytes (Empain and Lambinon 1975; Descy 1973). In addition, Remacle and co-workers (Anon. 1975) investigated the function of decomposers and nitrogen-cycle bacteria in the process of self-purification of polluted streams. From in situ and laboratory studies of self-purification, F. Evens, from the Rijksuniversitair Centrum Antwerpen, devised a new aeration technique to treat polluted waters.

Heavy metal pollution in agricultural ecosystems is being studied by A. Cottenie and co-workers at the Rijksuniversiteit Gent; soil-plant relationships and plant response to heavy metals have been investigated. A simulation model has also been worked out to express the variations of the contents of mineral compounds in natural waters (de Troch et al. 1976).

Radioecology

The field of radioecology has been well covered in Belgium as far as radionuclide cycling and food-chain contamination are concerned. R. Kirchmann and associates from the Centre d'Etudes Nucléaires at Mol published about fifty papers on this subject in the years 1960–1975. Of particular interest are real-sized experiments in the transfer of several radionuclides from soil, plants, and water to farm animals, and a unique study, with G. Cantillon and A. La Fontaine from the National Hygiene and Epidemiology Institute, of the contamination of a region with radium-226 from industrial effluents (Kirchmann et al. 1971). Kirchmann has also done pioneer work on environmental tritium contamination, by which he established the transfer of tritium from water to organic molecules (Kirchmann et al. 1973). He also worked jointly on specific problems of radiocontamination of freshwater courses with J. Lambinon (Liege), J. C. Micha (Namur), and others.

Ecological Theory

Finally, attention should be drawn to the contribution to ecological theory of I. Prigogine and his associate, R. Nicolis at the Université Libre de Bruxelles, in applying their concepts and discoveries on the thermodynamics of dissipative structures to ecological systems (Nicolis and Prigogine 1977).

Environmental Protection

Concern over environmental protection and resource conservation has given a great impetus to applied ecological studies. Government intervention, through funding and persuasion, has succeeded in integrating the efforts of ecologists and others interested in the environment in large-scale projects such as the North Sea model.

Summary

As the preceding paragraphs indicate, ecological research is fairly well developed in Belgium. As in other parts of the world, research concentrated initially on the descriptive aspects and classification of plant and animal communities. From the start, account was taken of possible applications to agriculture and forestry at home and in the Belgian Congo. More emphasis is now placed on ecosystems and function in terms of productivity and biogeochemical cycles, but autecological studies are not neglected. As elsewhere, ecology has become more sophisticated, making use of the advanced techniques of chemical analysis, applied statistics, and information theory.

INTERNATIONAL INVOLVEMENT

Belgium has been active in various international programs with an ecology component, such as the International Biological Program, the CCMS (Committee on Challenges to Modern Society) of NATO, SCOPE (Scientific Committee on Problems of the Environment) for which there is a national committee, and ICES (International Council for the Exploration of the Seas). It is also deeply involved in the environmental research effort of the European communities.

RESEARCH SUPPORT

Support of ecological research has always been essentially from public sources either directly or indirectly: university budgets, grants and contracts from the National Foundation for Scientific Research, the Foundation for Collective Fundamental Research, the Institute for Applied Research in Industry and Agriculture, the Ministry for Scientific Policy Programmation, provincial governments, and other agencies.

TEACHING

There is no degree major in ecology as such at the "License" (approximately Master's) level. Ecology is taught as part of the compulsory curriculum for botanists and zoologists, as well as for specialists in agriculture and forestry. However, doctoral degrees in botany and zoology can be granted in most universities on the basis of ecological research work.

Recently, graduate and postgraduate curricula have been set up in various aspects of the broad field of environment. They all include ecology courses.

One establishment, the "Fondation Universitaire Luxembourgeoise" in Arlon, is exclusively devoted to teaching and research in environmental sciences.

PUBLICATIONS

There are no ecological journals published in Belgium. However, ecological papers appear in French, Dutch, or English in the following periodicals: *Bulletin de la Société Royale de Zoologie de Belgique* and *Bulletin de la Société Royale de Botanique de Belgique.* Belgian ecologists also publish in foreign journals, such as *Oecologia Plantarum, Vegetatio, Journal de la Société d'Ecologie,* and so on.

REFERENCES CITED

Anonymous. 1975. *Modèle mathématique de la Sambre.* Rapport de synthèse aspects physiques, chimiques et biologiques. Programmation de la Politique Scientifique, 8 rue de la Science, Bruxelles 1040.

Descy, J. P. 1973. La végétation algale benthique de la Meuse belge et ses relations avec la pollution des eaux. *Lejeunia, N.S.* 69–58.

de Troch, F., A. Dhaese, and A. Cottenie. 1976. Modeling of mineral content variations in natural waters. In *System simulation in water resources,* ed. G. C. Vansteenkiste. Amsterdam: North Holland Publishing Co.

Duvigneaud, P. 1946. La variabilité des associations végétales. *Bull. Soc. R. Bot. Bel.* 78:107–134.

______. 1953. Les savanes du Bas-Congo. Essai de phytogéographie topographique. *Lejeunia, Mémoire* 10.

______. 1980. *La synthèse écologique.* 2d ed. Paris: Doin.

______ and S. Denaeyer-de Smet. 1975. Mineral cycling in terrestrial ecosystems. In *Productivity of world ecosystems,* pp. 133–154. Washington, D.C.: National Academy of Sciences.

______ and P. Kestemont, eds. 1977. *Productivité biologique en Belgique.* Paris-Gembloux: Duculot.

Empain, A. and J. Lambinon. 1975. Les bryophytes aquatiques et subaquatiques en tant que bioindicateurs de la pollution des eaux douces. *Société Botanique de France, Colloq. Bryol.* 121:257–264.

Kirchmann, R., A. La Fontaine, G. Cantillon, and R. Boulenger. 1971. Transfert dans le chaîne alimentaire de l'homme du radium-226 provenant d'effluents industriels déversés dans les cours d'eau. *Proceedings of the International Symposium on Radioecology Applied to the Protection of Man and His Environment,* Rome, (7–10 September 1971) pp. 203–222.

______, J. van den Hoek, G. Koch, and V. Adam. 1973. Studies on the food chain contamination by tritium. In *Tritium Symposium,* ed. A. A. Moghissi and M. V. Carter, pp. 341–348. Messenger Graphics.

Lebrun, J. 1947. *La végétation de la plaine alluviale au sud du lac Edouard.* Institut des Parcs Nationaux du Congo belge. 2 vol.

———, A. Noirfalise, P. Heinemann, and C. vander Berghen. 1949. *Les associations végétales de Belgique.* Gembloux.

——— and G. Gilbert. 1954. *Une classification écologique des forêts du Congo.* Bruxelles: INEAC.

Lebrun, P. 1971. Ecologie e biocénotique de quelques peuplements d'arthropodes édaphiques. *Mémoire Institut Royal des sciences naturelles de Belgique.* No. 165.

Lefebvre, C. 1976. Breeding system and population structure of *Armeria maritima* on a zinc-lead mine. *New Phytol.* 77:185–190.

Louis, J. and J. Lebrun. 1942. *Premier aperçu sur les groupements végétaux en Belgique.* Gembloux.

Nicolis, G. and I. Prigogine. 1977. *Self-organization in non-equilibrium systems.* New York: Wiley.

Nihoul, J. and L. de Coninck, eds. 1977. *Projet Mer. Rapport Final.* Vol. 7. Programmation de la Politique Scientifique, 8 rue de la Science, Bruxelles 1040.

Podamo, J. 1976. Ecometabolism of a shallow marine lagoon at Ostend (Belgium). Parts I to V. *Proceedings of the 10th European Symposium of Marine Biology* 2:485–562.

8

CZECHOSLOVAKIA

Milena Rychnovská, Editor

INTRODUCTION

Milena Rychnovská

Within the boundaries of the Czechoslovakia of today, the science of ecology emerged in the second half of the nineteenth century from the taxonomic and descriptive natural sciences of botany, zoology, geology, and geography. Following the example of the strict separation of these university disciplines, ecology advanced separately along the narrow fronts of plants, animals, and microorganisms mainly at the Charles University in Prague. At that time, practical ecological aspects were already in operation in applied fields, notably in forestry, agriculture, and fish farming, and aimed at disclosing actual connections between the organisms under consideration and the environment. Although the results of these studies were based on intuition and empirical approaches and did not provide for understanding the mechanisms and functions involved, the findings brought light to a number of problems. Thus, in addition to a perfect training system in these disciplines, the work contributed to the traditionally high standards of forestry, agriculture, and fish farming.

Under these conditions, intellectual fundamentals and ecological schools were developed mainly in the individual scientific disciplines; their integration did not occur until fifty years later. The academic approach was principally concerned with problems of taxonomy and classification, which in these early years were of great importance, but this emphasis impeded the development of integrated ecology in the second half of the twentieth century. However, the knowledge and experience obtained through these descriptive disciplines made a sound factual basis for the development of contemporary functional ecology.

The years after the First World War were characterized by a rapid growth of research centers and by the foundation of new universities and colleges outside Prague. At that time, the first attempts were made to introduce integrated ecology and landscape ecology to the universities and even to make the public aware of the new approaches. In 1923, Professor V. Úlehla (Úlehla 1947) started this endeavor at the University of Brno. Professor H. Lundegårdh (Sweden), an outstanding ecologist of that period, was invited as a visiting professor for one semester. His course in Brno gave an impetus to his ecological textbook, which was revised frequently and used for more than thirty years throughout Europe (Lundegårdh 1957).

Another group of young plant ecologists at Charles University in Prague produced some original ecological studies. One comprehensive work, published by M. Deyl (1940), tackled the problem of vegetation on a Carpathian mountain in relation to climate, soil, soil microorganisms, and animals and also taking into account new ideas in plant physiology.

After 1939, the Second World War, the closure of the universities, and the persecution of their teachers and students interrupted the development of all the sciences. Integrated ecology had to await its resurrection until the start of the International Biological Program in the early 1960s.

In the years before the Second World War, ecological research work was financed by the state and only to a small degree by private resources. Since 1945, the state has provided money for all research work, irrespective of the institutions performing it. Questions of quantitative ecology are being solved in a number of ecological departments at the various institutes mainly belonging to the Czechoslovak or Slovak Academies of Sciences. Ecological papers appear in botanical, zoological, and other journals. The results of synthetic research work in Czechoslovakia are published mostly in specialized collections of papers or in monographs.

DEVELOPMENTS IN PLANT ECOLOGY

J. Jeník

Developmental Periods

Development in plant ecology in Czechoslovakia can be divided into five periods:

1. During the second half of the nineteenth century, the first studies on

phytogeography were published either in the form of monographs or as chapters in local floras. The studies described plant formations and their dependence on conditions of the atmospheric and soil environments.

2. In the years 1901 to 1918, more details became available on the populations of which plant formations are made, and the first numerical data were published on the physical and chemical properties of the environment.

3. In the period between 1918 and 1945, marked progress was made in synecologic and phytosociological studies. Some of these resulted in comprehensive monographs discussing the relationships between plants and the environment on the basis of long-term measurements and experiments. Several authors were already using simple statistical methods in their classification of plant communities.

4. From 1945 to 1970, conditions became more favorable for the gradual emergence of more integrated forms of ecological research work, in which numerous factors of the atmospheric and soil environment were considered. From that period came detailed monographs dealing with the plant cover in various areas or with a certain type of ecosystem, e.g., forests, grasslands, mountains, water plants, and others. Simultaneously, considerable advances were made in the mapping and classification of plant cover. In the years 1955 to 1975, a newly designed method of reconstructional vegetation mapping made it possible to produce a detailed geobotanical map of the whole territory of Czechoslovakia. In this respect, Czechoslovakia is the leading country in the world (Mikyška 1965). Considerable progress was also made in field measurements, and in autecological and synecologic experiments.

5. The last period of development in plant ecology, 1970 onward, is characterized by the commencement of integrated ecology based on the concept of the ecosystem. This work is carried out mainly in the Botanical Institute CAS, founded in 1954.

Principal Theoretical and Methodological Contributions

In the development of plant ecology after the Second World War, A. Zlatník (1954) proposed an original system for the classification of forest ecosystems, based on phytocenology and ecology; his system was accepted mainly in the eastern parts of Czechoslovakia. In the early 1950s, a detailed analysis was made of the conditions of growth and the stands in a small clearing of a mixed deciduous forest. This was the first integrated ecological study made in Czechoslovakia. The results indicated that conditions in the forest are complicated and varied.

S. Hejný (1960) elaborated a theory on the forms of life of water plants and on ecophases, ecoperiods, and ecocycles, showing the dynamics of water and shore ecosystems within the course of changes in the water table during one year and for a period of several years. The terms introduced by Hejný enable a more accurate designation of the spatiotemporal relationships of plants in standing and running waters.

In the theory of anemo-orographical systems, J. Jeník (1961) defined the dependence of the mountain ecosystem on climate (wind and snow), soil, and relief. The theory explained the origin of the sites richest in mountain flora and brought forth practical measures for nature conservation in the Czech mountains.

A new ecophysiological method for a causal interpretation of phytogeographical phenomena was developed. Using *Corynephorus canescens* and the genus *Stipa,* M. Rychnovská and B. Úlehlová (1975) demonstrated that the distribution of plant species could be explained by their inherited physiologic properties and the degree of their adaptability to critical factors of the stand. A new classification of wet meadows and determination of the indicative value in species on the basis of dynamic soil parameters, notably fluctuations in the level of groundwater, was proposed. A new method for classifying the development of unstable ecosystems on a floristic-statistical basis (enabling the classification of stands in which the "characteristic" species were absent) was also developed. In the past ten years, a number of theses at the Charles University in Prague have been devoted to the complex research of dry grasslands and fallows.

The main journals publishing papers on the plant ecology are: *Folia Geobotanica et Phytotaxonomica* (Prague), *Preslia* (Prague), *Biologia Plantarum* (Prague), *Photosynthetica* (Prague), *Acta Scientiarum Naturalium Academiae Scientiarum Bohemoslovacae Brno* (Prague), and *Biológia* (Bratislava).

ECOLOGY OF VERTEBRATES

J. Pelikán

Vertebrate ecology is a comparatively recent subject in Czechoslovakia. In the years between the two world wars, attention was given merely to applied investigations of fishes and their production in fish ponds. Autecological studies on birds were scarce; studies on the ecology of mammals, reptiles, and amphibians were utterly neglected.

After the Second World War, development in the ecology of vertebrates progressed considerably. It became an important subject for study at the newly founded Institute of Vertebrate Zoology of the Czechoslovak Academy of Sciences, and at the universities and research institutes of agriculture and forestry. A marked shift took place from autecological studies to investigations at the level of populations, communities, and ecosystems. Within the framework of the International Biological Program (IBP) and Man and the Biosphere (MAB) program, research concentrated on trophic chains, population dynamics, reproduction, and growth and production of fishes, birds, and mammals. In recent studies, attempts have been made to obtain a quantitative characterization of functions of these vertebrates in the various ecosystems.

Fishery institutes show great interest in studies on the ecology of fishes in fish ponds and dam lakes as it relates to management of the fishes. The ecology of fishes in running waters is the main concern of research workers at the Institute of Vertebrate Zoology of the Czechoslovak Academy of Sciences, Brno. At first, studies were made in the growth of fishes, their reproductive potential, age structure, and sex ratio. Later, their production was studied, and the quantity of fish obtained by sportfishing was evaluated. At present, intensive studies are being made on the ecology and management of fish communities in artificial reservoirs. The ecology of fishes of the Danube River is the concern of the Laboratory of Fishery in Bratislava.

Investigations on the ecology of game animals, mammals, and birds are performed at the Institute of Forestry and Wildlife at Zbraslav, near Prague. Wildlife management is highly advanced in Czechoslovakia. The ecology of carnivorous mammals is investigated in Slovakia; game animals of high mountains are studied in the High Tatra Mountains.

Research work on the ecology of birds has been developed significantly by members of the Institute of Vertebrate Zoology of the Czechoslovak Academy of Sciences, Brno. After 1950, a complex investigation of the ecology of birds and mammals was part of the research program on infections from the epidemiological point of view. The results of these investigations were used in studies on populations of birds and mammals over a wider range of ecological factors. Raptorial birds and owls were examined as predators of small mammals to determine their function in the grazing-predatory food chain. Later, research work concentrated on waterbirds, mainly geese and ducks, with emphasis on their population dynamics, nesting ecology, migration, trophic relationships, and their function in the reed-swamp ecosystem. At present, investigations are concerned with the ecology of synanthropic birds in towns, villages, and agricultural agglomerations.

The Institute of Vertebrate Zoology of the Czechoslovak Academy of Sciences is engaged in large-scale investigations of the ecology of small mammals (Kratochvíl 1959). The research program includes studies on the ecology of abundant species that are of economic and medical importance, such as the common vole *Microtus arvalis,* mice of the genus *Apodemus,* and the water vole *Arvicola terrestris.* Of importance are newly designed methods of sampling mammalian populations and determining the trophic requirements of small mammals. Other investigations have been concerned with a breeding storm in the hamster and the population ecology of the common mole (*Talpa europaea*) and of other terrestrial mammals. As part of the IBP and MAB projects, mammalian communities have been examined in reed ecosystems, various forest types, in the grassland ecosystem, and in large-scale agriculture (Pelikán et al. 1974).

An outstanding personality of Czechoslovak ecology was F. J. Turček (1915–1977), who worked in Slovakia. He was among the first to treat the science of ecology from the standpoint of the ecosystem, and proposed modern trends for research work in this country. His studies were mainly concerned with such topics as the relationships of birds and mammals with forest trees and trophic relationships of animals in forest stands (Turček 1961).

The journals publishing articles on the ecology of animals are: *Acta Entomologica Bohemoslovaca* (Prague), *Věstník Československé společnosti zoologické* (Prague), *Folia Zoologica* (Brno), *Acta Scientiarum Naturalium Academiae Scientiarum Bohemoslovacae Brno* (Prague), and *Biológia* (Bratislava).

ECOLOGY OF INVERTEBRATES INCLUDING PARASITOLOGY

V. Skuhravý and K. Novák

In the years between the two world wars, studies on the ecology of invertebrates were concerned with the autecology of several insect pests, for example, the forest pest *Lymantria monacha* and several pests of the sugar beet.

Advances in Czechoslovak ecology were considerable after the Second World War as a result of several factors: the foundation of numerous specialized institutes of the Czechoslovak Academy of Sciences (the Entomological Institute, the Institute of Parasitology, and the Institute of Landscape Ecology); the establishment of the Institute of Experimental Biology and Ecology in the Slovak Academy of Sciences; an increase in the network of universities and colleges; and the foundation of a number of specialized institutions concerned with problems of agriculture and forestry. In Czechoslovakia, forty to seventy publications each year are concerned with invertebrate ecology.

The subject for most studies on insect ecology is the autecology of individual pests occurring in agriculture and forestry (Hodek 1973). Autecological studies cover 80 percent of published papers, the remaining 20 percent being concerned with ecological investigations of communities. At present, studies are available on the ecology of the following agricultural pests: *Hyphantria cunea, Phtorimea ocelatella, Leptinotarsa decemlineata, Melolontha melolontha, Contarinia medicaginis, Aphis fabae, Pegomya betae,* pests of cereals (notably *Oscinella frit*), and stored food pests. In forestry, pest studies have been done on mainly *Lymantria monacha* and *L. dispar, Thecodiplosis brachyntera, Epiblema tedella, Cacoecia murunana, Operophtera brumata, Tortrix viridana,* and members of the family Scolytidae.

Investigations of communities have focused mainly on agrocenoses, such as entomocenoses of potato, clover, sugar beet, tobacco, and alfalfa (Skuhravý and Novák 1957; Weismann and Vallo 1963).

In the years 1955 to 1966, ecological research was carried out on more than 1,200 sites in Czechoslovakia on the distribution of some groups of water insects (Ephemeroptera, Trichoptera, Plecoptera). The results, compared with the present distribution of the representatives of these orders, enables the tracing and recording of changes in the natural environment of standing and running water in Czechoslovakia.

Investigations of the soil mesofauna have concentrated on the dynamics and composition of communities in grassland and forest soils, and on the influences on these communities. The bio-indicative value of the soil fauna and the influence of fauna on the formation and development of soils have been examined.

Sophisticated experimental procedures are used in investigations of the influence of several abiotic factors on the development of insects. Studies have been made on the diapause of several insect species and on relationships between predators and hosts, and parasites and hosts.

An increasing amount of apparatus is being used in ecological research work in the laboratory and the field. Ecologists collaborate closely with physicists and chemists, and employ radioisotopes, pheromones, and acoustic signals in the solution of problems that they could not solve without the assistance of these experts and sophisticated technologies.

After 1950, a marked development appeared in medical arachnoentomology as a result of an investigation of natural focuses of infections that required information on susceptible periods in the ecology of blood-sucking arthropods for the purpose of vector control. The investigation started with a thorough examination of the biotopes and acquisition of statistical data on the incidence of parasites in various biotopes and on individual hosts. This was followed by experimental research work in the laboratory and in the field. A further contribution to ecological investigations of medical problems associated with arachnids is the complex of expeditionary methods designed for investigation of natural focuses and employed successfully in expeditions to Yugoslavia, Albania, Bulgaria, and Mongolia. In studies on parasitic worms of animals and humans, parasitologists have elucidated a number of ecological relationships between the parasite and its host.

At present, numerous pests of economic importance can be successfully controlled on the basis of profound knowledge of their ecology. The same applies to integrated protection of plants and to the solution of problems concerned with influences on the entire external environment.

DEVELOPMENTS IN UNDERSTANDING TERRESTRIAL ECOSYSTEMS

Milena Rychnovská

The rapid escalation in development of quantitative integrated ecology of terrestrial biomes in Czechoslovakia is undoubtedly associated with participation in the IBP. Investigations of the entire ecosystem were preceded by analytic studies on the production ecology of natural phytocenoses and population ecology of animals and soil microorganisms. On the basis of the data obtained in this way, it was relatively easy to apply an integrated investigation to the entire ecosystem.

Several of the IBP projects at first concentrated on an interdisciplinary approach (1965), but later developed into integrated projects having a clearly defined intention of explaining the structure, productivity, and functioning of the ecosystem (1968–1974). These projects were concerned with:

1. Grassland ecosystems (Lanžhot project), involving studies on abiotic factors, the structure and dynamics of primary producers, production processes (photosynthesis, respiration, transpiration), decomposition processes, and, to a small degree, studies on consumers (soil fauna). The results of these projects have been presented in approximately 150 publications and international syntheses of the IBP. They enabled the design of a static model of the energy flow in four grassland subsystems (Rychnovská 1979*a*) and of a dynamic simulation model of primary production based on photosynthesis, abiotic factors, and the structure of the stand. Information was obtained on the intensity of transpiration in grassland stands. Mineral cycles were studied by means of analyses concerning the biomass of plants, soils, soil water, and rainwater (Úlehlová et al. 1976). In addition to an understanding of the energetic balance of a grassland stand, other results provided an understanding of the surprisingly high efficiency of grassland production and its regenerative importance in the quality of superficial waters and the soil.

Another grassland ecosystem project was started in 1973 within the framework of MAB project No. 91: Function of grasslands in spring region—Kameničky project. The aim of this integrated project is the evaluation of productivity and other functions of meadow ecosystems in the densely inhabited uplands in central Europe. The region under study is heavily cultivated and serves as an important source of water. The results are supposed, on the one hand, to contribute to ecological theory and, on the other hand, to assist in the agricultural management of the region. More than ten research institutions are involved in this integrated project under the coordination of the ecology department, Institute of Botany, Czechoslovak Academy of Sciences. The bibliography of the project so far comprises 137 items; it is part of a progress report (Rychnovská 1979*b*) in which the main interim results have been presented. These results are an important step toward a final synthetic view of the functioning of the ecosystem under study, as well as of its productivity, stability, and ecological role in the landscape.

Although restricted in its extent, the Banská Štiavnica research project, concerned with the ecology of mountainous Nardetum, was highly sophisticated. While the Kameničky project sought to analyze the structures and functions of producers and decomposers, an attempt was made in the Banská Štiavnica project to obtain a complete understanding of the trophic chain of consumers. This resulted in a complete synthesis that has not yet been published, but which has been used as a basis for a number of theories on, for example, the ecological penetration in ecosystems.

2. Wetland ecosystems (Nesyt and the Třeboň Basin projects). These studies were concerned with the reed belt in the littoral of fish ponds extending on one side into open water, on the other side into wet meadows. The subjects for study in these projects were abiotic factors, the structure and dynamics of primary producers, production processes (photosynthesis, respiration, water regime, mineral nutrition), dynamics of consumers (rodents, birds, insects), decomposition processes, and cycles of mineral elements. The results of these studies were published in about 200 papers in addition to a national synthesis at the level of the projects (Dykyjová and Květ 1978; Květ et al. In press) and an international IBP synthesis. The inputs, i.e., abiotic factors (notably the regime of radiation), structural parameters, and parameters of photosynthesis, made it possible to design a mathematical simulation model of primary production. Cycles of geobioelements were assessed partly by means of analyses of water, soil, and biomass in natural stands, partly from cultures in hydroponics. An understanding of these fundamental properties was important both in explaining interactions between land and water and in the practical management of fish ponds. The final outcome was an integrated investigation of the area (Třeboň Basin) listed among biosphere reserves (MAB Project No. 8).

3. Forest ecosystems, examined in two IBP projects, Lednice and Báb. Investigations were made of energy flow and the cycles of geobioelements. In addition to forest communities, the Lednice project was concerned with production characteristics of the secondary communities, i.e., adjacent meadow and field cultures. The abiotic factors, the structure and dynamics of producers (tree, shrub, and herb layers), consumers (insects, rodents, birds), several production processes (photosynthesis, respiration, water regime), and decomposition processes were examined. The cycle of geobioelements was studied dynamically on the basis of analyses of plants (all layers), soils, and soil water. Syntheses have been made for the individual compartments (Biskupský 1975; Penka and Vašíček 1974; Vyskot 1976). The results can be used in forest cultivation and environmental ecology.

Not all integrated projects were designed for the purpose of disclosing

Table 8.1. **Publications of the Department of Ecology, Botanical Institute of the Czechoslovak Academy of Sciences (in percent)**

Years	Phytocenology, Taxonomy, Physiology	Synecology (coincidence of vegetation with habitat factors)	Quantitative ecology in 1 to 3 trophic levels	Mathematical models, syntheses
1955 to 1959	72	21	7	0
1960 to 1964	79	13	8	0
1965 to 1969	60	17	23	0
1970 to 1974	28	14	57	1
1975 to 1979	9	8	65	18

structures and functions of a certain ecosystem; some covered a smaller vertical range and a bigger horizontal range, and vice versa. In this respect, attention should be drawn to two investigations. In one, organized by the Grassland Research Institute in Banská Bystrica and carried out since 1965 in meadows and pastures of all mountain areas of Czechoslovakia, abiotic factors and their complexes, primary production, and a number of aspects of soil ecology in both naturally and artificially fertilized stands were examined. Another integrated series of investigations, carried out by the scientific staff of the Forest Management Research Institute at Zbraslav, was designed to obtain an understanding of the water-economy function of forests and the elucidation of the influence of industrial emissions on forest stands.

Further development of ecological projects is directed toward a wider integration to include socioeconomic aspects, as well as the ecological factors elaborated in the MAB projects. These lines have been followed in an elaboration of projects on wood- and grasslands based on preliminary models comprising all compartments of the various trophic levels. The intended result is the design of a mathematical model illustrating the functioning of ecosystems and a determination of the limits of their homeostasis. All those involved in this work have been trained in systems analysis, and an adequate number of computers has been provided.

The emergence of functional and integrated ecology from descriptive and observational ecology, or from classifying phytocenology, can be illustrated by the structure of publications of the ecology department, Botanical Institute, Czechoslovak Academy of Sciences, founded in 1955 (Table 8.1).

INVESTIGATION OF FRESHWATER BIOTA

J. Hrbáček

Investigations of the Elbe oxbows and of ponds and lakes in Bohemia, incorporating both the physical environment and all groups of water organisms except bacteria, started in the last third of the nineteenth century. Investigations by a group headed by Professor Frič resulted in a qualitative description of biota with suggestions of possible interactions. For example, the new stock of fish in a lake previously without fish was observed to feed on a species of Cladocerans that later disappeared. At about the same time, the biota in ponds were observed by the manager of the most important area of fish ponds in southern Bohemia; from the organisms present in the stomach of various fish species, researchers concluded that there was a competition for food among these species. It was also observed that manure had influenced the food organisms of fish and hence the fish productivity of ponds.

Studies performed at that time at the universities were concerned with detailed investigations of the taxonomy, morphology, and autecology of various freshwater organisms; they disregarded a broad approach. This attitude continued at the universities until the 1950s.

A new impetus for studying freshwater biota from the standpoint of the habitat came in the 1930s. This arose from a need to evaluate the effect of pollution on running waters and that of manure and fertilizers on ponds. In both cases, a qualitative approach, called biological indication, was developed and is still practiced (Sládeček 1973).

After the Second World War, the number of university research workers steadily increased for about twenty years. This enabled the formation of teams without which a more complex quantitative investigation is virtually impossible. In the late 1940s, one of these teams, headed by J. Hrbáček and O. Oliva, started the first investigation of the Elbe oxbows to compare the present biota with the earlier observations (Hrbáček 1962; Hrbáček and Straškraba 1966, 1973). In the early phase of these quantitative studies, the basic assumption of the fish management, namely, that these waters were understocked by fish, was found to be erroneous. To show that a large number of small fish were present but not harvested by anglers, the research group used fish toxicants. After eradication of fish, considerable changes occurred in the biota of these oxbows, the most striking of which was a change in the zooplankton during which small species were replaced by larger ones. Transparency increased almost twice. Later, comparative studies made on both oxbows and fish ponds suggested that this change was due to changes in the dominant predator and not to the toxicants used; in this way, the leading role of the top predator in the species composition and metabolism of standing waters was recognized. This finding was so different from the well-established paradigm concerning the leading role of the concentration of nutrients that it took some time before it was accepted as a principle and tool in the management of ponds and reservoirs for water supply. Other investigations of ponds supported the findings, as did a study on the biota of oxbows and the main stream of the Danube River (Ertl and Tomajka 1973).

Studies on reservoirs were characteristic of those conducted by Czechoslovak hydrobiologists in the 1950s. This resulted from the construction during these years of dam lakes, built partly for power generation, partly for water supply. As there are no natural lakes in the hills and lowlands of Czechoslovakia, there has been little practical knowledge available of the management of these man-made lakes. This necessitated intensive research work, which was descriptive at first; later, the use of computers for statistical evaluations of the data enabled the disclosure of some interactions. Recently, mathematical modelling (Straškraba 1976), and the results of investigations of the oxbows, have successfully been applied in the solution of some management problems.

The biota of the sewage treatment plants have also been investigated in the last twenty years, and some interactions between the composition of the biota and the effectiveness of the sewage plants have been recognized.

CONTEMPORARY TRENDS IN TRAINING IN ECOLOGY

J. Jeník

Ecology is a subject read at universities and colleges of agriculture and forestry within the teaching program of various subjects, e.g., physiology, geobotany, biogeography, hydrobiology, and parasitology. At some universities, plant ecology and animal ecology are read as separate subjects. At Charles University in Prague, courses on integrated ecology are available for specialists only.

Postgraduate training in ecology, as a form of postgraduate scientific education, is offered by universities, colleges of agriculture and forestry, and, to a major extent, by the Czechoslovak Academy of Sciences. In spite of the introduction of the specialization "Ecology," training has been conducted along the more narrow lines of either plant or animal ecology (or hydrobiology). Ecology is part of postgraduate training for the protection of the natural environment. Discussions are under way on the introduction of integrated ecology to university courses and secondary schools, but no decision has been reached. An accelerating factor is the general feeling that a synthetic knowledge of the environment at all its levels is one of the today's major necessities.

ACKNOWLEDGMENT

The authors wish to express their sincere thanks to Dr. V. Landa, corresponding member of the Czechoslovak Academy of Sciences, for his valuable advice and criticism.

REFERENCES CITED

Biskupský, V., ed. 1975. *Research project Báb.* IBP progress report II. IBP report no. 5. Bratislava: Veda.

Deyl, M. 1940. Plants, soil and climate of Pop Ivan. Synecological study from Carpathian Ukraina. *Opera Bot. Čechica* 2:1–288.

Dykyjová, D. and J. Květ, eds. 1978. *Pond littoral ecosystems. Structure and functioning.* Ecological studies no. 28. Berlin-Heidelberg-New York: Springer-Verlag.

Ertl, M. and J. Tomajka. 1973. Primary production of the periphyton in the littoral of the Danube. *Hydrobiologia* 42:429–444.

Hejný, S. 1960. *Ökologische Charakteristik der Wasser- und Sumpfpflanzen in der Slowakischen Tiefebenen (Donau- und Theissgebiet).* Bratislava: Vydavatel'stvo SAV.

Hodek, I. 1973. *Biology of Coccinellidae.* The Hague: W. Junk.

Hrbáček, J. 1962. Species composition and the amount of the zooplankton in relation to the fishstock. *Rozpravy Cesk. Akad. Ved Rada Mat. Prir. Ved* 72:1–115.

______ and M. Straškraba, eds. 1966, 1973. *Hydrobiological studies* 1, 2, 3. Prague: Academia.

Jeník, J. 1961. *Alpine Vegetation des Riesengebirges, des Glatzer Schneeberges und des Hochgesenkes (Theorie der anemo-orographischen Systeme).* Prague: Nakladatelství ČSAV.

Kratochvíl, J., ed. 1959. *Hraboš polní* (Microtus arvalis). Prague: Nakladatelství ČSAV.

Květ, J., A. Szczepánski, and D. F. Westlake, eds. In press. *Ecology of wetlands. International Biological Program No. 20.* Cambridge: Cambridge University Press.

Lundegårdh, H. 1957. *Klima und Boden in ihrer Wirkung auf das Pflanzenleben.* 5th ed. Jena: Gustar Fischer Verlag.

Mikyška, R., ed. 1968. *Geobotanische Karte der Tschechoslowakei. 1. Böhmische Länder (Böhmen, Mähren und Schlesien).* Vegetace ČSSR A 2. Prague: Academia.

Pelikán, J., J. Zejda, and V. Holišová. 1974. Standing crop estimates of small mammals in Moravian forests. *Folia Zool.* 23:197–216.

Penka, M. and V. Vašíček, eds. 1974. *Ecosystem study on floodplain forests in south Moravia.* IBP report No. 4. Brno: University of Agriculture.

Rychnovská, M., ed. 1979*a*. Temperate seminatural meadows and pastures. In *Grassland ecosystems of the world. International Biological Program no. 18,* ed. R. T. Coupland. Cambridge: Cambridge University Press.

______, ed. 1979*b*. *Function of grasslands in spring region—Kameničky project.* Progress report on MAB project no. 91. Brno: Botanical Institute CAS.

______ and B. Úlehlová. 1975. *Autökologische Studie der tschechoslowakischen Stipa-Arten.* Vegetace ČSSR A 8. Prague: Academia.

Skuhravý, V. and K. Novák. 1957. Entomozönose des Kartoffelfeldes und ihre Entwicklung. *Rozpravy Cesk. Akad. Ved Rada Mat. Prir. Ved* 67:1–50.

Sládeček, V. 1973. System of water quality from the biological point of view. *Ergeb. Limnol.* 7:1–218.

Straškraba, M. 1976. Development of an analytical phytoplankton model in the parameters empirically related to dominant controlling variable. In *Umwelt Biophysik. Arbeitstagung veranstalltet von der Gesellschaft fur Physikalische Biologie und der Biologischer Gesellschaft der DDR von 29.10. bis 1.11. 1973 in Kühlungsborn.* Berlin: Akademie Verlag.

Turček, F. J. 1961. *Ökologische Beziehungen der Vögel und Gehölze.* Bratislava: Vydavatel'stvo SAV.

Úlehla, V. 1947. *Napojme prameny.* Prague.

Úlehlová, B., E. Klimo, and J. Jakrlová. 1976. Mineral cycling in alluvial forest and meadow ecosystems in southern Moravia, Czechoslovakia. *Int. J. Ecol. Environ. Sci.* 2:15–25.

Vyskot, M. 1976. Tree store biomass in lowland forests in south Moravia. *Rozpravy Cesk. Akad. Ved Rada Mat. Prir. Ved* 86:1–166.

Weismann, L. and V. Vallo. 1963. *Voška maková* (Aphic fabae Scop.). Bratislava: Vydavatel'stvo SAV.

Zlatník, A. 1954. Methodik der typologischen Erforschung der tschechoslowakischen Wälder. *Angew. Pflanzensoziol.* (Festschrift E. Aichinger) 2B:916–955.

9

GREAT BRITAIN

Andrew G. Duff and
Philip D. Lowe

Britain is justifiably regarded as the home of one of the major schools of ecology, and in this necessarily brief account, there is space to mention only the most important institutional and theoretical advances, particularly those which have attained international recognition. Consequently, our choice of topics has been somewhat eclectic, and we are aware that other historians might paint a rather different picture. Nevertheless, we hope that our interpretation will provide a basis for comparison with other countries treated in this volume, and will lead toward a more adequate history of contemporary British ecology.

BRITISH ECOLOGY IN THE MAKING, 1900–1949

Ecology originated more or less simultaneously but independently in a number of different countries. This is especially marked in comparing British and American developments during the formative years of ecology from about 1900 to 1914.

Plant Ecology

The earliest thoroughgoing work on ecology in Britain was the phytogeographic surveys initiated around the turn of the century by Robert Smith (1899) and his brother William. Interest in the survey of vegetation grew rapidly, and local surveys were soon being conducted in a number of areas throughout Britain. Initially these were uncoordinated efforts and there was little agreement on the appropriate units of vegetation or how to represent them graphically.

In order to secure uniformity in vegetation survey work, the pioneers of British ecology began to associate into a community of ecologists. The Central Committee for the Survey and Study of British Vegetation (later shortened to the British Vegetation Committee) was formed in 1904, bringing together the leading investigators. The collaboration fostered by this committee bore fruit in a paper by C. E. Moss (1910), which established the basis for an agreed upon terminology and system of units. These were employed in the synoptic volume *Types of British Vegetation,* edited on behalf of the committee by A. G. Tansley (1911). The book stimulated widespread interest in vegetation studies among botanists, both amateur and professional.

Although some attempts were made to relate the distribution patterns of vegetation to environmental factors, this initial phase of British ecology was essentially a branch of plant geography. By contrast, American ecologists of the period were more interested in the dynamics of the organism-environment relationship; these researchers emphasized change and causality, as in Clements's studies on the succession of plant communities. American ecology also tended to be more utilitarian and experimental, whereas the outlook of British ecologists tended to be disinterested and observational. Such national differences in the style of ecology were no doubt due in part to the different cultural and institutional resources available to scientists in particular contexts.

Despite growing interest, the progress of regional survey work was dogged by the considerable expense involved in producing colored vegetation maps. The British Vegetation Committee explored various avenues to secure financial support, including a plan to the government for a national vegetation survey. After protracted negotiations from 1906 to 1911, the treasury finally refused to sanction the necessary finances for the project.

The failure to place the production of vegetation maps on a permanent footing was a severe blow to the British Vegetation Committee. Without the security of publication, survey work ceased, signalling the end of the descriptive phase of British ecology. Ecological work was beginning to broaden in diverse directions and to be taken up with enthusiasm by university students. It was decided to dissolve the Vegetation Committee and to form instead a society with its own journal and open to anyone interested in ecology. In 1913, the British Ecological Society was founded and its *Journal of Ecology* launched—both were the first of their kind in the world (Salisbury 1964).

From the description of extensive tracts of vegetation, the focus of ecological research turned toward correlations between plant communities and habitat factors. This required training in physiology and some familiarity with habitat-measuring instruments, factors which tended to estrange amateur involvement in ecology (Lowe 1976). As British ecology left behind its amateur associations and adopted a more analytical approach, ecologists' ideas of nature changed. The work of F. W. Oliver and his students at University College London on the geomorphology and ecology of coastal habitats came into the mainstream of ecological research and introduced a dynamic viewpoint. In 1920, an expression of this growing interest in the development of plant communities was Tansley's elaboration of the quasi-organismic theory of vegetation, in which the pattern of change in the community was recognized as the basis for a classification of vegetational units.

In the period between the wars, plant ecologists were largely occupied with studies of the dynamics of vegetation, attempting to elucidate the causal relations between the plant community and its habitat. Clements' vitalistic model of succession, though very influential among British investigators, was increasingly called into question during this period, first with the demonstration of retrogressive changes in peat-moor communities and then in 1929 with Godwin's finding, from his studies of the vegetation of Wicken Fen, that succession could be experimentally deflected onto a new course.

Institutionally, the interwar years were a hiatus for British plant ecology. There were no posts specifically for ecologists either in the universities or in government. Therefore, the maintenance of the discipline depended largely on the personal commitment of individual academics. Gradually, courses in ecology were introduced into university botany degrees. However, without specific posts, there was no incentive to train in ecology; indeed, Arthur Tansley, the leading British plant ecologist in the interwar years, actively discouraged students from specializing in the subject.

Animal Ecology

If anything, the prospects of animal ecology, though a more recent arrival on the scene, were brighter. Research in animal ecology did not get under way in Britain until the interwar period. Important institutional developments included the founding of the Freshwater Biological Association in 1930, which opened a laboratory on Lake Windermere under the direction of W. H. Pearsall (1964), and the establishment of the Bureau of Animal Population at Oxford in 1932 under Charles Elton. Gathering interest and research in the subject prompted the British Ecological Society to launch the *Journal of Animal Ecology* in 1932 with Elton as its editor.

In contrast with plant ecology, the government seemed prepared to recognize the general utility of supporting investigations in animal ecology. Animal ecologists tended to be more pragmatic in their ideas and concepts. Furthermore, their central concern with animal numbers intersected with such practical responsibilities of government as pest control and fisheries management. Indeed, much of the research on animal ecology, for example in economic entomology and marine fisheries, was of an applied nature and occurred outside the universities in government laboratories and research institutes.

The most significant work in giving coherence to the new discipline was Elton's research (1927) on the causes of fluctuations in animal populations. Studies of the trophic relations of organisms led him to formulate the notions of the food-web and pyramid of numbers; both concepts have been very influential in the development of ecological theory. The early work of Lack also belongs to this period and is exemplified by his studies of habitat selection in the birds of the English Breckland heaths. Investigations by both Elton and Lack were also important in providing empirical evidence of the ecological niche concept.

The growing realization of the important role that animals could play in determining the direction of plant succession was embodied in Tansley's conception of the ecosystem, formulated in 1935, which envisaged the fundamental unit of ecological study as the complex of plants, animals, and habitat (Tansley 1935, 1939). The ecosystem concept did not, however, make much impact on analysis and theory until the advent of systems analysis in ecology in the 1950s and the rise of production ecology.

Thus, the period between the wars forms a definite second phase in the history of British ecology, marked by the development of an analytic approach, the rise of a British school of animal ecology, and the general adoption of a dynamic conception of the organism and its environment.

World War II

The Second World War, like the First, severely disrupted the work and careers of many British scientists. For their part, ecologists were anxious to contribute to the war effort but also to avoid the tragic waste of talent that had occurred in the First War, when promising young biologists had been sent to the trenches to fight as ordinary soldiers. At least initially, however, the government did not seem to regard biology as one of the sciences particularly relevant to winning the war. In 1940, the annual meeting of the British Ecological Society passed a resolution calling for greater use of biologists in the war effort. Nevertheless, it was two and a half years after the beginning of the war before some central direction for mobilizing biological knowledge was provided by the cooperation of the Association of Applied Biology, the British Ecological Society, and the Society for Experimental Biology in establishing the Biology War Committee (the forerunner of the Institute of Biology).

Despite the exigencies of war time, this was a period when many groups and organizations looked to the future, and, with official sanction, reviewed their role in British society and their potential contribution to a viable and prosperous peace. Ecologists were no exception. Proposals for utilizing ecology became absorbed into the development of official thinking on the post-war planning and reconstruction of Britain. In essence, the case for ecology became attached to that for nature reserves and wildlife protection, which in turn was associated with the wider cause of preserving the British countryside—a cause which had gathered momentum and public support in the 1920s and 1930s and which now commended itself to the government for its obvious symbolic value in helping sustain morale during a period of intense national sacrifice.

Through a series of committees and investigations, beginning in 1941, the government was presented with a detailed plan for the designation and maintenance of a national system of nature reserves, which paralleled recommendations for a similar system of national parks. The drive for a system of nature reserves started with a concern over postwar wildlife preservation, initiated by the voluntary wildlife organizations, but with the growing involvement of senior members of the British Ecological Society, the plan became a coherent set of policies for nature conservation. The society established its own committee in 1943, under Tansley's chairmanship, to investigate the need for nature reserves and nature conservation. This committee reasoned that the formulation and implementation of nature conservation policies must be based on sound ecological advice. Therefore, it recommended the formation of an Ecological Research Council, which would take charge of nature reserves but would also undertake biological surveys and conduct fundamental ecological research.

These and other suggestions were considered by two official committees: one for England and Wales, under the chairmanship initially of Julian Huxley with Tansley as his deputy, which reported in 1947; and the other for Scotland, under James Ritchie, which reported in 1949. These committees drew up lists of proposed nature reserves. They stressed the importance of managing reserves on scientific principles and, therefore, recommended setting up an official "biological service." The government acted favorably on their recommendations, establishing, in 1949, the Nature Conservancy (Sheail 1976). This new government agency combined the functions of conducting and sponsoring ecological research, giving advice and information on nature conservation, and acquiring and managing nature reserves. Undoubtedly, its creation is the most significant milestone in British ecology, for it marks the great blossoming of ecological work in this country. A small staff and budget in its early years delayed its full impact. Nevertheless, in the creation of the Nature Conservancy, the government formally recognized the significance of ecology and secured the institutional basis of the discipline.

In the postwar period, British ecologists have been able to exploit the conservancy's unique institutional structure. Its combination of research and practical conservation has facilitated the application of ecological knowledge and techniques, and the development of applied ecology. The fusion of pure and applied science enabled ecology to break out, much more quickly than other disciplines, from the ivory tower mentality that had characterized academic biology prior to 1939. At first through nature conservation, then through a broadening range of functions, the social role of ecology has been established and gradually extended.

THE RISE OF MODERN ECOLOGY, 1950–1980

The period since 1950 has witnessed the rise of modern ecology. Institutional developments have gathered pace and research interests have diversified. These two aspects have been closely associated and are considered in turn below.

Institutional Developments

The most important institutional feature of the postwar period has been the emergence and growth of an ecological profession. This has been intimately linked with the implementation of the Nature Conservancy's program and is most conveniently described in relation to the evolution of the Conservancy.

Much of the Conservancy's first decade was occupied with initiating its primary tasks of reserve acquisition and of research, as well as securing its position in the face of considerable ignorance and some mistrust of its novel functions. The first national nature reserve, Beinn Eighe in Wester Ross, was declared in 1951, and by 1960 there were eighty-four in England, Scotland, and Wales covering about 140,000 acres. In 1953 and 1954, the first two of the Conservancy's research stations were opened: at Merlewood in the Lake District, as the base for moorland and woodland research; and at Furzebrook on Poole Harbour, in Dorset, as the center of physiographic research.

The Conservancy's planned development was inhibited by a shortage of suitably qualified staff. There were very few trained ecologists, and their background was university research, not practical conservation. In effect, the Nature Conservancy had to create a conservation profession sui generis.

As part of its support for academic research, the Conservancy began awarding studentships for postgraduate training in ecology, initially about ten to twelve per annum. This was the first systematic provision for the training of ecologists. More than a hundred studentships were awarded during the 1950s. The expansion of the Nature Conservancy provided posts for some of the newly trained ecologists; its scientific personnel rose from nine in 1950 to eighty-one in 1960, and about a fifth of the latter were former holders of studentships. Most, however, went into the traditional area of university teaching and research, in Britain and overseas.

As regards conservation, the Nature Conservancy had to generate its own internal training for staff, largely on the job. In 1953, it appointed its first regional officers, comprising an embryonic field staff, who began to accumulate the expertise, skills, and techniques necessary for the tasks of reserve management, the safeguarding and control of wildlife on other sites, and the provision of practical conservation advice to private and public landowners.

Difficulties in recruiting staff were compounded by cuts in the projected buildup of the Conservancy's grant. These arose from the economic crisis of the mid-fifties and the stringency imposed on the national budget by the rearmament of the Cold War. In addition, the general political climate was somewhat adverse. The Conservancy had been created by a Labor government. However, throughout the 1950s, in its formative years, the Conservancy faced a Conservative government that exhibited little sympathy for nature conservation, was determined to restrict at least non-military public expenditure, and was attuned to the interests of private landowners, among whom a small but influential element was intensely suspicious of the Conservancy's intentions and powers in acquiring and designating land. The Conservancy faced a precarious future. The period of uncertainty culminated in an investigation of the agency by the Select Committee on Estimates of the House of Commons in 1958. After searching examination, this parliamentary committee authoritatively endorsed the Conservancy's purpose and its program of work.

The experience of the Conservancy's first decade was that further progress promoting conservation policies would require considerable effort in informing and influencing public opinion and in expanding the political support for the objectives of conservation. The lesson was quickly absorbed, particularly by Max Nicholson, who was the very able director-general of the Nature Conservancy between 1952 and 1966. With its primary tasks in hand and its own position now reasonably secure, the Conservancy was able to turn its attention outward, to develop its advisory, information, and educational services, and its public relations. From the late 1950s through the 1960s, it spearheaded a concerted and highly successful campaign to arouse greater national commitment to conservation and to raise the status of ecology. Having established its expertise in applying ecology to the maintenance of nature reserves, the Conservancy was well placed to foster the extension of ecological knowledge and conservation techniques to other types of land and resource use (Nicholson 1976).

The 1960s was the decade of applied ecology (Warren and Goldsmith 1974). The discipline steadily expanded its political and institutional support, a process which took it far beyond its existing base in reserve management and as a minor feature of university research. Indeed, the general mood of the discipline changed radically, becoming expansive and outward-going. Ecologists actively popularized their subject, making very effective use of radio, television, and the press. They also looked for new outlets and applications for their skills. Specifically, expansion occurred in a number of realms:

public awareness of the value of ecology and conservation; the position of ecology in general education; training and employment opportunities for ecologists; and the international role of British expertise.

It is possible to review only briefly some of the major events of this period. The emergence of a large and well-organized conservation lobby has been both an expression of, and stimulus to, the growth of popular interest in nature conservation. New groups have been established and existing ones revived; all have experienced rapid membership growth. For example, the Royal Society for the Protection of Birds went from 8,000 members in 1959 to 300,000 in 1980. Up to 1955, only three county naturalists' trusts had been formed. During the 1960s, trust development spread across the country, such that, by 1980, there were forty-one trusts, with an aggregated membership of 125,000 and a total reserve acreage of 100,000. In managing local reserves and promoting conservation policies and field studies with local government, the trusts have complemented the regional work of the Nature Conservancy.

Public interest in ecology and conservation has grown with the intensification of pressures on the environment (Nicholson 1970). The industrialization of agriculture and the increasing recreational use of the countryside, for example, have made it quite evident that measures to conserve wildlife populations could not be confined to nature reserves. Particular catastrophes have drawn conservationists into considering these wider environmental issues. For instance, mass casualties of birds and mammals in 1959, 1960, and 1961 in areas subject to spraying with agricultural chemicals were recorded by naturalists. The Nature Conservancy took up the issue and, in negotiations with the manufacturers of pesticides, agreed on voluntary restrictions on their use. A program of research on the effects of toxic chemicals on wildlife was also initiated at the Conservancy's new experimental station at Monks Wood, near Huntingdon, and the results have led to further controls. Similar disasters that projected conservationists into the news included major oil spillages such as the Torrey Canyon incident of 1967 and the Irish Sea bird wreck of 1969.

Associated with the increasing public support for conservation has been an expanding role for ecology in education (Lambert 1967). "The key to informing the general public about nature conservation must lie with the schools," concluded the annual report for 1959 of the Nature Conservancy. This was the prelude to a series of major initiatives to establish a prominent position for ecology in general education, as part of an effort to modernize and improve the status of biology teaching. Pressure from school biology teachers, the Nature Conservancy, the Field Studies Council (founded in 1943), and the British Ecological Society created an atmosphere conducive to the reform of school biology incorporating a greater role for ecology and field studies. In 1960, the Nature Conservancy established a Study Group on Education and Field Biology, which brought together interested organizations and sponsored experimental trials of ecological teaching materials. The results showed that the ecological approach could be integrated into the normal school program of biology teaching and examinations, and that field studies could be an important complement to laboratory instruction.

Major conferences organized by the Nature Conservancy and by the British Ecological Society maintained the momentum of interest and pressure for change. The Nuffield biology course reflected the new climate of opinion and was designed to introduce students eleven to sixteen years of age to basic ecological and physiologic processes through a series of elementary experiments. Gathering interest in field studies stimulated a rapid growth in field centers, nature trails, and educational reserves. In the early 1970s, this movement to reform the biology curriculum was overtaken by mounting concern over pollution and resource depletion, which precipitated widespread interest in environmental education on a much broader basis and led to a spate of new courses focusing on the relationship between man and his natural environment.

This was particularly marked in higher education. The new universities and polytechnics provided fresh soil in which novel and previously fringe subjects could grow. Some of the new universities were particularly well situated to study the natural environment and conduct fieldwork through being located in rural surroundings, and schools of environmental science (or studies) were set up across the country. In a number of instances, they have proved an ideal institutional setting for ecological research and teaching because they often combine, within the one unit, geologists, geographers, soil scientists, and biologists, as well as ecological specialists. Ecology also claimed a larger place in the botany and zoology departments of well-established institutions, as well as in other subjects.

The major development in postgraduate education was the introduction of courses giving advanced training in conservation and ecology. The first such course was established, with the encouragement of the Nature Conservancy, at University College London in 1960; others followed later in the decade. These courses represented the beginning of formal vocational education in ecology. By the mid-sixties, it was estimated that the production of ecologists from the new courses and through the traditional mechanism of postgraduate research degrees was running at about 150 per annum.

Career opportunities were also growing and diversifying. Appointments in universities and other sectors of education grew apace. In addition, however, applied research in such fields as agriculture, fisheries, and pest control generated a steady demand for ecologists. Opportunities in conservation continued to expand, mainly within the Nature Conservancy. By the end of the decade, some of the voluntary organizations with considerable landholdings were also employing small numbers of ecologists in conservation work, as were certain landowning statutory bodies, such as the Forestry Commission. The investigation and management of fish stocks, both marine and freshwater, were the other established practical outlets for ecological skills.

Overseas demand for ecologists in the areas of teaching, applied research, and conservation was buoyant. Indeed, Britain's traditional overseas links have provided her ecologists with experience of a range of ecological conditions and conservation problems in both developed and developing countries. Consequently, Britain's ecologists have been well placed to take the lead in promoting international cooperation, for example, through the International Union for the Conservation of Nature and Natural Resources and the International Biological Program.

The keynote of ecology in the 1960s, that of expansion, has been maintained into the 1970s. In the early 1970s, completely new demands for ecologists have appeared. Stimulated by mounting environmental concern, the expanding horizons of applied ecology have continued to encompass ever more novel tasks in the fields of environmental management and resource conservation: for example, pollution control, land-use planning, recreation and amenity management, water conservation, landscape design, and land reclamation. The new employers include local government, the Countryside Commission, and regional water authorities.

The last decade also brought major institutional reforms that may shape the development of British ecology for many years to come. For example, there have been various attempts to organize applied ecologists on a professional basis. Thus, the concern of the previous decade to promote and popularize ecology has given way to a new preoccupation with the integrity and credibility of professional expertise, including an emphasis on standards and efforts to consolidate recent occupational advances.

The other major change relates to the structure of government support for ecology. In 1973, as part of the reorganization of civil science, following the proposals of Lord Rothschild, the research and conservation functions of the Nature Conservancy were separated. A new statutory body, the Nature Conservancy Council, was established, responsible for nature conservation to the Secretary of State for the Environment. The research stations that had formed part of the Conservancy were reconstituted as a new Institute of Terrestrial Ecology, remaining within the Natural Environment Research Council (which since its formation in 1965 had subsumed the Nature Conservancy).

Undoubtedly, the new arrangements have increased and diversified the access enjoyed by ecologists to the financial and political resources of the central government. However, the combination of pure and applied science within one organization, which did so much to facilitate the development of an ecological profession in Britain, has been formally disrupted. It may well be that such a division is now appropriate. For nature conservation is not just a matter of applied ecology but must involve policy contributions to and from planning, economics, education, industry, and agriculture. In addition, the future expansion of the role of ecology in British society will depend on the exploitation of new outlets for ecological skills and research findings, apart from nature conservation. It may well be that ecologists will find themselves hampered in this endeavor by being stereotyped through too exclusive an identification in the public mind with a specific set of conservationist attitudes. It is too early to predict what the impact of the change will be on the direction of research, though it seems likely that the exigencies of the Nature Conservancy Council will preserve the distinctive empiricist tradition of British ecology.

Conceptual Developments

In terms of its conceptual development, two important trends are discernible in the style of ecological research since 1950, namely, the rise of an experimental approach and the increased mathematical sophistication of ecologists. It is no coincidence that such intellectual pragmatism should have emerged in an era of ecological managerialism, when ecologists have increasingly been called upon to give specialist advice in conservation and land management. As the editors of the newly launched (1964) *Journal of Applied Ecology* commented: "In applied ecology, which is intended to lead to recommendations for action, it is particularly to be expected that measurement and experiment should be characteristic features, since experiment is essential to test the soundness of practical advice, and in any practical operation estimates of cost, duration or yield must depend on quantitative information."

In other respects, the period since 1950 is notable for the great diversification of research interests among British ecologists, concomitant with ecology's expanding institutional base and the growing number of practitioners. This plurality of research fields makes any concise historical appraisal doubly difficult, so we have focused our attention on two developments that seem to be of particular importance in an international context, quantitative plant ecology and population dynamics. Other salient research interests of British ecologists will be summarized at the end of the chapter.

Quantitative Plant Ecology. Plant ecologists have been in the vanguard in applying quantitative techniques within ecology. The rationale behind the use of objective statistical methods to characterize plant communities was neatly put by Harberd (1962):

> Regardless of the derivation of the technique it should stand or fall on whether or not it is useful. . . . A competent field ecologist with experience of the local vegetation could probably arrange the lists in a very similar fashion with a lot less labour. On the other hand, there is likely to be more agreement between a group of technicians applying the methods as described than between a group of experienced field ecologists relying on their own judgement.

The early 1950s was a watershed in the transition from the use of subjective phytosociological methods of community classification to statistical methods of analysis. At British Ecological Society meetings in 1954 and 1955, the relative merits of the two approaches were hotly debated. Realizing the significance of this debate, C. B. Williams (1964) remarked that "the old and somewhat anecdotal Field Natural History has changed into the science of ecology largely by increased knowledge, increased accuracy of observations, and increased use of measurement." Williams was an exponent of statistical methods in ecology, for example, in measuring species diversity using captures of insects in light-traps and in using the logarithmic series to analyze frequency distributions. He viewed favorably any attempts at mathematization of the discipline, but acknowledged that the application of statistical methods in biology was still in its infancy.

In the 1950s, M. E. D. Poore (1955) provided a lengthy critical assessment of the Braun-Blanquet system of phytosociology, which, he argued, had been unjustly neglected by British plant ecologists. For example, it had been summarily dismissed by Tansley in his monumental work on *The British Islands and their Vegetation,* published in 1939. Against the usual practice of British ecologists of naming a plant community by its dominant or codominant species, Poore argued that the Continental system enabled communities to be described in some detail and, therefore, more realistically. His own major contribution was to combine some of the best features of the Zurich-Montpellier and Scandinavian schools. Many British workers, however, felt that descriptive plant sociology was too subjective and too static, and that it ignored the problem of the nature of vegetation. Advances in statistical methods made such arguments seem redundant.

Goodall (1952) pioneered the application of statistical techniques in the distinction and classification of vegetation units, initially using discontinuous presence-or-absence data but later scoring species for cover or prominence, which enabled the use of orthodox multivariate techniques, such as factor analysis and the discriminant function. Following from the early work of Goodall, Hopkins produced evidence, from species-area curves over a range of habitats, that undermined the phytosociologists' "minimal area" concept by showing instead that species diversity varies continuously with area. These studies laid the foundation for the considerable development of multivariate methods by W. T. Williams and Joyce Lambert in the 1960s, and their paper introducing the use of an electronic digital computer for association-analysis in 1960 was a milestone in the application of computers in ecology. Finally, some mention should be made of the important work of Greig-Smith (1957) and co-workers at Bangor on the analysis of pattern in the plant community, which complemented the development of statistical methods of community classification.

Population Dynamics. The second major development in British ecology has been in the study of population dynamics. A paper by A. S. Watt (1947) stimulated plant ecologists in this direction. Watt was able to draw on a long experience of research, including his studies of Breckland vegetation since the 1920s. He adduced evidence from seven plant communities to show that pattern in a community can result from the life history of the dominant members of that community. For example, in a *Calluna* heath, the cyclic process of maturation and decay of individual *Calluna* plants produces a mosaic of bare areas and vegetation, which in turn form respectively favorable and unfavorable situations for associate lichen species. Another example presented by Watt is the well-known "hummock-and-hollow" cycle of *Festuca* grassland. In cases such as these, Watt presented a picture, previously overlooked by ecologists, of dynamic interaction between plant populations at particular stages in a succession.

However, the study of plant population dynamics has not been as vigorously pursued by British ecologists as has research into animal populations. Under the direction of Charles Elton, Wytham Woods near Oxford has become a center for intensive ecological research, to the extent that this ninety-hectare piece of land has been more thoroughly investigated ecologically than perhaps any other of comparable size. Elton (1966) introduced a technique whereby casual observations of animal behavior and species interactions could be entered directly onto record cards, incorporating full information on the position of the organism in the community. Over the years, this has enabled a complex model to be built up of the trophic relations of a woodland ecosystem. The work of Lack at Oxford (1954) on the population dynamics of birds deserves special mention, notably his seminal studies of the robin (*Erithacus*) and the breeding ecology of tits (*Parus*), which has demonstrated the adaptive response of clutch size to food availability in these species. These and related studies were interpreted by Lack as empirical support for the Nicholsonian model of density-dependent, biotic control of animal populations.

Lack himself adopted an approach that set his ecological studies firmly in the tradition of Darwinian evolutionary theory, and this Darwinian focus has also informed the work of J. L. Harper in his studies of plant competition. In the 1950s, Harper carried out a series of elegant experiments on the environmental factors affecting seedling development in maize (*Zea*), conducted at the Department of Agriculture at Oxford University. Harper went on to study the effects on production of growing different species together and in isolation, under controlled environmental conditions and different nutrient regimes. His research led to the idea of "ecological combining ability," the notion that production may be maximal in diverse, rather than simple, communities (depending on niche availability), an idea which has had important consequences both in agriculture and in nature conservation. As recently as 1967, however, in a stimulating review article, Harper was able to point out that despite the practical importance of this research, the experimental study of plant population dynamics still sadly lagged behind the work of animal ecologists in this direction.

Other Research Areas. Whereas quantitative plant ecology and the study of population dynamics have been the two major growth points in British ecology since 1945, other research interests of British ecologists in this period at least deserve a cursory mention.

An interest in autecology remains strong in this country (Clapham 1956). British ecology is rooted in the tradition of amateur natural history, and the inductivist approach of the naturalist informs a continuing series of biological monographs of the British flora, published in the *Journal of Ecology.* Started in 1941, these have appeared at a rate of four or five a year, on average, without a break to the present. Although having little impact on ecological theory, these studies have been of some use in the management of nature reserves. Production ecology has been pursued on a modest scale, stemming from the later work of W. H. Pearsall and particularly identified with the name of J. D. Ovington and the stimulus of the International Biological Program. However, in Britain there has not been so intense an interest in this field and the related developments in theoretical modelling and systems analysis as has been shown by American ecologists. Some contributions have been made by British workers to advances in microecology, especially in microclimatological technique, but this also remains a minor speciality. Tropical ecology has been of growing interest in Britain, signified by the inception of a Tropical Ecology Group of the British Ecological Society in 1961, in which the name of P. W. Richards has figured prominently. This last development doubtless reflects a growing degree of contact with foreign ecologists, as well as more opportunities to travel abroad owing to the improved institutional support for British ecology generally.

Finally, mention should be made of two fields that are strictly only marginal to British ecology, but that have nevertheless made significant contributions to it. Fisheries research, especially the work of the Fisheries Laboratory in Lowestoft, has added to ecologists' understanding of animal population dynamics. The growing field of ecological genetics is also noteworthy, particularly studies of the selective advantage of different phenotypes under field conditions, such as the classic case of industrial melanism in the pepper moth *Biston betularia.*

Summary

Since 1950 British ecology has extended its institutional support and diversified its research interests. This has coincided with the increasing involvement of ecologists in practical affairs, especially in nature conservation, which has tended to bolster ecology's public image, as well as its academic standing. The extent to which this model of the growth of ecology has been repeated in other countries is a topic of more than passing interest to the historian of ecology.

ACKNOWLEDGMENTS

We would like to thank David Allen, Tom Cairns, Dr. Bryn Green, Dr. Derek Ratcliffe, and Professor Gerald Wibberley for reading an earlier draft of this chapter. One of us (A. D.) gratefully acknowledges the financial support of the Science Research Council; the other (P. L.), of the Social Science Research Council.

REFERENCES CITED

British Ecology in the Making, 1900–1949

Elton, C. S. 1927. *Animal ecology.* London: Sidgwick and Jackson.

Godwin, H. 1929. The sub-climax and deflected succession. *J. Ecol.* 17:144–147.

Lowe, P. D. 1976. Amateurs and professionals: The institutional emergence of British plant ecology. *J. Soc. Bibliogr. Nat. Hist.* 7:517–535.

Moss, C. E. 1910. The fundamental units of vegetation: historical development of the concepts of the plant association and the plant formation. *New Phytol.* 9:18–53.

Pearsall, W. H. 1964. The development of ecology in Britain. *J. Ecol.* 52 (suppl.): 1–12.

Salisbury, Sir Edward. 1964. The origin and early years of the British Ecological Society. *J. Ecol.* 52 (suppl.):13–18.

Sheail, J. 1976. *Nature in trust: the history of nature conservation in Britain.* Glasgow and London: Blackie.

Smith, R. 1899. On the study of plant associations. *Nat. Sci.* 14:109–120.

Tansley, A. G., ed. 1911. *Types of British vegetation.* Cambridge: Cambridge University Press.

———. 1920. The classification of vegetation and the concept of development. *J. Ecol.* 8:118–149.

———. 1935. The use and abuse of vegetational concepts and terms. *Ecology* 16:284–307.

———. 1939. British ecology during the past quarter-century: the plant community and the ecosystem. *J. Ecol.* 27:513–530.

———. 1947. The early history of modern plant ecology in Britain. *J. Ecol.* 35:130–137.

The Rise of Modern Ecology, 1950–1980

Clapham, A. R. 1956. Autecological studies and the "Biological Flora of the British Isles." *J. Ecol.* 44:1–11.

Elton, C. S. 1966. *The pattern of animal communities.* London: Methuen.

Goodall, D. W. 1952. Quantitative aspects of plant distribution. *Biol. Rev.* 27:194–245.

Greig-Smith, P. 1957. *Quantitative plant ecology.* London: Butterworths Scientific Publications.

Harberd, D. J. 1962. Application of a multivariate technique to ecological survey. *J. Ecol.* 50:1–17.

Harper, J. L. 1967. A Darwinian approach to plant ecology. *J. Ecol.* 55:247–270.

Lack, D. 1954. *Natural regulation of animal numbers.* Oxford: Clarendon Press.

Lambert, J. M., ed. 1967. *The teaching of ecology.* Oxford and Edinburgh: Blackwell Scientific Publishers.

The Nature Conservancy. 1959. *The first ten years.* London: The Nature Conservancy.

Nicholson, M. 1970. *The environmental revolution.* London: Hodder and Stoughton.

———. 1976. The ecological breakthrough. *New Sci.* 72 (25 November):460–463.

Poore, M. E. D. 1955. The use of phytosociological methods in ecological investigations. *J. Ecol.* 43:226–269.

Tansley, A. G. 1939. *The British Islands and their vegetation.* Cambridge: Cambridge University Press.

Warren, A. and F. B. Goldsmith, eds. 1974. *Conservation in practice.* London: Wiley.

Watt, A. S. 1947. Pattern and process in the plant community. *J. Ecol.* 35:1–22.

Williams, C. B. 1964. *Patterns in the balance of nature.* London: Academic Press.

Williams, W. T. and J. M. Lambert. 1960. Multivariate methods in plant ecology. II. The use of an electronic digital computer for association-analysis. *J. Ecol.* 48:689–710.

10

GREECE

Pantazis A. Gerakis

HISTORICAL BACKGROUND

To the Greeks of the Golden Age and the Byzantine Era, the word *ecology* would be meaningless as would be most modern scientific terms that have been coined from Greek stems and roots since the advent of modern science. Even a few years ago, a layman in Greece would most likely explain the word *ecology* as the "discourse about houses"; this shows how misleading the coinage of a scientific term may be when based on a superficial knowledge of Greek. The tracing of the first ecologically significant concepts in the works of Hesiod, Aristotle, Theophrastus, and the historians of Byzantium would be an interesting venture. However, since such a history bears little relevance to the immediate objectives of the article, only a brief account of the social, economic, and scientific developments related to ecology from the emergence of modern Greece as a free state one and a half centuries ago to the Second World War will be given as a background necessary for understanding the developments since 1950.

Modern Greece emerged as a free nation in 1928 after a long war of independence, which left the country devastated. The young state started with a decimated and starving population depending mainly on crop and animal husbandry systems differing only slightly from the ones practiced by their ancestors three millennia earlier. Since 1928, the inevitable progress achieved by introducing Western European technology and education was felt more in industry, shipping, and crop production than in animal production and silviculture. With particular reference to the latter, Greece suffered a gradual destruction of its forests: it has been estimated that just over a century ago, forests covered about 40 percent of the country, while now they cover only 19 percent. The main causes of this destruction were the rapidly increasing population, which pressed for forest clearance in favor of new fields even in areas marginal for crop production, forest fires caused by shepherds wishing to extend their grazing lands, and government inefficiency in formulating policies and imposing controls for forest and range land use. Perhaps the major cause was that the people considered forests as a common resource open to uncontrolled exploitation by virtually anybody since almost all forests and wildlands in Greece are government property (Tsoumis 1976).

In a way, the history of ecology in Greece seems to be reflected in the history of the recognition of forestry as an economic entity and scientific discipline. As cardinal events in forestry history, we should note the establishment of a School of Forestry in the Athens Technical University in 1917. The school was moved to Thessaloniki in 1927 to be incorporated with the newly created University of Thessaloniki. Also, a separate and distinct Forest Service was organized in the Ministry of Agriculture in 1922. These two events contributed markedly to the accumulation of a background of applied ecological information related to silviculture and environmental conservation.

The establishment of the first Higher School of Agriculture in Athens in 1920 promoted also an awareness of the concepts of ecology as applied to food and fiber production. The most notable single ecological work in agricultural sciences was a monograph on crop ecology by the plant breeder J. Papadakis in the 1930s, in which the soil and climatic conditions of Greece were shown to be related to the response of the main field crops; crop ecological zones were also distinguished. This monograph formed the basis of a more general book published by the same author in Spanish (Papadakis 1954).

Apart from the Schools of Agriculture and Forestry, ecological work was also done at the Schools of Physics and Mathematics (known also as Schools of Natural Sciences) of the Universities of Athens and Thessaloniki, and especially at the Chairs of Botany, Plant Systematics and Plant Geography, and Zoology. However, the emphasis was in taxonomy, physiology, and mapping of the flora and fauna of various parts of Greece, rather than in the dynamics of plant and animal communities. Typical of this line of work is the paper by Ganiatsas (1936) on the allophytic vegetation in Greece.

Progress in the disciplines related to ecology, the realization of the need to study the biology of plants and animals in the field at a population and community level, and the slow but distinct progress in phytosociological work stopped abruptly with the advent of the Second World War, which was followed, in turn, by the Greek Civil War (1940–1949). The period between 1940 and 1949 was marked by a devastation of forested areas and wildlife directly by combat activities in certain areas and indirectly by the collapse of any control measures against forest and range fires and overgrazing. Similarly, Greek universities and research stations were plagued by lack of funds and qualified personnel.

THE POST-SECOND WORLD WAR AND CIVIL WAR YEARS

For the purposes of this paper, the years between 1950 and 1980 may be divided broadly into three periods, first from 1950 to 1962, second from 1963 to 1972, and third from 1973 to 1980.

First Period (1950–1962)

The beginning of the 1950s found the Greek economy totally shattered. Destruction was also shown by the vast areas of forest, shrub, and wildlands that were burned. Thousands of people were homeless. Large slums cropped up in the periphery of the major industrial cities, mainly in Athens, Piraeus, and Thessaloniki, with refugees fleeing combat zones. Universities and research stations were just barely functioning. Nevertheless, recovery came soon after the establishment of peace. Universities and research stations were funded again, new facilities were programmed and equipped, and many young scientists of all disciplines were provided scholarships for graduate studies abroad. Higher education and research resumed their prewar level.

Education

According to the traditional university structure in Greece, the importance of a scientific field or discipline is indicated by whether this field is (in increasing order) a part of a course, a whole course, a separate chair, and even by the number of persons working in a chair.

During this first period, ecology was still far from being generally recognized as a distinct field. No separate courses in ecology were taught. Ecological information was given as supplementary information in numerous related courses (e.g., botany, zoology). Teaching of theoretical ecological concepts was low-played because there were no chairs of ecology in the two older Universities of Athens and Thessaloniki nor in the newly created University of Patras. There were very few professors in the natural sciences for the rapidly increasing student population. Thus, the demands on their time and energy did not allow anything but a few basic courses in zoology and botany.

Applied ecological teaching started to expand, improved markedly in the School of Agriculture and Forestry, and was given by professors in such disciplines as silviculture, agronomy, forest management, forest botany, and horticulture. Also, in general, the quality of university textbooks on natural sciences, forestry, and agriculture was raised.

Research

Basic ecological research was still lacking for two reasons. First, the government had little interest in basic research in any field and instead made a strong effort to support research applied to the production of food, fiber, forest, and animal products. Second, Greece, being an undeveloped country at that time, did not have a modern autochthonous tradition in the natural sciences but had to import both technology and science from abroad, especially from the central European countries. Thus, since ecology even in those countries was still a subject studied by a relatively small number of botanists and zoologists, it was to be expected that the attention to and importance of ecology in Greece would be smaller by far.

Notably, part of the research work carried out during this period in fields closely related to ecology, and especially in the taxonomy, mapping, and geography of the flora and fauna of Greece, was done by foreigners (mainly central Europeans) alone or in collaboration with local scientists. This was because the unique species richness and diversity of the flora and fauna of Greece attracted the specialists from central European universities and because the great majority of their Greek counterparts had done their postgraduate work in central Europe. This is shown by the several papers on Greek flora and fauna published in German as indicated in the bibliographic lists compiled by Kanellis (1966) and Economidou (1976).

As representative of the type of research carried out during this period, the phytosociological work of Lavrentiadis (1956) may be mentioned. Several others on the same line followed later on, e.g., Anagnostidis (1961), Ganiatsas (1963), Lavrentiadis (1961, 1964), Debazac and Mavrommatis (1971), Dafis (1973), Voliotis (1973), Economidou (1974), Yannitsaros and Economidou (1974), Tsianacas (1975), Babalonas (1976, 1979), Economou-Amilli (1976), Hararas (1976), Pavlides (1976), and Drossos (1977). Of these, the works of Debazac and Mavrommatis (1971), Dafis (1973), and Voliotis (1973) present an overall picture of the vegetation zones of Greece.

Environmental Awareness

Environmental awareness during this period was low. People worked hard for the barest necessities. Construction of houses progressed rapidly and soon became the number one industry. New factories were built to provide work for the hundreds of thousands of peasants who had concentrated in the large cities during the war. Not only did these peasants refuse to return to their villages, many others were abandoning agriculture because their land holdings were too small to make a decent living. The significance of this radical change in Greek economy and social life was that ekistic and industrial growth was very poorly planned. For example, sewage disposal, whenever there were any facilities at all, was primitive.

Although the existence of a pollution problem in Greece has been recognized officially since 1959 and a special committee for its study was formed by the Minister of Public Works, no serious government restrictions were imposed against effluents and emissions from factories. Even highly polluting industrial plants were tolerated close to or within cities and towns. Not only politicians but the public and the press welcomed the increasing number of huge chimney stacks as a sign of the rising economic vigor of postwar Greece.

In spite of the people's disinterest in environmental issues, a few efforts to create an awareness about the long-range perils of such unplanned growth were made by small groups of scientists and laymen. The Athens International Center of Ekistics, created by the Greek city planner C. A. Doxiadis, was one of the first groups to focus on the environmental problems of Athens. Certain semi-scientific societies were formed by environmentalists; the Hellenic Society for the Protection of Nature, established in 1951, was to become one of the two leading such societies in Greece.

Second Period (1963–1972)

During this period, Greek universities and research stations completely overcame the setback of war. Also, the adverse effects of unplanned industrialization and urbanization on the quality of life started to be felt by more and more people.

Education

The relatively large numbers of scientists who were sent abroad for graduate studies not only in Europe but also in the United States resulted in a marked improvement in the quality of university education, in spite of the student population explosion. All universities increased their number of schools and the number of chairs per school. Job openings for university instructors increased threefold. The improvement was felt probably more in the natural sciences, agriculture, forestry, and veterinary medicine. Funds for buildings, books, and equipment reached a satisfactory level for the first time in contemporary Greek history.

The Schools of Physics and Mathematics, in which the chairs of zoology, biology, and botany belong, did not yet give ecology the status and prestige of a chair or even of a course. Principles of general ecology continued to be taught as integral parts of the various zoological and botanical courses, but, with some exceptions (e.g., Ganiatsas 1967), ecological principles were not strongly emphasized.

Education in the School of Agriculture and Forestry (University of Thessaloniki) took a decisive turn toward a fuller recognition of the need to apply the internationally developing dynamic concepts of ecology to the study of range management, silviculture, agronomy, and plant breeding. Thus, in 1963 the first course in range management that discussed the ecosystem concept and its relevance to the course was taught to forestry students (Biswell and Liakos 1962). This was followed by the creation of a separate chair on range management in 1965. Also, more emphasis started to be given to ecological teaching by the Chair of Silviculture when the first textbook on forest phytosociology was published by Dafis in 1967. This textbook was soon followed by a longer one on forest ecology by the same author (Dafis 1969*a*). (A fuller textbook on phytosociology was published by Athanasiadis in 1978.) From the conservation point of view, the creation and filling of the Chair of Forest Protection is also noteworthy.

In the agricultural sciences, three significant events must be mentioned. First, an extensive monograph on the ecological adaptability of cultivated crops in Greece was published (Fasoulas and Senloglou 1966); this helped to raise the level of ecological education of agronomists. Second, the ecological information included in the new courses on crop production by Sficas (1970) and by Farthis (1970), given respectively at the School of Agriculture and Forestry (University of Thessaloniki) and at the Higher School of Agriculture (Athens), was markedly increased. Third, a graduate course in the School of Agriculture and Forestry was planned that would be devoted entirely to general and physiologic ecology.

Research

There was still not one single research agency in Greece totally devoted to ecology at this time. On the other hand, research relative to ecology was carried out by several agencies, but it was almost always either on strictly applied subjects or on subjects distantly related and useful as background ecological information.

Ecological studies with some emphasis on theory were very few; at least two seem particularly relevant. The first (Ignatiades 1969) was a short study on species diversity and succession on phytoplankton. The second (Vamvakas 1972) was a study of bottom benthic biocenoses; this is also valuable because it contains an extensive literature review on methodology and an effort to translate ecological terms into Greek.

As characteristic examples of the rising level of applied ecological research, the studies of Kotoulas (1965, 1969) on the biological and technical aspects of a serious soil and water conservation problem, and of Dafis (1966, 1969*b*) on the primary productivity of Greek forests may be mentioned. Also, the work of Liakos and Moulopoulos (1967) is characteristic because it is probably the first major attempt in Greece to study the producers and consumers of Greek wildlands as a unit. Finally, in the work of Mavrommatis (1971), an effort was made to apply computer programming for forest vegetation mapping.

Environmental Awareness

The results of the rapid eutrophication of the Gulfs of Saronicos, Thermaicos, and Pagasiticos adjacent to the large industrial and urban centers of

Athens, Thessaloniki, and Volos, respectively, started to be felt by the ordinary citizen, who, after having solved the food problem, was now interested in a better quality of life. The miles of polluted beaches increased every year. Certain kinds of seafood disappeared and some became health hazards (e.g., mussels). Air pollution also caused concern. The results of the first determinations of air pollutants in Athens were finding an increasingly prominent place in the press, together with reports from the international environmental movement.

The government's tendency at first was to ignore the environmental problems. In certain cases, the military regime of the late 1960s tried to refute the reliability of actual measurements of pollutants and even put pressure against some scientists who published alarming reports. However, events like the internationally publicized deterioration of the Acropolis monuments and the public's outcry against pollution in specific urban areas, gradually changed the government's attitude but not to the degree of taking consistent measures.

The beginning of the 1970s found Greece in a state of environmental concern. Ecology had become a household word, not in its original context but as a synonym or substitute for protection of nature, environmental conservation, and pollution control. Previously established environmental societies increased their membership and sometimes were effective in exerting pressure on the government. The Hellenic Society for the Protection of Nature succeeded in the first steps toward establishing a national park in the Prespa Lakes (northern Greece). New environmental societies and clubs cropped up not only in Athens but also in smaller cities. Some of those societies fell into inertia while one, the Hellenic Society on Environmental Pollution, established in 1971, was to become strong in membership and in activities. Several review articles and editorials, mostly on pollution, but also on more general aspects of environmental conservation, appeared in various technical and popular magazines, and in the daily press. Some of them offered concrete solutions to specific pollution problems (e.g., Pikoulis 1969). Also, lectures, exhibitions, and television programs did much to expose scientists and laymen to the problems of environmental conservation. Certain specialists in botany, zoology, forestry, and agriculture, as well as nonspecialists, emphasized publicly the need for increased university education on ecology and environmental conservation.

Third Period (1973–present)

Education

The administrative procedure of creating a new course or a new chair in Greece often takes a very long time. Although the first special course in ecology was planned and proposed in 1969, it did not materialize until 1973. The course was given at the School of Agriculture and Forestry, University of Thessaloniki. It is noteworthy that this course was first taught at the graduate level to students specializing in plant breeding and agronomy. This was because graduate programs (which, by the way, are very few) in Greek universities have a greater elasticity than undergraduate programs. Half of the course was devoted to the principles of general ecology and the other half to plant ecophysiology. At first, Odum's *Fundamentals of Ecology* was used as a textbook, supplemented by several review papers in English; later on, the teaching material was further supplemented by specially prepared lecture notes in Greek (Gerakis 1975).

As a result of the general recognition of the need for more education in ecology and environmental sciences, the government approved the establishment of the first Chair of Ecology in the School of Agriculture and Forestry, University of Thessaloniki. This chair was, at the beginning, directed temporarily by Dr. L. G. Liakos (professor of range management) who taught the first undergraduate course devoted entirely to the principles of ecology to second-year forestry students in 1974–1975. Later on, in 1976, Dr. P. A. Gerakis was elected and appointed as first professor of ecology and took over from Dr. Liakos. Since 1976, general ecology has been taught to the undergraduates of agriculture and forestry, and to the graduate students of plant breeding and agronomy.

In addition to the aforementioned chair, four new ones were established during the period 1976–1980, one each at the Higher School of Agriculture, Athens; School of Physics and Mathematics, the University of Thessaloniki; School of Physics and Mathematics, the University of Patras; and School of Veterinary Medicine, the University of Thessaloniki. The former two chairs have been filled by Professors M. Karandinos and N. S. Margaris, respectively, while the remaining two are still open. The terms of reference of the two chairs belonging to the Schools of Physics and Mathematics are understandably more theoretical, while the other three emphasize applied aspects of ecology and conservation. However, the establishment of five chairs on one discipline within such a short period of time is without precedent in the history of Greek higher education and can only be attributed to pressure from a generally growing environmental awareness. Lecture notes on general ecology were prepared by Karandinos (personal communication), Lykakis (1977, 1979), Margaris (1979), and Kilikidis (1979). The book by Karayiannis (1979), although entitled *General Ecology,* is a concise encyclopedia of environmental science, rather than an ecological text in the ordinary sense. Similarly, Triantaphyllidis' work (1977) is almost entirely a sanitary engineering text in spite of its title *Ecology, Sanitary Engineering.*

Several other courses and chairs devoted to applications of ecology in environmental conservation were created. The new chairs of mountain water management and control, and of wildlife and fisheries in the Schools of Agriculture and Forestry are fundamentally chairs on conservation. Also, two chairs were created recently on floriculture and landscape architecture, which include among their terms of reference environmental planning. In addition, old chairs like silviculture, agronomy, range management, forest protection, agricultural chemistry, soil science, hydraulics and land reclamation, forest botany, and plant breeding devoted considerably more time to the discussion of applied ecological problems. One new course on pollution, with emphasis on soil and water pollution, was planned by the School of Agriculture and Forestry and another by the School of Veterinary Medicine (University of Thessaloniki). These two courses are being taught presently to graduate students.

University libraries were enriched by the purchase of several hundreds of books and periodicals on ecology and environmental conservation. The collections of the Schools of Agriculture and Forestry are the strongest in ecological material. Other libraries that spent considerable funds on ecological and environmental literature are those of the Schools of Physics and Mathematics (Athens, Thessaloniki, and Patras universities), the Higher Schools of Agriculture (Athens), the Democritus Nuclear Research Center, and the Hellenic Association on Environmental Pollution.

Research

The establishment of the new chairs of ecology and conservation have not yet had a great impact on the development of ecological research because of the slow procedures of staffing and equipping these chairs. Any progress achieved so far in research of ecological and related subjects was due mainly to the older chairs and to the existing research institutes.

In general, there was a marked progress in scientific and scholarly research in Greece during this period, in spite of the poor coordination and administration of the various research agencies. In particular, ecology benefitted considerably from the appearance of young qualified scientists in all scientific disciplines. A characteristic feature of the majority of the ecological research projects is that they originated from a distinct case of environmental concern. It was this environmental concern that prompted many scientists with or without formal training in ecological theory to focus their attention on the principles of ecology as they tackled specific problems of pollution. The following case is typical of numerous others and illustrates this point well.

In 1975, a group of scientists headed by Dr. S. D. Kilikidis from the Chair of Food Hygiene, School of Veterinary Medicine, University of Thessaloniki, was asked to explain the sudden and massive death of fish in the very small brackish water lake of Porto Koufo in northern Greece. The group, with previous research experience in pesticide residues (Panetsos et al. 1971; Panetsos and Kilikidis 1973; Panetsos et al. 1975*a*, 1975*b*), examined the problem and identified high chlorinated pesticide residues in the dead fish. However, these scientists, far from rushing to attribute the death of fish to pesticide action alone, proceeded into an elegant discussion of all possible causes; in conclusion, they stressed the need for a thorough and long-term study of all components of the lake ecosystem and their interactions (Panetsos et al. 1976). The study of this lake was not continued because attention had to be shifted to a similar but much more economically important case, that of the serious deterioration of the secondary productivity of Lake Vistonis (4,000 hectares). At this time, the same scientists started an ambitious long-term research project, which is still in progress, to collect qualitative and quantitative information on the biotic and abiotic factors and dynamic processes of the system. Thus, concern about pollution and resource deterioration caused the launching of one of the more interesting ecological research projects so far in Greece. Another notable example is the concern about the severe flood problem of Greece, analyzed extensively by Kotoulas (1980), which caused the study of the behavior of *Spisula subtrumcata* (Da Costa) in the area adjacent to the delta of the flooded rivers (Koukouras and Hintiroglou 1980, personal communication). Other similar cases are represented by the work of Papazafiriou (1975) and Zarkanellas and Bogdanos (1977).

In addition to the dangers due to pollution, the concern about the conservation of the flora and fauna of Greece has started several ecologically interesting studies. The work of Papageorgiou (1974), funded by U.S. sources, on the population energy relationships of the agrimi (*Capra aegagrus cretica*) may be considered as a cardinal event in the history of Greek ecological research. Other conservation-oriented studies are typified by the work of C. P. Panetsos (1975) and Athanasiadis and Gerasimidis (1978), stressing the need for the protection of certain plant species. A list of 313 plant species needing protection has been prepared recently by various specialists. Work is under progress in the various chairs of zoology, in the Chair of Wildlife and Fisheries, and in the Forest Service of the Ministry of Agriculture to study protection measures for Greek fauna. Fire ecology has received a growing attention during this period as indicated by the work of Liacos (1974, 1977), Kailidis et al. (1975), Papanastasis (1977), and Arianoutsou and Margaris (In press).

Applied ecological studies on various aspects of forest and agricultural production have multiplied during this period and are too numerous to be mentioned. These are typified by the works of Papanastasis (1976), Tsaftaris (1976), Galanopoulou-Sendouka (1977), Apatsidis (1977), Papanastasis and Liacos (1980), and C. P. Panetsos (In press). Also, studies on identification and monitoring of pollutants have increased both in number and in quality.

One of the few ecological studies that did not start from a specific point of environmental conservation or plant production concern is the detailed study of a phryganic ecosystem by Margaris (1976), who was at that time a lecturer in the Chair of General Botany, University of Athens.

Studies using the mathematical approach are very few. Except for the work of Papazafiriou (1975) on the modelling of water ecosystem processes, one can only mention so far the work of Stamou (personal communication) on the temporal and spatial changes of soil fauna. The Chair of Ecology in the Higher School of Agriculture, Athens (filled just recently by Prof. M. Karandinos) is the strongest in mathematical ecology. In addition to the papers by Ignatiades (1969) and Vamvakas (1972), extensive discussions of theory can be found in the work of Fasoulas and Tsaftaris (1975) and Fasoulas (1975), who attempt a theoretical treatment of competition, and Margaris (In press) on the adaptive strategies in plants of Mediterranean-type ecosystems.

Environmental Awareness

The environmental problems that emerged during the previous period now became more acute and public concern was further increased. The government that followed the fall of the military regime in 1974 took some measures to combat pollution and protect wildlife, although these measures were considered inadequate by the environmental societies and clubs. Anyhow, more funds were provided for pollution research. Perhaps the area where pollution research became more active was the marine environment (see below). Biological pest control enjoyed increased attention by entomologists because, except for its strictly economic advantages, the practice became of interest to all environmentalists (see below).

Since it is understandable that air, water, and soil pollution problems are difficult to study, and more difficult to solve because of many serious economic constraints, one would expect that the activities for wildlife protection would be more successful. In fact, little has been done, compared with what could be achieved. Except for the establishment of such important national parks as the ones at Vikos and Prespa and the biological wildlife station at the Evros Delta, progress has been slow.

At present, there is pressure by various environmental conservation societies and the press for a national environmental protection agency to supervise and coordinate all pertinent efforts, e.g., monitoring of pollutants on a national scale and management of national parks. An encouraging sign in the environmental movement of the late 1970s in Greece is that it is becoming, no matter how slowly, a minor political issue.

RESEARCH FUNDING AND RESEARCH AGENCIES

In Greece, research in all scientific fields is carried out mainly by the various chairs of the universities and university colleges, and by various government research institutes and stations. Virtually all funding is from the government. This is true for any kind of research, including that on ecology and environmental conservation.

All universities are funded by the Ministry of Education. Occasionally, some chairs receive extra funds for specific projects from other sources. For example, several agricultural and forestry chairs have received funds from the Ministry of Agriculture.

The great majority of the non-university research agencies are concerned with agriculture and forestry. They belong administratively to and are funded by the Ministry of Agriculture. The Tobacco Institute is an exception because, although an agricultural institute, it belongs to the Ministry of Commerce.

A recent source for research funding is the Scientific Research and Technology Service of the Ministry of Coordination. It acts independently and provides funds for scientists and scholars, irrespective of their professional status or affiliation, to carry out specific research projects.

The major non-agricultural and non-forestry institutes of ecological interest are the Democritus Nuclear Research Center and the Institute for Oceanographic and Fisheries Research. The former is, in every way, the largest single research agency in Greece and includes large biological sections whose research activities are not always linked with such areas as nuclear chemistry and physics.

During the last decade, some research funds have come from international agencies. Examples are the projects on the forest resources of Greece and on the Mediterranean Sea (United Nations Special Fund) and the Project on the Mediterranean-Type Ecosystems.

Industrial and other business firms do not contribute any substantial funds for research. As an exception, the establishment of the Botanical Museum at Kifissia, Athens, by the Goulandris firm of shipowners must be mentioned. This museum is also credited with some excellent natural science and conservation publications.

Coordination among the various research agencies (university chairs, institutes) is not very efficient, one of the reasons being that there is no national research council. A noteworthy effort to keep record of research publications about Greece was made by the Ministry of Culture and Science, which has established a modern documentation center. This service has issued a catalog of recent publications on environmental subjects (1976), which is very useful for anyone working on ecology and environmental science.

An agency of growing importance in Greece is the Planning and Environment Service of the Ministry of Coordination. Although it does not provide funds for research, its activities indirectly help the research workers who deal with ecological and environmental problems by, for example, the publication of material on natural resources and wetlands (Ministry of Coordination 1978, 1979).

MARINE BIOLOGY, ECOLOGY, AND POLLUTION

In spite of the geographic features of Greece and the historical affinity of the Greek people with the sea and with marine life, the attention paid to water ecosystems was very small until the end of the 1960s. Only sporadic and more or less brief studies were made previously. Among the first serious attempts to study the life of water systems was that by Anagnostidis, and his associates in the Universities of Athens and Thessaloniki, who published articles on the algae of Greece (e.g., Anagnostidis 1961). Several other studies followed by the scientists of the Democritus Nuclear Research Center, the Institute for Oceanographic and Fisheries Research, and the chairs of zoology in the Universities of Athens, Thessaloniki, and Patras. Most of these were published in the 1970s (e.g., Moraitou-Apostolopoulou 1971, 1972; Economides 1972; Kattoulas et al. 1972; Koukouras 1972; Yannopoulos and Yannopoulos 1972; Kiortsis 1973; Bogdanos et al. 1974; Yannopoulos and Barrois 1975; and Yannopoulos 1976). These articles deal mostly with systematics because the marine organisms of the eastern Mediterranean are not well known as compared with the ones of the western Mediterranean, which were studied by the scientifically more advanced nations of France and Italy.

The first research efforts on marine ecosystems were mostly short-term primary productivity studies (e.g., Becacos-Kontos 1968). Other characteristic studies were by Ignatiades (1969); Becacos-Kontos and Ignatiades (1970); Vamvakas (1972); Becacos-Kontos (1973*a*, 1973*b*, 1977); Yannopoulos (1978); Haritonidis (1978); Koukouras (1979); and Zarkanellas (1980). These studies did not have pollution effects as their main concern. Some emphasis on theoretical considerations was given by Ignatiades (1969) and the most recent authors.

Environmental concern caused the launching of several studies on the effects of pollution on marine organisms (e.g., Hatzistelios and Grimanis 1969; Dugdale et al. 1970; Ignatiades and Becacos-Kontos 1970; Kovatsis and Nitsos 1972; Papadopoulou 1972; Edipidis 1973; Hopkins et al. 1973; Friligos 1974; Skoullos 1974; Papazafiriou 1975; Grimanis et al. 1976; Ignatiades and Mimicos 1977; Zarkanellas and Bogdanos 1977; and Kilikidis et al. 1980).

Many marine studies were made by the Hydrobiology Group and the Radioanalytical Laboratory of the Democritus Nuclear Research Center. Scientists of this center have also tried to develop and improve analytical techniques for determining pollutants in water ecosystems (e.g., Hatziestelios and Grimanis 1969; Hatzistelios and Papadopoulou 1969; Hopkins et al. 1973). In the same center, computer simulation studies have been carried out on plankton growth in cooperation with the Department of Oceanography, University of Washington (U.S.A.). The nature of this cooperation and the subjects investigated are described by Becacos-Kontos and Dugdale (1971), who pointed out that the conditions of the east Mediterranean and especially of the Saronicos Gulf are ideal for marine eutrophication studies because the low ambient nutrient levels ensure a low background. Therefore, the effects of the municipal and industrial effluents on the marine ecosystem are easier to study. Some recent detailed papers on marine biology and ecology (e.g., Yannopoulos 1978; Koukouras 1979; Zarkanellas 1980) were carried out by the zoology chairs of Athens and Thessaloniki.

Research on freshwater biology and ecology has thus far been scarce and short, one reason being that Greek freshwater bodies are few and of relatively minor importance for recreation. However, there is a growing interest in the freshwater bodies of northern Greece as a result of disturbing signs of accelerated eutrophication and pollution (Becacos-Kontos 1971; Karvounaris 1972; Ocevski 1975; Ocevski et al. 1975; Panetsos et al. 1976; Mourkidis et al. 1978; Kilikidis 1980, personal communication).

INSECT ECOLOGY AND BIOLOGICAL CONTROL

Numerous applied ecological studies on insects of economic importance have been carried out in Greece. Most of the earlier studies were conducted at the Benaki Phytopathological Institute and published in the annals of the institute, in French and English. Entomological research started to progress more rapidly as a result of the formation of an increasingly stronger group of entomologists in the above institute and in the Democritus Nuclear Research Center and because of better staffing of the Chairs of Entomology in the Schools of Agriculture. Most of the insect ecology research concerned the effects of various environmental factors. These were studied, more often than not, in isolation. Thus, they were more or less "single-factor ecology" studies (e.g., Tzanakakis 1964; Fletcher and Zervas 1977) and behavioral studies (e.g., Procopy et al. 1975; Procopy and Economopoulos 1976; and Ifantidis 1978). Papers touching subjects about the population dynamics of insects are very few (e.g., Orphanidis and Soultanopoulos 1962; Fletcher and Economopoulos 1976). There are as yet no published papers reporting entomological research carried out in Greece to indicate that mathematical approaches have been used to a high degree for the study of insect populations. Perhaps the only entomological paper with a strong mathematical emphasis is that by Zouros (1969). Recently, the Chair of Ecology and Environmental Protection in the Higher School of Agriculture in Athens has been focusing some of its activities on the subject.

The study of biological control is relatively well developed in Greece and is mostly concentrated toward the control of the olive fruit fly. Information on the progress made in this field in Greece until the early 1970s may be found in a report by Tzanakakis (1972) and in a more recent one by Economopoulos in the ninth volume of the International Biological Program series (Delluchi 1976).

SOCIETIES AND JOURNALS RELATED TO ECOLOGY

In March 1980, about forty scientists were assembled at Volos to establish the first professional ecological society in Greece, the Association of Greek

Ecologists. In the first session, open to the general public, an analysis was made by Professors M. Karandinos and N. S. Margaris of the term *ecology*, and the pertinence of this discipline to common environmental problems was explained. The main objectives of the association were outlined, the advancement of ecology and the promotion of the professional status of ecologists. Prior to the discussion of association affairs, ten presentations of research papers were given. Among the resolutions of the assembly was the formation of a committee to prepare a Greek glossary of ecological terms. The majority of the members were from the various chairs of ecology, zoology, and botany. Several of the participants belong also to North American and European ecological societies.

There are two main nonprofessional societies in Greece fully devoted to the environmental movement. These have helped in many ways to raise the interests of various scientists in ecology. One is the Hellenic Society for the Protection of Nature (69, Anagnostopoulou Street, Athens 135, Greece). The aim of the society, formed in 1951, is to assist in the protection of the flora and fauna of Greece and of the natural environment in general. It helps various scientists in their studies. It has established and maintains a biological station in the delta of the River Evros. This society cooperates closely with the International Union for the Conservation of Nature and with other similar Greek and foreign societies. Also, it represents in Greece the European Information Center for the Conservation of Nature sponsored by the Council of Europe. One of the major successes of this society was the organization of a Conference on the Protection of the Flora, Fauna, and Biotopes of Greece, held in 1979 and inaugurated by the President of the Greek Republic.

The second nonprofessional environmental society is the Hellenic Association on Environmental Pollution (14, Xenophontos Street, Athens 118, Greece). The goals of this society are, first, to assist in the study of problems of water, air, soil, and noise pollution by cooperating with government and other agencies and individuals who are concerned about these problems, and second, to collect and disseminate information on pollution based on international and national literature by publishing pertinent material and by organizing various activities to raise environmental awareness. The society has an impressive record in drawing the attention of the general public to the cause of pollution control and in fighting for specific environmental issues. It has also acted as a catalyst to increase environmental awareness on the part of other scientific societies whose primary interest was not in ecology and environmental conservation.

There are several other societies and groups that are much smaller both in membership and in social impact than these two. These include the Alpine Club, Association of Friends of the Beaches and Coasts, Association of the Friends of the Forest, Federation of Touring Clubs, Touring and Automobile Club, and Helleniki Etairia. Recently, most of these societies, together with the two abovementioned large ones, have joined forces to form the Coordinating Committee of Societies for the Protection of the Environment. Although this committee has concentrated its attention on specific environmental problems of the Athens Greater Area, it has also tried to stimulate the interest of the government and of the people toward environmental conservation and ecological education in general.

Apart from the abovementioned environmental groups and societies, there are two large organizations of professional people that have formed special committees for the environment. These are the Technical Chamber and the Geotechnical Chamber, semi-governmental organizations comprising the graduates from the technical faculties in the first instance, and the graduates from the faculties of agriculture, forestry, and veterinary medicine in the second.

There is not one journal in Greece devoted entirely to ecology. Ecological information may be found in scientific journals of various other disciplines and societies and as separate publications (e.g., doctoral dissertations). Examples of such journals are *Chimica Chronica,* issued by the Association of Chemists; *The Forest,* issued by the Association of Foresters; *Technica Chronica,* issued by the Association of Graduates of Technical Faculties; *Geoponika,* issued by the Association of Agricultural Scientists of Northern Greece; and the scientific annals of the various university schools. Ecological information is occasionally published in various journals of human and veterinary medicine. Articles in all these journals are generally published in Greek with extensive summaries in English, German, or French. An old periodical research publication that occasionally contains papers on the ecology of insects and diseases is the *Annals of the Phytopathological Institute Benaki.* The articles of this publication, found in many libraries abroad, are in French and in English. Another recently issued journal of interest to ecologists is the *Biologia Gallo-Hellenica,* which publishes papers in French and English. All research institutes issue annual reports in Greek, with occasional summaries in English, French, or German.

The bulletins issued by the two major environmental societies of Greece, namely, *Physis* by the Hellenic Society for the Protection of Nature, and *Information Bulletin* by the Hellenic Association on Environmental Pollution, only rarely contain research papers. They are published in Greek, with extensive English summaries, and contain news, society activities, review articles, and short notes. The latter publication is more extensive and provides valuable information on important ecological and environmental conservation publications and activities in Greece and abroad.

A major part of the research work on ecology and related subjects carried out in Greece by native and foreign workers has been, and still continues to be, published in foreign journals. In the past, most of these papers were published in German and French because most zoologists, botanists, foresters, and agriculturists used to go for graduate studies to the German-speaking countries of central Europe. Recently, preferences are shared among the German, French, and English languages.

Ecological and environmental journals that may be found in Greek libraries are *Ecology, Ecological Monographs, Journal of Ecology, Journal of Applied Ecology, Journal of Animal Ecology, Oecologia, Oecologia Plantarum, Journal of Environmental Quality, Soil and Water Conservation, Agroecosystems, Archives and Bulletin of Environmental Contamination and Toxicology, Water Pollution, Environment Abstracts, Pollution Abstracts,* and *Applied Ecology Abstracts.* Numerous other journals related to ecology are also available in the fields of botany, zoology, limnology, marine biology, agriculture, forestry, statistics, and meteorology. The Universities of Athens and Thessaloniki have the largest collections. From the point of view of richness in ecological and related publications, these two libraries are nearly comparable to the libraries of many Western European or North American universities. However, both libraries are difficult to use because at present they suffer from a lack of space and trained personnel.

ACKNOWLEDGMENTS

I am thankful to Drs. N. Athanasiadis, S. Dafis, A. Economopoulos, A. Fasoulas, S. D. Kilikidis, D. Kotoulas, A. Koukouras, G. Lavrentiadis, L. Liakos, N. Margaris, G. Mavrommatis, C. P. Panetsos, N. Papageorgiou, V. Papanastasis, and M. Tzanakakis for providing me with information related to this article.

BIBLIOGRAPHY

Dafis, S. A. 1966. *Site and forest productivity research on coppice forests of oak and chestnut in Northeastern Chalkidiki, Greece.* Thessaloniki: School of Agriculture and Forestry, University of Thessaloniki. (In Greek, German summary). (The specific ecological interest of this paper lies in the phytosociological section. The author, instead of concentrating his attention on the detailed systematic classification of plant communities, as done in many previous studies, preferred to base his division of phytosociological units on ecological and floristic criteria, as proposed by Schlenker (1950) and Ellenberg (1956, 1962). This approach differs from the Braun-Blanquet method in that combinations of groups of characteristic species were used to differentiate between units, instead of individual characteristic species. The author discusses the advantages of his approach in terms of the facility with which ecological interpretations can be drawn).

Fasoulas, A. and N. A. Senloglou. 1966. *The adaptability of field crops in Greece.* Thessaloniki: University of Thessaloniki. (In Greek). (This extensive monograph provides an overview of the biologically significant physical environment of Greece and relates and explains the response of most field crops grown commercially or experimentally to this environment. The monograph tries also to establish the thesis that unless one has a thorough picture of the productivity of the major crop communities it would be erroneous to set any agronomic research priorities).

______ and A. S. Tsaftaris. 1975. *An integrated approach to plant breeding and field experimentation*. Pub. No 5. Thessaloniki: Department of Genetics and Plant Breeding, University of Thessaloniki. (An important part of this paper is devoted to the examination of the concept of competition. The authors suggest that the existing literature on the interactions within a population of plants is often confusing to the plant breeder, especially regarding competition effects and density effects. They try to resolve this confusion theoretically, providing their own experimental data in support for their conclusions. The terms *isocompetition* and *allocompetition* are proposed and defined, and their usefulness in approaching theoretical problems of controlled and natural plant evolution is discussed).

Galanopoulou-Sendouka, S. 1977. Growth and development of cotton (*Gossypium hirsutum* L.) under different plant populations and sowing dates. Doctoral dissertation, School of Agriculture and Forestry, University of Thessaloniki. (In Greek, English summary). (The genotype × climate × population interactions were studied in the field. The title designates a commonly followed line of applied agronomic research. This paper is unique in Greece in that it employs fully and for the first time the ecophysiological approach for the analysis of the productivity components of a cotton community).

Ignatiades, L. 1969. Annual cycle, species diversity, and succession of phytoplankton in lower Saronikos Bay, Aegean Sea. *Mar. Biol.* 3:196–200. (The theoretical model of species succession, proposed by Margalef on the organization of plankton, was affected by the poor nutritional conditions of the water ecosystem studied. Low species diversity levels prevailed during the spring phytoplankton bloom and increased in later succession stages. Besides its applied ecological value, the study is notable because it is probably the first attempt in Greece of a theoretical ecological approach to study one component of a marine ecosystem).

Kotoulas, K. D. 1965. *Pinus brutia* plantations in the watersheds of Greece. Doctoral dissertation, School of Agriculture and Forestry, University of Thessaloniki. (In Greek, German summary). (The problem of watershed management and torrent control, one of the most serious conservation problems of Greece, is analyzed. The mountains and hills of Greece are characterized by severe water erosion. The study concentrates on the use of *Pinus brutia* as a cover species against surface runoff and water erosion and as a means of influencing the hydrological cycle of a watershed).

Koukouras, A. 1979. Bionomic study of the macrofauna of the mediolittoral soft substratum in the Strymonikos and Thermaikos Gulfs. Doctoral dissertation, School of Physics and Mathematics, University of Thessaloniki. (In Greek, English summary). (Three communities were identified. The composition of each is given and comparisons are made between the two gulfs. Differences are discussed and related to ecological factors. The temporal and spatial changes of one of these communities are described).

Lavrentiadis, G. I. 1956. On the hydrophytes of Greek Macedonia. Doctoral dissertation, School of Physics and Mathematics, University of Thessaloniki. (In Greek, English summary). (This study is one of the first thorough phytosociological studies by the postwar generation of scientists and is typical of several later ones by the same and other plant scientists. The author discusses, although very briefly, the relationship of some of the plant communities to the animal communities living in the water bodies investigated).

Liakos, L. G. and C. Moulopoulos. 1967. *Contribution to the identification of some range types of* Quercus coccifera *L.* Res. Pub. 16. Thessaloniki: Ministry of Agriculture, Forest Research Institute. (In Greek, English summary). (Information on the primary productivity and the range capacity of the Greek evergeen brushlands for goats based on a five-year study is presented. It is one of the first studies on range ecology in Greece that gives special consideration to the conservation role of brushlands and to the interactions between natural vegetation and browsing animals).

Margaris, N. S. 1976. Structure and dynamics in a phryganic (east Mediterranean) ecosystem. *J. Biogeogr.* 3:249–259. (The study was carried out in an 800 m^2 area on Mt. Hymettus a few kilometers from Athens. Data on the structure of this ecosystem included total biomass, nitrogen, and chlorophyll content of plants at the beginning and end of a growth period; microbial populations of leaf canopy; and kind and biomass of soil microbes. The dynamic aspects were studied by obtaining data on net primary productivity and root turnover, growth characteristics, and nitrogen and chlorophyll content throughout the year, microbial activity, and carbon and nitrogen flow. This is the second attempt for a detailed terrestial ecosystem analysis made in Greece, the first being that of Papageorgiou (1974). However, it is the first such study in Greece in which due attention was paid to the role of microorganisms not only of the soil but also of the canopy).

Mavrommatis, G. 1971. Recherches phytosociologiques et écologiques dans le massif de l'Ossa (Grèce) en vue de sa gestion forestière. Thèse pour le grade de Docteur-Ingenieur en Ecologie, University of Science and Technology, Languedoc, Montpellier, France. (This research work is based on the premise that vegetation is the expression of the total conditions of an ecological environment. Thus, the study of vegetation is the easier way to learn about the abiotic factors of an ecosystem. This does not preclude the direct study of some of these factors whenever possible. This study was the first of its kind in Greece to attempt to apply information theory and one of the few in which data were analyzed by using specially prepared computer programs).

Panetsos, A. G., S. D. Kilikidis, and J. E. Psomas. 1976. Pollution of a sea water collection by chlorinated pesticides. *Bull. Greek Soc. Vet. Med.* 27:20–29. (In Greek, English summary). (The results of an investigation to find out the possible causes of the massive and sudden death of fish in a small shallow water body are reported. Only a preliminary investigation, it pointed out clearly the hazards of pesticide misuse on water organisms. It identified, and stressed, the need for a thorough investigation of the interactions taking place in this lake ecosystem to obtain reliable explanations of major disturbances in biotic communities).

Panetsos, C. P. 1975. Natural hybridization between *Pinus halepensis* and *Pinus brutia* in Greece. *Silv. Genet.* 24:163–168. (This paper examines the ecological consideration of the interactions between populations of *Pinus halepensis* and *P. brutia*. The implications of natural hybridization and introgression in terms of evolution of these two species are also discussed. Finally, the role of fire and climate is analyzed to predict the future of natural hybridization between populations of the species studied in various biotopes of Greece).

Papageorgiou, N. K. 1974. Population energy relationships of the agrimi (*Capra aegagrus cretica*) on Theodorou Island, Greece. Ph.D. thesis, Department of Fisheries and Wildlife, Michigan State University. (The objectives of this work were to appraise primary productivity and the pattern of vegetational changes associated with ungulate grazing and to collect data on the standing crop, energy assimilation, and other aspects of secondary productivity of agrimi. This is the first detailed study in Greece that applied the concepts of biological energetics to a conservation problem by examining the dynamic interaction between the primary productivity of the ecosystem and the secondary productivity of a known herbivore population. A unique feature of this island ecosystem was that the whole agrimi population could be captured, thereby enabling the precise and actual measurement of all population parameters).

Papanastasis, V. P. 1977. Fire ecology and management of phrygana communities in Greece. In *Proceedings of the Symposium on Environmental Consequences of Fire and Fuel Management in Mediterranean Ecosystems,* Palo Alto, Ca., Aug. 1–5, 1977. USDA Forest Service, Gen. Techn. Rep. WO-3, pp. 476–482. (The author distinguishes five phrygana subtypes and analyzes their adaptations to fire as regards flammability, stump sprouting, and seed germination. He discusses successional aspects of these communities and attempts to evaluate both the environmental hazards of fire in the phrygana and the potentialities of using fire as a range management practice. Also, a compartmental model of the phrygana ecosystem is proposed, the inclusion of which suggests the gradually increasing tendency in recent Greek ecological papers to stress the dynamic aspects of ecosystems and communities).

Papazafiriou, Z. G. 1975. *Modeling the variations in time and space of water ecosystem processes by selected sets of differential equations.* Thessaloniki: School of Agriculture and Forestry, University of Thessaloniki. (In Greek). (A quantitative evaluation of events taking place in water ecosystems is attempted by developing a system of differential equations that describe the behavior of the system's quality constituents. These equations are numerically solved by a variation on Taylor's method for solving ordinary differential equations. The model used is simple and inexpensive. A hypothetical application of the model to a lake ecosystem receiving effluents from a small city during a four-month period in the summer is given, and the predictive value of the model is demonstrated. It is one of the first papers in Greece to demonstrate the use of mathematical modelling for the analysis of structural and functional components of an ecosystem and for problem solving in environmental conservation).

Tsaftaris, A. S. 1976. The interference of competition on the selection of superior genotypes of wheat. Doctoral dissertation, School of Agriculture and Forestry, University of Thessaloniki. (In Greek, English summary). (Competition effects on the evaluation of wheat genotypes and on the performance of wheat populations of the same genotype were assessed. The author showed that in segregating dense populations, variance due to competition was twice that due to environmental factors. No variance due to competition was found in genotypically uniform dense populations because all individuals were influenced uniformly by high population pressure. The ultimate task of the author was to contribute to the development of plant breeding methodology. The first half of his research, however, is a theoretical and mathematical approach to the problem of competition).

Vamvakas, K. N. 1972. Contribution to the study of marine soft bottom benthic biocoenoses in the Western Bay of Saronicos, near Athens, Greece. Doctoral dissertation, School of Physics and Mathematics, University of Athens. (In Greek, English and French summaries). (Information is provided on the geographic distribution of the benthic organisms in Greek marine waters. The study is also informative in its attempt to analyze the mutual relationships among the communities investigated and the effect of biotopic factors on the spatial distribution of the benthic species and on the species composition of these communities. It also provides a critical evaluation of the method used in studying the benthic communities).

Zarkanellas, A. I. and C. D. Bogdanos. 1977. Benthic studies of a polluted area in the upper Saronikos Gulf. *Thalassographica* 1:155–177. (This study provides an initial qualitative and quantitative description of the macrobenthic fauna and its relationships to several environmental parameters. The effects of sewage disposal on the diversity, abundance, biomass, and species composition of the area studied are assessed. This is another example of the beneficial impact of the growing concern about pollution on the development of ecological research).

REFERENCES CITED

Anagnostidis, K. 1961. *Investigations on the blue algae in thermal waters in Greece.* Thessaloniki: Chair Syst. Bot. Plant Geogr., Univ. Thessaloniki.

Apatsidis, L. 1977. Natural regeneration of black pine: research on the most appropriate regeneration methods in relation to site-ecological conditions. Doct. Diss., School Agr. Forest., Univ. Thessaloniki.

Arianoutsou, M. and N. S. Margaris. In press. Fire induced nutrient losses in a phryganic (East Mediterranean) ecosystem. *Biol. Plant.* (Prague).

Athanasiadis, N. 1978. *Forest phytosociology.* Thessaloniki: Univ. Thessaloniki.

______ and A. Gerasimidis. 1978. *Drosera rotundifolia* L., *Drosera intermedia* Hayne, two new species of Greek flora. *Sci. Ann. Forest. Section,* Univ. Thessaloniki 21:67–82.

Babalonas, D. 1976. Über die Vegetation der östlichen Kavala-Küsten Nordgriechenland). I. Salzbödenvegetation. *Sci. Ann. School Phys. Math.,* Univ. Thessaloniki 16:265–306.

______. 1979. Phytosociological study of the vegetation of the Evros delta. Doct. diss. School Phys. Math. Univ. Thessaloniki.

Becacos-Kontos, T. 1968. The annual cycle of primary production in the Saronikos Gulf (Aegean Sea) for the period November 1963–October 1964. *Limnol. Oceanogr.* 13:485–489.

______. 1971. Hydrobiological observations on Greek lakes. *Proc. Inst. Oceanogr. Fish. Res.* 10:469–472.

______. 1973*a*. Environmental factors affecting production in Saronikos Gulf, Aegean Sea. *Bull. Inst. Océanogr. Monaco* 71:1423.

______. 1973*b*. Primary production investigations in the Saronikos Gulf, 1965–1967. *Rapp. Comm. Int. Mer Medit.* 21:325–329.

______. 1977. Primary production and environmental factors in an oligotrophic biome in the Aegean Sea. *Mar. Biol.* 42:93–98.

______ and R. C. Dugdale. 1971. Pollution in Greek waters. *Mar. Pollut. Bull.* 2:158–160.

______ and L. Ignatiades. 1970. Primary biological chemical and physical observations in the Corinth Canal area. *Cah. Océanogr.* 22:259–267.

Biswell, H. H. and L. G. Liakos. 1962. *Range management.* Thessaloniki.

Bogdanos, C. D., K. N. Vamvakas, and T. Koussouris. 1974. *Report on the distribution of benthic organisms.* Athens: Inst. Oceanogr. Fish. Res., Saronikos Systems Project., Data Rep. No. 14.

Dafis, S. A. 1966. *Site and forest productivity research on coppice forests of oak and chestnut in northeastern Chalkidiki, Greece.* Thessaloniki: School Agric. For., Univ. Thessaloniki.

______. 1967. *Lectures in forest phytosociology.* Thessaloniki: School Agr. Forest, Univ. Thessaloniki.

______. 1969*a*. *Lectures in forest ecology.* Thessaloniki: School Agr. Forest., Univ. Thessaloniki.

______. 1969*b*. Site quality studies in oak forests. *Sci. Ann. School Agr. Forest,* Univ. Thessaloniki 13:1–48.

______. 1973. Classification of the forest vegetation in Greece. *Sci. Ann. School Agr. Forest,* Univ. Thessaloniki 15:75–78.

Debazac, E. F. and G. Mavrommatis. 1971. Les grandes divisions écologiques de la végétation forestière en Grèce continentale. *Bull. Soc. Bot. Fr.* 118:429–452.

Dellucchi, V. L., ed. 1976. *Studies in biological control.* International Biological Program, Vol. 9, pp. 11–49. Cambridge: Cambridge University Press.

Drossos, E. G. 1977. Contribution to the study of the *Atropetum beladonae* plant communities of Greece. Doct. diss., School. Phys. Math., Univ. Thessaloniki.

Dugdale, R. C., J. C. Kelley, and T. Becacos-Kontos, 1970. The effects of effluent discharge on the concentration of nutrients in the Saronikos Gulf. *Proceedings of the FAO Conference on Marine Pollution, Rome,* 1970.

Economides, P. S. 1972. Inventory of the fishes of Greece, *Hellenic Oceanol. Limnol.* 11:421–598.

Economidou, E. 1974. *Euphorbia acanthothamnos* Heldr. and Sart. Recherches sur sa biologie et son écologie. *Candollea* 29:267–279.

______. 1979. Bibliographie botanique sur la Grèce (Plantes Vasculaires-Végétation). *Veroeff. Geobot. Inst. Eidg. Tech. Hochsch. Stift. Ruebel Zuer.* 56:190–242.

Economou-Amilli, A. 1976. On diatoms from thermal springs of Greece: taxonomic, ecological floristic and phytogeographical research. Doct. diss., School Phys. Math., Univ. Athens.

Edipidis, T. 1973. *Some observations on the environmental pollution in northern Greece.* Athens: Hellenic Assoc. Environ. Pollut.

Ellenberg, H. 1956. Aufgaben und Methoden der Vegetationskunde. In *Einführung in die Phytologie,* ed. H. Walter. Vol. IV, No. 1. Stuttgart: Eugen Ulmer Verlag.

——— and H. Rehder. 1962. Natürliche Waldgesellschaften der aufzuforstenden Kastanienflächen in Tessin. *S.Z.F.S.* 128–142.

Farthis, A. G. 1970. *Lectures in comparative agriculture.* Part I. Physical environment (crop ecology). Athens: Higher School of Agriculture.

Fasoulas, A. 1976. Principles and methods of plant breeding. Pub. No. 6. Thessaloniki: Dep. Genet. Plant Breeding, Univ. Thessanoliki.

——— and N. A. Senloglou. 1966. *The adaptability of field crops in Greece.* Thessaloniki: University of Thessaloniki.

——— and A. S. Tsaftaris. 1975. *An integrated approach to plant breeding and field experimentation.* Publ. No. 5. Thessaloniki: Department of Genetics and Plant Breeding, Univ. of Thessaloniki.

Fletcher, B. S. and A. P. Economopoulos. 1976. Dispersal of normal and irradiated laboratory strains and wild strains of the olive fly *Dacus oleae* in an olive grove. *Entomol. Exp. Appl.* 20:183–194.

——— and G. A. Zervas. 1977. Short term and long term acclimation of different strains of the olive fly (*Dacus oleae*) to low temperatures. *J. Insect Physiol.* 23:649–653.

Friligos, N. 1974. Eutrophication in the western basin of the Saronikos Gulf (Jan. 1973). *XXIV CIESM Congress, Monaco.*

Galanopoulou-Sendouka, S. 1977. Growth and development of cotton (*Gossypium hirsutum* L.) under different plant populations and sowing dates. Doct. diss., School of Agric. For., Univ. Thessaloniki.

Ganiatsas, C. A. 1936. Untersuchungen über die Vegetation auf den Salzböden bei Saloniki. *Berichte der Deutschen Botanischen Gesellschaft.*

———. 1963. *Vegetation and flora of the Athos Peninsula.* Athoniki Politeia, Sp. Pub. for the 1000 years since the establishment of the religious state of Athos. Thessaloniki: Univ. Thessaloniki.

———. 1967. *Plant geography.* Thessaloniki: Univ. Thessaloniki.

Gerakis, P. A. 1975. *Lectures in ecology.* Thessaloniki: School Agr. Forest. Dep. Grad. Studies, Univ. Thessaloniki.

Grimanis, A. P., D. Zafiropoulos, and M. Vassilaki-Grimani. 1976. Trace elements in *Sargus annularis* and *Gobius niger* from polluted and non-polluted areas of the Aegean Sea. *XXVe Congr. Assemblés Plenière de la CIESM* 22–30 October 1976.

Hadzistelios, I. and A. P. Grimanis. 1969. *Simultaneous determination of arsenic, antimony and mercury in biological materials by neutron activation analysis.* U.S. National Bureau of Standards, Sp. Pub. 312, Vol. 1, p. 184.

——— and C. Papadopoulou. 1969. Radiochemical microdetermination of manganese, strontium and barium by ion-exchange. *Talanta* 16:337–344.

Hararas, K. G. 1976. Research on the bryophytes of the island of Corfu (Ionean Islands): floral, ecological and phytogeographical study. Doct. diss., School Phys. Math., Univ. Athens.

Haritonidis, S. 1978. Contribution to the study of the benthic macro-algae of the Thermaikos Gulf. Doct. diss., School Phys. Math., Univ. Thessaloniki.

Hopkins, T., A. P. Grimanis, G. Papakostidis, and T. Papadopoulos. 1973. Neutron activation techniques in a pollution study of Saronicos Gulf sediments. *Thalassia Jugosl.* 9:219.

Ifantidis, M. D. 1978. Wabenorientirung in Nest der Honigbiene (*Apis mellifera* L.). *Apidologie* 9:57–73.

Ignatiades, L. 1969. Annual cycle, species diversity, and succession of phytoplankton in lower Saronikos Bay, Aegean Sea. *Mar. Biol.* 3:196–200.

______ and T. Becacos-Kontos. 1970. Ecology of fouling organisms in a polluted area. *Nature* 225:293–294.

______ and N. Mimicos. 1977. Ecological responses of phytoplankton on chronic oil pollution. *Environ. Pollut.* 13:109–118.

Kailidis, D. S., D. Theodoropoulou, and G. Papazoglou. 1975. Fire risk of plant zones and forest and grazing land fires in Greece. *Sci. Ann. School Agr. Forest.*, Univ. Thessaloniki 18:194–230.

Kanellis, A. 1966. *Bibliographia faunae Graecae. List of publications on Greek fauna, from 1800–1966.* Thessaloniki: Chair Gen. Biol., Univ. Thessaloniki.

Karayiannis, A. B. 1979. *General ecology,* Vols. I & II. Athens.

Karvounaris, D. 1972. Osservazioni sull'idrobiologia e la pesca nel Lago Doirani. *Hellenic Oceanogr. Limnol.* 11:665–714.

Kattoulas, M., P. S. Economides, and A. Koukouras. 1972. Benthic fauna of the Evoia coasts and Evoia Gulf. I. Barnacles (Crustacea). *Sci. Ann. School Phys. Math.*, Univ. Thessaloniki 12:331–338.

Kilikidis, S. D. 1979. *Ecology (structure, function, and pollution of ecosystems).* Thessaloniki: Univ. Thessaloniki.

______, A. P. Kamarianos, T. Kousouris, and I. Tsingkounakis. 1980. Effects of various chemicals on the behaviour and health of fishes (*Epinephelus*) in the Kisamos Gulf, Crete. ICEM/UNEP Workshop on Pollution of the Mediterranean, Cagliari, Italy.

Kiortsis, V. 1973. Quelques considérations sur l'écologie du zooplancton en Mer Egée. Repartition géographique et variations saisonnières. *Rapp. Comm. Int. Mer Medit.* 22:139–141.

Kotoulas, D. C. 1969. *The torrents of northern Greece. Classification and control principles.* Thessaloniki: School Agr. Forest., Univ. Thessaloniki.

______. 1980. *The flood problem of Greece in view of flood damages in central Macedonia* (Nov. 1979). Commun. 4 from Lab. Mountain Water Manage. and Control, Univ. Thessaloniki.

Kotoulas, K. D. 1965. *Pinus brutia* plantations in the watersheds of Greece. Doct. diss., School Agric. For., Univ. Thessaloniki.

Koukouras, A. 1972. A contribution to the study of the decapod crabs of Greece. *Hellenic Oceanol. Limnol.* 11:745–769.

______. 1979. Bionomic study of the macrofauna of the mediolittoral soft substratum in the Strymonikos and Thermaikos Gulfs. Doct. diss., School Phys. Math., Univ. Thessaloniki.

Kovatsis, A. V. and C. V. Nitsos. 1972. Research on the pollution from industrial discharges of the Gulf of Thessaloniki based on the determination of lead in shellfish. *Journées Etud. Pollution, CIESM, Athens.*

Lavrentiadis, G. I. 1956. On the hydrophytes of Greek Macedonia. Doct. diss., School Phys. Math., Univ. Thessaloniki.

______. 1961. *Research on the flora, plant geography and plant sociology of the Cassandra Peninsula.* Thessaloniki: School Phys. Math., Univ. Thessaloniki.

———. 1964. The ammophilus vegetation of the western Peloponnesos coasts. *Vegetatio* 12:223–287.

Liakos, L. G. 1974. Present studies and history of burning in Greece. *Proceedings of the 13th Annual Tall Timbers Fire Ecology Conference,* pp. 237–277.

———. 1977. Fire and fuel management in pine forest and evergreen brushland ecosystems of Greece. In *Proceedings of the Symposium on Environmental Consequences of Fire Fuel and Management in Mediterranean Ecosystems.* Palo Alto, CA., Aug. 1–5, 1977. USDA Forest Service, Gen. Techn. Rep. WO-3, pp. 289–298.

———. 1980. Livestock grazing in Mediterranean forests. Paper presented at Italian Min. Agr. Forests. Intern. Meetings Soil, Veg., Fauna: Safeguard and Restoration of Environm. Equilibrium and Reg. Planning of Med. Region. Palermo, Sicily.

——— and C. Moulopoulos. 1967. *Contribution to the identification of some range types of* Quercus coccifera *L.* Res. Publ. 16. Thessaloniki: Ministry of Agriculture, Forest Research Institute.

Lykakis, J. J. 1977. *Lectures in ecology.* Patras: Univ. Patras.

———. 1978. *Ecology: biological communities and ecosystems.* Patras: Univ. Patras.

Margaris, N. S. 1976. Structure and dynamics in a phryganic (east Mediterranean) ecosystem. *J. Biogeogr.* 3:249–259.

———. 1979. *Introduction to ecology. Part I. Ecosystems, the natural environment of organisms.* Thessaloniki: Univ. Thessaloniki.

———. 1980. *Introduction to ecology. Part II. Soil, plant water relationships, land ecosystems.* Thessaloniki: Univ. Thessaloniki.

———. In press. Adaptive strategies in plants dominating Mediterranean type ecosystems. In *Maquis and chaparral,* eds. F. di Castri and M. Specht. Amsterdam: Elsevier.

Mavrommatis, G. 1971. Recherches phytosociologiques et écologiques dans le massif de l'Ossa (Grèce) en vue de sa gestion forestière. Thèse pour le grade de Docteur-Ingenieur en Ecologie, University of Science and Technology, Languedoc, Montpellier, France.

Ministry of Coordination, Planning and Environment Service. 1978. *A list of agencies dealing with natural resources.* Athens.

———. 1979. *The main wetlands of Greece.* Athens.

Ministry of Culture and Science. 1976. *List of publications and studies on environmental subjects.* Service for Sci. Res. and Development, Athens.

Moraitou-Apostolopoulou, M. 1971. The pelagic copepods fauna of the Aegean Sea. Doct. diss., Univ. Athens.

———. 1972. Occurrence and fluctuation on the pelagic copepods of the Aegean with some notes on their ecology. *Hellenic Oceanol. Limnol.* 11:325–402.

Mourkidis, G. A., G. E. Tsikritsis, S. E. Tsiouris, and U. Menkisoglou. 1978. The lakes of northern Greece. I. Trophic status, 1977. *Sci. Ann. Agric. Section,* Univ. Thessaloniki 21:93–131.

Ocevski, B. 1975. Vertical characteristics of the bacterial paysage in the pelagic water of Castoria lake. *Ekologija* 10:171–181.

———, G. Kazarov, and I. Serafimova-Hadzisce. 1975. Distribution and characteristics of bacteria phytoplankton and zooplankton in Lake Castoria. *Symp. Biol. Hung.* 15:233–245.

Orphanidis, P. S. and C. D. Soultanopoulos. 1962. Observations préliminaires sur les courbes de densité de la population de certains insects vivant dans les oliveraies en 1961. *Ann. Inst. Phytopathol. Benaki* (N.S.) 4:148–154.

Panetsos, A. G. and S. D. Kilikidis. 1973. Toxicity and residues of Phostoxin. *Chim. Chron.* 38:146–149.

______, S. D. Kilikidis, and A. Mantis. 1971. Isolation and identification by polarography of benzene hexachloride in veal. *Hellenic Vet. Med.* 14:97–104.

______, S. D. Kilikidis, and J. E. Psomas. 1975*a*. Placental transfer of organochlorine pesticides in rabbits. *Proc. 20th World Vet. Congr.* 1:415–419.

______, S. D. Kilikidis, and J. E. Psomas. 1975*b*. Organo-chlorine pesticides residue in human milk in Greece. *Proc. Pediatric Clinic,* Univ. Thessaloniki 4:243–252.

______, S. D. Kilikidis, and J. E. Psomas. 1976. Pollution of a sea water collection by chlorinated pesticides. *Bull. Greek Soc. Vet. Med.* 27:20–29.

Panetsos, C. P. 1975. Natural hybridization between *Pinus halepensis* and *Pinus brutia* in Greece. *Silv. Genet.* 24:163–168.

______. In press. Monograph of *Pinus halepensis* (Mill.) and *P. brutia* (Ten.). *Yugosl. Acad. Sci., Ann. Forest.*

Papadakis, J. 1954. *Ecologia de los coltivos.* Buenos Aires.

Papadopoulou, C. 1972. Contribution to the radioecology of the Greek seas: trace element determination in edible mollusks. Doct. diss., School Phys. Math., Univ. Athens.

Papageorgiou, N. K. 1974. Population energy relationships of the agrimi (*Capra aegagrus cretica*) on Theodorou Island, Greece. Ph.D. thesis, Dept. Fisheries and Wildlife, Michigan State University.

Papanastasis, V. P. 1976. *The role of fire and sheep grazing in the* Phlomis fructicosa *L. communities in Thesprotia, Greece.* Pub. 81. Thessaloniki: Forest Res. Inst.

______. 1977. Fire ecology and management of phrygana communities in Greece. In *Proceedings of the Symposium on Environmental Consequences of Fire and Fuel Management in Mediterranean Ecosystems,* Palo Alto, Ca., Aug. 1–5, 1977. USDA Forest Service, Gen. Techn. Rep. WO-3, pp. 476–482.

______ and L. G. Liacos. 1980. Productivity and management of kermes oak brushlands for goats. Browse Symp., Adis Ababa, Ethiopia.

Papazafiriou, Z. G. 1975. *Modeling the variations in time and space of water ecosystem processes by selected sets of differential equations.* Thessaloniki: School Agric. For., Univ. Thessaloniki.

Pavlides, G. A. 1976. The flora and vegetation of the Sithonia peninsula, Chalkidiki, Greece. Doct. diss., School Phys. Math., Univ. Thessaloniki.

Pikoulis, S. D. 1969. The protection of the coasts of Greece from pollution by simple means. *Technica Chronica,* December 1969.

Procopy, R. J. and A. P. Economopoulos. 1976. Color responses of *Ceratitis capitata* flies. *Z. Angew. Entomol.* 80:434–437.

______, A. P. Economopoulos, and M. W. McFadden. 1975. Attraction of wild and lab-cultured *Dacus oleae* flies to small rectangles of different hues, shades and tints. *Entomol. Exp. Appl.* 18:141–152.

Schlenker, G. 1950. Forstliche Standortskartierung in Wüttemberg. *Allg. Forstztg.* 40/41.

Sficas, A. G. 1970. *General agronomy*. Thessaloniki: School Agr. Forest., Univ. Thessaloniki.

Skoullos, M. I. 1974. *Some effects of pollution on marine life. Contribution to the study of the Elefsis Gulf ecosystem.* Athens: Hellenic Assoc. Environ. Poll.

Triantaphyllidis, C. 1977. *Ecology, sanitary engineering.* Athens: Technical Univ.

Tsaftaris, A. S. 1976. The interference of competition on the selection of superior genotypes of wheat. Doct. diss., School Agric. For., Univ. Thessaloniki.

Tsianacas, D. T. 1975. Contribution a l'étude écologique de la végétation de la Chalcidique Nord-Orientale (Grèce). Doct. diss., Univ. Sci. Med., Grenoble, France.

Tsoumis, G. T. 1976. *The forests of Greece and Cyprus.* Thessaloniki: Chair of Forest Utilization, Univ. Thessaloniki.

Tzanakakis, M. E. 1964. Preliminary observations on the effect of certain light conditions on the pupation of the olive fruit fly *Dacus oleae* (Gmelin) outside the fruit. *Z. Angew. Entomol.* 55:94–99.

———. 1972. Current status and prospects of applying the sterile insect release method against *Dacus oleae.* Presented at FAO/IAEA Panel Meeting on the Practical Use of the Sterile Mole Technique for Insect Control. Vienna, 13–17 November 1972.

Vamvakas, K. N. 1972. Contribution to the study of marine soft bottom benthic biocoenoses in the Western Bay of Saronicos, near Athens, Greece. Doct. diss., School Phys. Math., Univ. Athens.

Voliotis, D. 1973. Beziehungen zwischen Klima, Boden und Vegetation und Vegetations-zonen in Griechenland. *Sci. Ann. School Phys. Math.,* Univ. Thessaloniki 13:221–239.

Yannitsaros, A. and E. Economidou. 1974. Studies on the adventive flora of Greece. I. General remarks on some recently introduced taxa. *Candollea* 29:111–119.

Yannopoulous, C. 1976. The annual regeneration of the Elefsis bay zooplanktonic ecosystem, Saronikos Gulf. *Rapp. Comm. Int. Mer Medit.* 23:109–111.

———. 1978. Secondary production and pollution in an oligotrophic marine ecosystem. Doct. diss., School Phys. Math., Univ. Athens.

——— and J. M. Barrois. 1975. Ecologie marine de la region de l'Eubée du Nord. I. Donées préliminaires sur le zooplancton et l'ichtyoplancton. *Biol. Gallo-Hellenica* 6:125–133.

——— and A. Yannopoulos. 1972. The Saronikos and the South Evoicos Gulfs, Aegean sea zooplankton standing stock and environmental factors. Presented at XXIIIth CIESM Congress, Athens.

Zarkanellas, A. I. 1980. Ecological study of macrobenthos of Thermaikos Gulf. Doct. diss. School Phys. Math., Univ. Thessaloniki.

——— and C. D. Bogdanos. 1977. Benthic studies of a polluted area in the upper Saronikos Gulf. *Thalassographica* 1:155–177.

Zouros, E. G. 1969. On the role of female monogamy in the sterile-male technique of insect control. *Ann. Inst. Phytopathol. Benaki* (N.S.) 9:20–29

11

HUNGARY

János Balogh and
Tibor Jermy

HISTORICAL ANTECEDENTS AND INTELLECTUAL TRADITIONS

The foundation of ecological research in Hungary goes back to the second half of the nineteenth century when intensive research was carried out on the flora and fauna of the Carpathian Basin. By the beginning of the twentieth century, the distribution of about 4,000 plant and 20,000 animal species was known on a territory of about 300,000 km^2. The results were summarized in the *Fauna Regni Hungariae* (1896–1918) and in a series of publications on the results of limnological studies of Lake Balaton carried out by a working group under the leadership of L. Lóczy (1897–1921), as well as in Jávorka's book on the flora of Hungary (1924–1925). This was followed by a series of floristic and phytocenological publications (see Soó 1960). The publication of a series of handbooks for identifying animal species, *Fauna Hungariae,* was launched in 1955; 138 issues appeared by 1980 covering about 16,000 taxa under the editorship of V. Székessy and later Z. Kaszab (1955–1980). This detailed taxonomic, biogeographic, and hydrobiological exploration of the territory serves as a solid base for ecological investigations.

In the nineteenth century, several outstanding ecological studies were issued. In 1863, A. Kerner published his book *Pflanzenleben der Donauländer,* which dealt with vegetation types and was one of the first publications on succession in plant communities. O. Herman (1876–1879) was probably the first in the world to develop a system of animal life forms in his study on the spider fauna of Hungary. He was also a pioneer of bromatological investigations in ornithology and the first in Europe to organize an observatory system for bird migration.

At the beginning of the 1930s, the Hungarian plant geography school was founded at the University of Debrecen by R. Soó, following the line of Braun-Blanquet and also of Meusel and Gams. Taking into consideration characteristic species, researchers have established a system of plant communities that was suitable for practical use also. Emphasis was laid on the quantitative analysis of plant communities and on the process of succession, as well as on the interactions between vegetation and environment. The results were summarized in the handbook on taxonomy and geography of the Hungarian flora and vegetation by Soó (1964–1979) and in a series of books on the vegetation of Hungary edited by B. Zólyomi (1957–1977).

It is common knowledge that ecology developed simultaneously in several centers of the world. A "Continental," a "British," and an "American" school are generally distinguished. Based on the concepts of biocenose by Möbius and biotope by Dahl, the Continental school aimed at a synthesis of abiotic and biotic ecological components, and developed the concept of higher units of nature, which are characterized by self-regulation. According to Palmgren, the flow of energy is the most important process in these self-regulating systems, and the ecological branch dealing with it was called *production biology*.

The British school did not use the concepts of biocenose and biotope. The food chain was regarded as the most important characteristic of a community forming the "ecological pyramid" or "Elton's pyramid." For the ecological unit, Tansley introduced the term *ecosystem*.

Contrary to the more space-centered approach of the Continental school, the American school concentrated on the time aspect, the result of which was a more dynamic approach. It stressed ecological processes; consequently, it was related to the production biological branch of the Continental school and to the food chain principle of the British school. Although the Continental school is the oldest, ecologists today use the terminology of the two other schools.

In Hungary, animal ecology research did not follow any of these lines exclusively but tried to amalgamate Thienemann's, Elton's, and Hutchinson's ideas; in that way, it succeeded in avoiding the controversies that for a long time divided the Continental and the Anglo-Saxon ecological schools. At the University of Budapest, L. Winkler developed world renowned, and still used, methods for the chemical analysis of natural waters. The first center of applied hydrobiological studies was the Experimental Station for Fish Physiology and Sewage-water Analysis (later, Research Institute for Fish Production) founded in 1906, and headed from 1933 to 1952 by R. Maucha, the outstanding representative of production biology research (see below).

In 1927, the Biological Research Institute was established in Tihany, on the shore of Lake Balaton, primarily for hydrobiological studies on the lake. G. Entz and O. Sebestyén (1946) summarized the results of two decades' investigations. Their work is regarded as a fundamental study in limnology of great shallow lakes.

Studies on the hydrobiology of the Danube became well coordinated in 1958 when the Hungarian Danube Research Station was established in Göd. The station cooperates with several foreign research institutions in the Danube Research Workshop of the International Limnological Society.

In 1955, G. Kolosváry started comprehensive biological research on the Tisza River, the second longest river of the country, and its tide lands. The valuable results help to determine the changes caused by the building of barrages.

The Research Institute of Plant Protection, Budapest, became the most important center of applied animal ecology. Here, the ecology of agricultural pests, mainly insects, has been studied continuously since 1880. From the beginning of the 1950s, ecological research has been extended in the directions of: (1) experimental studies on ecological factors influencing the life cycle (diapause), as well as fecundity, in insects; (2) insect—host-plant relationships; and (3) theoretical and field studies of agro-ecosystems.

The complete bibliography of ecological literature published in Hungary or by Hungarian authors abroad between 1900 and 1972 has been compiled by Soó (1978).

SIGNIFICANT ADVANCES IN THEORY AND METHODOLOGY

In plant ecology, the above-mentioned analytical type of research predominated until the 1960s when, under the influence of the International Biological Program (IBP), the study of the processes of production biology in plant communities became more pronounced with the application of the systems approach. At the same time, the huge amount of data gathered during the analytical period induced the introduction of modern statistical methods, principle component, and factor analyses in ecological research (Précsényi 1958, 1961; Juhász-Nagy 1963; Fekete and Szujkó-Lacza 1973; Szőcs 1971, 1973). On the other hand, by means of different types of models and systems (set theory, relations, functions, and probability theory), the elements of axiomatic modelling synbotany have been developed (Juhász-Nagy, 1966–1968, 1970, 1976).

In terrestrial zoocenoses, extensive studies on production biology were carried out well before the beginning of the IBP, mainly revealing quantitative aspects of the decomposition of oak forest litter. At the same time, the first synthesis of theoretical production biology was developed by Balogh (1963). His book is also the first publication to summarize methods of field ecology.

Unfortunately, the book appeared in German and is hardly known in English-speaking countries.

In the 1960s, the method of rearing detritophagous animals in a cave laboratory was introduced by A. Zicsi. The cave is used like a cheap and reliable "zootron," with a constant temperature of 10°C, 95–100 percent relative humidity, and total darkness, thus imitating exactly the ecological situation of Hungarian soils during the period from September to May when the activity of soil animals is highest. Zicsi was the first to determine by this means the quantitative activity of several soil-inhabiting animal groups (Lumbricidae, Enchytraeidae, Diplopoda, Isopoda, and Diptera larvae) and their feeding preferences toward different forest litter. As a result, the optimal complex of tree species in establishing forests for environmental protection with an optimal development of soil fertility has been determined. These experiments substantiated the introduction of certain earthworm species into the soils of afforested areas as in the Vértes-Cserhát Project, with excellent results (Zicsi 1975).

MAJOR TRENDS IN THEORETICAL AND APPLIED RESEARCH

Productivity Ecology

Ecology in the post–World War II period has been dominated in Hungary mostly by research on biological production. Maucha (1949, 1953) summarized the results of the fundamental and experimental work carried out during a quarter of a century in limnology. He showed that primary production of phytoplankton was maximal at comparatively low light intensities. This explained why maximum densities of phytoplankton occur close to the surface in arctic seas while they are deeper in tropical ones; as a consequence, arctic seas are more productive because of optimal spectral composition of light at the surface. Maucha further demonstrated that potential primary production can be estimated in monofocal aquatic communities by measuring only the available amount of carbon dioxide. Complementing the theoretical considerations of Hutchinson and Lindeman on the energy turnover of limnic biocenoses, a formula for the optimal planting of fish ponds was developed by Maucha as well.

In the 1930s, a center of animal ecology, developed at the University of Budapest under the leadership of E. Dudich, concentrated on food chains and energy turnover of terrestrial communities. In 1932, Dudich published his work on the energy budget of cave communities, the first to emphasize the autarky or self-supporting nature of them. Contemporaneous was the publication of the fundamental papers of Palmgren, the European pioneer on production biology of terrestrial communities. From Dudich's school, Balogh (1935) published one of the first ecological monographs dealing with the quantitative analysis of a life form (the spiders) within a terrestrial community.

An attempt to join the schools of Soó and Dudich is reflected in the investigations on birds (Udvardy 1943), Orthoptera (Nagy 1950), and Rhynchota (Koppányi 1960, 1961). These several studies analyzed the distribution, occurrence, and other aspects of the species composition of these animal groups in relation to the plant communities in the Hortobágy-puszta and the Tihany peninsula.

The contemporary theories on biological production, mainly considering terrestrial biocenoses, were surveyed and compiled by Balogh (1953, 1958, 1963). Balogh emphasized the importance of the quantitative relations of the three directions (sustenance, storing, and waste) in which energy flows at each link of the food chain with the further parts of the chain. He has shown that in each group of life forms there are only a few, or even a single, species with high dominance and constancy, representing the overwhelming majority of the biomass; that is, there are few main channels through which most of the energy flows.

Jermy (1957) pointed out that in production biology, the effect of a given population on the energy turnover of others (transformation potential) has to be taken into consideration.

Dudich, Balogh, and Loksa (1952) studied the validity of Bornebusch's "surface law" in different arthropods from the point of view of its use for estimating energy turnover in communities.

Balogh (1953) and Woynárovich (1954) introduced the notion of "recuperation," by which was meant the function of organisms transforming dead organic matter into living matter. Thus, symmetrical to Juday's pyramid of consumers, a pyramid of recuperating organisms can be built up; this is the so-called rule of the double pyramid.

As early as 1956, G. Gere measured the three directions of energy turnover in lepidopterous larvae using calorimetry, and introduced a new grouping of organisms according to their characteristics of production biology (Gere 1957).

Jermy (1958) framed two laws of energy flow in communities; the heterotrophic food chain tends to minimize the free energy content of the biocenose (i.e., for minimum entropy), or the "law of free energy minimum"; on the other hand, autotrophic organisms tend to bind the highest possible amount of solar energy which, together with the former process, results in maximal activity of life, or the "law of maximal biocenotic work."

Szelényi (1955) developed a system of categories and a nomenclature of zoocenoses, which took into consideration the energy base and trophic relations of populations. He differentiated five feeding-biological groups of heterotrophic organisms and four hierarchic categories of zoocenoses.

Special attention has been paid by Balogh's soil biology school to the process of forest litter decomposition. The role of arthropods and microbes in decomposition has been studied, and the amount of litter from twenty-three different types of Hungarian forests has been determined (Gere 1966). Extensive studies were carried out on the role of earthworms in mixing cultivated soils, their suitability for the bioindication of soil and vegetation types, and the effect of fertilizers and cultivation methods on their density (Zicsi 1967, 1968) as well as their role in the decomposition of forest litter. The ecology of enchytraeids, especially their litter-decomposing activity, has been investigated by Dózsa-Farkas (1973). The relation between the species composition of litter-inhabiting arthropods and the type of vegetation has been reported in detail by Loksa (1966). Andrássy (1953) found that the species composition of nematode communities in the rhizosphere of plants largely depends on the species of the plant. A method for the determination of the biomass of soil nematodes has been developed (Andrássy 1967). The characteristics of the nematode fauna in riparian soils and river beds turned out to depend on the chemical composition of the water and on the size of sand particles (Andrássy 1962).

Plant Ecology

Several important works have resulted from the analytical efforts in plant ecology. Detailed analyses of the vegetation types and their environmental conditions in different regions of Hungary have been published in a series of books edited by Zólyomi (1957–1977). Comparative studies have been carried out on woodland and grassland vegetation by means of computer classifications (Simon 1977). A close correlation between calcium, potassium, and humus content, as well as pH of the soil, and the occurrence of *Lithospermum purpureo-coeruleum* has been found (Zólyomi 1963; Fekete and Szujkó-Lacza 1973). More generally, researchers have made use of indicator plant species for the characterization and classification of habitats (e.g., water balance and pH of the soil, heat conditions) and of phytocenoses (Zólyomi and Précsényi 1964).

Jakucs (1972) discovered the successional processes of vegetation and soil in the contact zone of woodland and grassland, the so-called margin effect, and their importance in the formation of forest-steppe mosaics. He also stressed the importance of "polycormons" in succession. This notion was introduced by Pénzes (1958). Close interrelations between the different factors of soil and community structure of woodlands, as well as ecological gradients in the case of contact stands have been analyzed by Kovács (1975 in Zólyomi 1957–1977).

The results of the Hungarian plant geography school were applied and developed in vegetation, bioclimatological, and epiphyta phytomass production studies on the tropics (Borhidi et al. 1979; Pócs 1974, 1976).

As regards production biology in plant ecology, the grassland communities on sandy soils of the Great Hungarian Plain became one of the main targets of research in the 1960s. The coordinated effort of nine research institutions is directed to the pattern and structure of vegetation, ecological genetics of dominant plant species, dynamics of organic material and mineral nutrients, and productivity of flowering plants and moss-lichen synusia important in our steppe meadows. The effect of such environmental factors as temperature, precipitation, radiation, soil moisture, and available nutrients on phytomass production has been determined (Kovács-Láng and Szabó 1973; Kovács-Láng 1974, 1975; Simon and Szerényi 1975; Simon and Kovács-Láng 1976).

Extensive IBP productivity studies were carried on in the forest-steppe communities on loess soils. Detailed analyses of phytomass production of salt pastures in comparison with that of agricultural lands planted in maize or wheat, studies on energy budget, and turnover of communities have been performed. Statistical methods have been employed in the correlations between structural (weight-dominance, diversity) and functional (productivity efficiency, energy flow, turnover) characteristics of the community (Máthé et al. 1967; Précsényi 1970, 1973, 1975; Máthé and Précsényi 1971). For the above-mentioned communities, a few animal components and their ecology have been investigated also (Szelényi et al. 1974).

Studying the energy budget of a salt pasture, Précsényi (1975) revealed the relationships between dry matter production and meteorologic factors, as well as between structural and functional characteristics in steppe meadows. Data on the primary production of Hungarian grassland communities have been included in the grassland synthesis volume of the IBP.

Ecological aspects of the afforestation of the Great Hungarian Plain has been worked on by Magyar (1960–1961).

The most complex interdisciplinary ecosystem study, the Sikfőkut Project, was undertaken by Jakucs (in press) with the cooperation of forty-odd institutions. The aim is to analyze the material and energy turnover of an oak forest typical of the hilly regions of the country. Results have been published on the relation between weather conditions and primary production (Jakucs and Papp 1974; Jakucs and Virágh 1975), amount of food elements in leaching waters (Szabó 1977), caloric value of dominant primary producers (Papp 1975), homeostasis between light regime of different strata and the structure of pigments (Fekete and Tuba 1977), speed of litter decomposition (J. A. Tóth 1974), and the role of insect feces, produced at an outbreak of phytophagous insects, on the intensity of primary production (Varga et al. in Jakucs in press).

Long-range investigations on the structure and function of two agro-ecosystems, corn fields and apple orchards, were begun in 1976 under the guidance of the Research Institute for Plant Protection with participants from several institutions (Jermy et al. 1979).

Theoretical Ecology

In the field of theoretical ecology, important results have been achieved. Based on a new system of models in information theory, a family of functions has been developed representing such qualities as spatial processes and heterogeneity, and interconnecting a number of basic phenomena such as diversity, similarity, and preference (Juhász-Nagy et al. 1971–1973).

The role and order of intensity of environmental effects on the structure and productivity of different plant communities has been revealed by the use of statistical models for the study of relations between phenomena and acting factors (Précsényi 1971; Szujkó-Lacza and Fekete 1971).

Using multivariate analyses, G. Fekete and co-workers studied interspecific correlations of population triplets and published a series of papers on niche research in plant communities of Hungary (Fekete and Szujkó-Lacza 1973; Fekete et al. 1976–1979).

The autecological background of primary production has been studied by an analysis of the influence of different spectral ranges on the tissues of assimilation and transport, as well as on the accumulation of assimilata in cultivated plants (Horváth 1972). Also, a correlation between the photosynthetic system, PS II, and the ultrastructural differentiation of plastids has been shown (Keresztes et al. 1976), as has the relation between alkaloid production and environmental conditions with several plant species (Máthé 1962; Máthé and Máthé 1970).

Insect Autecology

As regards research on insect autecology, Jermy and Sáringer (1956) showed that short photophase not only induced imaginal diapause in the Colorado potato beetle, but also reduced fecundity of females originating from larvae that developed under short-day illumination. This effect has also been found in several species of Microlepidoptera by Deseő and Sáringer (1975).

The role of extreme winter temperatures in the survival of spider mite eggs, as well as the changes of ecological factors in time and space influencing the population dynamics of the San José scale, was investigated by Kozár (1974, 1978).

Theoretical and practical aspects of insect–host-plant relationships have been studied by Jermy (1976) and Nagy (1976, 1977). The presumable importance of intraspecific insect biotypes evolving in different ecosystems has been dealt with by Nagy and Jermy (1975).

Monographic studies on the main insect pests in Hungary contain valuable data on the ecology of the fall webworm, the Colorado potato beetle, *Hoplocampa* spp., and *Grapholitha funebrana,* among others. Extensive studies have been carried out on the ecology of pollinating Hymenoptera (Móczár

1959; Benedek 1971, 1972) and on moth communities of fruit orchards (Reichart 1977). Data on the autecology of pest species have been successfully used for forecasting in plant protection (Mészáros 1967; Benedek 1970).

Aquatic Ecology

Based on Maucha's work, Woynárovich (1956) developed a theory and practical method for the C-fertilization of fish ponds. Dvihally (1971) determined seasonal changes in the light, climate, and hydrochemistry of soda ponds with special regard to their primary production. Hydrobiological and zoological studies carried out on rice fields in Hungary succeeded in revealing several basic characteristics of astatic shallow waters (Berczik 1972, 1973, 1977).

Eutrophication of Lake Balaton has become one of the most important questions of hydrobiology in Hungary. The Biological Research Institute in Tihany gathered data on the process of eutrophication and analyzed several anthropogenic factors influencing the biological state of the lake (Tóth et al. 1961; Oláh 1971; Biró 1973; Zánkai and Ponyi 1974; Herodek and Tamás 1975; Entz 1976; also other papers published mainly in Volumes 22 to 43 of the *Ann. Biol. Tihany*). Sebestyén (1970) studied the subfossil relics of water organisms, thus commencing the paleolimnological exploration of the lake. Zánkai and Ponyi (1974) determined the feeding-biological characteristics of the main members of the zooplankton, as well as their place in the material turnover of the community.

The Hungarian part of the Danube has a length of 420 km. The team of the Hungarian Danube Research Station in Göd has carried out a detailed biological and chemical analysis of the river and surveys continuously the changes occurring in it with special emphasis on the bioindication of water pollution (Dudich 1967; Szemes 1969; Berczik 1971; Bothár 1974; J. Tóth 1974; Bereczky 1975; Kozma 1975; Dvihally 1977; and other papers published in the series *Danubialia Hungarica* from 1958 on).

The Workshop for Tisza River Research investigates the biology of the river with special regard to the effect of newly built barrages (Kolosváry 1958; Bodrogközy 1965; Ferencz 1969; Marián 1975; Uherkovich 1975; and other papers published mainly in the journal *Tiscia* in Szeged).

RELATIONS AND INTERACTIONS WITH OTHER DISCIPLINES

The more recent ecosystem studies necessarily induced close cooperation between ecology on the one hand and biosystematics, physiology, meteorology, pedology, geography, agricultural sciences, as well as computer science, on the other. For example, models of an oak forest ecosystem in the Sikfőkut Project, of Lake Balaton, and of a sewage receiver are being developed in cooperation with the Institute of Computer Science and Automatization, Budapest. Further, as an aid to research in ecology, the Hungarian Committee of the International Institute of Applied Systems Analysis has been formed.

The increasing importance of ecological research in the future welfare of mankind is beginning to strengthen ecology's connections with the economic and social sciences in Hungary. Representatives of the economic and social sciences have become more aware that priority has to be given to ecological aspects in making decisions about regional development of the country.

SOURCES AND LEVELS OF GOVERNMENT AND PRIVATE SUPPORT

From the beginning, ecological research has always been supported through government budgets, since it has been concentrated at universities maintained by the state and at state research institutions.

There was an urgent need to develop research in physiology, biochemistry, and molecular biology after the Second World War, so that only a small portion of the available funds was left for extending ecological research. However, it is planned that after 1980 ecology will get increased support.

The Hungarian Academy of Sciences, like the academies of other socialist countries, plays not only a consultative role in science, but also an organizational and financial one; the academy can be regarded partly as a ministry of science. The Hungarian Academy of Sciences aims to concentrate and, by a moderate increase of financial support, to strengthen ecological research.

During the last several decades, several socialized enterprises, such as state farms, have made contracts with research institutions and university departments for special research in applied ecology (e.g., increasing production).

TEACHING AND TRAINING IN ECOLOGY AT UNDERGRADUATE AND GRADUATE LEVELS

Regular training in ecology at undergraduate level is carried out at the following university departments:

Eötvös Loránd University, Budapest—Departments of Plant Systematics and Ecology, Animal Systematics and Ecology, and Microbiology.

Kossuth Lajos University, Debrecen—Departments of Botany, Zoology, and Ecology.

József Attila University, Szeged—Departments of Botany and Zoology.

Biology students are obliged to deal with ecology and ecological problems in the following subjects: general ecology, plant ecology, animal ecology, pedology, climatology, microbiology, biometry, and hydrobiology.

At the graduate level quite recently in the Budapest and Debrecen universities, students have had the possibility of specializing in different fields that may be characterized by some combination of subjects. These fields are: ecology-environment conservation-human ecology; ecology-environment conservation-soil biology and hydrobiology. Unfortunately, there is no regular postgraduate training in ecology at the moment, but there are some advanced seminars in the Budapest university; in addition, selected individuals can gain scholarship for a two-year Ph.D. period. The Hungarian Academy of Sciences also provides certain opportunities for postgraduate training.

JOURNALS AND SOCIETIES

No special journal of ecology is issued in Hungary. Ecological studies are published in the journals *Allattani Közlemények, Botanikai Közlemények,* and *Magyar Tudományos Akadémia Biológiai Tudományok Osztálya Közleményei.* These are edited in Hungarian with a summary in foreign languages. The following journals are edited in foreign languages: *Abstracta Botanica, Acta Agronomica Academiae Scientiarum Hungaricae, Acta Biologica Academiae Scientiarum Hungaricae, Acta Botanica Academiae Scientiarum Hungaricae, Acta Microbiologica Academiae Scientiarum Hungaricae, Acta Phytopathologica Academiae Scientiarum Hungaricae, Acta Zoologica Academiae Scientiarum Hungaricae, Acta Biologica Debrecina, Acta Geobotanica Hungarica, Annales Universitatis Scientiarum Budapestinensis, Aquila, Opuscula Zoologica, Tiscia,* and *Annales Instituti Biologici (Tihany) Hungaricae Academiae Scientiarum.*

The sections of botany, zoology, and ecology of the Hungarian Biological Society are the main forums in which discussions on ecological problems take place. The Hungarian Hydrobiological Society and the Biological Institute at Tihany organize an annual "Meeting of Hydrobiologists." Twice a year since 1973, the results obtained in the Sikfökut Project are discussed in special meetings.

All important sources published abroad on the achievements in ecology are consulted.

BIBLIOGRAPHY

Balogh, J. 1963. *Lebensgemeinschaften der Landtiere.* Budapest: Akadémiai Kiadó, Berlin: Akademie Verlag. (The author gives a critical evaluation of the theories on general biocenology, production biology, and characterization of zoocenoses, with an explanation of his own theoretical considerations. Two-thirds of the volume deals with methodology and field ecology.)

Deseő, K. V. and G. Sáringer. 1975. Photoperiodic regulation in the population dynamics of certain lepidopterous species. *Acta Phytopath. Acad. Sci. Hung.*

10:131–139. (The authors review their research on the photoperiodic regulation of fecundity.)

Dudich, E. 1967. Systematisches Verzeichnis der Tierwelt der Donau mit einer zusammenfassenden Erläuterung. In *Limnologie der Donau,* Vol. 3, ed. R. Liepolt, pp. 43–69. (This is a survey of the fauna of the Danube with ecological characterization of the species.)

Dvihally, Z. 1971. Die Dynamik der chemischen und optischen Veränderungen in ungarischen Natrongewässern. *Sitzungsber. Oesterr. Akad. Wiss. Math. Naturwiss. Kl.* 197:192–203. (The author reports results of chemical and optical investigations on very shallow and turbid ponds containing hydrated sodium carbonate, with special regard to primary production.)

Entz, B. 1976. Regional and circadian oxygen determinations in Lake Balaton concerning eutrophication of the lake. *Ann. Biol. Tihany* 43:69–82. (The method to determine the productivity of different sections of Lake Balaton by oxygen measurements is suitable because of its simplicity, speed, and valuation in situ by semi-synchronic studies.)

Entz, G. and O. Sebestyén. 1946. Das Leben des Balaton-Sees. *Ann. Biol. Tihany* 14:179–391. (This summarizes twenty years of hydrobiological investigations on Lake Balaton following Thienemann's ecological approach; it also includes a program for further research.)

Fekete, G., I. Précsényi, E. Molnár, and E. Melkó. 1976–1979. Niche studies on some plant species of a grassland community, I–IV. *Acta Bot. Acad. Sci. Hung. Budapest* 22:321–354; 23:193–218, 367–374; 25:63–73. (Niche breadth and overlap, and distance of niche centers were measured in grassland communities on sandy soil. The results were analyzed by different indices and compared with the data gained for the same parameters by different methods.)

Gere, G. 1957. Productive biologic grouping of organisms and their role in ecological communities. *Ann. Univ. Sci. Budapest,* Sect. Biol. 1:61–69. (Considering production-biological characteristics, the author distinguishes two types of organisms: constructive and transferring ones. The latter are divided into consuments and recuperants containing the further subgroups of actively and passively storing organisms, respectively.)

Herman, O. 1876–1879. Magyarország pókfaunája. (The spider fauna of Hungary), Vols. I–III. (This is the earliest work on a system of animal life forms.)

Herodek, S. and G. Tamás. 1975. The primary production of phytoplankton in the Keszthely Basin of Lake Balaton. *Ann. Biol. Tihany* 42:175–190. (The illumination, as well as composition, biomass, and production, of the phytoplankton were studied in the basin in 25, 100, 200 and 275 cm depths throughout a whole year.)

Jakucs, P. 1972. *Dynamische Verbindung der Wälder und Rasen.* Budapest: Akadémiai Kiadó. (The author has discovered the dynamic processes of soil, microclimate, and vegetation characteristic in the contact zone of woodland and grassland, and their significance in formation of forest-steppe mosaics.)

———, ed. In press. *Studies on the oak forest ecosystem of the Pannonicum. Results of Sikfőkut Project, I.* Budapest: Akadémiai Kiadó. (The first results of complex, interdisciplinary research on the structural and functional characteristics of the trophic levels in these oak forest ecosystems are discussed.)

Jermy, T. 1958. Ein Beitrag zur produktionsbiologischen Betrachtung der terrestrischen Biozönosen. *Acta Zool. Acad. Sci. Hung. Budapest* 4:135–155. (The laws of free energy minimum and of maximal biocenotic work in communities are framed.)

———, ed. 1976. The host-plant in relation to insect behavior and reproduction. *Symp. Biol. Hung.* 16. (This presents papers read at an international symposium on the relationships between insects and their host-plants, held in Tihany, Hungary, June 1974.)

Juhász-Nagy, P. 1966–1968. Some theoretical problems of synbotany, I–III. I. Primary considerations on a conceptual network. II. Preliminaries on an axiomatic model-building. III. The importance of methodology. *Acta Biol. Debrecina* 4:59–81; 6:65–77. (The papers aim to provide a proper foundation of methodology based on set theory, relation theory, probability theory, and so on.)

———, I. Dévai, and K. Horváth. 1971–1973. Some problems of model-building in synbiology, I–II. I. Spatial diversity process of the binary type in a simple situation. II. Associatum process in a simple situation. *Annal. Univ. Sci. Budapest,* Sect. Biol. 13:19–32; 15:39–51. (Based on a new system of models in information theory, the main achievement is a family of functions representing spatial processes and heterogeneity, and interconnecting a number of basic phenomena such as diversity, similarity, and preference.)

Lóczy, L. 1897–1921. *A Balaton tudományos tanulmányozásának eredményei.* (The results of scientific studies of the Lake Balaton). Budapest. (The foundation of research on Lake Balaton as an ecosystem based on the geologic, geographic, hydrobiological, and limnological exploration of the lake and its surroundings, is presented with many botanical and zoological data.)

Loksa, I. 1966. *Die bodenzoologischen Verhältnisse der Flaumeichen-Buchenwälder Südosteuropas.* Budapest: Akadémiai Kiadó. (The relations between phyto- and zoocenoses are shown by the analysis of the arthropod fauna found in the litter of Orno-cotinion forests in southeast Europe.)

Magyar, P. 1960–1961. *Alföldfásitás,* I–II. (Afforestation of the Great Hungarian Plain.) Budapest: Akadémiai Kiadó. (This practical handbook emphasizes the ecological aspects of the afforestation of the Great Hungarian Plain.)

Maucha, R. 1953. A vizek produkciósbiológiája és a halászat. (Production biology of waters and the fishery) *MTA Biol. Oszt. Közlem.* 2:393–455. (A new approach is presented to several basic questions of the physico-chemistry of primary production in waters with special reference to fish production.)

Précsényi, I. 1975. *Szikespusztai rét növényzetének produktivitása.* (Productivity of a meadow on salt-affected soil) Budapest: Akadémiai Kiadó. (The book covers the main results of IBP studies carried on in salt pastures in central Hungary; phytomass productivity, ecological efficiency, turnover, and correlations between the productivity and climatical factors are discussed.)

Simon, T. and E. Kovács-Láng. 1976. Phytomass production and environmental conditions of grasslands on sand soil at Csévharaszt (IBP experimental area in Hungary). *Pol. Ecol. Stud.* 2:121–127. (The authors give a short account of the results of investigations in relation to the productivity of grassland communities on sands.)

Soó, R. 1964–1979. *Synopsis systematico-geobotanica florae vegetationisque Hungariae,* I–VI. (Handbook of the Hungarian flora and vegetation) Budapest: Akadémiai Kiadó. (The series of books contains a detailed analysis of cormophyteous flora and vegetation of Hungary with ecological characterizations of the species and vegetation units concerned.)

______. 1978. *Bibliographia synoecologica scientifica hungarica 1900–1972.* Budapest: Akadémiai Kiadó. (This is a complete bibliography of ecological literature published in Hungary or by Hungarian authors abroad between 1900 and 1972.)

Székessy, V. and Z. Kaszab, eds. 1955–1980. *Fauna Hungariae.* Budapest: Akadémiai Kiadó. (A series of issues [138 by 1980] has dealt with the taxonomy of the fauna of Hungary and also contains many ecological data.)

Szelényi, G. 1955. Versuch einer Kategorisierung der Zoozönosen. *Beitr. Entomol.* 5:18–35. (A new system of hierarchic categories of zoocenoses and their nomenclature is given based on the trophic relations of animal populations.)

Zicsi, A. 1975. Zootische Einflüsse auf die Streuzersetzung in Hainbuchen-Eichenwäldern Ungarns. *Pedobiologia* 15:432–439. (Based on the distribution, abundance, and feeding biological characteristics of big earthworm species, a method for the investigation of zoogenic factors in ecosystem is shown.)

Zólyomi, B., ed. 1957–1977. *Die Vegetation ungarischer Landschaften.* Vols. 1–7. Vol. 1, Simon, T. 1957. *Die Wälder des Nördlichen Alföld;* Vol. 2, Pócs, T. et al. 1958. *Vegetationsstudien in Őrség.;* Vol. 3, Kovács, M. 1962. *Die Moorwiesen Ungarns;* Vol. 4, Horánszky, A. 1964. *Die Wälder des Szentendre-Visegráder Gebirges;* Vol. 5, Fekete, G. 1965. *Die Waldvegetation im Gödöllőer Hügelland;* Vol. 6, Kovács, M. 1975. *Beziehung zwischen Vegetation und Boden;* Vol. 7, Simon, T. 1977. *Vegetationsuntersuchungen im Zempléner Gebirge.* Budapest: Akadémiai Kiadó. (The series is a result of extensive geobotanical and ecological research carried out in different parts of Hungary and on different types of vegetation by the members of the Hungarian plant geography school.)

______ and I. Précsényi. 1964. Methode zur ökologischen Charakterisierung der Vegetationseinheiten und zum Vergleich der Standorte. *Acta Bot. Acad. Sci. Hung.* 10:377–416. (On the basis of the indicator theory, the authors have worked out a quantitative method to characterize the different plant communities.)

REFERENCES CITED

Andrássy, I. 1953. Die Wirkung der verschiedenen Pflanzenarten auf die Zusammensetzung der in der Rhizosphäre lebenden Nematodengemeinschaften. *Ann. Hist.-Nat. Mus. Natl. Hung.* 3:92–99.

______. 1962. Nematoden aus dem Ufergrundwasser der Donau von Bratislava bis Budapest. *Arch. Hydrobiol. Suppl. Donauforschung* 27:91–117.

______. 1967. The determination of volume and weight of nematodes. In *Selected East European papers in nematology* (English translation), pp. 73–84. East Wareham.

Balogh, J. 1935. *Die Spinnenfauna des Sashegy*. Budapest.

———. 1953. *Grundzüge der Zoozönologie*. Budapest: Akadémiai Kiadó.

———. 1958. On some problems of production biology. *Acta Zool. Acad. Sci. Hung.* 4:89–114.

———. 1963. *Lebensgemeinschaften der Landtiere*. Budapest: Akadémiai Kiadó, Berlin: Akademie Verlag.

Benedek, P. 1970. The Hungarian countrywide light-trap network in service of plant protection forecasting. *EPPO Publications,* Ser. A, No. 57, pp. 163–167.

———. 1971. Flower visiting habits of colletid and melittid bees (Hym. Apoidea) based on data originating from Hungary. *Mushi* (Fukuoka) 45:65–79.

———. 1972. The role of honeybees in the pollination of lucerne in relation to the activity of wild bees. *Z. Angew. Entomol.* 70:174–179.

Berczik, A. 1971. Die Chironomiden und ihre Lebensstätten auf dem ungarischen Donauabschnitt. *Limnologica* 8:61–71.

———. 1972. Zur Populationsdynamik der Mesofauna der Reisfelder. *Sitzungsber. Oesterr. Akad. Wiss. Math. Naturwiss. Kl.* 179:299–302.

———. 1973. Periodische Aspektenveränderungen der Zoozönosen auf Reisfeldern in Ungarn. *Verh. Int. Verein. Limnol.* 18:1742–1750.

———. 1977. Untersuchungen der Frassintensität der reisblattminierenden Chironomiden. *Opusc. Zool. (Budap.)* 13:31–35.

Bereczky, M. 1975. Die ökologische Charakterisierung einiger Ciliaten-Organismen des Ungarischen Donauabschnittes. *Ann. Univ. Sci. Budapest,* Sect. Biol. 17:123–136.

Biró, P. 1973. The food of pike perch (*Lucioperca lucioperca* L.) in Lake Balaton. *Ann. Biol. Tihany* 40:159–183.

Bodrogközy, Gy. 1965. Die Vegetation des Theiss-Wellenraumes. *Tiscia* 1:5–31.

Borhidi, A., O. Muniz, and E. Del Risco. 1979. Classificacion fitocenologica de la vegetacion de Cuba. *Acta Bot. Acad. Sci. Hung.* 25:263–310.

Bothár, A. 1974. Horizontale Planktonuntersuchungen an der Donau von Rajka bis Turnu Severin. *Ann. Univ. Sci. Budapest,* Sect. Biol. 16:157–162.

Deseő, K. V. and G. Sáringer. 1975. Photoperiodic regulation in the population dynamics of certain lepidopterous species. *Acta Phytopath. Acad. Sci. Hung.* 10:131–139.

Dózsa-Farkas, K. 1973. Saisondynamische Untersuchungen des Enchytraeiden-Besatzes im Boden eines ungarischen *Quercetum petreae cerris*. *Pedobiologia* 13:361–367.

Dudich, E. 1932. Biologie der Aggteleker Tropfsteinhöhle "Baradla" in Ungarn. *Speläolog. Monogr. Wien* 13:1–246.

———. 1967. Systematisches Verzeichnis der Tierwelt der Donau mit einer zusammenfassenden Erläuterung. In *Limnologie der Donau,* Vol. 3, ed. R. Liepolt, pp. 43–69.

———, J. Balogh, and I. Loksa. 1952. Produktionsbiologische Untersuchungen über die Arthropoden der Waldböden. *Acta Biol. Acad. Sci. Hung.* 3:295–317.

Dvihally, Z. 1971. Die Dynamik der chemischen und optischen Veränderungen in ungarischen Natrongewässern. *Sitzungsber. Oesterr. Akad. Wiss. Math. Naturwiss. Kl.* 197:192–203.

———. 1977. Die Änderung der chemischen Verhältnisse des Donauwassers zwischen 1964–1974. *Ann. Univ. Sci. Budapest.* 18:29–33.

Entz, B. 1976. Regional and circadian oxygen determinations in Lake Balaton concerning eutrophication of the lake. *Ann. Biol. Tihany* 43:69–82.

Entz, G. and O. Sebestyén. 1946. Das Leben des Balaton-Sees. *Ann. Biol. Tihany* 14:179–391.

Fekete, G., I. Précsényi, E. Molnár, and E. Melkó. 1976–1979. Niche studies on some plant species of a grassland community, Parts I–IV. *Acta Bot. Acad. Sci. Hung. Budapest* 22:321–354; 23:193–218, 367–374; 25:63–73.

——— and J. Szujkó-Lacza. 1973. Interspecific correlation of plants in oak wood at increasing block sizes. *Acta Biol. Acad. Sci. Hung.* 24:31–42.

——— and Z. Tuba. 1977. Supraindividual homogeneity of photosynthetic pigments: a study on community structure. *Acta Bot. Acad. Sci. Hung.* Vol. 23.

Ferencz, M. 1969. Occurrence of *Hypania invalida* in the Tisza. *Tiscia* 5:69–71.

Gere, G. 1956. Investigations concerning the energy turnover of the *Hyphantria cunea* Drury caterpillars. *Opusc. Zool.* (*Budap.*) 1:29–32.

———. 1957. Productive biologic grouping of organisms and their role in ecological communities. *Ann. Univ. Sci. Budapest,* Sect. Biol. 1:61–69.

———. 1966. Festbestellung der Gesamtmenge des Falllaubes in den Wäldern Ungarns. *Opusc. Zool.* (*Budap.*) 6:119–137.

Herman, O. 1876–1879. *Magyarország. pokfaunája,* Vols. I–III.

Herodek, S. and G. Tamás. 1975. The primary production of phytoplankton in the Keszthely Basin of Lake Balaton. *Ann. Biol. Tihany* 42:175–190.

Horváth, I. 1972. A study on the products of photosynthesis in connection with the primary production. *MTA Biol. Oszt. Kozl.* 15:71–77.

Jakucs, P. 1972. *Dynamische Verbindung der Wälder und Rasen.* Budapest: Akadémiai Kiadó.

———, ed. In press. *Studies on the oak forest ecosystem of the Pannonicum. Results of Sikfőkut Project, I.* Budapest: Akadémiai Kiadó.

——— and M. Papp. 1974. Production investigations of the undergrowth (herbaceous layer) of a *Quercetum petraeae cerris* forest ecosystem. *Acta Bot. Acad. Sci. Hung.* 20:295–308.

——— and K. Virágh. 1975. Changes in the area and weight of light- and shade-adapted leaves and shoots of *Quercus petraea* and *Quercus cerris* in Hungarian oak forest ecosystems. *Acta Bot. Acad. Sci. Hung.* 21:25–36.

Jermy, T. 1957. Der Pflanzenschutz aus produktionsbiologischem Gesichtspunkt betrachtet. *Ann. Inst. Prot. Plant. Hung.* 7:23–33.

———. 1958. Ein Beitrag zur produktionsbiologischen Betrachtung der terrestrischen Biozönosen. *Acta Zool. Acad. Sci. Hung. Budapest* 4:135–155.

———, ed. 1976. The host-plant in relation to insect behavior and reproduction. *Symp. Biol. Hung.* Vol. 16.

———, K. Balázs, F. Kozár, S. Mahunka, Z. Mészáros, I. Szarukán, F. Szentkirályi, Gy. Sziráki, and I. Varga. 1979. Vergleichende Untersuchungen an Gliederfüssler-Gemeinschaften der intensiven bzw. herkömmlichen Betriebsapfelanlagen und der Hausgärten. *VII. Int. Symp. Entomofaunistik Mitteleur. Verhandlungen. Leningrad*, pp. 82–87.

______ and G. Sáringer. 1956. Die Rolle der Photoperiode in der Auslösung der Diapause des Kartoffelkäfers (*Leptinotarsa decemlineata* Say.) und des amerikanischen weissen Bärenspinners (*Hyphantria cunea Drury*). *Acta Agron. Acad. Sci. Hung.* 5:419–440.

Juhász-Nagy, P. 1963. Investigations on the Bulgarian vegetation. Some hygrophilous plant communities, I–II. *Acta Biol. Debrecina* 2:47–70.

______. 1966–1968. Some theoretical problems of synbotony, Parts I–III. *Acta Biol. Debrecina* 4:59–81; 6:65–77.

______. 1970. Need for an operative ecology. *MTA Biol. Oszt. Kozl.* 12:441–464.

______. 1976. Spatial dependence of plant populations. Part I. Equivalence analysis. *Acta Bot. Acad. Sci. Hung.* 22:61–78.

______, I. Dévai, and K. Horváth. 1971–1973. Some problems of model-building in synbiology, Parts I–II. *Ann. Univ. Sci. Budapest,* Sect. Biol. 13:19–32; 15:39–51.

Keresztes, A., M. R. Davey, and F. Láng. 1976. Freeze-etched membrane faces and photosynthetic activity in normal and mutant *Tradescantia* chloroplasts. *Protoplasma* 90:1–14.

Kerner, A. 1863. *Das Pflanzenleben der Donauländer.* Vienna.

Kolosváry, G. 1958. Die Tierwelt der Tisza auf Grund neuerer Sammlungen und Beobachtungen. *Acta Biol. Szegedina* 4:203–235.

Koppányi, T. 1960. Zoozönologische Untersuchungen über Heteropteren und Homopteren in Kleegrasbeständen. *Folia Entomol. Hung.* 13:125–162.

______. 1961. Fragen der biozönologischen Forschungen. *Acta Zool. Acad. Sci. Hung.* 7:191–211.

Kovács-Láng, E. 1974. Examination of dynamics of organic matter in a perennial open sandy steppe-meadow (*Festucetum vaginatae danubiale*) at the Csévharaszt IBP sample area (Hungary). *Acta Bot. Acad. Sci. Hung.* 20:309–326.

______. 1975. Distribution and dynamics of phosphorus, nitrogen, and potassium in perennial open sandy steppe-meadow (*Festucetum vaginatae danubiale*). *Acta Bot. Acad. Sci. Hung.* 21:77–90.

______ and M. Szabó. 1973. The effect of environmental factors on the phytomass production of sandy meadows. *Ann. Univ. Sci. Budapest,* Sect. Biol. 13:115–126.

Kozár, F. 1974. The role of extreme temperature fluctuations in the population dynamics of overwintering eggs of *Panonychus ulmi* Koch. *Acta Phytopathol. Acad. Sci. Hung.* 9:363–367.

______. 1978. Some questions on the population dynamics of the San José scale, *Quadraspidiotus perniciosus* Comstock (Homoptera: Coccoidea) *Acta Phytopathol. Acad. Sci. Hung.* 13:179–195.

Kozma, E. 1975. Über die organischen Stoffgehaltveränderungen des Donauwassers beim Strkm. 1669. *Ann. Univ. Sci. Budapest* 17:39–46.

Lóczy, L. 1897–1921. *A Balaton tudományos tanulmányozásának eredményei.* Budapest.

Loksa, I. 1966. *Die bodenzoologischen Verhältnisse der Flaumeichen-Buchenwälder Südosteuropas.* Budapest: Akadémiai Kiadó.

Magyar, P. 1960–1961. *Alföldfásitás,* Parts I–II. Budapest: Akadémiai Kiadó.

Marián, M. 1975. The part of flood in the formation of the avifauna in the flood area of the Tisza. *Tiscia* 10:85–88.

Máthé, I. 1962. Die Veränderung der Entwicklung und der Wirksamen-Substanz der Kamille nach den verschiedenen Jahrgängen und Gebieten. *Bot. Kozl.* 49:280–288.

——— and I. Máthé, Jr. 1970. The alkaloid content of *Solanum dulcamara* L. populations in Hungary. *Herba Hung.* 11:5–22.

——— and I. Précsényi. 1971. Plant biomass production of maize grown on a forest-steppe area. *Acta Agron. Acad. Sci. Hung.* 20:378–384.

———, I. Précsényi, and B. Zólyomi. 1967. Phytomass investigations in different ecosystems at Ujszentmargita. *Acta Bot. Acad. Sci. Hung.* 13:239–257.

Maucha, R. 1949. Einige Gedanken zur Frage des Nährstoffhaushalts der Gewässer. *Hydrobiologia* 1:225–237.

———. 1953. A vizek produkciósbiológiája és a halászat. *MTA Biol. Oszt. Kozl.* 2:393–455.

Mészáros, Z. 1967. Lebensform-Gruppen schädlicher Lepidopteren und Prognose einzelner Arten mittels Lichtfallen. *Acta Phytopathol. Acad. Sci. Hung.* 2:251–266.

Móczár, L. 1959. The activity of wild bees (Hym. Apoidea) in Hungarian lucerne fields. *Acta Agron. Acad. Sci. Hung.* 9:237–289.

Nagy, B. 1950. Quantitative and qualitative investigation of the Saltatoria on the Tihany peninsula. *Ann. Biol. Tihany* 19:95–222.

———. 1976. Host selection of the European corn borer (*Ostrinia nubialis* Hbn.) populations in Hungary. *Symp. Biol. Hung.* 16:191–195.

———. 1977. Presence and use of natural food sources of the coding moth (*Laspeyresia pomonella* L.) in Hungary. *Coll. Int. CNRS* 265:211–225.

——— and T. Jermy. 1975. Habitat as a factor inducing diversity of populations in the codling moth and other orchard pests, and its relevance to genetic control method. In *Sterility principle for insect control*, pp. 537–542. Vienna: IAEA.

Oláh, J. 1971. Weekly changes of the bacterio- and phytoplankton standing stock in Lake Balaton and in the highly eutrophic Lake Belső. *Ann. Biol. Tihany* 38:167–175.

Papp, L. B. 1975. Caloric values of the dominant species in an oak forest (*Quercetum petraeae-cerris*) near Sikfőkut, north Hungary. *Acta Bot. Acad. Sci. Hung.* 21:347–352.

Pénzes, A. 1958. A survival of stoloniferous plant colonies (polycormons) of a relict character. *Biologia SAV, Bratislava* 13:253–264.

Pócs, T. 1974. Bioclimatic studies in the Uluguru Mountains (Tanzania, East Africa), I. *Acta Bot. Acad. Sci. Hung.* 20:115–135.

———. 1977. The role of the epiphytic vegetation in the water balance and humus production of the rain forest of the Uluguru Mountains, East Africa. *Boissiera* 24:299–503.

Précsényi, I. 1958. Über die interspezifische Korrelation. *Acta Bot. Acad. Sci. Hung.* 4:155–158.

———. 1961. Structure investigations in *Festucetum vaginatae. Acta. Bot. Acad. Sci. Hung.* 7:409–424.

______. 1970. A study on the energy budget in *Artemisio-Festucetum pseudovinae*. *Acta Bot. Acad. Sci. Hung.* 16:179–185.

______. 1971. Relationship among the dry matter production of natural plant communities and weather elements. *Acta Climat. Szegedina* 10:69–75.

______. 1973. Relationship between structural and functional characteristics in steppe-meadows in Hungary. *Acta Bot. Acad. Sci. Hung.* 18:155–162.

______. 1975. *Szikespusztai rét növényzetének produktivitása.* Budapest: Akadémiai Kiadó.

Reichart, G. 1977. Data to the knowledge of moth communities occurring on fruit trees and shrubs in Hungary. *Acta Phytopathol. Acad. Sci. Hung.* 12:359–373.

Sebestyén, O. 1970. Calcareous microfossils in the sediments of Lake Balaton. *Ann. Biol. Tihany* 37:281–289.

Simon, T. 1977. Vegetationsuntersuchungen im Zempléner Gebirge. (Abgrenzung zönologischer Einheiten unter Anwendung quantitativer und rechnentechnischer Methoden; Vorstellung der Zytozönologischen Analyse). *Die Vegetation ungarischer Landschaften,* Vol. 7. Budapest: Akadémiai Kiadó.

______ and E. Kovács-Láng. 1976. Phytomass production and environmental conditions of grasslands on sand soil at Csévharaszt (IBP experimental area in Hungary). *Pol. Ecol. Stud.* 2:121–127.

______ and G. Szerényi. 1975. Moss ecological investigation in the forest-steppe associations of the IBP area at Csévharaszt. *Acta Bot. Acad. Sci. Hung.* 21:117–136.

Soó, R. 1960. Bibliographia phytosociologica: Hungaria. *Excerpta Botanica,* Sect. B, Sociologica Vol. 2, No. 3, 93–160.

______. 1964–1979. *Synopsis systematico-geobotanica florae vegetationisque Hungariae*, Parts I–VI. Budapest: Akadémiai Kaidó.

______. 1978. *Bibliographia synoecologica scientifica hungarica 1900–1972.* Budapest: Akadémiai Kiadó.

Szabó, M. 1977. Nutrient content of throughfall and stemflow water in an oak-forest (*Quercetum petreae-cerris*) ecosystem. *Acta Agron. Acad. Sci. Hung.* 26:241–258.

Székessy, V. and Z. Kaszab, eds. 1955–1980. *Fauna Hungariae.* Budapest: Akadémiai Kiadó.

Szelényi, G. 1955. Versuch einer Kategorisierung der Zoozönosen. *Beitr. Entomol.* 5:18–35.

______, B. Nagy, and G. Sáringer. 1974. Zoocenological study of animal communities of Csévharaszt sandy steppe area (middle Hungary). *Abstr. Bot. Budapest* 2:47–69.

Szemes, G. 1969. The phytoplankton of the Hungarian reach of the Danube during the winter months. *Ann. Univ. Sci. Budapest* 11:75–117.

Szőcs, Z. 1971. The beechwoods of the Vértes Mountains. II. An investigation of the interspecific correlations. *Bot. Kozl.* 58:47–52.

______. 1973. On the botanical application of some multivariate analyses, II. *Bot. Kozl.* 60:29–33.

Szujkó-Lacza, J. and G. Fekete. 1971. The correlation of species and habitat factors in a xerothermic oak forest stand. *Feddes Rep. Berlin* 82:263–286.

Tóth, J. 1974. The distribution of the stock and the trend of the cathes of carp in the Hungarian Danube section. *Ann. Univ. Sci. Budapest* 16:207–215.

Tóth, J. A. 1974. Litter decomposition studies in the frame of MAB project "Sikfőkut." *MTA Biol. Oszt. Kozl.* 17:449–465.

Tóth, L., L. Felföldy, and E. Szabó. 1961. On some problems of production measurements in Phragmitatea in Lake Balaton. *Ann. Biol. Tihany* 28:169–178.

Udvardy, M. 1943. Pontus Palmgren's quantitative method in ornithology. *Állattani. Kozl.* 40:252–259.

Uherkovich, G. 1975. Taxonomisch-ökologische Übersicht der Chlorophyten-, Rhodophyten-, Schyzomyceten- und Mycophyten- Organismen der Theiss und ihrer Nebengewässer. *Tiscia* 10:15–37.

Woynárovich, E. 1954. Generalized diagrammatic illustration of food and energy cycles in waters. *Állattani. Kozl.* 44:279–286.

______. 1956. Das Carbon Düngungs-Verfahren. *Dtsch. Fisch. Ztg.* 3:48–52.

Zánkai, N. and J. Ponyi. 1974. On the seasonal fluctuation of the food incorporation of *Eudiaptomus gracilis. Ann. Biol. Tihany* 41:357–362.

Zicsi, A. 1967. Die Auswirkung von Bodenbearbeitungsverfahren auf Zustand und Besatzdichte von einheimischen Regenwürmern. In *Progress in soil biology,* pp. 290–298.

______. 1968. Ein zusammenfassendes Verbreitungsbild der Regenwürmer auf Grund der Boden- und Vegetationsverhältnisse Ungarns. *Opusc. Zool.* (*Budap.*) 8:99–164.

______. 1975. Zootische Einflüsse auf die Streuzersetzung in Hainbuchen-Eichenwäldern Ungarns. *Pedobiologia* 15:432–439.

Zólyomi, B., ed. 1957–1977. *Die Vegetation ungarischer Landschaften,* Vols. 1–7. Budapest: Akadémiai Kiadó.

______. 1963. Synökologische Untersuchung einer basiphil-kalziphilen Indikator-Waldpflanze. *Acta Bot. Acad. Sci. Hung.* 9:461–472.

______ and I. Précsényi. 1964. Methode zur ökologischen Charakterisierung der Vegetationseinheiten und zum Vergleich der Standorte. *Acta Bot. Acad. Sci. Hung.* 10:377–416.

12

ICELAND

Sturla Fridriksson

BACKGROUND

Increased knowledge in every field of ecology is important to all nations that wish to live in full harmony with the environment and to use their natural resources wisely. This is a particular concern of the Icelandic nation, which to a great extent depends on biological products of sea and land.

The Icelanders live in a country where the natural forces, ice and fire, constantly mold the environment and where all living beings are highly influenced by the fickleness of the cold-tempered climate. The relationships of various peoples to their particular environment and to their native country may differ somewhat, but inhabitants of islands are in many ways closely tied to nature and have a patriotic feeling for their country with its sharp ecological boundaries.

Iceland is a remote island far out in the North Atlantic. It was not discovered and settled until the ninth century, long after humans were well established in other parts of Europe. The settlers, some of whom were Norse and some from the British Isles, came to a country that was hitherto uninhabited. It was an island where the flora and fauna had reached a certain climax, and where a rather stable ecological balance existed, having developed for the nine thousand years since the land emerged from under an icecap that had covered the island during the last glaciation. These early settlers and their livestock utilized natural resources and accumulated produce from yet untouched vegetation and wildlife, causing changes in the native flora and fauna and a severe degradation of the country's virgin soil.

Iceland, Europe's second largest island (103,000 km^2), is volcanic in origin. Approximately 10 percent is covered with postglacial lava and 12 percent with glaciers. Only 20 percent of the total area is covered with vegetation, of which one percent is cultivated. The ocean surrounding the island is abundant in fish, especially over the continental shelf, and where the ocean currents of different temperatures meet. Although the climate was harsh and the country mountainous, conditions were favorable for farming, since grassland was available for cattle, sheep, and pony grazing. Thus, shortly after the country's discovery, there were five thousand homesteads scattered around the lowland.

Ever since earliest times, farming and fishing have been the major occupations of the Icelanders, and they have lived in close contact with nature as a farming community. Only in the twentieth century with the use of hydroelectric and geothermal energy did industry begin to have any effect on the country's economy. At the end of the nineteenth century, the population was approximately seventy thousand, having shown no increase during the first thousand years of settlement. The population then began to increase and villages developed. In 1977, Iceland had a population of two hundred twenty thousand individuals, half of whom live in the capital city, Reykjavík, and its neighborhood.

Education in Iceland has always been on a relatively high level. The early Icelanders were saga writers, historians, and great keepers of annals. Literacy was highly valued, even during the "dark" Middle Ages, although people were at that time more poetically minded and superstitious than scientific.

Among scholars, natural history was given some attention, and it is remarkable how accurately some natural phenomena were recorded. Descriptions of Icelandic nature by Bishop Oddur Einarsson (1559–1630) and Arngrimur Jónsson the wise (1568–1648) are outstanding, although these writings were mostly composed in Latin and were thus not accessible to the public.

Icelandic eighteenth-century scientists were general naturalists with a broad interest covering many fields of science. Their treatises on climate, geology, botany, zoology, agriculture, and human sciences were pioneering works, presented in a manner that was ecological in many ways. Such are the writings of Hannes Finnsson, Sveinn Pálsson, Eggert Ólafsson, and Bjarni Pálsson.

At the same time, foreign scientists were also beginning to show interest in Icelandic nature, especially in its geology and botany. Many books written by travellers in Iceland include descriptions of its nature and wonders. During the nineteenth century, the first major area survey was carried out by Björn Gunnlaugsson, but there was no general awakening of interest in the natural sciences at that time such as occurred in many neighboring countries.

In the early 1900s, there was an increased specialization in the mode of scientific investigation in Iceland through research in the classical fields of the sciences and publications of classification of flora and fauna and geologic phenomena. The most outstanding Icelandic scientists of the time include the geologists Thorvaldur Thoroddsen and Helgi Pétursson, the botanists Stefán Stefánsson, Ólafur Davidsson, and Helgi Jónsson, and the zoologist Bjarni Sæmundsson. These scientists laid the foundations in their field within the classical sciences and molded natural history in Iceland. They were educated abroad and, upon returning to Iceland, had to adapt their knowledge to local conditions to study Icelandic problems, which, in many ways, were totally different from what they had previously encountered. Natural history was taught at the lower level in schools, but any advanced study had to be done in other European countries. A university was established in Reykjavík in 1911, but a department of natural sciences was not established until 1968. Scientific institutions were almost nonexistent until the twentieth century.

PROFESSIONAL SOCIETIES AND GOVERNMENT AGENCIES

A society of natural sciences was founded in 1887. A museum, created in the same year, later developed into an institute of natural sciences specializing in marine biology, ornithology, botany, geology, and geography.

Meteorologic records had been kept since the middle of the 1800s, first at only one station, but by the end of that century, there were already several established stations spread around the lowland. The Icelandic Meteorological Service was founded in Reykjavík in 1920 and has carried out various climatological investigations.

The Icelandic Agricultural Society was founded in the late nineteenth century and, between the years 1902 and 1905, three agricultural research stations were established, the forerunners of an institute in agricultural sciences.

In the latter part of the 1700s, men began to realize that the country's vegetation had been and was still being severely damaged by bad land management. However, it was not until the year 1894 that district boards were empowered by laws to protect lymegrass and take measures against erosion. In 1907, laws were passed to prevent erosion and, in 1914, others were passed concerning the reclamation of sandy areas. The laws concerning reclamation were later revised in 1923 and 1941; and, in 1965, they were again altered to promote the control of soil erosion and protection of vegetation. The Soil Conservation Service has its headquarters at Gunnarsholt, Rangárvallasýsla, in a district that was badly eroded.

At the end of the nineteenth century, people also began to realize the urgent need to protect the remnants of the country's birch forests. Protection of the forests was an important factor in the fight against soil erosion, which was becoming a major threat to agriculture. Laws concerning afforestation were passed in 1907, along with provisions against erosion. In the following years, the youth associations began to awaken interest in afforestation and, in

1930, the Icelandic Forestry Society was founded. An Icelandic Forestry Service also had been established and carried out various experiments by importing different varieties of trees, building nurseries and an experimental station, and promoting the protection of the country's forests. Its head office is in Reykjavík.

During the 1930s and 1940s, interest in applied sciences increased resulting in the establishment, by law, of the University Research Institute in 1935. It began operation in the first research building in 1937. This was an institute of applied sciences with divisions in industry, agriculture, and fisheries. Later, by an act in 1965, separate institutes were established in Reykjavík: the Marine Research Institute, for marine biology and oceanography; the Agricultural Research Institute, for basic and applied research in agricultural sciences; the Industrial Research and Development Institute, for research and services for industry; the Building Research Institute; and the Icelandic Fisheries Laboratories.

Freshwater fishing had been controlled by law, and according to a law passed in 1946, a director general of freshwater fishing was to supervise limnological studies and regulate fishing in lakes and rivers. The Institute of Freshwater Fishing has its head office in Reykjavík, as well as a hatchery where research and breeding experiments are performed.

The Icelandic Geodetic Survey was established in 1956. Prior to that time, geographic mapping of the country had been done in cooperation with the Danish Geodetic Institute.

The investigation of rivers and streams, as well as hydroelectric activities, has been directed since 1947 by the director general of the State Electricity Authority. In 1967, this was reorganized into two institutes, one dealing with electrical production and transport, while the other, The National Energy Authority, carries out the research work. The latter consists of two departments, one for electric power, the other for geothermal heat. It carries out various hydrological measurements such as those of drainage of glaciers and run-off of rivers and, in addition, does preparatory studies for the construction of power stations using both hydropower and thermal energy.

National Research Council

The first National Research Council was founded in 1939, mainly as a coordinating and advisory body. The laws were revised in 1965. The following are among the council's objectives:

1. Strengthening and coordinating applied and basic research in Iceland.
2. Conducting studies on the utilization of the country's natural resources for new industries.
3. Making proposals to the government about appropriations for research.

4. Procuring funds, in addition to government appropriations, for research in general.
5. Having on file reports on research in the field of Icelandic science funded by the government, and ensuring that the results are made public. The National Research Council publishes reports annually on research activities in the country.
6. Promoting a scientific and technical information service.
7. Cooperating with corresponding foreign institutions in the coordination of Icelandic participation.
8. Undertaking activities that are found desirable for coordinating research.

The National Research Council controls permits and handles applications from foreigners who wish to undertake scientific research in Iceland. The permits are issued under the authority of the Ministry of Culture and Education, or the Ministry of Fisheries in the instance of foreign marine research. The council is advised on all applications for research in the fields of basic geology, geography, botany, and zoology by the Icelandic Museum of Natural History.

LAW AND ENVIRONMENTAL PROTECTION

Various precautionary measures were taken early in Iceland regarding treatment of the environment, as is shown by provisions concerning precautions in burning wilted grass and in the changing of water courses. Regulations were also made governing fishing. In 1849, an ordinance was published concerning limitations on egg collecting and seal hunting on breeding grounds. The reindeer, introduced from Norway, had already been protected from time to time, and was sometimes altogether off-limits for hunters. The eider-duck had been declared a protected species and, in 1913, laws concerning the protection of several other birds were passed. These laws were revised in 1930, 1954, and 1966. Laws are also now in force to protect nearly all birds during the egg-laying period; the exceptions are the raven, black-backed gull, and a few other species of sea gulls. The island of Eldey, off the southwestern coast, where one of the world's most remarkable gannet colonies is found, was also made into a reservation because of its bird life.

Laws to limit salmon fishing were set in 1886 and similar laws for trout fishing in 1904, as well as regulations concerning fishing methods in lakes and rivers. In 1923, further limitations were placed on fishing and on use of fishing tackle in rivers and lakes. Laws passed in 1932 governing salmon and trout fishing, for example, banned salmon fishing in the ocean. Laws governing fish-breeding societies were made in 1929, and fishing laws were further revised in 1957 and 1970. These laws contain provisions for protection of spawning fish, and fishing of all but a specific size of fish in banned.

Seal catching was permitted in estuaries and rivers to protect freshwater fish (c.f. laws from 1912), and legislation on seal shooting in the breeding areas was passed in 1925. Laws limiting the fishing of whales within territorial waters were made in 1928, these protective measures were made more far-reaching in 1949 when killing of whale calves and females with calves was banned. Mink had been introduced and became wild. Mink breeding was banned in the years 1951–1970, and the legislature once more took in hand the extermination of foxes in the years 1957–1964.

Attempts have also been made to protect plant and animal life from imported diseases. The import of animals has been strictly regulated by the veterinarian-in-chief by law since 1948 to prevent importation of livestock diseases. Regulations concerning import of plants were made in 1927 to prevent plant diseases from being brought to the country. Regulations were also made in 1970 concerning the import of seed and are, among other things, intended to limit the import of weed seeds to Iceland. In addition, twenty-five rare plant species in Iceland have been declared protected.

RESERVATIONS

From one point of view, it could be said that Icelanders have lived on the edge of a national park for eleven hundred years without fully realizing it, such is the size of the country compared with its number of inhabitants.

It is only with the advanced technology of travel in recent years that people in general have begun to appreciate the country's size and its unique situation for outdoor life. With increased public interest in leisure-time observation of nature and the out-of-doors, the need for protection of unique areas and special natural features has also increased. The need for improved facilities of traffic and supervision to avoid overtaxing and damage to the natural features has likewise grown.

In the first decades of this century, the question was raised whether to make Thingvellir, where the ancient Icelandic parliament (Althing) had been held, into a national park. From the point of view both of history and of natural history, there were good reasons for awarding this spot some distinction. Thus, Thingvellir was declared a national park in 1930 by laws dating from 1928. The region, which is about 27 km^2, extends over the old assembly place and its surroundings, between the large crevices, Hrafnagjá and Almannagjá. The national park was protected from grazing and various human encroachments, and the life in the region was declared protected.

In the forestry reservations, the public has been provided with facilities for outdoor life, and many patches of forest are at the same time public parks. In collaboration with the city of Reykjavík, the Forestry Commission has seen to the protection and planting of trees on Heiömörk, an outdoor area near the city.

In laws passed in 1971, provision was made for setting up public parks where the public would have free right of passage. Limited rules concerning enclosure and exploitation of resources, such as gravel excavation and grazing, apply to these areas. Laws concerning nature conservation were passed in the parliament in 1956 and revised in 1971. The purpose of these laws is to promote contact between humans and nature in such a way that life and land are not damaged unnecessarily, nor are sea, water, and air polluted. The laws are intended to ensure as far as possible the natural development of the Icelandic countryside and the protection of what is unique or historical, as well as to make it easier for the people to enjoy the country's natural amenities and increase their knowledge of them.

The Nature Conservation Council is the executive authority in matters concerning conservation. Some of the protected areas and the actions of the committee will be mentioned here. In 1966, a proposal was introduced to make a national park in Skaftafell in Öræfi. The region was put under the authority of the Ministry of Education and a national park established with support from the World Wildlife Fund. In 1973, the scenic canyon of the large glacial river Jökulsárgljúfur was declared a national park. The Myvatn-Laxá area was designated by special law in 1974 to be partly protected, so that any construction or disruption in the area is prohibited without the Council's permission. A field research station has been built next to Lake Myvatn, administered by the council and with cooperative research carried out by the University of Iceland and the Museum of Natural History.

Other reserves of unique landscapes are the highland oases of Hvannalindir, Herdurbreidarlindir, and Lónsöræfi; and the fjord districts of Vatnsfjördur and Hornstrandir on the northwestern peninsula of Iceland. Of smaller areas or biotopes that the Council has made into reservations, the following are examples: the Rauðhólar pseudo-volcanoes; the islands Eldey, Surtsey, Flatey, and Melrakkaey; and special natural phenomena, like the geyser in Haukadalur and the geyser Grýta, the hot springs area of Hveravellir and in the central part of the highland, and the volcano Grabrok in Borgarfjordur and the Eldborg by Drottning on Hellisheidi together with several other craters.

The Nature Conservation Council has also discussed a large number of issues and projects concerning conservation and protection. It is sufficient to mention here its intervention over Myvatn, Laxá and the þjórsár-basin at the threat of engineering works that could have had an effect on the environment and life in these unique bird breeding areas.

Furthermore, district societies for protection of nature and their associations have been founded, and these have particularly taken in hand the protection of regions within specific fields. These nature protection agencies have become involved especially with protection on the district level of unique natural features or local regions in Iceland.

ADVANCES IN ECOLOGICAL STUDIES

The science of ecology and environmental research is relatively new in Iceland. As previously mentioned, many of the earlier scientists had an overall view of natural sciences and described the harmony of land, flora, and fauna, as well as utilization of the natural resources by humans and their subsistence in the country. In the first part of the twentieth century, there was a period of specialization of scientific studies in the classical disciplines. It was not until the 1960s and 1970s that ecological approaches were practiced in scientific research in Iceland. However, it may be considered that some of the early marine biological studies were ecological, such as the studies of food chains, population size, and development of fish by Bjarni Sæmundsson, Árni Fridriksson, and Hermann Einarsson in the first half of this century. Similarly, there were studies of behavior, migration, and feeding habits of birds even in the late nineteenth century. The Swedish entomologist Carl H. Lindroth investigated the invertebrate fauna of Iceland in 1930, partly from an ecological standpoint. In the early 1940s, the Danish zoologist S. L. Tuxen carried out limnological studies of animal life in warm springs in Iceland using an ecological approach.

Some of the early botanical investigations were also ecological. Studies of zonation of the marine vegetation and the overwintering of plants were done by the botanist Helgi Jonsson; a classification of plant communities in Iceland was carried out by Mölholm Hansen, and later by Steindór Steindórsson, who studied the distribution of plants in Iceland and their association.

In 1962, a cooperative ecological study directed by C. H. Lindroth was carried out at Skaftafell in Öræfi in the vicinity of the glacier Vatnajökull in southeastern Iceland, a site which later became a national park. The expedition published the reports of this pioneer research work in the Scandinavian ecological journal *Oikos* in 1965.

On November 14, 1963, submarine volcanic activities started in the ocean south of Iceland that resulted in the formation of an island, later named Surtsey. This provided a unique ecological laboratory and aroused great interest among scientists both in Iceland and abroad. The island was protected for scientific research in 1965, and visits to it were restricted. The Surtsey Research Society was established to organize the scientific work on the island. During the island's first years of existence, extensive geologic study was performed followed by a major ecological program, which included the surrounding islands. The results are published in the Surtsey Research Society Reports.

However, it was not until after the middle of this century that an increased interest in the relationships of plants and animals with the environment arose, as well as interest in their communities as integrated ecological complexes. This ecological interest developed partly through marine research and the realization that the fish population had been over-exploited, and partly through studies in soil conservation problems and overgrazing of the native vegetation by sheep. At the same time, rapidly developing industrial activities with increased demands for hydroelectric power threatened many of the larger rivers with damming and the destruction of ecologically valuable areas, rare species, breeding grounds of birds, grazing areas for livestock, and scenic landscapes.

It was also realized that rapid industrialization brought increased dangers to the country's hitherto unpolluted environment. Iceland was taking part in various international activities concerned with the protection of nature. The general worldwide movement and interest in the protection of the environment came at an appropriate time and was readily received by Icelandic scientists and public.

Marine Research

The country's most valuable natural resources are the rich fishing grounds in the surrounding ocean. Marine research has been recognized as the highest priority in scientific research in Iceland. Understanding the development of marine organisms and fluctuations in their population sizes was considered a necessary prerequisite for proper management of the various commercially valuable marine species. It was the task of the Marine Research Institute to conduct the diverse oceanographic studies. It organized a broad survey and, since 1958, regular measurements have been taken all around Iceland, covering hydrographic and plankton recordings, as well as studies of fertility of various species, their rate of growth, and abundance of year classes.

By measuring the potential plankton productivity, energy flow, and efficiency of conversion of the plankton at various steps in the food web, and by following the flow toward the larger predatory organisms at the far end of the food chain, researchers have obtained an overall ecological view of the natural processes involved and have demonstrated the decisive factors acting on the whole ecological pyramid of marine life in these northern waters.

Marine researchers demonstrated that the large stock of the Atlanto-Scandinavian herring was depleted in the late 1960s by overfishing and unfavorable environmental conditions, and these researchers warned that the same fate was threatening the cod stock. They advised the government to put fishing on a national basis and enforce a total allowable catch of cod. This was a difficult step to take, since it conflicted with both local and foreign enterprise. To enforce these measures, Iceland extended its fishing limits to two hundred miles.

Agriculture and Land Management

The task of the Agricultural Research Institute was to investigate soil erosion and grazing management problems. Many of the Icelandic soils are of volcanic origin and, following the destruction of the woodland and deterioration of the grassland from overgrazing by the livestock, these were readily eroded by wind and water. This devastation was furthermore accelerated by the deterioration of the climate in the 1800s and 1900s and by the effect of ash fall from erupting volcanoes. During the eleven hundred years since man discovered Iceland and settled there, approximately half of the original vegetation cover has been lost. At the same time, there has been a drastic change in the composition of plant species in vegetated areas. Icelandic agriculture depends largely on the open rangeland; therefore, it was extremely important to find means to stop erosion, measure the carrying capacity of the rangeland, and find methods to improve the grassland and increase its fodder production. Similarly, winter-killing of grass on Icelandic hayfields is a complex problem. In some years, winter-killing takes a heavy toll of the country's annual haycrop, thus necessitating an ecological investigation of soils, vegetation, pathology, management, and climatic conditions.

Various societies and youth organizations have assisted the Soil Conservation Project in reclamation work, and wide public interest has been aroused for the protection of vegetation. In 1969, a society was founded to continue to support this national interest; this later became the Icelandic Environment Union (Landvernd). The society encouraged public participation in nature conservation and has played an active part in organizing campaigns for cleaning up the countryside and in advocating better environmental management. It has organized various conferences and seminars on environmental problems and published valuable informative booklets on the same subject that have been widely distributed in the country.

This national movement for conservation of soil and vegetation was highlighted in 1974 by a statute of the Althing to commemorate the eleven hundred years of Icelandic settlement in the country. This statute set aside a part of the annual budget for the next five years to be used for soil conservation and reclamation. Part of these funds were used by the Agricultural Research Institute to support ecological studies in connection with soil erosion and land improvement. It launched programs to study the effect of application of large amounts of fertilizers on the vegetation and animal life in sandy areas, and the effect of extensive draining of bogs.

In 1977, the Agricultural Society realized the need for an increased knowledge of proper land utilization and better land management, and included such a program in its extension service.

INDUSTRY AND POWER NEEDS

The major industrialization and technological development of modern times have upset the harmony of natural processes and caused more disturbances in the various ecosystems than ever before encountered. To this end, it has been the responsibility of the National Energy Authority to provide the country with electricity. This has been done by harnessing the water power of numerous rivers or by using geothermal energy. However, in these processes, many ecologically valuable areas are being threatened. Preparatory studies have been performed at the proposed sites of future dams and in reservoir areas. The resulting conflict between ecologists, landowners, and engineers over the use of such land has delayed some plans and curtailed others such as the damming of the river Laxá in northern Iceland. It is believed that damming this river would have posed a severe threat to salmon fishing and destroyed the vegetation and animal life in one of Iceland's most scenic valleys.

Similarly, a huge dam project in the upper parts of Thjórsá, the longest glacial river in Iceland, would inundate the large interior oasis of Thjórsárver, which is the largest known breeding ground for the pink-footed goose (*Anser brachyrhynchus*). The project is not being continued for the moment, and the area is under investigation by ecologists using models and computers.

Other projects also being studied from an ecological point of view are such proposed dams as that of the river Blanda in northern Iceland and the lowland near Lake Lagarfljot in eastern Iceland. Such damming programs and the opposition they have met have shown the necessity of having a thorough ecological investigation of an area before decisions are made to proceed with major engineering and construction activities that may reshape the landscape and have various side effects on the environment. The National Energy Authority, the Road Construction Authority, and other major construction bodies have lately met this challenge by requesting thorough ecological surveys of proposed building sites of highways, power plants, and dams before engineering activities are started.

INDUSTRY AND POLLUTION

In the early twentieth century, there was limited industrialization in Iceland, and the small discharge of pollutants from fish processing plants and slaughterhouses was of an organic nature. The middle of the century brought a marked change, however, with the introduction of heavy industry. A nitrogen fertilizer factory near Reykjavík, a cement factory, a factory for production of diatomaceous earth from Lake Myvatn, and an aluminum smelter near Reykjavík all had some effect on their immediate environment.

The aluminum smelter, jointly owned and operated by the Icelandic Aluminum Company and Alusuisse, emitted fluoride into the environment. Its polluting effect has been investigated since 1969 by a fluorine commission appointed both by the government and the company. The commission confirmed that the fluorine content in the vegetation in the plant's vicinity has increased markedly since the factory started operating.

This new threat of industrial pollution to the environment aroused a strong reaction from the public and a demand for the protection of the clean water, soil, and air of Iceland. Various antipollution measures have been carried out, as has ecological research in the vicinity of some of the factories. Thus, scientific studies have been made on the effects of the diatom factory and its increased accompanying human activity on the ecosystem in and around Lake Myvatn. This study was considered necessary to protect the whole area partly because of its natural beauty, and partly for its importance for trout fishing and as a breeding place for many European ducks. A report on this study is given in the Scandinavian ecological journal *Oikos* in 1978. Prior to that, only a few limnological studies had been performed, but from 1971 onward, several other lakes and rivers were the subjects of studies, such as Lake Thingvellavatn, the largest lake in Iceland, which is partly situated in the oldest national park in Iceland.

It is now compulsory for all major industrial plants to have an operation permit from the Ministry of Health, subject to rather strict regulations and terms to secure a clean environment and the greatest possible level of sanitation in the factory. This is in accordance with order No. 164 of 1972 concerning protection against pollution by poisonous and dangerous substances, and Act No. 85 of 1968 concerning the handling of poisonous and dangerous substances. The abovementioned permit also stipulates the support by industry of an ecological study in the immediate environment.

POLLUTION CONTROL

In spite of this new industrialization, pollution in Iceland is minimal. However, sometimes during southerly winds, industrial smog may be carried to Iceland by air masses coming from the continent of Europe. During such weather conditions, a low acidity has been measured in the precipitation. A regular survey of air pollutants is carried out by the Icelandic Meteorological Service. The program was originally launched by the Organization for Economic Cooperation and Development as the cooperative work of many European countries, in which Iceland participated with other Nordic nations under the supervision of Nordforsk. Similarly, Nordforsk has organized multiple research in the Nordic countries including pollution in rivers and lakes. This survey was carried out in Iceland by the Industrial Research and Development Institute in the Ellidaá and Ölfusá-Hvítár river basins.

For the protection of the marine environment, Iceland has ratified and implemented international agreements on measures aiming at minimizing marine pollution. Regarding oil pollution, Iceland has ratified the 1954 Convention on the Prevention of Oil Pollution of the Sea, as well as the 1962 and 1969 amendments thereto. These very well known conventions focus on operational discharges of oil from ships. In order to extend the same principles as outlined in these conventions to other possible oil polluters of the sea, national regulation No. 8, from 1971, prohibits any deliberate discharge of oil or oily residue from land-based sources, such as storage stations for oil, oil loading terminals, and other industrial activities, into the Icelandic marine environment.

Iceland has also figured prominently in international work related to the global convention on the prevention of marine pollution by dumping of wastes and other matter (London Dumping Convention), as well as the regional Oslo Dumping Convention on the same subject. These conventions have both been ratified and implemented in Iceland. The Icelandic government institution responsible both internally and internationally for the prevention of oil pollution of the sea, as well as for the global convention on dumping, is the Directorate of Shipping, Reykjavík.

The increased usage of various synthetic and toxic materials in modern society is dangerous to a large number of life forms and upsets natural balances; therefore, great caution must be exercised in the handling of these poisons, and care taken regarding cleanliness, so that the environment will not be impaired. In Iceland, the legislature has tried to secure a clean and healthy environment by passing various acts. According to Act No. 12 from 1969, the health committees in various districts are responsible for sanitation control under the direction of the National Institute of Environmental Health. The health committees are concerned with various environmental and health problems, such as securing a healthy environment in and around human habitats, air and water sanitation, and disposal of wastes, sewage, and all pollutants including water.

As previously mentioned, the Institute of Environmental Health issues operation licenses, according to regulation No. 164, 1972, to factories to secure a healthy environment in their respective vicinities and to prevent emission of poisonous materials. The institute is a member of the Nordic Technical Environmental Control Committee and cooperates with the committee in research and techniques in pollution control. A special committee on toxic substances also deals with the use of poisonous pesticides. It regulates imports and issues permits to those allowed to handle such substances, for example, insecticides against agricultural pests or poisons in rodent control.

EDUCATION

The teaching of natural sciences at the lower levels in Icelandic schools has recently been revised to include an introduction to ecological approaches, where pupils are, for example, trained to carry out limnological studies and introduced to various problems in relation to special ecosystems.

At the junior college level, the students receive a general ecological training by reading Icelandic translations of international textbooks or an Icelandic volume. In addition, the students are advised to read various local articles and books on ecology in Iceland.

Ecology was introduced as an independent field of study at the university level in 1970, and a professoriate in Ecological Sciences was established in 1973. Courses are offered in general ecology, plant sociology, and geobotany, as well as in marine and freshwater ecology. Ecological seminars are also offered. The students get practical training in fieldwork and are particularly acquainted with such ecosystems as those of tidal zones, rivers and lakes, or various dry land communities.

Field excursions are organized by the university, and it has an access to a field station at Lake Myvatn. Special study projects are supervised by scientists at institutes dealing with the respective ecological problem. The university's Institute of Biology organizes ecological surveys of special areas in which undergraduate and graduate students may participate. Some of these projects are undertaken at the request of the Icelandic Nature Conservation Council.

Study toward a B.S. degree in biology normally takes three years. If one more year is added, the student is awarded a degree comparable to the British B.S. Honors degree.

SCIENTIFIC JOURNALS

The Icelandic Natural Sciences Society has published a journal of natural sciences, *Náttúrufræðingurinn,* since 1931. In it have appeared a number of articles on ecological subjects, especially on soil erosion, grazing, and various plant and animal associations. The articles are in Icelandic with English summaries.

Scientists in northern Iceland, in cooperation with the Museum of Natural History at Akureyri and Neskaupstadur, launched the biannual journal *Tyli* in 1971. It publishes papers on natural sciences with special emphasis on ecological subjects, environmental problems, and on protection of nature.

The Glaciological Society publishes the journal *Jökull,* which covers mostly geologic and glaciologic matter, but includes ecological and environmental subjects, such as the effect of drift ice on the Icelandic ecosystem.

The Museum of Natural Sciences has published *Acta Naturalia Islandica* since 1946. This journal has covered ecological subjects such as plant geography, feeding habits of sea gulls, habitat preferences of some intertidal amphipods in Iceland, and the effects of volcanic outbreaks on the environment.

The Institute of Freshwater Fishing publishes miscellaneous papers on limnology and studies of fish management in Icelandic lakes and rivers.

The Marine Research Institute has published various results of marine research in its journal *Rit Fiskideildar* since 1940 and in its annual reports *Hafrannsoknir* since 1968. Miscellaneous mimeographic papers (*Fjölrit*) appeared during 1952–1956 and again since 1975. In these are presented articles on marine ecological problems covering hydrographic and marine biological studies.

More popular articles on marine research appear in *Ægir* published by the Fisheries Association of Iceland and in other local journals.

The Forestry Society has published Arsrit (annual reports) since it was established in 1930. The first issue covers the years 1930–1933. The reports include articles on the management of forests, the use of forests as public parks, land use, erosion problems and various ecological subjects of Icelandic forests.

The National Energy Authority (Orkustofnun) and the State Electric Power Works (Rafmagnsveitur ríkisins) have published various papers on miscellaneous subjects relevant to the programs for harnessing water power and geothermal energy. These cover, among other things, reports on geological, hydrological, biological and soil studies, some of which are of ecological nature and have been performed in collaboration with other institutes. In a few cases, specific studies have been organized and reported on at the request of different departments of the government.

The Icelandic Metereological Office publishes monthly and annually summaries of weather observation in *Iceland Veðráttan* and popular articles on climatic conditions and their effects appear in the journal *Veðrið*.

Occasional popular articles on grazing management, land utilization and erosion problems may appear in the farmers' journal *Freyr* published by the Icelandic Agricultural Society.

The Agricultural Research Institute has published reports since 1938 and the *Journal of Agricultural Research in Iceland* since 1969, as well as miscellaneous papers that include plant sociological and ecological subjects in relation to agriculture. The Icelandic Science Society (Societas Scientiarum Islandics) publishes, among others, *Rit* (since 1923) and *Greinar* (since 1935) covering reports on, for example, plant sociology, bird habitats, and effects of volcanic eruptions.

The Surtsey Research Society has published the *Surtsey Research Progress Report* since 1964. It has covered all research carried out on the volcanic island Surtsey since the eruption in 1963, and includes various ecological subjects.

The Research Institute Nedri-Ás, Hveragerdi, has sent out its reports since 1969 on such problems as winter-killing and plant sociology.

The Akureyri Museum of Natural History has published mimeographed reports since 1971, including reports on limnology and pollution.

BIBLIOGRAPHY

Of note are the four volumes published in Icelandic by the Icelandic Environment Union (Landvernd):

Mengun. 1971. A collection of papers on pollution.
Grodurvernd. 1972. A treatise on erosion and range management by Ingvi Thorsteinsson.
Landnýting. 1973. A collection of twenty-three papers on different land uses in Iceland.
Votlendi. 1975. A collection of papers, edited by Arnthor Gardarsson, on subjects concerning formation, life, and use of bogs and other wetlands in Iceland.

Other noteworthy articles and books include:

Bjarnason, Ágúst. 1975. *Almenn vistfræði*. Reykjavík: Iðunn.
Einarsson, Markús Á., ed. 1969. *Hafisinn*. Almenna bókafélagið, Reykjavík. (A book in Icelandic with articles on sea ice and its various effects.)
Einarsson, Thorleifur. 1968. *Jarðfræði*. Saga bergs og lands. Mál og menning, Reykjavík, 335 pp. (A book on Icelandic geology.)
Eythorsson, Jón and Hlynur Sigtryggsson. 1971. The climate and weather of Iceland. The Zoology of Iceland. Reykjavík, 62 pp.
Fridriksson, Sturla. 1973. *Lif og land*. Reykjavík: Vardi. (A book on ecology in Iceland, written in Icelandic, covering mainly terrestrial ecology and soil erosion problems.)
Fridriksson, Sturla. 1975. *Surtsey, Evolution of Life on a Volcanic Island*. London: Butterworths. (Describes the volcanic activities of the newly formed island, Surtsey, and associations of various life forms and developments in the island's ecosystem.
Iceland, A Human Environment Sensitive to Climatic Changes. A contribution by the Ministry of Foreign Affairs, Iceland, to the United Nations Conference on the Human Environment, Stockholm. June 1972 (mimeographic 48 pp.).
Karlsson, Thorbjörn, ed. 1972. *Sea Ice* 1972. Proc. Int. Conv., Reykjavík National Research Council, 72–4. (With articles on sea ice.)
Stefansson, Unnsteinn. 1961. *Hafið*, Almenna bókafélagið, Reykjavík.
Stefansson, Unnsteinn. 1962. *North Icelandic Waters*. Rit Fiskideildar III. (Describes conditions in Icelandic waters.)
Steindórsson, Steindór. 1964. *Gróður á Íslandi*. Almenna bókafélagið, Reykjavík. (In Icelandic. A description of the associations of higher plants in Iceland.)

Articles of pertinence include:

Fridriksson, Sturla. 1969. The effects of sea ice on flora, fauna and agriculture. *Jökull* 19:146–157. (Discusses problems of ecological nature effected by climatic changes.)
Fridriksson, Sturla. 1972. Grass and grass utilization in Iceland. *Ecology* 53:785–796. (Deals with erosion problems and its effect on the productivity of the ecosystem and the human population.)
Jakobsson, Jakob. 1978. The north Icelandic herring fishery and environmental conditions 1960–1968. ICES. Symp. Biol. Basis Pelagic Fish Stock Management, 30.
Jónsson, Pétur M., Aðalsteinsson, Hákon, Hunding, Carsten, Lindegaard, Claus,

and Jón Ólafsson. 1977. Limnology of Iceland. *Folia Limnologica Scand.* 17:111–1123.

Malmberg, Svend-Aage. 1979–80. Hydrographic conditions and fish stocks in Icelandic waters. *Ægir* 72–73, 7, 9, 11 and 4.

Thordardottir, Thorunn. 1977. Primary production in north Icelandic waters in relation to recent climatic changes. Polar Oceans, Proc. Pol. Oc. Conf. Montreal, 1974.

13

ITALY

Oscar Ravera

BACKGROUND

In Italy, the widespread study and teaching of pure and applied ecology is a recent phenomenon, occurring within the last ten years. Previously, ecological studies were done in a few institutes of entomology, zoology, botany, and limnology and were carried out by a few isolated researchers. As an example, V. Volterra (1926) developed one of the first mathematical models to be applied to quantitative ecology.

LITERATURE AND JOURNALS

Because of the lack of an ecological tradition, Italian books on the subject of ecology are very few and recently published; recent translations from French and English are generally adopted by university students.

Italian journals concerning the ecological field are the following: *Pubblicazioni della Stazione Zoologica di Napoli; Memorie dell'Istituto Italiano di Idrobiologia; Rivista d'Idrobiologia* (Perugia); *Bollettino di Pesca, Piscicoltura e Idrobiologia* (Roma); *Quaderni dell'Istituto di Ricerca sulle Acque (IRSA)* (Roma); *Pubblicazioni dell'Istituto Sperimentale Talassografico* (Trieste); *Inquinamento: Acqua, Aria e Suolo* (Milano); *Ingegneria ambientale, Inquinamento e Depurazione* (Politecnico Milano); *Giornale di Fisica Sanitaria e di Protezione contro le Radiazioni* (Torino); *Rivista di Parassitologia* (Messina); *Atti della Società Italiana di Biogeografia* (Siena); *Bollettino del Laboratorio di Entomologia Agraria* (Portici); *Annuali dell'Istituto Sperimentale per lo Studio e la Difesa del Suolo* (Firenze); *Memorie di Biologia Marina e di Oceanografia* (Messina); *Bollettino di Fitosociologia* (Bologna); and *Archivio di Oceanografia e Limnologia* (Venezia).

RESEARCH CENTERS

In 1872, the German scientist Anton Dohrn founded in Naples the first sea laboratory in the world, called Stazione Zoologica. He decided to establish a large public exhibition, Aquarium, and to finance the running of the planned institute for marine biology with the help of entrance fees. Soon thirty-eight scientific institutions and governments from all over the world participated in the "working tables" system of the Stazione Zoologica, in which work areas were rented in exchange for money. For more than one hundred years the Stazione Zoologica has been one of the most important centers in Europe for research in marine biology. Dohrn introduced three well-known publications: (1) *Mitteilungen der Zoologischen Station in Neapel* (now called *Pubblicazioni della Stazione Zoologica di Napoli*); (2) *Zoologischer Jahresbericht;* and (3) *Fauna und Flora des Golfes von Neapel.*

After the First World War, the station was brought under the control of the Italian Ministry of Education, but the direction and administration lay in the hands of Anton's son Reinhard. The library of the Zoological Station is the most comprehensive international library for marine biology in Europe. Attached to the Zoological Station is the Department of Ecological Research at Porto d'Ischia (Naples).

In 1938, Mrs. Rosa Curioni De Marchi founded at Pallanza on the shore of Lake Maggiore (northern Italy) an institute of hydrobiology called Istituto Italiano di Idrobiologia Marco De Marchi. Since 1977, this institute has become one of the institutes of CNR (National Research Council). The first director was E. Baldi (1939–1951), followed by V. Tonolli (1951–1967). Tonolli was succeeded by his wife, L. Tonolli (1967–1979), and at present the director is E. Grimaldi. The research carried out in this institute during the last 40 years has been concerned with the most important topics in limnology, with particular emphasis on the lakes of northern Italy. Twenty scientists and more than twenty technicians constitute the staff of the institute. The library, specialized in limnology, contains 4,773 books, 712 journals, and 39,728 publications. The publications of the institute are collected in the journal *Memorie dell'Istituto Italiano di Idrobiologia*. Thirty-eight volumes have been published to date. Each year Italian and foreign scientists carry out research in this institute which has been the school for almost all Italian limnologists.

More recently, in 1954, the Istituto di Idrobiologia of Perugia was founded. The first director was G. P. Moretti, later succeeded by Giannotti. The research work of this institute is mainly concerned with the Lake Trasimeno (central Italy).

In the most important cities, studies concerning ecology are carried out in museums and aquaria, such as the Museo Civico di Scienze Naturali of Verona, Milan, and Venice, and the Acquario Civico e Stazione Idrobiologica of Milan. Some small institutes for the study of marine biology and fishery are located along the Thyrrenian and Adriatic Sea.

In addition, the Centro di Ecologia, attached to the University of Parma, was recently founded and is directed by A. Moroni. The aims of this center are the development of the theoretical and practical studies in the ecology and the diffusion of ecological principles by courses and seminars.

The effects of pollutants on aquatic organisms is the most important aim of the research carried out by the Istituto di Ricerca sulle Acque (IRSA), CNR, directed by R. Marchetti and established at Brugherio (Milan).

For more than thirty years, the laboratory of CISE (Centro Informazioni Studi ed Esperienze) in Milan has carried out advanced research in the radioecological field in marine, terrestrial, and flowing water environments. Studies in the same field are carried out by the Laboratorio per lo Studio della Radioattività Ambientale CNEN (National Committee for Nuclear Energy) in Rome and the Laboratorio per il Controllo della Radioattività del Mare, Fiascherino (northern Italy).

Other important institutes, stations, and research centers in which ecological research is carried out are the following: Laboratorio Centrale di Idrobiologia, Roma; Istituto di Ecologia dell'Università di Parma; Istituto di Idrobiologia e Piscicultura dell'Università di Messina; Istituto di Selvicoltura dell'Università di Padova; Laboratorio di Ricerche Ambientali ENEL, Trino (Vercelli) and Milan; Ufficio Centrale Ecologia Agraria del Ministero Agricoltura e Foreste, Roma; Istituto Superiore di Sanità, Roma; Istituto di Ricerca sulle Acque (IRSA) CNR, Bari and Roma; Istituto di Biologia del Mare CNR, Venezia; Laboratorio di Tecnologia della Pesca CNR, Ancona; Laboratorio di Radiochimica ed Ecofisiologia Vegetale CNR, Roma; and Centro di Genetica ed Ecologia Quantitative CNR, Bologna.

More recently some important industries have established ecological departments with the main purpose of studying air and water pollution and improving methods of reducing environmental pollution.

The efforts of the region Emilia-Romagna (northern Italy) in studying and reducing pollution levels in the Adriatic Sea should be mentioned. For example, last year this region established a small Institute of Marine Biology at Cesenatico on the Adriatic Sea.

EDUCATION

In 1924, at the University of Perugia, the first Chair of Ecology was established. Very recently about twenty chairs of ecology have been established at the following universities: Florence (ecology, forestry, plant ecology), Genova (hydrobiology, fish culturing), Messina (hydrobiology, fish culturing, marine biology), Milan (ecology), Padova (ecology, zoogeography, animal ecology), Parma (animal ecology), Pavia (ecology, animal ethology), Perugia (hydrobiology, fish culturing), Rome (human ecology, ecology, animal ethology), Siena (hydrobiology, fish culturing, ecology) and Trieste (plant ecology).

Although in the universities the introduction of courses concerning the environment is only recent, there are thirty-eight courses distributed over nineteen universities as follows: Bari (ecology, agricultural ecology, forestry), Bologna (ecology, agricultural ecology), Camerino (ecology), Ferrara (ecology), Florence (plant ecology, phytogeography, forestry), Genova (animal ecology), L'Aquila (ecology, phytogeography), Messina (ecology), Milan (ecology, phytogeography, hydrobiology, fish culturing), Padova (phytogeography, plant ecology, zoogeography, animal ecology, hydrobiology, fish culturing), Parma (ecology, animal ecology), Pavia (animal ecology, ethology, phytogeography, plant ecology), Perugia (ecology), Pisa (agricultural ecology), Pontificia Universitas Lateranensis (ecology), Rome (ecology, animal ecology, ethology, human ecology, plant ecology, zoogeography), Siena (ecology), Turin (ecology, agricultural ecology, prehistoric ecology), and Venice (ecology).

ECOLOGICAL SOCIETIES AND GROUPS

The most important national societies involved in ecology are Associazione Italiana di Oceanologia e di Limnologia (AIOL), Società Italiana di Biogeografia, and Gruppo di Ecologia della Società Botanica Italiana.

In 1976, SITE (Società Italiana di Ecologia, Italian Society of Ecology) was founded. At present, the president is A. Buzzati-Traverso, the vice-president O. Ravera, and the secretary F. Bruno (Istituto di Botanica, Università di Roma). This society is structured on the basis of working groups and has the following aims: promoting both theoretical and applied ecological research; diffusing ecological knowledge; and collaborating with national and foreign societies, agencies, and organizations involved in the ecological field. Today there are more than one hundred Italian members, but the society is also open to foreign scientists. In October 1980, SITE will organize the First Italian Congress of Ecology (Salsomaggiore, northern Italy).

In 1970, some scientists in Milan founded the Gruppo di Ecologia di base G. Gadio, for the development in Italy of research and training in the field of fundamental ecology.

RESEARCH SUPPORT

At present the greatest part of Italian research is supported by the CNR (National Research Council) and considerable support for the ecological studies is given by the same council by means of oriented programs: "Programmi finalizzati per la promozione della qualità dell'ambiente." This program consists of five projects, namely, (1) description of ecosystems; (2) water; (3) air; (4) soil; and (5) mathematical methodology. Started in 1976, this program is in progress and is carried out in collaboration with ministries, public administrators, universities, and industries.

INTERNATIONAL ACTIVITIES

Italian researchers and organizations involved in ecology have had connections in various ways with the following organizations and agencies: CEC, OECD, UNESCO, WHO, NATO, IAEA, and UNEP. Also, Italian collaboration with the UNESCO Program, Man and the Biosphere (MAB), is noteworthy.

The Research Center of Ispra (Varese, northern Italy) belongs to the abovementioned organization CEC (Commission of the European Communities). It is the largest of the four establishments composing the JRC (Joint Research Center), and its staff amounts to seventeen hundred employees of whom eight hundred are researchers and technicians. The main areas of its research programs are nuclear safety, new energies, and environment and resources.

In addition, the program Education and Training is implemented through the organization of courses and seminars (Ispra Courses). Since 1976, seven courses concerning environmental problems have been organized. Most of the studies of the program Environment and Resources are carried out in Italy, in part with the collaboration of Italian universities and firms. This program started in 1972 and, with several modifications, will continue until 1984. It consists of projects concerning anthropogenic contribution to particle formation in the air and dispersion of pollutants; eutrophication processes; biological indicators; marine pollution detected by means of satellites; data bank of environmental pollutants; ecological and biochemical effects of heavy metals; heavy metals from fossil-fueled power plants; and soil moisture and heat balance studied by satellites. The aim of this program and that of external contracts of the CEC (Indirect Actions), is to give a scientific support to the actions of the commission in the environmental field.

GENERAL COMMENT

Finally, as has been mentioned, ecological research and teaching in Italy is not very diffuse and rich, but in recent years, some efforts in this field have been made. One of the most important events promoting the collaboration among Italian ecologists was the discussions of basic concepts and points of view of the environmental sciences at the first and second Colloquia of Ecology, held at the University of Parma (Institute of Ecology) in 1974 and 1976, respectively.

REFERENCE CITED

Volterra, V. 1926. Variazioni e fluttuazioni del numero di individui in specie animali conviventi. *Mem. Acad. Lincei.* 6:31–113.

14

THE NETHERLANDS

AQUATIC ECOLOGY

Karel F. Vaas*

Marine Hydrobiology

During the nineteenth century, considerable faunistic, floristic, and taxonomic research was done in the coastal zone and inland waters of the Netherlands. The first investigations of ecological significance concerned fishery problems. In 1884 (Anonymous), a committee of the Nederlandse Dierkundige Vereniging (NDV) (Netherlands Zoological Society), published a report in Dutch on oysters and oyster culture. This report contains data on ecology and sexuality of the oyster.

Hydrobiological work received a strong stimulus from the Zuiderzeewet (Zuderzee law) passed by parliament in 1918. This law ordered the reclamation of a large brackish-water bay (3,450 km²) in the center of the country. The NDV reacted with a plan for a description of the rich living community in the region. In 1922, a report was published under the title, *Flora en Fauna der Zuiderzee, Monografie van een Brakwatergebied* (Flora and Fauna of the Zuiderzee, Monograph of a Brackish-Water Region) by H. C. Redeke (1922) as editor, with contributions from twenty biologists. This work, intended as an inventory, showed elements of ecology in the modern sense insofar as zones

*Deceased April 28, 1980.

with different salinity were distinguished with their characteristic species. This brackish-water classification system designed by Redeke has since served internationally until the thirteenth Congress (1956) of the Société Internationale Limnologique at Helsinki, where the system was acknowledged as a landmark in brackish-water research and factually as its beginning.

Twenty years after the closing of the Zuiderzee in 1932, the work was followed up by a report, *Veranderingen in de Flora en Fauna van de Zuiderzee (thans Ysselmeer) na de afsluiting* (Changes in the Flora and Fauna of the Zuiderzee [Now Lake Yssel] after the Closing). Edited by L. F. de Beaufort (1954), this work, intended as a description just as its predecessor, also contained important indications about the ecology of both vanishing and newly colonizing species.

Comparable initiatives were taken after catastrophic floodings (about 2,000 km^2) in the delta region of the Netherlands in 1953. The government decided to close several estuaries in this area by dikes (721 km^2). In 1957, a special institute was founded to follow the hydrobiological consequences of this large-scale operation. This Delta Instituut voor Hydrobiologisch Onderzoek (Delta Institute for Hydrobiological Research) is far better equipped than the Zuiderzee Committee of 1920, but its object is far more complex. Moreover, its work is not restricted to the distribution and ecology of distinct species, but concerns whole ecosystems of open and closed estuaries, sometimes transformed into stagnant salt or brackish lakes. In this type of work, concepts such as primary and secondary production (referring to the carbon cycle) and turnover of nutrients are applied (Wolff 1973, 1976, 1977; Nienhuis 1970; Vegter 1976). K. Vaas (1975) studied migrating species and fishes. Investigations on the ecology of separate species were published by C. den Hartog (1964) on proseriate flatworms, S. Parma (1977) on chironomids, and on the alga *Rhizoclonium riparium* (Roth.) Harv. by P. H. Nienhuis (1975).

The Wadden Sea, between the Frisian Islands in the north and the Zuiderzee dike in the south, is another important subject for hydrobiologists in the Netherlands. The Wadden area represents a large tidal zone of about 10,000 km^2 divided over the Netherlands and the Helgoland Bight extending into Danish waters. In the nineteenth century, research work was done there by members of the NDV. In 1890, this society succeeded in establishing a zoological station near the harbor of den Helder at the southwest edge of the Wadden region. In the beginning, this work was mainly faunistic and taxonomic but, during the 1920s, more attention was gradually paid to the physiology and ecology of sea organisms, and especially during summer courses for university students. W. H. van Dobben (1935) studied jaw mechanisms of fishes from a functional point of view. In 1931, J. Verwey became director of the station, strongly promoting ecological observations on species of the tidal zone. G. J. Broekhuysen (1936) described development, growth, and distribution of *Carcinides* (= *Carcinus*) *maenas* (L.). D.

Kreger (1940) and I. Kristensen (1957) studied *Cardium edule* L., and M. Broekema (1941) published a report on seasonal movements and osmotic behavior of the shrimp. Much later, this work was continued by D. H. Spaargaren (1971). Work on elver migration was initiated before the war and finally published by F. Creutzberg (1961), who also worked on crab migration (1973). J. Verwey (1942) studied periodicity and displacement of jellyfish. During the same period, P. Korringa (1941) worked in the delta region on juvenile stages and setting of the oyster in relation to fishery problems. Much of the work from this period was published after World War II, e.g., studies of Verwey (1954) on the ecology of cockles and mussels and on the migration of sea animals (1958).

After the war, the station was transformed into the Nederlands Instituut voor het Onderzoek der Zee (NIOZ) (Netherlands Institute for Sea Research) by an extension of the program to several oceanic problems in a purely scientific context. It was transferred to Texel Island, where a new laboratory was built. The research program now encompasses autecological investigations and ecosystems research as well. A number of groups study several aspects of marine life: H. Postma (1961) has published reports on primary production, J. J. Beukema (1976) on biomass of macrobenthic animals, H. J. Vosjan (1977) and G. C. Cadée (1977) on microbial processes. Much of this NIOZ work on production has been summarized in the final report of the Netherlands contribution to IBP issued in 1974.

It has been established that production in the Wadden Sea is enhanced considerably by the import of organic matter from the North Sea. Further investigations intend to quantify the significance of the Wadden Sea for the growth of juvenile fish of species that are important for North Sea fisheries (J. J. Zijlstra 1972) and for the food supply of migrating birds. An April count in the Netherlands part of the area showed one million birds, including waders, ducks, and gulls, feeding along shores and tidal flats (G. C. Boere et al., 1973). Boere has also established that many arctic, subarctic, and boreal species accomplish their moult or at least the moult of distinct feather parties during a stay in the Wadden region. The status of several of these species clearly depends on the Wadden Sea as a food and rest area, and as an important winter quarter as well.

At NIOZ, much research work is done on the import of silt, nutrients (such as phosphate), and toxic substances (heavy metals, chlorinated hydrocarbons) carried by large rivers, especially the Rhine, into the North Sea. A substantial part enters the Wadden Sea, causing eutrophication and serious damage to wildlife. During the 1960s, the population of sandwich terns dropped from several ten thousands of pairs to six hundred pairs because of chlorinated hydrocarbon discharges into the Rhine estuary (J. H. Koeman, 1971).

NIOZ investigations on the autecology of sea organisms have been published by P. de Wolf on *Balanus* larvae (1973), G. C. Cadée on *Arenicola marina* L. (1976), J. J. Beukema on *Macoma baltica* (L.) (1976), K. Everards on *Mytilis edulis* (L.) (1973), B. R. Kuipers on *Pleuronectes platessa* (L.) (1973), and C. Swennen on the eider duck (*Somateria mollissima* L. (1977). J. Dorgelo, of the University of Amsterdam, works on salt tolerance in crustaceans (1978).

The discharges of wastewater into the Wadden Sea is being investigated by separate research groups, especially formed for the purpose. Discharges by agro-industries (potato flour, straw cardboard) consist mainly of organic matter with crude protein. The role of bacteria during natural purification and the effect of benthic diatoms are being studied by working groups of the University of Gronigen. Fieldwork is supplemented by laboratory experiments with continuous cultures. The effects on the Wadden ecosystem at large are also under investigation (Essink 1978). (For further discussion see the section below on Microbial Ecology.)

Applied work on fisheries is now a responsibility of the institute on fishery research (RIVO) at Ymuiden. Here, the dynamics of fish stocks are studied: P. Korringa (1970) published a report on shellfish farming, and N. Daan (1975) one on the ecology of the cod (*Gadus morrhua* L.). Recently, extensive research work on the ecology of algae in marine and brackish habitats has been initiated by Dutch scientists, especially in the Universities of Leiden and Nygmegen under the direction of C. den Hartog (1973), the University of Groningen under the direction of C. van den Hoek (1970, 1975), and the Free University, Amsterdam, under M. Vroman. At the University of Groningen, P. J. G. Polderman studied algal communities (1976), H. Rietema *Bryopsis* species and *Derbesia teniussima* (de Not.) (1975), W. T. Stamm et al. *Phormidium* species (1975), and A. M. Cortel-Breman et al. *Acrosymphyton purpuriferum* (J. Ag.) Sjöst. and *Elachista fucicola* (Velt.) (1975). J. Simons, of the Free University, Amsterdam, studied the ecology of *Vaucheria* species (1976).

Limnology

Freshwater research has an old tradition in the Netherlands. The pioneer work of seventeenth-century scientists as J. Swammerdam and A. van Leeuwenhoek, the discoverer of microbes, was mainly devoted to water organisms. In 1927, W. Beyerinck, of the Agriculture University of Wageningen, presented a thesis on distribution and periodicity of phytoplankton in small oligotrophic fens in a heathland biotope. In 1948, a posthumous manuscript of H. C. Redeke (1948) was published. It summarized many observations on taxonomy and distribution of freshwater organisms with details of ecological importance.

In 1957, an institute for hydrobiology was established at Nieuwerslius with the special purpose of developing ecological research work in freshwater systems. Since 1968, it has operated under the name Limnologisch Instituut. Investigations are mainly focused on two lakes: an isolated deep sand pit (Vechten) and a shallow lake of the Frisian polder system (Tjeukemeer). The work is designed as ecosystems research in which primary and secondary production are studied in relation to the cycling of nutrients (Beattie 1978; Vijverberg 1976; Gulatie 1972, 1975; van Densen 1976). Adsorption of nutrients, especially phosphates to sediments; exchange between sediments and water; and the role of organisms in these processes were investigated by H. L. Golterman (1969) and Golterman and Clymo (1962). In addition, autecological and demographic work is carried out with some important species, notably by J. Vijverberg on *Daphnia* sp. (1976) and J. R. Moed on diatoms (1972,1975). The fieldwork is supplemented by experimental laboratory work with cultures of several plankton species and bacteria (see also section below on Bacterial Ecology). The program of the institute also has many points of contact with environmental problems, such as eutrophication and the special role of phosphate in the occurrence of algal bloom. The effect of thermal pollution from a recently established power plant at a Frisian lake (Bergumer meer), otherwise comparable with the Tjeukemeer, is under investigation.

The limnological laboratory of the University of Amsterdam is another center for fundamental research. Work with aquatic microsystems is developed here under the direction of J. Ringelberg; in this connection, K. Kersting (1973) studied energy flow in a *Daphnia* population. Fieldwork concerns stratification of lakes (R. Lingeman 1975) and diversity in phytoplankton systems (G. M. Hallegraeff 1976).

At the Laboratory of Microbiology of the University of Amsterdam, work on *Scenedesmus* is done under direction of L. Mur (1971). Competition and light-limited growth of algae are studied with the help of continuous cultures (1976). Light sensitivity seems to inhibit algal bloom (H. J. Gons 1977). Another working group of the University of Amsterdam is investigating the effect of thermal pollution on the life cycle of parasitic trematodes. At the Zoological Laboratory of the University of Amsterdam, the autecology of the water mite *Hydrachna conjecta* was studied by C. Davids (1973) and of *Gammarus tigrinus* Sxt. by S. Pinkster (1975). P. J. Schroevers (1966), P. Leentvaar (1967), and J. F. M. Geelen (1969) studied plankton systems with trophic differences. H. J. Over (1967) presented a thesis on the ecology of the amphibian liver fluke snail *Lymnea truncatula* Müll. At the Free University, Amsterdam, the ecology of *Limnea stagnalis* (L.) is being studied under direction of W. J. van der Steen (1973).

Hydrobiological Work Overseas

During colonial times and thereafter, scientists from the Netherlands have been active in Indonesia and the West Indies. Before World War II, the

Botanical Garden at Buitenzorg (Bogor), with its Zoological Museum and the Treub laboratory, was the most important center of biological research in the tropical zone. In Jakarta, the Laboratory for the Investigation of the Sea, with its seawater aquarium (Pasar Ikan), was a center of hydrobiological work. A. Sunier (1922) investigated brackish-water ponds used for fish growing. Phycological work has been summarized by J. S. Zaneveld (1951). Applied studies with regard to fishery and fish production were published by Vaas et al. (1949, 1953, 1959).

The Caribbean Marine Biological Institute (CARMABI) on the island of Curaçao was founded in 1955. Annually, the volumes containing the collected papers by the staff and visitors of CARMABI are representative of the ecologic, economic, and taxonomic studies of the locally occurring marine and brackish-water organisms [e.g., molluscs by H. E. Coomans (1958, 1969), crustaceans by L. B. Holthuis (1958), Polyplacophora by P. Kaas (1972), copepods by J. H. Stock (1973), and fish and fisheries by J. S. Zaneveld (1961)]. In another publication, *Studies on the Fauna of Curaçao and Other Caribbean Islands,* edited by P. Wagenaar Hummelinck (1940), special attention was given to faunistic, ecological studies of the saltwater lagoons of the Antillean islands. The breeding and feeding behavior of the flamingo (*Phoenicopterus ruber*) was investigated by J. Rooth (1965, 1969). The preservation of underwater life around the islands, as well as the establishment of submarine nature parks and trails, were stimulated beginning in the early 1950s by J. H. Westermann (1953) and since 1978 by the Foundation for the Establishment of National Parks in the Netherlands Antilles. Typology and production of algae on coral reefs in the Caribbean area were studied by J. W. B. Wanders et al. (1974) and C. van den Hoek, of the University of Groningen (1972, 1975).

Research work on the artificial Brokopondo reservoir in Surinam has been published by P. Leentvaar (1976) and J. van der Heide (1971).

TERRESTRIAL ANIMAL ECOLOGY

Kornelius Bakker

The Pioneers

Before the Second World War, ecology as a scientific discipline was already beginning to emerge in the Netherlands. In those days, the University of Leiden harbored a few scientists who had an open eye for the importance of studying organisms in their natural environment. The plant physiologist L. G. M. Baas Becking wrote in his classic book *Geobiologie* in 1934: "However precisely one might analyse the phenomena of life in the laboratory, the organism is bound to the earth and its vicissitudes are, hence, intertwined with those of the earth." The animal morphologist and theoretical biologist C. J. van der Klaauw promoted new developments in biology, and published a paper in 1936 in which he claimed a place for ecology amid the various disciplines of zoology (van der Klaauw 1936). Later, he became one of the most important initiators of ecology in the Netherlands. The gifted field biologist J. Verwey was first trained as a parasitologist in Leiden. He, too, belonged to the small group of zoologists that promoted Dutch ecology in its childhood (see further discussion in the section on Aquatic Ecology).

Of the research workers outside Leiden who contributed much to the emergence of ecology in the Netherlands, the animal physiologist H. J. Jordan, in Utrecht, realized that for animal functions to be fully understood, they had to be studied in the field.

An important initiative was taken in 1912 at Wageningen. G. Wolda, a teacher in mathematics who was interested in the significance of birds for the prevention of insect pests in woods, started a large-scale investigation on hole-nesting birds with the aid of nestboxes. He collected data on first eggs, clutch size, and fluctuations in numbers of titmice. Later, he was appointed ornithologist at the Plantenziektenkundige Dienst (Phytopathological Service) in his residence. In 1924, H. N. Kluyver, a young student of the Agricultural University at Wageningen, became his part-time assistant. In 1928, Kluyver joined the scientific staff of the service to work on the significance of birds for agriculture. He was one of the first workers in this field who realized that the naive approach which held that predation always leads to a lowered prey density was untenable. This was illustrated in his thesis "Biology and ecology of the starling during its reproductive period" (1933). In 1934, Kluyver assumed the work on hole-nesting birds from Wolda, and extended it to an example of modern research on population dynamics. The main results were published after World War II.

Other work done before the war, but published afterwards, was a study of W. H. van Dobben (1952) on the food of the cormorant. He observed that, from a roach population 6.5 percent of which was infected by the large tapeworm *Ligula intestinalis,* the fish captured by the birds showed a 30 percent infection. With Schierbeek (see below), M. F. Mörzer Bruijns was one of the first workers in the Netherlands to recommend research of the terrestrial life-community as a whole. In his thesis "On biotic communities" (1947), he gave examples of zoological inventories of some vegetation units.

The Rise of Ecology after the Second World War

During the war, most scientific activity was at a standstill. In 1948, a committee was formed to stimulate and coordinate biological research in one of the few more or less natural landscapes in the Netherlands, the dunes along the North Sea coast. The Stichting Wetenschappelijk Duinonderzoek (Foundation for Scientific Dune Research) established two field stations: Weevers' Duin on the island of Voorne, and Schellingerland on the island of Terschelling. They had, however, no permanent staff.

University of Leiden

Under C. J. van der Klaauw, the field of zoology at the University of Leiden was extended in 1947 with his student Niko Tinbergen as professor of ethology. Tinbergen may be considered as one of the founders of Dutch field biology, and his ethological work contained many ecological elements.

In 1950, D. J. Kuenen was appointed professor of animal ecology. Kuenen's main field of interest at the time was applied entomology. He initiated a line of research on the importance of predators for populations of phytophagous mites in orchards (1947, 1962). The role of foodplant quality for the development of fruit tree red spider mite populations was studied by his student A. Post (1962). The investigations of M. van de Vrie (1974) and, later, Fransz and Rabbinge at the Agricultural University are directly related to this (see below).

Kuenen was also interested in the problem of the ecological aspects of the development of resistance to insecticides, and in the adaptive characteristics for life on the land in the land isopods (1959). The significance of activity patterns in the woodlouse *Porcellio scaber* in relation to humidity and water balance was studied by his pupil P. J. den Boer (1961).

In the debate on the theories of the regulation of animal numbers, Kuenen (1958) drew attention to some sources of misunderstanding between the adherents of the different schools. He pointed out that in the famous example of *Thrips imaginis,* the increase of the population is correlated with weather factors, but the decrease is density dependent. Recently, a bibliography of Kuenen's work appeared (Bakker 1980).

Dune research had started long before the Second World War. The initiator was Schierbeek, who lectured on the history of biology, his main interest, at the University of Leiden. His studies on Van Leeuwenhoek and others made him famous. In addition, he started a large-scale and long-term research project on the flora and fauna of the dune area called Meijendel, near The Hague. This research project, started in 1923, was planned as an attempt to unravel the "web of life" of this unique ecosystem and was, therefore, very modern in its approach. Initially, the work was mainly restricted to an inventory of the flora and fauna. In 1952, the Meijendel research, which had been interrupted by the war, got a new impulse through an initiative of the Dune Water Company of The Hague, which intended to infiltrate the area with water from the Rhine to replenish the groundwater supply that was being exploited. This exploitation had been going on for about seventy-five years, and had changed the vegetation, flora, and fauna dramatically. The infiltration would again bring about changes, but these might now be studied. It was necessary to acquire information on the distribution and the abundance of animals before the infiltration started. Therefore, a large sampling program was carried out, initially under the guidance of P. J. den Boer, the results of which are still being worked out. An analysis of the distribution of wolfspiders has been given by P. J. M. van der Aart (1973) and by van der Aart and Smeenk-Enserink (1975) by means of principal component analysis, and of diplopods by C. A. Barlow (1957). Intra- and interspecific competition in shrews was studied by N. Croin Michielsen (1966), who showed that both species maintained intraspecific individual territories in winter, but that the territories of the two species overlapped. This is ascribed to a separation of the layers in which the species are active, an example of vertical habitat differentiation. New research on this problem by F. J. M. Ellenbroek (1979) demonstrated that this separation is not caused by direct competition between the species. The dominant *Sorex araneus* lives in the lower layer, which is richest in food and provides more protection. When *S. araneus* has been removed from enclosures, the density of *S. minutus* has remained the same. Also, in Ireland, where only *S. minutus* occurs, it occupies the same upper layers in the same densities as on the mainland.

G. J. de Bruyn (1978) and de Bruyn and Mabelis (1972) studied different aspects of ant ecology. They produced evidence that nest densities of the red wood ant are regulated by mutual predation during spring. In his study on the significance of wood ant wars, A. A. Mabelis (1979) showed that there is no behavioral difference between aggression and predation, and that the main function of these wars, in which thousands are victimized, is the provision of food for the queens and the brood in times when other prey is scarce.

G. De Bruyn (1980) published a model in which the conditions are given for the coexistence of competitors.

The relationship between ragwort (*Senecio jacobaea*) and its monophagous enemy, the cinnabar moth (*Tyria jacobaeae*), was described by E. van der Meijden (1971). Later, he showed (1979) that local populations of the biennial ragwort frequently become extinct and that new populations appear. The role of the herbivore, though important, is not generally decisive. The plant-herbivore system survives because of the heterogeneity of the dune environment and the heterogeneity of suitability of the plant populations.

On the occasion of the centennial of the Dune Water Company of The Hague in 1974, a book on the biological research in the area appeared (N. Croin Michielsen 1974).

When Kuenen left Leiden in 1970 to become director of the Rijksinstituut voor Natuurbeheer (RIN), his pupil K. Bakker succeeded him. Bakker's interest lies mainly in the evolutionary aspects of ecology. Hence, processes like competition, selection, and adaptation attracted him, as witnessed by his work on competition for food in larvae of *Drosophila* (1961, 1969). The outcome of competition between strains could be fully explained by factors governing food requirements and food acquisition; the rate of feeding appeared the decisive characteristic. This study links up with the theory of competition as expounded by C. T. de Wit for plants (see the section on Vegetation Science). G. de Jong (1976) constructed a mathematical model on competition for food, illustrated by the results of Bakker's experiments. Bakker (1964) took part in the heated discussions concerning the importance of density-dependent factors in population dynamics in a paper, "Backgrounds of controversies about population theories and their terminologies."

During the last decade, a field of study that had been trodden before World War II has been explored further, i.e., the ecology of hymenopterous parasites (Jacobi 1939; Caudri 1941). In this connection, the work on host discrimination (van Lenteren 1976) should be mentioned. It was discovered that newly hatched wasps (*Pseudeucoila bochei*) that had never met unparasitized hosts (larvae of *Drosophila*) oviposited freely in parasitized hosts. Only after encountering and ovipositing in unparasitized hosts did they avoid parasitized ones (van Lenteren and Bakker 1975). Other work in this group concerns the population dynamics of parasite-host interactions. It was discovered that parasitic wasps may show a sigmoid functional response to the density of their hosts (van Lenteren and Bakker 1978). A recent expansion of this work, which was mainly done on parasites of *Drosophila* species, is the field and laboratory study of asparagus, its two monophagous herbivores (*Crioceris asparagi* and *C. duodecimpunctata*), and their parasites (*Tetrastichus*) (van Alphen 1980).

An applied aspect of the research on parasite-host relations is the biological control of glasshouse pests in various crops (tomato, cucumber, eggplant, sweet pepper, and others). The pests studied are mainly whiteflies, leaf miners, and aphids.

As in Tinbergen's work, the importance of behavioral studies for the solution of ecological problems is emphasized, resulting in growing cooperation between ecologists and ethologists. The ethologist J. van den Assem studied intraspecific competition for territories in the three-spined stickleback (1967) and is now involved in research on ecological and ethological aspects of parasite-host interactions. It was discovered that female wasps (*Lariophagus distinguendus*) in some way "measure" the size of their hosts, larvae of *Sitophilus granarius,* living in wheat kernels (1971). This results in a higher percentage of unfertilized (male) eggs in the smaller hosts. However, the difference between "small" and "large" hosts, as far as sex ratio of offspring is concerned, is not fixed; it depends on the relative sizes of the hosts present. Together with E. L. Charnov, van den Assem and co-workers tested Charnov's sex allocation model and have prepared a paper on sex ratio evolution in a patchy environment (Charnov et al. In press).

H. Dienske (1979) studied the importance of social interactions and habitat in competition between the two species of voles, *Microtus agrestis* and *M.*

arvalis. When both species are present, they appear to occupy different habitats, *M. arvalis* living in terrains with short vegetation, *M. agrestis* in higher vegetation. Dienske discusses the various pros and cons of these habitats for the voles and analyzes the behavioral adaptations to these habitats and the interactions at encounters.

University of Groningen

Lukas Tinbergen, a younger brother of Niko, graduated under Van der Klaauw in 1946 in Leiden presenting a thesis, "The sparrowhawk as a predator of passerine birds" (1946). In 1949, he went to the University of Groningen, where his main work concerned the dynamics of bird and insect populations. After his untimely death in 1955, his important paper on the natural control of insects in pine woods was published in 1960. The first part, on the factors influencing the intensity of predation by songbirds (1960), was nearly completed at the time of his death; the second, on the conditions for damping of Nicholson oscillations in parasite-host systems (1960), had to be compiled mainly from notes he left, a task taken up by H. Klomp. One of Tinbergen's major discoveries was the density-dependent mortality of prey animals due to selective learning on the part of the predators (searching images). One of his students, N. Prop (1960), studied the various ways in which sawfly larvae protect themselves against attack by birds and parasites. Threat displays, spacing out, and color patterns play a role in the different species studied. Herrebout et al. (1963) made a similar study on caterpillars feeding on Scots pine.

Tinbergen was succeeded by L. de Ruiter, who graduated on a paper on the adaptive significance of countershading in caterpillars (1956). Later, he wrote a paper on the ecology and evolution of mimicry (1958). De Ruiter started research on the polymorphic landsnail *Cepaea nemoralis,* later taken over by H. Wolda who showed that the variation of this species as regards growth rate, which is partly genetic, has considerable influence on its population dynamics (1963, 1971). Wolda left Groningen in 1971 to study the fluctuation of tropical insect populations at the Smithsonian Research Institute in Panama (1978, 1979). His pupil L. M. Oosterhoff published a thorough analysis of growth rate in *Cepaea* and showed that the rate is related to activity and dispersal and is partly density dependent (1977).

Wolda's successor, R. H. Drent, is mainly interested in the feeding ecology of birds. His research particularly concentrates on fieldwork concerning three aspects often not adequately incorporated in current optimal foraging theories: (1) the necessity for continuous sampling of the feeding habitat in relation to possible changes in food supply, (2) the importance of food quality as distinct from caloric value only, and (3) the role of interference by conspecifics. The work concerns mainly the starling (Westerterp 1973; Tinbergen 1976), waders (Hulscher 1974, 1976), and geese (Drent and Swierstra

1977). Emphasis is put on the assessment of the energy budget in field conditions to evaluate the adaptiveness of feeding strategies in terms of costs and benefits.

S. Daan has embarked on an analysis of adaptive significance of circadian rhythms in the feeding ecology of both predator and prey. There is close cooperation with ethologists G. P. Baerends and J. P. Kruyt and physiologists L. de Ruiter and P. R. Wiepkema in the department, and with the plant ecology group at Groningen, including D. Bakker.

An interesting new development is the integration between population ecology and population genetics now being pursued by Van Oortmersen and co-workers in the house mouse.

The biomathematician J. Reddingius published "Gambling for existence," a critical paper on the various attempts to demonstrate the action of density-dependent factors in natural populations (1971).

The Institute for Ecological Research

After an initiative by Mörzer Bruijns, a committee formed by the Royal Netherlands Academy of Sciences reported in 1953 on the status of ecological research in the Netherlands. It recommended the foundation of separate institutions for purely scientific work in the fields of terrestrial and aquatic ecology. The new Instituut voor Oecologisch Onderzoek (Institute for Ecological Research) was founded in 1954, and Kluyver became its first director. Several lines of research were brought together here. The work on bird migration (Stichting Vogeltrekstation), begun by G. F. Makkink, W. H. van Dobben, L. Tinbergen, A. C. Perdeck, and others, was incorporated.

The reclamation of polderland in the former Zuiderzee presented an unique opportunity for the study of immigration, settlement, and succession of the species that would eventually inhabit the new land. From the series of publications on animals in the new polders, the work by J. Haeck on the mole (1969) and on carabids (1971), by J. Mook on various animals (1971) and *Lipara* (1967), and by A. J. Cavé on the kestrel (1968) may be mentioned.

Kluyver himself extended his work on titmice, especially on the great tit. Together with Klomp's work on the pine looper, this work is among the best long-term studies on natural populations of animals. A first large paper on the population ecology of the great tit appeared as early as 1951. In Kluyver's opinion, territorial behavior played an important role in the regulation of numbers, and together with L. Tinbergen, he wrote a classic paper on this subject (1953). These ideas were confirmed in a series of experiments on a fairly well isolated island (Vlieland) where an artificial strong reduction of reproduction hardly influenced the population size, since adult survival increased. The work on tits is being continued by J. H. van Balen, who published on the breeding ecology in different habitats (1971). P. J. Drent makes a detailed study of territorial behavior of individual birds, and the energy requirements and thermal conditions of incubation were investigated by J. A. L. Mertens (1977). The latest development in this research program is the attempt to analyze the genetic component of clutch size and time of laying in the great tit (A. J. van Noordwijk). This research is only possible because the birds have been marked and followed over such a long period. Ecological work on other bird species concerns the coot and the collared turtle dove.

The research on dune communities, done at the biological station Weevers' Duin, was incorporated in the new institute. Before this takeover, B. M. Lensink worked here on the analysis of the distribution of grasshoppers (1963), but the vast majority of research done was and is botanical.

Free University, Amsterdam

At the Free University at Amsterdam, ecological work started in 1958 when L. Vlijm was appointed reader. During the first years, the investigations were focused on the ecology of carabids (L. Vlijm et al. 1961; van Dijk 1972, 1973) and wolf spiders (Vlijm and Kessler-Geschiere 1967). Distribution and aerial dispersal attracted special attention (Richter 1970). Here, too, a project has been started to study settlement of animals in a newly reclaimed area, the polder in the former Lauwerszee, a bay that was closed off from the sea in 1969 (Miejer 1974, 1977, 1980).

E. N. G. Joosse-van Damme leads a group working on the population ecology of springtails (Collembola), of which many aspects are studied. The ecophysiological basis of the population phenomena is receiving attention, and the importance of springtails for the ecosystem of the soil is being investigated. Hunger during drought (summer) or cold (winter) (Joosse and Testerink 1977) leads to reductions of energy-requiring processes, like growth, moulting, reproduction, and mobility. Other adaptations to drought and cold are reduction of evaporation and the ability to "commute" between wet and dry places (Verhoef and Witteveen 1980). Predation on springtails, especially by the carabid *Notiophilus biguttatus*, is being studied by G. Ernsting (Ernsting and Jansen 1978). Research on interference between species shows this to be a significant factor for distribution. A recent discovery is the existence of aggregation pheromones (Verhoef et al. 1977; Joosse and Koelman 1979).

Led by Vlijm, a group is working on community ecology, with particular stress on functional and structural relationships (1974).

The ornithologist Voous works with his group on the problem of ecological isolation in owls and birds of prey (Smeenk 1972; van Beusekom 1972; Schipper 1973, 1977, 1979).

University of Utrecht

The small animal ecology group at the University of Utrecht is working on the settlement and maintenance of epidaphic arthropod populations (e.g., carabids) and on autecology of bats (Sluyter 1971; Sluyter et al. 1956).

Catholic University, Nijmegen

The Department of Ecology started in 1964. It specializes in autecology and population ecology of amphibians and reptiles, in studies by H. C. J. Oomen, J. J. van Gelder, and co-workers (van Gelder and Oomen 1970; van Gelder 1973). In this work, ethological aspects are investigated, e.g., vocalization (van Gelder and Hoedemaekers 1971; van Gelder et al. 1978). Further, the ecological implications of the differentiation in the *Rana esculenta* complex receive attention (Wijnands and van Gelder 1976).

Agricultural University, Wageningen

Animal ecology is studied here mainly from the applied side. Research in the Department of Entomology, of which J. de Wilde is director, is in large part focused on the physiology of feeding, growth, development, reproduction, and diapause, and on the significance of photoperiodicity and insect hormones on these phenomena. In addition, insect-plant relations, as well as parasite-host relations, are being investigated. For example, L. M. Schoonhoven studied host-parasite synchronization in the pine looper, *Bupalus piniarius,* and the tachinid *Eucarcelia rutila* (1962).

Research on the ecology of the onion fly (Loosjes 1976) and the use of sterile males (Ticheler) may be mentioned as an example of new ways of pest control. A recent review is *Integrated Control of Insect Pests in the Netherlands,* edited by A. K. Minks and P. Gruys (1980).

At the Department of Theoretical Production Ecology, pioneer work was done on the simulation of ecological processes with the help of dynamic mathematical models under the direction of C. T. de Wit (de Wit and Goudriaan 1974). H. G. Fransz (1974) and R. Rabbinge (1976) applied simulation techniques in studies on the interactions between populations of phytophagous mites and their predators, among others predaceous mites; J. van den Bos and R. Rabbinge (1976) simulated the fluctuations of larch bud moth populations.

Biological Station at Wijster

The Biological Station at Wijster is a part of the Agricultural University of Wageningen. After leaving Leiden in 1958, P. J. den Boer came here and continued his work on the distribution ecology and population dynamics of carabid beetles, work which had already caught his attention when he worked in the dunes of Meijendel. He was strongly impressed by the patchy distribution of carabids, and attached much importance to the apparent frequent extinction and renewed founding of populations and thus to the significance of dispersal powers. The occurrence of wing polymorphism and dimorphism, its genetic background, and its possible evolution are important topics in this respect (den Boer et al. In press). Dispersal is considered as an autonomous phenomenon, i.e., without obvious proximate causes. M. A. Baars (1979*a*) studied patterns of movement of radioactive-labelled carabids and did simulation experiments on this subject (1979*b*).

Den Boer's paper summarizing much of his work on carabids appeared in 1977, "Dispersal power and survival: carabids in a cultivated countryside," in which special attention is given to the importance of the fragmentation of the habitat by human activity. The heterogeneity of populations and their environments, as well as the large numbers of factors influencing the populations, were the basis of his ideas set forth in his paper "Spreading of risk and the stabilization of animal numbers" (1968). He recognized many parallels between his ideas and those of Andrewartha and Birch. Reddingius and den Boer published a paper in which these ideas were illustrated by simulation experiments (1970).

Research Institute for Nature Management, Arnhem

A. D. Voûte, former director of Itbon (Institute for Applied Giological Research, Arnhem), became known for his work on the tropics. He wrote a classic paper on density regulation of insects in virgin forests and cultivated woods (1946), in which he stressed the idea of a relationship between the diversity of a virgin forest and its resistance against pests. In 1968 he published his views on the teleological nature of ecology as a science.

In 1969, Itbon and the Institute for Nature Conservancy at Zeist (Rivon) were combined into one Research Institute for Nature Management (RIN). This institute participated in the International Biological Program on productivity of an oak forest and on decomposition of organic matter in the soil, where soil fauna plays a major part. Current research is being done on the influence of habitat deterioration and pesticides, especially on bird populations (e.g., raptores) and on ecology of raptores in general, especially breeding ecology, feeding ecology, and niche differentiation. P. Opdam (1975, 1979) worked on goshawk and sparrowhawk.

Research is also being done on the ecology of the fox in relation to rabies by Niewold, the decline of the seal population in the Wadden Sea by van Haaften and by P. J. H. Reijnders (1980), fluctuations in hare populations by Broekhuizen, muskrats and their control by Doude van Troostwijk (1976), the distribution of several mammal species by van Wijngaarden, and food selection and habitat use in the red deer by H. E. van de Veen (1979). J. van der Drift (1951) reported on the animal community in a birch forest floor. A. Spaans (1971) has shown that the recent increase in numbers of the herring gull can be ascribed to bad management of garbage dumps. W. J. Doude van Troostwijk (1964) proved that intensive hunting during winter had no influence on the density of breeding wood pigeons in the following season. An early staff member of Itbon (later RIN) was H. Klomp, whose thesis upon graduation from Leiden was "Habitat selection in the lapwing" (1954). In this work, he combined ecology and functional morphology (i.e., of the locomotory system) to explain the preference of the birds for meadows with a low vegetation. This interest in ornithology has not waned; he has published a review of the fascinating problem of the determination of clutch size in birds (1970) and on density regulation by territorial behavior (1972).

The long-term study by Klomp on the dynamics of the pine looper, *Bupalus piniarius,* begun in 1950, is still going on. The pine looper was chosen because it was rather common, even though it never appeared to show the drastic outbreaks seen in other countries such as Germany. The main question concerns the mechanism of population regulation, and problems studied include the causes of the fluctuations, the analysis of density-dependent phenomena, and the interaction with parasitoids. An important survey appeared in 1966.

Klomp's pupil W. M. Herrebout investigated the interaction between the pine looper and its tachinid parasite *Eucarcelia rutila* (1969). P. Gruys, another pupil of Klomp and de Wilde, made a study of the effects of interference in larvae of *Bupalus.* He discovered (1970) that contacts between caterpillars during their nocturnal feeding activities inhibited growth, which leads to a lower adult weight and, eventually, in females to a lower fecundity. However, this lowered fecundity was not considered an important regulating mechanism. Gruys put forward the hypothesis that moths emerging from pupae that are small as a result of density-related larval growth reduction have a more favorable wing load and hence an advantage in dispersal to areas with lower mortality rates. This hypothesis was tested in an extensive paper by Botterweg (1978) and had to be rejected. Studies on color polymorphism in *Bupalus* by M. H. den Boer (1971) showed that the variation present in populations may have ecological significance. In the work on *Bupalus,* the point has been reached where a population approach from both ecology and genetics may be fruitful. As a convinced adherent of the regulationist school, Klomp (1962) took part in the international debate following the publication of the famous books by Andrewartha and Birch and by Lack.

Tropical Research

Traditionally, Dutch biologists often worked in the tropics, i.e., the Netherlands East Indies, work that was reviewed by K. G. Eveleens (1976). After the independence of Indonesia, this tradition was not lost, and ecological research, often of a more or less applied nature, is still being done. An example is the study of the population dynamics of the red locust by C. W. Stortenbeker (1967).

Research is mostly connected with agriculture, often guided by the Laboratory of Entomology of the Agricultural University at Wageningen (J. de Wilde), or with tropical medicine. In the latter case, the Laboratory of Tropical Medicine and Parasitology in Leiden (C. F. A. Bruyning) or the Tropical Institute in Amsterdam is often the initiator.

Research in the tropics is also being supported by Stichting voor Wetenschappelijk Onderzoek van de Tropen (WOTRO) (Netherlands Foundation for the Advancement of Tropical Research). Its annual reports are published in English and give a list of publications.

The research programs are very diverse and, as far as terrestrial animal ecology is concerned, the following projects may be mentioned: (a) H. Kruuk (1966, 1972) studied the behavior and population dynamics of the spotted hyena, and D. A. Kreulen et al., the use of vegetation and migration by wildebeests in the Serengeti Plain, Tanzania; (b) the Gunung Leuser Reserve, on Sumatra, Indonesia, is an area where research is being done on rhinoceros (N. J. van Strien), orangutan (Rijksen, 1978), and other endangered species; (c) in Surinam, the ecological conditions for birds on the coastal plains were studied by A. L. Spaans and his co-workers; (d) on the Antilles, the flamingo population of Bonaire received attention (Rooth 1965); and (e) birds of prey in East Africa were studied by C. Smeenk (1974).

General Conclusion

During the last five to ten years, a clear reappraisal of autecology is evident in Dutch ecological work. Not satisfied by pure correlative research in population dynamics, many investigators return to studying the morphological, physiologic, and behavioral properties of the individual animals, and try in this way to explain population phenomena. A further noteworthy development is the growing cooperation between ecologists and geneticists, as has been realized in the Working Group on Population Biology.

VEGETATION SCIENCE

Samuel Segal

Introduction

The earliest notion of plant ecology in the Netherlands was not to be found in science and theory, but in practice. This was particularly manifest in many forms of agriculture, forestry, land reclamation, and dune fixation and management. There was a fair knowledge of the most favorable composition of cultured and semicultured grasslands and woods, and a practical knowledge of how to influence and manage them.

During the nineteenth century, F. Holkema's 1870 study on dunes and salt marshes, *De plantengroei der Nederlandse Noordzee-eilanden*, was an interesting forerunner of vegetation science, but continuation of the scientific study of vegetation did not start until about 1930. The term *phytosociology* was generally used during the following twenty or thirty years, and later was gradually replaced by *vegetatiekunde* (vegetation science). The development of this field was originally stimulated by Scandinavian approaches (like those of Du Rietz, Nordhagen, and Raunkiaer), and soon also by the Zurich-Montpellier approach (Braun-Blanquet, Tüxen).

Dutch phytosociologists have always paid considerable attention to the theoretical foundations of their science including the basic concepts of vegetation, plant community, and vegetation units recognized by their floristic composition, structure, and relationships with the environment.

A review of Dutch ecological literature through 1959, which included 1,433 references, was published by V. Westhoff (1961). Ecology has become a popular study at the university level since that time, and the literature has increased substantially. A new literature review by W. A. Schenk will be published soon (In press). A special number of *Wentia* (no. 15, 1966) contained papers on research in progress at that time. Recently, the new developments were treated by several authors in M. J. A. Werger (1973).

The First Period

One of the earliest vegetation studies was conducted by J. Bijhouwer (1926) in a dune region where soils rich and poor in limestone meet, and he constructed one of the earliest vegetation maps.

Based on Scandinavian methods, with a prevailing interest in dominance of species, were studies performed by D. M. de Vries (1929), A. Scheygrond (1932), and J. W. van Dieren (1934). De Vries applied a frequency method originally developed by Raunkiaer. The simple statistical methods used at that time developed into three-dimensional models in which the ecological correlation between grassland species made it possible to distinguish correlation classes (1954). The methods closely resemble modern statistical methods such as cluster analysis. After some years, De Vries advocated integration of promising elements of Scandinavian and Zurich-Montpellier approaches. Scheygrond studied march vegetation, distinguishing vegetation layers and horizontal patches as separate units within a vegetation complex. Unlike the studies of De Vries, his efforts had no following. Van Dieren made an interesting study on dune formation which is in part of interest to physical geographers.

W. Feekes (1936) studied vegetation development in a newly reclaimed polder and performed dissemination experiments with seeds to assess their radius of action.

The methods of the Zurich-Montpellier school are mainly based on floristic composition, and the concept of the character species played an important role, especially in earlier studies in which many monographs followed the hierarchic system of plant communities. The first research based on this method was performed on dune vegetation by W. C. de Leeuw (1936) and on woodland vegetation by E. Meyer Drees (1936), W. H. Diemont (1938), and J. Vlieger. Diemont developed a climax theory (1937). Vlieger was the first to produce a survey on phytosociological units of higher ranks in the Netherlands.

An important landmark was the much more elaborate survey of vegetation units by Westhoff in 1946 (after an edition with small circulation in 1942), which currently has a historical interest especially since a profound review appeared in 1969. Meanwhile the number of the higher associated units described had increased considerably: from eighteen to thirty-eight classes, from twenty-seven to fifty-four orders, and from thirty-nine to eighty-five alliances, all grouped in thirteen formations, and including epiphytic communities.

Another important landmark was the first introduction to plant sociology by J. Meltzer and V. Westhoff in 1942 after a less extensive edition in 1940. This served as a source of inspiration for the next twenty years in the Netherlands; in addition to information on Braun-Blanquet techniques, it summarized studies and views up to that moment.

Field Studies after the Second World War

Only a very small portion of the studies on vegetation can be enumerated here; the starting point will be the theses, since they give a quite good idea about the problems under study. For example, Westhoff studied dune and marsh vegetation along the coast (1947), and his careful description of the vegetation units combined with life-form analyses and biosystematic research served as a high standard for many later studies. This thesis demonstrated that proper phytosociological studies may include synecology of communities.

The Braun-Blanquet approach found many followers, and methods and concepts were elaborated further. Gradually, the methods of the Scandinavian and Anglo-American approaches were integrated, at least after about 1960, so that the "differential species," still a Braun-Blanquet concept, became more important, and more stress was laid on dominance next to structure, and on constant species combinations. Community units (associations) as basic concepts for vegetation description were maintained, but intermediate combinations of species along environmental gradients, often comprising rare and highly indicative species, drew more and more attention. Transitions between the units also increased information on and comprehension of the relation of species and environment.

Simultaneously, the use and development of more objective classification and ordination methods was stimulated, as was habitat research. There was greater interest in structure, including growth forms, in life forms and adaptation, and in autecological problems. During the last ten years, vegetation science became an important tool in landscape planning and evaluation, partly by means of vegetation mapping. It was acknowledged that a hierarchic system of plant communities often bears a regional validity, so that the classification and ordination method is, in a sense, of relatively great importance. It has been shown in practice that this method can be used successfully under quite different conditions, such as tropical vegetation, as has been shown by M. J. A. Werger (1973) and by Hogeweg and Brenkert-van Riet (1969). A study of shrub, dwarf shrub, and terricolous lichen vegetation in southeast Greenland by F. J. A. Daniels is in press.

After Westhoff, a series of monographs on Dutch types of vegetation and their environment followed. G. Sissingh (1950) studied weed vegetation. Many students worked wholly or partly under Westhoff's guidance, like F. M. Maas (1959), J. H. A. Boerboom (1960), I. S. Zonneveld (1960), J. van Donselaar (1961), H. Doing (1962), W. G. Beeftink (1965), E. van der Maarel (1966), G. Londo (1971), N. M. Schoof-van Pelt (1973), and J. M. Sloet van Oldruitenborgh (1976).

Among typological dune studies belong those of Boerboom and Sloet van Oldruitenborgh; Londo studied succession in a superficial duneslack; and Van der Maarel gave a theoretical exposition on structure, vegetation relations, and systems based on research of a small area of dune grassland. Beeftink performed a study on coastal salt marshes in the southwestern part of the Netherlands.

An important study on the soil and the marsh vegetation of a freshwater tidal delta, a rare phenomenon throughout the world, was carried out by Zonneveld. This study has historical interest since the area recently has been cut off from the sea, with cessation of tidal movements. Studies on marsh vegetation in former river beds were published by Van Donselaar et al.

Maas studied springs, spring brooks, and spring woods, while H. Doing studied wood and shrub vegetation, both using sociological groups of species and structure as diagnostic characters for the discrimination of vegetation units.

Schoof-van Pelt studied certain amphiphytic communities in western Europe. Studies on aquatic vegetation have been influenced by C. den Hartog and S. Segal (1964), who worked out a growth form system for aquatic macrophytes. L. de Lange (1972) studied ditch vegetation. P. Hogeweg and A. L. Brenkert-van Riet gave an account of types and structure of Indian aquatic vegetation (1969).

S. Segal (1969) studied wall vegetation in western and parts of southern Europe using objective data processing to classify twelve hundred site descriptions containing many transitions to "typical" vegetation units. J. T. de Smidt studied heathlands in western Europe. Since heathlands are only natural in coastal regions, but covered considerable areas in the nineteenth century as a result of sheep grazing, burning and mowing have to be applied in order to conserve some areas.

Studies were also made on epilithic algae along the Dutch coast by C. den

Hartog (1959) and on cryptogamic epiphytes by J. J. Barkman (1958). The latter study is not only important for its detailed description of vegetation units but also for its elaborate views on methodology and theory (for example, on the synusial approach and on structure) and, by information, on the relationship between the distribution of species, especially lichens, and air pollution. This information has subsequently been applied in landscape planning.

An excellent review of Dutch landscape and vegetation, their history, ecology, and relation to man, was given in the finely illustrated three-volume *Wilde planten* (1970–1973).

Developments organized within the International Society for Vegetation Science toward an elaborate system of plant communities are culminating in a European *prodrome* under the direction of R. Tüxen; Dutch scientists are involved in this project. The first volume, by W. G. Beeftink and J. M. Géhu, dealt with *Spartina* vegetation (1973). A special working group prepared an extensive and documented code of phytosociological nomenclature (1976). Another working group is concerned with data processing (1976).

Attention has been paid to autecological aspects by several vegetation scientists, and is integrated in several studies (Westhoff 1947; van Donselaar 1961; Beeftink 1965; Segal 1969). Some other studies include those made on *Listera cordata* by V. Westhoff (1959), *Carex buxbaumii* by S. Segal and V. Westhoff (1959), *Betula* (1963) and other tree species by H. Doing, *Scirpus planifolius* by V. Westhoff and C. G. van Leeuwen (1966), and on some wetland and aquatic species, and ferns by S. Segal. Such information has been systematically presented in the ecological paragraphs of the species descriptions in the *Flora Neerlandica* since 1948 (published at Leiden, still in progress).

Theoretical Approaches

Apart from the items already mentioned, some theoretical aspects will be treated here. The interest in structural problems, a somewhat neglected aspect in phytosociology, is manifest by several systems for or additions to growth and life forms, e.g., J. J. Barkman (1958) for epiphytic bryophytes and lichens, E. van der Maarel (1966) for rooted terrestrial species, and C. den Hartog and S. Segal (1964) for macrophytes, using also structural features for associated systematic reasons, like H. Doing (1962). The above authors also elaborated the analysis of stratification and horizontal patterns. J. J. Barkman developed new ideas about minimum area and microcommunities, and reviewed synusial approaches (1973).

Refinement of the Braun-Blanquet methods for quantitative vegetation analysis, using critical weights for layering, coverage, abundance, sociability, and other features, were published by J. J. Barkman (1964). Some of these proposals have been widely adopted in the Netherlands. Views on the

Braun-Blanquet school were given by several authors, including V. Westhoff and E. van der Maarel (1973).

Dutch interest in numerical methods was first expressed by D. M. de Vries (e.g., 1954), and later by several authors (Barkman 1958; van der Maarel 1966; Segal 1969); some new or modified computer programs for handling vegetation data were elaborated, e.g., by L. F. M. Fresco (1971), J. G. M. Janssen (1975), W. M. Kortekaas (1976), H. van Gils and A. J. Kovács (1977), and C. P. van Schaik and P. Hogeweg (1977). Other effective approaches dealt with vegetation succession and gradient theory, e.g., by E. van der Maarel (1972), as put forward by Whittaker.

C. G. van Leeuwen (1966) developed a theory in which the relations between spatial and temporal variation in ecosystems were treated, and in which the overall importance of environmental dynamics for the establishment of species and communities is stressed. According to this theory, pioneer species in succession generally grow in coarse patterns and show a short lifetime. During the course of succession, vegetation changes tend to slow down, whereas spatial differentiation increases. Special attention was drawn to the specificity of different types of borders and zonations between vegetation types. Van Leeuwen's ideas were strongly influenced by the specific situation of nature reserves in the Netherlands. Here, the vegetation is often the result of old agricultural practices, such as grazing and hay-making on non-fertilized areas or on peat. To preserve the fine patterns and botanical richness in such areas, changes in handling have to be avoided so that, in several cases, the maintenance of a certain instability is profitable. The theory had a great influence on many students and on management in nature conservancy.

Applications of phytosociology to landscape ecology have been developed also by vegetation mapping. G. Nijland reviewed vegetation maps in print up to 1974. I. S. Zonneveld (1972) developed and stimulated application by photo interpretation, especially in tropical and subtropical regions. Several reports of Dutch regional areas were published. Recently, a vegetation map of the Netherlands appeared, based on types of potential natural vegetation by J. Kalkhoven (1977).

Research in Progress

Recent developments can be presented in the newly adopted framework of the foundation BION (biological research in the Netherlands), an advisory council to the government organization for scientific research. Within the BION framework, activities are concentrated within a "working community" for plant ecology and vegetation science, and are organized into two project groups. The one on associated systematics and synchorology prepares a new integrated system of plant communities in the Netherlands in which full tabular documentation will be presented on a numerical basis, and structural and ecophysiological data will be incorporated. The project group on structure and dynamics is concerned with short- and long-term changes in vegetation and plant populations in relation to environmental patterns and processes, especially in semi-natural ecosystems.

Most research is performed by university institutes. Dune vegetation is studied in several centers (for example, Wageningen, Nijmegen), and the biological station Weeversduin at Oostvoorne has some tradition in the relations to pedology and microclimatology. Salt marshes are studied in Groningen and the Delta Institute of the Royal Netherlands Academy of Arts and Sciences at Yerseke. Heathland vegetation is studied at Utrecht and at the biological station at Wijster, where detailed investigations on several aspects of *Juniperus* scrub are performed, including mycosociology and microclimatology (J. J. Barkman). Investigation of the mycoflora in various plant communities, including dry heathlands, coniferous wood types, acid oak woods, and grasslands, are also carried out at Wijster (R. N. A. Kramer, A. Janssen, P. Ypelaar, E. J. M. Arnolds); some papers on these investigations, including a general introduction of the problems, appear in J. J. Barkman (1976). Woods and scrub are investigated in Wageningen (H. Doing, E. C. J. Ott). Epiphytic and epilithic cryptogamous communities are studied in Utrecht and Wijster (F. J. A. Daniels, M. Arnolds). Patterns in limestone grasslands are determined by means of vegetation handling experiments in Utrecht (J. H. Willems, In press).

Ecological fen studies (G. van Wirdum) and alder brook vegetation (J. Smittenberg) are performed at RIN. Research on nature conservancy is carried on by the Rijksinstituut voor Natuurbeheer (RIN) at Leersum, and at Wageningen and Utrecht. Special interest is focused on vegetation mapping, landscape ecology, and evaluation by several teams. The International Institute for Aerial Survey and Earth Sciences (ITC) at Enschede specializes in vegetation problems in tropical and subtropical regions.

Acknowledgment

The author owes much to Dr. E. van der Maarel who provided information about recent research.

EXPERIMENTAL PLANT ECOLOGY

Willem H. Van Dobben

Introduction

Pioneer work was done by M. J. Adriani on the ecology of halophytes. In his thesis (1945), he gives experimental support to the idea of A. F. W. Schimper, expressed in his 1898 book *Pflanzengeographie auf physiolo-*

gischer Grundlage (Plant Geography on a Physiological Basis), that the xeromorphy of halophytes can be explained as an adaptation to water stress in salt media. In 1943, G. L. Funke published a book in the Dutch language, *Experimentele Plantensociologie.* This book is exclusively dedicated to phenomena of allelopathy, the mutual interference of plants by excretions. This past work has had no follow-up. Since 1950, investigations in plant ecology have increased steadily.

Life History Studies

This type of research work is based on the supposition that most properties of organisms can be explained as adaptations to specific niche relationships. Autecological investigations are not restricted, of course, to experimental work; field observations can furnish much information about the life history and demography of plant species. A combination of field studies and experimental work appears particularly fruitful. In this connection, pioneer work was done by D. Bakker on a number of weed species. At the time, Bakker served in the biology department of the authority for the IJssellake polders (Zuiderzee reclamations), and later introduced this type of work at Groningen University. Since 1960, other institutions have followed this lead. Ecological field studies, supplemented with experimental work, were published on the following species: *Tussilago farfara* L. (Bakker 1951); *Cirsium arvense* L. (Bakker 1960); *Senecio congestus* (R.Br.) DC. (Bakker 1960); *Centaurium littorale* (D. T.) Gilmour (Freysen 1962); *Caltha palustris* L. (Smit 1962); *Spergularia media* and S. *marina* (L.) (Sterk 1971); *Rumex acetocella* L. (Stork et al. 1971); *Rhinanthus serotinus* (Schonh.) Oborny. (ter Borg 1972); *Phragmitis australis* (Cav.) (van der Torn 1972); *Elytrigia repens* (L.) (Neuteboom 1975); *Sonchus arvensis* L. (Pegtel 1976); and *Plantago* species (Blom 1976).

Studies in progress include the following: hemiparasitic Scrophulariaceae, *Juncus compresous* Jacq. and *gerardii* (Lois.) at the University of Groningen; *Rubus sectio* Ebatus, *Scirpus planifolius* Grimm., *S. rufus* (Huds.), *Carex flava* L., *C. distans* L., and *C. extensa* (Good.), and *Juncus bufonius* L. at the University of Nijmegen; *Rumex acetocella* L., and *Anthyllus vulneraria* L. at the University of Amsterdam; *Linum catharticum* L. and *Blackstonia perfoliata* (L.) at the University of Utrecht; and *Ranunculus sceleratus* L., *Cotula coronopifolia* L., *Catabrosa aquatica* (L.), and *Plantago* spec. at the Institute for Ecological Research, Arnhem.

Studies in population biology, demography, and plant-animal relations have been published on the following species: *Senecio jacobaea* L. and its relations to *Tyria jacobaeae* L. (van der Meijden 1970); *Chamaenerion angustifolium* (L.) Scop. (van Andel 1975); *Glaux maritima* L. (Rozema 1975); and *Anthyllus vulneraria* L. (Sterk 1975). Studies in progress in population biology include: hemiparasitic Scrophulariaceae, *Salicornia* sp. at the University of Groningem; *Asparagus officinalis* L. and its relations to *Criocerus* sp., the biennials *Cirsium, Echium* and *Cynoglossum* in dune areas at the University of Heiden; *Juncus bufonius* L., *Taraxacum* sp., and *Aster tripolium* L. at the University of Amsterdam; species of wood clearings, dunes, and coastal areas at Free University, Amsterdam; *Limonium vulgare* Mill. and its parasitic fungi at the Agricultural University, Wageningen; and *Phragmitis australis* (Cav.) and its insect phytophages.

Ecophysiology

This discipline interprets the specific vital functions of organisms as adaptations. It may be considered a branch of autecology in the comparison between species with different niche relationships. Ecophysiology tries to explain field situations by way of physiological experiments mainly carried out in the laboratory. The investigations refer to a broad spectrum of environmental factors.

Mineral nutrition, tolerance. Published studies include investigations in halophytes (Adriani 1945), *Centaurium littorale* (D. T. Gimour) (Freysen 1975*a,b*), and *Glaux maritima* L. (Rozema 1975). Reactions to heavy metals (Ernst 1975), reactions to nitrogen (van Andel 1975). Work in progress includes reactions to phosphate and potassium by M. J. Veerkamp at the Agricultural University, Wageningen, and P. C. J. Kuiper, at the University of Groningen.

Water relations. Work in progress continues on water transport and variable root resistance by R. Brouwer, at the University of Utrecht, and on water relations in light and shadow plants by F. Kuiper, at the Agricultural University, Wageningen.

Aeration. A study of the influence of soil aeration on growth and respiration of roots of *Senecio* sp. has been published (Lambers 1976). Work in progress at the University of Utrecht includes influence of soil aeration on growth and aerenchyma formation.

Analysis of Growth. Areas of interest include the distribution of dry matter between organs of a plant as influenced by water stress, mineral deficiencies, light conditions, and aeration. The concept of functional equilibria between plant parts has been developed by R. Brouwer (1963) and relative growth rates of *Senecio* sp. by W. H. van Dobben (1967*a*). Work in progress includes runner- and stolon-forming sedges and grasses by R. Brouwer and T. Teitema at the University of Utrecht.

Productivity. Results have been published on productivity in the following areas: salt marsh (Ketner 1972); salt grassland (Alberda 1974); oak woodland (van der Drift 1974); and Stratoites vegetations (Segal 1973). Influence of light conditions on productivity of natural communities has been studied by E. C. Wassink (1969).

Light Intensity and Quality, Photoperiod. Published reports have appeared on: photoperiodicity in ecotypes of *Trifolium pratense* L. (van Dobben 1967*b*); photosynthesis function in light and shadow plants (Groen 1973); and physiology of shade plants in ash coppice (Pons 1976, 1977). Work in progress continues on shade plants at the Agricultural University, Wagenegen, and the University of Utrecht.

Germination and Establishment. Influence of soil compaction and trampling on *Plantago* sp. (Blom 1976), winter annuals on sandy patches (Janssen 1974), and grassland species in a sward (Oomes 1976) have been studied.

Micro-meteorology, Leaf Temperatures. Measurements in vegetation were taken by P. Stoutjesdijk (1966, 1970), and simulation models were prepared by J. Goudriaan (1977).

Mutual Interference. Experimental work on completion received a strong impulse by a publication of C. T. de Wit (1960). de Wit developed a characteristic for the relative competitive power of plant species by analogy with the theories underlying multicomponent distillation that treat the "competition" of liquid phases for evaporation. The "activity coefficients" of liquids in a mixture find their counterparts in "crowding coefficients," which quantify the outcome of competition of two species for the same requisites ("space" in the sense used by de Wit). The basic equations developed in this way are based on the supposition that the species grow simultaneously, and that the growth curves are of the same form, apart from a multiplying factor. They appear to be a particular solution of the Lotka-Volterra equations on competition. Furthermore, de Wit showed that the effect of spacing within one species can be treated as a special form of competition. Thus, a bridge is thrown from interspecific to intraspecific competition.

On the basis of de Wit's work, much research has been done in the competition of grassland species; in fact, his work was the impetus for such studies. For example, J. P. van den Bergh (1969) developed the concept of the relative yield total (RYT); this is the sum of the relative yields (yield in mixture divided by yield in monoculture) of two competing species. When these species are competing for exactly the same space, the RYT is one. What one species loses, the other gains. An RYT greater than one indicates that the species do not compete for exactly the same room. The RYT, therefore, makes it possible to quantify niche differentiation. An RYT less than one indicates that the two species have unfavorable interrelations, e.g., because of disease transfer.

For the evaluation of the competition between perennial grasses that are harvested periodically, the concept of relative replacement rate was developed. This is the quotient of the relative yields of two species at two successive harvests. Plotted on a logarithmic scale against time, the relative replacement rate gives a "course line," which may show a gradual replacement of one species by another. The outcome depends very much on conditions such as water relations, mineral supply, pH, and grassland management; the influence of such conditions on the outcome of competition can now be quantified. Work along these lines is in progress at the Center for Agrobiological Research (CABO) and the Agricultural University, Wageningen.

MICROBIAL ECOLOGY*

Jan W. Woldendorp

Microbial ecology in the Netherlands has a tradition that goes back to the end of the nineteenth century when, in 1888, Beijerinck isolated the root nodule-forming bacteria of leguminous plants in pure culture. In those years, Beijerinck developed the principles of modern microbiology by applying ecological concepts. His enrichment cultures were based on the principle of competition, and his isolations of a number of bacterial species, like sulfate-reducing bacteria (1895) and free-living, nitrogen-fixing bacteria (1901), are clear-cut examples of the niche concept. The basic ideas of Beijerinck were developed further by Kluyver and Van Niel, who became well known from their studies in a broad field of microbial ecology and physiology. Both investigators, whose publications can be found in every textbook on microbiology, worked at the Laboratory of Microbiology at Delft, which became a leading center in microbiology during the years before and immediately after the Second World War. This development has been described by C. B. van Niel (1949) in "The Delft school and the rise of general microbiology."

Now, research in the field of microbial ecology is centered at the University of Groningen, the Agricultural University, Wageningen, and a few ecological institutes. The investigations are mainly carried out in two fields: autecological studies on the relations between microorganisms and their environment, and the role of microorganisms in ecosystems in the cycling of elements and in the flow of energy. Major contributions have been made on the following subjects: the nitrogen cycle, the sulfur cycle, and the use of continuous culture techniques as a tool in ecological research. A survey of recent publications is given below.

*Literature survey completed March 1978.

Growth of Microorganisms

Work on enrichment cultures of procaryotic organisms was summarized by H. Veldkamp (1970*a*). The use of the continuous culture method in ecological studies has been studied by Veldkamp (1972, 1976*a*, 1977) and W. Harder (1977). Studies on competition between microorganisms in mixed cultures were carried out by Veldkamp (1976*b*) and H. van Gemerden (1974). Studies on productivity of microorganisms were made by A. H. Stouthamer (1976).

Energy Flow and Decomposition

Energy flow and decomposition of organic matter in freshwater sediments were studied by T. E. Cappenberg (1977), who also published on methane formation in bottom deposits of freshwater lakes (1976). Decomposition of cellulose was studied by G. W. Harmsen (1943), of pectin by K. T. Wieringa (1963), of chitin by Veldkamp (1955), of DNA by J. Antheunisse (1972), and of ethylene by J. A. M. de Bont (1976*a*). The formation of cellulose fibrils by bacteria during flocculation in wastewater treatment was investigated by M. H. Deinema and L. P. T. M. Zevenhuizen (1971). Decomposition processes in the rumen of a large number of herbivores were studied by R. A. Prins (1977). The effects of oxygen on anaerobic and micro-aerophilic bacteria were investigated by W. de Vries (1972).

Sulfur Cycle

Investigations of sulfate reduction in freshwater lakes were carried out by Cappenberg (1975) and in the sediments of the Wadden Sea by J. H. Vosjan (1975). Oxidation of sulfurous compounds has been studied by G. J. Kuenen (1972, 1975, 1977), T. A. Hansen (1974), and H. van Gemerden (1971).

Nitrogen Cycle

Nitrate reduction (denitrification) in soil was studied by W. Verhoeven (1952) and J. W. Woldendorp (1973), and in water and activated sludge by J. F. van Kessel (1976) and J. Krul (1976). The immobilization and mineralization of nitrogen in soil has been investigated by J. L. M. Huntjens (1972) and G. W. Harmsen and G. J. Kolenbrander (1965).

A large number of studies on the fixation of atmospheric nitrogen has appeared, and only the most important ones will be cited. Symbiotic nitrogen fixation by leguminous plants was investigated by Lie (1971, 1975, 1978*a,b*), E. G. Mulder (1977), and A. W. S. M. van Egeraat (1972). Studies on symbiotic nitrogen fixation by non-legumes were published by A. D. L. Ackermans (1971, 1977), J. H. Becking (1970), and C. van Dijk (1976). Nitrogen fixation by free-living nitrogen-fixing bacteria was studied by Mulder (1975) and Becking (1974*a,b*). Nitrogen fixation in the surface of leaves (phyllosphere) was investigated by J. Ruinen (1975) and E. P. M. Bessems (1973). Studies on nitrogen fixation by methane-utilizing bacteria were made by J. A. M. de Bont (1976). Most of the above aspects of nitrogen fixation are covered in a book by A. Quispel (1974).

Miscellaneous Papers

The ecology of the important group of coryne bacteria has been investigated by H. Veldkamp (1976*b*) and by E. G. Mulder and J. Antheunisse (1963, 1966). The oxidation of iron manganese was studied by Mulder and W. L. van Veen (1963, 1973).

ORGANIZATION OF RESEARCH WORK, SOURCES OF FINANCIAL SUPPORT, SCIENTIFIC SOCIETIES AND JOURNALS

Hans M. van Emden

Ecological research in the Netherlands is concentrated in the universities, the institutes of the Royal Academy of Arts and Sciences, and government institutes. The structure of and criteria for financial support are rather complicated and, therefore, will be only briefly mentioned here.

Most research in ecology is done at the universities and the agricultural university, and is directly financed by the government. In addition; the Netherlands Organization for Pure Scientific research (ZWO) and, more specifically, its Foundation for Biological Research (BION) contribute about 10 percent of total costs. The foundation promotes the cooperation and quality of research. BION works with research groups, formed by staff members of universities and institutes, around several themes. These groups can make proposals for research project grants for a three-year period.

Ecological research is done at the following government institutes: the Netherlands Institute for Sea Research, Texel (NIOZ); the Research Institute for Nature Management, Arnhem (RIN); the Institute for Fisheries Research (RIVO); the State Institute for the IJssellake Polders (RIJP), and the Institutes of the Royal Academy—the Institute for Ecological Research, Arnhem (IOO); the Delta Institute for Hydrobiological Research, Yerseke; and the Limnological Institute, Nieuwersluis. A close cooperation exists among these institutes and the universities. Other institutes involved with ecological research belong to the Organization for Applied Research (TNO) or to the agricultural university and the Ministry for Agriculture and Fishery and to the Ministry of Public Works. Besides these institutes, a lot of study groups, committees, and working groups deal with objects in the field of ecology, e.g., the Study and

Information Center for Environmental Research and the Foundation for the Dunes.

The contribution from industries to ecological research is small. However, the Research Institute of Electric Utilities (KEMA) has to be mentioned here because of hydrobiological investigations with respect to thermal pollution.

Scientists in the field of ecology are well organized. The "Ecological Circle," although linked with the Netherlands Zoological Society (NDV), includes members of the Royal Netherlands Botanical Society (KNBV) and other biological societies as well.

The *Acta Botanica Neerlandica,* the official journal of the KNBV, and the *Archives Néerlandaises de Zoologie* (from 1968 onward, *Netherland Journal of Zoology*), the journal of the NDV, both publish many papers with an ecological character. The same applies to the two journals of the Netherlands Entomological Society, *Entomologia Experimentalis et Applicata,* and *Tijdschrift voor Entomologie.* Publications of the Institute for Sea Research and the Fishery Research Institute are partly published in the *Netherlands Journal for Sea Research.* Finally, studies of the Netherlands Ornithological Union and of others on birds are published in *Ardea* and *Limosa*; the latter contains papers mainly in the Dutch language. Other journals with mainly or only Dutch articles are *Natura* and *Natuur en Landschap.*

REFERENCES CITED

Aquatic Ecology

Anonymous. 1884. Leiden: Brill.

Beattie, D. M. 1978. *Hydrobiologia* 58:49–64.

de Beaufort, L. F., Ed. 1954. *Den Helder.* Amsterdam: De Boer.

Beukema, J. J. 1976. In *Proc. 10th Europ. Mar. Biol. Symp. Oostende,* ed. G. Persoone and E. Jaspers.

Beyerinck, W. 1927. Thesis, University of Wageningen.

———. 1976. *Neth. J. Sea Res.* 10:236–261.

Boere, G. C. et al. 1973. *Limosa* 48:74–81.

Boere, G. C. 1977. *Ardea* 64:210–291.

Broekema, M. 1941. *Arch. Néerl. Zool.* 6:1–100.

Broekhuysen, G. J. 1936. *Arch. Néerl. Zool.* 2:257–360.

Cadée, G. C. 1976. *Neth. J. Sea Res.* 10:440–460.

———. 1977. *Neth. J. Sea Res.* 11:24–41.

Coomans, H. E. 1958. *Stud. Faun. Curafçao* 8:42–111.

———. 1969. *Malacologia* 9:79–84.

Cortel-Breman, A. M., et al, 1975. *Acta Bot. Néerl.* 24:111–127.

———. 1976. *Phycologia* 15:107–117.

Creutzberg, F. 1961. *Neth. J. Sea Res.* 1:257–338.

———. 1973. *Neth. J. Sea Res.* 7:94–102.

Daan, N. 1975. *Neth. J. Sea Res.* 9:24–55.

Davids, C. 1973. Thesis, University of Amsterdam.

van Densen, W. T. L. 1976. *Neth. J. Zool.* 26:444.

van Dobben, W. H. 1935. *Arch. Néerl. Zool.* 2:1–72.

Dorgelo, J. 1978. *Biol. Rev.* 51:255–290.

Essink, K. 1978. Thesis, University of Groningen.

Everards, K. 1973. NIOZ Report, 1973-2.

Geelen, J. F. M. 1969. Thesis, University of Nijmegen.

Golterman, H. L. 1969. *Proc. Soc. Int. Limnol.* 17:467–479.

______ and R. S. Clymo, eds. 1967. *Chemical environment in the aquatic habitat.* Amsterdam: Noord-Hollandsche Uitg. Mij.

Gons, H. J. 1977. Thesis, University of Amsterdam.

Gulatie, R. D. 1972. *Freshwater Biol.* 2:37–54.

______. 1975. *Proc. Soc. Int. Limnol.* 19:1202–1210.

Hallegraeff, G. M. 1976. Thesis, University of Amsterdam.

den Hartog, C. 1964. *Proc. R. Neth. Acad. Sci.* C67:10–34.

______. 1973. *Proc. 7th Int. Seaweed Symp. Sapporo,* pp. 274–276.

van der Heide, J. 1971. *Proc. Soc. Int. Limnol.* 18.

van den Hoek, C. 1970. *Acta Bot. Neerl.* 19:341–362.

______. 1972. *Proc. R. Neth. Acad. Sci.* 2–61, 1–72.

______. 1975. *Aquat. Bot.* 1:269–308.

Holthuis, L. B. 1958. *Rijksmus. Nat. Hist. Leiden, Zool. Bijdr.* 3:1–26 (D,E).

Kaas, P. 1972. *Stud. Faun. Curaçao* 43:1–162.

Kersting, K. 1973. Thesis. University of Amsterdam.

Koeman, J. H. 1971. Thesis, University of Utrecht.

Korringa, P. 1941. *Arch. Néerl. Zool.* 5:1–249.

______. 1970. *J. Mar. Biol. Assoc. India* 3:818–823.

Kreger, D. 1940. *Arch. Néerl. Zool.* 4:157–200.

Kristensen, I. 1957. *Arch. Néerl. Zool.* 12:351–453.

Kuipers, B. R. 1973. *Neth. J. Sea Res.* 6:376–388.

Leentvaar, P. 1967. *Hydrobiologia* 24:441–489.

______. 1976. *Brokopondo Res. Rep.* 1967.

Lingeman, R. 1975. *Proc. Soc. Ont. Limnol.* 19:1193–1202.

Moed, J. R. 1972. *Proc. Soc. Int. Limnol.* 18:192.

______. 1975. *Freshwater Biol.* 5:159–165.

Mur, L. 1971. Thesis, University of Amsterdam.

______. 1976. *Int. Symp. Exp. Alg. Cult. Sandefjord.*

Nienhuis, P. H. 1970. *Neth. J. Sea Res.* 5:20–49.

______. 1975. Thesis, University of Groningen.

Over, H. J. 1967. Thesis, University of Utrecht.

Parma, S. 1977. *Hydrobiologia* 52:117–126.

Pinkster, S. 1975. *Hydrobiol. Bull.* 9:131–138.

Polderman, P. J. G. 1976. *Coll. Phytosoc. IV, Lillie,* pp. 479–484.

______. 1976. *Acta Bot. Neerl.* 25:121–123.

Postma, H. 1961. *Neth. J. Sea Res.* 4:148–190.

Redeke, H. C. 1948. *Hydrobiologie van Nederland, de Zoete Wateren.* Amsterdam: De Boer.

Rietema, H. 1973. *Phycologia* 12:11–16.
______. 1975. Thesis, University of Groningen.
Rooth, J. 1965. *Natuurwiss. Studiekr. Sur., Ned. Ant.* 41:1–151.
______. 1969. *Natuurwiss. Werkgr. Ned. Ant.* 18:1–28.
Schroevers, P. J. 1966. *Wentia* 15:163–190.
Simons, J. 1976. *Acta Bot. Neerl.* 25:19–20.
Spaargaren, D. H. 1971. *Neth. J. Sea Res.* 5:275–333.
Stamm, W. T. et al. 1975. *Acta Bot. Neerl.* 24:379–390.
van der Steen, W. J. 1973. *Proc. R. Neth. Acad. Sci.* C76:245–256.
Stock, J. H. 1973. *Stud. Faun. Curaçao* 43:22–41.
Sunier, A. 1922. *Treubia* 2:159.
Swennen, C. 1977. *Ardea* 64:311–371.
Vaas, A. 1975. *Hydrobiol. Bull.* 9:114–119.
Vaas, A. et al. 1949. *Comm. Gen. Agr. Res. Sta. Buitenzorg,* No. 97.
______. 1953. *Contr. Int. Fish. Res. St. Djakarta-Bogor,* No. 3
______. 1959. *Hydrobiologia* 12:308–392.
Vegter, F. 1976. In *Proc. 10th Europ. Mar. Biol. Symp. Oostende* (ed. G. Persoone and E. Jaspers).
Verwey, J. 1942. *Arch. Neerl. Zool.* 6:363–468.
______. 1954. *Arch. Néerl. Zool.* 10:171–239.
______. 1958. *Arch. Néerl. Zool. Suppl.* 8:418–445.
______. 1973. *Neth. J. Sea Res.* 6:1–129.
Vijverberg, J. 1976. *Freshwater Biol.* 6:334–345.
______. 1976. *Hydrobiologia* 51:99–108.
Vosjan, H. J. 1977. *Neth. J. Sea Res.* 11:1–13.
Wagenaar Hummelinck, P. (ed.) 1940. *Studies on the fauna of Curaçao and Other Caribbean Islands.*
Wanders, J. W. B. et al. 1974. *Br. Phycol. J.* 9:223–224.
Westermann, J. H. 1953. *Found. Sci. Res. Surinam Neth. Ant.* 9:1–107.
de Wolf, P. 1973. *Neth. J. Sea Res.* 6:1–129.
Wolff, W. J. 1973. *Zool. Verh. Leiden* 126:1–242.
______. 1976. *Proc. 10th Europ. Mar. Biol. Symp. Oostende,* (ed. G. Persoone and E. Jaspers), pp. 653–689.
______. 1977. In *Ecology of marine benthos,* ed. B. C. Coull, pp. 267–280. Columbia: University of South Carolina Press.
Zaneveld, J. S. 1951. *Org. Sci. Res. Indonesia* 21:1–16.
______. 1961. *Gulf and Caribb. Fish. Inst. 14th Ann. Sess.* pp. 137–171.
Zijlstra, J. J. 1972. *Symp. Zool. Soc. London* 29:233–258.

Terrestrial Animal Ecology

Aart, P. J. M. van der. 1973. *Neth. J. Zool.* 23:266–329.
______ and N. Smeenk-Enserink. 1975. *Neth. J. Zool.* 25:1–45.
Alphen, J. J. M. van. 1980. *Neth. J. Zool.* 30:307–325.
Assem, J. van den. 1967. *Behaviour* suppl. 16:1–164.
______. 1971. *Neth. J. Zool.* 21:373–402.
Baars, M. A. 1979*a*. *Oecolgia* 44:125–140.

______. 1979*b*. Oecologia 41:25–46.
Bakker, K. 1961. *Arch. Néerl. Zool.* 14:200–281.
______. 1964. *Z. Angew. Entomol.* 53:187–208.
______. 1969. *Neth. J. Zool.* 19:541–595.
______. 1980. *Neth. J. Zool.* 30:145–150.
Balen, J. H. van. 1971. *Ardea* 61:1–93.
Barlow, C. A. 1957. *Tijdschr. Entomol.* 100:349–426.
Beusekom, C. F. van. 1972. *Ardea* 60:72–96.
Boer, M. H. den. 1971. *Neth. J. Zool.* 21:61–116.
Boer, P. J. den. 1961. *Arch. Néerl. Zool.* 14:283–409.
______. 1968. *Acta Biotheor.* 18:165–194.
______. 1977. Dispersal power and survival: carabids in a cultivated countryside. Miscellaneous papers. Landbouwhogeschool Wageningen 14.
______, et al. In press *Entomol. Gen.*
Bos, J. van den and R. Rabbinge. 1976. *Simulation of the fluctuations of the grey larch bud moth.* Simulation Monographs. Wageningen: Pudoc.
Botterweg, P. F. 1978. *Neth. J. Zool.* 28:341–464.
Bruyn, G. J. de. 1978. *Neth. J. Zool.* 28:55–61.
______. 1980. *Neth. J. Zool.* 30:345–368.
______ and A. A. Mabelis. 1972. *Ekol. Pol.* 20:93–101.
Caudri, L. W. D. 1941. *Arch. Néerl. Zool.* 5:413–498.
Cavé, A. J. 1968. *Neth. J. Zool.* 18:313–407.
Charnov, E. L. et al. In press *Nature.*
Croin Michielsen, N. 1966. *Arch. Néerl. Zool.* 17:73–174.
______, ed. 1974. *Meijendel, duin-water-leven.* Den Haag: Baarn.
Dienske, H. 1979. *Behaviour* 71:1–126.
Dijk, T. S. van. 1972. *Oecologia* 10:111–136.
______. 1973. *Oecologia* 12:213–240.
Dobben, W. H. van. 1952. *Ardea* 40:1–63.
Doude van Troostwijk, W. J. 1964. *Ardea* 52:13–29.
______. 1976. *Rin Verhandeling* nr. 7.
Drent, R. H. and P. Swierstra. 1977. *Wildfowl* 28:15–20.
Drift, J. van der. 1951. *Tijdschr. Entomol.* 94:1–168.
Ellenbroek, F. J. M. 1979. *Verh. Dtsch. Zool. Ges.* 1979:253.
Ernsting, G. and J. W. Jansen. 1978. *Oecologia* 33:173–183.
Eveleens, K. G. 1976. *Contr. Centr. Res. Inst. Agr. Bogor* 19:26.
Fransz, H. G. 1974. *The functional response to prey density in an acarine system.* Simulation Monographs. Wageningen: Pudoc.
Gelder, J. J. van. 1973. *Neth. J. Zool.* 23:86–108.
______ and H. C. J. Oomen. 1970. *Neth. J. Zool.* 20:238–252.
______ and H. C. M. Hoedemaekers. 1971. *J. Anim. Ecol.* 40:559–568.
______, P. M. G. Evers, and G. J. M. Maagnus. 1978. *J. Anim. Ecol.* 47:667–676.
Gruys, P. 1970. *Agricultural Research Report No. 742.* Wageningen: Pudoc.
Haeck, J. 1969. *Neth. J. Zool.* 19:145–248.
______. 1971. In *Dispersal and dispersal power of carabid beetles.* Miscellaneous papers. Landbouwhogeschool Wageningen 8:39–52.
Herrebout, W. M. 1969. *Neth. J. Zool.* 19:1–104.

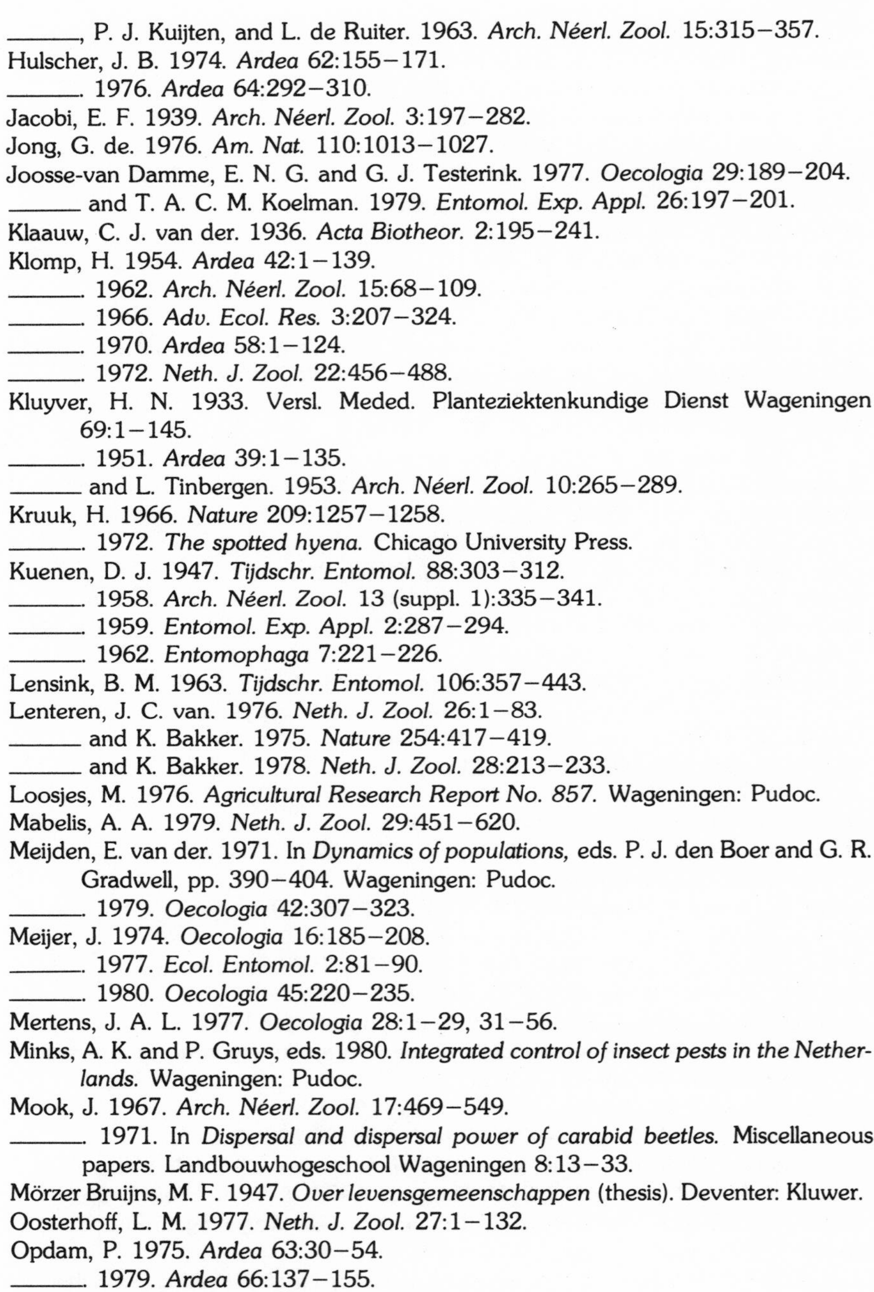

———, P. J. Kuijten, and L. de Ruiter. 1963. *Arch. Néerl. Zool.* 15:315–357.
Hulscher, J. B. 1974. *Ardea* 62:155–171.
———. 1976. *Ardea* 64:292–310.
Jacobi, E. F. 1939. *Arch. Néerl. Zool.* 3:197–282.
Jong, G. de. 1976. *Am. Nat.* 110:1013–1027.
Joosse-van Damme, E. N. G. and G. J. Testerink. 1977. *Oecologia* 29:189–204.
——— and T. A. C. M. Koelman. 1979. *Entomol. Exp. Appl.* 26:197–201.
Klaauw, C. J. van der. 1936. *Acta Biotheor.* 2:195–241.
Klomp, H. 1954. *Ardea* 42:1–139.
———. 1962. *Arch. Néerl. Zool.* 15:68–109.
———. 1966. *Adv. Ecol. Res.* 3:207–324.
———. 1970. *Ardea* 58:1–124.
———. 1972. *Neth. J. Zool.* 22:456–488.
Kluyver, H. N. 1933. Versl. Meded. Planteziektenkundige Dienst Wageningen 69:1–145.
———. 1951. *Ardea* 39:1–135.
——— and L. Tinbergen. 1953. *Arch. Néerl. Zool.* 10:265–289.
Kruuk, H. 1966. *Nature* 209:1257–1258.
———. 1972. *The spotted hyena.* Chicago University Press.
Kuenen, D. J. 1947. *Tijdschr. Entomol.* 88:303–312.
———. 1958. *Arch. Néerl. Zool.* 13 (suppl. 1):335–341.
———. 1959. *Entomol. Exp. Appl.* 2:287–294.
———. 1962. *Entomophaga* 7:221–226.
Lensink, B. M. 1963. *Tijdschr. Entomol.* 106:357–443.
Lenteren, J. C. van. 1976. *Neth. J. Zool.* 26:1–83.
——— and K. Bakker. 1975. *Nature* 254:417–419.
——— and K. Bakker. 1978. *Neth. J. Zool.* 28:213–233.
Loosjes, M. 1976. *Agricultural Research Report No. 857.* Wageningen: Pudoc.
Mabelis, A. A. 1979. *Neth. J. Zool.* 29:451–620.
Meijden, E. van der. 1971. In *Dynamics of populations,* eds. P. J. den Boer and G. R. Gradwell, pp. 390–404. Wageningen: Pudoc.
———. 1979. *Oecologia* 42:307–323.
Meijer, J. 1974. *Oecologia* 16:185–208.
———. 1977. *Ecol. Entomol.* 2:81–90.
———. 1980. *Oecologia* 45:220–235.
Mertens, J. A. L. 1977. *Oecologia* 28:1–29, 31–56.
Minks, A. K. and P. Gruys, eds. 1980. *Integrated control of insect pests in the Netherlands.* Wageningen: Pudoc.
Mook, J. 1967. *Arch. Néerl. Zool.* 17:469–549.
———. 1971. In *Dispersal and dispersal power of carabid beetles.* Miscellaneous papers. Landbouwhogeschool Wageningen 8:13–33.
Mörzer Bruijns, M. F. 1947. *Over levensgemeenschappen* (thesis). Deventer: Kluwer.
Oosterhoff, L. M. 1977. *Neth. J. Zool.* 27:1–132.
Opdam, P. 1975. *Ardea* 63:30–54.
———. 1979. *Ardea* 66:137–155.
Post, A. 1962. *Tijdschr. Planteziekten* 68:1–110.

Prop, N. 1960. *Arch. Néerl. Zool.* 13:380–447.

Rabbinge, R. 1976. *Biological control of fruit tree red spider mite.* Simulation Monographs. Wageningen: Pudoc.

Reddingius, J. 1971. *Acta Biotheor.* 20 (suppl. 1):1–208.

——— and P. J. den Boer. 1970. *Oecologia* 5:240–284.

Reijnders, P. J. H. 1980. On the causes of the decrease in the harbour seal (Phoca vitulina) population in the Dutch Wadden Sea. Thesis, Wageningen.

Richter, C. J. J. 1970. *Oecologia* 5:200–214.

Rijksen, H. D. 1978. *A field study on Sumatran orang utans.* Meded. Landbouwhogeschool Wageningen 78-2.

Rooth, J. 1965. The flamingos on Bonaire. *Natuurw. Studiekring Suriname-Ned. Antillen,* Utr. 41; RIVON Verh. 1.

Ruiter, L. de. 1956. *Arch. Néerl. Zool.* 11:285–341.

———. 1958. *Arch. Néerl. Zool.* 13 (suppl. 1):351–368.

Schipper, W. J. A. 1973. *Le Gerfaut* 6:17–20.

———. 1977. *Ardea* 65:53–72.

———. 1979. *Ardea* 66:77–102.

Schoonhoven, L. M. 1962. *Arch. Néerl. Zool.* 15:111–174.

Sluyter, J. W., P. F. van Heerdt, and J. J. Bezem. 1956. *Arch. Néerl. Zool.* 12:63–88.

Sluyter, J. W. 1971. *Decheniana Beih.* 18:1–44.

Smeenk, C. 1972. *Ardea* 60:1–71.

———. 1974. *Ardea* 62:1–97.

Spaans, A. 1971. *Ardea* 59:73–188.

Stortenbeker, C. W. 1967. *Agriculture Research Report No. 694.* Wageningen: Pudoc.

Tinbergen, J. M. 1976. *Ardea* 64:155–170.

Tinbergen, J. 1946. *Ardea* 34:1–212.

———. 1960. *Arch. Néerl. Zool.* 13:265–336.

Tinbergen, L. and H. Klomp. 1960. *Arch. Néerl. Zool.* 13:344–379.

Veen, H. E. van de. 1979. Food selection and habitat use in the red deer (*Cervus elephas* L.). Thesis, Groningen.

Verhoef, H. A., C. J. Nagelkerke, and E. N. G. Joosse. 1977. *J. Insect Physiol.* 23:1009–1013.

Verhoef, H. A. and J. Witteveen. 1980. *J. Insect Physiol.* 26:201–208.

Vlijm, L., L. Hartsuijker, and C. J. J. Richter. 1961. *Arch. Néerl. Zool.* 14:410–422.

——— and A. M. Kessler-Geschiere. 1967. *J. Anim. Ecol.* 36:31–56.

———, C. van de Kraan, and W. K. R. E. van Wingerden. 1974. *Rev. Ecol. Biol. Soc.* 11:511–518.

Voûte, A. D. 1946. *Arch. Néerl. Zool.* 7:435–470.

———. 1968. *Acta Biotheor.* 18:143–164.

Vrie, M. van de. 1974. *Proceedings of the FAO Conference on Ecology in Relation to Pest Control,* Rome, 1972, pp. 145–160.

Westerterp, K. 1973. *Ardea* 61:137–158.

Wijnands, H. E. J. and J. J. van Gelder. 1976. *Neth. J. Zool.* 26:414–424.

Wit, C. T. de and J. Goudriaan. 1974. *Simulation of ecological processes.* Simulation Monographs. Wageningen: Pudoc.

Wolda, H. 1963. *Arch. Néerl. Zool.* 15:381–471.
______. 1971. In *Dynamics of populations,* eds. P. J. den Boer and G. R. Gradwell, pp. 98–108. Wageningen: Pudoc.
______. 1978. *Am. Nat.* 112:1017–1045.
______. 1979. *J. Anim. Ecol.* 49:277–290.

Vegetation Science

Barkman, J. J. 1958. *Phytosociology and ecology of cryptogamic epiphytes.* Assen. (Reprinted 1969).
______. 1964. *Acta Bot. Neerl.* 13:394–419.
______. 1973. In *Handbook of vegetation science,* Vol. 5, ed. R. H. Whittaker, pp. 435–491. The Hague.
______. 1976. *Coolia* 19:57–66.
Beeftink, W. G. 1965. *Meded. Landbouwhogesch. Wageningen* 65 no. 1.
______ and J. M. Géhu. 1973. Spartinetea maritimae. *Prodrome des groupements végétaux d'Europe,* Vol. 1. Lehre.
Bijhouwer, J. 1926. *Geobotanische studie van de Berger duinen.*
Boerboom, J. H. A. 1960. *Meded. Landbouwhogesch. Wageningen 60* no. 10.
Daniels, F. J. A. In press. Vegetation of the Angmagssalik district of southeast Greenland. IV. Shrub, dwarf shrub and terricolous lichen vegetation. *Medd. om Grnl.*
Diemont, W. H. 1938. *Mitt. Flor.-soz. Arbeitsgem. Niedersachsen* 4.
______. 1937. *Jahresber. Naturh. Ges. Hannover* 88/89:73–87.
van Dieen, J. W. 1934. *Organogene Dünenbildung.* The Hague.
Doing, H. 1962. *Wentia* 8.
______. 1963. *Jaarb. Dendr. Ver.* 22:97–125.
van Donselaar, J. 1961. *Wentia* 15.
Feekes, W. 1936. *Ned. Kruidk. Arch.* 46:1–295.
Fresco, L. F. M. 1971. *Acta Bot. Neerl. 20:*589–599.
van Gils, H. and A. J. Kovacs. 1977. *Vegetatio* 33:175–186.
den Hartog, C. 1959. Wentia 1.
______ and S. Segal. 1964. *Acta. Bot. Neerl.* 13:367–393.
Hogeweg, P. and A. L. Brenkert-van Riet. 1969, *Trop. Ecol.* 10:139–162.
Holkema, F. 1870. *De plantengroei der Nederlandse Noordzee-eilanden.* Amsterdam.
Janssen, J. G. M. 1975. Vegetatio 30:67–71.
Kalkhoven, J. 1977. *Landelijke milieukartering.* The Hague.
Kortekaas, W. M. 1976. *Vegetatio* 33:51–60.
de Lange, L. 1972. *An ecological study of ditch vegetation in the Netherlands.* Amsterdam.
de Leeuw, W. C. 1936, *Ned. Kruidk. Arch.* 46:359–393.
van Leeuwen, C. G. 1966. *Wentia* 15:25–46.
Londo, G. 1971. *Patroon en proces in duinvegetaties langs een gegraven duinmeer in de Kennemerduinen.* Nijmegen.
van der Maarel, E. 1966. On vegetation structures, relations and systems, with special reference to the dune grasslands of Voorne, the Netherlands. Mimeographed. Zeist.

______. 1972. In *Basic problems and methods in phytosociology,* E. van der Maarel and R. Tüxen eds., pp. 183–190. The Hague.
Maas, F. M. 1959. *Meded. Landbouwhogesch. Wageningen* 59.
Meltzer, J., and V. Westhoff. 1942. *Inleiding tot de plantensociologie.* The Hague.
Meyer Drees, E. 1936. *De bosvegetatie van de Achterhoek en enkele aangrenzende gebieden.* Wageningen.
Nijland, G. 1974. *Meded. Landbouwhogesch. Wageningen* 74 no. 20.
van Schaik, C. P. and P. Hogeweg. 1977. *Vegetatio* 35:65–80.
Schenk, W. A. 1980. In press. *Excerpta Bot.,* Section B: Sociologica.
Scheygrond, A. 1932. *Ned. Kruidk. Arch.* 42:1–184.
Schoof-van Pelt, N. M. 1973. *Littorelletea, a study of the vegetation of some amphiphytic communities of Western Europe. Nijmegen.*
Segal, S. 1969. *Ecological studies on wall vegetation.* The Hague. (Reprinted 1972).
______ and V. Westhoff. 1959. *Acta Bot. Neerl.* 8:304–329.
Sissingh, G. 1950. *Versl. Landbouwk. Onderz.* 56 no. 15.
Sloet van Oldruitenborgh, J. M. 1976. *Duinstruwelen in het Deltagebied.* Wageningen.
Various authors. 1976. *Vegetatio* 32:65–72; 131–185.
de Vries, D. M. 1929. *Ned. Kruidk. Arch.* 39:145–403.
______. 1954. *Vegetatio* 5/6:105–111.
Werger, M. J. A. 1973. *Phytosociology of the upper Orange River valley, South Africa.* Pretoria.
______, ed. 1979. *The study of vegetation.* The Hague.
Westhoff, V. 1947. *The vegetation of dunes and salt marshes on the Dutch islands of Terschelling, Vlieland and Texel.* The Hague.
______. 1959. *Acta Bot. Neerl.* 8:422–448.
______. 1961. *Excerpta Bot.,* Section B: Sociologica 3, no. 2–3:81–220.
______. 1969. *Plantengemeenschappen in Nederland.* Zutphen.
______ and C. G. Leeuwen. 1966. In *Anthropogene vegetation,* ed. R. Tüxen pp. 156–172. The Hague.
______ and E. van der Maarel. 46. 1973. In *Handbook of vegetation science,* Vol. 5, ed. R. H. Whittaker, pp. 617–726.
Willems, J. H. In press. An experimental approach to the study of species diversity and above-ground biomass in chalk grassland. *Proc. Kon. Ned. Akad. Wet. Series C.*
Zonneveld, I. S. 1960.*Bodemkundige Studies* 4. (With a number of soil and vegetation maps).
______. 1972. *Land evaluation and land(scape) science.* ITC Textbook of Photointerpretation. Enschede.

Experimental Plant Ecology

Alberdo, T. 1974. *Neth. Contr. IBP, Final Report* 1966–67, pp. 24–25.
van Andel, J. 1975*a*. *Oecologia* 19:329–337.
______. 1975*b*. *Oecol. Plant.* 10:413–428.
Andriana, M. J. 1945. Thesis, University of Amsterdam.
Bakker, D. 1951. Thesis, University of Groningen.

——— 1960*a*. In *The biology of weeds,* ed. J. L. Harper. Oxford.
——— 1960*b*. *Acta Bot. Neerl.* 9:125–259.
van den Bergh, J. P. 1968. Thesis, Agricultural University, Wageningen.
Bloom, C. W. P. M. 1976. *Oecol. Plant.* 11:225–241.
——— 1977. *Oecol. Plant.* 12:363–381.
ter Borg, S. J. 1972. Thesis, University of Groningen.
Brouwer, R. 1962. *Neth. J. Agr. Sci.* 10:361–367.
——— 1963. *Yearbook IBS,* pp. 31–39.
van Dobben, W. H. 1967*a*. *Yearbook IBS,* pp. 75–83 (comm. 346).
——— 1967*b*. *Yearbook IBS,* pp. 61–73 (comm. 345).
van der Drift, J. 1974. *Neth. Contr. IBP, Final Report* 1966–71, pp. 26–32.
Ernst, W. H. O. 1975. *Int. Conf. Heavy Metals, Toronto.* Abstr. C 145; *Int. Bot. Congr., Leningrad.* Abstr. XII, p. 143.
Freysen, A. H. J. 1967. Thesis, University of Utrecht.
——— 1975*a*. *Acta Bot. Neerl.* 24:7–22.
——— 1975*b*. *Progr. Report 1974,* 100:34–36.
Gourdriaan, J. 1977. Thesis, Agricultural University, Wageningen.
Groen, J. 1973. Thesis, Agricultural University, Wageningen.
Janssen, J. G. M. 1974. Thesis, University of Nijmegen.
Ketner, P. 1972. Thesis, University of Nijmegen.
Lambers, J. T. 1976. *Physiol. Plant.* 37:117–123.
van der Meijden, E. 1970. In *Dynamics of populations,* eds. P. J. den Boer and G. R. Gradwell, pp. 309–404. Wageningen: Pudoc.
Neuteboom, J. H. 1975. *Med. LH (Proc. AUW).*
Oomes, M. J. M. 1976. J. Oecol. 64:745–755.
Pegtel, D. M. 1976. Thesis, University of Groningen.
Poms, T. L. 1976. *Acta Bot. Neerl.* 25:457–472.
——— 1977. *Acta Bot. Neerl.* 26:29–42, 251–263.
Rozema, J. 1975. *Oecol. Plant.* 10:317–329.
——— 1975. *Acta Bot. Neerl.* 24:407–416.
Segal, S. 1973. *Pol. Arch. Hydrobiol.* 20:195–205.
Smit, P. J. 1967/68. *Proc. R. Neth. Acad. Sci.* C 70–71:500–510, 280–292.
Sterk, A. A. 1968. Thesis, University of Utrecht.
——— 1975. *Acta Bot. Neerl.* 24:315–337.
——— and J. C. M. Den Nijs. 1971. *Acta Bot. Neerl.* 20:100–106.
Stoutjesdijk, P. 1966. *Wentia* 15:191–203.
——— 1970. *Acta Bot. Neerl.* 19:918–925.
van der Toorn, J. 1972. Thesis, University of Groningen.
Wassink, E. C. 1969. *IBP/PP Techn. Meet. Prod. Photosynth. Syst. I. Models and Methods* pp. 561–566.
de Wit, C. T. 1960. *On competition.* Versl. Landbk. Onderz. (Comm. Agr. Res.) 66.8. Wageningen: Pudoc.

Microbial Ecology

Ackermans, A. D. L. 1971. Thesis, University of Leiden.
——— 1977. In *Interactions between soil microorganisms and plants,* eds. Y. R. Dommergues and S. Krupa.

Atheunisse, J. 1972. *Antonie van Leeuwenhoek* 38:311–327.

Becking, J. H. 1970, *Plant Soil* 32:611–654.

______. 1974*a*. In *Bergey's manual of determinative bacteriology, 8th ed.* pp. 253, 256–261, 286, 288–289, 702–706, 871–872.

______. 1974*b*. *Soil Sci.* 118:196–212.

Bessems, E. P. M. 1973. Thesis, Agricultural University, Wageningen.

de Bont, J. A. M. 1976*a*. *Antonie van Leeuwenhoek* 42:59–71.

______. 1976*b*. Thesis, Agricultural University, Wageningen.

Cappenberg, T. E. 1975. Thesis, University of Utrecht.

______. 1976. In *Microbial production and utilization of gases,* eds. H. G. Schegel et al., pp. 125–134. Göttingen: E. Goltze-Verlag.

______. 1977. In *Proc. Int. Microbiol. Ecol. Symp.,* eds. J. A. R. Miles and M. W. Loutit Berlin: Springer-Verlag.

van Dijk, C. 1976. *New Phytol.* 77:73–91.

van Egeraart, A. W. S. M. 1972. Thesis, Agricultural University, Wageningen.

van Gemerden, H. 1971. *Arch. Mikrobiol.* 79:345–353.

______. 1974. *Microbial Ecol.* 1:104–119.

Hansen, T. A. 1974,. Thesis, University of Groningen.

Harder, W. 1977. *J. Appl. Bacteriol.* 43:1–24.

Harmsen, G. W. 1948. Thesis, Agricultural University, Wageningen.

Huntjens, J. L. M. 1972. Thesis, Agricultural University, Wageningen.

van Kessel, J. F. 1976. Thesis, Agricultural University, Wageningen.

Krul, J. 1976. *J. Appl. Bacteriol.* 40:245–260.

Kuenen, G. J. 1972. Thesis, University of Groningen.

______. 1975. *Plant Soil* 43:49–76.

______. 1977. *Microbial Ecol.* 3:119–130.

Lie, T. A. 1971. *Plant Soil,* special vol., pp. 117–127.

______. 1975. In *Symbiotic Nitrogen Fixation in Plants,* ed. P. S. Nutman pp. 319–333. Cambridge: Cambridge University Press.

______. 1978*a*. In *Nutrition and foods,* ed. M. Rechiigl. Cleveland: CRC Press.

______. 1978*b*. In *Proceedings in life science,* Berlin: Springer-Verlag.

Mulder, E. G. 1975. In *Nitrogen fixation by free living microorganisms,* ed. W. D. P. Stewart. IBP vol. 6, pp. 3–28.

______. 1977. In *A treatise of dinitrogen fixation,* eds. R. W. F. Hardy and A. H. Gibson pp. 221–242. New York: John Wiley and Sons.

______ and J. Antheunisse. 1963. *Ann. Inst. Pasteur, Paris,* 105: 46–74.

______ and J. Antheunisse. 1966. *J. Appl. Bacteriol.* 29:44–71.

______ and W. L. van Veen. 1963. *Antonie van Leeuwenhoek* 29:121–153.

______ and W. L. van Veen. 1973. *Antonie van Leeuwenhoek* 39:657–662.

Marmsen, J. L. M., and G. L. Kolenbrander. 1965. *Agronomy* 10:43–92.

van Niel, C. B. 1949. *Bacteriol Rev.* 13:161–174.

Prins, R. A. 1977. In *Microbial ecology of the gut,* eds. R. T. J. Clarke and T. Bauchop pp. 73–183. New York: Academic Press.

Quispel, A. 1974. *The biology of nitrogen fixation.* Amsterdam-New York: North Holland Publ. Co.

Ruinen, J. 1975. In *Nitrogen fixation by free living microorganisms,* ed. W. D. P. Stewart. IBP, vol. 6, pp. 85–100.

Stouthamer, A. H. 1976. *Yield studies in microorganisms.* Durham, U.K.: Meadowfield Press.

Veldkamp, H. 1955. *Meded. Landbauwhhogesch. Wageningen* 55:127–174.

______. 1970*a*. In *Methods in microbiology,* vol. 3A, eds. J. R. Norris and D. W. Ribbons, pp. 305–361. New York: Academic Press.

______. 1970*b*. *Rev. Microbiol.* 24:209–240.

______. 1972. *J. Appl. Chem. Biotechnol.* 22:105–123.

______. 1976*a*. *The continuous culture in microbial ecology and physiology,* Durham, U.K.: Meadowfield Press.

______. 1976*b*. In *Int. Symp. Continuous Culture, Oxford,* pp. 315–328. Chichester, U.K.: Ellis Horwood, Ltd.

______. 1977. *Adv. Microbial Ecol.* 1:59–94.

Verhoeven, W. 1952. Thesis, Technical University of Delft.

Vosjan, J. H. 1975. Thesis, University of Groningen.

de Vries, W. 1972. *J. Gen. Microbiol.* 71:515–524.

Wieringa, K. T. 1963. *Antonie van Leeuwenhoek* 29:84–88.

Woldendorp, J. W. 1973. Thesis, Agricultural University, Wageningen.

Zevenhuizen, L. P. T. M. 1971. *Arch. Microbiol.* 78:42–57.

15

NORWAY

Frans-Emil Wielgolaski, Egil Baardseth, Torleiv Brattegard, Eilif Dahl, Eystein Paasche, and Arne Semb-Johansson

BACKGROUND

Up to the Second World War, Norwegian biology was largely influenced by German scientific tradition. In this tradition, ecology was not considered a separate branch of biology but an aspect of other branches, such as morphology, physiology, and biogeography; it was divided into various subjects as botany, microbiology, invertebrate and vertebrate zoology, all both on land and in water. The ecosystem concept was then virtually unknown. The part of ecology that mainly deals with animal organisms has its chief historical roots in research with practical goals: the exploitation of fish and wildlife, and especially factors which influence population size.

Research activities in marine ecology and fisheries biology have been influenced by Norway's unique coastline stretching from 58°N to 71°N (21,100 km of shoreline and fjords as deep as 1,300 m), its closeness to some of the world's richest fishing areas, and the importance of its fisheries for the national economy.

Internationally known Norwegian wildlife biologists, marine biologists, and fisheries biologists have gained their reputation more by scientific work of a descriptive or applied nature than by making important contributions to theoretical ecology. These lines are also clearly seen in ecological activities after 1945, but other aspects and new fields of ecology have increased the diversity of ecology in recent years.

TEACHING AND TRAINING

Teaching in ecology started at the University of Oslo in the 1920s. The first courses were given for students in botany, but this teaching went on for only a few years. Normal courses in ecology for zoologists were given after World War II, and for botanists from the early 1960s. Recently, teaching in terrestrial ecology at the undergraduate level has been combined for all biologists and has dealt with more general and applied problems. Teaching and training in marine ecology and fisheries biology at the graduate level also started early at the University of Oslo although the first courses in these disciplines at the undergraduate level were given at the University of Bergen in the early 1960s and somewhat later at the University of Oslo. Undergraduate courses in both general and terrestrial ecology have been given at the Agricultural University of Norway at Ås since 1964. From the mid-1970s, instruction in both terrestrial and aquatic ecology has been given at all the universities of Norway (Oslo, Bergen, Ås, Trondheim, and Tromsø, at the last two universities from their establishment). At most of the universities, courses in ecology are now required for students in biology, and at some universities, the ecological parts of various subjects are brought together in integrated courses.

The Nordic countries (Denmark, Finland, Norway, Sweden, and later also Iceland) have cooperated within ecology through the Nordic Council for Marine Biology since 1956, through the Nordic Council for Terrestrial Ecology (now Nordic Council for Ecology, incorporating freshwater ecology also) from the early 1960s, and through the Nordic Council for Wildlife Research. The councils function as cooperative bodies for research training and arrange, for example, summer courses for graduate students and young scientists; these groups also conduct fellowship programs. Many of the courses and other activities have been carried out at the several biological field stations built particularly during the last fifteen to twenty years. In Norway, about twenty terrestrial and aquatic field stations are found from the far south to the north of the country. They have been of the greatest importance for ecological field training and research in Norway.

Most of the textbooks in ecology were in German before 1940, but from 1945 to 1950, British and American books were used. During the last few years, textbooks in Scandinavian languages have become common for undergraduate courses in both general and terrestrial ecology.

Research, development, and teaching in ecology are mainly financed by the government by direct contributions from the ministries of education, environment, fisheries, agriculture, and industry to the research institutes and the universities, all of which belong to the state. In addition, funds are channelled through the Norwegian research councils (science and humanities, scientific and industrial research, fisheries, agriculture). Other ecological funding organizations and private industry contribute a small percentage of the total, which amounted in 1973 to about N. kr. 15 million, or about 3 million U.S. dollars. The same year the funding for all environmental research in Norway was somewhat above N. kr. 50 million ($10 million U.S.).

SOCIETIES AND JOURNALS

There are societies in Norway within the various disciplines of biology, and many of them may be seen as ecologically oriented. Important in this respect is the Norwegian Ecological Society, which was founded in the beginning of the 1960s. The society cooperates with the Scandinavian sister organizations in Denmark and Sweden on the publication of the journal *Oikos;* it is also involved through the Scandinavian Ecological Association, Oikos, in the new journal *Holarctic Ecology,* which replaced some of the national ecological journals and publishes more descriptive ecological papers than *Oikos.* Ecology is, of course, also part of the interest of the Norwegian Botanical and Norwegian Zoological Societies, as well as of the Norwegian Ornithological and Norwegian Entomological societies. They all have or have had their own journals (*Blyttia, Fauna, Sterna,* and *Norw. Journal of Entomology*), mostly in the Norwegian language and with more popular articles, partly of ecological interest.

Marine ecology and fisheries biology are related to and interact with other disciplines of oceanography. Cooperation in oceanography is, therefore, necessary and has long traditions. It was mostly secured on an informal basis, as long as the number of scientists and institutes was low. In 1949, the Association of Norwegian Oceanographers was founded to promote and improve cooperation among the increasing number of oceanographers of all disciplines and between oceanographic institutes of all types. Its main activity has been to assemble a symposium every year but it has also been active in policy making on oceanographic research in the country. Since 1971, the Norwegian Oceanographic Committee (NOK), which is an ad hoc committee to the Norwegian Research Council for Science and the Humanities (NAVF), has been the main coordinating organization on the national level, as well as promoting communication and cooperation with international organizations (e.g., IOC, ICES, SCOR). Through memberships held by the Norwegian Academy of Science and Letters and national committees, contact is also kept with several international organizations dealing with ecological problems, such as SCAR, SCOR, SCOPE, and ICIPE.

In addition to the journals mentioned above, more popular ecological papers are found in about ten other Norwegian journals. The various museums, scientific institutes, and universities have their own yearbooks and other publications, often with ecological articles. The Norwegian Academy of Science and Letters, and the Royal Norwegian Society of Science and Letters have published some major papers on ecology. In forestry and agriculture, important ecological articles are presented in *Meldinger fra Norges landbrukshøgskole* (Reports from the Norwegian Agricultural University), *Forskning og forsøk i landbruket* (Research and Experiments in Agriculture), and *Meddelelser fra Norsk Institutt for Skogforskning* (Reports of the Norwegian Forest Research Institute), while articles on applied wildlife ecology often are presented in *Meddelelser fra Statens Viltundersøkelser* (Reports from the State Game Research Institute). Pollution problems resulting from acidification are often published in reports from the Acid Precipitation Project. Papers on Norwegian arctic ecology are sometimes published in *Norsk Polaninstitutts skrifter* (Reports from the Norwegian Polar Institute), while alpine ecology of Norway, for example, from research done during participation in the International Biological Program, often is published in temporary publications as *IBP i Norden;* some, however, appear in *Rapporter fra Høyfjellsøkologisk Stasjon, Finse* (Reports from the High Mountain Ecology Research Station, Finse), which is published at irregular intervals.

Articles on marine ecology and fisheries biology appear mostly in the following Norwegian journals: *Sarsia,* devoted to contributions on Norwegian and North Atlantic marine organisms and their environment; *Fiskeridirektoratets Skrifter, serie Havundersøkelser* (Reports from the Directorate on Fisheries, series Open Sea Studies), devoted to contributions on marine organisms or environments related to fisheries; *Hvalrådets Skrifter* (Reports from the Whaling Advisory Board), devoted mainly to contributions on whales and seals but also plankton; and *Fisken og Havet* (The Fish and the Open Sea), consisting of reports and articles (in Norwegian) issued at irregular intervals by the Institute of Marine Research, Bergen.

Other Norwegian journals that may contain articles of interest to ecologists are *Astarte* and *Nytt Magasin for Naturvitenskapene* (1945–1951) = *Nytt Magasin for Zoologi* + *Nytt Magasin for Botanikk* (both 1952–1970) = *Norwegian Journal of Zoology* + *Norwegian Journal of Botany* (1971–1980).

Some journals published in the other Scandinavian countries (Sweden and Denmark) get financial support from Norway and may also contain papers of ecological interest, e.g., *Acta Agriculturae Scandinavica, Acta Zoologica, Entomologica Scandinavica, Ornis Scandinavica,* and *Zoologica Scripta.* Norwegian ecologists present their results in these and other Nordic journals, often also in other foreign journals. The literature service in Norway is good, and most journals with ecological articles are readily available and used.

TERRESTRIAL ECOLOGY

As ecological research in Norway is based historically on various subjects of biology, it is natural first to look separately on ecology related to botany, zoology, and other subjects. Advances in ecological research have especially been associated with developments in phytogeography and zoogeography.

Botany

In botany, two important lines of research have been present, one in the study of plant communities, the other in the study of plant distribution.

Norwegian tradition in phytosociology goes back to the Uppsala school, but the approach was later modified by Nordhagen (1936, 1943) to encompass impulses from the Zurich-Montpellier school. This line was followed by Gjæevoll (1956) and others. However, Dahl (1956) was more influenced by central European tradition, and the approach of Kielland-Lund (1973) is almost entirely that of Braun-Blanquet. Thus, the earlier sharp division between the Uppsala and the Zurich-Montpellier schools is, at least in Norway, replaced by a gradient. Important in the theoretical discussions has been the concept of homogeneity of stands and the corresponding concept, homotoneity (Nordhagen 1943; Dahl 1956) when different stands are compared.

The classification of vegetation by these and several other Scandinavian studies has led to a Scandinavian agreement on a vegetation classification system for mapping purposes (Wielgolaski 1971). Vegetation mapping for conservation purposes and regional planning has developed rapidly during the last years.

The spatial pattern of different plant communities can be related to environmental factors. Vestergren (1902) stressed the importance of unequal snow cover in winter to alpine vegetation. His observations have been confirmed and elaborated on (Nordhagen 1943; Gjærevoll 1956; Dahl 1956) and are of importance to road engineers as a guide in summer to snow conditions in winter. Other important variables are solifluction, drainage, and soil fertility. Discriminant analysis is used to detect significant differences in soil chemical variables between forest communities, either based directly on the measurements (Dahl et al. 1967; Bjørnstad 1971) or on principal components derived from the measurements (Aune 1973).

The study of plant distribution in relation to environmental factors has long traditions in Norway. Holmboe (1913) made a detailed dot map of the distribution of *Ilex aquifolium* and demonstrated the close correlation between its range limit and the 0°C isotherm of the coldest month. Similar patterns are exhibited by many species with a distribution termed oceanic, and it is believed that many of them are restricted because of their sensitivity to frost (Fægri 1960). Lye (1970) studied the distribution of vascular plants, hepatics, mosses, and lichens along a transect from the coast inland in southwest Norway. He concluded that the distribution of most oceanic vascular plants is restricted by low winter temperatures, while the distribution of most hepatics is restricted by low precipitation and air humidity, mosses and lichens taking a position between.

Dahl (1951) suggested that the distribution of many alpine plant species is restricted by their sensitivity to high summer temperatures. This hypothesis was supported by a comparison of range limits of several species with isotherms of yearly average maximum summer temperatures calculated for the highest points in the landscape.

Many plant species are restricted to areas with relatively warm summers. The limit most closely studied is the alpine and arctic timberline. It is long known that this limit correlates well with the mean temperature of the three or four warmest months.

Dahl and Mork (1959) suggested that growth in *Picea abies* near its altitudinal limit is restricted by low production of ATP by respiration when temperatures are low. They compared measured growth of spruce with sums of temperature weighted according to the effect of temperature on respiration, called respiration equivalents, and found very good correlations between growth and respiration equivalents. Skre (1972) calculated respiration equivalents for Scandinavian meteorologic stations and compared isolines of respiration equivalents with northern and altitudinal limits of many species, producing improved correlations between the distribution limit of many species and meteorologic data.

Zoology

Many vertebrate populations show more or less regular three-to-four-year cycles, and since the days of Collet (1895), these cycles have attracted the interest of ecologists. Fluctuations in microtines have been analyzed with regard to periodicity and regional distribution (Wildhagen 1952), and in recent years also to reproduction, nutrition, and bioenergetics. The possibility of keeping colonies of native small rodents, especially the Norwegian lemming (*Lemmus lemmus*), in captivity has, since the beginning of the 1960s, added an experimental approach to the studies of population fluctuations.

Correlated with microtine cycles are variations in populations of other animals, e.g., the willow grouse (*Lagopus lagopus*). Investigations started in the 1920s were centered around the problem of population fluctuations (Olstad 1932). In later years, intensive studies on local willow grouse populations (Myrberget 1974) with the addition of work on captive grouse have brought forth valuable data.

Much of our knowledge, based on Norwegian research, about the role of predators in regulating the population density of rodents and game animals was brought together by Hagen (1952), who placed the predators in their true ecological position. Many of these ecological studies on terrestrial birds and mammals are organized by the Norwegian State Game Research Institute. This institute has also centered research around the cervids, and especially the management of populations of wild reindeer (*Rangifer tarandus*) in southern Norway. The practical aim has been a balance between the reindeer populations and their food supply, especially the carrying capacity of the mountain areas during the winter season, in order to prevent overgrazing.

The study of ecological conditions in the mountain areas has a long tradition in Norway, facilitated by the establishment of research stations in alpine areas. The mountain research (also freshwater studies) comprises both population fluctuations, productivity studies, and ecophysiological adaptations to these severe environments (Østbye et al. 1975).

Norwegian arctic research has for many years centered around the Spitzbergen Islands. The recent interest in arctic research is partly caused by the increased influence of humans on arctic ecosystems. Much of this research is part of international programs, e.g., the work on the polar bear (*Ursus marinus*). Besides different aspects of population ecology, work has been mainly on the ecophysiological adaptation of this animal to an arctic environment (Øritsland 1976). This ecophysiological tradition goes back to K. Schmidt-Nielsen, and was continued by F. Scholander and later by J. Krogh at the University of Oslo.

Another aspect of ecophysiology is represented by the work of Sømme (1977) and his group at the University of Oslo on cold-hardiness in insects, especially their ability to supercool and survive freezing. At the Zoological Museum at the University of Bergen, Kauri and his co-workers have carried out ecophysiological investigations on invertebrates, such as respiration studies in various groups (published in Wielgolaski 1975), as well as studies on dynamics of invertebrate groups.

Ecological studies on terrestrial invertebrates have also centered on noxious insects, their biology and ecology (Norwegian Plant Protection Institute), and the possibility of using biological control methods (Zoological Institute, Norwegian Agricultural University). The work by Bakke (1977) and co-workers on the pheromones of bark beetles is very interesting. Parts of the work on spruce insects has been a joint Nordic project.

In the first decades after 1945, work on parasitology was mainly centered around A. Brinkmann and his group in Bergen, but in later years, a helminthological group has developed around Vik at the Zoological Museum in Oslo. In addition to life history descriptions, work has included quantitative studies. Thus, the regulation of the size of a parasite population in an individual host has been found to be density dependent and to be an effect of the negative interaction between the parasites (e.g., Halvorsen 1976).

Several papers dealing with niche segregation between sympatric species of birds are of general ecological interest, especially the studies by Haftorn (1953–1956) working at the University of Trondheim on food biology and the storing of surplus food by tits (*Parus* spp.), tree-creepers (*Certhia familiaris*), and goldcrests (*Regulus regulus*). These are studies that deserve to be better known internationally.

Recent years have seen the emergence of evolutionary ecology. Voltinism and life-cycle strategies in different environments have been described for copepods (Elgmork) and for several insects. In this connection, special mention must be made of the recent work of Stenseth (1977) on theoretical studies on fluctuating populations, especially of rodents.

Microbiology

Traditionally, microbiologists have been working on physiologic aspects of bacteria and fungi, among others, but ecological studies have been carried out on soil microbes at the Norwegian Agricultural University. In later years, Goksøyr and co-workers at the University of Bergen have carried out microbiological investigations in ecophysiology, for example, in connection with ecosystem studies in alpine areas (published in Wielgolaski 1975).

Ecosystem Studies

Such studies need integrated research among several types of scientists and are, therefore, very expensive. During the IBP period (International Biological Program), a terrestrial ecosystem project was carried out in the alpine region at Hardangervidda in southern Norway in 1968–1974. During this period, a new mountain research station was built at Finse in the same area, and the station became important for the fieldwork within the project. The aim of the project was to look at energy flow and nutrient cycling through the systems, to examine the potential of the area for increased grazing by sheep and cattle in the future, and to get an impression of the carrying capacity for the reindeer population of the various communities compared.

It was necessary to employ workers on climatology, pedology, phytosociology, production ecology (plants and animals), ecophysiology (nutrition, translocation, photosynthesis, and respiration of plants and animals), agriculture, wildlife, decomposition and microbiology, as well as on modelling. The methods used were discussed both nationally and internationally in an attempt to link the results from the various subject groups within the country and to compare the results between countries. Many of the data and results are published in Wielgolaski (1975). After the end of the IBP, a Man and Biosphere program in the islands of Svalbard was begun and continues to study human influence on arctic and alpine ecosystems and particularly the ecology and management of arctic reindeer populations. The ecosystem of a coastal heath area in western Norway is also being studied in the so-called Lindås project.

FRESHWATER ECOLOGY

Strøm, who started out as an algologist, later placed particular emphasis on the physical and chemical factors in freshwater ecology. The investigations by him and his collaborators have, in many ways, formed the basis for modern freshwater ecology in Norway. He made regional surveys of Norwegian lakes and always viewed lakes as an integral part of the landscape. He made valuable contributions to our understanding of oxygen stratification and its relation to productivity and lake morphology. A broad surveying approach is evident in the studies of Økland (1964), who spent nineteen seasons in the field to analyze about fifteen hundred lakes and rivers. He uses the system of the European Invertebrate Survey for presentation of his material, not only for the fauna, like gastropods, but also for the physical and chemical factors.

A totally different approach, i.e., a holistic view of the freshwater lake as an ecosystem, was particularly evident in the large IBP teamwork studies of Øvre Heimdalsvann on a lake situated 1,090 m above sea level in the mountains of southern Norway. Here both energy flow and nutrient cycling, as well as other aspects of freshwater ecology, were studied over the entire year. Results from this work are presented in a separate volume of the journal *Holarctic Ecology* edited by Vik (1978). A synthesis and summary is given in a paper by Larsson et al. (1978).

Historically, freshwater ecology in Norway has its roots in the studies of fish populations. Among the pioneers in these studies are K. Dahl (1910) who in the first decades of this century gave valuable contributions to fish ecology. These studies, with special emphasis on the brown trout (*Salmo trutta*), have been continued to the present (Jensen 1977). Among other salmonids, the char (*Salmo alpinus*) has received much attention. After many years of intensive fieldwork and experimentation, Nordeng (1977) and his co-workers have proposed a pheromone hypothesis for homeward migration of anadromous salmonids.

The exploitation of water power for electricity started in Norway just after 1900. Before World War II, papers on the effects of the exploitation mostly covered the bottom fauna and subsequent consequences for the brown trout populations; after 1945, papers have dealt with several salmonid species in the reservoirs, the interaction between the species and their food resources, and the effect of stocking (Aass 1973). In 1975, a research group began a weir project to determine the ecological consequences when rivers are regulated for hydroelectric power supply and weirs are built. A study of the river Aurlandselven in western Norway was started by a group from the University of Bergen in 1965 before the river was regulated for hydroelectric power and has continued since the regulation. A similar study of the water system in the Voss area was a joint project between the local community and the University of Oslo.

Recent years have also brought other environmental threats against fish populations. A decrease, and even total extinction, of trout populations in many lakes in southwestern Norway have been linked to the increase in acid precipitation in these regions. A multidisciplinary research project has looked into these problems since the early 1970s.

MARINE ECOLOGY

Botany

Primary producers in the sea are benthic and planktonic algae, two quite different groups ecologically. Although the divisions overlap somewhat, the development of phytobenthic marine ecology in Norway may be categorized into descriptive, quantitative, and experimental ecology.

Descriptive Ecology

Descriptive phytobenthic ecology has a long tradition in Norway. It usually describes the seaweed vegetation qualitatively by dissecting it into associations or zones, each part with more or less "natural" boundaries and uniform appearance. The influence of environmental factors on the vegetation is often judged subjectively.

The effect of pollution has been studied in the Hardangerfjord by Alstadsæther (1954), the Oslofjord by Sundene (1953) and Grenager (1957) among others, and Nordåsvannet south of Bergen by Munda (1967). In all cases, an increasing dominance of green algae with increasing pollution was noted, with a simultaneous gradual disappearance of the fucoids. Sundene (1953) stressed the effect of wave action, salinity, and pollution. Pollution is often associated with reduced salinity, and the effects of these two factors are sometimes difficult to separate. An extreme case of industrial pollution (Iddefjorden) is described by Lein, Rueness, and Wiik (1974).

The benthic vegetation of the Hardangerfjord was studied by Jorde and Klavestad (1963). They found an impoverishment of the flora and a rise of the lower border of the vegetation toward the inner part of the fjord. Some species showed the best development in the outer fjord area (e.g., *Laminaria hyperborea*), whereas others (*Stictyosiphon*) had an inner fjord distribution. Similar studies have been carried out on other localities.

Although both areas face the Arctic Sea, the vegetation of Spitsbergen (Svendsen 1959) differed markedly from that of Finnmark, northern Norway (Jaasund 1965). The usual perennial fucoids of Finnmark were not found in the littoral region of Spitsbergen, which consisted mostly of quick-growing annuals. Furthermore, several species typical of the littoral zone in Finnmark are confined to the sublittoral region in Spitsbergen. These differences are explained by the ice cover at Spitsbergen.

Quantitative Ecology

Quantitative phytobenthic ecology, in which vegetation is measured by weight samples and these put in relation to external factors, started in the early 1950s with the establishment of the Norwegian Institute of Seaweed Research in Trondheim. At the beginning, the aim of this institute was purely practical, namely, to estimate the amount and the state of raw material available for a seaweed industry in Norway. The estimated seaweed quantities, however, could profitably be linked with certain external factors in order to reduce the sampling errors.

The densities of seaweed beds (fresh weight per unit area) in different districts along the Norwegian coasts are published in several reports from the institute. An objective delimitation of the beds, together with a random sampling procedure, was found to be of prime importance in order to get reproducible results. The use of hydrographic lines was found to give more objective results than the traditional division of vegetation into associations.

Extensive forests of oarweed (*Laminaria hyperborea*) exist all along the Norwegian coast. Their greatest density is found between 0 and 10 m with a gradual decrease to zero at about 30 m (e.g., Kain 1971).

Investigations on littoral fucoids (*Ascophyllum, Fucus serratus,* and *F. vesciculosus*) were limited to the area between high- and low-water springs. A two-stage sampling system permitted the density variation of these beds to be analyzed as resulting from accidental, local, and regional causes. Varying degrees of exposure to waves were found to have an important local effect, and a quantitative measure of this factor was developed. A much higher (seven times) quantity of *Ascophyllum* at 64–66°N than at 60°N seemed to be caused by the increase in tidal amplitude toward northern latitudes. The weight usually had a maximum in late summer and a minimum in June, immediately after the shedding of the fruit bodies (Baardseth 1970).

Experimental Ecology

Experimental ecology is the best method to show the effect of external factors on a single species. In Norway, Sundene (1962–1964) did the pioneer work on phytobenthic experimental ecology. By means of many cultures grown both in the laboratory and in the sea, and by transplantation of specimens from one part of the coast to another, he found, for example, that the summer sea temperature determines the distribution of *Alaria,* whereas *Chorda tomentosa* appeared to be controlled by the winter temperature.

Investigations on variation in chemical constituents of seaweeds with external factors are taken up by the Norwegian Institute of Seaweed Research. Researchers from the institute have shown that with increasing salinity the phenol content increases while the content of niacin, biotin, carotene, and chlorophyll decreases.

Another discovery of recent years is the reaction of fucoids toward heavy metal contamination of the water. In the Hardangerfjord, heavy metal levels as high as twenty to fifty times normal were found in seaweeds growing in highly polluted areas (Haug et al. 1974). It thus seems that a metal analysis of certain seaweeds is a useful and inexpensive method for evaluating the state of a marine recipient with regard to heavy metal contamination. Transplantation studies on *Ascophyllum* showed, for example, that the zinc content of new tissue was fairly quickly accommodated to new surroundings, whereas old tissue maintained its zinc content for a much longer time (Myklestad et al. 1978).

The study of marine phytoplankton in Norway represents an unbroken academic tradition dating back to the beginning of the century. Professor H. H. Gran (1870–1955) was one of the founders of plankton ecology, and his work at the University of Oslo was continued by his pupil Trygve Braarud (1903–), whose activities as a teacher and organizer had a strong influence on the developments taking place in the country from 1945 to 1970. In his own work, Braarud combined a thorough knowledge of phytoplankton species with an exceptional ability to extract relevant information from hydrographic data. Under his direction, a considerable number of larger and smaller investigations were completed, all of them based on a detailed quantitative analysis of the phytoplankton standing stocks by the inverted microscope.

The goal of this type of investigation was to arrive at an understanding of the dynamics of phytoplankton communities. Despite the fact that quantitative estimates of populations are found in all the published papers, the approach remained an essentially qualitative one, since no attempt was made to express the dynamic relations in mathematical terms. A representative paper from this period is the large-scale investigation of the spring phytoplankton in the North Sea (Braarud et al. 1953), the only reasonably complete mapping to date of the phytoplankton in this important area. There are a series of corresponding papers by Braarud and by his students on Norwegian coastal waters and on the Norwegian Sea. This work forms a valuable background for any future development of a quantitative plankton ecology in these areas. Therefore, Norway is one of the few countries for which a fairly adequate floral description of its coastal waters is available.

Since about 1970, work has commenced at two of the Norwegian universities (Trondheim and Oslo) in phytoplankton ecophysiology. This reflects a general tendency elsewhere, with the foremost exponents in the United States, to look for relationships between the growth rates of individual species and the physical and chemical variables in the environment. In this type of work, experiments on selected plankton algae in the laboratory are combined with analyses of plankton populations in the field. A quantitative mathematical approach to phytoplankton ecology had not yet been initiated in Norway by 1975.

Zoology and Fisheries Biology

In the Norwegian research traditions, marine zoology and fisheries biology are almost inseparable from marine ecology. Marine zoology started as a science with Michael Sars (1805–1869) who initiated studies in causal marine zoogeography. His son, Georg O. Sars (1837–1927), made important contributions to fishery biology (e.g., discovered that cod and mackerel have pelagic eggs), biology and faunistics of the deep Norwegian Sea (The Norwegian North-Atlantic Expedition 1876–1878), and systematic zoology. His monumental *An Account of the Crustacea of Norway* (1895–1928) will forever remain an international standard work of reference. Johan Hjort (1869–1948) was one of the first to emphasize the importance of the environment for fish behavior and fish migrations. His special interest was the study of yearly fluctuations in fish stocks and, using demographic methods, he found that these fluctuations were coupled to the size of specific year classes. He stressed the importance of studies of the fate of eggs and larvae. Together with Sir John Murray, he made important contributions to deep-sea biology in the book *The Depths of the Oceans* (1912). Hjalmar Broch (1882–1969) continued the research in marine zoogeography and systematics as founded by M. Sars and G. O. Sars. Gunnar Rollefsen (1899–1976) and Johan T. Ruud (1903–1970) are outstanding representatives of marine biologists and fisheries biologists bridging the traditional and the modern marine biological sciences in Norway.

Marine research activity, especially in fisheries biology, was hampered by lack of suitable vessels in the 1920s and 1930s, but increased considerably when ocean-going research vessels became available, the first *G. O. Sars* in 1949, and other vessels in the 1950s. Especially since the 1960s, research activity in marine zoology has gradually shifted toward field-oriented experimental ecology, population ecology, and systems ecology paralleling advances in general ecological theory, instrumentation, and computer science.

In fisheries biology, the main trend has been to concentrate efforts on problems of optimal use of living resources by increasing research efforts in studies of fish population dynamics, in the methodology of estimating standing stock by acoustic techniques, and in developing the scientific basis for marine aquaculture in Norwegian waters. Research interests in studies of pollutants and their effects on ecosystems and commercially important species are increasing because of an awareness of the potential dangers of dumping industrial wastes and excessive amounts of sewage. These interests are, however, mainly triggered by the development of oil production in the North Sea and by changes in the seasonal supply of fresh water to fjords and coastal waters because of construction of large hydroelectric power plants (Skreslet et al. 1976).

The number of marine zoologists and fisheries biologists at the universities and government research institutes increased rapidly from 1945 and reached about 120 at a dozen institutes and departments in the late 1970s. This growth has also caused a significant increase in activity. Important papers published during the first years after 1945 are those by Sætersdal (1952, 1953), who carried out important work on the haddock in Norwegian waters, and by Wiborg (1954) and Østvedt (1955), who made important zooplankton investigations in coastal and offshore waters of Norway. The work by Beyer (1958) merits special ecological interest, as it gives a general discussion of the life conditions of the fjord deeps.

The number of multidisciplinary projects, of which marine ecology has been an important part, has also increased in recent years. However, the Hardangerfjord investigations to study the natural history of a typical Norwegian fjord, started in 1955, have been going on for several years (Brattegard 1966). The pollution problem was one of the reasons for the Oslofjord investigations (1962–1966), with studies of the influence of domestic sewage and industrial wastes (Beyer 1968). From the late 1960s and into the 1970s, several multidisciplinary projects have been under way. The Trondheimfjord projects (Borgenfjord 1967–1974; the main fjord 1972–1974) comprised general ecological studies of plankton and benthos, and studies of the influence of domestic sewage and industrial wastes. In the investigations of the Skjomenfjord (phase I, 1970–1973) and the Ryfylkefjords (phase I, 1973–1975), the influence of changes in freshwater output due to construction of hydroelectric power plants has been studied. The Fensfjord investigations (1971–1973) concentrated on studies to evaluate possible effects of dumping of red mud from a proposed aluminum production plant (Brattegard and Høisæter 1972, 1973). In the Korsfjord project (1971–), ecological studies are carried out on the deep-water pelagic community with emphasis on trophic relations (Matthews and Bakke 1977). The same year (1971) a project was started in an attempt to model a total marine ecosystem (the Lindåspolls project) (Lie et al. 1978). In the Coastal Current Project (1974–), processes in the Norwegian coastal current are described and modelled.

REFERENCES CITED

Aass, P. 1973. Some effects of lake impoundments in salmonids in Norwegian hydroelectric reservoirs. *Acta Univ. Upsal, Abstr. Uppsala Diss. Fac. Sci. 234,* 14 pp.

Alstadsæter, I. 1954. Algological observations in the Hardangerfjord. *Nytt. Mag.* 2:101–116.

Aune, E. I. 1973. Forest vegetation in Hemne, Sør-Trøndelag, Western Central Norway. *Miscellania* 12:87 pp.

Baardseth, E. 1954. Kvantitative tare-undersøkelser i Lofoten og Salten sommeren 1952. *Norw. Inst. Seaweed Res. Report no. 6.* Oslo.

———. 1955. A statistical study of the structure of the Ascophyllum zone. *Norsk institutt for tang- og tare-forskning. Report n. 11.* Oslo.

———. 1958. A method of estimating the physode content in brown algae. *Norw. Inst. of Seaweed Res., Report no. 20,* Trondheim.

———. 1970. Seasonal variation in *Ascophyllum nodosum* (L.) Le Jol. in the Trondheimsfjord with respect to the absolute live and dry weight and the relative content of dry matter, ash and fruit bodies. *Botanica Marina* 13:13–22.

______. 1970. Synopsis of biological data on knobbed wrack *Ascophyllum nodosum* (L.) Le Jol. *FAO Fisheries Synopsis no. 38.* Rome.

______. 1970. A square-scanning, two-stage sampling method of estimating seaweed quantities. *Norw. Inst. Seaweed Res. Report no. 33.* Trondheim.

______ and B. Grenager, 1961. A method of assessing seaweed quantities. *Norw. Inst. of Seaweed Res. Rep no. 25,* Trondheim.

Bakke, A., P. Frøyen, and L. Skattebøl. 1977. Field response to a new pheromonal compound isolated from *Ips typographus. Naturwiss.* 64:98–99.

Beyer, F. 1958. A new, bottom-living Trachymedusa from the Oslofjord. Description of the species, and a general discussion of the life conditions and fauna of the fjord deeps. *Nytt. Mag. Zool.* 6:121–143.

______. 1968. Zooplankton, zoobenthos, and bottom sediments as related to pollution and water exchange in the Oslofjord. *Helgoländer wiss. Meeresunters.* 17:496–509.

Bjørnstad, A. 1971. A phytosociological investigation of the deciduous forest types in Søgne, South Norway. *Norw. J. Bot.* 18:191–214.

Braarud, T., K. R. Gaarder and J. Grøntvedt. 1953. The phytoplankton of the North Sea and adjacent waters in May 1948. *Rapp. P.-v.Réun. Cons. perm. int. Explor. Mer.* 133:1–87.

Brattegard, T. 1966. The natural history of the Hardangerfjord. 7. Horizontal distribution of the fauna of rocky shores. *Sarsia* 22:1–54.

______ and T. Høisæter 1972. Undersøkelse av Fensfjordens dype bløtbunners dyreliv. *Report to Norsk Hydro A. S.* Oslo. 88 pp. Limited distribution.

______. 1973. Supplerende undersøkelser av Fensfjordens dype bløtbunners dyreliv. *Report to Norsk Hydro A. S,* Oslo. 71 pp. Limited distribution.

Collett, R. 1895. *Myodes lemmus* its habits and migrations in Norway. *Forh. Vidensk. Selsk. Christ.* 1895, *3,* 63 pp.

Dahl, E. 1951. On the relation between summer temperature and the distribution of alpine vascular plants of Fennoscandia. *Oikos* 3:22–52.

______. 1956. Rondane mountain vegetation in South Norway and its relation to the environment. *Skr. Norske Vid. Akad. Oslo. 1. Mat.-Naturv. Klasse* 3:374 pp.

______, O. Gjems and J. Kielland-Lund. 1967: On the vegetation types of Norwegian conifer forests in relation to chemical properties of the humus layer. *Medd. N. Skogfors. vesen* 23:505–531.

______ and E. Mork 1959. On the relationships between temperature, respiration and growth in Norway spruce (*Picea abies* [L.] Karst.). *Medd. Norske Skogforsøksvesen* 53:83–93 (Norwegian with English summary).

Dahl, K. 1910. *Alder og vekst hos laks og ørret belyst ved studiet av deres skjæl.* 115 pp. (in Norw.)

Elgmork, K., J. P. Nilssen, T. Broch, and R. Øvrevik. 1978. Life cycle strategies in neighbouring populations of the copepod *Cyclops scutifer* Sars. *Vehr. Internat. Verein. Limnol.* 20:2518–2523.

Fægri, K. 1960. *Coast Plants.* Oslo. 134 pp.

Gjærevoll, O. 1956. The plant communities of the Scandinavian alpine snow-beds. *Skr. Kgl. Norske Videnskabers Selsk.* 1956 (1), 405 pp.

Grenager, B. 1952. Kvantitative undersøkelser av tang-og tareforekomstene på Hustadfeltet 1951. *Norw. Inst. of Seaweed Res. Report no. 1,* Oslo.

———. 1953. Kvantitative undersøkelser av tareforekomster på Kvitsøy og Karmøy 1952. Ibid. 3. Oslo.

———. 1954. Kvantitative undersøkelser av tareforekomster på Tustna 1952 og 1953. Ibid. 5. Oslo.

———. 1955. Kvantitative undersøkelser av tareforekomster i Sør-Helgeland 1952 og 1953. Ibid. 7. Oslo.

———. 1956. Kvantitative undersøkelser av tareforekomster i Øst-Finmark 1953. Ibid. 13. Oslo.

———. 1957. Algological observations from the polluted area of the Oslo fjord. *Nytt Mag. Bot.* 5. Oslo.

———. 1958. Kvantitative undersøkelser av tareforekomster i Helgøy, Troms 1953. *Norw. Inst. Seaweed Res. Report no. 21,* Oslo.

———. 1964. Kvantitative undersøkelser av tangog tareforekomster i Nord-Frøya herred 1954 og Jøssund herred 1956. Ibid. 28. Oslo.

Haftorn, S. 1954–6. Contribution to the food biology of tits especially about storing of surplus food. Part I. *Kgl. Norsk. Vid. Selsk. Skr.* 1953, 4, 123 pp. Part II. *Kgl. Norsk. Vid. Selsk. Skr.* 1956, 2, 52 pp. Part III. *Kgl. Norsk. Vid. Selsk. Skr.* 1956, 3, 79 pp. Part IV. *Kgl. Norsk. Vid. Selsk. Skr.* 1956, 4, 54 pp.

Hagen, Y. 1952. *Rovfuglene og viltpleien.* Oslo. 603 pp.

Halvorsen, O. 1976. Negative interaction amongst parasites, pp. 99–114 in Kennedy, C. R. (ed), *Ecological Aspects of Parasitology.* Amsterdam. 474 pp.

Haug, A., S. Melsom, and S. Omang. 1974. Estimation of heavy metal pollution in two Norwegian fjord areas by analysis of the brown alga *Ascophyllum nodosum. Environ. Pollut.* 7:179–192.

Holmboe, J. 1913. Knisttornen i Norge. *Bergen Mus. Arb.* 1913:7, 91 pp.

Jaasund, E. 1965. Aspects of the marine algal vegetation of North Norway. *Bot. Gothoburgensia* 4:1–174.

Jensen, K. W. 1977. On the dynamics and exploitation of brown trout, *Salmo trutta,* in lake Øvre Heimdalsvatn, Southern Norway. *Inst. Freshw. Res. Rep.* 56, 69 pp.

Jorde, I. 1966. Algal associations of a coastal area south of Bergen, Norway. *Sarsia* 23. Bergen.

——— and N. Klavestad, 1963. The natural history of the Hardangerfjord. 4. The benthonic algal vegetation. *Sarsia* 9:1–99.

Kain, J. M. 1967. Populations of *Laminaria hyperborea* at various latitudes. *Helgoländer wiss. Meeresunt.* 15. Germany.

———. 1971. The biology of *Laminaria hyperborea.* VI. Some Norwegian populations. *J. mar. biol. Ass. U.K.* 51.

———. 1971. Synopsis of biological data on Laminaria hyperborea. *FAO Fisheries Synopsis no. 87.* Rome: 1–9.

Kielland-Lund, J. 1973. A classification of Scandinavian forest vegetation for mapping purpose. *In* IBP/CT-symposium on vegetation classification and vegetation mapping. 27.-28.sept. 1972, Ås, Norway (ed. E. Marker). *IBP i Norden* 11:171–206.

Klavestad, N. 1957. An ecological study of the vegetation in Hunnebunnen, an old oyster poll in South-eastern Norway. *Nytt Mag. for Botanikk,* 5. Oslo.

Larsen, B., and A. Haug. 1958. The influence of habitat on the chemical composition of *Ascophyllum nodosum* (L.) Le Jol. *Norw. Inst. Seaweed Res. Rep. no. 20.* Trondheim.

Larsson, P., J. E. Brittain, L. Lien, A. Lillehammer, and K. Tangen. 1978. The lake ecosystem of Øvre Heimdalsvatn. *Holarct. Ecol.* 1:304–320.

Lein, T. E., J. Rueness and Ø. Wiik. 1974. Algologiske observasjoner i Iddefjorden og Singlefjorden. *Blyttia* 32:155–168.

Lie, U., O. Dahl, and O. J. Østvedt. 1978. Aspects of the life history of the local herring stock in Lindåspollene, western Norway. *Fisk. Dir. Skr. Ser. HavUnders.* 16:369–404.

Lye, K. A. 1970. The horizontal and vertical distribution of oceanic plants in South West Norway in relation to their environment. *Nytt. Mag. Bot.* 17:25–48.

Matthews, J. B. L., and J. W. Bakke. 1977. Ecological studies on the deep-water pelagic community of Korsfjorden (western Norway). The search for a trophic pattern. *Helgoländer wiss. Meeresunters.* 30:47–61.

Munda, I. 1967. Observations on the benthic marine algae in a landlocked fjord (Nordåsvannet) near Bergen, Western Norway. *Nova Hedwigia* 14:519–548.

Myklestad, S., I. Eide, and S. Melsom. 1978. Heavy metal exchange by *Ascophyllum nodosum* (L.) Le Jol. (Phaeophyceae) plants *in situ. Proc. Int. Seaweed Symp.* 9:143–151.

Myrberget, S. 1974. Variations in the production of the willow grouse *Lagopus lagopus* (L) in Norway, 1963–1972. *Ornis Scand.* 5:163–172.

Nordeng, H. 1977. A pheromone hypothesis for homeward migration in anadromous salmonids. *Oikos* 28:155–159.

Nordhagen, R. 1936. Versuch einer neuen Einteilung der subalpinen-alpinen Vegetation Norwegens. *Yearb. Bergen Museum, Naturvidenskapelig rekke* 7:88pp.

______. 1943. Sikilsdalen og Norges Fjellbeiter. *Skr. Bergen Museum* 22:607pp.

Olstad, O. 1932. Undersøkelser over lirypens forplantningsforhold. *Medd. Stat. viltunders.* 1 (1), 71 pp.

Økland, J. 1964. The eutrophic lake Borrevann (Norway)—an ecological study on shore and bottom fauna with special reference to gastropods, including a hydrographic study. *Folia Limnol. Scan.* 13, 337 pp.

Øritsland, N. A., and D. M. Lavigne. 1976. Radiative surface temperatures of exercising polar bears. *Comp. Biochem. Physiol.* 53 A:327–330.

Østbye, E., et al. 1975. Hardangervidda. *Ecol. Bull.* 20:225–264.

Østvedt, O. J. 1955. Zooplankton investigations from Weather Ship "M" in the Norwegian Sea 1948–49. *Hvalråd. Skr.* 40:1–93.

Rueness, J. 1973. Pollution effects on littoral algal communities in the inner Oslofjord, with special reference to *Ascophyllum nodosum. Helgol. Wiis. Meeresunt.* 24. Germany.

Sætersdal, G. S. 1952. The haddock in Norwegian waters. I. *Fisk. Dir. Skr.* 10 (4):1–14.

______. 1953. The haddock in Norwegian waters. II. *Fisk. Dir. Skr.* 10 (9):1–46.

Skre, O. 1972. High temperature demands for growth and development in Norway spruce (*Picea abies* [L.] Karst.) in Scandinavia. *Meld. NLH* 51:1–29.

______. 1979. The regional distribution of vascular plants in Scandinavia with requirements for high summer temperatures. *Norw. J. Bot.* 26:295–318.

Skreslet, R., R. Leinebo, J. B. L. Matthews, and E. Sakshaug (eds.). 1976. Fresh water on the sea. Proceedings from a symposium in 1974. The Association of Norwegian Oceanographers. 246 pp.

Sømme, L., and E.-M. Conradi-Larsen. 1977. Cold-hardiness of collembolans and oribatid mites from windswept mountain ridges. *Oikos* 29:118–126.

Stenseth, N. C. 1977. Evolutionary aspects of demographic cycles: the relevance of some models of cycles for microtine fluctuations. *Oikos* 29:525–538.

Stokke, K. The red alga *Gracilaria verrucosa* in Norway. *Nytt Mag. for Botanikk,* 5. Oslo.

Sundene, O. 1953. The algal vegetation of Oslofjord. *Skr. Norske Vid. Akad. Oslo.* 1. *Mat.-Naturv. Klasse* 2:1–244.

______. 1962. Growth in the sea of *Laminaria digitata* sporophytes from culture. Ibid. 9.

______. 1962. The implications of transplant and culture experiments on the growth and distribution of *Alaria esculenta. Skr. Norske Vid. Akad.* 9:155–174.

______. 1963. Reproduction and ecology of *Chorda tomentosa.* Ibid. 10.

______. 1964. The ecology of *Laminaria digitata* in Norway in view of transplant experiments. *Skr. Norske Vid. Akad.* 11:83–107.

Svendsen, P. 1959. The algal vegetation of Spitsbergen. *Skr. Norsk Polarinst.* 116:1–49.

Vestergren, T. 1902. Om den olikformiga snöbetäckningens inflytande på vegetationen i Sarekfjällen. *Bot. Notiser* 1902:241–268.

Vik, R. (ed.). 1978. The lake øvre Heimdalsvatn, a subalpine freshwater ecosystem. *Holarct. Ecol.* I: 81–320.

Wiborg, K. F. 1954. Investigations on zooplankton in coastal and offshore waters of western and northwestern Norway. *Fisk. Dir. Skr.* 11 (1):1–246.

Wielgolaski, F. E. (ed.). 1971. Nordisk vegatationsklassifisering för kartlägging. *IBP i Norden* 7:76 pp.

______. (ed.) 1975. Fennoscandian tundra ecosystems. Part 1 Plants and microorganisms. 366 pp. Part 2. Animals and systems analyses. 337 pp.

Wildhagen, Aa. 1952. Om vekslingene i bestandene avsmågnagere i Norge 1871–1949. *Statens Viltundersøkelser.* 192 pp.

16

POLAND

Zdzisław Kajak and Ewa Pieczyńska

THE ORIGIN AND DEVELOPMENT OF ECOLOGICAL STUDIES

Ecological aspects of the distribution of plants and animals can be found in Polish literature on natural history as early as the second half of the nineteenth century. In 1891, and more extensively in 1896, the famous Polish geobotanist J. Paczoski formulated in his paper in Polish *Collective Life of Plants,* for the first time in the world the aims and scope of the new branch of science named phytosociology.

Broader ecological studies, mainly hydrobiological and phytocenological, date from the years 1920 to 1930. The developing applied sciences of fishery, forestry, and agriculture were also important for theoretical ecology. One of the main hydrobiological centers in the interwar period was the Hydrobiological Station at Lake Wigry, which was established in 1920 and functioned until the outbreak of World War II. Plant ecology also developed at the time in several institutes, and a number of phytosociological works appeared between 1920 and 1930. The first center of marine research was the Marine (Baltic) Station on the Hel Peninsula, established in 1920.

Polish ecologists, like other Polish scientists, suffered great losses during World War II. After the war, ecological studies had to be organized almost from the beginning.

Four periods can be distinguished in the development of Polish ecology after 1945:

1. Research in the earliest post-war period concentrated around autecology

(e.g., ecological valence of different aquatic and terrestrial organisms), biocenology (mainly descriptions of communities in different environments), and population problems. It also included some practical problems like the effects of chemicals used in agriculture, chemical and biological control of pests, and water pollution problems.

2. The second period was dominated by population and biocenotic studies. Theoretical aspects of structure and functions of population and communities were of great interest from 1950 to 1960. Simultaneously, much information on communities of different terrestrial and aquatic ecosystems was gathered. These studies provided valuable data on the functioning of ecosystems and also for later studies on productivity and mineral cycling.

3. From 1960 to 1975 was a period of intense studies on ecological productivity and of ecosystem studies connected with the International Biological Program (IBP). Studies on small mammals, ecological bioenergetics, and production of lakes, ponds, grasslands, and forests were carried out; ecological investigations of agro-ecosystems also began.

4. Finally, there is the most recent period of intense "landscape" studies and research on ecological bases for the protection and management of the environment. Studies on such topics as potential natural vegetation, synanthropy, and recultivation of degraded environments have been carried out for many years. Recently, much attention has been paid to mineral cycling in multi-ecosystem units with consideration of hydrologic, pedologic, and biogeochemical factors. The ecology of plants and animals in several types of landscapes typical for Poland is also receiving considerable attention. Studies are being conducted on the natural bases for environmental management and the protection of waters and forests; urban ecology, recultivation of damaged areas, and ecological monitoring are also receiving emphasis. At the same time, research on the structure and functioning of populations and biocenoses is continuing.

PRESENT ORGANIZATION, STAFFING, AND FINANCING OF RESEARCH

Universities and Institutes

Ecological studies in Poland are conducted at the universities, institutes of the Polish Academy of Sciences, and other institutes. As regards the universities, the majority of ecological investigations, especially on the theoretical aspects, are conducted at the University of Warsaw, the Jagiellonian University in Krakow, University of Nicholas Kopernik in Torun, University of Lodz, and the University of Adam Mickiewicz in Poznan. Studies on terrestrial and aquatic ecosystems are also carried out along with population, biocenotic, and landscape research. The University of Gdansk concentrates on oceanographic studies.

Ecologists also work at other universities, like the Silesian University in Katowice, the Maria Curie-Skłodowska University in Lublin, and the University of Wroctaw, among others.

Many practical ecological aspects, especially those connected with plant and animal productivity, are being analyzed in the agricultural academies. Other schools at the university level, including the medical academies and technical universities, also participate to some extent in ecological research, mainly with regard to protection of the environment. Some ecologists also work in the physical education academies and pedagogic universities.

The Institute of Ecology of the Polish Academy of Sciences is the largest in Poland, and one of the largest in the world. The institute was established in 1952; has about 300 staff members, of whom about 130 are scientists, and several field stations; and publishes three journals. Recently, the Arctowski Field Station was established on King George Island for ecological investigations on Antarctica. The institute, the first in the world to be named an "institute of ecology," has gathered specialists on plant and animal ecology, and on aquatic and terrestrial environments, and has had an important and stimulating role in the development of ecology in Poland.

Ecological studies are also conducted by other institutions of the Polish Academy of Sciences: Laboratory of Water Biology in Krakow, Mammals Research Laboratory in Białowieża, Institute of Botany in Krakow, and Institute of Zoology in Warsaw. A number of specialized institutes deal with ecological problems, mainly practical ones. The most important of these institutes are: Institute of Inland Fisheries, Marine Fishery Institute, Institute of Landscape Management, Institute of Soil Science and Cultivation of Plants, Institute of Plant Protection, Institute of Land Reclamation and Grasslands, Institute of Cultivation and Acclimatization of Plants, Institute of Pomiculture, and Institute of Vegetable Growing.

On the basis of the number of institutes, Warsaw is the greatest center of ecological studies.

Number of Ecologists

It is difficult to give precise estimations of the number of Polish ecologists since modern ecology has so wide a range of activities and is connected with so many other fields. There are approximately one hundred scientists taking active part in the broadly understood field of ecology; about 50 percent work in the universities, and about 30 percent are in institutions of the Polish Academy of Sciences.

Financing Research

Generally, scientific studies in Poland are financed by the government, but there are different methods of allocating the grants. Each scientific institution receives a budget for research or other activities such as teaching. Some percentage of grants is also allocated for selected research problems and is then given to different institutions working on those projects.

Scientific institutions can also obtain funds from industry or local administrations to solve some practical matters.

In the last few years, there has been a tendency to concentrate the allocation of grants on scientific problems considered by state authorities as especially important for the national economy. Research on these problems is conducted by a number of institutions all over the country. The first ecological research of this kind, conducted between 1971 and 1975, dealt with biological productivity of both the natural ecosystems (forests, grasslands, lakes and rivers), including those transformed by man, and the artificial ones (artificial meadows, fish ponds, and so on). The second project (1976 to 1980) is concentrating on the natural bases of environmental management with a focus on mineral cycling in multi-ecosystem units and ecological processes in ecosystems under different kinds and degrees of anthropo-pressure. This program will be continued with appropriate modifications from 1981 to 1985. Problems of water management and the purity of natural surface waters, including essential hydrotechnical reconstruction of the rural and industrial landscape of the Vistula River, will be studied. The Institute of Ecology of the Polish Academy of Sciences coordinates most of these types of ecological projects.

Role of Committees and Societies

Committees and scientific associations are very important in the development of ecology in Poland. Since 1951, the Committee of Ecology of the Polish Academy of Sciences has coordinated scientific activity in ecology and partly financed selected (mainly theoretical) scientific research. The Polish Hydrobiological Association, now with six hundred members, was established in 1962. Both organizations hold congresses, symposia, and conferences. There is also the Committee of Man and the Environment of the Polish Academy of Sciences that functions contemporaneously with the national committee of the international program, Man and the Biosphere. The Polish Committee of the International Biological Program (IBP) was important to the organization and coordination of research from 1963 to 1973.

Ecological problems are also dealt with in the activities of other Polish Academy of Sciences committees, such as the Botanical Committee, and the committees of protection of nature and its resources, forest sciences, ecology of man, pedology and agricultural chemistry, land reclamation, plant protection, parasitology, and management of montane areas. Scientific associations specializing in botany, entomology, and pedology, among others, are also active.

International Activities

Polish ecologists actively participate in various international programs, and several international scientific meetings were held in Poland. Among the most significant are: International Limnological Congress (SIL, Warsaw, 1965), several symposia of the International Biological Program and Man and Biosphere Program (e.g., on parasitology and ichthyology), Baltic Conferences, Paleolimnological Symposium (1977), ornithological conferences, and others.

At the beginning of IBP activity, Poland was asked to organize the international symposium to work out the conception, notions, and methods in studies of energy flow and mineral cycling in terrestrial ecosystems (Jabłonna 1967). Polish hydrobiologists organized the symposium within the freshwater section of IBP where the essential international research was summed up by Kazimierz Dolny (1972).

Poland was also an international center coordinating the research on small mammals and granivorous birds. Polish specialists participated in steering committees of the freshwater section of IBP and the section of grassland ecosystems. K. Petrusewicz was the vice-president of IBP.

International IBP meetings were also held to synthesize the achievements as regards: ecology of wetlands (at Mikołajki, 1972); human influence on energy flow and mineral cycling in grassland ecosystems (at Warsaw, 1973); productivity of granivorous birds (at Dziekanów Leśny near Warsaw, 1973); small mammals (at Dziekanów Leśny near Warsaw, 1973); and social insects (at Warsaw, 1970). Also, two symposia of the section on human adaptability were held in Poland, one in 1966 and the other in 1968.

The Polish Committee of IBP cooperated in preparing three conferences that were held in other countries: Working Group of Small Mammals (at Oxford, 1968, and Helsinki, 1970), and Working Group on Granivorous Birds (at The Hague, 1970).

Polish specialists had the essential role in elaborating several IBP synthesis volumes (Kendeigh and Pinowski 1977; Golley et al. 1975; Breymeyer and Van Dyne in press). Polish ecologists also participated in several other IBP monographs. Polish achievements within the IBP are briefly summarized in the volume, *Polish Participation in the International Biological Programme*, published in Warsaw in 1975.

At present, Poland actively participates in six projects of the Man and the Biosphere program. Out of six research projects of INTECOL, the coordination of two, agro-ecosystems and granivorous birds, will be done in Poland. The Third INTECOL Congress will be held in Poland in 1982.

Finally, within the Council for Mutual Economic Aid, Poland coordinates the problems of mineral cycling in the landscape, plant protection, and ecological monitoring.

TEACHING AND TRAINING

Ecology is a subject of lectures and classes of all biological faculties in the universities. Biological courses include not only the special pedagogic branch, which encompasses four years of study, but also four specializations requiring four and one-half years to complete. These are biochemistry, general biology (with division to botany and zoology), microbiology, and environmental biology. Students of environmental biology can prepare their masters of science theses from various ecological fields in different departments, depending on the organizational structure of the university. For example, in Warsaw University, they can specialize during the last one and one-half years of study in five departments in the fields of animal ecology, plant ecology (with phytosociology), hydrobiology, and environmental microbiology.

For many years, postgraduate courses in ecology, requiring three to four years to complete, have been conducted in the universities and in the Polish Academy of Sciences. For example, in the Institute of Ecology, Polish Academy of Sciences, several postgraduates each year can obtain the Ph.D. in various fields of ecology. Working essentially on their theses for three to four years, they get interdisciplinary training in various departments of the institute at the same time and, if necessary, in other institutions also. They also take the course of philosophy.

The increasing interest in problems of environmental protection has resulted in new specializations in the medical academies and technical colleges where lectures on ecology are now included.

Significant for training are the special courses for scientific staff and summer practicums for students. These courses are regularly organized by different ecological institutions. In addition, international courses on productivity and bioenergetics have been organized.

Ecological matters are also in the program of the secondary schools and are popularized by competitions and other activities.

ECOLOGICAL LITERATURE

The library of the Institute of Ecology has most of the world's literature concerning ecology, whereas libraries of several other institutes have the basic ecological literature. A number of ecological textbooks written by such authors as W. C. Allee et al., E. P. Odum, N. P. Naumov, W. Tischler, A. P. Šennikov, R. MacArthur and J. Connell, P. Duvigneaud, Collier et al., Simmons, and other specialists have been translated into Polish.

Many textbooks written by Polish authors have been published in Polish. Among these are: D. Szymkiewicz 1932. *Plant Ecology;* W. Słakwiński 1947. *An Introduction to Phytosociology;* A. Lityński 1952. *General Hydrobiology;* J. Motyka 1962. *Plant Ecology;* J. Prończuk 1966. *Agricultural Ecology of*

Plants; W. Michajłow 1973. *Protection of Man's Natural Environment;* J. Mikulski 1974. *Biology of Inland Waters;* T. Górny 1975. *Zooecology of Forest Soils;* T. Puchalski and Z. Prusinkiewicz 1975. *Ecological Grounds of Forest Habitats;* P. Trojan 1975. *General Ecology;* K. Starmach, S. Wróbel, and K. Pasternak 1976. *Hydrobiology;* Z. Obmiński 1977. *Forest Ecology;* K. Petrusewicz 1978. *Individual, Species, Population;* and Kajak 1978. *Eutrophication of Lakes.* In addition, there are a number of other more specialized and practical books published in Polish.

Polish ecologists are also co-authors of international manuals on methods of investigating productivity, which are in the IBP handbook series published by Blackwell Scientific Publishers: Petrusewicz, K. and A. Macfadyen. 1970. *Productivity of Terrestrial Animals. Principles and Methods,* IBP Handbook No. 13; Grodziński, W., R. Z. Klekowski, and A. Duncan. 1975. *Methods for Ecological Bioenergetics,* IBP Handbook No. 24; and Edmondson, W. T., and G. G. Winberg, eds. 1971. *A Manual on Methods for the Assessment of Secondary Productivity in Fresh Waters.* IBP Handbook No. 17.

POLISH ECOLOGICAL JOURNALS

General ecological and hydrobiological journals and their dates of founding include the following (**Note:** *A,* English or other congress language; *B,* Polish with summary and descriptions of figures and tables in English or other congress languages; *C,* Polish with summaries in English or other congress languages; *r,* articles, reviews, discussions, and so on: *Ekologia Polska* (Polish Journal of Ecology), 1953A; *Polish Ecological Studies,* 1975A; *Wiadomości ekologiczne* (Ecological News), 1955B, r; *Phytocenosis,* 1972A or B; *Polskie Archiwum Hydrobiologii* (Polish Hydrobiological Archives), 1953A. [A continuation of *Archiwum Hydrobiologii i Rybactwa* (Archives of Hydrobiology and Fisheries) founded in 1926]; and *Acta Hydrobiologica,* 1959A or B.

Results of ecological studies are published also in journals dealing with subjects such as botany, zoology, agriculture, forestry, and nature protection (see code in preceding paragraph): *Studia Naturae,* 1967A; *Ochrona Przyrody* (Nature protection), 1920B; *Roczniki Nauk Rolniczych* (Annals of Agricultural Sciences), 1905A or B, 5 series; *Roczniki gleboznawcze* (Pedological Annals) 1950B; *Sylwan,* 1820C; *Zeszyty Problemowe Postępów Nauk Rolniczych* (Problems in the progress of agriculture), 1956C; *Fragmenta Floristica et Geobotanica,* 1953A or B; *Acta Agrobotanica,* 1953B; *Acta agraria et silvestria,* 1961B; *Acta Theriologica,* 1955A; *Arboretum Kórnickie* (Kórnik arboretum), 1946A or B; *Archiwum Ochrony Srodowiska* (Archives of Environment Protection), 1975C; *Floia Forestalia Polonica,* 1959C; *Polish Journal of Soil Science,* 1968A; *Pamiętnik Pulawski—Prace Instytutu Uprawy, Nawożenia i Gleboznawstwa* (papers of Institute of Soil Science and Cultivation of Plants), 1921B; and several others.

From 1952 to 1975, the *Polish Ecological Bibliography* was published annually in English or other congress languages; it contains brief information about papers on ecology in the broad sense of the word. Every few years, the *Polish Phytosociological Bibliography* is published.

REVIEW OF STUDIES

Ecological studies conducted in Poland cover all the main fields of ecology. Research is conducted in different terrestrial (forests, meadows, agrocenoses), freshwater (lakes, rivers, ponds, dam reservoirs), and marine (Baltic, oceans) ecosystems. A review of this research follows.

Population Studies

In the 1950s, these studies resulted in an elaboration of an original theoretical concept of population as a real ecological unit. On the basis of field and laboratory investigations, mainly of small mammals, a set of notions has been worked out concerning the organization of population according to factors such as social structure and intrapopulation migrations; this has been widely discussed in the world literature. Attempts were also made to determine the regulatory role of population organization in both natural and experimental populations. Dynamics of small-mammal populations, the role of various generations, reproduction control, and the influence of the life area on population density have been thoroughly examined.

Studies on population bioenergetics are well established. Methods for determining the energy budget of natural populations, well-known internationally, allowed studies on population productivity to proceed and studies on the role of populations in ecosystems to be initiated. Methods of analysis of numbers and migrations have also been elaborated.

Population studies were also applied in practical problems and have contributed to the development of research on rational game management—for example, a quick and easy method to determine the allowed intake of hare. Studies on factors controlling pests, parasites, and other populations are also important.

Agricultural and forest sciences provided abundant material on plant populations including autecology of several species of forest trees, population dynamics, intraspecific competition, and soil-plant interactions. Considerable progress has also been made in the ecology of the reed *Phragmites*.

Community Studies

At first, biocenotic studies were mainly descriptions of biocenoses of different environments in various regions. Interest in the functional aspect and integration of ecology of plants and animals in terrestrial ecology has increased since the IBP research. In hydrobiology, integration has existed for a long time. At present, plant ecology includes good information on, classification of, and estimation of the degree of deformation of phytocenoses. Numerous geobotanical monographs for various regions of the country have been elaborated.

The ecology of animals is well documented for only some regions and types of environment, but a lot has been done on the characteristics of animal associations, their structure and integration via competition, trophic relations (including predator-prey and parasite-host relations), and regulation of numbers. Scientists have investigated these problems experimentally to a great extent, giving special attention to creating conditions that approximate the natural ones.

Results of biocenotic papers are closely connected with management practices, such as plant protection, pest control, forestry, intense agriculture, urbanization, and industrialization. Comparative characteristics of biocenoses subjected to anthropo-pressure of different kinds are very significant.

Productivity Studies

The development of these studies took place during IBP activities. A significant increase in cooperation and coordination of studies within Poland and with other countries was observed during this period. The most important results gathered during productivity studies are the following:

—Energy pathways in over twenty ecosystems (lakes, ponds, fields, and forests) were estimated.
—Analyses have been made of food rations, food selectivity, production efficiency in various trophic conditions of a number of species, as well as analysis of predator-prey relations, significance of specialized and non-specialized predators, competitive relations, and effect of elimination on production.
—Bioenergetic balances of several tens of species from different systematic groups have been investigated. Several important technical and methodological solutions have been offered in calorimetry and respirometry.
—Great progress has been made in methods for quantitative estimation of distribution and biological processes of organisms in ecosystems. Experimental techniques in situ and under conditions maximally close to natural ones were widely introduced.

Some of the methods elaborated in Poland are being commonly applied elsewhere, for example, the method for estimating the numbers of small mammals, some techniques for quantitative sampling of aquatic organisms, and some techniques of bioenergetics.

Landscape Studies

Complex studies on biogeochemical cycles in multi-ecosystem units have begun only recently in Poland. Earlier studies dealt mainly with the interactions of water and land ecosystems and, in particular, included the influence of drainage basins on lakes, rivers, and reservoirs. Recently, multidisciplinary studies have been carried out on biogeochemical cycles in different areas typical of Poland, such as agricultural-forest-lake moraine landscape; areas of intense wide-scale agriculture; forest areas, not much transformed but under strong pressure from industrial pollution of the atmosphere; densely populated areas under strong pressure from industry and mining; and swampy areas varying as to the drainage extent.

Ecology and Practice

A number of theoretical investigations have practical aspects and, conversely, applied studies contribute considerably to the theory of ecology. Many studies concern the comparative characteristics of natural ecosystems and those variously transformed by such factors as intense mineral and organic fertilization, change of water relations, different cultivation methods, and means of plant protection.

In forestry, agriculture, and grassland management, pedologic and phytosociological studies are widely applied as an ecological basis for practice by the Institute of Land Reclamation and Grasslands, the Forestry Research Institute, and several institutions of the Polish Academy of Sciences and the universities.

In ponds and lakes, the effects of different pure stocks of carp, and mixed stocks of phytophagous, planktonivorous fish, and carp, were estimated and results utilized for a proposal of proper fishery management by the Institute of Inland Fisheries, Institute of Ecology of the Polish Academy of Sciences, and the Department of Hydrobiology of Warsaw University.

Recently analyzed by most of the hydrobiological institutes have been different aspects of pollution on freshwaters, such as the influence of agriculture, the effects of thermal pollution, and the impact of domestic and industrial sewage. Simultaneously, studies are being conducted on the utilization of diluted sewage in fish farming and on the effect of mineral fertilizers and dung on the functioning of pond and lake ecosystems. This work has been conducted by the Institute of Inland Fisheries and the Laboratory of Biology of Waters of the Polish Academy of Sciences. The establishment of fisheries in lakes is based on special scientific diagnosis for each lake in studies carried on by the Institute of Inland Fisheries.

Methods for using algae for treatment of mineral nitrogen sewage have been also elaborated by the Institute of Microbiology of Warsaw University.

Much has been done by the Institute of Land Reclamation and Grasslands and others on the agricultural use of sewage for soil improvement and for protection of waters.

Many investigations deal with restoration of destroyed lakes by the removal of the hypolimnion waters (for the first time in the world), aeration, and biorecultivation with the help of different stocks of fish. Such work is conducted by the Agricultural-Technical Academy in Olsztyn, the Institute of Inland Fisheries, the Institute of Ecology, and others.

Important results, theoretically and practically, have been obtained in experiments on enclosed sections of various-sized natural ecosystems such as grasslands, forests, and lakes.

A number of population and biocenotic results have been obtained in studies concerning the biological methods of plant protection by the Institute of Plant Protection, Institute of Vegetable Growing, Institute of Pomology, institutions of the agricultural academies, and others. Internationally recognized achievements have been obtained in complex studies on agro-ecosystems by the Department of Agricultural Biology and Institute of Ecology.

Restoration and rational management of areas degraded by industry and mining are heavily investigated by the Institute of Soil Science and Cultivation of Plants, Institute of Landscape Management, Institutes of Dendrology and of Botany of the Polish Academy of Sciences, and others. The project "Ecological grounds for management of environment," coordinated by the Institute of Ecology and conducted in typical regions of the country, has provided essential information on rational land management.

Polish ecologists have made an inventory of types of natural, semi-natural, and anthropogenic phytocenoses for the entire country. Assuming that the phytocenosis is the easiest ecosystem indicator that allows for spatial delimitation of the ecosystem, this inventory provides a basis for studies on the ecology of landscape and allows the division of the country into ecological-biogeographic regions.

A significant achievement is the elaboration of soil characteristics for the entire country by the agricultural academies, Institute of Soil Science and Cultivation of Plants, Institute of Landscape Management, and others. This is true also of maps of potential natural and vicarious vegetation and studies on synanthropy of plants conducted by the Institute of Botany, Warsaw University, and others. This information can serve as the basis for rational use of ecosystems and adaptation of agricultural, hydrological, urban, and recreation demands to the tendencies and possibilities of nature.

Intense studies have been conducted on urbanized areas by the Institute of Landscape Management, Institute of Zoology of the Polish Academy of Sciences, and others. Ecologists cooperate in works on innovative urban-ecological projects of new housing estates. Extensive, complex research is also conducted by the ecological institutions in Cracow and in Silesia, the Institute of Ecology, and others on areas under strong industrial pressure and in regions of intense agriculture.

Plans have been made by the Institute of Landscape Management to join the nature reserves and protected areas into one spatial system.

Ecological monitoring is being carried out, with Poland coordinating several international projects in eastern Europe. Monitoring has included most of the rivers, which has resulted in publication of atlases of river purity, many lakes (also with an atlas), and air. Proposals for monitoring of terrestrial ecosystems and landscapes are being prepared.

Extensive ecological studies and research on environmental protection have been conducted on the Baltic, more recently in some regions of the Antarctic, and, with the help of Russian expeditions, on other oceans by the Institute of Marine Fisheries, Institute of Ecology, and Institute of Landscape Management. Polish marine hydrobiologists cooperate actively with those of the Baltic countries and international organizations.

More and more frequently, although still far from sufficiently, ecologists cooperate in programs such as landscape planning of large industrial and other enterprises and offer opinions with a view toward environmental protection.

BIBLIOGRAPHY

To illustrate this review of Polish ecological investigations, several papers from various ecological fields are listed and annotated here in chronological order. Preference has been given to recently published papers that sum up complex and long-term investigations.

Petrusewicz, K. 1963. Population growth induced by disturbance in the ecological structure of the population. *Ekol. Pol.* 11:87–125. (This is an essentially new approach to the role of population structure with regard to numbers and dynamics. In isolated populations of white mice a few females were either added or taken away for a week. In most of these populations, the number of individuals rapidly increased as a result of higher rates of fertility and survival of young. These changes are considered to be the result of destruction of the previous population structure.)

Kaczmarek, W. 1963. An analysis of interspecific competition in communities of the soil macrofauna of some habitats in the Kampinos National Park. *Ekol. Pol.* 11:421–483. (A model of competitive relations was constructed that takes into consideration the direct and indirect effects of environmental factors on the numbers of animals. The concept of multi-specific competing associations is based on the differentiated ecological valence. Further studies on the subject are in the paper by M. Kaczmarek 1975. *Ekol. Pol.* 23:265–293).

Szafer, W. and K. Zarzycki, eds. 1972. Vegetation of Poland. Two volumes in Polish. Warsaw: PWN (English translations: Pergamon Press and PWN–Polish Scientific Publishers, International Series of monographs in pure and applied biology, Vol. 9). (A list and characteristics of plant communities in Poland with regard to the type of soil and climate environment are given. Discussed are history and present state of vegetation, and factors determining plant distribution including the effect of anthropo-pressure. Paper contains the description of the vegetation cover, the geobotanic regions, distribution of more important trees and shrubs, and national parks and reserves, and includes a comprehensive bibliography.)

Various Authors. 1973. Experimentally increased fish stock in the pond-type Lake Warniak. *Ekol. Pol.* 21:1–643. (The volume contains results of investigations of the Institute of Inland Fisheries, Institute of Ecology, and Department of Hydrobiology of Warsaw University. In fourteen detailed papers and one of summary by Z. Kajak and J. Zawisza, the authors discussed the effect of doubling the fish biomass, by introduction of carp, on the physico-chemical conditions, biomass, production of phyto- and zooplankton, benthos, and epiphytic fauna, and also on the feeding of fish, their state of infestation, and pressure on food components. Qualitative changes of all components of biocenosis were observed, as well as a decrease of biomass and phytoplankton production and an increase of decomposition in water, all probably owing to disturbance of the bottom by fish, thus creating higher turbidity.)

Ryszkowski, L., ed. 1974. *Ecological effects of intensive agriculture.* Warsaw: PWN-Polish Scientific Publishers. (This publication consists of four papers, which synthesize ecological problems of agro-ecosystems of rye and potato fields on the basis of complex research carried out for some years. Discussed are environmental problems, energy flow and matter cycling, and the role of invertebrates and vertebrates. Special attention is paid to the role of mechanization, chemical means of plant protection, and mineral fertilization on the functioning of agro-ecosystems.)

Various Authors. 1974. Analysis of a sheep pasture ecosystem in the Pieniny Mountains (the Carpathians). *Ekol. Pol.* 22:475–732. (The volume contains sixteen detailed papers, and one of summary by A. Kajak, on the results of investigations coordinated by the Institute of Ecology. The structure and function of ecosystems are compared on areas grazed by sheep and those grazed and intensely fertilized with sheep dung. Specific and dominance structure of plant and animal associations were analyzed, as well as production, decomposition, activity of fauna, and contribution of predators. A diagram of the carbon flow through the ecosystem is given.)

Faliński, J. B. 1975. Anthropogenic changes of the vegetation of Poland. *Phytocenosis* 4:97–115 + map. (This is a brief synthesis, based on many phytosociological publications, of studies on anthropogenic changes of the vegetation cover in Poland and on the extent of deviation from natural vegetation. The data, in the form of a map, present important information about the extent of changes in the environment and provide natural grounds for some decisions in environmental management.)

Grodziński, W. and Z. Pucek, eds. 1975. The role of large herbivore mammals in woodland ecosystems. *Pol. Ecol. Stud.* Vol. 1. (The volume contains nine papers on food resources, numbers of animals, their food demand and selectivity, energy budgets, estimation of the role of large mammals in the functioning of woodland ecosystem, and a mathematical model of the optimization of roe deer production. This is also an attempt to apply ecological studies for practical purposes, i.e., for game management and the influence of large herbivores on woodlands.)

Klekowski, R. Z. and Z. Fischer. 1975. Review of studies on ecological bioenergetics of aquatic animals. *Pol. Arch. Hydrobiol.* 22:345–373. (A review and synthesis of bioenergetics research of the Department of Biological Bioenergetics of the Institute of Ecology on protozoans, rotifiers, nematodes, crustaceans, and fishes. It presents energy budgets in individual life cycles depending on trophic conditions, temperature, oxygen concentration, and also on the presence of pesticides. Original calculations and theoretical considerations are included in the paper.

Mikulski, J. S. et al. 1975. Basic regularities of productive processes in the Iława Lakes and in the Gopło Lake from the point of view of utility values of the water. *Pol. Arch. Hydrobiol.* 22:101–122. (Results of several years of complex research comparing the production and decomposition in three eutrophic lakes are presented. In one of the lakes, primary phytoplankton production is used mainly by zooplankton, in the others mainly by benthos. Diagrams of energy flow through ecosystems of two lakes are given.)

Andrzejewski, R. and M. Mazurkiewicz. 1976. Abundance of food supply and size of the bank vole's home range. *Acta Theriol.* 21:237–253. (This is an important contribution to the problems of home ranges. While *Clethrionomys glareolus* was feeding on natural food only, its home ranges increased during the season, but while it was additionally and constantly fed with oats, the home ranges were smaller and constant. The home ranges overlapped more because of the higher density of the population. Generations appearing later in the season had smaller home ranges than the earlier ones.)

Pieczyńska, E., ed. 1976. *Selected problems of lake littoral ecology.* Warsaw: Wyd. UW (Publications of the University of Warsaw). (The volume consists of fourteen chapters, in which different ecological problems of the lake littoral are discussed. Analyzed are: environmental conditions, inflow of allochthonous matter, abundance and distribution of macrophytes, benthos and periphyton, fish and their role, production and decomposition processes, and influence of sewage on the littoral. General regularities in the functioning of lake littoral are discussed.)

Traczyk, T., ed. 1976. The effect of intensive fertilization on the structure and productivity of meadow ecosystems. *Pol. Ecol. Stud.* Vol. 2 No. 4; *and,* 1978. Matter cycling in meadow ecosystems in relation to intensive mineral fertilization. *Pol. Ecol. Stud.* Vol. 4 No. 1. (These two volumes sum up the complex research on the structure and function of meadow ecosystems under different doses of mineral fertilization. There are forty-seven papers thoroughly discussing the structure and functioning of these ecosystems and dealing with environmental conditions, matter cycling, primary and secondary production, chemical and structural characteristics of the majority of components, decomposition, trophic relations, and the role of animals.)

Zimka, J. R. and S. Stachurski. 1976. Vegetation as a modifier of carbon and nitrogen transfer to soil in various types of forest ecosystems. *Ekol. Pol.* 24:493–514. (The economy and circulation of nutrients in six forest ecosystems has been compared. Three types of nutrient economy were distinguished, namely, mixed forest, alder-ash carr and wet alder wood, and oak-hornbeam forest. Decomposition and other processes and properties of the soils were characterized.)

Gliwicz, Z. M. 1977. Food size selection and seasonal succession of filter-feeding zooplankton in a eutrophic lake. *Ekol. Pol.* 25:179–225. (The paper describes the mechanisms of both seasonal succession and long-term eutrophic changes in lake plankton communities. Filtering rate and, consequently, feeding rate, fecundity, and numbers are more strongly limited by low available food concentration in some filter-feeding crustacean species, while in other species too high concentrations of large and filamentous algae have this effect. A high concentration of net algal forms is discussed as a selective working factor, modifying the final result of competition between the more efficient and the less efficient filter-feeding species in the lake. This study is important for understanding the processes of eutrophication.)

Hillbricht-Ilkowska, A. 1977. Trophic relations and energy flow in pelagic plankton. *Pol. Ecol. Stud.* 3:3–98. (This is a synthetic discussion of trophic relations in plankton on the basis of the author's investigations and world literature. Discussed are: food selectivity, biomass, consumption and elimination of food, and zooplankton production in different trophic types of lakes. It was found that the production efficiency of consumers increases to some level of primary production and then decreases, showing a considerable scatter.)

Various Authors. 1977. Nitrogen-phosphorus fertilization of isolated parts of ponds. *Rocz. Nauk Roln. Ser.* D Monogr. Vol. 98 No. 1. (The volume contains eight papers and a recapitulation of results of investigations coordinated by the Institute of Inland Fisheries on the effects of different mineral fertilizers and their dosage on environment, bacteria, phyto- and zooplankton, benthos, production, and health of fry. Complex studies of this problem have been carried out in four complexes of fish ponds in different regions of the country that have different properties of bottom and water quality. The results provide significant information about the reaction of different ecosystems to the same nutrient load.)

Kajak, Z. 1978. Characteristics of a temperate, eutrophic, dimictic lake (Lake Mikołajskie, Northern Poland). *Int. Rev. Ges. Hydrobiol.* (This paper, presented at plenary session of the 20th Congress of the Societas Internationalis Limnologiae, Copenhagen, is a synthesis of complex, long-term research on biological production and balance of phosphorus as the main factor in eutrophication. A general description of the lake ecosystem and of its main components is given. Described are the regularities of biological production and quantitative occurrence of organisms over a year, changes connected with the progress of eutrophication, inflow of phosphorus from the drainage basin, and the distribution and fate of phosphorus in the ecosystem. Trophic relations are especially thoroughly discussed.)

Various Authors. 1978. The influence of silver carp (*Hypophtalmichthys molitrix* Val.) on eutrophication of the environment of carp ponds. *Rocz. Nauk Roln.* Ser. H Vol. 99. (The volume contains seven papers including a recapitulation of the complex studies of the Institute of Inland Fisheries concerning the environmental conditions, phyto-, zoo- and bacterioplankton, benthos, and the health of fish. The higher density of seston-feeding fish, silver carp, resulted in higher phytoplankton biomass and primary production; the probable reason is that this fish consumed more detritus and zooplankton than phytoplankton, and thereby stimulated the circulation of nutrients. The fish grew less in dense stocks, although the biomass of phytoplankton, the potential food of silver carp, was higher. This paper contributes considerably to the knowledge on the functioning of freshwater ecosystems based on the example of fish ponds.)

Lomnicki, A. 1978. Individual differences among animals and natural regulation of their number. *J. Anim. Ecol.* (47:461–475). (A theoretical paper on the significance of individual differentiation (genetic, possibly strengthened by phenotype) for population control. The simulation made on a model population shows that individuals higher in the hierarchy survive in a given habitat under conditions of the deficiency of requisites and those lower in the hierarchy emigrate; if there is no such possibility, i.e., a closed habitat, they die or stop reproducing. As a result of migration, the equilibrium with the environment is more stable than when there is no migration.)

Siudziński, K., ed. 1979. Productivity of the Baltic ecosystem. *Pol. Ecol. Stud.* (in press). (A synthesis is elaborated of the numbers, biomass, and production of all trophic levels of the Baltic with special consideration of their differentiation and variability in time against the differentiation and variability of environmental factors. The paper is the result of many years of team research.)

REFERENCES CITED

Breymeyer, A. and G. Van Dyne, eds. In press. *Grassland systems analysis and man.* IBP synthesis volume. Cambridge: Cambridge University Press.

Dolny, K. 1972. In *Productivity problems of fresh waters,* eds. Z. Kajak and A. Hillbricht-Ilkowska. Warsaw-Krakow: PWN–Polish Scientific Publishers.

Golley, F. B., K. Petrusewicz, and L. Ryszkowski. 1975. *Small mammals: their productivity and population dynamics.* IBP synthesis volume 5. Cambridge: Cambridge University Press.

Jabłonna. 1967. In *Secondary productivity of terrestrial ecosystems: principles and methods,* ed. K. Petrusewicz, 2 Vols. Warsaw-Krakow: PWN–Polish Scientific Publishers.

Kendeigh, S. C. and J. Pinowski, eds. 1977. *Granivorous birds in ecosystems: their evolution, energetics, adaptations, impact, and control.* IBP synthesis volume 12. Cambridge: Cambridge University Press.

17

SWEDEN

Hugo Sjörs

EARLY DEVELOPMENT

Ecological thought is traceable in the Swedish literature of the eighteenth century during which practical economy was the goal of much of the scientific endeavor inspired by Linnaeus himself, a keen observer of nature, and other members of the newborn Swedish Academy of Sciences. For over a century, botanists remained heavily absorbed in descriptive taxonomy and floristics. Göran Wahlenberg, however, was one of the fathers of regional vegetation geography, and to some extent ecology in the early nineteenth century. The second ecologist in Sweden might be said to have been Hampus von Post, working in the middle of that century with organic soils and other items. The rise of ecology in Denmark and elsewhere closer to the turn of the century largely bypassed Sweden, although Rutger Sernander, Henrik Hesselman, and several other students of peatlands and forests soon brought Sweden back to the front line.

From about 1910, the prevailing traditions were peat stratigraphy and vegetation history (R. Sernander, L. von Post, E. Granlund, G. Lundqvist); forest ecology (H. Hesselman, L.-G. Romell, C. Malmström); and plant sociology (T. C. E. Fries, G. E. Du Rietz, H. Osvald). Although contact between groups was poor and even occasionally hostile, Malmström managed to deal with all three branches, and a good deal of hydrology in addition. Romell, and also H. Lundegårdh and M. G. Stålfelt, were among the few to connect ecology with plant physiology, and G. Turesson's "ecotypes" connected ecology to genetics. From the 1920s, limnology developed as a fourth branch (E. Naumann, later W. Rodhe, and many others).

VEGETATION STUDIES

History of Vegetation

As just mentioned, Swedish scientists contributed early and in an important way to the progress of vegetation history studies. However, in Sweden this discipline is largely regarded as a branch of Quaternary geology rather than botany. Even though Sweden can no longer be regarded as the leading nation it once was, especially in the days of L. von Post, the pioneer of pollen statistics, much research has been carried out and is still going on in this field.

Description of Vegetation

World War II meant scientific isolation in Sweden, but in 1950, the first postwar International Botanical Congress met in Stockholm, involving an almost exhausting effort among Swedish botanists. The congress was a success in every respect (except the delayed publication of the proceedings), and the contact with ecologists from nearly all countries stimulated not least a younger generation of students of vegetation.

Ecology in Sweden at the time of the congress was more descriptive and less experimental than it is today, but the designation of "experimental ecology" was at that time much misused for investigations using instruments rather than experiments. True experiments were then mainly made in applied ecology, in which the use of experimental plots has a long tradition.

Vegetation ecology, however, remained greatly absorbed by the problems of delimiting and classifying plant communities, although increasing attention was paid to environmental factors and their determination, and to regional differentiation. The "vegetation regions" (later, "biotic regions") have traditionally been in the focus of vegetation, as well as floristic, research in Sweden, because of the pronounced differences between south and north in this "elongated" country.

In 1965, rather unintentionally, the epitaph of the predominantly descriptive vegetation research era was written, with the publication of the book *The Plant Cover of Sweden* dedicated to Du Reitz by his many pupils. Nevertheless, a tradition of careful observation and the giving of full descriptive details of the scene of investigation fortunately remains in Swedish ecology.

Autecology

Autecological studies have never been in vogue in Sweden, in contrast to Denmark. A decrease in the knowledge of plant morphology is apparent among botanists in general, not only ecologists, and this would hamper any true revival of autecology. However, the work by C. O. Tamm (1953) on *Hylocomium* and that by J. Flower-Ellis (1971) on *Vaccinium myrtillus* are examples of autecological investigations.

Floristics

Interest in floristics and plant geography on the species level is still strong in Sweden, a feature among amateur naturalists and young field biologists as much as among professional botanists. For this we very much thank the mass media, which have done much to raise interest in open air biology, including ecology. A typical product is the "provincial flora," a type of publication with a very long tradition in Sweden, dating back to Linnaeus. An even more important work than the various recent provincial floras was the atlas of plant distributions in all Fenno-Scandinavia by E. Hultén (1950).

PREVALENCE OF DYNAMIC ECOLOGY

Through the last thirty years, there have been various trends in ecology. One is the shift of interest from static to dynamic ecology. This involves a striking present-day dominance of investigations into changing rather than relatively stable environments, the preference especially of the early plant sociologists in Sweden but also of most ecosystem analysts (see below). A pioneer of the dynamic trend was B. Pettersson, who in 1958 published a work on dynamics and constancy in the flora and vegetation of Gotland Island.

Ecosystems

Thirty years ago, the so-called Uppsala school of phytosociology knew nothing about ecosystems, thinking it even absolutely necessary to investigate vegetation separately from environmental factors. The first Swedish work in which an equivalent of the ecosystem, the holocene of Friedrichs, was used was by E. Julin (1948), who investigated plant communities, biomass, root systems, soils, and earthworms, a remarkably full combination for that time. Later single-author efforts to study ecosystems or synusial systems included those of C. O. Tamm (*Hylocomium* carpets), H. Sjörs (1954) (wooded hay-meadows), N. Malmer (1962–1963) and Å. Persson (1961–1962) (mire ecosystems), and F. Andersson (1970) (deciduous woodland).

The International Biological Program (IBP) meant increased contacts among ecologists all over the world, not least inside Fenno-Scandinavia. However, mainly because of a lack of sufficient funds, the various IBP contributions in Sweden did not reach full ecosystem level. Late offsprings of the IBP are the studies at Andersby north of Uppsala by H. Hytteborn (1975), H. Persson (1975) and several other botanists and zoologists (deciduous woodland), and a tundra biome study made on a subalpine mire with permafrost in the bog part at Stordalen near Lake Torneträsk (Sonesson 1967, 1969, 1970). In the latter case, the team, which was led by M. Sonesson, T. Rosswall, T. Flower-Ellis, and others, included several microbiologists.

The Swedish Coniferous Forest Project was launched after the IBP years with ambitions to study a few related ecosystems from aspects of system analysis and synthesis. These studies include bioclimate; ecophysiology of growth, water economy, and other factors; biomass changes; consumption and decomposition; fine roots; soil organisms; and transformation of nitrogen. Intensely studied plots were selected mainly for their exceptional stand and soil homogeneity.

Most ecologists tend to avoid the problems of clustering, spatial diversity, and heterogeneity in nature where homogeneous communities, random dispersions in space, and normal distributions of quantitative properties are rarely found but eagerly searched for by investigators. The modern dominance of a statistical, quantitative approach has, of course, also befallen Swedish ecology, but what is too-seldom realized is that the divergences from averages and regularity are the really interesting features in nature, these hardly ever being random deviations. Maybe increased research into patterning and heterogeneity will be among the aims of prospective theoretical ecology.

Production Ecology

During the early part of the period under consideration, production and biomass were studied almost exclusively in applied ecology. Thanks to the IBP, these features of vegetation also became highlighted in basic research. Experiences with biomass determination, and even worse, with yearly increment studies in plant parts other than stem wood, have made us aware of how laborious this branch of ecology is. Since labor is far from cheap in Sweden, we can probably expect a decline in production studies.

CONSERVATION

Sweden has experienced the same explosion in interest in nature conservancy and protection of the environment as other nations where the problems of human mass survival can still be watched on the television screen rather than experienced in the streets. Environmental problems were already partly known thirty years ago, although some have been added later, such as mercury and PCB as environmental poisons. The worsened large-dimensional acid air and rain pollution over most of Europe includes southwest Sweden, and urban and industrial areas elsewhere in the country. A large fraction of present-day ecological investigations is devoted to effects of pollution and environmental poisons.

Rather unfortunately for plant ecology, the public interest in environmental questions is more and more centering on the human's own environment. This is, of course, natural to human thought, but only biologists realize to what extent we are dependent on, and bear responsibility for, our fellow creatures on this planet.

Present-day plant ecology is deeply involved in the analysis of environmental changes largely brought about by shifting land use and human behavior. The richness of the country—which may or may not have passed its peak already—has led to persistent abuse of natural resources and unnecessarily hard exploitation of living nature. The unique still-natural northern rivers with their well-preserved shore zonation are, for example, threatened by the ever-increasing demand for energy from a population that is among the highest energy consumers in the world. Although Sweden has more forest per capita than most other countries, the demand for wood by the wood-processing industry is well above the present production potential. This leads forestry people to ask for drainage and afforestation of much of the remaining wetlands, even though one-half of the wetlands area is climatically unfit for economical afforestation. Other threats may come from future peat-processing industry for energy production, and from the idea of planting, for the same purpose, so-called energy wood, i.e., mini-rotation coppicewood, onto drained wetlands.

Such pressures on remaining natural features in the nearly completely exploited Europe of today call for ecological surveys with rapid methods suited to deal with numerous objects of large combined area. However, present-day ecology has deviated from regional research and become more and more involved with intensive studies in small plots or special research areas where facilities may be good but an overall view is lacking. It may be necessary to go back to less sophistication before it is too late to save those ecosystems that still function largely by means of natural factors.

TEXTBOOKS

Northern ecological conditions were poorly treated in ecological textbooks of the past. Therefore, H. Sjörs wrote *Nordic Plant Geography* (1956), largely inspired by Du Rietz's teaching. The *Living Landscape of Sweden* (1955) was magnificiently described by S. Selander, a poet and man of letters, as well as a botanist. *Plant Ecology* (1960) by Stålfelt has been widely used. It has a logical sequence of chapters, the last of which highlights the human influence, but since he did not use the ecosystem approach, the book now seems slightly old-fashioned. Later, H. Sjörs wrote another textbook called *Ecological Botany* (1971). (N.B. All these books are in Swedish.)

Swedes read Norwegian without difficulty and O. Gjaerevoll's *Plant Geography* (1973) is used also in Sweden. It contains a good deal of general plant geography, as well as Scandinavian material. We are still lacking a textbook in which the orientation is toward northern areas and plant, animal, and microbial ecology are treated in an integrated manner. If not too bulky, such a book would be ideal to use in undergraduate biological education, since non-Scandinavian ecological textbooks are still deficient in their treatment of boreal conditions.

JOURNALS AND SERIES OF MONOGRAPHS

An unusual feature of Swedish ecology is the possibility of publishing substantial monographs. Ecology deals with a complicated environment, with factors usually variable over both space and time, and often with very intricate interactions between the environment and living beings forming populations and communities, including interactions among the living beings themselves. Therefore, reporting a large ecological investigation requires plenty of space, normally not available in scientific journals. It is fortunate that the monographic form can still be used in spite of high printing costs, problems of dissemination and marketing, and a bias for specialized journals among many scientists involved in the publication business.

The oldest series of monographs is the *Acta Phytogeographica Suecica,* which has now issued sixty-seven volumes. It is not strictly confined to phytogeography nor to Sweden; for instance, production studies and African material has been included. It has been recently supplemented with a smaller series called *Växtekologiska Studier* issued also by the Swedish Phytogeographical Society, which is located in Uppsala. Earlier, the *Opera Botanica* in Lund took ecological articles but, unfortunately, no longer does so. On the other hand, a new series called *Wahlenbergia* has been started at Umeå University. The *Ecological Bulletin of NFR* (see below) occasionally prints papers read at symposia. There are also special publishing facilities, e.g., for nature conservancy and forest ecology.

Only rather short papers are normally accepted by the leading Fenno-Scandinavian ecological journal *Oikos.* A new journal, *Holarctic Ecology,* has been launched recently. The *Svensk Botanisk Tidskrift* now takes only popularized ecology and floristics. Popular writing can also be published in the journal and yearbooks *Sveriges Natur,* of the Swedish Association for Protection of Nature, and in *Fauna och Flora.* Popularization on a more sophisticated level is possible in the journal *Ambio* dealing with the environment. Most papers are now in English; papers of local or popular or political interest are still mostly in Swedish, though normally with English summaries.

FUNDS

As in many other countries, ecological investigations are supplied with the necessary funds in three ways. One is by employment as university staff, including that of the new Agricultural University, which has a Faculty of Forestry (derived from the former School of Forestry) as well as a Faculty of Agriculture where, for instance, landscape planning is taught. There are, in addition, museums, institutes of the Royal Academy of Sciences, and other institutions, in which some ecology is carried out. Unfortunately, the money allocated for running the scientific institutes is insufficient for the research per se, being swallowed up by the ever-increasing costs for salaries and keeping the institutes in a workable state.

The second source of money is project money for basic research given from certain sources, of which the Natural Science Research Council (NFR) is the most important. However, since most of this money goes to a few "big" projects and also since most ecological research today will be regarded as applied rather than basic, this resource does not support ecology as heavily as could be expected.

Much more important are the funds available for applied research of a sectorial but more or less ecological character. This includes a large fraction of the money bestowed from the research branch of the Swedish Nature Conservancy Board (SNV), as well as many of the grants from the Research Council for Forestry and Agriculture. Several other sources are also available, as is occasionally some earmarked money directly from the government. These sources in principle disfavor basic research, a regrettable practice. Over the latter half of the period under consideration (i.e., about fifteen years), more and more of the ecological research has shifted toward the immediate solution of problems selected for their urgency as to public affairs rather than for their scientific interest. A plea for more long-term ecology is often heard, but both the university structure at doctorate and postdoctorate level and the grant system for project money make such planning difficult.

Although fundamental ecological limitations to social development are frequently witnessed under the conditions of poverty in developing countries, only an insignificant part of Sweden's aid goes to ecological research. The mostly rather gloomy auspices honestly forwarded by ecological investigators do not look pleasing to politicians at home and overseas, the false glamor of technical enterprises being preferred.

The total sum allocated to ecological research in the wide sense, including environmental investigations in general, has increased greatly over the years, even if corrected for inflation. In reality, however, the greater part of this money goes back to the government as taxes and charges of many kinds, which have also increased throughout this period. This is, of course, not a problem confined to ecology in Sweden.

More threatening in the future, in the long run, will be the forthcoming state of growthless economy with gradually developing deficiencies foreseen not the least by many ecologists. It seems unavoidable that such a state will prevent future ecologists in Sweden and elsewhere from carrying out large-scale investigations at the ecosystem level, and will call for studies of less complexity and expenditure. Such studies may, nevertheless, be directed toward essential scientific problems, as well as toward the ecological background of human welfare. Maybe ecology would be even more badly needed under such conditions.

BIBLIOGRAPHY

The number of more or less scientific papers in Swedish plant ecology of the three last decades may be well above five thousand. A great number of works were listed in *The Plant Cover of Sweden* (1965) and in the bibliography of environmental sciences by Dahlström-Ekbohm (1975). It is striking that only a small fraction was published outside Fenno-Scandinavia, and only few authors were non-Swedish. This national character is also reflected in the large number of papers devoted to local floristics. Much of the development of analytical and classification methods was recorded only in descriptive papers and monographs about local areas.

It is impossible to give an adequately selected bibliography in a limited space, so only a few rather arbitrarily chosen titles are added below to those quoted in the text. Only works from the last thirty-two years are listed. Vegetation history, limnology, and marine botany have been omitted.

Ammar, M. Y. 1978. Vegetation and local environment on shore ridges at Vickleby, Öland, Sweden. An Analysis. *Acta Phytogeogr. Suec.* Vol. 64.

Berglund, B., ed. 1969. Impact of man on the Scandinavian landscape during the Late Post-Glacial. *Oikos* Suppl. 12.

Björkman, E. 1970. Forest tree mycorrhiza—the conditions for its formation and the significance for tree growth and afforestation. *Plant and Soil* 32:589–610.

Du Rietz, G. E. 1949. Huvudenheter och huvudgränser i svensk myrvegetation. *Svensk Bot. Tidskr.* 43:274–309.

Elveland, J. 1976. Myrar på Storön vid Norrbottenskusten. *Wahlenbergia* Vol. 3.

Ericson, L. 1977. The influence of voles and lemmings on the vegetation in a coniferous forest during a 4-year period in northern Sweden. *Wahlenbergia* Vol. 4.

——— and Wallentinus, H.-G. 1979. Sea-shore vegetation around the Gulf of Bothnia. *Wahlenbergia* Vol. 5.

Holmen, H. 1964. Forest ecological studies on drained peat land in the province of Uppland, Sweden I–II. *Stud. Forest. Suec.* Vol. 16.

Ingestad, T. 1974. Towards optimum fertilization. Ambio 3:49–54.

Malmer, N. 1969. Organic matter and cycling of minerals in virgin and present ecosystems. In "Impact of man on the Scandinavian landscape during the Late Post-Glacial," ed. B. Berglund. *Oikos* Suppl. 12:79–86.

———. 1976. Acid precipitation: chemical changes in the soil. *Ambio* 5:231–234.

Påhlsson, L. 1976*a*. Relationship of soil, microclimate, and vegetation on a sandy hill. *Oikos* 25:21–34.

———. 1976*b*. Influence of vegetation on microclimate and soil moisture on a Scanian hill. *Oikos* 25:176–186.

Persson, H. 1979. Fine-root production, mortality and decomposition in forest ecosystems. *Vegetatio* 41:101–109.

———. 1980. Spatial distribution of fine-root growth, mortality and decomposition in a young Scots pine stand in central Sweden. *Oikos* 34:77–87.

Rühling, A., and G. Tyler. 1973. Heavy metal deposition in Scandinavia. *Water, Air Soil Pollut.* 2:445–455.

Sjörs, H. 1948. Myrvegetation i Bergslagen. *Acta Phytogeogr. Suec.* Vol. 21.

——— and C. Nilsson. 1976. Vattenutbyggnadens effekter på levande natur. *Vaxtekol. Stud.* Vol. 8.

Skye, E. 1968. Lichens and air pollution. A study of cryptogamic epiphytes and environment in the Stockholm region.*Acta Phytogeogr. Suec.* Vol. 52.

Tamm, C. O. 1956. Survival and flowering of some perennial herbs. Part I. *Oikos* 7:273–292.

———. 1972. Further observations on the survival and flowering of some perennial herbs. Parts II and III. *Oikos* 23:23–28, 23:159–166.

———. 1976. Acid precipitation: biological effects in soil and on forest vegetation. *Ambio* 5:235–238.

———, H. Holmen, B. Popović, and G. Wiklander. 1974. Leaching of plant nutrients from soils as a consequence of forestry operations. *Ambio* 3:211–221.

Tyler, G. 1971. Distribution and turnover of organic matter and minerals in a shore meadow ecosystem. *Oikos* 22:265–291.

———. 1972. Heavy metals pollute nature, may reduce productivity. *Ambio* 1:57–59.

———. 1975, 1975, 1977. Effects of heavy metal pollution on decomposition in forest soils. Parts I, II, III. Stockholm: National Swedish Environmental Protection Board (SNV), PM 443E, 542E, 861.

Waldemarson Jensén, E. 1979. Successions in relationship to lagoon development in the Laitaure delta, north Sweden. *Acta Phytogeogr. Suec.* Vol. 66.

Wielgolaski, F. E., ed. 1975. Fennoscandian tundra ecosystems. Parts I, II. *Ecol. Stud.* Vols. 16 and 17.

Zackrisson, O. 1977. Influence of forest fires on the north Swedish boreal forest. *Oikos* 29:22–32.

REFERENCES CITED

Those citations listed in the preceding section are omitted here.

Andersson, F. 1970. Ecological studies in a Scanian woodland and meadow area, southern Sweden. Parts I and II. *Opera. Bot.* Vol. 27; *Bot. Notiser* 123:8–51.

Dahlström-Ekbohm, Y. 1975. Svensk Miljövårds- och omgivningshygienlitteratur 1952–1971. Bibliografi och analys. *Vaxtekol. Stud.* Vol. 6.

Flower-Ellis, J. G. K. 1971. *Age structure and dynamics in stands of bilbery* (Vaccinium myrtillus *L.*). Dept. of Forest Ecology and Forest Soils, Royal College of Forestry, Stockholm. Research Notes Vol. 9.

Gjaerevoll, O. 1973. *Plantegeografi*. Oslo.

Hultén, E. 1950 (2d ed. 1971). *Atlas över växternas utbredning i Norden*. Stockholm.

Hytteborn, H. 1975. Deciduous woodland at Andersby, eastern Sweden. Aboveground tree and shrub production. *Acta Phytogeogr. Suec.* Vol. 61.

Julin, E. 1948. Vessers udde. Mark och vegetation i en igenväxande löväng vid Bjärka-Säby. *Acta Phytogeogr. Suec.* Vol. 23.

Malmer, N. 1962–1963. Studies on mire vegetation in the Archaean area of southwestern Götaland (south Sweden). Parts I–III. *Opera. Bot.* Vol. 7, Nos. 1 and 2; *Bot. Notiser* 116:249–256.

Persson, Å. 1961–1962. Mire and spring vegetation in an area north of Lake Torneträsk, Torne Lappmark, Sweden. Parts I and II. *Opera. Bot.* Vol. 6, Nos. 1 and 3.

Persson, H. 1975. Deciduous woodland at Andersby, eastern Sweden: field-layer and below-ground production. *Acta Phytogeogr. Suec.* Vol. 62.

Pettersson, B. 1958. Dynamik och konstans i Gotlands flora och vegetation. *Acta Phytogeogr. Suec.* Vol. 40.

Plant Cover of Sweden. 1965. *Acta Phytogeogr. Suec.* Vol. 50.

Selander, S. 1955 (2d ed. 1957). *Det levande landskapet i Sverige*. Stockholm.

Sjörs, H. 1954. Slåtterängar i Grangärde finnmark. *Acta Phytogeogr. Suec.* Vol. 34.

———. 1956 (2d ed. 1967). *Nordisk växtgeografi*. Stockholm.

———. 1971. *Ekologisk botanik*. Stockholm.

Sonesson, M. 1967, 1969, 1970, 1970. Studies on mire vegetation in the Torneträsk area, northern Sweden, Parts I–IV. *Bot. Notiser* 120:272–296; *Bot. Notiser* 122:481–511; *Opera. Bot.* Vol. 26; *Bot. Notiser* 123:67–111.

Stålfelt, M. G. 1960 (2d ed. 1965, 1969). *Växtekologi*. Stockholm.

Tamm, C. O. 1953. Growth, yield and nutrition in carpets of a forest moss (*Hylocomium splendens*). *Medd. Statens Skogsforskningsinst.* 43:1–140.

18

SWITZERLAND

Andreas Gigon, Frank Klötzli, and Urs Rahm

THE ECOLOGICAL SETTING OF SWITZERLAND AND EARLY ECOLOGICAL OBSERVATIONS

Situated in the middle of Europe around the central part of the Alps, Switzerland has a landscape that is diverse in relief, climate, and geology. The immigration paths from all parts of Europe and the Mediterranean region are short. Along these paths immigrated not only different plants and animals but also Celtic, Roman, and Germanic settlers with their own special crop plants and methods of agriculture. Several millennia of agriculture and other human activities have influenced almost all the regions below the timberline. All this gave great richness of species and distinct ecosystems that often show sharp boundaries (forest/grassland; north/south slope; siliceous/calcareous soil). This diversity, which is most pronounced in the Alps, fascinated even the early naturalists. To preserve it for the future is one of the major tasks for contemporary ecologists.

Probably the first scientific description of a mountain was that of C. Gessner, a doctor and naturalist living in Zurich in the sixteenth century. In *Descriptio montis fracti* (1555), he noted that there are four altitudinal zones, of which the lowest has all four seasons and the topmost only one, winter. He also observed that mountain plants differ from lowland plants in morphology and phenology. Various catalogs of plants and animals (by Scheuchzer, von Haller, and Bauhin, among others) published in the following centuries contain considerable information on habitats and other ecological aspects.

In the nineteenth century, bases for the development of ecology were laid by O. Heer, a scientist with a broad view ranging from entomology to vegetation science, particularly paleobotany; by F. v. Tschudi with his *Animal Life of the Alps;* and by F. A. Forel, who wrote a monograph on Lake Geneva (Le Léman). In *Physiologie végétale,* A. P. de Candolle gives a list of possible influences of the environment on plants: light, electricity, heat, atmosphere, water, soil, cultivation, chemicals, animals, and parasites. His son Alphonse published *Géographie botanique raisonnée* (1855), in which he tried to compile definitions and exact data on phytogeography. The *Pflanzenleben der Schweiz* by H. Christ (1879) is the first comprehensive book on the vegetation of Switzerland; it describes the different altitudinal zones, climate, plant geography, and history.

The works just mentioned show that in the nineteenth century, unfortunately, specialization was leading to a botanical and a zoological approach to ecology. There were, however, instances where representatives of the different disciplines worked together, namely, in the foundation of the Swiss League for Protection of Nature (1908) and the Swiss National Park (1914). Another ecologically important decision of those years was the Federal Forest Protection Act (1902), by which the percentage of forested area of Switzerland must be kept at 25 percent.

PLANT ECOLOGY

The Development of the Zurich-Montpellier School of Phytosociology

The ecological view of plant science was much promoted by C. Schröter, professor of botany in Zurich from 1879 to 1925. His major publications were on the moorlands of Switzerland, written with Früh, on the meadows and pastures of Switzerland, in collaboration with Stebler, with much useful information for agronomists; vegetation monographs of different lakes and alpine valleys; and, most important, *Das Pflanzenleben der Alpen* (first ed. 1904–1908, second ed. 1926). This monograph contains most of the knowledge of the time on the influence of elevation, soil, climate, and other environmental factors on alpine plants and plant communities. Floral biology, plant dispersal, and plant history were treated by his collaborators. Schröter can be considered as one of the first to consistently use the concept of the plant community for describing vegetation. This new approach, and the stimulating and serene personality of Schröter, influenced a whole generation of botanists, particularly in Zurich, in the direction of ecology. Among these was H. Brockmann-Jerosch, who studied the relation between timberline and climate, wrote a vegetation of Switzerland, and compiled one of the first maps of the vegetation of the earth. Later, P. Jaccard, A. U. Däniker, and F. Chodat, the latter in Geneva, were very active in the whole field of botany, but particularly in ecology. The coefficient of Jaccard is still used today as a simple means of expressing the similarity of plant communities. Under the influence of Schröter, the wealthy chemist and businessman E. Rübel became so enthusiastic about plant ecology that he founded, in 1918, a private institute for research in what he called geobotany, i.e., plant geography, ecology, and history. In 1958, this institute was donated to the Swiss Federal Institute of Technology and thus became the Geobotanisches Institute ETH, Stiftung Rübel in Zurich. Of the major publications of Rübel, one may mention several studies on the alpine flora and vegetation, the *Pflanzengesellschaften der Erde* (1930), many papers on the theory of plant ecology and vegetation mapping, as well as one of the first books on methods in plant ecology.

Much influenced by Schröter was J. Braun-Blanquet, assistant in Rübel's Geobotanical Research Institute from 1915 to 1926. In that year, he founded his own Station Internationale de Geóbotanique Méditerranéenne et Alpine (SIGMA) in Montpellier, France. In 1928, he published the *Pflanzensoziologie* (3d ed. 1964), which was the basis for the breakthrough of the so-called Zurich-Montpellier school of phytosociology.

The major concepts of the Zurich-Montpellier school are:

—Vegetation consists of discrete plant communities, i.e., assemblages of species always occurring together if the habitats are similar. (It is not surprising that this view of vegetation developed in Switzerland and Europe because here ecosystems with sharp boundaries are a reality.)
—The association is deinfed as the "fundamental unit for phytosociology, being a plant community of certain floristic composition, of uniform habitat, and of uniform physiognomy." Different associations contain different character species.
—Associations are described by means of vegetation tables, consisting of *relevés,* i.e., complete species lists with estimation of the cover or abundance, or both, of the species in the particular stand. The associations are given names composed of the root of the Latin name(s) of important species and the ending *-etum* (e.g., the association of the *Fagus* forests is called *Fagetum*).
—Similar associations can be grouped into a so-called vegetation alliance, alliances in an order, orders in a class, and so on, a hierarchic system of vegetation units, each with character species.

The methods of the Zurich-Montpellier school, widely used today in many parts of Europe and other continents, allow a quick understanding of the vegetation. These methods are a cheap system for vegetation mapping for agriculture and forestry, for example. The concepts of hierarchy in the vegetation units and that of the character species are now regarded as rather artificial and are often replaced by the concepts of differentiating species and ecological groups of species.

As might be expected, Braun-Blanquet was very active in using his method of phytosociology. Alone, or with co-authors, he published about forty papers on the vegetation and flora of the Swiss alpine canton (state) of the

Grisons. One of the more recent major works is on the vegetation of the dry central alpine valleys. As were many other Swiss ecologists, particularly Rikli (*Das Pflanzenkleid der Mittelmeerländer*), Braun-Blanquet was fascinated by the vegetation of the Mediterranean region and published a large number of phytosociological studies on that subject.

Transition to the 1960s

This period is characterized by a series of about fifty monographic studies of individual plant communities (associations) or the whole vegetation of particularly interesting parts of the country. (Palynology was another active field of research but will not be treated in the present essay.) These monographs contain vegetation tables, studies of the soil, climate, and human influences, and often also information about plant geography, history, and conservation. Examples are monographs on the beech forests (Moor 1952; the soils were studied by Bach 1950), the floristically rich *Bromus erectus* grasslands (Zoller 1954), alluvial fens, subalpine grasslands, and weed communities. Vegetation monographs, often with vegetation maps, were compiled by W. Koch (1926) on the alluvial plain of the Linth river, by Gams (1927) in part of the alpine valley of the Valais, by Etter on the forests of the Swiss midland, and by Kuoch on subalpine forests. Also to be mentioned was the work of Furrer, who was very active in many branches of plant ecology and who as early as 1923 had published a plant geography of Switzerland.

An intensively researched region is the Swiss National Park in the eastern Alps. Here, good collaboration between plant ecologists and soil scientists led to the classic investigations of Braun-Blanquet and Jenny (1926) on the development of vegetation and soil in the alpine zone, and to the studies on the subalpine forest and shrub communities by Braun-Blanquet, Pallmann, and Bach (1954). The vegetation of the park was mapped by Campbell and Trepp, and a flora giving much ecological information was published by Zoller et al. In an investigation lasting nearly three decades, Stüssi (1970) studied the influence of the enormous increase of the deer population (due to total protection) on the vegetation of the park.

More or less independent from the Zurich-Montpellier school, E. Schmid developed an approach in which plant communities are characterized not only by the species lists and cover/abundance, but also by the combination of life forms and phytogeographic relations (vegetation belts). Several vegetation monographs were developed with this approach. The main work of Schmid's small school is his vegetation map of Switzerland in the scale 1:200,000 (1943–1950 and 1961).

Among the few ecophysiological investigations before 1960, the more important are the study of Welten on the water relations of plants, and the investigations of Nägeli on the effects of wind and light.

A precursor of the modern approach of ecology was W. Lüdi, Director of Rübel's Geobotanical Research Institute in Zurich from 1931–1958. In his monograph of the alpine vegetation near Interlaken (1948) are contained results of investigations on not only phytosociological relations, soil, and climate, but also the whole ecosystem. In this work, he collaborated with many specialists: Ochsner for moss ecology, E. Frey for lichens, Stöckli, Gisin, and Heinis for soil fauna, and Düggeli for soil bacteria. The main goal was to establish the causal relations between the abiotic and biotic environmental factors and the plant communities. Lüdi also carried out experiments with different types of fertilizer and cutting regimes, as well as studies on the natural or artificial regeneration of the vegetation (also succession on glacier fields). These investigations lasted for several decades and may be considered as one of the first steps establishing an experimental ecology independent from agriculture and forestry. In addition, Lüdi was very active in many other fields, notably palynology and nature conservation.

Present Lines of Research in Plant Ecology

For the last twenty years, ecological research in vegetation science has mainly concentrated on assessing nutrient regimes, competition, and limiting factors of plant communities. Apart from this, several synopses of groups of plant communities, e.g., grasslands and woodlands, have been elaborated. Some specialists have worked on basidiomycetes or other groups of cryptogams.

"Pure" phytosociological work in this period is quite rare. Major publications (partly compilations) are, for example, on heath lands (Hofer 1970), alpine heath and pine scrub (Schweingruber 1972), grasslands (Béguin 1972; Dietl 1972, 1977), reedlands and swamp sites (Klötzli 1969*a*), and forest communities and forest habitats of Switzerland (Ellenberg and Klötzli 1972). Less frequent communities of more extreme sites on steep slopes, alluvial flats, or marginal areas of beech forest were described, for example, by J. L. Richard (1961), Zoller (1974), and others. Sophisticated numerical methods were tried out on forests and other relevé data by, for example, Hegg (1965), van Groenewoud (1968), and, considering various techniques, on bogs (Wildi 1977). A general account on middle-European forests including alpine vegetation is given in Ellenberg (1978).

The general site conditions of special groups of plant communities were analyzed by Béguin and Pochon (1971) for Jurassic acid meadows on calcareous subsoil; for reed stands by Ammann-Moser (1975), Klötzli and Grünig (1976), and Lachavanne and Wattenhofer (1975); and by Wildi (1977) for raised bog complexes. Ellenberg gave an abstract of details on indicator plants in agriculture; this was enlarged to contain all Swiss vascular and some cryptogamic plant species and most site factors by Landolt (1977).

A number of workers concentrated on the water and nutrient regime. Thus, León and Williams analyzed wet meadows [compare also Gigon, Yerly, and Antonietti on forests in the Italian-speaking southern part of the country (compilation in Ellenberg 1977)]. In this context, it was essential to gain some knowledge of the far-reaching effects of fertilized grasslands on oligotrophic straw meadows and other wetlands, valuable representatives of vanishing plant communities (Boller-Elmer 1977). From 1971 until 1973, some of these meadows and rare fen types were even transplanted with new elaborate techniques when a new runway had to be constructed through wetlands at Zurich airport (Klötzli 1975*a*). Revegetation of roadside slopes with dry meadows was investigated by Klein (1980).

Several studies dealt with the carrying capacity or limiting factors (nitrogen, phosphorus, water, mechanical factors), or both, of different ecosystems. By these investigations, the limits between beech and fir forests were characterized in altitude and seem to be due to edaphic factors (Pfadenhauer 1973; compare also Hainard 1969). Similar procedures were used to delimit the pine and the oak woodlands, as well as the beech and the yew mixed forests (Burnand, Roth, and Leuthold in compilation by Klötzli 1975*b*). Factors responsible for the great floristic and physiognomic differences between alpine grasslands on acid and on calcareous soils were studied in detail by Gigon (1971) in an analysis of edaphic and climatic factors, competition, and germination experiments. Some patterns of the ecology of these grasslands were expressed in simple cybernetic models.

What happens to certain species groups if distinct separating elements between different altitudinal belts are eliminated was experimentally tested by Landolt (1967) and Landolt et al. (1975). The opening of the forests between, for example, dry meadow sites in the interior alpine valleys and alpine meadows gave rise to the hybridization of related species, forming common meadow plants [e.g., *Scabiosa columbaria* = *S. lucida* (alpine) × *S. gramuntia* (dry valley)]. For many years, the ecological behavior and evolution (ecological genetics) of closely related taxa have been studied in culture and in the field by Urbanska-Worytkiewicz (see, for example, the investigation on the *Cardamine pratensis* group by Urbanska-Worytkiewicz and Landolt 1974 and Urbanska-Worytkiewicz 1980). Similar studies for endemic plants have been carried out for many years by Favarger and his school in Neuchâtel.

Very specialized works on cryptogamic groups of plants have been published by Horak (1963) on the ecology of certain mycorrhiza-forming basidiomycetes, by Cosandey (1964) on bog-dwelling phytoplanktonic algae, and by Vareschi (1936) and Züst (1977) on epiphytic lichens in and near anthropogenic "lichen deserts" in Zurich.

A relatively new line of specialization is ecophysiology (see, for example, the detailed investigations of the leaf energy budgets and temperature by Eller 1971).

Further research will be carried out on:

—the composition of certain groups of communities (e.g., subalpine spruce forests, alpine meadows, alluvial woodlands, and wetlands of higher altitudes);
—the limits between important forest communities;
—the carrying capacity of certain vegetation types: lake shores, Jurassic meadows, and particularly, different subalpine and alpine ecosystems more or less influenced by man (Man and the Biosphere projects in four regions of the Swiss Alps);
—successional trends on glacier fields and fallows or abandoned fields;
—the effects of game or domestic animals (sheep) on certain meadow types or birds on alluvial communities, valuable in the sense of nature conservancy; and
—a number of definite site factors (isolation, fire, extreme parent rock, such as serpentine), all with the general trend toward ensuring the existence of endangered plant communities and trying to assess the limits of and between certain communities and species by causal analysis.

Vegetation Mapping and Applied Ecology

Under the influence of a growing knowledge of plant communities in forests and cultivated lands and the requirements of these communities regarding environmental factors, mapping has become increasingly appreciated in applied ecology. One of the major works since the early days in mapping is a comparison of different methods on the same object (Ellenberg 1967; see also Rogers 1970). Mapping is now done to guarantee the best management techniques in many critical circumstances (e.g., delimitation of nature conservation areas, separation of forest and pasture, unstable slopes) or just for better use of available land. These maps, at a scale of 1:5,000 up to 1:10,000, are mostly unpublished. For purposes of nature conservancy and planning, a special computerized method was developed to present maps on a grid system showing the distribution of all major plant communities, diversity, singularities, and human influence (Béguin et al. 1978).

Phenology and its applications in forestry and agriculture were treated by Kuhn (1967, forest communities of the region of Zurich), Schreiber (1968), and Häberli (1968). These authors also worked out several phenological maps of smaller regions and of the whole country (scale 1:200,000) (Schreiber et al. 1977).

Soil maps are also produced in increasing numbers, but so far only in critical areas and mainly by three groups of soil scientists (Bach, Frei, and Richard; compare, e.g., Frei and Bach 1966; Frei and Juhasz 1963). A humus and soil classification system was worked out by Pallmann (between 1933 and 1954) and Frei et al. (since 1944), whereas Bach concentrated on clay chemistry (since 1950) and Richard (1945, 1953; Richard et al. 1978) and his school on soil physics (water regime, desorption curves, drainage, and diffusion of oxygen). Soil biology is treated by comparatively few scientists at present (see, e.g., Jäggi 1973). Of outstanding interest for the conservation of fertile soils in cultivated areas is the principle of "fungistasis," the inhibition of the development of fungal spores, a subject treated by Schüepp and Green (1968). The breakdown of certain organic substances (e.g., higher fatty acids) is a topic followed by Wanner and his school.

Applied ecology has gained increasing esteem in forestry and agronomy. In the early days, researchers concentrated on the influence of forests on water regime, climate, and soil, elaborating one of the first dual watershed experimental programs in the world (see Engler 1919; Burger 1943) and conversely, on the influence of meteorologic conditions on forests (Primault 1957). Now chiefly investigated are problems of nutrient regime and fertilizing, including also the effects of legumes, and interrelations with the rest of the organisms and soil (see, e.g., Gisiger 1966; Nösberger 1964; Künzli 1967; Dietl 1977). In forestry, special topics include: the effects of fungal infections, air pollution (fluorine and sulfur dioxide), and other factors on trees (T. Keller 1970, 1977); the influences of forests on the water and nutrient regime of whole areas (e.g., H. M. Keller 1970); and the influence of roe deer and other cervidae on forest and grassland communities (Eiberle 1959; Klötzli 1965), and of *Zeiraphera* on *Larix* populations (e.g., Benz 1974; Auer 1977). Intrinsic dynamics were studied in riparian forests (Heller 1969), at the alpine timberline (Kuoch and Amiet 1970), and in other different forest situations by, among others, Leibundgut (1966) and Ott (1965). The special issue of the *Swiss Journal of Forestry,* May 1968, gave a general account of global and Swiss forest ecology (compare also Leibundgut 1976; Schütz and Badoux 1979).

Since the rather isolated early work of Baumann (1911) on hydrology, limnology, and climatology of Lake Constance, applied ecology is finally getting more attention. The effects of currents or eutrophication on organisms (absorption of nutrients, seasonal fluctuations) were investigated by Zimmermann (1961), Thomas (1949, 1966), Ambühl (1964, see especially 1975), Gächter and Furrer (1972), Eichenberger (1972), Wattenhofer (1980) and many others. In biogeochemical ecology, Stumm and Morgan (1970) have been tracing the pathways of pesticides, fertilizers, and heavy metals.

In climatology, investigations treat such important ecological problems as the reafforestation at timberline (Turner 1966) and such effects of condensing towers of nuclear power plants on the environment as the changes in nebulosity and hoar frost frequency (Turner 1974). Here open questions are still concerned with the accumulation of heavy metals, including radionuclides in food chains, and also with the long-term effects of these substances. Similar investigations are carried out with pesticides. Gradually, alternative methods in agronomy are being tested by different university departments or other institutions.

ANIMAL ECOLOGY

Before 1900, zoological studies in Switzerland were mainly descriptive with occasional information on ecology. During the first half of this century, research was concerned with morphology, evolution, genetics, ontogeny, and experimental zoology. Only a few ecological observations were carried out, mostly in connection with faunistic studies (Universities of Fribourg and Basel: hydrobiology and entomology). Together with the inventory of the fauna of the Swiss National Park, some ecological problems were treated as well.

The impetus in ecology began about twenty five years ago, and research activity in this field has increased, especially during the last few years. Most scientists are studying a single species (autecology); some research teams are working on ecosystems (synecology). Ethological studies played an important role in activating ecological research. Many programs were promoted by the Wildlife Management, the Conservation of Nature, and the Federal Forestry Departments. Applied ecology also became important in solving environmental problems and the pollution of lakes and rivers.

Autecology of Animal Species

Studies on mammals include sociological ecology, food consumption, migration, population dynamics, altitudinal and habitat influence, and distribution. Mammals involved in these programs are wild boar, red deer, roe deer, ibex, chamois, rabbit, hare, alpine marmot, beaver, fox and badger. This work is carried on in the universities of Basel, Bern, and Zurich, and at ETH-Zurich. Research on the ecology of small mammals (Muridae and Soricidae) is done by the ETH-Zurich, the universities of Lausanne and Zurich, as well as the Federal Agricultural Research Station near Nyon. Some of this research is related to the damage caused by these animals to forests and agriculture. Another problem under examination is the increasing population of some of these species in nature reserves (e.g., national park and others).

Food ecology, population dynamics, breeding conditions, and the environmental influence of some bird species are also studied. Priority is given to endangered species. Basic and applied ecological research on fish populations is mainly the task of EAWAG-Dübendorf and the Lake Research Institute at Kastanienbaum (Lucerne). Population density and dispersion of some freshwater molluscs (*Dreissena, Limnaea, Anadonta*) are studied in some lakes.

The ecology of arthropods became very important in connection with new cultivation methods; Acarina and Collembola are research objects in Bern, Basel, Liebefeld, and ETH-Zurich. Researchers at Neuchâtel are especially interested in ticks; other insects are studied in Zurich (*Drosophila*), Bern (termites), Fribourg (*Aphis*), and ETH-Zurich. Tropical insects are a research object at the Swiss Tropical Institute in Basel. The ecology of *Hydracarina* is a main subject of research by the Natural History Museum in Basel.

Synecology of Animals

Several small ecosystems are being studied including moist habitats, dry regions, montane grassland, lakes, and ponds. Another subject is the influence on animals of civilization, for example, the construction of highways. The Ornithological Station at Sempach has research programs on the relation between bird fauna and vegetation. A special radar technique was developed in Sempach and at the Natural History Museum in Basel for studies on bird banding and migration. A main task is the conservation of bird sanctuaries in a landscape as strongly influenced by civilization as is the Swiss midlands.

Related to this is the study of lake ecosystems, which is seen as very important in regard to water pollution. The protection of ponds and other suitable places for amphibians is quite popular in Switzerland. Agriculture needs more data on the edaphic fauna, and this field of research will be developed.

TEACHING, RESEARCH, AND PUBLICATIONS

Teaching and Research

Teaching and research of botanical and zoological ecology is carried out to a larger or smaller degree at all seven universities and at the federal institutes of technology (ETH-Zurich and ETH-Lausanne). Research programs exist also at the Federal Institute of Forestry Research, the Federal Research Stations for Agronomy, the Federal Institute for Water Resources, the Swiss Ornithological Station, and at several natural history museums. Several agrochemical and planning firms are involved in applied ecological research. Furthermore, Switzerland has research facilities at a few institutes in foreign countries or owns small laboratories (e.g., Banyuls-sur-Mer and Roscoff, France; Naples, Italy; Adiopodoumé, Ivory Coast; Ifakara, Tanzania; Crete).

International relations are furthered by the fact that the United Nations Environmental Program (UNEP), the International Union for Conservation of Nature (IUCN), the World Wildlife Fund (WWF), and other international organizations have their headquarters in Switzerland. From the Geobotanisches Institute ETH in Zurich are organized the International

Phytogeographical Excursions (IPE), of which the latest, the sixteenth, was to the Carolinas in the United States (see Lieth and Landolt 1979).

For research, most grants are given by the Swiss National Science Foundation and by the cantons (states) through their support of the universities. Other funds come from the Federal Forestry Department, the National Foundation for the State Economy (Volkswirtschafts-Fonds), the Swiss League for Protection of Nature, the World Wildlife Fund, the natural history museums, and other institutions.

In the course of the implementation of some projects on a national scale, the collaboration between the universities and the different disciplines is becoming more and more intensive. An interdisciplinary approach is used for research in the national park, inventories of nature conservation areas, the MAB-project on "Impact of human activities on mountain ecosystems" (four test areas in Switzerland), and other projects.

Scientific Societies

Scientific societies with activities in ecology include: Schweizerische Botanische Gesellschaft, Société Suisse de Zoologie, Schweizerische Entomologische Gesellschaft, ALA Schweizerische Gesellschaft für Vogelkunde und Vogelschutz, Schweizerische Hydrologische Gesellschaft, Bodenkundliche Gesellschaft der Schweiz, Gesellschaft für Oekologie (of the German-speaking countries), Schweizerischer Naturschutzbund, Schweizerische Arbeitsgemeinschaft für Umweltforschung, and Schweizerische Gesellschaft für Umweltschultz.

Journals

Major journals containing papers on ecological topics are: *Ergebnisse der wissenschaftlichen Untersuchungen im Schweizerischen Nationalpark, Beiträge zur Geobotanischen Landesaufnahme der Schweiz, Veröffentlichungen (und Berichte) des Geobotanischen Institutes ETH, Stiftung Rübel, Mitteilungen (und Berichte) der Eidg. Anstalt für das forstliche Versuchswesen, Bulletin der Bodenkundlichen Gesellschaft der Schweiz, Berichte der Schweizerischen Botanischen Gesellschaft, Revue Suisse de Zoologie, Mitteilungen der Schweizerischen Entomologischen Gesellschaft, Der Ornithologische Beobachter, Schweizerische Zeitschrift für Hydrologie, Environmental Conservation,* and *Dokumente und Informationen zur Schweizerischen Orts-, Regional- und Landesplanung (DISP).*

There are several journals on agriculture and forestry (including the *Schweizerische Zeitschrift für Forstwesen*), as well as journals of the scientific societies of the different cantons (states). The languages of publication are German, French, Italian, and English.

General Reference Publications

Bibliographies containing almost all papers on plant ecology of Switzerland were compiled by Oefelein (1960) and Klötzli (1969*b*); a list of the recent literature is in preparation. Lists of references on game research have been published regularly since 1972. Merian and co-workers (1980) compiled a catalog of all projects on environmental sciences presently being carried out in Switzerland. It contains 1,462 projects and groups of projects ranging from recycling, energy problems, agronomy, nature conservation, and ecology to educational, sociological, economical, and many other aspects of environmental sciences.

REFERENCES CITED

Ambühl, H. 1964. Die Nährstoffelimination aus der Sicht des Limnologen. *Schweiz. Z. Hydrol.* 26:569–594.

———. 1975*a*. Versuch der Quantifizierung der Beeinflussung des Oekosystems durch chemische Faktoren: Stehende Gewässer. *Schweiz. Z. Hydrol.* 37:35–52.

———. 1975*b*. Die Krankengeschichte schweizerischer Seen. *NZZ* (5.3.75) 53:45–47.

Ammann-Moser, B. 1975. Vegetationskundliche und pollenanalytische Untersuchungen auf dem Heidenweg im Bielersee. *Beitr. Geobot, Landesaufn. Schweiz* Vol. 56.

Auer, C. 1977. Dynamik von Lärchenwickler-Populationen längs des Alpenbogens. *Mitt. Eidg. Anst. Forstl. Vers'wes.* 53:70–105.

Bach, R. 1950. Die Standorte jurassischer Buchenwaldgesellschaften mit besonderer Berücksichtigung der Böden (Humuskarbonatböden und Rendzinen). *Ber. Schweiz. Bot. Ges.* 60:51–152.

Baer, J. G. 1952. *Ecology of animal parasites.* Urbana: Univ. Illinois Press.

Baumann, E. 1911. Die Vegetation des Untersees (Bodensee)—Eine floristischkritische und biologische Studie. *Arch. Hydrobiol.* Suppl. 1.

Béguin, C. 1972. Contribution à l'étude phytosociologique et écologique du Haut Jura. *Beitr. Geobot. Landesaufn. Schweiz* Vol. 54.

——— and M. Pochon. 1971. Contribution à l'étude pétrographique et géochimique des sols des nardaies jurassiennes Nardetum jurassicum. *Bull. Soc. Neuchatel. Sci. Nat.* 94:67–76.

———, O. Hegg, and H. Zoller. 1978. Kartierung der Vegetation der Schweiz nach einem Kilometer-Raster. *Geogr. Helv.* 33:45–48.

Benz, G. 1974. Negative Rückkoppelung durch Raum- und Nahrungskonkurrenz sowie zyklische Vëranderung der Nahrungsgrundlage als Regelprinzip in der Populationsdynamik des grauen Lärchenwicklers, *Zeiraphera diniana. Z. Angew. Entomol.* 76:196–228.

Boller-Elmer, K. 1977. Stickstoff-Düngungseinflüsse von Intensiv-Grünland auf Streu- und Moorwiesen. *Veroeff. Geobot. Inst. Eidg. Tech. Hochsch. Stift. Ruebel, Zu.* Vol. 63.

Braun-Blanquet, J. 1964. *Pflanzensoziologie,* 3d ed. Vienna: Springer. (English translation of the 1st ed. by G. D. Fuller and H. S. Conard. 1932. *Plant sociology.* New York: McGraw-Hill).

——— and H. Jenny. 1926. Vegetationsentwicklung und Bodenbildung in der alpinen Stufe der Zentralalpen. *Denkschr. Schweiz. Naturforsch. Ges.* 63:183–349.

———, H. Pallmann, and R. Bach. 1954. Pflanzensoziologische und bodenkundliche Untersuchungen: Vegetation und Böden der Wald- und Zwergstrauch gesellschaften (Vaccinio-Piceetalia). *Ergeb. Wiss. Unters. Schweiz. Nationalpark* Vol. 4 (N.F.).

Burger, H. 1943. Stand und Ziele der forstlichen Grundlagenforschung. *Beih. Z. Schweiz. Forstver.* 21:40–64.

Christ, H. 1879. *Das Pflanzenleben der Schweiz.* Zurich: Schulthess.

Cosandey, F. 1964. La tourbière des Tenasses sur Vevey. *Beitr. Geobot. Landesaufn. Schweiz* Vol. 45.

Dietl, W. 1972. Die Vegetationskartierung als Grundlage für die Planung einer umfassenden Alpverbesserung im Raume Glaubenbüelen (Obwalden). Dissertation, ETH-Zurich.

———. 1977. Vegetationskunde als Grundlage der Verbesserung des Graslandes in den Alpen. In *Handbook of vegetation science,* Vol. 13. *Application of vegetation science to grassland-husbandry,* ed. W. Krause, pp. 405–458. The Hague: W. Junk.

Eiberle, K. 1959. Sylviculture et prévention des dommages que peut causer le gibier. *La Foret* 12:150–159.

Eichenberger, E. 1972. Oekologische Untersuchungen an Modellfliessgewässern 4. *Schweiz. Z. Hydrol.* 34:173–189.

Ellenberg, H., ed. 1967. Vegetations- und bodenkundliche Methoden der forstlichen Standortskartierung. *Veroeff. Geobot. Inst. Eidg. Tech. Hochsch. Stift. Ruebel, Zu.* Vol. 39.

———. 1977. Stickstoff als Standortsfaktor, insbesondere für mitteleuropäische Pflanzengesellschaften. *Oecol. Plant.* 12:1–22.

———. 1978. *Vegetation Mitteleuropas mit den Alpen in ökologischer Sicht,* 2d ed. (1st ed. 1963). Stuttgart: Ulmer.

——— and F. Klötzli. 1972. Waldgesellschaften und Waldstandorte der Schweiz. *Mitt. Schweiz. Anst. Forstl. Vers'wes.* 48:589–930.

Eller, B. 1976. *Energiebilanz und Blattemperatur.* Dissertation, Universität Zurich. Zurich: Juris.

Engler, A. 1919. Untersuchungen über den Einfluss des Waldes auf den Stand der Gewässer. *Mitt. Schweiz. Zentralanst. Forstl. Vers'wes.* Vol. 12.

Frei, E. and P. Juhasz. 1963. Beitrag zur Methodik der Bodenkartierung und der Auswertung von Bodenkarten unter schweizerischen Verhältnissen. Gebiet: Reckenholz. *Schweiz. Landwirtsch. Forsch.* 2:249–307.

——— and R. Bach. 1966. Bodenkarte der Schweiz 1:1,000,000. Erläuterungen zur Karte und zur Systematik der Böden der Schweiz. *Schweiz. Landwirtsch. Forsch.* 5:537–551.

Furrer, E. 1923. *Kleine Pflanzengeographie der Schweiz.* Zurich.

Gächter, R. and O. J. Furrer, 1972. Der Beitrag der Landwirtschaft zur Eutrophierung der Gewässer der Schweiz. *Schweiz. Z. Hydrol.* 34:41–70, 71–93.

Gams, H. 1927. Von den Follatères zur Dent de Morcles. *Beitr. Geobot. Landesaufn. Schweiz* Vol. 15.

Gigon, A. 1971. Vergleich alpiner Rasen auf Silikat- und auf Karbonatboden. *Veröff. Geobot. Inst. Eidg. Tech. Hochsch. Stift. Ruebel Zuer.* Vol. 48.

Gisiger, L. 1966. Ergebnisse eines langjährigen Versuches über die Phosphorsäurenachlieferung eines Wiesenbodens unter Berücksichtigung der übrigen Nährstoffe. *Schweiz. Landwritsch. Forsch.* 5:481–523.

Glutz von Blotzheim, U. N. 1962. *Die Brutvögel der Schweiz.* 2nd ed. Aarau. 648 pp.

Van Groenewoud, H. 1965. Ordination and classification of Swiss and Canadian coniferous forests by various biometric and other methods. *Ber. Geobot. Inst. Eidg. Tech. Hochsch. Stift. Ruebel Zuer.* 36:28–102.

Häberli, R. 1968. Levé cartographique agricole des stations végétales de la Côte (canton de Vaud, Suisse). Dissertation, ETH-Zurich.

Hainard, P. 1969. Signification écologique et biogéographique de la répartition des essences forestières sur l'adret valaisan. *Boissiere* Vol. 15.

Hegg, O. 1965. Untersuchungen zur Pflanzensoziologie und Oekologie im Naturschutzgebiet Hohgant (Berner Voralpen). *Beitr. Geobot. Landesaufn. Schweiz* Vol. 46.

Heller, H. 1969. Lebensbedingungen und Abfolge der Flussauenvegetation in der Schweiz. *Mitt. Schweiz. Anst. Forstl. Vers'wes* Vol. 45.

Hofer, H. 1970. Ueber die Zusammenhänge zwischen der Düngung und der Konkurrenzfähigkeit ausgewählter Naturwiesenpflanzen. Dissertation, ETH-Zurich.

Hofmann, A. and B. Nievergelt, 1972. Das jahreszeitliche Verteilungsmuster und der Aesungsdruck von Alpensteinbock, Gemse, Rothirsch und Reh in einem begrenzten Gebiet im Oberengadin. *Z. Jagdwiss.* 18:185–212.

Horak, E. 1963. Pilzökologische Untersuchungen in der subalpinen Stufe (Piceetum subalpinum und Rhodoreto-Vaccinietum) der Rätischen Alpen (Dischmatal, Graubünden). *Mitt. Schweiz. Anst. Forstl. Vers'wes.* Vol. 39.

Jäggi, W. 1973. Beziehungen zwischen bodenbiologischer Aktivität und Bodenfruchtbarkeit. *Schweiz. Landwritsch. Monatsh.* 51:264–298.

Keller, H. M. 1970. Der Chemismus kleiner Bäche in teilweise bewaldeten Einzugsgebieten in der Flyschzone eines Voralpentales. *Mitt. Schweiz. Anst. Forstl. Vers'wes.* 46:113–155.

Keller, T. 1970. Wuchsleistung, Gaswechsel, Ueberlebensprozente und Schneeschimmelpilzbefall gedüngter Ballenpflanzen an der oberen Waldgrenze. *Mitt. Schweiz. Anst. Forstl. Vers'wes.* 46:1–32.

______. 1977. Der Einfluss von Fluoremissionen auf die Nettoassimilation von Waldbaumarten. *Mitt. Eidg. Anst. Forstl. Vers'wes.* 53:161–198.

Keller, W. 1979. Ein Bestimmungsschlüssel für die Waldgesellschatten der Schweiz. *Schweiz. Z. Forstw.* 130:225–249.

Klein, A. In press. Die Vegetation an Nationalstrassenböschungen der Nordschweiz und ihre Eignung für den Naturschutz. *Veroeff. Geobot. Inst. Eidg. Tech. Hochsch. Stift. Ruebel Zuer.*

Klötzli, F. 1965. Qualität und Quantität der Rehäsung in Wald- und Grünland-

Gesellschaften des nördlichen Schweizer Mittellandes. *Veroeff. Geobot. Inst. Eidg. Tech. Hochsch. Stift. Ruebel Zuer.* Vol. 38.

———. 1969*a*. Die Grundwasserbeziehungen der Streu- und Moorwiesen im nördlichen Schweizer Mittelland. *Beitr. Geobot. Landesaufn. Schweiz.* Vol. 52.

———. 1969*b*. Bibliographia Phytosociologica: Helvetia, Part II. *Excerpta Bot.* Sect. B. 10:1–92.

———. 1975*a*. Naturschutz im Flughafengebiet—Konflikte und Symbiose. *Flughafen Information* 1975(3):3–12.

———. 1975*b*. Oekologische Besonderheiten Pinus-reicher Waldgesellschaften. *Schweiz. Z. Forstwes.* 126:672–710.

——— and A. Grünig. 1976. Seeufervegetetion als Bioindikator. *Daten und Dokumente zum Umweltschutz* 19:109–131.

Koch, W. 1926. Die Vegetationseinheiten der Linthebene. *Jb. Natw. Ges. St. Gallen* Vol. 61.

Künzli, W. 1967. Ueber die Wirkung von Hof- und Handelsdüngern auf Pflanzenbestand, Ertrag und Futterqualität der Fromentalwiesen. Schweiz. Landwirtsch. Forsch. 6:34–130.

Kuhn, N. 1967. Natürliche Waldgesellschaften und Waldstandorte der Umgebung von Zürich. *Veroeff. Geobot. Inst. Eidg. Tech. Hochsch. Stift. Ruebel Zuer.* Vol. 40.

Kuoch, R. and R. Amiet. 1970. Die Verjüngung im Bereich der oberen Waldgrenze der Alpen. *Mitt. Schweiz. Anst. Forstl. Vers'wes* 46:159–328.

Lachavanne, J. B. and R. Wattenhofer. 1975. *Les macrophytes du Léman.* Genèva: Conservatoire Bot.

Landolt, E. 1967. Gebirgs- und Tieflandsippen von Blütenpflanzen im Bereich der Schweizer Alpen. *Bot. Jb.* 86:463–480.

———. 1977. Oekologische Zeigerwerte zur Schweizer Flora. *Veroeff. Geobot. Inst. Eidg. Tech. Hochsch. Stift. Ruebel Zuer.* Vol. 64.

———, F. Grossmann, A. Gigon, and M. Meyer. 1975. Konkurrenzuntersuchungen zwischen nah verwandten Arten von Scabiosa columbaria L.s.l. *Ber. Geobot, Inst. Eidg. Tech. Hochsch. Stift. Ruebel Zuer.* 43:83–142.

Leibundgut, H. 1966. *Die Waldpflege.* Bern: Haupt.

———. 1976. Grundlagen zur Jungwaldpflege. Ergebnisse zwansigjähriger Untersuchungen. *Mitt. Eidg. Anst. Forstl. Vers'wes.* 52:311–371.

Lieth, H. and E. Landolt, eds. 1979. Contribution to the knowledge of flora and vegetation of the Carolinas. Part I. *Veroeff. Geobot. Inst. Eidg. Tech. Hochsch. Stift. Ruebel Zuer.* Vol. 68.

Lüdi, W. 1948. Die Pflanzengesellschaften der Schinigeplatte bei Interlaken und ihre Beziehungen zur Umwelt. *Veroeff. Geobot. Inst. Eidg. Tech. Hochsch. Stift. Ruebel Zuer.* Vol. 23.

Merian, E., et al. 1980. *Umweltforschung in der Schweiz,* 2d ed. Vol. 4a. *Einleitung und Verzeichnisse;* Vol. 5. *Bestandeskatalog.* Bern: Bundesamt für Umweltschutz.

Moor, M. 1952. Die Fagion-Gesellschaften des Schweizer Jura. *Beitr. Geobot. Landesaufn. Schweiz* Vol. 31.

Nösberger, J. 1964. Blattfläche und Trockensubstanzproduktion von Kleebeständen in Abhängigkeit von den Umweltbedingungen. *Ber. Schweiz. Bot. Ges.* 74:108–164.

Oefelein, H. 1960. Bibliographia Phytosociologica: Helvetia. *Excerpta Bot.* Sect. B. 2:161–324.

Ott, E. 1965. Ueber den Einfluss der Durchforstung auf ökologische Faktoren. Dissertation, ETH-Zurich.

Pfadenhauer, J. 1973. Versuch einer vergleichend-ökologischen Analyses der Buchen-Tannen-Wälder des Schweizer Jura. *Veroeff. Geobot. Inst. Eidg. Tech. Hochsch. Stift. Ruebel Zuer.* Vol. 50.

Primault, B. 1957. Contribution à l'étude des réactions végétales aux éléments météorologiques. *Bull. Soc. Neuchatel. Sci. Nat.* 80:115–162.

Richard, F. 1945. Der biologische Abbau von Zellulose- und Eiweiss-Test-schnüren im Boden von Wald- und Rasengesellschaften. *Mitt. Schweiz. Anst. Forstl. Vers'-wes.* 24:297–397.

______. 1953. Ueber die Verwertbarkeit des Bodenwassers durch die Pflanze. *Mitt. Schweiz. Anst. Forstl. Vers'wes.* 29:17–37.

______, P. Lüscher, and T. Strobel. 1978. *Physikalische Eigenschaften von Böden der Schweiz.* Vol. 1. Birmensdorf: Eidg. Anst. Forstl. Vers'wes.

Richard, J.-L. 1961. Les fôrets acidophiles du Jura. Etude phytosociologique et écologique. *Beitr. Geobot. Landesaufn. Schweiz* Vol. 38.

Rogers, D. J. 1970. A preliminary ordination study of forest vegetation in the Kirchleerau area of the Swiss midlands. *Ber. Geobot. Inst. Eidg. Tech. Hochsch. Stift. Ruebel Zuer.* 40:28–78.

Rübel, E. 1930. *Pflanzengesellschaften der Erde* (with map of vegetation of the earth by H. Brockmann-Jerosch). Bern/Berlin: Huber.

Schmid, E. 1943–1950 and 1961. Vegetationskarte der Schweiz 1:200,000. Bern:Huber; and Erläuterungen zur Vegetationskarte der Schweiz. *Beitr. Geobot. Landesaufn. Schweiz* Vol. 21.

Schreiber, K.-F. 1968. Ecologie appliquée à l'agriculture dans le Nord Vaudois. *Beitr. Geobot. Landesaufn. Schweiz* Vol. 50.

______ et al. 1977. Wärmegliederung der Schweiz 1:200,000. Der Delegierte für Raumplanung, EJPD Bern.

Schröter, C. 1926. *Das Pflanzenleben der Alpen,* 2d ed. Zurich.

Schüepp, H. and R. J. Green. 1968. Indirect assay methods to investigate soil fungistasis with special consideration of soil pH. *Phytopath. Z.* 61:1–28.

Schütz, J.-P. and E. Badoux. 1979. Production de jeunes peuplements de chênes en relation avec la station. *Mitt. Eidg. Anst. forstl. Vers'wes.* 53:4–176.

Schweingruber, F. H. 1972. Die subalpinen Zwergstrauchgesellschaften im Einzugsgebiet der Aare. *Mitt. Schweiz. Anst. Forstl. Vers'wes* 48:197–504.

Stumm, W. and J. J. Morgan. 1970. *Aquatic chemistry.* New York: Wiley-Interscience.

Stüssi, B. 1970. Naturbedingte Entwicklung subalpiner Weiderasen auf Alp La Schera im Schweizer Nationalpark während der Reservatsperiode 1939–1965. *Ergeb. Wiss. Untersuch. Schweiz. Nationalpark* XIII, Vol. 61.

Thomas, E. A. 1949. Regionallimnologische Studien an 25 Seen der Nordschweiz. *Verh. Int. Verein. Limnol.* 10:489–495.

______. 1966. Der Pfäffikersee vor, während und nach künstlicher Durchmischung. *Verh. Int. Verein. Limnol.* 16:144–152.

Turner, H. 1966. Die globale Hangbestrahlung als Standortsfaktor bei Aufforstungen in der subalpinen Stufe (Stillberg im Dischmatal, Kt. Graubünden). *Mitt. Schweiz. Anst. Forstl. Vers'wes.* 42:109–168.

______. 1974. Umweltprobleme bei Naturzug-Nasskuhltürmen grosser Kernkraftwerke in der Schweiz. *Verh. Ges. Oekol.* 3:261–271.

Urbanska-Worytkiewicz, K. 1980. Reproductive strategies in a hybridogenous population of *Cardamine* L. *Acta Oecol. Oecol. Plant.* 15:137–150.

______ and E. Landolt. 1974. Biosystematic investigations in *Cardamine pratensis* L.s.l. Part 1. Diploid taxa from central Europe and their fertility relationship. *Ber. Geobot. Inst. Eidg. Tech. Hochsch. Stift. Ruebel Zuer.* 42:42–139.

Vareschi, V. 1936. Die Epiphytenvegetation von Zürich. *Ber. Schweiz. Bot. Ges.* 46:445–488.

Wattenhofer, R. 1980. L'assimilation-fixation de nutriments avec une culture expérimentale de macrophytes (*Phragmites australis*) dans le but d'épurer des eaux usées. *Gas-Wasser-Abwasser* 60:190–195.

Wildi, O. 1977. Beschreibung exzentrischer Hochmoore mit Hilfe quantitativer Methoden. *Veroeff. Geobot. Inst. Eidg. Tech. Hochsch. Stift. Ruebel Zuer.* Vol. 60.

Zimmermann, P. 1961. Experimentelle Untersuchungen über die ökologische Wirkung der Strömungsgeschwindigkeit auf die Lebensgemeinschaften des fliessenden Wassers. *Schweiz. Z. Hydrol.* 23:1–81.

Zoller, H. 1954. Die Typen der Bromus erectus-Wiesen des Schweizer Juras. *Beitr. Geobot. Landesaufn. Schweiz* Vol. 33.

______. 1974. Flora und Vegetation der Innalluvionen zwischen Scuol und Martina (Unterengadin). *Ergebn. Wiss. Untersuch. Schweiz. Nationalpark* Vol. 12.

Züst, S. 1977. Die Epiphytenvegetation im Raume Zürich als Indiktor de Umweltbelastung. *Veroeff. Geobot. Inst. Eidg. Tech. Hochsch. Stift. Ruebel Zuer.* Vol. 62.

19

WEST GERMANY

Christian Kunze and Helmut Lieth

Ecology has a distinguished past in Germany. Not only did the use of the name *ecology* have its origin in Germany, chosen by Ernst Haeckel about a century ago, but substantial contributions were made to the field from various directions. In the beginning of this century, when the field clearly emerged out of taxonomical or physiologic work, names like Möbius, Friederichs, and Thinemann gained international recognition. Almost all other fields of biology (e.g., morphology, cytology, and plant chemistry) included ecological aspects in their treatments.

This interest in ecology was largely lost during the 1920s. Descriptive work changed generally into analytical investigations. Nevertheless, great innovations and impulses to the field of ecology took place during that time in spite of the fact that the contributors did not consider themselves ecologists. The latter point makes it somewhat difficult to render justice to the scientists who brought innovations to the attention of ecologists. Who was the more important, the innovator of a method or the one who put the innovation into general use?

The special political conditions of Central Europe create another difficulty for our analysis. Post-World War I saw Germany as the recipient of numerous refugees from Russia and Eastern Europe. Are these people to be considered Germans or not? Post-World War II saw many Germans emigrating to other parts of the world. Are their contributions to the field now to be credited to the pool of German scientists or to the new home countries of the emigrants' choice? We are more than aware of these difficulties and, in many cases, would not even be able to tell whether a particular contribution was made by a scientist of German citizenship, origin, or extraction. Any historic treatment of this kind must necessarily be spotty at best and ought to be considered as a contribution to, rather than as complete coverage of, the topic.

Finally, both authors of this article are plant ecologists. This probably results in a better coverage of contributions to plant ecology than other areas within ecology.

MAJOR AREAS OF RESEARCH

Regardless of all difficulties, we shall enumerate several concepts and present treatments of subject areas important to the field of ecology as we circumscribe it today. Important innovations from Germany during the last half century, which are described below, were made to the following fields: phytosociology, geoecology, environmental analysis, phenology and biorhythmics, autecology, animal behavior, modelling, energy budgets, matter cycles, and special projects.

Phytosociology

This area was initiated in Europe by several scientists, including Du Rietz, Braun-Blanquet, Kulćinsky, Sørensen, and Jaccard, to name a few. (See discussion of this topic by Dansereau 1968). It was, however, the immense organizational power of Tüxen that won general acceptance for Braun-Blanquet's statistical vegetation analysis in Europe. The consistent application of this method by Tüxen and many of his students gradually included the vegetation of all of Europe. This is the main reason why European ecologists know their plant associations in such enviable detail. The importance of Tüxen's work was recently confirmed by the adoption of one of his papers by McIntosh (1978) in his benchmark collection of contributions to phytosociology.

Geoecology

Germany has long been a major force in geoecology. During the last several decades, major contributions were added by Troll and his students in vegetation climatology and comparative high-mountain vegetation geography. To the first topic, Walter and Lieth (1960–1967) contributed the climate diagram world atlas, following the initial idea of the French scientist Gaussen for the construction of such diagrams. A significant contribution to geoecology was the first global net primary productivity map by Lieth (1964).

The most important recent German contribution in plant geography is probably Walter's *Die Vegetation der Erde* (1964, 1968), which started out as a revised edition of Schimper von Faber's work. For animal geography, ecology, and biology, Grzimeck's *Tierleben* (1973) is an important work.

Germans have always been prolific organizers of handbooks. A new idea in this respect was initiated in 1970 by K. Springer with his ecological studies series. This is now an American-German co-production in both publishing and editing, and is international with regard to contributing authors.

Environmental Analysis

Environmental parameters are among the most important items to be investigated, measured, and understood by ecologists. Numerous contributions to this field originated in Germany, such that it is difficult to single out any particular ones. However, two that deserve that distinction are the concept of microclimate by Geiger (1961) and the invention of the infrared gas analyzer by several engineers at the Badische Anilin und Sodafabrik (BASF) and its consistent introduction into ecophysiologic work by Seybold (1942) and Egle and Schenk (1951).

Responses of plant and animal functions and distributions to environmental parameters was developed to a high standard in Europe during the last fifty years. German ecologists adopted the term *ecological causal analysis* for this type of work, which introduced many students of ecology after World War II into the field. Typical studies were concerned with the distribution of plant species along environmental gradients, analyzed distribution patterns in the field, or established absolute environmental thresholds for the functioning or distribution of species. One of the earlier major studies of this type was Ellenberg's contribution, "The indicator value of weeds and meadow plants in southern Germany."

Phenology and Biorhythmics

These areas in ecology and physiology received strong impulses from German investigators. In phenology, Schnelle's book (1955) was the single outstanding guide for decades, and perhaps every plant and animal physiologist knows Bünning's book *The Biological Clock* (1963).

Plant Autecology and Synecology

These areas received strong impulses from Leick, Huber, Stocker, and Walter during the second quarter of this century. While many of the initial ideas for experimental ecological work came from Denmark and Sweden, these German authors contributed many new concepts and methods, mainly in fields of water stress analysis and carbon dioxide assimilation. In recent years, this work was continued by Langue and his associates and students.

One of the major achievements of this group was the development of a fully climatized cuvette.

Animal Behavior

The psychological and physiologic analysis of animal behavior conducted by German scientists received the most outstanding international distinction. Von Frisch (1950) analyzed the communication system of bees and the chemical nature of some warning systems in fish schools. Many new concepts were introduced by Lorenz (e.g., 1966) to the field of ethology and behavior and were well received and tested worldwide. They form the baseline for ecological work in animal behavior so important for the understanding of population dynamics in some species.

Ecological Modelling

This area is probably rightly regarded as a genuine American invention. Little is known, however, about the early German contribution to this field by E. A. Mitscherlich and L. V. Bertalanffy. Mitscherlich (1949) developed a yield model for crops in dependence on different amounts of fertilizers, and Bertalanffy (1951) developed various models for growth and functioning of animals and plants as a result of internally changing conditions.

Budgets

A discussion of energy budgets, water budgets, and matter cycles brings us to the most recent development in ecological work in Germany. Ecological budgets and cycles, including the matter cycles of entire ecosystems, were the subject of the International Biological Program (IBP). As in many other countries, the IBP was the single most important event for German ecologists in the last decade. When this program finally started in 1964 after four years of planning, West Germany concentrated on one single project: experimental ecology in the Solling. Known worldwide as the "Solling project," the aim of this interdisciplinary study was a comparative analysis of several land ecosystems close to each other.

The Solling is a centrally located mountain range of about 500-m elevation covered widely with one of the most common broad-leaved forests in Germany, the *Luzulo-Fagetum*. Besides the natural beech-forest, several managed vegetation types were investigated: spruce plantations (*Picea abies*) of different ages, meadows of different managements intensities, and cultivated fields with various crops. Ecosystems more disturbed by human activities were left for a later program now under way as part of Man and the Biosphere, which concentrates on problems in urban and industrial ecosystems.

The Solling project combined the efforts of about fifty scientists from various disciplines, which were mainly experimental and, therefore, the title "experimental ecology" was chosen for the entire project, in contrast to the internationally adopted "systems ecology" for similar projects. The project covered a wide range of botanical, zoological, and environmental analyses. The total range of investigations carried out during the project is given by Ellenberg (1971). Synthesis volumes digesting and interpreting the immense data pool are in preparation.

Projects parallel to the effort in the Solling were carried out in the Ebersberger forest near Munich, headed by Baumgartner. This project investigated the matter and energy balance of a spruce forest in connection with microclimate and seasonal weather pattern. Another large cooperative effort was the Lake Constanz project, headed by Elster, which analyzed the biological functioning of the lake as a system. This was especially convenient since numerous individual investigations were done either in Lake Constanz itself or in similar lakes. Lake Constanz is one of the most important types of water bodies in the region around the Alps with the region's heavy burdens of population and industrial wastes.

Other Research

Besides these integrated, large-scale ecological projects, numerous other studies have been carried out in recent years. In order to gain an insight into the range and depth of ecological studies in central Europe and to find possible deficiencies, two questionnaires were distributed, one by Halbach and Müller in 1975 for zoo-ecologists and one by Steubing and Kirschbaum in 1976 for plant ecologists. When the results of both questionnaires were combined, the following tabulations of focal points for ecological work in Germany emerged:

Faunal inventories of ecosystems.

Population dynamics of different species of animals (e.g., insects, rotatories, and small mammals).

Predator-prey systems; food chains.

Influence on organisms of abiotic factors, such as daily periodical temperature fluctuations on insects, different types of roads on the ground fauna of roadside ecosystems, heavy metal stress on limnic ecosystems including their organisms, deposition and effect of poisonous substances in the body of amphibia and fishes as well as in ecosystems, and so on.

Structural analysis of ecosystems.

In plant ecology, the following additional topics emerged:

Plant sociological investigations.

Ecophysiology of plants, especially water budget and matter production as influenced by temperature, drought, and soil salinity (i.e., adaptation to different habitat conditions).

Responses of higher and lower plants to different environmental stresses (i.e., plants as bio-indicators) in aquatic and terrestrial ecosystems including salt stress in seaweeds and higher plants, and reactions of lichens and mosses to poisonous gaseous or particulate substances.

The activity of soil microorganisms in ecosystems.

Energetic considerations of ecological factors.

This list of research topics gives an approximate idea about the subjects presently treated at West German universities but may not offer a comprehensive picture of all the ecological activities in Germany. We may assume also that the range of themes will change and expand, especially since ecology has recently been given appropriate recognition in Germany.

SOCIETIES AND JOURNALS

The Gesellschaft für Ökologie (Ecological Society), founded in 1970 in Giessen, aims to represent the interests of ecology. This society has held an annual scientific meeting since 1971. Ecologists of all disciplines present papers, and the reports of the meetings have become the standard literature for ecologists. The members of the society, whose membership exceeded 650 in 1978, come mainly from Germany, with smaller numbers from other German-speaking countries.

The Ecological Society resolved in 1971 to raise ecology to a more important position in schools and universities. This position was supported during the 1976 annual meeting of the German Botanical Society, where it was resolved that ecological courses ought to become compulsory for each biology curriculum.

In 1972, the Gruppe Ökologie (Ecological Club) was founded in Heiligenstadt. This "open circle" intends to link ecologists with the mass media and organizations concerned with protection of the environment and nature.

German ecologists publish their papers in various European and international journals. No single journal is specifically reserved for German ecological papers. Standard journals for botany, zoology, limnology, or oceanography are as frequently used as are journals for pedology, meteorology, agriculture, and forestry. Most journals used are listed in *Current Contents,* and regular reviews of the ecology literature appear as sections in Springer's review series, namely, "Fortschritte der Botanik" and "Fortschritte der Zoologie."

BIBLIOGRAPHY

The following list contains the most important ecological literature that has appeared in Germany in recent years. Many more recent ecological publications by German publishers are not included because the authors are from other countries and their books may be found in the literature cited for other countries.

Bertalanffy, L. v. 1951. *Theoretische Biologie,* Vol. 2, 2d ed. Bern: A. Francke.

Bornkamm, R. 1971. Grundprinzipien der Ökologie. Mathem. *Naturwiss. Unterr.* 24:467–472.

Buchwald, K. and W. Engelhardt. 1978. *Handbuch für Planung, Gestaltung und Schutz der menschlichen Umwelt.* Munich.

Bünning, E. 1963. *Die biologische Uhr.* Berlin-Heidelberg-New York: Springer-Verlag.

Dansereau, P. 1968. The continuum concept of vegetation: responses. *Bot. Rev.* 34:253–332.

Ecological Studies Vol. 1 1970, Vol. 22 1977. Berlin-Heidelberg-New York: Springer-Verlag.

Egle, L. and Schenk. 1951. Die Anwendung des URAS in der Photosyntheseforschung. *Ber. Dtsch. Bot. Ges. 64:180–196.*

Ellenberg, H., ed. 1971. *Integrated experimental ecology. Methods and results of ecosystem research in the German Solling project.* Ecological studies, Vol. 2. Berlin-Heidelberg-New York: Springer-Verlag.

______. 1972. Ökologische Forschung und Erziehung als gemeinsame Aufgabe. *Umschau* 72:53–54.

______, ed. 1973. *Ökosystemforschung.* Berlin-Heidelberg-New York: Springer-Verlag.

______. 1978. *Vegetation Mitteleuropas mit den Alpen.* Stuttgart: Ulmer Verlag.

Elster, H. J. 1974. Das Ökosystem Bodensee in Vergangenheit, Gegenwart und Zukunft. *Schriftenreihe VG Bodensee* 92:233–250.

______. 1974. History of limnology. *Mitt. Int. Ver. Limnol.* 20:7–30.

Frisch, K. v. 1950. *Bees, their vision, chemical senses, and language.* Ithaca: Cornell University Press.

Geiger, R. 1961. *Das Klima der bodennahen Luftschicht,* 4th ed. Braunschweig.

Grzimeck, B. 1973. *Tierleben.* Zurich: Kindler Verlag.

Halbach, U. 1976. Beziehungen zwischen Humanökologie und Ökologie. *Verh. Ges. Oekol. Goettingen,* pp. 483–490.

Kandler, O. 1976. Beifräge anlässlich des Rundgespräches "Ökologische Lehrveranstaltungen" im Rahmen der Tagung der Deutschen Botanischen Gesellschaft 1976 in Zürich. *Ber. Dtsch. Bot. Ges.* 89:197–216.

Kreeb, K. 1974. *Ökophysiologie der Pflanzen.* Jena: Gustav Fischer Verlag.

______. 1977. *Methoden der Pflanzenökologie.* Jena: Gustav Fischer Verlag.

Leser, H. 1976. *Landschaftsökologie.* Stuttgart: Ulmer Verlag.

Lieth, H. 1964–1965. Versuch einer kartographischen Darstellung der Produktivität der Pflanzendecke auf der Erde. *Geographisches Taschenbuch,* pp. 72–80. Wiesbaden; M. Steiner.

Lorenz, K. 1966. *On aggression.* London: Methuen.
McIntosh, R. P. 1978. *Phytosociology.* Benchmark papers in ecology, Vol. 6. Stroudsburg, Pa: Dowden, Hutchinson, and Ross.
Mitscherlich, E. A. v. 1949. *Bodenkunde,* 5th ed. Halle: Max Niemeyer.
Olschowy, G. 1977. *Natur- und Umweltschutz in der Bundesrepublik Deutschland.* Hamburg: Parey.
Osche, G. 1973. *Ökologie.* Freiburg-Basel-Vienna: Herder.
Overbeck, J. 1977. Zur Geschichte und Methodik der limnischen Ökosystemforschung. *Verh. Ges. Oekol., Kiel,* pp. 145–147.
Remmert, H. 1978. *Ökologie.* Berlin-Heidelberg-New York: Springer-Verlag.
Schnelle, F. 1955. *Pflanzenphänologie.* Leipzig: Akadem. Verlagsgesellschaft.
Schwenke, H. 1977. Hundert Jahre marine Ökosystemforschung. *Verh. Ges. Oekol., Kiel,* pp. 13–18.
Schwertfeger, F. 1963, 1968, 1975. *Ökologie der Tiere.* Vols. 1–3. Hamburg, Berlin.
Seybold, A. 1942. Pflanzenpigmente und Lichtfeld als physiologisches, geologisches und landwirtschaftliches Problem. *Ber. Dtsch. Bot. Ges.* 60:46–85.
Steubing, L. 1965. *Pflanzenökologisches Praktikum.* Berlin-Hamburg: Parey.
———. 1972. Ökologie als Grundlage des Umweltschutzes. *Umschau* 72:40.
——— and C. Kunze. 1972. *Pflanzenökologische Experimente zur Umweltverschmutzung.* Biol. Arbeitsbücher, Vol. 11.
Tischler, W. 1965. *Agrarökologie.* Jena: Gustav Fischer Verlag.
———. 1976. *Einführung in die Ökologie.* Stuttgart-New York.
Tuexen, R., ed. 1949. *Mitteilungen Flor.–soziol Arbeitsgemeinschaft.* N.F. Stolzenau/Weser.
Ulrich, B. 1968. Das System Boden-Pflanze in ökologischer Sicht. *Goettinger Bodenk. Ber.* 1:33–56.
Walter, H. 1964, 1968. *Die Vegetation der Erde in öko-physiologischer Betrachtung.* Vols. 1, 2. Stuttgart-Jena.
———. 1977. *Die ökologischen Systeme der Kontinente.* Stuttgart-Jena: Gustav Fischer Verlag.
——— and H. Lieth. 1960–1966. *Klimadiagramm-Weltatlas.* Jena: Gustav Fischer Verlag.
Wilmanns, O. 1971. Ökologie und moderner Naturschutz. *Biol. unserer Zeit* 1:147–156.
———. 1973. *Ökologische Pflanzensoziologie.* Heidelberg: Verlag Quelle und Meyer.
Winkler, S. 1972. *Einführung in die Pflanzenökologie.* Stuttgart: Gustav Fischer Verlag.

REFERENCES CITED

Bertalanffy, L. v. 1951. *Theoretische Biologie,* Vol. 2, 2d ed. Bern: A. Francke.
Bünning, E. 1963. *Die biologische Uhr.* Berlin-Heidelberg-New York: Springer-Verlag.
Dansereau, P. 1968. The continuum concept of vegetation: responses. *Bot. Rev.* 34:253–332.

Egle, L. and Schenk. 1951. Die Anwendung des URAS in der Photosyntheseforschung. *Ber. Dtsch. Bot. Ges.* 64:180–196.

Ellenberg, H., ed. 1971. *Integrated experimental ecology. Methods and results of ecosystem research in the German Solling project.* Ecological studies, Vol. 2. Berlin-Heidelberg-New York: Springer-Verlag.

Frisch, K. v. 1950. *Bees, their vision, chemical senses, and language.* Ithaca: Cornell University Press.

Geiger, R. 1961. *Das Klima der bodennahen Luftschicht.* Vol. 4. Auflg: Braunschweig. Friedrich Vieweg und Solin.

Grzimeck, B. 1973. *Tierleben.* Zurich: Kindler Verlag.

Lieth, H. 1964–1965. Versuch einer kartographischen Darstellung der Produktavität der Pflanzendecke auf der Erde. *Geographisches Taschenbuch,* pp. 72–80. Wiesbaden: M. Steiner.

Lorenz, K. 1966. *On aggression.* London: Methuen.

McIntosh, R. P. 1978. *Phytosociology.* Benchmark papers in ecology, Vol. 6. Stroudsburg, Pa.: Dowden, Hutchinson, and Ross.

Mitscherlich, E. A. v. 1949. *Bodenkunde,* 5th ed. Halle: Max Niemeyer.

Schnelle, F. 1955. *Pflanzenphänologie.* Leipzig: Akadem. Verlagsgesellschaft.

Seybold, A. 1942. Pflanzenpigmente und Lichtfeld als physiologisches, Geologisches und landwirtschaftliches Problem. *Ber. Dtsch. Bot. Ges.* 60:46–85.

Walter, H. 1964, 1968. *Die Vegetation der Erde in öko-physiologischer Betrachtung,* Vols. 1, 2. Stuttgart, Jena: Gustav Fischer Verlag.

Walter, H. and H. Lieth. 1960–1967. *Klimadiagramm-Weltatlas.* Jena: Gustav Fischer Verlag.

Soviet Union

20

SOVIET UNION

W. Carter Johnson and
Norman R. French

INTRODUCTION

Authors who write about scientific developments in other countries are often considered by their domestic colleagues as doing a service by informing them of scientific discoveries hidden by language, cultural, and sometimes political barriers. On the other hand, these same authors expose themselves to criticism from their foreign colleagues, some of whom actually participated in or observed the developments being described. Potential sins frequently committed by foreign authors include errors of omission, overgeneralization, and differing emphasis because of different training or divergent cultural points of view. We have tried to minimize the first two of these by personally interviewing Soviet ecologists who differ widely in age and scientific training: O. Bauer, M. Boch, V. Fedorov, T. Frey, M. Ghilarov, T. Gilmanov, J. Martin, G. Nahutrishvili, T. Rabotnov, L. Rodin, J. Ross, V. Sokolov, V. Vasilevich, O. Zalensky, and R. Zlotin. Their viewpoints on this subject are included in this chapter, along with those of Soviet authors who have documented their own historical development (e.g., Trass 1976; Shvartz 1970; Naumov 1970; Rafes 1970). We cannot escape completely (and do not want to) from the last of these sins. Thus, sprinkled throughout this chapter are our assessments of Soviet ecology and how it compares and contrasts with American ecology. Perhaps different training and points of view are prerequisites to selecting the Soviet studies that are most relevant to the current work of English-speaking scientists.

The contents of this chapter need some preliminary explanation. First, the word *ecology* is used in its broad, Western sense. Many Soviet scientists, on the contrary, equate ecology more narrowly with autecology. We consider the Soviet sciences of phytocenology, geobotany, and biogeocenology as counterparts to or subdivisions of ecology, and hence, developments in these fields are reviewed below as contributions to Soviet ecology. Second, the word *Soviet* is used rather than the unfortunate and often incorrect word *Russian*. Only about one-half of the people of the Soviet Union are Russian, with the remainder constituting nearly one hundred nationalities such as Ukrainian, Estonian, Northeast Asian "small peoples," Georgian, and Tadjik, all of which have different cultural and ecological backgrounds and, in most cases, different languages. Moreover, in addition to the very powerful All-Union Soviet Academy of Sciences, each of the fifteen republics of the U.S.S.R. has a republic-level academy. Understanding the Soviet concept of nationality is vital for the understanding of the structure of Soviet science. Third, this chapter deals mainly with the development of Soviet ecology, but other topics have purposefully been included to assist Western scientists in understanding and interpreting this development. This was done because, to the authors' knowledge, there are no existing books or papers in English that comprehensively treat the conduct and terminology of ecological sciences in the Soviet Union.

The tremendous bulk of Soviet literature published in Russian made it impossible to treat some components of ecology (e.g., physiological ecology) or the parallel development of many related disciplines (e.g., microbiology). We review what we consider to be mainline ecology in the Soviet Union: animal ecology, plant ecology (geobotany, phytocenology), ecosystem science (biogeocenology), and systems ecology. The unified nature of studies conducted during the International Biological Program suits their separate consideration.

PLANT ECOLOGY AND VEGETATION MAPPING

The field of plant ecology, as practiced by Western ecologists, corresponds roughly to the Soviet fields of geobotany (a science about vegetation cover) and phytocenology (a science about vegetation communities). Despite the apparent differences in the Greek roots, the sciences are now considered by many to be very similar (Voronov 1973). Geobotany has been defined by Voronov (1973) as a science concerning phytocenoses, their structure, interrelationships with the environment, dynamics (origin, growth, material exchange, phenology), classification, and interaction with other phytocenoses. Sukachev (1956) similarly defined the science of phytocenology as a division of botany studying the laws of the formation, development, and distribution of the earth's plant aggregations (phytocenoses or plant communities). These sciences represent the traditional line of development of plant ecology, which originated during the latter half of the nineteenth century. However, they do not constitute a holistic ecological approach because of the frequent exclusion of heterotrophic-autotrophic interactions and systems-level processes. The more holistic Soviet science of biogeocenology appeared during World War II as an outgrowth of phytocenology and geography.

General Trends

Trass (1976) has reviewed the developmental history of plant ecology in the Soviet Union. His developmental periods four, five, and six include the past three decades of Soviet plant ecological research. During period four (1920s to early 1950s), research on vegetation communities widened and deepened, and comprehensive work began on the classification of phytocenoses and the dynamics and mapping of vegetation. Period five (early 1950s–1960s) was a time of reappraisal and introduction of new quantitative methods. Ordination and gradient analysis, developed earlier by Ramensky and others, were reintroduced into Soviet ecology, and debate concerning the continuum concept was prevalent. During the end of this developmental period, quantitative and statistical techniques were being applied in many plant ecological investigations. A modern, synthetic period (period six) began with the mid-1960s, although it is not sharply separated from the former period. It began with the evaluation of new techniques to study the vegetation cover, including the adoption of concepts of cybernetics and systems analysis. Investigations were strongly stimulated by the International Biological Program and by a growing network of field stations. The overall developmental trend of Soviet plant ecology has been toward shorter periods, characteristic of a modern, rapidly developing science.

Trass (1976) has also identified significant research products of the past several decades. These include the printing of several major vegetation maps (Lavrenko 1950; Lavrenko and Sochava 1956) with a two-volume text accompanying the 1956 map, a description of the dominants in the vegetation cover of the U.S.S.R. (Bikov 1960–1965), initiation of the series *Field Geobotany* to review research progress (Lavrenko and Korchagin 1959, 1960, 1964, 1972, 1976), publication of a major geobotany textbook (Yaroshenko 1961), a classic text on biogeocenology (Sukachev and Dylis 1964), and texts of statistical methods in geobotany (Vasilevich 1969*b*) and vegetation classification (Aleksandrova 1969).

Descriptive Phase

A review of recent Soviet plant ecological literature reveals considerable description of vegetation and environment for small locales or regions, especially in Siberia and Central Asia. This descriptive phase of Soviet plant ecology has persisted because there is so much fundamental vegetation work yet to be done. Year-round travel to field sites has been limited by the vastness of the Soviet territory, the harsh climatic conditions in the Soviet hinterlands, and the location of population and scientific centers mostly in the European portion of the U.S.S.R. Examples of regional, descriptive syntheses are: for Siberia, Kuminova (1963), Utkin (1965), Kuminova (1971), Scherbakov (1975), Nazimova (1975); mountains, Stanukovich (1973), Gulisashvili et al. (1975); European forest and forest-steppe, Rysin (1975), Molchanov (1975); Central Asia, Nechayeva (1970), Ovchinnikov et al. (1973), Konnov (1974), Lavrenko (1977), and Gunin and Dyedkov (1978).

A good review of Soviet geobotany is the *Field Geobotany* series, which now includes five volumes. Volumes I–III have been reviewed by Raney (1965, 1966). Volume IV (Lavrenko and Korchagin 1972) is comprised of papers on seasonal dynamics of plant communities, fluctuations (annual variation), and surveying vegetation. The most recent volume, V, (Lavrenko and Korchagin 1976) is devoted to plant community structure. Principles and results of experimental phytocenology which has developed slowly in the U.S.S.R. because of a paucity of precision equipment (Trass 1976), have been discussed by Karpov (1969).

Statistical Period

Through the 1950s, there was comparatively little work on the statistical-mathematical analysis of vegetation in Soviet geobotany. The turning point came in the early 1960s with a new generation of geobotanists who demonstrated the need for the statistical approach. A major product of this period was Vasilevich's book (1969*b*) on statistical methods in geobotany, which has chapters on sampling, basis statistical measures, species patterns in phytocenoses, correlation, characteristics of vegetation, comparative analysis of methods of describing vegetation, coefficients of similarity, division into homogeneous groups, homogeneity of vegetation, methods of analyzing vegetation continua, and analysis of boundaries between phytocenoses. Vasilevich's book is excellent, original, and wide-ranging (Major 1975). Development of statistical techniques and application to the study of vegetation has continued (Vasilevich 1970*a*, 1972; Ipatov 1970; Ipatov et al. 1974; Aleksandrova 1975).

Classification and Mapping

During the first three decades of this century, the principles of the Russian school of classification were formalized. Briefly, the Russian approach to classification most closely parallels the northern tradition (Whittaker 1962).

Associations of phytocenoses, the fundamental vegetation unit, are defined by stratal dominants, the ecological-physiognomic approach of Lavmeko. The Russian use of the stratal approach to classify into associations closely resembles that of the Uppsala school and in large measure was derived from it, although "association" in the Russian school replaced "sociation" of the Uppsala school. This is the essential difference separating Soviet geobotany from the school of Braun-Blanquet; in the latter, the separation of taxonomic units of vegetation is based on diagnostic species (Aleksandrova 1969). The philosophy and techniques of modern classification in the U.S.S.R. date principally to the foundation laid by Sukachev in the years 1908–1910 and 1928–1931 (Aleksandrova 1969). Sukachev's hierarchic system of taxonomic units of vegetation (phytocenose, association, group of associations, formation, group of formations, type of vegetation) is now a tradition in Soviet geobotany. The association is treated abstractly, as a type of phytocenose. This is similar to the practice of the Braun-Blanquet school, but differs from the Scandinavian school where the association is considered as concrete. These conceptual differences are reflected as differences in methodology.

The most distinctive feature of the Russian school is the practice of organizing associations along environmental gradients to form patterns of ecological series. This early form of gradient analysis was used by Sukachev (1927) for spruce and pine forests along gradients of soil moisture and nutrients. This approach emphasized the importance of environmental gradients and ecological relationships between habitat and vegetation and hence contributed greatly to the development of a natural classification system. Ecological series and gradient analysis obviously include the ideas of the continuum and individualistic concepts of species in vegetation.

The Russian phytocenologist L. G. Ramensky was a critic of the association concept, one of the first, along with Gleason, Negri, and Lenoble, and perhaps the most eloquent. In 1924, he advanced the principles of both vegetation continuity and species individuality, believing that the goal was not to classify but to link biocenoses into a unified coordinate scheme. Ramensky attempted to test individuality by developing a cenocenter for each species in ordered groups of stands. He found that these centers differed for each of seventy species and hence considered the test as adequate to substantiate individuality. John Curtis' examination of the continuum forty years later was conceptually similar to Ramensky's test.

The conflict between advocates of association and continuum views in the U.S.S.R. in the 1920s and early 1930s was a precursor of the international debate of the 1960s (cf. McIntosh 1967). Despite the fact that Sukachev, the leading Soviet geobotanist, saw little conflict between Ramensky's continuity of the vegetation cover and the association as an abstract unit, Ramensky's views were not popularized or utilized by Soviet geobotanists and, in fact, were generally not included in Soviet geobotanical textbooks prior to the international debate of the 1960s (Ponyatovskaya 1961). However, since the worldwide popularization of the individualistic concept, Ramensky's work is now proudly included in Soviet geobotanical texts (e.g., Voronov 1973) and a collection of Ramensky's work has been published posthumously (Vasilevich et al. 1971).

Disagreement among Soviet vegetation scientists over the continuum concept was especially strong, primarily because of the close connection in the U.S.S.R. between the study and mapping of phytocenoses. The main and persistent criticism of the continuum lay primarily in its lack of established utility for the classification of vegetation, not its conceptual inadequacies, although there has been general criticism of Curtis and other continuum proponents on the grounds that the existence of the continuum is a relative matter (i.e., there are degrees of natural continuity) and depends to a certain degree on the scale of investigation (i.e., quadrat, stand sizes) (Vasilevich 1969*a*; Aleksandrova 1969). The difficulty in establishing a vegetation classification system based on continuum theory has been the main obstacle to its full acceptance in the U.S.S.R. Soviet theoreticians and statisticians generally accepted the continuum concept from the outset (Vasilevich 1969*a*) and contributed significantly to the development and application of statistical techniques to analyze vegetation pattern (Vasilevich 1963, 1966, 1967; Frey 1966).

Although the tenets of the Russian school of vegetation classification were developed during the first three decades of this century, it is only in the last three decades that these tenets and methods have been put into practice and the results used to develop small-scale vegetation maps of the U.S.S.R. Aleksandrova (1969) describes this postwar reconnaissance and vegetation sampling effort as colossal, embracing all distant corners of the country. She is less enthusiastic about the lack of standardized methodology used by the large number of investigators that took part in the development. Objective methods of processing lists of taxa for the separation of associations, formations, and other units were, unfortunately, not developed, and the now classic work of Ramensky was largely ignored. Moreover, classification methods used by the respective geobotany departments at universities were not published or documented; this made cross-comparison and generalization difficult.

Regardless of these inconsistencies, Lavrenko and Sochava (1956), of the Botanical Institute in Leningrad, were able to coordinate and integrate the available material into two maps (one vegetation, one geobotanical) at the scale of 1:4,000,000. Kuchler (1957) noted that these maps reflected the enormous progress made by Soviet geobotanists, and by comparison with earlier maps, they no longer showed only abstract schematic vegetation zones but portrayed altitudinal, longitudinal, and latitudinal conditions with local details. Unfortunately, these maps have long been out of print and practically unavailable to new students of Soviet vegetation. Currently, work is being conducted in the Vegetation Mapping Laboratory in Leningrad to complete maps of the U.S.S.R. vegetation at a scale of 1:2,500,000.

Another significant development in Soviet vegetation mapping was the set of global vegetation maps prepared under the direction of Sochava and included in the *Physical-Geographical Atlas of the World* (1964). The accuracy of this map, particularly for North America, has been evaluated by Major (1967). A most effective use of Sochava's map was by Bazilevich and co-workers (Bazilevich, Drozdov, and Rodin 1971; Bazilevich and Rodin 1971; Bazilevich, Rodin, and Rozov 1971) who assigned biomass and productivity values to the major formations and computed estimates for the globe.

We would be remiss not to mention several other important contributors to the development of plant ecology in the Soviet Union. A. P. Schennikov (1950, 1964) was a major figure in the Leningrad geobotanical school and the teacher of many of the Soviet Union's leading geobotanists. A. P. Ilinski was one of the first organizers of the Department of Geobotany in Leningrad and is perhaps best known for his 1937 book, *Vegetation of the Earth,* which put the classification of vegetation on an ecological basis. Reviews of geobotanical research at the Komarov Botanical Institute in Leningrad are periodically published (e.g., Levina 1971, 1978). V. V. Alekhin headed the famous Moscow school of geobotany, and N. I. Vavilov pioneered work on the geographic ecology of cultivated plants (Vavilov 1957).

BIOGEOCENOLOGY

Definition

The most widely cited definition of biogeocenosis (and certainly the longest) is "an assembly on a specific area of land surface of homogeneous natural elements (atmosphere, mineral strata, vegetation, animals and microorganisms, soils and hydrological conditions), with its own specific inter-relationships among these components and a definite type of inter-change of materials and energy among themselves and with other natural phenomena and representing an internally-contradictory dialectical unity, being in constant movement and development" (Sukachev and Dylis 1964). Clearly from this definition, biogeocenosis and ecosystem are similar concepts; both are commonly understood as natural units comprised of interacting living and nonliving elements in which materials cycle and energy cascades or flows. The biogeocenological concept, however, was consistent with the historical development of Russian and Soviet science, and hence did more than the ecosystem concept to provide many Soviet disciplinarians with a new holistic view of natural systems.

Roots

The emergence and practice of the science of biogeocenology represent the most significant development in Soviet ecology in recent times. The term *biogeocenose* was first advanced by Sukachev during the early 1940s, although similar concepts had been advanced earlier by others (e.g., Forbes, microcosm; Morozoev, biocenosa; Tansley, ecosystem). The term became widely known outside the U.S.S.R. as a result of international symposia (e.g., Ninth International Botanical Congress in Stockholm, symposium on forest ecosystems, see *Silvica Fennica* 1960, No. 105) and the English translation (1968) of Sukachev and Dylis (1964).

Biogeocenology has its roots in geography and phytocenology (geobotany), and Sukachev, who originally formalized the concept as a geobotanist and a landscape scientist, later found it most accurate not to consider biogeocenology as part of either biology or geography, but as a separate science (Sukachev and Dylis 1964). Because *ecology* has a much narrower meaning in the Soviet Union than in the West (it generally refers to autecology, not synecology or the study of ecosystems), Soviet biogeocenology as a science is much broader in its scope and actually includes ecology as a discipline. Graduate degrees in ecology at Moscow State University are titled "ecology and biogeocenology," further pointing out the separation of these fields in Soviet academic circles.

Sukachev advanced the concept during the time when there was much effort being expended over the development of a classification system of landscape units. The biogeocenose was proposed to represent the most fundamental landscape unit of the biogeosphere, the biotic and abiotic components of which exhibit a high degree of spatial uniformity. Units of land smaller than the biogeocenose were considered not to encompass all interacting components. Components of larger land units were only loosely interactive and spatially heterogeneous (i.e., adjacent stands of *Picea* and *Acer* exhibit divergent patterns of nutrient cycling). It is this melding of spatial (geographic) and biologic-environment concepts that distinguishes the biogeocenose from most other related terms in ecology. It is quite natural that this specific concept should have arisen in the U.S.S.R., since the Soviet sciences of geography, soils, and vegetation have by world standards not only been well developed historically, but they have developed so closely with one another.

The development of animal ecology in the U.S.S.R. in the post-World War II period is intimately connected with advances in knowledge of geography of the Soviet Union. Work on the distribution of natural resources was intensified in this period for practical reasons. If industrial centers could be established near the source of supply of the mineral resources, the very difficult problems of distribution could be partially overcome. The vast reaches of the eastern portions of the Soviet Union, primarily Siberia, represented a huge untapped and largely unknown source of many natural resources. Therefore, there was much emphasis on exploration and evaluation of the territories within the boundaries of the U.S.S.R. The distribution of timber resources had to be determined, as well as other such resources that were very much needed within the country. In addition, many natural resources were important exports, and the need for exploitation and management of these unique resources was recognized. Such resources included the valuable fur of the sable, which from the very earliest explorations of Siberia had been a valuable trade item with China, and later with the Western world. Not to be overlooked was the demand, continuing to this day, of other Asiatic countries for the horns of certain game animals, which are believed to have medicinal qualities. Such items are even today cultivated by state farms in Siberia solely for export.

Biogeocenose or Ecosystem?

Clearly, the major difference between the Western usage of ecosystem and the Soviet understanding of biogeocenose is that of spatial scale. The Anglo-American usage of ecosystem applies to a hierarchy of spatial scales; as some say, ecosystems come in a variety of sizes, ranging from a rabbit pellet to the biosphere. Not so, however, for the biogeocenose. As indicated above, the borders of the biogeocenose are limited by criteria of homogeneity. Soviet ecologists, principally biogeocenologists, believe the term *ecosystem* to be imprecise when applied to concrete land units. They cite numerous attempts to add spatial descriptors as evidence of its imprecision (e.g., micro-ecosystem, meso-ecosystem, macro-ecosystem). In short, Soviet biogeocenologists would say that all biogeocenoses are ecosystems but not all ecosystems qualify as biogeocenoses. The biogeocenose is an ecosystem the borders of which are those of the phytocenose (Lavrenko and Dylis 1968). Moreover, the common Western references to structural-functional units as separate ecosystems (e.g., soil ecosystems, urban ecosystems), violates the holistic criteria of biogeocenotic theory. Thus, Sukachev and Dylis (1964) write of soils, atmosphere, vegetation, microorganisms, and animals as only components of biogeocenoses, and consider it quite incorrect to identify these as specific biogeocenoses. Descriptors such as soil biogeocenoses or urban biogeocenoses rarely occur in Soviet literature.

Full acceptance of the biogeocenotic concept has, however, not occurred in the U.S.S.R., and for a variety of reasons, many Soviet ecologists prefer the more flexible ecosystem concept, which can be applied to any natural complex regardless of such parameters as size, age, and complexity. Some Soviet ecologists refrain from using the term *biogeocenosis* because they say it is a tongue-twister. Some zoologists use biogenocenosis "to designate actual communities, homogeneous in structure and occupying a definite area; and the term ecosystem is used in a general sense to designate any broad community type without structural and territorial limitations" (Zlotin and Khodashova 1974). Historically, many Soviet animal ecologists have used ecosystem rather than biogeocenose because (1) the Western concept of the ecosystem was introduced early by the excellent animal ecology textbook of Kashkarov (1944) and later by Naumov (1963), (2) the spatial homogeneity criterion for the definition of biogeocenose was primarily based on vegetation and applied poorly to home range and territory concepts of animal ecology, and (3) the traditional academic separation of animal and plant ecology facilitated the adoption of separate concepts and terminology.

Developmental Stages of Biogeocenology

Soviet biogeocenological literature over the past three decades reflects periods of formalization, application and geographic extension, and examination and re-evaluation. During the postwar years, Sukachev attempted to formalize biogeocenology as a discipline distinct from either geography or biology. Later, concepts were tested and advanced through the establishment of a network of biogeocenological field stations. With the rapid worldwide increase in the popularity of ecosystem sciences (rather than biogeocenological sciences) in the mid- to late-1950s and the evolution and testing of the continuum concepts of vegetation, the tenets of biogeocenotic theory were re-examined. The more traditional methods and procedures of biogeocenology have been re-evaluated to determine why such a holistic science (in theory) has produced so few truly holistic results.

Period I Formalization The birth of biogeocenology from the sciences of geography and biology has been referred to earlier. Along with the geographic studies that emphasized the character of vegetation cover and studies of the relationship between vegetation and climate (e.g., Sochava 1948), there were two excellent studies in the arctic regions, one by Grigoryev (1966), which analyzed interrelated processes of subarctic regions including energy balance ranging from inflow of solar radiation to biological productivity, and one by Formozov (1946), in which the insulative properties of snow cover were evaluated along with its implication for activity of birds and mammals in arctic regions. The latter study had great influence on the development of the ecological trend in zoogeography.

Important early work that helped to consolidate efforts in animal zoogeography includes Bobrinsky (1946) and later Isakov and Formozov (1963) on questions of ecological zoogeography in the U.S.S.R. The ecological trend was continued in tundra studies by Tikhomirov (1959) of the relation of animals to plant cover of the tundra, in which tundra food webs were diagrammed.

The process of formalization, however, took place during and shortly after World War II, the most difficult period of Soviet history. Some 20 million people, including thousands of scientists and technicians, were killed; cities such as Leningrad, where Sukachev lived and worked, were under siege for years; and many scientists either served at the front or in war factories (Trass 1976). As Rashevsky (1948) said of the appearance of two editions of Kashkarov's animal ecology textbook during the war, one is "inclined to a feeling of amazement rather than criticism" regarding Soviet research productivity during wartime.

The immediate postwar period was no less difficult. State control of science (e.g., Lysenkoism) was at its peak, and applied research was greatly emphasized. There arose distrust and conflict between applied and basic scientists, well-portrayed in Leonor's novel, *The Russian Forest.* It was also during the first decade after the war that plans were laid for the massive steppe reforestation and virgin lands projects. The first of these was to successfully establish forest shelterbelts in the southeastern European steppe to improve crop production by reducing evapotranspiration and erosion. Some shelterbelts (e.g., the Kamyshin-Volgograd state shelterbelt) were 250 km in length, with an area of four thousand to five thousand hectares. However, shortly after planting in 1949–1953, extensive die-off occurred, and by 1953 nearly half of the Kamyshin-Volgograd belt had died (Karchinsky 1971). A review of the causes of tree mortality by Karchinsky (1971) shows that some of the 1949 mandatory instructions for planting shelterbelts were wrong: cultivation was too shallow, trees were spaced too closely, relative drought resistence and compatability of species were poorly known, rows were too close to allow mechanical cultivation without bark injury, and others. Despite strict adherence to scientific guidelines and considerable human effort, the project failed for lack of advance research, both basic and applied.

On the heels of the reforestation failure came the virgin lands project, another massive effort to increase crop production by cultivating vast areas of virgin steppe in northern Kazakhastan, western Siberia, and eastern Russia (Eckholm 1976). It was assumed that the Soviet weather roulette, with frequent drought in one region or another, was risky, but two good harvests out of three would repay the investment many times over. Forty million hectares of virgin land, three times the size of England, were put under the plow, producing a 50 percent increase in grain production by 1960. However, wind erosion accelerated because of the small proportion of land in fallow. Suggestions to keep one-third of the land out of production each year, thus maintaining long-term productivity at the expense of short-term increases in yield, went unheeded. By the early 1960s, 17 million hectares were damaged by wind erosion, with 4 million hectares of these lost to production altogether. Despite yield predictions of 2 tons/hectare by 1963, peak production was only 1.1 tons/hectare and only 0.64 tons/hectare during the 1963 drought.

The ability of Sukachev and others to gain increasing government support for biogeocenological studies was in part due to the failure of the steppe reforestation and virgin lands projects. A lack of ecological understanding of natural and agricultural systems was clearly evident, and the importance of basic research in identifying scientific principles from which to plan large-scale technological projects was more fully realized. Currently, shelterbelt planting on a sound scientific basis is continuing in the steppe regions, and agricultural research has converted the virgin lands project from a liability to a moderate success.

The suggestion of a new scientific discipline with its own institutions whose work actually included disciplines of botany, zoology, microbiology, soils, and geography met with strong opposition from the established scientific community, and many of Sukachev's early papers were spent trying to promote the ideas. This posture was still very much in evidence in Sukachev and Dylis (1964): some fifty pages are spent in analyzing the term biogeocenology in relation to other "false" or "lesser" concepts such as the bioecos, diatopes, facies, and ecosystem.

Soviet ecologists who worked during this period of formalization say that Sukachev's greatness lay not only in his scientific abilities (he published over five hundred scientific papers during his lifetime), but also in his administrative and organizational skills, which were necessary to get biogeocenological field stations and laboratories established. During Sukachev's active years, the degree to which holistic studies of biogeocenoses could be conducted were limited by a lack of technical equipment (e.g., computers, portable field instruments). Although this situation has improved in recent years, and sophisticated equipment and techniques for the analysis of biogeocenoses are available in the U.S.S.R. on a limited basis, some Soviet scientists argue that the absence of an energetic, forceful leader to replace Sukachev now retards further advancement of holistic studies by biogeocenologists.

The practical trend in ecology in the Soviet Union resulted in the development of another important area, that of the ecology of diseases and disease control. The original 1964 work of Pavlovsky (1966) defined the biological basis of disease transmission involving animal vectors and laid the foundation for the work at a network of stations and institutes throughout the Soviet Union where emphasis on such problems was encouraged. Pavlovsky pointed out that certain diseases occur naturally and exist as a nidus or a nest or focus of infection in natural wildlife and arthropod vectors. It is from these locations that diseases can spread and be transmitted to man. The steppes of Russia were the ancient home of plague that swept periodically through Western Europe with such devastating results. Other wildlife diseases, such as rinderpest, were maintained there, and spread by epidemics through other parts of the world. Opening of the eastern regions of the U.S.S.R. brought humans into contact with diseases such as encephalitis and leishmaniosis. Although the concept of endemic diseases was not new, the emphasis placed on it by Pavlovsky provided a tremendous stimulus for ecological research on vector organisms in the Soviet Union.

Period II Application and Extension Following the period of formalization of the science of biogeocenology came one of application, in which the concepts of biogeocenology could be tested and advanced. Instrumental to this goal was the establishment of biogeocenological field stations and "outposts." Prior to World War II, most Soviet geobotanical and phytocenological investigations in Siberia, Central Asia, and the Far East, comprising about 80 percent of the total land area, were expeditionary in nature. The major scientific centers were located far off-center to the west in the European part of the U.S.S.R., primarily in Leningrad, Moscow, and Kiev. In addition to the enormous amounts of travel time required and difficulties in preparing and shipping samples, a major scientific drawback of the lack of permanent facilities was that observations in non-growing season months, which are often necessary to interpret ecosystem behavior, could not be made.

Thus, the establishment of a network of stations and outposts was instrumental in expanding geographically biogeocenological investigations during the postwar period by greatly improving the logistical support for investigations in the vast Soviet hinterlands. The stations and outposts have served not only as facilities where near-in, intensive experiments can be conducted, but as a logistical base for regional studies. Sukachev was instrumental in securing government support for new stations, but equally important, he obtained support for new scientific institutes and laboratories of biogeocenology as well (e.g., Laboratory of Biogeocenology of the Institute of Forests and Wood in Moscow and an affiliate branch of the Academy of Sciences in Krasnoyarsk, Siberia).

Field stations generally carry out biogeocenological investigations over many years according to a broad program, while outposts investigate specific regional questions and individual components of biogeocenotic systems. There are now several hundred stations and posts, with about fifty in each of the major vegetation zones. Some long-established stations are part of the network (for example, Repetek Desert Station established in Central Asia in 1928), but most have been added since World War II. The results of investigations in the network are periodically reviewed (e.g., Dylis et al. 1974). A list of the major stations and outposts, together with their geographic locations, institutional affiliation, and scientific program, is given in Dylis et al. (1976). In 1974, an official network of biogeocenotic stations and outposts was organized. The network includes both conservation and experimental properties operated by several government agencies, thus resembling the system of Experimental Ecological Reserves and UNESCO Biosphere Reserves recently established in the United States. The organization of these sites in the major natural zones again points out the close collaboration between the sciences of ecology and geography in the Soviet Union. As will be shown later, the establishment of these stations on a geographic plan was a great asset to Soviet studies during the International Biological Program.

Period III Examination and Re-evaluation The most recent period in the development of the science of biogeocenology was influenced significantly by the international debate of the continuum concept and the rise in popularity of the study of ecosystems. The effect of the former on the science of phytocenology has already been discussed; its effect was similar on the study of biogeocenoses because the limits of the biogeocenose are those of the phytocenose. Considerable energy was expended by biogeocenologists defending or evaluating their criteria in drawing boundaries and stressing the advantages of the biogeocenological approach over that of the ecosystem. The product of the international debate over these issues was that the concept and methods of the study of ecosystems made inroads into Soviet science such that now both approaches, although not always opposing viewpoints and methodology, are well represented in Soviet science. Generally speaking, most Soviet biogeocenologists are skilled in plant and soil sciences, while their ecosystem counterparts are younger and more broadly trained in ecology and mathematics.

The younger, quantitative Soviet ecologists of today quarrel not over the concept of biogeocenology but how it is commonly practiced. Some argue that biogeocenotic investigations are largely either plant- (especially) or animal-oriented and that despite the holistic concept of the biogeocenosis, investigations still reflect the traditional separation of plant and animal ecology. Ecosystem studies appear to them to more adequately address systems-level processes and better integrate biological and environmental sciences. There has also been a general reluctance by biogeocenologists to utilize and contribute to the development of the rapidly growing battery of quantitative techniques for the analysis of ecosystems. The failure of Soviet biogeocenologists to satisfactorily address questions about the whole biogeocenose has been mentioned by Lavrenko and Dylis (1968) and others.

The most popular ecology textbook in the Soviet Union today is the Russian translation of Odum's third edition of *Fundamentals of Ecology*. The book by Sukachev and Dylis (1964) is now somewhat outdated and is more suited for use by rising professionals rather than beginning students. There are many Soviet texts of phytocenology and animal ecology, but none that satisfactorily combines them.

Explanations for the paucity of results in Soviet biogeocenology pertaining to whole systems are varied but generally relate to: (1) strong disciplinarian traditions in the biological sciences; (2) some administrative difficulty in forming multidisciplinary groups (botanical and zoological institutes of the Soviet Academy of Sciences are separate and inter-institute research has often been a lower priority than the programmed research of each respective institute); (3) quantitative training of working biogeocenologists was mediocre, and, because the demand for students with good quantitative ability and skills has been high in the physical sciences, ingrowth of new personnel into ecology with the necessary quantitative skills has been slow; (4) precision, automatic equipment needed for monitoring ecosystem parameters has been limited, primarily because the highest quality instruments produced in Western Europe and North America can be purchased only with hard currency, which is in short supply; and (5) computer facilities are limited geographically, and ecologists do not have priority for their use.

Recent changes, however, have been made. For example, the Soviet Academy of Sciences agreed in 1976 to establish an Institute of Ecology. A new chair of ecology, in the Biology Faculty, has also been instituted at Moscow State University, and a new integrated course entitled "Ecology and Nature Preservation" is being team-taught by Naumov (animal ecologist), Rabotnov (plant population ecologist), and Fedorov (aquatic systems ecologist). It is a general course for all biology students and includes material on simulation modelling, biogeochemical cycling, ecosystem energetics, pollution, and other topics. Moreover, special training seminars and courses are being conducted in Moscow to improve the quantitative skills of practicing ecologists. A mathematician heads the "school," and ecologists well versed in quantitative methods lecture on a wide array of subjects.

The difficulties inherent in studying entire biogeocenoses contributed to the recent popularity in the U.S.S.R. of studying more manageable subunits called consortia. A consortium is composed of a central plant species, the determinant, and of associated species dependent on the central species for energy or physical support (Rabotnov 1972). A large number of papers have been published on the conceptual basis of consortia (e.g., Rabotnov 1973, 1974; Dylis 1973), but few detailed field investigations have been carried out as yet. Assessment of the potential benefits of studying consortia to the understanding of biogeocenoses is premature.

MODERN BIOGEOCENOLOGY AND ECOSYSTEM SCIENCE

Complex Investigations

Concurrent studies of biogeocenotic components by groups of specialists are called "complex" investigations by Soviet ecologists. Such studies have been especially common during the last decade, having been carried out at biogeocenological stations and by expeditions to remote areas within the Soviet Union, such as the Eurasian steppes and Central Asian deserts, and beyond (e.g., Mongolia). The ultimate goal has been to understand the structure and function of various biogeocenoses, but most studies remain descriptive. A recent example is that of Lavrenko and Borisova (1976), who were part of an expeditionary team conducting complex studies in the desert steppes of central Kazakhastan. Because little was known scientifically about this remote region of the Soviet Union, their results are primarily descriptive and include data on plant phenology, structure, community composition, ash composition of plant fractions, soils, and microorganisms. With respect to biota, estimates of species' abundance was emphasized.

Despite the current tendency for the bulk of Soviet complex investigations to be descriptive and inventory in nature (e.g., Lavrenko and Borisova 1976), there are many good examples of process-oriented biogeocenological research, the best from steppe (e.g., Kovalev 1974; Titlyanova 1973), desert (Chepurko et al. 1972; Miroshnichenko 1974), and forest-steppe (Goryshina 1974*a,b*) field stations. These studies are discussed later in the context of research conducted during the International Biological Program.

Soviet ecologists have emphasized study of the processes of productivity and decomposition and the combined role of the processes in mineral cycling. This emphasis has followed naturally from the strong Russian and Soviet tradition in soil science, especially from historic interest in the role of vegetation cover in the soil-formation process. A lesser, but growing, emphasis has been placed on the functional role of animals in the regulation of biogeocenological processes. Animal ecology in the U.S.S.R. has focused on the geographic distribution of animals, the preservation of important species such as sable, and the relation of animals to disease and other environmental factors.

Most ecological research in the Soviet Union is carried out by members of the Academy of Sciences of the U.S.S.R., and to a lesser extent by the Ministry of Agriculture and universities. University graduate students are assigned to the academy or ministries for summer research experience. The Academy of Sciences is doubtless the largest scientific organization in the world. It is made up of numerous institutes and laboratories, each with some mission or set of missions. The workers in these institutes and laboratories have advanced through a highly competitive education system, and professional positions are attained largely through the influence of one major professor. There is not a great deal of movement between positions for different people, although there is a slight concentration gradient that leads toward institutes in Moscow. After securing a position, a professional ecologist or biologist may remain for a long period of time, perhaps his entire career, in the same institute or laboratory. There is some inducement to work in those locations where the need is greatest or the population of scientists lowest.

Because of their work location workers in Siberia receive a 20 percent higher wage and pay lower rates for housing and other services than workers in less remote areas of the country.

A great tradition among Soviet scientific workers is the expedition to field stations during summer months. This is the period when considerable data collecting and field observations are made, and there is great pride and enthusiasm associated with this type of activity. Indeed, if one visits laboratories and institutes during the summer season, one is fortunate to find 10 percent of the staff on hand. There is also some financial inducement. While in the field, scientific workers receive an additional increment to their pay to compensate for working under adverse conditions that often require living in tents and cooking meals in the field.

Modern Process Studies in Biogeocenoses

Desert Extensive biogeocenological studies, emphasizing productivity and mineral cycling, have been carried out at the Repetek Station in the Kara-kum Desert of Central Asia in Southeastern Turkmenia. Vegetation in undisturbed parts of these sandy deserts includes small trees (*Haloxylon, Ammondendron*), shrubs (*Ephedra, Calligonum*), semi-shrublets (*Artemisia, Salsola, Anabasis*), and an abundant sedge (*Carex physodes*). Extensive data on phytomass and productivity have been collected over the past decade; phytomass is approximately 30 t/hectare and net primary production 2 t/hectare per year (Miroshnichenko 1974; Rodin 1975; Gunin and Dyedkov 1978). Two-thirds of the phytomass is below ground.

Extensive data have also been collected on elemental concentrations in plant and soil fractions, nutrient uptake, and litterfall such that mineral cycling patterns are well understood. Studies point out the importance of mineral cycling relationships to vegetation pattern and soil formation. To illustrate, two species of *Haloxylon* (*persicum, ammondendron*) occur at the Repetek Station; the former species occupies dunes and sand ridges and the latter low plains with a high water table. Total litterfall from each species is comparable, but *H. ammondendron* litterfall contains almost twice as much ash and nitrogen as *H. persicum*. About 2,600 mg-eq/m^2 of cations and only 201 mg-eq/m^2 of anions are returned under *H. ammondendron*. Upper soil layers are sharply alkalized (pH 9–10) under the influence of salts released from the litterfall under *H. ammondendron* canopies. Such high alkalinity prevents all plants from growing beneath the canopy, and only *Suaeda* grows at the canopy edge. What appears to be an effect of shading (competition for light) is, in fact, the result of biochemical interference.

The results of a decade of study at Repetek have been used to construct a trophic-functional scheme of the sand desert biogeocenose at Repetek (Rodin 1975). Additionally, a simple mathematical model of *H. ammondendron* population growth was constructed and used to simulate stem density over time and identify deficiencies in data bases.

Meadow-steppe at Karachi Some of the most detailed biogeocenological process studies have been carried out at the Karachi Field Station in the forest-steppe of western Siberia (Bazilevich 1975; Kovalev 1974; Titlyanova 1977). Research has emphasized the effects of environmental factors on the rates of net primary production and patterns of mineral cycling. The zonal vegetation at Karachi is designated as meadow-steppe, rather than true steppe, because plants receive at least some moisture from groundwater or uphill surface runoff during the growing season. Soviet ecologists define true steppe as short grasses occurring on well-drained sites receiving no moisture from the water table or its capillary fringe. Therefore, the interchange of the terms *prairie* and *steppe,* as is commonly done in the West because of their similar physiognomy, is not altogether acceptable.

Several biogeocenoses were investigated in detail during 1968–1973 at Karachi, including meadow-steppe, *Calamagrostis* meadow, and grassy marsh, as well as solonchak and solonetz steppe. Peak aboveground phytomass ranged narrowly from 1.4–3.0 t/hectare, being greatest in the marsh and least in solonetz steppe. Belowground phytomass ranged widely from 10 to 48 t/hectare with the highest belowground phytomass and root-shoot ratio (1:15–1:20) in the grassy marsh. Lowest phytomass and ratio (1:6–1:7) were in the meadow-steppe. Two phytomass peaks occurred in the steppe types, one in early summer and one in later summer–early autumn. The second peak was greatest and corresponded to a late July–August peak in precipitation. Phytomass of the other types peaked in late summer. Belowground net primary productivity was considerably higher than aboveground, with maximum in the meadow-steppe and minimum in the solonchak and solonetz steppe.

Annual patterns of net primary production, shoot mortality, and decomposition for the *Calamagrostis* meadow (chernozem soils) during 1968–1972 are given in Bazilevich (1975). Despite considerable annual variation in meteorologic conditions, net primary productivity of aboveground phytomass from year to year varied less than 20 percent. Greatest variability occurred in litter decomposition rates (from 7.3 to 2.7 t/hectare per year), but over a four-year average, annual production of organic matter (4.3 t/hectare per year) and amount of litter decomposed (4.2 t/hectare per year) were balanced.

These and other data collected at the Karachi Station (Titlyanova 1973, 1977) have been used to construct a functional model of exchange processes in the meadow-steppe biogeocenosis, the zonal vegetation type. The biogeocenosis is viewed as an assembly of compartments among which organic matter or energy or both are transferred. Estimates of both pool sizes and fluxes were made. Carbon and nitrogen dynamics were characterized separately in the model; other (potassium, sodium, calcium, magnesium, iron, aluminum, manganese, silicon, titanium, phosphorus, sulfur, chlorine) were lumped in various ways. The biogeocenose was divided into eight compartments or state variables; aboveground living green phytomass, living roots and other belowground organs, standing dead, litter, dead belowground vegetation residues, soil with sub-compartments representing soil humus, subsoil, and ground water. Similar descriptive models were constructed for other biogeocenoses at Karachi. With one notable exception (Gilmanov 1977), mathematical simulation models of the Karachi biogeocenoses or their subsystems have not, as yet, been completed.

Meadow-Steppe at Kursk Excellent results have accrued from the many years of investigations at the Central Chernozem Reserve near Kursk. The Central Chernozem Reserve lies in the middle of the broad belt of rich chernozem soil that extends across European Russia south of Moscow and north of the Crimea from Hungary to the Ural Mountains. A rich humus layer 1.3 m deep is underlain by a calcareous zone. The profile shows burrows of the mole rat (*Spalax*) and of lumbricids to a depth of 3 m. The meadow-steppe, never ploughed, is mowed four years out of five; a portion is never mowed. Since 1963, there has regularly been extensive defoliation of oak forests by the oak leaf roller (*Tortrix*). More recently, there has been extensive damage to the undergrowth by increasing populations of moose (*Alces*) and roe deer (*Capreolus*). Mounds made by marmots (*Marmota*), absent from the region for at least one hundred years, still are evident on the steppe. Mounds of earth pushed up by *Spalax* are conspicuous, as are areas of localized concentrations of the vole *Microtus arvalis.*

In contrast to the studies at Repetek and Karachi, the biogeocenological investigations at the Kursk Field Station emphasized temporal changes in vegetation structure and the functional role of animals in biogeocenoses. Perhaps most important, these units of study at Kursk were small watersheds, some of which were well equipped for measuring hydrologic parameters and nutrient loss. Types of data collected on primary producers were similar to those at Karachi, except that species phenology and seasonal changes in vertical structure were examined. For biogeocenoses at Kursk, aboveground phytomass ranged from 3–6 t/hectare with root/shoot ratios about 1:7–1:10 (Bazilevich 1975). Seasonal dynamics of phytomass, standing dead, litter, and living and dead roots and organs were also determined. Total net primary productivity was estimated at 8.4 t/hectare. Of this total, roots contributed 7.2 t/hectare. Compartment totals of carbon, nitrogen, and other elements have been estimated for Kursk biogeocenoses, but data on fluxes at Kursk are less complete than at Karachi.

In steppe ecosystems of the Russian plain, the biomass of animal populations is about 1 percent of plant mass on a dry weight basis (Zlotin 1969).

Greater than 90 percent of the zoomass is comprised of soil organisms, primarily invertebrates. In non-saline soils, earthworms constitute 90 percent of the zoomass; in saline soils, the zoomass of earthworms declines sharply. Soil invertebrate microfauna are extremely numerous (microarthropods: 100,000/m^2; Nematoda: 5–35 million/m^2) but comprise only about 20 percent of the total zoomass. Zoomass distribution is extremely spotty but is usually dominated by microarthropods and nematodes.

Distribution of trophic groups in the Russian plain is even more unbalanced: over 90 percent are saprophages, about 7 percent phytophages, and 1 percent predatory and parasitic. Efflux of carbon dioxide from soils at Kursk is about 1 g/m^2 per hour; about 70 percent of the total carbon dioxide efflux is from humus being decomposed by bacteria, 30 percent from root respiration, and 0.5–2.0 percent liberated by soil fauna. About 5–6 percent of the annual primary production is utilized by vertebrate and invertebrate animals; about 70 percent of that amount is transformed by invertebrates.

Many of these results have been synthesized and summarized by Zlotin and Khodashova (1974) and Green and Utekhin (1976). The former volume presents the dynamics of production, consumption, and decomposition processes in oak forest and meadow-steppe focusing particularly on the effects of outbreaks of leaf-eating insects (*Tortrix*) in the forested regions of the reserve. Other consumers are also considered, including the belowground consumers. The role of saprophages in promoting nutrient cycling in the system has been quantitatively evaluated, and the total participation of animals in promotion of biological cycling and the effect on total production of the system is emphasized. The volume by Green and Utekhin includes separate papers on the structure, community dynamics, and production of plants in the meadow-steppe, the role of invertebrates in nutrient cycling, the dynamics of bird populations, and some data on agricultural crops of the region; it also includes two papers on simulation modelling of changes in the forest-steppe boundary and in the spatial distribution of plant communities. This volume contains papers with excellent details of investigations of plant productivity, including live and dead plant material below ground, a detailed evaluation of soil invertebrates and their quantitative activity and consumption in terms of moving chemical elements, and results of a twenty-year breeding bird census of a ten-hectare plot in the oak forest.

Despite the small proportion of the annual production used directly by consumers, the effect of small mammals on specific synusia and plant species was significant. For example, mole-rats (*Spalax*) use up to 25 percent of the annual production of roots and rhizomes of several species of plants, thus consuming a large part of the plants' stored reserves. Zlotin and Khodashova (1973) agree with current thinking that the percent utilization of primary production by animals is not a full reflection of their effect on biogeocenoses because it leaves out the important aspect of their potential to regulate biotic and abiotic processes. The total loss of primary production due to consumer activity was estimated to be 20 percent (Zlotin and Khodashova 1974). Such activity stimulates primary production by augmented cycling of nutrients in the biogeocenosis. During periods of heavy defoliation of oaks by insect larvae, productivity of the understory increased by a factor of two. Consumer activity in the steppe biogeocenosis leads to more complex community development, thus contributing to stability. By contrast, in areas of the Central Chernozem Reserve that have been protected from grazing and mowing, litter accumulates, decomposition processes are slow, and species composition changes; these factors further reduce the numbers of invertebrate and small vertebrate herbivores, accompanied by reduction in primary production and biological cycling.

Forest-Steppe—Les na Vorskle Complex studies have been carried out at the Les na Vorskle Station (Forest on the Vorskla River) near Kharkov, at the southern end of the forest-steppe. At this station, Sukachev initiated his complex biogeocenological studies of forests. The vegetation consists of natural forest islands formerly surrounded by steppe, but now by crops; it is thus similar in aspect to the oak woods of southern Wisconsin. Many aspects of biogeocenological research have been studied, including soil moisture, microclimate dynamics, primary productivity, photosynthesis, decomposition, and mineral cycling, and are reported in Goryshina (1974*a,b*). Perhaps the most detailed and significant results pertain to the importance of the herbaceous layer to forest biogeochemical cycling (Goryshina 1976).

Above ground, phytomass of the herb layer is about 1,000–1,100 kg/hectare dry weight with a comparable amount below ground. The herb layer constitutes less than 1 percent of the total phytomass of the forest and about 10 percent of its total annual net primary production. However, herb litter is 15–20 percent of the total litterfall (excluding tree boles) and, in contrast to leaf litterfall from trees, is more evenly distributed during the year because of staggered phenological peaks. Herb litter is higher in ash elements and nitrogen per gram dry weight than tree leaf fall. Ephemerals such as *Aegopodium podagraria* are especially rich in phosphorus and potassium, the latter making up more than half the ash weight of the annual litterfall. Thus, herbs return the most important nutrients to the soil in greater proportions than all other types of litterfall. The herb cover supplies 58 percent of the total potassium, and the results of lysimeter studies show that only about 7 percent of the potassium is leached beyond the herb root zone. Thus, the herbaceous cover subsequently contributes to the retention of potassium and other mobile nutrients, especially in the early spring (ephemerals) when nutrients would otherwise be leached during snow melt. An equally important role is played in nitrogen turnover. About one-third of the total nitrogen returned in litterfall is contributed by the herbaceous layer.

Goryshina (1976) warns of modern "recreation loads" in forests near Moscow where trampling has destroyed the herbaceous layer. The most sensitive components are the spring ephemerals, which disappear completely with trampling and soil compaction. Destruction of herbaceous cover, while not initially decreasing total productivity, eventually reduces the system's ability to conserve and recycle elements for sustained growth.

Babatag Mountain Ridge A comprehensive approach is being taken to characterize some of the more than 110 nature reserves of the U.S.S.R. by the Central Laboratory of Nature Conservation under the Ministry of Agriculture. An example of quantitative evaluation of plant productivity, as well as numbers and biomass of invertebrate and vertebrate organisms, is provided by Vtorov and Makeev (1976). In their evaluation of a grassland site on the Babatag mountain ridge in Tadjikistan, plant biomass at their sample locations varied with altitude and east or west exposure, and ranged from 2,700 to 5,300 g/m^2, with shoot:root ratios of 1:26 and 1:2. Among microfauna in the 0- to 5-cm layer, mites were most numerous at nineteen hundred meters elevation (720 mg/m^2 live weight), and collembolans were most abundant at eighteen hundred and one thousand meters elevation (607 and 720 mg/m^2). Enchytraeid worms were also important (60–280 mg/m^2). Among the mesofauna, scarab beetles (94–785 mg/m^2) and diptera (*Asilidae*) larvae (4–40 mg/m^2) were most numerous in the 0- to 20-cm level. Important reptiles included a tortoise, *Testudo horsfieldi* (1,200–12,000 g/hectare), and lizard, *Agama lehmanni* (434–847 g/hectare). Number and biomass of birds at each of several stations are given, as are estimates of the daily kilocalories consumed by each species per kilometer. Highest values reported were for *Falco cherrug* (up to 4,000 g/km^2, 480 kcal/km^2 per day), *Columba livia* (5,400 g/km^2, 972 kcal/km^2 per day), *Alectoris kakelik* (6,000 g/km^2, 972 kcal/km^2 per day), and *Ammoperdix griseogularis* (2,860 g/km^2, 572 kcal/km^2 per day).

Other studies The role of arthropods and other invertebrates in mineralization and litter decomposition is being pursued by the Laboratory of Soil Zoology in the Institute of Evolutionary Morphology and Ecology of Animals in Moscow. Building on a long tradition of invertebrate morphology and systematics, these workers are now oriented to quantitative evaluation of invertebrate groups in ecosystems and their energy utilization and processing of organic material. Striganova and Rakhmanov (1972) and Striganova (1975) have determined diplopod density (up to 248/m^2) and assimilation efficiencies (14–83 percent) of different species and the amount of litter decomposition or processing (59–719 mg/m^2 per day). In laboratory experiments, Striganova has determined that species with high assimilation efficiencies show low consumption rates.

Krivolutsky (1975) has worked extensively with oribatid mites in different ecosystems of the U.S.S.R. Densities are: tundra, 10,000–20,000/m^2; taiga, 60,000–100,000; broadleaf forests, 40,000; steppe to desert regions, a decline from 20,000 to 200/m^2. Along an altitudinal gradient in the Tien Shan Mountains, the population densities were highest at middle altitudes in the forest soils of the *Picea schrenkiana* zone. Pokarzhevsky and Krivolutsky (1975) have evaluated the role of soil animals (Lumbricidae, Araneida, Insecta, Vertebrata) in calcium and alkaline-earth element storage and turnover. Although the majority of the calcium is in the soil and litter compartments of the system, the Lumbricidae contain significant amounts, as do certain arthropods. The values are similar to those that have been found in U.S. forest soils.

Chernov et al. (1975) have worked extensively with invertebrates in the tundra regions of the U.S.S.R., determining numbers and biomass, and estimating oxygen consumption or energetics. Taimyr tundra sampling has indicated that nematodes are the most abundant organisms (1 million–4 million/m^2) followed by Collembola (19,000–44,000/m^2), Oribatid mites, Gamasid mites, and Enchytraeid worms (1,000–2,000/m^2).

Studies of vertebrates have been extensive in the Soviet Union. The probable development of arctic and alpine bird species has been reconstructed by Kistchinski (1976*a*), results of which have important bearing on the North American fauna because of the Pliocene-Pleistocene connection between Asia and North America referred to as Beringia. Recent common groups of sheep, marmots, pikas, ground squirrels, pipits, and rosy finches developed there. Additional breadth of these studies is given in results of work analyzing the role of birds in subarctic ecosystems (Kistchinski 1974, 1976*b*). Birds in tundra ecosystems occupy top levels of the trophic pyramids, where their main role is in regulating energy flows between various trophic chains, rather than in augmenting the movement of energy through the chains, and in transporting energy and matter between different types of ecosystems (terrestrial-marine) by their movements. V. R. Dolnik (1975) has made extensive studies of migration, distribution, and energetics of passerine birds. His efforts have also contributed to understanding the role of pest species in the agricultural areas of the U.S.S.R.

Much of the recent research in the U.S.S.R. on mammals has been summarized in the two volumes of abstracts (in English) prepared for the First International Theriological Congress in 1974. For example, detailed investigations of the little suslik (ground squirrel) in deserts and semi-deserts have been conducted by Kuznetzov (1976), and Abaturov and Kuznetzov (1976*a, b*). Field and laboratory studies of *Citellus pygmaeus* indicate very high values of assimilation efficiency (80 percent), secondary production, and consumption (20 percent of aboveground vegetation). Abaturov (1968, 1972) has estimated quantities of soil moved to the surface by burrowing animals, which may cover 36 percent of ground surface in the case of *Talpa europaea* near Moscow, and of the numerous chemical elements brought to the surface in this process. Extensive studies of the vole *Arvicola terrestris* have been conducted by Panteleyev and Terekhina (1976). In addition to preparing studies of morphological and ecological characters, they have raised hypotheses concerning spatial distribution of these peculiarly interesting and large Old World voles. Zimina and Saint-Giron (1976) are currently involved in collaborative studies that compare mammal distributions in the Caucasus Mountains with those in the Alps. Studies of small mammals in northern latitudes have been conducted by Shvartz et al. (1969), who have documented dynamics of numbers of the northern populations, and by Smirnov and Tokmakova (1971), who have investigated the relationship among population size, plant consumption, and production. Recent work by Shvartz, Khodashova, Zlotin, Zimina, and others indicates that Pitelka's (1969) assessment of Soviet animal ecology (especially in the arctic) as unquantitative and descriptive with incomplete or scanty data is less characteristic of current research than it may have been of research in the 1950s and 1960s.

Systems Ecology

To the present, comparative analysis of systems properties of biogeocenoses has primarily been done by comparing fluxes, pool sizes, and flux pool ratios (in the sense of Bazilevich 1975). Dynamic analyses and use of systems analysis have generally not been utilized as in the West despite compatible data from some of the biogeocenological stations and much interest by Soviet investigators. One exception is work by Gilmanov (1977), who developed a dynamic model of the meadow-steppe ecosystem of western Siberia and utilized data from the Karachi site for validation (see earlier discussion of Karachi Station). Gilmanov (1977) emphasizes the plant submodel, especially the belowground portion. The model is highly aggregated, but the output showed good agreement with the Karachi field data. Gilmanov (1978) has also written a review of mathematical modelling of biogeochemical cycles in grassland ecosystems, the first of its kind to be published in the U.S.S.R. Landscape ecosystem structure and topology have been treated theoretically by Sochava (1970).

Many reasons for limited use of systems analysis techniques by Soviet ecologists parallel those discussed earlier for quantitative techniques in general. Another reason relates to Soviet computer hardware. Soviet computer technology is sufficienty advanced (Ershov 1975) so that the unavailability of machines has not in itself been a main reason for the lack of use of systems techniques. The majority of machines are still second generation, including the BESM-6, which is the most powerful computer built in the Soviet Union. Its American counterpart is the CDC 3600. The ES EVM third-generation series (1020–1060) is newer and jointly produced by seven socialist countries. All ES EVM machines can be hooked up in series. The IBM 360/75 is the U.S. counterpart to the ES EVM 1060. However, demand for computer time in the U.S.S.R. exceeds supply, and ecologists are behind physical scientists in the queue. The general lack of remote terminals at most universities and many institutes has not improved user efficiency. Day-to-day jobs run by ecologists are in batch mode.

SOVIET IBP

Soviet scientists participated actively in the International Biological Program (IBP). The Soviet effort involved more than 250 institutes including the Soviet Academy of Sciences as the major organization, republic academies, universities, and institutes of several ministries (e.g., Ministry of Agriculture). Of the republic academies, the Estonian, Lithuanian, Belorussian, Turkmenian, and Azerbaijanian were the most active. Clearly, in terms of institute and staff participation, the Soviet program was the largest of all national programs. Participation was voluntary, as no supplemental government funds were provided specifically for IBP research; hence, in many instances, it was difficult to separate related ongoing work from that which was unilaterally directed toward IBP goals and objectives. Operational costs of the Soviet IBP program (i.e., costs for projects identified as "IBP") reached a maximum in 1971 and were estimated to be 10 million rubles (Bychovsky and Bauer 1975).

Research emphasis during the Soviet IBP was clearly on productivity and mineral cycling on zonal biogeocenoses (that is, those representative of the broad climatic-vegetation zones), especially desert and tundra, patterns of which were not well known prior to IBP investigations. Complex studies were also undertaken at all trophic levels, especially those in need of research such as belowground processes. Use of quantitative, standardized methods was stressed in order to eventually construct mathematical models of ecosystem productivity (Bychovsky and Bauer 1975). The goal of Soviet hydrobiologists during the IBP was to investigate energy flow and the productivity of freshwater communities representative of different climatic zones of the U.S.S.R.

Thousands of publications were produced, most in Russian but a significant number in English (e.g., Rodin 1975; Estonian Republic Committee for IBP 1971; Laasimer 1975). Three IBP synthesis volumes have been published in Russian. The first (Rodin and Smirnov 1975) includes results of IBP sections PT (terrestrial productivity) and PP (production processes). The second volume (Bauer and Smirnov 1976) includes synthesized results of the photosynthesis subsection (section production processes) and the sections on productivity of marine (PM) and freshwater (PF) communities, and biological control (UM). Soviet research on human adaptability (HA) is synthesized in volume 3 (Barbashova 1976).

Terrestrial Productivity and Mineral Cycling

At the "beginning" of the IBP, the book by Rodin and Bazilevich (1965) was published in Russian. It represents an extensive synthesis of published productivity and mineral cycling data from mostly natural ecosystems around the world, and hence could rightly be considered the first synthesis volume directed toward the IBP goals of understanding global patterns of productivity. It has since been commonly used as a reference outside the U.S.S.R. after being translated into English in 1967. For Soviet ecologists, the synthesis provided an advance start on IBP problems of productivity and made it easier to identify areas where knowledge was limited and effort should be focused.

Russian and Soviet research interest in productivity and mineral cycling predates the advent of the IBP. Larin (1936) conducted an early study of the dynamics of vegetation production and nutrients in meadows in various zones of the U.S.S.R. His work was the prototype for terrestrial productivity research during the IBP. (For a review of Larin's work, see Larin 1969). As stated earlier, productivity-mineral cycling research was organized on a geographic basis with the goal of obtaining rather uniform sample coverage of the major biomes of the Soviet Union. Naturally, the biogeocenological field stations and outposts, which were distributed throughout the natural zones, were centers for many IBP investigations.

Most Soviet productivity-mineral cycling studies conducted during the IBP attempted to measure phytomass (above and below ground) by fraction (e.g., foliage, small-large stems, boles); productivity (above ground, some below ground); litterfall by fraction (e.g., leaves, fruits, bud scales); litter mass; and their respective elemental composition. Animal investigations were less common and emphasized species composition and mass of soil and litter fauna. Detailed meteorological measures were even less common, but some outstanding investigations were conducted at some sites (e.g., Ross 1975). In addition to the site-specific, complex studies, a number of geographic syntheses were made for certain biotic groups (e.g., Aristovskaya 1975; Ghilarov and Chernov 1975). Methods for investigating biological cycling have been reviewed in detail by Bazilevich et al. (1978).

The final synthesis chapter on productivity of desert communities by Rodin (1975) includes data from six Central Asian stations, including the data reviewed earlier from Repetek. These sites represent a wide variety of environmental conditions and are well described. Total phytomass ranged from 5–34 t/hectare, with maximum total net primary productivity near 7 t/hectare. Minimum was only 0.13 t/hectare (above ground) in the central Gobi Desert of Mongolia (Bulgan Station). Litterfall also varied widely, from 0.7–12 t/hectare. Elemental concentrations in plant, litter, and soil fractions were determined at three of the stations. Biomass of animals was only studied at Repetek, where a trophic-functional conceptual model was constructed for the sand desert ecosystem (Rodin 1975). A much more exhaustive synthesis of the productivity patterns of Central Asian deserts based on IBP studies during 1965–1974 has since been published by Rodin (1977, 1978).

IBP results for the steppe zone synthesized by Bazilevich (1975) are primarily those discussed earlier from the Kursk and Karachi Stations. Data were collected at an additional site, Tambovsky Station; thus, the steppe region was represented by only three stations. The geographic coverage is sparse, but some of the most complete biogeocenological data, sufficient to construct mathematical models of belowground processes (Gilmanov 1977), are available from the Kursk and Karachi sites in the steppe. A very recent review of the function of herbaceous ecosystems has been published by Bazilevich and Titlyanova (1978).

The largest number of investigations and sites occurred in the forest zones. Gortinsky et al. (1975) synthesized productivity results from forests in the European part of the U.S.S.R., including northern, middle, and southern taiga subzones, coniferous-broadleaved forests, and broadleaved forests of the forest-steppe. The comparative analysis of productivity among subzones was made by selecting data considered representative for each region and belonging to a fundamental type of community with specific age characteristics. Within the taiga zone, phytomass and productivity increase with decreasing continentality of the climate in a southwesterly direction. Greatest phytomass occurs in spruce stands of the Valday region of Estonia and near Moscow. Maximum phytomass is greater than 460 t/hectare, and maximum productivity exceeds 10 t/hectare. Maximum productivity of oak stands of the forest-steppe also exceeds 10 t/hectare. Uptake of nitrogen and mineral elements in larch forests was measured to be four times greater than uptake in spruce and pine forests.

The synthesis by Gortinsky et al. (1975) is especially sparse. A large portion of the IBP results in forests were not included or reviewed. Noteworthy additions include studies by Petrov (1971) and Goryshina (1974*b*) in the forest-steppe discussed earlier. Productivity of two oak woods with differing histories of use was carefully measured, and the tally of production components, especially the understory stratum, was especially complete.

Other comprehensive forest IBP productivity studies in the European part of the U.S.S.R. include those by Molchanov (1973, 1974), Smirnov (1971), Karpov (1973), and Rysin (1975). Extensive data on pine standing crop by synusial fractions were collected and analyzed in Belorussia by Yurkevich and Yaroshevich (1974). Productivity and mineral cycling patterns for eighteen spruce stands comprising a soil moisture and stand age gradient were compiled by Kazimirov and Morozova (1973). Frey (1971) and researchers from other Estonian IBP projects estimated productivity of mature Norway spruce (*Picea abies*) at 17–18 t/hectare, about twice that reported by Rodin and Bazilevich (1965) and others. Although differences in methodology and stand age were responsible for part of the disparity, much of the difference is real. Thus, prior to the IBP, spruce forest production in the western U.S.S.R. was severely underestimated.

Results of IBP investigations in Siberian forests have been synthesized by Pozdnyakov (1975). Again, representative plots were used to characterize the forests growing in the large territory from the east slope of the Urals eastward to central Yakutia, and from the steppes and semi-desert regions of Tuva north to the Arctic Circle. Phytomass in the northern taiga zone averaged 70–80 t/hectare, with a maximum near 100 t/hectare. In the middle taiga, phytomass reaches 100–130 t/hectare near the Urals and drops to 60–70 t/hectare in the strongly continental climate of Yakutia. Pine forests in the southern taiga and forest-steppe exhibit phytomass levels that exceed 250 t/hectare. The ratio of foliage mass to total aboveground phytomass increases with intensifying continentality of the climate. Foliage mass comprises 2–3 percent of the total phytomass in the southern taiga, about 4 percent in the middle taiga, 4–5 percent in Tuva and Kazakhastan, and 5–6 percent in Yakutia. Few IBP data on the rich forest ecosystems of the Far East were collected and reported.

Results of IBP forest productivity studies in mountain communities have been synthesized by Malinovsky (1975). His synthesis includes studies of phytomass, primary and secondary productivity, and mineral cycling of pine forests in the Tien-Shan Mountains (*Pinus sylvestris* plantations), the Carpathians (*Pinus mughus*), the Caucasus (*Pinus sosnovsky*, with *Abies nordmanniana* and *Picea orientalis*), spruce forests of different ages and elevations in the Carpathians (*Picea abies*), and wild apple woodlands (*Malus sieversii*) in the Tien-Shan.

Additional IBP results not reviewed by Malinovsky (1975) include studies of pistachio woodland (*Pistacia vera*) in the Pamir Alai of Central Asia (Zapryagaeva 1976), the Central Asian tugai or mountain floodplain woodlands (*Elaeagnus, Populus, Platanus*) in Tadjikistan (Molotovsky and Kabilov 1973), and the lesser Caucasus forests in Azerbaijan (Gasanov 1966, Aliev and Gasanov 1971). Except for limited study of oak forests of Tallish (southern Azerbaijan along the Caspian Sea, Safarov and Djalilov 1973), few data were collected on Soviet subtropical forests. Data from a number of the forest and woodland studies listed above have been included in the IBP woodlands data set (DeAngelis et al. In press).

Prior to IBP studies, productivity data were most lacking from desert and tundra biogeocenoses. IBP studies of tundra and forest tundra have been synthesized by Shamurin et al. (1975) and Gorchakovsky and Andreyashkina (1975). Studies were generally more extensive and less intensive than those reported earlier for the Central Asian deserts. Production estimates were made for more than a dozen tundra regions including tundra, shrub-tundra, lichen-shrub tundra, and forest-tundra. Data from the forest-tundra station

Harp were summarized separately by Gorchakovsky and Andreyashkina (1975). Additional details of IBP tundra research are available in Tikhomirov (1971) and Aleksandrova and Matveyeva (1979). A synthesis of IBP results on secondary productivity of the subarctic was completed by Danilov and Olshvang (1976), and was based primarily on studies at Tareye and Harp stations. Numbers and biomass of secondary producers were measured along with seasonal and annual dynamics. Energetic and functional roles of animals in biogeocenoses were addressed. These authors reside at the Institute of Plant and Animal Ecology in Sverdlovsk (Urals), which is said to be the closest to an integrated ecological institute in the U.S.S.R. Additional work of note from this institute is that of Shvartz et al. (1969), who documented the dynamics of numbers of northern small mammal populations, and Smirnov and Tokmakova (1972), who have investigated the relationship of population levels to plant consumption and production.

Other Terrestrial Studies

Ecosystem properties other than production and mineral cycling were examined during the IBP of Soviet ecologists, although not emphasized in the research plan. A sampling of ecophysiological research in the arid zones of the U.S.S.R. and Mongolia is available in Rodin (1972). Studies of photosynthesis were reviewed by Nichiporovich and Shulgin (1976). An outstanding contribution of environmental studies of biogeocenoses during the IBP was the work of Ross (1975) on the radiation regime and architectronics of the vegetation cover. Ross' work includes a quantitative theory of the transfer of solar radiation within plant stands. Also, the influence of the optical properties of leaves and the structure of incident radiation on the radiation regime in plant stands was examined. The book is highly regarded by the few specialists outside the Soviet Union who have seen it, although it has not as yet been translated into English.

Aquatic Studies

Results of Soviet freshwater investigations were reviewed by Winberg (1976) at the close of the IBP and earlier by Winberg and Bauer (1971). Some results are available in English (e.g. Winberg 1969, 1970). The overall goal of freshwater studies was to determine the patterns of productivity of natural communities and ecosystems across the broad geographic zones of the U.S.S.R. Considerable attention was given to developing new methodology and standardizing techniques among sites (Edmondson and Winberg 1971). The national program had two themes: to conduct complex investigations of all trophic levels in several reservoirs, and to conduct special investigations of productivity in a broad range of freshwater communities.

Results of twelve aquatic sites constituted the Soviet synthesis (Winberg 1976), although results from many sites are still pending, including those from Lake Baikal. Natural lakes studied include some near the White Sea, in Belorussia, and in Central Asia near Alma-Ata. The sites in Belorussia exhibit a range from mesotrophic to eutropic. Two reservoirs near Kiev and Moscow were studied extensively.

Estimates of net primary productivity for the twelve lakes ranged from 21 to 1,758 kcal/m^2 per year, representing an eighty-four-fold range from the least productive Lake Zelenyetskoye near the Bering Sea to Batorin in Belorussia (Winberg 1976). Geographic trends in production characteristics were evaluated by computing, for each site, p/b coefficients for all trophic levels and a series of other ratios. Energy exchange rates among trophic components (phytoplankton, bacterioplankton, and zooplankton) were also computed for the twelve sites.

IBP studies were also conducted in inland seas and open oceans. An extensive study of the biological productivity of the Caspian Sea, including the effects of both natural and anthropogenic factors, was completed by Marty and other researchers (Marty 1974). Results of marine studies have been briefly reviewed by Beklemishev (1976). More detailed information is available on marine ecosystem function (Petipa 1976), vertical distribution of phytoplankton (Semina 1976), and marine benthos (Golikov and Skarlato 1976; Neyman 1976; Yablonskaya 1976).

Soviet Assessment of IBP

Published commentary by Soviet scientists has been especially positive toward the IBP program. There is no question that the international nature of the program enabled increased contact between Soviet and foreign scientists and improved the exchange of scientific results. From the Soviet perspective, this has improved the chances of standardizing sampling and analytical procedures, thus enabling improved cross-comparability of results. Privately, some Soviet ecologists were disappointed about the Soviet IBP feeling that the overall goal of multidisciplinary research leading to a better understanding of whole ecosystems or biogeocenoses was generally not attained, except perhaps for a small number of studies conducted by ecologists at the Institute of Animals and Plants in Sverdlovsk and research discussed earlier at Karachi and Kursk.

SOVIET CONTRIBUTIONS TO WORLD ECOLOGY

Russian and Soviet scientists have contributed greatly to the development of ecology. The work of Dokachaev, Gause, Ramensky, Ivlev, and others is internationally recognized and has stimulated the formation of several ecological disciplines. Insufficient time may have passed to identify with certainty major Soviet contributions since World War II; the passage of time makes generalization easier. However, during recent trips to the U.S.S.R., we asked many Soviet ecologists to identify the most important research papers and books that, in their opinion, have influenced or will influence world ecology. The lists were noticeably mixed as would be expected from a group of ecologists, but some consensus was evident. Books by Sukachev and Dylis (1964) and Rodin and Bazilevich (1965) were universally noted. The textbooks by Naumov (1963) and Shvartz (1970) were mentioned frequently by animal ecologists, and plant ecologists listed Sochava (1976) and Aleksandrova (1969). Statistical-quantitative ecologists universally referenced Vasilevich (1969*b*). Three new books (Ross 1975; Budyko 1977; Laisk 1977), although differing widely in scope, have recently caused considerable excitement among Soviet ecologists.

Soviet ecology has made at least three major contributions to world ecology in recent years. First, the Soviets are becoming the world's synthesizers of ecological research. The syntheses by Rodin and Bazilevich (1965) and Aleksandrova (1969) include all relevant research regardless of national origin. Rodin and Bazilevich (1965) include some 550 references with over 200 from outside the Soviet Union, with few relevant omissions (Major 1970). Perhaps it is only the Soviets who could perform the task of international synthesis, given that so few Western ecologists read Russian, and costs to translate even a small proportion of Soviet research into English would be prohibitive. The subsequent translation of Soviet syntheses into English has provided a global view of ecological research that would otherwise scarcely be available to Western ecologists.

Second, by combining their knowledge of the world's ecological literature with historic interest in linking ecology and geography, Soviet scientists have provided a much clearer view of the geographic variability of ecosystem parameters such as productivity and mineral-cycling patterns. To illustrate, Soviet ecologists computed early estimates of the productivity of the main world ecosystems (Bazilevich et al. 1971*a*, *b*, *c*; Bazilevich 1974; Rodin et al. 1975). Even though they estimated "potential" amounts that are high relative to actual estimates from resource inventories, the Soviet geographic syntheses have been extensively used and cited by Americans studying the effect of biota on the global carbon dioxide balance (Baes et al. 1977; Woodwell et al. 1978). The Soviet ecologists' extensive knowledge of soils suggests that future contributions may be made regarding soil carbon pool sizes, which are now only being estimated crudely.

Third, Soviet ecologists have not lost sight of the need to develop standardized classifications and maps based on strong theoretical principles. It is likely that our current difficulty in extrapolating beyond experimental sites could be improved by a greater emphasis on classification and mapping.

Aleksandrova's synthesis (1969) shows that there is still much to be learned, and that new developments will likely come from research at Soviet mapping laboratories.

ACKNOWLEDGMENTS

The authors thank Jack Major, of the University of California-Davis, and Leonid E. Rodin, of the Komarov Botanical Institute in Leningrad, for carefully reviewing the manuscript. The National Academy of Science, through the U.S.-U.S.S.R. Scientific Exchange Program, and the Department of Energy enabled the authors to travel to the Soviet Union and organize the material for this chapter.

REFERENCES CITED

All references are in Russian unless otherwise designated. Readers should realize, however, that some Soviet journals are routinely translated (e.g., Soviet Geography, Pochvovideniye), and therefore, some Russian references are also available in English. Titles of Soviet periodicals have been translated, but where they translate identically to the title of an English periodical (e.g., *Ecologiya* to *Ecology*), transliteration of the Russian has been used.

Abaturov, B. D. 1968. Importance of the digging activity of the mole (*Talpa europaea* L.) on soil cover and vegetation in broadleaf-fir forest. *Pedobiologia* 8:239–264.

______. 1972. The role of burrowing animals in the transport of mineral substances in the soil [in English]. *Pedobiologia* 12:261–266.

______ and G. V. Kuznetzov. 1976*a*. A study of the intensity of food consumption by rodents. *Zool. J.* 55:122–127.

______ and G. V. Kuznotzov. 1976*b*. Formation of secondary production of little susliks (*Citellus pygmaeus*). *Zool. J.* 55:1526–1537.

Aleksandrova, V. D. 1969. *Classification of vegetation. A survey of the principles of classification and the classification systems in the various schools of phytoceonology*. Leningrad: Nauka Publ.

______. 1975. *Statistical methods for the investigation of natural complexes*. Moscow: Nauka Publ.

______ and N. V. Matveyeva, eds. 1979. Arctic tundra and polar deserts of the Taimyr. Leningrad: Nauka Publ.

Alieva, G. A. and K. N. Gasanov. 1971. Cycling of ash elements in broadleaved forests of the south-east slope of the Greater Caucasus. In *Biological productivity and cycling of chemical elements in vegetation communities,* Soviet Academy of Sciences, pp. 255–258. Leningrad: Nauka Publ.

Aristovskaya, T. V. 1975. Numbers, biomass and productivity of soil bacteria. In *Resources of the biosphere,* Vol. 1., eds. L. E. Rodin and N. N. Smirnov, pp. 241–259. Leningrad: Nauka Publ.

Baes, C. F., Jr., H. E. Goeller, J. S. Olson, and R. M. Rotty. 1977. Carbon dioxide and climate: the uncontrolled experiment [in English]. *Am. Sci.* 65:310–320.

Barbashova, Z. I., ed. 1976. *Resources of the biosphere.* Vol. 3, Human Adapability. Leningrad: Nauka Publ.

Bauer, O. N. and N. N. Smirnov, eds. 1976. *Resources of the biosphere.* Vol. 2. Leningrad: Nauka Publ.

Bazilevich, N. I. 1974. Energy flow and biogeochemical regularities of the main world *ecosystems,* ed. P. Duvigneaud, pp. 354–353 [in English]. Paris: UNESCO. 182–185. [in English].

———, ed. 1975. Productivity of steppe, meadow and marsh communities of the forest-steppe. In *Resources of the biosphere,* Vol. 1, eds. L. E. Rodin and N. N. Smirnov, pp. 56–95. Leningrad: Nauka Publ.

———, A. V. Drozdov, and L. E. Rodin. 1971. World forest productivity, its basic regularities and relationship with climatic factors. In *Productivity of forest ecosystems,* ed. P. Duvigneaud, pp. 354–353 [in English]. Paris: UNESCO.

——— and L. E. Rodin. 1971. Geographical regularities in productivity and the circulation of chemical elements in the earth's main vegetation types. *Sov. Geogr.* 12:24–53.

———, L. E. Rodin, and N. N. Rozov. 1971. Geographical aspects of biological productivity. *Sov. Geogr.* 12:293–317.

——— and A. A. Titlyanova. 1978. Functional patterns of herbaceous ecosystems (some results of IBP work in the USSR and other countries). *J. Gen. Biol.* 34:34–51.

———, A. A. Titlyanova, V. V. Smirnov, L. E. Rodin, N. T. Nechaeva, and F. I. Levin. 1978. *Methods of the study of biological cycling in different natural zones.* Moscow: Mesyel Press.

Beklemishev, K. V. 1976. Some results of the Soviet marine studies for the IBP. In *Resources of the biosphere,* Vol. 2, eds. O. N. Bauer and N. N. Smirnov, pp. 56–59. Leningrad: Nauka Publ.

Bikov, B. A. 1960–1965. *Dominants in the vegetation cover of the Soviet Union.* 3 Vols. (I-1900, II-1962, III-1965). Alma-Ata.

Bobrinsky, N. A. 1946. *Geography of animals.* Moscow: Nauka Publ.

Budyko, M. I. 1977. *Global ecology.* Moscow: Mesyel Press.

Bychovsky, B. E. and O. N. Bauer. 1975. Participation of Soviet scientists in the studies for the IBP. In *Resources of the biosphere*, Vol. 1, eds. L. E. Rodin and N. N. Smirnov, pp. 5–11. Leningrad: Nauka Publ.

Chepurko, N. L., N. I. Bazilevich, L. E. Rodin, and Y. M. Miroshnichenko. 1972. Biogeochemistry and productivity of *Haloxyloneta ammondendroni* in the southeastern Kara-kum Desert. In *Eco-physiological foundation of ecosystem productivity in the arid zone*, ed. L. E. Rodin, pp. 198–202 [in English]. Leningrad: Nauka Publ.

Chernov, Y. I., ed. 1975. Soil invertebrates in the tundra of western Taimyr. Selected articles from *Biogeocoeneses of the Taimyr tundra and their productivity.* International Tundra Biome Translation 12, part 1 [in English]. University of Alaska.

Danilov, N. N. and V. N. Olshvang. 1976. Secondary productivity of the subarctic. In

Resources of the biosphere, Vol. 2, eds. O. N. Bauer and N. N. Smirnov, pp. 221–234. Leningrad: Nauka Publ.

DeAngelis, D., R. Gardner, and H. Shugart. In press. The Woodlands IBP data set. In *Woodlands IBP synthesis*, Vol I D. Reichel, ed. [in English]. Cambridge: Cambridge University Press.

Dolnik, V. P. 1975. *Migrational condition of birds.* Moscow: Nauka Publ.

Dylis, N. V. 1973. *On the structure of consortia. J. Gen. Biol.* 34:575–580.

______, V. I. Ermakov, and N. I. Pyavchenko, eds. 1976. *Current status and perspectives on the development of biogeocoenological investigations.* Petrozavodsk: Karelian Branch of Soviet Academy of Sciences.

______, L. V. Motorina, L. M. Nosova, N. I. Pyavchenko, and T. A. Rabotnov. 1974. On biogeocoenological investigations in the U.S.S.R. in 1972. *Ser. Biol.* 1:111–124.

Eckholm, E. P. 1976. *Losing ground* [in English]. New York: W. W. Norton & Co., Inc.

Edmondson, W. T. and G. G. Winberg, eds. 1971. *Productivity of freshwaters* [in English]. Warsaw-Krakow.

Ershov, A. P. 1975. *A history of computing in the U.S.S.R.* [in English]. Datamation 21:80–88.

Estonian Republic Committee for IBP. 1971. *Estonian contributions to the International Biological Program*. Progress Report III [in English]. Tartu.

Formozov, A. N. 1946. Snow cover as an integral factor of the environment and its importance in the ecology of mammals and birds. English translation, *Occas. Papers* 1, *Boreal Inst., Univ. of Alberta,* 1964.

Frey, T. 1966. Several aspects of the phytocoenological significance of species in the vegetation community. *Bot. J.* 51:1073–84.

______. 1971. Productivity of Norway spruce stands deserves a coordinated ecological study (Project PICEA). In *Estonian contributions to the IBP.* Progress Report III, ed. Estonian Republic Committee for the IBP, pp. 7–18 [in English]. Tartu.

Gasanov, K. N. 1966. Forest litter layer and its role in soil processes in forests of the southeast slope of the Greater Caucasus. *Papers of the Academy of Sciences of the Azerbaijan SSR.* No. 5:65–71.

Ghilarov, M. S. and Y. I. Chernov. 1975. Soil invertebrates in communities of the temperate zone. In *Resources of the biosphere,* Vol. 1, eds. L. E. Rodin and N. N. Smirnov, pp. 218–240. Leningrad: Nauka Publ.

Gilmanov, T. G. 1977. Plant submodel in the holistic model of a grassland ecosystem (with special attention to the belowground part) [in English]. *Ecol. Model.* 3:149–163.

______. 1978. *Mathematical modeling of biogeochemical cycles in grassland ecosystems.* Moscow: Moscow State University Press.

Golikov, A. N. and O. A. Skarlato. 1976. Results of studies of distribution patterns of life in the upper shelf zones of U.S.S.R. seas. In *Resources of the biosphere,* Vol. 2, eds. O. N. Bauer and N. N. Smirnov, pp. 95–105. Leningrad: Nauka Publ.

Gorchakovsky, P. L. and N. I. Andreyashkina. 1975. Studies in primary production of communities at the station "Harp." In *Resources of the biosphere,* Vol. 1, eds. L. E. Rodin and N. N. Smirnov, pp. 25–33. Leningrad: Nauka Publ.

Gortinsky, G. B., A. A. Molchanov, M. A. Abrazhko, A. D. Vakurov, I. I. Gusev, I. V. Zaboeva, U. N. Neshataev, V. V. Smirnov, and A. I. Utkin. 1975. Productivity of forests of the European part of the U.S.S.R. In *Resources of the biosphere*, Vol. 1, eds. L. E. Rodin and N. N. Smirnov, pp. 34–42. Leningrad: Nauka Publ.

Goryshina, T. K. 1974*a*. Investigations of biological productivity and its factors in forest-steppe oak < Les na Vorskle >. *Ekologiya* 3:5–10.

———, ed. 1974*b*. *Biological productivity and its factors in forest-steppe oak. Series of Biological Science No. 53.* Leningrad State University Press.

———. 1976. Research of biological productivity of the herbaceous cover in the oak-wood of the forest-steppe zone [in English]. *Pol. Ecol. Stud.* 2:135–145.

Green, A. M. and V. D. Utekhin. 1976. *Biota of the main geosystem of the central forest-steppe.* Moscow: Institute of Geography.

Grigoryev, A. A. 1946. *Principles of development and structure of geographic systems.* Moscow: Nauka Publ.

Gulisashvili, V. Z., L. B. Machatadze, and L. I. Prilipko. 1975. *Vegetation of the Caucasus.* Moscow: Nauka Publ.

Gunin, P. D. and V. P. Dyedkov. 1978. Ecological regimes of desert biogeocoenoses. Moscow: Nauka Publ.

Ilinski, A. P. 1937. *Vegetation of the earth.* Moscow-Leningrad: Academy of Sciences.

Ipatov, V. S. 1970. Certain problems of the theoretical organization of vegetation cover. *Bot. J.* 55:184–195.

———, L. A. Kurikova, and Y. I. Samoilov. 1974. Several methodological aspects of the construction of species' ecological amplitudes. *Ekologiya* 1:13–23.

Isakov, Y. A. and A. N. Formozov, eds. 1963. *Questions of ecological zoogeography.* Moscow: Geogr. Inst. Acad. Sci. USSR.

Karchnisky, N. A. 1971. Reasons for the widespread withering of forest plantations in the southeastern European U.S.S.R. and their renewal. *Pochvovedeniye* 3:99–114.

Karpov, V. G. 1969. *Experimental phytocoenology of dark-coniferous taiga.* Leningrad: Nauka Publ.

———, ed. 1973. *Structure and productivity of spruce forest of south taiga.* Leningrad: Nauka Publ.

Kashkarov, D. N. 1944. *Fundamentals of animal ecology.* Leningrad.

Kazimirov, N. I. and R. M. Morozova. 1973. *Biological cycling of material in spruce forests of Karelia.* Leningrad: Nauka Publ.

Kistchinski, A. A. 1974. Birds in subarctic ecosystems. In *Abstracts of 16th International Ornithological Congress, Canberra*, pp. 141–142 [in English].

———. 1976*a*. Basic elements of mountain faunas in northeast Siberia and northwest America: main stages of formation based on biogeographic evidence. In *Beringia in the Cenozoic,* pp. 368–375. Vladivostok: Far-Eastern Scientific Center of the USSR Acad. of Sci.

———. 1976*b*. Number and biomass of birds and their energy transformation in subarctic ecosystems. *Ekologiya* 5:71–78.

Konnov, A. A. 1974. *Juniper forests of Tadjikistan.* Dushanbe: Donish Press.

Kovalev, R. V., ed. 1974. *Structure, function and evolution of Baraba biogeocoenoses.* Vol. I. Novosibirsk: Nauka Publ.

Krivolutsky, D. A. 1975. Oribatid mite complexes as the soil type bioindicator. In *Progress in soil zoology*, pp. 217–221 [in English]. Prague: Academia Publ. House of the Czech. Acad. of Sci.

Kuchler, A. W. 1957. The new Soviet vegetation maps (book reviews) [in English]. *Ecology* 38:671.

Kuminova, A. V., ed. 1963. *Vegetation of steppe and forest-steppe zones of western Siberia*. Novosibirsk: Soviet Academy of Sciences.

______. 1971. Geobotanical investigations in western and central Siberia. Novosibirsk: Nauka Publ.

Kuznetzov, G. V. 1976. Energy metabolism of a population of little susliks in semi-deserts of the North Caspian region. *Zool. J.* 55:1061–1072.

Laasimer, L., ed. 1975. *Some aspects of botanical research in the Estonian S.S.R.* [in English]. Tartu: Acad. Sci. Estonian S.S.R.

Laisk, A. K. 1977. *Kinetics of photosynthesis and photorespiration of C_3 plants.* Moscow: Nauka Publ.

Larin, I. V. 1936. Material on the dynamics of vegetation mass and nutrient materials in grasslands during the growing season in different zones of the U.S.S.R. *Papers of the Inst. of Phys. Geogr., Soviet Academy of Sciences.* Vol. 21.

______. 1969. Biological and ecological principles of grassland management. pp. 14–56. in I. V. Larin, *Grassland and pasture management*, ed. Leningrad: Kolos Press. 549 pp.

Lavrenko, E. M. 1950. Map of the vegetation of the European part of the U.S.S.R. at a scale 1:2,500,000, plus explanatory text. Leningrad.

______, ed. 1977. *The vegetation and animal world of Mongolia.* Leningrad: Nauka Publ.

______ and I. V. Borisova, eds. 1976. Biocomplex investigations in Kazakhastan. Vol. III. Leningrad: Nauka Publ.

______ and N. V. Dylis. 1968. Achievements and current tasks in the investigation of terrestrial biogeocoenosus in the U.S.S.R. *Bot. J.* 53:155–168.

______ and A. A. Korchagin, eds. 1959, 1960, 1964, 1972, 1976. *Field geobotany.* 5 Vols. Leningrad: Nautka Publ.

______ and V. B. Sochava, eds. 1956. *Vegetation cover of the U.S.S.R.* Vols. 1 and 2. Leningrad: Soviet Academy of Sciences.

Levina, F. Y. 1971. *Geobotany in the Komarov Botanical Institute of the Academy of Sciences of the U.S.S.R.* (1922–1964). Leningrad: Nauka Publ.

______. 1978. *Geobotany in the Komarov Botanical Institute of the Academy of Sciences of the U.S.S.R.* (1965–1972). Leningrad: Nauka Publ.

Major, J. 1967. World maps of vegetation (book review) [in English]. *Ecology* 48:328–329.

______. 1970. Essay review of Rodin and Bazilevich: the illusive mineral equilibrium (book review) [in English]. *Ecology* 51:160–163.

______ 1975. Quantitative study of vegetation (book review) [in English]. *Ecology* 56:255–256.

Malinovsky, K. A., ed. 1975. Productivity of mountain communities in the U.S.S.R. In *Resources of the biosphere,* Vol. 1, eds. L. E. Rodin and N. N. Smirnov, pp. 167–198. Leningrad: Nauka Publ.

Marty, U. U., ed. 1974. *Biological productivity of the Caspian Sea.* Moscow: Nauka Publ.

McIntosh, R. P. 1967. The continuum concept of vegetation [in English]. *Bot. Rev.* 33:130–187.

Miroshnichenko., Y. M. 1974. *Biological productivity of the Association Haloxylon ammodendron-Carex physodes* in the eastern Kara-kum Desert. *Vegetation Resources* 10:329–336.

Molchanov, A. A. 1973. *Productivity of the organic mass of forests in the different natural zones*. Moscow: Nauka Publ.

———, ed. 1974. *Productivity of the organic and biological mass of forests*. Moscow: Nautka Publ.

———. 1975. *Oak forest steppe from a biogeocoenological perspective.* Moscow: Nauka Publ.

Molotovsky, U. I. and R. S. Kabilov. 1973. Moisture-salinity characteristics of soils in several phytocoenoses of the reserve Tigrovaya Balka. *Papers of the Tadjikistan S.S.R. Academy of Scineces, Branch of Biological Sciences.* 3:3–14.

Naumov, N. P. 1963. (1972) *The ecology of animals.* Moscow: Nauka. English translation by F. W. Plous, Jr., edited by N. D. Levine. Urbana: University of Illinois Press.

———. 1970. Advances of population concepts in animal ecology. In *Essays on the history of ecology,* eds. G. A. Novikov, S. S. Shvartz, and L. V. Chesnova, pp. 106–146. Moscow: Nauka Publ.

Nazimova, D. I. 1975. *Mountain dark-coniferous forests of Western Sayan*. Leningrad: Nauka Publ.

Nechayeva, N. T., ed. 1970. *Vegetation of the central Kara-kum and its productivity.* Ashkhabad: Ylym Publ.

Neyman, A. A. 1976. The Soviet studies of benthos of the open shelf during the IBP. In *Resources of the biosphere,* Vol. 2, eds. O. N. Bauer and N. N. Smirnov, pp. 106–116. Leningrad: Nauka Publ.

Nichiporovich, A. A. and I. A. Shulgin. 1976. Photosynthesis and assimilation of solar radiation energy. In *Resources of the biosphere,* Vol. 2, eds. O. N. Bauer and N. N. Smirnov, pp. 6–55. Leningrad: Nauka Publ.

Ovchinnikov, P. N., G. T. Sidorenko, and N. G. Kaletkina. 1973. *Vegetation of the Pamir-Alaia.* Dushanbe: Donish Press.

Panteleyev, P. A. and A. N. Terekhina. 1976. Investigation of internal population fluctuations of the vole. In *Fauna and ecology of rodents.* Issue 13. Moscow State University.

Pavlovsky, E. N. 1966. *Natural nidality of transmissible diseases, with special reference to the landscape epidemiology of zooanthropuses.* English translation by F. Plous, Jr., edited by N. D. Levine. Urbana: University of Illinois Press.

Petipa, T. S. 1976. Food relations of communities and functioning of marine ecosystems. In *Resources of the biosphere,* Vol. 2, eds. O. N. Bauer and N. N. Smirnov, pp. 60–75. Leningrad: Nauka Publ.

Petrov, O. V., ed. 1971. *Complex research of the forests on the Vorskla River.* Series of Biological Science No. 52. Leningrad State University Press.

Physical-geographical atlas of the world. 1964. Moscow: Soviet Academy of Sciences.

Pitelka, F. A. 1969. Ecological studies on the Alaskan arctic slope. [in English]. *Arctic* 22:333–340.

Pokarzhevsky, A. N. and D. A. Krivolutsky. 1975. The role of pedobionts in biogeochemical cycles of calcium and strontium 90 in the ecosystem. In *Pro-*

gress in soil zoology. pp. 249–254 [in English]. Prague: Academia Publ. House of the Czech. Acad. of Sci.

Ponyatovskaya, V. M. 1961. On two trends in phytocoenology [in English]. *Vegetatio* 10:373–385.

Pozdnyakov, L. K. 1975. Productivity of the forests of Siberia. In *Resources of the biosphere,* Vol. 1, eds. L. E. Rodin and N. N. Smirnov, pp. 43–55. Leningrad: Nauka Publ.

Rabotnov, T. A. 1972. Consortia, the importance of their study for phytocoenology [in English]. *Folia Geobot. Phytotaxon.* 7:1–8.

______. 1973. Several questions of the study of consortia. J. Gen. Biol. 34:407–416.

______. 1974. Consortia as the structural unit of the biogeocoenose. *Priroda,* pp. 26–35.

Rafes, P. M. 1970. Development of biogeocoenose theory. In *Essays on the history of ecology,* eds. G. A. Novikov, S. S. Shvartz, and L. V. Chesnova, pp. 147–194. Moscow: Nauka Publ.

Raney, F. C. 1965. Methods in geobotany (book review). [in English]. *Ecology* 46:570–571.

______. 1966. Field geobotany (book review) [in English]. *Ecology* 47:174.

Rashevsky, N. 1948. A Russian text of ecology (book review) [in English]. *Ecology* 29:394–395.

Rodin, L. E., ed. 1972. *Eco-physiological foundation of ecosystem productivity in the arid zone.* [in English]. Leningrad: Nauka Publ.

______, ed. 1975. Productivity of desert communities. In *Resources of the biosphere,* Vol. 1, eds. L. E. Rodin and N. N. Smirnov, pp. 128–166. Leningrad: Nauka Publ.

______, ed. 1977. *Productivity of vegetation in the arid zone of Asia.* Leningrad: Nauka Publ.

______, ed. 1978. *Management of vegetation in the arid zone of Asia.* Leningrad: Nauka Publ.

______ and N. I. Bazilevich. 1965 (1967). *Production and mineral cycling in terrestrial vegetation.* Leningrad: Nauka Publ. English translation by Scripta Technica Ltd., edited by G. E. Fogg. London: Oliver and Boyd.

______, N. I. Bazilevich, and N. N. Rozov. 1975. pp. 13–26, In *Productivity of world ecosystems,* eds. D. E. Reichle, J. F. Franklin, and D. W. Goodall [in English]. Washington, D.C.: National Academy of Sciences.

______ and N. N. Smirnov, eds. 1975. *Resources of the biosphere* Vol. 1. Leningrad: Nauka Publ.

Ross, J. K. 1975. *Radiation regime and architectonics of vegetation cover.* Leningrad: Hydromet Publ.

Rysin, L. P. 1975. *Pine forests of the European part of the U.S.S.R.* Moscow: Nauka Publ.

Safarov, I. S. and K. G. Djalilov. 1973. Biological productivity of Talish oak forests. *Lesovideneye* 3:40–46.

Schennikov, A. P. 1950. *The ecology of plants.* Moscow.

______. 1964. *Introduction to geobotany.* Leningrad State Univ. Press.

Scherbakov, I. P. 1975. *Forest cover of the northeastern U.S.S.R.* Novosibirsk: Nauka Publ.

Semina, G. T. 1976. Vertical distribution of phytoplankton in the typical biotopes of the open ocean. In *Resources of the biosphere*, Vol. 2, eds. O. N. Bauer and N. N. Smirnov, pp. 76–94. Leningrad: Nauka Publ.

Shamurin, V. F., V. D. Aleksandrova, and B. A. Tikhomirov. 1975. Primary production of tundra communities. In *Resources of the biosphere,* Vol. 1, eds. L. E. Rodin and N. N. Smirnov, pp. 12–24. Leningrad: Nauka Publ.

Shvartz, S. S. 1970. History of the major concepts of modern ecology. In *Essays on the history of ecology,* eds. G. A. Novikov, S. S. Shvartz, and L. V. Chesnova, pp. 89–105. Moscow: Nauka Publ.

______, V. N. Bolshakov, V. G. Olenev, and O. A. Pyastolova. 1969/1970. Population dynamics of rodents from northern and mountainous geographical zones. In *Energy flow through small mammal populations,* eds. K. Petrusewiez and L. Ryszkowski, pp. 205–220 [in English]. Warsaw: PWN, Polish Sci. Publ.

Smirnov, V. V. 1971. *Organic mass in some forest phytocoenoses in the European part of the U.S.S.R.* Moscow: Nauka Publ.

______ and S. G. Tokmakova. 1971. Preliminary data on the influence of different numbers of voles on forest tundra vegetation [in English]. *Ann. Zool. Fenn.* 8:154–156.

______ and S. G. Tokmakova. 1972. Influences of consumers on variation in natural production of phytocoenoses. In *Tundra Biome Proceedings IV International Meeting of the Biol. Prod. of Tundra. Stockholm*. pp. 122–127 [in English].

Sochava, V. B. 1948. Geographical relationships of the vegetation cover in the U.S.S.R. *Trans. Gertzen Pedagog. Inst.* (Leningrad) 3:3–51.

______, ed. 1970. *Topology of steppe ecosystems.* Leningrad: Nauka Publ.

______, ed. 1976. *Temporal studies of the steppe geosystem.* Novosibirsk: Nauka Publ.

Stanyukovich, K. V. 1973. *Mountain vegetation of the U.S.S.R. (a botanical-geographical outline).* Dushanbe: Donish Press.

Striganova, B. R. 1975. Dispersion patterns of diplopods and their activity in the litter decomposition in the Carpathian foothills. In: *Progress in soil zoology.* pp. 167–173. [in English]. Prague: Academia Publ. House of Czech. Acad. Sci.

______ and R. R. Rakhmanov. 1972. Comparative study of the feeding activity of diplopods in Lenkoran Provinces of Azerbaijan [in English]. *Pedobiologia* 12:430–433.

Sukachev. V. N. 1927. *Short handbook for the investigation of forest types.* Moscow.

______. 1956. Several modern problems in the study of the vegetation cover. *Bot. J.* 41:476–86.

______ and N. V. Dylis. 1964. (1968). *Funamentals of forest biogeocoenology.* English translation by J. M. MacLennan. Edinburgh: Oliver and Boyd, Ltd.

Tikhomirov, B. A. 1959. *Relationship of the animal world and plant cover of the tundra.* Bot. Inst. Acad. Sci. U.S.S.R.

______, ed. 1971. *Biogeocoenoses of Taimyr tundra and their productivity.* Leningrad: Nauka Publ.

Titlyanova, A. A. 1973. Exchange processes and balance of chemical elements in meadow biogeocoenoses. In: *Topological aspects of the study of behavior of matter in geosystems,* ed. V. Sochava. Irkutsk.

———. 1977. *The biological cycling of carbon in grassland biogeocoenoses.* Novosibirsk: Nauka Publ. (English translation edited by N. R. French, in press. Stroudsburg, PA.: Dowden, Hutchinson and Ross).

Trass, H. 1976. *Geobotany. History and contemporary trends of development.* Leningrad: Nauka Publ. (English translation edited by W. C. Johnson, in press. Stroudsburg, PA.: Dowden, Hutchinson and Ross Publ.)

Utkin, A. I. 1965. *Forests of Central Uakutia*. Moscow: Nauka Publ.

Vasilevich, V. I. 1963. An experiment of morphological analysis of the meadow continuum. *Bot. J.* 48:1653–1659.

———. 1966. Study of the continuity of the vegetation cover. *Trans. Moscow Soc. Naturalists* 27:59–69.

———. 1967. Continuum in coniferous-small leaved forests of Karelia. *Bot. J.* 52:45–53.

———. 1969*a*. Continuum concept of vegetation: responses [in English]. *Bot. Rev.* 35:321–322.

———. 1969*b*. *Statistical methods in geobotany.* Leningrad: Nauka Publ.

———. 1970*a*. Method of autocorrelation for the study of vegetation dynamics. *Trans. Moscow Soc. Nat.* 38:17–23.

———. 1970*b*. The spatial homogeneity of plant communities and methods of estimation. *Bot. J.* 55:376–385.

———, ed. 1971. *L. G. Ramensky—collected works, problems and methods of the study of the vegetation cover.* Leningrad: Nauka Publ.

———. 1972. Methods of estimating the correlation between abundant species. *Trans. Moscow Soc. Nat. Biology Branch* 77:139–144.

Vavilov, N. I. 1957. *Agroecological survey of principle field crops.* Moscow-Leningrad: U.S.S.R. Academy of Sciences Publ.

Voronov, A. G. 1973. *Geobotany.* 2d ed., revised and supplemented. Moscow: Higher Education Press.

Vtorov, P. P. and V. M. Makeev. 1976. Characterizing a territory as a first step in biosphere evaluation (example for a study of the Babatag Mountain Range). In *Scientific elements of nature conservation*, ed. E. E. Syroyetchkovski, pp. 5–77. Moscow: Central Laboratory of Nature Conservation, U.S.S.R. Ministry of Agriculture.

Whittaker, R. H. 1962. Classification of natural communities [in English]. *Bot. Rev.* 28:1–239.

Winberg, G. G. 1969. Energy flow in aquatic ecosystems [in English]. *IBP News* 12:21–24.

———. 1970. Energy flow in aquatic ecological systems [in English]. *Pol. Arch. Hydrobiol.* 17:11–19.

———. 1976. Results of studies in productivity of freshwater communities of all trophic levels In *Resources of the biosphere,* Vol. 2, eds. O. N. Bauer, and N. N. Smirnov, Leningrad: Nauka Publ.

——— and O. N. Bauer. 1971. Biological productivity of continental waters in the U.S.S.R. *Bull. Moscow Soc. Nat.* 76:34–45.

Woodwell, G. M., R. H. Whittaker, W. A. Reiners, G. E. Likens, C. C. Delwiche, and D. B. Botkin. 1978. The biota and the world carbon budget [in English]. *Science* 199:141–146.

Yablonskaya, E. A. 1976. Studies in trophic interrelations of bottom communities of the southern seas. In *Resources of the biosphere,* Vol. 2, eds O. N. Bauer and N. N. Smirnov, pp. 117–144. Leningrad: Nauka Publ.

Yaroshenko, P. D. 1961. *Geobotany.* Leningrad: Nauka.

Yurkevich, I. D. and E. P. Yaroshevich. 1974. *Biological productivity of types and associations of pine forests.* Minsk: Nauka and Technica Publ.

Zapryagaeva, V. I. 1976. *Forest resources of the Pamir-Alai.* Leningrad: Nauka Publ.

Zimina, R. P. and M. C. Saint-Giron. 1976. Comparative characteristics of the biogeography of the Alps and the Caucasus. In *Biogeography and soil geography*. ed. I. P. Gerasimov, pp. 57–61 [in French].

Zlotin, R. I. 1969. Zonal patterns of biomass of soil invertebrates in the open landscapes of the Russian plain. In *Problems of soil zoology*. pp. 75–77. Moscow.

______ and K. S. Khodashova. 1973. Effect of animals on the autotrophic component of the nutrient cycle. In *Problems of biogeocoenology*. pp. 105–117. Moscow.

______ and K. S. Khodashova. 1974. *The role of animals in biological cycling of forest-steppe ecosystems.* Moscow: Nauka. (English translation edited by N. R. French, in press. Stroudsburg, PA.: Dowden, Hutchinson and Ross).

Oceania

21

AUSTRALIA

Raymond L. Specht

INTRODUCTION

In an island-continent the size of Australia (7.7 million km^2), with a population only recently exceeding 13.5 million, ecological studies have been undertaken by a small band of research workers located in the eight capital cities. The task was formidable. Most ecological research in Australia has been tackled by individuals rather than by teams. Consequently, only a portion of an ecosystem has been studied in any project, initially at a descriptive level. In a few cases, some dynamic processes within the ecosystem have been investigated over a period of time. More recently, a few multidisciplinary studies have attempted integration at the ecosystem level.

EMERGENCE OF ECOLOGY IN AUSTRALIA

Even though Australia is located on the opposite side of the world from Europe, the cradle of ecological thought, its scientists have by no means been isolated. Early in the twentieth century, Ludwig Diels, of the Berlin Herbarium, visited southwestern Australia and wrote a comprehensive treatise on the *Pflanzenwelt von West-Australien* (1906). Karel Domin, of the Czechoslovak University, Prague, collected extensively in Queensland and presented a paper (1911) on the plant associations of Queensland and their ecological relationships. Members of the British Association for the Advancement of Science held their 1914 meeting in Australia and thus stimulated several

Australian botanists to write ecological reports on the vegetation of the continent. Lilian S. Gibbs, a British ecologist/explorer, climbed Mount Kinabalu in Borneo (1910), the Arfak Mountains in New Guinea (1913), Bellenden Ker in north Queensland (1914), and the mountain summits of Tasmania (1914) as part of her studies on the "Antarctic element" in the Australasian flora (Gibbs 1917, 1921). W. A. Cannon, of the Carnegie Institution of Washington, D.C., visited Australia in 1918 to further his studies on arid-zone vegetation (Cannon 1921). During 1922, R. S. Adamson, with a grant from the Royal Society of London, spent six months with T. G. B. Osborn, of the Department of Botany, University of Adelaide; during that time, Adamson and Osborn examined the arid-zone vegetation at Ooldea and the ecology of the forest vegetation of the Mount Lofty Ranges.

The visits of international experts in the new discipline of ecology, plus the initiation of the *Journal of Ecology* in 1913, stimulated a number of Australian botanists who, after World War I, turned their attention to the study of Australian plant communities. A. A. Hamilton (1917) of the Botanic Gardens, Sydney, appears to have been the first botanist to use the word *ecology,* in studying the salt marsh vegetation around Port Jackson, New South Wales. Before long, many authors were using the term—Adamson and Osborn (1922 and 1924) and Ising (1922) in Adelaide, and Collins (1923), the Linnean Macleay Fellow in Botany, at the University of Sydney. In 1923, the Sydney University Botanical Society initiated an ecological study of the vegetation of Mount Wilson (Brough et al. 1924), in which the authors stressed the point that, although the study of plant ecology had developed with great rapidity in Britain, on the Continent, and in America, little ecology had been undertaken in New South Wales, despite the fact that innumerable fascinating and important problems existed.

Plant ecology in Australia emerged during the 1920s and has continued to expand since then (Table 21.1). The discipline has been strongly developed in South Australia, New South Wales, and Queensland and in the last two decades has spread to all states.

Animal ecology lagged behind plant ecology throughout the world (Specht 1976). Although many early studies on insect and vertebrate pests should probably be classed under the discipline of ecology, it was not until the appearance of Charles Elton's stimulating book, *Animal Ecology,* in 1927 that formal works on animal ecology emerged in Australia. Both the Council of Scientific and Industrial Research (CSIR), Division of Economic Entomology at Canberra (established 1927) and the entomology department within the Waite Agricultural Research Institute, at Adelaide (established by Act of Parliament, December 1927) were concerned with the relationships between weather conditions and outbreaks of insect pests. Over a period of years, systematic records were made of the seasonal behavior of the more important economic insects, and this information was related to climatic control. J.

Table 21.1. **Plant Ecological Studies, Other Than Regional Surveys, Conducted in the Seven States and Territories of Australia from 1916 to 1975[a].**

State/Territory	1916–1925	1926–1935	1936–1945	1946–1955	1956–1965	1966–1975
New South Wales and Australian Capital Territory	8	7	22	24	51	445
Northern Territory	—	—	—	1	18	9
Queensland	4	15	15	22	34	272
South Australia	10	13	6	8	26	36
Tasmania	2	3	2	3	3	9
Victoria	3	9	8	6	17	45
Western Australia	3	3	6	12	16	90
Total	30	50	59	76	165	906[b]

[a]Data up to 1961 extracted from Specht and Specht 1962; after 1961, compiled from a recent survey.

[b]The figures for 1966–1975 include about 350 publications dealing with the autecology of weeds and crop and pasture plants.

Davidson of the Waite Institute summarized his ecological approach to the seasonality of insect populations in articles published in 1933 and 1935. A. J. Nicholson, of the CSIR, was concerned with the ecological balance of animal populations (Nicholson 1933; Nicholson and Bailey 1935).

Until the 1950s, most research in terrestrial animal ecology in Australia was confined to the study of insect pests. After that date, studies on vertebrates of economic importance developed. Many Australian zoologists ignored the land and focused their attention on marine intertidal ecology.

Australian ecologists have kept in touch with European and American research through the wide range of ecological journals acquired by most libraries. As only limited postgraduate training was provided by Australian universities until the 1950s, many Australian scientists studied for their Ph.D. abroad. Regular study leave was, and still is, encouraged for research staff at the universities. Research organizations such as CSIRO (formerly CSIR, established in 1926) and some state government organizations have encouraged overseas visits by ecologists, sometimes to work in another laboratory for an extended period. In this way, there was a continual influx from abroad of current thought on the discipline of ecology.

DEVELOPMENT OF ECOLOGY IN AUSTRALIA

Regional Surveys

Australia was first settled by Europeans in 1788, less than 200 years ago. Since then, botanists and zoologists have been active in exploring the continent, collecting and studying its diverse and fascinating flora and fauna. New impetus to this phase of biology has been given to taxonomists in museums, herbaria, and universities by the establishment in 1977 of the Australian Biological Resources Study (Ride 1978). As part of this study of the taxonomy of Australian animals and plants, detailed studies of the ecology of certain species and regions are being encouraged, including vegetation mapping of the state of Western Australia, and surveys of the Prince Regent and Drysdale River areas of northwest Western Australia and of Cape York Peninsula, Queensland, all of which are areas little-known biologically.

Long before this current program to survey australian biological resources, regional surveys were initiated that aimed at defining and mapping the vegetation of sections of the continent and interrelating the plant communities to dominant environmental factors (climate, soils, animals) (Table 21.2). A strong school developed between 1920 and 1955 in the University of Adelaide, initially in the botany department but later combined with the agronomy department and Soils Division of CSIR, both in the Waite Agricultural Research Institute of the University of Adelaide. The impetus was an academic interest in the landscape, strengthened by (a) problems of overgraz-

Table 21.2. **Regional Surveys of Plant Communities and Their Ecology, Conducted in the Seven States and Territories of Australia and in Papua New Guinea from 1916 to 1975**

State/Territory	1916–1925	1926–1935	1936–1945	1946–1955	1956–1965	1966–1975
Papua New Guinea	—	—	—	—	4	12
New South Wales and Australian Capital Territory	—	—	1	4	3	3
Northern Territory	—	—	—	2	4	4
Queensland	—	—	1	3	6	19
South Australia	5	2	6	10	6	8
Tasmania	—	—	3	1	2	1
Victoria	—	—	2	1	3	24[a]
Western Australia	—	—	1	1	6	18
Total	5	2	14	22	30	77

[a]Including eight reports by the Land Conservation Council of Victoria surveying 104,000 km^2 (45 percent) of that state.

ing and soil erosion in the northern arid zone of the state and (b) land development in the southern humid zone following the discovery that much of this zone could be converted to pasture, crop, and forest by the correction of trace element deficiencies.

Ecological surveys in other states developed during the 1930s and 1940s in response to soil erosion problems in the arid zone that had been accentuated by drought and overgrazing (Zimmer 1937, in northwest Victoria; Blake 1938, in Western Queensland; and Beadle 1948, in western New South Wales) and in the Australian Alps (Costin 1954). Patton (1933–1951) in the University of Melbourne developed a series of ecological studies of eight major plant communities characteristic of Victoria.

A surprising area of landscape in southern Australia was studied by individual ecologists both in university and government departments; the contributions of C. D. Boomsma, J. E. Coaldrake, R. L. Crocker, R. W. Jessup, R. A. Perry, R. L. Specht, and J. G. Wood are worthy of mention. After World War II, the CSIRO (then CSIR) initiated a section, under C. S. Christian, for land research and regional survey in northern Australia, an activity later extended to Papua New Guinea. Instead of sending a lone ecologist into the field, a balanced team of experts was assembled: a plant ecologist, geomorphologist, and pedologist, supported by a climatologist with or without a hydrologist. The aim of the team was to map land systems, patterns of topography, soils, and vegetation that recurred over considerable areas of land (Christian 1952). Air photo interpretation, followed by extensive ground control, formed the basis of the surveys. Since 1946, the multidisciplinary teams have surveyed some 2,135,000 km^2 of the Australian landscape (28 percent of the continent) and 151,000 km^2 of Papua New Guinea (32 percent of that country). Many distinctive plant communities in northern humid and central arid Australia have been defined and their ecological relationships with environmental factors described (CSIRO 1952–1977).

In the 1960s, the Victorian Soil Conservation Authority (under R. G. Downes and later A. Mitchell) adopted the land system approach to the study of the landscape of Victoria. Fifteen major surveys have been completed, over an area totalling 142,300 km^2, 62 percent of the state.

The Queensland Department of Primary Industries (formerly the Department of Agriculture and Stock) which, over the years, had worked in close cooperation with the CSIRO land survey teams, embarked on its own survey of western Queensland, using plant ecologists, pedologists, and others on its staff. Part I of the report on the western arid region of Queensland, covering 15 million hectares, was published in 1974 (Queensland Dept. of Primary Industries 1974). Parts II–IV, embracing a further 65 million hectares, will be completed by the end of 1981.

In recent years, a Vegetation Survey of Western Australia has been initiated. Since 1972, two maps have been published by F. G. Smith, of the

Western Australian Department of Agriculture, and eighteen maps by J. S. Beard (1974–1976), supported by grants from mining companies and the Australian Biological Resources Study. The vegetation of most of Western Australia has now been mapped at scales of 1:1,000,000 and 1:250,000 (Ride 1978).

The large task of synthesizing all these regional surveys into a vegetation map of Australia was undertaken by Williams (1955) and Carnahan (1976) for the *Atlas of Australian Resources,* first and second series, respectively, published by the Department of National Resources, Canberra. Crocker and Wood (1947), Keast et al. (1959), Burbidge (1960), and Keast (1980) made assessments of the phytogeography of the Australian region as more floristic and ecological data became available.

The problem of establishing a satisfactory network of reserves conserving representative Australian ecosystems has fostered the idea of an ecological survey of Australia. In 1975, the CSIRO Division of Land Use Research (formerly the Division of Land Research and Regional Survey) embarked on a feasibility study of the project using LANDSAT imagery. The state of South Australia, with many detailed ecological studies already published, was selected as a trial area. The state was divided into eight provinces, and interpretations of LANDSAT images were made with ground survey; close liaison was maintained with the ecological survey team developed in the South Australian Department of Environment. The multi-volumed *Environments of South Australia* has been published recently (Laut et al. 1977).

Local Surveys

Regional surveys aimed at showing Australian vegetation and its environmental interrelations in perspective. As a result, an overview of the structure and composition of the major plant communities and their ecological relationships has been achieved. Much of the work has been tackled by CSIRO, state government research groups (agriculture, forestry, soil, and nature conservation departments) and, to a lesser extent, by university groups. The University of Adelaide "school of regional survey" (1920–1955) could be regarded as an exception among Australian universities.

Most university departments adopted a less ambitious approach to plant ecology; their studies can be classed as "local surveys." Groups or individual research workers organized expeditions to interesting areas, described the vegetation, often in detail, and appended some notes on the climate and soils of the area. Often, little more could be gained from the study because the area was so small that little of a significant pattern could be distinguished. A considerable number of descriptive papers resulted from this approach (Table 21.1).

Many of the local surveys produced valuable statistical data, but the subdivision of vegetation into plant communities by Australian ecologists was largely subjective. The rigid classificatory techniques of the Zurich-Montpellier school of phytosociology went virtually unnoticed. However, in 1953, D. W. Goodall, of the University of Melbourne, published on the use of positive interspecific correlation for the classification of vegetation, based on his studies of the Victorian mallee communities (Goodall 1953). Computing by hand or by slow electric calculators deterred most plant ecologists from using Goodall's revolutionary classificatory technique, although Patricia Rayson (1957) and Helene A. Martin (1961) used the technique as a tool in their ecological studies.

In England, W. T. Williams adapted and modified Goodall's classificatory technique for high-speed computer (Williams and Lambert 1959, 1960). On his appointment to the CSIRO in Australia in 1966, he developed classificatory strategies even further with the assistance of G. N. Lance, Chief of the CSIRO Division of Computing Research (e.g., Lance and Williams 1968).

The availability of such high-speed classificatory techniques caused a virtual explosion of ecological papers on local survey, mostly by young graduates who had little understanding of the "magic classificatory package." In many cases, the cynical ecologist would point out that the techniques only showed the obvious; often, various classificatory techniques had to be tried until one technique agreed with a subjective decision. This may be just criticism for relatively simple plant communities, but one of the greatest contributions of the techniques is to the clearer definition of structure and pattern in rain forests of eastern Australia (L. J. Webb et al. 1970, of the CSIRO, Rain Forest Ecology Unit, Brisbane). Biogeographic patterns in the distribution of birds throughout Australia have also been defined (Kikkawa and Pearse 1969).

Nevertheless, the classificatory techniques still produced only descriptive studies. They are only tools to define the limits and nature of a plant community and are not concerned with processes nor with integration at the ecosystem level.

"Process ecology" in Field and Laboratory

The continent of Australia extends from the tropics to the cool temperate region of the Southern Hemisphere. Rainfall tends to be markedly seasonal—in summer in the monsoonal north, in winter in the Mediterranean south, and much more uniformly distributed on the eastern coast. However, only the northern, eastern, and southern coastal areas may be classified as humid; the continent becomes more and more arid toward the center, though never less than a mean annual rainfall of 100 mm. Seasonal and long-term water deficit is thus a major problem in Australian ecology.

Over much of the continent, many of the soils are remnants of ancient soils formed during the seasonal subtropical climate of the Tertiary. Most plant nutrients have been leached from the soil profiles. Water and mineral deficiencies thus create frequent stress conditions in Australian ecosystems. The larger Australian herbivores, such as kangaroos, which evolved with the nutrient-poor ecosystems, exert a minor grazing pressure on the native vegetation; cattle, sheep, horses, and rabbits, introduced by European settlers, have imposed a major grazing stress on the ecosystems for the first time in their long period of evolution.

The coincidence of these environmental stresses (water, nutrients and, more recently, grazing) in Australian ecosystems appears to be unique in the world. Australian ecologists, in order to provide advice on the long-range management of the ecosystems of the continent, must understand the processes operating within these ecosystems. These scientists cannot borrow ideas from studies on similar ecosystems overseas because such ecosystems do not exist.

The ecological processes to be investigated have to be defined and field experiments testing various hypotheses carefully designed. The experiments need to be sustained over relatively long periods before results emerge. The continuity of such long-range research is difficult to maintain in the university environment in which the staff is highly mobile; long-range research may be easier in government research organizations where staff are more permanent, but is not encouraged because of the need to produce results. Long-term research investigating the effect of grazing on ecosystems has been initiated as follows:

1925: *Atriplex-Maireana* shrub steppes (regeneration following exclosure) on Koonamore Vegetation Reserve (now the T. G. B. Osborn Reserve), by the botany department, University of Adelaide, South Australia. (Initiated by T. G. B. Osborn, J. G. Wood, and T. G. Paltridge). See Osborn et al. (1932, 1935), Wood (1936), Hall et al. (1964).

1937: *Maireana* shrub steppe (grazing trial) on Yudnapinna Station, by the agronomy department, Waite Agriculture Research Institute, South Australia. (Initiated by H. C. Trumble and K. Woodroffe).

1941: *Astrebla* tussock grassland (grazing and exclosure trial), Gilruth Plains, Cunnamulla, Queensland, by CSIRO Division of Plant Industry, Canberra.

1945: *Poa* tussock grassland and alpine heathland (regeneration following exclosure) on Bogong High Plain, Victoria, by the botany department, University of Melbourne and Victorian Soil Conservation Authority, Victoria. (Initiated by J. S. Turner and S. G. M. Carr). See Carr and Turner (1959).

1954: *Atriplex* shrub steppe on Fowlers Gap, near Broken Hill, New South Wales, by the botany department, University of New England (later by the geography department, University of New South Wales). (Initiated by N. C. W. Beadle).

1965: *Acacia aneura* (mulga) tall shrubland transect (effect of grazing), Charleville, Queensland, by the Queensland Department of Primary Industries, Charleville Pastoral Laboratory. (Initiated by W. H. Burrows and I. F. Beale).

Early in the 1950s, several experiments were established in various parts of Australia to study the effect of fire on *Eucalyptus* forest ecosystems. At least one of these long-term experiments is still in progress.

1952–1953: *Eucalyptus maculata–E. drepanophylla* open forest (fire ecology—unburnt, annual, 3-year cycle) near Maryborough, Queensland, by the Queensland Department of Forestry. (Initiated by N. B. Henry).

Long-term studies on population dynamics within open forest (dominated by species of *Eucalyptus, Acacia, Callitris*) and tropical-subtropical rain forest ecosystems have been initiated. Alpine-subalpine communities, and recently wetlands in the monsoonal north of Australia, have been included.

1949–1973: Victorian *Eucalyptus* forests (regeneration plots), Wallaby Creek, 1949–1952; Kinglake West, 1964; Wilson's Promontory, 1964; Lake Mountain, 1966; Brisbane Ranges, 1968; Melton, 1969; Ocean Grove, 1973; Mount Donna Buang, 1970 by the botany department, University of Melbourne. (Initiated by D. H. Ashton (1976) and postgraduate students).

1949: *Eucalyptus pilularis–E. grandis* open forest (thinning experiment), Pine Creek State Forest near Coffs Harbour, New South Wales by the Australian Forestry School, Canberra. (Initiated by M. R. Jacobs).

1953: Subtropical rain forest (population dynamics), Wian Wian State Forest, northern New South Wales by CSIRO, Rainforest Ecology Unit and Division of Soils, Brisbane. (Initiated by L. J. Webb, J. G. Tracey, G. B. Stirk, and R. Trebble).

1957: Alpine-subalpine plant communities (population dynamics), Kosciusko National Park, New South Wales by CSIRO, Division of Plant Industry, Canberra. (Initiated by A. B. Costin). See Wimbush and Costin (1979).

1958: Subtropical rain forest (regeneration studies), Mount Glorious, Queensland by CSIRO, Rainforest Ecology Unit, Brisbane. (Initiated by L. J. Webb and J. G. Tracey).

1963: Subtropical rain forest (population dynamics), Lamington National Park, Queensland by CSIRO, Rainforest Ecology Unit, Brisbane. (Initiated by J. H. Connell, L. J. Webb, and J. G. Tracey).

1963: Tropical rain forest (population dynamics), Davies Creek, Lamb Range, North Queensland by CSIRO, Rainforest Ecology Unit, Brisbane. (Initiated by J. H. Connell, L. J. Webb, and J. G. Tracey).

1963: *Acacia harpophylla* (brigalow) open forest (regeneration study), Theodore, Queensland by the Queensland Department of Primary Industries, Brigalow Research Station. (Initiated by R. W. Johnson).

1975: Wetland ecosystems (study on the interaction of feral animals with indigenous flora and fauna), Kapalga, between the West and South Alligator Rivers, Northern Territory by CSIRO, Division of Wildlife Research.

Long-term research on mineral nutrition of ecosystems was initiated on Dark Island heathland near Keith, South Australia in 1950 by the botany department, University of Adelaide (Specht 1963; Heddle and Specht 1975). Less extensive studies were initiated at Beerwah, Queensland in 1952 (Connor and Wilson 1968) and transferred to North Stradbroke Island, Queensland in 1968 (Specht et al. 1977).

Studies on water balance in plant communities have not been continued over the long periods of time involved in experiments concerned with grazing and mineral nutrition. The water balance of heathlands has been studied by Specht (1957) in South Australia and Specht and Jones (1971) in Victoria; of eucalyptus open forest in the Mount Lofty Ranges, South Australia by Martin and Specht (1962); of mulga tall shrubland by Slatyer (1965) and Turner (1965) at Alice Springs, Northern Territory, and by Pressland (1976) at Charleville, Queensland. Of particular note is the long-term hydrologic study, before and after the disastrous 1939 bushfire, of the *Eucalyptus regnans* (mountain ash) forests on the Melbourne and Metropolitan Board of Works, Water Catchment Reserve at Maroondah, Victoria (Langford 1976). A paper by Specht (1972*a*) attempted to summarize the water use of perennial evergreen plant communities in Australia.

To develop a clear understanding of the behavior of the ecosystems under long-term experimental study, it is necessary to appreciate the seasonal behavior (the growth and flowering rhythms) and the structural changes (cyclical processes) that may occur during the life cycle of the plant community. Since the 1950s, such supporting research has been developed in the botany departments of the University of Adelaide (heathlands under R. L. Specht and arid-zone plants under R. L. Lange), University of Melbourne (eucalyptus forests, *Acmena* and *Nothofagus* rain forests under D. H. Ashton), Australian National University (subalpine communities to lowland eucalyptus forest under R. O. Slayter); University of Queensland (eucalyptus forests and heathlands under R. L. Specht and others), and University of Western Australia (arid-zone and heathland plants under B. J. Grieve).

In a few research centers, laboratory studies on mineral nutrition and water relations of key native plant species have been initiated. The botany department, University of Adelaide, continued active research in both these fields from 1920 to 1960, with studies of the water relations of arid-zone and heathland plants, the phosphorus nutrition of heathland plants, and the sodium nutrition of arid-zone plants supervised by J. G. Wood and later R. L. Specht. Similar ecophysiological studies on mineral nutrition and water balance were developed in the botany department, University of Sydney, between 1950 and 1960 under N. C. W. Beadle (1953, 1968). Physiological studies on the water relations of arid-zone and heathland plants were developed in the botany department, University of Western Australia, under B. J. Grieve and in the CSIRO Division of Land Research and Regional Survey under R. O. Slayter. After 1960, the mobility of staff and young graduates around Australia ensured a steady trickle of these ecophysiological studies.

Study of the ecological significance of community structure on the interception and utilization of solar energy by crops and pastures was a highlight of the agronomy department, Waite Agricultural Research Institute, during the 1950s and 1960s under C. M. Donald and J. N. Black (see Davidson and Donald 1958, among others). This fostered further work in this field in Canberra, Melbourne, and Brisbane. Multidisciplinary studies were initiated as part of the International Biological Program (IBP) between biometerologists and ecologists interested in community structure and dynamics. The studies strongly influenced Australian ecologists concerned with the analysis of structure of native plant communities; a significant advance in the classification of plant communities resulted. The conclusions of an IBP working group were presented in the fourth edition of *The Australian Environment* by Specht (1970).

Conservation

The conservation movement, since its initiation at the turn of the century, has been actively supported by taxonomists and ecologists. In 1959, the Australian Academy of Science, National Parks Committee, with M. F. Day as chairman, initiated an Australia-wide survey of national parks and nature reserves. A number of important state reports resulted and eventually, in 1968, Australian Academy of Science Report No. 9, *National Parks and Reserves in Australia,* was published. The state committees, and the widespread work they undertook in each state, came at a critical time in nature conservation activities in Australia. The establishment of the Australian Conservation Foundation in 1965, largely due to the drive and wisdom of Dr. F. N. Ratcliffe, was one of the many results of these activities.

Conservation studies on the plant communities in South Australia (Specht and Cleland 1961) and in Victoria (Frankenberg 1971) formed part of the program of the Academy's National Parks Committee. These surveys were expanded in 1964 under the aegis of the IBP to cover the whole continent of Australia and Papua New Guinea. The cooperative work of many biologists enabled a comprehensive report to be published, *Conservation of Major Plant Communities in Australia and Papua New Guinea* (Specht et al. 1974). A strong plea to create a national system of ecological reserves in Australia has been made by the Australian Academy of Science (Fenner 1975). Already, much research toward this aim has been initiated at federal and state levels.

Regional survey and ecological research toward wise management of conservation areas have emerged in the last decade as a major function of the state national parks and wildlife services.

Ecosystem Studies

Although the concept of an ecosystem was clearly defined by Tansley as long ago as 1935, it was not until the development of high-speed computers that ecosystem studies, in toto, became feasible. The IBP (1964–1974) promoted the study of ecosystems throughout the world. Australia, although lacking sufficient funds, made some contributions to the ecosystem program. Among these are: arid-zone grazing study at Alice Springs, North Territory by CSIRO Rangeland Ecology Unit; grassland ecosystem study at Uralla, New South Wales by CSIRO Division Plant Industry (Pastoral Research Laboratory, Armidale); grassland ecosystem study in Shoalhaven area, New South Wales by CSIRO Division Plant Industry (Ecology Unit).

Projects that predated IBP (during the 1950s) but lacked the support of ecosystem modellers and high-speed computers were: Dark Island heathland studies near Keith, South Australia by the botany department, University of Adelaide; mulga shrubland studies near Alice Springs, North Territory by CSIRO Division of Land Research and Regional Survey, Canberra.

The studies on the mulga ecosystem made by ecologists at the Queensland Department of Primary Industry, Charleville Pastoral Laboratory (established 1966) could form the basis of an ecosystem study. The series of studies on the soils, vegetation, and fauna of the coastal lowland of southeastern Queensland, made by ecologists of the University of Queensland and CSIRO, would be ideal for integration.

Population Ecology

The threat of weeds and insect and vertebrate pests to Australian agriculture and forestry has been a constant stimulus to ecological research, aimed at biological control.

Insects

Australia probably produced the classic example of biological control when the cochineal insect (*Cactoblastis cactorum*) was introduced to exterminate the prickly pear (*Opuntia stricta* and *O. inermis*), which had been introduced from Central and South America and had invaded some 250,000 km^2 of New South Wales and Queensland. Destruction of prickly pear had been urged by the Queensland state government entomologist, Henry Tryon, as far back as 1899. In 1912, the Prickly Pear Travelling Commission (H. Tryon and T. H. Johnson) sent back cochineal insects from Ceylon, which, in a few years, destroyed the species of prickly pear (*O. monacantha*) that had invaded northern Queensland. These species of cochineal insects from Ceylon would not attack *Opuntia inermis* or *O. stricta,* however. In 1920, the Commonwealth government, with the New South Wales Department of Agriculture and the Queensland Prickly Pear Land Commission, renewed the attack on the prickly pear. In 1925, the eggs of *Cactoblastis cactorum* were sent from Argentina; the caterpillars thrived only on the prickly pear and rapidly destroyed the extensive infestation. The success of *Cactoblastis* against the prickly pear stimulated research into many pest and weed populations with a view to biological control.

The newly formed Council for Scientific and Industrial Research established a Division of Economic Entomology in 1927. Initial projects involved the underground grass-grubs in Tasmania, the buffalo-fly pest, insect pests of dried fruit, codling moth, lucerne flea in South Australian pastures, sheep blowfly pest, and the biological control of ragwort (*Senecio jacobea*) and Saint-John's wort (*Hypericum perforatum*). By 1949, the Division of Economic Entomology (now the CSIRO Division of Entomology) was still concerned with most of these initial problems, but had added plague locusts and grasshoppers, earth-mites, cattle ticks, and termites to their list of problems.

The same problems still existed in the 1970s and bush flies, forest insects, and orchard pests were added to the list. The biological control of *Lantana,* skeleton weed (*Chondrilla juncea*), and other pest species is being tackled. For example, dung beetles had been introduced into Australia to speed the decomposition of cattle droppings and to reduce the buffalo-fly problem.

The entomology department, established by Act of Parliament within the Waite Agricultural Research Institute in December 1927, tackled pest problems pertinent to South Australia, often in close cooperation with the CSIR Division of Economic Entomology.

From these studies, two strong schools of thought on population ecology developed, one under A. J. Nicholson of CSIR (see Nicholson and Bailey 1935 and subsequent papers), the other under H. G. Andrewartha and L. C. Birch (summarized in their book, published in 1954; also Andrewartha 1961). A controversy developed that centered around the control of insect populations either by resource limitations or by built-in hormonal response under crowding. Further insight into the exciting development of population ecology in Australia may be gained from the book *The Ecology of Insect Populations in Theory and Practice* by Clark et al. (1967) and in the paper by Hughes and Gilbert (1968).

Vertebrates

The CSIRO Wild Life Section (later Division of Wildlife Research) was formed in 1949, with a charter to investigate native and introduced mammals and birds of economic importance. Over the twenty-five years of its existence, the division (under F. N. Ratcliffe and later H. J. Frith) has investigated (a) the biology of animals of economic importance: mammals (dingo, kangaroo, rabbit) and birds (black cockatoo, cormorant, galah, ibis, magpie, magpie goose, mutton bird, wedge-tailed eagle, wild duck, among others); (b) the biology and distribution of native fauna, with emphasis on management and conservation; (c) bird banding and bird migration; and (d) fundamental studies on population ecology, physiology, and animal behavior. Some idea of the direction of ecological research within the division may be gained from the following papers: Frith (1957), Carrick (1963), Meyer and Parker (1965), Newsome (1965), and Ealey (1967).

Australian universities have developed active schools in marsupial ecology (zoology department, University of Western Australia under A. B. Main), behavioral ecology (zoology department, University of New England, under J. le G. Brereton), bird and mammal ecology (zoology department, University of Queensland, under Jiro Kikkawa), and vertebrate ecology (zoology department, Monash University under A. J. Marshall).

Weeds

As the dominant elements of the native vegetation of southern Australia appear to be a subtropical flora stranded in a warm, temperate, Mediterranean environment (R. L. Specht 1975), many exotic plant species, better adapted to the present climate, have invaded the region. Over the last one hundred years, approximately one new naturalized plant has been recorded every two months.

The CSIR/CSIRO Division of Plant Industry (under R. M. Moore) developed studies on weed ecology often in association with the Division of (Economic) Entomology, which is concerned with biological control. Weed research was also tackled by the agronomy department of the Waite Agricultural Research Institute (1940s–1950s); the botany department, University of Melbourne (1960s) in conjunction with the Vermin and Noxious Weeds Destruction Board of Victoria; the agronomy department, University of Sydney (late 1960s); and the CSIRO Woodland Ecology Unit and the botany branch of the Queensland Department of Primary Industries in southeastern Queensland.

Weed ecology focused on the biology of the species, population studies, and competition with or without weed killers of: *Amsinckia* spp., blackberry (*Rubus fruticosus*), bulrush (*Typha* spp.), cape tulip (*Homeria breyniana*), galvanized bur (*Bassia birchii*), groundsel bush (*Baccharis halimifolia*), hoary cress (*Cardaria draba*), mintweed (*Salvia reflexa*), mistletoe (Loranthaceae), nut grass (*Cyperus rotundus*), potato weed (*Heliotropium europaeum*), Scotch thistle (*Onopordon*), skeleton weed (*Chondrilla juncea*), sour sob (*Oxalis pes-caprae*), Saint-John's-wort (*Hypericum perforatum*), water hyacinth (*Eichhornia crassipes*), water reed (*Phragmites communis*), wild turnip (Brassica tournefortii), and many other introduced weeds.

Most weed species appear to be reduced, or even eliminated, in well-managed perennial pastures, but unfortunately, the weeds survived outside these areas. The weeds are still with us! The success of *Cactoblastis* against prickly pear is still the shining example of biological control.

Palaeo-ecology

Palynology, the study of changes with depth, and hence with age, in the species composition of pollen preserved in peat bogs, had been developed in Europe in the 1920s and 1930s. Initial attempts during the 1940s to study pollen in peat samples from Tasmania, South Australia, and Western Australia failed, probably because the acetolysis treatment was too strong. Studies on vegetation changes were, therefore, confined to descriptions of macrofossils and fossil pollen grains found in older geologic deposits, especially in brown coals from the early Tertiary era. Most of the work was done by Isobel C. Cookson and her associates in the botany department, University of Melbourne.

In the late 1950s, D. M. Churchill (1957) of the botany department, University of Western Australia, used milder acetolysis on peat samples from that area and obtained fine spectra of fossil pollen grains. With this success in mind, the Quaternary Landscapes Committee of ANZAAS (1958–1959) actively promoted palynology in Australia. Groups were established in the Department of Biogeography and Geomorphology of the Australian National University under D. Walker, the botany departments of the University of Sydney under A. R. H. Martin and University of New South Wales under H. A. Martin, and at Monash University under D. M. Churchill. Further palynologic studies have been tackled in the botany departments of the Universities of Adelaide and Queensland. Many of these palynologists are indebted to Professor H. Godwin of Cambridge University, England, for their training.

These palynological investigations are gradually giving some insight into the changes in the vegetation in the Pleistocene or Recent epochs, as well as patterns of change from the early Tertiary.

Fire Ecology

Scientific investigation of the behavior of plant species in relation to fire began in Australia with a study by Phyllis H. Jarrett and A. H. K. Petrie (1929) on the responses of the flora of the mountain forests of Victoria after the 1926 bushfires. N. C. W. Beadle's paper (1940) on the effect of different fire intensities on the sclerophyllous flora of the Hawkesbury Sandstone near Sydney is another landmark in the development of the subject. The studies of R. L. Specht et al. (1958) on pyric succession in South Australian heathland developed Beadle's observations on the Sydney sclerophyllous flora.

During the 1950s, active research programs were developed by the state forestry departments, on the effect of fire on the eucalyptus forests of Western Australia, Tasmania, New South Wales (and the Australian Capital Territory), southeastern Queensland, and the Northern Territory. Bushfire research and control programs were also fostered by the state authorities, together with the Commonwealth Forestry and Timber Bureau and the CSIRO Bushfire Section under R. G. Vines.

In the last decade, fire ecology, as distinct from bushfire research and control, has gained momentum. Both animal and plant ecologists are now realizing the importance of fire in the Australian ecosystems; many important studies on fire ecology are emerging (see Gill et al. 1980).

TRAINING OF ECOLOGISTS IN AUSTRALIA

From the first, Australian universities have been active in ecological research in all fields. In many cases, close cooperation has been maintained with ecological research organizations at the state and federal level. Ecologists in Australian universities have attempted to keep pace with the expansion in the horizons of the discipline, provide undergraduate students with satisfactory "building-block" subjects, and develop courses emphasizing the holistic thinking necessary to study ecosystems. Table 21.3 shows how this progression in training has developed since the 1930s. Australian universities still have a long way to go in developing an holistic, integrative attitude in budding ecologists. Bold experiments in training ecologists have been initiated recently in the newer universities, namely, Griffith University in Brisbane, Queensland; University of New England, Armidale, New South Wales; and Murdock University, Perth, Western Australia.

Field studies (for example, excursions and expeditions) have stimulated many students to undertake ecological research. Field laboratories, centers for excursions, have played an integral role in the training of undergraduates and stimulated ecological research among both staff and postgraduate students. The following field laboratories have been established by Australian universities: Arrawarra Headland, Coff's Harbour, New South Wales (University of New England, 1960); Dark Island/Mount Rescue, South Australia (University of Adelaide, 1950); Dunwich, North Stradbroke Island, Queensland (University of Queensland, 1960); Fowlers Gap, Broken Hill, New South Wales (University of New England, 1954; University of New South Wales 1966); Garden Island, Western Australia (University of Western Australia, 1960); Heron Island, Great Barrier Reef, Queensland (Great Barrier Reef Committee, University of Queensland, 1951); Jandakot, Western Australia (University of Western Australia, 1970); Koonamore Vegetation Reserve, now T. G. B. Osborn Reserve, South Australia University of Adelaide, 1925); Lizard Island, North Queensland (Australian Museum, Sydney 1973); McLennan Laboratory, Wilson's Promontory, Victoria (University of Melbourne, 1961); Pemberton,

Table 21.3. Undergraduate Courses Studied by Practicing Australian Ecologists[a]

Graduating Class	1934-1945	1946-1955	1956-1965	1966-1975
Number of ecologists				
Agriculture	3	4	4	4
Forestry	1	6	5	5
Science	5	8	8	13
Total	9	18	17	22
Undergraduate courses	%	%	%	%
General botany/Systematics	100[b]	94[b]	100[b]	100[b]
Plant physiology	89[b]	94[b]	100[b]	95[b]
General zoology/Systematics	78	44	65	91
Animal physiology/Behavior	33[b]	28[b]	47[b]	77[b]
Geology/Geomorphology	78	78	76	59
Soils	67[b]	89[b]	76[b]	73[b]
Climate/Meteorology	33	61[b]	41[b]	59[b]
Statistics	67[b]	83[b]	82[b]	95[b]
Ecological studies				
Plant ecology	78	89[b]	88[b]	86[b]
Population (animal) ecology	11[b]	11[b]	29[b]	68[b]
Excursions	100	100	100	100
Ecosystems	—	17[b]	41[b]	41[b]
Ecochronology	11	39[b]	53[b]	50[b]
Palaeo-ecology	—	6	18[b]	27[b]
Community physiology	—	28	29[b]	41[b]
Ecosystems analysis	—	—	—	41[b]

[a] Results are expressed as a percentage of the total replies to questionnaires from ecologists who completed their undergraduate studies in the decades 1934–1945, 1946–1955, 1956–1965, and 1966–1975.

[b] More than half of these ecologists studied advanced (third or fourth year) courses in these fields.

Western Australia (University of Western Australia—Murdoch University, 1976); Rottnest Island, Western Australia (University of Western Australia—Western Australia Department of Fisheries and Wildlife, 1952); Tutanning, Western Australia (University of Western Australia—Western Australia Department of Fisheries and Wildlife, 1967); Warrah, north of Sydney, New South Wales (University of Sydney, 1952). Several other areas (for example, Middleback Station near Whyalla, South Australia) have been used as base camps for field studies.

Expeditions organized jointly by staff and by postgraduate and undergraduate students have also played a strong role in developing field experience and a lifelong interest in ecology. Among the more significant of these are: University of Adelaide (Expeditions to the Nuyt's Archipelago and the Investigator Group, 1920–1924); University of Adelaide, Tate Society (Swan

Reach, 1937; Deep Creek, 1938; Flinders Chase, Kangaroo Island, 1939); University of Melbourne, McCoy Society (Lady Julia Percy Island, 1935–1936; Sir Joseph Banks Islands, 1936; Sunday and Clonmel Islands, Corner Inlet, 1938 and 1947; Cathedral Ranges, 1951, Crater Lake near Colac, 1952; Waterloo Bay, Wilson's Promontory, 1958); University of Melbourne, botany department expeditions (Black's Spur, 1928; Bogong High Plain, 1945–1958); University of Queensland, Science Students' Association (Bird and Goat Islands, 1938; Somerset Dam, 1939; Green Island, Moreton Bay, 1940; Myora, Stradbroke Island, 1941; Fraser Island, 1942; Myora, Stradbroke Island, 1946; Noosa Heads, 1947; Mount Barney, 1948; Fraser Island, 1949; Coolum Beach, 1950; Mount Ballow, 1951; Darlington, 1952); University of Sydney, Botanical Society (Mount Wilson, 1923 and following years); Rover Crew and Biological Society (Myall Lakes, 1935; Narabeen, 1936).

A number of Australian scientists, now interested in all aspects of the ecosystem, made their first real contact with field problems on one of these expeditions. It is noteworthy that, as soon as the university population began to increase rapidly after World War II, few multidisciplinary expeditions have been organized.

From 1950 to 1975, the number of Australian universities increased from 7 to 18. Postgraduate studies in Australian universities increased continuously after World War II, rising from about 60 master's and no Ph.D. degrees awarded in 1950 to 1,353 master's and 814 Ph.D. degrees awarded in 1973 for the whole of Australia. An increasing number of graduates elected to study in ecological fields (see Table 21.4 for statistics of ecological degrees awarded from 1966 to 1975). Between 1966 and 1975, there were 273 Ph.D. degrees awarded for ecological studies, 4 percent of the Australian total. In a recent survey of practicing ecologists, a subjective inquiry was made as to how successful their postgraduate studies had been in enabling them to achieve some in-depth level of integration between the seven major building-blocks of ecology [climate, relief, soils, plant communities, animal populations, time (short-term), and time (geologic)]. The results of this inquiry are presented in Table 21.5 for ecologists who graduated in the decades from 1935 to 1975. If the data (Tables 21.3 and 21.5) give a true picture of the situation, Australian universities appear to be experimenting increasingly with more integrative approaches to the training of ecologists at the undergraduate level, but may be failing at the postgraduate level. A possible reason for this failure is the selection of research topics for the master's or Ph.D. degree. In the 1940s and 1950s, integrative topics, such as "regional surveys" (see above), tended to be selected; now "local surveys," descriptive ecology, or a small subsection of the ecosystem tend to be studied. A narrow, rather than a broad, front is often selected for research, and the student gains less experience at integrating results.

Table 21.4. **Postgraduate Degrees and Publications in Ecology Produced by Australian Universities (41[a]), CSIRO (9[a]), and State Government (23[a]) Research Organizations, 1966–1975**

	Degrees awarded			Publications		
Field of ecology	**Honor's**	**Master's**	**Ph.D.**	**University**	**CSIRO**	**State Government**
Plant ecology						
Survey	26	9	2	46	49	22
Biogeography	—	1	2	31	22	5
Autecology						
Native plants	55	25	31	126	41	26
Crop/pasture	8	28	24	87	107	12
Weeds	7	8	5	12	19	7
Synecology	25	28	13	75	60	32
Community physiology	5	13	21	111	13	—
Succession	7	2	3	9	4	2
Palaeo-ecology	3	3	10	39	7	—
Conservation/Pollution	11	3	1	27	24	8
Animal ecology						
Survey	21	4	3	43	31	59

Biogeography	4	4	9	59	3	4
Behavioral ecology	50	20	23	82	81	47
Physiological ecology	65	24	36	126	45	—
Population ecology	72	36	53	183	188 + 41[b]	13
Community ecology	3	3	6	21	—	—
Palaeo-ecology	—	—	—	8	1	—
Conservation	4	1	2	40	21	7
Soil ecology						
Microbial	5	6	3	19	11	21
Animals	6	1	3	11	12	1
Other	9	—	3	10	—	3
Ecosystems						
Ecosystem studies	10	4	8	50	13	6
Range management	2	1	4	8	29	2
Ecosystem modelling	2	—	1	7	3	—
Theoretical ecology	—	—	2	22	66	1
Methodological ecology	—	2	1	26	11	—
Biometeorology	1	1	4	23	21	—
Total	401	227	273	1301	923	278

[a]Number of replies to questionnaire.
[b]Biological control.

Table 21.5. Number of Fields[a] between which Practicing Australian Ecologists Considered that They Had Achieved Some In-depth Level of Integration at the End of Their Postgraduate Studies

Number of fields between which integration achieved	Percentage of total number of graduating class			
	1934–1945	1946–1955	1956–1965	1966–1975
7	—	6	6	—
6+	11	17	6	5
5+	33	39	30	19
4+	55	67	48	51
3+	88	89	72	78
2+	100	100	100	100

[a]Fields: Climate, relief, soils, plant communities, animal populations, time (short-term), time (geological).

CONCLUSIONS

Ecological research in Australia has sprung naturally from the many environmental problems of the continent. First, there was a desire to know more about the unique flora and fauna and their ecological relationships. Special problems such as seasonal and long-term drought, low levels of soil nutrients, and minimal grazing pressure exerted by native marsupials, in contrast to that of the introduced herbivores, have produced distinctive trends in ecological research in Australia as applied to agriculture, forestry, rangeland, and conservation management. Second, the special problems of animal pests, both insect and vertebrate, and weeds have been given high priority.

Descriptive ecology has dominated the research output. "Experimental manipulation" of ecosystems was developed as an ecological research tool in the study of arid-zone vegetation on Koonamore (now T. G. B. Osborn) Vegetation Reserve in the mid-1920s, and has been used in a number of other ecosystems since then. More recently, intensive studies on the processes operating within ecosystems and populations have been explored. Much more research is needed into the ecophysiological processes controlling the structure (leaf canopy, the partitioning of photosynthates between stems and roots, and the development of flowers and fruits) of the plant community and energy flow into consumers and decomposers.

In the opinion of the author, the late T. G. B. Osborn (University of Adelaide, 1912–1928; University of Sydney, 1938–1937) and J. G. Wood (University of Adelaide, 1923–1959) must be regarded as the "father and son" of ecological studies in Australia. It is because of their enthusiasm and wisdom through the 1920s and 1930s that the holistic discipline of ecology attained such strength. One may point, as an example, to the little-known paper of Wood published in 1939 in which ecological concepts, based on physiological processes within the ecosystem, were examined in relation to classification—the result of many years of intensive study in both descriptive ecology and ecophysiology (see the handbook, *The Vegetation of South Australia,* Wood 1937). It is in the Adelaide and Sydney schools of holistic ecology that eight ecologists who became leaders in ecological studies during the 1950s and 1960s received their training. These students attempted to approach the study of the ecosystem in toto, not just fragmented into parts. In effect, they espoused the approach enunciated by Major (1951) and Crocker (1952) in which the various ecophysiological facets of the ecosystem, *Vegetation = function (climate, parent material, relief, organisms, time),* were explored and integrated by *one* scientist. This was a formidable scientific exercise, but publications show that it was achieved by quite a number of Australian ecologists of the 1940s and 1950s. Later, teams of specialists (e.g., CSIRO Division of Land Research and Regional Survey, and subsequent ecosystem modelling teams under an holistic ecologist) have advanced into a higher level of integration.

It may be argued that the true ecologist must be holistic in his approach. Animal ecology in Australia as developed by H. G. Andrewartha, L. C. Birch, J. Davidson, and A. J. Nicholson advanced on a much narrower front of population ecology, and, in later years, behavioral ecology. It is only in recent years that the training of animal ecologists has become more holistic in some Australian universities.

The training of ecologists in Australian universities is being strengthened in all fields of the discipline (Table 21.3). Field studies, an important part of this training, appear to be neglected as the university population increases. Courses to stimulate the integrative thought essential in ecology are now being offered. It may be questioned whether many current postgraduate studies are achieving the holistic level of thought necessary to answer the ecological management problems the graduate will face in later life (Table 21.5).

Australian ecologists have kept in close contact with European and American colleagues through reading the literature and making frequent visits abroad. International research programs, sponsored by UNESCO and ICSU, have had their influence—for example, UNESCO Arid Zone Research Program in the 1950s; the ecosystem, productivity, and conservation studies promoted by the IBP (1964–1974); the SCOPE project on "Fire and the Australian Biota" (Gill et al. 1980); and the Man and the Biosphere (MAB) program—have each made a mark through the Australian Academy of Science. It must be stressed, however, that throughout all these programs, Australian ecologists have staunchly maintained their individuality. The preparation of articles for books such as *Biogeography and Ecology in Australia* (Keast et al. 1959), *Australian Grasslands* (Moore 1970), *Heathlands and Related Shrublands of the World* (Specht 1979–1980), and *Ecology and Biogeography of Australia* (Keast 1980) has forced Australian ecologists to examine their discipline critically. The establishment in 1976 of the professional journal, *Australian Journal of Ecology,* provides a national publishing outlet for Australian ecological research. Recently, environmental impact studies have occupied the attention of many ecologists, diverting professional ecologists from scientific studies.

It is of interest to note the careers of the forty people who undertook postgraduate research in plant ecology and who published in this field between 1930 and 1955. Half of these scientists opted out of field studies, seventeen becoming taxonomists or experimental taxonomists and three becoming plant physiologists. Of the remaining twenty plant ecologists, four died relatively early in their careers, nine have retired from research and teaching, often some years before the retirement age of sixty-five, to become environmental consultants, and seven are still active in the field of plant ecology, although subjected to considerable pressures to devote most of their time to environmental consulting and conservation.

The rigors of fieldwork, dissatisfaction with the slow results of long-term ecological experiments, lack of job opportunities, and eventually, the conflict between fieldwork and family life probably influenced many to turn to laboratory-based research. Social pressures concerning the environment and conservation have had a disturbing influence on senior plant ecologists who have diverted their attention to immediate applied consulting away from the long-range research studies on which consulting is based. Although it is probably a truism that the best ecological consultants are people who have been practicing research workers with long experience, the current switch from research to consulting is leaving a gap at a time when Australia most needs long-term ecological research.

It can only be hoped that the younger generation (post-1955) will fill the gap, but there is little encouragement in this sphere. The discipline of holistic ecology is still uncomprehended and unappreciated within the scientific fraternity. It is a field requiring long-term, integrative thought; quick results and rewards cannot be expected. Yet it would seem more and more necessary that sophisticated, long-term experimentation on an analysis of processes operating within ecosystems be persistently pursued.

Many long-term manipulative studies on the dynamics of Australian ecosystems are already underway (see above). The results of these experiments should be collated and assessed nationally at regular intervals. It is essential that the trends and conclusions from these experiments be published in readily available handbooks.

Australian ecological thought and planning can then be based on local experience, as well as on expertise from abroad, the latter often based on the behavior of ecosystems quite atypical of those stranded, geologically speaking, on the island-continent of Australia.

The Australian landscape presents many extreme stress situations where disjunctions are found between ecosystems: closed and open communities; *Eucalyptus*- and *Acacia*-dominated communities; treed and treeless communities; perennial and annual grass communities; grassy and heathy communities; summer- and spring-growing communities (both native and exotic); calciphobe and calciphile communities; saline, semi-saline, solodized, to non-saline communities; and waterlogged and well-drained communities. It is at these interfaces, where sharp changes occur in ecological control, that basic ecological principles are more likely to emerge from future ecological research.

Overlaying the sharp discontinuities between ecosystems (listed above) is the seasonal response of the plant and animal populations to the annual progression of climate. A phenological atlas of Australian ecosystems is essential for the understanding and management of Australian land systems, which show phenophases markedly different from the seasonal rhythms observed in similar homoclimes overseas.

ACKNOWLEDGMENTS

This article is based on replies to two questionnaires forwarded to over one hundred Australian ecologists and to all ecological research institutes in Australia; the cooperation and tolerance of all these ecologists and organizations are gratefully acknowledged. I take full responsibility for the interpretation of the statistics and apologize if certain aspects on the development of ecology in Australia have been omitted or distorted.

REFERENCES CITED

Adamson, R. A. and T. G. B. Osborn. 1922. On the ecology of the Ooldea district. *Trans. R. Soc. S. Aust.* 46:539–564.

______. 1924. The ecology of the *Eucalyptus* forests of the Mount Lofty Ranges (Adelaide district), South Australia. *Trans. R. Soc. S. Aust.* 48:87–144.

Andrewartha, H. G. 1961. *Introduction to the study of animal populations.* London: Methuen (2d ed., 1970, London: Chapman & Hall).

______ and L. C. Birch. 1954. *The distribution and abundance of animals.* Chicago: University of Chicago Press.

Ashton, D. H. 1976. The development of even-aged stands of *Eucalyptus regnans* F. Muell. in central Victoria. *Aust. J. Bot.* 24:397–414.

Beadle, N. C. W. 1940. Soil temperatures during forest fires and their effect on the survival of vegetation. *J. Ecol.* 28:180–192.

______. 1948. *The vegetation and pastures of western New South Wales, with special reference to soil erosion.* Sydney: Government Printer.

______. 1953. The edaphic factor in plant ecology with special note on soil phosphates. *Ecology* 34:426–428.

______. 1968. Some aspects of the ecology and physiology of Australian xeromorphic plants. *Aust. J. Sci.* 30:348–355.

Beard, J. S. 1974–1976. *Vegetation survey of Western Australia.* Nedlands, W. Aust.: University of Western Australia Press.

Blake, S. T. 1938. The plant communities of western Queensland and their relationships with special reference to the grazing industry. *Proc. R. Soc. Qd.* 49:156–204.

Brough, P., J. McLuckie, and A. H. K. Petrie. 1924. An ecological study of the flora of Mount Wilson. Part 1. The vegetation of the basalt. *Proc. Linn. Soc. N.S.W.* 49:475–498.

Burbidge, N. T. 1960. The phytogeography of the Australian region. *Aust. J. Bot.* 8:75–212.

Cannon, W. A. 1921. *Plant habit and habitats in the arid portions of South Australia.* Publ. Carnegie Institution Washington, Publ. No. 308.

Carnahan, J. A. 1976. Natural vegetation. In *Atlas of Australian Resources,* Second Series. Canberra: Department of National Resources.

Carr, S. G. M. and J. S. Turner. 1959. The ecology of the Bogong High Plains. *Aust. J. Bot.* 7:12–63.

Carrick, R. 1963. Ecological significance of territory in the Australian magpie, *Gymnorhina tibicen. Proc. XIII Int. Orn. Cong.* pp. 740–753.

Christian, C. S. 1952. Regional land surveys. *J. Aust. Inst. Agric. Sci.* 18:140–147.

Churchill, D. M. 1957. A method for concentrating pollen grains and small fossil remains from fibrous peats and moss polsters. *Nature, Lond.* 18:1437.

Clark, L. R., P. W. Geier, R. D. Hughes, and R. F. Morris. 1967. *The ecology of insect populations in theory and practice.* London: Methuen.

Collins, M. I. 1923. Studies in the vegetation of arid and semi-arid New South Wales. Part 1. The plant ecology of the Barrier District. *Proc. Linn. Soc. N.S.W.* 48:229–266.

Connor, D. J. and G. L. Wilson. 1968. Response of a coastal Queensland heath community to fertilizer application. *Aust. J. Bot.* 16:117–123.

Costin, A. B. 1954. *The ecosystems of the Monaro region of New South Wales with special references to soil erosion.* Sydney: Government Printer.

Crocker, R. L. 1952. Soil genesis and the pedogenic factors. *Quart. Rev. Biol.* 27:139–168.

______ and J. G. Wood. 1947. Some historical influences on the development of the South Australian vegetation communities and their bearing on concepts and classification in ecology. *Trans. R. Soc. Aust.* 71:91–136.

CSIRO (Aust.). 1952–1977. Land Research Series Nos. 1–39. Canberra.

Davidson, J. 1933. Effect of rainfall-evaporation ratio on insects inhabiting the soil surface. *Nature* 131:837–838.

______. 1935. Some aspects of climate and insect ecology. *J. Aust. Inst. Agric. Sci.* 1:105–108.

Davidson, J. L. and C. M. Donald. 1958. The growth of swards of subterranean clover with particular reference to leaf area. *Aust. J. Agric. Sci.* 9:53–72.

Day, M. F. 1968. *National parks and reserves in Australia. Report of the National Parks Committee.* Australian Academy of Science Rep. No. 9, Canberra.

Diels, L. 1906. *Die Vegetation der Erde.* Vol. 7. *Die Pflanzenwelt von West-Australian südlich des Wendekreises.* Leipzig: Engelmann.

Domin, K. 1911. Queensland's plant associations. *Proc. R. Soc. Qd.* 23:57–74.

Ealey, E. H. M. 1967. Ecology of the euro, *Macropus robustus* (Gould), in northwestern Australia. *CSIRO (Aus.) Wildl. Res.* 12:9–80 and subsequent papers.

Elton, C. 1927. *Animal ecology.* Oxford: Sidgwick and Jackson.

Fenner, F. 1975. *A national system of ecological reserves in Australia.* Australian Academy of Science Rep. No. 19.

Frankenberg, J. 1971. *Nature conservation in Victoria,* ed. J. S. Turner. Melbourne: Victorian National Parks Association.

Frith, H. J. 1957. Breeding and movements of wild duck in inland New South Wales. *CSIRO (Aust.) Wildl. Res.* 2:19–31.

Gibbs, L. S. 1917. The phytogeography of Bellenden-Ker. *J. Bot., Lond.* 55:297–301.

______. 1921. Notes on the phytogeography and flora of the mountain summit plateaux of Tasmania. *J. Ecol.* 8:1–17, 89–117.

Gill, A. M., R. H. Groves, and I. R. Noble eds. 1980. *Fire and the Australian biota.* Canberra: Australian Academy of Science.

Goodall, D. W. 1953. Objective methods for the classification of vegetation. I. The use of positive interspecific correlation. *Aust. J. Bot.* 1:39–63.

Hall, E. A. A., R. L. Specht, and C. M. Eardley. 1964. Regeneration of the vegetation on Koonamore Vegetation Reserve, 1926–1962. *Aust. J. Bot.* 12:205–264.

Hamilton, A. A. 1917. Topographical, ecological and taxonomic notes on the ocean shoreline vegetation of the Port Jackson district. *J. R. Soc. N.S.W.* 51:287–355.

Hughes, R. D. and N. Gilbert. 1968. A model of an aphid population—general statement. *J. Anim. Ecol.* 37:553–563.

Ising, E. H. 1922. Ecological notes on South Australian plants. Part I. *Trans. R. Soc. S. Aust.* 46:583–606.

Jarrett, P. H. and A. H. K. Petrie. 1929. The vegetation of the Black's Spur region. A study in the ecology of some Australian mountain *Eucalyptus* forests. II. Pyric succession. *J. Ecol.* 17:249–281.

Keast, A. 1980. *Ecology and biogeography of Australia.* Monogr. Biol. Vol. 32 The Hague: W. Junk.

______, R. L. Crocker, and C. S. Christian, eds. 1959. *Biogeography and ecology in Australia.* Monogr. Biol. Vol. 8 The Hague: W. Junk.

Kikkawa, J. and K. Pearse. 1969. Geographical distribution of land birds in Australia—a numerical analysis. *Aust. J. Zool.* 17:821–840.

Lance, G. N. and W. T. Williams. 1968. A note on new information statistics classificatory program. *Comput. J.* 11:195.

Langford, K. J. 1976. Changes in yield of water following a bush fire in a forest of *Eucalyptus regnans. J. Hydrol.* 29:87–114.

Laut, P. et al. 1977. *Environments of South Australia.* Provinces 1–8. (7 volumes). Canberra: CSIRO (Aust.), Div. Land Use Res.

Major, J. 1951. A functional, factorial approach to plant ecology. *Ecology* 32:392–412.

Martin, H. A. 1961. Sclerophyll communities at the Inglewood district, Mount Lofty Ranges, South Australia. *Trans. R. Soc. S. Aust.* 85:91–120.

——— and R. L. Specht. 1962. Are mesic communities less drought resistant? A study on moisture relationships in dry sclerophyll forest at Inglewood, South Australia. *Aust. J. Bot.* 10:106–118.

Meyer, K. and B. S. Parker. 1965. A study of the biology of the wild rabbit in climatically different regions in eastern Australia. I. Patterns of distribution. *CSIRO (Aust.) Wildl. Res.* 10:1–32 and subsequent papers.

Moore, R. M., ed. 1970. *Australian grasslands.* Canberra: Australian National University Press.

Newsome, A. E. 1965. The abundance of red kangaroo, *Megaleia rufa* (Desmarest), in central Australia. *Aust. J. Zool.* 13:269–287 and subsequent papers.

Nicholson, A. J. 1933. The balance of animal populations. *J. Anim. Ecol.* 2:132–178.

——— and V. A. Bailey. 1935. The balance of animal populations. *Proc. Zool. Soc. Lond.* 1935:551–603.

Osborn, T. G. B., J. G. Wood, and T. B. Paltridge. 1932. On the growth and reaction to grazing of the perennial saltbush, *Atriplex vesicarium.* An ecological study of the biotic factor. *Proc. Linn. Soc. N.S.W.* 57:377–402.

———. 1935. On the climate and vegetation of the Koonamore Vegetation Reserve to 1931. *Proc. Linn. Soc. N.S.W.* 50:392–427.

Patton, R. T. 1933–1951. Ecological studies in Victoria. Parts I –VIII. *Proc. R. Soc. Vict.* 45:205–218; 46:117–129; 47:135–157; 48:172–191; 49:293–307; 54:131–144; 61:35–51; *Vict. Nat.* 68:57–62.

Pressland, A. J. 1976. Effect of stand density on water use of mulga (*Acacia aneura* F. Muell.) woodlands in southwestern Queensland. *Aust. J. Bot.* 24:177–191.

Queensland Department of Primary Industries, Division of Land Utilization. 1974 and 1978. *Western arid region land use study.* Parts I and IV. Tech. Bull. Nos. 12, 23.

Rayson, P. 1957. Dark Island heath (Ninety-Mile Plain, South Australia). II. The effects of microtopography on climate, soils and vegetation. *Aust. J. Bot.* 5:86–102.

Ride, W. D. L. 1978. Towards a national biological survey. *Search* 9:73–82.

Slatyer, R. O. 1965. Measurements of precipitation interception by an arid zone plant community (*Acacia aneura* F. Muell.). *UNESCO Arid Zone Res.* 25:181–192.

Specht, M. M. and R. L. Specht 1962. Bibliographia Phytosociologica Australia. *Excerpta Bot.* Sect. B. 4:1–58.

Specht, R. L. 1957. Dark Island heath (Ninety-Mile Plain, South Australia). V. The water relationships in heath vegetation and pastures on the Makin sand. *Aust. J. Bot.* 5:151–172.

———. 163. Dark Island heath (Ninety-Mile Plain, South Australia). VII. The effect of fertilizers on composition and growth, 1950–1960. *Aust. J. Bot.* 11:67–94.

———. 1970. Vegetation. In *The Australian environment,* 4th ed., ed. G. W. Leeper, pp. 44–67. CSIRO. Melbourne: Melbourne University Press.

______. 1972*a*. Water use by perennial evergreen plant communities in Australia and Papua New Guinea. *Aust. J. Bot.* 20:273–299.

______. 1975. A heritage inverted: our flora endangered. *Search* 6:472–477.

______. 1976. The history and contemporary state of life sciences in Australian universities. II. Terrestrial ecology. *Aust. Univ.* 14:99–113.

______, ed. 1979, 1980. *Ecosystems of the world.* Vol. 9A & B. *Heathlands and related shrublands.* Amsterdam: Elsevier Scientific Publ. Co.

______ and J. B. Cleland. 1961. Flora conservation in South Australia. I. The preservation of plant formations and associations recorded in South Australia. *Trans. R. Soc. S. Aust.* 85:177–196.

______, D. J. Connor, and H. T. Clifford. 1977. The heath-savannah problem: the effect of fertilizer on sand-heath vegetation of North Stradbroke Island, Queensland. *Aust. J. Ecol.* 2:179–186.

______, E. M. Heddle, M. E. Jackman, and P. Rayson. 1957, 1958, 1963, 1975. Dark Island heath (Ninety-Mile Plain, South Australia). I–VIII. *Aust. J. Bot.* 5:52–114, 137–172; 6:59–88; 11:67–94; 23:151–164.

______ and R. Jones. 1971. A comparison of the water use by heath vegetation at Frankston, Victoria, and Dark Island Soak, South Australia. *Aust. J. Bot.* 19:311–326.

______, E. M. Roe, and V. H. Boughton. 1974. Conservation of major plant communities in Australia and Papua New Guinea. *Aust. J. Bot. Suppl.* No. 7.

Turner, J. C. 1965. Some energy and microclimate measurements in a natural arid zone plant community. *UNESCO Arid Zone Res.* 25:63–69.

Victoria Soil Conservation Authority. 1963–1975. *Technical Communications* Nos. 1–10.

Webb, L. J., J. G. Tracey, W. T. Williams, and G. N. Lance. 1970. Studies in the numerical analysis of complex rain-forest communities. V. A comparison of the properties of floristic and physiognomic-structural data. *J. Ecol.* 58:203–232.

Williams, R. J. 1955. Vegetation regions. In *Atlas of Australian resources,* First Series. Canberra: Department of National Development.

Williams, W. T. and J. M. Lambert. 1959. Multivariate methods in plant ecology. I. Association-analysis in plant communities. *J. Ecol.* 47:83–101.

______. 1960. Multivariate methods in plant ecology. II. The use of an electronic digital computer for association-analysis. *J. Ecol.* 48:689–710.

Wimbush, D. J. and A. B. Costin. 1979. Trends in vegetation at Kosciusko. I–III. *Aust. J. Bot.* 27:741–871.

Wood, J. G. 1936. Regeneration of the vegetation on the Koonamore Vegetation Reserve, 1926 to 1936. *Trans. R. Soc. S. Aust.* 60:96–111.

______. 1937. *The vegetation of South Australia.* Adelaide: Government Printer (See 2d ed., revised by Specht, 1972).

______. 1939. Ecological concepts and nomenclature. *Trans. R. Soc. S. Aust.* 63:215–223.

Zimmer, W. J. 1937. *The flora of the far northwest of Victoria. Its distribution in relation to soil types, and its value in the prevention of soil erosion.* Melbourne: Forests Comm. Victoria.

22

NEW ZEALAND

Alan F. Mark

INTRODUCTION

Since it is an isolated and small country of some 268,000 km^2, with a population only slightly exceeding 3 million and an economy based chiefly on the production of pasture and timber, New Zealand inevitably has applied its ecological activities primarily to agriculture and exotic forestry, with research sponsored predominantly by the government. Nevertheless, the many ecologically interesting features of the country's diverse natural ecosystems, which have been complicated only relatively recently by man's arrival, provide ample scope for most lines of ecological investigation, some of them unique. Unravelling the ecological impact of up to a thousand years of occupation by Polynesians prior to the more obvious modification of the European settlement that began in earnest about the mid-eighteenth century has been a complex but rewarding undertaking, the significance of which has been appreciated only within the last few decades. As in most developed countries, evaluating the ecological impact of both actual and proposed agricultural, industrial, and resource development is now receiving emphasis but is severely limited by constraints of finance, manpower, and politics. As an adjunct to this, there is concern for the reservation of unique indigenous ecosystems, particularly lowland forests (Fleming 1977), tussock grasslands (Scott 1979), and wetlands in the face of continued pressure for land development.

New Zealand is renowned ecologically for many successes among a range of introduced plants and animals, especially mammals, which not only have become established but also have displayed remarkable biological success in the favorable and diverse New Zealand environment. Many of the introduced mammals—several deer species, chamois, thar, opossum, rabbit, and hare—have seriously modified habitats of native species and created problems in agriculture, forestry, and particularly, catchment protection and stability. A few introduced mustelids, particularly stoats, have seriously depleted populations of native birds. Introduced trout (*Salmo* spp.) have also found favorable habitats in New Zealand. Among the plants, gorse (*Ulex europeaus*), broom (*Cytisus scoparius*), sweet brier (*Rosa rubiginosa*), and Saint-John's-wort (*Hypericum androsaemum*) proved particularly aggressive on non-arable land, and limited applied ecological studies have achieved control of only the last species.

Because of the remarkable ecological perspective and enthusiasm of Leonard Cockayne during the first third of this century, and the important contacts he established with the most prominent contemporary botanists of Great Britain and Europe (see Moore 1967), many of the special ecological features of the New Zealand biological region have been firmly established in the literature for at least half a century (Cockayne 1898, 1900, 1909, 1910, 1912, 1921, 1926, 1928).

PUBLICATIONS

Most of the early papers on various aspects of New Zealand ecology by Cockayne and others appeared in the *Transactions of the New Zealand Institute,* first published within a few decades of European settlement in 1868 with the geologist Sir James Hector as editor. The institute's function, as an incorporation of scientific societies, was taken over by the Royal Society of New Zealand in 1933, which continued the publication, but as *Transactions of the Royal Society of New Zealand* from 1935 and, since 1971, as the *Journal of the Society.*

Other scientific journals have appeared intermittently to cope with the steady increase in information being offered for publication. Most have been government financed, and for ecologists, those generally used have been publications of the government's Department of Scientific and Industrial Research; these included bulletins together with the *New Zealand Journal of Science and Technology* (1918–1957), which diversified into the current *New Zealand Journals of Science* (1958–), *Geology and Geophysics* (1957–), *Agricultural Research* (1958–), *Botany* (1963–), *Marine and Fresh Water Research* (1967–), *Experimental Agriculture* (1973–), and *Zoology* (1974–). The New Zealand Forest Service initiated the *New Zealand Journal of Forestry Science* in 1971, which partly superseded the *New Zealand Journal of Forestry,* a publication of the New Zealand Institute of Foresters which dates from 1925. The New Zealand Ornithological Society has published its own journal, *Notornis,* annually since 1943, and the New Zealand Ecological Society its own *Proceedings* since 1953, which it replaced with its *Journal* in 1978. Wellington's Victoria University Biological Society has published some valuable articles in its journal, *Tuatara* (1947–). The larger museums also publish results of scientific work.

SOCIETIES

Most New Zealand ecologists belong to one or more of the following specialist societies: The New Zealand Institute of Foresters founded in 1927, the New Zealand Ornithological Society (1939), the New Zealand Ecological Society (1952) with a current membership of 422, the New Zealand Marine Sciences Society (1960) with more than 200 New Zealand members, and the New Zealand Limnological Society (1968) with about 190 members. Professional ecologists, however, probably do not exceed 300 and few are self-employed. Many have been recruited from abroad, and most are employed by one of five government departments and hence are largely involved with some aspect of applied research.

TEACHING

Teaching of ecology in both schools and universities experienced a surge within the last decade in New Zealand. A New Zealand Ecological Society symposium on this topic was published in the society's 1969 proceedings (Vol. 16). The six universities all employ one or more ecologists, and all provide general undergraduate training with facilities for graduate research in certain aspects of the subject. The earlier trend of students venturing abroad for postgraduate study, traditionally to Great Britain but more recently also to the United States, Canada, or Australia, has declined considerably within the last decade. Almost all ecological research in New Zealand, including that conducted by universities, is sponsored by the government, private support being rare; a significant exception is the support given by the Miss E. L. Hellaby Indigenous Grasslands Research Trust initiated in 1959.

GENERAL TRENDS

As with any country, developments in ecology in New Zealand are a reflection of the combined effects of current trends in the field generally, the number, ability, and diversity of available ecologists, their research facilities, and the particular problems or fields of ecological endeavor the country presents. For its size, New Zealand has an unusual wealth of both interesting and important ecological phenomena. There is an extremely wide range of natural ecosystems, from coastal to nival and rain forest to arid grassland; true desert is absent. Settlement by Europeans within the last 140 years introduced a wide range of mammals into the ecosystems, which previously had evolved a reptile and bird fauna that proved vulnerable to the direct or indirect influences of many such introductions.

Two fairly comprehensive recent treatises on the natural history and ecology of New Zealand (Williams 1973; Kuschel 1975) provide the broad ecological background on which this aspect of my account is based.

Within the general field of terrestrial ecology, important contributions are being made in several spects:

1. Understanding the dynamics of natural vegetation in both space and time, particularly relationships to fluctuations in climate, dispersal limitations of important components of the indigenous flora, and the influence of introduced animals among other aspects of the recent impact of humans;

2. Highlighting a range of ecological anomalies in the New Zealand biota, e.g., a low incidence of winter dormancy (Dumbleton 1967), scarcity of protective overwintering buds (Wardle 1963b; Bliss and Mark 1974), importance of the divaricating shrub life form (Greenwood and Atkinson 1977), irregular flowering (Connor 1966; Mark 1970), generally slow assimilation and growth rates particularly in relation to those of many introduced plants (Mark 1965*a*, 1975). Only relatively small contributions have been made to date in understanding the physio-ecological processes of native species and their role in ecosystems (Green 1979; Mark 1975).

Among animal studies, those involving the unusual but endangered birds and reptiles, which invariably implicate one or more successful members of the alien fauna, are of special interest and importance. Interactions of native and introduced species in many groups have continued to receive attention and formed a symposium topic of the New Zealand Ecological Society in 1960 (published in its 1961 proceedings, Vol. 8). Similarly, the unique ecology of New Zealand's subantarctic islands was a topic published as a conference symposium of the society in its 1965 proceedings (Vol. 12).

Applications of ecology to forestry and agriculture traditionally have received strong research input from the government, the School of Forestry at the University of Canterbury, and the two agricultural faculties in New Zealand. More recently, this has extended into studies of eutrophication problems associated with intensive agriculture. These fields will be discussed briefly, as will the general aspects of freshwater and marine ecology.

PLANT ECOLOGY

Leonard Cockayne's comprehensive qualitative descriptions of New Zealand vegetation compiled fifty years ago (Cockayne 1921, 1928) showed clearly and convincingly the dynamic nature of the indigenous vegetation and the possible non-climax nature of several important associations, i.e., kauri forest, coniferous-broad-leaved forest. This concept of forest instability was brought into sharp focus by Holloway (1954) in his ecological assessment of the South Island forests resulting from a national forest survey undertaken following World War II. Holloway described anomalies of both forest species and forest type distributions, particularly those involving interactions between beech (*Nothofagus*) species and the longer lived conifers (mostly podocarps), as well as the regeneration deficiencies of certain predominant conifers in many of the coniferous-broad-leaved forests. These anomalies he accounted for in terms of a climatic change some time around the twelfth century. Patterns of active migration and redistribution of dominant forest species were described from several forested regions, the delayed response being accounted for in terms of restricted dispersal potential of the invading beeches, the relative longevity of the supplanted conifers, and the lack of any cultural interference to hasten or conceal the response.

Subsequent efforts to more critically assess Holloway's hypothesis, based on detailed studies of age-class distribution patterns of the conifers in several forested regions (Wardle 1963*c*), have established a regeneration gap in many localities, which peaked between A.D. 1600 and 1800 (assuming that growth rings are annual). Assessment by study of current regeneration of the various species in critical areas has been frustrated by the serious modification caused by introduced red deer, which now have spread through essentially all forested regions. Population dynamic studies of forests have also revealed more recent regeneration gaps attributable to high densities of deer (Ogden 1971*b*). Prior to the establishment of red deer on Secretary Island in the rain forests of Fiordland, however, quantitative sampling indicated that conifer regeneration under the most favorable conditions near sea level is even more successful than that of beeches, while above about 300 m, near the upper altitudinal limits of the lowland conifers, the reverse trend is apparent (Baylis and Mark 1963; P. Wardle et al. 1970). Continued studies of this type on the 80-km^2 Secretary Island have been jeopardized unfortunately by the recent establishment of a breeding population of red deer, while extremely difficult terrain and a high proportion of forest cover have so far thwarted efforts to eliminate the deer. Attempts to document the marked food selection exhibited by these animals during the initial stages of establishment in unmodified New Zealand forest have been made there (Mark and Baylis 1975) since this stage had passed undocumented in other areas. The observations do not always agree with browse indices devised to record such preferences in nearby forests that have been subjected to these browsing animals for a longer period (J. Wardle et al. 1971).

In addition to damage by deer, which tends to be lessening because of recent substantial reduction in numbers associated with a lucrative overseas venison market, there is continuing complementary damage to forests inflicted by expanding populations of the Australian opossum (*Trichosurus vulpecula*), which potentially is probably the most troublesome of our introduced mammals. The opossum's impact on the vegetation is being documented with simple but effective improved browse indices (Meads 1976).

Vegetation Instability

Holloway's classic paper, together with that of his contemporary pedologist Raeside (1948), first drew attention to major changes in vegetation in pre-European times, particularly deforestation, which had been widespread on the drier downlands, leeward of the Southern Alps on South Island. Deforestation and replacement by tussock grassland was assumed by both scientists to have been initiated by the twelfth-century climatic change, although the possible importance of fire was not discounted. Holloway's evidence as to timing was based on tree aging, whereas Raeside adopted the Northern Hemisphere chronology of climatic change. Subsequently, both estimates were verified from radiocarbon dating of surface logs and buried charcoals. The charcoals have been intensively studied by Molloy (Molloy et al. 1963) to clarify further this obviously important historical aspect of New Zealand ecology, which curiously had largely evaded Cockayne (1928, p. 426). Although these recent studies obviously implicate the early Polynesian settlers in most of the deforestation that occurred prior to European settlement, some charcoal dates from parts of Otago and Canterbury far predate known Maori settlement of South Island and are assumed to have been of natural origin (Molloy and Cox 1972). Conflicting opinions have been offered as to the composition of these earlier destroyed forests, ranging from mixed podocarp forest (Holloway 1954; Wardle 1963*a*) or open Woodland (Burrell 1965) to beech forest with a minor podocarp component (Holloway 1948; Wells 1972). Clarification awaits the identification of charcoals, now being actively researched.

Quaternary Research

Other aspects of Quaternary research are being pursued in New Zealand because of both the scope for such studies available here and their importance in understanding present ecosystems and landscapes (Fleming 1975*a*). In unravelling the chronology of the Pleistocene in New Zealand (Gage and Suggate 1958), considerable stimulus was provided by the Ninth INQUA Congress held here in 1973. Of particular significance to ecology has been the dating of several moraines of the many receding glaciers present in South Island using a range of methods, often in combination, for example, lichenometry (Burrows and Orwin 1971; Burrows and Maunder 1975), radiocarbon dating (Wardle 1973*a*), and plant cover (Burrows 1973). The important and obvious disjunctions, noted by Cockayne, in distribution of *Nothofagus* and several lesser species, particularly involving the northwestern and southwestern corners of South Island, have been much more fully documented (Wardle 1963*a*, Burrows 1965, 1969), extended to certain native invertebrates (Fleming 1975*b*), and explained in terms of Pleistocene extinction and subsequent events in the central portion of the island.

Palynology continues to make substantial contributions to the understanding of both paleoecologic and current patterns of vegetation. The initial classic study of Cranwell and von Post (1936) in southern New Zealand established the general pattern and was consistent with findings from contemporary studies abroad of a postglacial climatic sequence of warming and cooling. The culmination in warming supported coniferous-broad-leaved forest, and subsequent deterioration was associated with regional differentiation and establishment of *Nothofagus* in many areas. Subsequent studies, particularly by Moar (1971, 1973) and incorporating carbon-14 dating, have revealed a much greater complexity of vegetation history, establishing important regional differences in chronology and floristics of the various vegetation phases, particularly the pre-forest shrubland and forest-dominant phases. Of particular significance was Moar's information on rates of southward extension of *Nothofagus* into coniferous-broad-leaved forest in north Westland, of the order of 1.6 to 5.6 km per century; these rates presumably depended on dispersal limitations of the beeches and the competition provided by the established forest, rather than on concurrent climatic changes. The few studies of vegetation representation as pollen have revealed limited application for R=values and other anomalies that are not necessarily related to wind versus insect pollination (Pocknall 1978).

In assessing other ecological effects of Quaternary climates, Wardle (1963*a*) dismisses Cockayne's (1912) thesis that the curious physiognomic form of the divaricating shrub (combining stiff, wiry, closely interlacing, wide-angled branches and microphyllous leaves), a distinctive feature of New Zealand's woody flora, is a persistent adaptation to extremely arid Pleistocene climates. Wardle, by contrast, claims that the concentration of the divaricating habit in forest and mesic scrub suggests that this curious life form, together with other puzzling heteroblastic juvenile forms in several unrelated members of the woody flora, is an adaptation to "still-existing, albeit dryish, forest environments"; development of mesomorphic foliage in adult trees is attributed to "development of larger, deeper and more efficient root systems." More tenable perhaps, with several lines of circumstantial evidence but certainly as speculative, is the recent suggestion by Greenwood and Atkinson (1977) that this peculiar habit, involving about 10 percent of the woody flora (some fifty-three species, twenty genera, and sixteen families), represents a strategy to resist browsing by the recently extinct group of flightless ratites, the moas, which once were numerous and diverse, and would have had some 70 million years of co-evolution with the flora. Greenwood and Atkinson stress that introduced deer cannot be considered as an ecological equivalent to moas since they browse so differently.

Plant Succession

In addition to the studies of glacial primary succession, several other important successions have also been documented. Cockayne, by describing in 1898 the early stages of succession following fire in mixed subalpine vegetation near the crest of the Southern Alps, initiated the longest recorded and best documented example of plant succession in our ecological literature. An extensive fire in 1890, associated with a railway survey, destroyed areas of subalpine mountain beech (*N. solandri* var. *cliffortioides*) forest and adjoining mixed subalpine scrub and *Chionochloa* tussock grassland near Arthur's Pass (930 m), which Cockayne (1898) described eight years later with detailed semiquantitative comparisons of unburned and burnt vegetation from five sites. Thirty-four years later, Cockayne and Calder (1932) gave comparative descriptions and photographs, and about this time, Calder also established ten permanent belt transects, which were remapped and rephotographed in 1965–1966 to reveal that "the most complex succession after fire is that leading towards tall scrub or low forest. By combining the information from several transects, one can see that development is marked by successive dominants with increasing stature and longevity and decreasing growth rate" (Calder and Wardle 1969).

Another secondary succession, following clearing of North Island coniferous-broad-leaved forest and cultivation by Maori tribes early in the nineteenth century (Cameron 1960), involves a vegetation sequence of fern (*Pteridium*) to shrubland (*Leptospermum*) to broad-leaved species and, by fifty years, establishment of seedling conifers, which require a further fifty years to emerge through the deteriorating mixed broad-leaved forest. Primary forest successions following landslides (Mark et al. 1964) and around bog (pakihi) margins (Mark and Smith 1975) have emphasized the important role of the most tolerant member of the woody flora, *Leptospermum scoparium* (Burrell 1965; Mark et al. 1972; Cook et al. In press). Earlier, Dansereau (1964) discussed the important role of *Leptospermum* in New Zealand forest successions, which he claims are foreshortened because of the nearly complete lack of light-demanding woody species with the exclusive function of building up sub-climax forests, a feature he claims is common abroad. Stevens' (1968) study of a soil chronosequence of the receding Franz Josef Glacier in lowland Westland provided an important basis for documenting and assessing changes in phosphate fractions and availability during pedogenesis (Walker and Syres 1976). This concept is now being extended to certain other nutrients to explain complex mosaics of alpine *Chionochloa* grasslands in relation to soil maturity on North Island's Tararua Range (Williams 1975) and in the highly dissected topography of Fiordland (Williams et al. 1976).

Community Descriptions and Relationships

Vegetation descriptions for one or more purposes, such as defining community relationships in space or time or defining species distribution or environmental relations, continue to receive attention. New Zealand has not been immune from involvement with traditionally opposed viewpoints of vegetation being patterned as discrete communities or as continuua. Altitudinal patterns have been studied in several areas, most recently on North Island's perhumid volcanic cone of Mount Egmont (2,518 m) where Clarkson (1977), using a gradient analysis approach with similarity indices and the average linkage clustering technique of multivariate analysis, in general supported the previously described zonation patterns for this mountain. In particular, the tree shrub and shrub tussock grassland ecotones, which appear relatively diffuse in the absence of beech (*Nothofagus*) species, were shown to exhibit a spectrum of species distributions ranging from continuua to discontinuities at different locations. Moreover, Clarkson stresses that continuities or discontinuities may be physiognomic and structural, as well as floristic, as earlier studies had assumed. This study generally reinforced conclusions from several other less-detailed ones made previously in other parts of New Zealand involving forest (Scott et al. 1964; Wells and Mark 1966; Ogden 1971*a*), grassland (Daly 1967), and alpine vegetation (Mark and Burrell 1966).

Among other approaches to vegetation description, the Braun-Blanquet method of sociological analysis has been successfully applied to characterizing the flora of important tussock grassland communities of the Canterbury mountains on South Island, and through this, has been used to trace the vegetation history of the grasslands from their origin following forest destruction several centuries ago to their currently modified condition associated with more recent use for extensive grazing (Connor 1964, 1965). By contrast, careful measurements and photographic records of vegetation by a single observer over almost thirty years have revealed a successional sequence of important changes in the plant cover of once severely depleted tussock grassland of a semiarid intermontane basin on northeastern South Island (Moore 1976).

Quantitative studies in forest bryoecology in New Zealand offer considerable scope and, despite many sampling problems (Scott 1971), have revealed complex mosaics of ground and epiphytic communities. Forest floor patterns reflect small-scale variations in such environmental factors as substrate, drainage, humidity, litter, and light, while epiphytic assemblages have been shown to vary in relation to height, tilt, girth, exposure, rain tracks, and species of phorophyte (Scott and Armstrong 1966; Scott 1970; Scott and Rowley 1975).

Vegetation Sampling

Relatively little New Zealand research has been invested in developing, critically assessing, or improving the various quantitative sampling methods. However, the point-contact method was a New Zealand innovation (Levy and Madden 1933), which continues to receive attention (Radcliffe and Mountier 1964*a*, *b*; Mountier and Radcliffe 1965). A height-frequency method was devised for sampling the tall grasslands and scrub vegetation (Scott 1965), and has been modified by Williams (1975) to estimate the mass of vegetation and litter in a tussock grassland stand. Studies by Batcheler (1973) have been aimed at improved density estimates from certain plotless methods. The point-centered quarter method of plotless sampling has fallen into disrepute, at least for forest sampling, since it was found to substantially exaggerate tree basal areas in many New Zealand forests. The problem appears to be associated with the wide range of size classes that characterize most New Zealand forests; the method tends to over-represent the large trees since the area potentially available to a tree (which measures its ability to catch the sample points) generally increases with tree size (Franklin 1967; Mark and Esler 1970).

Autecology

Autecological studies have not featured prominently in New Zealand, although several are under way or have been completed recently. Studies by Wardle (1965, 1971, 1973*b*) on the features, phenology, and environmental limitations associated with tree line in New Zealand, particularly the most common form involving one of two species of *Nothofagus,* have led to his current explanation that tree line represents the highest altitude at which shoots can both grow and ripen under the air temperatures prevailing at the height of tree canopies. Wardle's most convincing evidence comes from experiments using local tree line species and various overseas counterparts grown together in a series of gardens both above and below the natural tree line (1,340 m) in Canterbury. Winter killing of beech seedlings in grassland below inverted tree lines on valley floors also stresses the importance of winter hardiness, although in this situation, North American tree line conifers proved tolerant. Experimental verification of low-temperature tolerances of three woody subalpine groups (Wardle and Campbell 1976) explains some important aspects of their present and assumed Quaternary ecology. Recently, Sakai and Wardle (1978) confirmed Cockayne's earlier claim that the indigenous woody flora is relatively intolerant of low temperatures: tolerance limits range from −4° to −25°C among the forty-two species tested and correlated with geographic ranges.

Of the important forest dominants, only *Nothofagus solandri,* the most widely tolerant of the beeches and an irregularly flowering species, has been intensively studied throughout much of its range (Wardle 1970). A significant finding in this study was that stands of mountain beech (var. *cliffortioides*) forest are effectively closed with a basal area of 45–60 m^2 per hectare that may be achieved with stands of mixed size or even-age either by a few large stems or many small ones. The release of understory beech stems is achieved only with tree basal areas less than these values.

Among the herbaceous species, the best studied group is the pair of eastern South Island alpine snow tussocks, *Chionochloa rigida* and *C. macra.* Only recently separated taxonomically, these species dominate extensive areas of the subalpine and alpine zones. These studies, while aimed at overall ecological appraisals (Mark 1965*a, b*; Connor 1966; O'Connor et al. 1972), have been significant in clarifying the separate responses to burning and grazing (O'Connor and Powell 1963; Mark 1965*c*; Rowley 1970) that previously had been confounded by field observations of their deleterious combined effects (Tussock Grassland Research Committee 1954). The irregular flowering of these exceptionally long-lived tussock grasses appears to be unique, at least among grasses, in that induction in midsummer is promoted by relatively high temperatures combined with long days (Mark 1965*b*), the critical temperature showing some ecotypic differentiation among altitudinal populations (Mark 1965*d*; Greer 1979). The inflorescences overwinter partly developed, as with many other alpine species (Mark 1970). A long-term study has revealed that some of the physiological changes, in leaf elongation, new leaf and tiller production, flowering, and nonstructural carbohydrates, which burning initiates in alpine species of *Chionochloa* and which are pronounced during the early years after fire, may persist for up to fifteen years (Payton and Mark 1979).

Several other important indigenous species have been subject to partial autecological studies. Initiation of a "Biological Flora of New Zealand" series by Wardle (1966), along the lines of the British series, has drawn attention to achievements and deficiencies in this important ecological field. To date, "Flora" have been compiled for seven species.

Physiologic Ecology

A limitation of facilities and adequate training has severely restricted physio-ecological studies of the New Zealand flora, although commercially valuable exotic species, particularly *Pinus radiata, Trifolium repens,* and *Lolium perenne,* have been intensively studied. Limited gas exchange studies have shown uniformly low photosynthetic capacities for native herbaceous (Scott et al. 1970; Mark 1975) and woody species (D. Scott 1970; Benecke et al. 1976). Further unpublished studies have reinforced the ecological strategy so far revealed for the alpine Chionochloas regarding the "ecological advantages of the evergreen habit coupled with low energy requirements in coping with cold windy environments" (Mark 1975), which characterize the alpine zone in New Zealand.

The few tree ring studies to date have revealed mostly complacent indicators of climatic variables (Scott 1972; Wells 1972), although a recent extensive study produced twenty chronologies from seven species, four in excess of five hundred years (Dunwiddie 1979). Rings were also used to date the recent volcanic history (within the last five hundred years) of Mount Egmont on the west coast of North Island (Druce 1966).

The ecological importance of phycomycetous mycorrhizae in the New Zealand vegetation has been established by Baylis (1967, 1972) and his students somewhat in advance of the growing appreciation of the global significance of these associations. A major exception is *Nothofagus*, which has ectotrophic mycorrhizae. The slow dispersal of *Nothofagus* already mentioned may be due in part to the major change in soil microbiology that is involved. Inoculation experiments indicate that the mycorrhizal phycomycetes have a wide host range but may be specific to soil type, while the hosts show no distinct preferences as growth responses for particular endophytes (Johnson 1977). The suggested substitution of root hairs for mycotrophy in the effective uptake of phosphorus from phosphate-deficient soils and the possible importance of water relationships in determining alternative evolutionary strategies (Baylis 1975) are ecologically far-reaching hypotheses developed on the basis of New Zealand studies. Root hair development in rushes and sedges has freed them altogether from dependence on mycorrhizal symbionts (Powell 1975).

ECOSYSTEM PRODUCTION

Comprehensive, whole ecosystem studies have not yet been attempted in New Zealand, because of lack of funds and research teams of adequate scope. Nevertheless, several studies have contributed to an understanding of the functioning of indigenous ecosystems. Forest productivity estimates have been restricted almost entirely to measurements of annual litterfall, which is somewhat greater in lowland coniferous–broad-leaved forest, 6,865 kg per hectare or 32 $\times$ 10^6 kcal per hectare (Daniel 1975) than in beech forest. Values for *Nothofagus* forest range from 6,050 to 4,970 kg per nectare or 26 to 23 $\times$ 10^6 kcal per hectare in lowland forests (Miller 1963; Bagnall 1972) with considerable annual variation related particularly to irregular flowering, to values to 3,718 to 3,062 kg per hectare in subalpine mountain beech stands at 1,036 m and 1,340 m, respectively (Wardle 1970). Values for total annual dry matter net production (minus bark values) for these two stands have been estimated at 7,788 kg per hectare and 5,833 kg per hectare, respectively (Wardle 1970).

For the tussock grasslands, the problem of a relatively large evergreen biomass (5.1–8.7 kg/m^2), coupled with conservation problems associated with adequate destructive sampling, has only recently been overcome with the use of a combination of destructive and nondestructive sampling, with the individual tiller rather than the whole plant as the unit of measurement (Williams 1977*a*; Meurk 1978). These methods have established a 148-to-267-day growing season, a total aboveground net annual production of 0.346 kg/m^2 to 0.797 kg/m^2 among seven grasslands stands in Canterbury and Central Otago, with estimated total annual net productions of 1.263 kg/m^2 to 0.726 kg/m^2. Both turnover times for aboveground biomass (10–20 yr) and growing season efficiency ratings (0.5–1.2 percent) increased with altitude in these snow tussock grasslands. Williams (1977*b*) has also established the macro-element pools and fluxes in the aboveground live and dead as well as belowground components of these two grassland ecosystems. A substantial proportion of the aboveground calcium is located in the dead compartment of each stand (77 and 76 percent), whereas for potassium the values are much less, 35 and 23 percent. Turnover of the aboveground components in these grasslands is slow, at about seven to eight years.

Information on secondary productivity remains sketchy, except for studies on native grasshoppers (Acrididae) by Batcheler (1967) and White (1978). Population densities may reach 48,900 per hectare (live biomass of 25.56 kg per hectare) in tussock grassland depleted by introduced deer and chamois (Batcheler 1967), but usually the densities are much lower, with herbage consumption usually no more than 3 percent of annual leaf production (White 1978). Nevertheless, for preferred species, up to 59 percent of foliage biomass may be removed causing local death of up to 11 percent total ground cover.

In a more severe environment of the high-alpine zone in Central Otago at 1,220–1,390 m, Bliss and Mark (1974) combined periodic harvests of pure stands of the more important species with their percentage cover values to establish annual net aboveground production ranging from 0.126 kg/m^2 (cushion) to 0.208–0.255 kg/m^2 (herbfield). In the absence of overwintering bud scale scar references to delimit the new season's growth, plants of each species were tagged to follow seasonal growth increments. The production is somewhat higher than for many physiognomically similar communities abroad although, with an extended growing season (about 150 days), daily net productivity and efficiency (0.18–0.35 percent) approximate many overseas values with phenological events much more extended. Turnover of aboveground biomass is very slow (7.6–15.3 years). As with the snow tussock grasslands, an unusually large proportion of the standing crop is aboveground, up to two-thirds for most species, perhaps reflecting the relatively mild winter temperatures of New Zealand's mountain climate.

ANIMAL AND WILDLIFE ECOLOGY

Studies of vertebrate ecology in New Zealand have largely centered around an understanding of the limited range of native vertebrates, particularly the unusual avifauna in relation to the generally more successful introduced fauna. Second, there have been ecological studies of the various introduced mammals aided by unusually large samples that are possible with unrestricted hunting. Third, studies have been conducted on the management of harvestable species, both native and introduced.

Richdale's classic studies, many published privately, embraced population ecology, behavior, and breeding biology of a wide range of birds, including the yellow-eyed penguin (*Megadyptes antipodes*), royal albatross (*Diomedea epomorpha*), Buller's mollymawk (*D. bulleri*), and sooty shearwater (*Puffinus griseus*) (Richdale 1951, 1957, 1963). More recently, studies of seabirds, both on mainland New Zealand and its off-lying islands, including those of the subantarctic as well as in New Zealand's Antarctic territory, have been continued by Westerskov (1963), Stonehouse (1967), Mills (1969), Warham (1971), Young (1976), and others.

Among the now-rare species, the flightless kakapo (*Strigops habroptilus*) in the precipitous glaciated country of Fiordland (Williams 1956) and the presumed-extinct flightless rail or notornis (*Notornis mantelli*), rediscovered in Fiordland in 1948, have recently stimulated more intensive studies. In the case of notornis, these studies were aimed initially at breeding behavior and population dynamics (Williams 1960; Williams and Miers 1958; Reid 1967). More recent studies of both kakapo and notornis have extended to their habitats and seasonal diets. Food preference studies on notornis were based initially on cuticle analyses of feces; these have been replaced by more direct studies of nutrient contents that have revealed an ability for selection both among and between species for the more nutritious plants. This ability is also shared by introduced red deer, which appear to be offering serious competition (Mills and Mark 1977). Ecological studies of another avifaunal curiosity, the kiwi, have been relatively minor, although the species, unlike many others, appears to be less endangered.

New Zealand's primitive endemic reptile, the tuatara (*Sphenodon punctatus*), now confined to islands close to the mainland, appears from age distribution and density studies to be declining on those islands where it occurs in conjunction with and in competition with the Polynesian rat or kiore (*Rattus exulans*). This decline is even apparent on certain islands without such competition (Crook 1973).

New Zealand has provided an excellent research facility for studying population explosion among many of the introduced mammals, although for several of these the documentation has been only partial. Introductions have been detailed by Wodzicki (1950), and a general account of their impact has been provided by Howard (1965). The economic consequences of extremely high rabbit numbers encouraged serious scientific work, initially by Wodzicki; subsequent researchers concentrated on reproduction and population ecology (Tyndale-Biscoe 1955; Watson 1957; Bull 1964). Similar studies were made of red deer (*Cervus elaphus*) (Caughley 1971) and thar (*Hemitragus jemlahicus*) (Caughley 1970*a*); in both cases, a kidney fat index was found to indicate the level of population well-being (Caughley 1970*b*). Caughley (1963) also determined dispersal rates for nine ungulate species that ranged from 0.6 km/yr for wapiti (*Cervus canadensis*) to 8.6 km/yr for chamois (*Rupicapra rupicapra*). In addition, he studied the eruption of thar in New Zealand by sampling populations at different distances from the point of liberation (Caughley 1970*c*); these studies showed fluctuations in the eruption spanning fifty years.

An extended breeding season has given the rabbit (*Oryctolagus cuniculus*) reproductive advantage over the hare (*Lepus europaeus*) in New Zealand, but hares have shown a greater tendency to penetrate and establish above the tree line where they live year-round. Though widespread, hares generally cause less damage than red deer or chamois, but population assessment of hares by pellet counts was complicated by relatively slow and variable decay rates, namely, half-lives of seven months at 610 m to over three years at 1,520 m (Flux 1967).

Most of the introduced mammals show definite preferences in their diet although, not surprisingly, a large proportion of the New Zealand flora appears generally palatable. The preference of opossum for important dominants such as species of *Metrosideros* and *Weinmannia* (Kean and Pracy 1953) means that where these trees clothe the steep montane slopes of central Westland under conditions of frequent high-intensity rainfall, land stability is being seriously impaired. Studies of the three species of mustelids have only recently been intensified to provide a full ecological perspective, but these have not yet been published.

Despite several ecological studies aimed at the elucidation of possible control measures (Riney and Caughley 1959), the control of all noxious mammals in New Zealand, in the absence of any significant predation, has depended on direct killing operations chiefly by one or two methods, poisoning or shooting. Some 110,000 deer carcasses were exported in 1970–1971, while 13 million rabbit skins were exported annually during the decade prior to introduction of a killer policy in 1949.

Ecological studies applied to the management of several game species have received considerable attention and have provided important basic information. Of significance are the studies of California quail (Williams 1963, 1967), pheasant (Westerskov 1956), grey ducks and mallards (Balham and Miers 1959; Williams 1969), and pukeko (*Porphyro melanotus*).

Ecological studies of New Zealand passerines generally have received lower priority, although the study by Kikkawa (1966) is notable. Among the most recent investigations, consequences of reduction and modification of indigenous forests have received increasing attention (McLay 1974).

Among the sizable invertebrate fauna, with the exception of the grasshopper studies previously mentioned, effort has been directed largely to application to agriculture, particularly the beneficial effects of earthworms (Stockdill 1966) and the deleterious effects of certain insect larval stages on pasture grasses (Wightman 1974).

LIMNOLOGY

Early limnology in New Zealand cannot be recognized as a discipline distinct from the taxonomic and general biological studies that characterized field projects until the 1920s and 1930s. The appointment of E. J. Percival to the University of Canterbury in 1929 and of B. J. Marples to the University of Otago in 1936 gave the initial stimulus to the study of inland waters, and, although these two workers did not publish a great deal, their interest and encouragement stimulated students both inside and outside the universities. Percival was interested in trout and salmon ecology and lake studies (1932, 1937, 1952), while Marples involved himself in the general biology of a wide range of organisms that led to the publication of the first book on New Zealand freshwater life (1962). A further early classic was the work of K. R. Allen (1951) on the trout population of the Horokiwi Stream that quantified the higher levels of production in a small stream.

The number of workers in universities and government departments increased steadily during the 1950s and 1960s, and the spread of interest led to the formation in 1968 of the New Zealand Limnological Society. This society, coming into existence at a time when environmental problems were receiving increasing attention from government and the general public, has acted as a further stimulus to limnological studies. A number of broad areas of effort can be traced over the last twenty years.

General and non-applied studies of lakes and rivers have developed along various lines, and the lake studies resulted in a major publication (Jolly and Brown 1975). Studies on rivers are more scattered (Winterbourn 1974, 1976). Within the last ten to fifteen years, however, the development of applied studies has accelerated markedly. The effects of insecticides on fish and invertebrates has received attention (Hopkins et al. 1969; Dacre and Scott 1971, 1973), while organic pollution of rivers has also been studied (Winterbourne et al. 1971; Scott 1973).

Eutrophication has attracted considerable attention from the 1960s onward. Mitchell (1971, 1975) and Burnet and Wallace (1973) used a carbon-14 technique to estimate primary production, while Fish (1975) emphasized the nutrient budget of enriched lakes. In 1969, the Department of Scientific and Industrial Research (DSIR) set up a freshwater research unit with particular emphasis on eutrophication and metabolism of nitrogen and phosphorus in lakes and streams. A research section within the Ministry of Works and Development is studying the basic ecology and physiology of planktonic algae, nutrient budgets for lakes, and modelling oxygen and chlorophyll concentrations in lakes and rivers. Factors influencing nutrient runoff are being investigated by the DSIR Soil Bureau, and extensive bathymetric surveys of lakes have been conducted by the Oceanographic Institute of DSIR. Macrophytic vegetation in lakes and rivers has reached nuisance proportions, and factors controlling its distribution have been studied (Chapman et al. 1971, 1974). Algal blooms have also been recorded where none were present twenty years ago (Burns and Mitchell 1974). The systematics and biology of New Zealand freshwater crustacea have been reviewed recently by Chapman and Lewis (1976).

While basic studies are not being neglected in New Zealand, it is obvious that the main developments are determined by those applied aspects that appear to warrant significant financial support.

MARINE ECOLOGY

As with many other parts of the world, results of the H.M.S. *Challenger* expedition of 1872–1876 made the first and most substantial contributions of the nineteenth century to marine biology, particularly on the deep-sea fauna of the New Zealand region. Overseas scientific expeditions, some including local scientists, have continued to make important contributions to the field (Putnam 1977).

With the turn of the century, marine biology and ecology received considerable impetus with the establishment in 1904, through government and local fundings, of a field station (Portobello) on Otago Harbour for fisheries research. However, the total research investment remained minimal until after the Second World War. Following its decline, the Portobello station was given to the University of Otago in 1951, and since then, there has been continued investment in facilities and research staff in other centers, as well as an improved coordination of activities (Dell 1976). Three other field stations were established by universities in the 1960s and now provide opportunities for a representative coverage. In addition, staff of the government's Oceanographic Institute, as well as its Fisheries Research and Management Divisions, are also involved, particularly with applied aspects of marine ecology. Moreover, there are eight research vessels available, owned privately (1) or by government (5) or universities (2). Nevertheless, limitations of trained staff and funds have meant that contributions from this important field have fallen far short of national needs.

Lucrative commercial exploitation of crustaceans [rock lobster (*Jasus* spp.)] and molluscs [dredge oyster (*Ostrea lutaria*), scallop (*Pecten novae zelandiae*), green-lipped mussel (*Perna canaliculus*), abalone or paua (*Haliotis iris*), and toheroa (*Paphies ventricosa*)] has been inadequately regulated and only recently have studies begun to provide adequate biological and ecological information. Moreover, available information has not always been applied to management of these species (Kensler 1969). Major stocks of all of them have been depleted, some seriously so.

With the systematics and biology of New Zealand seashore biota now reasonably well known, advances in understanding the ecology of this zone, as well as the successional patterns, are now possible, and the scope for experimental and physiological aspects of ecology are now becoming apparent (Morton and Miller 1968). Studies have recently been initiated on the ecology and seasonal succession of several intertidal algae and the life histories of some common invertebrates, particularly bivalves, gastropods, and decapod crustacea, as well as fishes. University of Auckland studies, using SCUBA, have made important contributions to understanding the mechanics of shallow sublittoral communities in the North Auckland region. The recent introduction of commercial shellfish farming (green-lipped mussel and northern rock oysters) has provided impetus for appropriate applied research. Biological production is yet to be measured in any seashore habitat in New Zealand. The intertidal and shallow-water fauna and flora have been related to the prevailing hydrologic conditions of the New Zealand marine environment by Knox (1963).

Although phytoplankton production is likely to be high because of mixing associated with strong tides and convergences around the New Zealand coast, few substantiating studies have been made (Cassie 1960; Cassie and Cassie 1960; Bradford and Roberts 1977). This latter study of waters around New Zealand has revealed chlorophyll *a* concentrations (surface to 10-m depth) of about 1.0 mg/m^3 from spring through autumn, a surface primary productivity of 0.25–2.0 mg/m^3 per hour, and integrated primary production of 0.25–1.0 g/m^2 per day. Zooplankton biomass is mostly within the range of 25–300 mg/m^3 except for much of the Tasman Sea to the west, where values less than 25 mg/m^3 have been recorded. An important finding was the significant correlation between reactive phosphorus and primary productivity of the surface waters that contrasts with some results from tropical waters of the Pacific Ocean where no such correlation was established. Similarly, there was evidence that fluctuations in phytoplankton are out of phase with those of zooplankton, a phenomenon that is becoming accepted for the high latitudes, yet is not a feature of low-latitude oceanic ecosystems. The values for primary production and zooplankton biomass established by Bradford and Roberts

(1977) are within the ranges previously recorded for other upwelling regions, but information on seasonal variation is still unavailable.

Measurements of secondary productivity have been negligible except for the work of Bradford and Roberts (1977) and earlier studies on distribution and density of zooplankton, although faunal benthic communities of the relatively narrow continental shelf extending out to about about 180 m have been described and defined by McKnight (1969).

Commercial harvesting of inshore fish has been relatively limited by New Zealand-operated boats (although beyond the twelve-mile limit of the territorial sea it has been intensive by foreign vessels), and the input of applied research has been limited. In the last decade, there have been quite extensive studies of most common, traditionally exploited marine fishes, especially snapper, tarakihi, gurnard, and flat fish, as well as others that are readily available, such as trevally and horse mackerel. In recent years, oceanic-pelagic fishes have begun to be fished and studied by New Zealanders. Big-game fishing, although an important activity off the northeast coast, has not yet been subject to any serious ecological investigations.

Although much remains to be done, and financing and facilities are both still severely limited, considerable momentum has been generated. Establishment of a 200-mile economic management zone around the New Zealand coast has sustained continuing acceleration in this important field of marine ecology.

Studies involving computer simulation and systems modelling are increasing, although few have yet been published.

Many professional ecologists in New Zealand, as in most developed countries, are expressing concern with those aspects of development that have serious ecological implications, as well as stressing the importance of an ecological perspective to future planning (Fordham and Ogden 1974).

ACKNOWLEDGMENTS

The assistance of Drs. J. B. Jillet, S. F. Mitchell, D. Scott, and K. E. Westerskov, Zoology Department, University of Otago, in the fields of marine, lacustrine, stream, and wildlife ecology, respectively, is recorded with thanks.

REFERENCES CITED

Allen, K. R. 1951. The Horokiwi Stream. *Fish Bull.* (Wellington, *N.Z.*) 10:1–231.

Bagnall, R. G. 1972. The dry weight and caloric value of litter fall in a New Zealand *Nothofagus* forest. *N.Z. J.Bot.* 10:27–36.

Balham, R. W. and K. H. Miers. 1959. *Mortality and survival of grey and mallard ducks banded in New Zealand.* N.Z. Dept Internal Affairs Wildlife Pub. No. 5.

Batcheler, C. L. 1967. Preliminary observations of alpine grasshoppers in a habitat modified by deer and chamois. *Proc. N.Z. Ecol. Soc.* 14:15–26.

———. 1973. Estimating density and dispersion from truncated or unrestricted joint point-distance nearest-neighbour distances. *Proc. N.Z. Ecol. Soc.* 20:131–147.

Baylis, G. T. S. 1967. Experiments on the ecological significance of phycomycetous mycorrhizas. *New Phytol.* 66:231–243.

———. 1972. Fungi, phosphorus and the evolution of root systems. *Search* 3:257–258.

———. 1975. The magnolioid mycorrhiza and mycotrophy in root systems derived from it. In *Endomycorrhizas,* eds. F. E. Sanders, B. Mosse, and P. B. Tinker, pp. 373–389. London: Academic Press.

——— and A. F. Mark. 1963. Vegetation studies on Secretary Island, Fiordland. Part 4. Composition of the beech-podocarp forest. *N.Z. J. Bot.* 1:203–207.

Benecke, U., W. Havranek, and I. McCracken. 1976. Comparative study of water use by tree species in a mountain environment. *Proc. Soil and Plant Water Symposium,* pp. 191–199. Dept. Scient. Indust. Res., Palmerston North, N.2.

Bliss, L. C. and A. F. Mark. 1974. High-alpine environments and primary production on Rock and Pillar Range, Central Otago, New Zealand. *N.Z. J. Bot.* 12:445–483.

Bradford, J. M. and P. E. Roberts. 1977. Distribution of reactive phosphorus and plankton in relation to upwelling and surface circulation around New Zealand. *N.Z. J. Mar. Freshwat. Res.* 11:131–144.

Bull, P. C. 1964. Ecology of helminth parasites of the wild rabbit *Oryctolagus cuniculus* (L.) in New Zealand. *N.Z. Dept. Sci. Indust. Res. Bull.* Vol. 158.

Burnet, A. M. R. and D. A. Wallace. 1973. The relation between primary productivity, nutrients and the trout environment in some New Zealand lakes. *N.Z. Fish. Res. Bull.* 10:1–28.

Burns, C. W. and S. F. Mitchell. 1974. Seasonal succession and vertical distribution of phytoplankton in Lake Hayes and Lake Johnson, South Island, New Zealand. *N.Z. J. Mar. Freshwat. Res.* 8:167–209.

Burrell, J. 1965. Ecology of *Leptospermum* in Otago. *N.Z. J. Bot.* 3:3–16.

Burrows, C. J. 1965. Some discontinuous distributions of plants within New Zealand and their ecological significance. Part 2. Disjunctions between Otago-Southland and Nelson-Marlborough and related distribution patterns. *Tuatara* 13:9–29.

———. 1969. Alpine grasslands. In *The natural history of Canterbury,* ed. G. A. Knox, pp. 133–166. Wellington: Reed.

———. 1973. Studies of some glacial moraines in New Zealand. 2. Ages of moraines of the Mueller, Hooker, and Tasman Glaciers (S79). *N.Z. J. Geol. Geophys.* 16:831–855.

——— and B. R. Maunder. 1975. The recent moraines of the Lyell and Ramsay Glaciers, Rakaia Valley, Canterbury. *J. R. Soc. N.Z.* 5:479–491.

——— and J. Orwin. 1971. Studies of some glacial moraines in New Zealand. 1. The establishment of lichen-growth curves in the Mount Cook area. *N.Z. J. Sci.* 14:327–335.

Calder, J. W. and P. Wardle. 1969. Succession in subalpine vegetation at Arthur's Pass, New Zealand. *Proc. N.Z. Ecol. Soc.* 16:36–47.

Cameron, R. J. 1960. Natural regeneration of podocarps in the forests of the Whirinaki River Valley. *N.Z. J. For.* 8:337–354.

Cassie, V. 1960. Seasonal changes in diatoms and dinoflagellates of the east coast of New Zealand during 1957 and 1958. *N.Z. J. Sci.* 3:137–172.

Cassie, R. M. and V. Cassie. 1960. Primary production in a New Zealand west coast phytoplankton bloom. *N.Z. J. Sci.* 3:173–199.

Caughley, G. 1963. Dispersal rates of several ungulates introduced into New Zealand. *Nature* 200:280–281.

______. 1970*a*. Liberation, dispersal and distribution of Himalayan thar (*Hemitragus jemlahicus*) in New Zealand. *N.Z. J. Sci.* 13:220–239.

______. 1970*b*. Fat reserves of Himalayan thar in New Zealand by season, sex, area and age. *N.Z. J. Sci.* 13:209–219.

______. 1970*c*. Eruption of ungulate populations, with emphasis on Himalayan thar in New Zealand. *Ecology* 51:53–72.

______. 1971. Demography, fat reserves and body size of a population of red deer, *Cervus elaphus,* in New Zealand. *Mammalia* 35:369–383.

Chapman, M. A. and M. H. Lewis. 1976. *An introduction to the freshwater crustacea of New Zealand.* Auckland: Collins.

Chapman, V. J., J. M. A. Brown, F. I. Dromgoole, and B. T. Coffey. 1971. Submerged vegetation of the Rotorua and Waikato Lakes. *N.Z. J. Mar. Freshw. Res.* 5:259–279.

______, J. M. A. Brown, F. Hill, and J. L. Carr. 1974. Biology of excessive weed growth in the hydro-electric lakes of the Waikato River, New Zealand. *Hydrobiologia* 44:349–363.

Clarkson, B. D. 1977. Vegetation change along an altitudinal gardient, Mount Egmont, New Zealand. Unupb. M.Sc. thesis, University of Waikato.

Cockayne, L. 1898. On the burning and reproduction of subalpine scrub and its associated plants with special reference to Arthur's Pass district. *Trans. N.Z. Inst.* 31:398–418.

______. 1900. A sketch of the plant geography of the Waimakariri River basin, considered chiefly from an oecological point of view. *Trans. N.Z. Inst.* 32:95–136.

______. 1909. The ecological botany of the Subantarctic Islands of New Zealand. In *The Subantarctic Islands of New Zealand,* ed. C. Chilton, pp. 182–235.

______. 1910. *New Zealand plants and their story.* Wellington: Government Printer.

______. 1912. Observations concerning evolution, derived from ecological studies in New Zealand. *Trans. N.Z. Inst.* 44:1–50.

______. 1921. *The vegetation of New Zealand.* Leipzig: W. Engelmann.

______. 1926. Monograph on the New Zealand beech forests. Part 1. The ecology of the forests and taxonomy of the beeches. *N.Z. State For. Serv. Bull.* Vol. 4.

______. 1928. *The vegetation of New Zealand,* 2d ed. Leipzig: W. Engelmann.

______ and J. W. Calder. 1932. The present vegetation of Arthur's Pass (New Zealand) as compared with that of thirty-four years ago. *J. Ecol.* 20:270–283.

Connor, H. E. 1964. Tussock grassland communities in the Mackenzie country, south Canterbury, New Zealand. *N.Z. J. Bot.* 2:325–351.

______. 1965. Tussock grasslands in the middle Rakaia Valley, Canterbury, New Zealand. *N.Z. J. Bot.* 3:261–276.

______. 1966. Breeding systems in New Zealand grasses. VII. Periodic flowering of snow tussock, *Chionochloa rigida*. *N.Z. J. Bot.* 4:392–397.

Cook, J. M., A. F. Mark, and B. F. Shore. In press. Responses of *Leptospermum scoparium* and *L. ericoides* to waterlogging. *N.Z. J. Bot.*

Cranwell, L. M. and L. von Post. 1936. Post-Pleistocene pollen diagrams from the Southern Hemisphere. 1. New Zealand. *Geogr. Ann.* 3–4:308–347.

Crook, I. G. 1973. The tuatara, *Sphenodon punctatus* Gray, on islands with and without populations of the Polynesian rat, *Rattus exulans* (Peale). *Proc. N.Z. Ecol. Soc.* 20:115–120.

Dacre, J. C. and D. Scott. 1971. Possible DDT mortality in young rainbow trout. *N.Z. J. Mar. Freshw. Res.* 5:58–65.

______. 1973. Effects of dieldrin on brown trout in field and laboratory studies. *N.Z. J. Mar. Freshw. Res.* 7:235–246.

Daly, G. T. 1967. Ordination of grassland and related communities in Otago. *Proc. N.Z. Ecol. Soc.* 14:63–70.

Daniel, M. J. 1975. Preliminary account of litter production in a New Zealand lowland podocarp-rata-broadleaf forest. *N.Z. J. Bot.* 13:173–187.

Dansereau, P. 1964. Six problems of New Zealand vegetation. *Bull. Torr. Bot. Club* 91:114–140.

Dell, R. K. 1976. Post-war developments of New Zealand oceanography: a personal view. *N.Z. J. Mar. Freshw. Res.* 10:1–14.

Druce, A. P. 1966. Tree-ring dating of recent volcanic ash and lapilli, Mt Egmont. *N.Z. J. Bot.* 4:3–41.

Dumbleton, L. J. 1967. Winter dormancy in New Zealand biota and its palaeoclimatic implications. *N.Z. J. Bot.* 5:211–222.

Dunwiddie, P. W. 1979. Dendrochronological studies of indigenous New Zealand tree species. *N.Z. J. Bot.* 17:251–266.

Fish, G. R. 1975. Lake Rotorua and Rotoiti: their trophic status and studies for a nutrient budget. *Fish. Res. Bull.* 8:1–70.

Fleming, C. A. 1975*a*. The Quaternary record of New Zealand and Australia. In *Quaternary studies,* eds. R. P. Suggate and M. M. Cresswell, pp. 1–20. Wellington: Royal Society of New Zealand.

______. 1975*b*. The geological history of New Zealand and its biota. In *Biogeography and ecology in New Zealand,* ed. G. Kuschel, pp. 1–86. The Hague: W. Junk.

______. 1977. The history of life in New Zealand forests. *N.Z. J. For.* 22:249–262.

Flux, J. E. C. 1967. Hare numbers and diet in an alpine basin in New Zealand. *Proc. N.Z. Ecol. Soc.* 14:27–33.

Fordham, R. A. and J. Ogden. 1974. An ecological approach to New Zealand's future. *Supplement to Proc. N.Z. Ecol. Soc.* Vol. 21.

Franklin, D. A. 1967. Basal area as determined by the point-centered quarter method. *N.Z. J. Bot.* 5:168–169.

Gage, M. and R. P. Suggate. 1958. Glacial chronology of the New Zealand Pleistocene. *Bull. Geol. Soc. Am.* 69:589–598.

Greenwood, R. M. and I. A. E. Atkinson. 1977. Evolution of divaricating plants in New Zealand in relation to moa browsing. *Proc. N.Z. Ecol. Soc.* 24:21–29.

Greer, D. H. 1979. Effects of long-term preconditioning on growth and flowering of some snow tussock (*Chionochloa* spp.) populations in Otago, New Zealand. *Aust. J. Bot.* 27:617–630.

Holloway, J. T. 1948. The vegetation and soils of Otago. In *The face of Otago,* ed. B. J. Garnier, pp. 26–35. Dunedin: Whitcombe and Tombs.

———. 1954. Forests and climates in the South Island of New Zealand. *Trans. R. Soc. N.Z.* 82:329–410.

Hopkins, C. L., S. R. B. Solly, and A. R. Ritchie. 1969. DDT in trout and its possible effect on reproductive potential. *N.Z. J. Mar. Freshw. Res.* 3:220–229.

Howard, W. A. 1965. *Control of introduced mammals in New Zealand.* N.Z. Dept. Sci. Indust. Res. Invo. Series No. 45.

Johnson, P. N. 1977. Mycorrhizal Endogonaceae in a New Zealand forest. *New Phytol.* 78:16–70.

Jolly, V. H. and J. M. A. Brown. 1975. *New Zealand lakes.* Auckland: Auckland University Press.

Kean, R. I. and L. Pracy. 1953. Effects of the Australian opossum (*Trichosurus vulpecula* Kerr) on indigenous vegetation in New Zealand. *Proc. 7th Pacif. Sci. Cong.* 4:696–705.

Kensler, C. B. 1969. Commercial landings of the spiny lobster *Jasus edwardsii* (Hutton) at Chatham Islands, New Zealand (Crustacea: Decapoda: Palinuridae). *N.Z. J. Mar. Freshw. Res.* 3:506–517.

Kikkawa, J. 1966. Population distribution of land birds in temperate rain forest of southern New Zealand. *Trans. R. Soc. N.Z.* 7:215–277.

Knox, G. 1963. The biogeography and intertidal ecology of the Australiasian coasts. *Oceanogr. Mar. Biol.* 1:341–404.

Kuschel, G., ed. 1975. *Biogeography and ecology in New Zealand.* The Hague: W. Junk.

Levy, E. B. and E. A. Madden. 1933. The point method of pasture analysis. *N.Z. J. Agric.* 46:267–279.

McKnight, D. G. 1969. Infaunal benthic communities of the New Zealand continental shelf. *N.Z. J. Mar. Freshw. Res.* 3:409–444.

McLay, C. L. 1974. The species diversity of New Zealand forest birds: some possible consequences of the modification of beech forests. *N.Z. J. Zool.* 1:179–196.

Mark, A. F. 1965*a*. The environment and growth rate of narrow-leaved snow tussock, *Chionochloa rigida,* in Otago. *N.Z. J. Bot.* 3:73–103.

———. 1965*b*. Flowering, seeding, and seedling establishment of narrow-leaved snow tussock. *N.Z. J. Bot.* 3:180–193.

———. 1965*c*. Effects of management practices on narrow-leaved snow tussock, *Chionochloa rigida. N.Z. J. Bot.* 3:300–319.

———. 1965*d*. Ecotypic differentiation in Otago populations of narrow-leaved snow tussock, *Chionochloa rigida. N.Z. J. Bot.* 3:277–299.

———. 1970. Floral initiation and development in New Zealand alpine plants. *N.Z. J. Bot.* 8:67–75.

———. 1976. Photosynthesis and dark respiration in three alpine snow tussocks (*Chionochloa* spp.) under controlled environments. *N.Z. J. Bot.* 13:93–122.

——— and G. T. S. Baylis. 1975. Impact of deer on Secretary Island, Fiordland, New Zealand. *Proc. N.Z. Ecol. Soc.* 22:19–24.

——— and J. Burrell. 1966. Vegetation studies on the Humboldt Mountains, Fiordland. Part 1. The alpine tussock grasslands. *Proc. N.Z. Ecol. Soc.* 13:12–28.

——— and A. E. Esler. 1970. An assessment of the point-centered quarter method of plotless sampling in some New Zealand forests. *Proc. N.Z. Ecol. Soc.* 17:106–110.

———, P. N. Johnson, J. R. Crush, and C. D. Meurk. 1972. Applied ecological studies of shoreline vegetation at Lakes Manapouri and Te Anau, Fiordland. Parts 1 to 4. *Proc. N.Z. Ecol. Soc.* 19:100–157.

———, G. A. M. Scott, F. R. Sanderson, and P. W. James. 1964. Forest succession on landslides above Lake Thomson, Fiordland. *N.Z. J. Bot.* 2:60–89.

——— and P. M. F. Smith. 1975. A lowland vegetation sequence in South Westland: pakihi bog to mixed beech-podocarp forest. Part 1. The principal strata. *Proc. N.Z. Ecol. Soc.* 22:76–92.

Marples, B. J. 1962. *An introduction to freshwater life in New Zealand.* Christchurch: Whitcombe and Tombs.

Meads, M. J. 1976. Effects of opossum browsing on northern rata trees in the Orongorongo Valley, Wellington, New Zealand. *N.Z. J. Zool.* 3:127–139.

Meurk, C. D. 1978. Alpine phytomass and primary productivity in Central Otago, New Zealand. *N.Z. J. Ecol.* 1:27–50.

Miller, R. B. 1963. Plant nutrients in hard beech. III. The cycle of nutrients. *N.Z. J. Sci.* 6:388–413.

Mills, J. A. 1969. The distribution of breeding red-billed gull colonies in New Zealand in relation to areas of plankton enrichment. *Notornis* 16:180–186.

——— and A. F. Mark. 1977. Food preferences of takahe in Fiordland National Park, New Zealand and the effect of competition from introduced red deer. *J. Anim. Ecol.* 46:939–958.

Mitchell, S. F. 1971. Phytoplankton productivity in Tomahawk Lagoon, Lake Waipori, and Lake Mahinerangi. *Fish Res. Bull.* 3:1–87.

———. 1975. Some effects of agricultural development and fluctuations in water level on the phytoplankton productivity and zooplankton of a New Zealand reservoir. *Freshwat. Biol.* 5:547–562.

Moar, N. T. 1971. Contributions to the Quaternary history of the New Zealand flora. 6. Aranuian pollen diagrams from Canterbury, Nelson, and North Westland, South Island. *N.Z. J. Bot.* 9:80–145.

———. 1973. Late Pleistocene vegetation and environment in southern New Zealand. In *Palaeoecology of Africa, the surrounding islands, and Antarctica,* ed. E. M. van Zinderen Bakker Sr., pp. 181–198. Cape Town: Balkena.

Molloy, B. P. J., C. J. Burrows, J. E. Cox, A. Johnston, and P. Wardle. 1963. Distribution of sub-fossil forest remains, eastern South Island, New Zealand. *N.Z. J. Bot.* 1:68–77.

——— and J. E. Cox. 1972. Subfossil remains and their bearing on forest history in the Rakaia Catchment, Canterbury, New Zealand. *N.Z. J. Bot.* 10:267–276.

Moore, L. B. 1967. The Cockayne Memorial Lecture, 1965. Leonard Cockayne, botanist. *Trans. R. Soc. N.Z. (General)* 2:1–18.

———. 1976. The changing vegetation of Molesworth Station, New Zealand, 1944 to 1971. *N.Z. Dept. Sci. Indust. Res. Bull.* Vol. 217.

Morton, J. E. and M. C. Miller. 1968. *The New Zealand sea shore.* London: Collins.

Mountier, N. S. and J. E. Radcliffe. 1965. Problems in measuring pasture composition in the field. 4. Observer variation with the point method. *N.Z. J. Bot.* 3:242–253.

O'Connor, K. F., H. E. Connor, and B. P. J. Molloy. 1972. Response of four species of *Chionochloa* and two introduced grasses to soil amendment. *N.Z. J. Bot.* 10:205–224.

——— and A. J. Powell. 1963. Studies on the management of snow-tussock grassland. I. The effects of burning, cutting and fertilizer on narrow-leaved snow tussock (*Chionochloa rigida* (Raoul) Zotov) at a mid-altitude site in Canterbury. *N.Z. J. Agric. Res.* 6:354–367.

Ogden, J. 1971*a*. Studies on the vegetation of Mount Colenso, New Zealand. 1. The forest continuum. *Proc. N.Z. Ecol. Soc.* 18:58–65.

———. 1971*b*. Studies on the vegetation of Mount Colenso, New Zealand. 2. The population dynamics of red beech. *Proc. N.Z. Ecol. Soc.* 18:66–75.

Payton, I. J. and A. F. Mark. 1979. Long-term effects of burning on growth, flowering and carbohydrate reserves in narrow-leaved snow tussock (*Chionochloa rigida*). *N.Z. J. Bot.* 17:43–54.

Percival, E. 1932. The depreciation of trout-fishing in the Oreti (or New River), Southland. *Fish. Bull.* (Wellington) 5:1–48.

———. 1937. New species of Copepoda from New Zealand lakes. *Rec. Canterbury Mus.* 4:169–175.

———. 1952. Some aspects of limnology in New Zealand. *N.Z. Sci. Rev.* 10:83–84.

Pocknall, D. T. 1978. Relative pollen representation in relation to vegetation composition, Westland, New Zealand. *N.Z. J. Bot.* 16:379–386.

Powell, C. L. 1975. Rushes and sedges are non-mycotrophic. *Plant Soil* 42:481–484.

Putnam, G. 1977. A brief history of New Zealand marine biology. *Tuatara* 22:189–212.

Radcliffe, J. E. and N. S. Mountier. 1964*a*. Problems in measuring pasture composition in the field. Part 1. Discussion of general problems and some consideration of the point method. *N.Z. J. Bot.* 2:90–97.

——— and N. S. Mountier. 1964*b*. Problems in measuring pasture composition in the field. Part 2. The effect of vegetation height using the point method. *N.Z. J. Bot.* 2:98–108.

Raeside, J. D. 1948. Some post-glacial climatic changes in Cantebury and their effect on soil formation. *Trans. R. Soc. N.Z.* 77:153–171.

Reid, B. E. 1967. Some features of recent research on the Takahe (*Notornis mantelli*). *Proc. N.Z. Ecol. Soc.* 14:79–87.

Richdale, L. E. 1951. *Sexual behavior in penguins.* Kansas: Kansas University Press.

———. 1957. *A population study of penguins.* London: Oxford University Press.

———. 1963. Biology of the sooty shearwater, *Puffinus griseus. Proc. Zool. Soc. London* 141:1–117.

Riney, T. and G. Caughley. 1959. A study of home range of a feral goat herd. *N.Z. J. Sci.* 2:157–170.

Rowley, J. 1970. Effects of burning and clipping on temperature, growth, and flowering of narrow-leaved snow tussock. *N.Z. J. Bot.* 8:264–282.

Sakai, A. and P. Wardle. 1978. Freezing resistance of New Zealand trees and shrubs. *N.Z. J. Ecol.* 1:51–61.

Scott, D. 1965. A height frequency method for sampling tussock and scrub vegetation. *N.Z. J. Bot.* 3:253–260.

———. 1970. Comparison between lodgepole pine and mountain beech in establishment and CO_2 exchange. *N.Z. J. Bot.* 8:357–360.

———. 1972. Correlation between tree-ring width and climate in two areas in New Zealand. *J. R. Soc. N.Z.* 2:545–560.

———. 1973. Animal indicators of organic pollution. Proc. Pollution Research Conference. *Dept. Scient. Indust. Res. Info. Series Bull.* 97:445–456.

———. 1979. Use and conservation of New Zealand native grasslands. *N.Z. J. Ecol.* 2:71–75.

———, P. H. Menalda, and J. A. Rowley. 1970. CO_2 exchange of plants. 1. Technique, and response of seven species to light intensity. *N.Z. J. Bot.* 8:82–90.

Scott, G. A. M. 1970. Vegetation studies on Secretary Island, Fiordland. Part 2. Epiphytic and ground cryptogamic vegetation on the northern slopes. *N.Z. J. Bot.* 8:30–50.

———. 1971. Some problems in quantitative ecology of bryophytes. *N.Z. J. Bot.* 9:744–749.

——— and J. M. Armstrong. 1966. The altitudinal sequence of climax vegetation on Mt Anglem, Steward Island Part 2. Ground and epiphytic vegetation. *N.Z. J. Bot.* 4:283–299.

———, A. F. Mark, and F. R. Sanderson. 1964. Altitudinal variation in forest composition near Lake Hankinson, Fiordland. *N.Z. J. Bot.* 2:310–323.

——— and J. A. Rowley. 1975. A lowland vegetation sequence in South Westland: pakihi to mixed beech-podocarp forest. Part 2. Ground and epiphytic vegetation. *Proc. N.Z. Ecol. Soc.* 22:93–108.

Stevens, P. R. 1968. A chronosequence of soils near Franz Josef Glacier. Unpub. Ph.D. thesis, Lincoln College, New Zealand.

Stockdill, S. M. J. 1966. The effect of earthworms on pastures. *Proc. N.Z. Ecol. Soc.* 13:68–74.

Stonehouse, B. 1967. The general biology and thermal balances of penguins. *Adv. Ecol. Res.* 4:131–197.

Tussock Grassland Research Committee. 1954. The high-altitude snow-tussock grassland in South Island, New Zealand. *N.Z. J. Sci. Tech.* A36:335–364.

Tyndale-Biscoe, C. H. 1955. A study of natural mortality in a wild population of the rabbit, *Oryctolagus cuniculus* L. *N.Z. J. Sci. Tech.* B36:561–580.

Walker, T. W. and J. K. Syers. 1976. The fate of phosphorus during pedogenesis. *Geoderma* 15:1–19.

Wardle, J. 1970. The ecology of *Nothofagus solandri*. Parts 1–4. *N.Z. J. Bot.* 8:494–646.

———, J. Hayward, and J. Herbert. 1971. Forests and scrublands of northern Fiordland. *N.Z. J. For. Sci.* 1:80–115.

Wardle, P. 1963*a*. Evolution and distribution of the New Zealand flora as affected by Quaternary climates. *N.Z. J. Bot.* 1:3–17.

———. 1963*b*. Growth habits of New Zealand subalpine shrubs and trees. *N.Z. J. Bot.* 1:18–47.

———. 1963*c*. The regeneration gap of New Zealand gymnosperms. *N.Z. J. Bot.* 1:301–315.

———. 1965. A comparison of alpine timberlines in New Zealand and North America. *N.Z. J. Bot.* 3:113–135.

———. 1966. Biological flora of New Zealand. 1. *Weinmannia racemosa* Linn. f. (Cunoniaceae). Kamahi. *N.Z. J. Bot.* 4:114–131.

———. 1971. An explanation for alpine timberline. *N.Z. J. Bot.* 9:371–402.

———. 1973*a*. Variations of the glaciers of Westland National Park and the Hooker Range, New Zealand. *N.Z. J. Bot.* 11:349–388.

———. 1973*b*. New Zealand timberlines. *Arctic Alp. Res.* 5:A127–A135.

——— and A. D. Campbell. 1976. Seasonal cycle of tolerance to low temperatures in three native woody plants, in relation to their ecology and post-glacial history. *Proc. N.Z. Ecol. Soc.* 23:85–91.

———, A. F. Mark, and G. T. S. Baylis. 1970. Vegetation studies on Secretary Island, Fiordland. Part 9. Additions to Parts 1, 2, 4, and 6. *N.Z. J. Bot.* 8:3–21.

Warham, J. 1971. Aspects of breeding behavior in the royal penguin *Eudyptes chrysolophus schelgeli. Notornis* 18:91–115.

Watson, J. S. 1957. Reproduction of the wild rabbit, *Oryctolagus cuniculus* (L.) in Hawke's Bay, New Zealand. *N.Z. J. Sci. Tech.* B38:451–482.

Wells, J. A. 1972. Ecology of *Podocarpus hallii* in Central Otago, New Zealand. *N.Z. J. Bot.* 10:399–426.

——— and A. F. Mark. 1966. The altitudinal sequence of climax vegetation on Mt Anglem, Stewart Island. Part 1. The principal strata. *N.Z. J. Bot.* 4:267–282.

Westerskov, K. E. 1956. *Productivity of New Zealand pheasant populations.* N.Z. Dept. Internal Affairs Wildlife Pub. No. 40B.

———. 1963. Ecological factors affecting distribution of a nesting Royal Albatross population. *Proceedings of the 13th International Ornithology Congress, U.S.A.*, pp. 795–811.

White, E. G. 1978. Energetics and consumption rates of alpine grasshoppers (Orthoptera:Acrididae) in New Zealand. *Oecologia* 33:17–44.

Wightman, J. A. 1974. Rearing *Costelytra zelandica* (Coeloptera: Scarabaeidae). 4. Some effects of different larval densities and food availability on larval survival and weight change. *N.Z. J. Zool.* 1:217–223.

Williams, G. R. 1956. The kakapo (*Strigops habroptilus,* Grey), a review and reappraisal of a near-extinct species. *Notornis* 7:29–56.

———. 1960. The takahe. A general survey after ten years (*Notornis mantelli* Owen). *Trans. R. Soc. N.Z.* 88:235–258.

———. 1963. Four-year population cycle in California quail in the South Island of New Zealand. *J. Anim. Ecol.* 32:441–459.

———. 1967. The breeding biology of California quail in New Zealand. *Proc. N.Z. Ecol. Soc.* 14:88–99.

———, ed. 1973. *The natural history of New Zealand: an ecological survey.* Wellingon: Reed.

——— and K. H. Miers. 1958. A five-year banding study of the takahe (*Notornis mantelli* Owen). *Notornis* 8:1–16.

Williams, M. J. 1969. Courtship and copulatory behavior in grey ducks. *Notornis* 16:23–32.

Williams, P. A. 1975. Studies of the tall tussock (*Chionochloa*) vegetation/soil systems of the southern Tarrarua Range, New Zealand. 2. The vegetation/soil relationships. *N.Z. J. Bot.* 13:269–303.

______. 1977. Growth, biomass and productivity studies of tall-tussock (*Chionochloa*) grasslands, Canterbury, New Zealand. *N.Z. J. Bot.* 15:

______, P. Ness and K. F. O'Conner. 1977. Macro-element pools and fluxes in tall-tussock (*Chionochloa*) grasslands, Canterbury, New Zealand. *N.Z. J. Bot.* 15:443–474.

______, J. L. Grigg, P. Nes, and K. F. O'Connor. 1976. Vegetation/soil relationships and distribution of selected macroelements within the shoots of tall-tussocks on the Murchison Mountains, Fiordland, New Zealand. *N.Z. J. Bot.* 14:29–53.

Winterbourn, M. J. 1974. The life histories, trophic relations and production of *Stenoperla prasina* (Plecoptera) and *Deleatidium* sp. (Ephemeraptera) in a New Zealand river. *Freshw. Biol.* 4:507–524.

______. 1976. Fluxes of litter falling into a small beech forest stream. *N.Z. J. Mar. Freshw. Res.* 10:399–416.

______, P. Alderton, and J. J. Hunter. 1971. *A biological evaluation of organic pollution in the lower Waimakariri River system 1970–71*. N.Z. Marine Department Technical Report No. 67.

Wodzicki, K. A. 1950. Introduced Mammals of New Zealand. *N.Z. Dept. Sci. Indust. Res. Bull.* Vol. 98.

Young. E. C. 1976. The overlapping breeding territories of several shore bird species. *Proc. N.Z. Ecol. Soc.* 23:38–44.

Africa

23

EGYPT

Mohamed El-Kassas

EARLY BEGINNING

Egypt has for many centuries attracted explorers and travellers who recorded their observations on various aspects of its natural history. The first treatise on the flora of Egypt was published in 1775 by Petrus Forskål. Records of the Egyptian flora made during the Napoleonic expedition to Egypt were published by A. R. Delile in 1809 and 1812.

The early beginnings of plant ecological studies in Egypt extend to the mid-nineteenth century. Two traditions may be recognized. The first was general exploration and survey, for which one name may be mentioned as symbolic: Georges-Auguste Schweinfurth (1836–1925), a German scientist and explorer who lived in Egypt from 1863 to 1914. From Egypt, he travelled to various African and Middle Eastern countries. His 464 publications in such fields as biology, geology, cartography, and archeaology are listed and reviewed in a special volume by Keimer (1926).

The second tradition was ecophysiological and was aimed at explaining plant life in the dry habitat of the desert. G. Volkens' (1887) work remains a classic study on xerophytism. Among other classic studies on the physiology of drought are O. Stocker's *Der Wasserhaushalt aegyptischer Wüsten und Salzpflanzen* (1929), and A. Seybold's "Untersuchungen über die Transpirationswiderstände und über die Temperatur aegyptisch-arabischer Wüstenpflanzen" (1929).

For a review of botanical literature of this era, see Vivi Laurent-Täckholm's "Bibliographical Notes on the Flora of Egypt" (1932).

These two traditions were maintained and expanded in further phases of ecological developments that were associated with the establishment of the Egyptian University in 1925 (now the University of Cairo). The first professor of botany was the Swede, Gunnar Täckholm (1925–1929). He died young, and his wife Vivi Laurent-Täckholm devoted her life to studies of the flora of Egypt and gave leadership and inspiration to plant taxonomic studies in Egypt for some fifty years. She died in 1978. *Taeckholmia,* a journal published by the University of Cairo and O. Koeltz Science Publishers, bears her name and memory.

The second professor of botany was F. W. Oliver (1929–1935) (see Oliver 1945–1946), one of the fathers of plant ecology in Britain. On his retirement from the Chair of Botany in Cairo, he made Egypt his home and lived in Borg-el-Arab (45 km west of Alexandria) until 1956, shortly before his death. His house in Borg-el-Arab is now a field station of the University of Alexandria. F. W. Oliver was succeeded by another British ecologist, F. J. Lewis (1935–1947). This episode saw the beginning of plant ecological studies by Egyptian scientists in two principal traditions.

ECOPHYSIOLOGY OF WATER RELATIONSHIPS

The first two plant ecologists, A. M. Migahid and A. H. Montasir, started their postgraduate work (1931–1933) on transpiration and stomata in desert plants. Their paper on the subject summed their joint M.S. thesis and was published in 1934. Later, Migahid developed this research trend and established a school of research students dealing mainly with such ecophysiological problems as water relationships and drought resistance. His paper "Drought Resistance of Egyptian Desert Plants" was presented to the UNESCO Madrid Symposium on Plant-Water Relationships, the proceedings of which were published (1962). The principal ideas in this paper may be summarized as follows:

1. Desert soils (surface deposits), if deep enough, conserve a certain amount of moisture in deep-seated layers; the depth of this layer varies according to physical attributes of soil. The maintenance of this layer is a result of a number of factors: formation of a dry, protective surface layer (dust mulch); in deeper layers of soil (below 50 cm), a nearly constant temperature maintained throughout the day, whereas surface layers show remarkable variations with a daily range that may exceed 40°C in summer days; differences in temperature of successive soil layers, which may produce vapor pressure gradients that cause downward movement of water vapor and its condensation in the cooler layer (internal dew); dew fall, especially in seasons of high atmospheric humidity.

2. Root developments extensively (horizontally) or intensively (vertically) represent important morphological attributes of desert perennials.

3. Desert plants have morphological and physiological attributes that enable them to maintain a favorable water balance: high root/shoot ratio, anatomic xeromorphic structures, high osmotic pressure, and high content of bound water (hydrophilic colloids) of cell sap and cytoplasm, which are mechanisms for control of transpiration.

Migahid led expeditions (1946–1955) to study plant life in the great swamps of the Sudd region (southern Sudan). Apart from general surveys of the vegetation, Migahid and his associates made extensive studies on evapotranspiration in the reed swamps (*e.g., Cyperus papyrus*) of the region. They used large tanks (10×10 m) to compare evaporation from water with evapotranspiration from water occupied with reed growth. Their results show that evapotranspiration may be three times that of evaporation.

Several Egyptian and visiting scientists contributed to this kind of study. From 1953 to 1955, the Swede I. Arvidsson (Arvidsson and Hellström 1956) carried out studies on dew condensation and methods of harvesting dew. The German W. Kausch (1960) carried out studies on root development in desert plants in the 1950s. T. M. Tadros (1935) and his associates studied osmotic pressure of cell sap of various ecological groups of plants, transpiration in *Cyperus papyrus,* and water relationships of barley and of a number of wild plants, notably *Plantago* spp. Nevertheless, Tadros' principal contribution, as will be noted later, was in the field of phytosociology.

Disciples of Migahid established a number of research schools that elaborated studies on plant-soil-water relationships in both wild and cultivated crops and trees. At the University of Cairo, A. A. Abdel-Rahman (1952) and K. H. El-Batanouny and co-workers (1971–1973) carried out studies on olive, almond, and several desert plants. E. M. El-Sharkawi, of the University of Assiut, investigated drought tolerance of crop plants at successive stages in the life cycle, and M. N. El-Shourbagi (1980), of the University of Tanta, studied the ecophysiology of salt tolerance. It may be noted that ecophysiological studies started with wild plants, but eventually evolved to deal with crop plants, the applied aspect of this research area.

SYNECOLOGY (PHASE 1, 1930–1950)

During the late twenties and early thirties, the staff of the newly established departments of biology in the university made several field expeditions to various parts of Egypt: oasis of the Libyan Desert, Red Sea coastal lands, and mountains including Gebel Elba (mist oasis on the Sudano-Egyptian border). Collections of biological materials and ecological observations were made, and the scope of ecological studies was gradually outlined.

M. Hassib summed up his lifetime observations in one volume, titled *Distribution of Plant Communities in Egypt* (1950). This survey covered the principal subdivisions of Egypt: Eastern (Arabian) and Western (Libyan) deserts,

Sinai, Mediterranean coast, Red Sea coastal lands, Gebel Elba, Nile Valley, and the oases. He appended his study with life-form analyses, following Raukiaer's system, and phytogeographical notes.

Modern synecological studies, inspired by Oliver and resulting from the closer links between the Egyptian and British universities, started with Montasir. In 1934, he carried out a plant ecological survey on Lake Manzala (northeast of the Nile Delta) (Montasir 1937). He later expanded his survey to cover other parts of Egypt (Montasir 1938). As would be expected, the interpretation of data was not easy in these pioneer studies because of the paucity of information about ecological attributes of individual species. The initiative taken by the British Ecological Society in 1940 to produce a British biological flora, and the publication of guidelines for such contributions (*Journal of Ecology* 29:358–360, 1941) had their influence on research programs carried out by Montasir and his many students. From 1944 onward, he embarked on a program of autecological studies that dealt with several genera of the Egyptian flora: *Alhagi, Fagonia, Zilla, Zygophyllum, Farsetia, Haplophyllum,* and *Heliotropium.* Other genera were examined by other research groups: *Leptadenia* (University of Assiut), *Plantago* (University of Alexandria), and *Panicum* (Desert Research Institute). Montasir summed up his experiences in this extensive program in his paper "Habitat Factors and Plant Distribution in Egypt" (1954), in which he enumerated twenty general conclusions, among which are the following:

1. Theraphytes comprise about 50 percent of the Egyptian flora, nanophanerophytes 5 percent.

2. Seven phytogeographic regions can be recognized in Egypt; they differ in their climatic particulars: temperature, relative humidity, evaporation, rainfall, and soil moisture.

3. Soil temperature affects several biological processes in plants: absorption, germination, root development, and activity of soil organisms. Daily temperature range near the soil surface is notable; the range diminishes downward and is minimal at 30-cm depth (this is elaborated in Abdel Rahman 1952).

4. Desert soils are poor in their humus (0.1–3.6 percent) and nitrate content.

5. Desert soils are alkaline (pH: 7.2–9.1).

During this phase, Oliver published a number of papers on plant life in Mareotis and on dust storms and their ecological consequences. J. Ball published his book *Contributions to the Geography of Egypt* (1938). R. A. Bagnold (1941) reported on his classic studies in the Western (Libyan) Desert of Egypt. In 1950, the Egyptian Department of Meteorology published the first *Climatological Normals for Egypt.* These studies paved the way for the further development of ecological studies in Egypt as they helped to elucidate the geomorphological setting in the deserts of Egypt.

SYNECOLOGY (PHASE 2, 1950–1970)

About 1950, two schools of research emerged; these were mainly concerned with (1) surveys of natural vegetation and (2) phytosociological analysis of plant communities and their ecological relationships. One was centered in the University of Alexandria and led by T. M. Tadros (1910–1972), who followed the Zurich-Montpellier school. He carried out phytosociological studies on the vegetation of the Mediterranean semidesert belt of northern Egypt. His 1935 paper was to be the first of a series of research reports by this pioneer ecologist and his students that constituted a notable contribution to the ecology of the vegetation of Egypt. In 1968, he presented a paper, "Vegetational Studies Accomplished and Problems Conceived in the North Western Desert of Egypt," to the International Biological Program Hammamet (Tunisia) Symposium. Publication of the proceedings of this symposium was not completed. In this paper, Tadros summed up his findings and made two principal points: (1) associations of semiarid vegetation of the coastal Mediterranean lands are syntaxonomically related, and the associations described in Egypt can fit within associations and alliances recognized by Braun-Blanquet and his followers; (2) there is a scheme of successional relationships of hydrophytic and halophytic communities.

The second school of research was centered in the University of Cairo and led by M. Kassas, who followed the Anglo-American school of thought. He and his associates carried out a vegetational survey of the desert between the Nile Valley and the Red Sea coast in both Egypt and the Sudan. His 1952 paper introduced a series (1952–1970) under the general title Habitat and Plant Communities in the Egyptian Desert. The objective of this series was to understand patterns and processes in desert vegetation. Kassas' 1966 paper on desert plant life sums up the following general conclusions:

1. Plant life in desert habitats is closely associated with landform patterns, including features of surface deposits. Eco-geomorphological units represent keys to understanding vegetational pattern.

2. Successional changes in desert vegetation are mainly allogenic as a result of gradual cumulative changes in the habitat produced essentially by physical processes independent of plant growth. Successional progressive and retrogressive changes are recognized. Elaboration of the concept of allogenic succession benefitted from geomorphological studies by a number of Egyptian geologists and geographers and from detailed studies on soil moisture distribution in relation to depth by Rahman (1952). He showed the presence of a deep-seated layer of soil kept moist throughout the year. The depth of soil (surface deposits) that allows for the formation of this layer depends on texture and structure of the deposits. The building up of surface deposits is a physical process that is the principal cause of vegetational succession.

3. Desert plant communities may be defined on the following bases:

a. Each community type is characterized by one or more dominant species, which is the most abundant perennial and the growth of which gives the vegetation its apparent homogeneity.
b. The floristic assemblage of each community type comprises a number of associate species that are present in the majority of the stands (sample plots) but not necessarily confined to a particular community type.
c. The main difference between the plant growth of the various community types is related to differences in the relative abundance and density of the species and not necessarily to differences of absence or presence of species. Fidelity concept does not apply.
d. Each community type needs to be referred to a discrete habitat type as a prerequisite of its identity. Plant growth (phytocenosis) alone, although of special importance, is not enough to provide terms for recognizing entities.

4. In his 1970 paper, "Geographical Facies of Plant Communities," Kassas adds:

e. More than one phytocenose type may occupy the same habitat type; this is due to differences in geographic ranges of the dominant species. However, phytocenose types occupying similar habitat types bear structural resemblances (i.e., similar vegetation form).
f. The phytocenose type may have more than one facies because of differences in the geographic ranges of the associate species.

An important feature of this phase was the establishment of the Desert Research Center in 1950, which provided a focal point for promoting integrated research programs in the Egyptian desert. The publication of the *Bulletin de L'Institut du Désert D'Égypte* provided an organ for publishing research reports on desert studies, including a number of monographic studies on groundwater resources, soil and plant life, and other topics.

This phase of synecologic developments witnessed the establishment of several new universities in the Middle East, and several Egyptian botanists went to work temporarily in various countries of the region: Libya, Sudan, Saudi Arabia, Gulf States, and Iraq. On their return, they brought with them rich collections of herbarium materials and expanded experiences in ecological studies. Reference may be made to studies by Kassas in Sudan and in particular to his 1970 paper.

THE SEVENTIES

Research studies in ecophysiological and synecologic fields continue with refined methodologies and the creation of new research units in the several provincial universities. A new development emerged in the University of Alexandria as M. A. Ayyad and his associates led research programs in the field of statistical ecology. During 1970–1974, Ayyad explored the application of the point-centered quarter method and ordination techniques, procedures of mathematical analyses made possible by the availability of computers, in studies of vegetation of the coastal areas west of Alexandria (Mareotis). In 1974, he established a multidisciplinary team of research workers for a desert biome study, Systems Analysis of Mediterranean Desert Ecosystems of Northern Egypt (SAMDENE). This is an internationally supported research program (University of Alexandria, U.S. Environmental Protection Agency, Ford Foundation, and UNESCO). Five annual reports have been issued (Ayyad 1974–1979) and a wealth of research papers has been published. Beginning in 1979, this program developed toward application and finding solutions for problems of arid land development [Regional Environmental Management of Mediterranean Desert Ecosystems of Northern Egypt (REMDENE)].

Education

Of late, interest in ecological and environmental studies has begun to emerge. The Institute of African Studies (University of Cairo) created a new department for natural resources and established a two-year course leading to a postgraduate diploma. This was an innovation, a multidisciplinary course open to graduates of various faculties. The first-year courses cover basic ecological sciences of climatology, pedology, plant and animal ecology, hydrology, geology, and geomorphology; the second-year courses cover applied ecological sciences related to surveys and management of natural resources with special reference to Africa.

Societies

The Egyptian Academy for Scientific Research and Technology was established in 1971. It created a National Council for Environmental Studies (now, Commission on Environmental Research), a National Committee for the United Nations Conference on the Human Environment, and in 1976 a National Committee for Conservation of Nature. The National Commission for UNESCO formed an Egyptian Committee for the Man and Biosphere (MAB) program, and the academy formed an Egyptian Committee for SCOPE. At the non-government level, several societies were formed: the Tree Lovers (1973), Egyptian Society for Protection of Nature (1975), and the Egyptian Society for Environmental Sciences (ESES) (1976). The proceedings of the ESES Symposium on Ecological Studies on the River Nile (April 1978) was published in a special issue of *Water Supply and Management* (Kassas and Ghabour 1980).

REFERENCES CITED

Arvidsson, I. and B. Hellström. 1956. A note on dew in Egypt. Publ. No. 36. l'Association International d'Hydrologie 1:416–424.

Ayyad, M. A., ed. 1974–1979. *Systems Analysis of Mediterranean Desert Ecosystems of Northern Egypt (SAMDENE).* Progress Reports 1–5. University of Alexandria.

Bagnold, R. A. 1941. *Physics of blown sand and desert dunes.* London: Methuen.

Ball, J. 1938. *Contributions to the geography of Egypt.* Cairo: Government Press.

Batanouny, K. H., et al. 1971–1973. Eco-physiological studies on desert plants. Parts I–VIII. *Oecologia* (Austria) Vols. 7–11.

Delile, A. R. 1809–1812. *Description de l'Egypt: histoire naturelle,* Vols. 1 and 2. Paris: Imprimérie Impériale.

Egyptian Department of Meteorology. 1950. *Climatic normals for Egypt.* Cairo: Government Press.

El-Shourbagi, M. N. 1980. Effect of constant and gradual exposure to sodium chloride stress on DNA, RNA, protein and certain protein-amino acids in two varieties of barley. *Phyton* (Austria) 20:37–45.

Forskål, Petrus. 1775. *Flora Aegyptiaco-Arabica.* Post mortem actioris, edidit C. Niebuhr, Hauniae.

Hassib, M. 1950. Distribution of plant communities in Egypt. *Bull. Fac. Sci., Univ. Cairo* 29:59–261.

Kassas, M. 1966. Plant life in deserts. In *Arid lands: a geographical appraisal,* ed. E. S. Hills, pp. 145–180. London: Methuen.

———. 1970. Desertification versus potential for recovery in circum-Saharan territories. In *Arid lands in transition,* ed. H. E. Dregne, pp. 123–142. AAAS.

——— and S. I. Ghabour, eds. 1980. The Nile and its environment. *Water Supply Manage.* 4:1–113.

———, et al. 1952–1970. Habitat and plant communities in the Egyptian desert. Parts I–VIII. *J. Ecol.* Vols. 40–58.

Kausch, W. 1960. *Bericht über die Ökologischen Untersuchungen der Wüstenvegetation in der Ägyptisch-arabischen Wüste.* UNESCO Document: NS/914/58.

Keimer, M. L. 1926. Bibliographie des ouvrages de G. Schweinfurth: 1858–1925. *Bull. Soc. R. Geogr. d'Egypt* 14:73–112.

Migahid, A. M. and A. H. Montasir. 1934. Transpiration and stomata in desert plants. *Bull. Fac. Sci., Univ. Cairo* No. 1.

———. 1962. Drought resistance of Egyptian desert plants. *UNESCO Arid Zone Research* 16:213–233.

Montasir, A. H. 1937. Ecology of Lake Manzala. *Bull. Fac. Sci., Univ. Cairo,* No. 12.

———. 1938. Egyptian soil structure in relation to plants. *Bull. Fac. Sci., Univ. Cairo,* No. 15.

———. 1954. Habitat factors and plant distribution in Egypt. *Bull. Inst. Desert d'Egypt* 4:36–63.

Oliver, F. W. 1945–1946. Flowers of Mareotis. *Trans. Norfolk Norwich Nat. Soc.,* pp. 130–164.

Rahman, A. A. 1952. Studies in the water economy of the Egyptian plants. Ph.D. thesis, University of Cairo.

Seybold, A. 1929. Untersuchungen über die Transpirationswinderstände und über die Temperatur aegyptisch-arabischer Wüstenpflanzen. *Planta Arch. Wissenschaftliche Bot.* 9:270–314.

Stocker, O. 1929. *Der Wasserhaushalt aegyptischer Wüsten und Salzpflanzen.*

Botanische Abhandlungen, Vol. 13, pp. 1–200. Jena: Verlag von Gustav fischer.

Täckholm, V. L. 1932. Bibliographical notes on the flora of Egypt. *Festskrift till Verner Söderberg,* pp. 193–208.

Tadros, T. M. 1935. A phytosociological study of halophylous communities from Mareotis (Egypt). *Vegetatio* 4:102–124.

Volkens, G. 1887. *Die flora der aegyptisch-arabischen Wüste auf Grundlage anatomisch-physiologischer Forschungen.* Berlin: Gebrüder Borntraeger.

24

MAURITIUS

A. W. Owadally

INTRODUCTION

Mauritius is the oldest of the islands in the Mascarene Archipelago and lies at latitude 20°20′ south, longitude 57°30′ east. The sea floor of the western Indian Ocean has recently been studied (Fisher et al. 1967), and isotopic dating of the volcanic rocks has been done by McDougall and Chamalaun (1969). The island was formed through volcanic activity some 6.8 to 7.8 million years ago, and two series of lava flows took place between 3.5 and 0.2 million years ago, with breaks of 2 and 0.7 million years in between.

With time, the rocks weathered, leaving isolated, beautifully shaped peaks and a fairly fertile soil that were colonized by plants and animals, giving rise to an interesting fauna and flora with many endemic species. On the other hand, the marine plants and animals were more cosmopolitan and did not give rise to many endemic species.

The island, which was rediscovered by the Portuguese in the sixteenth century, had long been known to the Arabs, but it was colonized only in the seventeenth century by the Dutch.

In 1528, the Portuguese released monkeys (*Cynamolgus fascicularis*) from Timor and, in 1550, pigs (*Sus scrofa*) and goats (*Capra hircus aegarus*) from India. Over the years, these animals have had a marked influence on the ecology of the island. The Portuguese also may have inadvertently released the rats, which later caused serious problems to health and cultivation.

In 1598, Admiral Wybrant van Warwick, together with a group of men, came to Mauritius, spending seventeen days. He left the first known records dealing with, among other things, the marine life and vegetation of the island. In his interesting description of the vegetation he writes:

> The land is uninhabited and very mountainous. The soil is extremely rocky but fertile as can be judged from the large number of trees which are so close to each other that one can hardly walk in the forest. The trees are mostly black ebony and yellow and red ebony are also common. There are also a large number of palms—the palmites and the palmistes which are edible.

Wybrant van Warwick was also impressed by the abundance of animal life in the lagoons, particularly the large fish populations. One of his nets caught so many fish that to lift it and its catch from the water, the men had to throw away the majority of the fish.

The Dutch left records of a type of vegetation occurring in the north and the west where palms were frequent. This vegetation was probably a palm savanna, which is now extinct on the mainland but remnants of which can be seen on Round Island. The newcomers virtually led to the extinction of this lowland palm community by burning, by using the palm heart for food and palm leaves for thatching material, and by tapping the sap in the production of arrack. They introduced the Javanese deer (*Cervus unicolor russa*) and many useful plants, such as sugarcane, tobacco, and sweet potatoes (Owadally and Butzler 1973). Dutch activities led to the extinction of the land tortoises and a few large birds, such as the dodo (*Raphus cucullatus*) and the *Aphanapteryx*. However, the large number of rats and monkeys roaming around at that time may have been more responsible for this destruction than men and wild pigs (Brouard 1963).

In 1715, the French took possession of the island, and subsequently, almost half of its surface was conceded to French settlers. They cleared about half of this mostly flat area for the growing of food and other crops. The population rose from 800 in 1735 to 75,000 in 1810 when the French lost the island. The French introduced many important exotic trees and shrubs like *Albizia lebbek, Sysygium jambos, Artocarpus communis, Eugenia fragrans,* which either spread naturally or were widely planted. Subsequently, some like the *Psidium cattleyanum* and *Ravenala madagascariensis* spread widely and rapidly and became a threat to the native forest. Legislation was enacted to safeguard forest and water conservation.

The British took possession of the island in 1810, and the sugar plantations that had been firmly established expanded to cover almost half of the island. The population rose rapidly to reach the present level of about 900,000. These events meant large-scale clearing of the forest to make room for sugarcane planting, habitation, roads, and various infrastructures for the production of food, timber, and fuel.

OBSERVATIONS BY NATURALISTS

After the descriptions given by casual visitors, Mauritius was fortunate in having the observations of more competent naturalists. For example, Philibert de Commerson, who reached Mauritius in 1768, painted and described our fishes whose efforts Lacépède based most of his work on for his *Histoire Naturelle des Poissons.* Commerson also collected plant materials, which were partly used by Boucherville (1871). Baker (1877) refers to Boucherville as the father of Mauritian botany.

In 1773, Bernadin de St. Pierre wrote *Voyage à l'Ile de France,* in which he deals with, among other things, the fauna and flora of the island. Du Petit-Thouars (1801) wrote on the plants of Ile de France (now Mauritius), Ile de Bourbon (now Réunion), and Madagascar. Shortly thereafter, Bory de Saint Vincent (1804), through his informative writings, made an important contribution to Mascarene botany.

Furthermore, in 1873, Nicholas Pike described his personal experiences and adventures while wandering in and around Mauritius, including two visits to Round Island. Pike left some interesting records on the vegetation of the islands, the richness of the fauna, and the reefs. W. Botting Hemsley (1886), who formed part of the H.M.S. *Challenger* expedition (1884–1885), made a report on the vegetation of Diégo Garcia and Chagos Archipelago. In addition, he wrote on the flora of Aldabra (1919) in collaboration with some other naturalists. Very interesting, too, are J. Horne's notes on Round Island plants (1870) and Flat Island (1887). He gives an idea of the island vegetation, some varieties of which have completely disappeared.

Among other activities by naturalists, there are the following: H. H. Johnston (1895*a*) reported on the flora of the outlying islands in Mahebourg Bay, Mauritius; Pitot (1905) gave some descriptions of fish, birds, forests, and traffic in ebony (*Diospyros tesselaria*) and other timber trees during the Dutch period; Fryer (1911) gave some notes on the flora and fauna of Aldabra Island; Tafforet's brief account of the vegetation of Rodrigues about 1726 has been published by Dupon (1973); Pierre Sonnerat's (1748–1814) voyages around the world have been described by Ly-Tio-Fane (1973), who shows how they had caused hundreds of weeds and exotic plants and animals to become established in many countries.

PREPARATION OF CHECKLISTS AND CATALOGS

Various checklists and catalogs of plants, terrestrial and marine animals, birds, and invertebrates have been compiled. For example, Liénard (1877) gave a list of molluscs including marine gastropods from Mauritius; the first comprehensive and annotated list of Mauritius plants was written by W. Bojer (1837), who endeavored to discriminate between indigenous and exotic species; Nylander (1857) had compiled a general list of lichens and had tried to work out their geographic distribution; R. E. Vaughan (1937) prepared a catalog of the flowering plants found in the Mauritius Institute Herbarium including an annotated list of species with their vernacular names. More recently, that is, since the 1950s, checklists of birds (Rountree et al. 1952), reptiles (Vinson and Vinson 1969), butterflies (Vinson 1939), beetles (Vinson 1956), fishes (Baissac 1950–1956), crabs (Michel 1964), and planktonic diatoms and diflagellates (Sournia 1965) have been prepared.

FLORAS AND IDENTIFICATION KEYS

The preparation of checklists and catalogs ought to have led to the writing up of floras and identification keys. The work done on these lines, however, has been very slow indeed. It is evident from the introduction of the work by Richard (1828) that he contemplated writing a flora of Mauritius and Réunion, but he never achieved it. Using herbarium specimens, Baker (1877) wrote the *Flora of Mauritius and the Seychelles,* assisted by Balfour. The flora section is preceded by a preface giving short notice on some explorers and collectors visiting Mauritius, and there are brief synoptic tables showing the distribution of Mascarene species. Baker never visited Mauritius or the Seychelles, so his flora does not give much information on the habitat and the color of the plants or flowers. Although Baker had to rely on the description given by others, his is still the classic work in this field. It is, of course, much out of date except that there have been some additions to the flora (Johnston 1895*b*) and some work done more recently on the grasses of Mauritius and Rodrigues (Hubbard and Vaughan 1940). Since 1976, three fascicles of a long-awaited flora of the Mascarenes have been published (*Flore des Mascareignes* 1976). These fascicles cover sixteen families, among which are Iridaceae, Amarylidaceae, Goodeniaceae, and Campanulaceae. It may take a decade or so to complete this series, which has been financed by the British government through Kew, the French government via ORSTOM in Paris, and the Mauritius government.

ECOLOGICAL STUDIES

The first true land ecological studies started in the late 1930s by Vaughan and Wiehe (1937, 1939, 1941, 1947) when they set about mapping the vegetation. They explained plant succession using charts for both primary and secondary vegetations. Very little comparative work has been done along the same line, even though almost forty years have elapsed. A proper quantitative assessment of the vegetation needs to be undertaken with statistical analysis. Although we do not expect spectacular results, such an analysis will no doubt show certain features that so far have passed unnoticed.

Because of various factors, the native vegetation is not regenerating naturally (Owadally 1973) and, in order to safeguard some of the rare species, enrichment planting may have to be resorted to.

Various autecological studies of weeds have been done (Rochecouste and Vaughan 1959; Vaughan and Autrey 1973; Vaughan and McIntyre 1975). These have one aim in view, that is, the elimination of weeds in sugarcane plantations because of the harm the weeds cause to an economic crop. In a series of leaflets, the authors give botanical descriptions, ecology, and distribution of certain weeds and their control measures.

The palms of the Mascarene Islands have been studied by Moore (1978*a,b*; Moore and Guého 1980). The ecology of the plant communities of Rodrigues Island has been studied by Wiehe (1949), and this again is rather descriptive; no applied ecology has been undertaken so far. It will be worthwhile to find out the effects of the activities of humans, goats, fire, drought, and various cyclones on the vegetation of Rodrigues and compare these with Wiehe's observations. Recently, the vegetation of the high altitude of Réunion Island has been the object of an investigation by Cadet (1974).

Jonathan Sauer (1961) has studied the coastal plant geography of Mauritius. He has been fortunate to repeat the studies just after a severe cyclone and has shown the destructive effects of a cyclone on the vegetation along the coast (1962), publishing photographs of the same site before and after the cyclone. Brouard (1967), too, has explained the damages caused by tropical cyclones to forest plantations in Mauritius. He shows that there are far more trees that are actually broken than windblown, pointing out the various species of exotic timber trees, both of low altitude and on the plateau in Mauritius, that are wind resistant.

A broad picture of the various marine habitats and life has been compiled by Baissac et al. (1962). On the other hand, Hodgkin and Michel (1963) have provided useful discussion on the ecology of rocky shores. Here, too, more comprehensive research work remains to be done.

Faure (1975) did a comparative study of coralline reefs of the Mascarene Archipelago. His work consists of three sections: a brief survey of environmental factors; a descriptive study of the main reef structures, analyzed in terms of morphology and ecology; and a discussion on the common features and on the peculiarities of each island forming a part of the Mascarene group.

Michel (1979) has described the various facets of marine biology and explains the relationships that exist between the various sea creatures and their environment.

A comprehensive bibliography of all the marine biology studies made in Mauritius has been compiled (Michel 1974), and this will no doubt greatly help anyone wishing to venture into this field. The uninitiated must know systematic marine biology fairly well, however, to be able to find his or her way around in this bibliography.

In a fairly extensive work, Starmühlnur (1979) describes and comments on the different biotopes of running water courses of the Seychelles, Comores, and the Mascarene Archipelago.

The Javanese deer (*Cervus unicolor russa*), which has been in the island for over three centuries and is a source of protein, has been the subject of study (Owadally and Butzler 1973). Its biology, social behavior, and habitat have been observed in some detail. The ecology and behavior of the crab-eating macaque, *Macaca fascicularis* syn. *Cynomolgus fascicularis,* are presently being investigated by Sussman and Tattersall, though a preliminary report (1977) has already been prepared.

The endemic birds of Mauritius have been described by Staub (1976). Most of these birds are extremely rare and some of them, like the *Falco punctatus, Nesoenas mayeri,* and *Psittacula echo,* are listed in the red data book of endangered species. Carl Jones (in press *a, b, c*) is making critical reviews of all the work done so far on these birds, together with his own observations, with a view to save them from extinction.

In order to protect the fauna and flora of Mauritius, the government has created fifteen nature reserves to a total extent of 4,768 hectares. In addition, native birds are being bred in captivity in an aviary constructed by the government of Mauritius.

THE TEACHING OF ECOLOGY

Not much attention has been given to the teaching of ecology in schools, but wherever it is taught, traditional foreign textbooks are being used. Unfortunately, these do not have much relevance to the local context for several reasons. First, there are no local textbooks to provide local examples. Second, the teachers, who are mostly trained abroad, are not themselves familiar with the local ecology; that they do not pay enough attention to what is around them and use their observations in their teachings may be due to lack of time and interest. Last, the teachers have to follow the syllabus set by the Cambridge Examinations Syndicate; however, this can be modified to suit our needs.

There is now a tendency to teach social sciences, instead of history and geography, in primary and secondary schools. Integrated sciences will form part of the curriculum of primary schools and secondary schools up to Form III, that is, pupils of up to fifteen years of age. In this respect, it is worthwhile mentioning the textbook written by Michael Atchia (1977) for the Mauritius Institute of Education; the text deals with ecology, natural resources, pollution, conservation, and population problems, among other topics.

Owadally and Michel (1975) have written a popular book, *Our Environment, Mauritius,* in which they describe the geological formation of Mauritius, various sources of pollution, fauna and flora, and the duties of the public and the government to protect our national heritage. A list of the existing legislation related to the environment is also included. Michel (1966) has published a popular book on our fauna at his own cost. Scientific publications of popular interest should be financed by government or international bodies. UNESCO may have to help to publish books with color photographs on natural history. These will help both teachers and pupils.

Gerald Durrell's book, *Golden Bats and Pink Pigeons* (1977), dealing with his visits to Mauritius and relating some of his encounters with the Mauritian fauna, can be used as a textbook for English literature. This will, without doubt, reveal to the younger generation some of the unique creatures that are found in Mauritius and promote the cause for conservation among the students.

The University of Mauritius does not teach such pure sciences as botany and zoology. Historically, the university ought to have taken more interest in the teaching of ecology and in carrying out ecological research. Some topics on which research could be carried out have been set by Owadally (in press). Being an island, Mauritius may in the future have to rely a lot on the sea. Research ought to be undertaken on marine resources, and the university ought to have a school of marine biology. It may play a leading role in this field in this part of the world.

PUBLICATIONS AND SOCIETIES

The *Mauritius Institute Bulletin,* published by the board of directors of the Mauritius Institute, and the *Proceedings of the Royal Society of Arts and Sciences of Mauritius,* published by the society, are the two worthwhile journals in the field of ecology. So far, they have been devoted to papers on the flora and fauna of the Mascarenes, especially Mauritius and its dependencies. The *Proceedings* sometimes deals with historical topics as well. The *Revue Agricole et Sucrière de l'Ile Maurice,* published by the Conseil d'Administration de la Revue, sometimes has articles dealing with the fauna and flora.

All leading international scientific journals dealing with ecology are consulted regularly.

The two local societies of world reputation are The Royal Society of Arts and Sciences and The Société de Technologie, Agricole et Sucrière de Maurice.

CONCLUSION

Although there has been a fair share of basic research done in ecology, there have not been significant advances in theory and methodology, nor has there been any major trend in applied research. It is hoped that with the teaching of integrated sciences in the primary and secondary schools with a strong emphasis on the local context, ecological research will find new outlets. The University of Mauritius should take a lead in ecological research; otherwise, research in this field may come to a standstill or will remain a field for amateurs, instead of professionals.

REFERENCES CITED

Atchia, M. 1977. *The human environment.* Mimeographed. Department of Science, Mauritius Institute of Education, Réduit, Mauritius.

Baissac, J. B. de. 1950–1956. Contribution à l'étude des poissons de l'Ile Maurice, IV to VI. *Proc. R. Soc. Arts Sci. Mauritius* 1.

———, P. Lubet, and C. Michel. 1962. Les biocénoses benthiques littorales de l'Ile Maurice. *Rec. Tranv. St. Mar. End.* 25:253–291.

Baker, J. G. 1877. *Flora of Mauritius and the Seychelles: A description of the flowering plants and ferns of those islands.* Reeve & Co.

Bernardin de St. Pierre, J. H. 1773. *Voyage à l'Ile de France, à l'Ile de Bourbon, au Cap de Boone Espérance etc.* Amsterdam. (An English edition, translated by John Parish, appeared in 1775.)

Bojer, W. 1837. *Hortus Mauritianus.* Port Louis, Mauritius.

Bory de Saint Vincent, J. B. G. M. 1804. *Voyage dans des quatre principales îles des Mers d'Afrique.* 4 Vols. Paris.

Boucherville, A. de. 1871. L'herbier de Commerson. *Rev. Coloniale* 1:64–66.

Brouard, N. R. 1963. *A history of woods and forests in Mauritius.* Mauritius: Government Printer.

———. 1967. *Damage by tropical cyclones to forest plantations with particular reference to Mauritius.* Port Louis, Mauritius: Government Printer.

Cadet, T. L. 1974. Etude sur la vègètation des hautes altitudes de L'Ile de la Réunion (Océan Indien). *Vegetatio* 29:121–130.

Du Petit-Thouars, L. M. A. A. 1801. Sur les plantes des Iles de France, de Bourbon et de Madagascar. Bull. Soc. Philom. Paris 34:41–42.

Dupon, J. F. 1973. Relation de l'Ile Rodrigue. *Proc. R. Soc. Arts Sci. Mauritius.* New Series 4:1–16.

Durrell, G. 1977. *Golden bats and pink pigeons.* London: William Collins and Co. Ltd.

Faure, G. 1975. Etude comparative des recifs corraliens de l'Archipel des Mascareignes (Océan Indien). *Bull. Mauritius Inst.* 8:1–26.

Fisher, R. L., G. L. Johnston, and B. C. Hezer. 1967. Mascarene plateau Western Indian Ocean. *Bull. Geol. Soc. Am.* 78.

Flore des Mascareignes, La Réunion, Maurice, Rodrigues. 1976. Three fascicles comprising sixteen families. Published by SIRI, Mauritius; Royal Botanic Gardens, Kew; and ORSTOM, Paris. Mauritius: Government Printer.

Fryer, J. C. F. 1911. The structure and formation of Aldabra and neighbouring islands with notes on their flora and fauna. *Trans. Linn. Soc. Lond. (Zool.)* 2d Series, 14:397–442.

Hemsley, W. Botting. 1886. Report on the vegetation of Diego Garcia, Chagos Archipelago. *J. Linn. Soc. (Bot.)* 22:332–340.

______, et al. 1919. Flora of Aldabra's: notes on the flora of the neighbouring islands: *Kew Bull.* pp. 108–153.

Hodgkin, E. P. and C. Michel. 1963. Zonation of plants and animals on rocky shores of Mauritius. *Proc. R. Soc. Arts Sci. Mauritius* 2:121–145.

Horne, J. 1870. Notes on Round Island plants collected by His Excellency Sir Henry Barkly, K.C.B. *Trans. R. Soc. Arts Sci. Mauritius.* New Series 4:135–138.

______. 1887. Notes on flora of Flat Island. *Trans. R. Soc. Arts Sci. Mauritius.* New Series 19:116–151.

Hubbard, C. E. and R. E. Vaughan. 1940. *The grasses of Mauritius and Rodrigues.* London: The Crown Agents for the Colonies.

Johnston, H. H. 1895*a*. Report on the flora of the outlying islands in Mahebourg Bay, Mauritius. *Trans. Bot. Soc. Edinb.* 20:353–374.

______. 1895*b*. Addition to the flora of Mauritius as recorded in Baker's "Flora of Mauritius and the Seychelles." *Trans. Bot. Soc. Edinb.* 20:391–403.

Jones, C. G. In press *a*. The echo parakeet: the world's rarest bird. *Oryx.*

______. In press *b*. The Mauritius kestrel. Its biology and conservation. *The Hawk Trust Annual Report.*

______. In press *c*. The pink pigeon. Its biology and conservation.

Liénard, E. 1877. *Catalogue de la faune malacologique de l'Ile Maurice et de ses dependances.* Paris.

Ly-Tio-Fane, M. 1973. The career of Pierre Sonnerat (1748–1814); a re-assessment of his contribution to the arts and to the natural sciences. Ph.D. thesis, University of London.

McDougall, I. and F. H. Chamalaun. 1969. Isotopic dating and geomagnetic polarity studies on volcanic rocks from Mauritius, Indian Ocean. *Bull. Geol. Soc. Am.* 80:1419–1442.

Michel, C. 1964. Check-list of the Crustacea Brachyra (crabs) recorded from Mauritius. *Bull. Mauritius Inst.* 6:1–48.

______. 1966. *Notre faune.* Mauritius: Alpha Printing.

______. 1974. Notes on marine biology studies made in Mauritius. *Bull. Mauritius Inst.* 7:1–284.

______. 1979. La vie dans nos mers. *Enda Océan Indien,* Document No. 1. Mauritius: Alpha Printing.

Moore, H. E. 1978*a*. The genus *Hyophorbe* (Palmae). *Gentes. Herb.* 2:215–245.

______. 1978*b*. *Tectiphiala,* a new genus of Palmae from Mauritius. *Gentes. Herb.* 2:284–290.

______ and L. J. Guého. 1980. *Acanthophoenix* and *Dictyosperma* (Palmae) in the Mascarene Islands. *Gentes. Herb.* 12:1–16.

Nylander, W. 1857. Enumération générale des liches, avec l'indication sommaire de leur distribution géographique. *Mem. Soc. Nat. Sci. Cherbourg* 5:85–146. Supple. pp. 332–339.

Owadally, A. W. 1973. Les forêts naturelles de l'Ile Maurice. *Info-Nature. Société Protectrice Réunionaise et d'Etude de la Nature. Numero Special La Forêt,* pp. 88–94.

______. In press. Some forest pests and diseases in Mauritius. *Rev. Agri. et Suc. Ile Maurice.*

______ and W. Butzler. 1973. *The deer in Mauritius.* Mauritius: Alpha Printing.

——— and C. Michel. 1975. *Our environment, Mauritius.* Port Louis, Mauritius: Super Printing.

Pike, N. 1873. *Sub-tropical rambles in the land of the Aphanapteryx.* London: Sampson Low.

Pitot, A. 1905. *T'Eylandt Mauritius. Esquisses historiques 1598–1710.* Port Louis, Mauritius: Coignet Frères et Cie.

Richard, A. 1828. *Monographie des Orchidées des Iles de France et de Bourbon.* Paris: J. Tastu.

Rochecouste, E. and R. E. Vaughan. 1959–1966. Weeds of Mauritius. *Bidens pilosa,* Leaflet No. 1. Mauritius Sugar Industry Research Institute (1956); *Cassia occidentalis,* Leaflet No. 2 (1959); *Oxalis latifolia* and *Oxalis dilibis,* Leaflet No. 3 (1960); *Agemone mexicana,* Leaflet No. 4 (1962); *Artemisia vulgaris,* Leaflet No. 5 (1963); *Ambrosia psilostachya,* Leaflet No. 6 (1963); *Hydrocotyle bonariensis* and *H. sibthorpioides,* Leaflet No. 7 (1963); *Centella heliotropium amplexicaule,* Leaflet No. 8 (1963); *Plantago lanceolata,* Leaflet No. 9 (1964); *Eleusine indica,* Leaflet No. 10 (1965); and *Sectaria barbata* and *S. pallidefusca,* Leaflet No. 11 (1966).

Rountree, F. R. G., R. Guerin, S. Pelte, and J. Vinson. 1952. Catalogue of birds of Mauritius. *Bull. Mauritius Inst.* 3:135–217.

Sauer, J. D. 1961. *Coastal plant geography of Mauritius.* Louisiana State University Studies. Coastal Studies Series No. 5. Baton Rouge: Louisiana State University Press.

———. 1962. Effects of recent tropical cyclones on the coastal vegetation of Mauritius. *J. Ecol.* 50:275–290.

Sournia, A. 1965. Premier inventaire du phytoplacton littoral de l'Ile Maurice. *Bull. Mus. Hist. Nat. Paris.* 2d Series 37:1046–1050.

Starmühlner, F. 1979. Results of the Austrian Hydrobiological Mission, 1974, to the Seychelles, Comores and Mascarene Archipelagos. *Ann. Naturhistor. Mus. Wien.* 82:621–762.

Staub, F. 1976. *Birds of the Mascarenes and Saint Brandon.* Labama House, Port Louis: Organisation Normale des Entreprises Ltée.

Sussman, R. W. and I. Tattersall. 1977. A preliminary study of crab-eating macaque *Macaca fascicularis* in Mauritius. Mimeographed.

Vaughan, R. E. 1937. Catalogue of the flowering plants in the Mauritius Institute Herbarium. *Bull. Mauritius Inst.* 1:1–120.

——— and J. C. Autrey. 1973. Weeds of Mauritius. *Ageratum conyzoides,* Leaflet No. 12. Mauritius Sugar Industry Research Institute; *Ageratum houstonianum,* Leaflet No. 13; *Paedaria tomentosa,* Leaflet No. 13; *Laurentia longiflora,* Leaflet No. 14.

——— and G. McIntyre. 1975. Weeds of Mauritius. *Colcoasia antiquorum,* Leaflet No. 15; *Paspalum paniculatum, P. commersonii,* Leaflet No. 16. Mauritius Sugar Industry Research Institute.

———, and P. O. Wiehe. 1937. Studies on the vegetation of Mauritius. I. A preliminary survey of the plant communities. *J. Ecol.* 25:289–343.

———. 1939. Studies on the vegetation of Mauritius. II. The effect of environment on certain features of leaf structure. *J. Ecol.* 27:263–281.

———. 1941. Studies on the vegetation of Mauritius. III. The structure and development of the upland climax forest. *J. Ecol.* 29:127–160.

———. 1947. Studies on the vegetation of Mauritius. IV. Notes on the internal climate of the upland climax forest. *J. Ecol.* 34:126–136.

Vinson, J. 1939. Catalogue of the Lepidoptera of the Mascarene Islands. *Bull. Mauritius Inst.* 1:1–69.

———. 1956. Catalogue of the Coleoptera of Mauritius. *Bull. Mauritius Inst.* 4:1–299.

——— and J. M. Vinson. 1969. The saurian fauna of the Mascarene Islands. *Bull. Mauritius Inst.* 6:203–320.

Wiehe, P. O. 1949. The vegetation of Rodrigues Island. *Bull. Mauritius Inst.* 2:279–304.

25

NIGERIA

James K. Egunjobi

HISTORICAL BACKGROUND

Description of Plant Communities

Prior to the outbreak of the Second World War, a Cambridge Botanical Expedition visited Nigeria to make detailed ecological studies of the tropical rain forest of Southern Nigeria. Although a number of ecological studies had been undertaken and published before this, the Cambridge Botanical Expedition (January to May, 1935) heralded the systematic study of plant communities in Nigeria. The expedition visited the Shasha Forest Reserve in western Nigeria and made intensive studies of the structure and environmental conditions of the forest. Two accounts arising from this study were published in 1939 (*Journal of Ecology,* Volume 26). Although these studies fall outside the period under review (1945–1975), reference to them throws more light on the subsequent development of ecology. The third part of the Cambridge Botanical Expedition studies was not published until fifteen years later, in 1954, in the same journal. The study, "Ecological studies in the rainforest of Southern Nigeria (III). Secondary succession in the Shasha Forest Reserve" (Ross 1954), was published within the time period under review, although the study had been completed earlier.

Between 1947 and 1948, another Cambridge Botanical Expedition was launched to discover other aspects of the ecology of the tropical rain forest in Nigeria. This study, "Ecological studies in the rainforest of Southern Nigeria

(IV). The plateau forest of the Okomu Forest Reserve," was designed to cover areas not studied in the earlier expedition, namely, forest regeneration, horizontal pattern of major species, and plant associations. The study was not published until several years later (Jones 1955, 1956).

The ecological studies of the rain forest of Southern Nigeria, published from the Cambridge Botanical Expeditions, were purely descriptive accounts of the ecology of the areas described, including aspects such as climate (rainfall, temperature, and humidity), site descriptions (topography, geomorphology, and soil) and vegetation (floristic composition and structure). During the two decades that followed (1945–1965), studies of a similar nature were published on the nature and distribution of plant communities in various ecological zones within the country. Notable among these are the studies by Keay (1947, 1949), Richards (1957), Clayton (1961, 1963), Jones (1963), and Hambles (1964).

Following these descriptive accounts of plant communities, there started to appear in the literature objective methods of characterizing plant communities. The earliest attempt at such an objective approach was the study of Jones (1955), in which he employed Poisson distribution for the analysis of horizontal pattern of plant species, and χ^2 analysis of 2×2 contigency tables to determine species association in the community. He also employed the product correlation coefficient (r) to determine association between pairs of species.

Analysis of horizontal patterns of plant species, although popular in the British schools during this period, did not feature prominently in Nigerian plant ecology. Quantitative investigations of small vegetation patterns are suitable for communities that have been well defined but find little use in areas less well known, as is the case with Nigeria.

The most important quantitative descriptions of plant communities during the period under review are those of Ramsay (1964), Ramsay and de Leeuw (1964, 1965), Kershaw (1968), and Hall (1973). These studies made use of advanced statistical techniques, such as principal component analysis, and computer methods in classifying or ordering vegetation units. These methods involve a large amount of computation, and their usage has been made possible by the availability of computers with large memories.

Ecosystem Studies

A large part of the ecological studies in Nigeria had been devoted to description of plant communities. However, in recent years, studies on various aspects of ecosystem processes have been published. Notably, studies on litterfall and litter disappearance were published by Hopkins (1966), Madge (1966), Egunjobi (1974), and Egunjobi and Fasehun (1972). There are also a few studies on primary productivity (Rees and Tinker 1963; Kassam and

Kawal 1973; Egunjobi 1973, 1974, 1975). Integrative energy flow and mineral cycling studies as pioneered by Lindeman, Ovington, and Odum have not been undertaken during the period 1945–1975. There is evidence, however, that studies of this nature are now being undertaken.

Ecological Traditions of Influence

In his review on the classification of natural communities, Whittaker (1962) identified five major regional ecological traditions, namely, the southern and northern of Western Europe centered around Zurich-Montpellier (south) and Uppsalla (north); the Russian; the British; and the American. As noted earlier, a large proportion of published ecological studies in Nigeria during the period 1945–1975 are descriptions of plant communities. A critical appraisal of these studies indicates a strong influence of the British and American traditions. The two traditions, which have been influenced considerably by the works of Cooper, Clements, and Cowles in America, and of Tansley in Britain, have developed along similar lines and differ considerably from the traditions of Western Europe.

The best known of the European traditions is the Zurich-Montpellier school, dominated by Braun-Blanquet and his associates. The Braun-Blanquet system recognized the association as the basic unit of vegetation. Associations were delimited on the basis of "character species," *i.e.*, species with restricted ecological amplitude that also show a high degree of presence. Each association was thus characterized by a number of "character species" or species of high "fidelity." Furthermore, associations were arranged in a hierarchy patterned after the linear system of plant taxonomy.

Unlike the Braun-Blanquet school, which devoted time to the studies of plant communities for the purpose of classification, the British-American traditions studied plant communities in relation to habitat. The British-American schools classified plant communities into types on the basis of physiognomy and dominant species. Another feature of the British-American tradition, not seen in the European tradition, is the recognition of the dynamic nature of plant communities. Thus, the literature on Nigerian ecology is full of descriptions of plant communities in terms of dominant species groups, *e.g.*, *Anogeissus-Strychnos-Combretum* open savanna woodland (Keay 1949), *Bombax-Diospyros-Ficus* inselberg association (Kershaw 1968). The dynamic nature of vegetation has been shown by studies on secondary succession (Ross 1954; Clayton 1958) and the recognition of seral phases in plant communities (Keay 1949). The use of character species or fidelity of the Zurich-Montpellier school never featured in the ecological literature in Nigeria.

It is not just a matter of chance that the British-American traditions dominated ecological inquiry in Nigeria; it is a result of the English language and the British connection. Until 1960, Nigeria was a British Protectorate, and

British influences and traditions are bound to be rife. A survey of the published work on plant ecology during the period 1945–1975 shows that over 95 percent was written by people raised in the British educational traditions.

The British-American schools rejected the concept of "character species" with the hierarchic classification of plant communities because of its subjectivity and because the concept did not take into account the dynamic nature of plant communities; thus, effort was devoted to finding objective methods of classification. The search for objective methods of grouping vegetation into units started with the various indices of similarity (e.g., Jaccard, modified by Gleason and Sørensens), which were followed by indices of association based on constancy and χ^2 analysis of 2 × 2 contingency tables of presence/absence data by De Vries. The search for more objective methods culminated finally in the work on classification of Goodall and of William and Lambert and ordination of vegetation of Curtis, McIntosh, and Bray.

Objective methods used in grouping vegetation in Nigeria have been based on the classificatory and ordination approaches developed by the British-American schools. Thus, Ramsay and de Leeuw (1964) used χ^2 analysis of presence/absence data, and a modified form of the Sørensens coefficient of similarity to group savanna vegetation in North-Eastern Nigeria into noda and groups (in the sense of Poore). Ordination techniques using principal component analysis of coefficients of association have also been used to order vegetation in a similar way (Ramsay and de Leeuw 1965; Kershaw 1968; Hall 1973).

Although the methods of the European schools were never seriously applied in Nigerian community ecology, there is sufficient evidence to show that ecologists working in Nigeria understood those methods. A number of terms and methods developed by European schools are found in the literature. A few examples are the use of Raunkiaer's life-form classification (Hopkins 1965 *a,b,c*), Raunkiaer's leaf-sizes classification (Keay 1949), Domin's cover abundance scale (Kershaw 1968), Chevalier's classification of West African savanna (Keay 1949), and Sørensen's coefficient of similarity (Ramsay 1964; Hall 1972).

ADVANCES IN THEORY AND METHODOLOGY

Ecological inquiry in Nigeria has remained an offshoot of the British-American effort. As shown in the preceding section, the philosophy of the British-American tradition has dominated the field. Generally, the evolution of ideas and methodologies has evolved out of institutions of higher learning. Such institutions are very young in Nigeria, the oldest being only thirty years of age. Besides, such institutions until recently depended for their staffing on British and sometimes American personnel. No significant advances in theory and methodology can be said to have evolved independently in the country.

Effort has so far been devoted to extending the use of British-American methodologies and ideas, sometimes with a view to finding their applicability to the region.

Margalef (1968) has lamented the dearth of ecologists in the tropics. Theories and practices in ecology may have been different had the discipline evolved in the tropical rain forest zones with its diversity of species.

RELATIONS AND INTERACTION WITH OTHER DISCIPLINES

Plant ecology as a scientific discipline has borrowed considerably from a number of other sciences, among others soil science, pedology, chemistry, geography, forestry, agriculture, climatology, and mathematics. The importance of plant ecology as a tool in the management of renewable resources is owing largely to the influences of these other disciplines. Thus, statistics and mathematics, with the aid of computer technology, have made it possible to predict the reaction of terrestrial ecosystems to a number of manipulations.

In Nigeria, the greatest contribution to plant ecology has been made in the context of forestry (silviculture and forest inventory) and land-use surveys. It is mainly in these two areas of resource use and inventory that plant ecology has been found to interact actively with other disciplines. A survey of published ecological studies indicates that as many as 50 percent were devoted to such studies.

The need for interactions with disciplines such as mathematics, statistics, and computer science is beginning to be felt as recent advances in plant ecology are based on an understanding of these disciplines. As a result, relevant courses have been designed in some of the universities to meet the need of future ecologists.

FUNDING

Financial support for ecological research in Nigeria has hitherto come from three main sources, the government, the universities, and foreign donors.

Government funding of ecological research has been mainly through annual subventions to the Forestry Department and Land-use Division of the Ministries of Agriculture and Natural Resources. The studies of Keay (1949), Clayton (1958, 1963), and Ramsay and de Leeuw (1964, 1965) were funded in this way. The Ramsay and de Leeuw studies were part of a preliminary soil survey of the research division of the Ministry of Agriculture of the former Northern Nigeria. The government has sometimes funded research directly by giving funds to individuals or groups in the university. A study on the ecology and control of Siam weed (*Eupatrorium odoratum* L.) was funded in this way with a subvention to a university department at Ibadan. Recently, the government has set up a Science and Technology Development Agency

(STDA) with powers to give grants on research that relate to development. This body also constitutes a funding agency for ecological research in the country.

Universities also provide small grants for research to individuals or departments. Such grants are, however, not as generous as those from the ministries. Hopkins' ecological studies (Hopkins 1962, 1965*a*, *b*, 1966, 1968, 1970*a*,*b*) on the vegetation of the Olokemeji Forest Reserve were funded by the universities. The author has also received a similar grant to study the ecology of introduced pines.

The third source of funds comes from foreign donors. This may take the form of aid from governments or funds from learned societies. The most important of the foreign donors is the British government through its colonial office until 1960 or its successor, the Ministry of Overseas Development. Most of the soil survey work, including ecological survey, in the country has been partly funded in this way. Learned societies have also contributed funds directly or indirectly to ecological research in the country. Such contributions have been through grants to individuals or in the form of a travel grant. A well-known example of such a learned society is the Royal Society of England which bore the major part of the cost of the Cambridge Botanical Expedition to Nigeria.

TEACHING AT THE UNIVERSITY LEVEL

All the universities in the country offer courses in biology, zoology, and botany. Courses in these subjects often include one or two in basic ecology at the undergraduate level. At the University of Ibadan, the oldest of the universities and where the author has taught ecology for eight years, courses in plant ecology are offered in three departments, namely, botany, forestry and agricultural biology. The courses in the applied departments of forestry and agricultural biology are integrated, and include such topics as: introduction to ecology; quantitative approaches to synecology; biological productivity and biogeochemical cycles; ecology of forest and savanna; and weed ecology and control.

Similar courses are offered in the other universities, although emphasis differs from place to place depending on the ecology of the area and the background of the professor in charge. An example of such background influence is the course on the ecology of epiphytes in one of the universities where expertise on epiphytes was readily available. Elsewhere, this would probably have been a course in phycology.

Of the thirteen universities in the country, three are known to offer graduate courses in various aspects of plant ecology. At Ibadan, the graduate courses are offered in the applied departments of forestry and agricultural biology; at Ife, in the Department of Biological Sciences; and at Nsukka, in the Department of Botany. At Ibadan, the graduate courses include the following: advanced quantitative methods in the analysis of plant and animal communities; resource ecology and management; population ecology and genetics; and mathematical modelling and systems analysis. At the University of Ife, where the courses are run by the Department of Biological Sciences, courses are given in: mathematical ecology; environmental pollution and conservation; ecology of soil animals; weeds and colonizers; ecology of epiphytes; and physiological plant ecology.

Development of graduate courses in ecology has been hampered to a considerable extent by the dearth of indigenous ecologists. Of the fifteen or so university teachers in ecology in the country that have attained the level of Ph.D. or its equivalent, less than half are Nigerians. As a result, some universities have to depend on foreign personnel. One of the universities, with well-defined courses in ecology, depends on the services of visiting lecturers from Britain to run its graduate courses. Although such short-term visitations from other universities enrich the institutions mutually, the lack of a core of staff often leads to discontinuity in course development.

Although the graduate courses are becoming popular, they attract fewer students than fields such as plant pathology, physiology, and bacteriology because of increasing interaction of the field with mathematics and statistics. Few students in the biological sciences, forestry, and agriculture have sufficient mathematics beyond the high school level to go into graduate school. To obviate this, students proceeding to graduate school are encouraged to take remedial courses in mathematics, especially calculus, before proceeding to graduate work. At Ibadan, a new first-year course, "Mathematics in Agriculture," designed to perform a similar function, was recently introduced in the Department of Agriculture. The effect of these steps is yet to be assessed, but it is bound to reduce the number of candidates opting for ecology at the graduate level because of the increased load of mathematics.

JOURNALS AND SOCIETIES

Nigeria is a nation of many languages. Although three of these are spoken by as many as 90 percent of the people, English is the official language of communication. There are no journals published in the native language. However, a number of indigenous journals published in the English language exist in the country and publish papers of ecological nature. These include:

Farm and Forest (now defunct) published by the Department of Forestry 1940–1952;

The Nigerian Field, published by the Nigerian Field Society based in England, publishes a variety of articles ranging from ecology and natural history to cultural art;

West African Journal of Science, published by the West African Science Association;

Forestry Research Memoirs, published by the Department of Forest Research; *Nigerian Journal of Science,* published by the Nigerian Science Association; *Nigerian Forestry Journal,* published by the Nigerian Forestry Association; and *Savanna,* published by the Ahmadu Bello University.

Apart from these journals, local ecologists publish in and routinely refer to the following foreign journals: *Journal of Ecology, Journal of Applied Ecology, Tropical Ecology, Oikos, Oecologia, Oecologia Plantarum, Annals of Botany, Ecology, Ecological Monographs, Plant and Soil, Pedobiologia, Journal of Tropical Geography,* and *Turrialba.* Over 80 percent of the world's ecological research is published in these journals.

MAJOR RESEARCH PAPERS

The following section contains a synopsis and indicates the significance of thirteen publications out of the many published during the period 1945–1975. The choice has been guided by a number of factors, including availability of literature and personal bias. Effort has been made to cover the whole spectrum of plant ecology, but much of this survey has been in the area of synecology. That is where most of the action has been. [All scientific names are after Hutchinson and Dalziel (1963–1968)].

Keay, R. W. J. 1949. An example of Sudan zone vegetation in Nigeria. *J. Ecol.* 37:335–364.

This publication concerns the vegetation of a typical Sudan savanna. Most of the vegetation of the area is secondary, and the author described the plant communities as a "complex mosaic of seral communities . . . influenced by different biotic factors or combinations of factors superimposed on a mosaic of several soil factors." The paper noted that in these mosaics of communities, the abundance of the three most important tree species (*Anogeissus leocarpus, Combretun glutinosum,* and *Strychnos spinosa*) is affected by soil conditions as well as biotic factors. The most important soil influences are depth and water-retaining ability, whereas fire and grazing are the most important biotic factors. These factors determine the community type or plant association. Soils with water-retaining properties (e.g., high clay content) favor *A. leocarpus,* whereas *C. glutinosum* and *S. spinosa* tend to dominate on the drier sandy soil. Fire eliminates fire-tender species and favors fire-resistant species, especially *C. glutinosum* and *S. spinosa.* Grazing of the herb layer by cattle creates "fire breaks" and the subsequent protection from fire tends to favor regeneration of trees, especially *A. leocarpa,* which is not grazed by cattle.

The author considered the likely occurrence of community types depending on the combination of actions of soil and biotic factors. Under the influence of these factors, the three co-dominants segregate to form four communities. As the vegetation was mainly secondary, the author attempted to construct the climatic climax of the area, from the vegetation of inaccessible rocky hills.

The significance of this paper lies in its recognition of the interplay between edaphic and biotic factors in secondary succession.

Ross, R. 1954. Ecological studies on the rainforest of Southern Nigeria. III. The secondary succession in the Shasha Forest Reserve. *J. Ecol.* 42:259–282.

The paper concerns the course of plant succession from plots aged five, fourteen, and seventeen years after cultivation in a tropical rain forest area. To obtain information on the initial phase of colonization, part of the clear ground at the base camp (though not cultivated) was studied for species composition. The course of succession was studied by making enumeration of sample plots in each of the stands. The paper established that the ligneous species colonizing successional stands fall into two categories, namely, primary forest species native to the area, and secondary forest species. The former are made up of primary forest undergrowth and the emergents. The latter consist of quick-growing, soft-wooded trees with short life spans and trees characteristic of secondary forest.

In the recently cleared plot, *Trema guineense* appeared as the main colonizing species, even though in some places *Vernonia conferta* appeared to be the first colonist. In the five-year-old stand, 87 percent of all ligneous species 5 cm in diameter and above were secondary forest species. *Musanga cecropoides* was the most prominent species with a few individuals of *Discoglypremna caloneura* and *Macaranga barteri*. In the fourteen-year-old plot, *M. cecropoides* remained the dominant species, with a few individuals of *Phyllanthus discoides, Sarcocephalus diderichii,* and *Rinorea oblongifolia.* In the seventeen-year-old stand, *M. cecropoides* was no longer dominant, and senescent plants of the species were commonly found. Few individuals of the primary forest type had grown to reach the upper story.

The author also described environmental conditions such as carbon dioxide concentration, light, temperature, and humidity within the forest.

This is the most comprehensive study on secondary succession made in the forest zone of Nigeria. Its limitation lies in the fact that the history of the cultivated areas, prior to abandonment, is not well known. Furthermore, the areas concerned are relatively small and surrounded by high forest. These conditions are likely to influence the speed of succession. The course of succession in large areas, removed from major sources of propagules, is likely to be different from this.

Jones, E. W. 1955, 1956. Ecological studies on the rainforest of Southern Nigeria. IV. The plateau forest of the Okomu Forest Reserve. *J. Ecol.* 43:564–594 and *J. Ecol.* 44:83–117.

The study concerns the pattern of species distribution, regeneration of the forest, and the stability of the rain forest, particularly in relation to the theory of "mosaic" structure. The author distinguished the following vegetation types: (a) high forest, (b) phases derived from high forest, (c) young secondary forest, and (d) gully margin forest.

Using various quantitative methods for the analysis of horizontal pattern of plant species, the author concluded that emergents were distributed more nearly at random than are the lower story species, which tended to aggregate with decreasing size. Some species were distributed in patchwork design on a large scale, although randomly distributed on a small scale. Jones also studied associations between species to detect any well-defined mosaic of species. Only very few pairs of species tended to associate, as they should if there were well-defined communities. About half the emergent species are wind dispersed, while the remaining are animal dispersed. In the lower story species, the proportion of wind-dispersed species is smaller than those of animal-dispersed species. Observation of seedlings indicates that they occur in patches or near mature trees. The author noted that in emergent species, stems of medium size tend to be less abundant than large-sized ones; he attributed this to a discontinuous recruitment. On the other hand, all sizes of the shade-tolerant species of the middle and lower stories are well represented, indicating a continuous regeneration.

The importance of this study lies in the use of statistical methods in the analysis of pattern and determination of plant association. Hitherto, subjective methods had been used in this type of study in Nigeria.

Clayton, W. D. 1958. Secondary vegetation and the transition to savanna near Ibadan, Nigeria. *J. Ecol.* 46:217–238.

Ecological work has hitherto been directed at forest vegetation in protected areas. This study differs in that it was carried out in cultivated areas; the objective was to show that, although it may be impossible to precisely define clear-cut associations in secondary bush, it is still possible to distinguish certain "nodal" communities. The study combined vegetation analysis with soil survey and land-use pattern, and herein lies its importance.

Studying land use and vegetation of seral communities on different soil types (clay soils, sandy soils, poorly drained or swampy soils), the author noted that secondary succession may either be progressive or regressive, depending on the intensity of cultivation. Observations indicate that succession tends to be regressive in the Ibaden area. The situation is further complicated by soil factor.

Ramsay, D. M. and P. N. de Leeuw. 1964. An analysis of the Nigerian savanna. I. The survey area and the vegetation developed over Bima sandstone. *J. Ecol.* 52:233–254.

The study was part of a quantitative vegetation survey carried out during a preliminary soil survey in North-Eastern Nigeria. The Bima sandstone formation covers approximately one sixth of the 18,200 km^2 survey area; the aim of the study was to determine vegetation groups that could be used as mapping units.

Ninety-two 0.2-hectare sampling plots and the fifty-six most frequent species out of ninety were used to perform a χ^2 analysis of presence/absence data; thirty-nine species each showed significant association of occurrence with at least two other species. When the thirty-nine species were plotted on a constellation diagram, groups of associated species could be identified, including four groups that have ecological interpretation. Such groups were shown to have different environmental preferences as well as practical value as mapping units.

Correlation between soil association and vegetation communities was found to be satisfactory.

The significance of the study lies in the application of simple ecological methods as an aid in preliminary soil survey.

Ramsay, D. M. 1964. An analysis of Nigerian savanna. II. An alternative method of analysis and its application to the Gombe sandstone vegetation. *J. Ecol.* 52:457–466.

The author discusses the limitations of using presence/absence data for association analysis and proposes an alternative method based on a modified form of Sørensen's coefficient of similarity:

$$K = \frac{2\ \mathrm{Jmin}}{DD_A + DD_B} \times 100,$$

where DD_A is the sum of the relative density plus relative dominance of all species in plot A and DD_B the same for plot B. Jmin is the minimum joint occurrence of one species in both plots. The value of the coefficient ranges between one hundred for perfect association to zero for complete lack of association.

Interplot coefficient of association K between all pairs of plots was calculated and presented in a matrix of coefficients. Values of $K \geqslant 70$ were chosen to delimit group noda and subnoda; K values of 60–69 indicate between noda linkages, while K values 50–59 delimit within group links. A group nodum was defined as the central core of plots that form the nucleus of a group, while a group is the whole assemblage of plots based on a nodum. The K values were used to construct a constellation diagram from which three noda and groups emerged. The groups so defined were found to agree closely with the empirical classification of the vegetation during field survey. A comparison of the method with the χ^2 method used on the Bima formation showed similar, although slightly different, divisions. The main disadvantage of the method described in this paper is the impossibility of assigning any statistical level of significance to the results.

The significance of this study lies in the modification of Sørensen's method. Methods in plant sociology developed by the European school of phytosociology have not always found acceptance in areas where the British-American traditions have dominated. The present use of the method, together with its modification, was part of the effort during the late 1950s at finding more objective methods in community ecology.

Ramsay, D. M. and P. N. de Leeuw. 1965. An analysis of Nigerian savanna. IV. Ordination of vegetation developed on different parent materials. *J. Ecol.* 53:661–677.

The objective of the study was to correlate the vegetation developed on different geological parent materials to determine whether differences found within the vegetation could be ascribed to differences in soil parent material. The 18,200-km^2 study area was constituted of soil from seven different parent materials, on which twenty-six vegetation noda and nineteen groups had been delineated.

Each nodum was compared with all other noda, and the coefficient of association of all pairs of noda ordinated on a two-dimensional axis, according to the method of Bray and Curtis. Ordination relates all plots to a series of axes (in this case, two) that reflects the plot interrelationship; ordination also relates the plots to the environmental factors controlling them. The nineteen groups were ordinated by a similar method, but the ordination of noda was preferred since groups show a greater degree of interrelationship. The ordination produced five distinct floristic units showing the influence of soil, water availability, and human interference, rather than soil parent material per se. In both cases, the x-axis of the ordination seems to represent an edaphic gradient from light-textured, shallow, freely drained soils to heavy-textured, poorly drained soils, while the y-axis depicts a physiognomic gradient from shrub savanna to woodland.

Kershaw, K. A. 1968. Classification and ordination of Nigerian savanna vegetation. *J. Ecol.* 56:467–482.

The author described two objective methods of grouping vegetation associations in a Guinea savanna, vegetation originally grouped by subjective methods into eighteen plant associations. The vegetation was sampled from 433 (30 × 12 m) plots. The objective methods used were: (a) a classificatory method using χ^2 analysis of presence and absence data for both pairs of plots and pairs of species, and (b) an ordination method using the similarity coefficient of Bray and Curtis. The similarity coefficients were calculated for all pairs of plots and the resultant matrix of coefficients analyzed by principal component analysis.

Taking arbitrary levels of χ^2, there was a remarkable agreement between the associations created by the χ^2 analysis and those created subjectively by the method of Braun-Blanquet. There was, however, a tendency for the χ^2 analysis to subdivide the data into small units of little or no ecological significance, a problem that did not occur in the subjective classification. Similarly, plot ordination indicated a high level of agreement with the subjective method; however, species ordination, although indicating similar groupings, suffered from a high variance in the data. Such a variance could, however, be reduced by eliminating the less common species or by a square-root transformation of the coefficients.

This paper is a unique example of the preoccupation during the middle and late 1960s with the search for objective methods in synecology. The use of statistics and mathematics in ecology developed rapidly with the availability of high-speed computers during this period.

Kassam, A. H. and J. M. Kawal. 1973. Productivity of crops in the savanna and rainforest zones of Nigeria. *Savanna* 2:39–49.

The authors assessed potential crop productivity in the savanna and rain forest zones of Nigeria using De Wit's model of gross photosynthesis. Mean net photosynthesis throughout the year in the savanna zone is 20–40 percent greater than in the forest zone; 55 percent of the gross photosynthesis is lost through respiration in the forest zone, while in the savanna zone the proportion is 49 percent.

Net photosynthesis of C_3 plants in the savanna zone is 19–27 percent greater than in the forest zone, while C_4 plant photosynthesis is 30–35 percent greater. During the growing season, the corresponding figures are 19–27 percent and 27–30 percent, respectively.

The authors showed that actual rates of dry matter production of some selected crops (maize, cotton, kenaf, and reselle) in the savanna are twice as high as in the forest zone. They explained that lower radiation intensities and higher night temperatures in the forest zone reduced potential photosynthesis below that in the savanna zone. Furthermore, actual economic yield of crops was further reduced by higher rates of leaching and greater pest and disease pressures.

This paper is one of the few papers on agricultural ecology from the region, and vividly demonstrates the relationship between plant physiology, agronomy, and ecology.

Madge, D. S. 1965. Leaf fall and litter disappearance in a tropical forest. *Pedobiologia* 5:273–288.

The author described leaf fall and the process of litter disappearance in a tropical rain forest. The sequence of leaf fall in the seven most important species (*Bosquea angolensis, Sterculia tragacantha, Alstonia congensis, Trichilia leudelotti, Funtumia africana, Theobroma cacao, Alchornea cordifolia*) indicate that except for *Alchornea,* which shed its leaves during the middle of the wet season, all other species shed their leaves mostly during the dry season in December to February. *Alstonia congensis,* however, showed two peaks of leaf fall, one in January and a lesser one in mid-May. Annual litterfall was estimated at 5,600 kg/hectare, of which leaves account for two-thirds. The litter on the ground averaged 2,450 kg/hectare, and this disappeared at the rate of 0.6 percent per day during the dry season and 1.5 percent per day during the wet season.

The author also investigated the activity of the soil and litter fauna on the disappearance of the fallen leaves in relation to climate. A good relationship was established between leaf area eaten and the total number of microathropods, mainly mites and collembola. Although numerous worm casts were produced during the wet season by the species *Hypericodrilus africanus* (Beddard), they do not appear to consume the litter unlike earthworms in temperate regions.

This is perhaps the first detailed study in tropical Africa showing what species of soil and litter fauna participate actively in the disappearance of litter.

Hopkins, B. 1968. Vegetation of the Olokemeji Forest Reserve, Nigeria. V. The vegetation on the savanna site with special reference to its seasonal changes. *J. Ecol.* 56:97–115.

The study, one of a series on the ecology of the Olokemeji forest, was concerned with the changes in the herb layer of the savanna vegetation following burning. Growth commences soon after the burning and before the onset of the rains. There is an increase in both dry weight and height during the season with growth rate remaining steady until October, when the grasses that dominate the herb layer change from a vegetative to a reproductive phase. The maximum dry weight attained by the herb layer during the year averaged 6.8 tons/hectare at which time the maximum leaf area index (LAI) was about 6.0.

Fifty-five species representing 66 percent of the vegetation were found to be flowering during ten years of observation. Most geophytes flower early with the arrival of the rains and, with the exception of *Sporobolus* which flowers from mid-April to mid-September, most other grasses flower from mid-October to mid-November. The dicotyledons flower over a longer period, from April to mid-December, with most coming into flower between mid-August to mid-October.

An ordination of relative frequency data from monthly quadrat samples of vegetation by principal component analysis of the weighted similarity coefficient of Orloci showed a distinct seasonal trend and between-year differences. A normal association analysis of the same data gave thirteen common groups, most of which changed their frequency seasonally. The usefulness of this method in this type of study is not readily obvious.

Hopkins, B. 1970. Vegetation of the Olokemeji Forest Reserve Nigeria. VI. The plants of the forest site with special reference to their seasonal growth. *J. Ecol.* 58:765–793.

The study addressed seasonal changes in the growth of nineteen forest species. Each species has its own seasonal growth pattern. Growth occurs mainly between February and March, and until May in some cases. Cambial activity takes place between May and September, while most leaf fall and radial shrinkage occur between December and February. A general relationship between rainfall and growth exists, although this is not causal; the most likely factor controlling extension growth is photoperiod, although moisture may exert a limiting effect. Growth rates were generally low in all the species, and this was attributed to lack of water.

Egunjobi, J. K. 1974. Litterfall and litter mineralization in a stand of teak (*Tectona grandis* L.). *Oikos* 25:222–226.

The author presented estimates of litterfall and its mineral content and discussed the rate of mineralization of the litter in a young plantation of teak, an exotic in Nigeria. The mean annual litterfall was 9,024 ± 882 kg/hectare, over 63 percent of which fell between December and March; 90 percent was leaf litter, the rest being twigs, flowers, and seeds. The mean annual return of plant nutrients in the litter was 91N, 10P, 7K, 188Ca, 22Mg, and 2Na. The seasonal litterfall accumulates during the dry months of December to March, but completely disappears between June and October. The quantities of minerals in the annual litterfall therefore represent the yearly return of nutrients in the biogeochemical cycle.

With the exception of a preliminary account of litterfall in *Pinus caribaea* L. (Egunjobi and Fasehun 1972) earlier litterfall studies (Hopkins 1966; Madge 1966) had been limited to organic matter. This study incorporated the nutrient element. The study also showed the similarity between teak and native forest in the pattern of leaf fall.

REFERENCES CITED

Clayton, W. D. 1958. Secondary vegetation and the transition to savanna near Ibadan, Nigeria. *J. Ecol.* 46:217–238.

______. 1961. Derived savanna in Kabba province, Nigeria. *J. Ecol.* 49:595–604.

______. 1963. The vegetation of Katsina province, Nigeria. *J. Ecol.* 51:345–351.

Egunjobi, J. K. 1973. Studies on the primary productivity of a regularly burnt tropical savanna. *Ann. Univ. Abidjan Series E (Ecologie)* 6:157–170.

______. 1974. Litterfall and litter mineralization in a stand of teak (*Tectona grandis* L). *Oikos* 25:222–226.

______. 1975. Dry matter production by an immature stand of *P. caribaea* L. *Oikos* 26:80–85.

______ and F. E. Fasehun, 1972. Preliminary observations on the monthly litterfall and nutrient content of *P. caribaea* L. litter. *Nig. J. Sci.* 6:37–44.

Hall, J. B. 1971. Environment and vegetation on Nigeria highlands. *Vegetatio* 23:339–359.

______. 1973. Vegetation zones of the southern slopes of Mount Cameroon. *Vegetatio* 27:49–69.

Hambles, D. J. 1964. The vegetation of granitic outcrops in western Nigeria. *J. Ecol.* 52:573–594.

Hopkins, B. 1962. The vegetation of the Olokemeji Forest Reserve, Nigeria. I. General features of the reserve and the research sites. *J. Ecol.* 50:559–598.

______. 1965*a*. *Forest and savanna.* Ibadan-London: Heinemann.

______. 1965*b*. Vegetation of the Olokemeji Forest Reserve, Nigeria. II. The climate with special reference to its seasonal changes. *J. Ecol.* 53:109–124.

______. 1965*c*. Vegetation of the Olokemeji Forest Reserve, Nigeria. III. The microclimate with special reference to the seasonal changes. *J. Ecol.* 53:125–138.

______. 1966. Vegetation of the Olokemeji Forest Reserve, Nigeria. IV. The litter and soil with special reference to their seasonal changes. *J. Ecol.* 54:687–703.

______. 1968. Vegetation of the Olokemeji Forest Reserve, Nigeria. V. The vegetation of the savanna site with special reference to its seasonal changes. *J. Ecol.* 56:97–115.

______. 1970*a*. Vegetation of the Olokemeji Forest Reserve, Nigeria. VI. The plants on the forest site with special reference to their seasonal growth. *J. Ecol.* 58:765–793.

______. 1970*b*. Vegetation of the Olokemeji Forest Reserve, Nigeria. VII. The plants of the savanna site with special reference to their seasonal growth. *J. Ecol.* 58:795–825.

Hutchinson, J. and J. M. Dalziel. 1963–1968. *Flora of West Tropical Africa.* London.

Jones, E. W. 1955, 1956. Ecological studies on the rainforest of southern Nigeria. IV. The plateau forest of the Okomu Forest Reserve. *J. Ecol.* 43:564–594; 44:83–117.

______. 1963. The forest outliers in the Guinea zone of northern Nigeria. *J. Ecol.* 51:415–434.

Kassam, A. H. and J. M. Kawal. 1973. Productivity of crops in the savanna and rainforest zones of Nigeria. *Savanna* 2:39–49.

Keay, R. W. J. 1947. Notes on the vegetation of old Oyo Forest Reserve. *Farm For.* 8:36–47.

______. 1949. An example of Sudan zone vegetation in Nigeria. *J. Ecol.* 37:335–364.

Kershaw, K. A. 1968. Classification and ordination of Nigerian savanna vegetation. *J. Ecol.* 56:467–482.

Madge, D. S. 1966. Leaf fall and litter disappearance in a tropical forest. *Pedobiologia* 5:273–288.

Margalef, R. 1968. *Perspectives in ecology.* Chicago: University of Chicago Press.

Ramsay, D. M. 1964. An analysis of Nigerian savanna. II. An alternative method of analysis and its application to the Gombe sandstone vegetation. *J. Ecol.* 52:457–466.

______ and P. N. de Leeuw. 1964. An analysis of Nigerian savanna. I. The survey area and the vegetation developed over Bima sandstone. *J. Ecol.* 52:233–254.

______ and P. N. de Leeuw. 1965. An analysis of Nigerian savanna. IV. Ordination of vegetation developed on different parent materials. *J. Ecol.* 53:661–677.

Rees, A. R. and P. B. H. Tinker. 1963. Dry matter production and nutrient content of plantation oil plam in Nigeria. I. Growth and dry matter production. *Plant Soil* 19:19–32.

Richards, P. W. 1957. Ecological notes on West African vegetation. I. The plant communities on Idanre Hills, Nigeria. *J. Ecol.* 45:563–577.

Ross, R. 1954. Ecological studies on the rainforest of southern Nigeria. III. Secondary succession in the Shasha Forest Reserve. *J. Ecol.* 42:259–282.

Whittaker, R. H. 1962. Classification of natural communities. *Bot. Rev.* 20:1–239.

26

REPUBLIC OF SOUTH AFRICA

Gerrit de Graaff

INTRODUCTION

Climatology and Hydrology

Because of its limited water resources, South Africa is committed to policies that will ensure the optimum use of those resources. The Department of Water Affairs is responsible for all matters relating to water in the country. The National Institute for Water Research (NIWR) of the Council for Scientific and Industrial Research (CSIR), established in 1958, has the primary objectives of improving water quality and utilization and developing techniques for the reuse of water and prevention of water pollution (Cillié and Hofmeyr 1975). Estuaries are the subject of extensive research by the NIWR, and it has undertaken extensive research into the effects of pollution on river fauna and flora and efficient purification of waste water.

In arid areas with a high evaporation rate, the availability and quality of ground water resources need to be assessed. In many cases, such sources are highly mineralized and unsuitable for human and animal consumption. Extensive research by the CSIR, the Geological Survey, and the Department of Water Affairs has resulted in the compilation of a water map of southwest Africa indicating sources and potability. In addition, research on the desalination of mineralized waters, including seawater, by the CSIR with subvention by the Water Research Commission through the NIWR, is making steady progress. The Hydrological Research Institute (HRI), of the Department of Water Affairs, is investigating the feasibility of electrostatic precipitation of moisture from low clouds on mountain ranges (cloud milking) and has also undertaken extensive surveys of silt loads in surface runoff, which can lead to the rapid silting of dams (Cillié and Hofmeyr 1975).

Soils and Pedology

Four major soil zones are recognized in South Africa, the first of which contains the unleached alkaline soils characteristic of the arid regions in the north and northwest of the country; this zone corresponds to a vegetational zone consisting mainly of desert shrub. A second category is the thin immature soils of the winter rainfall area in the southwest part of the country, consisting of the grey sandy soils of the Table Mountain sandstone areas, which are mainly acidic and deficient in humus, and the clayey Bokkeveld and Malmesbury soils which have a higher plant-food content, are less acidic, and have a more loamy texture. Both soils are predominantly associated with sclerophyllous bush. A third group is the podzolic soils occupying the southern part of the summer rainfall region and including the soils of the prairie highveld, eastern Cape and Natal midlands, and Natal coastal belt. Vegetationally, these soils are associated with grassland. The fourth group are the lateritic soils, consisting of true laterites and ferruginous lateritic soils. This group is well developed in the north and northeast portions of the country, occupying an almost continuous belt from the Soutpans Mountains in the north to the Transkei in the south, all along the eastern plateau slopes. The dominant vegetation consists of evergreen forest or savanna. There is also a group of unleached subtropical soils in the north and northeast of the country that do not really fit into any of the four main groups.

More than two centuries after the first European settlement in South Africa, the population depended largely on farming of a pastoral nature. With the discovery of diamonds, and afterwards gold, enormous changes were introduced that led to marked and rapid industrial growth, which had far-reaching repercussions on the farming economy. Emphasis was placed on economic production with little regard to the eventual fate of soil, vegetation, and water resources. Grazing was without interruption, and arable lands were overtaxed; soil depletion and veld deterioration finally gave rise to widespread soil erosion, which is now a formidable national problem (Ross 1974). It may be said that soil erosion has been South Africa's greatest ecological problem (Sullivan and Sullivan 1977). Reliable figures on the extent of soil loss in South Africa due to erosion are lacking, but a rough estimate places it at not less than 300 million tons annually (Ross 1974).

FRESHWATER ECOLOGY

Basic and Applied Research

Until recently, very little was known of the ecology of inland waters in South Africa; however, steady progress is now being made in unravelling the complexities of freshwater ecology. Allanson (1963) described the hydrobiological aspects of inundation of river basins, a factor of particular importance in contemporary South Africa with the development of the Orange River Project and its associated dams. In a subsequent paper, Allanson (1965) discussed the significance of the thermocline in the biology of developing reservoirs, comparing temperature stratification results obtained for the great lakes of Africa with what little is known of South African waters.

A survey of the limnological investigations of the Orange River system discussed by Van Zinderen Bakker (1965) forms part of the proceedings of symposia on the Orange River Development Project, held under the auspices of the South African Association for the Advancement of Science in 1963 and 1964.

Work on freshwater fishes was begun by J. D. F. Gilchrist in 1895, continued by Barnard after 1911, and brought to monographic stage by Jubb, (1967) whose handsome and comprehensive monograph entitled *Freshwater Fishes of Southern Africa* remains the authoritative work on freshwater fishes of this area. Similarly, conservation agencies are also concerned with research into freshwater fish and the management of this important resource (Pienaar 1968). The placid-flowing waters (rivers and streams) of the Kruger National Park, as well as the seasonal pools and larger dams, afford sanctuary to some forty-six species of freshwater fishes. The province of Transvaal, in which the Kruger Park is located, has a wealth of species that do not occur further south; consequently, freshwater angling is more important in this province than in any other part of the Republic of South Africa (Le Roux and Steyn 1968).

An account of the ecological changes brought about in South African rivers by human activities in the past and the known effects of the changes on the biology is dealt with by Chutter (1973). Probable future changes in rivers are described against trends in population growth, agricultural practice, and water consumption. The last three hundred years have witnessed a deterioration in the quality of South African rivers; many perennial rivers have become seasonal, most rivers carry increased silt loads, and in recent years the chemical nature of the water has been altered through the discharge of various effluents. Formerly, most of a downpour was retained where it fell, but in areas presently denuded of vegetation, the bulk of the water rushes over the surface and along erosion channels to empty itself and its siltload into the nearest river. Enormous masses of silt are deposited in the larger irrigation dams built by the state at great cost, and this process threatens to render them worthless eventually (Ross 1974). In the Republic of South Africa, there are some twenty-one drainage regions and 114 principal dams (Robertson 1974).

In addition to silting, pollution is also a threat to South Africa's freshwater resources. A diversity of substances ranging from industrial wastes to household detergents often find their way into the rivers. Eutrophication has become a major problem in many places in the republic. Control of substances entering water systems is supported by legislation, and the South African Bureau of Standards is responsible for setting permissible levels of such substances. However, not enough research has been done locally to set standards for all substances; thus, there are no restrictions on substances like mercury and phosphorus, while standards on others (e.g., cadmium and nickel) are lenient by international standards (Sullivan and Sullivan 1977).

Research on the causes, consequences, and control of eutrophication was initiated in 1972 by the National Institute of Water Research (NIWR) under the sponsorship of the Water Research Commission. Guidelines were prepared for acceptable levels of phosphate and nitrogen in lakes and reservoirs, and a survey of some ninety-eight South African impoundments was undertaken. The results indicated that phosphate was the primary algal growth-limiting nutrient in about two-thirds of the cases; South African impoundments appear to be able to receive phosphate inputs of 0.3–0.7 grams of phosphorus per square meter per annum without developing symptoms of overabundant growth (Toerien 1977). The harvesting of freshwater fish, algae, or macrophytes, or all three, seems to be the most promising method of manipulating impoundments to produce desirable changes in water quality. The implementation of eutrophication control techniques is subject to economic and technological considerations and must be integrated with the long-term management of water supplies in South Africa (Toerien 1977).

More intensive studies on the ecology and hydrobiology of particular rivers and river systems have been undertaken for the Vaal River and the catchment of the Vaal Dam in Transvaal (Chutter 1963, 1970, 1971), for the lower Pongola River and its flood plain in northern Natal (Coke 1970), and for the Tugela River system in Natal (Oliff, Kemp, and King 1965; Kemp 1967). Similar studies on the Great Berg River in the western Cape Province were initiated by Harrison (1958*a*, *b*).

Universities and Museums

As noted above, different organizations are associated with ecological research matters pertaining to freshwater ecology in South Africa including government departments, provincial administrations, and statutory bodies.

As examples of university and museum participation, the Snail Research

Group, attached to the Potchefstroom University for Christian Higher Education, is working on the identification, distribution, and conditions for survival of freshwater snails, of concern in snail-borne parasites. Similarly, the Research Group for Freshwater Biology, founded at the Rand Afrikaans University in Johannesburg, conducts research into physiology and ecology of freshwater organisms in reservoirs and rivers, and pollution studies of rivers and impoundments affected by pesticides in water. At Rhodes University in Grahamstown, the Institute for Freshwater Studies undertakes limnological studies on coastal lakes and has recently entered into a contract with the Water Research Commission for research on the role of aquatic macrophytes in maintaining oligotrophic conditions in the open-water body of Swartvlei in the Wilderness area on the southern Cape coast. The Institute for Environmental Sciences at the University of the Orange Free State in Bloemfontein conducts research on physicochemical and biological studies of the Orange River system, as well as limnological investigations on the Memel and other pans occurring in the Orange Free State. Research is undertaken in the fields of freshwater ichthyology and freshwater invertebrates by the Albany Museum in Grahamstown, while the main research projects at the Port Elizabeth Museum include investigations of the plankton and ecology of South African estuaries.

MARINE ECOLOGY

Phytoplankton from the oceans surrounding South Africa was collected and studied from the latter part of the nineteenth century onward, especially by several of the great oceanographic expeditions that circumnavigated the southern tip of the African continent. More recently, material collected by ships of the South African Sea Fisheries Branch has been studied by Boden (1950) and Nel (1968), west coast and east coast, respectively.

According to Grindley (1973), the composition and density of the phytoplankton in the seas around South Africa vary remarkably from one region to another. In the southwestern Indian Ocean, there are usually fewer than one hundred thousand cells per liter, whereas in the richer and colder areas, at more than 40° south and in the region of upwelling in the Benguela Current, there are usually more than one hundred thousand cells per liter. The diversity of species is greater in the warmer waters of the Indian Ocean, and over one hundred species are frequently found in samples taken off the east coast; in contrast, about a quarter as many may be encountered in a sample from the cold waters of the west coast.

The patterns of distribution of phytoplankton around South Africa are not yet clear, and only a few measurements of productivity have been made so far, using the carbon-14 method. High values have been recorded in tropical waters of the Agulhas Current region: a value of 597 mg carbon per square meter per day off the Transkei Coast and values as low as 14 mg carbon per square meter per day in the more impoverished offshore waters of the western Indian Ocean (Grindley 1973). There is no obvious correlation between regions of highest productivity and the concentration of phytoplankton cells present in these areas. However, a concerted and intensive research effort is required before a clear picture of productivity of phytoplankton in South African seas will emerge. In order of importance and abundance, the South African marine phytoplankton consists of diatoms, dinoflagellates, coccolithophorids, and silicoflagellates.

Marine zooplankton is studied today by several organizations, including the Sea Fisheries Branch of the central government, the University of Cape Town, the South African Museum, and the Oceanographic Research Institute in Durban (Grindley 1975). The results of this research are published in the *Investigational Reports of the Division of Sea Fisheries* and in various other scientific journals.

The rich fisheries of South Africa's west coast are dependent on the wealth of plankton and other associated food chains that develop in the cold, fertile waters of the Benguela Current. As is the case in the phytoplankton, the zooplankton of the cold water of the Atlantic west coast is quite different from that found in the warmer waters near the Agulhas Current off the Indian Ocean coast of Natal; these differences are apparently due to differences in the temperature and fertility of the sea. Some seven different regions with characteristic plankton families may be recognized (Grindley 1975). The most abundant zooplankton organisms in South African waters are the crustacean copepods; over 300 species have now been recovered. Another important zooplankton group are the shrimplike Euphausiacea. These two groups are supplemented by other drifting crustaceans, coelenterids, salps, arrowworms, and protozoans, especially the Radiolaria and Foraminifera.

As earlier noted, the rich fishwaters of South Africa are influenced by two great ocean currents. Moving down the east coast to Cape Point is the warm Agulhas Current, containing more than 1,000 different fish species off the southwestern tip of the Cape; along the west coast, this current meets the cold Benguela Current flowing northward from the Antarctic drift. In the area where these two currents meet, and in the cold waters along the west coast, are found the pilchards (*Sardinops ocellata*), maasbankers (*Trachurus trachurus*), mackerel, anchovies, and other species on which a large part of the South African fishing industry is based. It appears that pilchard and anchovy are triggered to spawn by particular water conditions that also favor growth of planktonic food for the fish larvae (Field 1977).

Research into the resources of fish and their environment is done by the Sea Fisheries Branch of the Department of Industries, which is responsible for conservational and rational management of the exploited fish resources (Anonymous 1971*a,b*). Much of the basic research work is done in collaboration with the southern universities, especially the University of Stellenbosch (du Toit 1976).

The systematic study of fishes, both marine and freshwater, was initiated by J. D. F. Gilchrist in 1895, and his work stimulated a developing fishing industry. In 1911, K. H. Barnard joined the staff of the South African Museum in Cape Town and continued the work started by Gilchrist. His monograph on the marine fishes of South Africa is of fundamental importance to systematic ichthyology in South African waters. These developments were followed by the publication of a comprehensive monograph by Smith (1949) entitled *The Sea Fishes of Southern Africa* listing some 1,275 species; in the 1972 edition, the list exceeds 1,600 species. Smith's indefatigable productivity led to the establishment at Rhodes University of the J. L. B. Smith Institute of Ichthylogy, now under the directorship of his widow Margaret Smith. The study of freshwater fish and resultant research has also become a function of this institute. In addition, the four southern universities (Cape Town, Western Cape, Stellenbosch, and Port Elizabeth) are also unravelling the anatomy and physiology of marine and estuarine fishes, while the Oceanographic Research Institute in Durban is focusing its attention on fish species occurring along the east coast (du Toit 1976). A national marine pollution survey was launched in 1973 as part of the National Program of Environmental Sciences, to monitor sources of pollution along the coast and to establish a marine pollution data center (Oliff 1977).

TERRESTRIAL ECOLOGY

Plant Ecology

Historical

Botany in South Africa had its modest beginnings before the time Jan van Riebeeck landed at the Cape in 1652. Ships en route to and from the Far East called at Table Bay for supplies of fresh water; gradually plants found their way to Europe where they aroused much interest. The first South African plant to be illustrated, *Protea neriifolia,* appeared in a book published in 1605 in Holland. A thorough account of the history and development of botany in South Africa has been compiled by Levyns (1970), while an excellent overview of botanical research in South Africa was written by Dyer (1977).

It was not until the beginning of the twentieth century that the study of botany became firmly established in university colleges in South Africa. Through the teaching provided by these newly founded institutions of higher education, ecology became an integral part of training. An excellent example is the case of John William Bews (1884–1938) who arrived in South Africa to become professor of botany and geology at the University of Natal and who left behind a flourishing school of ecology in Natal, a school which still exists. At the time of Union (1910), agriculture and forestry were developing rapidly, and the Division of Botany was founded within the Department of Agriculture. Under the directorship of I. B. Pole Evans, the Botanical Survey was organized in 1918. In 1919, the results of the Botanical Survey began to be published in a series of *Memoirs,* which appeared as each piece of research was completed. In addition, two further periodicals were started in 1921: *Bothalia* was a medium for the publication of research carried out in the Division of Botany, while the *Flowering Plants of South Africa* (becoming the *Flowering Plants of Africa* in 1944), an annual publication, carried color illustrations and short descriptions of new or little-known South African plants.

In building up his organization for botanical research, Pole Evans gave a warning and directive about the veld to agriculturalists and botanists in his presidential address to the South African Association for the Advancement of Science (1920), and later published a vegetation map as *Memoir* no. 15 (1936), which remained the standard work of reference until J. H. P. Acocks' (1953) "Veld types of South Africa." From about 1935 to the present time, Acocks had been collecting extensively, recording species, mapping, and photographing the distribution of veld types, thereby greatly enhancing the value and impact of *Memoir* no. 40 (1975).

The former Division of Botany is today known as the Botanical Research Institute, and consists of three main sections dealing with classification, economic botany, and the Botanical Survey, respectively. In addition, an important undertaking being carried out by the institute is the compilation of a new *Flora of Southern Africa.*

Among other outstanding botanists was John Hutchinson, at the Royal Botanic Gardens, Kew, who recorded his experiences in his book, *A Botanist in Southern Africa* (1946). The original Botanical Survey Advisory Committee entrusted to E. P. Phillips the compilation of a record of *The Genera of South African Flowering Plants, Memoir* no. 10 (1926) and the revised edition (1951). Another illustrious botanist who became a member of the Botanical Survey Advisory Committee was John F. V. Phillips, who contributed a thesis on *Forest-Succession and Ecology in the Knysna Region* (1931) to the Memoir series (no. 14).

The history of botany (and therefore ecology) in southern Africa reveals the debt owed to men and women who, although not professional botanists, have contributed greatly to the knowledge of the subject: T. M. Salter, a retired naval officer, published his research on *Oxalis* (1944) and also contributed much as co-author to the *Flora of the Cape Peninsula* (1950); G. W. Reynolds, a businessman, devoted virtually all his spare time to the study of the genus *Aloe,* travelling widely in Africa and Madagascar to obtain plants and information (1950, 1966); H. Herre, who had the unique distinction of being the first to grow the famous *Welwitschia mirabrilis* from seed in 1928 to seed in the glasshouse of the University of Stellenbosch twenty-three years later, published a monograph on the typically South African family Mesembryanthemaceae (1971); and Eve Palmer, author of text, and Norah Pitman, artist, prepared three comprehensive volumes on *The Trees of Southern Africa* (1972).

Algae to Forests

In Cape Town, R. Simons has been working on a badly needed field guide to the marine algae, and his team is determining the growth rate and productivity of the giant kelp that forms part and parcel of the whole kelpbed ecosystem (Day 1977). At Rhodes University, where there is an established tradition of algology, Seagrief (1967) had produced a well-illustrated account of the seaweeds along the Tsitsikama coast and has prepared a checklist of South African algae as an aid to further studies (Day 1977). It is estimated that there are about 700 species around the coast of South Africa.

As far as the freshwater algae are concerned, mention must be made of the work done by Cholnoky (1954*a, b*) and Claassen (1956) who have made extensive contributions and laid sound foundations for future research and developments.

Ethyl M. Doidge, who was promoted to the post of principal pathologist of the Division of Botany in 1929, devoted herself largely to the completion of a near-encyclopedic record on *South African Fungi and Lichens* (1950).

Thomas Robert Sim (1858–1938), who arrived in South Africa in 1889 and eventually became conservator of forests in Natal, published an important work in 1907, *The Forests and Forest Flora of the Colony of the Cape of Good Hope,* which is still regarded as a standard work of reference.

Grasses and Pastures of South Africa, edited by Meredith (1955), includes as Part I a guide by Lucy K. A. Chippendall describing the distribution and usefulness of some 700 grasses occurring in South Africa; many ecological data are given. Part II is devoted to a discussion of pasture management, in many of its divergent phases, by fifteen leading experts including a discussion on the ecology of grasslands by Bayer (1955). Places like the Frankenwald Field Research Station, of the University of the Witwatersrand in Johannesburg, are doing some of the most vitally important research on grasses undertaken today. The harsh, indigenous grassveld of the Frankenwald Station, situated on poor granite-derived soil and growing under severe climatic conditions, has occupied a generation of ecologists studying grassland succession, overgrazing, veld burning, and other ecological occurrences to determine the balance between maximum economic production and veld spoilage (Roux 1969).

Botanical Paleoecology

Van Zinderen Bakker (1966) and Plumstead (1967*a, b,* 1969) put South Africa on the international palynology and paleobotanical maps, respectively.

Van Zinderen Bakker's pollen records prove that climatic changes caused major migrations of vegetation types and that the ebb flow of the vegetation caused dynamic changes in the floral compounds of the vegetation including the multiplication of species. Another exacting undertaking by Van Zinderen Bakker, of international importance, was the planning, direction, and publication of the results of a scientific expedition to Marion and Prince Edward Islands, 1965–1966 (1971).

In recent years, interesting finds in the coal-bearing beds at Vereeniging have revealed a new class of plant, Glossopterideae, with reproductive structures of an unfamiliar type and which dominated the ancient lands of the south millions of years ago (Levyns 1970). Plumstead has earned international standing in her subject particularly for her research into the classification of plant fossils from Antarctica (Dyer 1977).

Invertebrates

In addition to the work done by local scientists, knowledge of the invertebrates was considerably increased by an expedition from the Zoological Institute of the University of Lund (1950–1951) that collected extensively in South Africa, including Lesotho and southwest Africa. The results were published under the title *South African Animal Life,* which appeared in fourteen volumes between 1955 and 1970 (Hanström et al. 1955). The collections yielded only a couple of new species, but the many new distribution records added significantly to our knowledge of the fauna as a whole (du Toit 1976).

In comparison with the insect faunas of European countries, the South African insects have not received continuous attention over several centuries and have not been subjected to large numbers of trained specialists to work on smaller numbers of insects. As a result, the classification of the insect fauna has been overtaken by the human population explosion and the erosion of the environment by agriculture and pollution; this has led to a situation whereby species have probably become extinct before they could be recorded or described. Thus, the true number of indigenous forms can never be completely known. Lawrence (1977) has prepared an excellent account of the history of entomology, arachnology, and related matters.

Vertebrates

The establishment of the South African Museum in Cape Town in 1825 with Dr. Andrew Smith as its first superintendent, resulted in fairly detailed accounts of reptiles and amphibians occurring in South Africa. Much later, V. F. M. FitzSimons became the greatest authority on lizards and snakes in southern Africa, and his two monographs *The Lizards of South Africa* (1943) and *Snakes of Southern Africa* (1962) are noteworthy achievements in southern African herpetology; his 1970 field guide is a useful abridged version of the big monograph. Other herpetological publications since 1945 that have greatly added to our knowledge of the life histories, general biology, and ecology of reptiles and amphibians include those by Rose (1950), Wager (1965), Visser (1966), and Poynton (1964). For a more detailed discussion on the history of herpetology in South Africa, the reader is referred to Du Toit (1976).

The first attempt at a comprehensive account of the birds of South Africa was the volume on birds in Andrew Smith's series *Illustrations of the Zoology of South Africa* (1849). This landmark in the history of South African ornithology was incomplete, however, since Smith's travels did not cover the whole region. This effort was followed by Layard (1867), W. L. Sclater (1900–1901), and A. C. Stark (1901, 1903, 1906). In 1936, E. L. Gill, director of the South African Museum, 1925–1942, produced *A First Guide to South African Birds,* well illustrated by means of color illustrations. Roberts, of the Transvaal Museum in Pretoria, prepared a much more comprehensive book (1940), which proved to be a landmark in South African ornithology. Roberts was also instrumental in founding the South African Ornithological Society in 1929 and in launching its official Journal, *The Ostrich.* Other milestones in the ornithological literature of South Africa include the two magnificent monographs by Skead (1960, 1967), a field guide by Prozesky (1970), and a volume by Mackworth-Praed and Grant (1962).

Mammals

The first strictly zoological publication on the fauna of southern Africa was the systematic account of the mammals of the Cape Province published by Johannes Smuts in 1832. Sclater's two volumes of *Mammals of South Africa* were published in 1900 and 1901. Sclater was very modern in his approach, dealing not only with the systematics of mammals but also providing data on distribution and habits. The magnum opus on South African mammals is that by Roberts (1951). The 1953 publication by Ellerman, Morrison-Scott, and Hayman greatly reduced the number of species recognized by Roberts. These divergent interpretations were rectified in a complete and penetrating revision of all the groups of African mammals (Setzer and Meester 1971).

Beginning about 1950, a strong school of mammalian research developed at the Univeristy of Pretoria in which all aspects of mammalogy are covered with emphasis on ecology, ecological physiology, and ethology. The Mammal Research Institute, established in 1966, deals with the role of marine mammals in the bioenergetics of the Marion Island ecosystem in the South Atlantic. The ecology of mammals was further advanced at the University of Pretoria by the institution within the Department of Zoology of a postgraduate course in wildlife management in 1970. During this period, a Department of Nature Conservation was established (also in 1970) in the Faculty of Forestry at the University of Stellenbosch, dealing with water requirements of various antelope species, the relations of mammals to the practice of forestry, and the role of pheromones in mammal behavior. Physiological ecology has become a principal field of interest at the Department of Zoology at the University of Cape Town. Finally, the Medical Ecology Center in Johannesburg, under the auspices of the Department of Health, has played an important role in the study of the transmission of diseases by animals. In their study of bubonic plague, Davis (1964) and his colleagues have made important contributions to our knowledge of the taxonomy, distribution, and ecology of rodents and other small mammals.

Ecological research on mammals is not confined to universities alone. In many cases, a university cooperates closely with the particular Department of Nature Conservation in its province. In addition, the National Parks Board of Trustees, as well as the Natal Parks, Game and Fish Preservation Board, does a great amount of important ecological research on its own. This also applies to a varying degree to some state-aided (national and provincial) museums. The National Parks Board issues an annual journal *Koedoe* containing research results of importance to conservation, while the conservation authorities in Natal issue the *Lammergeyer,* a periodical serving the same purpose. Examples of museum publications carrying articles on mammals would be the *Annals of the Transvaal Museum, Annals of the South African Museum,* and *Annals of the Natal Museum.*

AGRICULTURE

According to Verbeek (1977), the Republic of South Africa is still traditionally regarded as a great, extensive country with more than sufficient land for all possible purposes. However, for all practical purposes, the land has been fully occupied and has become a scarce source of production under competition for different areas. The total area of the republic, including the developing territories, is approximately 122 million hectares, of which 102,871,000 (84%) are employed for agricultural purposes. Because of a low and uncertain rainfall, mountains and rolling landscape, poor, shallow, and brackish soils, as well as other factors, at most 15 percent of this area is suitable to tillage and cultivation of crops. The remainder can be used only as natural pasture in extensive stock farming systems.

The generally increased agricultural production in recent years has mainly been achieved by intensification. Because of the restricted nature and vulnerability of the South African agricultural resources, the increasing pressure on the ecosystems had a markedly harmful effect on the natural resources and overall appearance of the environment. Obvious damage and changes were caused by soil washaways, wind erosion, intrusion of alien (often harmful) plants, bush encroachment, as well as bracking and drowning of soils especially where irrigation is practiced. Of the several factors responsible for these effects is the practice of production systems that are not in harmony with and adapted to the natural environmental factors (Verbeek 1977).

This destruction of agricultural resources is regarded as serious by the state and led to the adoption in 1946 of the Soil Conservation Act (now Act No. 76 of 1969 as amended). The object of this legislation was to control and prevent soil erosion and to conserve, protect, and improve the soil, vegetation, and water resources of the republic. Next to the Soil Conservation Act, the subdivision of Agricultural Land Act of 1972 (No. 70 of 1970 as amended) is the most recent important measure taken to preserve land for production.

Prosperity depends to a large extent on an efficient methodology of agriculture and the continual improvement of these methods; this, in turn is rendered possible by research and can succeed only if the knowledge so acquired is communicated to and applied by agricultural producers. The purpose of agricultural research activities in the Republic of South Africa has always been to gather information on natural resources of use in agriculture, aiming at increased productivity while ensuring that natural resources are not placed in jeopardy by excessive production (du Plessis, 1970).

FORESTRY

The Republic of South Africa is poorly endowed with natural forests. Over 73 percent of the surface of the republic has an annual rainfall of less than 635 mm and the summer temperatures are high. Only about 8 percent of the country has a wet climate, with an annual rainfall of over 750 mm. Indigenous forests occur as an interrupted belt in the region of high rainfall extending east and northeast from Table Mountain in Cape Town to the northeastern Transvaal. The only really extensive wooded areas are in the George-Knysna region, where there are more than 48,000 hectares of timber forest on the narrow plateau between the Indian Ocean and the Outeniqua and Tsitsikama mountain ranges (Steyn 1971). A variety of species is encountered and the further east one travels, the more diversified the forest vegetation becomes. The actual timber forests are a combination of hardwood species and yellowwoods and, with a few exceptions, the forests are all evergreens.

Ecologically, three main types of forest can be distinguished and can be described as follows:

Mixed yellowwood and broad-leaved forest. In the past, an imposing array of useful timber varieties grew in the kloofs of Table Mountain including stinkwood, assegaiwood, Cape beech, keurboom, candlewood, and many others. When the first South African settlement was founded by the Dutch

East India Company in 1652, extensive use was made of the wood obtained from the small natural forests occurring in these wooded ravines. Today, the indigenous trees on Table Mountain have been reduced to mere thickets, and timber is no longer obtained there. Originally, these forests extended eastward to the George-Knysna region, where giant old yellowwoods (*Podocarpus* spp.) are still growing (reaching heights of some 43 meters and girths of 6–9 meters) surrounded by broad-leaved species, such as ironwood, knysna boxwood, white elders, and the Cape ash. It is sad to relate that these magnificent forests are now probably only half as large as they were two centuries ago (Hartwig 1971). Uncontrolled forest fires have also played their devastating role in diminishing the former range. Continuing eastward, the same type of forest is found with similar species composition, ranging along the Drakensberg escarpment in Natal and further northward to the Zoutpans mountains in the northern Transvaal. After the discovery of gold in the Transvaal (1886), a heavy demand arose for timber as pit-props. Loads of indigenous wood were required for making wagons to bring provisions to the Rand, while even more timber was demanded for building purposes. Wood for pit-props came from the bushveld in the central Transvaal, but large beams needed for construction purposes had to be supplied by the mountain forests referred to above. Fortunately, the railway to Johannesburg was completed in 1895, and alien timber was imported from overseas. Consequently, the market for indigenous timber collapsed; otherwise, the South African forests would in all probability have been completely eradicated (Hartwig 1971).

Coastal Forests from Alexandria to Zululand. In these forests, some species present in the yellowwood-broad-leaved forests are also encountered, including the Outeniqua yellowwood, assegaiwood, and ironwood. However, new and more subtropical species such as the Natal mahogany, the Umzimbeet and Cape ebony are present. What strikes one about these forests, especially in the Transkei and Natal, is the scarcity of young trees, which are systematically cut down by Africans for building their huts and abodes, a process which has become very perceptible over the past two decades. The original ecology of the area has, therefore, also been drastically influenced; further, the size of the original forests has been conspicuously reduced with the clearing of ground for the production of sugarcane, especially in Natal.

The Cedar Forests. The scattered trees on the Cedar Mountains near Clanwilliam in the southwestern Cape do not form true forests in the stricter sense of the word, since the trees occur singly or in small groups over a distance of some 48 km. They must once have occupied a much wider area but were gradually decimated by axe and fire (Hartwig 1971). Fortunately, these trees are now protected, and their augmentation is encouraged.

In addition to these three forest types, there are extensive areas in the northern and northeastern parts of South Africa where trees are encountered, but they are not sufficiently tall and dense to constitute forests (Hartwig 1971). In the low-lying bushveld of the eastern Transvaal, the trees attain a height of 5–9 meters and consist of Apiesdoring, sweet thorn, Transvaal boekenhout, marula, and other species. These extensive areas, which also occur in Swaziland and Zululand, include the Kruger National Park where the veld is park-like and covered with trees of a more subtropical and tropical character. Species include leadwood, kiaat, and the cabbage tree among some 150-odd species growing in the bushveld.

The protection and judicious use of natural and timber forests implies the planting, care, and use of trees, protection of plant and animal life occurring therein, conservation of water catchment areas, and necessary action to prevent soil erosion. Following the establishment of the Union of South Africa in 1910, a Department of Forestry was founded and charged with administering and protecting state-owned forests, establishing plantations, and managing them to meet future timber requirements of the country. Another task was to furnish advice and guidance to private individuals and undertakings in such matters as the establishment, management, and exploitation of plantations. In 1910, the state-owned plantations covered an area of 13,500 hectares; in 1960, the total wooded area privately and state owned was more than 850,000 hectares. About 252,000 hectares were still available for afforestation.

While many varieties of indigenous trees provide valuable timber, they supply only a small part of the country's needs. According to Hartwig (1971), dependence on imported timber was especially noticeable during the two world wars. Experience has shown, however, that it is very difficult to establish South African trees out of their natural habitat. The state has, therefore, experimented extensively with exotic trees, testing in different parts of the country some 900 varieties from all over the world. Several exotic species of trees, especially those from parts of the world where climatic conditions are similar to those in different parts of the Republic of South Africa, proved to be the most successful. Excellent results have been obtained with such species as *Eucalyptus saligna, E. maculata,* and *Acacia melanoxylon* from Australia, *Pinus patula* from Mexico, and *Pinus elliottii, taeda,* and *radiata* from the United States.

NATURE CONSERVATION

When the first white settlers arrived at the southern tip of the African continent in 1652 to establish a refreshment station under the leadership of Jan van Riebeeck, they encountered a unique diversity of fauna and flora which prompted Linnaeus, about 100 years later, to refer to the Cape as "that paradise upon earth." Over the years, naturalists, explorers, and big game hunters were drawn to southern Africa by similar laudations.

Early attempts at nature conservation can be seen in the proclamations of van Riebeeck (1656), Van der Stel (1677), Borghorst (1699) and the passing and enforcing of legislation with regard to species that constituted part of the indigenous fauna and flora. In this connection, reference may be made to Governor Ryk Tulbach who, in 1770, was concerned about the destruction of wildlife: anyone who killed a hippopotamus was liable to a fine of 1,000 guilders. A similar example is that of the bontebok (*Damaliscus dorcas dorcas*) in the southwestern Cape; in 1800 it was noticed that the numbers of bontebok were decreasing, and in 1836 Harris mentioned that the authorities imposed heavy penalties on anyone who killed a bontebok.

With the development and expansion of the settlement at the Cape and the gradual opening of the interior to the north of the Hottentotsholland Mountains, it is understandable that a gradual and constant decrease in the number of animals occurred. It is clear that opposing interests were at issue: attempts at organized agriculture on the one hand and at nature conservation on the other (de Graaff 1977). During this process, the indigenous fauna of South Africa was steadily forced deeper into the interior and confined to areas that were not yet available for economic and agricultural development, while unauthorized poaching was rampant. The inevitable result was that the days of plentiful game were beginning to belong irrevocably to the past. The march of civilization, development of organized agriculture and industry, and seemingly inherent human destructiveness all became (and still are) serious threats to the natural wealth of fauna and flora in the Republic of South Africa. Taxa such as Cape lion, quagga, and blue antelope have been exterminated while large mammals such as mountain zebra, black rhinoceros, white rhinoceros, hippopotamus, Cape buffalo, bontebok, tsessebe, and many other antelope are encountered today only in national parks and game reserves. The flora has suffered a fate similar to the fauna, although not to the same extent. Crop cultivation, overgrazing by stock, indiscriminate picking of wild flowers for commercial exploits, and similar retrogressive actions have contributed to an alarming decline of certain plant species, and there are indications that some species have become extinct.

Strange as it may seem, the other side of the coin tells a different story. Historical records indicate most positively that for the past three centuries inhabitants of South Africa have constantly been aware of the necessity of conserving the fauna and flora. The danger threatening the indigenous fauna of South Africa was apparently first realized clearly by S. J. P. Kruger who, in 1884, drew attention to the diminishing numbers of game in the Transvaal. He pleaded with the Volksraad to set aside an area in which measures for total protection could be applied, but deaf ears were turned to this first plea. In

1888, he repeated his arguments for an area in which the fauna and flora would be completely protected, and on this occasion, the motion was carried but not put into practice. Finally, the first game reserve in the Transvaal, the Pongola, was proclaimed in 1894, but after considerable opposition. On September 6, 1895, a motion that would eventually have far-reaching effects was again presented to the Volksraad. The authorities in Natal followed this example by proclaiming the Hluhluwe Game Reserve and the Umfolozi Game Reserve during 1897, while the area between the Crocodile and Sabie Rivers in the eastern Transvaal was proclaimed by Kruger as the Sabi Game Reserve on March 26, 1898. The latter reserve eventually became the well-known Kruger National Park in 1926.

The National Parks Board

After the Union of South Africa came into existence in 1910, protection of the country's indigenous fauna and flora became the responsibility of the four provincial councils, as authorized by the South Africa Act of 1909. In the meantime, the Sabie Game Reserve had survived some rough passages, and in 1926 some provincial reserves were proclaimed as national parks with responsibility resting in the newly formed National Parks Board, which came into being as a result of the National Parks Act of May 31, 1926. The four provinces retained responsibility for protection and conservation of fauna and flora throughout the rest of the country in areas which were not set aside as national parks.

After the establishment of the National Parks Board in 1926, and the redistribution of duties, nature conservation on the national level made rapid progress so that today the National Parks Board has ten national parks under its control.

It is the function of the board to control and preserve the fauna and flora within the national parks and to provide facilities for visitors. It is a government-subsidized body, which is financially also dependent on various other sources. In collaboration with private, provincial, and central government authorities, the National Parks Board conducts valuable ecological research into the problems associated with nature conservation. The Republic of South Africa is already accepted as a world authority in this field, and advice on the management of game and the administration of parks and reserves is constantly sought by foreign countries.

Nature Conservation by the Provinces

In addition to the approximately sixty provincial nature reserves in the republic, the provincial authorities are also responsible for the active utilization of wildlife, mainly by means of recreational hunting and angling. Each province has a Department of Nature Conservation whose activities consist of administration, law enforcement, breeding of fish, game birds, and other game, establishment of wild gardens, research, controlling beasts of prey and problem animals, and education concerned with nature conservation and the environment.

Nature Conservation by other Government Departments

Different government departments to a varying degree also play an important role in nature conservation in South Africa. The Division of Sea Fisheries, for example, is in control of the protection and development of fish life along the coasts, whereas the Division of Government Guano Islands accepts responsibility for seabirds and seals as well as for the administration of the important guano islands. Numerous areas, where the fauna is also protected, are controlled by the Department of Forestry, which also controls the vitally important catchment areas.

Land belonging to the state, and on which conservation is practiced to some extent, falls under the Department of Agricultural Credit and Land Tenure, whereas the Department of Water Affairs has control over all the natural and dammed waters in the republic. The Department of Agricultural Technical Services is responsible for soil conservation which in turn is closely related to wildlife and wildlife management while the Division of Veterinary Services of this Department is directly concerned with wild animals as disease vectors (de Graaff 1977).

Nature Conservation by Local Authorities and the Private Sector

The implementation of nature conservation and all the facets concerned with it, however, is managed not only at the national and provincial level or through government departments, but also through many nature reserves that have been proclaimed but are controlled by town or divisional councils. At least a hundred of these have particular merit in preserving some particular aspect of the flora and fauna (or both) for posterity. The private sector also fulfills a highly important function in nature conservation in South Africa; in the Transvaal alone, there are some 500 private nature reserves with a total area of 1,160,000 hectares. Examples of these are the well-known Sabie-Sand Game Reserve and the Timbavati, both situated on the western boundary of the Kruger National Park. Since South Africa is largely subdivided into farms, farmers naturally play an important role in nature conservation and control, and it is especially the task of the provincial authorities to provide guidance to interested farmers on nature conservation and the proper utilization of this resource. Lastly, mention should be made of the many societies, such as the South African Ornithological Society and South African Biological

Society, each in its own field and with its own aids, which disseminate ecological information and thereby contribute toward conserving the natural wealth and natural resources of the republic.

THE STRUCTURE OF ENVIRONMENTAL ADMINISTRATION IN SOUTH AFRICA

A brief but accurate overview of environmental administration in South Africa has been issued by the Department of Planning and the Environment Anonymous (1977). Various government departments, provincial administration, and local authorities are legally empowered to deal with divergent aspects of environmental conservation and the abatement of pollution in South Africa. The Department of Planning and the Environment is responsible for the application of sound principles of environmental protection in physical planning at national level, as well as for the coordinated gathering and dissemination of information on aspects of the environment. In addition, the department coordinates all action at the national level aimed at environmental conservation mainly by means of a Cabinet Committee on Environmental conservation and the South African Council for the Environment, previously known as the South African Committee on Environmental Conservation.

The Cabinet Committee on Environmental Conservation, established in 1972, functions under the chairmanship of the Minister of Planning and the Environment, while the Ministers of Transport, Water Affairs, Agriculture, Health, and Economic Affairs represent overall coordination; the committee attends to positive and remedial aspects of environmental issues while also identifying spheres of action and research. The Council for the Environment was set up to advise the cabinet committee. It consists of representatives of government departments, provincial administrations, and statutory bodies. The council concerns itself with all aspects of environmental conservation and pollution, prepares priorities for action, and advises on coordination. It also reviews existing legislation and advises interested bodies on investigations, studies, surveys, and research that have to be undertaken on aspects of environmental conservation. Several working groups have been established to assist the council in its coordinating task. Various experts and university and local authorities are co-opted wherever necessary.

There are some 200 voluntary organizations concerned with the environment in the Republic of South Africa. One of them, the National Veld Trust, has taken the initiative to coordinate the efforts of these organizations in one national front. To promote consultation, cooperation, and coordinated action among these organizations and between them as a group and various government and other bodies in matters pertaining to environmental conservation, the Council for the Habitat was established in 1974. The council acts as a consultative body on matters of common interest to its member organizations and may administer and act on behalf of them. It endeavors to coordinate all environmental actions by the private sector and strives for conservation, protection, and optimum utilization of the environment. To improve and implement functional liaison, the Council for the Habitat was given representation on the Council for the Environment.

Planning and Environmental Protection

Until the Second World War, the economy of South Africa had not developed much beyond the stage of agriculture and mining. There was very little physical planning, and the distribution of the population and growth or decline of urban centers were a direct result of the free interplay of economic factors (South Africa Yearbook 1976).

The discovery of gold in the Orange Free State and the large-scale development of industry expected to follow prompted the government to introduce legislation in 1947 to promote a better coordinated and more effective exploitation, development, and use of the country's natural resources. This resulted in the establishment of the Natural Resources Development Council (NRDC), which published several definitive reports that were of significant value to present action. It is a common phenomenon that in a rapidly developing country, industry, as well as the population, tends to be concentrated in a few large centers. It is known that ecologically such concentrations are undesirable, and consequently, the republic has embarked on a planned process of decentralization. New industries are encouraged to establish themselves in and existing industries to move to or expand in the less developed areas of the country. The main effort is at present being directed at the accelerated development of seventeen selected growth points based mainly on the availability of labor and the developmental potential of the area.

As the concept and scope of physical planning broadened, the need grew for a single comprehensive organization to coordinate the many facets of physical planning and development. In 1964, the Department of Planning was established as the NRDC was abolished; in 1973, the department assumed additional responsibility regarding the overall environment, and the name was changed to the Department of Planning and Environment.

Environmental Education

The entire system of education in the Republic of South Africa from primary school and secondary school to university has in recent years been geared to make students conscious of their environment. Curricula emphasize studies of most aspects of the environs, and schools actively participate in national campaigns. In the past, these campaigns included the "Festival of the Soil" (1968–1971), the "Water Year" (1971), the "Keep South Africa

Clean" (1972), and "Our Green Heritage" (1973). Educational tours bring scholars into contact with nature and make them aware of the need for the conservation of the country's overall heritage. It is safe to say that the schools are fast becoming centers for stimulating the environmental consciousness of the community that has become noticeable in recent years.

On the tertiary level, several universities have introduced new courses or adapted existing ones to study environmental conservation and planning on a multidisciplinary basis. These universities also cooperate closely with research institutions such as the Council for Scientific and Industrial Research (CSIR).

The Department of Planning and the Environment will in the future also play a leading role in promoting environmental awareness and education through a variety of media. It was actively involved in the "Our Green Heritage" program, which was produced in cooperation with the Departments of Agricultural Technical Services, Forestry, and Water Affairs; a highly informative color slide program was shown throughout the Republic. In 1973, the Republic Pavilion at the Rand Easter Show in Johannesburg was devoted to the same theme, and the theme for 1974 was "Environmental Conservation," presented by the Department of Information.

Several symposia, including ones on air pollution control, wildlife protection, oceanography, transportation, and planning for environmental conservation, were organized by various parties in 1973. These contributed in a marked degree to the stimulation of civic interest in circumjacent issues. Furthermore, South Africa shares in the effort to stimulate cognition of the environment by observing World Environment Day on June 5 each year.

Environmental Research

The CSIR coordinates the lion's share of environmental research in the republic through its National Committee for Environmental Sciences. At present, more than 380 research projects with bearing on environmental issues are being undertaken by various institutes, advisory committees, and working groups. These operate in close liaison with the South African Council for Environmental Conservation. The Atomic Energy Board, Fuel Research Institute, universities, various government departments, four provincial administrations, as well as the private sector are all contributing directly or indirectly to this research effort.

CONCLUDING REMARKS

In a somewhat controversial article, Huntley (1977) reviewed the position of terrestrial ecology in South Africa and stated that the environmental revolution of the late 1960s initiated a dramatic change in the role of ecologists in science and society, but the "apparent inability of South African ecologists to meet these demands is cause for concern. . . ." He states that although terrestrial ecology in South Africa enjoys wide support, the impact of the subject as a developing science has been insignificant. The ecological challenges in South Africa are immense but can be met only if radical changes are brought about in our current approach to the subject. Huntley lists five priorities for this change: (1) the need for a strong two-year postgraduate course in ecology at one or another campus that would provide a holistic framework, strong in advanced ecological theory and methods, and with adequate coverage of both earth and mathematical sciences; (2) the need for multidisciplinary research programs in the structure and function of selected ecosystems; (3) the consolidation of terrestrial ecologists, who are presently spread over forty-six government and statutory organizations, and the development of organized teams of research ecologists; (4) the use of multidisciplinary workshops to review and synthesize research findings and to identify future research needs, replacing the traditional conferences and symposia; and (5) the absence of a South African journal of ecology, which is regarded as "perhaps the most telling evidence of the lack of a seriously motivated body of ecologists in this country." Hitherto, research findings have been published in a wide array of journals, adding to the polarization of plant ecologists from animal ecologists.

The ideas, concepts, and activities alluded to in this paper can best be brought in perspective by recognizing that all this demands a rethinking of man's place in nature and of attitudes about the total environment, the development of a new ethic for the land and for survival, and of an ecological conscience for love, respect, admiration, and understanding for the total ecosystem of which we are a part (Kormondy 1976).

REFERENCES CITED

Acocks, J. P. H. 1953. Veld types of South Africa. *Mem. Bot. Surv.* 28.

Allanson, B. R. 1963. Inundation of River Basius. *S. Afr. J. Sci.* 59:491–498.

———. 1965. The significance of the thermocline in the biology of developing reservoirs. *S. Afr. J. Sci.* 61:132–136.

Anonymous. 1971*a*. Fishing research. *The standard encyclopaedia of southern Africa.* Cape Town: Nasou Ltd.

———. 1971b. Fishing administration. *The standard encyclopaedia of southern Africa.* Cape Town: Nasou Ltd.

———. 1977. Environmental administration and research in South Africa. Pretoria: Dept. of Planning and the Environment.

Bayer, A. W. 1955. The ecology of grasslands. In *The grasses and pastures of South Africa,* ed. D. Meredith. Johannesburg: Central News Agency.

Boden, B. P. 1950. Some marine plankton diatoms from the west coast of South Africa. *Trans. R. Soc. S. Afr.* 32:321–434.

Cholnoky, B. J. 1954*a*. Ein Beitrag zur Kenntnis der Algenflora des Mongolflusses in Nordost-Transvaal. *Oesterr. Bot. Z.* 101 (1/2).

———. 1954*b*. Diatomeen und einige ander Algen aus dem 'de Hoek'- Reservat in Nord-Transvaal. *Saertryck ur Botaniska Notiser* 3.

Chutter, F. M. 1963 Hydrobiological studies on the Vaal River in the Vereeniging area. Part 1. *Hydrobiologia* 21:1–65.

———. 1954*b*. Diatomeen und einige ander Algen aus dem 'de Hoek'-Reservat in Nord-Transvool. *Saertryck ur Botaniska Notiser* 3.

———. 1971. Hydrobiological studies in the catchment of Vaal Dam, South Africa. Part 2. *Int. Rev. Gesamten Hydrobiol.* 56:227–240.

———. 1973. An ecological account of the past and future of South African rivers. *Limnol. Soc. S. Afr.* 21:22–24.

Cillié, G. G. and H. P. Hofmeyr. 1975. Water research. *The standard encyclopaedia of southern Africa.* Cape Town: Nasou Ltd.

Claassen, M. I. 1956. *'n Bydrae tot die kennis van die inheemse alge-flora van die Provinsie Transvaal.* M.S. thesis, University of Pretoria.

Coke, M. 1970. The water requirements of the Pongolo flood plain pans. In *Proceedings of "Water for the Future" Convention.* Pretoria, Nov. 16–20, 1970.

Davis, D. H. S. 1964. Ecology of wild rodent plague. *Monogr. Biol.* 14:301–314.

Day, J. H. 1977. Marine biology in South Africa. In *A history of scientific endeavour in South Africa,* ed. A. C. Brown. Cape Town: Royal Society of South Africa.

De Graaff, G. 1977. Trends in the development of natural resources in the national and international field with special reference to nature conservation. *RSA 2000.* 2:10–18.

Doidge, E. M. 1950. The South African fungi and lichens. *Bothalia* 5:967–994.

Du Plessis, S. J. 1970. Agricultural research. *The standard encyclopaedia of southern Africa.* Cape Town: Nasou Ltd.

Du Toit, C. A. 1976. Zoology. *The standard encyclopaedia of southern Africa* Cape Town: Nasou Ltd.

Dyer, R. A. 1977. Botanical research in South Africa in the twentieth century. In *A history of scientific endeavour in South Africa,* ed. A. C. Brown. Cape Town: Royal Society of South Africa.

Ellerman, J. R., T. C. S. Morrison-Scott, and R. W. Hayman. 1953. *Southern African mammals 1758–1951: A reclassification.* London: British Museum Nat. Hist.

Evans, I. B. Pole. 1920. The Veld: its resources and dangers. *S. Afr. J. Sci.* 17:1.

———. 1936. A vegetation map of South Africa. *Bot Surv. Mem. S. Afr.* 15.

Field, J. G. 1977. Marine ecology. In *Oceanography in South Africa.* Pretoria: SANCOR, CSIR.

FitzSimons, V. F. M. 1943. The lizards of South Africa. *Transvaal Mus. Mem. 1.*

———. 1962. *Snakes of southern Africa.* Johannesburg: Purnell & Sons (SA).

———. 1970. *A field guide to the snakes of southern Africa.* London: Collins.

Gill, E. L. 1936. *A first guide to South African birds.* Cape Town: Maskew Millar.

Grindley, J. R. 1973. Phytoplankton. *The standard encyclopaedia of southern Africa.* Cape Town: Nasou Ltd.

———. 1975. Zooplankton. *The standard encyclopaedia of southern Africa.* Cape Town: Nasou Ltd.

Hanström, B., P. Brinck, and G. Rudebeck. 1955. *South African animal life: results of the Lund Expedition in 1950–1951.* Stockholm: Almqvist & Wilksell.

Harrison, A. D. 1958*a*. Hydrobiological studies on the Great Berg River, Western Cape Province. Part 2. *Trans. R. Soc. S. Afr.* 35:125–226.

______. 1958*b*. Hydrobiological studies on the Great Berg River, Western Cape Province. Part 4. *Trans. R. Soc. S. Afr.* 35:299–329.

Hartwig, G. L. F. 1971. Forests, indigenous. *The standard encyclopaedia of southern Africa.* Cape Town: Nasou Ltd.

Herre, H. 1971. *The genera of the Mesembryanthemaceae.* Cape Town: Tafelberg.

Huntley, B. J. 1977. Terrestrial Ecology in South Africa. *S. Afr. J. Sci.* 73:366–370.

Hutchinson, J. 1946. *A botanist in southern Africa.* London: P. R. Gawthorn Ltd.

Jubb, R. A. 1967. *Fresh water fishes of southern Africa.* Cape Town: A. A. Balkema.

Kemp, P. H. 1967. Hydrobiological studies on the Tugela river system. Part 6. *Hydrobiologia* 29:393–425.

Kormondy, E. J. 1976. *Concepts of ecology.* 2d Ed. Englewood Cliffs: Prentice-Hall.

Lawrence, R. F. 1977. Insects, arachnids and peripatus. In *A history of scientific endeavour in South Africa,* ed. A. C. Brown. Cape Town: Royal Soc. S. Afr.

Layard, E. L. 1867. *The birds of South Africa.* Cape Town: J.C. Juta.

Le Roux, P. and L. Steyn. 1968. *Fishes of the Transvaal.* Johannesburg: S. A. Breweries Institute.

Levyns, M. R. 1970. Botany. *The standard encyclopaedia of southern Africa.* Cape Town: Nasou Ltd.

Mackworth-Praed, C. W. and C. H. B. Grant. 1962. *Birds of the southern third Africa.* London: Longmans.

Meredith, D. 1955. *The grasses and pastures of South Africa.* Johannesburg: Central News Agency.

Nel, E. A. 1968. The microplankton of the southwest Indian Ocean. *Invest. Rep. Div. Sea Fish. S. Afr.* 62:1–106.

Oliff, W. D. 1977. Marine pollution. In *Oceanography in South Africa.* Pretoria: SANCOR, CSIR.

______, P. H. Kemp, and J. L. King. 1965. Hydrobiological studies on the Tugela river system. Part 5. *Hydrobiologia* 26:189–202.

Palmer, E. and N. Pitman. 1972. *Trees of southern Africa* Vols. 1–3. Cape Town: Balkema.

Phillips, E. P. 1926. The genera of South African flowering plants. *Mem Bot. Surv.* 10.

Phillips, J. F. V. 1931. Forest-succession and ecology in the Knysna region. *Mem. Bot. Surv.* 14.

Pienaar, U de V. 1968. The freshwater fishes of the Kruger National Park. *Koedoe* 11:1–79.

Plumstead, E. P. 1967*a*. A general review of the Devonian fossil plants found in the Cape System of South Africa. *Palaeontol. Afr.* 10:1–83.

______. 1967*b*. A general review of the Devonian fossil plants found in the Cape System of South Africa. *Palaeontol. Afr.* 10:1–83.

______. 1969. *Three thousand million years of plant life in Africa.* The Geological Society of South Africa. Alex L. du Toit. Memorial Lecture 11.

Poynton, J. C. 1964. The amphibia of South Africa: a faunal study. *Ann. Natal Mus.* 17:1–334.

Prozesky, O. P. M. 1970. *A field guide to the birds of southern Africa.* London: Collins.

Reynolds, G. W. 1950. *The aloes of South Africa.* Johannesburg: Aloes of South Africa Book Fund.

———. 1966. *The aloes of tropical Africa and Madagascar*- Johannesburg: The Aloes Book Fund.

Roberts, A. 1940. *The birds of South Africa.* Johannesburg: CNA.

———. 1951. *The mammals of South Africa.* Johannesburg: Trustees of "Mammals of S.A." Book Fund, CNA.

Robertson, T. C. 1974. Water. In *The conservation of our heritage,* ed. A. Du Plessis. Cape Town: Human & Rousseau.

Rose, W. 1950. *The reptiles and amphibians of southern Africa.* Cape Town: Maskew Millar Ltd.

Ross, J. C. 1974. Soil conservation. *The standard encyclopaedia of southern Africa.* Cape Town: Nasou Ltd.

Roux, E. 1969. *Grass. A story of Frankenwald.* Cape Town: Oxford University Press.

Salter, T. M. 1944. The genus *Oxalis* in South Africa. *J. S. Afr. Bot. Suppl.* Vol. 1.

Sclater, W. L. 1900–1901. *The mammals of South Africa.* 2 Vols. London: R.H. Porter.

Seagrief, S. C. 1967. *The seaweeds of the Tsitsikama Coastal National Park.* Pretoria: National Parks Board of Trustees.

Setzer, H. and J. A. J. Meester. 1971. *The mammals of Africa: an identification manual.* Washington: Smithsonian Institute Press.

Sim, T. R. 1907. *The forests and forest flora of the colony of the Cape of Good Hope.* Aberdeen: Taylor and Henderson.

Skead, C. J. 1960. *The canaries, seed-eaters and buntings of southern Africa.* Trustees, South African Bird Book Fund.

———. 1967. *The sunbirds of southern Africa; also the sugarbirds, the white-eyes and the spotted creeper.* Cape Town: Balkema.

Smith, J. L. B. 1949. *The sea fishes of southern Africa.* South Africa: Central News Agency Ltd.

South Africa 1976. *Official yearbook of the Republic of South Africa.* 3d ed. Pretoria: South African State Dept. of Information.

Stark, A. C. and W. L. Sclater. 1901, 1903, 1906. *The birds of South Africa.* London: Porter.

Steyn, J. W. 1971. Forestry. *The standard encyclopaedia for southern Africa.* Cape Town: Nasou Ltd.

Sullivan, D. and R. Sullivan. 1977. *South African environment.* Cape Town: Macdonald South Africa.

Toerien, D. F. 1977. A review of eutrophication and guidelines for its control in South Africa. *CSIR Special Report* WAT 48:1–110.

Van Zinderen Bakker, E. M. 1965. Limnological investigations of the Orange river system. *S. Afr. J. Sci.* 61:129–131.

———. 1966. *Palaeoecology of Africa.* Cape Town: Balkema.

———, J. M. Winterbottom, and R. A. Dyer, eds. 1971. *Marion and Prince Edward Islands: report on the South African biological and geological expedition 1965–1966.* Cape Town: Balkema.

Verbeek, W. A. 1977. Agriculture and landscape conservation. *Environment RSA* 4(11):1–4.

Visser, J. 1966. *Poisonous snakes of southern Africa and the treatment of snake-bite.* Cape Town: Howard Timmins.

Wager, V. A. 1965. *The frogs of South Africa.* Johannesburg: Purnell.

27

SUDAN

M. E. Beshir and M. Obeid

Interest in the role of the river Nile is probably as old as human life on its valley because it is indeed a life-giving artery to the inhabitants of its valley. Five thousand years ago, Menes, the first king of Egypt, dammed the river to build the city of Memphis, and since then much effort has gone into controlling the river on which life depends. The influence of humans became significant by turning Egypt and Sudan green by agriculture irrigated from this great river.

Further south in Sudan, interest in the role of the mighty river aroused Herodotus in 460 B.C. to turn his doubt into inquiry and undertake his journey to the second cataract to find out "where the water came from." The Arab penetration of Sudan beginning in A.D. 651 brought into the country many scholars, among them the famous Arab geographer Idrisi in the twelfth century, whose description of the country may be regarded as the first ecological account of the country, its people, and environment.

European explorers began visiting Sudan in the late eighteenth century, and with the European penetration, a new upsurge of interest in the Nile and its valley began. In the first half of the 1800s, antiquities of the Nile civilization captured most of the interest, but in the second half began the quest for the sources of the Nile.

Inasmuch as ecology is the study of the household of nature, it is not surprising that much of the ecological interest in Sudan centers in one way or another around the Nile, the life-giving household of nature. It was probably a Roman who succinctly coined the phrase "Aut Nilus aut nihil."

THE NILE AND LANDFORMS

The landforms of Sudan received the attention of the European travellers, and the river Nile, naturally, was prominent in their accounts and reports. By 1896, there began interest in recording and analyzing the physical characteristics of the Nile. Ball (1902) calculated the amounts of erosion in the cataract region of northern Sudan, while Lyons (1908) attempted a geological assessment of the changes in the river's course in southern Sudan and established that the present Nile includes portions of river systems of very different origin and date of evolution.

The work of Hurst and Phillips (1931, 1938) and Hurst (1946, 1950) has made the Nile one of the best-known rivers in the world with regard to its hydrology. Hurst (1957) states that "there is no other great river in the world upon which such an accurate and extensive system of measurements is carried out," and mentions further that in Egypt, records of the river level extend as far back as A.D. 660 and, with large gaps, to even much earlier periods.

The postwar years brought a number of different studies of the Nile. Fairbridge (1962), Butzer (1959), Nilson (1953), and Berry (1962*a, b, c*) made contributions to the geologic history and evolution of the Nile. The first two studies were concerned with the northern parts of the river, while the others dealt with the Nile in Sudan. The geologic history of the Nile in Sudan has been reviewed by Berry and Whiteman (1968), Butzer and Hansen (1968), and Whiteman (1971). Recent fieldwork by Williams and Adamson (1973) added considerable details to the knowledge of the age and origin of the Gezira clay plain between the Blue and White Niles, as well as the late Quaternary history of the two rivers.

Vegetation studies were no less important than the physical and hydrological investigations of the Nile. Wright (1949) assessed the distribution of vegetation of the White Nile flood plain and examined some of the probable effects on the ecology of the plain of the hydrological schemes proposed to conserve the Nile flood. In the Sudd swamp region, the most important ecological factors that determine the occurrence of plant species are hydrological conditions of the river, current velocity, depth, and seasonal duration of flooding. The importance of these factors was first diagnosed by Migahid (1947, 1952) during his botanical excursion to the Sudd, and the relationship between these factors and individual species was shown by Sutcliffe (1974). Although the study was conducted in the Aliab Valley in the southern stretch of the Sudd, its results are applicable to the whole area.

In 1938, an engineering plan known as the Equatorial Nile Project was proposed to conserve 50 percent of the annual average flow of the Nile waters that are estimated to be lost through evaporation on its northward journey through the Sudd swamps. The plan envisaged the elimination of the swamps by reversing the natural cycle of river fluctuations during the flood and low-flow period; this modification would lead to radical changes in the pattern of livelihood of the pastoral inhabitants of the region. The Sudanese government commissioned the Jonglei Investigation Team to examine the proposal and evaluate its impact on the environment of the Sudd. The Jonglei Investigation Report (Anonymous 1954) is a renowned ecological document. The investigation covered such aspects as the probable effects of the total elimination of the Sudd swamps on vegetation, climate, topography, riverian pastures, and fisheries, in addition to socioeconomic and human problems. The study recommended that seasonal fluctuations of the river must be maintained since these variations are the key ecological factor regulating the biological productivity of the river, as well as the livelihood of a population of one million pastoralists.

Away from the Nile, however, the inland areas of Sudan attracted the attention of the early German geographers, who used examples from Sudan for their investigations of desert and savanna. Walter (1912), whose work on the desert is a classic, carried out fieldwork in northern and eastern Sudan, especially in the Kassala area.

Later work on landforms resulted from an interest in applied ecology. The Soil Conservation Committee Report of 1954 marked this beginning. The relationship between the details of the physical landscape, land-use patterns, and human and animal populations became the new strategy for the policy of land development and protection. This new approach was necessitated by many examples of deterioration in the environment, such as sheet and gully erosion, soil deterioration due to overcropping and overgrazing, and forest degradation due to grazing and involuntary fires.

HYDROBIOLOGICAL RESEARCH

The Nile system with its length of 6,695 km is particularly interesting in view of the great range of physical conditions from a very swift torrent in southern Sudan, through the vast Sudd swamps where the current is reduced to a minimum and the huge floating mats of aquatic vegetation filter out much of the dissolved salts, to a sluggish river flowing through semidesert, and, finally, desert in the far north.

Brook (1954) began detailed studies of the plankton algae of the Blue and White Niles of Sudan. This study was a prerequisite to the ecological studies that were to follow, eventually developing into quantitative analysis of the annual cycles of plankton production in the two Niles (Rzoska, Brook, and Prowse 1955). It was found that in the two rivers, there was marked seasonal fluctuation in plankton density that was related to the hydrological conditions of the two rivers. Reduced current velocity, due to low river flow or storage in dams, was favorable to heavy growth, while flood conditions restricted plankton abundance.

The influence of the Jebel Aulia Dam Reservoir on the development of plankton in the White Nile was investigated by Brook and Rzoska (1954), who reported a hundredfold increase in phyto- and zooplankton in the reservoir. With the sequence of management from opening to closure of Jebel Aulia Dam, river conditions are followed by flowing lake conditions. Currents fall upstream and so does the capacity to transport sediments. The water clears gradually downstream, photosynthesis sets in and, along with the increase in algal abundance, zooplankton appears in pure form. This plankton suspension persists downstream. In view of the lack of adequate information on the ecology of long tropical rivers, this sequence was viewed as a "discovery."

Prowse and Talling (1958) gave a detailed account of seasonal growth and succession of planktonic algae in the White Nile. They showed that the sequence of development was related to the relative abundance of algae in the river water entering the reservoir, and that growth of algae produced an increase in pH and depleted the nitrate and phosphate concentrations. In addition, the influence of current velocity was examined, and estimates made of photosynthetic production. The rate of carbon fixation of 2.2 grams of carbon per square meter per day was comparable with the highest values previously recorded for phytoplankton populations.

About the same time, Talling (1957*a*) made a comparative study of the diurnal changes due to photosynthesis of plankton algae with the vertical distribution changes associated with intermittent thermal stratification in three locations of the Nile system (i.e., at Jebel Aulia Dam, a lagoon in the Sudd, and a bay of Lake Victoria). He showed that small diurnal changes of temperature in warm tropical waters may cause clear stratification, the maximum rates of photosynthesis were unusually high, and high temperatures were probably not the main cause.

The first detailed study of the longitudinal changes in physical and chemical characteristics of the Nile between Lake Victoria and Jebel Aulia was made by Talling (1957*b*). Data on water characteristics of the larger tributaries were collected by Rzoska in 1956. Talling's survey showed the presence of modifying influences on the Nile water on its northward journey, the most important being Lake Albert, which adds to the dissolved salts, especially phosphate, sulphate, and chloride, of the poorer Victoria Nile water. This survey confirmed the earlier reports of strong seasonal deoxygenation that takes place in the Sudd where half of the Nile water is lost through seepage and evaporation. A similar survey of the Blue Nile showed that the influence of the Sennar Dam Reservoir extended only a short distance upstream and that the plankton population persisted as true river plankton for a considerable stretch downstream.

Further investigations brought findings similar to those of Talling, but Bishai (1962) suggested that annual, as well as seasonal, changes occur in the amounts of dissolved salts in some sections of the White Nile. A longitudinal survey of Bahr El Ghazal showed significant changes in chemical characteristics compared with the White Nile and other tributaries. This was confirmed by the work of Moghraby (1975), who detected higher values for pH, alkalinity, calcium, magnesium, sodium, phosphate, nitrate, and nitrite nitrogen.

Recent work (Moghraby 1975) made a comparison of the results of Talling (1957*a*) and Bishai (1962) with new data to discover the impact of the water hyacinth sixteen years after it had invaded the White Nile system. A comparison of the factors of spatial succession of water characteristics and longitudinal succession of zooplankton showed that the longitudinal succession is more or less the same, but the presence of the hyacinth has brought about significant depletion of nutrients. On the other hand, the presence of the floating mats of the water hyacinth provided a favorable habitat for the development of zooplankton by slowing currents (Rzoska 1973; Monakov 1969; Yousif 1974).

THE WATER HYACINTH

Gay (1958) reported that *Eichhornia crassipes* (Mart.) Solms was first seen on the White Nile in March 1958 at a point 300 km south of Khartoum but was probably present further south in the Sudd swamps in 1956 or 1957. By 1962, the plant succeeded in infesting the whole stretch of the White Nile between Juba and the Jebel Aulia Dam (1,762 km); the Sobat (350 km), Bahr El Zeraf (270 km), and Bahr El Ghazal (200 km) rivers; Lake No, and many of the side lakes and lagoons especially in the Sudd swamps (Obeid 1975). The picture today is not much different from that of 1962, despite the expenditure of 2.5 million dollars annually on chemical control programs.

The water hyacinth was not unknown in the Nile system prior to 1958 when it was reported in Sudan. It had been present in the Nile Delta for many years (Muschler, 1912; Tackholm and Drar, 1950) but had not reached plague proportions in Sudan until 1958 or Egypt after 1973. The southward movement of the plant in Egypt was a consequence of the slowing down of the Nile current resulting from the Aswan High Dam.

The spread of the water hyacinth in the White Nile system has brought a number of harmful effects, including an increase in water loss compared to a free Nile surface (Desougi and Obeid 1978), restriction of fish breeding ground (Davies 1959), oxygen deficiency (Bishai 1961), and transport of freshwater snails (Desougi 1974).

The hazards that the hyacinth has created prompted research into the autecology of the plant with the view that such results might prove useful in its control or management. Thus, Tag El Seed (1972) studied the biology and life cycle of the hyacinth under Sudanese conditions with special reference to the factors affecting sexual reproduction and seed germination in an attempt to assess the significance of the seed in the dispersal of the plant. This work was much needed despite the wealth of knowledge on the ecology, biology, and control of the species accumulated in other parts of the world. With the advent of the water hyacinth into the Nile system in Sudan, the plant has for the first time entered a water system traversing great tracts of arid and semiarid climate, suggesting that further investigation might reveal new and interesting information about the species.

Freidel (1979) evaluated the factors contributing to the success of the species and aggravating the infestation of the White Nile and its tributaries. He studied such external factors as temperature, rainfall, relative humidity, wind speed, and direction and such hydrological factors as river discharge, water levels, and current velocity in the infested area. The internal factors included innate characteristics of the plant, such as mode of reproduction, life cycle strategy, and plasticity. The results of this investigation revealed that the population dynamics of the water hyacinth in the White Nile and its tributaries is regulated first by the discharge and water levels of the rivers and the wind speed, and second by relative humidity and wind quality.

Control measures against the infestation comprise chemical control, manual removal, public education, and legislative action. Owing to the lack of suitable machinery, mechanical measures have not been tried. Chemical control using 2,4-D at the rate of 1.8 kg per acre proved efficient. Only in the dry months of the year, December to March, could aerial spraying be conducted; during the rainy season, muddy soil conditions prevent use of landing strips for aircraft. The rainy season also coincides with the time when many food and cash crops are being established and would need protection from the spray drift.

The water hyacinth, one of the most successful of aquatic plants, has found in the White Nile and its tributaries a most favorable environment for spread. The vastness of the area infested, the prolific reproductive capacity, and the deceptive temporal and spatial distribution of the floating mats help to frustrate the efforts to combat the weed.

Many workers (e.g., Osman et al. 1975) considered methods of utilizing the weed in some way in order to recoup some of the loss involved in trying to eradicate it. Experiments have been carried out and ideas advocated to turn the plant into a crop, and the current view of the hyacinth infestation is to manage the weed rather than control it. Recent studies on using the water hyacinth (Philipp et al. 1978, 1979) indicated positive results for its use in agriculture and energy production. Water hyacinth ash gave significant yield increase on groundnuts. Digestibility, as well as feeding, trials showed that the plants can possibly be used in animal nutrition. The installation of different types of bio-gas generator systems allowed household appliances to be supplied with gas obtained from the anaerobic fermentation of the green plant material. The dried plants suited the pyrolysis process, yielding high solid residues, mainly carbon.

BIOGEOGRAPHY

Sudan extends across a range of vegetation zones from desert in the north to rainforest in some parts of southern Sudan. This grand progression over eighteen degrees of latitude has prompted a number of descriptive and analytic studies of the distribution of soils, plants, and animals.

Andrews (1948) and Harrison and Jackson (1958) made a general classification and outline of the distribution of plants in Sudan. Later investigators (Wickens 1975) considered the relationship between soil types and the distribution of plants, as well as the past history of vegetation distribution. A good deal of work assessed the character and distribution of vegetation in different ecological provinces. Worrall (1959, 1960*a, b*) commented on the nature of plant distribution in the arid environment of northern Sudan, and Kassas (1955, 1956, 1957) made regional studies of vegetation in the desert near Omdurman and along the Red Sea coast. Jackson (1962) outlined the vegetation zone of the Imatong mountains.

The distribution of riverian plants received much interest; many early comments were made on the characteristics of the Sudd vegetation and numerous papers carried accounts on this region. Nonetheless, the work of Migahid (1947, 1952) and Sutcliffe (1974), referred to above, is especially important.

The deterioration of plant cover as a result of human incursion and possibly climatic change has been a subject of interest. Booth (1952) reviewed the process of forest degradation as a result of wood cutting and burning, while Stebbing (1953) wrote a dramatic description of the encroachment of the desert. Halwagy (1961) concluded that the impact of man and animal grazing was the most important biotic factor contributing to deterioration of plant cover.

Soils of Sudan received a good deal of study, but much of this was carried out on a regional basis. Jewitt (1955) summarized the work on the Gezira heavy clay soil, and Worrall (1957) described the semidesert soil. Bunting and Lea (1967) investigated the soil characteristics of the Fung area in the central rainlands of Sudan. Detailed surveys of the soils of New Halfa, Nuba Mountains, Kenana, and along the White and Blue Niles have been made by the Soil Survey Administration. The aim of these surveys is soil productivity and classification analysis to determine land capability for agricultural production.

CROP ECOLOGY

In the early 1900s, there was need for subsistence and rehabilitation for a sizable proportion of the population that led to an early start of crop experimentation in food and cash crops and their production. With time, a wealth of largely unpublished information on the ecology of crop production has accumulated from field experiments on the agronomy and physiology of crops.

Many crops, of which cotton was to become the most important, were relatively new in the Sudanese environment, and all aspects of their culture needed to be established by experiment. Early research, therefore, addressed itself to methods of cultivation, such as sowing date, seed rate, spacing, times of watering, and manuring. Subsequent work assessed the importance of the main factors affecting crop yields, such as nitrogen fertilizer, irrigation frequency, spacing, and sowing date, and how the factors interacted with each other.

Analysis of yield in relation to plant characteristics and environmental factors also received attention. One of the most stimulating and unique features has been the relatively wide annual fluctuations of crop yields, particularly of cotton in the Gezira environment, that take place under conditions that appear uniform. For a time, cotton yield variation was shown to be associated with rainfall factors. High rainfall in the year before cotton sowing correlated with reduction in yield and high rainfall six weeks before sowing with an increase in yield. Further investigations identified two groups of factors, the controllable (fertilizer level, sowing rate, sowing time, insect pest levels) and the uncontrollable factors, such as presowing rains.

Because crop production depends on irrigation, the best use of water was to receive early investigation. Two aspects were important, the amount of water needed to produce maximum yield, and the minimum amount required for satisfactory yield. Both aspects have been determined for many crops, and it has been established that there is for many crops a wide range of water duty within which yields are not affected. This practical advantage was attributed to the characteristics of the heavy clay soil of central Sudan. Furthermore, data accumulated from water duty experiments have demonstrated that formal theories on soil water—crop behavior are not applicable to the clay soil of the Gezira, because of the characteristics of the clay and the absence of an effective field capacity (Farbrother 1972).

NATURAL RESOURCES

For some time now, Sudan has been developing its natural resources at a fairly rapid rate to enhance the socioeconomic life of its people. A number of major agricultural development schemes have been completed, among which are the Gezira, Managil, New Halfa, Suki, and Rahad irrigation schemes. Today, irrigated agriculture is being diversified, intensified, and extended through mechanization of land in the rainfed areas.

This era of economic development, with its consequent exploitation and interference with the natural environment, stimulated research in the field of natural resources and their management. Much of this fledgling research has originated in the University of Khartoum, but is being extended to other institutions. It was initiated by Kassas' 1968 re-examination of the distribution of the dominant tree species in comparison with the picture documented by Smith (1949). This important investigation showed that the various dominant trees are practicing a southeasterly shift into areas of higher rainfall: the semidesert species *Aracia ehrenbergiana* Hochst. ex A. Rich. and *A. nubica* Benth. have expanded into *A. mellifera* (Vahl) Benth. country; this species has expanded into *A seyal* Del.; and the latter has almost completely been replaced by *Combretum* woodland. Thus, species that had formerly flourished in lower rainfall areas failed to regenerate in their own habitats and are moving toward higher rainfall areas.

A. senegal Willd., the gum arabic-producing tree, is of great economic importance to Sudan, which produces 80 percent of the world demand; recent observations have shown the species to be retreating from many sites of its natural occurrence. Experimental evidence revealed that a high proportion of seed is destroyed before or at the time of germination, and only about 16 percent of the seed finds the chance for germination (Sief El Din 1969). Destruction of seedlings through grass fires, shade intolerance, browsing, and grazing contribute greatly to the decline in species numbers.

Cordia africana Lamb. produces one of the finest and most sought after timbers in Sudan. Like *A. senegal,* it has sustained heavy losses in density in its natural stands in western Sudan, and biotic and climatic factors play a significant role in its regeneration. Much experimental work was been directed toward assessing the effect of such factors as depth of sowing, shade tolerance, soil and seed bed conditions, competitive ability, intensity of grazing and browsing, and alternating temperatures on seed germination and establishment. The aim of this experimentation was to make sound recommendations for afforestation.

A second interest in natural resources management centered around soil moisture conservation and plant growth and rehabilitation in the arid zone of Sudan. The studies undertaken were directed toward finding suitable field techniques to conserve and increase soil moisture revenue. Also of interest was how soil moisture influences the survival, performance, and regeneration of both indigenous and introduced plant species. This work was needed because the arid and semiarid zones occupy 320 million feddans (134.4 million hectares), and much of the plant cover has been squandered by increasing human and animal populations.

The above theme is presently being extended to evaluate different systems of land utilization with the view of predicting the outcome of different systems of traditional land management.

CONCEPTS AND METHODS

At the turn of the century, modern scientific knowledge as we know it today was lacking in Sudan. What had accumulated by then was mainly drawn from explorers' observations, in addition to local traditions, methods, and experiences. The first modern research effort was, therefore, deployed to define in scientific terms the environment of the country so that its economic potential could be evaluated.

Because the immediate need in the country after the reconquest of Sudan in 1898 was for rehabilitation and subsistence, research efforts went to solve problems of agricultural production. The theme of research was the definition of the natural environment, the interaction of different crops with different environments, and the adjustment of environmental conditions by agricultural practice to improve agricultural output.

Knowledge of the environment was gained by surveys, rather than basic research. By the same token, the approach to ecology of crop production was made by testing in field experiments a range of crop varieties and agricultural practices. This approach, although admittedly broad and shallow, has helped to produce the results desired by the stated policy.

The policy of Nile water use has also led to an intensive study to assess the storage capacity required to extend irrigated agriculture to the maximum, irrespective of the annual variations in the Nile yield. This study culminated in *The Nile Basin,* twelve volumes with detailed accounts of the physical and hydrological characteristics of all tributary catchments of the Nile system and information and research results into the measurements of discharge as well as methods of computations of the required storage capacities necessary for expansion of irrigated agriculture in Sudan and Egypt.

Two lines of approach were used in measuring the discharge of the Nile (Hurst 1957): (1) experimental and statistical methods of collecting discharges and calculating storage capacity required to equalize the discharge in each case; and (2) a mathematical approach with the theory of probability, treating the variability of river discharges as chance events. Being statistical, the first approach required a mass of records of river discharges; since these were not available, rainfall statistics were used. Temperature and barometric pressure were included because they have similar frequency distributions. The longest series of such records did not cover 200 years, so measurements were taken of tree rings and the thickness of varves to get a longer series of figures. In all, seventy-five different phenomena were analyzed and 690 computations made of storage capacity. This very large amount of work yielded the required result for practical purposes.

The mathematical approach was used because river discharges can be treated as chance events. Under this assumption, it is theoretically possible to find a solution. A solution was found and confirmed by experiments with chance events. However, when this solution was compared with that calculated from river discharges or rainfall, the storage required in the case of natural events was greater than that which fits purely chance events. This was attributed to the tendency of natural events to group themselves in runs where high and low values are preponderant.

The methodology of research has, in general, drawn extensively from the experiences and concepts developed in Europe and North America. This is justified if one considers the lack of a long tradition of research and the fact that research personnel, whether local or expatriate, tend to bring home their school traditions, methods, and concepts. Thus, research on patterns of land use adopted the British tradition of land-use maps, but some attempts were made to tackle the problem on a country-wide basis, using the World Land Use Survey Program.

In other instances, concepts developed elsewhere were applied to discover how far they could provide satisfactory solutions to local problems. The catena concept, for example, was applied in southern Sudan and proved valuable in determining that the mosaic of soil and vegetation types was a complex result of topographic, climatic, and soil factors. On the other hand, theories on soil water–crop behavior were found not applicable to the predominantly heavy clay soil of the irrigated crop production schemes to which they were applied.

In the early days of crop production research, investigators used Fisher and Yates' design of experiments and the field plot technique with the analysis of variance. Studies of the physiology of crop production began with Gregory's technique of the leaf area index but were extended to include the ideas of Penman and Monteith and the microenvironmental factors. In later years, the strategy for the design and analysis of experiments was extended to the multivariate situation that enabled the analysis of within-year and between-year variations in crop yield, together with the definition of variance attributable to specified environmental factors.

The current outlook in ecological research, and particularly in the field of natural resources development, stems from the growing pressures of human and animal populations and the many efforts through land development to expand and modernize the economic and social life of the country. This realization has led to the adoption of the ideas and tactics espoused by the new science of ecology and resource management. In an era of accelerating economic development and exploitation of resources in huge development projects, this approach is considered vital. The aim is twofold: to synthesize basic ecological data as an important input before planning policies of land development, and to assess the likely changes that might accompany development and thereby guard against environmental risks.

REFERENCES CITED

Andrews, F. W. 1948. The vegetation of the Sudan. In *Agriculture in Sudan,* ed. J. D. Tothill, pp. 32–61. London: O.U.P.

Anonymous. 1954. *The Equatorial Nile Project* (Report of the Jonglei Investigation Team). Vols. I–IV. Sudan Gov.

Ball, J. 1902. The semna cataract or rapid of the Nile, a study in river erosion. *Q. J. Geol. Soc.* 59:65–79.

Berry, L. 1962*a*. Alluvial islands in the Nile. *Rev. Geomorph. Dyn.* 12:105–108.

———. 1962*b*. The characteristics and mode of formation of the Nile islands between Malakal and Sabaloka. *Eighth Annual Report of the Hydrobiological Research Unit,* pp. 7–13. University of Khartoum, Sudan.

———. 1962*c*. The physical history of the White Nile. *Eighth Annual Report of the Hydrobiological Research Unit.* University of Khartoum, Sudan.

——— and A. J. Whiteman. 1968. The Nile in the Sudan. *Geogr. J.* 134:1–37.

Bishai, H. M. 1961. The effect of the water hyacinth on the fisheries of the Sudan. *H.R.U., University of Khartoum. Annu. Rep.* 8:29–36.

———. 1962. The water characteristics of the Nile in the Sudan with a note on the effect of *Eichhornia crassipes* on the hydrology of the Nile. *Hydrobiologia* 19:359–382.

Booth, G. A. 1952. The forests of Upper Nile Province 1862–1950. *Sudan Notes and Records* 33:529–556.

Brook, A. J. 1954. A systematic account of the phytoplankton of the Blue and White Nile at Khartoum. *Ann. Mag. Nat. Hist.* 12:648–656.

——— and R. Rzoska. 1954. The influence of the Jebel Aulia dam on the development of Nile plankton. *J. Anim. Ecol.* 23:101–114.

Bunting, A. H. and J. D. Lea. 1967. The soils and vegetation of the Fung. *J. Ecol.* 50:529–556.

Butzer, K. W. 1959. Contributions to the Pleistocene geology of the Nile valley. *Erkunde Band* 13:46–67.

——— and C. L. Hansen. 1968. *Desert and river in Nubia: geomorphology and prehistory environments at the Aswan reservoir.* Madison: University of Wisconsin Press.

Davies, H. R. J. 1959. The effect of *Eichhornia crassipes* on the people of the Sobat and White Nile between Sobat and Kosti. *H.R.U., University of Khartoum, Annu. Rep.* 6:26–29.

Desougi, L. A. 1974. Some aspects of the biology and control of the water hyacinth [*Eichhornia crassipes* (Mart.) Solms]. M.S. thesis, University of Khartoum.

——— and M. Obeid. 1978. Some aspects of the evapotranspiration of *Eichhornia crassipes* and some other aquatic weeds. *Proc. EWRS Symp. on Aquatic Weeds* pp. 391–398.

Fairbridge, R. W. 1962. New radiocarbon dates of Nile sediments. *Nature* 196:108–110.

Farbrother, H. G. 1972. Field behaviour of Gezira clay under irrigation. *Cotton Grow Rev.* 49:1–27.

Freidel, J. W. 1979. Population dynamics of the water hyacinth [*Eichhornia crassipes* (Mart.) Solms] with special reference to the Sudan. Berichte aus dem Fachgebiet Herbologie der Universität Hohenheim, No. Heft 17.

Gay, D. A. 1958. *Eichhornia crassipes* in the Nile of the Sudan. *Nature* 182:538–539.

Halwagy, R. 1961. The vegetation of the semidesert northeast of Khartoum, Sudan. *Oikos* 12:87–110.

Harrison, M. N. and J. K. Jackson. 1958. Ecological classification of the vegetation of Sudan. *For. Bull.* New Ser. 2.

Hurst, H. E. 1946. *A short account of the Nile Basin.* Cairo: Gov. Press.

______. 1950. *The Nile Basin.* Vol. VIII. *The hydrology of the Sobat and White Nile and the topography of the Blue Nile and Atbara.* Cairo: Gov. Press.

______. 1957. *The Nile.* London: Constable.

______ and P. Phillips. 1931. *The Nile Basin.* Vol I. *General description of the basin. Meteorology, topography of the White Nile Basin.* Cairo: Gov. Press.

______ and P. Phillips. 1938. *The Nile Basin.* Vol. V. *The hydrology of the lake plateau and Bahr El Jebel.* Cairo: Gov. Press.

Jackson, J. K. 1962. The vegetation of the Imatong Mountains, Sudan. *J. Ecol.* 44: 47–66.

Jewitt, T. N. 1955. *Gezira soil.* Bull. 12. Ministry of Agriculture, Sudan.

Kassas, M. 1955. The mist oasis of Erkowit, Sudan. *J. Ecol.* 44:180–194.

______. 1956. Landforms and plant cover in the Omdurman desert. *Bull. Soc. Geogr. Egypte* 29:43–58.

______. 1957. On the ecology of the Red Sea coastal land. *J. Ecol.* 45:187–203.

______. 1968. Dynamics of desert vegetation. *Proc. of the conference organized by I.B.P.,* Tunis, March 1968.

Lyons, H. G. 1908. Some geographical aspects of the Nile. *Geogr. J.* 34:440–480.

Migahid, A. M. 1947. An ecological study of the Sudd swamps of the Upper Nile. *Proc. Egypt Acad. Sci.* 3:57–86.

______. 1952. *Velocity of water current and its relation to swamp vegetation in the Sudd region of the Upper Nile.* Cairo: Fouad I University Press.

Moghraby, A. I. 1975. Some effects of *Eichhornia crassipes* (Mart.) Solms on the productivity of the Nile. In *Aquatic weeds in the Sudan,* ed. M. Obeid, pp. 133–150. National Council for Research, Sudan and USA National Academy of Sciences.

Monakov, A. V. 1969. The zooplankton and zoobenthos of the White Nile and adjoining waters in the Republic of the Sudan. *Hydrobiologia* 33:161–187.

Muschler, R. 1912. *A manual flora of Egypt.* Vol. I. Berlin: R. Friedlander und Sohn.

Nilson, E. 1953. Contributions to the history of the Blue Nile. *Bull. Soc. R. Geogr. Egypte* 25:29–47.

Obeid, M. 1975. The water hyacinth—*Eichhornia crassipes* (Mart.) Solms. In *Aquatic weeds in the Sudan,* ed. M. Obeid, pp. 31–49. National Council for Research, Sudan and USA National Academy of Sciences.

Osman, H. E., et al. 1975. Studies on the nutritive value of water hyacinth [*Eichhornia crassipes* (Mart.) Solms], ed. M. Obeid, pp. 104–127. National Council for Research, Sudan and USA National Academy of Sciences.

Philipp, O., et al. 1978. Studies on the utilization of the water hyacinth [*Eichhornia crassipes* (Mart.) Solms] in the Sudan. *Proc. EWRS Symp. on Aquatic Weeds,* pp. 415–427.

______ 1979. Some studies and aims of the utilization of water hyacinth, *Eichhornia crassipes* (Mart.) Solms, in Sudan. In *Weed research in Sudan,* Vol. 1, eds. M. E. Beshir and W. Koch, pp. 106–115.

Prowse, A. G. and J. F. Talling. 1958. The seasonal growth and succession of plankton algae in the White Nile. *Limnol. Oceanogr.* 3:222–238.

Rzoska, J. 1973. The Upper Nile swamps: a tropical wetland study. *Freshwat. Biol.* 4:1–30.

———, A. J. Brook, and G. A. Prowse. 1955. Seasonal plankton development in the White and Blue Nile at Khartoum. *Proc. Int. Cong. Limnol.* 12:327–334.

Sief El Din, A. G. 1969. The natural regeneration of *Acacia senegal* Willd. M.S. thesis, University of Khartoum.

Smith, J. 1949. *Distribution of tree species in the Sudan in relation to rainfall and soil texture.* Bull. 4. Ministry of Agriculture, Sudan.

Stebbing, E. P. 1953. *The creeping desert in the Sudan and elsewhere in Africa.* Sudan: McCorquodale and Co.

Sutcliffe, J. 1974. A hydrological study of the southern Sudd region of the Upper Nile. *Bull. Sci. Hydrolog.* 19:237–255.

Tackholm, V. and M. Drar. 1950. *Flora of Egypt.* Cairo: Fouad I University Press.

Tag El Seed, M. 1972. Some aspects of the biology and control of *Eichhornia crassipes* (Mart.) Solms. Ph.D. thesis, University of Khartoum.

Talling, J. F. 1957*a*. Diurnal changes of stratification and photosynthesis in some tropical African waters. *Proc. R. Soc. Lond. B* 147:57–83.

———. 1957*b*. The longitudinal succession of water characteristics in the White Nile. *Hydrobiologia* 11:73–89.

Walter, J. 1912. *Das Gesetz der Wustenbildung.* Leipzig.

Whiteman, A. J. 1971. *The geology of the Sudan.* London: Oxford University Press.

Asia

28

INDONESIA

Kuswata Kartawinata

INTRODUCTION

The Indonesian Achipelago extends for about 5,000 km from west to east, and consists of a diversity of ecosystems. About 63 percent of the land surface consists of dry and swamp forest.

Biological investigations have barely scratched the surface, although they date back to the beginning of the eighteenth century. A historical account of the research undertakings to 1945 was summarized in *Science and Scientists in Netherlands Indies* (Honig and Verdoorn 1945) and later in *Chronica Naturae,* volume 106 (6) in 1950. Investigations were concerned primarily with floristic and faunistic exploration and inventory; ecological studies dealt mainly with descriptive accounts based on visual observations, natural history, and to a certain extent, with ecological factors. Most of these were published in *Tropische Natuur, Natuurkundig Tijdschrift voor Nederlandsch Indie, Treubia, Bulletin du Jardin Botanique de Buitenzorg, Annales du Jardin Botanique de Buitenzorg, Teysmannia, Nova Guinea,* and *Tectona.*

Primary succession after the eruption of Krakatau in 1883 received a great deal of attention, and there are quite a number of papers dealing with these (e.g., Treub 1888; Backer 1929; Ernst 1934; Docters van Leeuwen 1936). The article on the biology of mountain plants and animals by Docters van Leeuwen (1933) is a monumental work of ecological significance. Steenis' (1935) excellent work on the sketches of vegetation of Indonesia has never been surpassed; it forms the basis of the vegetation map in the *Atlas van tropische Nederland* (1938) and later *The Vegetation Map of Malaysia* (1958*a*). Results of the forest inventory and ecologically inclined studies of forestry were published in *Tectona.*

The present paper gives a brief account of the progress of ecological research during the period of 1945–1980. It is not my intent to enumerate all the pertinent literature; a number of publications have appeared in various journals or reports published in Indonesia and abroad, and much survey research carried out during the last ten years was published with limited circulation. Many of these publications and reports were unavailable to me and hence were not reviewed in this paper.

TERRESTRIAL ECOLOGY

Vegetation Studies

Dilmy and Kostermans (1958) gave an account of the progress of vegetation studies in Indonesia and pointed out various problems and difficulties contributing to the slow progress. In 1950, the Forest Planning Bureau of the Indonesian Forest Service compiled a vegetation map of Indonesia elaborating on that prepared by Steenis in 1938 and supplemented with field survey data. The map was further improved and extended to cover the Malaysian region (Indonesia, Malaysia, Philippines, and Papua New Guinea) and was published by UNESCO (Steenis 1958*a*). Using aerial photographs and field survey data, the Forest Planning Bureau is currently preparing a new vegetation map primarily emphasizing the timber volume of the forests.

Simple strip surveying of the forests that was initiated before 1935 is currently being continued, but the data produced are ecologically somewhat unreliable. The old tradition of describing vegetation based on visual observations and impressions has been continued. The lack of well-trained botanists and ecologists and the vastness of the country, where the total area of the forest alone covers about 122 million hectares, have hampered the study of vegetation in more details.

Steenis, who resided in Indonesia for about twenty years, contributed a great deal of knowledge on the ecology of plant species and communities. His knowledge on the ecology of mountain species and vegetation has been presented in great detail in his *Mountain Flora of Java* (1972); he is currently preparing information on the vegetation of Malaysia for the *Flora Malesiana,* vol. 2.

The use of Zurich-Montpellier and Scandinavian phytosociological methods in the analysis of vegetation was attempted but without satisfactory results (Steenis 1958*b*). This attempt failed because tropical vegetation, particularly the forests, not only is very complex and heterogeneous in species composition, but also changes gradually spatially. This makes it difficult to determine minimum area; even if the vegetation is relatively homogeneous, the minimum area is so large that it becomes impractical in the field. Steenis, therefore, favors the use of indicator species and physiognomy for characterizing vegetation.

Quantitative approaches in synecologic studies were initiated by Meijer (1959), who used enumeration methods in analyzing the montane rain forest at Cibodas, West Java. The trend toward using quantitative methods is currently increasing; participants of BIOTROP Training Course in Forest Ecology (1972) analyzed the lowland rain forest at the Ujung Kulon Nature Reserve, and Yamada (1975, 1976*a, b,* 1977) did the same in the montane forest at Cibodas. Kartawinata and his co-workers are currently working on quantitative analyses of various vegetation types. (Kartawinata 1977*a*, 1978*a*, in press; Kartawinata and Waluyo 1977; Kartawinata et al. 1980; Riswan 1979*c*; Sukardjo and Kartawinata 1979.)

Steenis (1957) has developed a classification scheme for the major climax vegetation of Indonesia and the adjacent region on the basis of distribution of rainfall in a year, quantity and quality of water, soil conditions, and topographic conditions. He (1958*c*) stressed that climate, particularly the distribution of rainfall, is the most important factor in the distribution and characteristics of vegetation types. Referring to the distribution of rainfall, he emphasized the significance of the number of rainy days in four consecutive driest months. This concept, developed by Mohr, was further refined by Schmidt and Ferguson (1951), who calculated the ratio between the number of dry months and wet months as the index of dryness to characterize the type of climate. Steenis also developed the concept of phytoclimate, namely, that the classification of climate should be approached from considerations of climate and plant geography; plants can be classed into various classes of tolerance to climatic conditions and these can be used as indicator species for phytoclimates. This has been successfully applied to plant life in Java (Steenis 1965).

Recently, Kartawinata (1976, 1977*b*, in press) proposed a scheme of ecological zonation of Indonesia using available data on vegetation, particularly those of Steenis (1935, 1957), soils, and climate. The scheme was developed following the biogeoclimatic criteria of Krajina (1965, 1973).

The swamp forests (peat swamp, freshwater swamp, and mangrove forests) cover about 15 million hectares but have been little investigated. A major work on mangrove forest was made before World War II (Becking et al. 1922; Haan 1931), but it dealt mainly with species composition and zonation. Steenis (1958*d*) synthesized existing knowledge on the ecology of mangrove and discussed the autecology, structure, and composition of forest, zonation, regeneration, physiology, and ecological factors. Recent works on mangrove appeared in various publications (Kartawinata and Waluyo 1977; Sukardjo and Kartawinata 1979; Soemodihardjo et al. 1979). The ecology and distribution of peat swamps have been briefly discussed by Polak (1950, 1952), and a detailed survey of peat swamps in South Sumatra was made by Team Institut Pertanian Bogor (1975). Recently, an interdisciplinary approach to ecological studies in the swamp forest area at South Sumatra was initiated by the Team Survei Ekologi IPB (1975). These studies were aimed at collecting ecological data that will be used as the basis for the management of swamp ecosystems in line with a government plan to convert these ecosystems into agricultural land (Hanson and Koesoebiono 1977; Sobur et al. 1977). Similar surveys were made by others in Jambi and Riau on the east coast of Sumatra and West Kalimantan (Borneo).

The "kerangas" (heath) forest in Indonesia was reviewed by Kartawinata (1978*b*), and results of recent studies were reported by Kartawinata (1980) and Riswan (1979*a, b, c,* 1980).

Some studies on hydrology in watersheds have been carried out experimentally and in the field (e.g., Bakker and van Wijk 1951; Surjono 1964). It is indicated that infiltration, runoff, and ground water reserves are related to the nature of soils, vegetation types, and the presence of terraces. Pine forest has a low evapotranspiration rate and is able to absorb about half of the rainfall but is not effective in reducing runoff.

During the last thirty years, few studies have been made on primary succession. Richards summarized data on primary succession on Krakatau and illustrated the trend diagrammatically. Additional data on Krakatau were recently collected by Borssum Waalkes (1960) on plant communities and Toxopeus (1950) on animal communities. Dilmy (1967) initiated studies of early succession after the eruption of Mount Agung in Bali, but since then no follow-up has been made.

Secondary succession after the destruction of primary lowland forests has currently received special attention in connection with the Man and Biosphere (MAB) project no. 1, which deals with the ecological effects of increasing human activities in tropical forest ecosystems. Kartawinata and his co-workers are at present working on this project in East Kalimantan, applying an interdisciplinary approach; parts of the results have been reported (Kartawinata et al. 1979; Rahayuningsih 1979; Rahayuningsih et al. 1979; Riswan 1979*a, b, c;* Riswan and Hadrijanto 1979).

A great deal of attention is now given also to the studies of the effects of mechanized logging activities in the lowland rain forests, particularly because during the last ten years logging activities have increased tremendously. Preliminary results have been recently reported in the Symposium on the Effects of Logging in Southeast Asia, in Bogor, 1975, and the Seminars on Afforestation and Reforestation, in Yogyakarta, (Anonymous 1975) and in the Second Round Table Conference on Dipterocarpaceae in Malaysia (Abdulhadi et al. 1980). The results indicate that damage of residual stands as a result of mechanized logging is up to 50 percent, and the destruction of the soil is up to 30 percent depending on the intensity of logging. Experimental studies of seedling growth indicate that, in some primary forest species, growth is enhanced by forest openings. Residual stands are invariably overgrown by forest weeds. The environmental effects of logging have been reported by Kartawinata (1979).

Openings occur also in primary forests as a result of the death of old trees, and succession will take place in such openings. Steenis (1958*b*) used the term *spotwise regeneration* to refer to recovery in these openings. Which primary forest species will invade and prevail is entirely dependent on chance. Species invading such openings are in general short-lived; Steenis calls these species the *nomadic species.* Steenis believes that the primary forest or climax forest is composed of mosaics of regenerating openings, which he assumes to be responsible for the heterogeneity of species within tropical rain forests.

Soil-vegetation relationships have been little investigated. The work of Soerianegara (1966, 1970, 1971) can be considered representative of such studies. He indicated that primary forest soils have moderate fertility but more so than soils under secondry forests. He pointed out also the relationship between soil properties and species distribution and, to a certain extent, vegetation zonation as well.

Data on timber volumes in various forests are available as the result of extensive strip surveys made by the Forest Service. This has led Soerianegara (1965) to make estimates of productivity of the lowland and montane tropical rain forests; relationships were found between productivity and rainfall, soil type, drainage condition, altitude, and species composition. Soerianegara (1973) further attempted to estimate forest productivity by using Paterson's CVP index but found no correlation between the estimated values and the actual ones, attributing this to variations in site factors and species composition. There has been no direct productivity measurement conducted so far in this country. Studies on litterfall and litter decomposition in montane and lowland forests have been initiated recently (Abdulkadir and Brotonegoro 1980).

Although it is somewhat incomplete, the state of knowledge on forest ecosystems in Indonesia has been summarized by Kartawinata (1974). He gave a brief but comprehensive review of vegetation types, functioning of ecosystems, water balance, erosion, nutrient cycling, relationship between man and the forest, problems and pattern of use, management policy, and the gaps in knowledge. Summaries of various ecological articles that are related to agriculture may be also found in series of publications of the Department of Agriculture entitled *Ringkasan Publikasi dan Laporan Penelitian Pertanian* (Summaries of Publications and Reports on Agricultural Research), which was initiated in 1971.

Studies on grasses and grassland have been concerned with floristic composition of natural grassland and with biological and ecological properties that are related to pasture improvement, utilization of species as cattle feed, and weed problems. Walandouw (1952) and Soerianegara (1970) have reviewed various aspects of grassland ecosystems in Indonesia.

Currently, inventories of ecosystem types; studies on ecology and dynamics of dipterocarp forests, comprising investigations of structure and composition, dynamics, growth and regeneration, phenology, reproductive biology, roles of animals in seed dispersal, nutrient cycling, and roles of microorganisms in forest ecosystems; and studies on ecology of home gardens. Preliminary results appear in various reports (Budiman and Kartawinata 1979, 1980).

An ongoing project on interactions between man and forests, a cooperative work between the Indonesian MAB and the United States MAB programs, is concerned with discovering and contextually describing people-forest interactions that will have practical significance for forests and that will improve the lives of the people. Another MAB project on environmental effects of different land uses, involving both social and biological scientists, is being carried out in East Kalimantan. Reports of preliminary results and general accounts appears in various papers (Kartawinata et al. 1977, 1980, in press; Vayda et al., in press).

ANIMAL ECOLOGY

Research on animal ecology is lagging behind that of plant ecology. Most animal studies have been concerned with taxonomy and geographic distribution. A study on the ecology of insect communities in grassland, forest edge, and river bank in the Ujung Kulon Nature Reserve was recently made by Adisoemarto (1974), who found that the difference in insect populations was attributable to habitat factors. In the same area, various zoologists have investigated the ecology of various wildlife under the sponsorship of the World Wildlife Fund. The most notable work is that of Schenkel and Schenkel-Hulligers (1969) on the ecology of the vanishing Javan rhinoceros. A general ecological account of various wildlife and vegetation in the Ujung Kulon Nature Reserve is given in detail by Hoogerwerf (1970). Recent studies on insect populations in primary and young secondary forests and cultivated lands were reported by Rahayuningsih (1979) and Rahayuningsih et al. (1979).

The World Wildlife Fund has active projects on wildlife research in various places in Indonesia. During the last ten years, studies of primates have been conducted by various scientists from the University of California, University of Washington, and Harvard University. Most of the results of these studies have been published elsewhere and were unfortunately not available to me. The ecology of orangutans received a great deal of attention (e.g., Borner 1976; MacKinnon 1973, 1977; Rijksen 1978). Recent studies and reviews on ecology and management were published in a symposium proceedings by McNeely.

The effects of logging activities on the primate population have been recently investigated by Wilson and Wilson (1975). They found that the effects depend on the degree of damage and the intrinsic nature of species themselves.

Most of the work on birds has been practically monopolized by Hoogerwerf and has dealt with taxonomy but very little ecology. Sody (1953, 1955, 1956) gave a descriptive ecological account of forest birds of Java and the association of birds with plant species. He showed that the altitudinal zonation of birds is related to that of plant communities. Migratory studies of various bird species, conducted within the framework of the Migratory Animal Pathological Survey, were initiated in 1967, and the results were incorporated in a publication entitled, *Migration and Survival of the Birds of Asia* (McClure 1974). Presently, quantitative analysis of bird communities is still in progress.

AQUATIC ECOLOGY

Marine

Hardenberg (1948) gave an account of various problems in marine research in Indonesia. He summarized briefly research accomplishments to that date and discussed problems covering almost all aspects of research in the tropical sea environment, such as light and temperature, population, biogeography, production capacity, water properties, and special properties of the estuaries. Research in the 1950s was concerned more with taxonomy and chemical and physical properties of the sea, and less with ecology.

Doty et al. (1963) initiated the study of productivity of the northwestern Indonesian waters and indicated that the shallow waters were as productive in organic matter as the most productive waters elsewhere in tropical Asia, New Zealand, or America, and more productive than deeper waters nearby or in the central Pacific. Doty and his co-workers indicated gaps in marine research that need further study; these include light measurement and standing crops of phytoplankton and periodic measurements to determine the potential productivity. Since then, systematic exploration and investigations of Indonesian waters have been undertaken by the National Institute of Oceanology. Results of the studies on chlorophyll distribution, planktonic flora and fauna, ecology of various animal species, and physical and chemical properties of the sea have been reported in the Institute's journals (*Marine Research in Indonesia* and *Oseanologi* di *Indonesia*), as well as in cruise reports. Results of recent studies were reported in the proceedings of a symposium on tropical shallow water communities (Soegiarto et al. 1977).

The Sea Fishery Research Institute has undertaken various surveys and research on the population and ecology of economically important marine animals, especially fish and shrimp. The results are reported in the *Report on Sea Fishery Research* (e.g., Ritterbush 1974).

Fresh Water

Studies on freshwater ecology are mostly concerned with or related to inland fishery problems and are carried out largely by the Inland Fishery Research Institute in Bogor. These studies deal with such aspects as planktonic flora and fauna, hydrochemistry, ecological factors affecting productivity, algal growth, effects of pesticides, and autecology in natural and artifical lakes and fishponds with special emphasis on economic potentials. Other studies are concerned with fish culture, improvement of fish production, and other practical aspects of fisheries. Results of the research are published primarily in the Institute's publications, *Contributions/Communications/Reports of the Inland Fishery Research Station Bogor* or in *Contributions/Communications of the General Agricultural Research Station Bogor* (e.g. Vaas et al. 1953). Research on the ecology of fishes, shrimps, and aquatic molluscs is handled also by the National Biological Institute in Bogor, Bogor Agricultural University, and BIOTROP Regional Center for Tropical Biology, Bogor.

Various articles on aquatic ecology, especially those related to fisheries, are from time to time published in the proceedings of the Indo-Pacific Fishery Council sessions. An annotated bibliography on aquatic biological resources, an important source of information containing over 700 entries, has been prepared by Soegiarto et al. (1975).

APPLIED ECOLOGY

A number of ecological research projects have been developed to support the solution of various problems in forestry, agriculture, fisheries, and pollution. The progress of such a study in forestry up to 1958 has been summarized by Moersaid and Soediarto (1960). The need for ecological research in forestry has been further emphasized by Soerianegara (1974), who indicated that at present only a few species are ecologically known and can be used in afforestation and reforestation programs. Silvicultural studies of various species in logged-over natural forests are being conducted by the Forest Research Institute. The publication of the results appear in the *Reports* or *Communications of the Forest Research Institute, Bogor.* The International Timber Corporation Indonesia, a subsidiary of the American-based Weyerhaeuser Company, is actively doing research in various ecological aspects of forestry; the results are published in the company's publications.

Weed and pesticide ecology has received a great deal of attention in agriculture (e.g., Soerjani 1970) with various research institutions undertaking investigations. The *Proceedings of the Indonesian Weed Science Conference* (e.g., Soerjani 1971) and *Proceedings of the Asia-Pacific Weed Science Society Conference* (Soerjani et al. 1977) included results of many such studies. Studies on crop plants themselves have been concerned mainly with physiological and agronomic aspects; only a few, such as that on fruit trees by Terra (1952), deal with crop ecology. Lately, the ecology of home gardens has been the focus of investigations by various research institutes and universities.

Pollution has become a great concern in Indonesia as a consequence of the rapid rate of economic development. Water pollution is the main problem and is particularly attributable to oil and chemical industries, as well as to the extensive use of pesticides. Research on pollution has just started and has been undertaken by various agencies, such as LEMIGAS (Oil and Gas Research Institute), LON (National Institute of Oceanology), LPPD (Inland Fishery Research Station), PPMPL (Environmental Research Center of Jakarta Municipality), various university centers for environmental studies and management, and the Institute of Ecology of Padjadjaran University. LEMIGAS (Anonymous 1974), in cooperation with the Smithsonian Institution, for example, made an oil pollution survey in Java, Sumatra, and Kalimantan. Hardjamulia and Kusumadinata (1974) studied the pesticide spread along irrigation canals and the effects of pesticides on fishery; and Koeman et al. (1974) investigated the contents of metals and chlorinated hydrocarbon pesticides in fish, duck eggs, crustaceans, and molluscs in west and central Java. Baseline studies monitoring the effects of industries on biotic communities have been initiated also by Romimohtarto and associates.

As has been indicated earlier, research in freshwater and marine ecology is mostly aimed at providing ecological information that will directly or indirectly support fishery practices, and in particular, production. On the more applied side, studies have been concerned with such aspects as artificial feeding, fingerling supply, domestication of wild species, improvement of fish culture, and utilization of ricefields, natural and artificial lakes, and coastal resources for aquaculture.

The Institute of Medical Research in Jakarta has been dealing with the ecology of various diseases and the application of ecological approaches in public health studies. The Institute is also working cooperatively with the U.S. Naval Medical Research Unit, executing various research projects such as the studies on schistosomiasis in central Sulawesi. Results have been published in the Institute's journal, as well as in Indonesian or foreign medical and scientific periodicals.

Various results of ecological studies were reported at the 5th International Symposium on Tropical Ecology at Kuala Lumpur, Malaysia in 1979. Papers on human environment were presented in a national seminar on the human environment in Jakarta in 1978 (Anonymous 1978).

RESEARCH ORGANIZATIONS

As indicated above, research is carried out by various government agencies or institutions, most of which are attached to government departments. The

National Biological Institute and the National Institute of Oceanology, however, are attached to the Indonesian Institute of Sciences, a government agency whose functions are roughly similar to the national academies of science elsewhere. Other institutions are divisions of state universities, such as the Institute of Ecology of the Padjadjaran University and the Center for Natural Resource Management and Environmental Studies of the Bogor Agricultural University. In the last few years other universities have also established centers for environmental studies and management. Various universities are engaged in research, and surveys are contracted out by various government departments. Thus, almost all research projects are financed by the government; however, grants and financial supports may also be received from non-government agencies, such as private companies, Ford Foundation, World Wildlife Fund, UNESCO-UNEP, and other UN agencies.

NATIVE AND FOREIGN JOURNALS

The major native journals that may publish ecological articles are:

Reinwardtia, a journal on plant taxonomy and ecology, is published irregularly in English by the Herbarium Bogoriense, National Biological Institute, LIPI, Bogor. It is the continuation of the *Bulletin of the Botanic Gardens, Buitenzorg* (1940–1949) and *Bulletin du Jardin Botanique de Buitenzorg* (1911–1940).

Annales Bogorienses, a journal on general botany, is published irregularly in English by the Laboratory for General Botany (Treub Laboratory), National Biological Institute, LIPI, Bogor. It is the continuation of *Annals of the Botanic Gardens, Buitenzorg* (1940–1949) and *Annales du Jardin Botanique de Buitenzorg* (1897–1940).

Treubia, a journal on systematic zoology and animal geography, is published irregularly in English by the Zoological Museum, National Biological Institute, LIPI Bogor.

BioIndonesia, a journal specially for papers on current biological problems in Indonesia presented in scientific meetings, is published irregularly in English or Indonesian by the National Biological Institute, LIPI, Bogor.

Bulletin Kebun Raya, a quarterly journal on general biology, is published in Indonesian or English by the Botanic Gardens, National Biological Institute, LIPI, Bogor.

Marine Research in Indonesia, a journal on marine sciences, is published irregularly in English by the National Institute of Oceanology, LIPI, Jakarta.

Oseanologi di Indonesia, a journal on marine sciences publishing articles of interest to both laymen and researchers and preliminary research and survey reports, is issued irregularly in Indonesian or English by the National Institute of Oceanology, LIPI, Jakarta.

Communications of the Forest Research Institute is published irregularly in Indonesian or English by the Forest Research Institute, Bogor.

Communications/Contributions of the General Agricultural Research Station is the aperiodic publication of the General Agricultural Research Station, Bogor.

Contributions of the Inland Fishery Research Station is published irregularly in Indonesian or English by the Inland Fishery Research Station, Bogor.

Berita Biologi, a journal on biology, is published irregularly in Indonesian or English by the Biological Society of Indonesia.

Proceeding Kongres Biologi dan Seminar Biologi is published biannually in Indonesian by the Biological Society of Indonesia.

Rimba Indonesia, a journal of forestry, is published irregularly in Indonesian or English by the Indonesian Society of Foresters, Bogor.

Penggemar Alam, a journal on natural history, was published annually until 1961 in Indonesian or English by the Indonesian Natural History Society. It was the continuation of *Tropische Natuur* (1912–1953).

Tectona, a forestry journal, was published quarterly in Dutch by the Society of Foresters (1900–1954).

Some of the major foreign journals that are routinely consulted include: *Ecology, Ecological Monographs, Journal of Ecology, Journal of Applied Ecology, Journal of Animal Ecology, Tropical Ecology, Oikos, Vegetatio, Environmental Conservation, Biotropica, Malayan Nature Journal,* and *Malaysian Forester.*

ECOLOGY TEACHING AND TRAINING

The teaching of ecology varies from one university to another, hence it is difficult to generalize. I will give an account of ecology teaching in three major universities, Institut Teknologi Bandung (Bandung Institute of Technology), Institut Pertanian Bogor (Bogor Agricultural University), and Gajah Mada University at Yogyakarta. These are three of five major universities that have been designated as model and leading universities.

At the Bandung Institute of Technology, the Department of Biology offers courses in ecology at the undergraduate level. Ecology teaching was initiated in 1949, and until 1959, ecology was offered as a part of biology with emphasis on reciprocal relationships between plants, animals, and their natural environment. The course was aimed primarily at stimulating students to be aware of natural phenomena taking place in their surroundings. During the 1960s, ecology teaching was initially directed toward forest ecology with emphasis on vegetation. During the later part of this period, the scope of ecology teaching was gradually broadened by stressing the role of ecology in applied fields. After 1970, this broadening was fully implemented by the introduction of a course on environmental science. The course, offered for two semesters during the first preparatory year and compulsory for all students of the university, is aimed at providing students with knowledge on the utilization and management of natural resources. For students majoring in biology, courses on ecology (plant and animal), advanced ecology, limnology, and field techniques in biology are also offered. In addition, a special course in ecology is also given in the graduate program in highway engineering. A concept of establishing a graduate program in environment and human settlement, an interdisciplinary program involving biology, ecology, chemistry, sanitary engineering, planning, and architecture, is currently being developed.

At Gajah Mada University, where biological sciences form a separate faculty or college, ecology teaching is not so well developed. In this school, ecology has been taught for many years; currently, only two courses on ecology are offered to biology students, general and advanced ecology, both offered in the fourth year of the undergraduate program. The College of Forestry also offers courses on forest ecology and related subjects.

At Bogor Agricultural University, ecology courses are offered by different faculties (agriculture, fishery, animal husbandry, veterinary medicine, and forestry) in the undergraduate program. These include plant ecology, crop ecology, animal ecology, environmental science, resource mangement, and limnology. At the graduate level, a degree program (M.S. and Ph.D.) in environmental and natural resource management has been initiated; it is an interdepartmental effort supported by other graduate programs. In this program, ecology and ecologically related courses are offered, including general ecology, environment and natural resource management, environmental planning and administration, and resource economics. Fields of specialization include water resources management, quantitative ecology, resource economics, land use, human ecology, conservation, and resource policy and administration. The university also offers training courses to administrators and planners of regional governments.

The Regional Center for Tropical Biology (BIOTROP) of the South East Asian Ministers of Education Organization (SEAMEO) in Bogor, regularly conducts six-week and six-month training courses in special topics concerning tropical forest ecosystems, aquatic ecosystems, and tropical pest biology. The six-week course is an intensive program covering lectures and practical work, whereas the six-month course is geared toward a training to conduct research.

UNESCO's Man and Biosphere program from time to time organizes training in various aspects of ecology, such as techniques of tropical vegetation analysis, environmental resource management, and human ecology, as well as environmental education for primary school teachers. Lectures in ecology or environmental management with special emphasis on the role of ecology in development are usually incorporated also in the curriculum of upgrading courses organized by various government departments.

ACKNOWLEDGMENTS

I wish to extend my gratitude to Prof. Gembong Tjitrosoepomo of Gadjah Mada University, Yogyakarta; Prof. Oetit Koswara of Bogor Agricultural University, Bogor; and Dr. R. E. Soeriatmadja of Bandung Institute of Technology, Bandung, for their kind cooperation in supplying information on ecology teaching in their respective universities.

BIBLIOGRAPHY

The following list includes research papers representing various aspects of ecology, including applied ecology:

Adisoemarto, S. 1974. A comparative study of three faunistic communities of Ujung Kulon Nature Reserve, West Java. *BIOTROP Bull.* 9:1–24. (A quantitative analysis of insect fauna in the grassland, forest edge, and river bank. The author discusses differences in density and daily fluctuation as related to the differences in habitat conditions.)

Anonymous 1974. *Coastal zone pollution in Indonesia with special emphasis on oil, a reconnaissance survey.* Study Group Pencemaran, Lembaga Minyak dan Gas Bumi, Jakarta and Office of International and Environmental Programs, Smithsonian Institution, Washington, D.C. (The result of a pollution survey made in 1972–1973 in Java, Sumatra, and Kalimantan aimed at determining the effects of oil and other activities related to oil industries on marine environment. Other aspects of pollution and a review on oil pollution in the tropics are presented.)

______. 1975. *Proceeding afforestation and reforestation.* Yogyakarta: Fakultas Kehutanan, Universitas Gadjah Mada. (A collection of papers dealing with the problems of afforestation and reforestation after selective logging activities in the lowland rain forests. It covers the silvicultural background and problems of rain forests, regulation and control measure of the Indonesian Selective Cutting System, review and evaluation of the selective cutting practices, results of studies of ecological effects of selective cutting practices, and other supporting topics related to the problems of rehabilitating the logged-over forests.)

______. 1978. Laporan hasil seminar nasional pengembangan lingkungan hidup, June 5–6, 1978, Jakarta. (A collection of papers and recommendations of a national seminar on human environment. The papers deal with the renewable natural resources, regional development and improvement of human environment, management of nonrenewable resources, and human resources in relation to improvement of human environment.)

Doty, M. S., R. E. Soeriatmadja, and A. Soegiarto. 1963. Observations on the primary marine productivity of northwestern Indonesian waters. *Mar. Res. Indon.* 5:1–25. (A study of productivity indicating that the shallow waters investigated are as productive in organic matter as the most productive waters elsewhere. The gaps in productivity study are indicated.)

Hanson, A. J. and Koesoebiono. 1977. *Settling coastal swamplands in Sumatra. A case study for integrated resource management.* PSPSL/Research Report/004.

Center for Natural Resource Management and Environmental Studies, Bogor Agricultural University. (A study on the formulation and implementation of an integrated resource management strategy of marginal coastal swampland transformed into agricultural lands. It reviews key issues likely to result in a pilot project area: concern for long-term stability of agricultural production, stable healthy human settlements, potentially non-sustainable resource uses, and environmental impact in the estuary-delta coastal zone.)

Kartawinata, K. 1974. Report on the state of knowledge on tropical forest ecosystems in Indonesia. Bogor: Herbarium Bogoriense, LBN-LIPI. (Mimeographed). [A brief but comprehensive review of forest ecosystems in Indonesia. Discussion topics include structure and composition of various forest types, dynamics of development, succession, primary productivity, water balance, erosion, nutrient cycling, interaction between man and the forests, pattern of utilization (conservation, logging, shifting cultivation, agriculture, and other conversion to man-made ecosystems), management policy, and the gaps of knowledge.]

Rijksen, H. D. 1978. A field study on Sumatran orangutans (*Pongo pygmaeus abelii* Lesson 1827). Ecology, behaviour and conservation. *Meded. Landbouwhogesch. Wageningen.* No. 78-2. (Results of field research on a relationship between orangutan behavior and rain forest environment. Detailed descriptions of habitat, feeding behavior, size and density of population, behavior in relation to social organization, and the conservation of orangutans and their habitat are presented.)

Ritterbush, S. 1974. *An assessment of the population biology of the Bali Strait lemuru fishery.* Jakarta: Direktorat Jenderal Perikanan and FAO/UNDP Fisheries Development Project for Indonesia. [A study on the growth, recruitment, mortality, fecundity, and feeding behavior of lemuru (*Sardinella longiceps*) to provide basic data for fisheries development on the Strait of Bali.]

Schenkel, R. and L. Schenkel-Hulligers. 1969. The Javan rhinoceros (*Rh. sundaicus* Desm.) in Udjung Kulon Nature Reserve. Its ecology and behaviour. *Acta Trop.* 26:98–135. (A result of a study on ecology and behavior made in 1967 and 1968. This report discusses the problems of field research, general conditions of the reserve as the habitat of rhinoceros, present population, and in more detail, the ecology and behavior of rhinoceros.)

Sobur, A. S., M. J. Chambers, R. Chamber, J. Damopolii, S. Hadi, and A. J. Hanson. 1977. *Remote sensing applications in the southeast Sumatra coastal environment.* PSPSL/Research Report/002. Center for Natural Resource Management and Environmental Studies, Bogor Agricultural University. (A time series analysis of aerial photographs and LANDSAT imageries of landform, vegetation pattern, sediment and erosion sites, land-use dynamics, settlement pattern, and albedo correlated with field data are used to indicate patterns of ecological constraints and resource use dynamics having implications for development of the eastern coastal swampland of Sumatra.)

Sody, H. J. V. 1956. De Javaansche bosvogel. *Indon. J. Nat. Sci.* 112:153–170. (An account of 265 bird species inhabiting forests of Java with notes on their breeding, ecology, distribution, and status. The correlation between bird species zonation and vegetation zonation is indicated.)

Soemodihardjo, S., S. A. Nontji, and A. Djamali, ed. 1979. Prosiding Seminar Ekosistem Hutan Mangrove. Panitia Program MAB Indonesia dan Lembaga Oseanologi Nasional, LIPI, Jakarta. (A collection of papers ranging from results of original research to reviews on biology, ecology, social aspects, utilization, management, and conservation of mangrove ecosystem in Indonesia, presented in a seminar.)

Soerianegara, I. 1965. The primary productivity of selected forests in Indonesia. *Rimba Indon.* 10:246–256. (A quantitative analysis of the stem biomass and productivity of selected lowland rain forest, montane forest, and *Agathis* forest. Stem biomass and productivity are estimated from standing volume, specific gravity, and growth increment. Relationships between stem biomass and productivity and habitat factors are indicated.)

______. 1970. The status of range research and management in Indonesia. *Rimba Indon.* 15:99–115. [Summary of results of various surveys and research on range ecology (distribution of rangeland, botanical explorations and surveys, nutritive values, carrying capacity, and production). Over 300 species of fodder plants and their nutritive composition are listed.]

Soerjani, M. 1970. Alang-lang, *Imperata cylindrica* (L.) Beauv. (1812). Pattern of growth as related to its problem of control. *BIOTROP Bull.* 1:1–88. (Field and laboratory experiments on physiology and ecology with special emphasis on growth. The studies include field surveys in different habitats to determine the yield of organic matter, effects of shading, slashing and water supply, relationship with other plant species and parasites, factors affecting the resprout of rhizomes, and herbicide effects on growth.)

Steenis, C. G. G. J. van. 1957. Outline of vegetation types in Indonesia and some adjacent regions. *Proc. 8th Pac. Sci. Congr.* 4:61–97. (A brief description of climax vegetation and its classification system based on climatic, edaphic, topographic, and altitudinal characteristics. Characteristic taxa within each vegetation type are indicated.)

______. 1958. Tropical lowland vegetation: the characteristics of its types and their relation to climate. *Proc. 9th Pac. Sci. Congr.* 20:25–37. (A discussion of the climatic types and classification and climate as the most important factor affecting the distribution and characteristics of vegetation. The concept of phytoclimate and the natural system of tropical lowland climaxes, based on climatic, structural, edaphic, and topographic characteristics, are discussed.)

______. 1965. Concise plant geography of Java. In *Flora of Java,* Vol. 2, eds. C. A. Backer and R. C. Bakhuizen Van Den Brink, Jr., pp. 1–72. [A phytogeographic analysis of the flora of Java, which includes a brief description of vegetation types (map included) and discussion on altitudinal zonation of flora and flora in relation to climate. Lists of indicator species for everwet and drought climates supplemented with altitudinal range and geographic occurrences are presented.]

______. 1972. *The mountain flora of Java.* Leiden. [A book primarily devoted to the ecology of species and communities in the mountain environment. The account is very detailed and covers the environmental factors (volcanism, climate, fire, and man), altitudinal zonation, plant formations, succession, flower biology, dispersal, phytogeography, and conservation.]

Terra, G. J. A. 1952. Some ecological requirements of Indonesian fruit trees. *Land-*

bouw 24:193–222. [An analysis of distribution of fruit tree species on Java in relation to climate, altitude, and soil properties; various centers are identified. The important factors (soil water availability in relation to length of drought, oxygen in the soil, length of dry season, and altitude) affecting the growth and the ecological requirements of various species are discussed.]

Team Survei Ekologi IPB 1975. Laporan akhir survei ekologi Delta Upang-Banyuasin. 2 Vols. Departemen PUTL dan Institute Pertanian, Bogor. (Mimeographed.) (An ecological analysis of the mangrove, peat swamp forest, and freshwater swamp forest that includes aspects of vegetation, soil, hydrology, aquatic biology, climate, geomorphology, animal husbandry, plant pests and diseases, and socioeconomics. The study is aimed at providing basic ecological data that can be used in defining the policy and management strategy of the area.)

Vaas, K. F., M. Sachlan, and G. Wiraatmadja. 1953. On the ecology of some inland waters along the rivers Ogan and Komering in southeast Sumatra. *Comm. Inl. Fish. Res. Sta.*, Bogor 3:1–31. (A result of studies on ecological conditions in nine sites along the rivers Ogan and Komering, which include the hydrochemical, plankton, and fishery aspects. A list of fish species grouped on the basis of feeding habits is presented.)

Yamada, I. 1975. Forest ecological studies of the montane forest of Mt. Pangrango, West Java. *Southeast Asian Stud.* 13:402–426. (A detailed quantitative analysis of floristic composition of forest, ground cover, epiphytes, and woody climbers and forest canopy stratification.)

———. 1976*a*. Forest ecological studies of the montane forest of Mt. Pangrango, West Java. II. Stratification and floristic composition of the forest vegetation of the higher part of Mt. Pangrango. *Southeast Asian Stud.* 13:513–534. (A phytosociological study of the upper montane rain forest and altitudinal distribution of species.)

———. 1976*b*. Forest ecological studies of the montane forest of Mt. Pangrango, West Java. III. Litterfall of the tropical montane forest near Cibodas. *Southeast Asian Stud.* 14:194–229. (A study on litterfall of various life forms and their components, and annual fluctuations, as well as notes on phenology of some trees, shrubs, herbs, climbers, and epiphytes.)

———. 1977. Forest ecological studies of the montane forest of Mt. Pangrango, West Java. IV. Floristic composition along the altitude. *Southeast Asian Stud.* 15:226–254. (A description of floristic composition of rain forest at different altitudes, and distribution and important species along the altitudinal gradients.)

REFERENCES CITED

Abdulhadi, R., K. Kartawinata, and S. Sukardjo. 1980. Effects of mechanized logging in lowland dipterocarp forest at Lempake, East Kalimantan. Paper presented at the International Working Group on Dipterocarpaceae Second Round Table Conference, Kuala Lumpur, Malaysia, June 27–July 3, 1980.

Abdulkadir, S. and S. Brotonegoro. 1980. Produksi dan penguraian serasah dalam hutan primer dan sekunder di Wanariset, Kalimantan Timur. In *Peningkatan penelitian dan pengembangan prasarana penelitian biologi.* ed. A. Budiman and K. Kartawinata, pp. 159–163. Bogor: Lembaga Biologi Nasional, LIPI. Laporan Teknik 1979–1980.

Adisoemarto, S. 1974. A comparative study of three faunistic communities of Ujung Kulon Nature Reserve, West Java. *BIOTROP Bull.* 9:1–24.

Anonymous. 1974. Coastal zone pollution in Indonesia with special emphasis on oil, a reconnaissance survey. Study Group Pencemaran, Lembaga Minyak dan Gas Bumi, Jakarta and Office of International and Environmental Programs, Smithsonian Institution, Washington, D.C.

Anonymous. 1975. Proceeding afforestation and reforestation. Yogyakarta: Fakultas Kehutanan, Universitas Gadjah Mada.

Anonymous. 1978. Laporan hasil seminar nasional pengembangan lingkungan hidup, June 5–6, 1978, Jakarta.

Backer, C. A. 1929. *The Problems of Krakatau as seen by a botanist.* The Hague.

Bakker, A. J. and C. L. van Wijk. 1951. Infiltration and runoff under various conditions on Java. *O.S.R. News* 3(9):56–69.

Becking, J. H., L. G. Den Berger, and H. W. Meindersma. 1922. Vloed of mangroveboschen in Nederlands Indie. *Tectona* 15:561–611.

BIOTROP Training Course Participants. 1972. A quantitative vegetational study of a tropical rainforest on the Peucang Islands, S.W. Java. *BIOTROP/Tr.F*/041.

Borner M. 1976. Sumatran orangutans. *Oryx* 13:290–293.

Borssum Waalkes, J. van. 1960. Botanical observations in the Krakatau Islands in 1951 and 1952. *Ann. Bogor* 4:5–64.

Budiman, A. and K. Kartawinata, eds. 1979. Peningkatan penelitian dan pengembangan prasarana penelitian biologi. Bogor: Lembaga Biologi Nasional, LIPI. Laporan Teknik 1978–1979.

———, eds. 1980. *Peningkatan penelitian dan pengembangan prasarana penelitian biologi.* Bogor: Lembaga Biologi Nasional, LIPI. Laporan Teknik 1979–1980.

Dilmy, A. 1967. Pioneer plants found one year after the eruption of Agung in Bali. *Pac. Sci.* 19:498–501.

——— and A. J. G. Kostermans. 1958. Research on the vegetation in Indonesia. *Proceedings of Kandy Symposium: Study of Tropical Vegetation.* pp. 28–31.

Docters van Leeuwen, W. J. M. 1933. Biology of plants and animals occurring in the higher parts of Mt. Pangrango-Gedeh in West Java. *Verhand. Akad. Wetensch. Amsterdam,* Sect. 2, 31:1–270.

———. 1936. Krakatau, 1883 to 1933. A. Botany. *Ann. Jard. Bot. Buitenzorg* 46–47:1–506.

Doty, M. S., R. E. Soeriatmadja, and A. Soegiarto. 1963. Observations on the primary marine productivity of northwestern Indonesian waters. *Mar. Res. Indones.* 5:1–25.

Ernst, A. 1934. Das biologische Krakatau Problem. *Vjschr. Naturf. Ges.,* Zurich 79: 1–187.

Haan, J. H. De. 1931. Het een en ander over Tjilatjapsche vloedboschen. *Tectona* 24:36–76.

Hanson, A. J. and Koesoebiono. 1977. *Settling coastal swamplands in Sumatra. A case study for integrated resource management.* PSPSL/Research Report/004. Center for Natural Resource Management and Environmental Studies, Bogor Agricultural University.

Hardenberg, J. D. F. 1948. The seas of the Indies, their research and their problems. *Chron. Nat.* 104:337–334.

Hardjamulia, A. and S. Kusumadinata. 1974. Preliminary experiments on the effects of thiodan and endrin in fish culture in Indonesia. *Proc. Indo-Pac. Fish. Counc. Sec.* 15, Sect. 3:56–65.

Honig, P. and F. Verdoorn. 1945. *Science and scientists in the Netherlands Indies.* New York: Board for the Netherlands Indies, Surinam and Curacao.

Hoogerwerf, A. 1970. *Udjung Kulon. The land of the last Javan Rhinoceros.* Leiden: E. J. Brill.

Kartawinata, K. 1974. Report on the state of knowledge on tropical forest ecosystems in Indonesia. Bogor: Herbarium Borgoriense, LBN-LIPI. (Mimeographed.)

Kartawinata, K. 1976. Penelaahan dasar-dasar penyusuran pedoman untuk menentukan jenis, jumlah, luas, lokasi serta prioritas penyelenggaraan wilayah suaka alam di darat. In *Lokakarya Perlindungan dan Pengawetan Alam,* eds. S. Adisoemarto and K. Kartawinata, pp. 1–12.

———. 1977*a*. Structure and composition of forests in some nature reserves in West Java, Indonesia. In *Papers presented at the 13th Pacific Congress, Vancouver, Canada, 1975,* pp. 59–68. Jakarta: Lembaga Ilmu Pengetahuan Indonesia.

———. 1977*b*. Ecological zones of Indonesia. *Papers presented at the 13th Pacific Congress, Vancouver, Canada,* 1975, pp. 51–58. Jakarta: Lembaga Ilmu Pengetahuan Indonesia.

———. 1978*a*. Fitososiologi belukar muda di Lempake, Kalimantan Timur. In *Peningkatan penelitian dan pengembangan prasarana penelitian biologi,* eds. A. Budiman and K. Kartawinata, pp. 153–155. Bogor: Lembaga Biologi Nasional, LIPI, Laporan Teknik 1977–1978.

———. 1978*b*. The kerangas (heath) forest in Indonesia. In *Glimpses of ecology,* eds. J. S. Singh and Gopal, pp. 145–153. Jaipur: International Scientific Publications.

———. 1979. An overview of the environmental consequences of the removal from the forest in Indonesia. In *Biological and sociological basis for a rational use of forest resources for energy and organics,* ed. S. G. Boyce pp. 129–140. Proceedings of International Workshop for the Man and the Biosphere Program, May 1979, Michigan State University, East Lansing. Ashville, N. C.: U.S. Department of Agriculture, Forest Service, Southeastern Forest Experimental Station.

———. 1980. A note on a kerangas (heath) forest at Sebulu, East Kalimantan. *Reinwardtia* 9:429–447.

———. In press. The classification and utilization of forests in Indonesia. *BioIndonesia.*

———, R. Abdulhadi, and T. Partomihardjo. 1980. A lowland forest stand at Wanariset, East Kalimantan. Paper presented at the International Working Group on Dipterocarpaceae Second Round Table Conference, June 27–July 3, 1980, Kuala Lumpur, Malaysia.

———, S. Adisoemarto, S. Riswan, and A. P. Vayda. In Press. The human impact on the lowland dipterocarp forest in East Kalimantan. *Ambio.*

———, S. Riswan, and S. Soedjito. 1979. The floristic changes after disturbances in lowland dipterocarp forest in East Kalimantan, Indonesia. Paper presented at V

International Symposium of Tropical Ecology, Kuala Lumpur, Malaysia, April 16–21, 1979.

——— and E. B. Walujo. 1977. A preliminary study of the mangrove forest on Pulau Rambut, Jakarta Bay. *Mar. Res. Indones.* 18:119–129.

———, A. P. Vayda, and R. S. Wirakusumah. 1977. East Kalimantan and the Man and Biosphere Program. *Berita Ilmu Pengetahuan dan Teknologi* 21:16–26.

Koeman, J. H., J. H. Pennings, R. Rosanto, and others. 1974. Metals and chlorinated hydrocarbon pesticides in samples of fish, sawah-duck eggs, crustaceans, and molluscs collected in west and central Java. *Publ. Ecol. Devel.* 2:1–14.

Krajina, V. J. 1965. Biogeoclimatic zones and classification of British Columbia. *Ecol. West N. Am.* 1:1–17.

———. 1973. Biogeoclimatic zonation as a basis for regional ecosystems. *Symposium on Planned Utilization of Lowland Tropical Forests, Cipayung, Bogor.* Pre-Congress Conference in Indonesia, Pacific Science Association, pp. 18–32.

MacKinnon, J. R. 1973. Orangutans in Sumatra. *Oryx* 12:234–242.

———. 1977. Rehabilitation and orangutan conservation. *New Sci.* 74:697–699.

McClure, H. E. 1974. *Migration and survival of the birds of Asia.* Bangkok: U.S. Army Medical Components, South East Asia Treaty Organization Medical Project.

Meijer, W. 1959. Plant sociological analysis of the montane rain forest near Tjibodas. West Java. *Acta Bot. Neerl.* 8:277–291.

Moersaid, K. and R. Soediarto. 1960. Silvicultural aspects of the tropical rainforest in Indonesia. *Proceedings of the Symposium on Humid Tropics Vegetation, Tjiawa, Indonesia,* pp. 285–294. UNESCO.

Polak, B. 1950. Occurrence and fertility of tropical peat soils in Indonesia. *Contr. Gen. Agric. Res. Sta.* No. 104.

———. 1952. Veenmos en veenbos. *Penggemar Alam* 32:69–77.

Rahayuningsih, Y. 1979. Perbandingan keanekaragaman populasi serangga di hutan primer, hutan sekunder dan ladang di Lempake, Kalimantan Timur. In *Peningkatan penelitian dan pengembangan prasarana penelitian biologi,* eds. A. Budiman and K. Kartawinata, pp. 225–230. Bogor: Lembaga Biologi Nasional, LIPI. Laporan Teknik 1978–1979.

———, W. Anggraitoningsih, and A. Adisoemarto. 1979. Perubahan susunan serangga ladang di Kalimantan Timur. Paper presented at Kongres Entomologi I, Jakarta, January 9–11, 1979.

Rijksen, H. D. 1978. A field study on Sumatran orangutans (*Pongo pygmaeus abelii* Lesson 1827). Ecology, behaviour and conservation. *Meded. Landbouwhogesch. Wageningen* No. 78-2.

Riswan, S. 1979*a*. Natural regeneration in lowland dipterocarp forest in East Kalimantan, Indonesia, with special reference to kerangas forest. Paper presented at the Symposium on Forest Regeneration in South East Asia, BIOTROP, Bogor, June 19–21, 1979.

———. 1979*b*. Nitrogen content of top soil in lowland tropical forest in East Kalimantan, Indonesia, before and after clear-cutting and burning. Paper presented at the UNU Workshop on Nitrogen Cycling in South Asian Wet Monsoonal Ecosystems, Chiang Mai, Thailand, November 5–10, 1980.

———. 1979*c*. Hutan kerangas di Samboja, Kalimantan Timur. In *Peningkatan penelitian dan pengembangen prasarana penelitian biologi,* eds. A. Budiman and K. Kartawinata, pp. 218–223. Bogor: Lembaga Biologi Nasional, LIPI. Laporan Teknik 1978–1979.

———. 1980. Hutan kerangas sekunder di Samboja, Kalimantan Timur. In *Peningkatan penelitian dan pengembangan prasarana penelitian biologi,* eds. A. Budiman and K. Kartawinata, pp. 164–167. Bogor: Lembaga Biologi Nasional, LIPI. Laporan Teknik 1979–1980.

——— and D. Hadrijanto. 1979. Lowland dipterocarp forest 30 years after pepper plantation in East Kalimantan, Indonesia. Paper presented at V International Symposium of Tropical Ecology, Kuala Lumpur, Malaysia, April 16–21, 1979.

Ritterbush, S. 1974. *An assessment of the population biology of the Bali Strait lemuru fishery.* Jakarta: Direktorat Jenderal Perikanan and FAO/UNDP Fisheries Development Project for Indonesia.

Schenkel, R. and L. Schenkel-Hulligers. 1969. The Javan rhinoceros (*Rh. sundaicus* Desm.) in Udjung Kulon Nature Reserve. Its ecology and behaviour. *Acta Trop.* 26:98–135.

Schmidt, F. H. and J. H. A. Ferguson. 1951. *Rainfall types based on wet and dry period ratios for Indonesia with Western New Guinea.* Djawatan Meteorologi dan Geofisika, Verhandelingen No. 42.

Sobur, A. S., M. J. Chambers, R. Chamber, J. Damopolii, S. Hadi, and A. J. Hanson. 1977. *Remote sensing applications in the southeast Sumatra coastal environment.* PSPSL/Research Report/002. Center for Natural Resource Management and Environmental Studies, Bogor Agricultural University.

Sody, H. J. V. 1953. Vogels van het Javanse djatibos. Met overwegingen over nut en schade voor dit bos. *Indones. J. Nat. Sci.* 109:125–172.

———. 1955. Enkele opmerkingen over vogelcultuuren op Java in het algemeen en over vogelplanten in het bijzonder. *Indones. J. Nat. Sci.* 111:178–196.

———. 1956. De Janaansche bosvogel. *Indones. J. Nat. Sci.* 112:153–170.

Soegiarto, A., S. Adisoemarto, S. Birowo, and K. Romimohtarto, eds. 1977. *Mar. Res. Indones.* Nos. 17, 18 and 19.

———, S. Soemodihardjo, and K. Soegiarto. 1975. *Bibliografi beranotasi: I. Sumber daya hayati; II. Udang.* Jakarta: Lembaga Oseanologi Nasional.

Soerianegara, I. 1965. The primary productivity of selected forests in Indonesia. *Rimba Indon.* 10:246–256.

———. 1966. Soils of Peucang Island, southwest Java. *Geoderma* 2:297–308.

———. 1970. Soils investigation on Mount Hondje Forest Reserve, West Java, Indonesia. *Rimba Indones.* 15:1–16.

———. 1971. Characterization and classification of mangrove soils of Java. *Rimba Indones.* 15:141–150.

———. 1973. The use of Paterson's CPV Index in characterizing forest vegetation. *Symposium of Planned Utilization of Lowland Tropical Forests, Tjipajung.* Pre-Congress Conference in Indonesia, Pacific Science Association, pp. 48–65.

———. 1974. Ecological researches relevant to current silvicultural problems. In *Coordinated Studies of Lowland Forest of Indonesia,* eds. K. Kartawinata and R. Atmawidjaja, pp. 151–160. Bogor: BIOTROP and IPB.

Soerjani, M. 1970. Alang-lang, *Imperata cylindrica* (L.) Beauv. (1812). Pattern of growth as related to its problem of control. *BIOTROP Bull.* 1:1–88.

———, ed. 1971. Tropical weeds: some problems, biology and control. *BIOTROP Bull.* 2:1–215.

———, D. E. Barnes, and T. O. Robson, eds. 1977. *Proceedings of the South East Asian-Pacific Weed Science Society Conference,* Jakarta, July 11–17, 1977. Vol. 1.

Steenis, C. G. G. J. van. 1935. Maleische vegetatieschetsen. *Tijdschr. Ned. Aardrk. Genoots.* 52:25–67, 171–203, 363–398.

———. 1938. Plantengeografie. In *Atlas van Tropisch Nederlands.* Amsterdam.

———. 1957. Outline of vegetation types in Indonesia and some adjacent regions. *Proc. 8th Pac. Sci. Congr.* 4:61–97.

———. 1958*a*. *The vegetation map of Malaysia.* UNESCO.

———. 1958*b*. Basic principles of lowlands forest sociology. *Proceedings of Kandy Symposium: study of tropical vegetation,* pp. 159–165. UNESCO.

———. 1958*c*. Tropical lowland vegetation: the characteristics of its types and their relation to climate. *Proc. 9th Pac. Sci. Congr.* 20:25–37.

———. ed. Ding Hou. 1958*d*. Ecology. In *Rhizophoraceae, Flora Malesiana* I, 5:431–441.

———. 1965. Concise plant geography of Java. In *Flora of Java,* Vol. 2, eds. C. A. Backer and R. C. Bakhuizen Van Den Brink, Jr., pp. 1–72. Groningen: P. Noordhaff.

———. 1972. *The mountain flora of Java.* Leiden: E. J. Brill.

Sukardjo, S. and K. Kartawinata. 1979. Mangrove forest of Banyuasin, Musi River estuary, South Sumatra. *BIOTROP Spec. Publ.* 10:62–83.

Surjono, R. 1964. Hutan *Pinus merkusii* ditinjau dari segi pengawetan tanah dan air. *Rimba Indones.* 9:311–318.

Team Institut Pertanian Bogor. 1975. Laporan survey dan pemetaan tanah daerah pasang surut Musi-Banyuasin. Departemen PUTL dan Institut Pertanian Bogor.

Team Survei Ekologi IPB 1975. Laporan akhir survei ekologi Delta Upang-Banyuasin. Departemen PUTL dan Institut Pertanian Bogor.

Terra, G. J. A. 1952. Some ecological requirements of Indonesian fruit trees. *Landbouw* 24:193–222.

Toxopeus, J. L. 1950. Over de pioneer fauna van Anak Krakatau, met eenige beschowing over het ontstaan van de Krakatau fauna. *Chron. Nat.* 106:27–34.

Treub, M. 1888. Notice sur la Bouvele flora de Krakatau. *Ann. J. Bot. Buitenzorg* 7:213–223.

Vaas, K. F., M. Sachlan, and G. Wiraatmadja. 1953. On the ecology of some inland waters along the rivers Ogan and Komering in southeast Sumatra. *Comm. Inl. Fish. Res. Sta.,* Bogor 3:1–31.

Vayda, A. P., C. J. Pierce Colfer, and M. Brotokusumo. In press. Interaction between people and forests in east Kalimantan. *Impact of Science and Society.*

Walandouw, P. H. 1952. Grassland in Indonesia. *J. Sci. Res.* 1:201–212.

Wilson, C. C. and W. L. Wilson. 1975. The influence of selective logging on primates in E. Kalimantan. *Folia Primatol.* 23:245–274.

Yamada, I. 1975. Forest ecological studies of the montane forest of Mt. Pangrango, West Java. *Southeast Asian Stud.* 13:402–426.

———. 1976*a*. Forest ecological studies of the montane forest of Mt. Pangrango,

West Java. II. Stratification and floristic composition of the forest vegetation of the higher part of Mt. Pangrango. *Southeast Asian Stud.* 13:513–534.

———. 1976*b*. Forest ecological studies of the montane forest of Mt. Pangrango, West Java. III. Litterfall of the tropical montane forest near Cibodas. *Southeast Asian Stud.* 14:194–229.

———. 1977. Forest ecological studies of the montane forest of Mt. Pangrango, West Java. IV. Floristic composition along the altitude. *Southeast Asian Stud.* 15:226–254.

29

Israel

Lawrence B. Slobodkin and Yossef Loya

HISTORICAL BACKGROUND

Modern ecology has an obvious genesis in the fusion of the taxonomic and biogeographic fields that started in the seventeenth and eighteenth centuries, the evolutionary theories that began in the nineteenth century, and the genetic and mechanistic biology of the early twentieth century. Since approximately 1925, ecology has existed as a recognizable subdiscipline of biology, comparable to physiology, genetics, and behavior. Ecologists, physiologists, and geneticists are well advised to use each other's information in their own work but to have distinct attitudes, problems, and theories. We are discussing a usual kind of history of a discipline.

Ecology in modern Israel compares well with ecology in Europe, Japan, and America. Israeli ecology is as much of a busy modern discipline as ecology is anywhere. It shares with other small countries limits on professional opportunities. The world looks different viewed from the hills of Jerusalem, the site of the Hebrew University, than from the plains of Tel Aviv, the site of the younger university. As in most small countries, a major aid to personal advancement is international reputation. Israeli academicians, therefore, usually make strong efforts to publish in non-Israeli (typically English-language) journals and symposia, and particularly some of the younger professors have attained well-deserved international reputations. The Second International Congress of Ecology was held in Jerusalem in 1978 with heavy local participation, demonstrating the high state of Israeli ecological research.

So far we might have been describing almost any small but "developed" country. There is, however, a curious and very interesting early history of Israeli ecology. This has not been discussed or considered by the general community of ecologists or historians of science nor by historians of Judaism and Zionism. The presentation of a complete study in this area is within the professional province of historians and not that of ecologists, so that all we will attempt here is to give something of what we have reconstructed of the flavor and background of early Israeli ecology in the hope that more qualified persons will take it from there.

We believe that even a brief discussion of the contrast between the role of ecology in Israel and its role in most other states may clarify the curious relation between ecological, political, and philosophical thought, which we believe exists in every country but is seen most clearly in the Israeli context.

In this abbreviated history, which is formally similar to that of almost any discipline, we tacitly assumed a long prehistory during which nationalism, empiricism, secularism, and a tradition of observational natural history had emerged. Certainly we should have gone back to at least the thirteenth century in England when leaves were carved on the pillars of Southwell Cathedral to see the beginnings of this prehistory, and we would have had to quote John Ray's seventeenth-century introduction to the *Botany of Cambridge* in which he extolls the virtues of *English* plants.

During these hundreds of years of the prehistory of ecology, people in what is now Israel (but which was then part of the province of Syria in the Turkish Empire) and the mass of the Jewish people (then located in Eastern Europe as well as the Middle East) were unaware of the intellectual ferment of the West.

According to Professor Mendelssohn, Director of the experimental zoo of Tel Aviv University and recipient of the Israeli distinguished achievement award, after the Second World War it was still believed that when the hyenas of Israel met strangers, they would place their forepaws on their chests and entrance them by urinating on them. In the trance the victims would follow the hyenas to their lairs with a peculiar gait which is imitated in the folk dance called the Debka. In their lairs the hyenas would suck out their victims' brains. Captured hyenas were blinded with hot irons in such a way as to leave the pupils enlarged and expose the green optic tapetum. The animals were then taken from fair to fair and market to market where, for a price, people could strike the animals with sticks to express their distaste for the unseemly behavior of hyenas. That was thirty years ago. Hyenas in Israel are now protected by stiff conservation laws and are objects of scientific research. This presents one dimension of the transition in the Israeli attitude toward nature.

Of course the Debka dance and the tale of the hyena were part of Arab folklore, but in 1969 Jewish Israeli children were terrified of touching the common harmless chameleon because when it is picked up it opens its mouth and makes a croaking hiss that they were told was a curse of great power.

But we know that some people in America still believe that toads cause warts, and that snakes don't die until sundown even if they are decapitated in the morning.

Further evidence of the development of the Israeli attitude toward nature is the strong indoctrination in wildlife protection that now occurs in kindergartens and elementary schools. Twenty years ago it was usual for children to gather large bunches of wild anemones every spring. Now that these children are parents, their children protest violently if they attempt to pick flowers. The young children of Israel now consider wild flowers as something to enjoy in the fields and reject any attempt to bring them home in bouquets.

There is a deeper and more interesting peculiarity in the early history of Israeli ecology. During the period of approximately five hundred years that it took to go from the herbal to the ecological research on the sand dunes near Chicago, there was the development of what is considered modernity in Europe, and ecological research went hand in hand with this modernity. In order to appreciate the interesting and curious properties of the history of Israeli ecology, it must be understood that except for Western Europe and Germany, most of the Jewish population of the world did not join this transition to the modern until the middle of the nineteenth century. In particular, the Jewish population of what is now Israel, while perhaps actually engaged in agriculture or agriculture-related pursuits, was not intellectually concerned with natural history or scientific studies of nature in any modern sense. Of course, the same kind of comments could be made for any agricultural community of the eighteenth and nineteenth centuries. The peasants of Poland, even though engaged in agricultural pursuit, were not concerned with the intellectual study of nature nor any particularly intellectual enterprise. There is, however, a critical and most curious difference. The Jewish population of the Mideast and Eastern Europe was literate and did have profound intellectual concerns. They were deeply concerned with the legalistic, moralistic, and philosophical issues of the Bible, Talmud, commentaries, responsa, etc. That is, in one sense the mass of the Jewish population of the eighteenth and nineteenth centuries was in the intellectual situation of the literate elite of Western Europe in the twelfth and thirteenth centuries, for whom the concern of the proper intellectual was to elucidate the full meaning of received texts. The surrounding natural and physical world was at best an accident, a nuisance, or a way to make a living. This background is critical in understanding the role that ecology played in the development of Israel.

The process of modernization of the Jews of the Mideast and Eastern Europe in the nineteenth and even twentieth centuries was a breaking out of a basically scholastic mind set. This involved a deep revolution within the Jewish community in attitudes toward nature, art, philosophy, religion, and values. For a young Jewish boy of Poland in the nineteenth century to collect rocks or beetles (as Darwin did) or to keep a pet snake or even to touch a dog was a major breach of normal behavioral standard. In the twentieth century, students in classical Jewish schools smuggled in the books of Darwin and texts on chemistry and geology and hid them inside of Talmud volumes to read them secretly.

The concern with nature and the rise of the Zionist movement itself were two aspects of the same revolution aimed, in a sense, at normalizing the structure of the Jewish people. Other aspects of this revolution included the development of the uniquely Jewish socialist movements.

The relation of the nineteenth-century Zionists to Israel was that with an idealized land preserved in literature, both sacred and secular. The relation of the Eastern European and Middle Eastern Jews to their own native landscape in Russia, Poland, or wherever was that of people who were there temporarily waiting to return to the landscape that they were *really* concerned with. The fact that prayers for rain have been said in synagogues for 2,000 years during the season when rain is appropriate for Israeli agriculture and not during the season when rain is locally appropriate is of particular interest here. This set a curious background to how Israeli landscape was going to be examined.

With the development of Jewish settlement, the non-idyllic realities of Israeli landscape impressed themselves most strongly. The country was not particularly hospitable, alternating from regions of excessive malarial wetness to excessive sterile aridity. There was a rapid development of the idea that land is something you construct by your own efforts, not a natural paradise. The rich landscape is a developed, settled, and controlled landscape. This is quite different from what was the American situation: the existence of millions of wild passenger pigeons, buffalo, turkeys, antelope, and so forth. The Hebrew word Pardes (whence the English Paradise) is a reference to an orchard, not a forest. The idea that a livable world is to be constructed by hard work rather than by being attuned to nature and accepting her bounty may have been reinforced by the Israeli landscape, but it was derived from Zionist theory, particularly as enunciated by Gordon and, in large part, from the same Russian revolutionary sources that inspired Tolstoy.

It should be understood we are discussing very recent history. Dr. Salo Jonas, father-in-law of the senior author, has described students from Eastern Galicia standing for their examinations in chemistry at the University of Halle in the 1920s and reciting the facts of chemistry in the chant of the Talmudist, to the great horror of the German professors. The chemistry was correct but the style was different. The senior author's grandmother was one of the founders of a Polish Jewish Socialist party but her father functioned as an exorcist. Both of the authors of this essay are the first members of their families ever to attend a Western-style college.

Among the Jews of Eastern Europe, concern with nature was seen as a revolutionary act equal in kind to the revolutionary concern with socialism and nationalistic reconstruction, and therefore deliberate analysis was made of how best a concern with nature might fit into revolutionary goals. It should be noted that while revolution was in the air of Europe, in the sense indicated above, the term revolution as used here has a more profound meaning than that of non-Jewish revolutionaries who could be more concerned with the merely political aspects of revolution.

There was no unanimity within the Jewish revolutionary movements on the shape revolution should take. For example, a Jewish revolutionary had to decide whether he was concerned with world revolution (e.g., Trotsky) or with local revolution (in, say, Poland or Germany or Russia), or whether his concern was with Jewish revolution. If a Jewish revolutionary was concerned with Jewish revolution—that is, if he opposed the notion of Jewish assimilation and insisted on the nationhood of Jews—was he concerned with that nationhood as a minority nation in Europe (i.e., Der Bund) or with Zionism (Blau-Weiss or Hashomer-Hatzair)?

Historical events in the twentieth century have promoted Zionism and the development of the Jewish National Homeland. It wasn't at all necessarily obvious to the mass of the Jewish people in the nineteenth or early twentieth century that this was the path that history should follow.

The idea of revolution as a normal activity may in itself seem surprising, particularly to the Americans and English, and may therefore require some explanation. With some exceptions the relation between the various governments of Europe and the Middle East and their Jewish populations was a warm mutual contempt during most of the last three hundred years. The rights of a citizen in many of these countries were limited at best and even these tenuous rights were (and in some cases still are) withheld from native Jewish populations. A Jew could therefore choose to endure patiently this situation or try to break out of it. Breaking out involved much more than social mobility as a consequence of industry and talent à la Horatio Alger heroes. From the standpoint of the local governments, there was often a set of laws designed to prevent the intrusion of Jews into the general population. Within the Jewish community there were institutionalized sanctions that restricted the type of education and behavior that was permitted. A concern with Zionism or with secular use of the Hebrew language often was seen as a violation of religious tenets by the "leaders" of the Jewish community. A concern with secular science not only disturbed local Jewish leaders but often was seen by the outside community as an intrusion by Jews into non-Jewish affairs. One of the biological pioneers in Israel told us that in Berlin in 1929 he wanted to study Invertebrate Zoology with a Professor Marcus and was told flatly that for him the proper study was Talmud not Zoology. Marcus was himself a kind of revolutionary in the sense that he had renounced Judaism in order to gain a university post—although the rise of the Nazis made it impossible for him to obtain a chair in Berlin, and he eventually became a Brazilian.

It was possible either to adapt to local circumstances or to attempt deliberate violation of the sanctions imposed by either the secular government, the Jewish community itself, or often by both simultaneously. This path contained real danger and required young persons to consider the nature of society and their individual and national role. It is out of this background that revolutionary activity became a kind of a norm. It was almost always the case that the early ecologists of Israel were therefore revolutionaries in the sense that they were Zionists, naturalists, and Hebraists. They often found themselves in simultaneous conflict with their own families, the "leader" of the Jewish community, their governments in Europe, or the Turkish or British rule in Israel. Even within the Zionist movement, the Tolstoyan philosophy of Gordon and other Zionist theorists, combined with the harsh realities faced by the early settlements, made any non-exploitative intellectual concern with nature suspect. It is in this setting that Israeli ecology was founded.

Therefore if a young Jew prior to 1930 decided to concern himself with the ecology of Israel, he had to have made a whole set of ancillary decisions. Was his biology to serve his professional advancement as a liberated citizen of Europe or America, or was biology to serve the agricultural or medical needs of humanity in general, or would his part in biology serve first the needs of the Jewish people? Would he be concerned with the biology of the place where he was or the place where the nation was to be rebuilt? Israeli ecology was founded by that last small category and can be identified with a very small number of names. The origins and history of ecology within Israel can be localized in a unique way.

The people who founded Israeli ecology (Bodenheimer, Aaroni, Margolin, Mendelssohn, Even-Ari) were those who had talent as biologists and had the good fortune to find in Israel a way of making a living which permitted them to develop that talent. This was a significant problem considering that there was only one university in the early days of the Jewish settlement.

Even if choices were made and a path to an education in biology was found, the wrong organisms and landscape were being studied if one were studying in Russia or Germany or Poland rather than in Israel.

We are speaking of people who literally or psychologically had fought their way through the problems of European politics and philosophy and had found, at least on a personal level, a kind of solution to what used to be called "the Jewish problem." Victoriously entering what Herzl called Alt-New-Land, these people were then confronted with the anonymity of the local flora and fauna. The first urgent problem for the new Israeli naturalists was to discover the names of organisms.

The spirit with which this was undertaken was beautifully expressed by Professor A. Barash, who in the 1920s recalled his arrival in Israel in a 1978 conversation. Translated and slightly paraphrased, he said:

> I used to envy deeply the Russian poets who could go out at night and look at the stars and know their names. In those days the Hebrew poets knew that there were birds and

all birds sang "cheep cheep"—because there was only one kind of bird. Patriotism and national desire turned to nature in those days. My motivation and desire in knowing nature was that there should be a homeland. With what enthusiasm I, a botanist, could announce this is *Capsella bursa-pastoris!* I sang the words! For me it was a wonder. Here was I, the Jew who *knew* such a thing! I know that tree and that one and that one. There were kinds of trees! An oak, acacia, a date palm. Suddenly the delight of "I know this thing" burst on the images of the poets of Israel!

The early ecologists of Israel (particularly Margolin, or "Uncle Joshua," as he was called by pupils) felt that there could be no normal people, no poetry, and therefore no homeland until the local flora and fauna of Israel had been woven into the rearing and education of a new generation. There could be no proper music or painting until the imagery of nature had been made concrete by biological knowledge.

It will be noticed immediately that this echoes strongly the history of Romanticism of the early nineteenth century in Western Europe. The intimacy of the interaction between nationalism, poetry, and science in German Romanticism is exemplified by the threefold careers of Novallis, Humboldt, and Goethe, each of whom was simultaneously naturalist, author, and man of political affairs, among other roles.

The new Jewish settlements were attempts to realize in actuality the visions of Goethe, Tolstoy, and the prophets of Zionism. Poetry, nationalism, religious imagery, and a sacramental Jewish ethnic combined into a revolutionary utopian movement and the naturalists of Israel undertook to weave this into the local landscape.

Almost as soon as settlements were established—after the sheds for housing the people and farm animals—came nursery and elementary schools. In most of these there was a plot of land set aside for animals and plants kept for the education of the children. The words *zoological* or *botanical garden* do not quite translate the Hebrew term used for these collections. The place housing the collections is known as the "Pinat-ha-chai," i.e., "the corner of life." These existed and still exist all over the country, perhaps with just a few goats, chickens, and pigeons but often with extensive local collections of living plants and animals requiring constant and meticulous labor and irrigation.

Some of these quickly became much more than adjuncts to elementary education. There was beginning, for example, in the heart of Tel Aviv in a rotting building that had once housed Tel Aviv's first synagogue, a somewhat larger collection with a small reference library, a taxidermist, and a small museum. Secondary-school teachers from the kibbutzim went there to learn how to teach their children and how to maintain and study organisms. There were other collections developing in other parts of the country: the teachers' training schools, seminar-ha-kibbutzim, near Tel Aviv and Oranim near Haifa, were among the most prominent. In addition, exhibition zoos in the European sense were developed, including the municipal zoo in Tel Aviv and the "Biblical Zoo" in Jerusalem.

The zoo started by Margolin in the old Tel Aviv synagogue with its associated botanical garden has a most curious history: it gave birth to a university. As the city developed, it moved to a south Tel Aviv slum area, Abu Kabir. There an area of a few acres, originally cleared for the building of a British hospital, were fixed. Apartments were rented as offices in the surrounding buildings, and a university began to rise around the zoo.

Students came to study zoology and botany, initially from the standpoint of what the Israelis call faunistics and floristics, namely ecology, taxonomy, anatomy, and behavior with a central theme of the plants and animals of Israel. With the support primarily of the Tel Aviv municipality, teachers, technicians, carpenters, and gardeners were supplied. Many of the students returned to secondary schools, kibbutzim, and government agencies. With the passage of time it became clear that a chemistry department was needed; for this, further space was purchased from the neighbors, who continued to let their chickens and donkeys wander through the classrooms and between the offices. A department of microbiology was added as were other departments until an infant university had appeared in the Abu Kabir slum. This eventually became independent of the municipal government. Now, a new, large, fully equipped and most impressive campus exists to the north of the city. The botanical gardens have been moved to the new campus. The buildings for the zoo are being constructed, and the experimental zoo is about to move from its pioneer location in the south of the city to elegant new quarters, all forming an excellent center for ecological research.

Like any successful revolution, however, the quality of excitement of the earliest phases is difficult to maintain. The "normalization" of the relation between the people of Israel and their landscape has succeeded to the extent that the early biology and ecology texts by Israeli authors (particularly Margolin and Bodenheimer) with their emphasis on local landscape and their (then) revolutionary motivation have been replaced in the Israeli high schools by translations of the texts developed by the Biological Sciences Curriculum Study in the United States. The focus of the secondary and elementary school teacher is now seen to be to motivate their students on an intellectual level, i.e., the Israeli educational system now sees itself as part of the world community of educators just as the science faculty of the seven universities of Israel see themselves a part of the world scientific community.

Their problems doubtless sound familiar to American educators and scientists. There is, however, still a living legacy of the revolutionary phase. The tiny "corners of life" persist in many of the village schools and kibbutzim. "Faunistics" and "Floristics" are still taught at the universities of Israel using the excellent living collections. There is a thriving set of organizations in which laymen, teachers, and scientists voice their concern for the natural history of Israel in an active way. Field trips to all parts of the country, conducted under the direction of trained naturalists, are a favored form of relaxation for a large fraction of the population. One of the few forms of alternative services available within the Israeli universal military conscription system is to work as a warden and guide at National Nature Reserves. In addition, there is a system of field schools initiated and maintained by the Israeli Association for the Protection of Nature. These consist of small laboratories and dormitories set in locations of particular ecological interest. Each is supervised by a trained naturalist of M.S. or Ph.D. level and is utilized by research workers, secondary schools, and the general public.

From the standpoint of the non-Israeli scientist, the country is a rich research source partially because of the Israeli scientific community and partly because of the curious biogeographic richness of the Israeli fauna and flora that combine African, Asian, and European elements. In addition, there is available for study a rich coral reef with an immediately adjacent, well equipped laboratory.

For the non-Israeli layman, the ecology of Israel is seen from the standpoint of the cultural, literary, and historic role of Israel itself. In a sense, any aware newcomer to Israel cannot avoid experiencing, to some degree, the excitement of the Israeli ecological pioneers. This is of more than sentimental importance. The interaction between particular people and their particular landscape and literature is a fact, a stimulus to thought, and a restraint on thought. To act as if the interaction does not exist is intellectually dangerous.

As Smoli wrote (*On Nature and on Agriculture.* Hora a't Ha-Tera, 11:3–4, 1962), "Children, what has happened? Why have they cut down the wood lot? . . . ." "Because of the cattle egrets. Their cries annoyed the neighbours. They dirtied (things) terribly. They carried sickness from cow to cow and barn to barn." "Children, doesn't it disturb you that they cut down the trees and drove away the egrets?"

"It's nothing to worry about. The paper mill paid well for the trees."

"It is not about the egrets and the trees that I worry, children . . . not about them. . . ."

THE SOCIETY FOR PROTECTION OF NATURE IN ISRAEL AND THE DEVELOPMENT OF "FIELD SCHOOLS"

At the end of the British mandatory regime in 1948, public opinion in Israel was entirely ignorant of the concept of nature conservation. In response, the Society for Protection of Nature in Israel (S.P.N.I.) was established in 1953. At that time, the prevailing notion was that it was almost a sin to preserve land for snakes and scorpions instead of developing it for the benefit of people with but one exception: with the drainage of the Hula swamp, a small area was set aside to become a Nature Reserve, the first in Israel. In 1963, the Knesset proclaimed laws of protected natural items and the Nature Reserves Authority was established, taking over the executive activity stemming from the law on Nature Conservancy.

Today, the S.P.N.I. has more than 30,000 members and operates twenty field study centers. The field study center combines the study of biology, ecology, and geography with education and research on these subjects, and actual conservation of nature in the area. The field study centers (Field Schools, in local jargon), are located at sites of interest all over the country, from Mount-Hermon in the north to Sharm-el-Sheikh at the southern tip of Sinai. Each field study center is situated in the vicinity of an important Nature Reserve, or in an area which combines natural values, scenery, and sites of historical significance. High school and university students use these centers year-round in their studies on the biology and ecology of animals and plants in the area, the teaching being carried out mainly through courses and seminars of four-six days on specific subjects. The field school instructors undertake research in ecology, geology, and related subjects on the Reserves and supervise protected animals and plants.

RECENT DEVELOPMENTS IN RESEARCH AND EDUCATION

During the last fifteen years, there has been an enormous advancement in ecological research and education in Israel. An increasing number of students is attracted to this field, and in the universities more than forty different courses dealing with various aspects of ecology are suggested to undergraduate and graduate students.

The major activity of ecological research takes place at the universities (Hebrew University at Jerusalem, Tel Aviv University, Haifa University, Bar-Ilan University and Ben-Gurion University of the Neger) and the research institutions (The Weizman Institute, The Technion-Technical Institute of Israel, Israel Oceanographical Limnological Research Institution and the Biological Institution at Nes-Ziona).

Ecological research engulfs a wide spectrum of subjects, among the general areas of which are: desert ecology (plant and animal adaptations to desert ecosystems); marine ecology (Mediterranean and Red Sea animal and plant communities); terrestrial ecology of plants and animals; salt marsh ecosystems; limnological research of Lake Kinneret; pollution studies (oil pollution, air pollution, sewage purification, pesticide and herbicide pollution, heavy metals, detergents, etc.); aquaculture research (fish, oysters, shrimp, algae); applied entomology and biological warfare; and theoretical ecology (population genetics, community and population ecology).

The major sources of governmental support for environmental studies are: the National Council for Research and Development (Prime Minister's Office), Administration for Research and Natural Resources (Ministry of Commerce and Industry), Environmental Protection Service (Ministry of the

Interior), Israeli Academy of Science and Humanities, and U.S.-Israel Binational Science Foundation.

JOURNALS

The major local scientific journals in ecology published in English are: *Israel Journal of Zoology* and *Israel Journal of Botany.* Semipopular journals published in Hebrew are *Teva-Va'aretz* (Nature and Land) and *Mada* (Science). As in other countries, research results also appear in English-language journals throughout the world.

The ecological literature is of such magnitude that to single out but a few salient and seminal contributions would be to do injustice to the many more not cited.

30

JAPAN

Makoto Numata

INTRODUCTION

For almost three hundred years before the Meiji Era (1868–1912), diplomatic relations between Japan and the West, with the exception of the Netherlands, had been completely cut off. As a result, modern Western biology was introduced into Japan for the most part after the beginning of the Meiji Era in 1868, the exception being some biological work introduced by way of the Netherlands.

Ecology was introduced into Japan at the end of the nineteenth century primarily by M. Miyoshi, a professor at Tokyo University, who had studied botany, particularly plant physiology, ecology, and taxonomy, in Germany. As he was the first scientist to introduce plant ecology to Japan, he was the one who called it *Seitaigaku,* the commonly accepted Japanese name for *ecology.* He wrote the first comprehensive books on ecology, *Plant Communities* (1903) and *General Plant Ecology* (1908), and he gave lectures on plant ecology at Tokyo University beginning in 1910. However, Miyoshi considered plant physiology to be a basic exact science, whereas plant ecology was not: according to his view, plant physiology clarifies the objective, analytical laws of plant life based on laboratory experiments; plant ecology only interprets the field life phenomena of plants based on those physiological laws. Miyoshi considered ecological interpretation to be subjective, teleological, and vitalistic, a view influenced by the teleological ecology in vogue in the late 1800s. Cowles, in 1910, criticized the nineteenth-century theory of adaptive response in his textbook of botany.

After Miyoshi, Y. Yoshii established a new course in plant ecology at Tohoku University (Sendai) in 1921. H. Nakano took over Miyoshi's post (plant physiology and ecology) at Tokyo University in 1934. Nakano in 1933 and Yoshii (1955) wrote leading books on research methods in plant ecology. The only independent courses of ecology before World War II were at Tohoku University (plant ecology) and Kyoto University (animal ecology), the latter established by T. Kawamura. The biology course at Kyoto University was established in 1919, two years before that at Tohoku University. Kawamura commenced his lectures on animal ecology in 1921 at Kyoto University simultaneously with Yoshii at Tohoku University, and Kawamura wrote monumental books on freshwater biology in 1918 and research methods of animal communities in 1939.

POSTWAR RE-ESTABLISHMENT OF ECOLOGY

Ecological viewpoints gradually penetrated the thinking of the younger generation of biologists. However, there continued to be subordination of ecology to physiology, following after Miyoshi, as seen in Nakano's *Experimental Methods in Plant Physiology and Ecology* (1933) and Koriba's *Plant Physiology and Ecology* (1953), where stress was laid on physiology.

After the Second World War, Numata stressed ecology as the biology of populations and communities, and K. Imanishi (1949) insisted on the habitat-segregation of specific societies as an ecological principle based on the individualistic concept. These books were the start of postwar ecology of Japan. Imanishi's school of ecologists tried field surveys to verify his view of nature related to habitat-segregation. They made expeditions to Ponape Island (1941), the Greater Khingan Mountain (1942), and the Himalayas (1952–1955). Imanishi's studies have developed in the fields of primatology and anthropology through animal sociology. During the same period, a symposium on "Biotic Populations and the Environment" was held in 1949. This was the opening of the postwar biological movement, particularly in relation to ecology.

Courses and lectures on ecology were few in prewar universities. After the war, lectures on ecology were held at most universities, particularly in the faculties of science. However, independent ecology courses are relatively few in number even today. Among the eighty-three national universities, thirty-two universities have a faculty of science, among which only eleven have independent laboratories for plant or animal ecology or both. Besides these, there are few applied ecology courses (for example, forest or grassland) and ecology-related courses, such as environmental biology, limnology, oceanography, entomology, and pathology.

JOURNALS

As for ecological journals, *Ecological Review* is the oldest, having been issued by Tohoku University (chief editor, Y. Yoshii) since 1935; it was an open journal until Vol. 12 (1949) after which it became the closed journal of the Mt. Hakkoda Botanical Laboratory, Tohoku University. Continuing as an open journal similar to *Ecological Review* was the *Bulletin of the Society of Plant Ecology* (1951–1953, 3 vols.) issued by the Plant Ecological Society (president, Y. Yoshii). *Annals of Phytoecology* (1941–1943, 3 vols.) was issued by the Phytoecological Society of Japan under the guidance of H. Nakano (successor, M. Monsi). The Ecological Society of Japan started under the guidance of D. Miyadi from two groups in plant ecology and a group of animal ecologists. As a result, the *Japanese Journal of Ecology* was begun, starting with Vol. 4 in 1954.

Besides the official journal of the Ecological Society of Japan, there are ecological journals, such as *Physiology and Ecology, Japan* published since 1949 and *Researches on Population Ecology* (published in Japanese with English summary from 1952 to 1956 and as an international journal in English starting with Vol. 4, 1962). There are also ecology-related journals, such as the *Botanical Magazine/Tokyo, Journal of the Japanese Forestry Society,* the *Japanese Journal of Grassland Science, Weed Research/Japan,* the *Japanese Journal of Applied Entomology and Zoology, Botyu-Kagaku* (Scientific Pest Control), *Kontyû* (Insects), *Miscellaneous Reports of the Yamashina Institute for Ornithology, Primates—Journal of Primatology,* the *Japanese Journal of Limnology, Bulletin of the Japanese Society of Scientific Fisheries, Biological Science/Tokyo, Acta Phytotaxonomica et Geobotanica, Hikobia—Journal of the Hiroshima Botanical Club,* and the *Journal of Botany* (also see Numata 1958).

MONOGRAPHS AND OTHER PUBLICATIONS

Since the war, there have been many other publications in the field of ecology: methodology and history of ecology (e.g., Imanishi 1949; Numata 1953; Ito 1959; Shibuya 1956, 1960, 1969; Research Group on Measuring Methodology of Freshwater Biological Production 1969); experimental and research methods (e.g., Yoshii 1955; Ecological Exercise Committee 1967; Microbial Ecology Research Group 1974; Okino 1976; Kitazawa et al. 1976–present); textbooks on ecology (e.g., Miyadi and Mori 1953; Yagi et al. 1960; Miyadi et al. 1961; Kawanabe et al. 1966; Numata and Utida 1963; Arasaki et al. 1976; Miyawaki 1977; Numata 1980); dictionaries (Numata 1974*b*, 1976*b*); ecological series (Numata 1970–1972; Kitawaza et al. 1972–1976; Numata et al. 1977–1978; Japanese Committee for the IBP 1975–1978); research on special themes (Miyake and Koyama 1964); proceedings (e.g., Theoretical Biology Research Group [ed.] 1950; Imanishi 1959); memorial issues for the dead, the ages of sixty and seventy, and retirement; ecological expeditions (e.g., Kihara 1955, 1956; Kira 1961–1976); ecological illustration of flora and vegetation (e.g., Numata and Asano 1969–1970; Numata 1974*a;* Miyawaki 1977); vegetation maps, climax, potential natural and actual; nature conservation and environmental science (e.g., Sasa and Yamamoto 1972–1977; Hogetsu et al. 1972; Numata 1976*a;* Miyawaki and Tüxen 1977); popular books; ecological essays (e.g., Shibuya 1956; Numata 1958; Ito 1975). Besides these, there are many translations of foreign textbooks and monographs.

IMPORTANT PROBLEMS FOR JAPANESE ECOLOGISTS

Important problems for Japanese ecologists have been suggested in many papers, books, debates, and discussions. The titles of symposia of the annual assembly of the Ecological Society of Japan indicate the most important of these:

1954 The development of ecology into an applied science
1956 Ecological problems in cultivation and breeding
1957 Biological periodicity
1958 The adaptability of biological populations
1959 How is the distribution of organisms determined?
1960 Coactions in biotic communities
1961 Methods and situation of animal sociology; interrelationships between the productive structure of organisms and productivity; problems in water pollution biology; lower units of plant associations; the basis of the theory of communities
1962 Vegetation unit theory and vegetation continuum theory in plant sociology; the meaning of foods in the life of animals; the difference of productivity and the productive relationship between plants and animals; the variation of the number of animals and the change of characteristics of individuals
1963 The future program for the development of ecology in Japan
1964 The present status and future of nature conservation; what is modelling?
1965 The future program of Japanese ecology; problems in measuring the productivity of terrestrial animal communities (a separate symposium following the annual assembly of the Zoological Society of Japan)
1966 Problems in water pollution biology microbiological problems of water pollution; can we recover from water pollution in the Yodo River?
1967 The ecology of estuaries; what is the productivity of biotic communities?
1968 How can we use the vegetation research for human life? the ecology of microorganisms in the soil, fresh water, ocean, and rumen
1969 Efficiencies of biological production
1971 Plants and water; the wildlife of mammals and its conservation; environmen-

tal disruption and the Ecological Society; the results of the International Biological Program
1972 Pollution and destruction of nature; regulation in ecology
1974 Environmental problems; ecology education
1975 Ecology and evolution
1976 Dynamics of ecosystems and their metabolism; problems in population dynamics
1977 Problems in habitat-segregation; structure and dynamics of urban ecosystems; feeding behavior and research on the population of animals; vegetation since the post-glacial period and pollen analysis
1978 Ecology of lucidophyllous forests
1979 Models in home range, predation strategy, migration and diffusion; is the coexistence of nature and human civilization possible?
1980 Ecological problems in the beech forest region; evolution of life history.

The Botanical Society of Japan has occasionally held ecological symposia listed as follows:

1958 How shall we study plant communities?
1959 The ecology of lower plants
1960 Succession in Japan
1963 The structure of plant communities
1964 The measurement of primary productivity
1968 The ecology of warm-temperate laurel-leaved forests
1969 The present state of nature destruction and the logic of nature conservation (Joint Symposium with the Zoological Society of Japan)
1970 Photosynthesis in forests
1971 Biogeography in and around the Japanese archipelago (Joint Symposium with the Zoological Society of Japan)
1976 Ecology and conservation of alpine and mountain vegetation in the Japanese archipelago
1978 Distribution and speciation of plants on islands.

The Zoological Society of Japan has had little interest in ecology whether it be in journals or meetings. However, recently it has begun to show an inclination toward having joint symposia with the Botanical Society of Japan, as it did in 1969 and 1971. The Zoological Society of Japan has also occasionally held ecological symposia listed as follows:

1952 Lake as an ecosystem; ecological studies in the rice-stem borer and its outbreak forecasting
1953 Methodology of ecology
1954 Concepts and terms of ecology
1955 Habitat segregation
1956 Geographical distribution and speciation of animals
1957 Animal life in individual and population levels

1958 Productivity
1960 Present status and problems in animal ecology
1961 Relationship of individuals in a population
1962 On the future plan of ecology
1963 Problems in the field survey of animal communities
1965 Problems in measuring productivity of terrestrial animal communities
1968 Productivity of communities
1973 Mechanism of fish migration
1975 Diurnal periodicity of animals.

The Ecological Society of Japan has several committees on planning for the future development of ecology, ecological education, nature conservation, and environmental problems. When the annual assemblies take place, there are small group meetings on plant communities, benthos, population ecology, the ecology of birds, the behavior and ecology of butterflies and dragonflies, soil animals, the ecology of seeds, microbial ecology, wildlife management, conservation education, environmental problems, organic evolution, small mammals, and development and environmental assessment.

Besides the Ecological Society of Japan, the Theoretical Biology Research Group of the Democratic Scientist's Society in Japan has played a great role in the development of Japanese ecology. As stated earlier, the first biological symposium after the war was convened by them on "Biotic Population and Environment" in 1949 (published in 1950). They held ecological symposia on "The Interactions Between Organisms and the Environment" in 1955 and "Problems Concerning the Life of Organisms" in 1958. These were published as special issues of *Biological Science/Tokyo.* This quarterly journal, edited by the Theoretical Biology Research Group, has published many contributions on methodological problems in ecology. In 1949 and 1950, there was an extended debate between Hatakeyama and Numata on the scientific character of ecology, with Numata's essay on modern biology as the keynote address. Many important problems were discussed, such as the history of ecology, applied ecology, measurement and evaluation of the environment, struggle for existence, intraspecific competition of higher plants, population ecology, criticism on Japanese ecology, estimation of population parameters from marking-and-recapture data, biogeochemical function of ecosystems, ecosystem models, ecological effects of military defoliation on the forests of South Vietnam, and environmental conservation.

DEBATES AND REMARKABLE TRENDS IN ECOLOGY

Ecology in Japan before the war followed the European ecological tradition. Since the war, the ecology of the United States and Soviet Union has influenced Japanese ecologists. Recently we have been receiving information on Chinese ecology.

Postwar ecology in Japan started with discussion on the definition, situation, and logic of ecology in biological sciences (e.g., Imanishi 1949). The principle of habitat-segregation as put forth by Imanishi was based on the mutually exclusive distribution of organisms in space and time. As a view of nature, this concept strongly affected young ecologists and was often used as a guideline for the description and interpretation of biotic society.

The concept of environment is approached from two standpoints: the total of external conditions (Umgebung), and influencing factors in terms of organisms (Umwelt). According to the latter, Morisita proposed a concept of environmental density, and Numata evaluated environmental effects on the distribution and growth of bamboo in relation to biological levels (formation, association, and stand levels). There was a debate between the two views of environment in a colloquium in Kyoto in which Numata supported the biocentric "subject-environment system" instead of the "ecosystem," i.e., that the subject is the master or host of the system (Numata 1953) and has a leading role in the system. In the concept of the ecosystem, such a structural viewpoint is weak. For example, the city can be studied as an anthropocentric man-environment system as well as a biocentric vegetation-environment or an animal-environment system. The difference in the subject (leading factor) results in a different structure and function of the ecosystem.

The ecological basis for the study of the material production of plant communities was put forth by Boysen-Jensen in 1932. Along this guideline, Monsi and Saeki wrote a paper in 1953 on the light factor in the plant community and its role in matter production. In this paper, they proposed the concept of the productive structure of a plant community, which comprised the distribution of leaves in the plant community and micro-environmental factors. The profiles of plant materials, i.e., of the photosynthetic and non-photosynthetic systems, were assessed by the stratified clip technique. Monsi and Saeki also tried to develop mathematical models of plant communities on the basis of Beer-Lambert's equation.

Plant sociology following the Zurich-Montpellier school was introduced by Tokio Suzuki in 1953. He discussed climax alliances and associations of humid East Asia in relation to climax forests in the Northern Hemisphere. Later, he proposed a preliminary system for Japanese natural forest communities and developed a vegetation map of Japan based on it (scale: 1/2,000,000). Miyawaki (1967, revised 1977) edited a *Vegetation of Japan* and with his colleagues is developing actual and potential natural vegetation maps for many areas of Japan. The first Japanese meeting of the International Society for Vegetation Science (secretary-general, Prof. Dr. R. Tüxen) was held in 1974 and encouraged Japanese plant sociologists very much.

The two trends of production ecology and plant sociology have been parallel; they do not associate with each other. In order for researchers to understand the ideas of each side, a symposium on "How to study plant communities?" was held in 1958 by the Botanical Society of Japan. However, it was difficult for each side to understand the other well.

To form a bridge between production ecology and plant sociology, Numata proposed the "degree of succession." The relationships between the seral stages of grassland vegetation and their productivity were clarified on the basis of plant sociology, i.e., different biomass-degree of succession curves were drawn depending on different subassociations and variants. One more bridge between production ecology and plant sociology uses the approach of quantitative ecology. Phytosociological characteristics and procedures following Braun-Blanquet in sampling method, coverage, and sociability were criticized from the stand point of quantitative plant ecology.

After World War II, Lysenko's agrobiology, particularly his criticism of Darwin's concept of intraspecific competition, was a temporary influence and caused confusion among young biologists. On the other hand, Kira and his colleagues (1953–1965) experimentally and theoretically analyzed intraspecific competition among higher plants, particularly in regard to their competition-yield-density interrelationship. The law of constant final yield introduced from the competition-density effect was a strong influence on agriculture and forestry.

Kira and his colleagues (1961–1974) shifted to tropical studies in Southeast Asia including the production ecology of tropical forest vegetation, monkeys and insects, as well as studies on freshwater productivity in a tropical lake. The results were published as a series, *Nature and Life in Southeast Asia*. Some of the studies were conducted cooperatively with Malaysia and the United Kingdom within the framework of the IBP.

A series of ecological studies in the Himalayas was conducted to compare vegetation types, animals, and human life styles (e.g., Numata 1965). There are many studies on the flora and fauna of the Himalayas, but few on ecology.

Divisions of climatic types have been proposed by many climatologists. In Japan, a new climatic classification based on warmth and coldness indices was proposed by Kira, a plant ecologist, in 1945. He applied this system to the climax forest zones of Japan and recently extended it to the world. Kira's classification of climate is widely used in Japan.

The law of geometric series, a mathematical representation of the relationship between the number of species and that of individuals in a community, was first formulated by Motomura in 1932. It was first applied to benthic biota of a Japanese lake and Swedish land snails, and then to sessile animal communities on the rocks of an intertidal zone, and later to insect populations collected by light, as well as on pioneer plant communities on bare ground. It is interpreted as a simplified form of the law of logarithmic series and of lognormality.

There are many indices of dispersion to express the mode of distribution, such as the variance-mean ratio or the abundance/frequency ratio. A coefficient of homogeneity (Numata), an I_{δ}-index (Morisita), and a modification of the index of mean crowding (Iwao) were proposed as measures of dispersion of individuals. The dispersive structure of communities and the mode of life of species in relationship to dominance, habitat, and succession may be interpreted on the basis of the dispersion of individuals.

Using the experimental population of insects, Utida distinguished three types of density effect: the *Drosophila* type, the intermediate type, and the Allee type in which the relationship was interpreted using a mathematical model by Fujita.

Kawamura, a founder of Japanese animal ecology, developed an important basis for freshwater ecology. He was followed by Miyadi, who was known for his energetic works in the 1930s on the development of benthic fauna in lakes. Kani (1944, see Kani 1970) and Imanishi (1949) established a methodology for interpreting the distribution and life of aquatic insects in rivers based on the concept of habitat-segregation. Tsuda (1964, 1974) and his colleagues developed a method for judging water quality using aquatic organisms as bioindicators. A research group on river ecology at Kyoto University has studied since 1950 the mode of life of fish in relation to their population density, food web, and biological productivity.

To establish a new ecology combining population ecology and production ecology, Morisita proposed a new concept, *the bioeconomic life table,* in 1973. This consists of a life table including various quantities of prey supply, the food consumed during their lifetime by dead animals, and so on. The difference between the quantity of prey captured and that of food consumed during their lifetime by the dead animals that did not survive to their adult stage results in the quantity of "wasted food."

For insects and small rodents, the methods of estimating the home range, population density, and biomass were developed early by Iwao and Tanaka, respectively. However, those of large mammals, such as the Japanese serow and bear, were very difficult to determine. The population density of large wild mammals is currently being estimated by feces and radiotelemetry.

The social behavior of monkeys and apes was investigated by field studies both in Japan and in foreign countries by Imanishi and his colleagues. Their studies were aimed not only at the social structure and life of colonies, but also at an estimation of the evolutionary process of human characteristics based on primate sociology.

Japan is a mountainous country with Mount Fuji and the Japan Alps being higher than 3,000 m. Some Japanese ecologists have considerable interest in high-mountain ecology, particularly in the Himalayas. This is because of the similarity of Himalayan flora and fauna to that found in Japanese mountains (e.g., Numata 1965). Despite the fact that there are many taxonomic studies of the flora and fauna on the Himalayas, Andes, and other mountains, there are still very few ecological studies.

Some ecologists, like Kitazawa, tried to study ecosystem metabolism and prepare flow diagrams for matter and energy in ecosystems. In opposition to this approach, some ecologists (for example, Ito) have adopted an approach in which they thoroughly study the population of a key species. In the view of these ecologists, measurement of the number of animals should be conducted on the basis of knowledge of the mode of distribution of each species and a strict sampling method depending on the mode of distribution. If not, accurate and reliable data will not be available for the study of ecosystem metabolism. Ito has criticized recent trends in Japanese ecology from the viewpoint of a population ecologist.

Since 1964, more than six hundred biologists have engaged in the research work of the International Biological Program (IBP), which was supported financially by the Ministry of Education as a special research project entitled "Studies on the Dynamics of the Biosphere." Its results are being published as a series of JIBP syntheses by the University of Tokyo Press, and some of them are included in international synthesis volumes published by Cambridge University Press. The direction and methodology were discussed in symposia of the Ecological Society of Japan, and advanced ideas and results were obtained on productivity, conservation, and human adaptability. The period 1973–1974 was devoted to phase III (synthesis and transfer) of IBP. During the period of IBP research, the *JIBP News* was published and attached to the *Japanese Journal of Ecology.*

The International Coordinating Council Meeting of the Program on Man and the Biosphere (MAB) was first held in 1971. The Ministry of Education supported research related to MAB under the title "Basic Approaches to the Environment in Relation to Human Survival" from 1971 to 1976. Starting in 1977, a new MAB-related research project, "Environmental Sciences," commenced under the sponsorship of the Ministry of Education; some Japanese ecologists are currently conducting regional and conservation-related studies in this project.

The Ecological Society of Japan frequently issued resolutions and recommendations to the government and appeals to the people on concerns such as nature conservation, environmental monitoring, ecological education, ecological problems of extensive or repeated use of herbicides in Vietnam, and environmental assessment. Groups from the Ecological Society of Japan published a *Manual on Ecological Exercises in Universities* in 1967 and *Environment and Biological Indicators* in 1975. The Ecological Society has two types of members, basic and general ecologists belonging to the Faculty of Science of universities, and applied ecologists belonging to the Faculty of Agriculture of universities and agricultural, forest, grassland, and fisheries experiment stations. Recently, some ecologists have been employed by the Environment Agency and Agency for Science and Technology. Some of them are employed in consulting companies doing environmental assessment work and as teachers. In 1977, the Science Council of Japan recommended that the government establish an Institute of Ecology as a national institute used jointly by various universities.

Ecology in Japan is a miniature copy of world ecology; however it has some special characteristics.

ACKNOWLEDGMENTS

The author wishes to extend his sincere thanks to Professors Emeritus D. Miyadi (Kyoto Univ.), M. Kato (Tohoku U.), S. Mori and M. Morisita (Kyoto Univ.), Professors T. Kira (Osaka City Univ.), S. Iizumi (Tohoku Univ.), M. Ono (Kyushu Univ.), and F. Takahashi (Hiroshima Univ.), Drs. I. Ikusima and Y. Yamamoto (Chiba Univ.), and Y. Ito (Nagoya Univ.) for their kind cooperation.

REFERENCES CITED

(* in English or with English summary)

Arasaki, M., M. Horikoshi, and T. Kikuchi. 1976. *Marine algae and benthos.* Tokai University Press.

Ecological Exercise Committee. 1967. *Manual on ecological exercises in universities.* Asakura-Shoten.

Hogetsu, K., T. Kira, and H. Iwaki, eds. 1972. *Science of environment.* NHK.

Imanishi, K. 1949. *The logic of biotic communities.* Mainichi-Shinbunsha.

______, ed. 1959. *Society and individuals of animals.* Iwanami-Shoten.

Ito, Y. 1959. *Comparative ecology.* Iwanami-Shoten.

______. 1975. *Animal ecology,* I, II. Kokon-Shoin.

Japanese Committee for the IBP. 1975–78. *JIBP synthesis.** 20 vols. University of Tokyo Press (not yet completed).

Kani, T. 1970. *Ecological papers of T. Kani.* Shisakusha.

Kawanabe, H. et al. 1966. *Ecology and evolution.* Iwanami-Shoten.

Kihara, H., ed. 1955. *Fauna and flora of Nepal Himalaya.** Kyoto: The Fauna and Flora Research Society.

______. 1956. *Land and crops of Nepal Himalaya.** Kyoto: The Fauna and Flora Research Society.

Kira, T. et al. eds. 1961–1976. *Nature and life in Southeast Asia,** 7 vols. Kyoto: The Fauna and Flora Research Society.

Kitazawa, Y. et al. eds. 1970–1976. *Lectures on ecology.* 19 vols. Kyoritsu-Shuppan.

______, ed. 1976–present. *Lectures on research methods in ecology.* 33 vols. Kyoritsu-Shuppan (not yet completed).

Koriba, K. 1953. *Plant physiology and ecology.* Yokendo.

Microbial Ecology Research Group. 1974. *Ecology of microorganisms.* University of Tokyo Press.
Miyadi, D. 1961. *Animal ecology.* Tokyo: Asakura-Shoten.
———, and S. Mori, 1953. *Ecology of animals.* Iwanami-Shoten.
Miyake, Y. and T. Koyama. 1964. *Recent researches in the fields of hydrosphere, atmosphere and nuclear geochemistry.** Maruzen.
Miyawaki, A., ed. 1977. *Vegetation of Japan.* Gakken.
——— and R. Tüxen, eds. 1977. *Vegetation Science and environmental protection.** Maruzen Co.
Numata, M. 1953. *Methodology of ecology.* Kokon-Shoin.
———. 1958. Japanese publications in the field of ecology.* *Ecology* 39:566–567.
———, ed. 1965. *Ecological study and mountaineering of Mt. Numbur in eastern Nepal.** Himalayan Committee of Chiba University.
———, ed. 1970–1972. *Research series on ecology.* 6 vols. Tsukiji-Shokan.
———, ed. 1974*a*. *The flora and vegetation of Japan.** Kodansha and Elsevier.
———, ed. 1974*b*. *Dictionary of ecology.* Tsukiji-Shokan.
———, ed. 1976*a*. *Handbook for nature conservation.* University of Tokyo Press.
———, ed. 1976*b*. *Glossary of ecology.* Tokyodo.
———, ed. 1980. *Ecology of grasslands and bamboolands in the world.* VEB Gustav Fischer Verlag.
———, et al. eds. 1977–1978. *Lectures on plant ecology,* 5 vols. Asakura-Shoten.
——— and S. Asano. 1969–1970. *Biological flora of Japan,** 3 vols. Tsukiji-Shokan.
——— and T. Utida, eds. 1963. *Applied ecology, 2 vols. Kokon-Shoin.*
Okino, T., ed. 1976. Surveying methods on eutrophication. Kodansha.
Research Group on Measuring Methodology of Freshwater Biological Production. 1969. *Research methods of freshwater biological production.* Kodansha.
Sasa, M. and T. Yamamoto, eds. 1972–1977. *Environment and human survival,* 4 vols. University of Tokyo Press.
Shibuya, T. 1956. *Problems on ecology.* Rironsha.
———. 1960. *Theoretical ecology.* Rironsha.
———. 1969. *Problems in history of ecology.* Horitsu-Bunkasha.
Special Committee for Environmental Problems, Ecological Society of Japan, ed. 1975. *Environment and biological indicators,* 2 vols. Kyoritsu-Shuppan.
Theoretical Biology Research Group, ed. 1950. *Biotic population and environment.* Iwanami-Shoten.
Tsuda, M. 1964. *Biology in polluted water,* Hokuryukan.
———. 1974. *Freshwater ecology.* Kyoritsu-Shuppan.
Yagi, N. et al. 1960. *New general ecology.* Yokendo.
Yoshii, Y. 1955. *Experimental methods in plant ecology.* Kenbunkan.

31

KOREA

Kye Chil Oh

BACKGROUND

In the Korean peninsula, six zones of forest communities (boreal-montane coniferous, montane coniferous, mixed northern hardwood, deciduous broad-leaved, mixed mesophytic, and evergreen broad-leaved) are distributed from north to south (Wang 1961). The vegetation is similar to Japan and the northeastern part of the United States. However, there is no beech forest except in the Ullyung Island far from the mainland. Throughout most of our history, agriculture, particularly rice cultivation, has been predominant. The agricultural life, distinct seasonal climatic rhythm, hilly land form, mostly old igneous rocks, and frequent invasion by neighboring countries decisively influenced Korean vegetation.

Such physical and biotic environmental characteristics might have helped Korean farmers to observe their surroundings as a matter of survival. They have a very long history of spreading oak shoots in rice paddies along with the usual green manure. From their long practice of rice cultivation, these farmers know the effects of different river water quality on the fertility of rice paddy soil. For example, river water of summer green forest origin is more valued than that from predominantly Korean red pine (*Pinus densiflora*) stands. However, for a thousand years the government adopted the forest management policy of maintaining red pine stands rather than climax forest of mostly deciduous broad-leaved forest. As is now well known, pine stands have higher productivity, usage, and homestead fuel value.

Rice cultivation might have been more helpful in keeping soil nutrients from being lost by soil erosion than other kinds of crop cultivation on hilly land. The distinctive monsoon climate and short river system in this small, hilly peninsula gave the Korean people a compelling need to use water resources rationally. This may be one of the reasons why Korea has one of the longest histories of rainfall and river flow measurements. The first rain gauge was invented about 1442 by King Sejong, and measurements of rainfall at meteorologic stations in Seoul and provincial governments have been made since 1639. (Yi-dynasty Official History from 1413 to 1865). Sanrimkyunzae (foresty and agriculture) by Man Sun Hong (1643–1715), Tackrichi (landscape and vegetation) by Chung Whan Lee (1751), and Jeunuzi (Korean fish ecology) by Yoo Geu Suh (1834) are representative of archives that are worthwhile for studying intellectual traditions and natural history of Korea.

Koreans in general have been inclined to learn literature and practice Confucian philosophy. In the seventeenth century, a strong Western influence through China on Korean scholars gave ardent impetus to the study of such practical subjects as agriculture, forestry, fisheries, irrigation, and transportation. These brilliant new scholars, many of them pioneer Korean Catholics, unfortunately did not have the opportunity to pursue their interests further on practical aspects of Korean life because of the feudalistic ruling group of Yi-dynasty.

SIGNIFICANT ADVANCEMENTS AND TRENDS IN ECOLOGICAL RESEARCH

Pre-Korean War

Until 1945 there were no ecology courses in Korean colleges. In junior colleges, ecology was taught as a part of biology. The biology department, College of Education of Seoul National University, which was founded in 1946, offered two courses, plant ecology and animal ecology. In the plant ecology course, Braun-Banquet's *Pflazensoziologie* and Weaver and Clement's *Plant Ecology* were used by Professor Choon Min Kim. In the animal ecology class, biology majors read Elton's *Animal Ecology* under Professor Ki Chul Choi's guidance. One of the students majoring in biology, Kye C. Oh, wrote a B.S. thesis with the title, "Soil moisture content and successional stages of dune plant communities near the River Hankang"; this was the first written thesis in the field of ecology in Korea.

Professor Kin's major motivation in studying ecology was to restore Korea's forest vegetation on what was almost devastated bare land. However, he had not majored in forestry but in botany at the Tohoku University, Sendai, Japan; his special training background was physiologic plant ecology. This might have been one of the reasons why he did not have interests in the more descriptive aspects of plant ecology. However, there were no experimental facilities for physiologic plant ecology in Korea in 1945, a situation that gave him an opportunity to review diverse aspects of ecology. One of his first works used Raunkiaer's life form spectrum analysis to elucidate the Korean phytoclimate.

Several riverian and coastal plant communities were described and identified quantitatively by some Korean botanists. However, the quality of these works is far below that of the earlier ecological work in the Tongnai River basin of northern Korea by Mills (1921), one of the earliest excellent publications on ecology in Korea.

Soil Nutrients

About the time Korean ecology was to enter a new era, the Korean War broke out (1950), lasting to 1953. The war did profound damage to the physical facilities, references, and specimens for the field of ecology. After the armistice, Kim's major interest centered on the effects of saline and alkaline salts on plant growth. These studies showed that minor differences of the two soil salts had strong influence on the internal components of radish, cabbage, and lettuce, but growth inhibitions by these salts were not significantly different (C. M. Kim 1958). His work on chestnut tree (*Castanea crenata*) growth in relation to soil nutrients showed that the amounts of foliar nitrogen and phosphorus were significantly correlated to elongation growth, and the amounts were inversely correlated with the soil calcium level. From this fieldwork, he has shown the possibility of indirect negative influence of the high amount of soil calcium on the elongation growth of the tree (C. M. Kim 1967).

Kim's fieldwork on the amount of ammonia and nitrogen dioxide liberated from the soils in *Pinus densiflora* (Korean red pine), *Quercus mongolica* (Mongolian oak), and *Zoysia Japonica* communities showed that the amounts of ammonia volatilization were 3.41 kg, 2.62 kg, and 1.84 kg per hectare per week, respectively; for nitrogen dioxide the amounts were 0.21 kg, 0.12 kg, and 0.19 kg per hectare per week, respectively, in the central part of the Korean peninsula (C. M. Kim 1973*a*). An attempt was made to compare soil nutrient-holding capacities by analyzing thirteen chemicals in eight kinds of forest communities (*Pinus desiflora, Abies holophylla, Quercus mongolica, Q. aliena, Q. variabilis, Q. acutae, Carpinus laxiflora,* and *Camellia japonica*) from four regions of the Korean peninsula, namely, Kwangnung, Kaya, Gili, and Haenam. Evergreen and deciduous broad-leaved forests seem to have higher soil nutrient-holding capacity than do pine forests, except for the Kwangnung forest, which has been conserved for the past four centuries, where there was no significant difference in the holding capacity among the forests (C. M. Kim 1965).

Decomposition

Study on the decomposition rate of pine and oak litter under the summer green forest in Kwangnung showed a loss constant of 0.13 and 0.28 for pine and oak litters, respectively. The half-life of the accumulated organic matter of pine and oak in decomposition was estimated to be 2.4 and 5.3 years, respectively, and the annual amount of different mineral nutrients such as nitrogen, phosphorus, potassium, and calcium returned to the forest soil was higher in oak than pine forest. The exception was magnesium (C. M. Kim 1966).

Kim's study under Professor Yoshii in the Department of Biology at Tohoku University from 1937 to 1940 and in 1951 and a period of brief study in the Department of Botany at Duke University strongly influenced his work. Likewise, he was influenced by the mineral cycling studies of Dr. Jerry Olson around 1960. Productivity studies supported by the IBP and the National Survey Project supported by the government of the Republic of Korea also had an impact on his research.

Succession

Research on ecological succession in summer green forest was initiated by Oh (1959). In contrast to the prevalent Korean red pine (*Pinus densiflora*) forest, hornbeam (*Carpinus erosa*) and chestnut oak (*Quercus grandulifera*) are found to be climax species in different regions of Korea. Broad-leaf oak (*Q. dentata*) or mongolian oak (*Q. mongolica*) seem to replace pine in the central part of Korea and at higher elevations in the southern part of Korea; the oaks are subsequently displaced by hornbeam and maples. However, the successional sequence of larch (*Larix dahurica*), Korean fir (*Abies holophylla*), and flat-leaf spruce (*Picea jezoensis*) had already been determined in detail by careful observation in northern conifer forests (Wilson 1918).

Pattern and Association Studies

The first studies on pattern and association for Korean red pine (*Pinus densiflora*) forest were made by Oh (1970), who suggested that pine trees were generally randomly distributed at basic units of 4 × 4 m, 2 × 2 m, and 1 × 1 m, although there were rarely regular or contiguous ones. Primary and secondary random groups were regularly distributed. Similar patterns were also found among *Quercus serrata, Q. accutissima,* and several other species in pine stands. It was also observed that most species pairs of shrub layer were negatively associated in one-to-eight-meter blocks, but they became significantly positively associated in eight-to-sixteen-meter blocks. Oh surmised that microedaphic variation within pine stands was not great enough to cause their distributional differences among relatively large pines in general. However, for pine seedlings and some shrub species, the microedaphic variation within pine stands might be great enough to cause differences in the distributional pattern.

A similar study on the shrub layer under summer green forest revealed that primary clumps with dimensions of 1 × 1 m or 1 × 2 m were a common occurrence. The clumps were distributed either regularly or randomly. In general, change of species association was unidirectional as plot size increased in the pine stands but not in the summer green forest (Oh 1972*a*). Oh's pattern study was related to his earlier work on beech stands in the Great Smoky Mountains, in the southeastern part of North America (Oh 1964), a study that was influenced chiefly by Greig-Smith's school in Britain.

Studies on the annual height growth of *Pinus densiflora* in young natural pine stands were made in the central Korean peninsula by Oh (1972*b*). The amount of annual height growth was estimated to be 14.9–35.4 cm, 9.0–54.4 cm, and 2.4–69 cm for stand, individual pine tree, and observation, respectively. The total mean value was 23.5 cm/year. Oh suggested that sampling efficiency for the height growth determination might be increased to 744 percent if measurements were made on fifteen trees per stand from twenty stands instead of twenty trees per stand from fifteen stands. The amount of readily soluble phosphorus, total nitrogen, loss on ignition, and pH of soils under the pine stands in central Korea was estimated to be 2.8 ppm, and 0.09, 5.4, and 4.6 percent, respectively. Oh also suggested that of the seven soil properties, readily soluble phosphorus seemed to have significant positive influence on annual height growth.

Extensive joint surveys on vegetation, climate, and geology have been made by Korean taxonomists, ecologists, and geologists with government support since 1955. Through this work, plant species and parent rocks were identified for several relatively well conserved forest regions, estuaries, and islands. The water balance analysis of Quelpart Island in terms of the Thornthwaite approach is noteworthy. The study suggested the possible reason why the southern part of the island has several waterfalls, while there are none in the northern part, and discussed the potential abundant water resources in the south (Oh 1968).

Production and Physiological Studies

Studies on production ecology of *Pinus rigida, P. densiflora, Quercus mongolica,* and mulberry were carried out by J. H. Kim (1971, 1972, 1975); the estimated annual net production per hectare was found to be 4.97–5.47 tons, 12.66 tons, 8.78 tons, and 9.06–12.54 tons, respectively. J. H. Kim (1964*a*) also carried out work on physiological ecology for *Panax ginseng* with special reference to relative light intensity. He found in field experiments that the minimum, maximum, and optimum relative light intensities were 3, 30, and 8 percent, respectively, during the growing season. The estimated annual gross production ranged from 1,091 g to 506 g/m^2; the estimated annual net production ranged from 129 g to 0 g/m^2 (J. H. Kim 1964*b*).

H. S. Choi (1972) estimated that the maximum apparent photosynthesis rate of the mature leaf of common mistletoe was 9 mg CO_2/ dm^2/ hr at 20°C. He suggested that the plant is parasitic not only for water and mineral requirements but also for carbon. Through productivity studies, Song (1975) estimated the amount of nitrogen demand and supply for different parts of sunflowers and suggested the ratio of amount of dry matter produced to the assimilated nitrogen per year might be sixty. These productivity process studies were influenced by the ecology group of the Botany Department, Tokyo University.

Aquatic Studies

Studies on freshwater ecology were initiated by Professor K. C. Choi (1969*a*) who found that 80 percent of the total fish caught in the Choonchon Reservoir consisted of four species, *Zacco platypus, Gobius similis, Opsarichthys bidens,* and *Microphysogobio koreensis.*

Extensive environmental studies at tidal sand flats on the clam *Tapes philippinarum* were made by Professor Choi (1964, 1965) with special reference to early developmental stages and physical environmental factors. After five years' fieldwork, Choi estimated that the specific gravity of sea water was 1.020; the difference of sea level was 2.5 to 10.1 m; the maximum current velocity was 53.8 cm/sec; and the proportion of coarse sand for the substrates at Kyunggi Bay (midwest coast of the Korean peninsula) was 30–80 percent. The life cycle, feeding habits, distributional pattern, and predators of *T. philippinarum* were also elucidated. Among the physical factors studied, sea water temperature and substrate stability were the most critical factors for population growth (Choi 1969*b*). Choi also estimated annual biomass for the tidal sand flat to be 110 ton/m^2 (fresh weight).

Nature Conservation

In recent studies on the relationship between size of island and number of vascular plant species in offshore islands (Oh 1978) and inshore islands (Oh 1979*a*) around the Korean peninsula, Oh indicated that Preston's *Z* values for the islands were 0.236 and 0.407, respectively. He also found that Preston's dissimilarity indices for the species in the offshore islands and inshore islands ranged from 0.57 to 0.84 and from 0.55 to 0.71, respectively.

In a study on the impact of trampling on soil compressibility and on grass performance around trails in terms of regression and correlation analysis, Oh found that the regression coefficients between distances from trail center to forest and soil compressibility were significantly different among sites, and that especially fertile sites showed higher regression coefficients than less fertile sites. In addition, the regression coefficients between distance from trail edge to forest and performance of *Miscanthus sinensis* were significantly different among sites. This study also indicated that soils of granite origin were more susceptible to trampling than those of gneiss origin (Oh 1979*b*).

Commentary

No distinct contribution to theoretical or methodological ecology has been made by Korean ecologists. Most of their efforts to apply Anglo-American ecological approaches did not bear fruit in terms of reproducibility, predictability, and reliability. Most of the work unfortunately falls short of high quality research in some aspects. The reasons are manifold: the short history of Korean ecology; lack of broad, reliable descriptive studies on plant communities, geomorphology, and pedology as mentioned earlier; only one B.S. degree holder in physiological plant ecology from the Imperial University of Tohoku; and no available single volumes or journals on ecology, except for partial volumes of *Ecological Review* from Tohoku University and certain others from Japan. Some part of these publications were of limited help but in general they were not useful or readable, not because of a language barrier but because of a conceptual one. For most Korean ecology students, the updated ecological concepts were almost impossible to grasp comprehensibly and accurately.

It is, of course, not difficult to understand that ecology, an integrative science, might be difficult to study without the guidance of able ecologists and experts in topics such as statistics, pedology, geology, geomorphology, systems analysis, and computer sciences. This also means that ecologists need a broader background and more foreign language training than biochemists or physical scientists. This might be one of the reasons there are few qualified ecologists among Koreans, in contrast to rather sizable numbers of biochemists, physicists, chemists, and engineers.

As mentioned earlier, Korean vegetation has been disturbed intensively in degree and extensively in scope for a long time. This fact made it far more difficult for Korean ecologists to discern any distributional pattern and to conduct competent ecological research.

Korea urgently needs qualified ecologists more than ever before because of rapid industrialization, overpopulation, and paucity of natural resources. For Korea it is vital to use, restore, and conserve natural resources rationally and intensively. The distinct Korean climate, rainfall pattern, igneous geology, and hilly land form require basic data to determine the urgent and important ecological problems and seek their solutions.

To identify, compare, and relate variables in ecological research, Korean ecologists particularly need to become familiar with designs of ecological sampling and field experimentation. It would be a great help to ecologists in developing countries if there were available a textbook in ecological methodology with special reference to design in ecological research. Recently published benchmark references and symposium volumes have been useful but may be less helpful than the suggested kind of book for the less well trained ecology student working with inadequate facilities.

RELATIONS AND INTERACTIONS WITH OTHER DISCIPLINES

Oh's works (1970, 1972*a*, *b*) on pattern analysis and species association were influenced almost entirely by the approach of Greig-Smith, perhaps one of the first applications of his methodology in the Far East. Oh's subsequent work on the relation between elongation of Korean red pine (*Pinus densiflora*) and soil properties (Oh 1972*b*) involved multiple regression analysis, the first example of electronic computer data processing applied to ecological research in Korea.

A large-scale soil map (1/25,000) prepared by the Research Institute of Forest Resources, Republic of Korea, in 1976 may be of great help to future ecological work. Interactions between ecology and applied fields, such as forestry, agronomy, civil engineering, and sociology, were not vigorous enough for mutual benefit, encouragement, and understanding because of different background, training, and less frequent professional association. Currently, the urgent necessities of reforestation, coastal land reclamation, water reservoir construction, and environmental pollution are giving strong impetus for these groups to work together. Korea needs to pay immediate attention to the training of ecologists who can play leading roles in planning comprehensive research programs, coordinating and integrating the outcomes from the different disciplines.

I have not discussed the tasks, responsibilities, and limitations of the Korean ecologist merely to delineate his role in the natural sciences; more importantly, this discussion strongly indicates the significance and usefulness of ecological research and education in developing a cooperative way of life among Koreans. Because of the distinctive nature of ecology as a integrative science, ecology can have a decisive influence not only on Korean science education but on general education, in establishing values or scientific attitudes among Koreans. In this respect, I believe the Korean ecology teacher has a unique position, task, and opportunity. This fundamental theme of ecology may be extended worldwide for a stable, peaceful, and harmonious future for all people of this planet.

SOURCES AND LEVELS OF GOVERNMENT AND PRIVATE SUPPORT

There is no specific support designated entirely for ecologists in Korea. They have, however, a relatively good opportunity to receive research funds from the Ministry of Education, Ministry of Science and Technology, and Ministry of Agriculture. The amount of funds for each project is about two thousand U.S. dollars annually. The Traders Scholarship Foundation also provides some research funds each year.

Private corporations, such as Hyundai and Younam, also provide relatively large amounts of research funds every year; in fact, they provide larger amounts per project than the government. The Korean Foundation of Nature and Natural Resources Conservation organizes several teams for regional preliminary surveys, providing travel funds and per diem to the survey participants; most of the results are published by the Ministry of Public Affairs or the Foundation. The Inchon Foundation of the Dong-a Ilbo Daily has annually provided supplementary research funds the past several years.

In general, ecologists in college-level institutions have an opportunity to receive research funds almost every year in Korea. Some larger or better universities also provide small amounts of funds every year to encourage staff research work. The forthcoming Science Foundation of Korea may play a significant role in developing science and technology in this country. In the future, ecologists in Korea may have better opportunities than are currently available for pursuing their own research.

In general, this support allows the conduct of small-scale, relatively less sophisticated field and laboratory work for Korean ecologists. For large-scale, intensive fieldwork, such as community classification or ordination with multivariate statistical techniques for natural plant communities, productivity, and systematically planned physiological plant ecology, the amount of research funds is not yet adequate. Considering physical facilities, references, and the experiences of most Korean ecologists, international cooperation with competent foreign ecologists will give strong advantages and greater opportunities to them.

LEGISLATION ON ENVIRONMENTAL PROTECTION AND ENVIRONMENTAL CONSERVATION MOVEMENT

In order to keep environmental quality and abate environmental pollution, the Republic of Korea promulgated the Environmental Preservation Law (July 1978) and the Marine Pollution Control Law (July 1978). The Office of Environment, founded in 1980, is responsible for the implementation of the laws.

The Natural Parks Law was enacted in 1980. The Ministry of Construction has responsibility for designation, development, and maintenance of natural parks. The Law for the Protection of Cultural Heritage and National Monuments was promulgated in 1962. For the implementation of these laws, the Ministry of Public Affairs has the highest responsibility so far as conservation of nature and cultural heritage in Korea is concerned.

The Korean Association for Conservation of Nature (1964), Environmental

Protection Association (1979), and Korean Council for Natural Environmental Preservation (1978) are promoting a nationwide movement for environmental research, protection, and conservation. The Ministry of Interior also subsidizes these organizations.

TEACHING AND TRAINING OF ECOLOGY AT UNDERGRADUATE AND GRADUATE LEVELS

Presently, there is no department of ecology among Korean higher education institutions. However, some fifteen biology departments offer at least introductory general ecology courses for biology majors. In particular, junior colleges for teachers put high emphasis on ecology in their general biology education. The Korean Biology Education Association adopted the Green Version of BSCS (Biological Sciences Curriculum Study); the book has been adapted to Korean situations through the generous help of the BSCS home office. The official curriculum of Korean high school biology is heavily influenced by the Green Version.

In graduate schools, several courses in ecology, such as introductory plant ecology, animal ecology, and advanced plant ecology, are offered. The number of ecology majors at Seoul National University ranges from one to five; there are approximately five to ten students per year nationwide. Teaching facilities and faculty manpower for ecology courses are not yet satisfactory in most higher institutions, compared to those for biochemistry and physical sciences.

JOURNALS, SOCIETIES, AND FOREIGN LITERATURE

The Ecological Society of Korea was founded in 1976. The society publishes quarterly the *Korean Journal of Ecology,* for which manuscripts can be written in any one of the European languages (such as English, French, and German) or Korean. To date, all the papers have been written in either Korean or English; in all cases, an abstract is prepared either in Korean or one of the European languages. A total of sixty active members of the society meet annually.

The Botanical Society of Korea, founded in 1958, has about two hundred active members and publishes quarterly the *Korean Journal of Botany.* The Zoological Society of Korea, also founded in 1958, publishes a quarterly journal, the *Korean Journal of Zoology;* it has approximately three hundred active members. Prior to the foundation of these societies, there was the Korean Biological Society, founded in 1940 but dissolved in 1958. The Microbiological Society of Korea was established in 1963 and has around two hundred active members; it publishes quarterly the *Korean Journal of Microbiology.* The Limnological Society of Korea, founded in 1968, has around two hundred active members and publishes a quarterly journal, the *Korean Journal of Limnology.* Before the foundation of the Ecological Society of Korea, most ecological works were published in the several journals mentioned.

The major textbooks and references used by ecology students are the contemporary American and British ones (e.g., Odum, Daubenmire, Krebs, Kershaw, Grieg-Smith).

Ecology, published by the Ecological Society of America, is the main journal subscribed to in Korea. *Ecological Monographs,* the journals of the British Ecological Society, and *Oikos* are available to a few Korean ecologists. Some Korean ecologists subscribe to the *Japanese Journal of Ecology.*

BIBLIOGRAPHY

Animal

Choe, S. 1965. On the morphological variation and special feature of the elongated and stunted forms in the short-necked clam, *Tapes japonica* [in Korean with English abstract]. *Korean J. Zool.* 8:1–7. (The elongated forms are frequently found on tidal flats where circulation of sea water is active and the salinity is high with narrow fluctuations of salinity and temperature; stunted forms are found frequently at the tidal flats where the physical factors are opposite those of the elongated form.)

Hong, H. K. 1967. Bionomics of *Anopheles sinensis* Wiedmann in western plain area in Korea [in Korean with English abstract]. *Korean J. Zool.* 10:76–22. (The habit, habitat, and cardinal temperature for the biting activity were observed in detail.)

Hyun, J. S. 1963. Development of storage fungi in polished rice infested with rice weevil, *Sitophilus orygae. Seoul Univ. J.* 13:77–86. (It is found that the moisture content of grain increased to 42 percent at the bottom level in weevil-infested cylinders; however, it was 12 percent in the control after twelve weeks.)

Jolivet, P. H. A., B. G. Yi, and H. I. Ree. 1974. A trial for application of phytoecological cartography to detect the mosquito breeding places on an island in the Yellow Sea, Korea. *Korean J. Entomol.* 4:15–25. (By phytoecological mapping, the breeding sites of mosquitoes were determined in the small island of Wido; eight vegetation units were selected, then subdivided into communities.)

Kim, C. W., Y. T. Noh, and Y. W. Chung. 1959. Relationship between the host and its natural enemy introduced into a new ecosystem. 1. Mortality of *Hyphantria cunea* Drary killed by *Podisus maculiventis* [in Korean with English abstract]. *Korean J. Zool.* 12:103–108. (Percentages of host attached by ten *Podisus masculiventis* were determined in net cage with different host densities of 200, 400, and 800; the percentages were 95, 91, and 62 for the first generation and 96, 94, and 67 for the second generation.)

Lee, T. J. 1966. On the polymorphism of color pattern in *Scaptomyza pallida* [in Korean with English abstract]. *Theses Collection, Chungang University*

11:425–436. (In natural *Scaptomyza pallida* populations, the color pattern is influenced by environmental factors as well as hereditary factors; during summer, the percentage of the light-colored forms increases.)

Tyson, E. L. 1967. Small mammals in relation to Korean hemorrhagic fever. *Korean J. Zool.* 10:35–38. (*Mus musculus* was more closely associated with the Korean hemorrhagic than any other mammals, for example, *Rattus rattus, Crocidura laisura,* and *C. suaveolens.*)

Won, P. O. and K. J. Rhee. 1965. Ecological notes on narcissus flycatcher, *Muscicapa narcissina zanthopygia* Hay [in Korean with English abstract]. *Korean J. Zool.* 8:121–127. (The nesting, feeding, and breeding habits of the narcissus flycatcher were observed by the collar method (wrapping the necks) at fifteen nest-boxes in two localities in central Korea; the flycatcher may be one of the effective approaches for forest pest control.)

Parasitology

Kim, I. S., Y. W., Lim and H. W. Lee. 1974. Studies on field rodents collected in the hyperendemic areas of Korean hemorrhagic fever [in Korean with English abstract]. *Med. J. Korea Univ.* 11:263–291. (Of the 759 field rodents collected in the hyperendemic areas of Korean hemorrhagic fever (KHF), *Apodemus agoarius coreae* was one of the most prevalent species (80 percent). Seasonal incidence of the field rodent was correlated with that of KHF patients with two peaks in late spring and winter. For several species of rodents, the weights of spleen, liver, kidney, and maxillary lymph nodes were determined.)

Rim, H. J. 1977. Control of clonorchiasis in Korea. *Korean J. Rural Med.,* 2:43–52. (Distribution, life cycle, host species such as snails and fishes, and measures to control clonorchiasis were discussed.)

Seo, B. S. 1978. Malayan filariasis in Korea. *Korean J. Parasitol.* (Supplement).[16] (This is the most comprehensive, analytical, as well as synthetic, review on the subject in terms of interactions among *Filaria bancrofti, Aedes togoi* and human population.)

Plant

Chang, N. K. 1968. The amounts of the available phosphorus in soils of Kwangnung forest. *Korean J. Bot.* 11:99–102. (There seems to be a significant difference in the amount of available phosphorus among fourteen plant communities in Kwangnung forest.)

Chung, Y. H. and J. H. Shim. 1969. A study on the brackish water type of the Han River estuary [in Korean with English abstract]. *Korean J. Bot.* 12:126–134. (Daily variations of salinity distribution and composition of various kinds of phytoplankton in the Han River estuary were observed.)

Hong, S. W., Y. C. Hah, and Y. K. Chai. 1970. Ecological studies of halophyte on the high saline soil [in Korean with English abstract]. *Korean J. Bot.* 13:25–32. (The estimated amount of chloride absorbed by the halophytes was 24,629 ppm/100 cm^2.)

Im, H. B. 1970. Study on the salt tolerance of rice and other crops in reclaimed areas (x). Response of rice population to varying plant density and N levels in reclaimed salty areas. *Korean J. Bot.* 13:105–120. (Suggested is the importance of interaction between nitrogen treatment and population density in rice cultivation by a series of factorial analyses with consideration of leaf area index, production structure, and ratio of non-assimilation parts to assimilation parts.)

Jin, H. S. 1972. Studies on the competition-density effect of some high plants [in Korean with English abstract]. *Korean J. Bot.* 15:49–61. (Relative growth rates and net assimilation rates of *Raphanus acanthiformis* var. *simoodaeguen, Brassica campestris* var. *pekinensis, Oryza sativa* f. *kimmajae,* and *O. sativa* f. *mangyeng* in higher density cultivation were lower than those of lower density cultivation. The relationship was the opposite for leaf area ratio.)

Kim, J. H. 1977. On the budget of mineral nutrients of ginseng plant [in Korean with English abstract]. *Korean J. Ginseng Sci.* 2:59–65. (Of the soil nutrients nitrogen, phosphorus, and potassium in a ginseng plantation, it is suggested that the amount of phosphorus seems to be one of the most limiting factors.)

Lee, I. K., H. J. Lee, and K. S. Lee. 1970. The studies on affinity between *Miscanthus sinensis* and other plants [in Korean with English abstract]. *Korean J. Bot.* 13:149–159. (Allelopathic effect of *Miscanthus sinensis* on some plants and the positive effect on other plants was suggested by field plot growth experiments.)

______, J. H. Lee, S. Y. Kang, and S. L. Lee. 1977. A study on the marine algae in the Kwang Yang Bay. 2. The residues of organichlorine pesticides in marine algae [in Korean with English abstract]. *Korean J. Bot.* 20:53–57. (For *Sargassum thumbergii, Ulva pertusa, Codium flagile,* and *Enteromorpha linga,* the amounts of different organochlorine pesticide residues were determined; the range was from 0 to 93 μg/kg dry matter in Kwang Yang Bay.)

Ma, S. K. 1974. Studies on the estimation of Korean white pine (*Pinus koraiensis)* productivity by the quantification of environmental factors and their relation to the tree growth [in Korean with English abstract]. *Res. Rep. For. Res. Inst., Seoul, Korea* 21:41–115. (Among ten soil properties studied, the amounts of soil organic matter, soil texture, and exchangeable calcium in surface soil were significantly correlated with forest tree volume.)

Oh, C. Y. 1971. A pollen analysis in the peat sediments from Pyung Taek county, Korea [in Korean with English abstract]. *Korean J. Bot.* 14:126–133. (Peat was formed approximately 3,000 ± 500 years ago when the climate was cooler and moister.)

Oh, M. S. 1980. Pattern of grasses within Mt. Chung-gae in central part of Korean peninsula [in Korean with English abstract]. M.S. thesis, Sogang University. (Interspecies association, dimension, and annual increment of rhizome system and performance of *Calamagrostis arundinacea, Miscanthus sinensis,* and *Spodiopogon sibiricus* were studied in terms of pattern analysis by Greig-Smith. Of the twelve soil properties studied, potassium and calcium had significant correlation with pattern and interspecies association.)

Park, B. K. 1966. The grassland type in Korea [in Korean with English abstract]. *Korean J. Bot.* 9:39–45. (The author suggests nine kinds of grass communities in Korea: *Sasamorpha, Carex, Miscanthus, Pteridium, Arundinella, Themeda, Festuca, Phragmites,* and *Zoysia.*)

Uhm, K. B., and H. J. Kim. 1974. Ecological studies of the Lake Chanjamot. II. Primary production in Lake Changjamot during spring season [in Korean with English abstract]. *Korean J. Bot.* 17:53–62. (The amount of chlorophyll-*a* per square meter ranged from 25 to 277 mg from January to September, and the amount of daily gross production of carbon per square meter ranged from 655 to 2,859 mg.)

Yim, Y. J. and T. Kira. 1975. Distribution of forest vegetation and climate in the Korean Peninsula. 1. Distribution of some indices of thermal climate. *Jpn. J. Ecol.* 25:77–88. (The value of Thornthwaite's potential evapotranspiration (PE) was almost linearly correlated with that of Kira's warmth indices (WI); maps of WI and CI (Kira's coldness index) were drawn, and close agreement was found between the indices and the vegetation map.)

REFERENCES CITED

(* in Korean with English summary)

Choi, H. S. 1972. Dry matter economy of common mistletoe, *Viscum album* var. *coloratum*. *Theses Collection, Kyung Hee University, Seoul* 7:217–230.

Choi, K. C. 1964. Observations on the snails drilling young bivalves of *Tapes philippinarum*. *Seoul Univ. J.* 15:15–22.

———. 1965. Ecological studies on early stage of *Tapes philippinarum*.* *Coll. Educ. Rev., Seoul Nat. Univ.* 7:161–234.

———. 1969*a*. Fish population dynamics in the Choon-chun impondment.* *Korean J. Limnol.* 2:31–38.

———. 1969*b*. Studies on the structure of tidal flat ecosystem for increasing commercial clam yield.* *Korean J. Limnol.* 2:1–121.

Kim, C. M. 1958. Effect of saline and alkaline salts on the growth and internal components of selected vegetable plants. *Physiol. Plant.* 11:441–450.

———. 1965. The nutrient-holding capacity of soils of different forest types in Korea. *Seoul Univ. J.* 16:148–172.

———. 1966. The decomposition rate of pine and oak litters affecting the amount of mineral nutrients of forest soils in Korea. *Seoul Univ. J.* 17:83–92.

———. 1967. Growth of the chestnut tree, *Castanea crenata,* in relation to soil nutrients in Korea. *Jpn. J. Ecol.* 17:143–148.

———. 1973*a*. Influence of vegetation types on the intensity of ammonia and nitrogen dioxide liberation from soil. *Soil Biol. Biochem.* 5:163–166.

Kim, J. H. 1964*a*. Physiological and ecological studies on the growth of ginseng plants (*Panax ginseng*). IV. Sun-and-shade tolerance and optimum light intensity for the growth.* *Seoul Univ. J.* 15:94–101.

———. 1964*b*. Physiological and ecological studies on the growth of ginseng plants (Panax ginseng). V. On the photosynthesis, respiration, and dry matter production.* *J. Kongju Teacher's Coll.* 2:1–16.

———. 1971. Studies on the productivity and the production structure of the forests. 1. On the productivity of *Pinus rigida* plantation.* *Korean J. Bot.* 14:19–25.

———. 1972. Studies on the productivity and the production structure of the forests.

II. Comparison between the productivity of *Pinus densiflora* and of *Quercus mongolica* stands located near Choon-chun city.* *Korean J. Bot.* 15:1–8.

———. 1975. On the measurement of biomass and the productivity of cultivated mulberry plants.* *Korean J. Bot.* 18:121–128.

Mills, R. G. 1921. Ecological studies in the Tongnai River Basin, northern Korea. *Trans. Korea Branch R. Asiatic Soc.* 12:3–78.

Oh, K. C. 1959. Synecological studies on several forest communities in Kwangnung. Part II. *Theses Collection, Chungang Univ., Seoul* 4:497–519.

———. 1964. The sampling, pattern, and survival of the higher elevation beech in the Great Smoky Mountains. Ph.D. dissertation, The University of Tennessee, Knoxville, TN.

———. 1968. The climate and vegetation of Halla Mountain of the Quelpart Island.* *Report of the survey of Mt. Hanlasan,* pp. 60–89. Ministry of Culture and Public Information. Republic of Korea.

———. 1970. Pattern and association within *Pinus densiflora* communities in Kyunggi province, Korea.* *Korean J. Bot.* 13:33–45.

———. 1972*a*. Pattern and association within shrub layer under summer green forest in central Korean peninsula. *Korean J. Bot.* 15:33–41.

———. 1972*b*. An analysis of the relationship of soil factors to the height growth of *Pinus densiflora* within the young natural stands in central Korea.* *Korean J. Bot.* 15:1–12.

Song, S. D. 1975. Studies on the nitrogen economy and production of *Helianthus annus* population. *Korean J. Bot.* 18:101–108.

Wang, Chi-Wee. 1961. *The forests of China.* Cambridge: Harvard University Press.

Wilson, E. H. 1918. The vegetation of Korea. *Trans. Korea Branch R. Asiatic Soc.* 9:1–16.

32

PAKISTAN

Abdur Rahman Beg

PHYTOSOCIOLOGY OF TERRESTRIAL HABITATS

Work has mainly been centered on broad vegetation types; integrated vegetation-soil-landform studies; diversity and behavior of species in seral plant communities; dynamics of vegetation on sand dunes, baralands, plains, and some aquatic habitats; effect of enclosure on vegetation; classification of wildlife habitats; role of plant cover in watershed management; and ecopathological significance of heavy irrigation in three plantations.

Studies on Vegetation Types

Champion, Seth, and Khattak (1965) gave a comprehensive account of forest types of Pakistan, including climatic, seral, and edaphic types, as well as the ecological factors responsible for their development and distribution in the country. Zeller, Kalande, and Beg (1969) made a preliminary survey of Baluchistan and the Indus valley and gave a general account of the site and vegetation types of the area as observed during the survey in 1967. Their findings provide a useful basis for subsequent vegetation surveys.

An attempt to classify the juniper forest of Ziarat according to ecological criteria was made by Zeller and Beg (1969*a*). These juniper forests are quite homogeneous, the vegetation type changing gradually with altitude yet often abruptly depending on parent rock and soil type. In an area where the monsoon-type climate and Mediterranean climate overlap, Zeller and Beg

(1969*b*) studied the vegetation types of Dir and Chitral for an altitudinal range between 600 and 3,600 meters. It was shown that vegetation types are distinct and depend on the prevalence of one or the other climatic type.

A vegetation survey of the Pat area was made by Zeller and Beg (1969*c*), who recommended that, in view of the extremely arid climate and heavy, compact, and saline soil, the area should be managed only as rangeland except for tree growth along canals and for agriculture where irrigation combined with drainage is possible.

Beg (1978) investigated the vegetation of the Swabi-Gadoon area, recording two vegetation zones with sixteen vegetation types, and made recommendations for development of the area. Beg (1976) also gave an account of the vegetation of the Tarbela catchment area, describing five vegetation zones and nineteen vegetation types.

Repp (1963) studied vegetation zonation in the Rakhiot and Naltar valleys of the Karakoram and compared the vegetation of the two aspects of a mountain in Naltar. Recommendations were made for raising plantations for fuelwood production, improvement of rangelands, and protection of watersheds for water regeneration in the river catchments. Repp and Khan (1958*a*) gave a brief account of topography, climate, soil, and vegetation of the coastal desert tract between Hyderabad and Karachi and suggested some measures for improvement of pastures; they also gave a brief account (1958*b*) of climate, soil, and vegetation of the Tharparkar area and made some recommendations for its development. The vegetation of Ayub National Park was classified by Hussain (1969*a*) into four categories: vegetation in and around ponds, on plains, on hillocks, and on canal banks. Information on climate and human influence was also added as were recommendations. Ahmad (1964) described the vegetation of the plains and sandstone and limestone hills in the Salt Range, giving a brief account of ecological factors.

Chaudhri (1952*a*) gave a brief account of the vegetation growing in the waterlogged areas of the Shaikhupura district and, in particular, the vegetation of ditches, drains, low-lying moist areas, dry areas, and raised places, together with their edaphic and biotic factors.

A classification of five types of grass cover of Pakistan was proposed by Johnston and Hussain (1963). They recommended that research be focused on producing more fodder for which *Dichanthium, Cenchrus, Elionurus,* and *Chrysopogon* types of grass have the greatest potential.

An account of vegetation in the Mangla catchment area recognizes four vegetation zones based on a number of samples of vegetation throughout the area (WAPDA 1961).

Said (1951) studied the effects of biotic interference, soil, and flora of Salt Range forests and classified the forests into five local types. He proposed that kau forest is the climatic climax for the Salt Range and not chir pine.

The vegetation of Kaghan valley, together with climatic conditions, geology, and soil, was described by Chaudhri (1960). He divided the vegetation of the valley in nine types and noted that the absence of moonsoon rains in the interior of the valley created an environment for growth of Mediterranean plants.

Integrated Vegetation-Soil-Landform Studies

Higgins and Ibrahim (1970) conducted an integrated soil and vegetation survey of Thal and briefly described the climate, geology, geomorphology, and hydrology of the area. Twenty-one soil series were described and thirty plant communities discussed in relation to them. Present, as well as proposed, land use for different soils was presented, together with their suitability rating for various crops.

The vegetation and soil of wastelands around Lahore was studied by Rutter and Shaikh (1962), who described eight vegetation types and discussed vegetation in relation to various soil characteristics. Beg and Bakhsh (1974) studied the vegetation of scree slopes in Chitral Gol valley, recognizing eight plant communities. A short account of geomorphology, climate, and biotic factors is also given. Beg (1966) also gave a brief account of various ecological factors such as geology, geomorphology, soil, and climate of Quetta and environs. A comprehensive description of the vegetation data, based on a phytosociological table after the method of Braun-Blanquet was given. Preliminary plant ecological groups were defined and described, together with the habitats they indicated. Some suggestions as to management possibilities were also given.

Zeller and Beg (1969*d*) carried out detailed soil and vegetation studies in the riverain areas of the Hyderabad region. An attempt was made to understand the links between incidence and duration of flooding and the vegetation types, especially forests. It was found that the change of the Indus water regime, especially the extent of flooding caused by the construction of bunds and irrigation schemes, has a decided effect on survival and productivity of the natural riverain forest. Suggestions for the management of riverain forests, including the selection of suitable species for each site, have been made.

Beg and Repp (1965) conducted a vegetation survey in close association with a geomorphologist and a soil scientist during the integrated survey of the Porali plain (Lasbela). Sampling of vegetation was based on criteria of land systems and land units as delineated by the geomorphologist, and the vegetation was described as it appeared in those units and systems. Synoptic tables for vegetation, soils, and landforms were prepared as was a vegetation–land use map.

Vegetation in relation to land systems and land units was recorded by Repp and Khan (1959) in an integrated survey of the Isplingi valley. The indicator value of some plants was given, as were recommendations on improvement of rangelands. Repp and Khan (1958*c*) previously reported on vegetation and ecological factors in the Maslakh project area. They discussed vegetation in relation to topography and soil and, in particular, in relation to various geomorphological features. Effects of closure on improvement of vegetation and soil were given; some suggestions for improvement of vegetation and introduction of forage plants were also made.

Khan (1975) surveyed the vegetation in six different forests of Chakwal Forest Subdivision of Salt Range; six plant communities were worked out. Suggestions were made for encouraging the growth of useful plants and eradicating, from the ecological point of view, less useful species. Khan (1978) recognized three plant communities (*Rhazya stricta-Salvadora oleoides, Acacia modesta-Olea cuspidata-Dodonaea viscosa,* and *Cymbopogon jwarancusa-Cenchrus ciliaris-Dodonaea viscosa*) in a preliminary study of vegetation made at Shaikh Badin Hills, Dera Ismail Khan.

Hussain (1964) studied the vegetation of Nagar Parkar in an integrated survey of the area, describing vegetation on eleven land units. Root and shoot relationships of a few species were also investigated, and recommendations for proper range management and propagation of some indigenous tree species were made.

Vegetation in the flood plains of the Indus River at Dera Ismail Khan was surveyed by Alizai and Naqvi (1976), who described five plant communities in relation to some soil characteristics and flooding. The flood plains mainly carry herbaceous and shrubby flora, while trees are scarce; some recommendations were also made.

Webster and Nasir (1965) have given a brief account of vegetation growing on four habitat types found in Baltistan; they also described six vegetation types for the Hushe valley and added a list of 250 vascular plants and 56 bryophytes, together with brief ecological notes for each species.

Chaghtai and Ghawas (1976) studied the effect of exposure in the Malakand pass area. Three plant communities were identified, of which two were found on the northfacing slope and the third on the southfacing slope.

A phytosociological survey along the Gilgit-Gopis-Yasin-Phandar area was carried out by Ahmad and Qadir (1976), who recognized ten plant communities. All ten communities are briefly discussed as are the various factors affecting the vegetation.

Diversity

Chaghtai and Yusuf (1976) made a study of diversity and behavior of species in the seral communities of Kohat and the relationship between species diversity and its components. Species diversity and its components were found to be correlated with the structural characteristics of the communities.

Shaukat and Khan (1979) found that in a moderately diverse desert vegetation, diversity is almost equally measured by McIntosh's index $\frac{I - \sqrt{\Sigma n_i^2}}{N}$ and Margalef's H. McIntosh's index

$$\frac{N - \sqrt{\Sigma n_i^2}}{N - \sqrt{N}}$$

shows a somewhat low variability. The equitability is best measured by

$$\frac{N - \sqrt{\Sigma n_i^2} - \{N - \sqrt{[N - (S - 1)]^2 + (S - 1)}\}}{N - N/\sqrt{S} - \{N - \sqrt{[N - (S - 1)]^2 + (S - 1)}\}}$$

although

$$\frac{N - \sqrt{\Sigma n_i^2}}{N - \sqrt{[N - (S - 1)]^2 + (S - 1)}}$$

appears to be substantially more advantageous than other currently used equitability indices. Equitability indices were insensitive to small sampling variability, and ordinary standard deviation was found to be an appropriate equitability measure in situations in which the relative abundance pattern was geometric or approximately geometric. The two indices of species richness ($S/\sqrt{N}$ and $S-1/\text{Log } N$) show similar statistical behavior.

Vegetation Dynamics

Monsi and Khan (1957) studied vegetation on sand dunes and levelled areas in the Thal area and discussed it in comparison with that in other areas of Pakistan with a view to evaluating the role of plant cover as a control for soil erosion. The plant cover on levelled areas is somewhat higher than on tops of sand dunes in these arid areas. Some physiological behaviors of plants in these areas, particularly stomatal opening and transpiration in relation to soil moisture, are discussed and explained as a reason for the difficulty in re-vegetating sandy areas of low rainfall.

The patterns of vegetation of sand dunes of Karachi have been described by Chaudri and Qadir (1958), who classified them into three categories, namely, embryo, intermediate, and inland. Periodicity was also studied. The authors recommend using *Casuarina equisetifolia, Pongamia glabra,* and *Erythrina indica* for fixing coastal dunes, along with *Euphorbia tirucalli,* which was being used for this purpose at the time. Khan (1974) did a preliminary survey of the vegetation of sand dunes in the Cholistan Forest Division and studied the successional trends, giving brief accounts of climatic, edaphic, and biotic factors. He concluded that stabilization of these dunes would be possible by protecting indigenous vegetation through restriction of grazing by livestock, development of water points, and use of plant barriers against wind erosion.

Chaudhri (1952*b*) described the Bara Land, its edaphic and biotic factors, and plant succession leading to the development of sand dunes. He correlated the natural flora with soil, worked out plant indicators of soils, and suggested that investigation may be made on *Suaeda fruticosa* as an agent for removing excessive salt. He also investigated (1957) the process of plant succession in the plains of Pakistan, recording four main series of succession leading to the climax vegetation and two series resulting in the degeneration of the climax in the area.

Hussain (1969*b*) studied hydrosere succession in the Wah garden and adjacent hills and classified the vegetation as that in and around streams and spring water, and that on the hills. Information on climate and soils was also given.

Enclosure Studies

Khan and Hussain (1960) evaluated an enclosure at Hazarganji Forest, Quetta. On the basis of a vegetation study inside and outside the enclosure, they found that, despite no strict control on biotic influences, vegetation inside the enclosure was definitely better and richer. There was an improvement in the vegetation by 26–28 percent in terms of coverage, and trees and palatable grasses, particularly perennial ones, are present only inside the enclosure. As against seventy species with well-developed plants inside the enclosure, there were only eight more common ones, including thorny species, outside. Some suggestions for improvement of vegetation inside the enclosure were made. Khan and Bhatti (1956) observed that wastelands of Pakistan have great potential for raising fodder grasses and stressed the need for proper management of lands. They studied the effect of closure on vegetation in five places in Murree Hills in comparison with that outside the closure. Irshad (1961) studied the density of *Haloxylon* inside and outside the project area in Maslakh. He enumerated the associated species and discussed the problem of eradication of this unpalatable plant. Beg and Repp (1966) made preliminary ecological observations in the juniper forests of Ziarat, Baluchistan, particularly the effect of enclosure on recovery of vegetation in Batsargi experimental area. They mainly discussed juniper regeneration problems largely attributable to heavy grazing. Among the remedial measures recommended were protection against livestock grazing and trampling, especially in regeneration areas; artificial sowing in furrows; addition of juniper humus, and shading; selective cutting of male trees; and vegetative propagation by layering.

Noor (1978) studied vegetation changes inside an enclosure at Sari, Kaghan, in 1977 after one year's closure to grazing. Vegetation coverage definitely increased, and there was a threefold increase in forage production.

While *Agrostis gigantea* and *Potentilla sibbaldia* behaved as decreasers in the grazed area, the reverse was true for *Poa alpina.*

Wildlife Habitats

Beg (1975) gave a synoptic account of wildlife habitats of Pakistan, using vegetation types, subtypes, and stages as the basis of identification; he recognized eleven major and a large number of minor habitat types. The scheme is based mainly on the account of vegetation types by Champion, Seth, and Khattak (1965).

Watersheds and Irrigation

Raeder-Roitzsch and Masrur (1968) studied surface runoff, erosion, soil water storage, and evapotranspiration for different types of ground cover in the chir pine forest floor in the Himalayan foothills. Zeller and Beg (1968) prepared a note on the contribution of upper course riverain forests to watershed management. Although riverain forests have practically disappeared in the upper course of the streams of West Pakistan, it is possible, by studying the relict vegetation, to form a reasonably clear picture of the natural riverain vegetation. The different stages of colonization and succession of vegetation on sand spits and gravel banks were described, and it was suggested that the natural riverain vegetation can contribute greatly to a consolidation of river banks that would result in a considerable reduction of stream sediments.

Khan and Repp (1961) made ecological observations on the problems of forest hygiene, occurrence of disease, monocultivation, weeds, and biological desiccation of waterlogged areas in irrigated plantations, as well as on the vegetation and soil in the riverain forests of Pakistan.

Khan et al. (1956) investigated the mortality of shisham and other trees in relation to edaphic factors and irrigation in the Khanewal plantation and opined that mortality in shisham and for most species was not due to any pathogen. Among the various factors considered for inquiry into the problem are rainfall, temperature, irrigation, soil, and water temperature during the irrigation period. An airborne fungal pathogen, *Hendersonula toruloidea,* was found responsible for mortality in mulberry and bakain.

General

Reviewing the literature on ecological research on arid and semiarid regions of Afghanistan, India, and Pakistan, Bharucha (1955) stated that, as compared with the Western countries, ecological research in these countries is poorly developed, even though there is a considerable amount of pure systematic work that will form the basis of future ecological research. For Pakistan, he identified two major problems, alkaline soils and soil erosion. While problems of soil erosion had been tackled by the Forest Department and much work on alkaline soils had been done before partition of British India, much still remains to be done, particularly in the Baluchistan and North-West Frontier Province, which are still almost scientifically undeveloped. Pakistan, an arid country, however, advanced its agriculture.

AUTECOLOGY OF PLANTS

Autecological work has been centered mainly on plants that grow in the arid to semiarid, industrially polluted, and salt-affected areas of the country. Ahmad (1959) recorded that *Haloxylon recurum* (Khar) grows in saline valleys bounded by sand dunes and prefers that habitat. It can survive severe desiccation and recovers when moisture again becomes available, producing viable seeds which ripen during December–January.

Qaiser and Qadir (1971, 1972) reported that *Capparis decidua,* a very slow growing species, is widely distributed in the arid to semiarid region of Pakistan. It grows well in heavy soils but performs poorly on light soils. Phenology of the plant is influenced by topographical factors and varies accordingly. The seeds gradually lose their viability with the lapse of time but have a high percentage of germination. Moderately warm temperatures are required for successful establishment of seedlings.

The effect of industrial pollution on seed germination in different species was studied by Iqbal and Qadir (1973), who found a variety of responses. While the polluted water had a stimulating effect on germination of seeds of some species, there was no response in others, and germination percentage in certain other species was even less than in the control. *Prosopis juliflora, Cassia holosericea,* and *Acacia senegal* are those that were not affected by pollution conditions at the germination stage. The polluted water and polluted soil extracts both had similar effects on seed germination.

Muftee (1966) investigated the autecology of *Cynodon dactylon* and *Eleusine flagellifera.* He recorded that the former species occupies low-lying areas, has roots more than 300 centimeters long, and turned out to be highly tolerant to soil salinity in controlled experiments. As to the latter plant, it prefers raised places, has roots more than 290 centimeters long, and can tolerate moderate salinity only at maturity, being highly sensitive at germination stages.

ECOLOGY OF AQUATIC HABITATS

Fresh Waters

Ali (1970*a,* 1975) studied the bottom fauna of water tanks, streams, and canals in Dera Ismail Khan and Peshawar in the spring season, and found that the productivity of the bottom fauna was very high in water tanks by number as well as by weight, whereas it was low in the streams and canals. Ali (1966, 1974*a*) and Ali et al. (1974) found that the productivity of bottom fauna is abundant when the water is clear and vegetation luxurious. Productivity of organisms depends on ecological conditions, including the chemical nature of the ponds from summer through early winter. It was found that the presence of bloom in the ponds was due to organic pollution. The pH value of the water varied from 8.0 to 12.5; when the pH was high, there were no fish in the ponds, and only frogs abounded in large numbers.

Ali (1968*a*, 1969) also studied the productivity of the bottom fauna of streams, comparing it with ponds. The bottom fauna per unit area by number and weight was high in some of the streams, while it was usually high in all ponds before rains. He suggested that fish production could be improved by the systematic study of the bottom organisms during different seasons. He also studied (1968*b*, *c*; 1971*a*, *b*) the bottom fauna of streams of Rawalpindi, Wah, Kohat, Thal, Parachinar, Kotli, and the southern region of Azad Kashmir, Korang Nallah, and Rawlakot in spring. It was found that streams with low and moderate gradient were highly productive both in number and weight, while those with high gradient were less productive. He compared the productivity of bottom fauna in the Korang stream during different seasons, finding it to be rich in two or three seasons at moderate and low gradient stations, with the highest number of organisms in the low gradient stations. Productivity by weight was poor at high and moderate gradient areas in all seasons, and was much higher in Rawlakot streams by number but poorer by weight than in those of Rawalpindi.

Ali et al. (1975*a*) conducted a study of the productivity and variation of bottom fauna in number and weight on a monthly basis for an entire year in a water tank of Ishaque Ice Factory, Rawalpindi. They found that it was the highest in number and weight in August and the lowest in January.

Akhtar and Ahmad (1975) recorded alkalinity ranges of 250–400 and pH ranges of 7.5–8.0 as most favorable for the productivity of fauna in Haro River, Hassanabadal on the basis of observations made from October to June. The presence of nitrates and higher oxygen content was found to accelerate the growth.

Ali (1968*d*) reported that summer rains did not retard the productivity of bottom fauna of streams and rivers of Hazara district as in the case of Rawalpindi district. He divided Hazara into three regions, namely, Haripur-Havelian, Abbottabad, and Mansehra. On the basis of number, productivity in Haripur was grade I and the others, grade III; by weight, the productivity of all regions was grade II.

Polluted Waters

Ali (1970*b*) studied the effects of water pollution on bottom organisms and found that, after the confluence of Leh Nallah, the organisms are greater in number and heavier in weight per unit area than those of the non-polluted water. In polluted water, there is a larger number of fish, which are also bigger in size. Some insects of ocean waters were also present in the polluted water; Ali suggested that this was probably due to the presence of sufficient dissolved oxygen.

Productivity of bottom fauna was lower where the water is polluted by the organic matter issuing from the butchery into the springs of Muzaffarabad (Ali 1974*b*). In the industrially polluted water, dissolved oxygen was generally absent; total hardness was much above the standard; chloride content was very high; and hydrogen sulphide was present in sufficient quantities (Ali et al. 1975*b*). Aquatic insects were few, productivity of the bottom fauna was low, and algal flora was absent in such polluted waters.

Inshore Waters

Baquai and Rehana (1974) found that *Diaptomus dorsalis* was dominant (28 percent) among the calanoid zooplankton population of Kinjher Lake throughout the year, being 38.3 percent of the total zooplankton during the peak season of July; other species were dominant only once in the year. The population of calanoids is at its lowest in September (2.1 percent) because of a high bloom of phytoplankton overshadowing the zooplankton.

Nazneed (1974) conducted an ecological survey of phytoplankton in Kinjher Lake at six different stations to ascertain seasonal variation at the surface and at various depths. The investigation revealed that *Microcystis aeruginosa* was dominant at surface level throughout the year, with a peak during summer, followed by *Melosira granulata* and *Spirogyra fuellbornei; M. aeruginosa* was also more abundant in slow-moving waters. Growth at various depths was found to be irregular; however, the highest concentration was in the month of March at one meter.

Baquai and Rehana (1973) observed seasonal fluctuation in copepods in Kinjher Lake and correlated it with physicochemical properties. Temperature was the only effective factor. The pH of the lake varied from 6.0 to 6.5; salinity level remained static except in February; oxygen content was 3.4–8.4 ppl. All these factors had no effect.

Ali and Arshad (1965) found that, in all the months of observation, Korangi creek inshore waters are much more productive in plankton. Baka, Bhit, and Manora inshore waters are uniform in their composition but have smaller populations as compared to creeks because of the pollution of water in fish harbor and shipyard areas. At Korangi, May and September are peak months, while at Manora, June is productive. Copepods are more numerous in September and October; during the rest of the months, Lucifer, cladocera, and other copepods are not present. In late May, June, July, and early October, decopod larvae are commonly found. During the period of investigation, temperature and salinity ranged from 23°–28°C and 34.5–37.0 percent, respectively.

Saifullah and Hassan (1973*a*, *b*) studied the taxonomy and some aspects of the ecology of three species of Goniaulax, namely, *G. monacantha, G. polyedra,* and *G. polygramma,* and seven species of the genus *Amphisolenia. Goniaulax* is next to diatoms in terms of abundance, and has been associated with asphyxiation and toxicity in marine animals, such as fish and molluscs. *G. polyedra* occurred in Manora channel within the salinity range (36.0–36.5 percent) and temperature range (24.9°–29.1°C), while *G. monacantha* occurred at a temperature range of 24.9°–29.1°C and salinity range of 29.4–36.7 percent. All three species inhabit warm waters. Most of the species of *Amphisolenia* were found during the months of September, November, and December, and all the species were recorded in a temperature range of 24.9°–29.1°C and salinity range of 28.12–36.67 percent, except for a few for which low salinity values were recorded.

Coastal Marine

Ali and Arshad (1966) made preliminary observations on the composition of zooplankton in coastal waters. They observed that areas near the shore are the richest in zooplankton, and copepods are dominant in the group. Higher oxygen content appears to promote their productivity.

ECOPHYSIOLOGY

Work has mainly centered on water relationships of forest trees and the response of selected agriculture plants to the effects of soil salts, poor soil aeration, and nutrient regime. Repp (1967) studied the water relationships of *Dalbergia sissoo, Morus alba,* and *Eucalyptus tereticomis* in the plains and *Pinus roxburghii, Olea cuspidata,* and *E. tereticomis* in the mountains under their respective habitat conditions. She compared their leaf morphology, diurnal march of transpiration, stomatal openings, water balance, and drought tolerance using conventional techniques. She found that *E. tereticomis* was the most xeric, while *D. sissoo* had the lowest protoplasmic desiccation tolerance and a high rate of transpiration. *Morus alba* behaved as an evaporation type with no control over its transpiration, while *O. cuspidata* and *P. roxburghii* proved well suited to their habitats in terms of water balance. Zaman et al. (1970) standarized relative turgidity methods for assessing leaf water content in *E. camaldulensis* under Peshawar conditions and found a period of six hours as the optimum time for floating leaf discs on the water to attain turgidity.

Khan and Shaikh (1976) investigated the effect of different concentrations of sodium chloride on seed germination of *Capsicum annum* var. *longum.*

They found that it is not truly salt tolerant since it was adversely affected by salinity during growth. Wahab (1961) conducted a similar type of study on different varieties of agricultural crops under laboratory conditions. The study was, however, limited only to germination stages. Hasnain and Shaikh (1976) compared the growth of *Capsicum annuum* var. *longum* under flooded and drained soil conditions and found that the plant had its best growth in the latter case.

Shamim and Shaikh (1975) studied the effects of different levels of nitrogen on the growth of *Hibiscus cannabinus* in culture solutions; they found that 50 ppm of nitrogen was the optimum level for growth in this species. Ramzan (1967) has studied the effect of soil salinity and SAR on nutrient uptake by rye seedlings. He found that increase in SAR and salinity adversely affected the plant growth; sodium uptake was increased, while calcium and magnesium uptake was decreased.

Quraishi et al. (1977) investigated the diurnal fluctuations in water balance parameters of *Arceuthobium oxycedri* in relation to its host, *Juniperus excelsa,* in nature. They found that the mistletoe has no restrictions on its water loss as compared to its host, even under severe stress from reduced water supply. In their investigations on water balance of *Juniperus excelsa, Caragana ambigua,* and *Perovskia abrotanoides,* growing in the juniper forest tract at Ziarat (1978), they found juniper to be the most highly adapted species to the habitat as compared with the other two, having better control of its water loss under both normal and abnormal conditions.

ALLELOPATHY

From a combined field and laboratory study of *Cenchrus ciliaris* Linn. and *Chrysopogon aucheri* (Boiss) Stapf, Akhtar et al. (1978) found that, besides toxic root exudates, water extracts from each plant contained substances that proved to be inhibitory not only to its own growth but also to that of other species used in the bioassays. In both cases, toxicity increased with increasing concentration and soaking time. *Cenchrus ciliaris* was potentially more allelopathic than *Chrysopogon aucheri,* but again in both cases, toxicity was found to be species related. In another study, Khanum et al. (1979) reported both *Chloris gayana* and *Panicum antidotale* as potentially allelopathic and even self-toxic. The root exudates, besides inhibiting the root's own growth, reduced growth of *Chloris.* Aqueous shoot extracts inhibited radicle growth of both of the aforementioned species, as well as that of *Pennisetum americanum* and *Chrysopogon aucheri.* The toxicity of each species, however, depended on the amount of material soaked, length of time soaked, freshness of the material assayed, and test species used. In still another work, Hussain et al. (1979) recorded that *Datura innoxia* significantly inhibited germination and growth of a number of test species by root exudates, aqueous extracts from various parts, leachates, and substances volatilizing from its shoots. Soil collected under and around it was also inhibitory against the test species, phytotoxicity depending on the part assayed, its age, the test species used, and the physiologic process involved.

REFERENCES CITED

Ahmad, I. 1964. Vegetation of the Salt Range. *Pak. J. For.* 14:36–64.

Ahmad, M. and S. A. Qadir. 1976. Phytosociological studies along the way of Gilgit to Gopis, Yasin and Phundar. *Pak. J. For.* 26:93–104.

Ahmad, S. D. 1959. Distribution, ecology, economics, physiology and propagation of Khar plant, *Haloxylon recurvum* Bunge. *Pak. J. For.* 9:267–272.

Akhtar, N., H. H. Naqvi, and F. Hussain. 1978. Biochemical inhibition (allelopathy) exhibited by *Cenchrus ciliaris* Linn. and *Chrysopogon aucheri* (Boiss) Stapf. *Pak. J. For.* 28:194–200.

Akhtar, S. and M. Ahmad. 1975. Productivity of bottom fauna and chemical nature of Haro River. *Bull. Hydrobiol. Res. Gordon Coll.,* Ser. I, No. 3:17–24.

Ali, M. and M. Arshad. 1965. Quantitative analysis of the Karachi inshore water planktons. *Agric. Pakistan* 16:213–222.

———. 1966. Preliminary observation on the composition of zooplankton along the Karachi coast. *Agric. Pakistan.* 17:227–237.

Ali, S. R. 1966. The productivity of bottom fauna in a pond of New Gordon College Campus, Rawalpindi. *Pak. J. Sci.* 18:202–204.

———. 1968*a*. Bottom fauna of the streams of Kohat District and Kurram Agency after winter rains. *Pak. J. Sci. Ind. Res.* 11:449–454.

———. 1968*b*. Bottom fauna in a stream of Raw-lakot, Azad Kashmir in late spring. *Pak. J. For.* 18:373–378.

———. 1968*c*. Bottom fauna of the Korang stream, Rawalpindi. *Pak. J. Sci.* 20:266–270.

———. 1968*d*. Bottom fauna in streams and rivers of Hazara District after summer. *Pak. J. Sci. Ind. Res.* 11:208–211.

———. 1969. Effects of rain on the bottom fauna of the streams of Rawalpindi and Wah. *Pak. J. For.* 19:227–234.

———. 1970*a*. Bottom fauna of freshwater bodies of Dera Ismail Khan District in spring. *Agri. Pakistan* 21:205–213.

———. 1970*b*. Effects of water pollution on the bottom fauna of Soan River, Rawalpindi. *Pak. J. For* 20:69–73.

———. 1971*a*. Bottom fauna of the streams in spring season in relation to food of fishes. *Pak. J. Sci.* 23:73–77.

———. 1971*b*. Bottom fauna of the streams of the southern region of Azad Kashmir in spring session. *Pak. J. For.* 21:61–66.

———. 1974*a*. Aquatic fauna of the ponds of Lahore [In Urdu]. 15th Annual Science Conference.

———. 1974*b*. Bottom fauna of springs of Muzaffarabad Azad Kashmir [In Urdu].

———. 1975. Bottom fauna of certain freshwater bodies of Peshawar during spring season. *Pak. J. For.* 25:77–86.

———, M. Ahmad, and N. Akhtar. 1974. The productivity and chemical nature of three ponds of churharpal, Rawalpindi. *Bull. Hydrobiol. Res. Gordon Coll.*, Ser. 1, No. 1:1–4.

———, M. Ahmad, and Z. Khalil. 1975*a*. Hydrobiological studies of a water tank of Ishaque Ice Factory, Rawalpindi. *Bull. Hydrobiol. Res. Gordon Coll.*, Ser. 1, No. 4:pp. 25–32.

———, M. Ahmad, and Z. Khalil. 1975*b*. Organisms found in industrially polluted waters. *Bull. Hydrobiol. Res. Gordon Coll.* Ser. 1, No. 6:40–52.

Alizai, I. A. and H. H. Naqvi. 1976. Phytosociological studies of flood plains of Dera Ismail Khan, Pakistan. *Pak. J. For.* 26:7–13.

Baquai, I. U. and I. Rehana. 1973. Seasonal fluctuation of freshwater copepods of Kinjher Lake, Sind and its correlation with physicochemical factors. *Pak. J. Zool.* 5:165–168.

———. 1974. Quantitative and qualitative studies of the freshwater calanoid zooplankton of Kinjher Lake. *Pak. J. Zool.* 6:69–72.

Beg, A. R. 1966. Preliminary study of vegetation of Quetta. *Proceedings of the West Pakistan Range Management Conference,* Oct. 5–7, 1966, pp. 6–17.

———. 1975. *The wildlife habitats of Pakistan.* Bulletin No. 5. Peshawar: Forest Institute.

———. 1976. Vegetation of Tarbela catchment area. Submitted to WAPDA for their feasibility report. (Unpublished).

———. 1978. Vegetation. In *Causes, effects, and remedies of poppy cultivation in Swabi-Gadoon area.* Vol. I. Resource base, pp. 269–300. Board of Economic Inquiry, N.W.F.P., University of Peshawar.

——— and I. Bakhsh. 1974. Vegetation of scree slopes in Chitral Gol. *Pak. J. For.* 24:393–402.

——— and G. I. Repp. 1965. *Vegetation in integrated surveys of Porali Plain, 1964–1965.* Report No. 3. Quetta. Arid Zone Research Section, Geophysiocal Institute.

——— and G. I. Repp. 1966. Preliminary ecological observations in the juniper forests of Ziarat. *Silvi. Conf.* pp. 245–253.

Bharucha, F. R. 1955. Afghanistan, India and Pakistan. In *Plant Ecology, Review of Research,* pp. 19–39. (Arid Zone Research No. 6). Paris: UNESCO.

Chaghtai, S. M. and I. H. Ghawas. 1976. The study of the effect of exposure on community set-up in Malakand pass, N.W.F.P., Pakistan. *Sultania* (Herbarium, PCSIR., Lab., Peshawar.) No. 2, pp. 1–8.

——— and M. Yusuf. 1976. A study of diversity and behavior of species in seral communities of Kohat. *Pak. J. For.* 26:249–255.

Champion, H. G., S. K. Seth, and G. M. Khattak. 1965. *Forest types of Pakistan.* Peshawar: Pakistan Forest Institute.

Chaudhri, I. I. 1952*a*. The vegetation of the waterlogged areas of District Sheikhupura of the Punjab. *Pak. J. For.* 3:74–83.

———. 1952*b*. Observations on the vegetation of Bara Land of the Punjab. *Pak. J. For.* 2:188–200.

———. 1957. Succession of vegetation in the arid regions of West Pakistan plains. In *Proceedings of the Karachi, UNESCO/FACP symposium on soil erosion and its control in arid and semiarid zones,* Karachi. pp. 141–155.

______. 1960. Vegetation of Kaghan valley. *Pak. J. For.* 10:285–294.

______ and S. A. Qadir. 1958. Sand dunes vegetation of coastal region of Karachi. *Pak. J. For.* 8: 337–341.

Hasnain, S. and K. H. Shaikh. 1976. Effects of flooding and drainage on the growth of *Capsicum annuum* L. *biologia* 22:89–120.

Higgins and Ibrahim. 1970. Integrated soil and vegetation report. *Thal Report* No. 10 and 11.

Hussain, F., B. Mubarak, I. Haq, and H. H. Naqvi. 1979. Allelopathic effects of *Datura innoxia* Mill. *Pak. J. Bot.* 11:141–153.

Hussain, S. S. 1969*a*. Vegetation survey of Ayub National Park, Rawalpindi. *Pak. J. For.* 19:339–348.

______. 1969*b*. Phytosociological survey of Wah Garden. *Agric. Pakistan* 20:309–325.

Iqbal, M. Z. and S. A. Qadir. 1973. Effect of industrial pollution on seed germination. *Pak. J. Bot.* 5:155–158.

Irshad, S. M. 1961. *Haloxylon* on Maslakh range. *Pak. J. For.* 11:302–304.

Johnston, A. and I. Hussain. 1963. Grass cover types of West Pakistan. *Pak. J. For.* 13:239–247.

Khan, A. H., A. G. Asghar, C. G. Rasul, and A. Hamid. 1956. Observations on the mortality of shisham (*Dalbergia sissoo* Roxb.) and other trees in Khanewal Plantation. *Pak. J. For.* 6:109–126, 203–220, and 289–301.

Khan, A. H. and A. G. Bhatti. 1956. Effect of closure on growth of grasses. *Pak. J. For.* 6:187–190.

Khan, A. H. and S. M. Hussain. 1960. Ecological studies in Hazarganji forest, Quetta. Proceedings of the 4th PIOSA Congress, Karachi, Section D.

Khan, A. H. and G. I. Repp. 1961. Some ecological observations in irrigated plantations and riverain forests of West Pakistan. *Pak. J. For.* 11:340–374.

Khan, M. H. 1974. A preliminary report on the sand dune vegetation of Cholistan. *Bitki Cilt* 1, *Sayi* 4:449–554.

______. 1975. Ecological observations of some halophytic communities in the Salt Range, Pakistan Forests. *Bitki Cilt* 2, *Sayi* 3:329–336.

______. 1978. Preliminary study of plant communities in Shaikh Badin Hills, D. I. Khan. *Pak. J. For.* 28:210–205.

Khan, S. S. and K. H. Shaikh. 1976. Effects of different levels of salinity on seed germination and growth of *Capsicum annuum* L. *Biologia* 22:15–60.

Khanum, S. E., F. Hussain, and H. H. Naqvi. 1979. Allelopathic potentiality of *Chloris gayana* Kunth and *Panicum antiodotale* Retz. *Pak. J. For.* 29:245–249.

Monsi, M. and A. H. Khan. 1957. Some ecological studies on natural vegetation in Thal. In *Proceedings of the Karachi,* UNESCO/FACP symposium on soil erosion and its control in arid and semiarid zones, Karachi. pp. 157–168.

Muftee, R. A. 1966. Soil water and salinity as factors in the ecology of *Gynodon dactylon* Pres. and *Eleusine flagellifera* Nees. *Pak. J. For.* 16:177–193.

Nazneen, S. 1974. Seasonal distribution of phytoplankton in Kinijher (Kalari) Lake. *Pak. J. Bot.* 6:69–82.

Noor, M. 1978. Comparison of grazed and ungrazed vegetation of subalpine ecological zone at Sari. *Pak. J. For.* 28:186–189.

Qaiser, M. and S. A. Qadir. 1971. A contribution to the autecology of *Capparis decidua* (Forsk.) Edgew. Seed germination and the effect of topographic conditions on the growth, abundance and sociability. *Pak. J. Bot.* 3:37–60.

———. 1972. A contribution to the autecology of *Capparis decidua* (Forsk.) Edgew. II. Effect of edaphic and biotic factors on growth and abundance. *Pak. J. Bot.* 4:137–156.

Quraishi, M. A., A. Khalique, S. Perveen, and P. Akhtar. 1977. Water relations of dwarf mistletoe, *Arceuthobium oxycedri* M. Bieb. in relation to that of its host, *Juniperus excelsa* M. Bieb. *Pak. J. For.* 27:198–202.

———. 1978. Ecophysiological investigations on the water balance of three important species of juniper forest tract at Ziarat (Baluchistan). *Pak. J. For.* 28:35–42.

Raeder-Roitzsch, J. E. and A. Masrur. 1968. Some hydrologic relationships of natural vegetation in the chir pine belt of West Pakistan. *Watershed Management Conference,* pp. 345–360.

Ramzan, M. 1967. Effect of salinity and SAR on the plant growth and cation uptake by rye seedlings from the equilibrated soils. *Agric. Pakistan* 18:479–500.

Repp, G. I. 1963. *Vegetation studies in the arid zone of the river catchments in Karokoram.* Technical Report No. 6. UNESCO Plant Ecological Project. Pakistan Forest Institute, Peshawar.

———. 1967. *Ecophysiological investigations on some forest trees in West Pakistan.* UNDP/FAO Report. No. 2. Pakistan Forest Institute, Peshawar.

——— and A. H. Khan. 1958*a*. *The coastal desert of Sind between Karachi and Hyderabad.* Technical Report No. 3. UNESCO Plant Ecological Project, West Pakistan Forest Institute.

——— and A. H. Khan. 1958*b*. *Tharparker area in Sind: climate, soil and vegetation.* Technical Report No. 2. UNESCO Plant Ecological Project, West Pakistan Forest Institute.

——— and A. H. Khan. 1958*c*. *Integrated plant ecological studies in Maslakh range improvement project.* Technical Report No. 8. UNESCO Plant Ecological Project, Pakistan Forest Institute.

——— and A. H. Khan. 1959. *Integrated survey of Isplingi Valley.* Technical Report No. 7. UNESCO Plant Ecological Project, Pakistan Forest Institute.

Rutter, A. J. and K. H. Shaikh. 1962. A survey of the vegetation of wastelands around Lahore and its relation to soil. *Biologia* 3:91–122.

Said, M. 1951. Ecology of Salt Range Forests. *Pak. J. For.* 1:310–323.

Saifullah, S. M. and D. Hassan. 1973*a*. Planktonic dinoflagellates from inshore waters of Karachi. Part I. *Goniaulax* Diesing. *Pak. J. Zool.* 5:143–148.

———. 1973*b*. Planktonic dinoflagellates from inshore waters of Karachi. Part II. *Amphisolenia* Stein. *Pak. J. Zool.* 5:149–156.

Shamim, G. and K. H. Shaikh. 1975. Effects of different levels of nitrogen on the growth of *Hibiscus. Biologia.* 21:125–141.

Shaukat, S. S. and D. Khan. 1979. A comparative study of the statistical behavior of diversity and equitability indices with reference to desert vegetation. *Pak. J. Bot.* 11:155–165.

Wahab, A. 1961. Salt tolerance of various varieties of agricultural crops at the germination stage. *UNESCO Arid Zone Research* 14:185–192.

WAPDA. 1961. Vegetation of the Mangla catchment. In *Mangla Watershed Management Study.* Vol. 2. General Report, pp. 11–17. Hunting Technical Services, Ltd.

Webster, G. L. and E. Nasir. 1965. The vegetation and flora of the Hushe valley (Karakoram Range, Pakistan). *Pak. J. For.* 15:201–234.

Zaman, M. B., A. H. Khan and A. Khalique. 1970. Determination of internal water balance in *Eucalyptus* under field conditions. *Pak. J. For.* 3:55–62.

Zeller, W. and A. R. Beg. 1968. The contribution of upper course riverain forests to watershed management. *Watershed Management Conference,* pp. 295–298.

———. 1969*a*. *Preliminary classification of the juniper forests in the Ziarat region.* Ecological papers, UNDP/FAO Project. Pak. Forest Institute, Peshawar.

———. 1969*b*. *Review of some vegetation types of Dir and Chitral.* Ecological papers, UNDP/FAO Project. Pak. Forest Institute, Peshawar.

———. 1969*c*. *Vegetation survey of Pat area.* Ecological papers, UNDP/FAO Project. Pak. Forest Institute, Peshawar.

———. 1969*d*. *Report on an ecological survey of the riverain forests of Hyderabad Region.* Ecological papers, UNDP/FAO Project. Pak. Forest Institute, Peshawar.

Zeller, W., P. Lalande, and A. R. Beg. 1969. *Reconnaissance survey of Baluchistan and the Indus Valley.* Ecological papers, UNDP/FAO Project. Pak. Forest Institute, Peshawar.

33

SINGAPORE

Kuan-hon Chow

INTRODUCTION

Singapore lies 137 km north of the equator and consists of a main island 41.8 km long and 22.5 km wide (584 km^2 in area), and fifty-four isles, about two dozen of which are inhabited. The main island, linked to Malaysia by a 1,056-m causeway, is generally low-lying and undulating with about 64 percent of the area lower than 15 m of elevation and only 10 percent higher than 30 m. The highest hill (Bukit Timah) reaches only 177 m. There are a few short and sluggish rivers, or rather streams. Singapore's coastline stretches 133.6 km and is mostly flat, consisting of fine sand and mud.

The climate of Singapore is essentially equatorial but equable and pleasant owing to the modifying influence of the sea. Yearly mean temperature is 26.6°C, and the temperature rarely falls below 21°C or rises above 35°C. Rainfall is abundant, about 2,500 mm per year, and fairly evenly distributed throughout the year; there are about 180 rainy days per year. Much of the rainfall is of convective origin and comes from large cumulus or cumulonimbus clouds. Such rainfall tends to be local in distribution so that while certain areas of the island are receiving heavy rainfall, nearby areas may be completely dry. The average relative humidity is 84.3 percent. Daylength in Singapore is constant; the difference between the shortest and the longest days of the years is only nine minutes. However, because of frequent cloudiness and rainfall, there is an average of only 5.6 hours of sunshine per day and 404 cal/cm^2 per day of incoming solar radiation. Singapore is untroubled by typhoons, cyclones, or earthquakes.

The population of Singapore was about 2.3 million in 1979. By origin, about 76 percent are Chinese, 15 percent Malays, and 7 percent Indians and Pakistanis; the remaining 2 percent belong to the other races. The majority of the population is urban, and a small percent is rural. Industrialization is already well advanced and is proceeding rapidly such that Singapore's standard of living is second in Asia, next to that of Japan. Most of its people are well fed, well housed, and well educated. In 1975, the population of Singapore had a birth rate of 2 percent, death rate of 0.5 percent for a population growth rate of 1.6 percent. Median age was 19.7 years, and life expectancy at birth was 67 years (Myers 1976). The number of children per woman by the end of her reproductive life-span was 2.5 in 1978 (IPPF 1979).

Before the Second World War, there was no science education in Singapore at the university level. The first university, then called University of Malaya, was founded in Singapore on October 8, 1949. The botany department was headed by Professor R. E. Holttum and was attended by twelve students in the first year. In 1950, a Department of Zoology, headed by Professor R. D. Purchon, was established. Ecology has been taught as a subject by the two departments since their establishment. The second university, Nanyang University, was officially declared open on March 15, 1956. At that time, it had two colleges, Arts and Science; biology was a department in the Science College. Ecology has been taught as a subject in the biology department. In July 1980, the two universities were merged to form the National University of Singapore.

NATURAL VEGETATION AND WILD ANIMAL LIFE

Natural Vegetation

Before the nineteenth century, the island was covered mainly by tropical rain forest. In 1819, the establishment of a trading post and settlement by the East India Company of London marked the beginning of changes in the original vegetation. Forests were cleared for settlement and cultivation, and by 1893, the government became seriously alarmed at the extent of forest depletion and passed legislation for its control. In 1895, a total of 5,028 hectares of forests were rescued and declared forest reserves. These made up about 9 percent of the total area of the island. However, due to the increased pressure for land, some of the forest reserves were released later for settlement and development. Today, the only original vegetation left is the sixty-six hectares of rain forest at Bukit Timah Hill. In addition, there are about 2,718 hectares of water catchment area confined to the center of the island; this consists mainly of secondary forests. A. Johnson (1973*b*) categorized the vegetation types in Singapore as follows:

A. Primary vegetation
   a. Lowland tropical evergreen forest: Tropical rain forest found in well-drained areas; freshwater swamp forest found in poorly drained areas; and riparian forest found rarely along some rivers.
   b. Mangrove forest.
   c. Beach vegetation.
   d. Freshwater aquatic vegetation found in ponds, streams.
B. Secondary vegetation
   a. Secondary forest, scrub and grassland: secondary forest and thicket; secondary scrub on eroded or exhausted soil; and lalang grassland.
   b. Cultivated land.
   c. Urban areas including buildings with their gardens and parks.
   d. Devastated areas including abandoned building sites, roads, and air fields.

Tropical Rain Forest Vegetation

The tropical rain forest in Singapore is lowland forest with the dominant trees belonging to the family Dipterocarpaceae. Nearly all the dipterocarps are big trees with resinous wood, alternate, simple leaves, and yellow or pink flowers. Some isolated trees, often seraya (*Shorea cutisii*), may rise above the dominate stratum. Apart from dipterocarps, trees belonging to other families are often encountered, such as jelutong (*Dyera costulata*), jumbu (*Eugenia* spp.), oaks (*Lithocarpus* spp.), *Colophyllum* spp., *Garcinia* spp., and *Koompassia malaccensis.*

The shrub layer of the rain forest consists chiefly of the tree seedlings mixed with certain shrubs or small tree ferns that never grow to great height; these include *Agrostistachya sessilifolia, Aporosa benthamiana, Calophyllum* spp., and *Garcinia parvifolia,* among others. Ground flora of the rain forest consists of some shade-tolerant herbaceous plants and ferns. Ferns are particularly abundant at the Bukit Timah Hill, which supports a sixty-six hectare patch of the original rain forest: among 168 fern species found in Singapore, about half are found there, with fifteen species strictly confined to it (Wee and Rao 1977). Epiphytes, lianas, and climbers are also abundant; Awan (1968) has given a detailed account of the epiphytes in Singapore. A group of botanists and ecologists organized by Wong Yew Kwan has undertaken a study of the composition, size, regeneration, and succession of the trees at the Bukit Timah Hill.

Mangrove Vegetation

Mangrove is found inside tidal river mouths and may spread along the coast with fine mud. Mangrove trees are relatively small in size and girth. Compared with the inland forests, there are remarkably fewer species in the mangrove forest owing to the peculiar conditions of their existence. The tree flora is almost confined to six families: Rhizophoraceae, Sonneratiaceae, Verbenaceae, Meliaceae, Combrataceae, and Rubiaceae. The Rhizophoraceae is the most important mangrove family; four genera (*Rhizophora, Bruguiera, Ceriops,* and *Kandelia*) are commonly found in the mangroves, and all of them have vivaparous seedlings. The Sonneratiaceae is represented by the genus *Sonneratia,* the Verbenaceae by *Avicennia,* Meliaceae by *Xylocarpus; Lumnitzera* and *Scyphiphora* are the representatives of Combrataceae and Rubiaceae, respectively. The important shrubs and climbers in the mangrove forest include *Acanthus ebracteatus, Ceripos lagal,* and *Derris* spp.

Beach Vegetation

Sandy beaches support a distinctive flora in Singapore. The upper parts of the sand may become invaded by some herbaceous plants with a spreading growth habit, which act as sand binders through their rhizomes. These plants belong mainly to grass species (such as *Dactyloctenium aegyptium, Ischaemum muticum, Brachiania distachya*) and sedge species (*Remirea maritima, Fimbristylis dichotoma,* and *Cyperus* spp.). The narrow band of sandy beach forest includes such tree and shrub species as *Hibiscus tiliaceus, Calophyllum inophyllum, Scaevola taccada, Cocos nucifera, Cerbera odollam, Breynia* sp., and *Derris* sp. In a recent visit to a sandy beach on Hantu Island, Rao and Wee (personal communication) produced a list of plants found there, including twenty-one natural species, sixteen weed species, eleven tree and shrub species, and sixteen introduced species.

Because of a shortage of land, Singapore has been reclaiming foreshore land for the development of industrial, housing, and recreational projects. The properties of the reclaimed land deviate far from the normal soil series. The soil of reclaimed land is highly compact and structureless, and poor in nutrients. The high intensity of light and wind promotes a drying affect on the plants, as well as to the soil surface. However, the major problem of plant growth on reclaimed land lies in drainage rather than in nutrition. Because the land is flat and highly compact, there is insufficient surface drainage and percolation. Remedial measures to improve plant growth on reclaimed land were suggested by Lee (1977).

Freshwater Vegetation

Though often ignored because of their small size, the algae are the most important freshwater plants. Most freshwater algae are green algae; other common groups are the diatoms and blue-green algae. Nah (1977) investigated the factors that may underlie the dominance of the blue-green algae, *Microcystis aeruginosa,* in Seletar Reservoir. He concluded that the dominance of this species was due to its high-yield production at low nutrient levels and its productive buoyancy.

Totally submerged higher plants in Singapore are few in number, and include ditch moss (*Hydrilla verticilla*), *Cryptocoryne affinis,* and bladderwort (*Utricularia flexuosa*). Emergent plants are numerous, including arrowhead (*Sagittaria sagittifolia* introduced), yellow burhead (*Limnocharis flava* introduced), short-leaved pipewort (*Eriocaulon truncatum*), common Malayan wallow herb (*Ludwigia suffructicosa*), common knotweed (*Polygonum barbatum*), sacred lotus (*Nelumbo nucifera*), and various freshwater sedges. Floating plants found in Singapore include water hyacinth (*Eichornia crassipes* introduced), hastate-leaved pond weed (*Monochoria hastata*), duckweed (*Lemna perpusilla*), rootless duckweed (*Wolffia arrhiza*), water lettuce (*Pistia stratioides*), and aquatic sensitive plant (*Neptunia oleracea*). *Azolla pinnate* and *Salvinia auriculata* (introduced) are common floating ferns.

Corner (1978) described the freshwater swamp-forests in Singapore and south Malaya, both by enumeration of the component species and by description of the communities that succeed each other along the upstream gradient. His book includes a great deal of new or important data on the form, behavior, and growth of individual species, among which were many previously undescribed species. The succession of riparian belts leading to the swamp-forest is described, as is that of the coastal belts leading to the interior swamp-forest.

Secondary Vegetation

Secondary vegetation is more widespread than is the tropical rainforest in Singapore. It occupies much of the area where land has been cleared for plantation. Subsequently, the land has been left uncultivated and forest has been regenerated. The trees of the secondary forest are, on the whole, shorter than those of the rain forest. They are often quite varied, although less so than those of the rain forest. There is usually an abundant undergrowth of shrubs, ferns, and saplings in the secondary forest.

Inland cleared lands are often covered with low scrub, which marks a stage in the succession to secondary forest; but, because of the poor and shallow soil, the succession has been more or less permanently arrested at this stage. D. S. Johnson (1964*b*) described the common shrubs found in the scrubs in Singapore.

Some abandoned lands are covered with a tall grass called lalang (*Imperata cylindrica*). D. S. Johnson (1964*b*) stated that the lalang grasslands that were left undisturbed were in the process of turning into scrub. With repeated cutting and occasional burning, the shrubs were exterminated and the lalang flourished. A number of herbaceous legumes occur naturally on the cleared lands and abandoned places. Chow (1974) described the morphology and ecology of twelve wild herbaceous legumes in Singapore. He also introduced sixteen herbaceous legumes from various tropical areas and evaluated their possible roles in soil fertility improvement and soil erosion control with secondary vegetation in Singapore (Chow 1964).

Marine Vegetation

The true seaweed flora is well developed on reefs, particularly in the southern islands of Singapore (Purchon and Enoch 1954). The most luxuriant growth of seaweed is found in the littoral region that is covered twice a day by high tide and in the upper sublittoral region below the limits of the lowest tide. The upper belt of seaweeds includes a green belt of sea lettuce (*Ulva reticulata*), together with the microphytic *Clapophora, Enteromorpha,* and other small species. Where a mud bank has drifted across the coral area, *Enhalus acoroides* may be encountered, but on pure coral there will normally be a brown seaweed zone with various species of *Sargassum, Turbinaria ornata, Cystoseira prolifera,* and *Padina commersonii.*

D. S. Johnson (1964*b*) stated that the most conspicuous marine plants are those forming weedbeds at and just below low-tide level. The most important on sandy and muddy beaches are the long-leaved *Enhalus acoroides* and *Sargassum,* which form similar beds on rocky shores and coral reefs. Other seashore algae include the green sea lettuce (*Ulva reticulata*), branching green species of *Caulerpa,* the stony green algae (*Halimeda* sp.), mermaid's fan (*Padina commersonii*), and the much-branched monkey's feathers (*Hydroclathros cancellatus*).

Wild Animal Life

Terrestrial Animal Life

Medway (1969) has given a detailed account of the mammals in Singapore and Malaya. The house shrew (*Suncus murinus*) is widespread in towns, and the greater treeshrew (*Tupai glis*) is common. The ordinary house rat (*Rattus diardii*), little house rat (*R. exulaus*), and house mouse (*Mus musculus*) are widespread in houses. The common red-bellied squirrel (*Callosciurus notatus*) and the slender little squirrel (*Sundasciurus tenuis*) seem to be the only tree squirrels present. The long-tailed macaque (*Macaca fasciata*) is the common monkey found in Singapore.

Among the members of Felidae, tigers (*Panthera tigris*) used to occur with some frequency in the last century. However, the last tiger shot in Singapore was in 1932. Leopards (*Panthera pardus*) used to occur but have not been recorded for many years. The leopard cat (*Felis bengalensis*) occurred until a few years ago and is probably still present in some number (Harrison 1966).

Among reptiles, snakes and house lizards are the most common. Tweedie

(1957) listed a total of well over a hundred species of land snakes in Malaya and Singapore; sixteen are venomous and five of these are dangerous to human life (Sharma 1973). House lizards are very common in Singapore; they do more good than harm by helping to keep the number of unwanted insects low. Chou (1975, 1976) reviewed the taxonomy and systematic status of the house lizards and studied the eggs, incubation period, hatchlings, growth rate of hatchlings, and tail regeneration rates of five species commonly found in Singapore. The most common species, *Hemidactylus frenatus,* had the shortest incubation period and the fastest tail regeneration rate.

Singapore is poor in birds in variety and absolute numbers. Glenister (1951) listed nearly 230 species occurring in Singapore; this list has subsequently been increased, but many of these species are occasional migrants or rare, or shy, skulking birds of forest and mangrove which are easily missed. In a particularly well situated garden comprising 0.8 hectares of mixed vegetation, only forty-eight kinds of birds were seen over a period of eighteen months, and only thirty were resident or regular visitors. Most Singapore gardens would yield a much smaller species count. D. S. Johnson (1964*b*) stated that birds seemed better able to adapt to the presence of humans than were mammals, and a considerable number of species are to be found in suburban gardens and even in the center of the town. He (1973*a*) described the birds of different habitats in Singapore.

Corbet and Pendlebury (1956) stated that about four hundred species of butterflies have been recorded from Singapore, and Morrell (1960, 1973) described the butterflies of nine families found in Singapore. He also stated that the moths are far too numerous for a list, and that the macrolepidoptera alone must number several thousands. Murphy (1973*a*) published an illustrated identification manual to 118 genera of ants, including all those known to occur in the wet equatorial region centered in Singapore.

Murphy (1973*b*) studied the animals in the forest ecosystems of Singapore. He reported that the vertebrates of the upper canopy were predominantly herbivores, such as the flying lemurs (*Cynocephalus veriagatus*), two species of squirrels (*Callosciurus notatus* and *Sundasciurus tenuis*), and a small troop of monkeys (*Macaca fascicularsis*); the lower canopy fauna consisted largely of such carnivores as snakes (*Chrysopelea* and *Aheatulla*), rats (*Rattus annadalei* and *R. surifer*), tree-shrews (*Tupaia glis*), tiny shrews (*Crocidura fuliginosa*), lizards (*Mabuya* and *Goniocephalus*), and tree frogs. The microarthropods in the upper canopy include scale insects and their predators such as eucyrtid wasps, coccinellid beetles, spiders, and twig and leaf-running ants (mostly species of *Crematogaster, Monomorium,* and *Gauromyrmex*), while those in the lower canopy are dominated by a variety of tetranychid and oribatid mites, ants, and spiders; Collembola (mainly species of *Epimetrura, Salina,* and *Willowsia*); Psocoptera (of which the most common is *Archipsocus*); and thrips, in roughly that order of importance. Flies, ants, Psyllidae, and other small Homoptera are also abundant. The animals of ground level and soil were also described and an account of the horizontal distribution of animals in the forest ecosystem in Singapore was also given (Murphy 1973*b*).

Marine Animal Life

Owing to the large amounts of freshwater discharged by the rivers of southern Johore, Singapore seawater is always less saline than that of neighboring open seas. Tham (1973*b*) divided the fish fauna around Singapore into four groups, based on their distribution, i.e., inshore waters up to the 18.5-m line in Singapore Straits, Johore Straits, and the coral reef area.

The fish fauna within the 18.5-m line in Singapore is very rich in species. There are more than 150 species from a little over fifty families; most of the species are small, plankton feeders, and only a comparatively few are benthos feeders. There appears to be a balance between the numbers of plankton-feeding fish and benthos-feeding fish (Le Mare and Tham 1954).

The fish fauna in Singapore Straits beyond the 18.5-m line is relatively limited in species, *Stolephorus* spp., *Caranx* spp., *Scomberomorus lineolatus,* and *Chirocentrus dorab* predominating (Tham 1973*b*). Khoo (1973) studied the fish fauna of Johore Straits and concluded that most species found in Singapore Straits were also found in Johore Straits; however, such species as *Tilapia mossambica, Toxotes jaculator, Batrachus* spp., *Antennarius commersonii,* and *Abudefduf* spp. were found only in the Johore Straits, not in the Singapore Straits.

Around the coral reefs, the fauna is distinctly different, in that certain species such as members of the Labridae and Scaridae are very common. Also, atherinids, siganids, *Pentapus* spp., serranids, and lutianids, including *Caesio* spp., may be very common (Tham 1973*b*).

Chuang (1973) divided the rocky shores around Singapore into three major biological zones. In the uppermost zone, the Littorinid or periwinkle zone, the sea slater (*Ligia vitiensis*) roam the shore around the high-water line, nibbling away the remains of plants and animals littered on the shore. The rocky shore below this is predominated by the periwinkles of the following species, *Littorina granularis, L. undulata, L. ventricosa,* and *Nodilittorina pyramidalis.* The next zone or barnacle zone is dominated by the undate nerite (*Nerita undata*) and barnacles (*Balanus amphitrite, Tetraclita porosa,* and *Chthamalus stellatus*). In favorable environmental conditions, this zone may extend more than 2 m along the height of the shore measured vertically. Associated with the barnacles and usually extending lower down are oysters (*Ostrea cucullata*). The irregular spaces between barnacles and oysters provide shelters for minute coelenterates, worms, and gastropods. The lowest zone of the rocky shores, the coral zone, is dominated by the more hardy species that can tolerate not only occasional heavy downpour at ebb tide during the rainy season but also some temporary burial in the coral sand that accumulates in the flatter part of the shore. The common coral species include actiniform mushroom coral (*Fungia actiniformis*), echinate mushroom coral (*F. echinata*), slimy snake mushroom coral (*Herpolitha limax*), yellow pore coral (*Porites lutea*), *Goniopora lobata,* and the honeycomb coral (*Favites abdita*).

Animal life on non-rocky shores in Singapore can best be described by the animals of mangrove swamps; these animals are divided conveniently into three groups: terrestrial forms, amphibious forms, and fully aquatic forms (D. S. Johnson 1973*c*). The terrestrial forms include a variety of birds, reptiles, and insects that live on the mangrove trees and shrubs. Amphibious forms can be classified further into three groups, namely, the quiescent group, active surface-crawling group, and the burrowing group. The quiescent group includes a variety of bivalves (species of *Enigmonia* and *Isognomon*), mussels (species of *Mytilus* and *Modiolus*), barnacles (*Balanus amphitrite* and *Chthamalus* spp.), and caterpillars of *Olethreutes leveri.* The surface-crawling group includes snails (*Littorina melanostoma, Telescopium telescopium,* species of *Cerithidea* and *Terebralia*), hermit crabs (*Chibanarius longitarsus* and *Clibanarius* spp.), and mudskippers (*Periophthalmodan schlosseri* and *Periophthalmus* spp.). The burrowing group includes the air-breathing crabs of the families Grapsidae and Ocypodidae, small crabs of the family Xanthidae, porcelain crabs of the genus *Petrolisthes,* edible crabs (*Scylla serrata*), and mud lobsters (*Thalassina anomala, Upogebia* spp.).

Fully aquatic forms include various "herrings" such as *Megalops cyprinoides,* lady fish (*Albula* sp.), mullets, several gobies, glassfishes (*Ambassis* sp.), half-beaks of several kinds, the archerfish (*Toxotes* sp.), deep-bodied scat (*Scatophagus argus*), crabs (*Varuna litterata*), water snakes (*Cerberus rhynchops*), and prawns (*Penaeus indicus, Metapenaeus ensis, M. burkenroadi,* and *M. brevicornis*).

Reef flats occur on the western part of Singapore Island and on most of the southern islands; here sponges, corals, and molluscs form the major groups of animals. The most common sponge on reef flats is the cork sponge (*Suberites inconstans*); less common are ramosa hircine sponge (*Hircinia ramosa*), lattice sponge (*Hyatella clathrata*), and the near relative of the bath sponge (*Hippiospongia* spp.). Many of the common corals of reef flats belong to the family honeycomb coral or Faviidae. The greatest diversity is found near the reef edge, especially where the current is strong and the water free from silt or other suspended matter. In this favorable habitat, more than forty different species of corals may be found (Chuang 1973).

Many molluscs find shelter in the numerous coral heads of the reef flat. A luxuriant growth of algae among the corals near the edge of a reef flat favors the mollusc population. Other molluscs filter the floating organisms and plankton, and still others feed on other molluscs. Crustaceans, annelids, and sea cucumbers form other major groups of animals on reef flats. Reef-flat crustaceans include many crab species, *Hippolyte* shrimps, talitrid amphipods, and small snapping prawns (species of *Alpheus* and *Synalpheas*). Reef-flat annelids comprise the tube-forming worms and the tubeless ones. Sea cucumbers on the reef flat around Singapore consist of the species *Holothuria vagabunda, Actinopyga lacanora, Halodeima edulis, Opheodesoma grisea.*

Freshwater Animal Life

Facilities for analysis of the major cations and anions of freshwater were not available in Singapore until the 1960s. By 1961, there were still insufficient chemical data available to indicate whether sudden fish mortality was due to deficits in oxygen or tuba fish poisoning (Johnson 1961). Johnson (1967) was able to make a report on the freshwater chemistry of Singapore and south Malaya. Streams in Singapore were found to contain dilute, anion rich, acid water with extremely low to undetectable calcium levels. Analysis of oxygen showed that the apparent oxygen tension might be high, while the actual oxygen content of the water was low and inadequate to support many organisms. Ammonium was absent, except for polluted water, and sodium was the dominant cation in two-thirds of the habitats. Potassium and magnesium were low except in a few areas.

Little was published on the freshwater fauna of Singapore until the 1960s owing to the lack of even the most basic literature and the inaccessibility of previous collections in Europe. By 1962, some accounts of aquatic insects (Fernando 1961), leeches (Sharma and Fernando 1961) and water fleas (Johnson 1962) had been published. In the 1960s, the Department of Zoology at the University of Singapore began to produce mimeographed keys to local freshwater animals including water bugs (Fernando and Cheng 1963), Coleoptera (Fernando and Gatha 1963), freshwater crabs (Fernando and Lim 1964), Cladocera (Johnson 1964*a*), and fishes (Lindsay 1963). In the early 1970s, students reading for higher degrees at the universities worked on the biology, physiology, and ecology of a number of freshwater animals. These animals include the common toad, *Bufo melanostichus* (Sit 1972); tree frog, *Rhacophorus leucomystax* (Ting 1970); a number of species of amphibia (Lee and Chen 1970; Low et al. 1972); euryhaline frog, *Rana cancrivora* (Chew and Elliott 1971; Chew et al. 1972; Dicker and Elliott 1972; Elliott 1974; Elliott and Karunakaran 1973; Elliott and Ong 1973); the snail, *Melancides tuberculate* (Sung and Johnson 1972); pygmy half-beak, *Dermogenes pusillus* (Soong 1969); and two-spot gourami, *Trichogaster trichoterus* (Tan 1970).

D. S. Johnson (1973*b*) stated that freshwater animal life in Singapore was dominated by a few groups such as fish, tadpoles, crabs, prawns, water bugs (Hemiptera), and dragonfly nymphs. There was a remarkable absence of small invertebrates and of most kinds of insects. Freshwater fishes were of considerable interest to the biologists, as well as to the general public. In 1966, Alfred studied the past records and his own collections from 1957–1964 in giving an account of the freshwater fishes of Singapore. Because of the economic value of aquarium fish, special studies have been made since 1960 on various species of particular interest; twelve local species and a host of exotics were bred for sale overseas. Although the value of the exports was less than half a million U.S. dollars a year in 1963, it rose to about 4 million U.S. dollars by 1972.

In 1963, there was a severe drought in Singapore and south Malaya from which considerable information was obtained on the tolerance of fish. The first rain flooded the streams with highly acid water, and surviving fish including *Rasbora einthovenii, Tilapia mossambica,* and *Anabas testudinaceus* had to contend with the acid water. The latter, which is an air-breather and can migrate overland, was by far the most common survivor. Khoo et al. (1977) carried out a limnological survey of Seletar Reservoir and described the relationships between weather conditions and water conditions. They also discussed the cause of mass fish mortality.

Two species of potamonid crab are common, *Paratelphusa maculata* and *Potamon johorense,* both somewhat amphibious. Like other species of the family, they have direct development. The small, square grapsid crab (*Geosesarma perracae*) is more terrestrial, while *G. ocypoda* is almost fully terrestrial. Freshwater prawns are more common than crabs in Singapore. The ability of the prawns, especially those of the genus *Cryphiops,* to survive at low alkalinity and very low calcium content was unexpected in view of the importance of calcium carbonate in the hardening of their exoskeleton. Certain species, such as *C. trompil* and *C. geron,* were extremely tolerant to the acid water of Singapore and south Malaya (Johnson 1966).

Most open-country weedy habitats have enough calcium to allow a few hardy species of snails to survive. The largest is the edible pond snail (*Pila scutata*); another very widely distributed species is the pointed snail (*Melanoides tuberculata*). *Lymnaea rubiginosa* is an air-breathing, somewhat amphibious species; it is most frequent where there is some organic pollution. The tiny whirlpool shell (*Gyraulus convexiusculus*) is usually found on the leaves of submerged plants (D. S. Johnson 1973*b*).

Plankton

Marine Plankton

The marine phytoplankton in Singapore Straits consists mainly of diatoms. They exist either as single cells or in the form of chains of cells, and are mainly species of *Coscindiscus, Biddulphia, Chaetoceras, Rhizosolenia, Thalassiothrix, Bacteriastrum,* and *Ditylum.* Their abundance during the different months of the year follows a characteristic pattern: for example, *Coscinodis-*

cus may be abundant during January to March and again during June to August; *Chaetoceras* is normally very abundant during April and May each year; *Biddulphia* may be common from July to September and *Rhizosolenia* during November. In certain years, there may be abundance of a blue-green algae, *Trichodesmium erythraem,* during the months of June to August, and in some years, this alga is so abundant in Singapore Straits that it is washed up and deposited on the beaches as a thin mat. It has been reported that chickens get sick after eating it (Tham 1973*a*).

The zooplankton in Singapore Straits is dominated by the Crustacea, copepods forming about 70 percent of the total population number. Among the more common copepods are species of *Paracalanus, Eucalanus, Acartia, Tortanus, Oithonia,* and *Euterpina;* species of *Euchaeta, Candacia, Centropages, Temora, Clytemnestra,* and *Oncaea* are among the less common or rare forms. Copepods are extremely abundant during April and May. Other members of the crustacean plankton (mysids, isopods, and amphipods) are occasionally present but not in large numbers. The decapod larvae are, however, fairly common, especially brachyuran or crab larvae, as are chaetognaths, or arrowworms, notably during March, April, July, and November. The pelagic *Oikopleura* spp. and salps are sometimes common. Fish eggs and larvae are never abundant (Tham 1973*a*).

The common protozoan forms are: tintinnids represented by species of *Tintinnopsis* and *Favella;* dinoflagellates by *Ceratium, Dinophysis,* and *Peridinium;* and *cytoflagellates* by *Noctiluca,* which are mainly responsible for the luminescence of the sea. The most common coelenterate siphonophores are the small *Diphyes* and *Lensia,* which are most abundant during March, April, October, and November. Of the ctenophores, the most common are *Pleurobrachia* and *Beroe.* Among the polychaete larvae, the post-trochophore stages appear to be fairly common at times; lamellibranch larvae are fairly common during April and November (Tham 1973*a*).

Freshwater Plankton

During the first half of the twentieth century, only four papers were published dealing with the freshwater phytoplankton of Singapore and Malaya, and most data had been limited to drainage and mosquito control. In 1957, Prowse collected 150 species of desmids from Singapore and Malacca and launched a serious study of the freshwater algae of the region. In 1958, he published a monograph on Euglenineae, containing descriptions of 125 species or forms, eleven of which were new to the region. The Euglenineae are extremely important in Singapore, particularly in eutrophic habitats where a lot of decay is taking place, or where there is abundant plant growth. Red blooms of *Euglena sanguinea* are particularly noticeable on fish ponds. Prowse's studies continued into the 1960s and covered other groups of flagellates, diatoms, plus some general accounts and floras (Prowse 1962*a, b,* 1969).

D. S. Johnson (1973*b*) stated that freshwater planktonic forms were seldom abundant in Singapore and never formed true water blooms. On the other hand, masses of filamentous algae and diatoms may accumulate around plants at reservoir margins. These may include: filamentous forms such as *Mougeotia, Spirogyra,* and *Oedogonium;* many striking desmids including certain filament-forming species; soft water diatoms such as *Eunotia* and *Frustulia;* and acid water blue-green algae such as *Tolypothrix.*

In 1973, A. Johnson published some information on the microflora of the University of Singapore pond. She recorded a total of 220 plankton species, including 19 blue-green algae, 105 green algae, 38 Euglenophyceae, and 18 diatoms (A. Johnson 1973*a*). Such diversity is common in equatorial freshwater habitats. However, the bottom flora of the pond was much less diverse because of the insufficient light intensity for most phytoplankton.

Freshwater zooplankton in Singapore includes a diverse assemblage of protozoans, rotifers, nematodes, water fleas, copepods, water mites, larvae of insects, and other small organisms. It is usually dominated by copepods, especially species of *Diaptomus* and *Mesocyclops.* Water fleas include the relatively large, transparent *Diaphanosoma excisum* and the tiny *Bosminopsis deitersi.* Rotifers such as *Keratella tropica* are also often common. A considerable variety of other copepods and water fleas may occur among the marginal weeds although only occasionally in large numbers. Other small arthropods that may be common among the weeds include: various water mites; water bugs such as *Ranatra micronecta,* and the minute *Plea;* small dytiscid and hydrophilid water beetles; dipteran larvae; dragonflies (*Crocothemis* and *Orthetrum*); damselflies (*Agriocnemis* and *Pseudagrion*); mayfly (*Chloeon*); and planktonic water boatmen (*Anisops*) (D. S. Johnson 1973*b;* A. Johnson 1975).

The larvae of mosquitoes live in freshwater, and *Aedes aegypti,* the primary vector of dangerous hemorrhagic fever which has replaced malaria as the most dangerous mosquito-borne disease in Singapore, breeds indoors in man-made containers such as water jars. *A. albopictus* tends to have a wider distribution in natural habitats including bamboo stems, tree holes, and ginger leaf axils (Goh and Chan 1974).

HUMAN INFLUENCE ON NATURE

Terrestrial

Singapore is a classic example of the overwhelming impact of humans on nature. During the last thirty years, there has been a rapid increase of population, and a fast progress in urbanization and industrialization has upset the conditions of the natural environment. Three broad classes of intensity of change on land may be distinguished (Hill 1973): areas where the original topography is unrecognizable, and the original soils have been either covered or removed; suburban areas where the original landform is still recognizable but is somewhat modified by cut and fill for buildings, roads, parks, and playing fields; and areas where the terrain is little modified by direct human action, although modification by accelerated erosion following deforestation may be significant.

The human effect on land vegetation in Singapore is great. A tropical rain forest covered about 80 percent of the land of Singapore one and a half centuries ago, but today only a small area of about 70 hectares in the center of the island remains in relatively unspoiled condition. Most of Singapore is covered with secondary vegetation today. When the tall trees of the primary forest are removed, the initial climate they control is altered since the soils and plants are exposed to direct sunshine and rain. Normal ground plants in the primary forest, which can exist in deep shade and high humidity, will disappear and be replaced by sun-loving plants. Furthermore, once the forest cover is removed, the organic matter in the soil decomposes rapidly and the soil may become eroded into deep furrows (A. Johnson 1973*b*).

Plant succession on land with natural vegetation removed follows three major stages. The first stage may be found on poor or heavily eroded soil where, according to Holttum (1954), the first colonizers are *Eriachne pallescens* and *Gahnia tristis.* Once the soil has become somewhat settled and humus has accumulated, numerous other plants will appear, such as *Dicranopteris linearis, Lycopodium cernuum, Nepenthes* spp., and some sedges, grasses, and orchids (Gilliland 1958). During the second stage of succession, these herbaceous plants will be replaced by bushy plants and trees such as *Melastoma malabrathricum, Wormia suffruticosa,* and *Ficus alba.* The scrub stage soon develops into the third or mature stage of succession, a secondary forest, in which the most common plant, *Adinandra dumosa,* is associated with *Fagraea fragrans, Eugenia longiflora,* and *Elaeocarpus* spp.

At least a quarter of Singapore Island consists of cultivated land, which is the main source of fresh leafy vegetables, pigs, poultry, and eggs. Cabbages (*Brassica* spp.), long beans (*Vigna sinensis*), ladies fingers (*Hibiscus esculentus*), amaranth (*Amaranthus mangostanus*), tomatoes (*Lycopersicum esculentum*), and cucumbers (*Cucumis sativus*) are the common vegetables grown in Singapore. The finest lawns in Singapore are of Serangoon grass (*Digitaria didactyla*) and Siglap grass (*Zoysia matrella*), but many private gardens have lawns of coarse grasses such as carpet grass (*Axonopus compressus*) and buffalo grass (*Paspalum conjugatum*), together with a few herbaceous legumes such as *Desmodium triflorum, D. heterophyllum,* and *Alysicarpus vaginalis* (Chow 1976). In gardens and parks and along roadsides, a large number of different trees and ornamental plants form the major components in the landscape. Many of them were introduced from other areas in the tropics and subtropics.

After the urbanization and encroachments on forest areas, some larger animals that were once indigenous and common in the forests have been reduced to the point of extinction. Most of these animals, of course, are of little economic value to humans. By contrast, pigs and chickens are reared on a large scale because of their economic value, and Singapore is not only self-sufficient in these animals, but also has a surplus for export. Smaller animals and insects inhabit the urban areas, and rats, shrews, flies, mosquitoes, and house lizards find the human urban environment to their liking. Protection is not the appropriate word for these animals.

Human activities have greatly reduced the habitats of many forest and mangrove birds, with many species being infrequent today. On the other hand, the increase in large tall buildings is likely to favor species, such as pigeons and swifts, which are natural cliff breeders; and the increase of residential areas has provided a large area of habitats suitable for coastal savanna and grassland birds.

Marine

The human effect on the sea around Singapore is remarkable. The amount of dissolved nutrients has increased, and the average phosphate content has almost doubled during the last twenty years. The water in Singapore Straits has a phosphate content ranging from 10 mg to 80 mg of phosphorus pentoxide per cubic meter, depending on the time of the year. In Johore Straits, which is enclosed to a greater extent than is Singapore Straits, the phosphate content varies from 33 mg to 230 mg of phosphorus pentoxide per cubic meter (Khoo 1966). The higher values in Johore Straits are the result of the substantial discharge from rivers draining into it. The nitrate content in Johore Straits ranges from 47 mg to 128 mg nitrate nitrogen/m^3. The effects of drainage may not be limited to the immediate estuary but may spread outwards. This pollution may have disastrous effects on certain living organisms.

The reclamation of seashore land and increased outflow of polluted discharge from the city and factories affect not only mangrove vegetation but also animal life. For instance, the erection of concrete embankments where mangroves once thrived destroys these together with the littorinids (*Littorina melanostoma, L. undulata, L. carinifera,* and *L. scabra*), other gastropods (*Monodonta labio, Terebralia sulcata, Ellobium aurismidae, Onchidium*), peanut worm (*Phascolosoma lurco*), and mangrove crab (*Scylla serrata* and *Upogebia*). However, the concrete embankments create a new environment suitable to other littorinids such as *L. ventricosa* and *Nodilittorina pyramidalis,* and also to barnacles and oysters. Chuang (1973) stated that the loss of the sandy beaches will bring about the decline and extinction of certain bivalves that could not stand the silt and mud.

Construction of wharves and dockyards, as well as reclamation, has caused changes in the shore environment. Concrete and wooden structures provide substrata for the attachment of typical rocky shore animals, such as periwinkles, barnacles, and oysters; wooden structures provide habitats for marine borers, such as shipworm (*Teredo*) and another bivalve borer, *Martesia*. Granite boulders in sandy mud areas provide appropriate habitats for certain rocky shore organisms, such as barnacles, crabs, solitary coral (*Culicia stellata*), ark shells, gastropods (*Euchelus atratus*), and bristle worms.

Being one of the busiest ports, Singapore had had marine oil pollution problems for a long time. The Oil Pollution Committee was established in July 1972 under the Port of Singapore Authority. As a result of the stricter control imposed by the committee, the number of oil spills around Singapore after 1973 has decreased considerably. However, whether this reduction also indicates lower amounts of oil spilled into the marine environment is not certain because the available data do not include information on the type and amount of oil spilled (Rahman and Chia 1977). Besides, no data on the effect of oil pollution on marine life in Singapore are available at present.

Fresh Water

Little attention was paid to the problem of freshwater pollution in Singapore before the Second World War. For over a hundred years, Singapore residents had thrown wastewater and solids into the open drains that lined every street of the city and that washed directly into the rivers and canals. Even in 1960, quite a number of flowing streams were classified as polysaprobic. Rochore Canal and Singapore River in 1961 were "dead conduits" without any apparent plant or animal life (A. Johnson 1976).

The heaviest polluted areas are in the city. Tan (1972) reported that the water pollution problem in Singapore was aggravated by the fact that of the 110–115 million gallons of water consumed every day, about half was discharged into open drains and was, therefore, discharged into the rivers or sea without proper treatment. There are an estimated forty thousand hawkers and some fifty private markets in the republic. Together, these discharge some 5–6 million gallons of wastewater into the canals and rivers daily. Industrial growth in the last two decades has worsened the water pollution by discharging insufficiently treated chemical wastes into the rivers and canals. In addition, silting poses a natural pollution problem in the rivers and canals; in nearly all rivers, the amount of silt brought down by the heavy rains is enormous.

The Ministry of Environment has taken serious steps to stop freshwater pollution and keep the problem within manageable bounds. An Anti-pollution Unit was established in 1970. A five-year plan for sewerage and drainage has been put forward to cover all existing open drains along the roads and to initiate massive education programs to stop people from doing what they have always done. Nearly all homes in Singapore now have modern sewerage facilities for human wastes and the sullage from washing. Future plans are designed to turn the island into a huge catchment area, a goal that will be possible only by a total prevention of pollution of drains and rivers (A. Johnson 1976).

Pollution of fresh water in Singapore was indicated by the appearance of the snails normally absent or very rare in unpolluted habitats. The occurrence of fish in polluted water is in part a result of many of them being air breathers (A. Johnson 1976). Alfred (1961, 1966) studied the freshwater fishes of Singapore and reported that of the seventy-three freshwater fishes recorded from Singapore in the past, only forty-two species remained in 1966. He believed that the other thirty-one species were excluded because of pollution from human and factory wastes. On the other hand, because of the aquarium fish industry, which began in the early 1960s, aquarium escapees, such as *Betta splendeus* and *Poecilia reticulata,* entered the streams and became widely distributed in Singapore.

D. S. Johnson (1973*b*) stated that *Hydrilla verticillata* is one of the most tolerant of plants and may persist in quite polluted water. Different algae may also be abundant in polluted waters, although restricted in species; a characteristic form is the small, branched green alga, *Stigeoclonium.* The blue-green alga, *Oscillatoria,* is often very abundant and may form dark mats on the bottom. Various small diatoms may also be common.

Air

In general, air pollution levels in Singapore, with the exception of the central business areas during the busy hours, are fairly low compared with big cities in developed countries. This is because there are considerable wind movements, especially during the northeast monsoon, and abundant rainfall. Chia (1972) stated that equatorial areas do not experience persistent large-scale anticyclones and are, therefore, in no danger of the more severe forms of air pollution. The buoyant air, assisted by strong surface heating during the day, promotes dispersion of air pollutants. However, during the night, air tends to be more sluggish and stable at low levels, so there is greater likelihood that sheltered areas near sources of discharge of pollutants will suffer from air pollution. Chia and Wong (1977) reviewed the problem of air pollution in Singapore through a consideration of the various sources of air pollution and the meteorologic factors that affect air pollution levels.

The major air pollutants in Singapore are carbon monoxide, hydrocarbons, sulphur oxides, nitrogen oxides, oxidants, and particulate matter. It has been estimated that about 67 percent of the air pollutants come from motor vehicles, about 26 percent from power generators, and about 7 percent from industry. Observations on carbon monoxide and hydrocarbons by the Anti-pollution Unit indicate that at present their concentration levels in most parts of the island are moderately low. There are, of course, some areas in the busy city center where concentration levels are quite high and have been found to exceed maximum safety levels for brief periods of times. The monthly average of sulphur dioxide concentration was 17.5 $\mu g/m^3$ in rural areas, 40 $\mu g/m^3$ in residential areas, and 65.5 $\mu g/m^3$ in commercial areas. The maximum allowable level set by the United States and WHO are 80 and 60 $\mu g/m^3$, respectively. Since motor vehicles are the major source of these two air pollutants in residential and commercial areas, more stringent measures against vehicle exhaust emissions have been taken. These include regulations enforced by the traffic police on smoke emissions, a high road tax on motor vehicles, and motor vehicle restriction on entering the central commercial areas during certain busy hours. Industries and power-generating stations are responsible for contributing 35 percent of total air pollution in Singapore. However, the use of tall chimney stacks for a more effective dispersal of atmospheric effluents has resulted in a relatively low ground-level pollution concentration in the industrial areas (Wong 1977).

The seasonal variation of air pollution levels in Singapore is significant. At certain times of the year or certain hours in a day when industrial and commercial activities have increased, and during periods of unfavorable meteorologic conditions, peak concentrations of pollutants may exceed the maximum allowable levels set by the United States and WHO. Furthermore, if the Singapore economy continues to grow at the rates achieved in the past decade, it can be expected that in the absence of proper controls, air pollution levels will rise with time. The Anti-pollution Unit enforced the Clean Air Act of 1971, the Clean Air Regulations of 1972, and the Clear Air (prohibition on the use of open fires) Order of 1973. The act was amended in 1975 to provide for greater control of air pollution, especially from construction sites; the regulations were amended again in 1978 to upgrade the emission standards of certain air pollutants. Through the enforcement activities of the Anti-pollution Unit, air pollution levels have been successfully controlled and reduced in Singapore. Clean air legislation in Singapore has been effective in controlling and reducing pollution levels particularly from industrial sources. Finally, the use of air pollution control equipment in industrial premises and motor vehicles, as well as the screening of new industries for their possible undesirable effects on the environment, have helped toward the prevention of large-scale increases in air pollutants.

ACKNOWLEDGMENTS

I am grateful to Professor A. N. Rao, Head, Department of Botany, and Associate Professor H. Keng for their valuable comments.

REFERENCES CITED

Alfred, E. R. 1961. Singapore freshwater fishes. *Malay Nat. J.* 15:1–19.

———. 1966. The freshwater fishes of Singapore. *Zool. Verh.* (Leiden) 78:1–68.

Awan, B. 1968. Autecology of epiphytes on *Fagraea fragrans* and *Swietenia macrophylla* in Singapore. Ph.D. thesis, Department of Botany, University of Singapore.

Chew, M. M. and A. B. Elliott. 1971. Fluid intake from intestine of the euryhaline frog, *Rana cancrivora,* as affected by the environment. *J. Physiol.* 225:62–63.

Chew, M. M., A. B. Elliott, and H. Y. Wong. 1972. Permeability of the urinary bladder of *Rana cancrivora* to urea in the presence of oxytocin. *J. Physiol.* 223:757–772.

Chia, L. S. 1972. Meteorological aspects of air pollution with special references to equatorial areas. *J. Singapore Natl. Acad. Sci.* 2:28.

——— and M. L. Wong. 1977. Atmospheric pollution and its control in Singapore. *Proceedings of the Symposium on Our Environment,* pp. 100–123. Singapore: Nanyang University.

Chou, L. M. 1975. Systematic account of the Singapore house geckos. *J. Singapore Natl. Acad. Sci.* 4:130–138.

———. 1976. Some studies on the morphology and biology of the common house Gekkonidae in Singapore. Ph.D. thesis, University of Singapore.

Chow, K. H. 1974. Morphology and ecology of some introduced herbaceous legumes. *Gard. Bull.* (Singapore) 27:85–94.

———. 1976. Morphology and ecology of some wild herbaceous legumes in Singapore. *J. Singapore Natl. Acad. Sci.* 5:20–30.

Chuang, S. H. 1973. Life of the seashore. In *Animal life and nature in Singapore,* ed. S. H. Chuang, pp. 150–174. Singapore: Singapore University Press.

Corbet, A. S. and H. M. Pendlebury. 1956. *Butterflies of the Malay Peninsula,* 2d ed. Edinburgh: Oliver & Boyd.

Corner, E. J. H. (1978). *The freshwater swamp-forest of south Johore and Singapore.* Singapore: Botanic Gardens.

Dicker, S. E. and A. B. Elliott. 1972. Neurohypophysial hormones and homeostasis in the crab-eating frog, *Rana cancrivora. Horm. Res.* 4:224–260.

Elliott, A. B. 1974. Neurohypophysial control of plasma urea as osmoregulatory mechanism in the euryhaline frog, *Rana cancrivora. Proc. Int. Union Physiol. Sci.* 11:113.

——— and L. Karunakaran. 1973. Diet of *Rana cancrivora* in freshwater and brackish water environment. *J. Zool. (Lond.)* 184:203–208.

——— and C. N. Ong. 1973. Oxygen consumption in vitro by skin and urinary bladder of the euryhaline frog, *Rana cancrivora. J. Physiol.* 233:23–24.

Fernando, C. H. 1961. Note on aquatic insects caught at light in Malaya with a discussion of their distribution and dispersal. *Bull. Natl. Mus. Singapore* 30:19–31.

——— and L. Cheng. 1963. Guide to genera of Malayan water bugs. Mimeographed. Department of Zoology, University of Singapore.

——— and S. Gatha. 1963. Guide to families of Malayan aquatic Coleoptera. *Guide to the fauna of the Malaysian region,* Vol. 5, pp. 1–29.

______ and A. W. Lim. 1964. A Guide to the freshwater crabs (Potamonidae) of Malaya. Mimeographed. Department of Zoology, University of Singapore.

Gilliland, H. B. 1958. Plant communities on Singapore Island. *Gard. Bull. (Singapore)* 17:82–90.

Glenister, A. G. 1951. *The birds of the Malaya Peninsula, Singapore and Penang.* Oxford: Oxford University Press.

Goh, E. H. and K. L. Chan. 1974. The 1973 dengue haemorrhagic fever outbreak in Singapore. *Singapore Publ. Health Bull.* 14:24–29.

Harrison, J. 1966. *An introduction to mammals of Singapore and Malaya.* Singapore: Malayan Nature Society.

Hill, R. D. 1973. Land and sea. In *Animal life and nature in Singapore,* ed. S. H. Chuang, pp. 9–26. Singapore: Singapore University Press.

Holttum, R. E. 1954. *Adinandra belukar. Malay. J. Trop. Geogr.* 3:27–32.

IPPF. 1979. *A 1979 people wallchart.* London: International Planned Parenthood Federation.

Johnson, A. 1973*a*. The microflora of the University of Singapore pond. *J. Singapore Natl. Acad. Sci.* 3:241–252.

______. 1973*b*. Vegetation. In *Animal Life and Nature in Singapore,* ed. S. H. Chuang, pp. 40–52. Singapore: Singapore University Press.

______. 1975. The microfauna of the University of Singapore pond. *J. Singapore Natl. Acad. Sci.* 4:100–105.

______. 1976. A quarter century of freshwater research in Singapore. *J. Singapore Natl. Acad. Sci.* 5:1–8.

Johnson, D. S. 1961. An instance of large-scale mortality of fish in a natural habitat in south Malaya. *Malay. Nat. J.* 15:160–162.

______. 1962. Water fleas. *Malay. Nature J.* 16:126–144.

______ *1964a.* Key to Malayan Cladocera. Mimeographed. Department of Zoology, University of Singapore.

______. 1964*b*. *An introduction to the natural history of Singapore.* Kuala Lumpur: Rayirath Publications.

______. 1966. Some factors influencing the distribution of freshwater prawns in Malaya. *Proc. Symp. Crustacea Mar. Biol. Assoc. India* 1:418–433.

______. 1967. On the chemistry of the freshwater in southern Malaya and Singapore. *Arch. Hydrobiol.* 63:477–496.

______. 1973*a*. Bird life. In *Animal life and nature in Singapore,* ed. S. H. Chuang, pp. 85–102. Singapore: Singapore University Press.

______. 1973*b*. Freshwater life. In *Animal life and nature in Singapore,* ed. S. H. Chuang, pp. 103–127. Singapore: Singapore University Press.

______. 1973*c*. Brackish water. In *Animal life and nature in Singapore,* ed. S. H. Chuang, pp. 128–139. Singapore: Singapore University Press.

Khoo, H. W. 1966. A preliminary study of the physical, chemical and biological characteristics of Johore Straits. M.S. thesis, Department of Zoology, University of Singapore.

______. 1973. Inshore fish fauna distribution in Singapore waters and their relation to environmental conditions. *J. Singapore Natl. Acad. Sci.* 3:45–49.

______, S. L. Yang, and C. J. Goh. 1977. A preliminary limnological study of Seletar Reservoir. *J. Singapore Natl. Acad. Sci.* 6:1–12.

Lee, S. H. and T. W. Chen. 1970. Artificial induction of ovulation and artificial insemination in *Rana limnocharis. J. Singapore Natl. Acad. Sci.* 1:59–67.

Lee, S. K. 1977. Problems of tree growth on reclaimed land in Singapore. *Proceedings of the Symposium on Our Environment,* pp. 76–80. Singapore: Nanyang University.

Le Mare, D. W. and A. K. Tham. 1954. On the inshore fish population of the Straits of Singapore. *Proc. Indo-Pacific Fish. Council, 5th Session, Bangkok.*

Lindsay, C. C. 1963. *Guide to the families of Malayan fish.* Mimeographed. Department of Zoology, University of Singapore.

Low, K. L., T. W. Chen, and C. K. Tan. 1972. Factors affecting the fertility and hatchability of *Bufo melanostichus* (Bloch and Schneider). *Nanyang Univ. J.* 6:78–86.

Medway, L. 1969. *The wild mammals of Malaya and offshore islands including Singapore.* Oxford: Oxford University Press.

Morrell, R. C. R. 1960. *Common Malayan butterflies.* London: Longmans, Green & Co.

______. 1973. Butterflies and moths. In *Animal life and nature in Singapore,* ed. S. H. Chuang, pp. 74–84. Singapore: Singapore University Press.

Murphy, D. H. 1973*a*. Guide to genera of Malayan ants based on the worker caste. *Guides to the fauna of the Malayan region,* No. 10, pp. 1–27. Singapore: University of Singapore.

______. 1973*b*. Animals in the forest ecosystem. In *Animal life and nature in Singapore,* ed. S. H. Chuang, pp. 53–72. Singapore: Singapore University Press.

Myers, P. E. 1976. *World population data sheet.* Washington: Population Ref. Bureau, Inc.

Nah, S. C. 1977. Some growth studies on three freshwater phytoplankton from a tropical reservoir. M.S. thesis, University of Singapore.

Prowse, G. A. 1957. An introduction to the desmids of Malaya. *Malay. Nat. J.* 11:42–58.

______. 1958. The Euglenineae of Malaya. *Gard. Bull. (Singapore)* 16:136–204.

______. 1962*a*. Diatoms of Malayan freshwaters. *Gard. Bull. (Singapore)* 19:1 –104.

______. 1962b. Further Malayan flagellata. *Gard. Bull. (Singapore)* 19:105–145.

______. 1969. Some new desmid taxa from Malaya and Singapore. *Gard. Bull. (Singapore)* 25:179–187.

Purchon, R. D. and I. Enoch. 1954. Zonation of the marine fauna and flora on a rocky shore near Singapore. *Bull. Raffles Mus.* 25:47–65.

Rahman, A. and L. S. Chia. 1977. A survey of oil pollution of water around Singapore. *Proceedings of Symposium on Our Environment,* pp. 208–230. Singapore: Nanyang University.

Sharma, R. E. 1973. Noxious and toxic animals. In *Animal life and nature in Singapore,* ed. S. H. Chuang, pp. 229–250. Singapore: Singapore University Press.

______ and C. H. Fernando. 1961. Leeches and their ways. *Malay. Nat. J.* 15:152–159.

Sit, K. H. 1972. Mineralcorticoid induced ovulation and development in the toad, *Bufo melanostichus* Schneider. *J. Singapore Natl. Acad. Sci.* 2:65–71.

Soong, M. 1969. Courtship behavior of the pygmy half-beak, *Dermogenes pusillus. J. Singapore Natl. Acad. Sci.* 1:46.

Sung, I. D. and D. S. Johnson. 1972. Tolerance to various aquatic factors by the common aquatic snail, *Melanoides tuberculata* (O.F. Muller) Gastropoda: Melaniidae. *J. Singapore Natl. Acad. Sci.* 2:56–64.

Tan, C. K. 1970. Some biological problems of the two-spot gourami, *Trichogaster trichopterus* (Pallas). M.S. thesis, Department of Zoology, University of Singapore.

Tan, G. 1972. Economic growth and the environment in Singapore. In *The Singapore environment,* eds. R. S. Bhathal and S. J. Chen, pp. 12–31. Singapore: University Education Press.

Tham, A. K. 1973*a*. The sea. In *Animal life and nature in Singapore,* ed. S. H. Chuang, pp. 140–149. Singapore: Singapore University Press.

______. 1973*b*. Sea fish. In *Animal life and nature in Singapore,* ed. S. H. Chuang, pp. 202–229. Singapore: Singapore University Press.

Ting, M. C. 1970. Table of the early development of *Rhacophorus leucomystax. J. Singapore Natl. Acad. Sci.* 2:38–46.

Tweedie, M. W. F. 1957. *The snakes of Malaya.* Singapore: Singapore Government Printers.

Wee, Y. C. and A. N. Rao. 1977. The ferns flora of Singapore. *Fern Society of Palm Beach County (Florida)* 1:5–26.

Wong, M. L. 1977. A survey of air pollution and its control in Singapore. Thesis, Department of Geography, University of Singapore.

34

TAIWAN

Chang-Hung Chou

INTRODUCTION

During the period from 1945 to 1980, ecological development in Taiwan, as in other parts of the world, was drastically changed: from being an almost ignored subject it became a modern science. Before the Second World War, Taiwan was occupied by the Japanese for fifty years (1895–1945); during those years, the Japanese established only one university, Taihoku Imperial University (now called National Taiwan University), three professional colleges, and many high schools. Although many Japanese scientists performed excellent scientific work, especially in the taxonomic study of the natural vegetation of Taiwan, ecological development was rather weak. Immediately after the war, almost all the Japanese scientists returned to Japan, resulting in a vacuum in scientific research. The return of Taiwan to China put it again under the traditional Chinese culture and its education system. So that the ecological developments in Taiwan since 1945 can be more easily understood, the period has been arbitrarily divided into 3 stages: 1945–1955, 1955–1965, and 1965–1980.

Scientific development including ecology was very weak from 1945 to 1955. Only a few of the botanists coming from mainland China conducted ecological investigations. The late Dr. S. C. Lee, a University of Chicago graduate, was probably the only well-qualified plant ecologist; his active research on coniferous and tropical forests in Taiwan was conducted through the Department of Botany, National Taiwan University. Fortunately, several eminent plant taxonomists, Professors H. L. Li, T. S. Liu, S. Keng, and Y. C. Liu, provided valuable taxonomic-ecological information. In particular, Professor Li (1963) published an excellent book on the *Woody Flora of Taiwan,* and Professor Liu (1962) published his two volumes, *Illustrations of Native and Introduced Ligneous Plants of Taiwan.* In addition, a six-volume *Flora of Taiwan* was recently published by botanists here and abroad (Li et al. 1979). This *Flora of Taiwan* is based on successive research efforts by botanists for more than seventy years and depicts the vegetation types from sea level to the highest alpine regions. Dr. H. L. Li and his colleagues also established the botanical journal *Taiwania,* which contained much ecological information. They also sought to build up the excellent herbarium, which had been started by the Japanese botanists, for the Department of Botany in the National Taiwan University. More than one hundred and seventy thousand specimens have been deposited so far. As indicated in Table 34.1, there were fewer than ten ecologists doing research or teaching ecology in the above-mentioned

Table 34.1. Research Institutes and Scientists Teaching and Doing Research in Ecology or Its Related Subjects 1945–1980

	Number of scientists		
Institute	**1945–1955**	**1955–1965**	**1965–1980**
Institute of Botany, Academia Sinica	NE[1]	0	3
Institute of Zoology, Academia Sinica	NE	NE	3
Department of Botany, National Taiwan University	1	1	2
Department of Zoology, National Taiwan University	1	1	2
Institute of Oceanography, National Taiwan University	NE	NE	3
College of Agriculture, National Taiwan University	1	1	5
Department of Biology, National Taiwan Normal University	1	1	2
Department of Botany, National Chung-Hsiung University	NE	1	1
College of Agriculture, National Chung-Hsiung University	1	1	1
Department of Biology, Tunghai University	NE	1	2
Department of Biology, Fu-Jen University	NE	NE	1
Taiwan Forestry Research Institute	0	2	3
Taiwan Sugarcane Research Institute	1	1	1
Others	2	2	5
Total	8	12	34

[1]NE: The institute was not established during this period.

institutions. Some who taught ecological courses during this period were not trained in ecology.

During the second stage, 1955–1965, ecological activity slightly increased; this coincided with science development in general. In 1959, an internationally known scholar, Dr. Hu Shih, former president of Academia Sinica, was appointed as chairman of the National Science Development Council of the Republic of China. Dr. Hu exerted great effort to develop science in Taiwan and planned long-term projects to furnish facilities for academic institutions; he also instigated a training program for sending young, promising scholars abroad to pursue advanced degrees. Many young scholars, under the auspices of the National Science Development Council, received their doctorates abroad and returned. Dr. Thomas S. C. Wang, the former director of Life Sciences Division of National Science Council, the late director, Dr. S. C. Hsu, and the present director, Dr. K. C. Hsieh, have exerted great efforts to develop biological research in Taiwan; Dr. S. L. Chien, president of Academia Sinica, has been particularly concerned about and supported the study of environmental problems. In addition, the Institute of Botany of Academia Sinica was re-established in 1960, and the Institute of Zoology, which was planned in 1957, was founded in 1970. Dr. H. W. Li, former director of the Institute of Botany, Academia Sinica, spent ten years developing the institute, which has now become one of the best research institutions in Taiwan. Later, two private universities were founded, Tunghai University and Fu-Jen University; these universities have biology departments, and the former has a graduate program. During this period, fewer than fifteen environmental scientists worked on ecological research (Table 34.1). However, active research was conducted by the Taiwan Forestry Research Institute, and applied agricultural ecological research was carried on in the Taiwan Agricultural Research Institute and by the Taiwan Sugarcane Research Institute.

In the last decade, ecology, as well as other fields of science, developed rapidly. People have become more concerned about environmental problems. At present, there are about thirty-four scientists working on different aspects of environmental research. The major influential institution is the Academia Sinica, which has organized several team projects. In 1972, the Republic of China National Scientific Committee on Problems of Environment (ROC/SCOPE) was established in Academia Sinica, and Dr. J. C. Su was appointed chairman of the committee. This committee consists of twenty scientists from various aspects of environmental studies. Several national representatives or correspondents were appointed, with Prof. T. C. Hung as the executive secetary; Dr. Hong-Chi Lin deals with biogeochemical cartography, Prof. Valient T. Liu with human impact on renewable natural resources, Dr. Yu-Lin Chen with environmental toxicology, and Dr. Chang-Hung Chou with ecological effects of fire. Under the auspices of Academia Sinica, the ROC/SCOPE has organized several academic conferences in an attempt to get all environmental scientists together to discuss and solve current environmental problems, some of which will be described in latter sections of this report. This committee also organized an international meeting, the "Colloquium on Aquatic Environment in Pacific Region" held in August 1978 in Taipei. More recently, an Asian Ecological Society has been organized by Dr. Edgar Lin of Tunghai University; the society was organized primarily by the several Christian universities in Asia. Our ecologists have also actively participated in many international conferences.

Since 1945, the higher education system in Taiwan has changed. As shown in Table 34.1, only a few academic institutes had ecological programs at that time. Now universities are giving graduate programs in ecology, and several members from Academia Sinica are serving as graduate advisors in the several universities listed. In the past thirty-five years, many students have received their M.S. degree from these universities and then went abroad to pursue work on advanced degrees or to do postgraduate research. An increasing number of ecologists received doctorates in Japan or Western countries and returned home to help their universities. In the future, universities in Taiwan may establish their own Ph.D. programs in ecology. The research facilities in the listed universities and research institutions are very good; they have modern, sophisticated analytical instruments. Since people and students are much more aware of the importance of environmental matters, the future for ecological development in Taiwan looks good.

There is no ecological society in Taiwan; however, many related societies have been founded since 1945. Ecological information thus far has appeared in the journals of the societies as listed below: The Botanical Society of the Republic of China, The Biology Society of China, The Agricultural Society of China, The Forestry Society of China, The Horticultural Society of China, The Plant Protection Society of the Republic of China, The Soil and Water Conservation Association of China, The Chinese Society of Animal Science, Taiwan Society of Fisheries, The Society of Soil Scientists and Fertilizer Technologists of Taiwan, The Environmental Protection Society of the Republic of China, and other related academic societies. These societies have published their journals in Chinese with an English summary, there being one, two, or four issues a year. In addition the *Botanical Bulletin of Academia Sinica, Taiwania,* and the *Bulletin of the Institute of Zoology Academia Sinica* are published semiannually in English with Chinese abstracts. These three journals have a high international reputation, and ecological papers have appeared in them since 1955. Furthermore, our ecologists have published not only in domestic journals but also in international ones. In Taiwan, when considered as a group, university libraries have subscribed to almost all international journals, although not every institute has done so. Many libraries interchange their magazines both domestically and internationally. Individual scientists also subscribe for personal copies.

The major force accelerating ecological activities in Taiwan is financial assistance. However, financial assistance for environmental research was insufficient in the early period from 1945 to 1965. The National Science Council of the Republic of China is the predominant agent providing research grants; in addition, the Joint Commission on Rural Reconstruction (JCRR) (now called Council for Agricultural Planning and Development), National Health Administration, Taiwan Provincial Government, Taiwan Power Company, China Foundation, and several private donors have to date contributed enough money to make some research possible. Recently, some private companies have also given funds to aid in applied ecological research. Of course, financial support for ecological research never meets the demand of scientists; nevertheless, this support has been drastically increased since 1945.

Ecological development in Taiwan is still in its infancy; we need more ecologists and greater financial support to make this child grown up. It is a science that is becoming conspicuously important in view of the rapid economic and technological growth of the region. By 1982, Taiwan hopes to reach the status of a developed nation, and it is hoped that ecology will come to be as greatly important here as in other developed nations of the world.

ECOLOGICAL BACKGROUND OF TAIWAN

Taiwan is located about 130 km off the southeastern coast of mainland China. The island has an area of approximately 35,960 km^2 and is 390 km long by 144 km wide at its widest point. About two-thirds of the island is occupied by mountains, particularly the Central Mountain Range, which extends from north to south. There are more than sixty peaks that exceed 3,000 m in elevation; Mt. Morrison (Yu Shan), the highest one, is 3995 m. The western part of the island is a vast plain with high agricultural productivity; about 80 percent of Taiwan's population lives here. On the eastern side, there are several coastal plains in the north and a long rift valley to the south, which separates the coastal range from the central range. The elevation of the coastal mountain range is about 1,680 m. Since the Tropic of Cancer passes through Chiayi, in the center of Taiwan, Taiwan has a subtropical and tropical climate with a long, warm summer and mild winter. Based on rainfall and temperature, the island can be divided into six climatic regions (Kao 1975); these fit well into the ecological zones proposed by Liu (1976). The mean monthly temperature ranges from 12.4° to 20°C as a maximum and from 9.9° to 13.3°C as a minimum. The annual precipitation ranges from 2,124 to 3,575 mm (Kao 1975). Inasmuch as these are favorable weather conditions, a luxuriant and diversified vegetation grows everywhere in Taiwan.

There is a great diversity of marine habitats in the area off the coast of Taiwan. The western coast of Taiwan is actually a continental shelf about 200–300 m deep, while the eastern side is bounded by the Pacific Ocean, which drops to at least 4,000 m below sea level. Many new tidal lands along the western coast of the island have been gradually formed; here there is great productivity of sea foods (e.g., oyster, shellfish, clams, and cultivated fishes). However, because of the high industrial development on Taiwan, the productivity of sea organisms has been seriously jeopardized in both the cultivated bed areas and off the west coast. However, on the eastern coast, productivity of marine organisms has been little affected.

CLASSICAL ECOLOGY

Concept of Plant Community

The luxuriant vegetation on Taiwan and great diversity of species found here attracted many botanists from mainland China after 1945. Professor S. C. Lee (deceased), H. L. Li, T. S. Liu, C. K. Wang, T. Liu, C. Y. Chang, C. H. Hu, S. Keng, L. M. Chang, and other botanists not so well known have been exerting their efforts in the community study. In addition, Dr. C. E. DeVol, an eminent American botanist, has contributed greatly to ecological taxonomic work at National Taiwan University on the pteriophytes. Although the studies have varied because of the different disciplinary aspects, a lot of information has accumulated.

In regard to the concept of plant community, C. K. Wang and T. Liu have provided evidence supporting Clements' concept of the monoclimax theory (Liu 1968, 1970; Wang 1975). With this theory as a base, they have attempted to classify the vegetation into several formations: alpine tundra (3,700–3,900 m), subalpine coniferous forest (3,000–3,700 m), cold-temperate montane coniferous forest (2,000–3,000 m), warm-temperate montane forest (300–2,500 m), tropical rain forest, littoral forest, tropical savanna, and warm-temperate rain forest. Detailed information concerning this classification can be found in papers by Liu (1968, 1970, 1971). It would be interesting to study plant communities using Whittaker's gradient analysis because the vegetation seems to be correlated with slope gradient.

The mechanism of plant succession has scarcely been investigated, although in recent years Chou has attempted to do so and to also study the dominance of several grassland species (Chou and Chung 1974; Chou and Young 1975). However, it is too early to draw any conclusions regarding concepts of plant community and community development.

Unfortunately, much of the natural vegetation has been destroyed by fire and unplanned logging. This may jeopardize the work of ecologists in doing community studies. Nevertheless, Green Island, a small island about twenty miles off the eastern coast of Taitung, still has its natural vegetation. Some studies on a reservation of a natural community have also been done; this will be described in the last section of this paper.

Fish Community

Since the last decade, Dr. K. H. Chang and his associates have extensively studied the fish community in some intertidal zones at Patouzu in the north and Maopitou in the south, these representing subtropical and tropical regions, respectively. Their findings indicate that the frequency distribution of species with different numbers of individuals in the intertidal fish community belongs to a logarithmic series distribution. Species composition between the two communities examined is quite different. These researchers also indicate that the diversity of the species in the intertidal community is controlled by both physical factors and biological accommodations, and the community of the tropic is more stable than that of the subtropic (Chang et al. 1973). They also investigated the distribution and feeding habitats of *Auxis tapeinosome,* a frigate mackeral, in the northeastern waters of Taiwan (Chang and Lee 1971). Additionally, a recent investigation on the evaluation of diversity and abundance of the fish assemblage of the reef limestone platform at Maopitou revealed a total of 194 species, this being nearly three times higher than that of the 1969 evaluation (Chang, Lee, and Wu 1977). Both the diversity and evenness in the recent investigation was greater than that of 1969.

In a more practical study of efforts to improve fisheries around the coastal water of Taiwan, Chang and his associates have constructed model artificial reefs at a depth of 10–14 m at Wanli in northern Taiwan since 1974. They reported that biomass and the number of fish species were higher in the multiple disc sampling apparatus than in the multiple pyramidal-frustum sampling apparatus (Chang, Lee, and Shao 1977). Isolated model reefs attracted more fish than those nearest the natural reefs. This model artificial reef has been used in many places along coastal areas (Chang 1979).

Algae Community

In recent years, Chiang (1960, 1962, 1973) has studied the marine algae of Taiwan. He reported that the marine algae along the coast of southern Taiwan differed markedly from that of northern Taiwan. In addition, Huang and Chiang (1974) reported the distribution and composition of phytoplankton along the southern coast of Taiwan. The concentration of chlorophyll *a* varied with the vertical profiles and was homogeneous at or near the surface area with a range of 0.05 μg/1 and average of 0.19 μg/1. However, the data showed that there was a distinct variation of chlorophyll *a* distribution with high values occurring along the coast and low values in the offshore waters. There were forth genera and 114 species of diatoms, and frequently occurring species were *Thalassionema nitzchioides, Thalassiothrix franenfeldii, Bacteriastrum varians, B. elongatum,* and *Chaetoceros atlanticus.* In addition, *Skeletonema costatum* was found throughout the coastal area, and

Trichodesmium erytheraeum was the dominant blue-green algae, the maximum cell number reaching 28.03 × 10^7 cells/m^3.

ECOSYSTEM RESEARCH

Primary Productivity

Inasmuch as luxuriant vegetation and productivity in Taiwan is exceedingly high, estimation of vegetation productivity and energy utilization efficiency becomes important research as far as the ecosystem is concerned. Several physiological ecologists have measured the primary productivity of natural and crop vegetation, as well as of the marine ecosystem. Following the models of Lieth (1973), Rosenzwig (1968), and Lieth and Box (1972), the net primary productivity (NPP) of agricultural ecosystem in Taiwan can be theoretically calculated to range from about 2,100 to 3,500 g/m^2 per year. The total NPP of Taiwan is approximately 7.81 × 10^7 ton/yr, agricultural production about 1.86 × 10^7 ton/yr, and forest production about 2.46 × 10^7 ton/yr. The energy conversion efficiency is about 0.96% (Chou and Chen, unpublished data). Compared with that of natural vegetation, the NPP of the rice plant, which is the major crop in Taiwan, is about 850 to 1,025 g/m^2 (Shieh 1977). This figure is somewhat lower than that obtained from the theoretical models mentioned. However, rice production has been more than sufficient for the people in Taiwan, and rice is even being exported to other countries.

The productivity of the marine ecosystem has been investigated by Hung (1975, 1977), who found that the daily NPP of the Kuroshio current surrounding Taiwan ranged from 0.07 to 0.62 g carbon per square meter per day. At the site of the most important culture beds for oysters and clams, productivity reached its maximum of 0.62 g carbon per square meter per day, while in the polluted area along the Keelung-Patoutzu coast, productivity was the lowest, namely, 0.07 g. Subsequent findings of related studies also have been reported (Hung et al. 1979).

Terrestrial and marine ecosystems in Taiwan have been gradually changing because of the rapid increase of human population and industrial development. It is extremely important for the nation to do more regarding these ecosystem studies since they will eventually tell us the dynamics and nature of the ecosystem in regard to the gross national product. It is important to emphasize, however, that we must keep the ecosystem balanced without jeopardizing the primary productivity of crops and natural vegetation in Taiwan.

Ecosystems Affected by Nuclear Power Plants

Two nuclear power plants at Chinshan (1977) and Kuosheng (1979) are located along the northern coast of Taiwan. Owing to the large quantities of cooling water intake and discharge from the reactors, biological activities in the surrounding ecosystems may be greatly affected. Thus SCOPE of Academia Sinica, under support of the Atomic Energy Council and Taiwan Power Company of the Republic of China, has initiated a long-term research program (three years each before and after the plant begins operation) to assess the dynamics of the ecosystems of the particular areas. The following investigations are being conducted: phytoplankton studies, hydrographic observations and water chemical analyses, zooplankton studies, benthos studies, fishery resources studies, radioactive substances in marine organisms, and near-shore ocean current studies. The samples are being taken by the *Chiu-Lien* research vessel and *Tung-Shan* experimental vessel in eleven cruises. The first three-year reports have been made (Su et al. 1975, 1976, 1979). The whole investigation will be carried out in the next three to four years; however, progress reports have been made (1979). After the study, the dynamics of the ecosystem in this area will be clear. The data will guide us in manipulating the nuclear power plants to limit the deleterious effects. Also, the findings of the research may suggest to engineers how to construct other nuclear power plants at the south end of Taiwan without causing detrimental effects to the ecological systems.

CHEMICAL ECOLOGY

In 1964, Ehrlich and Raven proposed a theory of co-evolution, a part of which was the concept that an organism often produced chemicals that are not directly related to the basic metabolic pathway but are considered as secondary waste metabolites. Many of the biologically active compounds produced by higher plants may find their way into another organism where they may take greater or lesser part in a multiplicity of important physiological processes. They often attract or repel and nourish or poison animals; they may stimulate or suppress the growth of microorganisms (Muller and Chou 1972). This newly developed subject of chemical ecology promotes an understanding of the interactions of organisms with their environment mediated by the chemicals they produce. Such relationships comprise all biotic communication both in aquatic and terrestrial ecosystems. This field of chemical ecology has recently been developed in Taiwan by Chou and other scientists to be mentioned later. Their findings contribute not only to general science but also to agriculture.

Allelopathy

The detrimental effect of one plant on another by means of chemical products released into the environment is termed *allelopathy* (Molisch 1937) and is recognized as a fundamentally ecological process (Muller 1974; Rice 1974). Cases of allelopathy have been found mostly in arid and semiarid areas, and are scarcely to be found in humid or subhumid areas. Since 1972, Chou and his co-workers have studied the allelopathy of natural vegetation in the humid zone of Taiwan. A native grass, *Miscanthus floridulus,* which is widely distributed on the mountains and hillsides of Taiwan, was investigated. Competition for physical factors fail to explain the aggressive action of *M. floridulus* on other weeds; however, allelopathy was proved to be a key factor for the dominance of this grass (Chow and Chung 1974). Chou and Young (1975) studied the dominance of twelve subtropical grasses and found that allelopathy was strongly exhibited between them; at least seven allelopathic constituents were identified in the dominant grasses. More recently, Chou and Chen (1976) studied the allelopathic potential of twenty-five common species in northern Taiwan and showed that at least five species strongly showed allelopathic potential.

Allelopathy vs. Agricultural Productivity

In cultivated fields, severe reduction of crop yield has been recognized as primarily owing to continuous monoculturing. The debris of crop plants in soil is not always beneficial but may be harmful to the growth of succeeding crops (Wang et al. 1967; Chou and Patrick 1976). Wang and his associates studied the decline of sugarcane yield in Taiwan, and found that five growth inhibitors were of plant origin and came from the decomposed debris of sugarcane. Similarly, productivity of rice in the second crop is generally lower than that in the first crop. Although there are many factors involved in determining the reduction of rice yield in the second crop, phytotoxic inhibition was proved to be one of the factors involved (Chou and Lin 1976). They demonstrated that seven allelopathic compounds were found during the decomposition of rice residues in soil. These substances are able to retard the growth of rice seedlings and to decrease the number of tillers, the panicle number, and the test weight, resulting in the reduction of rice yield (Chou et al. 1977, 1979).

Dr. Thomas S. C. Wang, an eminent soil chemist, has contributed greatly to the development of this field of study in Taiwan. His prominent research has been concentrated on plant growth inhibitors in the soil, and he has gained international recognition for his work. His current investigation on the ecology of humic acid in the soil makes this field an exciting subject, one which will be of great benefit to mankind (Wang et al. 1971; Wang and Li 1977; Wang and Ferng 1978; Wang and Huang 1978).

Pheromone Research

In recent years, pheromone research has become a very important subject, and the substantial findings have been reported in the *Journal of Chemical*

Ecology. These studies have also successfully shown that sex pheromones of insects, alone or in combination with other chemicals (pesticides), can be of value in pest control. These results have stimulated the need to elucidate these messengers in other arthropod groups. In Taiwan, the research has been actively carried on by Chow and his associates, who have identified several sex pheromones from the female brown dog tick, *Rhipicephalus sanguineus,* and the American cockroach, *Periplaneta americana* L. (Chow et al. 1975, 1976).

The almond moth *Cadra cautella* and the Indian meal moth *Plodia interpunctella* have become serious grain pests in storage bins in Taiwan. Chow, Mayer, and Tumlinson (1980) studied electroantennogram (EAG) response of *P. interpunctella* to its sex pheromone and wing gland extracts. Antennae of the male moth gave the strongest EAG activities in response to two components of its sex pheromone, (*Z, E*)-9,12-tetradecadienol acetate and (*Z, E*)-9,12-tetradecadienol, and relatively strong activity to the related structure (*Z*)-9-tetradecenol acetate. Electroantennogram study obtained from the antennae of female moths indicated that the females also were sensitive to these compounds, but the response was not dosage dependent. Extracts of wing glands from males elicited an EAG from female antennae above that of the control, but the EAG amplitude did not change with changes in concentration over a range of 5–150 male equivalents (Chow et al. 1980).

Although modern control techniques, such as sterile male release, sex pheromone, and juvenile hormone have been studied, no practical way of controlling the moths is known. Chow and his associates (1977) performed sex pheromone attraction experiments. When the female sex pheromones were used in combination with water, as solvent, and soap powder, a great number of males and fertilized females of these two species were caught. The increased catch was ascribed to the presence of a detergent in the water.

Water Repellency in Soil

In Taiwan, the majority of the mountain slopes are extremely steep, resulting in a serious erosion problem, which is particularly serious in logging and burned-over areas. After vegetation is burned or destroyed, a great deal of plant debris is left in the soil. Hydrophobic substances are released into the soil and often can restrict water movement, causing a water repellancy problem in the soil. Chou has studied water-repellent substances in various soils where natural vegetation has been destroyed or been burned over; he and his co-workers have found some soils, collected from various mountain slopes, that exhibited great water repellency. The repellent substances have been isolated but not yet identified (Chou and Tsai, unpublished data). This field of study will become very important to agricultural productivity and reforestation of mountain slopes.

PALEOECOLOGY

Researchers in paleoecology have focused on the relationship between humans and their environment, looking at systems of cultivation and their culture-ecological relationships to shed light on the history of plant domestication and agriculture. They have also focused on modern aborigines, comparing their land patterns with those of prehistoric people. Since the Second World War, analytical methods of radiocarbon dating and pollen analysis techniques have been greatly improved, and paleoecological studies can be carried on with precision. During the last decade, this research has been intensively carried on in Taiwan by Dr. T. C. Huang and his co-workers. His outstanding work in palynology resulted in publication of a monograph, *Pollen Flora of Taiwan* (1972); although this book is taxonomic, it has made it possible to study the pollen in peat bogs, giving us a knowledge of the past previously unknown. In recent years, Dr. Huang has collaborated with a distinguished anthropologist, Dr. K. C. Chang, professor of anthropology, Harvard University, in investigating the relationships between humans and their environment in Taiwan (Chung et al. 1973; Huang 1975; Huang and Huang 1975).

With regard to its paleoecological aspect, the vegetation in Taiwan differs from that on the mainland China because of differences in geologic formation of soil, the high central mountain range, and climatic conditions. From the Mesozoic era through the Cenozoic, the climate of the island was stable. Before the Cretaceous period, the plains area of the island was dominated by cryptogams, extending to the mountain slopes (Liu 1971). However, after the middle of the Cretaceous period, the plains area was dominated by angiosperms instead of coniferous forests, and the vegetation has been greatly changed by climate because of its elevation.

The unique vegetation types on Taiwan are the littoral forest, strand forest, mangrove, and tropical savanna; these are different in paleoecological aspects from those of mainland China. The warm-temperate forests of the island have been widespread on the slope of the mountains since the Oligocene. Many coniferous trees such as *Chamaecyparis, Cephalotaxus, Taiwania, Cunnighamia, Pseudotsuga, Calocedrus,* and *Metasequoia* appeared in North America, Europe, and Asia during the Oligocene. In addition, Huang and his associates have reported that in the Puli Basin, indicator pollen grains are those of *Cryptomeria, Cunnighamia,* and *Pinus,* and for crop cultivation are assemblages of *Plantago, Ipomoea, Cyperus, Carex, Gramineae,* and *Chenopodium* (Chung et al. 1973). Researchers using radiocarbon dating suggest that the initial deforestation of the area occurred between 5000 to 15,900 B.P. Evidences of pottery and lithic artifacts seem to indicate that Neolithic peoples of the Lunshanoid culture of southwest Taiwan and southeast China arrived in this area before 2381 B.P. (Chung et al. 1973).

POPULATION ECOLOGY

Wild Rice Population

L. Wu (1978), studying wild rice populations in Taoyuan County, Taiwan, indicated that there was great genetic variability regarding the degree of seed dormancy and claimed that the wild rice population may be a potential genetic resource for breeding a sprouting-resistant rice variety. In 1976, Wu and his co-workers visited the sites and found a small population of around seventy plants at Patu village, Taoyuan County. This population appeared on the edge of the pond on mud that had been brought up from dredging operations. However, Kiang, Antonovics, and Wu (1979) reported that this wild rice population disappeared in 1978. Kiang et al. studied the causes for its disappearance and suggested three possible causes: hybridization with cultivated rice, changes in water management, and pollution of water by heavy application of chemical fertilizer. They reported that Taiwan wild rice contains a large amount of genetic variability and may be a very valuable genetic resource for rice crop improvement. They also suggested that this genetic resource should be preserved in order to study the impact of changes in agricultural practice in Taiwan on ecological systems (Kiang et al. 1979).

Rice Adaptability

The mechanism of rice varietal yield adaptability was studied by Dr. H. P. Wu. He used five indica and five japonica types of rice cultivars to study their adaptative mechanism in various environmental regimes. Regarding the adaptability of yield and its components, the yield of the indica type was relatively high and unstable compared with the japonica type. He concluded that the indica-type rice, particularly Chianon native 11, exhibited high yield and stability in the first crop season, while the japonica type showed better adaptation in the second crop season (H. P. Wu 1978).

Insect Population

A unique insect population study was performed by Lin et al. (1977), who studied the population fluctuations of soybean miner, *Ophiomyia phaseoli* (Tryon), as affected by nine environmental parameters. The population density of *O. phaseoli* in six successive crop seasons during a period of two years showed two maximum peaks for each crop season in southern Taiwan; one peak is at germination time and the other at the flowering stage. The factors influencing the population density of *O. phaseoli* are soil moisture, soil pH, solar intensity, and relative humidity.

Lizard Population

There are about twenty species of lizards in Taiwan (Wang 1962; Y. M. Liu 1970; Liang and Wang 1976; Lin 1979). Recently, Lin (1979) comprehensively studied the reproductive biology and seasonal weight changes in the liver and fat bodies in female *Japalura swinhonis formosensis,* which is endemic to Taiwan and several closely associated islands. The population of this species was found in orchards and forests over most of the country from sea level to an elevation of over two thousand meters. Lin concluded that *Japalura swinhonis formosensis* has a cyclic reproductive pattern similar to lizards from temperate environments. Females reproduce synchronously with the males. The presence of fat bodies is inversely correlated with reproduction in both sexes, though the cyclic weight changes of fat bodies and livers show somewhat different patterns in males and females.

Methods of Estimating Plant Stability

Many methods are available to estimate the interaction between genotypic and environmental effects. However, the parameters of stability estimated from the modern methods frequently fail to evaluate the quadratic responses between genotypes and environments. Wu (1973) used *Arabidopsis thaliana* and the hybrids F_1 and F_2 to devise two estimation methods for the stability of quantitative characters of a population under different environmental conditions when the response function is quadratic in form.

ENVIRONMENTAL POLLUTION

As a result of the rapid population growth and industrial development in Taiwan in recent years, environmental pollution has become a severe problem. In regard to air pollution, most pollutants are released from automobiles, factories, and power plants. The National Health Administration, SCOPE of Academia Sinica, and several research institutions have organized research projects to assess environmental problems, and several outstanding works have been reported. Sung and Chuang (1973) indicated that the city of Taipei has heavy air pollution that reaches maximum peaks at 7–9 A.M. and 6–7 P.M. daily. Chang and Tang (1975) observed the effect of air pollution on natural vegetation and found that species of *Pinus massoniana, Diospyrus discolor, Liquidambar formosana, Alnus formosana, Fraxinus formosana, Swietenia macrophylla,* and *Melia azdarch* appeared to be severely damaged. In addition, the coastal protective vegetation, *Kanehira* and *Casuarina* spp. along the coast at Taoyuan and Hsinchu, has been damaged by sulphur dioxide and other pollutants, and as a result a secondary effect shows up in damage to rice growth by salt spray. In consequence, the yield of rice in the area is significantly lower.

In water pollution studies, Chou and his associates (Chou 1978; Chou and

Chiou 1979; Chou et al. 1979) indicated that many industrial waters severely injure the growth of numerous crop plants. In particular, rice growth was greatly affected in the areas around Shinchu, Taoyuan, Taufen, Chunan, and Kaohsiung; frequently, a reduction in rice yield of more than 30 percent was found in the polluted areas. In addition, ducks, fish, clams, and oysters grown in the polluted coastal areas were also severely jeopardized. Hung et al. (1975) reported that heavy metals were one of the significant factors causing the mass mortality of oysters and fish along the western coast of Taiwan. Toxic phenolics were also suspected as a key agent.

Another significant project on coastal waters was conducted by a group of scientists at the Institute of Oceanography, National Taiwan University. This team has very good facilities, and the research vessel *Chiu-Lien* makes investigation of waters surrounding Taiwan possible (Hung et al. 1978, 1979). Hung et al. (1974, 1975); and Hung and Lin (1976) reported that heavy pollution was found in Kaohsiung and Keelung harbors where the oxygen content is almost zero. In Kaohsiung harbor, the phenolic content ranged from 0.01 ppm to 1.20 ppm, and total oils ranged from 62 to 3,600 ppm. In addition, the total coliform count in Jen-Ai and Chien-Cheng rivers already exceeds the 1,000 counts/100 ml set up by the United States as a standard for water pollution in harbors.

Recently, a Mussel Watch Program was evolved as a surveillance of U.S. coastal pollution, and the expansion of the program worldwide has been considered. Professor Hung has also been involved in this program and has given a progress report on the activities related to mussel watch in Taiwan (1979).

In February 1977, a large accidental oil spill occurred one mile off the Keelung harbor; in consequence, the fishing area around the northern coast of Taiwan was greatly jeopardized. Dr. K. H. Chang of Academia Sinica organized a team to investigate the change of biota and the dynamics of the aquatic ecosystem in the area.

In the last decade, heavy use of synthetic pesticides, fungicides, and synthetic fertilizers has caused serious environmental problems related to agricultural productivity. The heavy use of these synthetic chemicals causes an ecological imbalance of the soil fauna and microflora in many of the agricultural lands of Taiwan. The staff of the Taiwan Plant Protection Center has attempted to understand this impact and tried to solve this problem.

ECOLOGICAL RESERVATIONS

The island of Taiwan used to be the preserve of luxuriant growth of natural vegetation, extensive wildlife, and many natural areas. However, owing to the rapid population growth and intensive use of natural resources, these natural areas are rapidly becoming limited and eventually will disappear if we do not make plans for natural reserves. In line with the movement promoted by the

International Union of the Conservation of Nature and Nature Resources (IUCN) and related agencies, the government of the Republic of China has prepared laws, which we hope will soon be enacted, to protect national parks and more than three hundred natural reserve areas.

Ecologists in Taiwan have also attempted to do some ecological investigation regarding the establishment of natural reservations. An intensive ecological study was carried out on the reserve area of Yuen-Yang Lake, a natural watershed located in the northeast part of Taiwan. The whole area encircling the lake is 2.2 hectares. The surrounding slopes are covered by evergreen forests. There are 108 seed plants, twenty-eight ferns, and many unidentified species of liverworts and mosses (Liu and Hsu 1973). These investigators also indicated that in their floristic investigation, four new records were found.

After the resolutions adopted by the General Assembly of IUBS held in Helsinki, Finland, in August 1979, the protection of rare and endangered species and conservation of genetic resources have received great attention here. Our botanists and environmental scientists have made a great effort to protect a rare plant, *Kandelia candel* (one of the mangroves in Taiwan), in Tamsui River. Premier Sun finally announced that the mangrove forests along the coast of Taiwan should be protected; thus, a big project of residential construction in the sixty-hectare area of mangrove forest was cancelled. This protection was the first case in Chinese history. In addition, Hsu and his colleagues (1980) made a list of the rare and endangered species in Taiwan. It is hoped that naturalists will make a real effort to preserve the natural vegetation of this area and make it a reservation for the generations to come.

DEDICATION AND ACKNOWLEDGMENTS

This is dedicated to my parents, Mr. and Mrs. F. K. Chou, for their seventieth birthday in 1978. The author would like to express his appreciation to Dr. Thomas S. C. Wang (Academician, Academia Sinica) and Dr. C. H. Muller (Professor Emeritus, UC Santa Barbara), for my initiation into the exciting field of plant ecology. Thanks are also due to my colleagues Professors K. H. Chang, Y. M. Chiang, Y. S. Chow, C. E. DeVol, K. S. Hsu, T. C. Huang, T. C. Hung, T. T. Kuo, C. Y. Lin, J. Y. Lin, F. J. Lin, Valiant T. Liu, J. C. Su, C. K. Wang, L. Wu, and H. P. Wu and visiting professors Drs. Janis Antonovics (Duke University, U.S.A.) and Y. T. Kiang (University of New Hampshire, U.S.A.) for their valuable information and suggestions during the preparation of the essay.

REFERENCES CITED

Chang, C. H. and C. E. Tang. 1975. *Study on air pollution affects on the growth of forest trees* [in Chinese]. Technical Bull. No. 136. Dept. of Forestry, National Chung-Hsiung University.

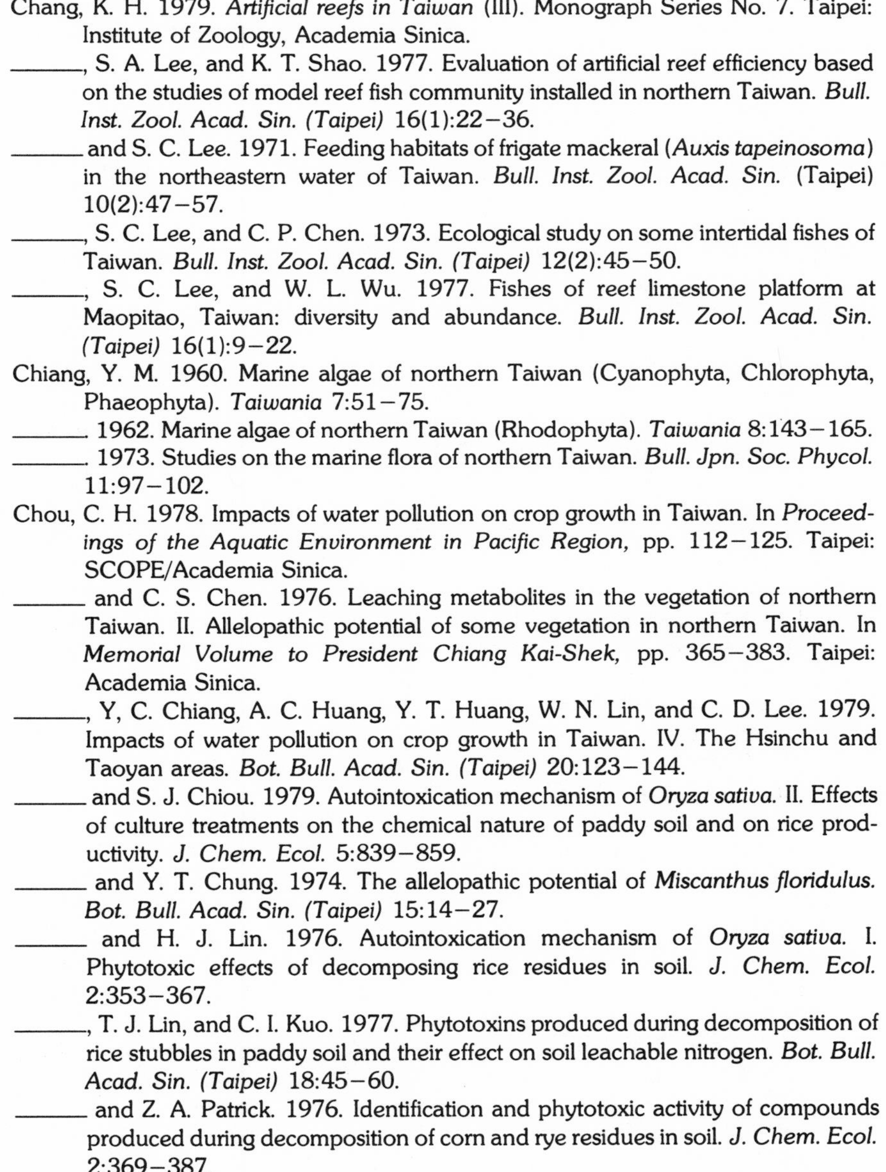

Chang, K. H. 1979. *Artificial reefs in Taiwan* (III). Monograph Series No. 7. Taipei: Institute of Zoology, Academia Sinica.

———, S. A. Lee, and K. T. Shao. 1977. Evaluation of artificial reef efficiency based on the studies of model reef fish community installed in northern Taiwan. *Bull. Inst. Zool. Acad. Sin. (Taipei)* 16(1):22–36.

——— and S. C. Lee. 1971. Feeding habitats of frigate mackeral (*Auxis tapeinosoma*) in the northeastern water of Taiwan. *Bull. Inst. Zool. Acad. Sin.* (Taipei) 10(2):47–57.

———, S. C. Lee, and C. P. Chen. 1973. Ecological study on some intertidal fishes of Taiwan. *Bull. Inst. Zool. Acad. Sin. (Taipei)* 12(2):45–50.

———, S. C. Lee, and W. L. Wu. 1977. Fishes of reef limestone platform at Maopitao, Taiwan: diversity and abundance. *Bull. Inst. Zool. Acad. Sin. (Taipei)* 16(1):9–22.

Chiang, Y. M. 1960. Marine algae of northern Taiwan (Cyanophyta, Chlorophyta, Phaeophyta). *Taiwania* 7:51–75.

———. 1962. Marine algae of northern Taiwan (Rhodophyta). *Taiwania* 8:143–165.

———. 1973. Studies on the marine flora of northern Taiwan. *Bull. Jpn. Soc. Phycol.* 11:97–102.

Chou, C. H. 1978. Impacts of water pollution on crop growth in Taiwan. In *Proceedings of the Aquatic Environment in Pacific Region,* pp. 112–125. Taipei: SCOPE/Academia Sinica.

——— and C. S. Chen. 1976. Leaching metabolites in the vegetation of northern Taiwan. II. Allelopathic potential of some vegetation in northern Taiwan. In *Memorial Volume to President Chiang Kai-Shek,* pp. 365–383. Taipei: Academia Sinica.

———, Y, C. Chiang, A. C. Huang, Y. T. Huang, W. N. Lin, and C. D. Lee. 1979. Impacts of water pollution on crop growth in Taiwan. IV. The Hsinchu and Taoyan areas. *Bot. Bull. Acad. Sin. (Taipei)* 20:123–144.

——— and S. J. Chiou. 1979. Autointoxication mechanism of *Oryza sativa*. II. Effects of culture treatments on the chemical nature of paddy soil and on rice productivity. *J. Chem. Ecol.* 5:839–859.

——— and Y. T. Chung. 1974. The allelopathic potential of *Miscanthus floridulus*. *Bot. Bull. Acad. Sin. (Taipei)* 15:14–27.

——— and H. J. Lin. 1976. Autointoxication mechanism of *Oryza sativa*. I. Phytotoxic effects of decomposing rice residues in soil. *J. Chem. Ecol.* 2:353–367.

———, T. J. Lin, and C. I. Kuo. 1977. Phytotoxins produced during decomposition of rice stubbles in paddy soil and their effect on soil leachable nitrogen. *Bot. Bull. Acad. Sin. (Taipei)* 18:45–60.

——— and Z. A. Patrick. 1976. Identification and phytotoxic activity of compounds produced during decomposition of corn and rye residues in soil. *J. Chem. Ecol.* 2:369–387.

——— and C. C. Young. 1975. Phytotoxic substances in twelve subtropical grasses. *J. Chem. Ecol.* 1:183–193.

Chow, Y. S., Y. M. Lin, and M. Y. Lee. 1976. Sex pheromone of the American cockroach, *Periplaneta americana* (L). I. Isolation techniques and attraction test for the pheromone in a heavily infested room. *Bull. Inst. Zool. Acad. Sin. (Taipei)* 15(2):39–45.

———, M. S. Mayer, and J. H. Tumlinson. 1980. Electroantennogram response of *Plodia interpunctella* to its sex pheromone and wing gland extracts. *Bull. Inst. Zool. Acad. Sin. (Taipei)* 19(1):27–31.

———, C. B. Wang, and L. C. Lin. 1975. Identification of a sex pheromone of a female brown dog tick, *Rhipicephalus sanguineus. Ann. Entomol. Soc. Am.* 68:485–488.

———, D. F. Yen, and S. H. Lin. 1977. Water, a powerful attractant for the gravid females of *Plodia interpunctella* and *Cadra cautella. Experimentia* 33:453–454.

Chung, T. F., T. C. Huang, and R. B. Stamps. 1973. Paleoecological study of Taiwan. (3) The Pu-Li Basin. *Taiwania* 18:179–193.

Ehrlich, P. R. and P. H. Raven. 1964. Butterflies and plants: a study in coevolution. *Evolution* 18:586–608.

Hsu, K. S., S. Y. Lu, Y. P. Yang, T. P. Lin, and H. C. Chang. 1980. Rare and nearly extinct plants in Taiwan. *Chin. Biosci.* 15:3–18.

Huang, R. and Y. M. Chiang. 1974. Phytoplankton along the southeastern coast of Taiwan. *J. Fish. Soc. Taiwan* 3(2):29–33.

Huang, S. Y. and T. C. Huang. 1975. Paleoecological study of Taiwan. (5) Toushe Basin. *Taiwania* 22:1–14.

Huang, T. C. 1972. *Pollen flora of Taiwan.* Taipei: National Taiwan University Press.

———. 1975. Paleoecological study of Taiwan. (4) Waichiataoken profile. *Taiwania* 20:1–22.

Hung, T. C. 1975. Primary production in the Kuroshio current surrounding Taiwan. *J. Oceanogr. Soc. Jpn.* 31:255–258.

———. 1977. Studies on primary productivity and chlorophyll *a* in the Kuroshio current surrounding Taiwan. *Proc. Nat. Sci. Counc., Republic of China* 10:169–184.

———. 1979. Brief report on the activities related to mussel watch in Taiwan. *Bull. Inst. Chem. Acad. Sin. (Taipei)* 26:55–65.

———, J. C. Chen, Y. M. Chiang, T. H. Tan, L. P. Lin, N. K. Liang, and H. T. Chang. 1979. *Environmental studies on Kaohsiung industrial coastal area.* Special Publication No. 22. Taipei: Inst. of Oceanography, National Taiwan University.

———, J. C. Chen, L. P. Lin, Y. M. Chiang, T. H. Tan, and N. K. Liang. 1978. *Studies on the coastal environment and estuary of Ta-Tu Chi Taichung, Taiwan, Republic of China.* Special Publication No. 17. Taipei: Inst. of Oceanography, National Taiwan University.

———, J. C. Chen, L. P. Lin, and N. K. Liang. 1975. *Pollution studies on shellfish-cultivating area of Taiwan western coast* [in Chinese]. Special Publication No. 6. Taipei: Inst. of Oceanography, National Taiwan University.

———, Y. H. Li, D. C. Wu, Y. M. Chiang, T. S. Tan, H. T. Chang, and P. C. Chu. 1974. *The aquatic environment and ecology of the Kaoshiung harbor* [in Chinese]. Special Publication No. 5. Taipei: Inst. of Oceanography, National Taiwan University.

——— and T. T. Lin. 1976. Study on mercury in the waters, sediments and benthonic organisms along Chia-I coastal area. *Acta Oceanogr. Taiwanica* 6:30–38.

Kao, P. C. 1975. Classification of Taiwan climatic regions based on rainfall temperature diagrams. pp. 368–375. *Proceedings of the 4th Pan-Pacific Conference on Regional Sciences.* Tamkang College, Taiwan.

Kiang, Y. T., J. Antonovics, and L. Wu. 1979. The extinction of wild rice (*Oryza perennis formosana*) in Taiwan. *J. Asian Ecol.* 1:1–9.

Li, H. L. 1963. *Woody flora of Taiwan.* Narberth, Pa: Livingston Publishing Co.

———, T. S. Liu, T. C. Huang, T. Koyama, and C. E. DeVol. 1979. *Flora of Taiwan,* Vols. 1–6. Taipei: Epoch Publishing Co., Ltd.

Liang, Y. S. and C. S. Wang. 1976. Review of the genus *Japalura (Lacertilia: Agamidae)* from Taiwan. *Q. J. Taiwan Mus.* 29(1&2):153–189.

Lieth, H. 1973. Primary production: terrestrial ecosystem. *J. Human Ecol.* 1:303–322.

——— and E. Box. 1972. Evapotranspiration and primary productivity. In *Papers on Selected Topics in Climatology,* Vol. 2, ed. J. R. Mather, pp. 37–44. New York: Elmer.

Lin, F. J., T. C. Wang, and C. Y. Hsieh. 1977. Population fluctuations of soybean miner, *Ophiomyia phaseoli* (Tryon). *Bull. Inst. Zool. Acad. Sin. (Taipei)* 17(1):69–76.

Lin, J. Y. 1979. Ovarian, fat body and liver cycles in the lizard *Japalura swinhonis formosensis* in Taiwan (*Lacertilia: Agamidae*). *J. Asian Ecol.* 1:29–38.

Liu, T. 1968. Studies on the classification of the climax vegetation communities of Taiwan. I. Classification of the climax formation of the vegetation of Taiwan. *Bull. Taiwan For. Res. Inst.* No. 166.

———. 1970. Studies on the classification of the climax vegetation communities of Taiwan. *Proc. Natl. Sci. Counc. Rep. China* 4(11):1–36.

———. 1971. Studies on the classification of the climax vegetation communities of Taiwan IV. *J. Agr. Assoc. China* 76:39–62.

———. 1976. Ecological zones of Taiwan. *Chin. For. Assoc.* 9:31–42.

——— and K. S. Hsu. 1973. Ecological study on Yuen-Yang Lake natural area reserve. *Bull. Taiwan For. Res. Inst.* No. 237.

Liu, T. S. 1962. *Illustration of native and introduced ligneous plants of Taiwan,* Vols. 1 and 2. Taipei: National Taiwan University Press.

Liu, Y. M. 1970. Studies on Taiwan lizards. *Biol. Bull. Taiwan Normal Univ.* 5:52–93.

Molisch, H. 1937. *Der Einfluss einer auf die andere—Allelopathie.* Jena: Gustav Fischer Verlag.

Muller, C. H. 1974. Allelopathy in the environmental complex. In *Handbook of Vegetation Science,* Part VI. *Vegetation and Environment,* B. R. Strain and W. D. Billings, eds. pp. 73–85. The Hague: Dr. W. Junk.

——— and C. H. Chou. 1972. Phytotoxins: an ecological phase of phytochemistry. In *Phytochemical Ecology,* J. B. Harborne, ed. pp. 201–216. New York and London: Academic Press.

Rice, E. L. 1974. *Allelopathy.* New York and London: Academic Press.

Rosenzwig, W. L. 1968. Primary productivity of terrestrial communities: production from climatological data. *Am. Nat.* 102:67–74.

Shieh, Y. J. 1977. Effect of planting density on community photosynthesis and on yielding components of rice plants. *Bot. Bull. Acad. Sin. (Taipei)* 18:153–168.

Su, J. C. et al. 1975. *An ecological survey on the water around the nuclear power plant sites in northern Taiwan I.* Taipei: SCOPE/Academia Sinica.

———. 1976. *An ecological survey on the waters adjacent to the nuclear power plants in northern Taiwan II.* Taipei: SCOPE/Academia Sinica.

———. 1979. *An ecological survey on the waters adjacent to the nuclear power plants in northern Taiwan (1974–1977).* Taipei: SCOPE/Academia Sinica.

Sung, F. C. and C. Y. Chuang. 1973. Air pollution in Taipei city. *J. Formosan Med. Assoc.* 72:267–278.

Wang, C. K. 1975. *Ecological study of the tropical strand forest of Hengchun peninsula.* Bio. Bull. No. 41. Taichung: Tunghai University.

Wang, C. S. 1962. The reptiles of Totel-Tobago (Orchid Island). *Q. J. Taiwan Mus.* 15:141–191.

Wang, T. S. C. and Y. L. Ferng. 1978. Catalytic polymerization of phenolic compounds by clay minerals. *Soil Sci.* 126:15–21.

——— and P. M. Huang. 1978. Catalytic polymerization of phenolic compounds by a latosol. *Soil Sci.* 126:81–86.

——— and S. W. Li. 1977. Clay minerals as heterogeneous catalysts in preparation of model humic substances. *Z. Pflanzenernaehr. Bodenkd.* 140:669–676.

———, T. K. Yang, and T. T. Chuang. 1967. Soil phenolic acids as plant growth inhibitors. *Soil Sci.* 103:239–246.

———, K. L. Yeh, S. Y. Cheng, and T. K. Yang. 1971. Behavior of soil phenolic acids. In *Biochemical interactions among plants,* pp. 113–120. Washington, D.C.: National Academy of Sciences.

Wu, H. P. 1973. Studies on the methods of estimating plant stability. *Bot. Bull. Acad. Sin. (Taipei)* 14:151–160.

———. 1978. Studies of the mechanism of rice varietal yield adaptability. In *Studies and Essays in Commemoration of the Golden Jubilee of Academia Sinica,* pp. 533–548. Taipei, Taiwan.

Wu, L. 1978. The seed dormancy of a Taiwan wild rice population and its potential for rice breeding. *Bot. Bull. Acad. Sin. (Taipei)* 19:1–18.

Applications of Ecology to the Solution of Environmental Problems

35

Applied Ecology

Jon Ghiselin

THE ORIGIN OF PRACTICAL ECOLOGY

Natural history in the eighteenth and early nineteenth centuries emphasized biology and the earth sciences. Linnaeus classified not only plants and animals, but minerals as well. Buffon studied zoology and geology. Hutton investigated geology and meteorology. Other areas of learning added also to a general body of scientific and technological knowledge. Malthus, a minister, contributed to both economics and biology by his study of the mathematics of the human population. An engineer, Ingenhousz, and another minister, Priestley, elucidated the respiratory interdependence of animals and green plants. Darwin and Wallace inherited a taxonomic profusion that was built largely by the contributions to biogeography of such explorers as Humboldt, Audubon, and Fremont. The great museum collections were being formed by the middle of the nineteenth century.

The importance of biogeography and systematics to the development of ecology is sometimes overlooked. Organic diversity began to be understood only after relationships were recognized. Organisms that were distant in both space and relationship could then be seen sometimes to respond to similar circumstances in analogous ways.

Recognizing the consequences of such convergence led to formulation of several partly opposing ideas about biotic communities. Such competing theories were the organismic and the individualistic: evidence is still accumulating that the individualistic viewpoint is probably nearer truth. Nevertheless, the comforting cosmology of the "superorganism" persists in two important ways.

The first is the public view of nature and of humanity's place in it. This seems to have been formed almost equally by the ideas of Theodore Roosevelt and Thornton W. Burgess, probably with some contributions from certain nineteenth-century poets. About 1900 this view led to an American conservation policy compounding preservation with the principle of sustained yield.

The second view is the functional. The names of life zones (Merriam 1898) are still used in describing habitats: kangaroo mice *(Microdipodops* spp.) are restricted to Upper Sonoran deserts, pine martens *(Martes americana)* principally to Canadian and Hudsonian forests. Government regulations often call for treating biotic communities in essentially organismic terms in the day-to-day practice of applied ecology.

CURRENT PRACTICE IN APPLIED ECOLOGY

Development of Applied Ecology as a Separate Specialty

Applied ecology can be interpreted as including all those aspects of the science that have some pertinence to practical human concerns. Such an interpretation could easily be stretched to include most human activities. As we shall see, something of the sort has actually occurred in judge-made law.

Applied ecology is restricted here to the area of ecology concerned with predicting the biological consequences of human actions undertaken with principal goals other than biological ones. Such a restriction conforms reasonably well to a consensus of those who regard themselves as applied ecologists. It excludes such well-defined fields as forestry, agronomy, and much of wildlife management and entomology. All of these fields and many others contribute special insights and techniques to the applied ecologist. Although practitioners of the specialties are consulted for their special knowledge, they are not included here as applied ecologists. On the other hand, many applied ecologists are strongly grounded in such practical specialties as fisheries biology or range management.

The applied ecologist practices—or attempts to achieve—synecological study, the goal of which is to predict the effects of postulated changes on biotic communities. This is approached in two general steps: a "baseline" study describes existing conditions; then, the effects of some change on those conditions are predicted.

Seral change and responses to such stresses as pollution must be identified during the baseline investigation because a baseline study deals with a changing system. In this sense, it is unfortunate that the term *baseline* was borrowed from engineering. When a surveyor establishes a base for triangulation, that line is permanent: its ends are marked, and its length determined precisely. Moreover, a surveyor's base can be measured repeatedly, but the ecologist can have no such certainty about an ecological baseline.

The applied ecologist's second major task is predicting changes and being accountable for those predictions. The difference between the applied ecologist and the academic lies just there. The standard of practice in applied ecology can best be elevated by improving predictive methods. Scientific theories are, or should be, expressed in testable hypotheses, and ecological prediction should be no different. Predictions should be testable, and they should be tested. A subsequent section will set forth some ideas about how this can best be done.

Ecology is an old science. Its component disciplines branched at several points from a root stock in natural history. Yet the whole structure of predictive, applied ecology discussed here became discrete only in the last quarter-century. Most growth has occurred since 1970. It is well to consider briefly why applied ecology grew up at all, before we discuss its future.

Public sentiment for conservation in the United States did not arise de novo in 1969 with the National Environmental Policy Act (NEPA). It has grown as a significant, organized force since the middle of the nineteenth century. For convenience, I date the obvious public movement from 1872, when Yellowstone National Park was designated, but public awareness goes back to Mosaic laws. As less remained to be conserved, insistence grew on restoration. The histories of the national forests and the national parks should provide sufficient examples, familiar enough that they need not be detailed here.

NEPA initiated the requirement for predicting environmental consequences of federal projects. State and other laws have since extended this to proposals of more local effect, and the courts have expanded the requirement beyond the purely ecological. Nevertheless, the need for ecological revelation is undiminished. In fact, because ecology is perhaps no less a discipline than a point of view, these changes in the interpretation of laws have increased the importance of the ecological outlook and emphasized the need for holistic thinking. NEPA, like most laws derivative from it, explicitly requires interdisciplinary participation in predicting the consequences of planned actions. Because of professional background, the applied ecologist is often responsible for integrating the information provided by an interdisciplinary effort.

Few laws requiring environmental impact statements provide for enforcement; they merely require responsible agencies to reveal fully the probable results of proposed actions. Comment by other agencies, combined with public reaction, should then lead to preventing or at least mitigating undesirable impacts. It is remarkable how well this mechanism has worked, and how far the interpretation of the law has led beyond what it seemed at first to require.

Jobs for Applied Ecologists

In the early 1970s, NEPA and its legal relatives created a demand for ecological information of a new type. Very few studies had attempted to inventory the organic diversity in single communities. The International Biological Program was only beginning its efforts at the analysis of ecosystems. Neither experience nor methodology was developed for the interdisciplinary study of biotic communities. At about that time, citizens' groups seized on NEPA and other laws to give them standing to sue in environmental matters that previously had been largely disregarded by the courts. The Calvert Cliffs decision of 1971 required the Atomic Energy Commission (AEC) to make its rules conform to NEPA. The AEC's revised procedures demanded full disclosure of the environmental consequences of proposed actions so that those consequences could be weighed and balanced against other costs and benefits during the agency's decision-making process. These rules led to the practice of filing vast environmental reports, abundantly buttressed by scientific information, to support proposals requiring federal approval at any level. The decision brought to prominence the legal specialty of environmental litigation and outlined the future of much of applied ecology. Onto the complexity of biotic communities the law now grafted the convolutions of industrial hygiene and socioeconomics as elements of the human environment.

Extensive environmental reports were soon required for many public projects, and often for private ones. Too few ecologists, economists, and others were in private practice to provide the information. In any case, individual investigators obviously could not produce the interdisciplinary studies that were suddenly needed. Faced with new requirements, power companies and highway builders turned to engineering firms for help, as they were accustomed to do in dealing with other impediments to construction.

Consulting engineering firms began competing for ecologists with the established ecological consultants and with the utilities themselves. Many biologists were hired; most were called ecologists, and some were. Some brought new bachelor's or master's degrees to their first jobs. This hurried staffing had probably unavoidable effects. Planning and direction of environmental studies usually were performed by engineers and others already established in consulting firms. Few were prepared by training, experience, or outlook either to design the ecological investigations now needed or to interpret the data that would result. Environmental reports were produced that often brimmed with undigested data, presented in volumes of species lists. The bulk often satisfied both clients and the public that environmental problems had been considered. Simultaneously, government agencies were unprepared to form the considered judgments for which the law now called. They retyped the species lists and reissued them as environmental impact statements. Requirements for predicting effects were simply dismissed. Although a baseline study properly should be a utilitarian means to a pragmatic end, it became an end in itself.

Improvement in the practice of applied ecology is coming slowly for three reasons. The first is continuing public pressure, often exerted through the courts. Begun in the tradition of conservation, this popular concern led in 1969 to NEPA, and since then to further laws, broader regulations, and a spreading realization in a variety of agencies that their responsibilities include environmental stewardship.

The second influence on the standards of applied ecology is internal. The profession is recognizing its own status and developing the self-assurance to assert the uniqueness of its special training and its special knowledge in a professional community populated by accountants, engineers, and lawyers. The qualifications of those who are labelled *ecologists* are being examined more critically, both within the profession and outside it. The research of applied ecologists, working in both private and governmental situations, continues to contribute improved techniques. New societies and journals meet special needs in applied ecology and related fields. The result of all this is that the ecological effects of proposed changes are being predicted with accuracy.

Third, the public increasingly identifies applied ecology as a discrete profession, as well as accepting the necessity to act as perpetual custodian of the environment. These developments are interacting to cause government agencies and regulated utilities to seek ecological advice through enlightened self-interest.

These trends for improvement can be perceived. The best standards of practice sometimes are actually applied, but the general level of design and execution in applied ecology remains less than the best.

THE ROLES OF APPLIED ECOLOGISTS

Practioners of such professions as forestry and wildlife management modify the environment by what they do themselves. These resource managers take actions for the sake of actions, but applied ecologists make predictions and recommendations principally about the actions of others. They often attempt to balance, if not to optimize, the potential consequences of several proposals with variously conflicting goals and effects. In this, they act as both scientist and arbitrator. This function as a practical mediator requires approaching negotiation in a way that calls particularly on the holistic outlook of the field of ecology.

Numerous processes involve concentrating, transporting, or converting energy or materials; all of these alter biotas and produce wastes. Many examples, therefore, could show the difficulty of predicting the effects of modifying natural systems. Such projects as sewer plants are meant to minimize environmental effects; others such as bridges have local or very specialized effects. Evaluating alternative sites for steam power plants requires a range of ecological considerations. It represents also the class of actions calling for cooperation of applied ecologists with other specialists.

The siting of power plants is limited both by the requirements of the plants and by the plants' environmental effects. Ecologists must understand the first in order to deal practically with the second. The nature of steam power stations presently restricts them to places where it is practicable to cool process steam. However ingeniously heat may be recovered in a power plant, some waste heat must be rejected to the environment. How this is done is basically immaterial to the mechanics of the power station, but the several possible means have very different environmental effects.

Because of its physical characteristics, water is a more convenient medium for transferring heat than is air. Consequently, water is used to cool condensers and other parts of a generating plant. Process water, used for steam and condensed for reuse, is expensively demineralized, and kept separate from the coolant. The easiest way to cool machinery is to pass cool water around it, and discharge heated water from the plant. The convenience of this "once-through" cooling accounts for the historic siting of thermal power plants on bodies of water. However, discharging heated effluents into a river or lake causes thermal effects on the natural water body. These effects range from "thermal enrichment," which may be seen as good, to "thermal pollution," which is usually seen as bad.

One way to avoid losing an argument is to evade the controversy. It appears that the way to avoid considering the fate of waste heat is to avoid returning hot water to a cool source. This requires that the waste heat be rejected elsewhere. Bodies of water reject heat ultimately to the air, and heat from a power plant is no different. If not transferred to the air by the medium of water, it can go directly. The questions, therefore, really concern not where the heat of a power plant goes, but how it gets there.

Two possibilities exist for transferring waste heat to the atmosphere. The first is dry cooling by radiation and convection from a surface over which air flows, but dry mechanisms usually cost more than the alternative of cooling by evaporation. Cooling towers cool water by evaporating part of it; most of the cooled water is reused, but some is returned to a river or lake at about the temperature at which it was withdrawn. Such evaporative systems cause increased salinity both in the water returned to the source and in water droplets entrained in the vapor rising from the cooling tower. Among other effects are inducing fog and increased precipitation, sometimes far from the cooling tower (Kramer et al. 1976).

However waste heat may be rejected ultimately to the atmosphere, the effects of using surface water for cooling include mortality of aquatic organisms that are entrained in the cooling water. Reducing the volume of water by evaporating part of it slows stream flow, and concentrating dissolved solids generally reduces water quality.

Other influences principally affect the land. Some terrestrial consequences of cooling devices have been mentioned. Coal-fired plants also produce a variety of air pollutants; ash and other solid wastes occupy extensive areas and may cause degradation of ground water. Nuclear plants produce far less solid waste than coal-fired units, but they share with them the hazard to flying birds of any large structure.

This simplified description of effects and alternatives suggests some of the variables that must be considered in evaluating the potential influences of power stations on their environments. It shows why limnology and meteorology are especially important for some kinds of projects.

Usually, new generating facilities built anywhere within a huge area could meet expected needs for service about equally well, and usually, several sites are available. Choosing among sites and among types of plants is usually beyond the unaided capabilities of a utility's operating staff. Consequently, utilities that expect to need additional capacity often seek the help of consultants early in the siting process. Many integrated engineering and consulting firms include siting among the services offered to the power industry. A siting study by such a firm provides an example of one role of the applied ecologist.

Engineering firms hire ecologists for two basic reasons: one is to save money for themselves and their clients by preventing blunders; and the other is to help their clients make money by increasing efficiency. The ecologist contributes predictive advice in both cases. Sometimes the advice is based on special knowledge of the probable effects of proposed actions. Siting studies usually fall in this class. Participation by ecologists in the earliest stages of such studies helps prevent the error of making a costly design effort when a site cannot be used. Later, when the choice of sites has been narrowed, consultation by ecologists and others with design engineers will continue to help preclude the expensive pursuit of futile plans.

Sites may be disqualified on ecological advice because rare organisms might be harmed. Plants and animals are placed on official lists of endangered species because their populations are too small to assure their survival. Rarity may result from overexploiting a population, as is the case with many marine mammals. The habitat may be reduced, like that of the eastern cougar *(Felis concolor couguar).* Or ranges may be very limited, like those of many desert fish. Whatever the reason for a species being rare, one can be sure that it cannot survive if its habitat is destroyed. Conversely, the apparent absence of a rare species from an area of appropriate habitat does not indicate that the possibility of that species' occurrence can be neglected. Some secretive species, such as the black-footed ferret (*Mustela nigripes*), are hard to find even where they are known to occur (Henderson et al. 1969). Others range so widely and occur so sporadically that their appearance in a particular spot in a particular year is unpredictable.

Such considerations are useful very early in evaluating plant sites that have been found acceptable for construction with regard to the availability of cooling water, for example, or distance from centers of population. The need at this stage is to discriminate biotic communities, either as potential habitats for particular plants or animals, or as unique in themselves. The more potential sites can be disqualified on such grounds as the pre-emption of critical habitats, the fewer will remain to be evaluated by such comparatively costly means as drilling to determine the suitability for foundations.

Other judgments also involve the suitability of habitats for particular organisms, but are more apt to find use in comparing potential sites. It is here that siting studies are sometimes more difficult than the baseline studies, which are conducted after a site has been chosen. The principal problem is the need to attempt the comparison of disparate values measured on incompatible scales. This is the dilemma of cost-benefit analysis as a mechanism for evaluating change. The difficulty is encountered both in environmental impact assessment and in other activities involving judgment among qualities of different sorts (Ghiselin 1978).

Baseline studies at chosen plant sites are meant to identify current conditions. This is prerequisite for two reasons. First, one must predict changes that would occur in the absence of a proposed facility. This usually requires anticipating the course of ecological succession and other environmental alterations throughout the probable lifetime of a project, and sometimes longer. Second, one must predict the effects of the facility if it were constructed. Baseline studies for most types of industrial or utility construction must provide for evaluating separately the effects of constructing and operating, as well as decommissioning or abandoning, the facilities.

Unfortunately often, mere species lists are submitted as sufficient studies of baseline ecological conditions. Such a list is an instantaneous catalog of the biota at a particular place, often made without regard to the relative abundance or seasonal appearance of organisms. The basis of most practical ecological study is discriminating communities of organisms. Describing lists of taxa without considering abundance cannot indicate communities (Shelford 1932). In this context, the rare organism is less important than the abundant one. Certainly, rarities do not ordinarily give special character to the communities in which they occur. While observing a species new to the hemisphere is exciting to the observer, it is rarely of vast moment for understanding how organisms interact. Making exhaustive lists necessarily takes time that may be better spent. Nonetheless, some agencies require such lists, and I have even known an agency to condense a more ample treatment to little more in its impact statement. I argue that it is a serious misapprehension to think such lists will serve where prediction is called for. Predictions must take into account changes that occur both in short cycles and over much longer periods. The most obvious cycles are those of the day and the year. Among the most subtle are seral changes in biotic communities. Populations of such lemmings as *Lemmus trimucronatus* and seventeen-year locusts *(Magicicada septendecim)* vary in ways that are harder to explain than the seasons but little less certain. Other natural variations seem to be at random, and human action may modify many other conditions. The ecologist must incorporate in a prediction both the more or less well understood cycles and trends, and the chance variations, which occur in all natural situations. The same great variability of living communities also leads ecologists to depend on statistical inference more than do those who work with more tractable materials.

To point this out seems needless to field ecologists and, one would think, to all biologists if not all scientists and engineers. Yet experience shows this is not the case: some need the reasons so baldy stated, and even then they may not believe.

Species lists are static, and by themselves almost meaningless. They predict neither the future of an area nor the changes that might be caused by any proposed activity. Yet prediction is the only reason for an environmental report under NEPA. One may go a bit further: prediction is the only reason for applied ecology.

The best one might hope of a species list is a basis for inference about community structure. For example, a listing that combines mountain mahogany *(Cercocarpus* sp.) with mule deer *(Odocoileus hemionus)* implies a general kind of community in western North America. Additions to the list may suggest further conjectures. Every step requires an increase in judgment and interpretation of data by the reader. Clearly, only an expert can base inferences on species lists, yet the expert who undertakes such an evaluation is at a major disadvantage by comparison with the earlier investigator who has worked with the biota where some change is proposed.

When the expert judges what a species list means, what is being done should have been done in preparing the list: interpreting data, rejecting most as presently immaterial, and inferring current conditions from various indicators. The attempt is to reconstruct a process that should have generated the species list, if at all, as a byproduct. So many guesses and approximations will be required, however, that the most expert judgment on species lists must be tenuous and tentative. Such inductive reasoning about community structure is inadequate to the degree that biotic communities are more than brushpiles. Descriptions of conditions made in this way are apt to be so insubstantial that they will have little use as foundations for prediction.

Expert judgment in regulatory agencies should detect such weaknesses. Environmental reports are meant to predict the consequences of proposed actions. Impact statements based on such reports should present expert and independent assessments of predictions made in the reports. If the expert in an agency has too little information to confirm an applicant's predictions, the agreement should not be certified. That inadequate reports sometimes are accepted indicates to my mind either that the putative expert is not actually expert, or that there is bowing to a less knowledgeable superior.

The principal activity of most applied ecologists presently is predicting the effects of proposed actions, which includes comparing the effects of using different sites for similar actions. Another predictive function is becoming increasingly prominent, namely, participating early in planning industrial and other developments. The goal of the applied ecologist in such planning is to predict and thus to control environmental effects. Technology is becoming more complex as its capabilities increase. The question before industry, government, and the public at large is now often not how to act, but rather whether to attempt something at all. Here the applied ecologist brings a unique outlook to planning a range of activities.

The ecologist's viewpoint differs from that, say, of the engineer because the perspective differs. It is probably as much as anything else an awareness of the error term that gives the ecologist a holistic outlook. Ecologists are accustomed to dealing with—or at least thinking about—situations in which feedback loops can be suppressed for many iterations before they unexpectedly become manifest. Biological training makes an ecologist recognize the complexity of the evolution and co-evolution of species, and impresses with the influence of stabilizing selection on the variance actually existing in phenotypically monomorphic populations (Dobzhansky 1970). This training forces the ecologist not only to realize the importance of time, but also to tolerate complexity, disorder, and uncertainty.

TOOLS OF APPLIED ECOLOGY

Applied ecology differs from other branches of the science in two chief ways, the objectives sought, and the time available to meet them. The apparatus of investigation and prediction is much the same.

One heritage of biology's origin from natural history is that biological investigation begins with description. Like other biologists, an ecologist may treat description as an end in itself. Having described a community, an ecologist may seek to explain its structure from its history, and in prognosticating to anticipate orderly succession.

Ecologists have usually been concerned with deviations from the seral course only when these arose from natural causes. Our materials are so complex and variable that we seek what stability we can by studying wildernesses and searching for relict communities. Some ecologists perhaps would hope at last to be buried in the oldest and most overgrown of cemeteries.

The applied ecologist deals with many of the same communities, with the same histories, as the purest academic. Further, there must be prediction of how such communities will change if left to themselves. Consequently the present ecology of an area must always be studied in some detail. This part of the job requires tools and techniques common to all ecologists. The literature of ecology, especially descriptions of wildernesses and neglected cemeteries, is irreplaceable for this work. Besides understanding the present and future of an area, however, the applied ecologist must predict what might happen if each of several possible changes were to be imposed upon it. In this, there is often little help from the traditional literature; there may be no existing analogues for the environmental effects of new technologies. Even having achieved an understanding of the mechanisms by which a community functions, the applied ecologist must often base predictions on little theory and no experience.

Dealing with such situations requires examining multitudes of interacting possibilities, and attempting to optimize the results. This is obviously a place for help from the systems ecologist. Other methods are particularly useful for the applied ecologist; for example, remote sensing of conditions ranging from overgrazing to thermal pollution is becoming increasingly routine. However, the most important advances in bringing applied ecology above the level of anecdote and guesswork will depend on strengthening theory to permit the applied ecologist to present predictions more often in the form of testable hypotheses.

MAKING ECOLOGY MORE PREDICTIVE

Ecology may be separating itself from natural history more slowly than other biological disciplines. Aspects of romanticism, perhaps even of mysticism, persist in several areas. These outwardly disparate *Weltanschauungen* share an unwillingness to see natural occurrences, and especially biotic communities, as they are, rather than as the observer wishes. Their manifestations form a variously entertaining continuum from Peter Rabbit through much of opera to the invention and manipulation of mathematical models. Their practical danger is obscuring actuality under more attractive fiction.

Applied ecology, however, needs pragmatic prediction. Ecologists' ability to anticipate certain consequences of construction gives their services unique value. Because their background may make their outlook somewhat broader than that of most other specialists, ecologists are especially useful in interdisciplinary planning teams. Yet, despite all this, or perhaps because of it, some co-workers, and some of the public, still suspect the ecologist.

The scientific method requires formulating empirically testable hypotheses. A hypothesis may originate subjectively, and intuition often has a principal part. To be testable, a hypothesis must be expressed in a form that in appropriate circumstances would permit it to be proved wrong. The distinction between being able in principle to falsify a prediction and actually doing so is especially important in ecology, because of the long periods that may be involved; the actual test may never come. Sometimes, a hypothesis may be intended and taken as a warning and consequently never tested. Warning of the unworkable or the hazardous is one of the applied ecologist's most important jobs.

Prediction is more difficult in applied ecology than in some other fields for several reasons. Two seem to stand out. First, one must depend in part on predictions in several other areas, each having its own special difficulties. In climatology, for example, long-term trends may be masked by fluctuations of greater amplitude but shorter period. Second, the tools of prediction cannot always include the panoply of devices offered by statistical inference. Eberhardt (1976) has shown that experimental techniques tend to be deficient in impact assessment because adequate replication of samples is often impossible.

Despite these difficulties, advanced current practice shows how the methods of ecological prediction can be improved; the means to do so are at hand. The ideas summarized here do no violence to the proven methods of science; rather, these ideas are intended to apply the scientific method strictly and with economy of effort. Nevertheless, they question some procedures that have become conventional without having had rigorous consideration of their merit.

We should ask first why some investigations are conducted at all. The U.S. Army Corps of Engineers (1974), for example, requires that environmental reports describe the range in the United States of every "biotic species" occurring in an area. I am at a loss to know why. The U.S. Nuclear Regulatory Commission (1976) requires quantitative data on the densities of some populations, but apparently nowhere defines acceptable statistical variances (σ^2). Such data cannot be interpreted as they stand; they have very limited value either in documenting baseline studies or in validating monitoring. Consequently, they cannot find much use in the prediction of environmental impacts, which is the only apparent reason for their being. I suggest that unless some benefit from gathering these data can be found, they should no longer be demanded.

What would be better? I think the experimental methods of natural science, left alone, would do. Let us not forget what the applied ecologist tries to do. Given a set of hypothetical modifications to an existing system, the attempt is to predict the consequences of those changes. Given a set of alternatives for action, the applied ecologist tries to predict the effects and the intensity of those effects for each. Many such predictions could be cast in experimentally testable form. It follows, in my view, that they should be, and where feasible, that they be put to the test.

Perhaps a didactic model will help here. It is proposed to site a power plant on a large river. The limited choices of the model are not constructing the plant, building it as planned, or building it at an alternate site. The predictions required are these. First, if the plant is not built, one must predict the course of succession at the unaltered site. A falsifiable hypothesis is that succession will progress from mudbank to willow *(Salix)* to a mature riparian forest dominated by black locust *(Robinia pseudoacacia)* and sycamore *(Platanus occidentalis)*. One cannot wait three centuries for the climax community, but the prediction can be partially confirmed by the appearance of willow in only a few years. [The appearance of saguaro (*Carnegiea gigantea),* for example, would falsify the hypothesis.] If a control area can be found nearby—and it will not be the same area, but perhaps it may resemble it closely enough for our purposes—where willow grows initially, then the evidence seems strong that succession to locust and sycamore on the control area presages a similar succession on the proposed plant site. Second, if the plant is built as planned, one falsifiable hypothesis is that the river temperature 100 m downstream from the discharge of cooling water will be increased no more than 2°C. A test of this can have meaning only if the conditions existing before the plant's construction are known. Testing that hypothesis is a reason for recording river temperatures at that place during the baseline study. Finally, one could frame similar questions in falsifiable terms about the alternate site.

Applied ecologists sometimes predict the effects of applying untried technologies. It is important for the progress of the discipline that this type of prediction be tested publicly. However, in a competitive atmosphere, clients or employers may require confidentiality; this is especially likely when the investigations deal with the feasibility of untested ideas and can reasonably be regarded as proprietary. Public disclosure of such predictions thus may occur only when disclosure is required for environmental impact statements, and these are prepared only when it is planned to actually employ the new methods. Predictions of severe effects may languish undisclosed and untested.

An analogous difficulty occurs in achieving disclosure of information that would test predictions. The laws now impose no general requirement that the results of environmental monitoring, performed during and after construction of an approved facility, be made available to the public. This is true even when such monitoring is required as a condition of licensing. Furthermore, when information of this kind is released, it is not required that it be related to predictions made before construction. Thus, the reliability of applied ecologists' predictions cannot be assessed except by special efforts, and comparison among predictions (and ecologists) is generally impossible.

It remains to be determined how failure of prediction, the only significant test of performance for an applied ecologist, could be turned to ensuring the competence of practitioners. Verifying a set of prognostications would have little significance in an individual case. Only if the police power of the government were invoked (perhaps through licensing) could the validity of predictions be tested, and then not immediately. The final test would seem to be in the competition of applied ecologists: the analogy of deaths among surgical patients is clear and appropriate.

ACKNOWLEDGMENTS

I thank Donald G. Frier, Charles E. Obold, and Patricia A. Pingel for advice about the manuscript.

REFERENCES CITED

Dobzhansky, T. 1970. *Genetics of the evolutionary process.* New York: Columbia Univ. Press.

Eberhardt, L. L. 1976. Quantitative ecology and impact assessment. *J. Environ. Manage.* 4:27–70.

Ghiselin, J. 1978. Perils of the orderly mind: cost-benefit analysis and other logical pitfalls. *Environ. Manage.* 2:295–300.

Henderson, F. R., P. F. Springer, and R. Adrian. 1969. *The black-footed ferret in South Dakota.* South Dakota Dept. Game, Fish and Parks, Pierre, S.D.

Kramer, M. L., D. E. Seymour, M. E. Smith, R. W. Reeves and T. T. Frankenberg. 1976. Snowfall observations from natural-draft cooling tower plumes. *Science* 193:1239–1241.

Merriam, C. H. 1898. Life zones and crop zones of the United States. *Biol. Surv., Dept. Agr. Bull.* 10:1–79.

Shelford, V. E. 1932. Basic principles of the classification of communities and habitats and the use of terms. *Ecology* 13:105–120.

U.S. Army, Corps of Engineers. 1974. Preparation of biological inventories. In *Preparation and coordination of environmental statements,* Appendix G, page G-1. ER 1105-2-507. (Also *Fed. Regist.* 38[220]:31638.)

U.S. Nuclear Regulatory Commission. 1976. *Preparation of environmental reports for nuclear power stations.* USNRC Regulatory Guide Series, Reg. Guide 4.2, Rev. 2.

36

Ecosystems Analysis And Land-Use Planning*

Herman H. Shugart, J. M. Klopatek, and William R. Emanuel

INTRODUCTION

The landscape around us is composed of a mosaic of ecosystems, both natural and man-made. As human intervention into ecosystem processes increases, a priori evaluations of future land-use planning commitments are needed. Any successful plan for the integrated management of a land area should be preceded by a characterization of the ecosystem(s) involved, study of the plan's probable impact on the environment, and evaluation of all possible management alternatives (T.I.E. 1972). Since the development of an ecological approach to land-use planning by Hills (1961), there has been an increasing tendency to incorporate environmental factors in such planning (McAllister 1974). The reasons for this development are as diverse as are the land-use problems facing society today (U.S. EPA 1974), but in the United States it can be attributed to three major factors: 1) an increase in environmental awareness that has spawned public support and interaction; 2) the passing of the National Environmental Policy Act (NEPA), which has forced environmental and ecological considerations into a broad spectrum of projects; and 3) the rise of systems in ecology whereby decisions and impacts

*Research sponsored in part by the Energy Research and Development Administration under contract with Union Carbide Corporation and in part by the Eastern Deciduous Forest Biome, funded by the National Science Foundation under Interagency Agreement AG-199, DEB 76-00761. Contribution No. 298, Eastern Deciduous Forest Biome, US/IBP publication No. 1074, Environmental Sciences Division, ORNL.

can be evaluated in terms of their functional interrelationships within the ecosystem. The first two factors need no belaboring here; the third factor is the focus of the following discussion.

As systems ecology and ecosystem analysis have developed over the past few years, there has been a concomitant increased interest in practical applications. The application of systems ecology to land-use planning has not reached maturity; however, systems ecology has its strength in the ability to deal with one element of a system (e.g., land-use type) in its functional interrelationship with the rest of the system (e.g., the surrounding region). Planning questions often require an extrapolation and refinement from traditional ecological dogma. By viewing an entire system, insight is gained into the relative importance of individual parts thus decreasing the likelihood of spending excessive time analyzing individual components that perhaps play only a minor role. Finally, systems ecology forms the basis for mathematical simulation models, which, when adequately calibrated, can be exercised to obtain predictions of future events. These models, through the universality of mathematics, allow interaction across disciplinary boundaries more readily than other types of information.

An additional point concerning the linkage of systems ecology and land-use planning stems from the regional scope of many of today's land-use problems and required policy decisions. Aside from the spatial aspect, a region should imply a functional entity. This means that a regional system possesses attributes not found at lower hierarchies, such as ecosystems and emergent properties unique to its level of scale. The magnitude and complexity of regional problems dictate that a systems approach be employed not only to assess the existing state but also to provide prognostications of land-use changes and associated impacts and conflicts. Three examples of developments will illustrate this intersection of systems ecology and land-use planning.

Forest Succession Modelling. Such modelling has developed over the past five to ten years into a useful management tool. The modelling approach generally attempts to mimic the behavior of a natural or near-natural ecosystem. The models, commonly implemented on a high-speed digital computer, usually simulate the ecological attributes of some relatively small (0.01 – 1 hectare) area of land. To apply the models in a regional context, one must assume that the simulated forest stands are in some way representative of the elements that make up a landscape. This latter procedure either may be in the interpretation of the implications of the model behavior, or it may constitute an additional modelling exercise (see "landscape-scale" models below). Forest succession models are a holotype for what may be a rich assemblage of fundamentally ecological models with utility in more applied contexts.

Energy Flow Studies. These have been important methods in ecosystem studies since the mid-1950s. Systems ecology as a subdiscipline in ecology was spawned in part by an intense interest in ecological energetics. Energy flow diagrams are paradigms in their own right, corresponding closely, but not exactly, to the diagrams used to program analog computers; in fact, energy flow modelling owes much of its early development to analog computation methods. Recently, ecologists have been increasingly interested in using energy flow analysis in modelling human-dominated or influenced ecosystems at the regional or county level. The methodology capitalizes on using energy as a commodity common to any real system to allow the modeler to explicitly develop functional relationships between different sectors of a modelled system.

Optimization Techniques. Although the two previously discussed techniques originated in ecology, the use of optimization techniques for land-use planning developed from general systems theory (operations research). Its inclusion here stems from its potential to solve the conflicts that arise from mixing ecological factors with more traditional considerations for planning. The methods usually require the high-speed digital computer to determine the best alternative, and the computational problem involves searching a complex response-surface for the best solution. Like the forest succession models, the approach of most optimization procedures is that a region is composed of a mosaic of mixed land uses, with the problem being identification of the most desirable pattern of this mosaic.

MODELLING FOREST SUCCESSION AT LANDSCAPE AND STAND LEVELS

Two frequently used spatial scales for the consideration of forest succession are the landscape (up to several thousand hectares) and the stand (small areas on the order of one hectare). Studies on either stands or landscapes dominate the literature on forest succession to the extent that there seems to be only limited interest in succession at other spatial scales. Scientists performing landscape studies infer a "temporal" pattern from the mosaic of information gathered at the stand level from different plant communities scattered over a region. In landscape-scale studies, the size of the region considered may relate directly to the area that one must examine to obtain enough different plant communities to piece together some reasonable temporal pattern. Data for the stand studies are frequently obtained by periodic remeasurement of the individual trees on a forest sample unit, the stand. Because stand studies are usually based on direct measurements, they are less abstract, less contestable, contain less extrapolation, and are often concerned with shorter time intervals than are landscape studies.

Large-Scale Simulators

A rationale for modelling landscape-scale forest succession was presented in an earlier paper (Shugart et al. 1973), and work on these types of models has been continued by colleagues (W. C. Johnson, Oak Ridge National Laboratory; D. M. Sharpe, Southern Illinois University; J. E. Hett, University of Washington). Our remarks will be confined to the more general aspects of large-area successional modelling.

Shugart et al. (1973) assumed that:

1. Land can be characterized as having some finite number of cover types (cover-states).
2. Effects of landscape heterogeneity on the dynamics of cover-states are reasonably constant over the time segments of interest, and model simulation may be less accurate in cases of altered heterogeneity. For example, in a region completely cleared of all forest (altered heterogeneity), the return of forest communities to the landscape might be retarded due to a lack of tree propagules.
3. The area of land in each cover-state in a regional successional system provides sufficient information to allow computation of future apportionments of land by area.
4. Cover-states have input-output relations that are superposable (*i.e.*, the system behaves as a linear system).

Cover-states represent stages of forest development along a successional gradient. The relationships between the cover-states and the densities (or mass) of various tree species found during succession are shown in Fig. 36.1. The changes in density or biomass of species in a given stand through time can be thought of as a trajectory through an n-dimensional hyperspace (Fig. 36.1a). Each dimension (axes on Fig. 36.1a) of this space is the density, or some other relevant quantifier, of one of the n species in the succession; the cover-state is a hypervolume in this n-space. Such data are available for many regions, and construction of successional models serves to collate these data (Johnson and Sharpe, 1976) and to transpose them into meaningful information.

Stand Studies

Over the past five years, several stand simulators have been developed independently (Arney 1972; Botkin et al. 1972; Ek and Monserud 1974). These models focus on tree ontogeny and function by keeping track of the birth, death, and growth of each individual tree in a forest stand. There are

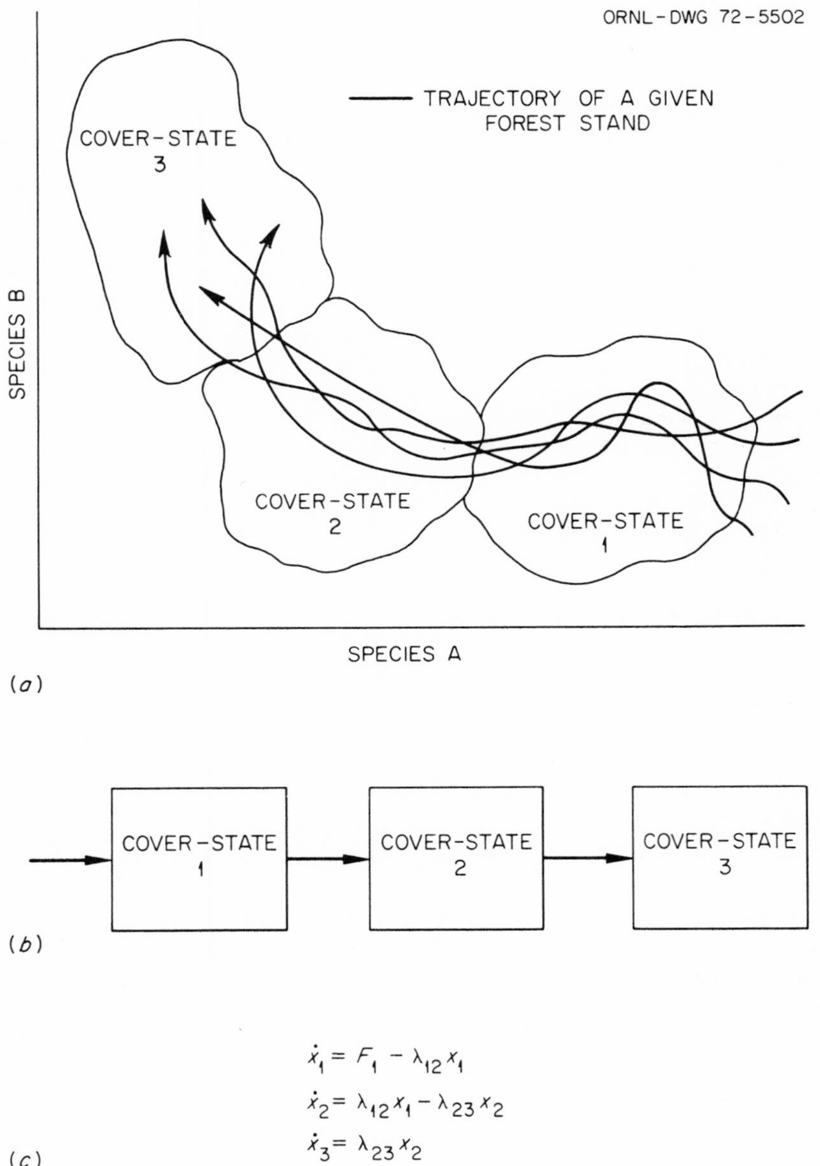

$$\dot{x}_1 = F_1 - \lambda_{12} x_1$$
$$\dot{x}_2 = \lambda_{12} x_1 - \lambda_{23} x_2$$
$$\dot{x}_3 = \lambda_{23} x_2$$

Figure 36.1. Three Equivalent Abstractions Representing Forest Succession in a Large Region. (a) Regional succession represented by a number of stand trajectories through a species-density hyperspace. (b) Compartment diagram showing transfers among cover-states. (c) System of differential equations indicating transfers between cover-states (figure from Shugart et al. 1973).

several problems associated with developing such models; for example, in our own efforts (Shugart and West 1977; Mielke et al. 1977) we have noted:

1. One must decide whether or not to consider explicitly the location of each tree or each seed tree in the stand. Several stand models developed to experiment with single-species management strategies (thinning and planting) consider the position explicitly (e.g., Ek and Monserud 1974; Mitchell 1971; Arney 1972), but most models do not keep track of the location of seed trees (e.g., Ek and Monserud 1974 reseed sources).
2. There are a multitude of assumptions that must be made regarding stand size, correct time scales for simulation, physiological characteristics of each species, and appropriate minimum size of tree to consider. Additional assumptions are made concerning the species of trees considered that relate both to computational considerations (computer time, core, input and output of information) and to the behavior of the models. There are currently no obvious general rules (theory) for determining the appropriateness of these assumptions.
3. Generally, one must select some mode(s) of principal interaction(s) that determines how individuals of various species compete and behave relative to one another. Obvious candidates are tolerance-growth characteristics of species (Botkin et al. 1972; Shugart and West 1977) and different water-use characteristics of species (Botkin et al. 1972; Mielke et al. 1977). This selection process is usually accompanied by problems in establishing factors to characterize species differences.

FORET, the stand-level simulator developed by Shugart and West (1977), simulates reproduction from seeds and vegetative growth and the death of trees larger than 1.27 cm on a one-twelfth-hectare plot. The model does not consider seed source, although it does consider seedling establishment in great detail, nor does it keep track of the position of individual trees. The trees interact directly by shading one another and interact indirectly according to differences in reproductive strategies. The model is developed on a rationale presented by Botkin et al. (1972). A sample of output from the FORET model illustrating the results of a model experiment involving adding and removing the American chestnut from the Tennessee forests is shown in Fig. 36.2. The stochastic nature of the model is reflected in the erratic small-scale changes in the curves tracing species biomass. The model is, as are most stand simulators, sensitive to the elimination of tree species, elimination of individual trees, and altered tree growth rates. These sensitivities parallel directly the model characteristics needed to simulate blights, harvesting, or pollutant effects. In an applied situation, the stand simulator model can be of unique value to the land-use planner for the elucidation of how policy decisions or actions will have long-term effects on a region's forests. Example situations include the consequences of additional timber harvesting or the effect of an increase in air pollution resulting from energy technology facilities. For this reason, a variety of these models have been developed by organizations with

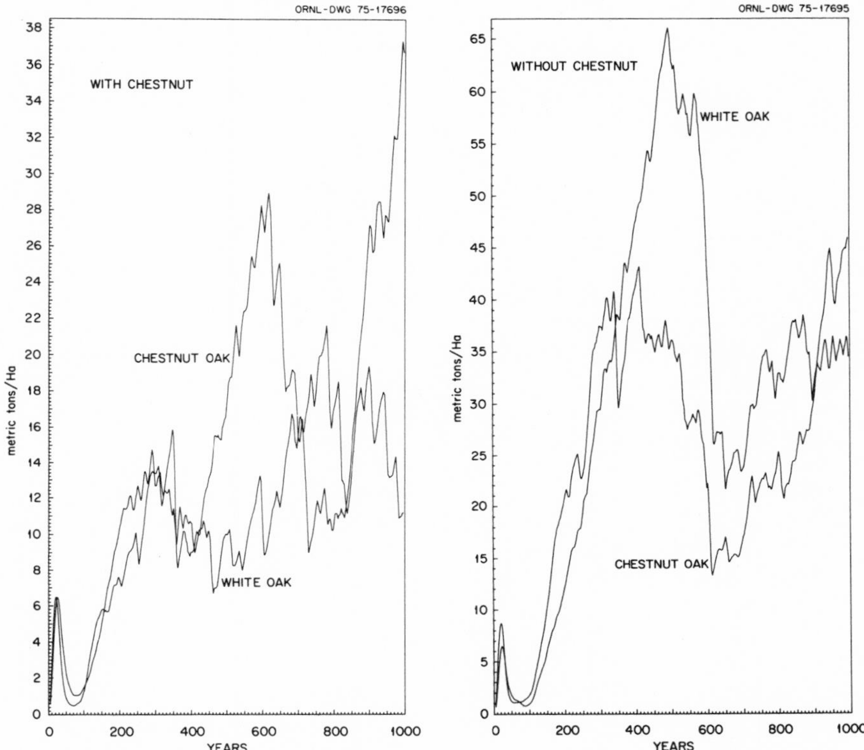

Figure 36.2. FORET Model Simulations of Chestnut Oak (*Quercus prinus*) and White Oak (*Quercus alba*) with (a) and without (b) American Chestnut (*Castanea dentata*) over 1,000 Simulated Years Starting from an Open Plot. Lines are the mean values from 100 simulated plots.

regional planning interests (e.g., USDA-Forest Service, the Energy Research and Development Administration, and several large timber companies).

Available Modelling Approaches

For illustrative purposes, we have described an example of a landscape-level simulator and a stand simulator. There are, in the recent literature, several alternate modelling approaches all directed toward similar goals (Table 36.1). We would advise those intending to use succession modelling for land-use planning to closely investigate the assumptions of whatever model is chosen. All the models listed are limited in the range of conditions they can be expected to simulate. Modelling of forest succession is a rapidly developing

Table 36.1. **Models of Potential or Realized Utility in Land-Use Related Studies**

Model Category	Description	Applications for Land Use	Examples and Notes
Single-species stand simulators	Usually very applied models using a variety of statistical or assumed functions for forest growth. Model output is usually in terms of yield of timber products as a function of time. The modelling techniques for these models are extremely varied, but the model goals are directed toward simulating outputs from managed stands.	Models are useful for simulating economic and forest product yields from managed forests. Some of the models are restricted in their ability to simulate altered conditions as they might affect the forests and some are less so. Some models simulate even-age stands, while others simulate all-age stands.	Newnham (1964): Douglas fir stands Clutter (1963): Loblolly pine stands Mitchell (1967): White spruce stands Lee (1967): Lodgepole pine stands Bella (1970): Aspen stands Dress (1970): General even-age stand simulator Bosch (1971): Redwood stands Mitchell (1971): Douglas fir stands Hatch (1971): Red pine stands Goulding (1972): Douglas fir stands

Population models	Frequently uses Markov processes as the modelling paradigm. Models are usually parameterized from stand remeasurement data or from theory of plant replacements. Although there are some Markov stand models used in forest economics, population models are generally considered by forest ecologists in a basic research context.	Since these models keep track of the number of trees of a given species in a forest, the models are useful for determining the composition of mixed-species, all-age stands. Some of the models should be able to simulate effects of altered regional conditions.	Leak (1970): Northern hardwoods Waggoner and Stephens (1970): Forests in Connecticut Penden et al. (1973): General Markov simulator Cassell and Moser (1974): General Markov simulator Hartshorn (1975): Tropical forests Horn (1975): Forests in New Jersey

(continued)

Table 36.1—Continued

Model Category	Description	Applications for Land Use	Examples and Notes
Stand simulators	Extremely detailed models that keep account of the species and diameter of each tree in a modelled stand. Models also may plant, harvest, or kill individual trees. Some of the models have been applied to plantation spacing problems; others have been used in basic research context.	Since these models use very mechanistic representations for competition and growth of individual trees, they tend to be able to simulate the effects of altered regional conditions on forest composition and yield.	Newnham (1964); Mitchell (1971); and Arney (1972): Stand simulators for economically important Douglas fir stands Botkin et al. (1972): Northern hardwood forest simulation used to predict clearcut effects Ek and Monserud (1974): Extremely detailed stand simulator of forests in Wisconsin Shugart and West (1977): Mixed mesophytic forest simulator used to assess blight in forests Mielke et al. (1977): Southern Arkansas upland forest simulator used to inspect management strategies for the Red-cockaded Woodpecker, an endangered species

Large-scale simulators	Differential equations used to simulate the changes in area of land in different forest type categories for a large region.	Models are regional in their development and can be used to assess the overall dynamics expected of the forests of a region.	Olson and Cristofolini (1966): Model simulates forest dynamics in the Oak Ridge, Tennessee vicinity Shugart et al. (1973): Model simulates northern lower Michigan regional forests Johnson and Sharp (1976): Model simulates Georgia Piedmont regional forests

field that has already produced several modelling approaches which are beginning to find application in practical landscape level problems.

Combining Stand and Landscape Studies

In our original consideration of the modelling rationale for landscape dynamics (Shugart et al. 1973), our intent was to develop a large-scale modelling technique that was relatively straightforward and would utilize general rules, if not actual data, for stand-level dynamics. In the rationale developed and depicted in Fig. 36.1, if one has a proper stand model, the appropriate landscape model is little more than a bookkeeping algorithm for the dynamics of several thousand stands. On the surface, it seems relatively easy to use stand simulators to generate "data" to obtain landscape simulators. Unfortunately, it takes a great deal of effort to construct a reasonable stand simulator, develop an acceptable classification scheme for a landscape's vegetation mosaic, and conduct a survey of the amounts of land in each category in some region. The step of starting with a stand model and generalizing upward to a landscape model has yet to be made. The primary obstacle at present seems to be the very size of the problem; by contrast, necessary conceptual steps have been formulated to allow regional modelling of forest ecosystems at a fairly high level of detail.

ENERGY FLOW STUDIES IN LAND-USE PROBLEMS

In general, the transition from the study of small-scale, natural, intact communities to the analyses of macroscale systems has been difficult to accomplish (Van Dyne and Abramsky 1974). Often, the problem can be attributed to the necessary, but perplexing, inclusion of humans as an integral part of the community (Barret et al. 1976). The U.S. International Biological Program realized the importance of incorporating humans as a component of the ecosystem and concluded that a prime method of integrating study of human communities with studies of ecosystems was through the implementation of energy flow studies (Jamison and Friedman 1974).

Methodologies

A pioneer of energy flow analysis, H. T. Odum (Odum 1971; Odum and Odum 1976), has combined energy principles with general systems theory to provide a unified methodology that can be employed to analyze systems at all levels of resolution. The methodology integrates principles of ecology, thermodynamics, and economics to address problems straddling the biological, physical, and social sciences. Underlying energy flow analysis is the concept that energy is the universal measure of work performed by humans and nature, and that energy units (e.g., joules, calories, BTUs) afford the best common denominator for evaluation and comparison. This is a concept that has been both vigorously praised and criticized by economists (Georgescu-Roegen 1971, 1977; Huettner 1976).

Energy analysis necessarily includes not only the measure of the amount of useful work obtained from a given process but also the energy requirements to facilitate that process. Direct and indirect flows of energy required for the production of goods and services, as well as the quality of energy, need to be accounted for. When energy flows are expressed in heat units, only the heat content of the flow is reflected, not the ability of the flow to perform work. Any energy flow can be degraded to heat with a 100 percent efficiency (e.g., 1,000 kcal of sunlight or 1,000 kcal of gasoline.) However, the ability of energy flow to do work, or to be harnessed, is dependent on how it is concentrated. For example, a farmer applies 100 kg/hectare of nitrogen to assist planted corn to capture and concentrate energy from sunlight, a very dilute form of energy. Production of nitrogen fertilizer requires approximately 11,500 kcal/kg, of which 10,000 comes from fossil fuel and 700 comes from electricity. However, approximately 3.89 units of fossil fuel are required to make one unit of electricity (Herendeen and Bullard 1974), and thus a total of 13,500 kcal are required to produce a kilogram of nitrogen fertilizer. The farmer, therefore, subsidizes the system with 1,350,000 kcal/hectare in the form of nitrogen fertilizer in addition to other fuel-based subsidies. The combination of subsidized energy plus the natural energy of sun and rain is then the total energy required to maintain this particular land-use type. It follows that energy flow analysis requires not only an evaluation of the energy embodied in goods and services, but also the quality of energy. Employing these criteria, one can evaluate the resources used or gained in any natural or human process according to their capacity to contribute useful work to the system in which they operate.

The strength of energy flow analysis is its ability to integrate ecological, as well as economic, costs based on economic-energetic linkages (Garvey 1972; Shatz 1974). Because of the deterministic nature of energy, complex interactions within any system can be readily modelled with a basic understanding of energy flow theory. Dynamic models that show energy flow throughout the system can be simulated to provide predictions of the future status resulting from impacts of projects or policy decisions. The fluxes and storages of energy can be measured within the system, and alternative decisions can be compared based on the predicted total useful work generated and dissipated.

Energy flow methodology thus has substantial utility as a framework for regional analysis and land-use planning. In fact, Lavine and Meyburg (1976), in a study prepared for the Highway Transportation Board of the National Research Council, have shown that the methodology appears to be better suited for environmental planning purposes than seventeen other leading methodologies with which it was compared.

The application of any methodology to land use requires a macroscale approach since proper evaluation of a specific land-use system must be done in relation to the region. At this level, linkages and feedback processes between natural and cultural phenomena are extremely complex. Because of this, many investigators have avoided empirical analyses because of their inability to accurately and comprehensively portray the entire system. The problems associated with the development of macrolevel models have been discussed by Van Dyne and Innis (1972) and stem from a host of factors, some of which were mentioned above. However, macroscale models do not have to be simulated to be useful. Rather, their utility lies in synthesizing ideas, organizing information, guiding data collection, comparing types of impacts, directing more in-depth microscale analyses at a level where simulation is valuable, and communicating results (Gilliland and Risser 1977).

Analysis of Specific Problems

To implement the modelling process, Odum (1972, 1975) has developed an energy flow language, which visually and mathematically conveys the structure and function of the system according to the laws of thermodynamics and Lotka's maximum power principle (Odum and Pinkerton 1955; Wesley 1974). The primary symbols used in this discussion are depicted in Fig. 36.3, and an in-depth explanation and mathematical description of the symbols can be found in Odum (1972, 1975). We will now describe examples of how energy flow analysis has been employed on a macrosystem level to deal with some specific land-use problems, which are intended to portray not only the versatility of the methodology but also the diversity of land-use problems that need to be addressed at the macrolevel.

Resource Depletion Antonini et al. (1974) used an interdisciplinary systems approach to land resource analysis to simulate land-use changes in predicting the outcome of certain policy decisions in the Dominican Republic. The investigation attempted to estimate the effects of increasing population pressures and changing land use on the resource base of the region and the possible synergistic relationship between land use and siltation of a proposed reservoir. In this example, land-use changes were simulated using a macroscale approach, and information derived from this analysis is utilized to key on specific related problems at lower levels of resolution.

Fig. 36.4a depicts the land-use model assembled for the particular watershed examined. In addition to depicting the energy relationships, the diagram also shows the major flows of land area within the watershed. The units that designate changes in land use are in area per time (Shugart et al.

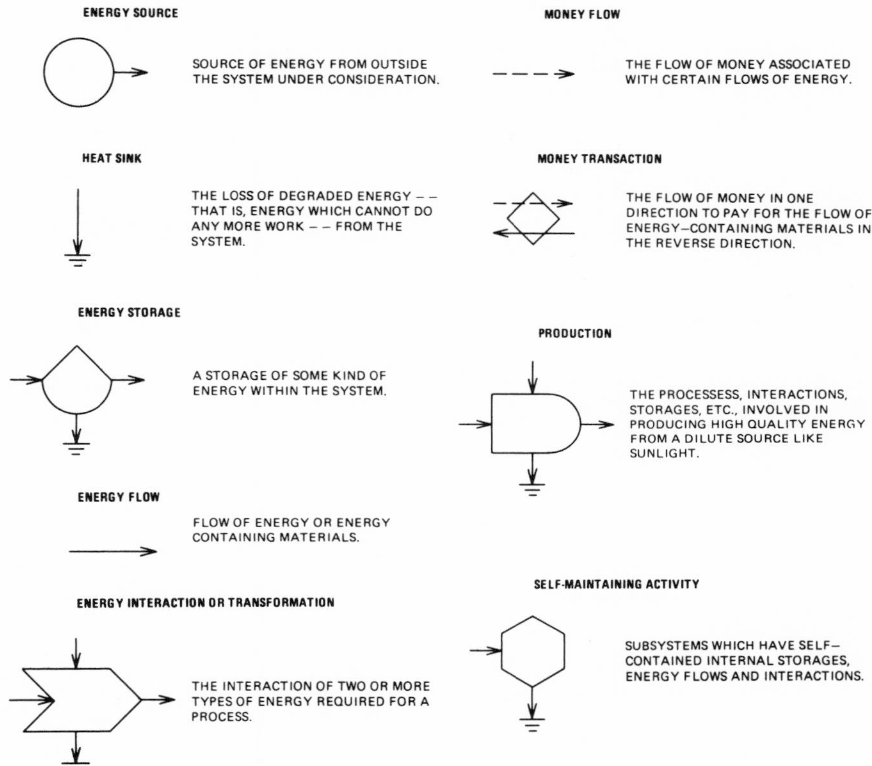

Figure 36.3. Description of the Principal Energy Language Symbols Employed in Figures 36.4 through 36.7. (After H. T. Odum 1972)

1973; Johnson and Sharpe 1976), while inputs (forest cutting, agricultural practices) and outputs (crop protection, timber) are expressed in units of energy. In this situation, Antonini et al. (1974) have modelled the land-use changes of the region and related them to the predominant forcing functions through the flow of energy. Although this study of forest succession was based on historical data, the forest succession modelling approach discussed previously (e.g. large-scale simulators, see Table 36.1) would have also been applicable. This would be especially true if one wanted somewhat greater detail on the effects of forest cutting on the regional forest mix.

Figure 36.4b depicts two of the possible changes in land use resulting from policy decisions. As indicated in Fig. 36.4a, the output from the land-use model was fed into a water balance model to address specific questions dealing with erosion and sedimentation resulting from depletion of tropical

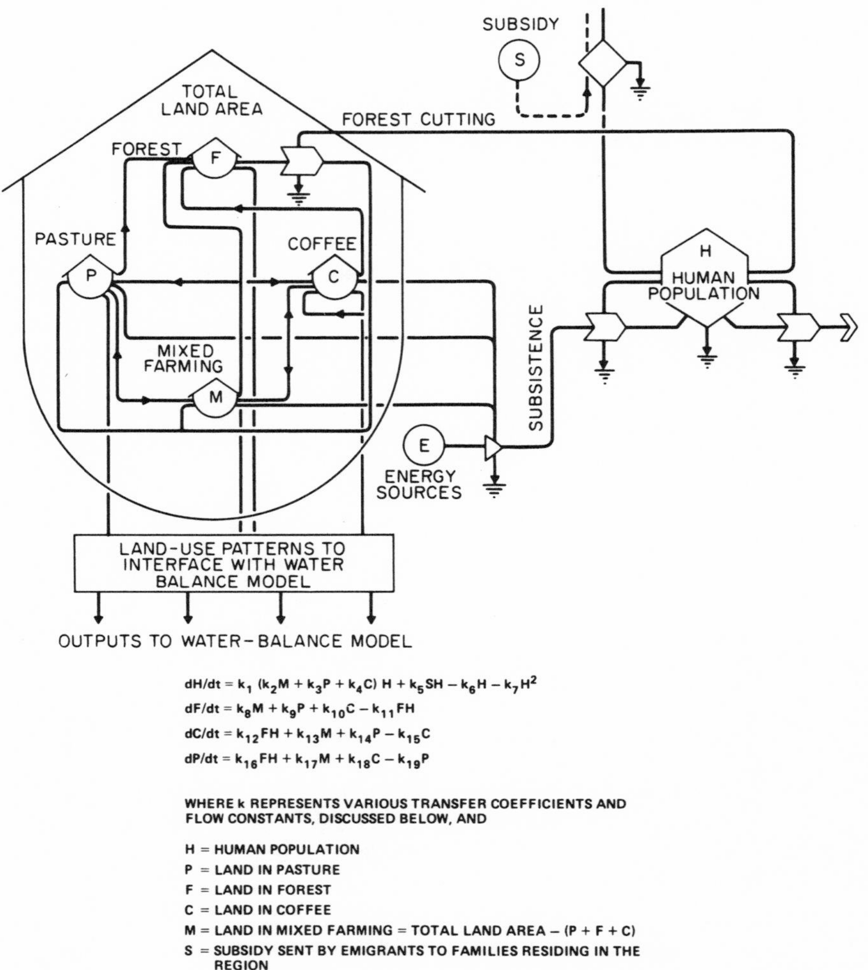

Figure 36.4. (a) The Energy Flow Model of Land-Use Changes and Population Growth in a Dominican Republic Watershed. The differential equations defining the changes are listed below the diagram. (After Anatonini et al. 1974)

forest resources. The energy flow diagram can also be thought of as a way of writing the differential equations that are an intermediate step to digital or analog simulation. The differential equations describing the changes occurring in the individual land-use categories are a composite of inflows and outflows of the storage compartments and thus are translations of the energy flow diagram. This does not mean that only compartments and associated flows need to be delineated. It should be understood that both expertise and re-

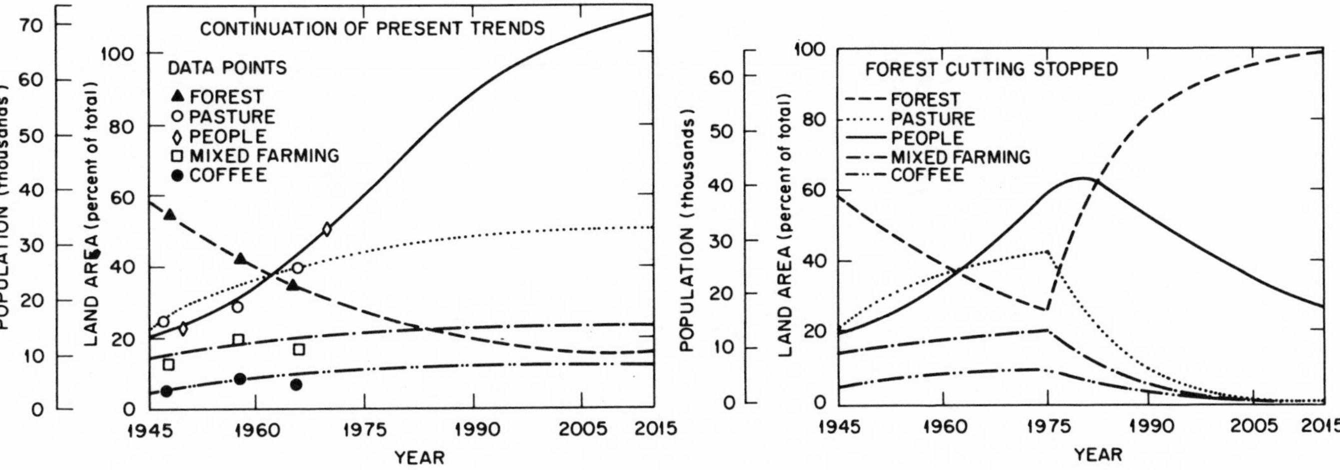

Figure 36.4. (b) Two examples of Output Obtained from an Analog Simulation of the Model Depicted in Fig. 36.4a.

search are required to compile the model, ascribe the interaction, and determine the coefficients.

Impact Analysis Gilliland and Risser (1977) have presented an excellent example of how energy flow analysis can be used at a macrolevel. Their procedures included five basic steps: 1) construction of a macroscale systems diagram representing the important cultural, technological, and natural functions and interactions within the system; 2) evaluation of pathways and storages; 3) analysis of data; 4) identification of impacts that require more detailed analysis; and 5) examination of the environmental impacts outside the boundaries of the system. Figure 36.5 is the energy flow system diagram for their study of the White Sands Missile Range (WSMR). The integration of natural and cultural causal factors or forcing functions is exemplified in this model. The focal point of the analysis centers on the impact that a particular land-use activity (a military base and associated operations) has on the surrounding natural and cultural systems. It is obvious that the level of presentation does not portray the entire complexity of the system but indicates the level of resolution the investigators wish to address. The methodology does not guarantee that all important flows and compartments have been evaluated, for this is still dependent on the knowledge of the investigators and also on the boundaries of the system. The quantification of this model showed that the stress of WSMR activities on the natural environment (pathways 19–22 and 42) was only about 1 percent of the natural energy flow. Transformed and evaluated in the context of the next higher system (a three-county region), the WSMR-developed energies (work done by nature and by humans) contributed 677×10^9 kcal/year (in fossil-fuel equivalents), while the loss of natural energy amounted to only 5×10^9 kcal/year. We mentioned previously that one of the attributes of approaching systems modelling with a macroscale approach is the indication of where detailed microscale anaylsis is necessary and simulation is valuable. Even from the macroscale level depicted in Fig. 36.5, the investigators ascertained that a principle stress on the system resulted from the high water-use rate of the WSMR complex. A detailed analysis and computer simulation was then carried out to assist in long-range planning for the area.

Carrying Capacity To predict future land-use conversions and consequences, one must decide how much economic development is compatible with a region's natural resources so that the regional economy remains vital while maintaining a high quality of life. In other words, how much cultural land use may be interspersed with the natural systems of a region? Or, what is the carrying capacity of the system? In a natural intact community, the problem can be addressed relatively simply by extrapolating information from similar communities that are in a steady state.

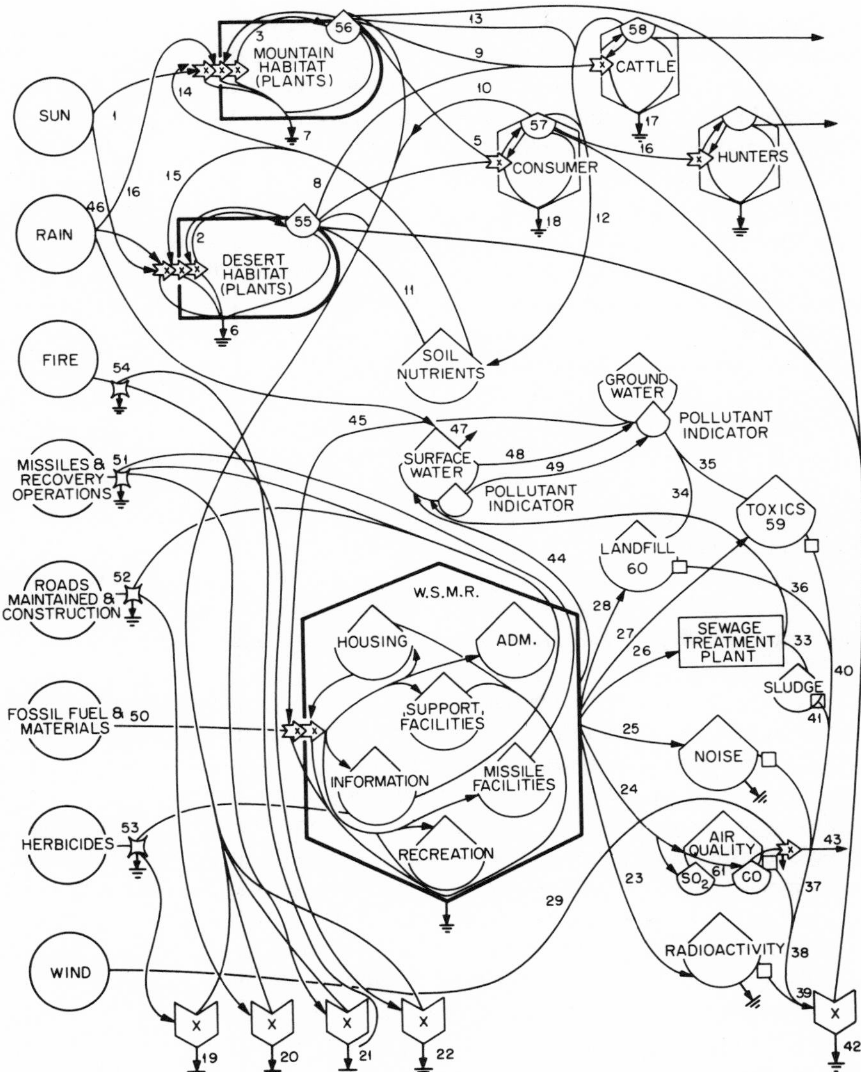

Figure 36.5. Energy Flow Systems Diagram of the Major Compartments Flows and Causal Factors for the White Sands Missile Range. (After Gilliland and Risser 1977)

A natural community is able to support only a given amount of biomass (structure) based on the available natural energies and resources. Over time, species composition may change but, after a peak level of structure is reached, the system's level of production is adjusted to coincide with the amount of structure it can support. Thus, ecosystem production is roughly equivalent to ecosystem maintenance. This level is, of course, not static and may exhibit minor fluctuations owing to natural environmental perturbations. Cultural systems, those dominated by humans, are not limited by naturally occurring energies; through human activities, these systems (e.g., cities, agriculture) are able to support a structure based on subsidized energies imported from outside the systems' boundaries. Natural systems have evolved over time to establish their structural limits, but cultural systems, which are developed through inputs of fuel-based energies, have not evolved such limits. Humans can and do develop systems that have an amount of structure which, over the long run, is unsupportable because of an unguaranteed level of energy subsidization required for the systems' maintenance. Present-day examples can be seen from New York City to the energy-intense agricultural areas of California to the feedlots of the Great Plains.

Perhaps the most intensive and extensive effort to deal with carrying capacity and land use on a regional basis has been the South Florida Study (Browder et al. 1976). A simplified macroscale mini-model of south Florida and the external causal forces are shown in Fig. 36.6, an example of how a large area can be modelled with energy flow analysis methodology. For a detailed discussion of the model parameters and output, see Odum and Brown (1975).

There is, of course, much more detail in the south Florida system than represented by the diagram, since a large number of individual studies were involved in the overall project. However, the key to a useful model in such a situation is to choose a level of complexity that includes the principal technological and natural interactions of concern. Results from computer simulation models showed that south Florida was already at or near its carrying capacity based on its naturally available energies and its predicted incoming fuel-based energies. While some areas within the region possessed growth potential, other areas, such as the Miami-Dade County urbanized subregion, could expect economic and structural decline (Zuchetto 1975).

If the systems that survive are those which maximize the incoming energy flow for useful work as proposed by Lotka (1924), and if useful work (e.g., power flow) can be measured, it can serve as the criterion for determining what combination of human-dominated and natural systems a region can support. The useful work, of course, stems from the available potential energy in a region coming from fossil-fuel-based energies and materials and natural energies of sun, wind, precipitation, and other elements. In combining the

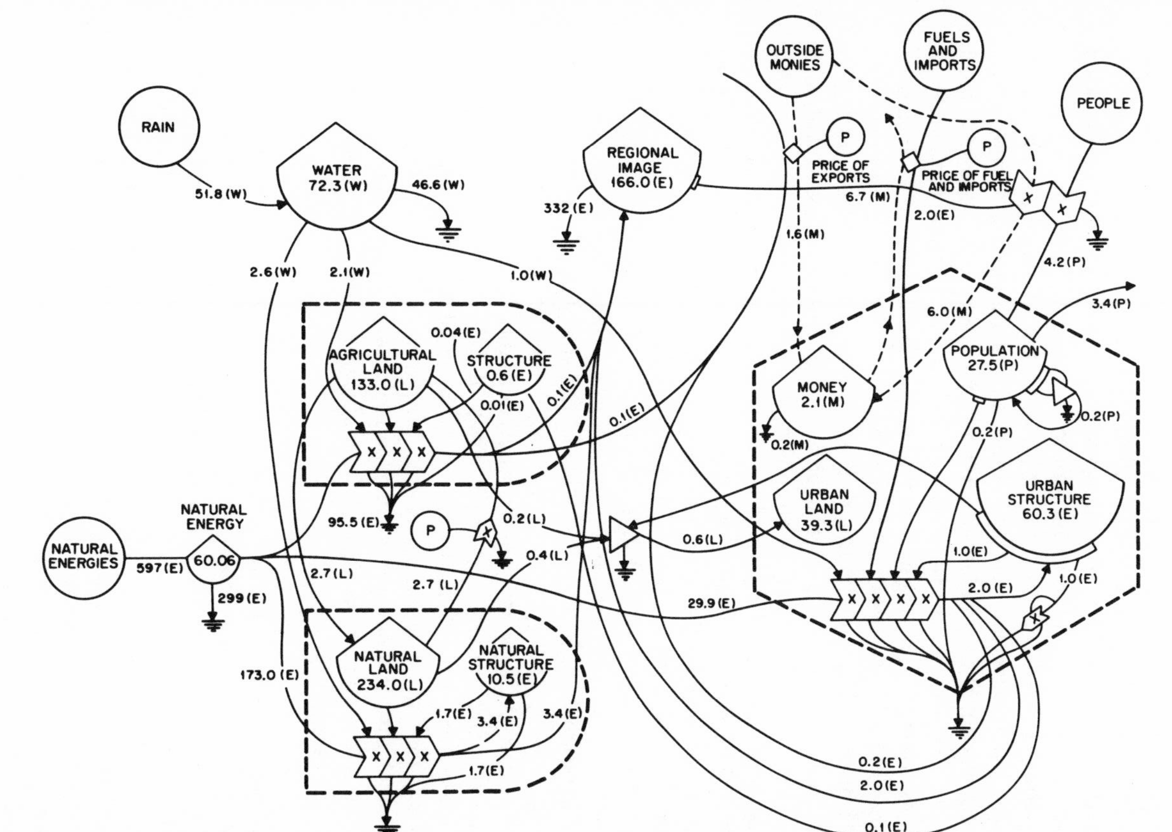

Figure 36.6. A Quantified Energy Flow Model of the Principal Interaction of Man and Nature in South Florida. (After Ahlstrom et al. 1975) (W)=Flow of water × 10^6 acre-ft/year; storage × 10^6 acre-ft. (L)=Flow of land × 10^8 m^2/year; storages × 10^8 m^2. (M)=Flow of money × 10^9 \$/year; storage × 10^9 \$. (P)=Flow of people × 10^5 people/year; storage × 10^5 people. (E)=Flow of energy × 10^{14} kcals/h; storages × 10^{14} kcal.

energies, a balance needs to be maintained between the free work done by the environment, or as Woodwell (1974) describes it, the public service function of nature, and that based on fossil fuels. In an earlier study, Odum and Odum (1972) showed that for south Florida, a combination of 50 percent developed land (e.g., urban, agriculture) and 50 percent natural land yielded the maximum value of the environment in terms of useful work.

E. P. Odum (1970) and his students showed that to maximize the natural energies in Georgia, while maintaining the current standard of living, would require 10 percent of the land in urban-industrial systems, 30 percent in food production, 20 percent in fiber production, and 40 percent remaining as natural environment. This is not meant to imply that the goal of each state or region should be a self-contained system based on the energy and materials within its borders. Rather, it is meant that for planning purposes the region must be evaluated in terms of available natural energy. Fossil-fuel-based energies, including the small contribution of nuclear fuels, coupled with natural energies can then be utilized not only to maintain a level of development within the system but also produce materials, foodstuffs, and services that can be exchanged for other energies and materials, with money as a mediator, necessary for the functioning of the system.

In regional analysis, all long-range planning should include a strategy for a steady-state future. Given a region, its naturally occurring energies, and a reasonable guaranteed level of fossil-fuel-based energies, a level of development (e.g., steady state) can be determined for the region that will best maximize the available energies and properties of the environment. This does not mean that the amount of specific types of development will be determined; these decisions will still be left up to the local planners. What it does mean is that for a given region, a level of development can be approximated beyond which further development can lead to severe oscillations or a decline in the level of the system because of the inability to guarantee stable energy inflows (Forrester 1971).

Land-Use Efficiency Besides identifying the supportive limit or carrying capacity of a region, a researcher must objectively determine the optimal uses of specific land types within that region. Figure 36.7 illustrates a quantitative mini-model for agricultural land in Texas County, Oklahoma. The overall complexity of interactions, the variety of crops, and different management strategies are not shown, but the diagram clearly depicts the tremendous energy-based subsidization of the agroecosystem. Using a common denominator of energy units of fuel equivalents, a scientist can calculate the total maintenance costs of the system and compare them in terms of the system's output and naturally occurring energies and hence the energy efficiency of land use.

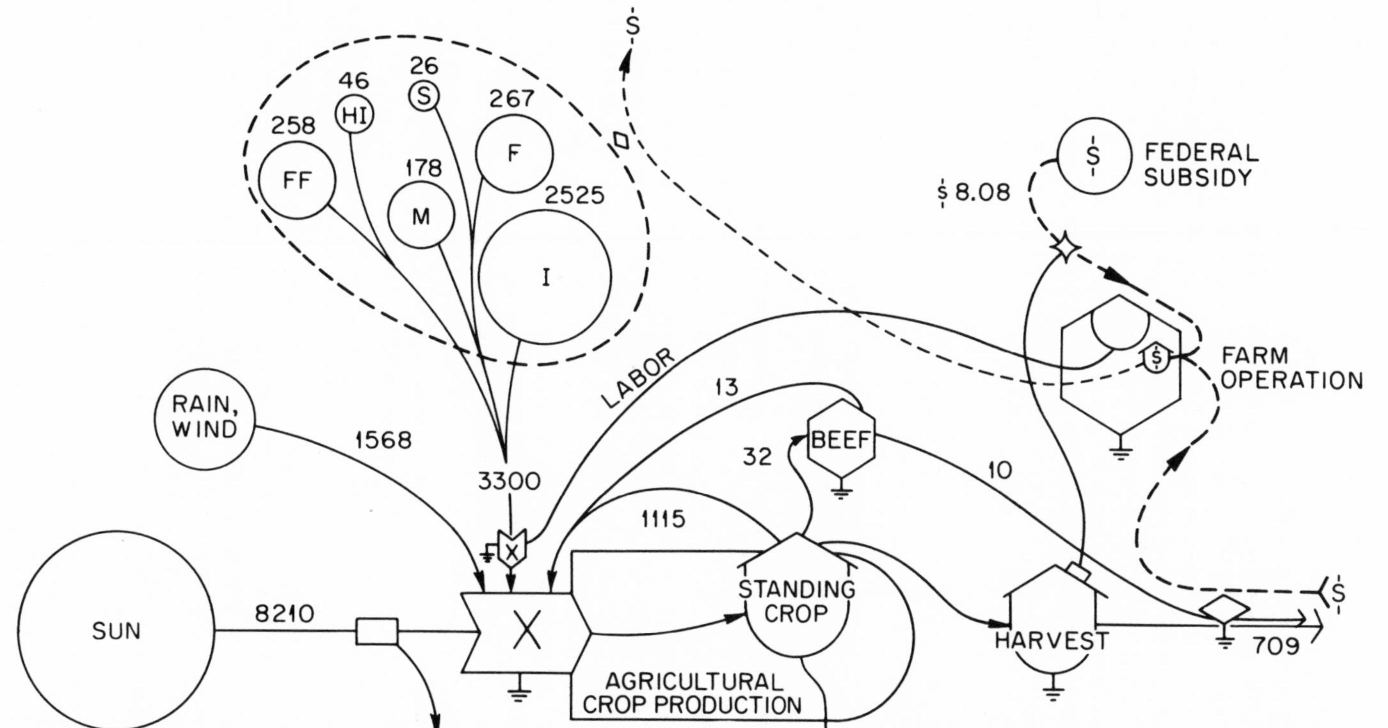

Figure 36.7. A Macroscale Minimodel of the Agroecosystems in Texas County, Oklahoma. All values are in 10^3 kilocalories of fuel equivalents. FF = fossil fuel; HI = herbicides and insecticides; S = seed; M = machinery; F = fertilizer; I = irrigation. Federal subsidy is in 1974 dollars per hectare. (After Klopatek 1977)

Concluding Comment As pointed out by Cooper and Vlasin (1974) the determining decisions on land use and development are usually made at the local level based on economic, political, and social considerations, not environmental ones. Energy flow analysis methodology affords a technique to span these various interests because it is based on a quantifiable theory of value that is applicable to both human-dominated and natural systems. Furthermore, the technique has the ability for integrating ecologic and economic analysis, allowing for consideration of costs and benefits across a broad array of parameters. Finally, the methodology can be used to simplify complex systems to produce models that accurately describe the important aspects of structure and function of humans and nature.

OPTIMIZATION IN LAND-USE ALLOCATION AND THE DISTRIBUTION OF MAJOR TECHNOLOGICAL FACILITIES

As discussed earlier, one of the major barriers to integrated land-use planning is the host of criteria that must be considered. One of the fundamental concepts that has evolved to simplify this complexity is the scaling down or decomposition of the landscape or region into smaller land units or cells. Amir (1976) presents the basic process of landscape decomposition and the subsequent rating of the individual land units based on their land-use potential. After the region has been subdivided into appropriate cells amenable to analysis, the optimization problem of land allocation and distribution of technological facilities can be clearly addressed. In general, it is desirable to determine the allocation of landscape elements and locations of major facilities for a given region that minimize a set of planning criteria, subject to constraints. It should be pointed out that the siting of technological facilities (e.g., industrial complexes, energy technology facilities) is one of the key land-use issues facing the United States today (U.S. EPA 1974).

Traditionally, planning criteria have been, and for the most part still are, economic-cost oriented. Thus, to a great extent, transitions between land-use categories have been driven toward a minimum dollar cost configuration. Cost-benefit analysis is also frequently employed to assist in environmental or land-use decision-making (Schramm 1973), although it should be emphasized that it is often extremely difficult to place dollar values on ecological variables. With an increasing emphasis on environmental implications of landscape allocation, planners have incorporated the use of econometric measures and analysis techniques. Isard (1972) has described in detail one such technique, that of input-output analysis, to describe economic-ecological linkages.

Although efforts have been made toward development of integrated systems analysis procedures synthesizing economic and environmental principles (e.g., Koenig 1972), approaches that have been totally acceptable to planners have not emerged. In the previous section, the applicability of energy flow analysis to these problems was discussed. However, no matter how comprehensive or how long-term a land-use plan is, it is difficult, if not impossible at times, to satisfy the diverse prerequisites of the ecologist, economist, developer, farmer, public official, and private citizen. In other words, the worth of a tract of land can be expected to be valued as diversely as the groups of individuals evaluating it.

The range of criteria that must be treated in land-use decisions is discussed by Welch (1976), who strongly advocates the necessity of a multi-dimensional approach in the assessment of these decisions. These same arguments provide a basis for the development of optimization approaches to land-use planning that incorporate multiple objective functions. An approach to land allocation decisions emphasizing quality-of-life has been proposed by Swartzman and Van Dyne (1975). The relative importance of a set of quality-of-life indicators, along with value standardization curves, is used as a means of expressing the indicators on an equivalent scale.

In what follows, a multiple objective optimization concept is invoked to form a framework for land allocation and the distribution of major facilities over the landscape of a region.

Let the region of interest be divided into a set of cells specified by the index

$$j = 1, 2, \ldots, p, \tag{1}$$

where p is the total number of cells required to span the area of the region. Land use in each cell is characterized by the assignment of a descriptor chosen from the set

$$U = \{U_1, U_2, \ldots, U_q\}, \tag{2}$$

where the descriptor U_i takes on the value 1 when category i is assigned; all other descriptors U_k, $k \neq i$, are set to zero. These descriptors provide a broad categorical characterization of land use, such as natural forest, managed forest, urban area, or agricultural land.

To further delineate the land-use mix and intensity for the broad category specified by U_i, a set of variables

$$Y_i = \{Y_{i1}, Y_{i2}, \ldots, Y_{ir_i}\}, i = 1, 2, \ldots, q \tag{3}$$

is associated with each descriptor. It should be noted that the number of variables, r_i, for each set Y_i is allowed to vary. For example, if the managed forest category is assigned by choice of descriptor, the variables Y_i might measure quantities such as timber yield, supporting population, or natural forest mix. The descriptors U and variables Y_i, when assigned for each cell, describe the land allocation pattern of the region. The land-use allocation for the region is constrained by the following equations:

$$g(U, Y_i) \leqslant 0,\ i = 1, 2, \ldots, q, \tag{4}$$

$$Y_{ik} \geqslant 0,\ i = 1, 2, \ldots, q,\ k = 1, 2, \ldots, r_i, \text{ and} \tag{5}$$

$$\sum_{l=1}^{q} U_l = 1 \tag{6}$$

for all cells $j = 1, 2, \ldots, p$. The equality constraint (6) requires that one and only one land-use category be assigned to each cell. The inequaltiy constraints (4) define relationships within cells and across the region that must be met by the allocation. An example is the allotment of sufficient land to agriculture to support the population of each cell or of the region.

The land-use allocation problem as presented here is to choose the descriptors U and the variables Y_i for each cell $j = 1, 2, \ldots, p$ such that all constraints (4), (5), and (6) are satisfied, and a set of planning criteria or objective functions (e.g., required energy subsidy or perturbation to successional dynamics) are in some sense minimized. The set of objective functions is given by

$$\{f_1\,(U, Y_i), f_2\,(U, Y_i), \ldots, f_n\,(U, Y_i)\}.$$

The simulation models described for natural and managed systems provide a mechanism for evaluation of objective functions. In other words, the simulation models provide the link between the land-use allocation described by U and the Y_i and planning criteria or objectives. The land-use allocation becomes a multiple objective optimization problem with continuous and integer variables. The nature of integer programming problems is described in detail by Garfinkel and Nemhauser (1972). Computer codes for solution of this type of problem are given by Gillett (1976).

In addition to the allocation aspect of land-use planning, the location of major facilities on a regional scale is of importance. Optimization techniques (e.g., Roberts 1975) have been used frequently to choose locations for facilities that minimize the distance to resources or product demand. The location of facilities to minimize the distance a user must travel to the facility, called the maximal covering location problem, has been considered by Church and ReVelle (1974). A fundamental concept in land-use planning relative to the distribution of facilities is the minimization of environmental impact (Nijkamp and Paelinck 1974), and the necessity of a multiple objective approach similar to that motivated for the land allocation problem has been stressed by Panagiotakopoulos (1975). The siting of energy facilities subject to the constraints of cooling-water temperature has been considered in a mixed-integer programming framework by Marks and Borenstein (1970). Siting of facilities incorporating air quality considerations in an urban area has been analyzed by Werczberger (1973), and O'Neill (1975) has suggested a coupling of the air dispersion characteristics with crop models. The following discussion will demonstrate the incorporation of facility siting in the land allocation framework developed above.

Let a subset of the cells spanning the region (1)

$$S = \{s_1, s_2, \ldots, s_v\} \tag{8}$$

be candidate sites for the location of major facilities. The s_l's chosen as facility locations take on the value 1; all others are zero. Associated with each candidate site is a variable specifying the activity level or size of facility assigned to the site. These activity variables are given by the vector

$$X = \{x_1, x_2, \ldots, x_v\}. \tag{9}$$

The use of a particular candidate site and the level of activity at the site is constrained by its suitability. These suitability constraints are written as

$$W(S, X) \leq 0. \tag{10}$$

The facility location problem is to choose the sites S and activity levels X such that (10) is satisfied and a set of objective functions (e.g., exposure to air pollutants)

$$\{Z_1(S, X), Z_2(S, X), \ldots, Z_m(S, X)\} \tag{11}$$

is in some sense minimized. Similar to the land allocation problem, equations (8) through (11) constitute a mixed-integer program.

To illustrate the formulation of objective functions for facility siting, an air quality exposure index for combustion power plant location is briefly described. A wind trajectory model developed by the National Oceanic and Atmospheric Administration (Heffter et al. 1975) is used for the analysis of long-range pollutant transport. This trajectory model makes use of wind data from monitoring stations in the region to develop the average trajectories of winds in the troposphere. Several mechanisms for deposition of pollutants are incorporated in the model. The trajectory model is used to estimate the ground level concentration of air dispersed pollutants in each cell $j = 1,2, \ldots, p$ due to a unit source at each candidate site S. These calculations provide a matrix of transfer coefficients

$$D = [d_{ij}], \tag{12}$$

where $j = 1, 2, \ldots, p$ and $i = 1, 2, \ldots, v$. This matrix serves as a parameterization of the air dispersion characteristics of the region. Ground level concentrations due to general sources (i.e., non-unit sources) are calculated by multiplying the transfer coefficients (12) by source models for each candidate site of the form

$$E_i = \alpha_i\, x_i,\ i = 1, 2, \ldots, v, \tag{13}$$

where E_i is the source strength at site *i and* α_i is the source model coefficient for site *i*. Using the source strength model (13) and the matrix of transfer coefficients (12), the average ground level concentration of pollutants in each cell due to sources at all candidate sites is given by:

$$R_j = \sum_{i=1}^{v} d_{ij} E_i. \tag{14}$$

The exposure of critical categories of land use to air dispersed pollutants is then

$$Z_1\,(S,X) = \sum_{j=1}^{p} \sum_{i=1}^{v} d_{ij} \alpha_i s_i x_i (U_c Y_{cl})_j, \tag{15}$$

where U_c is the land allocation descriptor for the critical land-use category being considered and Y_{cl} is a measure of intensity (e.g., timber yield from a managed forest). This objective function for exposure of critical categories of land use to air dispersed pollutants is typical of the set (11). Pantell (1976) provides further insight into formulation of environmental objective functions.

The two optimization models described here combine to form an optimization framework for land allocation and distribution of major facilities on a regional scale. The complete land-use optimization model is

$$\begin{aligned} \underset{U,Y_i,S,X}{\text{minimize}}\quad & \{f_1(U, Y_i), f_2(U, Y_i), \ldots, f_n(U, Y_i), \\ & Z_1(S, X), Z_2\,(S, X), \ldots, Z_m(S, X)\} \\ & g\,(U, Y_i) \leqslant 0,\ i = 1, 2, \ldots, q, \\ & Y_{ik} \geqslant 0,\ i = 1, 2, \ldots, q,\ k = 1, 2, \ldots, r_i, \\ & \sum_{l=1}^{q} U_l = 1, \\ & W\,(S, X) \leqslant 0, \\ & s_j = 1, 0,\ j = 1, 2, \ldots, v, \text{ and} \\ & x_j \geqslant 0,\ j = 1, 2, \ldots, v. \end{aligned} \tag{16}$$

This model is in the form of a mixed-integer program with multiple objective functions.

Perhaps the most important characteristic of the land-use optimization model (16) is the multiple objective function approach. However, when developed in the fashion presented here, additional insight is possible. A review of multiple objective programming techniques has been given by Cohon and Marks (1975). A particular technique, the surrogate worth trade-off method (Haimes and Hall 1974); its implications for the model (16) and land-use planning will be briefly reviewed.

The most significant characteristic of the multiple objective optimization model for land use (16) is that there is no optimal solution in the sense that there does not exist a set of values for the decision variables (i.e., land-use descriptors) which simultaneously minimize all objective functions while satisfying the constraint set. This condition leads to the necessity of a trade-off or compromise between objectives. This is the central issue of land-use decisions.

The nonexistence of an optimal solution leads to the definition of a non-inferior solution (Reid and Vemuri 1971), that is, one in which no improvement can be obtained with respect to any of the objectives without causing a simultaneous degradation in at least one of the other objectives. Any solution that does not satisfy this condition is referred to as inferior. Clearly, only non-inferior solutions are of interest, so that the problem becomes one of selecting preferred solutions from the set of non-inferior ones.

The selection of preferred solutions is based on indifference on the part of the decision-maker. The indifference band is defined to be the subset of the non-inferior set where the improvement of one objective function is equivalent in the mind of the decision-maker to the necessary degradation of the others (Haimes et al. 1975). Since no other solution can be demonstrated to be superior, solutions belonging to the indifference band will be considered preferred solutions. The surrogate worth trade-off method is based on the determination of a surrogate worth function, which has a value of zero when the decision-maker is indifferent concerning the trade-off between objectives.

Consider a trade-off rate function

$$T_{ij} = \left. \frac{\Delta f_i}{\Delta f_j} \right|_{*}, \tag{17}$$

where Δ denotes a differential change, and f_i and f_j are any two conflicting objective functions drawn from (16). The * specifies evaluation of (17) at some sort of optimal condition. The trade-off rate function given by (17) expresses the marginal worth of the ith objective function due to a unit change in the jth objective function. Haimes et al. (1975) have used the Kuhn and Tucker (1950) conditions for optimality of a general nonlinear programming problem to derive an expression for the trade-off rate function and develop numerical approaches to its evaluation.

The trade-off rate functions are used as a basis for forming a surrogate worth function Ω_{ij} between each pair of objective functions. The decision-maker is provided the value of the trade-off rate function and corresponding values of objective functions and expresses feelings about the improvement of objective i and the corresponding degradation of objective j in the following manner:

$$\Omega_{ij}\begin{cases} > 0 \text{ when } T_{ij} \text{ marginal units of objective } i \text{ are preferred over one marginal unit of objective } j; \\ = 0 \text{ when } T_{ij} \text{ marginal units of objective } i \text{ are equivalent to one marginal unit of objective } j; \\ < 0 \text{ when } T_{ij} \text{ marginal units of objective } i \text{ are not preferred over one marginal unit of objective } j. \end{cases}$$

The Ω_{ij} are monotonic functions of the trade-off rate functions. The values of decision variables corresponding to $\Omega_{ij} = 0$ are considered a preferred solution to the multiple objective optimization problem.

The surrogate worth trade-off method and similar approaches provide a method of reconciling the multiple objective dilemma through interaction with decision-makers. The trade-off rate functions provided by the analyst give the decision-maker sufficient information to express relative worths of objectives. Approaches such as this will provide a useful tool for future land-use decisions.

PROSPECTUS

Systems ecology has provided and should continue to provide valuable methodologies for land-use planning decisions. These methodological inputs are of two general types: Models and modelling philosophies of uniquely ecological perspective, and methods developed in physical and engineering sciences, used in ecology, and later translated a second time into a land-use context. Our first two examples (forest succession modelling and energy-flow analysis) correspond with the first type of input and the final discussion (optimization) is an example of the latter. Now we need to ask what the future role of the systems ecologists is either as originators or as translators of systems procedures for land use.

The past five years have, through a number of circumstances, generated a strong interest in land-use-related problems among systems ecologists. The International Biological Program in the United States, as well as elsewhere, provided research and funding for several young systems ecologists who are just now in the productive part of their careers. A decidedly applied shift in direction was evident in the latter part of the US/IBP program as ecologists looked for practical uses of their models. Much of this application was in land-use problems, and the work is just beginning to be published. At the same time, a number of U.S. federal agencies (notably Energy Research and Development Administration, Forest Service, Department of Interior, and

Environmental Protection Agency) have become interested in regional problems and have initiated research in this area. This work is in an embryonic state at present, but it shows promise of acceleration in the infusion of systems ecology into land-use considerations.

In terms of the translator role of systems ecology, we can also expect increased diffusion of methodologies from other sciences through systems ecology into land-use applications. First, there has been a large body of new numerical methodologies developed with the space program (NASA) and the advent of large computers at most research installations. Second, ecology has been colonized by scientists from methodologically rich disciplines. Third, the social importance of regional ecological problems is beginning to attract transdisciplinary scientists, many of whom are well versed in advanced analytical techniques.

If land-use planners continue to be a receptive in the near future as they have in the recent past, we can expect the next few years to be extremely exciting in regional ecology. If the potential for systems ecologist to contribute to land-use and regional plans is realized, we can expect both an exciting area of research to develop and a better allocation of uses of the landscpae to result.

REFERENCES CITED

Ahlstrom, T., S. Brown and H. T. Odum 1975. Overall model of south Florida and external causes. In *Carrying capacity for man and nature in south Florida,* eds. H. T. Odum and M. Brown, pp. 102–121. Gainesville: Center for Wetlands, University of Florida.

Amir, S. 1976. Land resources assessment framework: a tool for environmental policy-making. *J. Environ. Manage.* 4:1–13.

Antonini, G. A., K. C. Ewel and J. J. Ewel 1974. Ecological modelling of a tropical watershed: a guide to regional planning, pp. 51–74. In *Spatial Aspects of Development,* ed. B. Hoyle, pp. 51–74. London: John Wiley and Sons.

Arney, J. 1972. Computer simulation of Douglas fir tree and stand growth. Doctoral dissertation, Oregon State University, Corvallis.

Barret, G. W., G. M. Van Dyne, and E. P. Odum. 1976. Stress ecology. *BioScience* 26:192–197.

Bella, I. E. 1970. Simulation of growth, yield and management of aspen. Doctoral dissertation, University of British Columbia, Vancouver.

Bosch, C. A. 1971. Redwoods: a population model. *Science* 172:345–349.

Botkin, D. B., J. F. Janak and J. R. Wallis. 1972. Some ecological consequences of a computer model of forest growth. *J. Ecol.* 60:849–872.

Browder, J., C. Littlejohn and D. Young 1976. *South Florida: seeking a balance of man and nature.* Division of State Planning, Florida Department of Administration, Tallahassee, and Center for Wetlands, University of Florida, Gainesville.

Cassell, R. F., and J. W. Moser, Jr. 1974. *A programmed Markov model for predicting diameter distribution and species composition in uneven-aged forests.* Agricultural Experiment Station Research Bulletin No. 915. Lafayette, In: Purdue University.

Church, R. and C. ReVelle 1974. The maximal covering location problem *Pap. Regional Sci. Assoc.* 32:101–118.

Clutter, J. L. 1963. Compatible growth and yield models for loblolly pine. *For. Sci.* 9:354–371.

Cohon, J. L. and D. H. Marks 1975. A review and evaluation of multi-objective programming techniques. *Water Resour. Res.* 11:208–220.

Cooper, W. E. and R. D. Vlasen 1974. Ecological concepts and applications to planning. In *Environment: a new focus for land-use planning,* ed. D. M. McAllister, pp. 183–206. Washington, D.C.: RANN, National Science Foundation.

Dress, P. E. 1970. A system for the stochastic simulation of even-aged forest stands of pure species composition. Doctoral dissertation, Purdue University, Lafayette, Indiana.

Ek, A. R. and R. A. Monserud. 1974. *FOREST: a computer model for simulating the growth and reproduction of mixed species forest stands.* Research Report. Madison: University of Wisconsin.

Forrester, J. W. 1971. *World dynamics.* Cambridge, Mass.: Wright-Allen.

Garfinkel, R. S. and G. L. Nemhauser. 1972. *Integer programming.* New York: John Wiley and Sons, Inc.

Garvey, G. 1972. *Energy, ecology and economy.* New York: W. W. Norton and Co., Inc.

Georgescu-Rogen, N. 1971. *The entrophy law and the economic process.* Cambridge, Mass: Harvard University Press.

______. 1977. The steady state and ecological salvation: a thermodynamic analysis. *BioScience* 27:266–270.

Gillett, B. E. 1976. *Introduction to operations research.* New York: McGraw-Hill Book Company.

Gilliland, M. W. and P. G. Risser 1977. The use of systems diagrams for environmental impact assessment: procedures and application. *Ecol. Model.* 3:183-209.

Goulding, C. J. 1972. Simulation techniques for a stochastic model of the growth of Douglas fir. Ph.D. thesis, University of British Columbia, Vancouver.

Haimes, Y. Y. and W. A. Hall 1974. Multiobjectives in water resource systems analysis: the surrogate worth trade-off method. *Water Resour. Res.* 10:615–624.

Haimes, Y. Y., W. A. Hall and N. J. Freedman. 1975. *Multiobjective optimization in water resources systems.* New York: Elsevier Scientific Publishing Co.

Hartshorn, G. S. 1975. A matrix model of tree population dynamics. In *Tropical ecological systems,* eds. F. B. Golley and E. Medina. New York: Springer-Verlag.

Hatch, C. R. 1971. *Simulation of an even-aged red pine stand in northern Minnesota.* Minneapolis: University of Minnesota.

Heffter, J. L., A.D. Taylor and G. J. Ferber. 1975. *A regional-continental scale transport, diffusion, and deposition model.* NOAA Technical Memorandum ERL ARL-50. Silver Springs, Md.: National Oceanic and Atmospheric Administration, Air Resources Laboratories.

Herendeen, R. L. and C. W. Bullard, III 1974. *Energy cost of commerce goods, 1963 and 1967.* CAC Document No. 140, Center for Advanced Computation. Urbana-Champaign: University of Illinois.

Hills, G. A. 1961. *The ecological basis for land-use planning.* Research Paper 46. Tech. Series. Toronto: Ontario Dept. Lands and Forests.

Horn, Henry S. 1975. Forest succession. *Sci. Am.* 232:90–98.

Huettner, D. A. 1976. Net energy analysis: an economic assessment. *Science* 192:101–104.

Isard, W. 1972. *Ecologic-economic analysis for regional development.* New York: The Free Press.

Jamison, P. L. and S. M. Friedman, eds. 1974. *Energy flow in human communities. Proceedings of a Workshop.* University Park: Pennsylvania State University.

Johnson, W. C. and D. M. Sharpe 1976. An analysis of forest dynamics in the northern Georgia Piedmont. *For. Sci.* 22:307–322.

Koenig, H. E. and R. L. Tummala. 1972. Principles of ecosystem design and management. *IEEE Transactions on Systems, Man, and Cybernetics.* SMC-2:449–459.

Klopatek, J. M. 1977. The energetics of land use in three Oklahoma counties. Ph.D. thesis, University of Oklahoma, Norman.

Kuhn, H. W. and A. W. Tucker. 1950. Nonlinear programming. In *Proceedings of the Second Berkeley Symposium on Mathematical Statistics and Probability.* Berkeley: University of California Press.

Lavine, M. J. and A. H. Meyburg. 1976. *Toward environmental benefit/cost analysis: measurement methodology.* Washington, D.C.: National Cooperative Highway Research Program, National Research Council.

Leak, W. B. 1970. Successional change in northern hardwoods predicted by birth and death simulation. *Ecology* 51:794–801.

Lee, Y. 1967. Stand models for lodgepole pine and limits to their application. Ph.D. thesis, University of British Columbia, Vancouver.

Lotka, A. J. 1924. Contribution to energetics of evolution. *Proc. Natl. Acad. Sci.* 8:147–188.

Marks, D. H. and R. A. Borenstein. 1970. *An optimal siting model for thermal plants with temperature constraints.* Research Project RP-49, Report 6. Baltimore, Md.: Johns Hopkins University.

McAllister, D. M., ed. 1974. *Environment: a new focus for land-use planning.* Washington, D.C.: RANN, National Science Foundation.

Mielke, D.C., H. H. Shugart, and D. C. West. 1977. *User's manual for FORAR, A stand model for composition and growth of upland forests of southern Arkansas.* Oak Ridge, Tn.: ORNL/TM-5767 Oak Ridge National Laboratory.

Mitchell, K. J. 1967. Simulation of the growth of uneven-aged stands of white spruce. Ph.D. thesis, Yale University, New Haven.

______. 1971. *Description and growth simulation of Douglas fir stands.* Internal Report BC-25, Pacific Forest Research. Victoria, B.C.: Canadian Forest Service.

Newnham, R. M. 1964. The development of a stand model for Douglas fir. Ph.D. thesis, University of British Columbia, Vancouver.

Nijkamp, P. and J. H. P. Paelinck. 1974. An interregional model of environmental choice. *Pap. Reg. Sci. Assoc.* 33:51–71.

Odum, E. P. 1970. Optimum population and environment: a Georgian microcosm. *Curr. Hist.* 58:355–359.

——— and H. T. Odum. 1972. Natural areas as necessary components of man's total environment. In *37th North American Wildlife Resources Conference,* pp. 178–189. Washington, D.C.: Wildlife Management Institute.

Odum, H. T. 1971. *Environment, power and society.* New York: Wiley-Interscience.

———. 1972. An energy circuit language for ecological and social systems: its physical basis. In *Systems analysis and simulation in ecology,* ed. B. C. Patten, pp. 139–211. New York: Academic Press.

———. 1975. Computing energy laws and corollaries of the maximum power principle with visual mathematics. In *Ecosystem analysis and prediction,* pp. 239–263. Philadelphia: Society for Industrial Applied Mathematics.

——— and R. C. Pinkerton 1955. Time's speed regulator: the optimum efficiency for maximum power output in physical and biological systems. *Am. Sci.* 43:331–343.

———, and M. T. Brown, eds. 1975. *Carrying capacity for man and nature in south Florida.* Gainesville: Center for Wetlands, University of Florida.

———, and E. C. Odum 1976. *Energy basis for man and nature.* New York: McGraw-Hill.

Olson, J. S. and G. Cristofolini. 1966. *Model simulation of Oak Ridge vegetation succession.* ORNL-4007. Oak Ridge, Tn.: Oak Ridge National Laboratory.

O'Neill, R. V. 1975. Modeling in the Eastern Deciduous Forest Biome. In *Systems analysis and simulation in ecology,* Vol. III, ed. B. C. Patten, pp. 49–72. New York: Academic Press.

Panagiotakopoulos, D. 1975. A multi-objective framework for environmental management using goal programming. *J. Environ. Sys.* 5:133–147.

Pantell, R. H. 1976. *Techniques of environmental systems analysis.* New York: John Wiley and Sons.

Peden, L. M., J. S. Williams and W. E. Frayer 1973. A Markov model for stand projection. *For. Sci.* 19:303–314.

Reid, R. W. and V. Vemuri 1971. On the noninferior index approach to large-scale multi-criteria systems. *J. Franklin Inst.* 291:241–254.

Roberts, F. S., ed. 1975. *Energy: mathematics and models. Proceedings of a SIMS Conference on Energy.* Philadelphia: Society of Industrial and Applied Mathematics.

Schramm, G. 1973. Accounting for non-economic goals in benefit-cost analysis. *J. Environ. Manage.* 1:129–150.

Shatz, J. 1974. Cosmic economics. In *Energy: today's choices, tomorrow's opportunities,* ed. A. B. Schmalz, pp. 20–26. Washington, D.C.: World Future Society.

Shugart, H. H., T. R. Crow and J. M. Hett 1973. Forest succession models: a rationale and methodology for modeling forest succession over large regions. *For. Sci.* 19:203–212.

Shugart, H. H. and D. C. West 1977. Development of an Appalachian deciduous forest succession model and its application to assessment of the impact of the chestnut blight. *J. Environ. Manage.* 5:161–179.

Swartzman, G. L. and G. M. Van Dyne 1975. Land allocation decisions: a mathematical programming framework focusing on quality of life. *J. Environ. Manage.* 3:105–132.

T.I.E. (The Institute of Ecology). 1972. *Man and the living environment.* Madison: University of Wisconsin Press.

U.S. Environmental Protection Agency (U.S.EPA). 1974. Key land-use issues facing EPA. Document No. PB-235 345/6. Boston: Harbridge House, Inc.

Van Dyne, G. M. and G. S. Innis 1972. Macrolevel ecosystem models in relation to man: a preliminary analysis of concepts and approaches. U.S. IBP Grassland Biome Tech. Report No. 162. Ft. Collins: Colorado State University.

Van Dyne, G. M., and Z. Abramsky. 1974. Agricultural systems models and modelling: an overview. In *Study of agricultural systems,* ed. G. E. Dalton, London: Applied Science Publications.

Waggoner, P. E. and G. R. Stephens. 1970. Transition probabilities for a forest. *Nature* 225:1160–1161.

Wesley, J. P. 1974. *Ecophysics. The application of physics to ecology.* Springfield, Ill.: Charles C. Thomas, Publ.

Welch, H. W. 1976. Assessing environmental impacts of multiple use land management. *J. Environ. Manage.* 4:197–209.

Werczberger, E. 1973. A mixed-integer programming model for the integration of air-quality policy into land-use planning. *Pap. Reg. Sci. Assoc.* 31:141–154.

Woodwell, G. M. 1974. Success, succession, and Adam Smith. *BioScience* 24:81–87.

Zuchetto, J. J. 1975. Energy-economic theory and mathematical models for combining the systems of man and nature, case study: the urban region of Miami, Florida. *Ecol. Model.* 1:241–268.

37

The UNESCO Program on Man and the Biosphere (MAB)

Vernon C. Gilbert and
E. Jennifer Christy

BACKGROUND, DEVELOPMENT, AND ORGANIZATION OF THE PROGRAM

The increasing awareness, particularly in the last decade, that the world is faced with extremely serious environmental problems has caused nations to begin to work together to develop solutions to global problems. A major step in this direction was taken in 1968 when the UNESCO Conference on Use and Conservation of the Biosphere (the "Biosphere Conference") convened in Paris. The world drift toward environmental deterioration would become irreversible, the conference concluded, unless appropriate actions were taken in due time (UNESCO Paris 1970). More than a decade later, there is serious doubt that the necessary actions are underway. At the same time, some progress has been made in developing international efforts to obtain more adequate knowledge of the nature and consequences of human impact on the world's ecosystem. The realization by decision-makers that such efforts are necessary to create a sound basis for intelligent management of natural resources has had considerable influence on the growth of ecology, and major national and international programs are increasingly developing around this discipline.

An example is the UNESCO Man and the Biosphere (MAB) program, which was conceived at the Biosphere Conference in 1968 and is now coordinated by a secretariat in the Division of Ecological Sciences in UNESCO, Paris. MAB is a promising international research effort seeking solutions to environmental problems arising from man's interaction with the major ecosystems of the world.

Representatives of sixty-three nations and eight international organizations recognized the need for a program in which countries could work toward maintenance and improvement of the human environment. U.S. ecologist Stanley Cain (1970) expressed this global imperative in these words:

> We have come to a period of human history when there is a great need for, and some recognition of, what has been described by various terms notably "landscape planning" or "regional planning." What is implied is more than land planning, land-use planning, resource-use planning, city planning, park planning, etc., as usually undertaken. It is a multi-disciplinary, multi-agency, public-private joint planning effort that can stem only from a recognition of the existence and nature of natural and human ecosystems. Essentially it is "ecological planning."
>
> The felt need, such as it is (and it is presently only primordial), has resulted from the failure of traditional single-purpose approaches to human needs and the inability to wrest from nature the resources to meet them. The prevailing single-purpose planning by both public and private enterprises has changed the human condition. It has given some people and some nations affluence that all people would like to enjoy. It has produced a new hope for the poor, the disadvantaged, the downtrodden, but it has proven inadequate to meet the needs of humanity, in rich as well as poor countries, in cities as well as the countryside. What has been called "the revolution of rising expectations" is not being met in populous poor countries while in affluent nations the great cost of restoring and maintaining environments, fit for human needs is being met.

Based on information presented to the Biosphere Conference on various human impacts on the biosphere and based on the depletion of natural resources, the representatives agreed on a series of recommendations for future action. A major item called for preparation of a proposal for an international, interdisciplinary program focusing on the rational utilization and conservation of resources within the biosphere, a long-term effort including the participation of the appropriate private organizations. The plan would take into consideration the valuable progress made under the International Biological Program (IBP) and the the International Union for the Conservation of Nature and Natural Resources (IUCN) and would utilize the established networks of scientists who were active in these programs.

Following the Biosphere Conference, work began at UNESCO with consultation groups in cooperation with United Nations specialized agencies and appropriate non-government organizations, such as the IUCN and the International Council on Scientific Unions (ICSU), on drafting the long-term research and conservation effort that became known as the MAB Program.

During initial efforts to get MAB underway and later during implementation of the program, many individuals from a number of countries made major contributions. Among these, a few individuals in UNESCO, Michel Batisse

(France), Francesco di Castri (Italy), and Malcolm Hadley (U.K.) deserve special credit for their pioneering efforts.

MAB-WHAT IT IS AND HOW IT WORKS

The recommendation of the Biosphere Conference that a program be set up to deal with global environmental problems presented an immense task, yet there existed considerable experience and knowledge to build upon. A great deal of progress has been made in the development of environmental sciences, especially in the integrative, synthesizing science of ecology. Insights had been gained on the functioning of whole environmental systems, in large part resulting from research of the International Biological Program. Scientists had demonstrated the capability: (1) to characterize and understand the basic governing processes of ecosystems; (2) to develop models capable of simulating the behavior of whole ecosystems; and (3) to derive generalities about the structure and dynamics of ecosystems, all of which permitted extrapolation of knowledge to other environments (Reichle 1973). These advances and the tremendous amount of data available formed a significant foundation for MAB.

The draft outline for a MAB program was agreed on by the delegates when presented to the UNESCO General Conference in 1970. Subsequently, a MAB International Coordinating Council was established, consisting of scientific representatives from twenty-five nations (in 1976 the number was increased to thirty) plus observers from United Nations specialized agencies and appropriate non-government organizations. At its first session in 1971 the council, provided with valuable background material by the UNESCO secretariat, concentrated on developing the general scope and objectives of MAB and a framework of international scientific project areas, within which nations could begin to participate (UNESCO Paris 1971).

The general objective of MAB, as formulated by the council was:

To develop the basis within the natural and social sciences for the rational use and conservation of the resources of the biosphere and for the improvement of the global relationship between man and the environment; to predict the consequences of today's actions on tomorrow's world and thereby to increase man's ability to manage efficiently the natural resources of the biosphere.

The specific objectives agreed on were:

1) To identify and assess the changes in the biosphere resulting from man's activities and the effects of these changes on man.

2) To study and compare the structure, functioning and dynamics of natural, modified, and managed ecosystems.

3) To study and compare the dynamic interrelationships between "natural" eco-

systems and socio-economic processes, and especially the impact of changes in human populations, settlement patterns, and technology on the future viability of these systems.

4) To develop ways and means to measure quantitative and qualitative changes in the environment in order to establish scientific criteria to serve as a basis for rational management of nature, and for establishment of standards of environmental quality.

5) To help bring about greater global coherence of environmental research, by:

a) establishing comparable, compatible, and, where appropriate, standardized methods for the acquisition and processing of environmental data;

b) promoting the exchange and transfer of knowledge on environmental problems.

6) To promote the development and application of simulation and other techniques for prediction, as tools for environmental management.

7) To promote environmental education in its broadest sense, by:

a) developing background material, including books and teaching aids, for educational curricula at all levels;

b) promoting specialist training in appropriate disciplines;

c) stressing the interdisciplinary nature of environmental problems;

d) stimulating global awareness of environmental problems through public and other information media;

e) promoting the idea of man's personal fulfillment in partnership with nature, and his responsibility for nature.

Since MAB was intended to focus on specific management problems related to human interactions with particular natural systems, a framework of international projects was designed as follows:

1. Ecological effects of increasing human activities on tropical and subtropical forest ecosystems.
2. Ecological effects of different land uses and management practices on temperate and Mediterranean landscapes.
3. Impact of human activities and land use practices on grazing lands: savanna and grassland (from temperate to arid areas).
4. Impact of human activities on the dynamics of arid and semiarid zones' ecosystems, with particular attention to the effects of irrigation.
5. Ecological effects of human activities on the value and resources of lakes, marshes, rivers, deltas, estuaries, and coastal zones.
6. Impact of human activities on mountain and tundra ecosystems.
7. Ecology and rational use of island ecosystems.
8. Conservation of natural areas and of the genetic material they contain.
9. Ecological assessment of pest management and fertilizer use on terrestrial and aquatic ecosystems.
10. Effects on man and his environment of major engineering works.
11. Ecological aspects of urban systems with particular emphasis on energy utilization.
12. Interactions between environmental transformations and the adaptive, demographic, and genetic structure of human populations.
13. Perception of environmental quality.

In 1974 a 14th project was added entitled "Research on environmental pollution and its effects on the Biosphere" (UNESCO Paris 1975). The council intended that this list of projects be flexible both in content and approach, and that MAB national committees in each country would tailor the projects to their own needs. It was planned that in each country a MAB national committee would use this framework of projects to define and organize activities concerning particular national problems.

In the years following the council's definition of international MAB projects, expert panels and working groups of scientists and decision-makers have elaborated the content of each project area and provided the basis for implementation. Also, an international series of regional meetings was organized by UNESCO's MAB secretariat in cooperation with other agencies and national MAB committees. These meetings provided opportunities for dialogues and planning; a number of concrete research plans and activities have resulted.

The organization of MAB is shown in Table 37.1.

Table 37.1. Organization of the MAB Program

International Program	
UNESCO	**Cooperating Organizations**
International Co-ordinating Council (thirty nations)	**United Nations Environment Program (UNEP)** **Food and Agriculture Organization (FAO)** **World Health Organization (WHO)**
MAB Secretariat	**World Meterorological Organization (WMO)** **International Council of Scientific Unions (CSU)** **International Union for the Conservation of Nature and Natural Resources (IUCN)** **United Nations Development Program (UNDP)**

National Programs National MAB Committees (87 participating countries- 1979)	
Country	**Cooperating Organizations**
National Committee	**Government agencies** **Public and private organizations**
Project Committees	**Universities and colleges** **Individual scientists**
Secretariat	

PROBLEM AREAS IN MAB

There are obvious difficulties in activating an international program with such vast scope and ambitious objectives. Michel Batisse (1975), UNESCO, described some of these difficulties:

> The response to MAB at government level, particularly from the developing countries, was favorable from the start, yet it requires a very long time and much patient effort to get any project moving on a reasonably harmonious front at the international level. The reasons for this inertia are easy to understand. They relate to traditional suspicion in the older countries of anything "supranational," to the difficulties of fully conveying the concepts underlying a common objective in a multilingual and multicultural world and to the mere fact that not all countries are, to put it mildly, at the same stage of development and at the same level of capability. For those with no experience of the intricacies of international cooperation, this slow movement is thoroughly frustrating. For those aware of the problems, it is always a pleasant surprise when some progress is actually made.

Clearly, the commitment of funds and technical assistance by participating countries and international organizations has been insufficient to deal with these expensive and complex problems that include change of traditional (land use) methods and introduction of new technologies. Francesco di Castri, secretary of the International Coordinating Council, indicated in his report to the council in 1977 (UNESCO Paris 1978) that a main shortcoming of the MAB Program was in its organization of training activities for developing countries and in follow-up activities after training. This situation, considered with the increase in global environmental problems over time, makes the need for vigorous action all the more urgent.

MAJOR THRUSTS OF MAB

In 1978, the U.S. MAB assisted in a conference sponsored by the Department of State and U.S. Agency for International Development to develop a national plan to deal with deforestation problems. The major conclusion of a Strategy Conference on Tropical Deforestation (U.S. Department of State 1978) contains this warning:

> The world is being confronted by an extremely serious problem with immediate and long-range socio-economic and ecological consequences as the result of the accelerating loss of forest and vegetative cover in the humid and semi-arid lands within or near the tropical latitudes. Further, the community of nations must quickly launch an accelerated and coordinated attack on the problem if these greatly undervalued and probably irreplaceable resources are to be protected from virtual destruction by the early part of the next century.

Although there are activities underway in all fourteen project areas of MAB,

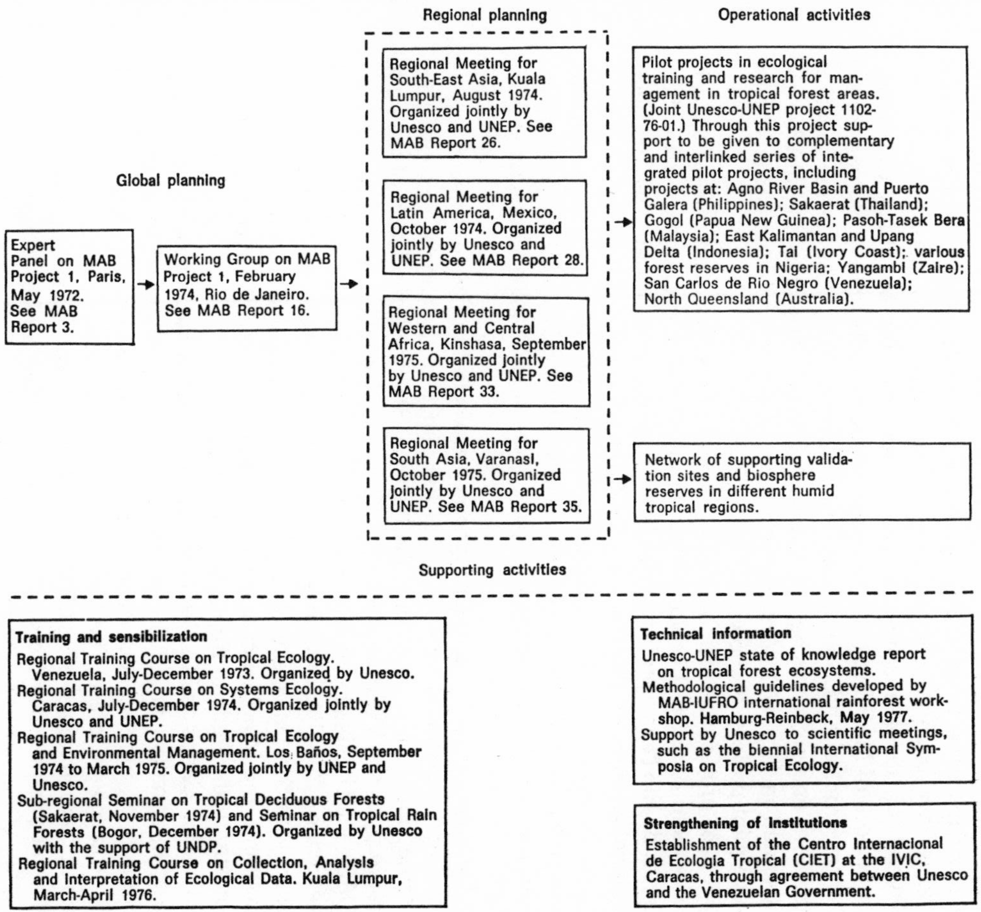

Global planning

Expert Panel on MAB Project 1, Paris, May 1972. See MAB Report 3.

→ Working Group on MAB Project 1, February 1974, Rio de Janeiro. See MAB Report 16.

Regional planning

Regional Meeting for South-East Asia, Kuala Lumpur, August 1974. Organized jointly by Unesco and UNEP. See MAB Report 26.

Regional Meeting for Latin America, Mexico, October 1974. Organized jointly by Unesco and UNEP. See MAB Report 28.

Regional Meeting for Western and Central Africa, Kinshasa, September 1975. Organized jointly by Unesco and UNEP. See MAB Report 33.

Regional Meeting for South Asia, Varanasi, October 1975. Organized jointly by Unesco and UNEP. See MAB Report 35.

Operational activities

Pilot projects in ecological training and research for management in tropical forest areas. (Joint Unesco-UNEP project 1102-76-01.) Through this project support to be given to complementary and interlinked series of integrated pilot projects, including projects at: Agno River Basin and Puerto Galera (Philippines); Sakaerat (Thailand); Gogol (Papua New Guinea); Pasoh-Tasek Bera (Malaysia); East Kalimantan and Upang Delta (Indonesia); Tai (Ivory Coast); various forest reserves in Nigeria; Yangambi (Zaire); San Carlos de Rio Negro (Venezuela); North Queensland (Australia).

Network of supporting validation sites and biosphere reserves in different humid tropical regions.

Supporting activities

Training and sensibilization

Regional Training Course on Tropical Ecology. Venezuela, July-December 1973. Organized by Unesco.
Regional Training Course on Systems Ecology. Caracas, July-December 1974. Organized jointly by Unesco and UNEP.
Regional Training Course on Tropical Ecology and Environmental Management. Los Baños, September 1974 to March 1975. Organized jointly by UNEP and Unesco.
Sub-regional Seminar on Tropical Deciduous Forests (Sakaerat, November 1974) and Seminar on Tropical Rain Forests (Bogor, December 1974). Organized by Unesco with the support of UNDP.
Regional Training Course on Collection, Analysis and Interpretation of Ecological Data. Kuala Lumpur, March-April 1976.

Technical information

Unesco-UNEP state of knowledge report on tropical forest ecosystems.
Methodological guidelines developed by MAB-IUFRO international rainforest workshop. Hamburg-Reinbeck, May 1977.
Support by Unesco to scientific meetings, such as the biennial International Symposia on Tropical Ecology.

Strengthening of institutions

Establishment of the Centro Internacional de Ecologia Tropical (CIET) at the IVIC, Caracas, through agreement between Unesco and the Venezuelan Government.

Figure 37.1 Planning Phases of MAB-1
Source: UNESCO, Paris 1977a.

two projects are chosen to illustrate the progress made since the program began.

MAB Project No. 1: Tropical Forests

The problems involved in the rational management of tropical forest ecosystems have been a priority concern of MAB since its inception, and efforts have been concentrated on the development of pilot field projects. Several of these research projects, launched by countries within the framework of MAB Project 1 (Ecological Effects of Increasing Human Activities on Tropical and Subtropical Forest Ecosystems), illustrate the types of situations and problems being examined. The planning phases of MAB-1 are illustrated in Fig. 37.1. A schematic representation of the characteristics of MAB pilot projects is shown in Fig. 37.2.

A pilot project that demonstrates a significant contribution toward the advancement of tropical ecology through international cooperation is the San Carlos de Rio Negro project in the Amazon territory of Venezuela. It has been undertaken through the International Center for Tropical Ecology of the Instituto Venezolano de Investigaciones Cientificas (IVIC), Caracas, which was created by the government of Venezuela and UNESCO in 1976. Prior to this, MAB had organized courses in tropical ecology and systems analysis at IVIC (UNESCO Paris 1977*a*).

Through the center, a vast program of ecological studies in Amazon forests has been developed with technical assistance and financial support from international sources, including the National Science Foundation of the Federal Republic of Venezuela (CONICIT), the Organization of American States (OAS), the U.S. National Science Foundation, and the Science Foundation of the Federal Republic of Germany. International cooperation has been established with the University of Georgia (as a part of the United States MAB Program), the Max Planck Institute of Limnology, and the World Institute of Forestry in the Federal Republic of Germany.

The San Carlos de Rio Negro project, in its first phase, focuses on gathering basic information about the structure and composition of the vegetation, productivity, nutrient cycling, and soils in undisturbed natural ecosystems of the Amazonian forest. The next phase, now underway, is to establish and monitor experimental plots for studies of nutrient cycling and recovery under different treatments and disturbances, such as slash and burn agriculture and plantation forestry (UNESCO Paris 1977*b*).

MAB Project No. 8: Biosphere Reserves

One other project can illustrate the progress that has been made in the MAB Program. MAB Project No. 8 "Conservation of Natural Areas and the

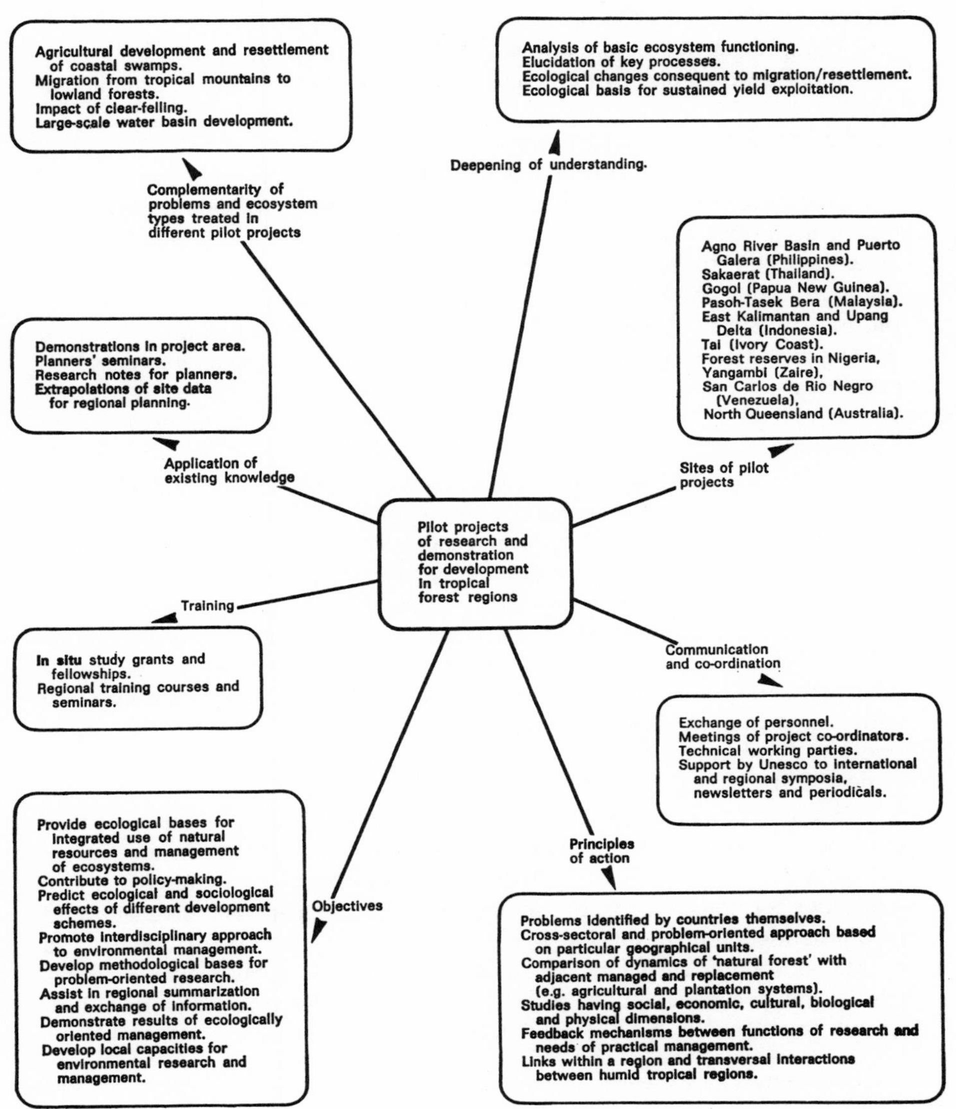

Figure 37.2 The Characteristics of MAB Pilot Projects (U.S. Dept. of State, 1978)

Genetic Material They Contain" is a core project that focuses on the development of an international network of biosphere reserves. These reserves preserve representative samples of the earth's ecosystems and conserve the genetic materials of the flora and fauna. These sites are used as standards, or benchmarks, in studies of the tolerance of ecosystems to human manipulation.

One of the major problems associated with traditional conservation practices, particularly in the less-developed nations, is the belief that conservation of nature is detrimental to development and exploitation of natural resources. Often, the public image of national parks and equivalent reserves is one of areas set aside strictly for the enjoyment of those who can afford to travel to see them. Thus, in countries where hunger still prevails, the idea of reserving productive lands is unacceptable to many. MAB Project 8 provides new dimensions in conservation, ones which recognize that sustainable development depends on our abilities to understand natural ecosystem processes and to maintain, or restore, the genetic diversity of species on which their continuing evolution depends (UNESCO Paris 1973).

At its first session in November 1971, the International Coordinating Council within UNESCO defined Project 8 and recognized that the establishment of reserves, protected and managed in various ways, is important to mankind through the role they can play in meeting scientific, economic, educational, cultural, and recreational needs. Such areas were regarded as essential for research in ecosystems of various kinds and of fundamental importance to the MAB program, since these areas represent baselines or standards against which environmental change can be measured and the performance of ecosystems judged. They also represent a means of maintaining the gene pools of their indigenous plants, animals, and microorganisms (UNESCO Paris 1973).

In September 1973, the Expert Panel on Project 8 decided on the scientific content of the project and urged immediate action toward the conservation of natural areas (UNESCO Paris 1974). The panel outlined general criteria and guidelines for conservation of natural areas and their genetic diversity, and recommended that a special group be convened to prepare criteria and guidelines for the selection and establishment of biosphere reserves. This special group crystallized the objectives of the international network of biosphere reserves (UNESCO Paris 1974):

(a) To conserve, for present and future human use, the diversity and integrity of biotic communities of plants and animals within natural ecosystems, and to safeguard the genetic diversity of species on which their continuing evolution depends.
(b) To provide areas for ecological and environmental research including, particularly, baseline studies, both within and adjacent to these reserves, such research to be consistent with objective (a) above.
(c) To provide facilities for education and training.

The essential criteria for selection of biosphere reserves are as follows (UNESCO Paris 1973, and 1974):

(a) *Representativeness.* This criterion is primary for selection. A reserve should represent as many of the characteristic features of the particular biogeographic regions as possible, so that information relating to the nature and dynamics of the reserve area can be extrapolated to similar areas throughout the region. The classification of biogeographic regions and natural regions of the world has been developed for IUCN (Dasmann 1973; Udvardy 1975).

(b) *Diversity.* Representative biosphere reserves should contain the maximum representation of ecosystems, communities, and organisms characteristic of the biome. Ecosystem-level diversity has the highest priority, so that primary concern is with the degree to which the range of habitats characteristic of the biome is present in any one area.

(c) *Naturalness.* Selection of representative samples of biomes in their natural state necessitates a high priority being placed on naturalness, the least modified areas being the most appropriate. In addition, sufficient areas of the same ecosystem should be available for comparative, manipulative types of research.

(d) *Effectiveness of an area as a conservation unit.* This criterion involves a number of factors, such as size, shape, and location with respect to natural protective barriers. Optimum size depends largely on the type of system and the requirements of the species involved. Studies of the minimum critical size and distribution of protected areas are being encouraged in the MAB Program. The ideal area is one sufficiently large to be self-regulating through the inclusion of all the interacting components. Also, there should be adequate buffer-zone compatibility ensuring that the land use of surrounding areas is compatible with the objectives of the reserve.

The MAB biosphere reserve concept recognizes that it is unrealistic, even impossible, to conserve every living organism; therefore, strategies are being developed whereby nations can act more effectively to conserve a greater diversity of ecosystems and their species. Efforts are underway now to identify the most significant and diverse ecosystems, within the broad scheme of biogeographic provinces of the world, on the basis of size and importance of the genetic loss that would occur should these ecosystems deteriorate completely.

Another means has been developed to determine high priority areas for conservation by identifying those biogeographic provinces that are poorly represented by protected areas such as national parks or equivalent reserves. According to the World Conservation Strategy (IUCN 1980), a review of the United Nations List of National Parks and Equivalent Reserves and the World Directory of National Parks and Other Protected Areas by IUCN indicates that of the 193 terrestrial biogeographic provinces listed by Udvardy (1975), seventy-three contain either no protected areas or are inadequately covered.

There are particular regions and ecosystems that should have the highest priority for conservation action and research. The World Conservation Strategy contains the following statement (IUCN 1980):

> 40% of the world's tropical rain forests—the richest environments on the planet—have been destroyed already. The rest are being felled and burned at the rate of 20 hectares a minute.
>
> 30 million km^2 (19% of the earth's land surface) are threatened with desertification. The world's drylands are being degraded at the rate of 44 hectares a minute.
>
> Coastal wetlands and shallows—the support systems of two-thirds of the world's fisheries—are being degraded or destroyed by dredging, dumping, and pollution just as fast.
>
> More than a thousand vertebrate species and 25,000 plant species are threatened with extinction.

The IUCN biogeographic province classification, as with other global classification schemes, is not detailed enough to reflect the diversity of ecosystems, especially in tropical and subtropical regions. However, it provides a useful and broad framework within which nations can begin to identify, for conservation and research purposes, the most significant ecosystems on the basis of size, naturalness, diversity of species, and the importance of potential genetic loss. This approach to international conservation enables nations and international organizations to concentrate their efforts in biogeographic provinces where there is the greatest need or where little has been accomplished.

Table 37.2 identifies the 144 sites, listed within the biogeographic provinces they represent, that have been officially designated by UNESCO as biosphere reserves as of May, 1979. Thirty-five nations have thus far established biosphere reserves. Only about one-third of the 193 biogeographic provinces

Table 37.2. Biosphere Reserves Designated by UNESCO as of May 1979

1. Tropical Humid Forests (18 provinces)		
Congo Rain Forest	**Reserve Floristique de Yangambi**	**Zaire**
	Parc National d'Odzala	**Congo**
	Basse Lobaye Forest	**Central African Empire**
Amazonian	**Reserve del Manu**	**Peru**
Madeiran	**Parque National Pilon-Lajas**	**Bolivia**
Guinean Rain Forest	**Tai National Park**	**Ivory Coast**
	OMO Reserve	**Nigeria**
Ceylonese Rain Forest	**Sinharaja Forest Reserve**	**Sri Lanka**

(continued)

Table 37.2—Continued

2. Subtropical and Temperate Rain Forests or Woodlands (10 provinces)		
Oregonian	Cascade Head Experimental Forest and Scenic Research Area	USA
	H. J. Andrews Experimental Forest	USA
	Olympic National Park	USA
Tasmanian	Southwest National Park	Australia
	Macquarie Island State Reserve	Australia

3. Temperate Needle-leaf Forests or Woodlands (4 provinces)		
Yukon Taiga	Mount McKinley National Park	USA
Subartic Birchlands	Silhote-Alin Reserve	USSR
Canadian Taiga	St. Hilaire	Canada

4. Tropical Dry or Deciduous Forests (including Monsoon Forests) or Woodlands (25 provinces)		
Thailandian Monsoon Forest	Sakaerat Environmental Research Station	Thailand
	Mae Sa Watershed	Thailand
	Hauy Tak Reserve	Thailand
Ceylonese Monsoon Forest	Hurulu Forest Reserve	Sri Lanka
Everglades	Everglades National Park	USA
Equadorian Dry Forest	Reserva del Noroeste	Peru
Northern Coastal	Prince Regent River Natural Reserve	Australia

5. Temperate Broad-leaf Forests or Woodlands, and Subpolar Deciduous Thickets (13 provinces)		
Eastern Forest	Coweeta Hydrological Laboratory and Experimental Forest	USA
	Great Smoky Mountains National Park	USA
	Hubbard Brook Experimental Forest	USA
British Islands	Braunton Burrows National Nature Reserve	UK
	Caerlaverock National Nature Reserve	UK
	Cairnsmore of Fleet National Nature Reserve	UK

(continued)

Table 37.2—Continued

British Islands	Dyfi National Nature Reserve	UK
	Moore House-Upper Teesdale National Nature Reserve	UK
	North Norfolk Coast Biosphere Reserve	UK
	St. Kilda National Nature Reserve	UK
	Silver Flowe-Merrick Kells Biosphere Reserve	UK
	Taynish National Nature Reserve	UK
	Claish Moss National Nature Reserve	UK
Boreonemoral	Luknajno Lake Reserve	Poland
Middle European Forest	Bialowieza National Park	Poland
	Slowinski National Park	Poland
	Reserve Srébarna	Bulgaria
	Krivoklatsko Reserve	Czechoslovakia
	Slovak Karst Reserve	Czechoslovakia
	Trebon Basin Reserve	Czechoslovakia
Pannonian	Neusiedler See-Osterreichischer Tel	Austria
6. Evergreen Sclerophyllous Forests, Scrubs or Woodlands (9 provinces)		
Californian	Channel Islands National Monument	USA
	San Dimas Experimental Forest	USA
	San Joaquin Experimental Forest	USA
Iberian Highlands	Ordesa-Vinamala	Spain
Eastern Sclerophyll	Kosciusko National Park	Australia
	Croajingolong National Park	Australia
Western Sclerophyll	Fitzgerald River National Park	Australia
Southern Sclerophyll	Murray Valley	Australia
Chilean Sclerophyll	Parque National Fray Jorge	Chile
Mediterranean Scherophyll	Repetek Reserve	USSR
7. Warm Deserts and Semideserts (18 provinces)		
Sonoran	Organ Pipe Cactus National Monument	USA
Thar desert	Lal Sohara National Park	Pakistan
Chihuahuan	Big Bend National Park	USA
	Jornada Experimental Range	USA
	Reserva de Mapimi	Mexico

(continued)

Table 37.2—Continued

Somalian	Mt. Kulal Reserve	Kenya
Mediterranean Sclerophyll	Reserve Nationale de Camargue	France
	Forêt domainale du Fango	France
	Forêt domainale du Circeo	Italy
	Reserva de Grazalema	Spain
	Parc National de l'Ichkeul	Tunisia
	Park National des Iles Zembra et Zembretta	Tunisia
	Velebit Mountain	Yugoslavia[a]
Central Desert	Ayers Rock–Mt. Olga National Park	Australia
Southern Mulga/ Saltbush	Unnamed conservation site (29°S; 130°E)	Australia
	Danggali Conservation Park	Australia
Deccan Thorn Forest	Mount Kenya Biosphere Reserve	Kenya
8. Cold-winter (continental) Deserts and Semideserts (6 provinces)		
Great Basin	Desert Experimental Range	USA
Turanian	Prioksko-Terrasni Reserve	USSR
Anatolian-Iranian	Hara National Park	Iran
Desert	Kuh-e-Geno National Park	Iran
9. Tundra Communities and Barren Arctic Desert (12 provinces)		
Aleutian Islands	Aleutian Islands National Wildlife Refuge	USA
Alaskan Tundra	Noatak National Arctic Range	USA
Arctic Desert	Northeast Greenland National Park	Denmark
Iranian Desert	Kavir National Park	Iran
	Turan Wildlife Refuge and Protected Area	Iran
Arctic Desert	Northeast Svalbard Nature Reserve	Norway
10. Tropical Grasslands and Savannas (6 provinces)		
11. Temperate Grasslands (8 provinces)		
Grasslands	Central Plains Experimental Range	USA

[a]Also in Central European Highlands

(continued)

Table 37.2—Continued

Atlas Steppe	Parc National de Djebel Bou-Hedma	Tunisia
	Parc National de Djebel Chambi	Tunisia
Eastern Grasslands and Savannas	Yathong Nature Reserve	Australia
Uruguayan Pamapas	Bañados del Este	Uruguay

12. Mixed Mountain and Highland Systems with Complex Zonation (22 provinces)

Rocky Mountains	Coran Experimental Forest	USA
	Fraser Experimental Forest	USA
	Glacier National Park	USA
	Rocky Mountain National Park	USA
	Yellowstone National Park	USA
Sierra-Cascade	Sequoia-Kings Canyon National Park	USA
	Stanislaus-Tuolumne Experimental Forest	USA
	Three Sisters Wilderness	USA
Madrean-Cordilleran	Beaver Creek Experimental Watershed	USA
	Reserva de la Michilia	Mexico
Scottish Highlands	Beinn Eighe National Nature Reserve	UK
	Isle of Rhum National Natural Reserve	
	Lock Druidibeg National Natural Reserve	UK
Central European Highlands	Collemeluccio-Montedimezzo	Italy
	Gurgler Kamm	Austria
	Gossenkoellsee	Austria
	Babia Gora National Park	Poland
	Lobau Reserve	Austria
	Berezinskij Reserve	USSR
	Velebit Mountain	Yugoslavia[b]
Balkan Highlands	Reserve Ecologique du Bassin de la Rivera Tara	Yugoslavia
	Reserve Kamtchia	Bulgaria
	Reserve Tchouprene	Bulgaria
	Reserve Boatine	Bulgaria
	Reserve Tsaritchina	Bulgaria
	Park National Steneto	Bulgaria
	Reserve Djendema	Bulgaria
	Reserve Bistrichko branichté	Bulgaria

[b]Also in Mediterranean Sclerophyll

(continued)

Table 37.2—Continued

Balkan Highlands	Reserve Parangalitza	Bulgaria
	Reserve Maritchini ezera	Bulgaria
	Reserve Baévi doupki	Bulgaria
Pamir-Tian Shan Highlands	Sary Chelek Reserve	USSR
Balkan Highlands	Reserve Alibotouch	Bulgaria
	Reserve Mantaritza	Bulgaria
	Reserve Koupena	Bulgaria
	Reserve Doupkata	Bulgaria
	Reserve Tchervenata sténa	Bulgaria
	Reserve Ouzounbodjak	Bulgaria
Caucaso-Iranian Highlands	Arasbaran Wildlife Refuge and Protected Area	Iran
	Arjan National Park	Iran
	Caucasus Reserve	USSR
	Lake Rezaiyeh National Park	Iran
	Miankaleh Wildlife Refuge	Iran
	Mohammed Reza Shah National Park	Iran
Yungas	Reserve del Huascaran	Peru
	Reserva del Manu	Peru
Puna	Reserva Biologica de Ulla Ulla	Bolivia
Southern Andean	Reserva del Huascaran	Peru
West Eurasian Taiga	Central-Charnosem Reserve	USSR

13. Mixed Island Systems (13 provinces)

Philippines	Puerto Galera Biosphere Reserve	Philippines
Java	Cibodas Reserve	Indonesia
Lesser Sunda Islands	Komodo Island Game Reserve	Indonesia
Celebes	Lore Kalamanta Game Reserve	Indonesia
Borneo	Tanjung Puting Nature Park	Indonesia
Southeastern Polynesian	Parque Nacional Juan Rernandez	Chile
	Atoll de Taiaro	France
Greater Antillean	Luquillo Experimental Forest	USA
Lesser Antillean	Virgin Islands National Park	USA

are included. About half of the reserves are in temperate forests and mixed mountain and highland systems. The most significant gaps exist in subtropical rain forests, temperate needle-leaf forests, cold winter deserts and semi-deserts, tropical grasslands and savannas, temperate grasslands, and aquatic systems.

This initial network of biosphere reserves is based, primarily, on areas that are already protected, although several have been established on previously unprotected areas. The significance and distinctness of the biosphere reserve network result from the increased cooperation between different nations and international organizations in research, monitoring, training activities, and exchange of information.

An example of this cooperation is the summit agreement in Moscow, July 1974, between the Union of Soviet Socialist Republics and the United States. Both countries agreed to designate biosphere reserves and to exchange results from pilot projects on ecological research and monitoring in these reserves. High priority in the U.S.-U.S.S.R. project is placed on: (1) monitoring and research aimed at understanding the structure and function of ecosystems and their components; (2) environmental consequences of various land management practices; and (3) ensuring the effectiveness of biological reserves in maintaining biotic diversity and gene pools by considering size, habitat heterogeneity, and external influences. The U.S.S.R. Hydrometerological Service is particularly interested in developing comparable environmental monitoring programs for various pollutants. (Franklin 1977).

The first of these pilot projects in the United States is taking place in the Appalachian Mountain Biosphere Reserve Cluster in Tennessee and North Carolina. This area demonstrates how MAB can work as a mechanism to marshall existing resources and expertise within a region to achieve common goals. The reserve cluster consists of the Great Smoky Mountains National Park and the Coweeta Experimental Forest, the staffs of which cooperate closely with that from the Oak Ridge Reservation administered by the Oak Ridge National Laboratory. The universities in the area, such as the Universities of Tennessee, Georgia, and Western Carolina have also contributed to a program of ecological research and monitoring in this moist, richly diverse example of the Eastern Forest Province. Through establishment of permanent vegetation plots, inventory of rare and endangered species, monitoring of exotic species populations and their effects, climatic measurements, and manipulation of forests at Coweeta Experimental Forest, researchers are accumulating a growing body of data to aid in understanding the southern Appalachian ecosystems as they are now, and as they respond to on-going internal and external influences.

Because of the progress of MAB activities in this biosphere reserve cluster, the units within the cluster were appropriate sites for an International Workshop on Long-term Ecological Monitoring, held in October 1978. Scientists from eleven nations and from UNESCO and the UNEP Global Environmental Monitoring System (GEMS) developed guidelines and recommendations for international long-term monitoring in biosphere reserves. For most types of data, three levels of monitoring were developed to fit the levels of funding, knowledge, facilities, and equipment available. The published guidelines (U.S. National Committee for Man and the Biosphere 1979) will be used in an international program of long-term ecological monitoring and exchange of information. Land use, climate, atmospheric deposition, carbon dioxide, and pesticide levels and other variables will be monitored in selected biosphere reserves of the world.

So the Biosphere Reserve Program, recognizing that conservation and ecological research must be an integral part of development, has set out to identify and protect the representative ecosystems of the world. Then these reserves, which remain under national administration and control, become platforms for research and the sharing of information and expertise in a coordinated international program.

SOURCES OF INFORMATION ON MAB

An information system has been established for the Biosphere Reserve Project and for all other project areas of MAB. A report (UNESCO 1978), which provides an index to all MAB field projects and tabulates the projects by country, themes of research, year of start and duration, source of funding, and major activities in addition to research, is available from the MAB Secretariat, UNESCO, 7 Place de Fontenoy, 75700 Paris, France.

For the U.S. biosphere reserves, pertinent ecological and climatological data for each reserve have been synthesized (Risser and Cornelison 1979). This is available from: Office of Science and Technology, National Park Service, Department of the Interior, Washington, D.C. 20240.

SUMMARY

Scientific programs directed toward solving environmental problems and reaching judicious decisions concerning natural resources have grown throughout the world. Yet our knowledge about the biosphere in which we live is still inadequate to cope with these problems and to avoid ultimate catastrophe. Greater concerted international action is needed, and the Man and the Biosphere Program of UNESCO seems to offer a promising channel for such action. This program has recognized that different disciplines and human systems, such as sociology and economics, must be understood as part of the total ecology of the planet. MAB is a program that deals with humanity as a natural part of Earth's ecology—at times seriously impacting, but never apart from, or free of, the physical, chemical, and biological laws that underlie all planetary processes.

REFERENCES CITED

Batisse, M. 1975. Man and the biosphere. *Nature* 256: 156–158.

Cain, S. A. 1970. Preservation of natural areas and ecosystems, protection of rare and endangered species. In *Use and conservation of the biosphere* from UNESCO Paris 1970 (see below).

Dasmann, R. F. 1973. *A system for defining and classifying natural regions for purposes of conservation.* IUCN Occasional paper Number 7. Morges, Switzerland.

Franklin, J. F. 1977. The Biosphere Reserve Program in the United States. *Science* 195:262–267.

IUCN. 1980. *World conservation strategy.* With UNEP and WWF. International Union for the Conservation of Nature and Natural Resources. Morges, Switzerland.

Reichle, D. E. 1973. *Advances in ecosystem science.* Paper presented at joint meeting of Interagency Coordinating Committee and U.S. National Committee for the International Biological Program, Washington, D.C.

Risser, P. G. and K. D. Cornelison. 1979. *Information Synthesis Project; MAB-8 Biosphere Reserves.* Norman: University of Oklahoma Press.

Udvardy, M. D. F. 1975. *A classification of the biogeographical provinces of the world.* IUCN Occasional paper Number 18. Morges, Switzerland.

UNESCO. 1978. *MAB information system.* Compilation 2.

UNESCO Paris. 1970. *Proceedings of the Intergovernmental Conference of Experts on the Scientific Basis for Rational Use and Conservation of the Resources of the Biosphere.* September 4–13, 1968, Paris, France.

———. 1971. *Final report of the first session of the International Co-ordinating Council on the Programme of Man and the Biosphere (MAB).* MAB Report Series Number 1.

———. 1973. *Final report of the expert panel on Project 8: Conservation of Natural Areas and of the Genetic Material They Contain.* MAB Report Series Number 12.

———. 1974. *Final report of the Task Force on: Criteria and Guidelines for the Choice and Establishment of Biosphere Reserves.* Organized jointly by UNESCO and UNEP. MAB Report Series Number 22.

———. 1975. *Final report of the International Co-ordinating Council of the Programme on Man and the Biosphere (MAB).* MAB Report Number 38.

———. 1977*a*. *Nat. resour.* 13 (2):18–21.

———. 1977*b*. *Nat. resour.* 13 (3):4–6.

———. 1978. *Final report of the International Co-ordinating Council of the Programme on Man and the Biosphere (MAB).* MAB Report Series Number 46.

U.S. Department of State. 1978. *Proceedings of a strategy conference on tropical deforestation.* Washington, D.C.: U.S. Department of State and Agency for International Development.

U.S. National Committee for Man and the Biosphere. 1979. *Long-term ecological monitoring in biosphere reserves.* Washington, D.C.: Department of State.

APPENDIX I

Major Ecological Journals

Title	Country of Publication
Abstracta Botanica	Hungary
Academia Sinica. Institute of Zoology. Bulletin	Taiwan
Acqua Aria	Italy
Acta Agraria et Silvestria	Poland
Acta Agrobotanica	Poland
Acta Agronomica Academiae Scientiarum Hungaricae	Hungary
Acta Amazonica	Brazil
Acta Biologica Academiae Scientiarum Hungaricae	Hungary
Acta Biologica Debrecina	Hungary
Acta Botanica Academiae Scientiarum Hungaricae	Hungary
Acta Botanica Neerlandica	Netherlands
Acta Cientifica Venezolana	Venezuela
Acta Geobotanica Hungarica	Hungary
Acta Hydrobiologica	Poland
Acta Microbiologica Academiae Scientiarum Hungaricae	Hungary
Acta Naturalia Islandica	Iceland
Acta Oceanographica Taiwanica	Taiwan
Acta Phytogeographica Suecica	Sweden
Acta Phytopathologica Academiae Scientiarum Hungaricae	Hungary
Acta Theriologica	Poland
Acta Zoologica Academiae Scientiarum Hungaricae	Hungary
Adansonia	France
Advances in Ecological Research	United Kingdom
Advances in Marine Biology	United States

(continued)

Title	Country of Publication
Agriculture and Environment	Netherlands
Agriculture Pakistan	Pakistan
Agro-Ecosystems	Netherlands
Agronomia Costarricense	Costa Rica
Allattani Közlemények	Hungary
American Birds	United States
American Journal of Botany	United States
American Midland Naturalist	United States
American Museum Novitates	United States
American Naturalist	United States
American Scientist	United States
American Zoologist	United States
Anales de la Escuela Nacional de Ciencias Biológicas	Mexico
Anales del Instituto de Biología (Series Botánica y zoología)	Mexico
Anatomical Record	United States
Animal Behavior	United States
Annales Bogorienses	Indonesia
Annales de Zoologie-Ecologie	United Kingdom
Annales Instituti Biologici (Tihany) Hungaricae Academiae Scientiarum	Hungary
Annales Universitatis Scientiarum Budapestinensis	Hungary
Annales Zoologici Fennici	Finland
Annals of Botany	United Kingdom
Annals of the Association of American Geographers	United States
Annals of the Missouri Botanical Garden	United States
Annals of the Phytopathological Institute Benaki	Greece
Annual Review of Ecology and Systematics	United States
Annual Review of Entomology	United States
Annual Review of Phytopathology	United States
Annual Review of Plant Physiology	United States
Annuali dell'Istituto Sperimentale per lo Studio e la Difesa del Suolo (Firenze)	Italy
Anzeiger der Öesterreichischen Akademie der Wissenschaften, Mathematisch—Naturwissenschaftliche Klasse	Austria
Applied and Environmental Microbiology	United States
Applied Ecology Abstracts	United Kingdom
Aquila	Hungary
Arboretum Kórnickie (Kórnik Arboretum)	Poland
Archiv für Hydrobiologie	W. Germany

(continued)

Title	Country of Publication
Archives of Environmental Contamination and Toxicology	United States
Archives of Microbiology	United States
Archivio di Oceanografia e Limnologia (Venezia)	Italy
Archiwum Ochrony Srodowiska (Archives of Environment Protection)	Poland
Arctic	Canada
Arctic and Alpine Research	United States
Ardea	Netherlands
Atti della Società Italiana di Biogeografia (Siena)	Italy
Auk (The)	United States
Australian Journal of Botany	Australia
Australian Journal of Ecology	Australia
Australian Journal of Science	Australia
Australian Journal of Zoology	Australia
The Australian University	Australia
Behavioral Ecology and Sociobiology	United States
Behavior Genetics	United States
Behaviour	United Kingdom
Beiträge zur geobotanischen Landesaufnahme der Schweiz	Switzerland
Berichte der Deutschen Botanischen Gesellschaft	W. Germany
Berichte der Schweizerische Botanischen Gesellschaft	Switzerland
Berita Biologi	Indonesia
Biochemica et Biophysica Acta	Netherlands
BioIndonesia	Indonesia
Biologia	Pakistan
Biologia Gallo-Hellenica	Greece
Biological Bulletin	United States
Biological Bulletin of Taiwan Normal University	Taiwan
Biological Conservation	United Kingdom
Biologicke Listy/Biological Review	Czechoslovakia
Biologie in Unserer Zeit	W. Germany
Biologist (The)	United States and United Kingdom
Biologiya Morya (Marine Biology)	USSR
Biometrics	United States
Biometrika	United Kingdom
BioScience	United States
Biótica	Mexico
Biotropica	United States

(continued)

Title	Country of Publication
Bois et Forets des Tropiques	France
Boletín, Brasilian Forest Service	Brazil
Boletín de la Sociedad Botánica de México	Mexico
Bollettino del Laboratorio di Entomologia Agraria (Portici)	Italy
Bollettino di Fitosociologia (Bologna)	Italy
Bollettino di Pesca, Piscicoltura e Idrobiologia (Roma)	Italy
Botanical Bulletin of Academia Sinica	Taiwan
Botanical Gazette	United States
Botanical Journal	USSR
Botanical Review	USSR
Botanikai Közlemények	Hungary
Botaniska Notiser	Sweden
Brenesia	Costa Rica
British Birds	United Kingdom
Brittania	United Kingdom
Bryologist (The)	United States
Buletin Kebun Raya	Indonesia
Bulletin de la Société Royale de Botanique de Belgique	Belgium
Bulletin de la Société Royale de Zoologie de Belgique	Belgium
Bulletin of the American Meteorological Society	United States
Bulletin of the American Museum of Natural History	United States
Bulletin of Marine Science	United States
Bulletin of the Geological Society of America	United States
Bulletin of the National Museum of Singapore	Singapore
Bulletin of the Taiwan Forestry Research Institute	Taiwan
Bulletins	Puerto Rico
Bulletins of the Ministry of Agriculture of Sudan	Sudan
California Fish and Game	United States
Cambridge Philosophical Society: Biological Reviews	United Kingdom
Canadian Entomologist (The)	Canada
Canadian Field Naturalist	Canada
Canadian Journal of Botany	Canada
Canadian Journal of Microbiology	Canada
Canadian Journal of Zoology	Canada
Caribbean Journal of Sciences	Puerto Rico
Castanea	United States
Ceiba	Honduras

(continued)

Title	Country of Publication
Chesapeake Science	United States
Chimica Chronica	Greece
Chung-hua Nung Hsueh Hui Pao (Journal of the Agricultural Association of China)	Taiwan
Chung-kuo Lin Yeh K'o Hsueh (Peking) (Chinese Forestry Science)	China
Ciencia, México	Mexico
Communications of the Forest Research Institute	Indonesia
Communications/Contributions of the General Agricultural Research Station	Indonesia
Condor	United States
Contributions of the Inland Fishery Research Station	Indonesia
Copeia	United States
CSIRO (Aust) Wildlife Research	Australia
Current Advances in Ecological Sciences	United States
Cytobios	United Kingdom
Der Ornithologische Beobachter	Switzerland
East African Wildlife Journal	United Kingdom
Ecologia Agraria	Italy
Ecological Bulletin of NFR (Natural Science Research Council)	Sweden
Ecological Modelling	Netherlands
Ecological Monographs	United States
Ecological Society of America Bulletin	United States
Ecologist (The)	United Kingdom
Ecology	United States
Ecology Law Quarterly	United States
Economic Botany	United States
Ecotoxicology and Environmental Safety	United States
Ekologia Polska (Polish Journal of Ecology)	Poland
Ekologiya	USSR
Entomologia experimentalis et applicata	Netherlands
Environment	United States
Environment Abstracts	United States
Environment and Behavior	United States
Environment International (International Journal of the Environment)	United States
Environment Reporter	United States
Environmental and Experimental Botany	United States
Environmental Conservation	Switzerland
Environmental Entomology	United States

(continued)

Title	Country of Publication
Environmental Law	United States
Environmental Law Reporter	United States
Environmental Management	United States
Environmental Pollution	United States
Environmental Research	United States
Environmental Review	United States
Environmental Science and Technology	United States
Ergebnisse der Wissenschaftlichen Untersuchungen im Schweizerischen Nationalpark	Switzerland
Evolution	United States
Excerpta Botanica, Sectio B	W. Germany
Experientia	Switzerland
Fauna und Flora des Golfes von Neapel	Italy
Fieldiana: Botany	United States
Fieldiana: Zoology	United States
Fish Bulletin	New Zealand
Fisheries Research Bulletin (Western Australia Marine Research Laboratories)	Australia
Fiskeridirektoratets Skrifter, Serie Havundersoekelser	Norway
Folia Entomologica Mexicana	Mexico
Folia Forestalia Polonica	Poland
Folia Zoologica	Czechoslovakia
Forest (The)	Greece
Forest Ecology and Management	Netherlands
Forestry	United Kingdom
Forestry Research Memoirs	Nigeria
Forest Science	United States
Fragmenta Floristica et Geobotanica	Poland
Freshwater Biology	United Kingdom
Geobios	India
Geographical Journal (Czasopismo Geograficzne)	United Kingdom
Geographical Review (The)	United States
Geoponika	Greece
Giornale di Fisica Sanitaria e di Protezione contro le Radiazioni (Torino)	Italy
Great Basin Naturalist (The)	United States
Greinar	Iceland
Helgolander wissenschaftliche Meeresuntersuchungen	W. Germany
Herpetologica	United States
Hilgardia	United States

(continued)

Title	Country of Publication
Holarctic Ecology	Denmark
Human Ecology	United States
Human Ecology Forum	United States
Hvalrådets Skrifter. Scientific Results of Marine Biological Research	Norway
Hydrobiologia	Netherlands
Hydrological Sciences Bulletin/Bulletin des Sciences Hydrologiques	United Kingdom
Ibis	United Kingdom
Indian Forester	India
Indian Journal of Ecology	India
Ingegneria ambientale, Inquinamento e Depurazione (Politecnico Milano)	Italy
Inquinamento: Acqua, Aria e Suolo (Milano)	Italy
Instituto Biologico. Arquivos	Brazil
Interciencia	Venezuela
International Journal of Ecology and Environmental Sciences	India
International Journal of Environmental Studies	United Kingdom
Internationale Revue der gesamten Hydrobiologie	E. Germany
Japanese Journal of Ecology/Nippon Seitai Gakkaishi	Japan
Jökull	Iceland
Journal fuer Ornithologie	W. Germany
Journal of Agricultural Research in Iceland	Iceland
Journal of Agriculture	Puerto Rico
Journal of Animal Ecology	United Kingdom
Journal of Applied Ecology	United Kingdom
Journal of Biogeography	United Kingdom
Journal of Chemical Ecology	United States
Journal of Ecology	United Kingdom
Journal of Economic Entomology	United States
Journal of Environmental Management	United States
Journal of Environmental Quality	United States
Journal of Environmental Sciences	United States
Journal of Experimental Biology	United Kingdom
Journal of Experimental Marine Biology and Ecology	Netherlands
Journal of Experimental Zoology	United States
Journal of Fish Biology	United States
Journal of Forestry	United States
Journal of General Biology	USSR

(continued)

Title	Country of Publication
Journal of Herpetology	United States
Journal of Hydrology	Netherlands
Journal of Mammalogy	United States
Journal of Marine Research	United States
Journal of Morphology	United States
Journal of Range Management	United States
Journal of the Fisheries Research Board of Canada	Canada
Journal of the Singapore National Academy of Science	Singapore
Journal of Soil and Water Conservation	United States
Journal of Soil Science	United Kingdom
Journal of South African Botany	S. Africa
Journal of the Australian Institute of Agricultural Science	Australia
Journal of the Fishery Society of Taiwan	Taiwan
Journal of the Formosan Medical Association	Taiwan
Journal of the Geological Society, London	United Kingdom
Journal of the Royal Society of New Zealand	New Zealand
Journal of Theoretical Biology	United Kingdom
Journal of Tropical Geography	Singapore
Journal of Wildlife Management	United States
Journal of Zoology	United Kingdom
Korean Journal of Botany	Korea
Korean Journal of Ecology	Korea
Korean Journal of Limnology	Korea
Korean Journal of Microbiology	Korea
Korean Journal of Zoology	Korea
Limnological Society of Southern Africa. Journal	S. Africa
Limnology and Oceanography	United States
Limosa	Netherlands
Linnaean Society. Botanical Journal. Biological Journal. Zoological Journal	United States
Magyar Tudományos Akadémia Biológiai Tudományok Osztálya Közleményei	Hungary
Malayan Nature Journal	Malaysia
Malaysian Forester	Malaysia
Mammalia	France
Marine Biology	United States
Marine Research in Indonesia	Indonesia
Mauritius Institute Bulletin	Mauritius
Meddelande Norske Skogforsøksvesen	Norway
Memorie dell/Istituto Italiano di Idrobiolgia	Italy

(continued)

Title	Country of Publication
Memorie di Biologia Marina e di Oceanografia (Messina)	Italy
Microbial Ecology	United States
Mitteilungen (und Berichte) der Eidg. Anstalt für das forstliche Versuchswesen	Switzerland
Mitteilungen der Schweizerische Entomologischen Gesellschaft	Switzerland
Mitteilungen—Internationale Vereinigung fuer Theoretische und Angewandte Limnologie	W. Germany
Monograph Series. Institute of Zoology, Academia Sinica	Taiwan
Monographiae Biologicae	Netherlands
Montes	Spain
Náttūrufræðingurinn (Journal of Natural Sciences)	Iceland
Natura	Netherlands
Natural Resources Journal	United States
Nature	Great Britain
Naturwissenschaften im Unterricht. Biologie	W. Germany
Natuur en Landschap	Netherlands
Netherland Journal of Zoology	Netherlands
Netherlands Journal for Sea Research	Netherlands
New Phytologist	United Kingdom
New Scientist	Great Britain
New York Fish and Game Journal	United States
New Zealand Department of Internal Affairs Wildlife Publication	New Zealand
New Zealand Department of Scientific and Industrial Research Bulletin	New Zealand
New Zealand Department of Scientific and Industrial Research Information Series	New Zealand
New Zealand Journal of Agriculture	New Zealand
New Zealand Journal of Agricultural Research	New Zealand
New Zealand Journal of Botany	New Zealand
New Zealand Journal of Forestry	New Zealand
New Zealand Journal of Forestry Science	New Zealand
New Zealand Journal of Geology and Geophysics	New Zealand
New Zealand Journal of Marine and Freshwater Research	New Zealand
New Zealand Journal of Science	New Zealand
New Zealand Journal of Science and Technology	New Zealand
New Zealand Journal of Zoology	New Zealand
New Zealand Science Review	New Zealand

(continued)

Title	Country of Publication
New Zealand State Forest Service Bulletin	New Zealand
The Nigerian Field	Nigeria
Nigerian Forestry Journal	Nigeria
Nigerian Journal of Science	Nigeria
Norwegian Journal of Botany	Norway
Norwegian Journal of Zoology	Norway
Notornis	New Zealand
Nova Hedwiga	W. Germany
Oceanography and Marine Biology. An Annual Review	United Kingdom
Ochrona Przyrody (Nature Protection)	Poland
Oecologia	United States
Oecologia Plantarum	France
Oikos	Denmark
Opuscula Zoologica	Hungary
Oseanologi di Indonesia	Indonesia
Pakistan Journal of Botany	Pakistan
Pakistan Journal of Forestry	Pakistan
Pakistan Journal of Science	Pakistan
Pakistan Journal of Scientific and Industrial Research	Pakistan
Pakistan Journal of Zoology	Pakistan
Palaeogeography, Palaeoclimatology, Palaeoecology	Netherlands
Pamiętnik Puławski—Prace Instytutu Uprawy, Nawożenia i Gleboznawstwa (Papers of the Institute of Soil Science and Cultivation of plants)	Poland
Papers of the Academy of Sciences of the Azerbaijan SSR	USSR
Papers of the Tadjikistan SSR Academy of Sciences, Branch of Biological Sciences	USSR
Pedobiologia	E. Germany
Pflanzenbau	W. Germany
Physiological Zoology	United States
Phytocenosis	Poland
Phytocoenologia	W. Germany
Plant and Soil	Netherlands
Planta	United States
Pochvovedeniye	USSR
Polish Ecological Studies	Poland
Polish Journal of Soil Science	Poland

(continued)

Title	Country of Publication
Pollution Abstracts	United States
Polskie Archiwum Hydrobiologii (Polish Hydrobiological Archives)	Poland
Population Studies	United Kingdom
Prairie Naturalist	United States
Prilozhna Mikrobiologiia (Applied Microbiology)	Bulgaria
Priroda	USSR
Proceeding Kongres Biologi dan Seminar Biologi	Indonesia
Proceedings of the Egyptian Academy of Sciences	Egypt
Proceedings of the Linnaean Society of New South Wales	Australia
Proceedings of the Natural Science Council of the Republic of China	Taiwan
Proceedings of the New Zealand Ecological Society	New Zealand
Proceedings of the National Academy of Science of the United States	United States
Proceedings of the Royal Society of Arts and Sciences of Mauritius	Mauritius
Proceedings of the Royal Society of London	Great Britain
Proceedings of the Royal Society of Queensland	Australia
Proceedings of the Royal Society of Victoria	Australia
Proceedings of the Symposium on Crustacea. Marine Biology Association of India	India
Proceedings United States National Museum	United States
Proceedings of the Zoological Society of London	Great Britain
Protection Ecology	Netherlands
Pubblicazioni della Stazione Zoologica di Napoli	Italy
Pubblicazioni dell'Istituto Spermentale Talassografico (Trieste)	Italy
Publicaciones (Instituto Mexicano de Recursos Naturalez Renovables)	Mexico
Publications in Botany. California University	United States
Publication in Zoology. California University	United States
Quaderni dell'Istituto di Ricerca Sulle Acque (IRSA) (Roma)	Italy
Quarterly Journal of the Taiwan Museum	Taiwan
Quarterly Review of Biology	United States
Quaternary Research	United States
Rapports et Proces—Verbaux des Reunions, Conseil International pour l'Exploration de la Mer	Denmark
Records of the Canterbury Museum	New Zealand

(continued)

Title	Country of Publication
Reinwardtia	Indonesia
Research Papers (U.S. Forest Service at Rio Piedras)	Puerto Rico
Researches on Population Ecology	Japan
Revista Ceres	Brazil
Revista de Agricultura de Puerto Rico	Puerto Rico
Revista de Biologia Tropical	Costa Rica
Revista Forestal Venezolana	Venezuela
Revista de la Sociedad Mexicana de Historia Natural	Mexico
Revista Turrialba	Costa Rica
Revue Agricole et Sucriere de l'Ile Maurice	Mauritius
Revue d'Ecologie et de Biologie du Sol	France
Revue de Geologie Dynamique et de Geographie Physique	France
Revue Suisse de Zoologie	Switzerland
Rimba Indonesia	Indonesia
Rit	Iceland
Rivista di Parassitologia (Messina)	Italy
Rivista d'Idrobiologia (Perugia)	Italy
Roczniki gleboznawcze (Pedological Annals)	Poland
Roczniki Nauk Rolniczych (Annals of Agricultural Sciences)	Poland
Rozpravy Ceskoslovenske Akademie Ved, Rada Matematickych a Prirodnich Ved	Czechoslovakia
Savanna	Nigeria
Schriften des Vereines zur Verbreitung Naturwissenschaftlicher Kenntnisse in Wien	Austria
Skrifter, Kongelige Norske Videnskabers Selskab (Publications, Royal Norwegian Scientific Society)	Norway
Skrifter, Norsk Polarinstitutt (Papers from the Norwegian Polar Institute)	Norway
Skrifter, utgitt av det Norske Videnskaps Akademi (Klasse)1: Matematisk—Naturvidenskapelig Klasse (Papers—Norwegian Academy of Sciences and Letters (Section)1: Mathematics—Natural Sciences Section)	Norway
Schweizerische Zeitschrift für Forstwesen	Switzerland
Schweizerische Zeitschrift für Hydrologie	Switzerland
Science	United States

(continued)

Title	Country of Publication
Science of the Total Environment	Netherlands
Scientific American	United States
Scientific Annals	Greece
Search	Australia
Series of Biology	USSR
Sheng Wu K'o Hsueh (Chinese Bioscience)	Taiwan
Society for the Bibliography of Natural History. Journal	United Kingdom
Soil Science	United States
South African Journal of Science	S. Africa
Southwestern Naturalist	United States
Soviet Geography	USSR
Soviet Journal of Ecology (English Translation of Ekologiya)	United States
Special Publications of the Institute of Oceanography, National Taiwan University	Taiwan
Stiftung Rübe	Switzerland
Studia Naturae	Poland
Sudan Notes and Records	Sudan
Surtsey Research Progress Report	Iceland
Svensk Botanisk Tidskrift	Sweden
Swedish Natural Science Research Council Ecological Bulletins	Sweden
Sylwan	Poland
Systematic Zoology	United States
Taiwania	Taiwan
Taxon	Netherlands
Technica Chronica	Greece
Technical Bulletins	Taiwan
Theoretical Population Biology	United States
Tijdschrift voor Entomologie	Netherlands
Tiscia	Hungary
Torreia—Cuba	Cuba
Torrey Botanical Club. Bulletin	United States
Transaction Gertzen Pedagogical Institute (Leningrad)	USSR
Transactions of the American Fishery Society	United States
Transactions of the Moscow Society of Naturalists	USSR
Transactions of the New Zealand Institute	New Zealand
Transactions of the Royal Society of Australia	Australia
Transactions of the Royal Society of South Africa	S. Africa
Treubia	Indonesia

(continued)

Title	Country of Publication
Tropical Ecology	India
Tuatara	New Zealand
Turrialba	Costa Rica
Tyli	Iceland
Umschau in Wissenschaft und Technik	W. Germany
Urban Ecology	Netherlands
Växtekologiska Studier	Sweden
Vegetatio	Netherlands
Vegetation Resources	USSR
Verhandlungen der Deutschen Zoologischen Gesellschaft	W. Germany
Verhandlungen der Gesellschaft für Oekologie, Jahresversammlung, 6th, Goettingen	W. Germany
Veröffentlichungen (und Berichte) des Geobotanischen Instituts ETH	Switzerland
Victoria Naturalist	Australia
Vie et Milieu (periodique d'ecologie generale)	France
Wahlenbergia	Sweden
Water, Air and Soil Pollution	Netherlands
Water Research	United States
Water Resources Research	United States
West African Journal of Science	Nigeria
Wiadomosci edologiczne (Ecological News)	Poland
World Health Organization Bulletin	United Nations
Zeszyty Problemowe Postepow Nauk Rolniczych (Problems in the Progress of Agriculture)	Poland
Zoologischer Jahresbericht	Italy
Zoology Journal	USSR
Zoomorphologie	W. Germany

Source: Foregoing essays and Ulrich's International Periodicals Directory, 18th Edition, 1979–80

APPENDIX II

Major Source Books in Ecology

Aleksandrova, T. D. 1975. *Statistical methods for the investigation of natural complexes.* Moscow: Nauka Pub.

Aleksandrova, V. D. 1969. *Classification of Vegetation. A Survey of the principles of classification and of classification systems in the various schools of phytocoenology.* Leningrad: Nauka Pub.

______ and N. V. Matveyeva. (eds) 1979. *Arctic tundra and polar deserts of the Taimyr.* Leningrad: Nauka Pub.

Arid Zone Research. 1955. *Plant Ecology, Review of Research.* Paris: UNESCO.

Balogh, J. 1963. *Lebengemeinschaften der Landtiere.* Budapest: Akademiai Kiado; Berlin: Akademie Verlag.

Barbashova, Z. I. (ed) 1976. *Resources of the Biosphere.* Vol. 3. Leningrad: Nauka Pub.

Bauer, O. N. and N. N. Smirnov. (eds) 1976. *Resources of the Biosphere.* Vol. 2. Leningrad: Nauka Pub.

Bazilevich, N. I., A. A. Titlyanova, V. V. Smirnov, L. E. Rodin, N. T. Nechaeva and F. I. Levin. 1978. *Methods of the Study of biological cycling in different natural zones.* Moscow: Mesyel Press.

Beadle, N. C. W. 1948. *The Vegetation and Pastures of Western New South Wales, with Special Reference to soil Erosion.* Sydney: Gov't. Printer.

Beard, J. S. 1974–76. *Vegetation Survey of Western Australia.* Nedlands, W. Aust.: Univ. of W. Aust.

Beg, A. R. 1975. *The Wildlife Habitats of Pakistan.* Bulletin No. 5. Peshawar: Forest Institute.

Biaggi, V. 1970. *Las Aves de Puerto Rico.* Rio Piedras: Editorial Universitaria.

Bikov, B. A. 1960–65. *Dominants in the Vegetation Cover of the Soviet Union.* 3 Vols. Alma-Ata.

Bobrinsky, N. A. 1946. *Geography of Animals.* Moscow: Nauka Pub.

Britton, N. L. *et al.,* 1916–1943. *Scientific Survey of Porto Rico and the Virgin Islands.* 18 Vols. New York: New York Academy of Sciences.

Buchwald, K. and W. Engelhardt. 1978. *Handbuch für Planung, Gestaltung und Schutz der menschlichen Umwelt.* München.

Champion, H. G., S. K. Seth and G. M. Khattak. 1965. *Forest Types of Pakistan.* Peshawar: Pakistan Forest Institute.

Chuang, S. H. 1973. *Animal Life and Nature in Singapore.* Singapore: Sing. Univ. Press.

Cockayne, L. 1928. *The Vegetation of New Zealand.* 2nd Edition. Leipzig: W. Engelmann.

Corner, E. J. H. 1978. *The Freshwater Swamp-Forest of South Johore and Singapore.* Singapore: Botanic Gardens.

Costin, A. B. 1954. *The Ecosystems of the Monaro Region of New South Wales with Special Reference to Soil Erosion.* Sydney: Gov't. Printer.

Dahl, K. 1910. *Alder og vekst hos laks og ørret belyst ved studiet av deres skjael.*

Dansereau, P. 1966. *Studies on the Vegetation of Puerto Rico.* Institute of Caribbean Sciences Special Publication #1. Mayaguez: University of Puerto Rico.

Duvigneaud, P. (ed) 1971. *Productivity of Forest Ecosystems.* Paris: UNESCO.

Dykyjová, D. and J. Květ (eds) (in press) *Pond Littoral Ecosystems. Structure and Functioning.* Ecological Studies #28. Berlin: Springer-Verlag.

Dylis, N. V., V. I. Ermakov and N. I. Pyavchenko (eds) 1976. *Current Status and Perspectives on the Development of Biogeocoenological Investigations.* Petrozavodsk: Karelian Branch of Soviet Acad. of Sci.

Ecological Papers. UNDP/FAO Project. Peshawar: Pakistan Forest Institute.

Ecological Studies. 1970, 1977. Vol. 1, Vol. 22. Berlin, Heidelberg, New York: Springer Verlag.

Ellenberg, H. 1978. *Vegetation Mitteleuropas mit den Alpen.* Ulmer Verlag.

——— (ed) 1973. *Ökosystemforschung.* Berlin, Heidelberg, New York.

——— (ed) 1971. *Integrated Experimental Ecology. Methods and Results of Ecosystem Research in the German Solling Project.* Ecological Studies 2. Berlin, Heidelberg, New York: Springer Verlag.

Ewel, J. S. and J. L. Whitmore. 1973. *Ecological Life Zones of Puerto Rico and the Virgin Islands.* Rio Piedras: Forest Service, USDA.

Faegri, K. 1960. *Coast Plants.* Oslo.

Franz, H. 1950. *Bodenzoologie als Grundlage der Bodenpflege.* Akademieverlag Berlin.

Geiger, R. 1961. *Das Klima der Bodennahen Luftschicht.* 4. Auflg: Braunschweig.

Gill, A. M., R. H. Groves and I. R. Noble (eds) 1980. *Fire and the Australian Biota.* Canberra: Australian Academy of Science.

Gilmanov, T. G. 1978. *Mathematical modeling of Biogeochemical Cycles in Grassland Ecosystems.* Moscow: Moscow State Univ. Press.

Green, A. M. and V. D. Utekhin. 1976. *Biota of the Main Geosystem of the Central Forest-Steppe.* Moscow: Institute of Geography.

Grzimeck, B. 1973. *Tierleben.* Zürich: Kindler Verlag.

Gulisashvili, V. Z., L. B. Machatadze and L. I. Prilipko. 1975. *Vegetation of the Caucasus.* Moscow: Nauka Pub.

Gunin, P. D. and V. D. Dyedkov. 1978. *Ecological Regimes of Desert Biogeocoenoses.* Moscow: Nauka Pub.

Hagen, Y. 1952. *Rovfuglene og viltpleien.* Oslo.

Harrison, M. N. and J. K. Jackson. 1958. *Ecological Classification of the Vegetation of Sudan.* Forests Bull. New Ser. 2.

Hartmann, F. 1952. *Forstökologie.* Wien: Georg Fromme & Co.

Hejný, S. 1960. *Ökologische Characteristick der Wasser—und Sumpfpflanzen in der Slowakischen Tiefebenen (Donau—und Theissgebiet).* Bratislava: Vydavatel'stvo SAV.

Holdridge, L. R. 1942. *Trees of Puerto Rico.* 2 Vols. Rio Piedras: Forest Service, USDA.

Hrbacek, J. and M. Straskraba (eds) 1966, 1973. *Hydrobiological Studies* 1, 2, 3. Prague: Academia.

Huang, T. C. 1972. *Pollen Flora of Taiwan.* Taipei, Taiwan: National Taiwan Univ. Press.

Jeffers, J. N. R. (ed) 1972. *Mathematical Models in Ecology.* Oxford: Blackwell Sci. Pub.

Jeník, J. 1961. *Alpine Vegetation des Riesengebirges, des Glatzer Schneeberges und des Hochgesenkes.* (*Theorie der anemoorographischen Systeme*) Prague: Nakladatelství CSAV.

Jolly, V. H. and J. M. A. Brown. 1975. *New Zealand Lakes.* Auckland: Auckland Univ. Press.

Kani, T. 1971. *Ecological Papers of T. Kani.* Shisakusha.

Karpov, V. G. (ed) 1973. *Structure and Productivity of Spruce Forest of South Taiga.* Leningrad: Nauka Pub.

______. 1969. *Experimental Phytocoenology of Dark-Coniferous Taija.* Leningrad: Nauka Pub.

Kashkarov, D. N. 1944. *Fundamentals of Animal Ecology.* Leningrad.

Kihara, H. 1956. *Land and Crops of Nepal Himalaya.* Kyoto: The Fauna and Flora Research Society.

Kira, T. *et al.* (eds) 1961–76. *Nature and Life in Southeast Asia.* 7 Vols. Kyoto: The Fauna and Flora Res. Soc.

Kovalev, R. V. (ed) 1974. *Structure, Function and Evolution of Baraba Biogeocoenoses.* Vol. 1. Novosibirsk: Nauka Pub.

Kreeb, K. 1977. *Methoden der Pflanzenökologie.* Jena.

______. 1974. *Ökophysiologie der pflanzen.* Jena.

Küchler, A. W. 1964. *Potential Natural Vegetation of the Conterminous United States.* Spec. Publ. 36. New York: Amer. Geographical Soc.

Kühnelt, W. 1970. *Grundriss der Okologie.* 2nd Edition. Jena and Stuttgart: Gustav Fischer.

______. 1950. *Bodenbiologie.* Wien: Herold.

Kuminova, A. V. (ed) 1963. *Vegetation of Steppe and Forest Steppe Zones of Western Siberia.* Novosibirsk: Soviet Acad. of Sci.

Kuschel, G (ed) 1975. *Biogeography and Ecology in New Zealand.* The Hague: Dr W Junk.

Larcher, W. 1972. *Ökologie der Pfanzen.* Stuttgart: Eugen Ulmer.

Larin, I. V. 1969. *Grassland and Pasture Management.* Leningrad: Kolos Press.

Lavrenko, E. M. (ed) 1977. *The Vegetation and Animal World of Mongolia.* Leningrad: Nauka Pub.

Leeper, G. W. 1970. *The Australian Environment.* 4th Edition. CSIRO Melbourne: Melbourne Univ. Press.

Leser, H. 1976. *Landschaftsökologie.* Stuttgart: Ulmer Verlag.

Li, H. L. 1963. *Woody Flora of Taiwan.* Narberth, PA: Livingston Publ. Co.

______, T. S. Liu, T. C. Huang, T. Koyama and C. E. DeVol. 1979. *Flora of Taiwan.* Vol. 1–6. Taipei, Taiwan: Epoch Publ. Co., Ltd.

Liu, T. S. 1962. *Illustration of Native and Introduced Ligneous Plants of Taiwan.* Vol. I & II. Taipei, Taiwan: National Taiwan Univ. Press.

Marty, U. U. (ed) 1974. *Biological Productivity of the Caspian Sea,* Moscow: Nauka Pub.

Meredith, D. (ed) 1955. *The Grasses and Pastures of South Africa.* Johannesburg: Central News Agency.

Microbial Ecology Research Group. 1974. *Ecology of Microorganisms.* Tokyo: Univ. of Tokyo Press.

Mikyška, R. (ed) 1968. *Geobotanische Karte der Tschechoslowakei.* 1. Böhmishe Länder (Böhmen, Mähren und Schlesien). Vegetace CSSR A2. Praha: Academia.

Mitscherlich, E. A. V. 1949. *Bodenkunde* (5th edition). Halle: Max Niemeyer.

Miyake, Y. and T. Koyama 1964. *Recent Researches in the Fields of Hydrosphere, Atmosphere and Nuclear Geochemistry.* Maruzen.

Miyawaki, A. (ed) 1977. *Vegetation of Japan.* Gakken.

Miyawaki, A. and R. Tüxen (ed) 1977. *Vegetation Sciences and Environmental Protection.* Maruzen Co.

Molchanov, A. A. (ed) 1974. *Productivity of the Organic Mass of Forests in the Different Natural Zones.* Moscow: Nauka Pub.

Nechayeva, N. T. (ed) 1970. *Vegetation of the Central Kara-kum and its Productivity.* Ashkhabad: Ylym Pub.

Numata, M. 1953. *Methodology of Ecology.* Kokon-Shoin.

——— (ed) 1965. *Ecological Study and Mountaineering of Mt. Numbur in Eastern Nepal.* Himalayan Comm. of Chiba Univ.

——— (ed) 1970–72. *Research Series on Ecology.* 6 Vols. Tsukiji-Shokan.

——— (ed) 1974. *Dictionary of Ecology.* Tsukiji-Shokan.

——— (ed) 1974. *The Flora and Vegetation of Japan.* Kodansha and Elsevier.

——— (ed) 1976. *Glossary of Ecology.* Tokyo.

——— (ed) 1980. *Ecology of Grasslands and Bamboolands in the World.* JEB Gustav Fisher Verlag.

——— and S. Asano. 1969–70. *Biological Flora of Japan.* 3 Vols. Tsukiji-Shokan.

——— and T. Utida (ed) 1963. *Applied Ecology.* I,II. Kokon-Shoin.

Obeid, M. (ed) 1975. *Aquatic Weeds in the Sudan.* Sudan: National Council for Research and USA: National Acad. of Sci.

Okino, T. (ed) 1976. *Surveying Methods on Eutrophication.* Kodansha.

Olschowy, G. 1977. *Natur-und Umweltschutz in der Bundesrepublik Deutschland.* Hamburg.

Osche, G. 1973. *Ökologie.* Freiburg, Basel, Wien.

Petrusewiez, K. and L. Ryszkowski (eds) 1969/70. *Energy Flow Through Small Mammal Populations.* Warsaw: PWN, Polish Sci. Pub.

Physical-geographical Atlas of the World. 1964. Moscow: Soviet Acad. of Sci.

Reidl, R. 1966. *Biologie der Meereshohlen.* Hamburg and Berlin: Paul Parey.

Remmert, H. 1978. *Ökologie.* Berlin, Heidelberg, New York: Springer Verlag.

Report of the Johglei Investigation Team. 1954. The Equatorial Nile Project. Vols. I–IV. Sudan: Sudan Gov't.

Research Group on Measuring Methodology of Freshwater Biological Production. 1969. Research Methods of Freshwater Biological Production. Kodansha.

Risser, P. G. and K. D. Cornelison. 1979. *Man and the Biosphere.* Norman, OK: Univ. of Oklahoma Press.

Rodin, L. E. (ed) 1972. *Eco-physiological Foundation of Ecosystem Productivity in the Arid Zone.* Leningrad: Nauka Pub.

______ and N. I. Bazilevich. 1965. *Production and Mineral Cycling in Terrestrial Vegetation.* Moscow-Leningrad: Nauka Pub. (Translated by Scripta Technica Ltd., GE Fogg (ed) 1967. London: Oliver and Boyd.

______ and N. N. Smirnov (eds) 1975. *Resources of the Biosphere.* Vol. 1. Leningrad: Nauka Pub.

Ruttner, F. 1962. *Grundriss der Limnologie.* 3rd Edition. Berlin: Walter de Gruyter & Co.

Rychnovská, M. and B. Úlehlová. 1975. *Autokölogische Studie der Tschechoslowakischen Stipa-Arten.* Vegetace ČSSR. A8. Praha: Academia.

Schmitschek, E. 1969. *Grundzüge der Waldhygiene.* Hamburg und Berlin: Paul Parey.

Schnelle, F. 1955. *Pflanzenphänologie.* Leipzig: Akadem. Verlagsgesellschaft.

Shugart, H. H. and R. V. O'Neill (eds) 1979. *Systems Ecology.* Benchmark Papers in Ecology, Vol. 9. Stroudsburg, PA: Dowden, Hutchinson and Ross.

Shultz, V. and A. W. Klement (eds) 1963. *Proceedings of the 1st National Symposium on Radioecology.* New York: Reinhold Publ. Co.

Sochava, V. B. (ed) 1976. *Temporal Studies of the Steppe Geosystem.* Novosibirsk: Nauka Pub.

______ (ed) 1970. *Topology of Steppe Ecosystems.* Leningrad: Nauka.

Soviet Academy of Sciences. 1971. *Biological Productivity and Cycling of Chemical Elements in Vegetation Communities.* Leningrad: Nauka Pub.

Specht, R. L. (ed) 1979,80. *Ecosystems of the World.* Vol. 9 A & B. *Heathlands and Related Shrublands.* Amsterdam: Elsevier Sci. Pub. Co.

______ 1972. *The Vegetation of South Australia.* 2nd Edition. Adelaide: Gov't. Printer.

Special Committee for Environmental Problems, Ecological Society of Japan. (ed) 1975. Environment and Biological Indicators. 2 Vols. Kyoritsu-Shuppan.

Stanyukovich, K. V. 1973. *Mountain Vegetation of the USSR.* Dushanbe: Donish Press.

Steubing, L. 1965. *Pflanzenökologisches Praktikum.* Berlin, Hamburg.

Steubing, L. and C. H. Kunze. 1972. *Pflanzenökologische Experimente zur Umweltverschmutzung.* Biol. Arbeitsbücher Bd. 11.

Suggate, R. P. and M. M. Cresswell (eds) 1975. *Quaternary Studies.* Wellington: Royal Society of New Zealand.

Sullivan, D. and R. Sullivan. 1977. *South African Environment.* Cape Town: Macdonald South Africa.

Tansley, A. G. 1939. *The British Islands and Their Vegetation.* Cambridge: Cambridge Univ. Press.

______ (ed) 1911. *Types of British Vegetation.* Cambridge: Cambridge Univ. Press.

Thorsteinsson, I. 1972. *Grodurvernd* (*Vegetation Protection*). Iceland Environment Union (Landvernd).

Tischler, W. 1976. *Einführung in die Ökologie.* Stuttgart, New York.

______ 1965. *Agrarökologie.* Jena.

Titlyanova, A. A. 1977. *The Biological Cycling of Carbon in Grassland Biogeocoenoses.* Novosibirsk: Nauka [Translated by NR French (ed) (in press) Stroudsburg, PA: Dowden, Hutchinson & Ross.]

Toerien, D. F. 1977. *A Review of Eutrophication and Guidelines for its Control in South Africa.* CSIR SPECIAL REPORT WAT 48.

Tothill, J. D. (ed) 1948. *Agriculture in Sudan.* London: OUP.

Turček, F. J. 1961. *Ökologische Beziehungen der Vögel und Gehölze.* Bratislava: Vydavatel'stvo SAV.

Van Dyne, G. M. (ed) 1969. *The Ecosystem Concept in Natural Resource Management.* New York: Academic Press.

Vavilov, N. I. 1957. *Agroecological survey of Principle Field Crops.* Moscow-Leningrad: USSR Acad. of Sci. Pub.

Walter, H. 1977. *Die Ökologischen Systeme der Kontinente.* Stuttgart, Jena.

——— 1964,1968. *Die Vegetation der Erde in Öko-physiologischer Betrachtung.* Bds. I, II. Stuttgart, Jena.

——— and H. Lieth. 1960–66. *Klimadiagramm-Weltatlas.* Jena: VEB Gustav Fischer Verlag.

Watt, K. E. F. (ed) 1966. *Systems Analysis in Ecology.* New York: Academic Press.

Wielgolaski, F. E. (ed) 1975. *Fennoscandian Tundra Ecosystems.* Part I: Plants and Microorganisms. Part II: Animals and Systems Analyses.

Wilmanns, O. 1973. *Ökologische Pflanzensoziologie.* Heidelberg: Verlag Quelle und Meyer.

Winkler, S. 1972. *Einführung in die Pflanzenökologie.* Stuttgart: Fischer Verlag.

Yoshii, Y. 1955. *Experimental Methods in Plant Ecology.* Kenbunkan.

Zlotin, R. I. and K. S. Khodashova. 1974. *The Role of Animals in Biological Cycling of Forest-Steppe Ecosystems.* Moscow: Nauka. [Translated by NR French (ed) (in press) Stroudsburg, PA: Dowden, Hutchinson & Ross.]

SOURCE: Identified by authors in foregoing essays

APPENDIX III

Bibliographic and Abstracting Services

Agency for International Development Research and Development Abstracts
Applied Science and Technology Index
Aquatic Sciences and Fisheries Abstracts
Australian Science Index
Bangladesh Agricultural Sciences Abstracts
Berichte Biochemie und Biologie
Bibliographic Index
Bibliographie der Pflanzenschutzliteratur
Bibliography of Agriculture
Biological Abstracts
Biological and Agricultural Index
Biology Digest
Bioresearch Index
Canadian Periodical Index
Commercial Fisheries Abstracts
Current Bibliography for Aquatic Sciences and Fisheries
Current Contents
Dissertation Abstracts
Deep Sea Research and Oceanographic Abstracts
Ecological Abstracts
Ecology Abstracts
Environmental Abstracts
Environmental Periodicals Bibliography
Environmental Quality Abstracts
Excerpta Botanica
Forestry Abstracts
Fortschritte der Botanik (W. Germany)
Fortschritte der Zoologie (W. Germany)
Indice Agricole de America Latina y el Caribe
Index to Scientific Reviews
Indian Science Abstracts
International Abstracts of Biological Sciences
Microbiological Abstracts
The Polish Ecological Bibliography (Poland)

The Polish Phytosociological Bibliography (Poland)
Science Citation Index
Science Research Abstracts
Water Research Centre Information
Water Resources Abstracts
World Fisheries Abstracts
Zoological Record

SOURCE: *Ulrich's International Periodicals Directory,* 18th Edition, 1979–80

APPENDIX IV

Major Professional Ecological Organizations

ALA Schweizerische Gesellschaft für Vogelkunde und Vogelschutz—Switzerland
American Society of Limnology and Oceanography—U.S.
Asociación Costarricense para la Conservación de la Naturaleza (ASCONA)— Costa Rica
Association of Greek Ecologists—Greece
Associazione Italiana di Oceanologia e di Limnologia (AIOL)—Italy
Bodenkundliche Gesellschaft der Schweiz—Switzerland
Botanical Society of Korea—Korea
Colegio de Biologos de Costa Rica—Costa Rica
Ecological Circle—Netherlands
Ecological Society of America—U.S.
Ecological Society of Korea—Korea
Entomological Society of Southern Africa—South Africa
Geological Society of South Africa—South Africa
Gesellschaft für Oekologie—Switzerland
Gesellschaft für Ökologie—W. Germany
Glaciological Society—Iceland
Gruppe di Ecologia della Società Botanic Italiana—Italy
Gruppe Ökologie—W. Germany
Gruppo di Ecologia di base G. Gadio—Italy
Hungarian Biological Society (Sections: Botany, Zoology, Ecology)—Hungary
Hungarian Hydrobiological Society—Hungary
Icelandic Natural Sciences Society—Iceland
Icelandic Science Society (Societas Scientiarum Islandics)—Iceland
Limnological Society of Korea—Korea
Limnological Society of South Africa—S. Africa
Microbiological Society of Korea—Korea
The Royal Society of Arts and Sciences—Mauritius
Schweizerische Arbeitsgemeinschaft für Umweltforschung—Switzerland
Schweizerische Botanische Gesellschaft—Switzerland
Schweizerische Entomologische Gesellschaft—Switzerland
Schweizerische Gesellschaft für Umweltschutz—Switzerland

Schweizerische Hydrologische Gesellschaft—Switzerland
Schweizerische Naturschutzbund—Switzerland
Sociedad Botánica de México (SBM)—Mexico
Sociedad Mexicana de Entomologia (SME)—Mexico
Sociedad Mexicana de Historia Natural (SMHN)—Mexico
Società Italiana di Biogeografia—Italy
Società Italiana di Ecologia (SITE)—Italy
The Société de Technologie, Agricole et Sucriére de Maurice—Mauritius
Société Suisse de Zoologie—Switzerland
Special Committee for the Environment of the Geotechnical Chamber—Greece
Special Committee for the Environment of the Technical Chamber—Greece
Swedish Phytogeographical Society—Sweden
Zoological Society of Korea—Korea

SOURCE: foregoing essays

APPENDIX V

Major Ecological Research Organizations

Agricultural Research Institute—Iceland
Argonne National Laboratory—U.S.
Biölogical Institute at Tihany—Hungary
Brookhaven National Laboratory—U.S.
Center for Natural Resource Management and Environmental Studies of the Bogor Agricultural University—Indonesia
College of Agriculture, National Chung-Hsiung University—Taiwan
College of Agriculture, National Taiwan University—Taiwan
Delta Institute for Hydrobiological Research, Yerseke—Netherlands
Department of Biology, Fu-Jen University—Taiwan
Department of Biology, National Taiwan Normal University—Taiwan
Department of Biology, Tunghai University—Taiwan
Department of Botany, National Chung-Hsiung University—Taiwan
Department of Botany, National Taiwan University—Taiwan
Department of Ecological Research at Porto d'Ischia (Naples)—Italy
Department of Zoology, National Taiwan University—Taiwan
Dirección de Estudios del Territorio Nacional (DETENAL)—Mexico
Facultad de Ciencias, Universidad Nacional Autónoma de México (UNAM)—Mexico
Fondation Universitaire Luxembourgeosie in Arlon—Belgium
Foundation for the Dunes—Netherlands
The Institute for Ecological Research, Arnhem (IOO)—Netherlands
Institute for Fisheries Research (RIVO)—Netherlands
Institute of Biology—Iceland
Institute of Botany, Academia Sinica—Taiwan
Institute of Ecology of the Padjadjaran University—Indonesia
Institute of Medical Research, Jakarta—Indonesia
Institute of Oceanograph, National Taiwan University—Taiwan
Institute of Zoology, Academia Sinica—Taiwan
Inventario Nacional Forestal (National Forest Inventory)—Mexico
Limnological Institute, Nieuwersluis—Netherlands
Los Alamos Scientific Laboratory—U.S.

Ministry for Agriculture and Fishery—Netherlands
Ministry of Public Works—Netherlands
National Biological Institute of the Indonesian Institute of Sciences—Indonesia
National Institute of Oceanology of the Indonesian Institute of Sciences—Indonesia
Natural Science Research Council (NFR)—Sweden
Netherlands Institute for Sea Research, Texel (NIOZ)—Netherlands
Netherlands Organization for Pure Scientific Research (ZWO)—Netherlands
Oak Ridge National Laboratory—U.S.
Organization for Applied Research (TNO)—Netherlands
Pacific Northwest Laboratory—U.S.
Research Council for Forestry and Agriculture—Sweden
Research Institute for Nature Management, Arnhem (RIN)—Netherlands
Research Institute of Electric Utilities (KEMA)—Netherlands
Research Istitute Nedri-Ás, Hveragerdi—Iceland
Sikfokut Project—Hungary
State Institute for the IJssellake Polders (RIJP)—Netherlands
Study and Information Center for Environmental Research—Netherlands
Surtsey Research Society—Iceland
Swedish Nature Conservancy Board (SNV)—Sweden
Taiwan Forestry Research Institute—Taiwan
Taiwan Sugar Cane Research Institute—Taiwan
Woods Hole Oceanographic Institute—U.S.

SOURCE: foregoing essays

Geographic and Thematic Index

About the Contributors

Egil Baardseth is Professor in the Institute of Marine Biology of the University of Bergen, 5065 Blomsterdalen, Bergen, Norway. From the University of Oslo he received the degrees of cand. real. and Ph.D. He was algologist with the NTNF from 1950 to 1970, at which time he assumed his present position. Among his major publications: A square-scanning, two-stage sampling method of estimating seaweed quantitites (1970); the marine algae of Tristan da Cuhna (1941); and synopsis of biological data on knobbed wrack, *Ascophyllum nodosum* (1970).

Kornelius Bakker is Professor in Animal Ecology, Department of Ecology, Zoological Laboratory, University of Leiden, Kaiserstraat 63, Leiden, The Netherlands. From the University of Leiden, he received the cadidaats examen in 1954, the doctoraal examen in 1957, and the doctor's degree in 1961. He has been a Reader in Animal Ecology at the University of Leiden since 1963. Dr. Bakker is a member of the Nederlandse Dierkundige Vereniging, British Ecological Society, and American Society of Naturalists. His major research papers include the following: 1961. *Arch. Neerl. Zool.* 14:200–281 (competition in *Drosophila* larvae); 1964. *Z. Ang. Ent.* 53:187–208 (controversies about population theories); 1969. *Neth. J. Zool.* 19:541–595 (growth selection in *Drosophila* larvae); 1972 (with others). *Oecologia* 10:29–57 (models of hymenopteran parasite on *Drosophila* larvae); and 1978 (with others). *Neth. J. Zool.* 28:213–233 (hymenoptera parasite behavior relative to *Drosophila* host). Dr. Bakker served as Secretary of the Organizing Committee of the Advanced Study Institute, "Dynamics of numbers in populations" in Oosterbeek, Netherlands, 1970.

János Balogh is University Professor and Chief of the Department of Systematic Zoology and Ecology, Eötvös Lorand University, H-1088 Budapest, Puskin u.3, Hungary. He has been at Eötvös Lorand University since 1936, is a member of the Hungarian Academy of Sciences and President of the Biological Department of the Academy. Since 1963 he has been a leader or participant in fifteen soil zoological expeditions in such tropical-subtropical regions as South America, Papua New Guinea, New Caledonia, and Hawaii. He is a recipient of the Kossuth Prize, a Hungarian distinction for merit in scientific activities. Among his major publications: *Gründzuge der Zoozönologie* (1953. Budapest); *Lebensgemeinschaften der Landtiere* (1958. Berlin-Budapest), and many papers on the ecology, cenology, and taxonomy of Oribatid mites and spiders.

Abdur Rahman Beg is Forest Botanist, Pakistan Forest Institute, Peshawar, Pakistan. He holds the B.S. Honors in Botany (1958) and M.S. Honors in Botany (1959); in 1964 he received the Ph.D. in Plant Ecology from the University of Montpellier. He was Lecturer in Botany, Islamia College, Peshawar University (1959–1960), Plant Taxonomist (1960–1974), and since 1974 Forest Botanist at the Pakistan Forest Institute. He is the author of a number of publications on the vegetation, notably forests, of Pakistan.

Mohamed El Mahdi Beshir is lecturer, Department of Biological Sciences, University of Gezira, P.O. Box 20, Wad Medani, Sudan. He received the B.S. in 1964 from the University of Khartoum, the M.S. in 1968 from the University of Wales, and the Ph.D. in 1975 from the University of Western Ontario. He served as Research Officer, Agricultural Research Division, Ministry of Agriculture, Sudan 1964–1966; Botanist, Agricultural Research Corporation, Sudan 1968–1971 and 1975–1977; Teaching Assistant at the University of Western Ontario 1971–1975; and Lecturer at the University of Khartoum 1975–1977. He has been a member of INTECOL since 1970. His publications include some fifteen papers dealing with distribution, management, and control of weeds, aquatic habitats in Sudan, and gravity flow irrigation impact on spread of aquatic plants.

Philippe F. Bourdeau is Head of the Environmental Research Programme, Commission of the European Communities, Directorate General Research, Science, and Education, 200 rue de La Loi, 1049 Brussels, Belgium. He is also Professor, Universite Libre de Bruxelles. He received the degree of Ingenieur agronome from Gemblous Belgique in 1949 and the M.S. (1951) and Ph.D. (1954) in ecology from Duke University. Dr. Bourdeau's past experience includes teaching at North Carolina State College (1954–1956) and Yale University (1956–1962), and research in biology at Euratom Joint Research Centre, Ispra, Italy (1962–1971). He is a member of the Ecological Society of America and Biometrics Society, among others, and has published about fifty papers on ecophysiology, radioecology, and pollution ecology.

Torleiv Brattegard is Assistant Professor (försteamanuensis) in the Institute of Marine Biology, University of Bergen, N-5065 Blomsterdalen, Norway. From the University of Bergen, he received the degree of Cand. real. in 1964. At the Institute of Marine Biology, he was Scientific Assistant from October 1964 to November 1965 and has been in his present position since that time. He was Nordic Fellow in Miami, Florida, January–June 1968. He is a member of the Norwegian Oceanographers Association, serving as its Secretary 1975–1977. Since 1969, he has published a series of papers on systematics, ecology, and distribution of Mysidacea (Crustacea), mostly of the Caribbean Sea and adjacent areas.

Robert L. Burgess is Program Manager, Environmental Sciences Division, Oak Ridge National Laboratory, Oak Ridge, Tennessee 37830. He received the B.S. from the University of Wisconsin-Milwaukee in 1957 and the M.S. in 1959 and Ph.D. in Botany in 1961 from the University of Wisconsin-Madison. Dr. Burgess taught at Arizona State University 1960–1963 and North Dakota State University 1963–1971, with the 1965–1966 year spent as Visiting Professor, Pahlavi University, Shiraz, Iran, before joining the Oak Ridge Laboratory. He is a member of the Ecological Society of America (serving on the Board of Editors since 1971), British Ecological Society, International Association for Ecology, International Society for Tropical Ecology, and Tennessee Chapter, The Nature Conservancy (serving on the Board of Directors since 1975). He was Deputy Director, Eastern Deciduous Forest Biome of the IBP, President of the North Dakota Natural Science Society 1967–69, and President of the North Dakota Academy of Science 1970–71. Since 1975 he has served as Professor of Ecology at the University of Tennessee. He was noted as the North Dakota Conservationist of the Year by the Wildlife Federation in 1969 and the 1970 North Dakota Conservationist of the Year by Safari Club International. He is the author of more than sixty publications dealing with such diverse topics as characteristics and utilization of desert plants, relations of forest overstory and environment, plant succession, and the IBP deciduous forest project.

Chang-Hung Chou is Research Fellow and Professor of Ecology, Institute of Botany, Academia Sinica, Nankang, Taipei, Taiwan 115. He received the B.S. (1965) and M.S. (1968) from the National Taiwan University, the M.S. (1970) and Ph.D. (1971) from the University of California-Santa Barbara. He assumed his present position in 1976. Dr. Chou is a member of the Ecological Society of America, Sigma Xi, Botanical Society of the Republic of China (Taiwan), Biological Society of China (Taipei), Biochemistry Society of China, and Society of Environmental Protection of the Republic of China, Taipei. Among his major publications are: Allelopathic mechanism of *Arctostaphylos glandulosa* var *zacaenis* (1972. *Amer. Midl. Nat.* 88:324–347); Phytotoxins: an ecological phase of phytochemistry (1972. In: *Phytochemical Ecology*, J. B. Harbourne (ed), pp. 201–206); Phytotoxic substances in 12 subtropical grasses (1975. *J. Chem. Ecol.* 1:183–193); Autointoxication mechanism of *Oryza sativa* I. (1976. *J. Chem. Ecol.* 2:353–367); Identification and phytotoxic activity of compounds produced during decomposition of corn and rye residues in soil (1976. *J. Chem. Ecol.* 2:369–387).

Kuan-hon Chow is Lecturer, Department of Botany, National University of Singapore, Singapore 10, Republic of Singapore. He holds the B.S. from National Taiwan University (1963), M.S. from the University of Hawaii (1968), and Ph.D. from Cornell University (1971). He has been in his present position since 1971. Dr. Chow is a member of the American Society of Agronomy, Crop Scientific Society of America, and the Tropical Grassland Society of Australia. He has published some fifteen major papers ranging from studies on hybridization, flowering behavior, and seed development to esterase isozyme patterns and solar energy utilization in herbaceous legumes, primarily *Desmodium.*

E. Jennifer Christy is a Ph.D. candidate in Plant Ecology, Department of Botany, Washington State University, Pullman, Washington 99164. She received the B.A. in 1972 from the University of New Hampshire and the M.S. in 1976 from the University of Georgia. She served as a Congressional Intern as a staff member of the Fisheries and Wildlife Conservation and the Environment Subcommittee and later of the Environment and Atmospheric Subcommittee on Science and Technology of the U.S. House of Representatives 1976–1977, and with the Man and the Biosphere program at the National Park Service 1977–1978. She is a member of the American Institute of Biological Sciences, Ecological Society of America, and Societies Internationalis de Plantarum Demographia. Her research has focused on vegetation of swamps receiving reactor effluents (1974. *Oikos* 25:7–13), turkey oak ecology (1977. *Amer. Midl. Nat.* 98:489–491), and marsh vegetation under different temperature regimes.

Eilif Dahl is Professor in the Botanical Institute, Agricultural University of Norway, N-1432, Ås-NLH, Norway. From the University of Oslo, he received the degrees of Cand. real. (1942) and Ph.D. (1957). He was Research Assistant in Oslo (1946–1951), studied in England (1952) and the United States (1953), and served as Research Associate (1954–1959), Associate Professor (1959–1965), and Professor (1965–) at the Agricultural University of Norway. He was Chairman of Norway's IBP/CT 1967–1974. Major publications include: Rondane mountain vegetation in South Norway and its relation to the environment (1957); Studies in the macrolichen flora of Southwest Greenland (1950); and a series of papers relating to historical and ecological biogeography, plant sociology, and environmental problems.

Gerrit de Graaff is Assistant Director, National Parks Board of Trustee, P.O. Box 787, Pretoria 0001, Republic of South Africa. He received the B.S. (1955), B. S. (hons.)(1956), M.S. (1959) from the University of Witwatersrand and the D.Sc. (1965) from the University of Pretoria. In addition to his present position, he serves as Associate Professor, University of Pretoria. He is a board member of the Transvaal Museum and the Zoological Society of Southern Africa, a past president of the South African Biological Society, and is a member of the South African National Council for Environmental Sciences and the South African Academy of Science and Arts. He is the author of some thirty research papers and an equivalent number of popular articles.

Willem H. van Dobben is Professor of Botanical Ecology, Agricultural University, Wageningen, De Dreyen 11, Wageningen, Netherlands. He received the Dr. Biology from the University of Utrecht in 1935. From 1932 to 1939 he conducted studies on bird migration in Texel; from 1938 to 1967, he served at what is now known as the Center for Agrobiological Research in Wageningen; from 1967 to 1972 he was Director of the Institute of Ecological Research, Arnhem; and from 1972 to the present, has served as Head of the Department of Botanical Ecology, Agricultural University, University of Wageningen. Dr. van Dobben was President of the Ecological Circle 1969–1975, and is a member of the Netherlands Ornithological Union and Royal Netherlands Society of Agricultural Science. Among his major papers are the following: Ueber den Kiefermechanismus der Knochenfische (1935. thesis); Bird Migration in the Netherlands (1953. *Ibis* 95); The food of the cormorant in the Netherlands (1952. *Ardea* 40); Management of cereals for improved yield and quality (1966.) In: *The Growth of Cereals and Grasses,* Milthorpe and Ivins, eds.); 1960–68, several short papers on plant and crop ecology in *Jaarboek IBS,* Wageningen.

Andrew G. Duff is Research Officer, School of Humanities and Social Sciences, Bath University, Claverton Down, Bath BA2 7AY, England. He received the B.S. in Biological Sciences from the University of East Anglia in 1974 and in 1975 the M.S. in Structure and Organization of Science and Technology from the University of Manchester. During 1975–1977, Mr. Duff pursued work for the Ph.D. in the history of ecology at the University of Manchester. His M.S. dissertation was, "Organismic and mechanistic styles of thought in ecology." With Philip Lowe, he has written a book on the history of ecology to be published shortly by Croom Helm.

James K. Egunjobi is in the Department of Agricultural Biology, University of Ibadan, Nigeria. He received the B.S. Hons. from the University of London and the Ph.D. from the University of Wellington, New Zealand. He served as Senior Research Officer (Ecology), Ministry of Agriculture-Western State, Nigeria 1968–1970 and as Senior Lecturer in Ecology, Department of Agricultural Biology, University of Ibaden, Nigeria from 1974–1978. He spent 1978–1980 with the Regional Office for Africa, United Nations Environment Program in Nairobi, subsequent to which he returned to his previous position. He is a member of the Nigerian Science Association and served as National Secretary for the Man and the Biosphere Program (MAB) and as Coordinator of the Grassland Research Project in MAB. His major research papers include: Ecosystem studies in a stand of *Ulex europaens* L. (ii) The cycling of chemical elements in the ecosystem. (1971. *J. Ecol.* 59:669–678); and Dry matter, nitrogen and mineral element distribution in an unburnt savanna during the year. (1974. *Oecol. Plantarum* 9:1–10). He was the recipient of a Rockefeller Fellowship for a course in systems analysis at Colorado State University.

William R. Emanuel is Research Associate, Environmental Sciences Division, Oak Ridge National Laboratory, Oak Ridge, Tennessee 37830. He received three degrees in Electrical Engineering from Oklahoma State University, the B.S. in 1971, M.S. in 1973, and Ph.D. in 1975. He has been at the Oak Ridge Laboratory since 1975. He is a member of the Ecological Society of America, American Association for the Advancement of Science, Sigma Xi, and Phi Kappa Phi. He has published a dozen papers largely on ecosystem analysis and modelling, among them: 1975. *Int. J. Systems Sci.* 6:965–976; 1976. *Int. J. Control* 24:807–820; and 1978. *Ecol. Modelling* 4:313–326.

Hans M. van Emden is Adj. Secretary, Biological Council, Royal Dutch Academy of Arts and Sciences, Kloveniersburgwal 29, Amsterdam, The Netherlands. His professional education was at the University of Amsterdam, 1967–1973 (drs.)

Luis Alberto Fournier-Origgi is Professor of Ecology and Dendrology in the School of Biology, University of Costa Rica, Costa Rica. His educational background includes: Ingeniero Agronomo from the University of Costa Rica in 1958, M.S. in Agronomy from the Interamerican Institute of Agricultural Sciences, Turrialba, Costa Rica in 1961, and Ph.D. in Botany from the University of California in 1964. At the University of Costa Rica he has served as Teaching Assistant (1959–1961), Assistant Professor (1964–1967), and since 1967 as Professor; he has been Visiting Professor at the Interamerican Institute of Agricultural Sciences in Turrialba, Costa Rica in 1968, 1969, 1972, and 1975. He is a member of the Colegio de Ingenieros Agronomos de Costa Rica, Colegio de Biologos de Costa Rica (and was its Vice-President 1968–1970), and Asociacion Latinoamericana de Fitotecnia. He was elected to the Board of Directors of Consejo Nacional de Investigaciones Cientificas y Technologicas de Costa Rica in 1976 and serves as Advisor in Conservation of Natural Resources to the Ministry of Agriculture, Costa Rica. He has published more than forty papers in botany, forest ecology, and nature conservation among which he regards the most significant to be: *Fundamentos de Ecologia Vegetal* (1970. University of Costa Rica, 174 pp.); Observaciones fenologicas en el bosque humedo de San Pedro de Montes de Oca Costa Rica (1976. *Turrialba* 26:54–59); La sucesion ecologica comoun metodo eficaz en la recuperacion del bosque (1977. *Agron. Costa.* 1:23–29).

Norman R. French is Professor of Zoology and Senior Research Ecologist, Natural Resource Ecology Laboratory, Colorado State University, Fort Collins, Colorado 80523. He received the B.A. from the University of Illinois (1949), the M.S. from the University of Colorado (1951), and the Ph.D. from the University of Utah (1954). From 1955 to 1959, he was Chief, Ecology Section, AEC Idaho Reactor Testing Station, and from 1959 to 1969 Research Ecologist, University of California-Los Angeles Laboratory of Nuclear Medicine and Radiation Biology. Dr. French is a member of the Ecological Society of America, Cooper Ornithological Society (currently Assistant Business Manager), and American Society of Mammalogists. He is a Fellow of the American Association for the Advancement of Science and Trustee, Bioscience Information Service (Biological Abstracts). He held a National Academy of Sciences Exchange Fellowship to the U.S.S.R. in 1977. Among his publications are: Small mammal energetics in grassland ecosystems (*Ecol. Monogr.* 46:201–220); Patterns of demography in small mammal populations. In: *Small Mammals, Their Productivity and Population Dynamics;* and Phenology studies and modelling in grasslands. In: *Phenology and Seasonality Modelling* (H. Lieth, ed).

Sturla Fridriksson is Head of the Agronomy Department, Agricultural Research Institute, Keldnaholt, Reykjavík, Iceland. His education includes: Cand. Phil., University of Iceland, 1942; B.A. (1944) and M.S. (1946) from Cornell University; and Ph.D. (1961) from the University of Saskatchewan, Canada. Major teaching and research positions include: Plant Breeder, University Research Institute, Reykjavík (1951–1965); Agronomist, Agricultural Research Institute, Reykjavík (1965–); Ecologist, Surtsey Research Society (1965–); Executive Director, the Genetical Committee, University of Iceland (1965–). He has held his present position since 1965. Dr. Fridriksson was President of the Society Scientiarum Islandica from 1965 to 1967 and has served as President of the Asa Wright Scientific Award Fund of Iceland since 1968. Major publications include: *Lif og land* (1975. Butterworths, London); *Ecology of Iceland* (1973. Vardi, Reykjavík); Grass and grass utilization in Iceland

1972. *Ecology* 53:785–796); and The effect of sea ice on flora, fauna, and agriculture (1969. *Jökull* 19:147–157).

Pantazis Alexandros Gerakis is Professor of Ecology, Laboratory of Ecology, School of Agriculture and Forestry, University of Thessaloniki, Thessaloniki, Greece. He received the B.S. in Agricultural Science from the University of Thessaloniki in 1957 and the Ph.D. in Horticulture from Michigan State University in 1968. He was Research Agronomist, UN Special Fund, Kordofan Project, Sudan (1962–1965), Lecturer in Agricultural Ecology (1969–1976), and Professor of Ecology (since 1976) at the University of Thessaloniki. He spent 1972–1973 at the Department of Agronomy and Range Science, University of California-Davis as an Associate Research Ecologist working with R. S. Loomis and W. A. Williams. Dr. Gerakis is a member of the American Society of Agronomy, Ecological Society of America, Soil Conservation Society of America, British Ecological Society, and Hellenic Society on Environmental Pollution. Among his major publications are: Rehabilitation of the Pediplain ("gardud") soils of the Central Sudan (with C. Z. Tsangarakis) (1968. *Agron. J.* 60:396–400); Adaptation of globe artichoke (*Cynara scolymus* L) to annual culture (1968. Ph.D. thesis, Michigan State University); Productivity of agricultural ecosystems (with R. S. Loomis) (1975. In: *Photosynthesis and Productivity in Different Environments,* J. P. Cooper (ed) IBP, Cambridge: Cambridge University Press, pp. 145–172); *Lectures in Ecology* (in Greek) (1975. University of Thessaloniki).

Jon Ghiselin is an independent resource management consultant residing at 1252 Woodcrest Drive, Kenhorst, Pennsylvania 19607. He received the B.S. (1955) and M.S. (1956) from the University of Utah and the Ph.D. in 1967 from the University of Wisconsin-Madison. In addition to various faculty appointments from 1962 to 1972, he was Research Biologist, US/IBP Desert Biome, Tunisia (1972); Project Ecologist (Wildlife Management), Dames and Moore, Cincinnati, Ohio 1973; and from 1974–1979 he was Senior Terrestrial Ecologist with Gilbert/Commonwealth, Reading, Pennsylvania. He is a member of the Ecological Society of America (Secretary, Applied Ecology Section, 1975–77), American Ornithologists' Union, American Society of Mammalogists, Animal Behavior Society, Cooper Ornithological Society, Sigma Xi, Wildlife Society, American Association for the Advancement of Science, and American Institute of Biological Sciences. In addition to numerous consulting reports, Dr. Ghiselin has published some twenty papers, largely on avian and mammalian ecology, and a number of reviews.

Andreas Gigon is on the staff of the Geobotanisches Institut of the Swiss Federal Institute of Technology, Stiftung Rübel, Zürichbergstrasse 38, CH-8044, Zürich, Switzerland. He is also Lecturer at the Swiss Federal Institute of Technology (ETH), Zurich and the University of Zurich. He received the Dipl. Natw. (1966) and Dr. sc. nat. (1971) from the Swiss Federal Institute of Technology. Dr. Gigon was Research Assistant at the Swiss Federal Institute of Technology (1966–1971) and since 1972 a Lecturer; in 1971–1972, he was Postdoctoral Fellow and lecturer at Stanford University. He is a member of the Swiss Botanical Society (currently its Secretary), INTECOL, Gesellschaft für Oekologie (Germany), and Schweizerische Arbeitsgemeinschaft für Umweltforschung. He received the Silver Medal of the Swiss

Federal Institute of Technology for an outstanding Ph.D. thesis. Major publications include: Stickstoff- und Wasserversorgung von Trespen-Halbtrockenrasen (1968); Vergleich alpiner Rasen auf Silikat- und auf Karbonatboden (1971, Ph.D. thesis); and Ecophysiology and convergence of Mediterranean shrub-types from California and Chile (in preparation).

Vernon C. Gilbert is Project Director, International Science and Technology Institute, Inc., 2033 M Street, Washington, D.C., 20036. He received the B.A. in Botany in 1950 and the M.S. in Plant Ecology in 1954 from the University of Tennessee. From 1965 to 1970, he taught at the College of African Wildlife Management in Tanzania. He was Chief, Environmental Education for the National Park Service 1971–1972 and served at UNESCO, Paris, as consultant on MAB 1973–1975 and as the U.S. MAB Coordinator 1975–1976; from 1978–1980 he was Associate Chief Scientist in the Natural History Division, Nation Park Services. Mr. Gilbert participated in preparation of UNESCO MAB reports and planning documents and published "Plants of Mount Kilimanjaro" for use by students at the College of African Wildlife Management. He serves as Co-chairman of MAB Project 8 in the United States, the National Park Service and Forest Service being co-lead agencies in the project.

Jaroslav Hrbáček is Head of the Hydrobiological Laboratory, Institute of Landscape Ecology, Czechoslovak Academy of Sciences, Vltavska 17, CS 151 05, Prague 5, Czechoslovakia. He received the degrees of RND and CSc. from Charles University in Prague respectively in 1948 and 1968. He served as Associate Professor (Docent) from 1954 to 1968 on the faculty of Natural Sciences of Charles University and has held his present position since that time. Professor Hrbácek has served as Chairman of the Czechoslovak Limnological Society, secretary of the Czechslovak National Committee for IBP, and Secretary of the Czechoslovak National Committee for Intergovernmental Program of UNESCO(MAB). He is the recipient of the Mendel Silver Medal of the Czechoslovak Academy of Science for Achievement in Biology. Dr. Hrbácek is the author of numerous papers dealing with the ecology of zooplankton relative to species composition, competition, and predation.

Jan Jeník is Research Professor, Botanical Institute, Czechoslovak Academy of Science, 379 82 Trebon, Czechoslovakia. He received the Ing. degree in 1952 from Prague Technical University, and the Ph.D. (1956) and Doc. (1961) from Charles University in Prague. At Charles University, he was successively Assistant Professor (1955–61), Associate Professor (1961–1964, and 1967–1971); he served as Senior Lecturer in the University of Ghana, 1964–1967 and assumed his present position in 1971. Dr. Jenik's major works include *Alpine Vegetation of the High Sudeten* (1961) (in Czechoslovakian), *Tropical Forest and Its Environment* (1974, jointly with K. A. Longman), and *Pictorial Encyclopaedia of Forests* (1979).

Tibor Jermy is Director Emeritus of the Research Institute for Plant Protection, H-1525, Budapest, Pf. 102, Hungary. He received a teacher's certificate in 1940 and the Ph.D. in 1942 from Pazmany Peter University of Sciences, Budapest. He was research chemist in the Research Institute for Viticulture, Budapest (1940–1948); at the Research Institute for Plant Protection, he was research entomologist from 1948 to

1969 and Director from 1969 to 1977. He is a member of the Hungarian Academy of Sciences (elected 1976), member of the Governing Board of the Hungarian Entomological Society, and Honorary President of the Hungarian Society for Plant Protection. He received a Ford Foundation Fellowship in 1966–1967, has been a Visiting Scientist at the Agricultural University of Wageningen, The Netherlands, and Visiting Expert at the U.S. Department of Agriculture's Agricultural Research Laboratory in Yakima, Washington. Among his major publications are: *The Colorado Potato Beetle* (1955. Budapest:Mezogazdasagi Kiado); *Biological Control of Plant Pests* (1967. Budapest: Mezogazdasagi Kiado); editor of *The Host Plant in Relation to Insect Behavior and Reproduction* (1976. Budapest: Hungarian Academy of Sciences and New York: Plenum Publishing Co.); Feeding inhibitors and food preference in chewing phytophagous insects (1966. *Ent. Exp. Appl. Amsterdam* 9:1–12).

W. Carter Johnson is Assistant Professor of Botany, Department of Biology, Virginia Polytechnic Institute and State University, Blacksburg, Virginia 24061. He received the B.S. from Augustana College (1968) and the Ph.D. from North Dakota State University (1971). He was Research Associate from 1971–1975 and Research Staff Member from 1975 to 1980 in the Environmental Sciences Division of the Oak Ridge National Laboratory. Dr. Johnson is a member of the Ecological Society of America. He was U.S.-U.S.S.R. Academies of Science Exchange Scientist to the Soviet Union (March-August 1975) and a member of the American delegation to the Soviet Union concerning UNESCO Biosphere Reserves, May 5–18, 1976. Among his major publications are: Forest overstory vegetation and environment on the Missouri River flood plain in North Dakota (1976. *Ecol. Monogr.*); An analysis of forest dynamics in the northern Georgia Piedmont (with D. M. Sharpe) (1976. *For. Sci.*)

Zdzisław Kajak is Assistant Professor and Head of Laboratory, Institute of Ecology, 05-150 Lomianki, Dziekanow Lesny k., Warsaw, Poland. He received the degrees of doctor (1958) and habilis doctor docent (1968) from the University of Warsaw. He has been Head of the Department of Hydrobiology, Institute of Ecology (1960–1973), Coordinator of Polish PF IBP (1966–1972), and Coordinator of Polish Problem on Productivity and Purity of Water (1970–1975); in addition, he has taught part-time at the University of Warsaw and Silesian University. Dr. Kajak is a member of the Societas Internationalis Limnologiae, Polish Ecological Committee (Vice-President of the Hydrobiological Section for four years), Polish Hydrobiological Society (Scientific Secretary for six years, currently Vice-President). He has been recognized with five awards from the Polish Academy of Sciences and two from the Polish Hydrobiological Society. Major publications include: Benthos of standing waters (chapter in IBP handbook); Experimentally increased fish stock in the pond type lake Warniak: The realtions between fish and other biocenotic components (1973. *Ekol. Pol.* 31:632–643); Influence of the silver carp on the plankton and benthos of the eutrophic lake (1975. *Pol. Arch. Hydrobiol.* 22:301–310); (ed) *Production Problems of Freshwaters* (1972. Warsaw-Krakow: A. Hillbricht-Ilkowska); The achievements of Polish ecology 1945–70: The state, needs, and perspectives (1971. *Sci. Rev.*, 71–89).

Kuswata Kartawinata is Senior Research Officer, Herbarium Bogoriense, National Biological Institute, Jalan Raya Juanda 22–24, Bogor, Indonesia. He received the

B.S. in 1959 from the University of Bogor, the B.S. (honors) in 1964 from the University of Singapore, and the Ph.D. in 1971 from the University of Hawaii. He was Research Assistant in Botany, Herbarium Borgoriense 1959–1962, Teaching Assistant, University of Hawaii 1965–1971, Scientist and Program Manager in Tropical Forest Biology, SEAMEO Regional Center for Tropical Biology (BIOTROP) 1972–1975, and has been in his present position since 1974. He is a member of the Ecological Society of America, British Ecological Society, Sigma Xi, International Society for Tropical Ecology, Association of Tropical Biology, Tropical Grassland Society of Australia, Hawaiian Botanical Society, Biological Society of Indonesia, and Western Society of Naturalists. He was a member of the Indonesian National Committee for MAB and has taught plant ecology part-time at the University of Indonesia, Jakarta, and Bandung Institute of Technology, Bandung. Among his major publications are: The genus *Planchonia* Blume (Lecythidaceae)(1965. *Bull. Bot. Surv. India* 7:162–187); Phytosociology and ecology of the natural dry-grass communities on Oahu, Hawaii (with D. Mueller-Dombois)(1972. *Reinwardtia* 8:369–494); *Jenis-jenis kayu Indonesia* (Some timber trees of Indonesia)(1977, with others); and *Sumber daya hayati Indonesia* (Biological Resources of Indonesia)(1977, with others).

Mohamed Abdel El-Kassas is Professor of Botany, Faculty of Science, University of Cairo, Giza, Egypt. He received the B.S. (Hons.) in 1944 and the M.S. in 1947 from the University of Cairo, and the Ph.D. in Plant Ecology from Cambridge University in 1950. He has been teaching and conducting research at the University of Cairo since 1950 except for the period 1964–1968 when he was Professor of Botany at the University of Khartoum. He served as Assistant Director General of Arab League Educational, Cultural, and Scientific Organization (ALESCO) 1972–1976, and has been Vice-President of SCOPE and a member of editorial boards of several international journals. He received the Egyptian State Prize for Biology Research in 1958. His research centers on desert plant ecology in Egypt and the Sudan.

Jeffrey M. Klopatek is Research Ecologist, Environmental Sciences Division, Oak Ridge National Laboratory, Oak Ridge, Tennessee 37830. He received the B.S. in 1971 and the M.S. in 1974 from the University of Wisconsin-Milwaukee and the Ph.D. in 1978 from the University of Oklahoma. He is a member of the Ecological Society of America, the International Association for Ecology, the American Institute of Biological Sciences, and the Interdisciplinary Group for Ecology, Development, and Energy (EDEN). He has published on the role of emergent macrophytes in freshwater riverine marshes and on the energetics of managed land-use systems.

Frank Klötzli is on the staff of the Geobotanisches Institut of the Swiss Federal Institute of Technology, Stiftung Rübel, Zürichbergrstrasse 38, CH-8044, Zürich, Switzerland. He is also Professor at the Swiss Federal Institute of Technology, Zurich and the University of Zurich. His degrees from the Swiss Federal Institute of Technology include the Dipl. Natw. (1959), Dr. sc. nat. (1964), and Priv. Doz. (Habilitation) (1969). At this same Institute, he was Research Fellow (1958–1959), Lecturer (beginning 1966), Privat-Dozent (beginning 1969), and Professor (beginning 1976). In between, he taught at the universities of Stockholm, Lund, Uppsala, and Bangor; he has conducted research in Ethiopia and Tanzania since 1971. Dr. Klötzli is a member of the German Botanical Society, Swiss Botanical Society, German Ecological Society, Schwisz. Arbeitsgemeinschaft für Umweltforschung, INTECOL, and International Society for Tropical Ecology. His major publications include: Quality and quantity of Roe deer browsing (1964. Ph.D. thesis); Soil water relations of meadow communities (1968); Forest communities and forest sites of Switzerland (1972); Site conditions of broad-leaved forests in the southern taiga zone (1975); On the causality of woodland steppe mosaigues in High-Semien, Ethiopia (1975); On transplantation experiments with mires (1975); Lake shore vegetation as an indicator (1976); Game and cattle influencing vegetation in puna ecosystems of Ethiopia (1977); and Range management in the coastal savanna of Tanzania (1977).

Edward J. Kormondy is Provost and Professor of Biology, University of Southern Maine, Portland, Maine 04103. He received the B.S. from Tusculum College in 1950 and the M.S. (1951) and Ph.D. (1955) from the University of Michigan. He was Instructor in Zoology and Curator of Insects, University of Michigan (1955–1957), Assistant to Professor of Biology, Oberlin College (1957–1968), Director of the Commission on Undergraduate Education in the Biological Sciences and Director, Office of Biological Education, American Institute of Biological Sciences (1968–1971); in addition to his faculty appointment in 1971, he served as Vice-President and Provost of The Evergreen State College from 1973–1978. Dr. Kormondy is a member of the American Association for the Advancement of Science (Fellow), American Society of Limnology and Oceanography, Ecological Society of America (Secretary, 1976–1978), National Association of Biology Teachers (Board of Directors 1974–1976, Executive Committee 1975–1976, President 1981), and Sigma Xi. He held a postdoctoral fellowship in Radiation Ecology at the University of Georgia in 1963–1964 and studied at the Center for Bioethics, Georgetown University in 1978–1979. He served as Senior Staff Associate, Directorate for Science Education, National Science Foundation in 1979. He is the author of some fifty research papers and reviews and ten books including *Readings in Ecology* (1966), *Concepts of Ecology* (1969, 1976), and *General Biology: The Integrity and Natural History of Organisms* (1977, with T. Sherman and others).

Wilhelm Kühnelt is a retired Professor of Zoology, II. Zoologisches Institut, University of Vienna, Dr. Karl Lueger-Ring 1, A-1010 Vienna, Austria. He received the Ph.D. from the University of Vienna in 1927 and taught general zoology and comparative anatomy at the University of Vienna from 1939 to 1950. He was Professor at the University of Graz from 1950 to 1953, subsequent to which he became Professor at the University of Vienna. He is a member of the Austrian Academy of Sciences and served as chairman of a number of its committees, including Urbanecology, Protection of Nature, Biological Oceanography, IBP, SCOPE, and Edition of the Catalogus Faunae Austriae. Among his important works are: *Bodenbiologie* (1950. Vienna: Herold) and *Grundriss der Ökologie* (1965, 1970. Jena and Stuttgart: Gustav Fischer). The former appears in English and Spanish editions, the latter in French.

Christian Kunze is University Professor of Botany, Institute of Botany, University of Giessen, Heinrich-Buff-Ring 38, D-6300 Giessen, Federal Republic of Germany. Professor Kunze studied at Justus Liebig University, Giessen, receiving the doctorate (rer.

nat.) in 1968. He served at the Institut for Plant Ecology at Justus Liebig University and in the Laboratory for Soil Ecology. His major research papers include: The importance of the enzymes to judge the biological activity of the soil. (1970. *Bakt. Zbl.* II. 125:385–393); and Microbial transformation of organic material in the soil, in *Ecological Studies. Analysis and Synthesis,* Vol. 2.

Helmut Lieth is Professor in the Lehrstuhl für Ökologie, FB-5, Universität Osnabrück, Postfach 44 69, D-4500 Osnabrück, Federal Republic of Germany. In addition to study in the Agricultural School of Lindlar and the Philosophical and Theological College in Bamberg, Dr. Lieth did undergraduate study and thesis work in the Botany Department of the University of Cologne, receiving the Ph.D. in 1953. He served as Scientific Assistant in the Botany Department, University of Cologne (1954–1955) and in the Botany Department, Agricultural University in Hohenheim (1955–1964, with interruptions); he was Guest Professor at the Universidad Central de Venezuela (1961) and at the Universidad del Tolima in Ibague, Colombia (1963–1964); in the Agricultural University, Stuttgart-Hohenheim, he was Senior Lecturer (1964–1966) and then Apl. Professor (1966); he was Professor of Botany, University of Hawaii (1967) and successively Associate Professor (1967–1970) and Professor of Botany (1970–1978) at the University of North Carolina. He was National Research Fellow in the Botany Department, Université de Montreal (1960–1961). Professor Lieth is a member of the Ecological Society of America, Deutsche Botanische Gesellschaft, International Society of Biometeorology, American Association for the Advancement of Science (fellow), INTECOL, and a number of other professional organizations. He was Biome Director and a member of the Phenology Committee, Tropical Forest Biome of the US/IBP and served as a member of the Board of Directors of the Organization for Tropical Studies. He is the author of five books, an atlas, and a substantial number of research papers on phenology, forest ecology, and primary productivity.

Philip D. Lowe is Lecturer in Countryside Planning, University College London, Gower Street, London WC1E 6BT, England. He received the M.A. from Oxford University in 1971 and the M.S. from the University of Manchester in 1973. Mr. Lowe did postgraduate research at the University of Sussex 1973–1974 and subsequently has been in his present position. With Andrew Duff, he has written a book on the history of ecology to be published shortly by Croom Helm.

Yossef Loya is Senior Lecturer, Department of Zoology, Tel Aviv University, Tel Aviv, Israel. He received the B.S. in 1965 and the M.S. in 1967 from Tel Aviv University, and the Ph.D. from the State University of New York at Stony Brook in 1971. He held a postdoctoral research fellowship at Woods Hole Oceanographic Institute, 1971–1972 and served as Lecturer in Ecology, Department of Zoology, Tel Aviv University, 1972–1977. He is a member of the Ecological Society of America, Ecological Society of Israel, and the Zoological Society of Israel, of which he was Chairman 1976–1977. He is the author of some fifteen research papers, largely on the corals of the Red Sea, among them: 1972. *Mar. Biol.* 13:100–123; 1975. *Mar. Biol.* 29:177–185; *Nature* 259:478–480; 1976. *Ecology* 57:278–289. He received the Rekanati Student Research Fellowship, Tel Aviv University 1964–1965, and served as research associate on a number of grants investigating reef corals.

Herminio Lugo Lugo is Director of the Colegio Universitario de Cayey, University of Puerto Rico, Cayey, Puerto Rico 00633. He received the B.A. from the Polytechnic Institute of Puerto Rico in 1939; from Cornell University he received the M.S. in 1948 and Ph.D. in 1954. He served as Professor of Biology on the Mayaguez Campus of the University of Puerto Rico 1948–1960, as Professor of Biology on the Rio Piedras Campus of the University of Puerto Rico from 1960–1978, at which time he assumed his present position. He is a member of the New York Academy of Sciences, Botanical Society of America, American Association for the Advancement of Science, American Institute of Biological Sciences, Ecological Society of America, National Science Teachers Association, and Puerto Rico Science Teachers Association, of which he was President for two years. He regards his Ph.D. thesis on the germination of vanilla seeds as his major research paper.

Alan F. Mark is Professor of Botany, University of Otago, Box 56, Dunedin, New Zealand. He received the B.S. (1953) and M.S. (1955) from the University of New Zealand and the Ph.D. in 1958 from Duke University. At the University of Otago, he was appointed Assistant Junior Lecturer (1955), Lecturer (1960), Associate Professor (1967), and Professor (1976). He was Research Fellow (1960–1965) and since 1966 Advisor on Studies to Hellaby Indigenous Grassland Research Trust; he was Visiting Assistant Professor at Duke University in 1966. He is a member of the New Zealand Ecological Society (Council 1968–1970, vice-President 1970), Royal Society of New Zealand-Otago Branch (Council 1970–1974, Vice-President 1975, President 1976), Ecological Society of America, Sigma Xi, and Phi Beta Kappa. He was recipient of a Fulbright Grant in 1955 and in 1975 of the Loder Cup, a New Zealand Conservation Award. Among his major publications are: *New Zealand Alpine Plants* (with N. M. Adams) (1973); an edition of the papers of A. H. and A. W. Reed dealing especially with the snow tussock grasslands of New Zealand; and studies on the vegetation of the Fiordland region of New Zealand.

J. Frank McCormick is Professor of Ecology and Director, The Graduate Program in Ecology, University of Tennessee, Knoxville, Tennessee 37916. He received the B.S. from Butler University in 1958 and the M.S. (1960) and Ph.D. (1961) from Emory University. He served as Instructor of Botany at Butler University 1958; Assistant Professor of Biology, Vanderbilt University 1961–1963; Assistant Professor of Zoology and Senior Research Investigator, Savannah River Ecology Laboratory, University of Georgia 1963–1964. At the University of North Carolina, Dr. McCormick served as Assistant Professor (1964–1965) and Associate Professor (1965–1970) of Botany; Director, Ecology Training Program (1967–1969); and Professor of Ecology and Botany (1971–1974). He has been in his present position since 1974 except for 1977–1978 when he served as Senior Ecologist, U.S. Department of the Interior, Fish and Wildlife Service, Office of Biological Services. He is a member of the Ecological Society (Secretary 1971–1976, Editorial Board 1967–1970, Chairman Education Committee 1976–1977), Association of Southeastern Biologists (Executive Committee 1976–1979), American Institute of Biological Sciences, American Association for the Advancement of Sciences, and Sigma Xi. His major research interests and more than seventy-five publications are in the areas of radiation, population, community, ecosystem, and tropical ecology. He received the University of North Carolina Tanner Award for "Excellence in Inspirational Teaching of Undergraduate Students" in 1969.

He has served as consultant to numerous national, foreign, and international groups including: World Health Organization (Pan American Health Organization), Mexico (nuclear power monitoring and safety program), Nicaragua (energy and natural resources development), Council on Environmental Quality, Environmental Protection Agency (effects of increased coal utilization), National Academy of Sciences (Committee on Energy, Natural Resources, and Environment), and President's Interagency Task Force on Environmental Data and Monitoring (Panel on Ecological and Living Resources).

Karel Novák is Research Scientist and Head of the Department of Insect Ecology in the Institute of Entomology, Czechoslovak Academy of Sciences, CS 128 00 Prague 2, Vinicna 7, Czechoslovakia. He received the RNDr. (1950) and Ph.D. (1956) from Charles University in Prague. Dr. Novak served as Assistant Professor in Charles University from 1950–1954 at which time he joined the Academy. He is Scientific Secretary of the Institute of Entomology of the Academy and a member of the Committee of the Czechoslovak Zoological Society. He is the author of 120 research papers and the co-author of three books as well as the editor of a book on methods of collecting and studying insects.

Makoto Numata is Professor and Dean of the Faculty of Science, Chiba University, Yayoi-cho, Chiba 280, Japan. After earlier education at Tokyo Bunrika University, he received the D.Sc. from Kyoto University in 1953. He was Lecturer at Tokyo Bunrika University 1948–1950, Professor at Tohoku University (Sendai) 1963–1973, and at Chiba University, he was Assistant Professor 1950–1963 and has been Professor since 1963. He has served as President of the Ecological Society of Japan, Board Member of INTECOL, and member of Ecology and Education Commission of IUCN. He received the Prize for Deserving Persons on Natural Monuments from the Japanese government in 1970. Among his major publications are: *Methodology of Ecology* (1953), *Standpoint of Ecology* (1958), *Plant Ecology (1959), Applied Ecology* (1963), *Nature Conservation and Ecology* (1973), *The Flora and Vegetation of Japan* (1974) and *Urban Ecology* (1974).

Mohamed Obeid is Vice Chancellor of the University of Gezira, Wad Medani, Sudan. He received both the B.S. and the M.S. from the University of Khartoum and the Ph.D. from the University of Wales. He has been Lecturer (1965–1971) and Reader (1971–1977) in the Department of Botany at the University of Khartoum, Secretary of the Arid Zone Research Unit, and Director of the Hydrobiological Research Unit. He has published more than thirty papers, guides, and books on the terrestrial and aquatic plant ecology of the Sudan.

Kye Chil Oh is Professor of Biology, Department of Biology, Sogang University, Seoul, Korea 121. He received the B.S. from Seoul National University in 1949 and the Ph.D. in 1964 from the University of Tennessee-Knoxville; he studied at the University of Oklahoma 1960–1961, and was an Advanced Exchange Scholar on a Fulbright-Hays Fellowship at the Oak Ridge National Laboratory, Oak Ridge, Tennessee 1976–1977. From 1971 to 1974, he was Chairman of the Department of Biology, Sogang University. Dr. Oh was Vice-President of the Botanical Society of Korea

1971–1972, Council Member of Nature Reserves of the Republic of Korea 1971–1976, and has been Editor of the Ecological Society of Korea since 1976. Among his major publications are: The sampling, pattern, and survival of the higher elevation beech in the Great Smoky Mountains (Ph.D. thesis); Annual height growth of *Pinus densiflora* in relation to the selected soil factors in central Korea (1971. *Pacific Science Association 12th Pacific Science Congress, Record of Proceedings*).

A. W. Owadally is Conservator of Forests, Forestry Service, Curepipe, Mauritius. He received the B.S. (hons.) in Forestry in 1964 from the University of North Wales and has served as a part-time lecturer at the University of Mauritius. Among his major publications are: *The Deer in Mauritius,* with W. Butzler (1972. Mauritius: Alpha Printing); *Our Environment, Mauritius,* with C. Michel (1975. Mauritius: Super Printing); and *A Guide to the Royal Botanic Gardens* (1976. Mauritius: Government Printer).

Eystein Paasche is Professor of Marine Biology, Avdeling for Marin Botanik, University of Oslo, Postboks 1069, Blindern, Oslo 3, Norway. He received the Ph.D. from the University of Oslo in 1965, at which time he assumed his present position. His publications are in phytoplankton ecology and algal physiology.

Jaroslav Pelikán is Associate Professor and scientific worker in the Institute of Vertebrate Zoology, Czechoslovak Academy of Sciences, Kvetna 8, 603 65 Brno, Czechoslovakia. He received the Ing. and Dr. Degrees from the College of Agriculture in Brno in 1949 and the degree of CSc. from the Biological Institute of the Czechoslovak Academy of Sciences in Prague in 1958. Dr. Pelikán was appointed Associate Professor in the College of Agriculture in Brno in 1968 and has been Head of the Mammalogical Research Group in the Institute of Vertebrate Zoology of the Academy of Sciences since 1953. He served as general secretary of the Symposium Theriologicum in Brno in 1960 and as secretary general of the II. International Theriological Congress in Brno in 1978. Professor Pelikán is the author of about 60 papers on the ecology of small mammals, especially microtine rodents, dealing with reproduction, population dynamics, and their role and function in different ecosystems.

Ewa Pieczyńska is Head of the Department of Hydrobiology and Vice Director of the Institute of Zoology, University of Warsaw, Nowy Swiat 67, 00-046 Warsaw, Poland. Trained as a biologist and ecologist, she received the doctor's degree in 1963 and the doctor habilis docent designation in 1971 from the University of Warsaw. She has been Head of the Department of Hydrobiology since 1969 and Vice-Director of the Institute of Zoology since 1974. Dr. Pieczyńska is Vice-President of the Ecological Committee of the Polish Academy of Sciences and a member of the General Council of the National MAB Committee. Among her major publications are: Ecology of the eulittoral zone of lakes (1972. *Ekol. pol.* 20:637–732) and editor of *Selected Problems of Lake Littoral Ecology* (1976. Warsaw: Wyd. University of Warsaw).

Urs Rahm is Vice-Director and Head of the Zoology Department, Natural History Museum, Augustinergasse 2, CH-4051 Basel, Switzerland. He received the Ph.D. in

Zoology from the University of Basel, which he now serves as Professor of Zoology. Dr. Rahm was Head of the Swiss Research Station, Ivory Coast (1952–1955), Research Assistant, Swiss Tropical Institute, Basel (1955–1958), and Director General, Research Institute in Central Africa, Zaire (1958–1969). He is a member of the Swiss Zoological Society, American Society of Mammalogists, International Council of Museums (currently Vice-President), and Research Foundation for Animals and Plants (currently President). He has published more than fifty papers on mammals (mostly African), some fifteen papers on entomology and parasitology, and five on hydrobiology.

Oscar Ravera is Senior Scientist of European Communities with responsibilities in the limnology section, Department of Biology, Joint Research Center-Commission of the European Communities, 21020 Ispra (Varese), Italy. He received the Doctorate in Natural Sciences with highest award from the University of Milan in 1949, was designated Qualified University Lecturer in Hydrobiology in 1962, and Full University Professor in 1976. Dr. Ravera was Assistant at the Istituto Italiano di Idrobiologia, Pallanza, Italy (1949–1956), Chief Micropaleontologist, Mining Section, EDISON Co., Italy (1956–1960), and Hydrobiologist, Comitato Nazionale Ricerche Nucleari Center of Ispra (1960–1961). He is President of Societa Malacologica Italiana (Milan) and a member of the Societa Ecologia Italiana, American Society of Limnology and Oceanography, Freshwater Biological Association, Malacological Society, Unitas Malacologica Europaea, International Association of Limnology, and INTECOL. He has published some eighty research papers and one book, *Introduzione allo studio della Radioecologia* (1971. Torino: Edizioni Minerva Medica).

Milena Rychnovská is Head of the Ecological Department, Botanical Institute, Czechoslovak Academy of Sciences, Stara 18, Brno, Czechoslovakia. She received the RNDr in Plant Physiology from the University of Brno in 1951 and the C.Sc. (Ph.D.) in Plant Ecology in 1959 from the Czechoslovak Academy of Sciences, Prague. In addition to being in her present position since 1962, she was Coordinator of the IBP Grassland Project (Project Kamenicky) 1975–1980. She has been a member of the Czechoslovak National Committee on IBP, Sect. PP-PT, head of the working group on Project No. 3 of the Czechoslovak National Committee for MAB, and Secretary of the Czechoslovak National Committee on IUBS. She has been active in international synthesis of IBP grassland studies as subeditor of the section on temperate seminatural meadows and pastures, in which she was author of the chapter on energy flow. In 1973 she received, with her working group, the prize of the Czechoslovak Academy of Sciences for ecosystem studies on alluvial meadows. Among her major publications are: Water relations on some psammophytes (1963. In: *The Water Relations of Plants,* J. Rutter (ed) pp. 190–198); Plant water relations in three zones of grassland (1972. *Acta Sci. Nat. Brno,* 1–38); and, *Autökologische Studie der Tschechoslovakischen STIPA-Arten.* (1975. Praha).

José Sarukhán is Senior Researcher, Departmento de Botanica, Instituto de Biologia, Universidad Nacional Autonoma de Mexico, Apdo. Postal 70-233, Mexico 20. D.F. His educational background includes: B.S., University of Mexico, 1961; M.S., National School of Agriculture, 1965; Ph.D., School of Plant Biology, University of North

Wales, 1972. He has served as Director, Comision de Dioscoreas, INIF, Mexico (1965–1968); Senior Researcher, Instituto de Biologia and Professor of Population Ecology, Faculty of Sciences of the Universidad Nacional Autonoma de Mexico since 1972. He is a member of the British Ecological Society, the Linnean Society of London, the Sociedad Botanica de Mexico (which he served as President, 1972–1975), and the Association for Tropical Botany. His major publications include: *Arboles Tropicales de Mexico* (with T. D. Pennington, 1968); Demographic Studies of Tropical Trees In: *The Biology of Tropical Trees* Tomlinson and Zimmerman (eds); 1973. *J. Ecol.* 61:675–716; 1974. *J. Ecol.* 62:151–177 and 921–936; and in press. *Ann. Mo. Bot. Gard.* 63.

Samuel Segal is in residence at Keizersgracht 776, 1017 BE Amsterdam, The Netherlands. He attended the University of Amsterdam 1953–1960 and presented his thesis in 1969. He has served at the University of Amsterdam 1960–1975 and at the Technical University at Eindhoven, 1971 to the present. Significant among his some forty-five publications are: Notes on wall vegetation (1969 and 1972. The Hague) and *Een vegetatieonderzoek van de hogere waterplanten in Nederland* (1965. Hoogwoud).

Arne Semb-Johansson is Professor of Zoology, University of Oslo, Blindern, Oslo 3, Norway. He attended Cornell University (1948–1949), University of Colorado (1954–1955), and Albert Einstein College of Medicine, Yeshiva University (1955); he received the Ph.D. in 1959 from the University of Oslo, at which time he assumed his present position. He is a member of the Norwegian Academy of Sciences and Letters, of which he has been Secretary-General since 1975, and currently serves as Vice-Chairman of the ICIPE Foundation. He has been honored with the War Participation Medal (1946), King's Medal for Courage in the Cause of Freedom (Britain, 1950), and King's Gold Medal (1952). Major publications include: Relation of nutrition to endocrine-reproductive functions in the milkweed bug, *Oncopeltus fasciatus* (Dallas) (Heteroptera:Lygaeidae) (1958. *N. Mag. Zool.* 7:1–132) and *Norges Dyr,* Vols. 1–6 (1969–72).

Herman H. Shugart is Ecologist, Environmental Sciences Division, Oak Ridge National Laboratory, Oak Ridge, Tennessee 37830. He received the M.S. (1966) and M.S. (1968) from the University of Arkansas and the Ph.D. in 1971 from the University of Georgia. In addition to his present position, which he assumed in 1971, Dr. Shugart has been Associate Professor of Botany, Graduate Program in Ecology, University of Tennessee-Knoxville since 1975. He is a member of the American Ornithologists' Union, Ecological Society of America, Wilson Ornithological Society, Sigma Xi, and Phi Kappa Phi. From the American Ornithologists' Union, he received the Josselyn Van Tyne Memorial Research Award in 1967 and the Marcia Brady Tucker Travel Award in 1969. He has published some fifty-five research papers and book chapters on such topics as niche theory and quantification, digital and analog computer modelling of energy and nutrient flows, population ecology of responses to various environmental gradients, and evolution of resource partitioning in various organisms.

Hugo Sjörs is Professor of Ecological Botany,Institute of Ecological Botany, Uppsala University, Box 559, S-75122, Uppsala, Sweden. He received the degree of Fil. Dr. from Uppsala University in 1948. He has been Docent at Uppsala University (1948–1952), Deputy Assistant Professor, University of Lund (1952–1955), and Assistant Professor, School of Forestry, University of Stockholm (1955–1962); he has held his present position since 1962. Professor Sjörs has been a member and Chairman of the Swedish Phytogeographical Society, a member of the Swedish Academy of Sciences, and has been recognized with the Starbäck Medal by the Swedish Association for the Protection of Nature. Major publications include: *Myrvegetation I Bergslagen* (1948), *Slåtterängar I Gragärde Finnmark* (1954), *Nordisk Växtgeografi* (1956, 1967), and *Ekologisk Botanik* (1971).

Vaclav Skuhravý is Research Scientist in the Institute of Entomology, Czechoslovak Academy of Science, Prague 2, Vinicna 7. He received the RnDR (1951) and Ph.D. (1960) from Charles University in Prague. Dr. Skuhravy was Assistant Professor at Charles University from 1952–1955 at which time he came to his present position. He is the author of 150 scientific publications and four books. His research interests lie in the ecology of insects, ecosystem studies, and the influence of insecticides.

Lawrence B. Slobodkin is Professor of Biology, Department of Ecology and Evolution, State University of New York at Stony Brook, Stony Brook, New York 11794. He received the B.S. from Bethany College in 1947 and the Ph.D. from Yale University in 1951. He was Chief Investigator (1951–1953) and Fisheries Research Biologist, U.S. Fish and Wildlife Service (1952–1953), Instructor to full Professor of Zoology, University of Michigan (1953–1968), after which he assumed his present appointment. He has served at SUNY-Stony Brook as Director, Ecology and Evolution Program (1968–1971) and Chairman, Department of Ecology and Evolution (1971–1974). He was Senior Visiting Scientist on a Guggenheim Fellowship at the Smithsonian Institution (1974–1975) and has continued as a Research Associate of the Institution since 1976. In addition to being named a Sterling Fellow at Yale University in 1950, Dr. Slobodkin received a Guggenheim Fellowship (1961) and a Fulbright Fellowship (1962) to study at Hebrew University, and another Fulbright Fellowship and Visiting Professorship, University of Tel Aviv 1965–1966. He has served on a number of national and international committees and panels and the editorial boards of *American Naturalist* and *Journal of Theoretical Population Studies.* He is the author of some ninety papers and of *Growth and Regulation of Animal Populations* (1961. Holt, Rinehart and Winston). Among his honors are the 1960 Distinguished Service Award from the University of Michigan and the 1961 Henry Russell Award for Research from the same university. He was designated Distinguished Visiting Scholar, University of Maryland 1975 and Visiting Scholar, University Center in Virginia in 1975.

Raymond L. Specht is Professor of Botany, University of Queensland, St. Lucia, Queensland, Australia 4067. From the University of Adelaide, he received the B.S. Hons. (1946), M.S. (1949), Ph.D. (1953), and D.Sc. (1974). Dr. Specht was Lecturer to Senior Lecturer in Plant Ecology, University of Adelaide (1950–1960) and Reader in Plant Ecology, University of Melbourne (1961–1965); he has been in his present post since 1966. He served as Australian Convener of the joint sections "Productivity, Physiological Processes, and Conservation of Terrestrial Communities" IBP from 1964–1974. He received Fulbright, Smith-Mundt, and Carnegie grants to the United States in 1954, the Royal Society-Nuffield Foundation Commonwealth Bursary in 1964, the Verco Medal of the Royal Society of South Australia in 1961, and the Research Medal of the Royal Society of Victoria in 1976. Among his major publications are: *Records of the American-Australian Expedition to Arnhem Land,* Vol. 3 *Botany and Plant Ecology* and Vol. 4 *Zoology* (1958–1964. Melbourne University Press); *The Vegetation of South Australia* (1972. Adelaide: Government Printer); Conservation of major plant communities in Australia and Papua New Guinea (1974. *Aust. J. Bot.* Suppl. No. 7); and *Ecosystems of the World,* one volume in the forthcoming *Heathlands and Related Shrublands* (Amsterdam: Elsevier Sci. Publ. Co.).

José G. Tundisi is Professor of Biological Sciences, São Carlos Universidade Federal, via Washington Luiz, Km 235, Brazil. From the University of São Paulo, he received the Bs.C. in Natural History in 1962, Licenciate in Natural History in 1963, the Ph.D. in Botany in 1969, and the D.Sc. in Ecology in 1977; he received the Ms.C. in Oceanography in 1965 from the University of Southampton. He served as Research Assistant (1961–1963) and Oceanographer (1963–1971) in the Oceanographic Institute of the University of São Paulo; at the Universidade Federal de São Carlos, he has been Associate Professor (1971–1972) and Professor of Biological Sciences (since 1972). He is a member of the Freshwater Biological Association, British Phycological Society, Societie Internationalis Limnologie, and Theoreticae et Applicatae. He serves as special advisor for ecology to the National Research Council of Brazil and Fundação de Ampara a Pesquisa do Estado do São Paulo. He has published fifteen papers, with an additional nine in preparation, and translated from English to Portuguese J. Phillipson Davies' *Ecological Energetics* and P. and A. Ehrlich's *Population, Resources, and Environment;* in preparation are two books, *Introduction to Ecology* and *Ecology of a Tropical Reservoir,* to be published by McGraw Hill of Brazil Limited.

Karel F. Vaas died on April 28, 1980, prior to which he was retired, living in Yerseke, The Netherlands. He received the Doctorate in Natural Philosophy from the University of Leiden in 1938. He served as advisor-laker Director, Laboratory of Inland Fisheries, Bogor, Indonesia from 1939 to 1958, and as Director of the Delta Institute of Hydrobiological Research, Royal Netherlands Academy of Science, Yerseke from 1958 to 1977. He was representative to SIL from 1970 to 1976 and has served as editor in chief of *Hydrobiologia* since 1970. Among his major publications are: Studies on the production and utilization of natural food in Indonesia carp ponds. (1959. *Hydrobiologia* 12:308–392); Lakes in Dutch reclamation schemes. (1966. In: *Man-made Lakes,* R. H. Lowe (ed), London: Academic Press); Studies on the fish fauna of the newly created lake near Veere. (1970. *Netherlands J. Sea Res.* 5:50–95); Studies on the black goby (*Gobius niger*) in the Verse Meer. (1975, with others. *Netherlands J. Sea Res.*); The osmotic concentration of the blood plasma of plaice (*Pleuronectes platessa*) from three habitats of different salinity. (1977, with others. *Netherlands J. Sea Res.* 11:168–183).

Frans-Emil Wielgolaski is Professor of Terrestrial Botanical Ecology, Institute of Biology and Geology, University of Tromsø, Box 790, 9001, Tromsø, Norway. His degrees include Cand. hort., Agricultural University of Norway (1957) and Mag. scient., University of Oslo (1964). He was Assistant and Associate Professor, University of Bergen (1965–1968) and University of Oslo (1969–1976) and has been in his present position since 1977. From 1967 to 1974, he served as Secretary General of the Norwegian IBP and as Secretary of IBP/PT-UM and IBP/CT; since 1972 he has been the Norwegian member in the IUCN Commission on Ecology. Major publications include: *Fennoscandia Tundra Ecosystems,* Vol. I and II (1975. Springer-Verlag); Biological indicators of pollution (1975. *Urban Ecol.* 1); Investigations on phenology and primary production in relation to environmental factors (in press).

Jan W. Woldendorp is Director of the Institute for Ecological Research, Kemperbergerweg 67, Arnhem, The Netherlands. He attended the Agricultural University, Wageningen receiving the Ir. in 1958 and the Dr. in 1963. In addition to a position at the Agricultural University, Wageningen, Dr. Woldendorp was head of the Biology Department of the Dutch States Mines. Among his research papers are those dealing with the nitrogen cycle in the soil, and extraction of proteins from wastewater.